Ireland

**Lou Callan
Fionn Davenport
Patrick Horton
Oda O'Carroll
Tom Smallman
David Wenk**

LONELY PLANET PUBLICATIONS
Melbourne • Oakland • London • Paris

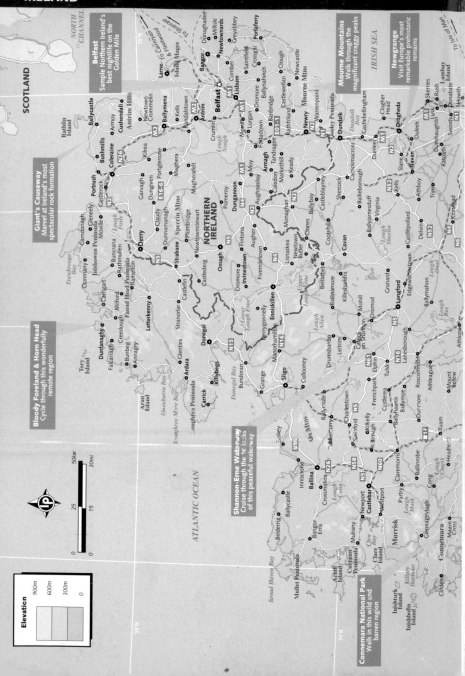

IRELAND

Giant's Causeway
Marvel at Ireland's most spectacular rock formation

Bloody Foreland & Horn Head
Cycle through this wonderfully remote region

Shannon-Erne Waterway
Cruise through the 16 locks of this peaceful waterway

Connemara National Park
Walk in this wild and barren region

Belfast
Sample Northern Ireland's best nightlife on the Golden Mile

Mourne Mountains
Walk through the magnificent craggy peaks

Newgrange
Visit Europe's most remarkable prehistoric remains

SCOTLAND

NORTH CHANNEL

NORTHERN IRELAND

ATLANTIC OCEAN

IRISH SEA

Elevation
900m
600m
300m
0

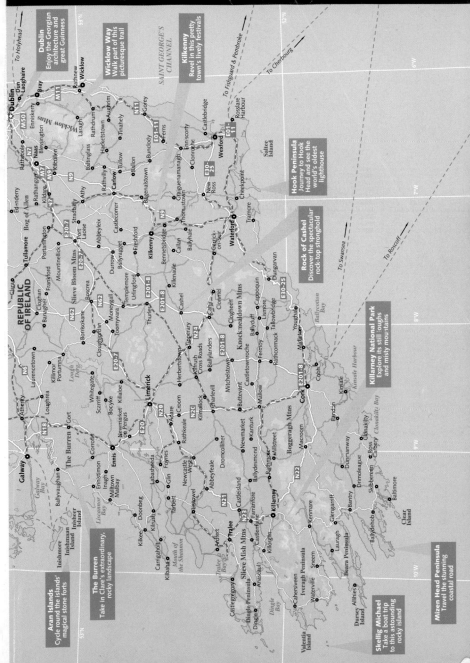

IRELAND

Dublin
Enjoy the Georgian architecture and great Guinness

Wicklow Way
Walk part of this picturesque trail

Killkenny
Revel in this pretty town's lively festivals

Hook Peninsula
Journey to Hook Head and see the world's oldest lighthouse

Rock of Cashel
Discover the spectacular rock-top stronghold

Killarney National Park
Explore its still loughs and misty mountains

Mizen Head Peninsula
Travel the stunning coastal road

Skellig Michael
Take a boat trip to this astounding rocky island

The Burren
Take in Clare's extraordinary, rocky landscape

Aran Islands
Cycle round the islands' magical stone forts

REPUBLIC OF IRELAND

Ireland
5th edition – March 2002
First published – January 1994

Six-monthly upgrades of this title available free on
www.lonelyplanet.com/upgrades

Published by
Lonely Planet Publications Pty Ltd ABN 36 005 607 983
90 Maribyrnong St, Footscray, Victoria 3011, Australia

Lonely Planet Offices
Australia Locked Bag 1, Footscray, Victoria 3011
USA 150 Linden St, Oakland, CA 94607
UK 10a Spring Place, London NW5 3BH
France 1 rue du Dahomey, 75011 Paris

Photographs
Many of the images in this guide are available for licensing from
Lonely Planet Images.
email: lpi@lonelyplanet.com.au
Web site: www.lonelyplanetimages.com

Front cover photograph
Ornate lampost in Dublin (Richard Cummins)

ISBN 1 86450 379 3

text & maps © Lonely Planet Publications Pty Ltd 2002
photos © photographers as indicated 2002

Printed by The Bookmaker International Ltd
Printed in China

4 Contents – Text

NORTHERN IRELAND 646

BELFAST 653

COUNTIES DOWN & ARMAGH 687

COUNTIES DERRY & ANTRIM 719

COUNTIES TYRONE & FERMANAGH 758

LANGUAGE 777

APPENDIX – PLACE NAMES 780

GLOSSARY 783

INDEX 790

MAP LEGEND back page

METRIC CONVERSION inside back cover

Contents – Maps

MAP INDEX

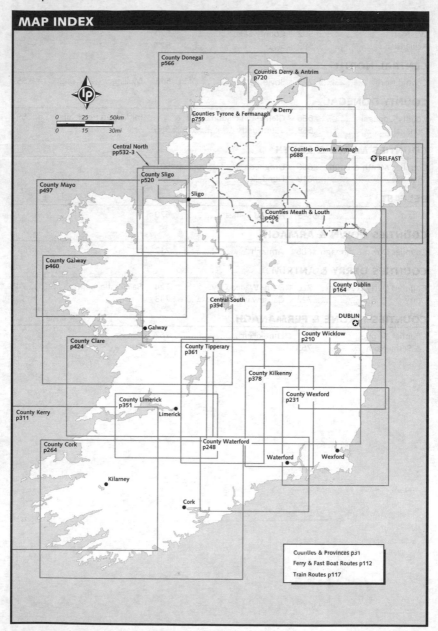

County Donegal
p566

Counties Derry & Antrim
p720

● Derry

Counties Tyrone & Fermanagh
p759

Counties Down & Armagh
p688

✪ BELFAST

Central North
pp532-3

County Sligo
p520

● Sligo

County Mayo
p497

Counties Meath & Louth
p606

County Galway
p460

County Dublin
p164

Central South
p394

DUBLIN
✪

County Clare
p424

● Galway

County Wicklow
p210

County Tipperary
p361

County Kilkenny
p378

County Wexford
p231

County Limerick
p351

● Limerick

County Kerry
p311

County Waterford
p248

County Cork
p264

● Waterford

● Wexford

● Kilarney

● Cork

0   25   50km
0   15   30mi

Counties & Provinces p31
Ferry & Fast Boat Routes p112
Train Routes p117

The Authors

Lou Callan

After completing a degree in languages, Lou bounced between a variety of jobs while completing further study in publishing and editing. After lots of strenuous book launch parties as Publicity Manager at Oxford University Press Australia, she found work as a contributing editor on *Australian Bookseller & Publisher*. In 1998, after four years at Lonely Planet as a phrasebook editor, Lou packed up and followed her husband, Tony, to the red dunes of the United Arab Emirates for a very long, hot 2½ years. Here she wrote Lonely Planet's *Dubai* and, with Gordon Robison, *Oman & the United Arab Emirates*, as well as contributing to *Middle East*. Other jobs have included contributions to the *England* and *Britain* guides. Lou is now very nicely situated in cool, shady Melbourne with Tony the husband and Ziggy the cat.

Fionn Davenport

Fionn was born and raised in Dublin – an idyllic youth interrupted only by jarring moves to Buenos Aires, Geneva and New York (thanks to his Dad's job) that left him incapable of spending more than a couple of years in any one place without uprooting and moving somewhere else. He stayed in Dublin long enough to complete a degree in French and History at Trinity College (but still took a year off somewhere in the middle) before moving to Paris and then New York. A series of odd jobs and adventures eventually landed him behind the editor's desk, and he spent three years editing other people's travel experiences. These days he splits his time between New York, Dublin and wherever the call of work and travel takes him. He has written about many destinations throughout the world and has previously worked on Lonely Planet's *Spain*, *Dublin*, *Ireland*, *Sicily* and *Britain* guides, as well as a host of pan-European books.

Partick Horton

Patrick, a writer and photographer, was born with restless feet. He travelled extensively in his native Britain before hitting the around-the-world trail in 1985. Since bringing his old British motorbikes out to Australia, he now calls Melbourne home. He finds his travels lead him to the more arcane areas of the world such as North Korea, Eritrea, Kosovo, East Timor and Tonga, or riding a motorcycle over the Himalaya. Patrick lives with his long-suffering partner, Christine, another ardent traveller, who he met in Paris. Patrick has had many photographs published in Lonely Planet guides and his contributions as an author include *Australia*, *Eastern Europe*, *Europe*, *Ireland* and *Mediterranean Europe*.

Oda O'Carroll

Born in Roscommon, in the windy mid-west of Ireland, Oda packed her knapsack for the big smoke of Dublin where she studied Communications until 1990. Since graduating she has worked as a television researcher and writer for the independent sector in Ireland. Oda also spent some time donkey working on film sets and made her own short film in 1998. She has travelled extensively in Europe and, last summer, chugged between America's coasts, with friends, in a clapped-out 1967 Cadillac (without air conditioning) and hopes to return soon for the northern route. She still lives happily in Dublin with her husband, Eoin.

Tom Smallman

Tom lives in Melbourne, Australia, and had a number of jobs before joining Lonely Planet as an editor. He now works full time as an author and has worked on Lonely Planet guides to *Britain*, *Scotland*, *Edinburgh*, *Australia*, *New South Wales*, *Sydney*, *Canada*, *Dublin* and *Pennsylvania*.

David Wenk

A creature of the outdoors at heart, David has spent much of the past three years holed up in Lonely Planet's London office, offering cartographic skills and technical know-how to the book production team. He frequently promises himself he'll get out more. Growing up without a television on a remote farmstead in upstate New York, David is well versed in the manufacture of goat's cheese and maple syrup, and once was a decent musician. Thankfully though, modesty precludes him from regaling the LP office staff with tales of aerial derring-do from his brief yet colourful career as a pilot. This update of *Ireland* is his fourth contribution to Lonely Planet as a writer.

FROM THE AUTHORS

Lou Callan Thanks should go to everyone, travellers and Irish alike, who provided so much information. Thanks also to the wonderful staff at Heron's Cove in Goleen on the Mizen Head Peninsula and to the people of Tacumshin who hauled our car out of a muddy ditch on that cold, wet St Patrick's Day. As always, special thanks to Tony Cleaver, my darling travel companion who makes it all seem so easy.

Fionn Davenport My efforts on this book would not have been possible without the help of dozens of people, who helped me out of professional courtesy and friendship. Travelling throughout Ireland with an obsessive curiosity and a need to gather information is always that bit easier thanks to them. However, my biggest thanks go to Sorcha O'Callaghan, without whose support, help, advice and encouragement (not to mention tolerance and patience) I wouldn't have managed it at all. You're always in my heart and, for that, I love you more than you can even imagine.

Partick Horton I would like to offer my thanks to the many people who have helped me in updating the Northern Ireland chapters. They're many but I'll mention a few: the staff of the Belfast Welcome Centre and all the Northern Ireland tourist offices; Helen Mark who introduced me to so many interesting and useful contacts; Bill Rolston, author of *Drawing Support* – a series of excellent books on the Northern Ireland murals; Geoff Hill and Paul McKillion of the *Belfast News*

Letter for background information; Tom Hartley, Belfast City councillor and cemetery tour guide; the staff of the Linen Hall Library – one of the nicest libraries I've ever visited; Patrick and staff of the Linen House, Belfast; Herman and Marion of the Flax Mill for the great *craic*; DriveAway Holidays, Sydney, for car hire; and lastly to my partner, Christine, who put up with and helped so much.

Oda O'Carroll My thanks go to Tom and Eileen Flynn in Cavan; Anthony in Athlone; Eileen in Strokestown; Kathleen Moffatt in Carrick tourist office; Noreen Dunne in Lanesboro; Michael Farren of Bord Fáilte; Stephanie Connolly in Mullingar tourist office; David O'Rourke, pizza-flipping savant in Monaghan; Nuala and Pat Dunne in Clonard and the lovely Louise for the Irish dancing lessons; Kevin Rooney; Laurent Mellet; Greg; Jay and Red for the book; Luan; Donal Dineen; Fionn Davenport, and David, Tim and Michala at the LP London office for all their support and good humour; Kate and Et for the endless babysitting (how are you fixed next Friday?) and endless other help; Mrs O (as she's fondly known); Eoin and little Esa for the giggles.

Tom Smallman My eternal gratitude to Sue Graefe for her enduring support. My deepest thanks also go to Eileen Maguire for her hospitality and the *craic* in Dublin; as always to the Ryan Rue family, Kathleen, Christy, Kathleen (and Seamus), Roger and Christy in Tipperary for being such wonderful people; to Jeanette on Inishmór for use of the bike; to Shay at Rich View Hostel for information on Achill Island; to Mary Sexton for the low-down on Galway city; to Marie at the Bundoran tourist office, Donegal; to Steve Fallon for additional information on Donegal; to all those people in the travel industry who patiently answered my questions; and to all those readers who wrote in with comments on the previous edition.

David Wenk First, thanks to my fellow authors. They're the ones who did the real legwork in the field. Despite numerous queries from me at a time when they were flat out writing up their own manuscripts, all responded graciously and helpfully. Elsewhere, Mary Egan at the Irish Tourist Board provided information and statistics on travel patterns. Susan Mangan helped with the section on Gulliver, the information and reservation system, and Miriam Burke provided details of Aer Lingus' services. Thanks also to Kevin Rooney for his piece on fishing and to Jonathan Wenk for advice on photography. I'm also grateful to Christina Tlustos of Dublin and Lonely Planet's own Rachel Suddart and Pelin Thornhill, all of whom offered their advice and expertise on the Getting There & Away chapter.

This Book

The 1st edition of *Ireland* was written by John Murray, Sean Sheehan and Tony Wheeler. The 2nd edition was updated by Tom Smallman, Sean Sheehan and Pat Yale. The 3rd edition was updated by Tom Smallman, Pat Yale and Steve Fallon. The 4th edition was updated by Tom Smallman, Fionn Davenport, Dorinda Talbot, Steve Fallon and Pat Yale.

For this 5th edition Lou Callan updated the Wexford & Waterford, Cork and Kerry chapters; Fionn Davenport updated the Dublin, Wicklow, Kilkenny, Central South and Meath & Louth chapters; Patrick Horton updated all of the Northern Ireland chapters; Oda O'Carroll updated the Introduction, Facts about Ireland, Getting Around, Republic of Ireland and Central North chapters – she also wrote the Music special section; Tom Smallman updated the Limerick & Tipperary, Clare, Galway, Mayo & Sligo and Donegal chapters; and David Wenk updated the Facts for the Visitor and Getting There & Away chapters.

FROM THE PUBLISHER

This book was produced in Lonely Planet's London office. Michala Green coordinated the editing, assisted by Claire Hornshaw, Jenny Lansbury, Sally Schafer, Arabella Shepherd and Sam Trafford. Mapping and design was coordinated by James Timmins, assisted by Ed Pickard, Simon Tillema and Joelene Kowalski. Annika Roojun designed the cover and Lachlan Ross drew the back-cover map. Emma Koch produced the language chapter and the illustrations were drawn by Jane Smith, Martin Harris, Matt King and Nicky Caven. Thanks to Mary Harte at Bus Éireann for last-minute help with bus fares, Lindsay Brown and Sandra Bardwell for walking advice, Steve Fallon for sharing his Irish-language expertise, and to all of the authors for their hard work and enthusiasm.

ACKNOWLEDGEMENTS

Grateful acknowledgement is made for reproduction permission: BMG/RCA for the Chieftains photo on p52; Anton Corbijn for the U2 photo on p55; Andy Earl of Curtain Call Ltd for the Cranberries photo on p57; and James Cumpsty for the David Holmes photo on p58. Thanks to Iain Moffat at www.playlouder.com, Yvonne McMahon at MCMA, Rainer Lindheim at www.cranberries.ie and Sandra McKay at RMP for help with sourcing these images.

The photograph of Achill Island on the Republic of Ireland title page, p123, is by Richard Mills and the photograph of the Carrick-a-rede rope bridge on the Northern Ireland title page, p645, is by David Tipling. Both images are available for licensing from Lonely Planet Images.

THANKS

Many thanks to the travellers who used the previous editions and wrote to us with helpful hints, useful advice and interesting anecdotes. Your names follow:

Joy Adams, Naomi Anders, Clare Anderson, Lydia Athmer, Jostein Austvik, Ted Baglin, Melanie Bale, Helena Battdrill, Patricia Bernard, Kathrin Besse, Jude Billard, Pat Bode, Jevan Brett, Baden Brown, Frank Bugeja, AGW Butler, Gerry Carden, Katrina Cartwright, Brent Cassidy, Claire Caulton, Kristina Chamberlain, Maria Chamberlain, Edward Chambers, Simone Clark, Debbie Cleaveley, Liz Cochrane, Cathie Coles, Peter Collins, Ellen Connelly, Dan Conroy, Cathleen Conway, Noel Conway, Alistair Craig, Jennifer Cropley, Rodger Crowe, Shelagh Cullity, Andrea Curtis, Jayne D'Arcy, Janice Day, Flo & Paul De Beer, Niamh M Dempsey, Colm Dolan, Jeffrey Donnelly, Mara d'Oriano, Kelly Douglas, MF Dowd, Shane Duffy, H Dunn, William Edwards, Sybil Ehrlich, Robin Ellis, Tim Entwistle, Caroline Evans, Aliza F, Rosemary Fairlain, Michael Falk, Rev. Pat Farnham, Katja Fedrowitz, Arnold Fieldman, Kerstin Finkhaeuser, B Finnerty, Tim FitzPatrick, Sean Flynn, Karen & Roberta For, Sally Forbes, Graham Ford, Barbara Fraser, Sue Frezza, Anna Frith, Sarah Garrison, Stephen Gilmore, Susan Gilpin, Allison Gordon, Marie Goss, Patricia E Graham, Diana Green, Michel Gregoire, Ron Griep, John Hamilton, Jacki Hatnett, Henry Haubert, Erin Heffron, Angela Heidrich, Lorenz A Heinze, KG Hellyen, Ellie Henk, Vincent Henry, Robert M Herbst, Nattanya Hewitt, Catherine Hovenden, Sabine Huba, Viktoria Huber, Terry Hunt, Jill & Rod Hunter, Jan Jaap van Lomwel, Danyane Johnston, Christine Kaegii, Daniel Kavanaugh, Victoria Kearns, Rachel Kelly, Judith Kiddlo, William Kirwan, Andrew Knight, Frank Kohns, Jenifer Kooiman, Henry Koster, Anke Kuhner, Abbi Lawrance, Tanya Lecut, Rob Lee, Evelyn Leeper, Jamie Lennahan, Tom R Linden, Par Longton Collis, Israel Luski, Marc Luthy-Gagliardo, Kathleen Madden, Valerie Maguire, Carolyn Mandersloot, Dan Manson, Tracey Marek, Chana & Shabtai Matzliach, Jim & Pat McAtee, Mandy McCabe, Carmel McCann, Jenny McCormick, Karen McGlinchey, Lisa McInnis, Peter McKenna, Kylie McKernan, Mary Medicus, JM Mellifont, David Monaghan, Christine Moon, Declan Moran, Thomas F Moran, Elaine Murphy, Hamish Murray, Beate Myran, John Naughton, Mary Naughton, Peter Neild, Victoria Newman Sumner, Christy Nickel, Melissa Nurczynski, Jean O Sullian, Kathy O'Brian, Con O'Conalll, John O'Connor, P Octay, Joe O'Dea, Tony Ogilvie, Giovanna Olivieri, Sharon O'Reilly, Stephen O'Reilly, Jen O'Shea, Derek Paterson, Ole P Pedersen, Heike Phillips, Ben Pickett, DC Piper, Klaus Podransky, Catherine Pyne, Joel Rane, Anne Rasmusen, David Reid, Katja Ritari, Marc Roede, Ellen Roffey, Christopher Romanet, Kris Rosar, Monica Rumpf, Nicky Rutherford, Emma Ryan, Roger Salinas, Patrick Samaey, Markus Schonherr, Rebecca Scott, Dan Sharp, Laurie Sheldon, Tom William Skarre, Eugene Sobka, PW Spencer, Helen Squires, Robert Stanley, Lou Stephenson, Yvonne Sterling, Judy Stern, Kathryn Stokes, David Taylor, Janice Teoh, Natalie T'Jampens, Miguel Trevinto, Jackie Trott, Mike C Tucker, AJ Turner, Chris Uphill, Sarann Forester Valentine, Marieke van Riet, Robert Vanover, Mirella Vaseley, Suzanne Vinci-Irwin, Rudy Volin, Sigrit Walloe, Aidan Walsh, Dara Ward, Phil Waring, Richard Watson, Anthony Webb, Julie Webb, Robert Webb, Alison Weir, Shannon White, Daryl Williams, David Wilson, Johannes Woern, Jessica Wolf, Leesa Yeo, Bram Zandbelt.

Foreword

ABOUT LONELY PLANET GUIDEBOOKS

The story begins with a classic travel adventure: Tony and Maureen Wheeler's 1972 journey across Europe and Asia to Australia. Useful information about the overland trail did not exist at that time, so Tony and Maureen published the first Lonely Planet guidebook to meet a growing need.

From a kitchen table, then from a tiny office in Melbourne (Australia), Lonely Planet has become the largest independent travel publisher in the world, an international company with offices in Melbourne, Oakland (USA), London (UK) and Paris (France).

Today Lonely Planet guidebooks cover the globe. There is an ever-growing list of books and there's information in a variety of forms and media. Some things haven't changed. The main aim is still to help make it possible for adventurous travellers to get out there – to explore and better understand the world.

At Lonely Planet we believe travellers can make a positive contribution to the countries they visit – if they respect their host communities and spend their money wisely. Since 1986 a percentage of the income from each book has been donated to aid projects and human rights campaigns.

Updates Lonely Planet thoroughly updates each guidebook as often as possible. This usually means there are around two years between editions, although for more unusual or more stable destinations the gap can be longer. Check the imprint page (following the colour map at the beginning of the book) for publication dates.

Between editions up-to-date information is available in two free newsletters – the paper *Planet Talk* and email *Comet* (to subscribe, contact any Lonely Planet office) – and on our Web site at www.lonelyplanet.com. The *Upgrades* section of the Web site covers a number of important and volatile destinations and is regularly updated by Lonely Planet authors. *Scoop* covers news and current affairs relevant to travellers. And, lastly, the *Thorn Tree* bulletin board and *Postcards* section of the site carry unverified, but fascinating, reports from travellers.

Correspondence The process of creating new editions begins with the letters, postcards and emails received from travellers. This correspondence often includes suggestions, criticisms and comments about the current editions. Interesting excerpts are immediately passed on via newsletters and the Web site, and everything goes to our authors to be verified when they're researching on the road. We're keen to get more feedback from organisations or individuals who represent communities visited by travellers.

> Lonely Planet gathers information for everyone who's curious about the planet – and especially for those who explore it first-hand. Through guidebooks, phrasebooks, activity guides, maps, literature, newsletters, image library, TV series and Web site we act as an information exchange for a worldwide community of travellers.

Research Authors aim to gather sufficient practical information to enable travellers to make informed choices and to make the mechanics of a journey run smoothly. They also research historical and cultural background to help enrich the travel experience and allow travellers to understand and respond appropriately to cultural and environmental issues.

Authors don't stay in every hotel because that would mean spending a couple of months in each medium-sized city and, no, they don't eat at every restaurant because that would mean stretching belts beyond capacity. They do visit hotels and restaurants to check standards and prices, but feedback based on readers' direct experiences can be very helpful.

Many of our authors work undercover, others aren't so secretive. None of them accept freebies in exchange for positive write-ups. And none of our guidebooks contain any advertising.

Production Authors submit their manuscripts and maps to offices in Australia, USA, UK or France. Editors and cartographers – all experienced travellers themselves – then begin the process of assembling the pieces. When the book finally hits the shops, some things are already out of date, we start getting feedback from readers and the process begins again…

WARNING & REQUEST

Things change – prices go up, schedules change, good places go bad and bad places go bankrupt – nothing stays the same. So, if you find things better or worse, recently opened or long since closed, please tell us and help make the next edition even more accurate and useful. We genuinely value all the feedback we receive. A well-travelled team reads and acknowledges every letter, postcard and email and ensures that every morsel of information finds its way to the appropriate authors, editors and cartographers for verification.

Everyone who writes to us will find their name in the next edition of the appropriate guidebook. They will also receive the latest issue of *Planet Talk*, our quarterly printed newsletter, or *Comet*, our monthly email newsletter. Subscriptions to both newsletters are free. The very best contributions will be rewarded with a free guidebook.

Excerpts from your correspondence may appear in new editions of Lonely Planet guidebooks, the Lonely Planet Web site, *Planet Talk* or *Comet*, so please let us know if you *don't* want your letter published or your name acknowledged.

Send all correspondence to the Lonely Planet office closest to you:

Australia: Locked Bag 1, Footscray, Victoria 3011
USA: 150 Linden St, Oakland, CA 94607
UK: 10a Spring Place, London NW5 3BH
France: 1 rue du Dahomey, 75011 Paris

Or email us at: talk2us@lonelyplanet.com.au

For news, views and updates see our Web site: www.lonelyplanet.com

HOW TO USE A LONELY PLANET GUIDEBOOK

The best way to use a Lonely Planet guidebook is any way you choose. At Lonely Planet we believe the most memorable travel experiences are often those that are unexpected, and the finest discoveries are those you make yourself. Guidebooks are not intended to be used as if they provide a detailed set of infallible instructions!

Contents All Lonely Planet guidebooks follow roughly the same format. The Facts about the Destination chapters or sections give background information ranging from history to weather. Facts for the Visitor gives practical information on issues like visas and health. Getting There & Away gives a brief starting point for researching travel to and from the destination. Getting Around gives an overview of the transport options when you arrive.

The peculiar demands of each destination determine how subsequent chapters are broken up, but some things remain constant. We always start with background, then proceed to sights, places to stay, places to eat, entertainment, getting there and away, and getting around information – in that order.

Heading Hierarchy Lonely Planet headings are used in a strict hierarchical structure that can be visualised as a set of Russian dolls. Each heading (and its following text) is encompassed by any preceding heading that is higher on the hierarchical ladder.

Entry Points We do not assume guidebooks will be read from beginning to end, but that people will dip into them. The traditional entry points are the list of contents and the index. In addition, however, some books have a complete list of maps and an index map illustrating map coverage.

There may also be a colour map that shows highlights. These highlights are dealt with in greater detail in the Facts for the Visitor chapter, along with planning questions and suggested itineraries. Each chapter covering a geographical region usually begins with a locator map and another list of highlights. Once you find something of interest in a list of highlights, turn to the index.

Maps Maps play a crucial role in Lonely Planet guidebooks and include a huge amount of information. A legend is printed on the back page. We seek to have complete consistency between maps and text, and to have every important place in the text captured on a map. Map key numbers usually start in the top left corner.

> Although inclusion in a guidebook usually implies a recommendation we cannot list every good place. Exclusion does not necessarily imply criticism. In fact there are a number of reasons why we might exclude a place – sometimes it is simply inappropriate to encourage an influx of travellers.

Introduction

The Ireland of today differs greatly from the country of a decade ago. Its huge economic renewal has transformed many aspects of modern Irish life.

Traditionally Ireland is well known for its lush green landscape and hugely varied scenery. From the unspoiled midlands with its lakes and mountains and many undiscovered treasures, to the magnificent cliffs of the wild Atlantic coast and its remote beaches, to the offshore islands inhabited for millennia, or the friendliness of the people, Ireland has much to offer. In spite of the huge recent social changes, many traces of traditional culture survive, especially in remote western areas, and there are still communities in which Irish is the first language.

Ireland's capital, Dublin, no longer the 'dirty old town' eulogised in The Pogues' anthem, has instead become one of Europe's most exciting and vibrant cities. Not only Dublin, but the whole country has woken up to a massive regeneration process. With almost half the population aged under 25 and one of the most highly educated young workforces in Europe, much of Ireland's new art and culture is reflected in this demographic.

Compared to other European countries Ireland's cities are relatively contained, so if you feel like getting away from the busy urban distractions, the calm of the countryside is never too far away, where the pace is yours to set. The glories of the past are easy to trace, from Stone Age passage tombs and ring forts, to ancient monasteries and castles, down to the great houses and splendid Georgian architecture of the 18th and 19th centuries.

Historically, Cromwell's merciless rampage of Ireland of 1649 and subsequent plantation of his supporters, and the horrific loss of over two million lives through death and emigration to a needless famine, has left an indelible mark on the nation's collective memory. But shaking off the shackles of its colonial past, Ireland is now truly emerging as a confident, credible and independent nation of the world.

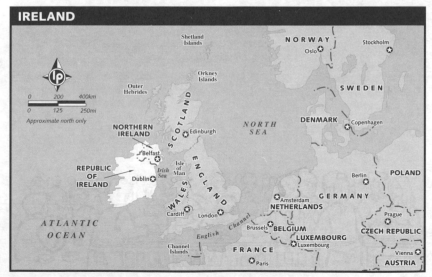

What's in a Name?

When the distinction between Ireland the island and Ireland the state needs to be made in this book, the state is referred to as the Republic of Ireland, the Republic or the South. You may also hear Ireland the state referred to as Eire, Southern Ireland or the Free State. In this book Northern Ireland is either referred to as such or as the North. You may also hear it dubbed the six counties or Ulster, though the latter is technically incorrect. The province of Ulster actually comprises nine counties, but at the time of partition in 1922 six of these (Derry, Antrim, Down, Armagh, Tyrone and Fermanagh) went into Northern Ireland and the other three (Cavan, Donegal and Monaghan) into the Republic.

After the Great Famine, Ireland's population only really began to grow in the 1960s, until the 1980s when high unemployment forced many of its talented young graduates abroad. The boom of the 'Celtic Tiger' stopped that exodus in its tracks and has enticed many to return. Another facet of this evolving nation is that Ireland's prosperity has also attracted, for the first time in its history, a wave of immigrants from Eastern Europe and Africa who have brought with them an energy and culture that add greatly to Ireland's own identity.

A new political era is dawning for Northern Ireland and it appears to be entering the last chapter of its turbulent history. A long-sought-after peace process has been gaining momentum since its inception and the 1998 Good Friday Agreement, and with it comes hope for a brighter future. The stability in the region has given a welcome boost to the North's business, industrial and arts communities. Northern Ireland's cities, towns and villages are remarkably friendly places and the countryside, especially along the Antrim coast, is some of Ireland's finest.

Above all, Ireland's reputation for being a sociable, friendly place remains. Its cities are lively with great pubs, a vibrant live-music scene, good theatres and – when it's not raining – cheerful street life. There's an incredible energy and excitement to be experienced in a country in a state of flux and this new, positive, forward-thinking, multicultural Ireland has never looked better.

Facts about Ireland

HISTORY
The First Settlers
Ireland was probably first settled by humans relatively late in European prehistory, about 10,000 years ago, at the end of the last Ice Age.

During the last Ice Age, there were land or ice bridges between Ireland and Britain, but conditions in Ireland would have been hostile to human migration until the glaciers receded. As the ice caps melted there was an enormous rise in the sea level and, about 9000 years ago, Ireland was cut off from Britain. Around this time the first humans had reached Ireland from Britain, possibly across the land bridge or in small hide-covered boats. These were Middle Stone Age (Mesolithic) hunter-gatherers. They lived in small family or tribal groups, collecting fruit and nuts and hunting any animals they could tackle.

Traces of these first Irish people are faint – just a few scattered middens (rubbish dumps) containing shells and the bones of small animals. Their weapons and tools included flint axes, which were used to hunt boar. The richest concentration of these early sites is in Northern Ireland, including one at Mountsandel Mt near Coleraine; they date from around 8000 to 6000 BC.

The First Farmers
While the first settlers were discovering Ireland, the greatest revolution in human history had already taken place in the fertile crescent of the Middle East. Yet it was another 2000 years before farming reached Ireland, around 4000 BC. Farming marked the arrival of New Stone Age (Neolithic) times.

A settlement from this era exists at Lough Gur near Grange in County Limerick. The traces of pottery, wooden houses and implements indicate a more prosperous, more settled way of life than before. At Céide Fields, near Ballycastle in northern Mayo, a remarkable complex of intact stone field walls dating from Neolithic times has been discovered hidden under a vast blanket of bog. Also around this time one of the first Irish exports was born. Tievebulliagh Mt near Cushendall in County Antrim has an outcrop of remarkably hard stone called porcellanite that formed the basis of a thriving stone-axe industry, examples of which have been found in the south of England.

These farmers had enormous respect for the dead and, from about 3000 BC, built the extraordinary passage graves found at Newgrange, Knowth and Dowth in the Boyne Valley. Over 1000 megalithic tombs survive from the Neolithic period.

The Bronze Age
Ireland's rich resources of gold and copper brought Bronze Age prospectors astute at finding sources of metal, and almost everywhere that modern geologists have discovered traces of copper and other metals, they have also discovered that someone was there about 4000 years previously, without the help of modern equipment and mapping.

Bronze Age mine workings can still be seen on Mt Gabriel near Schull in County Cork. St Kevin's Bed in Glendalough, County Wicklow, is thought by many to be an early mine.

Goldworking flourished during the Bronze Age and the quality of the craftwork and quantity of metal used say something about the wealth of Ireland at that time. The National Museum in Dublin contains the finest collection of prehistoric goldwork in Europe.

During the Bronze Age and the later Iron Age, the tentacles of trade spread out from Ireland. Torques and other jewellery were exported to the rest of mainland Europe. Blue faïence beads manufactured in Egypt were found in graves on the Hill of Tara in County Meath, as was amber from Scandinavia. The skeleton of a Barbary ape from Spain or Portugal was discovered in a site dating from 200 BC on Navan Fort in County Armagh.

The Celts

The Celts were Iron Age warrior tribes from Eastern Europe who conquered large sections of central and southern Europe between 800 and 300 BC. The Romans called them 'Galli' (Gauls) and the Greeks used the term 'Keltoi'. Both societies feared the Celts, who had a reputation for fierce brutality and were to plunder Rome in the 4th century AD.

Celtic warriors and adventurers probably reached Ireland around 300 BC, bringing the Iron Age with them, and were certainly well ensconced by 100 BC. They were a tall, fair-haired, imaginative race who put great store in spirituality and the supernatural and believed in an afterworld called Tír na nÓg (Land of Youth), the entrance to which they believed to be in the Oweynagat Cave in Tulsk, County Roscommon. They controlled the country for 1000 years and left a legacy of language and culture that survives today.

The Celts used a sophisticated code of law called the Brehon Law, which was in use until the early 17th century. Druids or priests, who also served as teachers and judges, were highly esteemed in society and their kings lived in *crannógs*, houses on sticks in lakes. Distinctive Celtic designs evident on artefacts of the time used swirls and loops to symbolise the permanence of life and immortality. Some good examples are the Broighter Collar in the National Museum in Dublin and the Turoe Stone near Loughrea in County Galway. The Irish language is Celtic in origin (see the Language section at the end of this chapter).

There are no written records for the early Celtic period but the florid oral tradition ensured their chieftains' heroic deeds and actions were passed on through (no doubt embellished) songs and stories for generations. The epic tales of Cúchulainn (pronounced coo-**hull**-in) and the Táin Bó Cúailnge (Cattle Raid of Cooley) are believed to have originated in this period. Cúchulainn is the consummate Celtic hero warrior. The Táin Bó Cúailnge may not be historically accurate but the stories give some idea of Irish society in the first two centuries AD. (For further details see the boxed texts 'Cúchulainn's Leap' in the County Clare chapter and 'The Táin Bó Cúailnge' in the Counties Meath & Louth chapter.)

Celtic Ireland was divided into five provinces: Leinster, Meath, Connaught, Ulster and Munster. Meath later merged with Leinster. The principal struggle for power, as reflected in the Táin Bó Cúailnge, was between Connaught and Ulster. Within the provinces there were perhaps 100 or more minor kings and chieftains controlling sections (known as Tuatha) of the country. Tara in County Meath became the base for some of the most powerful leaders and is still the site of many important legendary remains. Navan Fort in County Armagh, which was mentioned in the Táin Bó Cúailnge, is recorded on the map of Ireland as Isamnium, drawn in the 2nd century AD by the Egyptian scholar Ptolemy.

St Patrick & Christianity

Christianity arrived in Ireland between the 3rd and 5th centuries. Although St Patrick, Ireland's patron saint, is given the credit for proselytising the native Irish, there were certainly earlier missionaries. Some scholars dispute that there was a St Patrick at all and claim that the stories about him are really about these early clerics or are later inventions. However, evidence suggests that there was a St Patrick who lived in the 5th century and was kidnapped from Britain at the age of 16 by Irish pirates. During six years in Ireland as a slave tending sheep, Patrick found religion.

After escaping back to Britain, he was instructed by powerful visions to return to Ireland, where from 432 he spent his life converting the natives to Christianity. His base was the town of Armagh, probably chosen because of the symbolic pagan significance of nearby Navan Fort.

The westwards march of the Roman Empire halted in England. As the Empire declined and the Dark Ages engulfed much of the rest of Europe, Ireland in the 7th and 8th centuries became a 'land of saints and scholars', and attracted many scholars and kings from Britain and mainland Europe. Monasteries thrived and became hotbeds of creative activity where monks, oblivious to the plight of the rest of Europe, wrought beautiful objects in semiprecious metals, wrote in Latin and illuminated manuscripts, including the famous, intricately detailed Book of Kells (held in Trinity College, Dublin). Clonmacnoise in County Offaly and Glendalough in County Wicklow are outstanding examples of such monasteries.

The Vikings

By the end of the 8th century, Vikings had caught wind of the rumour that a handsome cache of booty was waiting to be plundered in Irish monasteries and duly set sail in their slim, powerful boats, arriving first at Lambay Island off Dublin in 795. Small, surprise attacks along the eastern coast were succeeded by strategic advances up rivers to inland terrain where they set up bases.

Although Irish weapons and soldiers proved no match for the superbly armed, ferocious Norsemen, it didn't deter the Irish themselves from joining in on the prosperous monastery raids, and intertribal squabbles often got in the way of establishing a unified Irish defence system. The monks, naturally keen to protect their wealth, built round-towers to act as lookout posts and places of refuge in the event of an attack.

During the 9th century the Vikings started to settle in Ireland and integrate. They founded Dubh Linn (Black Pool) or Dublin, which by the 10th century was a small Viking kingdom, and the towns of Wicklow, Waterford and Wexford.

The most decisive defeat for Viking ambitions was at the Battle of Clontarf in 1014, by Irish forces led by an elderly Brian Ború, king of Munster, who was killed in the process. Viking military power in Ireland had been broken but large numbers remained, marrying with the Irish and joining in the struggle against the next wave of invaders – the Normans.

The Norman Conquest

In 1066 the Normans, under William the Conqueror, invaded and conquered England. Former Vikings from France, they then turned their attention to neighbouring Ireland, ironically responding to an invitation from an Irish chief.

This came about because the king of Leinster, Dermot MacMurrough, and the king of Connaught, Tiernan O'Rourke, were arch rivals. Their relationship wasn't improved by MacMurrough's kidnapping of O'Rourke's wife in 1152 (although it seems she went willingly). O'Rourke defeated MacMurrough, who fled abroad in 1166 to search for foreign allies. Henry II of England, one of William's descendants, suggested MacMurrough seek help in Wales among his subjects.

There MacMurrough met Richard Fitz-Gilbert de Clare, better known as Strongbow, who agreed to muster an army to send to Ireland in return for the hand of Mac-Murrough's daughter in marriage and the inheritance of the kingship of Leinster on MacMurrough's death. MacMurrough accepted, and the stage was set for more than 800 years of English involvement in Ireland.

In May 1169, the first Anglo-Norman forces met MacMurrough in Bannow Bay, County Wexford, and took Wexford town and Dublin with ease. The following year Strongbow himself came and, after a bloody battle, took Waterford and a new bride, MacMurrough's daughter Aoife. Within twelve months MacMurrough had died and Strongbow claimed the final part of the bargain, his title as king of Leinster.

Meanwhile, Henry II was watching events in Ireland with growing unease. In 1154 he had been recognised by the pope as lord of Ireland so technically Strongbow was one of his subjects, but Strongbow's independence of mind and action worried him. In 1171 Henry II sailed from England with a huge naval force, landed at Waterford and declared the place a royal city. He took a semblance of control, but the new Norman lords still did pretty much as they pleased.

Just as the Vikings first settled and were then absorbed, so were the new Anglo-Norman intruders. Barons such as de Courcy and de Lacy set up independent power bases and, over the next 200 years, integration between the Anglo-Normans and native Irish was so successful that in 1366 the English Crown introduced the Statutes of Kilkenny, making intermarriage and the use of Irish language and customs illegal. It was too late: assimilation had gone too far. Over the following centuries English control gradually retreated to an area around Dublin known as 'the Pale'. Hence the expression 'beyond the pale' for an area beyond control.

Henry VIII

In the 16th century Henry VIII, wary of an invasion from the French or Spanish through Ireland, moved to reinforce English authority. However the defiant and worryingly influential Anglo-Norman Fitzgeralds, earls of Kildare, posed a serious threat to his supremacy. They had to be destroyed.

In 1534 Silken Thomas, son of the reigning earl, stormed Dublin and its English garrisons on the false pretext that his father had been executed by Henry in England. With greater aggression, Henry used this as an opportune moment to advance and quash the troublesome Kildares once and for all. The rebellion was a wash out and Thomas and his followers were subsequently executed in what became known as the 'pardon of Maynooth'. This pattern of retribution was to become familiar in the following centuries. In 1535, the Fitzgerald estates were divided among English settlers and an English viceroy was appointed.

Now with the Kildares' downfall in the bag, Henry was able to launch an assault on the affluent property of the Catholic Church, who he had fallen out with over his divorce from Catherine of Aragon. Over the next few years, Henry pillaged and plundered the Irish monasteries. In 1541 Henry ensured that the Irish Parliament declared him king of Ireland.

Elizabeth I

Under Elizabeth I, the English consolidated their power in Ireland. Strategically, Ireland was important as a possible back door for an invasion from England's enemies in mainland Europe.

English jurisdiction was established in Connaught and Munster despite a number of rebellions by the local ruling families. The thorn in Elizabeth's side was Ulster, the last outpost of the Irish chiefs. Hugh O'Neill, earl of Tyrone, was the prime mover in the last serious assault on English power in Ireland for centuries. O'Neill had been educated in London, and Elizabeth believed that he would be loyal. A story is told of O'Neill's ordering lead from England to reroof his castle; in reality the lead was for bullets. From 1594, O'Neill moved into open conflict with the English and thus began the Nine Years' War (1594–1603). He proved a courageous and crafty foe, and the English forces met with little success against him until 1601.

In September of that year, a Spanish force landed in Kinsale, County Cork, to join O'Neill. O'Neill was forced to march south to join them and, after an exhausting journey, ended up fighting just outside Kinsale in unfamiliar territory. The Irish were defeated by the English forces under Lord Mountjoy while the Spanish army was pinned down in Kinsale.

The Battle of Kinsale was the end for O'Neill and for Ulster, and signalled the demise of the old Gaelic way of life. Although O'Neill and his forces made it home, their power was broken, and 15 months later O'Neill signed the Treaty of Mellifont, surrendering to the English Crown. However, in 1607, after a number of frustrating years of subjugation and harassment, O'Neill and 90 other Ulster chiefs boarded a ship in Lough Swilly for Europe, leaving Ireland forever. This was known as the Flight of the Earls, and it left Ulster leaderless and open to English rule.

With the native chiefs gone, Elizabeth and her successor, James I, pursued a policy of colonisation known as the Plantation – an organised, ambitious confiscation of land that sowed the seeds for the division of Ulster that still exists. Huge swathes of land were taken from the Irish and given to English gentlemen 'undertakers' – among them Sir Walter Raleigh – who carved up the land and gave it to Scottish and English settlers. These new

Protestant landowners remained apart from the impoverished, angry population of native Irish and Anglo-Norman Catholics.

Oliver Cromwell

Ongoing plantations and fear of persecution from the Puritans in England fuelled Catholic insecurity and bitter anti-British feeling. The stage was set for a showdown and in 1641 a bloody rebellion ensued, with Irish and Anglo-Norman Catholics joining forces against the newly arrived Protestant settlers. Many lives were lost on both sides during the 10-year battle.

The English Civil War kept most of the English busy at home for much of the 1640s. In Ireland, the native Irish and Anglo-Norman Catholics, allied under the 1641 Confederation of Kilkenny, supported Charles I against the Protestant parliamentarians in the hope of restoring Catholic power in Ireland. After Charles' defeat and execution, the victorious Oliver Cromwell, leader of the parliamentarians, decided to go to Ireland and sort it out.

He arrived in 1649 and, after a ruthless massacre in Drogheda, rampaged through the country leaving a fearsome trail of death behind him. Word of his barbaric conduct spread quickly and many towns gave up without a fight when his army approached.

Under the 1652 Act of Settlement others were dispossessed and exiled, on pain of death, to the harsh, infertile lands of Connaught. Two million hectares of land were confiscated – more than a quarter of the country – and handed over to Cromwell's supporters.

The Battle of the Boyne

The 1660 Restoration saw Charles II, who kept his Catholic sympathies in check, on the English throne. In 1685 his brother James succeeded him. James II's more open Catholicism raised English ire. He was forced to flee the country for France at the beginning of 1689, intending to raise an army in Ireland and regain his throne from the Protestant William of Orange, who had been invited to sit on the English throne by Parliament.

In late 1688, with rumours spreading among Irish Protestants that Irish Catholics were about to rise in support of James II, the Protestant citizens of Derry heard that a Catholic regiment was to be stationed in their city. After furious debate among the local worthies, 13 apprentice boys purloined the keys to the city and slammed the gates in the face of James' soldiers.

In March 1689 James II himself arrived at Kinsale and marched north to Dublin, where the Irish Parliament recognised him as king and began to organise the return of expropriated land to Catholic landowners. The siege of Derry by James' forces began in earnest in April and ended, after mass starvation, with the arrival of William's ships in July. The Protestant slogan 'No Surrender!' dates from the siege, which acquired mythical status among Irish Protestants over the following centuries.

William of Orange landed in 1690 at Carrickfergus, just north of Belfast, with an army of up to 36,000 men. The Battle of the Boyne took place on 12 July. It was fought between Irish Catholics (led by James II, a Scot) and English Protestants (led by William of Orange, a Dutchman).

William's victory was a turning point and is commemorated to this day by Northern Protestants as a pivotal victory over 'popes and popery'. The final surrender came in 1691 when the Catholic leader Patrick Sarsfield signed the Treaty of Limerick. He and thousands of his troops went into exile in France.

Penal Times

The 1691 Treaty of Limerick contained quite generous terms of surrender for the Catholics but, as it turned out, wasn't worth the vellum it was written on. It was replaced by a harsh regime of penal laws in 1695. These scurrilously oppressive laws were passed by a Protestant gentry anxious to consolidate its powers and worried that Louis XIV of France might attempt an invasion of Ireland. Also known as a 'popery code', these laws set about disempowering Catholics who were now forbidden from buying land or stock worth over five pounds, bringing up children in their own religion or educating themselves and from entering any profession. All Irish culture, music and education were banned in the hope that Catholicism would be quashed. Lesser restrictions were imposed on Presbyterians and other nonconformists.

In response, Catholics organised open-air Masses at secret locations usually marked by a 'mass rock'. Illegal outdoor schools known as 'hedge schools' continued to teach the Irish language. Among the educated classes, many Catholics converted to Protestantism to preserve their careers and wealth.

From around 1715, strict enforcement of the religious sections of the penal laws eased off, although many of the restrictions to do with employment and public office remained. A significant majority of the Catholic population were now tenants living in wretched conditions. By the mid-18th century, Catholics held less than 15% of the land in Ireland, and by 1778 barely 5%.

The 18th Century

Meanwhile, Dublin thrived, ranking as Europe's fifth-largest city. The Irish ruling class were members of the established Protestant Episcopalian Church and were descendants of Cromwellian soldiers, Norman nobles and Elizabethan settlers. They formed a new, prosperous upper class known as the Protestant Ascendancy. There was a Protestant-only parliament, but laws still had to be approved by the British Crown and Parliament. It was from these Protestants that pressure first came for Ireland to be treated on an equal footing with Britain.

A strong Patriot Party calling for independence developed under the leadership of Henry Grattan (1746–1820) and Henry Flood (1732–91). When the American War of Independence broke out in 1776, Britain was in a difficult position. The majority of her forces were withdrawn from Ireland to fight in the colonies, leaving security in Ireland largely in the hands of Protestant 'volunteer' forces under the control of the landowners and merchant classes. To avoid further clashes with the increasingly inde-

pendent Irish Parliament, the British government in 1782 allowed the Irish what it considered complete freedom of legislation. The new Irish governing body was known as Grattan's Parliament. However, London still controlled much of what went on in Ireland through royal patronage and favours, and the Crown still had the power of veto.

To achieve prosperity in Ireland, Grattan had espoused improved conditions and rights for Catholics. Henry Flood and the majority of other Protestant members were not as sympathetic, and in the life of the Parliament – nearly 20 years – little progress was made.

The French Revolution

With the American War of Independence and – more shocking to Britain – the French Revolution of 1789, the ruling classes could no longer be complacent about the poverty-stricken masses.

In Ireland, an organisation known as the United Irishmen had been formed by Belfast Presbyterians; its most prominent leader was a young Dublin Protestant and republican, Theobald Wolfe Tone (1763–98). The United Irishmen started out with high ideals of bringing together men of all creeds to reform and reduce Britain's power in Ireland, but their attempts to gain power through straightforward politics proved fruitless.

MATT KING

Theobald Wolfe Tone (1763–98) led a failed French invasion of Ireland.

When war broke out between Britain and France, the United Irishmen found they were no longer tolerated by the establishment. They re-formed themselves as an underground organisation committed to bringing change by any means, violent or otherwise. Tone was keen to enlist the help of the French, who, fresh from their European victories, were easily persuaded.

At the same time, loyalist Protestants were worried by the turn of events and prepared for possible conflict by forming the Protestant Orange Society, which later became known as the Orange Order.

In 1796 a French invasion fleet, with thousands of troops and Wolf Tone aboard, approached Bantry Bay in County Cork. On shore, the local militia were ill equipped to repel them. However, a strong offshore wind frustrated attempts to land and the French were forced to return home with a disappointed Wolfe Tone in tow.

The government in Ireland began an effective nationwide campaign to hunt out United Irishmen. Floggings and indiscriminate torture sent a wave of panic through the population and sparked off the 1798 Rising. Wexford, a county not noted for its rebellious tendencies, saw the fiercest fighting, with Father John Murphy leading the resistance. After a number of minor victories the rebels were finally and decisively defeated at Vinegar Hill just outside Enniscorthy.

After another failed French invasion, a persistent Wolfe Tone himself arrived later in 1798 with a French fleet, but was defeated at sea. Wolfe Tone was captured and taken to Dublin where he committed suicide in his prison cell. It was the end for the United Irishmen and also, ironically, precipitated the demise of the independent Irish Parliament.

The Protestant gentry, alarmed at the level of unrest, was much inclined to accept the security of British authority. In 1800 the Act of Union, uniting Ireland politically with Britain, was passed, taking effect from 1 January 1801. Many wealthier Irish Catholics supported the Act, especially after the British prime minister, William Pitt, promised to remove the last of the penal laws, most of which had been repealed by 1793. The Irish Parliament voted itself out of existence and around 100 of the Members of Parliament (MPs) moved to the House of Commons in London.

As if to remind England of the rebellious nature of Ireland, a tiny and completely ineffectual rebellion was staged in Dublin in 1803, led by a former United Irishman, Robert Emmet (1778–1803). Fewer than 100 men took part and Emmet was caught, tried and executed. He gave a famous speech from the dock, which included the oft-quoted words: 'Let no man write my epitaph... When my country takes her place among the nations of the earth, then and not till then let my epitaph be written.'

The Great Liberator

In the meantime, a 28-year-old Catholic man from Kerry called Daniel O'Connell (1775–1847) was set on a course that would make him one of Ireland's greatest leaders.

In 1823 O'Connell founded the Catholic Association with the aim of achieving political equality for Catholics. The association soon became a vehicle for peaceful mass protest and action. In the 1826 general election it first showed its muscle by backing Protestant candidates who were in favour of Catholic emancipation.

In 1828 O'Connell himself stood for a seat in County Clare, even though, being a Catholic, he couldn't take the seat (the remaining penal laws had not been repealed, despite William Pitt's promise). O'Connell won easily, putting the British Parliament in a quandary. If they didn't allow O'Connell to take his seat, there might be a popular uprising. Many in the House of Commons favoured emancipation, and the combination of circumstances led them to pass the 1829 Act of Catholic Emancipation, allowing some well-off Catholics voting rights and the right to be elected as MPs.

After this great victory, O'Connell sought to secure further reforms. Ten years later he turned his attentions to the repeal of the Act of Union and the re-establishment of an Irish Parliament. Now that Catholics could become MPs, such a body would be very different from the old Protestant-dominated Irish Parliaments.

In 1843 the campaign took off, with O'Connell's 'monster meetings' attracting up to half a million supporters and taking place all over Ireland. O'Connell exploited the threat that such gatherings represented to the establishment, but he balked at a genuinely radical confrontation with the British. His bluff was called when a monster meeting at Clontarf was prohibited and he called it off.

O'Connell was arrested in 1844 and served a short spell in prison. After that, he quarrelled with the Young Ireland movement (which, having seen pacifism fail, favoured the use of violence) and never again posed a threat to the British. He died in 1847, while his country was being devoured by famine.

The Great Famine

One of Ireland's worst tragedies, the Great Famine of 1845–51, during which a staggering two million people died or were forced to emigrate, is all the more inconceivable given that the scale of suffering was attributable to human misdemeanour as much as natural causes. Potatoes were the staple food of a rapidly growing but desperately poor population and when a blight hit the crop, prices soared. The repressive penal laws ensured that farmers, already crippled with high rents, could ill afford the little subsistence potato provided. Inevitably, most tenants fell into arrears with little or no concession given by mostly indifferent landlords and were evicted or sent to the dire conditions of the workhouses.

Shamefully, during this time there were abundant harvests of wheat and dairy produce – the country was producing more than enough grain to feed the entire population and it's said that more cattle were sold abroad than there were people on the island. But while millions of its citizens were starving, Ireland was forced to export its food to Britain and overseas.

The Poor Laws in place at the height of the Famine deemed landlords responsible for the maintenance of their poor and encouraged many to 'remove' tenants from their estates by paying their way to America – many were sent unwittingly to their deaths on board the notoriously scourged 'coffin ships'. British Prime Minister Sir Robert Peel made well intentioned but largely inadequate gestures at famine relief, and it has to be said that some landlords did their best for their tenants. But many others ignored the situation from their homes in Britain, in line with the predominant *laissez-faire* economic theory of the time, which held that it was not the government's or, for that matter, the landowner's job to provide aid. The Quaker movement in Ireland provided crucial aid by establishing soup kitchens and employment funds.

Mass emigration continued to reduce the population during the next 100 years and huge numbers of Irish emigrants who found their way abroad, particularly to the USA, carried with them a lasting bitterness.

Parnell & the Land League

In spite of the bitterness aroused by the Famine, there was little challenge to Britain's control of Ireland for quite some time. One rebellion was the abortive Fenian (Irish Republican Brotherhood) rising in March 1867.

In 1875 Charles Stewart Parnell (1846–91) was elected to Westminster. The son of a Protestant landowner from County Wicklow, he had much in common with other members of the Anglo-Irish Ascendancy. But there were differences. Parnell's mother was American and her father had fought the British in the American War of Independence. Parnell's family supported the principle of Irish independence from Britain. He quickly became noticed in the House of Commons as a passionate, difficult member who asked awkward questions. At 31 he became leader of the new Home Rule Party, which advocated a limited form of autonomy for Ireland.

In 1879 Ireland appeared to be facing another famine as potato crops were failing once again and evictions were becoming widespread. Cheap corn from America had pushed down grain prices and with that the earnings of the tenants who grew grain on their plots. Michael Davitt, a Fenian, began to organise the tenants and early on found a sympathetic ear in the unlikely person of Parnell. This odd pair were the brains behind the Land League, which initiated widespread agitation for reduced rents and improved working conditions. The conflict heated up and there was violence on both sides. Parnell instigated the strategy of 'boycotting' tenants, agents and landlords who didn't adhere to the Land League's aims: they were treated like lepers by the local population.

The Land War, as it became known, lasted from 1879 to 1882 and was a momentous period. For the first time, tenants were defying their landlords en masse. William Gladstone's second term in power brought the Land Act of 1881, which improved life immeasurably for tenants, creating fair rents and the possibility of tenants owning their land.

A crisis threatened in 1882 when two of the Crown's leading figures in Ireland were murdered by nationalists in Phoenix Park, Dublin, and Parnell was tenuously and wrongly implicated. However, reform had been achieved, and Parnell turned his attentions to Home Rule. He had an extraordinary ally in William Gladstone, who was dependent on Parnell for crucial support in Parliament. But Gladstone and Parnell had their Home Rule Bill defeated, partly as a result of defections from Gladstone's own party.

The end was drawing near for Parnell. For 10 years he had been having an affair with Kitty O'Shea, who was married to a member of his own party. When the relationship was exposed in 1890, Parnell refused to resign as party leader and the party split. Parnell married O'Shea, was deposed as leader and the Catholic Church in Ireland quickly turned against him. The 'uncrowned king of Ireland' was no longer welcome. Parnell's health deteriorated rapidly and he died less than a year later, aged just 45.

Home Rule Beckons

Gladstone was elected as prime minister for a fourth term in 1892 and this time managed to get his Home Rule for Ireland Bill through the House of Commons, but it was thrown out by the House of Lords.

By now, eastern Ulster was quite prosperous. It had been spared the worst effects of the Famine, and heavy industrialisation meant the Protestant ruling class was doing nicely. While Gladstone had failed for the time being, the Ulster Unionists (the Unionist Party had been formed in 1885) were now acutely aware that Home Rule could resurface and were determined to fight if it became law. The unionists, led by Sir Edward Carson (1854–1935), a Dublin lawyer, formed a Protestant vigilante brigade called the Ulster Volunteer Force (UVF), which held a series of mass paramilitary rallies mustering strong opposition to Home Rule. Carson threatened an armed struggle for a separate Northern Ireland if independence was granted to Ireland. The British began to bend before this Ulster opposition and, in July 1914, Carson agreed that Home Rule could go through for Ireland, so long as Ulster was kept separate and thus Ireland's partition was established.

In Britain a new Liberal government under Prime Minister Asquith had removed the House of Lords' power to veto bills and began to put another Home Rule for Ireland Bill through Parliament – the political price being demanded by Irish Home Rule MPs for their support. The bill was passed (but not enacted) in 1912 against strident unionist and Conservative British opposition, which mounted in ferocity.

As the UVF grew in strength, a republican group called the Irish Volunteers, led by the academic Eoin MacNeill, was set up in the south to defend Home Rule for the whole of Ireland. They lacked the weapons and organisation of the UVF, however, which succeeded in large-scale gunrunning, and in 1914, with widespread support from the British army, civil war loomed ahead.

However, the Home Rule Act was suspended at the outbreak of WWI in August 1914 and the question of Ulster was left unresolved. Many Irish nationalists believed that Home Rule would come after the war and that by supporting the British war effort they could influence British opinion in their favour. John Redmond, the leader of the

Irish Home Rule Party, actively encouraged people to join the British forces to fight Germany.

The Gaelic Revival

While these attempts at Home Rule were being shunted about, something of a revolution was taking place in Irish arts, literature and identity.

The Anglo-Irish literary revival was one aspect of this, championed by the young William Butler Yeats. The poet had a coterie of literary friends such as Lady Gregory, Douglas Hyde, John Millington Synge and George Russell. They unearthed many Celtic tales and wrote with fresh enthusiasm about a romantic Ireland of epic battles and warrior queens. For a country that had suffered centuries of invasion and deprivation, these images presented a much more attractive version of history.

At the same time, people such as Douglas Hyde and Eoin MacNeill were doing their best to ensure the survival of the Irish language and the more everyday Irish customs and culture, which they believed to be central to Irish identity. They formed the Gaelic League (Conradh na Gaeilge) in 1893, which, among other things, pushed for the teaching of Irish in schools. In the 1890s the Gaelic League was primarily a cultural outfit and assumed a nationalistic aura only later.

Another strongly politicised organisation is the Gaelic Athletic Association (GAA), initially founded in 1884 to promote Irish sport and culture.

A small pressure group called Sinn Féin (literally 'we ourselves'; pronounced shin fain) was set up under the leadership of Arthur Griffith, founder of the *United Irishmen* newspaper. He proposed a stance of passive resistance whereby all Irish MPs should abandon the House of Commons in London and set up a Parliament in Dublin.

Socialism attracted support in Dublin among the hungry tenement dwellers, who endured some of the worst urban housing conditions in Europe. In 1913 Jim Larkin and James Connolly called the transport workers out on strike. Although the strike

JANE SMITH

Jim Larkin – founder of the Irish Citizens' Army

ended in a return to work, the employers failed to break the union and Larkin and Connolly had created the Irish Citizens' Army for self-defence. It now joined forces with the newly formed Irish Volunteers.

It must be said, however, that prior to 1916, the majority of Dubliners were probably more concerned with WWI: while some might have believed that independence from Britain was a good idea, their passions went no further.

The Easter Rising

Many Irishmen with nationalist sympathies went off to the battlefields of Europe believing their sacrifice would ensure that Britain stood by its promise of Home Rule for Ireland. However, a minority of nationalists in Ireland was not so trusting of British resolve. The Irish Volunteers split into two groups: those under John Redmond who adopted a wait-and-see approach, and a radical group that believed in a more revolutionary course of action.

Two small groups – a section of the Irish Volunteers under Pádraig Pearse and the Irish Citizens' Army led by James Connolly – staged a rebellion that took the country by surprise. Expecting British forces to be depleted with the onset of the war, the insurrection was also set to coincide with the arrival of a shipment of arms from Germany. But their plans were scuppered. The arms were intercepted by the British navy and Eoin MacNeill (the leader of the Irish Volunteers), annoyed that the rising had been planned without his knowledge attempted to call the whole thing off, resulting in very few turning up on the day. On Easter Monday 1916, the Volunteer group marched into Dublin and took over a number of key positions in the city, with the General Post Office on O'Connell St as headquarters. From its steps Pearse read out to nonplussed passers-by a declaration that Ireland was now a republic and that his band was the provisional government. Less than a week of fighting ensued before the rebels surrendered to the superior British forces. The rebels weren't popular and had to be protected from angry Dubliners as they were marched to jail.

So what might have been a real threat to British authority fizzled out completely. Many have said that Pearse, one of the main instigators, knew they didn't stand a chance but was preoccupied with a blood sacrifice, a noble gesture by a few brave souls that would galvanise the nation. Whether he believed this or not, a blood sacrifice was on the way.

The Easter Rising would probably have had little impact on the Irish situation had the British not unwittingly made martyrs of the leaders of the rebellion. Of the 77 given death sentences, 15 were executed. Pearse was shot three days after the surrender, and nine days later James Connolly was the last to die, shot in a chair because he couldn't stand on a gangrenous ankle. The deaths provoked a sea change in public attitudes to the republicans, for whom support henceforth climbed.

Countess Markievicz (see the boxed text) was one of those not executed, because she was female, and Eamon de Valera's (1882–1975) death sentence was commuted

Countess Markievicz

Born Constance Georgina Gore-Booth to a wealthy family in Lissadell, County Sligo, in 1868, the 'Red Countess' (as she later became known) played a pivotal role in the 1916 Easter Rising. Having her subsequent death sentence commuted to life, she went on to become the first woman elected to British Parliament – a seat she refused to take – and later the first female government minister in any modern democracy.

As a child Constance, displaying an early solidarity with the underdog, helped the peasants on her estate with their manual chores. At 19, the strident young woman was presented at court to Queen Victoria as 'the new Irish beauty' and entered society as a member of the Anglo-Irish landed gentry. Tired of the normal social whirlwind of hunts and balls and with aspirations to be a painter, Constance left Ireland to study at the Slade School and later to Julien's in Paris where she met and married Count Casimir Markievicz, a Polish Catholic landowner. They returned to Lissadell for the birth of her daughter.

By 1908 Constance was fully immersed in the Dublin theatrical scene – a vehicle for nationalist feeling – and inadvertently came across an article containing Robert Emmett's emotive speech from the dock. Constance was instantly propelled towards an all-consuming anti-British devotion. Keen to get to work immediately, she joined Inghinidhe na hÉireann (Daughters of Erin) and was soon on Arthur Griffith's council for Sinn Féin where she established the Fianna, a nationalist boy scout movement and military training ground for later Volunteers. As her military activities became more involved, her marriage deteriorated and, by the 1916 Rising, her husband had left a fully fledged republican activist in his wake. She was sentenced to death after the Rising but had it commuted to life imprisonment, and on her release a year later, she returned to Ireland unbroken, a Catholic and a national hero. Refusing her British Parliament seat two years later from the confines of Holloway prison, she opted instead for a seat as Minister for Labour of the newly formed Dáil Éireann under Eamon de Valera. Her continued fighting in the civil war, a spell in a workhouse and a hunger strike all contributed to her deteriorating health, and the maverick countess died in a slum hospital among Dublin's poor in 1927.

to life imprisonment because of his US citizenship; he was freed after an amnesty in 1917.

In the 1918 general election, the republicans stood under the banner of Sinn Féin and won a large majority of the Irish seats. Ignoring London's Parliament, where technically they were supposed to sit, the newly elected Sinn Féin deputies – many of them veterans of the 1916 Easter Rising – declared Ireland independent and formed the first Dáil Éireann (Irish assembly or lower house), which sat in Dublin's Mansion House under the leadership of Eamon de Valera. The Irish Volunteers became the Irish Republican Army (IRA) and the Dáil authorised them to wage war on British troops in Ireland: a lot more blood was about to be shed.

The Anglo-Irish War

The day the Dáil convened in Dublin in January 1919, two policemen were shot dead in County Tipperary. This was the beginning of the bitter Anglo-Irish War, which lasted from 1919 to mid-1921. This was the period when Michael Collins (1890–1922) came to the fore, a charismatic, ruthless leader who masterminded the campaign of violence against the British while at the same time serving as minister for finance in the new Dáil.

The war quickly became entrenched and bloody. On the Irish side was the IRA and on the other a coalition of the Royal Irish Constabulary, regular British army soldiers and two groups of quasi-military status who rapidly gained a vicious reputation – the Auxiliaries and the notoriously brutal Black and Tans, who were newly demobbed British soldiers. Their use of violence and corruption compounded resentment against the British and bolstered fervent support for the nationalist cause. The death from hunger strike of Terence MacSwiney, mayor of Cork, further crystallised Irish opinion. The IRA created 'flying columns', small groups of armed volunteers to ambush British forces, and on home ground they operated successfully. A truce was eventually agreed in July 1921.

After months of difficult negotiations in London, the Irish delegation signed the Anglo-Irish Treaty on 6 December 1921. It gave 26 counties of Ireland independence and allowed six largely Protestant Ulster counties the choice of opting out. If they did (a foregone conclusion), a Boundary Commission would decide on the final frontiers between north and south.

The Outbreak of Civil War

The Treaty negotiations had been largely undertaken on the Irish side by Michael Collins and Arthur Griffith. Both knew that many Dáil members wouldn't accept the loss of the north, or the fact that the British monarch would still be head of the new Irish Free State and Irish MPs would still have to swear an oath of allegiance to the Crown. Under pressure from Britain's Lloyd George and after a spell of exhausting negotiations, they signed the Treaty without checking with de Valera in Dublin.

Collins regarded the issue of the monarchy and the oath of allegiance as largely symbolic. He also hoped that the six northeastern counties wouldn't be a viable entity and would eventually become part of the Free State. During the Treaty negotiations he had been encouraged to think that the Border Commission would decrease the size of that part of Ireland remaining outside the Free State. He hoped that he could convince the rest of his comrades, but he knew the risks and declared: 'I may have signed my death warrant tonight.'

In the end Collins couldn't persuade his colleagues to accept the Treaty. De Valera was furious and it wasn't long before a bitter civil war broke out between comrades who, a year previously, had fought alongside each other. Michael Collins was shot in an ambush in County Cork and Arthur Griffith died from exhaustion and anxiety.

Ireland since Partition

For the history of Ireland since partition, see the introductory chapters to the Republic of Ireland and Northern Ireland sections.

GEOGRAPHY & GEOLOGY

Ireland is an island lying off the northwestern edge of the Eurasian landmass, separated from Britain by the Irish Sea and the

COUNTIES & PROVINCES

St George's and North channels (less than 18km at one point). The island's area is 84,421 sq km: 14,139 sq km in the North and 70,282 sq km in the South. It stretches 486km north to south and 275km east to west. The convoluted coastline extends for over 3100km.

Political Geography

Ireland is divided into 32 counties. The Republic of Ireland consists of 26 counties, and Northern Ireland of six. The northernmost point in the Republic (Malin Head in Donegal) is actually farther north than anywhere

in Northern Ireland. To confuse things further, the island has traditionally been divided into four provinces: Leinster, Ulster, Connaught and Munster. The six counties of Northern Ireland are often loosely referred to as Ulster, but three of the Republic's counties – Donegal, Cavan and Monaghan – were also in the old province of Ulster.

Landscape

It can be as little as 50km from the heart of one of Ireland's major cities to an isolated sweep of mountains and bogland. Most of the higher ground is close to the coast, while the central regions are largely flat. Almost the entire western seaboard from Cork to Donegal is a continuous bulwark of cliffs, hills and mountains with few safe anchorages. The only significant breaches in the chain are the Shannon Estuary and Galway Bay.

The western mountain ranges aren't particularly high but they're often beautiful. The highest mountains are in the south-west; the tallest mountain in Ireland is Carrantuohil (1041m) in Kerry's MacGillycuddy's Reeks.

The Shannon is the longest river in Ireland. It runs for 370km from its source in Cavan's Cuilcagh Mountains down through the midlands before emptying into the wide Shannon Estuary west of Limerick town. Lough Neagh in Northern Ireland is the island's largest lake, covering 396 sq km.

The midlands of Ireland lie above Carboniferous limestone deposited between 300 and 400 million years ago. On the surface, the flat landscape is mostly rich farmland or raised bogs, huge swathes of brown peat rapidly disappearing under the machines of the Bord na Móna (Irish Turf Board).

As you travel west from the midlands, the soil becomes poorer, the fields smaller and stone walls more numerous. The Cromwellian cry 'To hell or to Connaught' wasn't without foundation, as the land west of the Shannon can't compare with fertile counties such as Meath and Tipperary.

Before the Famine, the pressure on land was enormous; eight million people had to be fed and so they farmed in the most inaccessible places. Up the hillsides above today's fields, you may see the faint regular lines of pre-Famine potato ridges called 'lazy beds'.

Ice Age The last Ice Age, from 100,000 to just over 10,000 years ago, had a huge impact on the Irish landscape. Characteristic U-shaped valleys were carved out by glaciers, as were the small deep-set corrie lakes high on the mountainsides. The receding ice left behind many shallow lakes, mainly in the centre of Ireland. Most of the baked sedimentary rocks covering the Wicklow

Mountains were stripped away, exposing the underlying granite. In County Clare, limestone appeared when a layer of waterproof shale and sandstone was removed.

Many of Ireland's mountains and hills have a round, smooth profile, formed by the abrasive effect of moving ice. The ice also deposited soil in its wake, leaving a layer of boulder clay on many parts of the country. There is a large belt of drumlins (small round hills of boulder clay) across the country from County Cavan to Clew Bay in County Mayo.

CLIMATE

Ireland is farther north than either Newfoundland or Vancouver yet the country's climate is relatively mild for its latitude, with a mean annual temperature of around 10°C, because of the moderating effect of the Atlantic Gulf Stream. The temperature drops below freezing only intermittently during winter, and snow is scarce – perhaps one or two brief flurries a year. The coldest months are January and February, when daily temperatures range from 4° to 8°C, with 7°C the average. In summer, temperatures during the day are a comfortable 15° to 20°C. During the warmest months, July and August, the average is 16°C. A hot summer's day in Ireland is 22° to 24°C, although it can sometimes reach 30°C. There are about 18 hours of daylight daily during July and August and it's only truly dark after about 11pm.

One thing you can be sure of about Irish weather is how little you can be sure of. It may be shirtsleeves and sunglasses in February but winter woollies in March and even during the summer.

And then there's the rain. Ireland receives a lot of rain – about 1000mm each year, ranging from 750mm in the midlands to over 1300mm in the south-west. Certain areas get rain on as many as 270 days of the year. The prevailing winds over Ireland come from the south-west, bringing rain-bearing clouds from the Atlantic that dump their loads as soon as they meet high ground. The mountains of south-west Kerry are the wettest part of the country. The south-east is the driest area, enjoying something like a more southern continental cli-

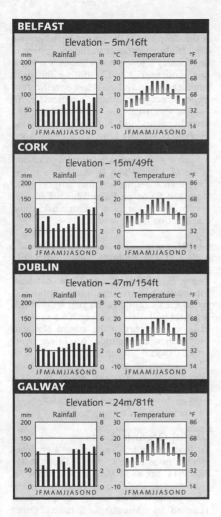

BELFAST

Elevation – 5m/16ft

CORK

Elevation – 15m/49ft

DUBLIN

Elevation – 47m/154ft

GALWAY

Elevation – 24m/81ft

mate. If you find the rain getting you down you might find some comfort in the Irish saying: 'It doesn't rain in the pub!'

ECOLOGY & ENVIRONMENT
Forests

At one time Ireland was largely covered by forests. Then, about 6000 years ago, the first farmers cleared small areas for their crops, the beginning of a long process of deforestation. Substantial tracts of natural oak wood survived until the mid-16th century, but the following 200 years saw the country stripped of its oak for ship timbers, charcoal, tanning and barrels, and by the mid-18th century almost all the country's timber was being imported.

In the 20th century, pine plantations were born out of the need for local timber and the desire to do something with what many people considered to be wasteland. There are now state subsidies for plantations, although the most widely used species – sitka spruce and lodgepole pine – are so fast growing and soft as to be unsuitable for high-quality wood products.

Today forests cover about 5.5% of the country and the percentage is slowly increasing, although much of the wood grown is for commercial purposes. Recognition of the need for native forest is found in places such as Glencree in County Wicklow, where there's a project to reforest part of the area with oak trees.

Agriculture

In the past, Ireland experienced limited industrialisation compared to other developed countries, leaving the beautiful Irish countryside mostly untouched. However, in the 1970s, the European Union (EU) encouraged intensive, specialised farming and the use of pesticides and chemical fertilisers. These caused serious pollution and land degradation in areas such as the Burren in County Clare. More recently, the EU and the Irish government have promoted environmental protection, less-intensive farming methods and the adoption of alternative practices or crops. The result has been a reduction in pollution, though it continues to occur in rivers and lakes.

In the same period the trend towards larger farms led to the destruction of many ring forts and stone walls.

Water Quality

A 1999 report by the Environmental Protection Agency graded most of Ireland's water supply as satisfactory. Nevertheless, much drinking water in remote rural areas, it said, was unfit for human consumption due to *E. coli* contamination caused by farm slurry pits and run-off from septic tanks. In January 2001 the EU Commission began legal proceedings against Ireland over the quality of its drinking water – the outcome of which was unknown at the time of writing.

However, it should improve following the introduction of water-management schemes by the Department of the Environment, the National Federation of Group Water Schemes and local authorities. Also, the EU Water Framework Directive – a 15-year Europe-wide plan to improve overall water quality – was initiated in December 2000.

Beaches

Unfortunately a number of Irish beaches suffer from pollution and despite EU directives on waste management, plastic containers and other landfill debris have found their way onto beaches. As part of a scheme to improve the situation, clean beaches are awarded the EU Blue Flag and encouragingly in 2001, over 70 beaches, including seven in Northern Ireland, were awarded a Blue Flag. An Taisce (National Trust for Ireland) keeps a list of these, or you can check them on ☒ www.blueflag.org.

The Urban Environment

Since the mid-1960s most Irish have lived in urban areas. Dublin in particular has grown enormously. Initially, little was done to tackle inner-city decay and population decline, but urban renewal programs have begun to turn things round. The emergence of Temple Bar as a living cultural and entertainment centre is one example.

To retain Dublin's character much redevelopment is in the form of refurbishment and restoration of existing buildings rather than the construction of new ones. Where new buildings occur their design is mostly in keeping with the surrounding architecture. Aided by current economic prosperity and finance from the EU and the International Fund for Ireland, this urban renewal is happening in other towns and cities across Ireland.

One consequence of Ireland's affluence is the steep rise in the ownership of private cars, leading to greater traffic congestion in the country's towns and villages. Combine this with tourist traffic during the peak summer season and you have a traffic controller's and town planner's nightmare. To combat this, roads are being upgraded and town bypasses built, but this doesn't please everybody. Kildare town is one of the worst bottlenecks in the country; construction of a bypass was suspended pending the outcome of a complaint by An Taisce to the European Commission that it threatened flora and fauna on Pollardstown Fen near Newbridge – the plan was modified and construction has now begun.

Litter

Sadly, in many places, litter, especially plastic, is a common sight. However, awareness of this as a problem (not least for tourism) is growing. Local authorities spend €25.4 million each year on preventing litter pollution, and over 700 towns and villages take part in the annual National Tidy Towns competition. An Taisce oversees the month-long annual National Spring Clean campaign and also implements the Green Schools program, which awards a Green Flag to primary schools that comply with environmental and litter guidelines, in an attempt to tackle the problem.

Useful Organisations

To find out more about Ireland's environment, a good place to start is Enfo (☎ 01-888 3911, fax 888 3946), 17 St Andrew St, Dublin, near the Dublin Tourism Centre. It's a public information service and opens 10am to 5pm Monday to Saturday. Other sources include:

An Taisce (National Trust for Ireland; ☎ 01-454 1786, ☒ www.antaisce.org) The Tailors Hall, Back Lane, Dublin. This nonprofit organisation is dedicated to the preservation of historical buildings and important natural sites.

Conservation Volunteers Ireland (☎ 01-498 2946, ☒ www.cvi.ie) 65a Harold's Cross Rd, Dublin. This organisation runs a number of volunteer conservation projects around the country.

Dúchas (☎ 01-647 2371, W www.heritageireland .ie) 51 St Stephen's Green, Dublin. Dúchas is the government body that oversees many parks, gardens, monuments, inland waterways and sites of natural, historic and cultural importance.

Earthwatch (☎ 01-478 5101, W www.iol.ie/ ~foeeire) 7 Upper Pembroke St, Dublin. This nonprofit organisation addresses waste management, climate and energy issues.

Irish Wildlife Trust (☎ 01-676 8588, W www .iwt.ie) 107 Lower Baggot St, Dublin. The Irish Wildlife Trust is focused on protection of wilderness and the designation of wilderness areas.

National Trust (Northern Ireland; ☎ 028-9051 0721, W www.nationaltrust.org.uk) Rowallane, Saintfield, Ballynahinch. This organisation performs a similar function to its counterpart in the South.

FLORA & FAUNA
Flora
After the end of the last Ice Age about 10,000 years ago, a shrubby flora similar to that found in modern Arctic tundra took hold. This was eventually replaced by oak forest, which established itself on most of the island. In the upland regions and on more exposed hillsides, the oak was mixed with or replaced by birch and pine. In the lower regions where the soil was richer there were also elm, alder, hawthorn and ash. Underneath the oak trees were smaller plants such as holly, hazel, ferns, mosses and brambles, which provided a rich habitat for animals. Many species of European flora failed to reach Ireland before it became an island.

Today, however, the Irish landscape and predominant flora are mostly the result of human influence (see Forests and Agriculture in the Ecology & Environment section earlier in this chapter). Only 1% of genuine native oak forest survives, making Ireland the least wooded country in Europe. There are remnants in Killarney National Park and in southern Wicklow near Shillelagh. Regimental columns of pine plantations are now a major feature of the Irish countryside and add little in the way of beauty.

In the 17th century hedges were introduced to the landscape to act as land boundaries. Native plants survive in the hedgerows

and in the wilder parts of the country. Because intensive agriculture arrived only comparatively recently, the range of surviving plant species is larger than in many other European countries.

The Burren limestone region in County Clare was covered in light woodland before the early settlers arrived. Now the area is almost all bare rock, but many of the original plants live on, a remarkable mixture of Mediterranean, alpine and arctic species.

The bogs of Ireland are home to a unique flora adapted to wet, acidic, nutrient-poor conditions and whose survival is threatened by the depletion of bogs for energy use. Sphagnum moss is the key bog plant and is joined by plants such as bog rosemary, bog cotton, black-beaked sedge (whose spindly stem grows up to 30cm high) and various types of heather and lichen. Carnivorous plants also thrive, such as the sundew, whose sticky tentacles trap insects, and bladderwort whose tiny explosive bladders trap aquatic animals in bog pools.

Fauna
Mammals The most common native land mammals of any size are foxes and badgers, but although there are plenty about you're unlikely to see any on a casual visit. Smaller mammals include rabbits – introduced by the Normans for food – hares, hedgehogs, red and grey squirrels, shrews and bats. Of the seven species of bat present, two common varieties – the lesser horseshoe bat and Leisler's bat – are considered rare in other parts of Europe. Red deer roam the hillsides in many of the wilder parts of the country, particularly the Wicklow Mountains, and in Killarney National Park, which holds the country's largest herd of native red deer. Other red deer have been introduced from abroad, including the Japanese sika deer.

Less common in Ireland are the elusive otter, stoat and pine marten, which are usually found in remote areas such as the Burren in County Clare or Connemara in County Galway.

Sea mammals include grey and common seals, which are found all around the coastline and can often be seen if you keep quiet

Ireland's Disappearing Bogs

There are three types of bogs (peatland) – raised bogs, fens and blanket bogs.

Raised ones are formed when sphagnum moss gains a foothold in a low-lying, waterlogged area. The moss accumulates as it dies, retaining a lot of water, and the bog starts to form. The centres of these bogs are higher than the edges, hence the term 'raised bog'. The most famous example in Ireland is the Bog of Allen, which once covered as much as 100,000 hectares. The bogs of the midlands have been worked by the Bord na Móna (Irish Turf Board) to create electricity, briquettes and, to a lesser extent, garden compost since 1932.

Fens are flat bogs found at the edges of lakes and in waterlogged areas supplied by mineral-rich waters. When that water supply is cut off, raised bogs develop over the top of fens.

The bogs found covering hills and valleys are known as blanket bogs. These develop on acidic soil in a very wet climate, which usually means 240 days or more of rain each year. There are good examples of still-surviving blanket bogs in Wicklow, Sligo, Antrim and the Slieve Bloom Mountains.

About 17% of Ireland's landscape was once made up of bogs, but it's now thought that at the present rate of destruction they could all be gone in the very near future, wiping out 10,000 years of accumulation. The phenomenon of bog conservation appeared only towards the end of the 20th century, as previously bogs were seen either as large tracts of potential fuel or as useless and dangerous ground. On top of this, no-one had much affection for them, because they were closely tied to the stereotype of the bog Irishman. Now that so many of these bogs have been almost obliterated, there is an urgent need to conserve some of what's left. Many European countries, having stripped away their bogs, now realise the importance of their preservation and have begun to artificially recreate conditions to encourage new bog growth. Ireland's oceanic raised bogs are the most important of their kind in Europe. It has been suggested that 4% should be earmarked for protection. Some argue that all bogs should be conserved, especially since they are home to their own unique family of plants and insects and provide an important habitat for bird life.

The preservation properties of bogs also make them a vital historical resource. Due to the acidity and lack of oxygen in the peat, fragile organic artefacts and pollen (which reveals information about the landscape of the time) that would otherwise have disintegrated long ago are occasionally preserved. The countless relics recovered, some of them 5000 years old, include Iron Age wooden highways, preserved bodies and wooden wheels and buckets. Among more recent items found were 300-year-old packets of butter. For more information contact the Irish Peatland Conservation Council (☎ 01-872 2397, e ipcc@indigo.ie, w www.ipcc.ie), Capel Chambers, Capel St, Dublin.

and know where to look. There are some substantial colonies of grey seals living on the uninhabited islands off County Mayo and around the shores of Strangford Lough in Northern Ireland. Dolphins often swim close to land, particularly in the bays and inlets off the western coast, and for many years Dingle Harbour has had a famous resident bottle-nosed dolphin called Fungie. There are whales in the sea off Ireland, but they tend to be so dispersed and stay so far out from land that they're rarely sighted.

Birds Ireland possesses fewer breeding species than mainland Europe because of its relative isolation, but its westerly location on the fringe of Europe makes it an ideal stopover point for birds migrating from North America and the Arctic. Out of 380 species of wild bird recorded in the country almost 40% breed in Ireland. In autumn the southern counties become temporary home to the American waders – mainly sandpipers and plovers – and warblers. Migrants from Africa, such as shearwaters, petrels and auks, begin to arrive in spring in the south western counties.

Of Ireland's own breeding land birds the reasonably rare corncrake, which migrates from Africa, can be found in the western

Colourful puffin colonies inhabit Ireland's rugged cliffs and islands.

counties, in Donegal and around the Shannon callows, and on islands such as Inisbofin in Mayo. Ireland is also home to the red-billed chough. In late spring and early summer, the rugged coastlines, particularly cliff areas and islands, become a haven for breeding seabirds, mainly puffin, gannet, kittiwake, Manx shearwater, fulmar, cormorant and heron. Sightings of rarer species such as cory and skua have also been recorded.

The lakes and low-lying wetlands attract large numbers of Arctic and northern European waterfowl and waders such as whooper swans, lapwing, barnacle, white-fronted geese and golden plover. The important Wexford Wildfowl Reserve holds half the world's population of Greenland white-fronted geese, and little tern breed on the beach there, protected by the dunes. Also found during the winter are teal, redshank and curlew. The main migration periods are April to May and September to October.

Birds of prey include hen harrier, sparrowhawk, falcon (peregrine, merlin and kestrel) and the odd buzzard. The magnificent peregrine falcon has been making something of a recovery and can be found nesting on cliffs in Wicklow and elsewhere. In 2001, a number of golden eagle chicks from Scotland were released into Glenveagh National Park in Donegal in an effort to reintroduce the species.

For details on the best places for bird-watching, see that section under Activities in the Facts for the Visitor chapter.

Fish The main fish to be found in Ireland are salmon and varieties of trout (brown, rainbow and sea), but there are other species, including mackerel and pollack, off the coast, and pike, bream, perch, roach and eel in lakes and rivers.

Other Fauna The spotted Kerry slug is found, as the name suggests, in Kerry. So is the natterjack toad, Ireland's only species of toad, which lives in sandy areas behind Inch Strand and near Castlegregory on the northern side of the Dingle Peninsula. In the Burren you'll find 28 of Ireland's 33 species of butterfly. The boglands too are home to large varieties of moths and butterflies as well as water skaters and water scorpions in its pools.

Endangered Species

All species native to Ireland's raised bogs are threatened with extinction if their habitat disappears in the next few years.

One of Ireland's rarest native birds is the corncrake, which used to be common in grasslands and meadows. For more on this elusive bird see the boxed text 'The Corncrake Crisis' in the County Donegal chapter.

Also rare, the chough – an unusual crow with bright-red feet and beak – can be seen in the west along coastlines with extensive sand dunes and on Clare Island in Mayo. Other endangered birds are the barn owl, Canadian brent goose, roseate tern, little tern and red-throated diver.

In the Ring of Kerry, the Kerry Bog pony is officially designated a rare breed (see the boxed text 'Kerry Bog Pony' in the Kerry chapter). Other endangered mammals are the whiskered bat, hedgehog, Irish hare, badger and otter. A rare ancient Irish fish and glacial relic, the pollan, found in Lough Derg amongst other places, is in danger of becoming extinct partly because the invasive zebra mussel, which was introduced to Irish waters attached to foreign boats, has colonised the pollan's spawning ground.

National Parks

Ireland has five national parks – The Burren (Clare and Galway), Connemara (Galway), Glenveagh (Donegal), Killarney (Kerry) and Wicklow Mountains (Wicklow) – with another blanket bog area under designation in Mayo. These have been developed to protect, preserve and make accessible areas of significant natural heritage. The parks open year round and each has its own information office. For general information contact Dúchas (see Useful Organisations in the Ecology & Environment section earlier in this chapter).

Forests & Forest Parks Coillte Teoranta (Irish Forestry Board) administers about 400,000 hectares of forested land, which includes designated picnic areas and 12 forest parks. These parks open year round and have a range of wildlife and habitats. Some also have chalets and/or caravan parks, shops, cafes and play areas for children. For further information contact Coillte Teoranta (☎ 01-661 5666, ✉ pr@coillte.ie), Leeson Lane, Dublin.

National Nature Reserves There are 66 state-owned and 10 privately owned National Nature Reserves (NNRs) in the Republic, represented by Dúchas. In Northern Ireland there are over 40 NNRs, which are leased or owned by the Department of the Environment. These reserves are defined as areas of importance for their special flora, fauna or geology and include the Giant's Causeway and Glenariff Glen in Antrim, Marble Arch in County Fermanagh and North Strangford Lough in County Down. More information is available from the Environment and Heritage Service (☎ 028-9054 6533, W www.nics.gov.uk/ehs), Commonwealth House, 35 Castle St, Belfast.

POPULATION & PEOPLE

The total population of Ireland is around 5.4 million. This figure is actually lower than 160 years ago. Prior to the 1845–51 Famine the population was around eight million. Death and emigration reduced the population to around five million, and emigration continued at a high level for the next 100 years. Not until the 1960s did this haemorrhaging slow down, but economic difficulties meant that even in the 1980s over 200,000 people joined the diaspora.

The Republic's population is 3.8 million. Dublin is the largest city and the capital of the Republic, with up to 1.5 million people – about 40% of the population – living within commuting distance of the city centre. The Republic's next largest cities are Cork, Galway and Limerick. A high proportion of the population of the Republic – 41% – is aged under 25. These figures (and population counts throughout the book) are based on the last census of 1996; a rise in most urban centres can be expected.

Northern Ireland has a population of about 1.6 million, and Belfast, the principal settlement, around 280,000.

Since the early 1990s there has been less emigration than immigration, which mostly consists of returning Irish but also immigrants from Britain, other EU countries and North America. The country has also admitted a small number of refugees from Eastern Europe and Africa.

EDUCATION

School attendance is compulsory and free up to and including the age of 16. Most schools at primary and secondary levels are run by religious denominations and receive state aid. Secondary schools are for children aged 12 and over, and those who successfully complete their education at this level receive the Leaving Certificate. There are also state-run vocational schools and privately run multidenominational schools as well as state-aided schools for minority religions.

At the tertiary level, there are four universities in the Republic: Dublin University, housed in Trinity College; the National University of Ireland (NUI), with colleges in Dublin, Maynooth (Kildare), Cork and Galway; Dublin City University; and the University of Limerick. Regional Institutes of Technology (ITs) provide tertiary vocational training.

Irish is a compulsory subject in primary and secondary schools and the growth of interest in the Irish language and traditional culture has led to a number of Irish-medium schools *(gaelscoileanna)*, mostly at primary level.

In Northern Ireland, education is modelled on the British system, though here, too, many schools are operated by religious denominations. There are two universities: Queen's University in Belfast and the University of Ulster, which has colleges in Belfast, Coleraine, Derry and Jordanstown.

With such a young population it's not surprising that over 25% of Ireland's populace is in full-time education, putting enormous pressure on facilities. The competition for tertiary places also means that there's a lot more pressure to succeed on young people, but with the current economic climate, for a growing number, that means opting for work after secondary school rather than further education.

ARTS
Dance
The most important form of dance in Ireland is traditional Irish dancing, performed communally at *ceilidhs* (**kay**-lees), often in an impromptu format and always accompanied by an Irish traditional band. Dances include the hornpipe, jig and reel. The west and south-west are strongholds of traditional dance. Irish dancing has received international attention and success through shows such as *Riverdance* and its offshoots.

Ireland doesn't have a national dance school, but there are a number of schools and companies around the country teaching and performing ballet and modern dance. The Dance Theatre of Ireland and the Irish Modern Dance Theatre are based in Dublin, while the Firkin Crane Centre in Cork is Ireland's only venue devoted solely to dance.

Literature
The Irish have always had a distinctive way of using their adopted tongue which differs from other English speakers, and it's this great oral tradition and love of language that contributes to Ireland's legacy of world-renowned writers and storytellers. If you took all the Irish writers off the university reading lists for English literature, the degree courses could probably be shortened by a year!

The first great work of Irish literature was the *Ulaid (Ulster) Cycle*, written down from oral tradition between the 8th and 12th centuries. The chief story is the *Táin Bó Cúailnge*, about a battle between Queen Maeve of Connaught and Cúchulainn, the principle hero of Irish mythology. Cúchulainn appears in the work of Irish writers right up to the present day, from Samuel Beckett to Frank McCourt.

Some of the more famous names born before 1900 include *Gulliver's Travels* author Jonathan Swift (1667–1745), poet and playwright Oliver Goldsmith (1728–74), *Dracula* creator Bram Stoker (1847–1912) and acclaimed dramatist Oscar Wilde (1854–1900). Equally enduring are socialist playwrights George Bernard Shaw (1856–1950), John Millington Synge (1871–1909), Sean O'Casey (1880–1964), poet WB Yeats (1865–1939) and, not least, James Joyce (1882–1941). Today there are plenty of talented young writers carrying the Irish literary torch into the new millennium.

Ireland can boast four winners of the Nobel Prize for Literature: George Bernard Shaw in 1925, WB Yeats in 1938, Samuel Beckett in 1969 and Seamus Heaney in 1995.

The Ireland Anthology edited by the late Seán Dunne, poet and literary editor of the *Examiner*, is a good introduction to Irish literature, though, as with any anthology, some might debate its inclusions and omissions. The *Oxford Companion to Irish Literature*, edited by Robert Welch, is a useful reference.

Fiction & Drama James Joyce (1882–1941) is regarded as probably the most significant Irish writer of the 20th century.

In 1904 three short stories appeared in an Irish farmers' magazine, written under the pen name Stephen Dedalus; later it formed part of *Dubliners*, which was published 10 years later. The final story in this remarkable collection, *The Dead*, was turned into a memorable film by John Huston.

On leaving Ireland with Nora Barnacle in 1904, Joyce spent most of the next 10 years in self-imposed exile in Trieste, Italy. Although he despised the conservatism and repression of the Catholic Church at home, his canon of work draws directly from his experiences of everyday life and people in Ireland, particularly Dublin. It was there he dreamt up his autobiographical novel *Stephen Hero*, which evolved into *A Portrait of the Artist as a Young Man*.

In 1918, extracts of his masterpiece *Ulysses* were published in a US magazine, but notoriety was already pursuing his epic work and censors prevented further episodes from being published until 1922 when, ironically, its sensational reputation contributed to its instant success. Though considered challenging because of its experimental literary style, there is much for a reader new to Joyce to relish on its pages. A testament to its enduring relevance, *Ulysses* has inspired a whole host of Dublin guides based on the events in the novel, and to this day Joycean admirers from around the world converge annually in Dublin to celebrate the time of its setting – Bloomsday, 16 June 1904. Joyce's most daunting but enjoyable work is *Finnegan's Wake*.

Recommended for anyone who wants to know more about Joyce's life is *Nora: A Biography of Nora Joyce* by Brenda Maddox, which was made into a film in 2000. It complements Richard Ellmann's more reverential biography of James Joyce himself.

Samuel Beckett (1906–89) came from an Anglo-Irish background and studied at Trinity College, before moving to Paris where he associated with Joyce. Influenced by the Italian poet Dante and French philosopher Descartes his work centres on fundamental existential questions about the human condition and the nature of self. He is probably best known for his play *Waiting for Godot* but his unassailable reputation is based on a series of stark novels and plays. A good taster of his work might be *Krapp's Last Tape*, a monologue about an old man listening irreconcilably to a tape of himself as a young, idealistic man talking about his dreams, or the black humoured novel *Molloy*.

The funny, absurdist novelist Flann O'Brien (1911–66), real name Brian O'Nuallain, published his first novel *At Swim-Two-Birds* in 1939 to critical acclaim. For years he wrote a popular, witty column in the *Irish Times* under the pseudonym Myles na gCopaleen which satirised figures of authority. *The Dalkey Archive* followed and his third novel *The Third Policeman* was published posthumously.

Playwright and novelist Brendan Behan (1923–64) led a turbulent life, which spawned powerful tragicomic writing. Grappling with alcoholism from an early age, he was expelled from school and when caught working as a courier for the IRA, was sent to reform school in Britain from where one of his most famous works, *Borstal Boy*, originates. A further incarceration, this time in Mountjoy prison, provided the backdrop for his acclaimed *The Quare Fellow*, a vehicle for Behan's vehement objections to capital punishment. *The Hostage* is one of his most enduring works, a fantastical mixture of slapstick and human anguish. Behan died, a local legend, from alcoholism in Dublin.

Haunting fiction writer and *Irish Times* literary editor John Banville (born 1945) won the Whitbread Award for his peculiar character-driven novel *Dr Copernicus*. His bestseller *The Untouchable* is a fictionalised biography of Cold War British spy Anthony Blunt.

Despite (or maybe because of) Ireland's tragic history, the comic vision has always been a characteristic of Irish writers. Comedy features strongly in the work of Roddy Doyle (born 1958), former school teacher and one of Ireland's most successful contemporary writers. His bawdy stories, set in the working-class world of northern Dublin, won him the Booker Prize in 1993 for *Paddy Clarke Ha Ha Ha*. *The Commitments* (1991) was made into an internationally successful film. *The Woman Who Walked into Doors* (1996) is a bleak, realistic story about domestic violence.

One of Ireland's most original contemporary writers, Patrick McCabe's (born 1955) brilliant, gruesome comedy, *The

Butcher Boy, about an orphaned Monaghan boy's descent into madness, received several awards and was made into a successful film. Another novel that made it to the screen was *The Field* by Kerry novelist and playwright John B Keane (born 1928), about life on the land in the 1920s. Joseph O'Connor (born 1963), brother of singer Sinead, has produced some fine novels that showcase his flair for descriptive realism.

The legacy of history – centuries of fighting the British, the destructive Civil War and the Troubles since the 1960s – has obviously affected Irish writers. *The Informer* by Liam O'Flaherty (1896–1984) is the classic book about the divided sympathies which plagued Ireland throughout its struggle for independence and the ensuing Civil War (he fought on the republican side).

One of Ireland's most important modern writers is John McGahern (born 1935). His simple, economical prose centres on well-drawn, complex yet familiar characters. His acclaimed *Amongst Women* deals with a west of Ireland family in the social aftermath of the War of Independence.

Frank McCourt's (born 1930) Pulitzer Prize-winning *Angela's Ashes* is the miserable story of his poverty-stricken Limerick childhood. His follow-up, *'Tis* (2000), picks up the story in 1949 when he returned to America.

One of the most outstanding playwrights of the last two decades is Frank McGuinness (born 1956), who has had a prolific output since the 1970s. His plays, such as *The Carthaginians*, explore the consequences of 1972's Bloody Sunday on the people of Derry. London-Irish young playwright Martin McDonagh (born 1971) uses the darker side of a romantic rural Irish idyll as his inspiration. Among his work, *The Leenane Trilogy* has been performed by Britain's National Theatre and on Broadway, where he has won a number of Tony Awards. *Dancing at Lughnasa* by Brian Friel (born 1929) was a great success on Broadway and in London and has been made into a film.

Other talented young playwrights to watch out for include Dubliner Conor McPherson, whose acclaimed play *The Weir* was commissioned by the Royal Court and who also scripted two Irish films, Donal O'Kelly *(Catalpa)* and Enda Walsh *(Disco Pigs)*.

The North The Troubles, not surprisingly, feature in much Northern writing. CS Lewis (1898–1963), from Belfast, is best known for *The Chronicles of Narnia*, a series of allegorical children's stories.

Cal by Bernard MacLaverty (born 1942) traces a life where the choices are miserable and the consequences terrible and inevitable. Those no-win political situations are also seen in *Lies of Silence* by Brian Moore (born 1921), which was shortlisted for the Booker Prize in 1990. *The Lonely Passion of Judith Hearne* was his first novel; it portrays the mid-life crisis of a Belfast woman.

In Glenn Patterson's (born 1961) amusing first novel, *Fat Lad* (a children's mnemonic for learning the names of the six counties of Northern Ireland), the political situation is a backdrop to a story that captures the feel of life in Belfast today. Colin Bateman (born 1961) daringly uses the Troubles and contemporary Northern life as an environment for his fast-paced, B-movie-style capers. His novels translate well to the screen and several, *Divorcing Jack* included, have been adapted.

Call My Brother Back by Michael McLaverty recounts growing up on Rathlin Island and the Falls Rd, Belfast, in the 1920s. From Sinn Féin president Gerry Adams (born 1948) comes *The Street*, a collection of stories dealing with life in west Belfast, where he grew up.

Belfast-born Robert McLiam Wilson (born 1964) is at the forefront of modern Irish writing. His first novel was the award-winning *Ripley Bogle*, which follows a west-Belfast tramp through London with flashbacks to his youth. The work of playwright and poet Damian Gorman (born 1962) has received considerable praise. *Broken Nails*, his first play, received four Ulster Theatre awards.

Women Ireland has produced its fair share of women writers. Earlier examples, mostly of the Anglo-Irish Ascendancy, were Lady Morgan (1776–1859), Maria Edgeworth

(1768–1849), literary team EO Somerville (1858–1949) and her cousin Violet Martin (1861–1915), who wrote under the pseudonym of Martin Ross and co-penned *The Irish RM*, and Elizabeth Bowen (1899–1973), whose work has been compared to that of Jane Austen. Bowen spent her formative years in the care of elderly relatives in England and this itinerant childhood lifestyle and sense of displacement influenced much of her work. She is best known for her portraits of alienated characters, notably children, and for her telling descriptions of life in the Big House in the twilight years of the Ascendancy. She lived for many years in one such house, the family home, Bowen's Court, County Cork – the setting for her acclaimed novel *The Last September* – before returning to England where she died.

The work of London-based Edna O'Brien (born 1932) has often been described as racy and explores the small-minded, hypocritical side of Irish life. In 1960 she enjoyed the accolade of having her *The Country Girls* banned. She's not afraid to confront contemporary issues and in 1997 she wrote *Down by the River*, based on the real-life controversy of a 14-year-old Dublin girl who was raped and went to England for an abortion. O'Brien added incest to the mix by making the girl's father the rapist.

The works of the prolific Iris Murdoch (1919–99) encompass fiction, drama, poetry and philosophy. Her novel *The Sea, The Sea* won the Booker Prize. The story of her descent into the throes of Alzheimer's disease and eventual death is lovingly chronicled by her husband John Bayley in a book simply titled *Iris*.

Caitlin Thomas (born 1913), nee MacNamara, wife of poet Dylan Thomas, subjugated her impulse to write under the weight of her husband's celebrity and her own addiction to alcohol. *Double Drink Story* is a brilliant, self-deprecating memoir of their love–hate relationship.

The Old Jest by Jennifer Johnston (born 1930) is set in Ireland between the wars. The protagonist is an Anglo-Irish girl growing up in the South at a time when change is about to sweep through the country and the Anglo-Irish Ascendancy is in its final days; a theme which runs through many of her books.

Molly Keane (1904–66) wrote several books in the 1920s and 1930s under the pseudonym MJ Farrell, then had a literary second life in her 70s when *Good Behaviour* and *Time after Time* came out under her real name.

In popular fiction Maeve Binchy (born 1940) is *the* writer of best-selling blockbusters that just rise above the sex and shopping genre. With a good ear for dialogue, she ably captures the often hilarious peculiarities of the quotidian. *Circle of Friends*, set in 1940s Dublin, was made into a film. Journalist Nuala O'Faolain's (born 1950) *Are You Somebody?* is a memoir of her childhood in Dublin in the 1950s and about coping in a male-dominated world.

Young novelists such as Emma Donoghue (born 1969) tackle once-taboo subjects; *Stir-fry* is a lesbian love story.

Poetry WB Yeats (1865–1939) was both playwright and poet, but it's his poetry that has the greatest appeal. His *Love Poems*, edited by Norman Jeffares, makes a suitable introduction for anyone new to his writing.

Pádraig Pearse (1879–1916) used the Irish language as his medium and was one of the leaders of the 1916 Easter Rising.

Patrick Kavanagh (1905–67), one of Ireland's most respected poets, was born in Inniskeen, County Monaghan. *The Great Hunger* and *Tarry Flynn* evoke the atmosphere and often grim reality of life for the poor farming community. You'll find a bronze statue of him in Dublin, sitting beside his beloved Grand Canal.

Seamus Heaney (born 1939) won the 1995 Nobel Prize for Literature. In 1997 Heaney added the Whitbread Book of the Year to his accolades for *The Spirit Level*. Some poems reflect the hope, disappointment and disillusionment of the peace process.

Paul Durcan (born 1944) boldly tackles awkward issues such as the oppressive nature of Catholicism and Republican activity in his trademark unconventional style.

Cork-born Irish-language poet Louis de Paor has had two of his collections win Ireland's prestigious Sean O'Riordan Prize. Tom Paulin (born 1949) writes memorable poetry about the North – try *The Strange Museum* – as does Ciaran Carson (born 1948). Many of Paula Meehan's (born 1955) magical, evocative poems speak of cherished relationships.

Other modern notables are Brendan Kennelly, Eavan Boland, Michael Hartnett and Derek Mahon. For a taste of modern Irish poetry try *Contemporary Irish Poetry* edited by Fallon & Mahon. *A Rage for Order* edited by Frank Ormsby is a vibrant collection of the poetry of the North.

Architecture

Ireland is packed with prehistoric graves, ruined monasteries, crumbling fortresses and many other solid reminders of its long, often dramatic, history. The principal surviving structures from Stone Age times are the graves and monuments people built for their dead, usually grouped under the heading of megalithic (great stone) tombs.

Megalithic Tombs Among the most easily recognisable megalithic tombs are dolmens, massive three-legged structures rather like giant stone stools, in which a number of bodies were interred before the whole structure was covered in earth. Most are 4000 to 5000 years old. Good examples are the Poulnabrone Dolmen in the Burren, Proleek near Dundalk, and Browne's Hill near Carlow town.

MATT KING

Massive megalithic dolmens were built by Stone Age people to inter their dead.

Court tombs, with a formal forecourt in front of the tomb, are found mostly in Ulster. Ossian's Grave at Cushendall in County Antrim is a good example.

Passage graves such as Newgrange and Knowth in Meath are huge mounds with narrow stone-walled passages leading to burial chambers. These chambers are enriched with spiral and chevron symbols and have an opening through which the rising sun penetrates on the winter or summer solstice, thus acting as a giant celestial calendar. They're surrounded by stone circles of unknown significance.

Also plentiful in Ireland are cist graves (chambers excavated in rock or formed of stones or a hollowed tree trunk) and gallery graves (tunnel-shaped tombs).

Ogham Stones These are peculiarly Irish standing stones dating from the 4th to 7th centuries AD. Ogham (o-am) was an early form of Irish script using a variety of notched strokes placed above, below or across a keyline, usually on stones. The stones mainly indicate graves and are inscribed with the name of the deceased. The majority are found in Counties Cork, Kerry and Waterford. Many have been moved: you may find them incorporated in walls, buildings or gateposts.

Forts The Irish names for forts – *dun*, *rath*, *caiseal/cashel* and *caher* – have ended up in the names of countless towns and villages. The Irish countryside is peppered with the remains of over 30,000 of them. The earliest known examples date from the Bronze Age but they have been built and used for many thousands of years since, some as late as the 17th century. The most common fort was the ring fort, with circular earth-and-stone banks, topped by a wooden palisade fence to keep out intruders, and surrounded on the outside by a moatlike ditch. Ring forts are found everywhere and were the basic family or tribal enclosure in Ireland for thousands of years. Outside Clonakilty in County Cork, the ring fort at Lisnagun (Lios na gCon) has been reconstructed to give some idea of its original appearance.

Some forts were constructed entirely of stone; Staigue Fort in Kerry and Cathair Dhún Iorais on Clare's Black Head are fine examples. Promontory forts were built on headlands or cliff edges, which gave natural protection on one side. The Iron Age fort of Dún Aengus on Inishmór (the largest of the Aran Islands) is a superb example.

The Normans used many ring forts to their full advantage by building inside them. A characteristic early Norman-built fort was the military motte and bailey. The motte was a small flat-topped hill surrounded by a ditch and earthen banks at the base for further protection; attached to and surrounding the motte was the bailey, an outer wall that enclosed animals and their keepers.

Crannógs Artificial islands built in many Irish lakes, crannógs are the equivalent of a ring fort on water. Estimates put the number of them in Ireland at over 250. They date back to the Bronze Age and, like the ring forts, were used right up to the 17th century. The Craggaunowen Project in Clare has a reconstructed example, and the lake near Fair Head in County Antrim has an easily spotted original.

The midland lakes have many crannógs, which today are usually overgrown, with little evidence betraying their artificial origins except perhaps the too-perfect circular outline. Sometimes they were built in bogs, or the original lake has since become a bog, so many are now hidden below the water level.

Monasteries & Churches After Christianity arrived in Ireland in the 5th century, the first monasteries were built, mainly of perishable materials, particularly wood. The early stone churches were often very simple, some roofed with timber, such as the 6th-century Teampall Bheanáin (Church of St Benen) on Inishmór of the Aran Islands, or built completely of stone, such as the 8th-century Gallarus Oratory on the Dingle Peninsula. Early hermitages include the small beehive huts and buildings on the summit of Skellig Michael off County Kerry.

As the monasteries grew in size and stature, so did the architecture. The cathedrals at Glendalough (12th century) and Clonmacnoise (10th to 15th century) are good examples, although they're tiny compared with European medieval cathedrals.

Round towers have become symbols of Ireland. These tall, stone, needle-like structures were built largely as lookout posts and refuges in the event of Viking attacks in the late 9th or early 10th centuries.

That other great Irish symbol, the Celtic cross, dates from between the 8th and 12th centuries, a fine example of which is Muiredach's Cross at Monasterboice in County Louth.

Ireland's early church architecture developed in isolation, as Europe was experiencing the Dark Ages. However, foreign influences began to appear in the 11th and 12th centuries. The Cistercians, a European order of monks, established their first Irish monastery at Mellifont, County Louth, in 1142. The strict and formal layout of these new establishments was radically different from the simple and relatively random layout of the traditional Irish monastery as exemplified by nearby Monasterboice, Glendalough in Wicklow and Clonmacnoise in Offaly. Cormac's Chapel (1127) at the Rock of Cashel in Tipperary shows strong foreign influence in its European Romanesque design, with its tunnel-vaulted nave and rib-vaulted chancel. Elaborately carved doorways are common in church architecture of the 12th century.

With the Normans in 1169 came the Gothic style of architecture, characterised by tall vaulted windows and soaring V-shaped arches. Fine examples of this can be seen in Christ Church Cathedral (1172) in Dublin, and St Canice's Cathedral (13th century) in Kilkenny.

Castles & Mansions The Normans first built temporary motte-and-bailey forts (see Forts earlier in this section), but once they had established themselves they built more permanent stone castles. The great castle at Trim (1172), County Meath, is the best example.

Many castles that you see today are the tall, thin tower houses built between the 14th and 17th centuries for local landlords or chieftains. The earliest of these tower houses are simple, small keeps with few embellishments, such as Bunratty Castle (15th century), while the later forms became more like large, fortified stone houses with sophisticated features, bigger windows and less emphasis on security.

From the 17th century on, as the established landowning families became wealthier and felt more secure, they began to build unfortified houses, and classical principles began to emerge, particularly in the less rebellious parts of the country around Counties Kildare, Meath, Dublin and Wicklow.

Cottages Authentic traditional thatched Irish cottages were built of limestone or clay to suit the elements, but weren't durable and have become rare. They contained an open fireplace for heating and cooking. Some cottages, called longhouses, sheltered animals as well as humans. The building of traditional cottages died out around the middle of the 20th century.

Georgian Houses In Georgian times, Dublin became one of the architectural glories of Europe, with simple, beautifully built Georgian terraces of red brick, with delicate glass fanlights over large, elegant, curved doorways. From the 1960s Dublin's Georgian heritage suffered badly but many buildings, in places such as Mountjoy Square, are being restored. You can see fine examples around Merrion and Fitzwilliam Squares. Georgian urban architecture wasn't confined to Dublin and you'll see other fine examples in places such as Cork and Limerick.

The Anglo-Irish Ascendancy built country houses such as Castletown House (1722) near Celbridge, and Russborough House (1741) near Blessington, which are both excellent examples of the Palladian style, with their regularity and classical correctness. Prolific German architect Richard Cassels (also known as Richard Castle), came to Ireland in 1728 and designed many landmark buildings including Powerscourt House in County Wicklow, Strokestown Park House in County Roscommon and Leinster House (home to Dáil Éireann, the Irish government) in Dublin.

Modern Architecture Ireland has little modern architecture of note. For much of the 20th century the pace of change was slow, and it wasn't until the construction of Dublin's Busáras Station in the 1950s that modernity began to really express itself. It was designed by Michael Scott, who was to have an influence on architects in Ireland for the next two decades. The poorly regulated building boom of the 1960s and 1970s, however, paid little attention to the country's architectural heritage and destroyed more than it created. From that period Paul Koralek's 1967 brutalist-style Berkeley Library in Trinity College, Dublin, has been hailed as Ireland's best example of modern architecture.

Since the 1980s more care has been given to architectural heritage and context, the best example of which has been the redevelopment of Dublin's previously near-derelict Temple Bar area.

Painting

Ireland's painting doesn't receive the kind of recognition that its literature and music do. Nevertheless, painting in Ireland has a long tradition dating back to the illuminated manuscripts of the early Christian period, most notably the Book of Kells.

The National Gallery has an extensive Irish School collection, much of it chronicling the people and pursuits of the Anglo-Irish aristocracy.

Like other European artists of the 18th century, Roderic O'Conor featured portraits and landscapes in his work. His postimpressionist style stood out for its vivid use of colour and sturdy brush strokes. James Malton captured 18th-century Dublin in a series of line drawings and paintings.

In the 19th century there was still no hint of Ireland's political and social problems in the work of its major artists. The most prominent landscape painter was James Arthur O'Connor.

Just as WB Yeats played a seminal role in the Celtic literary revival, his younger brother, Jack Butler Yeats (1871–1957), inspired an artistic surge of creativity in the early 20th century, taking Celtic mythology and Irish life as his subjects. (Their father, John Butler Yeats, had also been a noted portrait painter.) William John Leech (1881–1961) was fascinated by changing light, an affection reflected in his expressionistic landscapes and flower paintings. Born to English parents in Dublin, Francis Bacon (1909–92) emerged as one of the most powerful figurative artists of the 20th century with his violent depictions of distorted human bodies.

The pioneering work of Irish cubist painter Mainie Jellett (1897–1944) and her friend, modernist stained-glass artist Evie Hone (1894–1955), had an effecting influence on later modernists Barrie Cooke (born 1931) and Camille Souter (born 1929). Together with Louis Le Brocquy (born 1916), Jellett and Hone set up the Irish Exhibition of Living Art in 1943 to foster the work of nonacademic artists. In the 1950s and 1960s, a school of naive artists including James Dixon appeared on Tory Island, off Donegal.

Contemporary artists to watch out for include Felim Egan, New York-based Sean Scully and Fionnuala Ní Chíosain.

Experimental photographer Clare Langan's work has gained international recognition in recent years with her trademark ethereal images of primal landscapes.

Cinema

During much of the 20th century Ireland didn't have a particularly active film-making industry, partly because of the small home market, and it was often left to American or British film-makers to represent Ireland to the rest of the world (see Films in the Facts for the Visitor chapter).

This began to change in 1981 following the creation of the Irish Film Board and the spending of more money on a home-grown film industry, including some attractive tax-incentive packages for foreign film makers in Ireland.

Nevertheless, Irish actors do have a long tradition of appearances in film and quite a few have achieved extraordinary international success in the last couple of decades. Young Dublin soap actor Tim Farrell shot to stardom in 2001 following his naturalistic portrayal of a pre-Vietnam GI in US boot camp *Tigerland*; Jonathan Rhys-Meyers similarly enjoyed success in glam rock drama *Velvet Goldmine* and *The Age of Innocence*. Liam Neeson *(Schindler's List)* and Daniel Day-Lewis and Brenda Fricker *(My Left Foot)* have won Oscars; Belfast-born Kenneth Branagh's career has invited comparisons with Laurence Olivier's; Gabriel Byrne starred in a series of hits *(The Usual Suspects, Man in the Iron Mask)*; and Navan man Pierce Brosnan scored the coveted James Bond role. Other actors who achieved success in the same period include Aidan Quinn *(Legends of the Fall)*, Stephen Rea *(The Crying Game)* and Colm Meaney *(The Commitments)*. They have followed in the footsteps of the likes of Richard Harris *(The Guns of Navarone, The Field)*, Peter O'Toole *(Lawrence of Arabia)*, Milo O'Shea *(Barbarella)* and before them Greer Garson *(Goodbye, Mr Chips)* and Maureen O'Hara *(Jamaica Inn)*.

To this crop of acting talent can be added the screenwriter and director Neil Jordan, whose impressive body of work includes *Mona Lisa* (1986), *The Crying Game* (1992), *Interview with the Vampire* (1994), *Michael Collins* (1996) and *The Butcher Boy* (1998). *The Crying Game*, for which Jordan won an Oscar for best screenplay, is perhaps the most intriguing commercial film to feature the IRA. Jordan's powerful *Michael Collins* stars Liam Neeson and follows the life of Collins from the Easter Rising to the Civil War and his death in 1922 at the hands of his former comrades. *The Butcher Boy* was a successful translation of Patrick McCabe's novel.

Other important film-makers are producer Noel Pearson and director Jim Sheridan, who worked together on *My Left Foot* (1989) and *The Field* (1990). *My Left Foot* told the true story of Dublin writer Christy Brown, who was crippled with cerebral palsy. Noel Pearson's production of Brian Friel's play *Dancing at Lughnasa* (1998) is set in 1930s Donegal and stars Meryl Streep. Jim Sheridan's *In the Name of the Father* (1993), starred Daniel Day-Lewis as Gerry Conlon and Emma Thompson as his lawyer. It tells the story of the arrest and conviction of the Guildford Four for a pub bombing in England, then of the struggle to clear their names. In Sheridan's *The Boxer* (1997) Daniel Day-Lewis plays a Belfast man unable to escape the Troubles. Jim Sheridan also wrote the screenplay for Mike Newell's *Into the West* (1993), a romantic story of two children and a mythical white horse.

Pat O'Connor's credits as film director include Bernard MacLaverty's *Cal* (1984) and Maeve Binchy's *Circle of Friends* (1994). Young directors to watch out for are Damien O'Donnell and Enda Hughes.

Theatre

Dublin and Belfast are the main centres, but most sizeable towns, such as Cork, Derry, Donegal, Limerick and Galway, have their own theatres. Ireland has a theatrical history almost as long as its literary one. Dublin's first theatre was founded in Werburgh St in 1637, although it was closed only four years later by the Puritans. Another theatre, named the Smock Alley Playhouse or Theatre Royal, opened in 1661 and continued to stage plays for over a century.

The literary revival of the late 19th century saw the establishment of Dublin's Abbey Theatre, now Ireland's national theatre. Its role is to present works by former greats such as WB Yeats, JM Synge and Sean O'Casey, as well as to promote modern Irish dramatists. Also in Dublin, the Gate Theatre produces classics and comedies, while the Gaiety and Olympia Theatres present a range of productions, as does the Grand Opera House in Belfast. Dublin's Project Arts Centre offers a more experimental program.

SOCIETY & CONDUCT

Ireland's recent economic success, social changes and cultural resurgence are rapidly dispelling old stereotypes of the country as a predominantly poor, agrarian backwater. In reality, it has a young, expanding population, flourishing arts scene and a booming economy that has embraced high technology.

Social stratification exists, but movement between classes is fairly fluid and more to do with personal wealth than birth or background. Yet the gap between the 'haves' and 'have nots' has widened alarmingly. Booming property prices in Dublin have made housing unaffordable for a large proportion of the city's population and have sadly added to the rise in homelessness. Although unemployment has gone down to under 4% from 19% in the last decade, a minimum wage was only introduced in 2000 and the number of Irish living below the poverty line (set at 60% of the national average wage) rose from 31% in 1991 to 35% in 1997. Current estimates suggest that figure has been maintained; however, the government's plans to reduce poverty levels to below 5% by 2004 give some cause for hope.

With the decline in the power of the Church there has been a liberalising of sexual mores. Contraceptive pills and condoms are freely available, though in some areas they're still taboo subjects of discussion. In a 1995 referendum, divorce was narrowly, but finally, accepted.

The thorny abortion issue has been temporarily resolved in a typically Irish compromise. Abortion is still illegal but it's no longer illegal to provide information on abortion, and women who travel to Britain to terminate their pregnancies do so without fear of legal sanction. For more details see the boxed text 'The Abortion Debate' in the Republic of Ireland chapter.

Do's & Don'ts

On the whole, Irish of all political or religious persuasions are friendly and accommodating towards foreigners. However, religion and politics are inextricably mixed, especially in the North, and, whenever these subjects come up, as a visitor it's probably a good idea to make this a time to practise your listening skills – at least until you're sure of the situation.

There's a marked difference in opinion and outlook between the older, more 'traditional' generations and young people. While the former may recognise that contraception, divorce, abortion and homosexuality exist in modern Ireland, they are, nevertheless, often wary of entertaining a conversation on such subjects. Religious beliefs among older people, especially in rural areas, are still strong, and they might take offence at a foreigner who doesn't respect their opinions on these matters.

Younger Irish, on the other hand, have embraced social change as long overdue and are often extremely liberal, sometimes radically so, in their views.

As with any other nation, the Irish don't like to be reminded of their faults by anybody but other Irish. The best policy is to relax and accept the many good things that the people of Ireland have to offer.

RELIGION

The Republic of Ireland is nominally 92% Roman Catholic, but church attendance has fallen, especially among younger people. The rest of the population are 3% Protestant and 0.1% Jewish, while 4.9% either have no religious beliefs or belong to other religious groups, including Islam and Buddhism. In the North the breakdown is about 60% Protestant, 40% Catholic. Most Irish Protestants are members of the Church of Ireland, an offshoot of the Church of England, and the Presbyterian and Methodist Churches.

The Gaeltacht – Ireland's Heart & Soul

Were you to limit your travels in Ireland to what was once called the Pale (including Dublin, Counties Wexford and Waterford) or much of the east and south for that matter, you would be forgiven for thinking you were in a monolingual, English-speaking country. You might be surprised by all the street and road signs in both English and Irish or catch a bit of national news *as Gaeilge* (in Irish) on the radio, but you would seldom – if ever – hear it spoken on the streets.

That's not the case in the Gaeltacht, a word used collectively to describe the pockets of the Republic where Irish (or Gaelic as it is sometimes called) remains, at least in theory, the first language of communication and commerce among the majority of the population.

Sadly, the Gaeltacht represents only a tiny area of how Ireland used to appear linguistically. If you were to look at a map of Ireland dating from the early 19th century that had been shaded to show the areas in which Irish was spoken as a first language, and then compared it with one marking today's Gaeltacht, you would be shocked to see the extent that the language has lost ground over the past 200 years.

The older map would incorporate more than two-thirds of the island, representing some 2.4 million people. On the more recent map there would be just a dozen small smudges in seven counties mostly along the west coast. Some 86,000 people live in the Gaeltacht today, with the majority of them – just over 70% – *Gaeilgeoirí* (Irish speakers). But according to the most recent census (1996), only 21,000 adults there speak Irish on a daily basis.

The Gaeltacht is not the only place where Irish is spoken regularly in Ireland; if that were the case, the language would have given up the ghost long ago. More than 1.4 million people in the Irish Republic claim to have an ability to speak Irish, but the vast majority say so only because they were required to study it for up to 12 years at school. Most would be hard-pressed to rustle up even *cúpla focal* (a few words) if necessary. In reality, only about 50,000 adults outside the Gaeltacht borders use it every day.

The Gaeltacht remains, however, the last bastion where Irish is spoken as a community language – where ordering a pint, buying a newspaper and asking directions in Irish is as natural as the rain is here. The Gaeltacht is where the language can be allowed to grow and develop and, at the same time, where it can be protected.

The Catholic Church has always taken a strong conservative line on abortion, contraception, divorce and censorship, and opposed attempts to liberalise the laws on these matters. But the Church has been weakened by declining attendance, the fall in the number of young men and women entering religious life and by damaging sex scandals, particularly the abuse of children. In the late 1990s they launched a nationwide advertising campaign aimed at young people called 'Men in Black' parodying the American film of the same title, in an effort to encourage young people to join the priesthood.

The Church is now treated with a curious mixture of respect and derision by various sections of the community.

Despite its declining power, the Catholic Church still wields considerable influence in the South. It retains control of most schools and hospitals (which are funded by the state) and, in rural towns and villages, large numbers attend Mass every Sunday. Oddly enough, the primates of both the Roman Catholic Church and the Church of Ireland sit in Armagh, Northern Ireland, the traditional base of St Patrick. The country's religious history clearly overrides its current divisions.

LANGUAGE

In my cottage I have never heard a word of English from the women except when they are speaking to pigs or dogs.

JM Synge, *The Aran Islands*

The Gaeltacht – Ireland's Heart & Soul

These natural environments of a language that stretches back some 2500 years, and can claim to have the oldest vernacular literature in Europe, are thus important to a nation that, at least officially, encourages bilingualism among its citizens. To promoters and students of the language they are even more: 'holy' sites to which they make pilgrimages.

The Gaeltachts range in size and population from small to minuscule. By far the largest (population 34,000) and most dynamic is the Galway (or Connemara) Gaeltacht, which extends from just west of Galway City to the coast and includes the Aran Islands. The Donegal Gaeltacht, in the Republic's extreme north-western corner, counts some 24,000 people who speak a dialect of Irish that is closer to Scottish Gaelic than the others.

The Kerry Gaeltacht, centred at the western end of the Dingle Peninsula, is celebrated for having produced a wealth of modern Irish-language literature, including Muiris Ó Súileabháin's *Fiche Bliain ag Fás* (Twenty Years A-Growing) and Tomás Ó Criomhthain's *An tOileánach* (The Islandman). The Cork Gaeltacht is unique in that it is largely inland, centred in the quiet valleys of the Muskerry area.

The smallest Gaeltachts are in Counties Mayo, Waterford and Meath. The last is interesting for two reasons. It is the only one in the eastern part of the Republic and is, in fact, artificial – a planted community of Irish speakers brought here from impoverished and congested coastal Gaeltachts in the mid-1930s on the promise of land. It is centred around Rathcairn, near the town of Kells.

The Gaeltachts are in some of the most remote and beautiful parts of the Republic and well worth a visit for that reason alone. If you do want to hear Irish spoken in these most natural of environments, head for the village pub, the local shop or Mass on Sunday. And try to say a few words yourself, even a simple and hesitantly pronounced *Dia duit* (hello) or *Sláinte!* (cheers). To a people who have fought the good fight and remained loyal to their ancient language for all these centuries, it will sound like *ceol* (music).

Steve Fallon is the author of the Lonely Planet Journeys title *Home with Alice: Travels in Gaelic Ireland*

Although English is the main language of Ireland, it's spoken with a peculiar Irish flavour and lilt. Indeed the Irish accent is one of the most pleasant varieties of English to be heard. Some of the peculiarly Irish sentence constructions in English are closely related to the Irish language. For instance, the usual word order in Irish sentences is verb, subject, object. The present participle is also used more frequently, in constructions such as: 'Would you be going to Galway today?' Another peculiarity is the use of 'after' as in: 'I'm after going to the shop,' meaning: 'I've just been to the shop.' The Irish also make good use of scatological references in their speech – the word shite often finds its way into everyday conversation.

English is spoken throughout Ireland, but there are parts of western and southern Ireland known as Gaeltacht areas where Irish is the native language. Irish is a Celtic language, probably first introduced to Ireland by the Celts in the last few centuries BC. It is similar to Scottish Gaelic, and has much in common with Welsh and Breton.

The Republic of Ireland is officially bilingual, and many official documents and road-signs are printed in both Irish and English. The reality, however, is a little bit more complex.

Until the time of the Plantation in the late 16th and early 17th centuries, successive invaders had been assimilated and had adopted the Irish language. From the time of the Plantation, Irish was seen as the language of the old Irish aristocracy, the poor and the dispossessed; strenuous efforts were consequently made by the English to wipe it out. Social advancement meant giving up Irish. When independence was achieved in 1921 efforts were made to revive the language, but progress has been slow.

Irish is compulsory in both primary and secondary schools in the Republic, and most colleges and universities require prospective students to pass the subject in their school-leaving exams. Despite this – partly because too much emphasis is placed on the complex grammar and too little on speaking the language – most Irish school leavers would be hard pressed to hold a simple conversation in Irish, despite having just completed 12 years of daily classes in it. Many complain that it's a waste of time studying a difficult language that's not in everyday use.

However, attitudes are changing and speaking Irish no longer carries a stigma. Even in Dublin there's a revival, with several Irish-medium infant and junior schools, and a local radio station broadcasting in Gaelic. The national Irish-language radio station, Radió na Gaeltachta, broadcasts from Connemara; Telefis ná Gaelige is the national Irish-language TV station; and RTE, the Republic's state-sponsored broadcaster, has daily news bulletins and programs in Irish. An increasing number of people derive intense satisfaction from speaking and keeping alive an ancient aspect of Ireland's culture. Irish is also one of the official languages of the EU.

For pronunciation details and useful phrases, see the Language chapter at the end of this book. Lonely Planet's *Europe phrasebook* devotes a chapter to the Irish language.

IRISH MUSIC

The rock band U2 may be Ireland's biggest musical export but when people talk about Irish music they are generally referring to an older, more intimate style of traditional or folk music. For the visitor, the joy of Irish music lies in its sheer accessibility. The biggest names may play the same major venues as the rock stars, but almost every town and village seems to have a pub renowned for its music where you can show up and find a session in progress, or even join in if you feel so inclined.

New Music from Old Roots

The true origins of traditional Irish music are lost in the proverbial mists of time. However, clues to its humble roots lie in the instruments themselves. The *bodhrán*, the simple goatskin drum that resembles a giant cymbal, for example, was originally probably shaken to separate the corn from the chaff, while the small knuckle-ended beater was banged against it to frighten birds away from the fields.

Celtic traditional music may have found its way overland from Asia and India some 2000 years ago. The Irish harp may even have been developed in Egypt. Until around 1700, the harp was the most important instrument in Irish music. It was smaller than the version played today, had a wooden frame and wire strings that were sounded with the fingernails rather than the fingertips.

Just as the great painters of the Renaissance in Italy depended on the patronage of wealthy merchants, so the harpists found support and patronage among Ireland's Gaelic chieftains. Consequently, music suffered a serious setback in 1607 when the Flight of the Earls saw the chieftains flee the country, leaving the harpists to teach music to support themselves. The most famous of these itinerant musicians was Turlough O'Carolan (1670–1738), some of whose tunes are still played today. Traditionally, music was performed as a background to dancing, so the 17th-century penal laws did nothing to help by banning all expressions of traditional culture, including dancing. Music was forced underground, which goes some way towards explaining the homely feel of much Irish music today.

Until the late 18th century, Irish music was largely unwritten. In 1762, a book of 49 airs was published in Dublin. Then, in 1792, Edward Bunting attended a Belfast harp festival and wrote down the tunes he heard. His manuscripts are still housed in the library of Queen's University in Belfast.

The 1845–51 Famine dealt traditional music another blow as musicians either died, or emigrated in search of a better life. However, within the Irish diaspora the traditions lived on. To the standard repertoire of songs, new themes were added, as musicians sang nostalgically of the homeland and celebrated their new lives.

Eventually the tide turned. Recordings of the music being made in America in the 1920s travelled back across the Atlantic and sparked renewed interest in what had been lost. Copying the Irish-Americans, musicians at home also began to experiment by adding new instruments to the traditional line-up of fiddle, tin whistle, *uilleann* (elbow) pipes and drum.

In the 1960s, Seán O'Riada (1931–71) of Cork set up Ceoltóirí Chualann, a band featuring a fiddle, flute, accordion, bodhrán and uilleann pipes, and began to perform music to listen to rather than dance to. When his band performed at the Gaiety Theatre in Dublin, it gave a

BMG/RCA

whole new credibility to traditional music. Members of the band went on to form the Chieftains, who still play an important role in bringing Irish music to an international audience.

With added vocals come bands such as the Clancy Brothers and Tommy Makem; the Dubliners with their notorious drinking songs; the Wolfe Tones, who've been described as 'the rabble end of the rebel song tradition'; and the Fureys. Younger groups such as Clannad, Altan, Dervish and Nomos espouse a quieter, more mystical style of singing, while Kíla stretch the boundaries by combining traditional music with reggae, Eastern and new-age influences.

Skiffle, an off-shoot of rock and roll which used improvised instruments such as washboards, originated in working-class America in the 1950s and found its way to Ireland and England where Lonnie Donegan was its main exponent.

Irish Singer-Songwriters

Christy Moore is the most prominent of the contemporary singer-songwriters playing in a broadly traditional idiom. Moore has been performing since the 1960s and although a pivotal member of the influential bands Planxty and Moving Hearts, he's probably best known for his solo albums. Moore's younger brother, Luka Bloom, has carved out a solo career for himself too, as has Andy Irvine, who, like Moore, was once a member of Planxty.

The unique Van Morrison, native of Belfast, seems to have been going for ever. In the 1960s he was lead singer with Them, whose anthem *Gloria* was a Beatles-era classic. 'Van the Man' moved on to a solo career in the USA, and his *Astral Weeks*, recorded when aged only 22, was a landmark and is regularly listed by critics as one of the seminal records of the 1960s. Although he has never generated a mass audience, Van Morrison has always attracted a cult following. His latest solo album is *Back on Top* (1999).

Top Left: Still going strong – the Chieftains

Other male singer-songwriters to listen out for include Finbar Furey, Mick Hanly, Jimmy MacCarthy, Kieran Goss, Paul Brady and Davy Spillane.

Appealing to younger audiences, Paddy Casey has been compared to David Gray because of his melodic arrangements and intelligent lyrics.

The release of David Kitt's ambient-folk debut album *The Big Romance* in 2001 to rave reviews earmarks him as a name to watch, and in 2001 rock-folk singer Mundy released the catchy single *Mexico* and a first solo album after a string of successes with his band of the same name.

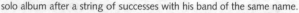

MARTIN HARRIS

Female singer-songwriters have an equally strong following. The mystical voice of Donegal's Enya, formerly of Clannad, has penetrated to a wide audience. Among the best-known contemporary female singers to look out for are sisters Mary and Frances Black, smoky-voiced Mary Coughlan, wild melodion-player Sharon Shannon, Dolores Keane and Eleanor McEvoy. Björkesque Nina Hynes' penetrative voice sets her apart from more traditional singers of the genre.

Popular Music

No account of contemporary Irish music would be complete without reference to the popularity of country music and to singer and boy-next-door Daniel O'Donnell, with huge album sales under his belt. Another perennial over-40s' favourite is dance-hall singer Joe Dolan who still packs them in at small venues around the country. Following in the steps of fellow-crooner Tom Jones, his music had something of a renaissance at the end of the 1990s with the timely release of Joe's Nineties – a cover album featuring songs by Neil Young, Pulp and Blur.

Ireland's phenomenal success rate in the Eurovision Song Contest is not to be sniffed at either. First in a long line to receive the honour was a fresh-faced, 16-year-old Dana from Derry in 1970 with *All Kinds of Everything*, followed by Johnny Logan (twice); Ireland won it for three consecutive years from 1992 to 1994, and again in 1996. It was also from that unlikely platform that *Riverdance* became the outstanding success it is today.

Rock Music

Although Ireland has a healthy track record in producing world-class popular musicians, this was not always the case. During the 1960s when America and Britain were producing revolutionary acts like the Doors, the Beatles, Led Zeppelin and the Rolling Stones, Ireland's contribution to contemporary music was far less evident. Though far from cutting-edge, Church-influenced, conservative Ireland had it's own genre of popular music – the showband. Dickie Rock, Brendan Boyer and the Big Eight and the Miami Showband gigged around the country playing

Top Right: Van 'the Man' Morrison

covers of Top 40 hits to large crowds in purpose-built dance halls.

It wasn't until the late 1960s and 1970s that Rory Gallagher's band Taste and Phil Lynott's Thin Lizzy put Ireland on the map. Rory Gallagher, from Donegal, started his musical career with the Fontana Showband but, unsurprisingly, felt constrained by the limitations of such an outfit. With a passion for the blues he formed his own three-piece rock band, Taste, in 1965. The release of their eponymous debut album in 1969 made them an international force to be reckoned with.

Around the same time, progressive rockers Skid Row, with a young Phil Lynott on vocals, were exploring new ground with their experimental psychedelic sound. The charismatic Lynott soon departed and formed Thin Lizzy in December 1969. The striking appearance and romantic lyrics of the half-Brazilian Dubliner set him apart from the word go. The definitive single *Whisky in the Jar* (1972) provided a showcase for Eric Bell's accomplished guitar work and, by the release of the internationally acclaimed album *Jailbreak* in 1976, Thin Lizzy were one of the best live acts around.

The lesser-known Horslips began making noises on the Irish circuit around 1971 and were said to have invented a new genre – Celtic rock – which boldly crossed traditional Irish tunes with psychedelic rock.

The punk explosion of 1976 saw bands such as the Clash, the Sex Pistols and the Damned grab headlines all over Britain while across the Irish Sea a similar but smaller movement, with bands like The Radiators from Space and the better-known Boomtown Rats, began making waves. The Boomtown Rats, fronted by an angry but eloquent Bob Geldof scored huge success with their singles *Rat Trap* and *I Don't Like Mondays*. Phil Chevron, songwriter and guitarist with the Radiators went on to join the Pogues.

In Northern Ireland, bands such as the Undertones and Stiff Little Fingers were spearheading the musical anarchy. The Undertones' radio-friendly *Teenage Kicks* stands out as an all-time classic single of that era. The harder-edged Stiff Little Fingers were based in Belfast and angry, politically fuelled songs such as *Alternative Ulster* were their stock in trade.

In 1978 a group of friends from the Artane suburb of Dublin (who had invented a private fantasy universe for themselves called Lypton village) formed two bands. Gavin Friday formed the avant-garde Virgin Prunes and later went solo with a rich cabaret style of music, while Bono, The Edge, Adam Clayton and Larry Mullen Jr formed The Hype, later known as U2.

U2's debut album *Boy* in 1980 was the first in a series of classic albums that decade. *War*, *The Unforgettable Fire* and *The Joshua Tree* followed as the band matured and went from strength to strength. A dramatic appearance at the massive Live Aid concert (organised by Bob Geldof) con-

MARTIN HARRIS

Left: Bob Geldof still doesn't like Mondays

solidated their place as a band to be reckoned with on an international scale. With Edge's idiosyncratic guitar playing, Clayton's and Mullen's driving rhythm section and Bono's fervent, emotive lyrics and vocal range, U2 were always primed to fill stadiums with their rock anthems *Sunday Bloody Sunday*, *New Year's Day* and *I Will Follow*. U2's ability to reinvent themselves from the overblown theatrics of 1993's *Zooropa* to the self-deprecating but no less indulgent *Popmart* tour of 1997 has been a factor in their enduring cross-the-board popularity. After a 'best of' album, the release of *All That You Can't Leave Behind* in 2000 saw a return to the more introspective, reflective tone of old.

The Blades, underrated contemporaries of U2, never got the commercial success they deserved. Paul Cleary, the lead singer, continued to write well-crafted, melodic tunes in his next band the Partisans with not much more success. A best hits album released in 2000 created a bit of a stir among those who fondly remembered the Blades' catchy sound.

In the early 1980s, London-based Irish rabble-rousers Pogue Mahone (the name is phonetically Gaelic for 'kiss my ass') emerged. After a ban by the BBC, the more tastefully rechristened Pogues, under the stewardship of singer Shane McGowan, continued to gain support with their punky patriotic songs. Unfortunately McGowan's drunken on- and off-stage antics often overshadowded his genuine, empathetic and lucid songwriting talent.

Around the same time, a 20-year old shaven-headed Dublin singer Sinead O'Connor was gaining attention with her spine-chilling voice

Right: Stadium rockers U2

ANTON CORBIJN

and sharp lyrics. After an auspicious first album in 1987 *(The Lion and the Cobra)* people began to take notice. However it wasn't until her emotional rendition of the Prince song *Nothing Compares 2 U* was released in 1990, with accompanying video of her painfully tearful face (she had just split up with her boyfriend), that her reputation as a powerful singer and songwriter was established. In more recent times her personal life, rather than musical offering, has been the focus of media attention. A series of controversial actions included, paradoxically, taking a full page ad out in the national newspapers asking the press to leave her alone and becoming a priest. Her *Faith & Courage* album (2000) was well received.

Dublin noise merchants My Bloody Valentine, formed in 1984, produced several brooding EPs in the mid-1980s to cult appeal. Mainly a studio band (they were known for their almost static live performances), their most noteworthy work was evident on their second ethereal album *Loveless*, released in 1991.

Former Dublin street buskers, the Hothouse Flowers formed in 1984 and were renowned for their energetic live performances. Singer Liam O'Maonlai's fluid piano playing mixed with stomping gospel strains, traditional folk music and rock created an earthy, vibrant blend. Their 1988 album *People* soared up the Irish charts and peaked at No 2 in the British charts.

In the wake of U2's phenomenal success, a rumour that had A&R people from record companies salivating in their swivel chairs, began circulating. Word had it that there were thousands of great, unsigned bands in Ireland waiting to be discovered and, while it was an exaggeration, U2's achievements had created a climate of (sometimes misplaced) confidence in young guitar-toting hopefuls. It seemed like every kid who'd ever brandished an air guitar came out of their bedroom to peddle their wares in the old venue, the Baggot Inn in Dublin. For many, that's as far as they got. However, that energy was not wasted, and a few truly talented musicians did emerge from that era. Among them the Limerick-based Cranberries, barely out of school, scored huge success with their brooding, indie guitar sound punctuated by Dolores O'Riordain's distinctive piercing voice. Their debut album *Everyone Else Is Doing It So Why Can't We?* in 1993 and follow ups *No Need to Argue* and *Wake Up and Smell the Coffee* provided a string of hits. Other bands rocking Irish stages around that time include The Stunning, A-House and That Petrol Emotion.

Northern Ireland has equally spawned a host of talented bands in recent years. Among them and probably the most successful to date are Downpatrick trio Ash, whose Undertones-influenced debut album *1977* went straight in at No 1 in the UK charts. They supported U2 on their *Popmart* tour and joined forces with the band again in 1997 in Belfast when they played a joint gig to endorse the nascent peace process.

Also from Downpatrick, accomplished act Relish wear their American 1970s soul and R&B influences unashamedly on their sleeves. Their singalong *Rainbow Zephyr* single became the festival anthem of summer 2001.

ANDY EARL – PHOTOGRAPHER © CURTAIN CALL LTD

Glasgow-based three-piece Snow Patrol, originally from Belfast, mix adrenaline-fuelled grunge with soul-baring melancholic lyrics, and have gained widespread respect.

Back in Dublin, indie trio JJ72 have been compared to Radiohead and Joy Division and are a young act to keep an eye on.

Pop

The demise of guitar-based rock music in the early 1990s paved the way for the emergence of boy bands, a formula with which Ireland has had unmitigated success. First off the school bus in 1993 and into the dance studio, with savvy manager Louis Walsh at the helm, were Boyzone, an innocuous five-piece from Dublin, headed by Ronan Keating. The combination of good-looks and tried and tested hits to cover was a sure-fire winner. Their first 12 singles reached the top 5 in Britain and, with a solid fanbase of adoring prepubescents, they went the way of all boy bands and split up. Undeterred, Ronan has gone on to have an equally successful career as a solo artist and – no better man – a boy-band manager. Walsh knew a good thing when he saw it and after lengthy auditions created a second lucrative prodigy, Westlife, who have equalled the Beatles' record of seven consecutive No 1 hits in the UK. The most recent addition to Walsh's books has been Dublin- er Samantha Mumba, a sultry half-Nigerian diva who became an overnight success with her sample of David Bowie's hit *Ashes to Ashes*. Easy on the eyes and ears, The Corrs, sisters and brother act from Dundalk, combine a touch of the traditional with American pop rhythms and harmonies. With *Forgiven Not Forgotten* and *Talk on Corners* they were the first Irish band to hold the top two positions in the UK album charts. Their *In Blue* album was released in 2000.

Top Right:
The Limerick-based
Cranberries

The London-based baroque pop act Divine Comedy, fronted by Derry-born lyricist Neil Hannon, successfully blend their jazzy, classical sound with a pure pop sensibility. Known for their tongue-in-cheek lyrics and Hannon's resonant, moody voice, they've produced eight albums and a string of radio-friendly singles such as *Generation Sex*.

The Dublin girl group B*witched, with their sunny Celtic-infused pop sound, were the first band ever to have their first four singles reach No 1 in the UK.

Punk-tinged bubblegum pop princesses The Chicks are a feisty Dublin three-piece whose Ramones and Blondie influences come across on their album *Criminales, Coches, Pistolas y Chicas*.

The Dance Scene

The emergence of a dance scene proper in Britain came about in the late 1980s and, like the arrival of punk, signalled a dissension with the music of the day – in this case excessive stadium rock – and the need for a fresh new sound. The underground scene aside, the impact of dance culture really only hit Ireland in the early 1990s, but it wasn't long before those thumping club beats were ubiquitous. Since then dance culture evolved and fragmented into distinct identifiable sub-cultures.

David Holmes from Belfast is probably Ireland's most commercially successful DJ. His Sugar Sweet night (now called Shake Ya Brain) in his home town was the first serious venue for dance music in Northern Ireland. In 1995 his debut album *This Film's Crap Let's Slash the Seats* received mixed reviews but his film score for the 1998 film *Out of Sight* set him in a league above the rest. Strains of northern soul, house, funk and jazz can be heard in his set but his outstanding reputation must be as a talented remixer. His third album *Bow Down to the Exit Sign* was released in 2000.

Young Dubliner Johnny Moy has been playing in clubs in Britain and Ireland and touring the major European festivals since 1990. His eclec-

JAMES CUMPSTY

tic taste in Detroit techno, soul and funk has kept him at the fore of the notoriously fickle dance scene in Ireland. Through his independent record label, Influx, he has put out a number of records, including a remix of U2's *Elevation* in 2001, which was used on the *Tomb Raider* film soundtrack and as the opening song on U2's 2001 world tour.

Other Irish notables to watch out for are Glen Brady, Matt Vinyl, Arveene and producer-DJ whizz kids-Decal.

Left: David Holmes – a leading light in the Belfast club scene

Facts for the Visitor

HIGHLIGHTS
Scenery, Beaches & Coastline

It's Ireland's scenery, encompassing a diverse landscape of soft green fields, awesome cliffs tumbling into the ferocious Atlantic, and the rocky, barren reaches of the far west, that constitutes visitors' most abiding memories of the island. Highlights include the beautiful and popular Ring of Kerry, the Dingle Peninsula, the curious limestone outcrops of the Burren, the rocky Aran Islands, and the pretty lakes that dot the north and south.

Stunning stretches of coastline are found in Connemara and Donegal, also at the wild, formidable Cliffs of Moher, at Cork's Mizen Head Peninsula, and along the Antrim coast road, which passes the Giant's Causeway.

The south-eastern coast has some fine beaches and marginally warmer water, while the north and north-western coasts are noted for their fantastic surfing. Sligo and Galway are home to some of the island's best sandy beaches.

Castles, Houses & Museums

Castles and forts of various types and sizes, and in various states of ruination, are scattered liberally across Ireland. The Aran Islands' Stone Age forts are quite interesting, but there are plenty of other ancient ring forts all over Ireland. Prime examples include Bunratty, Charles Fort, Birr and Kilkenny.

A legacy of the Anglo-Irish aristocracy is Ireland's wide selection of stately homes, many of which are open to the public. Castletown House, Malahide House, Mount Stewart and recently reopened Belvedere House are all recommended. Strokestown House in County Roscommon is an important example of Palladian architecture; Bantry House and Powerscourt Estate are both worth a visit for their wonderful gardens.

Ireland has a wealth of good museums. In Dublin there's the must-see Trinity College Library with its ancient Book of Kells, the National Museum, National Gallery, Dublin Castle's Chester Beatty Library, the Old Jameson Distillery and the Ceol interactive museum of traditional Irish music. In the North there's Belfast's excellent Ulster Museum and County Down's Ulster Folk & Transport Museum. Elsewhere, the Blasket Island's visitor centre is worth the sea crossing, the Hunt Museum in Limerick is particularly good, and the 1798 Visitor Centre near Wexford is much acclaimed.

Religious Sites

Stone circles, dolmens and passage graves are ubiquitous reminders of the days before Christianity reached Ireland. Newgrange's massive passage grave is the most impressive of the relics. Early Christian churches, many well over 1000 years old, are strewn across Ireland. Ruined monastic sites, often appearing with characteristic round towers, are also numerous. Clonmacnoise, Glendalough, Mellifont Abbey, Grey Abbey, Inch Abbey and Jerpoint Abbey are all interesting religious sites. Cashel's rock-top complex is rightfully one of Ireland's major tourist attractions. The beehive huts built by monks on Skellig Michael, off the Kerry coast, are also well worth visiting.

Islands

Lying off Ireland's coast are a multitude of islands, many of which are uninhabited save for flocks of migrating birds. Some of these islands are easily accessible, others require the hire of a private boat. Galway's Aran Islands and Mayo's Achill Island are the most visited, but it's easy enough to pick out the more isolated ones. A boat trip to the Skelligs is one of the highlights of a visit to Ireland, and their wildlife is fascinating. Also off the Kerry coast, the Blaskets can be glorious on a fine day. Tory Island, standing in often tempestuous seas off Donegal's coast, is home to a group of local artists. County Cork has a number of accessible islands, of which Clear Island is famous for its bird life.

SUGGESTED ITINERARIES

Any itinerary is very much a matter of personal choice. To do Ireland justice you'll want at least three to four weeks, but the country is small enough for you to cover a fair bit of territory even in a week. The following suggestions may help:

Three Days
Visit Dublin and perhaps a couple of places nearby: Powerscourt Estate and Glendalough to the south, or Newgrange passage grave, Mellifont Abbey and Monasterboice monastery to the north.
One Week
Visit Dublin, Newgrange, Mellifont, Kilkenny town, Killarney, Dingle and the Burren.
Two Weeks
As above, plus the Ring of Kerry and some of the sights of County Cork.
One Month
With a car or motorcycle you would have time to explore all of the above, adding places such as Connemara, Donegal and Antrim to the list, but you'd be moving quite quickly; on public transport this is still feasible but more difficult. A month allows time for some walking and cycling too.

PLANNING
When to Go

The weather is generally warm in July and August, when the daylight hours are long, but the crowds are greater, the costs higher and accommodation scarcer. If you go in winter there are fewer tourists and accommodation is cheaper, but you may get miserable weather, the daylight hours are short and many tourist facilities are shut. The best of both worlds falls between April and June or in September; it's less crowded than in the summer, and most attractions and tourist offices are open. Dublin and Belfast are welcoming destinations year round.

Festivals and other events occur throughout the year. For details see Public Holidays & Special Events later in this chapter.

What Kind of Trip?

Your particular interests will have a large bearing on the kind of trip you choose, as will the amount of time and money at your disposal. The longer you stay, the more

---

Upgrade This Book

The world can change a lot in a day. Borders may open, hotels close or currencies crash. So before you leave home, check out Upgrades on the LP Web site (www.lonelyplanet.com/upgrades) for significant changes that might have occurred since this book went to press. View or download them, print them and fold them to fit inside the guidebook.

Upgrades are available for over 60 guidebooks, including our most popular titles and those covering countries or regions that are changing rapidly. They are revised every six months until the new, thoroughly updated edition of the book is published.

---

likely it is you'll step outside the frequently superficial world of the tourist, and the lower your relative daily expenses will be.

Try to leave enough time to walk at least part of one or two waymarked ways, or to do some cycle touring somewhere off the beaten track. Some visitor attractions have no public transport, so walking or cycling could be your only way to see them.

Hiring a car for part of the trip could be useful if you're planning to visit some out-of-the-way places. There is a good public transport network, but many services in rural areas are infrequent, especially out of the main tourist season.

Many attractions can also be visited as part of a guided tour. This is often a good way to get a quick overview of areas you're unfamiliar with and allows you to consider your options should you wish to return.

Travelling alone is fine, provided you follow normal precautions, and is a great way to meet new people. Hostels, camp sites and caravan parks are good places to meet fellow travellers, and B&Bs allow you to meet locals, who may offer the kinds of insights unavailable at the local tourist office.

Maps

Many publishers produce good-quality maps of Ireland. Michelin's 1:400,000-scale Ireland map (No 923) is a good single-sheet map. The cartography is clear and comprehensive, and the map highlights most of the island's scenic roads. The four maps – North, South, East and West – that make up the Ordnance Survey Holiday map series at 1:250,000-scale are useful if you want more detail. Collins also publishes a range of maps covering Ireland.

For greater detail, the Ordnance Survey Discovery series covers the whole island in 89 maps at a scale of 1:50,000. They're available at the National Map Centre (☎ 01-476 0471), 34 Aungier St, Dublin, and many other bookshops around Ireland.

For details of Lonely Planet's *Dublin City Map* see Maps under Orientation in the Dublin chapter.

What to Bring

A travelpack – a combination backpack and shoulder bag – is the most useful means of carrying gear. A travelpack's straps zip away inside when not needed, making it easy to handle in airports and on crowded public transport. It also looks classier than a backpack and can be made thief-resistant by adding small combination locks.

A raincoat or an umbrella is a necessity (the former is better in windy weather), as are some warm clothes – even during good summer weather it gets chilly in the evenings. Walkers should be well prepared when in exposed or upland country. Dress is usually casual; you're unlikely to come across many jacket-and-tie-type regulations, apart from in some smarter Dublin bars.

Other worthwhile items to pack include a small medical kit (see the Medical Kit Check List in the Health section later in this chapter), a pocket knife, a compass, a torch, an alarm clock or watch with an alarm function, a universal adapter for electrical appliances, a universal bath/sink plug, sunglasses and an elastic clothesline.

RESPONSIBLE TOURISM

As tourist sites and paths become more popular, their surrounding environment comes under greater pressure. Ireland's system of walking paths, called waymarked ways, has been established with the cooperation and good will of various bodies, including pri-

vate landowners, local authorities and voluntary workers. Walkers therefore need to use the ways sensitively by minimising disturbance to farm animals and farmland, and by taking home all rubbish. For more information on conservation issues in Ireland see the Ecology & Environment section of the Facts about Ireland chapter.

TOURIST OFFICES

Bord Fáilte (the Irish Tourist Board) and the Northern Ireland Tourist Board (NITB) each operate a separate network of tourist information offices throughout Ireland and co-produce some joint publications and brochures.

Tourist offices offer a wide variety of services including accommodation reservations, reservation services for local attractions and exhibitions, route planning, bureau de change services (in the larger centres), map and guidebook sales and free publications.

Both national tourist boards feature a computerised tourist information and reservations service (Gulliver) which operates live in all the main tourist offices. Gulliver provides information on places to visit, visas, cultural information and events, transport and accommodation, and the service boasts a unique real-time accommodation reservation service. Gulliver is also available online at W www.ireland.travel.ie and W www.discovernorthernireland.com. Telephone reservations can be made on ☎ 1800 668 668 (Ireland), ☎ 800 398 4376 (USA/Canada) or ☎ 0800 783 5740 (UK).

Bord Fáilte's information service can be contacted on ☎ 1850 230 330 in the Republic, or ☎ 0800 039 7000 in the UK. Alternatively, visit W www.ireland.travel.ie or email e info@irishtouristboard.ie. The NITB's head office is at 59 North St, Belfast. Call them on ☎ 028-9023 1221 or email e visitorservices@nitb.com.

Local Tourist Offices

Both Dublin and Belfast have Bord Fáilte and NITB offices; Dublin and Belfast also have their own tourism agencies. Elsewhere in the Republic and the North there's a tourist office in almost every town big enough to have half a dozen pubs. For contact details of individual local tourist offices see the regional chapters of this book.

Local Bord Fáilte offices have become virtually indistinguishable from souvenir shops as a result of the pressure to be self-financing. They only book Bord Fáilte-approved accommodation or recommend attractions and services registered with them, and often know little about public transport. Consider this before joining the sometimes lengthy queues at their offices. Almost all pamphlets at Bord Fáilte tourist offices have a price tag and there's usually nowhere for local enterprises to advertise their services. Also, some offices open for only very limited periods. As a result, several local communities have set up their own tourist office separate from Bord Fáilte. Hostel and B&B owners are often more useful sources of local information for those on limited budgets.

In the bigger towns and more touristy areas opening hours are usually 9am to 5pm Monday to Friday, and 9am to 1pm on Saturday, but hours are often extended in summer. In other areas offices open seasonally only (from April, May or June to August or September) or for much shorter hours from October to April. Local tourist offices will find and book approved accommodation for walk-in customers; there's a €1.27/2.54 booking fee for this service, the higher price being applicable when you book nonlocal accommodation.

Tourist Offices Abroad

Irish tourist offices abroad include:

Australia
   Bord Fáilte: (☎ 02-9299 6177) 5th level, 36 Carrington St, Sydney, NSW 2000. It also has information on Northern Ireland.
Canada
   Bord Fáilte: (☎ 416-487 3335) 120 Eglinton Ave East, Suite 500, Toronto, Ontario M4P 1E2
   NITB: (☎ 416-925 6368) 2 Bloor St West, Suite 1501, Toronto, Ontario M5R 3J8
France
   Bord Fáilte: (☎ 01 70 20 00 20) 33 rue de Miromesnil, 75008 Paris

   NITB: (☎ 01 49 39 05 77) Centre PO 166, 23 rue Lecourbe, 77015 Paris
Germany
   Bord Fáilte: (☎ 069-6680 0950) Untermainanlage 7, 60329 Frankfurt-am-Main
   NITB: (☎ 069-234 504) Westendstrasse 16–22, 60325 Frankfurt-am-Main
Ireland
   Bord Fáilte: (☎ 028-9032 7888) 53 Castle St, Belfast
   NITB: (☎ 01-679 1977, 1850 230230 within the Republic) 16 Nassau St, Dublin
Italy
   Bord Fáilte: (☎ 02 4829 6060) Via Santa Maria Segreta 6, 20123 Milan
Netherlands
   Bord Fáilte: (☎ 020-504 0689) Spuistraat 104, 1012 VA Amsterdam
New Zealand
   Bord Fáilte: (☎ 09-379 8720) Dingwall Building, 2nd floor, 87 Queen St, Auckland
   NITB: (☎ 09-379 3708) 18 Shortland St, Private Bag 92136, Auckland
UK
   Bord Fáilte: (☎ 020-7493 3201) Ireland House, 150 New Bond St, London W1S 2AQ. Personal callers should go to the Britain Visitor Centre, 1 Regent St, London SW1Y 4PQ.
   NITB: (☎ 0870 155 5250) 24 Haymarket, London SW1 4DG; (☎ 0141-572 4030) 98 West George St, Glasgow G2 1PJ. Personal callers in London should go to the Britain Visitor Centre (see above).
USA
   Bord Fáilte: (☎ 800 223 6470) 345 Park Ave, New York, NY 10154
   NITB: (☎ 212-922 0101) 551 5th Ave, Suite 701, New York, NY 10176

VISAS & DOCUMENTS
Passport

UK nationals don't need a passport to visit the Republic, but are advised to carry one (or some other form of photo identification) to prove that they are a UK national. It's also useful to have a passport or photo ID when changing travellers cheques or hiring a car. EU nationals can enter Ireland with either a passport or a national ID card.

Visitors from outside the EU will need a passport, which should remain valid for at least six months after their intended arrival. If it's about to expire, renew it before you go. Applying for or renewing a passport can take from a few days to several months, so don't leave it until the last minute. Things will probably happen faster if you do everything in person, but check first on what you need to take with you to the passport office. Carry your passport at all times while travelling, and guard it carefully.

Visas

For citizens of EU states and most western countries, including Australia, Canada, New Zealand and the USA, no visa is required to visit either the Republic or Northern Ireland, but citizens of India, China and many African states do need a visa for the Republic. Full visa requirements for visiting the Republic are available online at W www.gov.ie/iveagh/services/visas; for Northern Ireland's visa requirements see W http://visa.fco.gov.uk

EU nationals are allowed to stay indefinitely, while other visitors can usually remain for three to six months. To stay longer in the Republic, contact the local *garda* (police) station or the Department of Foreign Affairs (☎ 01-478 0822, W www.gov.ie/iveagh), 80 St Stephen's Green, Dublin. To stay longer in Northern Ireland contact the Home Office (☎ 0870 606 7766), Immigration and Nationality Department, Lunar House, Wellesley Rd, Croydon CR9 2BY, UK.

Onward Tickets

Although you don't need an onward or return ticket to enter Ireland, it could help if there's any doubt that you have sufficient funds to support yourself in Ireland.

Travel Insurance

This not only covers you for medical expenses and luggage theft or loss, but also for cancellations or delays in your travel arrangements under certain circumstances (if, for instance, you were to fall ill just before departure). Ticket loss is also usually covered by travel insurance. There's a wide variety of policies and your travel agency will have recommendations. Cover depends on your insurance and type of ticket, so ask both your insurer and your ticket-issuing agency to explain where you stand.

If you're an EU citizen, an E111 form covers you for most medical care (excluding medication, dental examinations and X-rays). In the UK these forms are available from the post office. Otherwise, ask your health authority or travel agency. Other countries, such as Australia, also have reciprocal agreements with Ireland and Britain, but many countries do not.

If you do need health insurance, remember that some policies offer lower and higher medical-expense options, but the higher one is chiefly for countries such as the USA that have extremely high medical costs. Everyone should be covered for the worst possible case, such as an accident requiring an ambulance, hospital treatment or an emergency flight home. You may prefer a policy that pays healthcare providers directly rather than you having to pay on the spot and claim later.

Buy travel insurance as early as possible. If you buy it the week before you fly, you may find, for example, that you're not covered for delays to your flight.

Driving Licence & Permits

Unless you have an EU licence, which is treated like an Irish one, your driving licence is valid for 12 months from the date of entry to Ireland, but you should have held it for two years prior to that. If you don't hold an EU licence it's a good idea to obtain an International Driving Permit (IDP) from your home automobile association before you leave. Also, members of automobile associations should ask for a Card of Introduction, which entitles you to services offered by sister organisations (maps, information, breakdown assistance, legal advice etc), usually free of charge. See the Getting Around chapter for details on automobile associations in Ireland. If you take your own vehicle you should always carry a vehicle registration document as proof that it's yours.

Hostel Cards

Recommended for travellers on tight budgets, membership of Hostelling International (HI) will give you access to An Óige hostels in the South and Hostelling International of Northern Ireland (HINI) hostels in the North (see Hostels in the Accommodation section later in this chapter for details). You can become a member for about €15.25 by joining your national Youth Hostel Association (YHA). For details see HI's Web site at W www.iyhf.org. Alternatively, once in Ireland you can join by obtaining a guest card from a hostel and paying €1.90 per night for a stamp, on top of the nightly charge. When you have accumulated six stamps on your card you are a full HI member. Membership entitles you to a range of discounts on car rental, tours, admission fees and activities in Ireland.

Student & Youth Cards

The most useful is the International Student Identity Card (ISIC), a plastic ID-style card. With it you can get discounts on transport, commercial goods and services, and admission to museums and sights. If you're aged under 26 but not a student, you can apply for an International Youth Travel Card (IYTC) or a European Youth Card (EYC), also called a Euro<26 Card, which offer similar discounts. All these cards are issued by hostelling organisations, student unions and student travel agencies.

Seniors Cards

Senior citizens usually need show only proof of age to benefit from the many discounts available to them. These include reductions at museums and galleries, and free or subsidised public transport. The minimum qualifying age is usually 60 to 65 for men, and 55 to 65 for women.

Heritage Discounts

Many parks, monuments and gardens in the Republic are operated by Ireland's heritage organisation, Dúchas. For €19.05 (children and students €7.60) you can get a Heritage Card permitting free access to these sites for one year. For more information contact the Heritage Service, Dúchas (☎ 01-647 3000, fax 661 6764, e info@heritage.ie, W www .heritageireland.com), 51 St Stephen's Green, Dublin. In Northern Ireland, membership of the National Trust entitles you to free admission to its properties, but there are fewer

sites here so it only makes financial sense if you're touring Britain too. Membership costs £31/15/58 for adults/under-25s/families. For more information contact the National Trust Membership Department (☎ 0870 458 4000, W www.nationaltrust.org .uk), PO Box 39, Bromley BR1 3XL, UK.

You can also join Dúchas or the National Trust at most of their sites.

Copies

All important documents (passport data page and visa page, credit cards, travel insurance policy, air/bus/train tickets, driving licence etc) should be photocopied before you leave home. Leave one copy with someone at home and keep another with you, separate from the originals. If your documents are lost or stolen, replacing them will be much easier. You can store and protect vital information, that can then be accessed while travelling, in the eKno 'virtual' travel vault (see eKno Communications Service under Post & Communications later in this chapter).

EMBASSIES & CONSULATES
Irish Embassies & Consulates

Irish diplomatic offices overseas include:

Australia
   Embassy: (☎ 02-6273 3022, fax 6273 3741, e irishemb@cyberone.com.au) 20 Arkana St, Yarralumla, Canberra, ACT 2615
Canada
   Embassy: (☎ 613-233 6281, fax 233 5835) 130 Albert St, Suite 1105, Ottawa, Ontario K1P 5G4
France
   Embassy: (☎ 01 44 17 67 00, fax 01 44 17 67 60) 4 rue de Paris, 75116 Paris
Germany
   Embassy: (☎ 030-220 720, fax 220 72299) Friedrichstrasse 200, 10117 Berlin
Italy
   Embassy: (☎ 06 697 9121, fax 06 679 2354) Piazza di Campitelli 3, 00186 Rome
Netherlands
   Embassy: (☎ 070-363 0993, fax 361 7604, e embassy@irish-embassy.demon.nl) Dr Kuyperstraat 9, 2514 BA The Hague
New Zealand
   Embassy: (☎ 09-302 2867) 2nd floor, Dingwall Building, Queen St, Auckland

UK
   Embassy: (☎ 020-7235 2171, fax 7245 6961)
   17 Grosvenor Place, London SW1X 7HR
   Consulate: (☎ 0131-220 8226) City Base,
   1 St Colme St, Edinburgh EH3 6AA
   Consulate: (☎ 029-2023 0709) Jury's Hotel,
   Mary Ann St, Cardiff CF1 2EQ
USA
   Embassy: (☎ 202-462 3939, fax 232 5993)
   2234 Massachusetts Ave, NW, Washington, DC
   20008. There are also consulates in Boston,
   Chicago, New York and San Francisco.

UK (for Northern Ireland) diplomatic offices abroad include:

Australia
   High Commission: (☎ 02-6270 6666, fax 6270
   6606) Commonwealth Ave, Yarralumla,
   Canberra, ACT 2600
Canada
   High Commission: (☎ 613-237 1530, fax 237
   7980, Ⓦ www.britain-in-canada.org) 80 Elgin
   St, Ottawa, Ontario K1P 5K7
France
   Embassy: (☎ 01 44 51 31 00, fax 01 44 51 32
   88, Ⓦ www.amb-grandebretagne.fr) 35 rue du
   Faubourg St Honoré, 75383 Paris
Germany
   Embassy: (☎ 030-204 570, fax 2045 7574,
   Ⓦ www.britischebotschaft.de) Wilhelmstrasse
   70, 10117 Berlin
Italy
   Embassy: (☎ 06 4220 0001, fax 06 487 3324,
   Ⓦ www.ukinitalia.it) Via XX Settembre 80a,
   00187 Rome
Netherlands
   Consulate: (☎ 020-676 4343, fax 676 1069,
   Ⓦ www.britain.nl) Koningslaan 44, 1007 AE
   Amsterdam
New Zealand
   High Commission: (☎ 04-472 6049, fax 471
   1974) 44 Hill St, Wellington
USA
   Embassy: (☎ 202-588 6500, fax 588 7850) 3100
   Massachusetts Ave NW, Washington, DC 20008

Embassies & Consulates in Ireland

It's important to realise what your own country's embassy can and can't do to help you if you get into trouble. Generally speaking, it won't be much help if the trouble you're in is remotely your own fault. Remember that you are bound by the laws of the country you are in. Your embassy will not be sympathetic if you end up in jail after committing a crime locally, even if such actions are legal in your own country.

In genuine emergencies you might get some assistance, but only if other channels have been exhausted. For example, if you need to get home urgently, a free ticket is exceedingly unlikely – embassies expect you to have insurance. If you have all your money and documents stolen, it might assist with getting a new passport, but a loan for onward travel is out of the question.

Countries with diplomatic offices in Dublin include:

Australia
   Embassy: (☎ 01-676 1517, fax 661 3576,
   ⓔ austremb.dublin@dfat.gov.au, Ⓦ www
   .australianembassy.ie) 2nd floor, Fitzwilton
   House, Wilton Terrace, Dublin
Canada
   Embassy: (☎ 01-417 4100, fax 417 4101) 4th
   floor, 65–68 St Stephen's Green, Dublin
France
   Embassy: (☎ 01-260 1666, fax 283 0178) 36
   Ailesbury Rd, Dublin
Germany
   Embassy: (☎ 01-269 3011, fax 269 3946) 31
   Trimleston Ave, Booterstown, County Dublin
Italy
   Embassy: (☎ 01-660 1744, fax 668 2759,
   ⓔ italianembassy@eircom.net) 63 Northumberland Rd, Dublin
Netherlands
   Embassy: (☎ 01-269 3444, fax 283 9690) 160
   Merrion Rd, Dublin
New Zealand
   Consulate: (☎ 01-660 4233, fax 660 4228,
   ⓔ nzconsul@indigo.ie) 37 Leeson Park, Dublin
UK
   Embassy: (☎ 01-205 3700, fax 205 3890,
   ⓔ bembassy@internet-ireland.ie, Ⓦ www
   .britishembassy.ie) 29 Merrion Rd, Ballsbridge,
   Dublin
USA
   Embassy: (☎ 01-668 7122, fax 668 9946,
   ⓔ aedublin@indigo.ie) 42 Elgin Rd, Dublin

The following countries have consular representation in Northern Ireland:

Germany (☎ 028-7034 0403) Hillman's Way,
   Ballycastle Rd, Coleraine
Netherlands (☎ 028-9077 9088) c/o All-Route

Shipping (NI) Ltd, 14–16 West Bank Rd, Belfast

USA (☎ 028-9032 8239) Queen's House, 14 Queen St, Belfast

CUSTOMS

Duty-free sales are no longer available when travelling within the EU. Under the rules of the single market, goods bought in and exported within the EU incur no additional taxes, as long as duty or taxes have been paid somewhere in the EU – provided the goods are for personal consumption. Over certain limits you may have to show that they are for personal use. The amounts that officially constitute personal use are 800 cigarettes (or 400 cigarillos, 200 cigars or 1kg of tobacco) and either 10L of spirits, 20L of fortified wine, 60L of sparkling wine, 90L of still wine or 110L of beer. There's no customs inspection apart from those concerned with drugs and national security.

Travellers coming from outside the EU are allowed to import, duty free, 200 cigarettes, 1L of spirits or 2L of wine, 60mL of perfume or 250mL of toilet water, and other dutiable goods to the value of €180.

Apart from the usual bans on firearms, explosives and illicit drugs, it is illegal to bring into Ireland such things as oral smokeless tobacco, indecent or obscene books and pictures, all meat and meat products, and all plants and plant products (including seeds). Dogs and cats from anywhere outside Ireland and the UK are subject to strict quarantine laws. The UK's Pet Travel Scheme, whereby animals are fitted with a microchip, vaccinated against rabies and blood tested six months *prior* to entry, will eventually come into force in the Republic. In the meantime, animals arriving into Ireland are quarantined for six months unless they first pass through the UK and meet British criteria for entry. Contact the Department of Agriculture, Food and Rural Development in Dublin (☎ 01-607 2000) for further details.

MONEY
Currency

The punt is dead, long live the euro. In February 2002, after a short transition period, Ireland bid adieu to the punt and adopted the

Prices in This Book

This book was researched during the transition period, when not all prices were available in euros. Prices quoted by hotels, restaurants and entertainment venues in the Republic have been converted to euros at the fixed conversion rate (€1 is equal to IR£0.78, IR£1 is equal to €1.26) – these may undergo further change as the euro comes into use.

euro as its only currency; part of its ongoing commitment to greater European union. The other EU participants in the European Monetary Union (EMU) are Austria, Belgium, Finland, France, Germany, Greece, Italy, Luxembourg, the Netherlands, Portugal and Spain.

The euro (€) is divided into 100 cents. The notes come in denominations of €5, €10, €20, €50, €100, €200 and €500. There are coins of one, two, five, 10, 20 and 50 cents, as well as €1 and €2. The reverse side of the euro coins have a design particular to their country of issue (a Celtic harp in Ireland's case), but are legal tender in all countries that accept the euro. Remember that the UK is not a participant, so if you're travelling to Northern Ireland you'll have to change euros into UK pounds.

If for some reason you have a wad of Irish punts, don't fret. You can exchange them at any bank or bureau de change for euros, but only until 30 June 2002, after which the only place you can exchange punts is at the Central Bank in Dublin, but you'll be able to do so for an indefinite period.

The British pound sterling (£) is used in Northern Ireland, where it is known as the Northern Irish pound. Coins come in denominations of 1p ('p' for 'penny'), 2p, 5p, 10p, 20p, 50p, £1 and £2. Notes are printed in denominations of £5, £10, £20 and £50. Don't confuse Northern Irish pounds (issued by the First Trust Bank, Ulster Bank, Northern Bank and Bank of England) with old, pre-euro Republic of Ireland pounds (issued by the Central Bank of Ireland). 'Sterling' or 'Belfast' are giveaway words on the Northern Ireland notes. Northern Ireland notes, while equivalent in value to British pound notes, are not readily accepted in Britain, but British banks will swap them for you.

Exchange Rates

country	unit	euro	£
Australia	A$1	€0.55	£0.34
Canada	C$1	€0.69	£0.43
Japan	¥100	€0.90	£0.56
New Zealand	NZ$1	€0.45	£0.28
UK	£1	€1.61	–
USA	US$1	€1.11	£0.68

Exchanging Money

The best exchange rates are obtained at banks. In the Republic banks normally open 10am to 4pm on weekdays, and most stay open till 5pm on Thursday or Friday (on Thursday in Dublin). In Northern Ireland banks open 9.30am to 4.30pm on weekdays, and most open until 5pm on Thursday. In remote areas North and South some banks close for lunch from 12.30pm to 1.30pm and some may open only two or three days (or two or three hours) a week, so it's best to change money in larger towns.

Bureaux de change and other exchange facilities usually open for more hours than banks, but the rate and/or commission will be worse. Building societies often handle currency exchange and open longer hours than banks. Many post offices in both the Republic and Northern Ireland have a currency-exchange facility and have the advantage of opening on Saturday morning.

Cash & Travellers Cheques Nothing beats cash for convenience – or risk. It's still a good idea, though, to arrive with some local currency in cash, if only to tide you over till you get to an exchange facility.

Most major currencies of travellers cheques are readily accepted in Ireland, but carrying them in pounds sterling has the advantage that in Northern Ireland or Britain you can change them without exchange loss or commission.

American Express (AmEx) and Thomas Cook travellers cheques are widely recognised and offices don't charge commission

for cashing their own cheques. Eurocheques can also be cashed in Ireland. Keep a record of the cheque numbers and the cheques you have cashed in case of loss. Keep this list separate from the cheques themselves. Also, keep a note of the number to ring in case of loss or theft (you should be given this when you buy the cheques). Travellers cheques are rarely accepted outside banks or used for everyday transactions (as they are in the USA).

Take most cheques in large denominations. It's only towards the end of a stay that you may want to change a small cheque to make sure you don't get left with too much local currency.

ATMs & Credit Cards Plastic cards make the perfect travelling companions – they're ideal for major purchases and let you withdraw cash (using a personal identification number or PIN) from selected banks and automatic teller machines (ATMs). ATMs are usually linked to international money systems such as Cirrus, Maestro or Plus, so you can get instant cash from your account back home. Bear in mind, though, that there's a limit on how much you can withdraw and, unless your bank has a direct link with an Irish bank, each transaction incurs an automatic currency conversion fee.

Credit cards can be linked to an ATM network: ask your bank for a PIN and which ATMs in Ireland accept your credit card. But remember, withdrawing cash from a credit card account can incur immediate and exorbitant cash advance interest rate charges.

Charge cards such as AmEx and Diners Club don't have credit limits, but may not be accepted in small establishments or off the beaten track. Visa and MasterCard are more widely accepted, though many B&Bs and some smaller or remote petrol stations take cash only.

Remember to keep a note of the telephone number to ring if your card is lost or stolen (your credit card company will supply you with it).

International Transfers The most practical way to receive money from overseas is

€40/day X17 = £680
≈ $1000

by telegraphic transfer. There are two ways to do this. The first is through the banking system. Your bank sends money to an Irish bank nominated by you. You will need identification, most likely a passport (though in some cases a driving licence will do), before the money is paid to you in euros, minus the transfer commission, of course. This transfer can take up to eight days.

The quickest way to receive cash from home is to transfer it through AmEx, Thomas Cook or Western Union.

It is not practical to receive money by bank draft. Irish banks are notorious sticklers about drafts and won't allow you to cash them unless you first open a bank account, a small bureaucratic nightmare that involves obtaining proof of residence and address. Even then, it can take three weeks to clear. If you're not planning a long stay, stick to telegraphic transfers.

Security

Carry your money (only what you'll need for that day) somewhere inside your clothing rather than in a handbag or an outside pocket. You might want to stitch an inside pocket into your skirt or trousers to keep an emergency stash; keep at least €75 separate from the rest of your cash in case of emergency. Distribute your money in several places. Most hotels and hostels provide safekeeping, so you can leave money and other valuables with them.

Costs

Ireland is expensive, but costs are lower out of the chief tourist areas. A bed in a hostel dormitory costs €10 to €19 a night in the high season. A B&B will cost about €24 to €32 per person, while more luxurious B&Bs (usually with en suite bathroom), and B&Bs in Dublin, can cost anywhere from €60 per person. Many places to stay have different high- and low-season prices. In this book, unless it says otherwise, the prices quoted are for the high season. It's more economical, in terms of accommodation, to travel with another person, since many places charge a single-occupancy supplement. This means that solo travellers

often pay more than half the double or twin rate.

A modest meal at lunchtime costs €5 to €7, while dinner in a reasonable restaurant with a glass of wine or a beer costs from €13 to €20 (slightly more in Dublin). A pint of Guinness usually costs about €3.25; buying lots of drinks in a pub is a good way of spending a large amount of money in a remarkably short space of time.

Car hire is very expensive (see Rental under Car & Motorcycle in the Getting Around chapter for details). Petrol prices vary but generally basic unleaded petrol costs from €0.90 to €1 per litre. Petrol is more expensive in Northern Ireland at around 80p per litre.

Admission prices are often lower for children, seniors and students than for adults. In this book, unless otherwise stated, admission prices to museums and so on are given for adults/children.

If you stay at a hostel, eat a light pub lunch and cook your own meal in the evening, you could get by on €30 a day, plus transportation costs, but in practice the average budget traveller should be prepared to spend a bit more than this.

Tipping

Although tipping is less prevalent in Ireland than elsewhere in Europe, things are changing fast. Top-end hotels and restaurants usually add a 15% service charge and no additional tip is required. Simpler places usually don't add service, and if you decide to tip, it's acceptable to round up the bill or add 15% at most. You don't have to tip taxi drivers, but if you do 10% is fine. For hotel porters €1 or 70p per bag is acceptable.

Taxes & Refunds

Value-added tax (VAT) is a sales tax of 20% that applies to most goods and services in Ireland, excluding books and children's footwear. Residents of the EU cannot claim a VAT refund. Visitors from non-EU countries can claim back the VAT on large purchases that are subsequently exported from the EU through the Cashback scheme. If you're a resident of a country outside the EU and buy something from a store displaying a Cashback sticker, you'll be given a Cashback voucher with your purchase. This voucher can be refunded in US, Canadian or Australian dollars, British pounds or euros at Dublin or Shannon airport. Alternatively, you can have the voucher stamped at the ferry port and mail it back for a refund.

If you reclaim more than €255 on any of your vouchers you'll need to get the voucher stamped at the customs booth in the arrivals hall at Dublin or Shannon airport before you can get your refund from the Cashback desk.

In Northern Ireland, shops participating in the refund scheme will give you a form/invoice on request. This must be presented to customs with the goods and receipts when you leave. After customs have certified the form, it will be returned to the shop for a refund.

POST & COMMUNICATIONS
Post
Post offices in the Republic are run by An Post, the Irish Postal Service, and open 8.30am (9.30am on Wednesday) to 5.30pm or 6pm on Monday to Friday, and 9am to noon or 1pm on Saturday; small offices may close for lunch. Postcards and airmail letters weighing up to 25g cost €0.38 to Britain, €0.41 to continental Europe and €0.57 to the rest of the world.

Post offices in the North are run by Royal Mail and open 9am to 5.30pm on Monday to Friday, and 9am to 1pm on Saturday. Postcards cost 27p to Britain, 36p to continental Europe, and 40p to the rest of the world. Letters sent by 1st-class/2nd-class mail to Britain cost 27/19p as long as they weigh less than 60g. Airmail letters under 20g cost 36p to continental Europe and 65p to the rest of the world. You can also send airmail letters under 10g to the rest of the world for 45p.

You can also buy stamps from some newsagents and shops. All mail to Britain and Europe goes by air, so air-mail envelopes and stickers are unnecessary.

Both postal services are efficient: over 95% of mail posted to destinations within Ireland is delivered the next working day. Mail to Britain and continental Europe takes three to five days, to Australasia a week to 10 days, and to North America about 10 days. If you want to send mail to be held for collection to a post office in Ireland, mark it 'Poste Restante: Hold for Collection'. The post office will officially only hold this post for two weeks; you will need photo identification to claim your post.

Telephone
When calling the Republic of Ireland from abroad, dial your international access code, followed by 353, followed by the domestic number minus the initial '0'. When calling Northern Ireland from abroad, dial your international access code, then 44 28, and then the local number. To call Northern Ireland from Britain, dial 028, then the local number.

For a small country, Ireland has a remarkably sophisticated phone service and was one of the first countries in the world to make the switch to high-speed fibreoptic cabling. Consequently, you shouldn't have any problems making phone calls to anyone, anywhere. Irish phones offer a full range of services, including reverse-charge calls, operator-assisted calls, telemessages (formerly telegrams) and international directory enquiries.

Eircom is Ireland's largest telephone service provider. Deregulation of the telephone industry has seen the arrival of a number of other providers to Ireland, all of which, however, rent their lines from Eircom. Eircom's main competitor is ESAT, which in 2001 launched its first land-line service. In the North most public phones are owned by British Telecom (BT).

Peak per-minute charges for international calls from Ireland to selected countries include:

to	Republic	North
Australia	€0.85	49p
Canada	€0.19	24p
France	€0.38	29p
Germany	€0.38	29p
New Zealand	€0.85	49p
Italy	€0.48	36p
Netherlands	€0.38	29p
UK	€0.15	8p
USA	€0.19	24p

Mobile Phones

Mobile phone usage in Ireland has skyrocketed. They're the most convenient – and expensive – way to keep in touch. Ireland uses GSM 900/1800, which is compatible with the rest of Europe and Australia but not with North American GSM 1900 or the totally different system in Japan (though some specially equipped North American phones do work here). There are three service providers in Ireland. Eircell (087) is the most popular, followed by ESAT Digifone (086) and the latest arrival, Meteor (085).

All three service providers are linked with most international GSM providers, which will allow you to 'roam' onto a local service once you arrive in Ireland. This means you can use your mobile phone to make local calls, but you should be aware that you will be charged at the highest possible rate for all calls. A pitfall of using your mobile phone in Ireland is that should you receive a call from someone at home, they will be charged for the price of a local call to a mobile, and you will be charged the difference – in some cases an exorbitant amount.

If you're cost-conscious about mobile phone use, you may want to leave yours at home and get a prepaid phone on arrival in Ireland, known as a Ready-to-Go. For around €50 you will get a phone, your own number and anywhere up to €25-worth of air-time. As you use up your air-time, you simply buy more. Ready-to-Go phones are available at mobile phone shops throughout the Republic, while prepaid air-time cards are on sale at nearly all newsagents. Eircell, ESAT Digifone and Meteor have variations on this scheme. Similar schemes exist in Northern Ireland.

Prices are lower in the evening and at the weekend. The above prices are for calls placed from land-line phones to land-line phones; international calls to mobiles can cost significantly more. Phone calls from hotel rooms cost at least double the standard rate.

In the Republic, 1850-prefixed numbers cost €0.15 per call and 1800-prefixed numbers are free.

In Northern Ireland, 0870-prefixed numbers are billed at the national rate, 0845-prefixed numbers are billed at the local rate, and 0800-prefixed numbers are free.

Calls from the Republic Domestic callers simply dial the area code followed by the local number. To call Northern Ireland dial 048, followed by the eight-digit local number. For all other UK numbers dial 00 44, then the area code minus the initial '0', then the local number.

To call elsewhere overseas dial 00 followed by the country code, then the area code (dropping any leading '0'), and then the local number.

For directory enquiries dial ☎ 11811 for numbers within Ireland. For enquiries about numbers in Britain and elsewhere dial ☎ 11818. For international reverse-charge (collect) calls dial ☎ 114 and for operator-assisted calls dial ☎ 10.

Calls from Northern Ireland The area code for the whole of Northern Ireland is 028, so domestic callers need only dial the eight-digit local number. To call Britain dial the area code followed by the local number.

To place an international call or to call the Republic, dial 00 followed by the country code, then the area code (dropping any leading '0') and the local number.

For directory enquiries within the UK dial ☎ 192. For international directory assistance dial ☎ 153. For operator assistance on calls within the UK dial ☎ 100; for operator assistance on international calls dial ☎ 155.

Payphones Local telephone calls from a public phone in the Republic cost €0.25 for around three minutes, regardless of when you call. In Northern Ireland a local call costs a minimum of 20p. Try to avoid making phone calls in pubs, as in the Republic they usually cost €0.38 for the same time, and they're also more expensive than the basic payphone rate in Northern Ireland. National or trunk calls are more expensive (depending on where you're calling) than local-rate calls, but they work out at an average of about €0.63 (50p in Northern Ireland) for three minutes. Calls to mobile phones are dearer still, around €0.50 (75p in Northern Ireland) per minute at peak times and €0.25 (43p in Northern Ireland) at off-peak times.

New-generation prepaid phonecards, available in newsagents and post offices, work from all payphones and dispense with the need for coins. In the South, Eircom's Callcards come in units of 10 (€2.50), 20 (€4.50) and 50 (€10.20). In the North, BT's Phonecard Plus cards come in units of 15 (£3), 25 (£5), 50 (£10), and 100 (£20). Each unit is the equivalent of a local phone call. Many other companies sell their own phonecards. Some of these are limited to domestic or international use only; check the card's capabilities before you buy.

Direct Home Calls Rather than placing reverse-charge calls through the operator in Ireland, you can dial direct to your home-country operator and then reverse the charges or charge the call to a local phone credit card. To use the home-direct service dial the codes in the table below then the area code and, in most cases, the number you want. Your home country operator will come on the line before the call goes through.

eKno Communication Service Lonely Planet's eKno global communication service provides low-cost international calls – for local calls you're usually better off with a local phonecard. eKno also offers free messaging services, email, travel information and an online travel vault, where you can securely store your important documents. To join online, go to **W** www.ekno.lonelyplanet .com, where you will find the local-access numbers for the 24-hour customer-service centre. Once you have joined, always check the eKno Web site for the latest access numbers for each country and updates on new features.

Fax & Telegram

You can send faxes from post offices, most hotels or other specialist offices, but it's expensive: up to €1.50/£1 per page locally, €2.50/£1.50 to €4/£2.50 to Europe and approximately €5/£3 to such overseas destinations as Australia or the USA.

Phone the operator on ☎ 196 in the South to send international telegrams (known as telemessages); in the North call BT on ☎ 0800 190190.

Email & Internet Access

Travelling with a portable computer is a great way to stay in touch with life back home, but setting yourself up abroad can be fraught with problems. If you plan to carry your notebook or palmtop computer with you, remember that the power-supply voltage in the countries you visit may vary from that at home. Check the Electricity section later in this chapter and compare against your home power-supply

Direct Home Call Codes

to	from the Republic	from the North
Australia	☎ 1800 550061 + number	☎ 0800 890061 + number
France	☎ 1800 551033 + number	☎ 0800 890033 + number
Italy	☎ 1800 550039 + number	☎ 0800 890039 + number
New Zealand	☎ 1800 550064 + number	☎ 0800 890064 + number
Spain	☎ 1800 550034 + number	☎ 0800 890034 + number
UK – BT	☎ 1800 550044 + number	n/a
USA – AT&T	☎ 1800 550000 + number	☎ 0800 890011 + number
USA – MCI	☎ 1800 551001 + number	☎ 0800 890222 + number
USA – Sprint	☎ 1800 552001 + number	☎ 0800 890877 + number

ratings. To avoid frying your electronics, the best investment is a universal AC adapter, which will enable you to plug in anywhere. You'll also need a plug adapter for each country you plan to visit – often it's easiest to buy these before you leave home.

Also, your PC-card modem may or may not work once you leave your home country – and you won't know for sure until you try. Either check with your modem manufacturer, buy a reputable 'global' modem before you leave home, or consider buying a local PC-card modem if you're spending an extended time in any one country. Keep in mind that the telephone socket in each country you visit may be different from the one at home, so ensure that you have at least a US RJ-11 telephone adapter that works with your modem. You can almost always find an adapter that will convert from RJ-11 to the local variety. For more on travelling with portable computers visit W www.teleadapt .com or W www.roadwarrior.com.

Major Internet service providers such as AOL (W www.aol.com), CompuServe (W www.compuserve.com) and AT&T Business Internet Services (W www.attbusiness .net) have dial-in nodes throughout Europe; download a list of the dial-in numbers before you leave home. If you access your Internet email account at home through a smaller Internet service provider (ISP) or your office or school network, your best option is either to open an account with a global ISP, like those mentioned above, or to rely on cybercafes. You'll need to carry three pieces of information with you to enable you to access your Internet mail account: your incoming (POP or IMAP) mail server name, your account name and your password. Your ISP or network supervisor will be able to give you these. Armed with this information, you should be able to access your Internet mail account from any Net-connected machine in the world, provided it runs some kind of email software. It pays to become familiar with the process for doing this before you leave home. Alternatively, you can collect mail through cybercafes by opening a free Web-based email account such as those provided by Hotmail

(W www.hotmail.com) or Yahoo! (W http:// mail.yahoo.com).

You'll find cybercafes and/or cyberpubs in most major towns in Ireland. Addresses are listed in specific town sections. You can log on in a cybercafe for €6–9 per hour in the Republic, or about £4 per hour in the North.

DIGITAL RESOURCES

The World Wide Web is a rich resource for travellers. You can research your trip, hunt down bargain airfares, book hotels, check on weather conditions or chat with locals and other travellers about the best places to visit (or avoid!).

The best place to start your explorations is the Lonely Planet Web site (W www .lonelyplanet.com). Here you'll find succinct summaries on travelling to most places (including Ireland), postcards from other travellers, and the Thorn Tree bulletin board, where you can ask questions before you go or dispense advice when you return. You can also find travel news and updates to many of our most popular guidebooks, and the sub-WWWay section links you to the most useful travel resources elsewhere on the Web.

Bord Fáilte and the NITB have their own Web sites (see Tourist Offices earlier in this chapter); some other useful sites are:

CIE Group Public transportation links for the Republic.
W www.cie.ie
Doras An Irish search engine run by Eircom.
W www.doras.ie
EntertainmentIreland Information on entertainment around Ireland, including special events and exhibitions.
W www.entertainment.ie
GoIreland.com Information on accommodation, genealogy, holiday packages and more, with useful links.
W www.goireland.com
Government of Ireland Official government site of the Republic.
W www.gov.ie
Indigo A portal hosted by Ireland's biggest ISP, with good links to news and search engines.
W www.indigo.ie
Ireland.com An information-packed site featuring the *Irish Times* online.

W www.ireland.com

Ireland On-Line An Irish portal with good news, information and mapping links.

W www.iol.com

IrishFood.com Details on recipes, books and more.

W www.irishfood.com

Local Ireland An Irish portal providing information organised by county.

W www.local.ie

NiceOne A comprehensive Irish search engine.

W www.niceone.com

Northern Ireland Office Northern Ireland's official government site.

W www.nio.gov.uk

Translink Public transportation links for Northern Ireland.

W www.translink.co.uk

BOOKS

A glance in almost any bookshop in Ireland will reveal huge Irish-interest sections – fiction, history, current events – and numerous local and regional guidebooks. Many cities have more than one good bookshop, Waterstone's and Eason & Son being familiar names. Two independent shops of note that specialise in books on Ireland are Read Ireland (☎ 01-830 2997), 342 North Circular Rd, Phibsboro, Dublin, and Kenny's Bookshop (☎ 091-562739), High St, Galway.

See Literature in the Arts section of the Facts about Ireland chapter for information on works by Irish writers.

Lonely Planet

Lonely Planet also publishes *Dublin*, a detailed guide to the capital, *Walking in Ireland*, a comprehensive guide to walking Ireland's waymarked ways, and *World Food Ireland*, a full-colour exploration of the history and culture of Irish food and drink. Lonely Planet's *Europe phrasebook* has a chapter on the Irish language.

If you plan to travel more widely within Europe, try *Western Europe* or *Europe on a Shoestring*.

Guidebooks

Ireland, and Dublin in particular, has produced so many writers that you could easily plan a literary holiday. The *Oxford Illustrated Literary Guide to Great Britain*

and Ireland details the writers who have immortalised various towns and villages. Vivien Igoe's *A Literary Guide to Dublin* includes detailed route maps, a guide to cemeteries and an eight-page section on literary and historical pubs.

James Joyce groupies can plan their own Bloomsbury tour of Dublin with a number of books that follow the wanderings of *Ulysses*'s characters in minute detail. *Joyce's Dublin: A Walking Guide to Ulysses* by Jack McCarthy traces the events chapter by chapter with clear maps. *The Ulysses Guide: Tours Through Joyce's Dublin* by Robert Nicholson has easy-to-follow maps. It concentrates on certain areas and follows the events of various related chapters.

The *Irish Pub Guide* lists and describes a number of pubs across Ireland that are of particular interest. *The Hidden Gardens of Ireland* by Marianne Heron is an informative guide. For all sorts of minutiae about Dublin buildings and streets refer to the *Encyclopaedia of Dublin* by Douglas Bennett.

Travel

To understand the Anglo-Irish, read the novel *Woodbrook* by David Thomson, who, as a young man, went to the north-west as a tutor for an Anglo-Irish family.

Pete McCarthy's book, *McCarthy's Bar*, is a recommended account of the author's attempts to rediscover Ireland by way of taking a pint in every pub that bears his name.

For cycling visitors, Eric Newby's *Round Ireland in Low Gear* is a classic of travel masochism complete with lousy weather, high winds and predatory trucks. *Sealegs: Hitchhiking the Coast of Ireland Alone* by Rosita Boland tells the tale of an Irish woman's solo exploration of Ireland by thumb. Not content with simple challenges, Tony Hawks recounts his lunatic hitchhiking expedition in *Round Ireland with a Fridge*.

The Crack: A Belfast Year by Sally Belfrage is a reporter's account of a series of visits to Belfast in the 1980s.

In the mid-1970s, Irish travel writer Dervla Murphy jumped on her faithful bicycle Roz, which she had taken to India in the 1960s, and rode off to explore Northern Ireland. The result was *A Place Apart*. It's a highly readable book and makes an accessible introduction to such topics as Orangeism, Paisleyism and the problems in South Armagh.

History & Politics

For a thorough, detailed account of Irish history there's *The Oxford Companion to Irish History* edited by SJ Connolly. Mike Cronin's *A History of Ireland* is a thoroughly accessible history of the island from the 12th century to the present day. A shorter, very palatable introduction is Máire and Conor Cruise O'Brien's comprehensively illustrated *Ireland: A Concise History*. The more recently published *Ireland: A History* by Robert Kee, developed from a BBC/RTE TV series, covers similar ground in a similar format. Breandán O'hEithir's *A Pocket History of Ireland* is a concise account of Irish history.

Historian Roy Foster's new book *The Irish Story* takes a fresh look at the evolution of the country over the last four hundred years, and Terry Golway describes the vivid tale of Irish nationalism in *For the Cause of Liberty: A Thousand Years of Ireland's Heroes*.

Focusing on the 19th and 20th centuries, the three volumes of *The Green Flag* by Robert Kee offer a good introduction, although the emphasis is more on narrative than analysis. A collection of essays comprise *The Course of Irish History* edited by TW Moody & FX Martin.

The classic study of the 1845–51 Famine is *The Great Hunger* by Cecil Woodham Smith. A more recent analysis is Christine Kinealy's *This Great Calamity*. Liam O'Flaherty's novel *Famine* was based on the catastrophe, as was *The Hanging Gale*, from a BBC/RTE TV series.

Two important tomes on Ireland's more recent history are JJ Lee's controversial *Ireland 1912–1985* and the classic *Ireland since the Famine* by FSL Lyons. Lyons' book is the standard history for all students of modern Ireland; its author was a professor of history at Trinity College. However,

for books that include a look at contemporary Ireland, you're best off trying John Ardagh's *Ireland & the Irish – Portrait of a Changing Society*. It is a well written exploration of the complexities of a nation struggling to make changes while attempting to maintain its essence. Another excellent book on contemporary Ireland is *She Moves Through the Boom* by Anne Marie Hourihane, which looks at the country through a variety of different eyes, including those of asylum seekers. It is insightful and full of funny observations.

Two contrasting titles exploring the roots and results of Ireland's phenomenal economic success are *The Making of the Celtic Tiger* by Ray MacSharry and Padraic White, and *The Celtic Tiger: The Myth of Social Partnership in Ireland* by Kieran Allen. The former eulogises its success, which is hardly surprising considering that MacSharry was Minister of Finance in the 1980s. Allen's book is more interested in the cracks beneath the surface and argues that the economic 'miracle', though of benefit to many, has benefited far fewer than the government would have us imagine.

The North The problem with books about Northern Ireland's recent history is that they're in constant need of updating and it's difficult to find a truly impartial account of what has been happening.

A serious and far-reaching attempt to get to grips with Ulster's story is *A History of Ulster* by Jonathon Bardon. It's a thorough but readable account of Ulster from prehistory to the 1990s. Thomas Hennessey's more recent *A History of Northern Ireland* is also worth investigating. Brian Barton's *A Pocket History of Ulster* is a concise introduction to the history of the North.

German academic Sabine Wichert, a Belfast resident since the early 1970s, manages to bring an outsider's view to Northern Ireland's tumultuous history in *Northern Ireland since 1945*. US-based journalist and historian Jack Holland takes a more recent look in the acclaimed *Hope Against History: The Course of Conflict in Northern Ireland*. J Bowyer Bell's *The IRA, 1968–2000: Analy-*

sis of a Secret Army is one man's biography of the IRA. Gerry Adams, the president of Sinn Féin, gives his account of the Troubles in *Free Ireland: Towards a Lasting Peace*.

Jonathan Stevenson's *We Wrecked the Place* gets inside the minds of paramilitaries on both sides and tries to explain what motivates them.

Three books worth reading on life in Belfast during the Troubles are John Conroy's captivating *A Belfast Diary: War as a Way of Life*, Gerry Adams' *Falls Memories: A Belfast Life*, and Tony Parker's collection of interviews with Belfast people, *May the Lord in His Mercy Be Kind to Belfast*.

The prolific investigative journalist Martin Dillon has a slew of recent books out: *God and the Gun*, *The Dirty War* and *The Shankill Butchers* all cover various aspects of the Troubles.

Based on the BBC TV series, *Loyalists* by Peter Taylor draws back the veil on the complex story of loyalism, from the 17th century to the 1998 Good Friday Agreement and its aftermath.

General

The *Irish Almanac & Yearbook of Facts*, published annually, is a good reference, with lots of information on many different aspects of Irish life, on both sides of the border.

FILMS

If you'd like to get in the mood for your holiday by watching films that are set in Ireland or use Ireland as a backdrop, choose some of the following. For information on films by Irish directors and producers, which generally also have Irish settings, themes and casts, see Cinema in the Arts section of the Facts about Ireland chapter.

Hollywood came to Ireland in 1952 when John Ford filmed John Wayne as *The Quiet Man*, wooing Maureen O'Hara in Cong, County Sligo. You can take Quiet Man tours in Cong today. The 1970 David Lean epic, *Ryan's Daughter*, was filmed on the Dingle Peninsula in Kerry. The place and the film have been inextricably linked ever since: the Dingle Peninsula has simply become 'Ryan's Daughter country'.

The Tom Cruise and Nicole Kidman vehicle *Far and Away* (1992) provided some picturesque views of the western coast, and Dublin's Temple Bar stood in for late-19th-century Boston! *The Secret of Roan Inish* (1994) is a mystical tale set on the western coast of Ireland. Though filmed on the Isle of Man, *Waking Ned* (1998) is a whimsically humorous, but morally questionable, tale of Irish villagers claiming the lottery money of the deceased winner. *Hear My Song* (1991), about the Irish tenor Joseph Locke, was a surprise success.

Many films have been set in Dublin. Joseph Strick attempted the seemingly impossible task of putting *Ulysses* on screen in 1967. The film was promptly banned in Ireland. A 21st-century version is now in the works. Renowned director John Huston's final film, *The Dead* (1987), was based on a story from James Joyce's *Dubliners*. *The Commitments* (1991), by British director Alan Parker, was a wonderful, bright and energetic hit about a northern-Dublin soul band. *The Snapper* (1993) and *The Van* (1995), other books by Roddy Doyle, were also made into films. Following his convincing portrayal of an Irishman in *The Playboys* (1992), Albert Finney played a 1960s Dublin bus conductor who runs an amateur theatre group in *A Man of No Importance* (1994). The city also appeared in John Boorman's *The General* (1997), about the notorious Dublin gangster Martin Cahill, played by Brendan Gleeson.

The Troubles have spawned several films. An early one is *Odd Man Out* (1947) starring James Mason. *Some Mother's Son* (1996), starring Helen Mirren, deals with events surrounding the hunger strike of 1981 and the election of Bobby Sands as MP for Tyrone and Fermanagh shortly before his death. Other films are Channel 4's *A Further Gesture* (1996), about an IRA man escaping to Paris, and *Patriot Games* (1992) with Harrison Ford, an over-the-top tale of a man who thwarts an IRA assassination attempt in London and is then hunted by IRA agents seeking revenge.

Ireland has also been a pure and straightforward backdrop. The Powerscourt Estate in County Wicklow was the setting for films such as Laurence Olivier's *Henry V* (1943), Stanley Kubrick's *Barry Lyndon* (1975) and John Boorman's *Excalibur* (1980). Youghal in County Cork was Captain Ahab's port in John Huston's *Moby Dick* (1956). Cork and Donegal figure in *Disco Pigs*, a film about the bond that exists between twins. The Irish countryside was used for the WWI aerial epic *The Blue Max* (1966), and *Educating Rita* (1982) used Trinity College as its quintessentially English university! Dublin Castle can be spotted in the 1997 version of *Moll Flanders* starring Julia Roberts. Though set in Scotland, Mel Gibson's Oscar-winning *Braveheart* (1994) was mostly filmed in Ireland. Wexford's beaches stood in for Normandy's in Steven Spielberg's *Saving Private Ryan* (1997), and the town makes an appearance in *A Love Divided* (1999), a moving tale of the trials of an interdenominational relationship in 1950s Ireland.

NEWSPAPERS & MAGAZINES

In the Republic, the daily *Irish Times* (W www.ireland.com) is a bastion of liberal opinion and good journalism, and is considered by some to be one of the world's best newspapers. The biggest-selling paper is the *Irish Independent* (W www.independent.ie) and its Sunday equivalent. These both tend to be lighter in content, with more features and gossip. The *Irish Examiner* (W www.examiner.ie), formerly the *Cork Examiner*, has only recently started nationwide news coverage, but is remarkably good. The two main evening papers are the *Evening Herald*, published in Dublin, and Cork's *Evening Echo*. The *Sunday Tribune* has a liberal approach and claims to be good at investigating and breaking stories. One of the biggest sellers on Sunday is *Sunday World*, offering plenty of titillation. The *Sunday Business Post* concentrates on financial matters.

In the North you'll find the apolitical evening *Belfast Telegraph* (W www.belfasttelegraph.co.uk). The Sunday edition is called *Sunday Life*. Morning papers are the tabloid and staunchly Protestant *News Letter* and the pro-nationalist *Irish News* (W www.irishnews.com). *An Phoblacht/Republican News* (W http://irlnet.com/aprn) is published weekly by Sinn Féin.

Ireland has a range of magazines that cater for almost every interest, but the most popular is *RTE Guide*, the weekly radio and TV guide. For serious investigative journalism and opinion there's the current-affairs monthly *Magill*, and for a satirical viewpoint there's the fortnightly *Phoenix*.

British papers and magazines are readily available in both the North and the South. They sell at a slightly higher price in the South than in the North, but still undercut the Irish ones. There are sanitised Irish versions of the British daily tabloids in the South. The main European and US newspapers and magazines are sold in the larger newsagents in Dublin, Belfast and Cork.

RADIO & TV

The Republic has four Radio Telefís Éireann (RTE) state-run radio stations. Irish radio, AM or FM, varies in quality. Many of the morning programs consist of phone-ins. RTE Radio One (88–90 FM or 567/729 MW) has a good mix of documentaries, music and talk shows. Broadcasters such as Pat Kenny, Joe Duffy and Marian Finucane give an insight into the country's foibles. Also notable on RTE1 is John Bowman's *Questions & Answers* (Tuesday evenings), a lively current-affairs discussion. RTE's 2FM (92–93 FM or 612/1278 MW) is the national pop-music station and is a good forum for upcoming Irish rock talent. Lyric FM (96–99 FM) is a 24-hour classical-music and arts service. Radió na Gaeltachta (92.5–96 FM or 540/828/963 MW) is the national Irish-language service. It's possible to tune into British BBC radio and independent channels, though the farther west you go, the weaker the signal. Today FM (100–100.3 FM) is a very popular nationwide radio station (formerly Radio Ireland) that has been running for about five years. The Eamon Dunphy show from 5pm to 7pm weekdays is a relevant, topical – and nearly always controversial – talk show, hosted by sports journalist Dunphy (you either love him or hate him). The Pet Sounds show with Tom Dunne (7pm to 9pm weekdays), Donal Dineen's 10pm to 1am indie-music show, and the Sunday Show with *Irish Independent* journalist Sam Smyth (Sunday mornings) are all worth tuning in for.

There is a host of regional radio stations offering good local services. The most popular is Highland Radio in Donegal broadcasting on 94.7 FM; others include LM FM in Counties Louth and Meath on 95.8 FM, Radio Kerry on 97.6 FM, and Clare FM on 96.4 FM. In Dublin, 98 FM and FM 104 stations offer a diet of classic international rock and pop tunes.

The state-run TV channels in the Republic are RTE 1 and 2 and the Irish-language Telefís na Ghaelige (TnaG). British BBC and independent TV programs can be picked up in many parts of the country and offer a welcome substitute for the sometimes dreary Irish programming. In its defence, RTE isn't bad by international standards. It may appear parochial but local topics are always of limited interest to outsiders. TV3, Ireland's first commercial station, began broadcasting in September 1998.

A program worth watching is *The Late Late Show* (RTE 1), the longest-running chat show in the world, hosted by Pat Kenny. It has a good mix of celebrities and current affairs, and is often an interesting window into Irish life. Current-affairs programs such as *Prime Time* (RTE 1) are also worth a look. Watch out for Gaelic football and hurling matches broadcast at the weekend.

In Northern Ireland, there are two TV stations: BBC NI and Ulster TV (UTV), which mix their own programming with input from their parent networks in Britain (BBC and ITV, respectively). Britain's Channel 4 and Channel 5 also broadcast in Northern Ireland, and you can pick up Channel 4 and UTV throughout the Republic, too.

VIDEO SYSTEMS
Ireland uses the PAL system for video recorders and players, which is not compatible with NTSC or SECAM, standards in use elsewhere around the world.

PHOTOGRAPHY & VIDEO
Ireland has enough spectacular seascapes, ancient ruins, picturesque villages and interesting faces to keep any photographer or video-camera user happy.

Developing and printing a 24-exposure print film typically costs around €10.50 (£6.50 in Northern Ireland) for a one-hour service or from €6.50 to €8 (£4 to £5 in Northern Ireland) for a slower turnaround. Slide processing costs about €9 (£5.50 in Northern Ireland) per roll and takes a few days in most places.

Technical Tips
Irish light can be very dull, so to capture the sombre atmosphere use faster film, such as 400, 800, or even 1600 ASA. Fujicolor 800 is a suitable all-purpose choice. Lonely Planet's full-colour *Travel Photography: A Guide to Taking Better Pictures,* written by internationally renowned travel photographer Richard I'Anson, is full of handy hints and is designed to take on the road.

Restrictions
In the North, if you want to take photos of fortified police stations or army posts and other military or quasi-military paraphernalia, ask first to be on the safe side. Some tourist attractions either charge for taking photos or prohibit it altogether. Use of flash is annoying and it's often forbidden in museums to protect delicate pictures and fabrics. Video cameras may also be disallowed because of the inconvenience they can cause other visitors.

Airport Security
You'll have to put your camera and film through the X-ray machine at all airports. The machines are supposed to be film-safe, but you may feel happier if you put exposed films in a lead-lined bag to protect them. To err on the side of caution, get your photos developed before you travel.

TIME
In winter, Ireland is on Greenwich Mean Time (GMT), also known as Universal Time Coordinated (UTC), the same as Britain. In

summer, the clock shifts to GMT plus one hour. When it's noon in Dublin, Belfast and London, it is 3am in Los Angeles and Vancouver, 7am in New York and Toronto, 1pm in Paris, 8pm in Singapore, and 10pm in Sydney or Melbourne.

ELECTRICITY

Electricity is 220V, 50Hz AC. Plugs are of the three flat pin type, as in Britain.

WEIGHTS & MEASURES

Progress towards metrication in Ireland is slow and piecemeal. Green roadsigns give distances in kilometres, older white ones measure them in miles, and newer white ones give them in kilometres. Speed limits are given in miles per hour, food in shops is priced and weighed in metric units, and beer in pubs is served in pints and half pints. Some helpful metric–imperial conversions are given on the inside back cover of this book.

LAUNDRY

Most hostels and some cheaper hotels have inexpensive self-service laundry facilities. Otherwise, there are self-service laundrettes and dry cleaners in most sizeable towns. Washing a load costs about €4 (or about £3 in Northern Ireland) and drying it another €1.50 (£1.50 in Northern Ireland) or so. Laundrettes usually also offer a service-wash facility, where for €6.25–9 (more in Northern Ireland) they'll wash, dry and neatly fold your washing. Guesthouses and hotels sometimes offer a similar service in conjunction with a local laundry, tacking on a small handling fee.

TOILETS

Many Irish restaurants and bars display notices asserting that toilets are reserved for customers only. Given this fact and the money Ireland makes from visitors it wouldn't seem unreasonable to expect that decent facilities would be available elsewhere. Instead, public toilets are often fairly sordid. Even places with lots of visitors seem to regard keeping their facilities clean as a low priority.

Most toilets have signs indicating gender in English and Irish, but some may have a sign in Irish only. To avoid any embarrassment be warned that the Irish word 'mná', which looks like the English word 'man', does in fact mean 'women'; the Gaelic word for 'men' is 'fir'. The Irish word for 'toilet' is 'leithreas'.

The law states that all places open to the public should have facilities for the disabled (and quite a few of the newer bars and restaurants do have proper facilities), but many establishments have been slow to comply.

HEALTH

Apart from cholesterol, Ireland poses no serious threats to health. The Catholic distaste for contraception doesn't prevent condoms being sold, to those aged over 18, through pharmacies if the pharmacist isn't personally opposed. Condoms are also available from vending machines in many pubs and nightclubs. The pill is available on prescription only. For emergency phone numbers, see the Emergencies section later in this chapter.

Predeparture Planning

Immunisations No jabs are required to travel to Ireland, but it's wise to make sure routine vaccinations such as polio (usually administered during childhood), tetanus and diphtheria (usually administered together during childhood and updated every 10 years) are up-to-date. If you'll have stopovers in Asia, Africa or Latin America, check with your travel agency and doctor. Don't leave it till the last minute, as the vaccinations may have to be spread out over several weeks. Vaccinations should be recorded on an International Health Certificate, which is available from your physician or government health department.

Health Insurance Get adequate health insurance before you travel. For details see Travel Insurance in the Visas & Documents section earlier in this chapter.

Other Preparations Make sure you're healthy before you start travelling. If you wear glasses take a spare pair and your pre-

Medical Kit Check List

Following is a list of items you should consider including in your medical kit – consult your pharmacist for brands available in your country.

- ☐ **Aspirin or paracetamol (acetaminophen in the USA)** – for pain or fever
- ☐ **Antihistamine** – for allergies, eg, hay fever; to ease the itch from insect bites or stings; and to prevent motion sickness
- ☐ **Cold and flu tablets, throat lozenges and nasal decongestant**
- ☐ **Multivitamins** – consider for long trips, when dietary vitamin intake may be inadequate
- ☐ **Insect repellent, sunscreen, lip balm and eye drops**
- ☐ **Calamine lotion, sting relief spray or aloe vera** to ease irritation from sunburn and insect bites or stings
- ☐ **Antifungal cream or powder** – for fungal skin infections and thrush
- ☐ **Antiseptic (such as povidone-iodine)** – for cuts and grazes
- ☐ **Bandages, Band-Aids (plasters) and other wound dressings**
- ☐ **Water purification tablets or iodine**
- ☐ **Scissors, tweezers and a thermometer** – note that mercury thermometers are prohibited by airlines

scription. If you require a particular medication take an adequate supply, as it may not be available locally. Take part of the packaging showing the generic name, rather than the brand, which will make getting replacements easier. It's a good idea to have a legible prescription or letter from your doctor to show that you legally use the medication.

Basic Rules

Care in what you eat and drink and maintenance of personal hygiene are the most important health rules, wherever you travel. Many health problems can be avoided by just taking care of yourself. Wash your hands frequently. Tap water in Ireland is normally safe. Don't drink straight from a stream: you can never be certain there are no people or animals upstream.

Environmental Hazards

Cold Hypothermia occurs when the body loses heat faster than it can produce it and the core temperature of the body falls. It's easy to progress from very cold to dangerously cold due to a combination of wind, wet clothing, fatigue and hunger, even if the air temperature is above freezing.

Walkers in Ireland should be prepared for difficult conditions. It's best to dress in layers, and a strong, waterproof outer layer is essential. A hat is important, as a lot of heat is lost through the head. Carry basic supplies, including food containing simple sugars to generate heat quickly.

Symptoms of hypothermia are exhaustion, numb skin (particularly toes and fingers), shivering, slurred speech, irrational or violent behaviour, lethargy, stumbling, dizzy spells, muscle cramps and violent bursts of energy.

To treat mild hypothermia, first get the person out of the wind and/or rain, remove their clothing if it's wet and replace it with dry, warm clothing. Give them hot liquids – not alcohol – and some high-calorie, easily digestible food. Do not rub victims: instead, allow them to slowly warm themselves. The early recognition and treatment of mild hypothermia is the only way to prevent severe hypothermia, which is a critical condition – sufferers should get urgent medical attention.

Heat Exhaustion Dehydration or salt deficiency can cause heat exhaustion. In hot conditions (they do happen!), or if you're exerting yourself, make sure you get sufficient nonalcoholic liquids such as tea and drinks rich in mineral salts (such as clear soups, and fruit and vegetable juices). Salt deficiency is characterised by fatigue, lethargy, headaches, giddiness and muscle cramps. Salt tablets may help, but adding salt to your food is better.

Sexually Transmitted Diseases (STDs)

STDs include gonorrhoea, herpes and syphilis. Sores, blisters or rashes around the genitals, discharges, or pain when urinating are common symptoms. With some STDs, such as wart virus or chlamydia, symptoms may be less marked or not observed at all, especially in women. Chlamydia infection can cause infertility in both men and women before any symptoms have been noticed. Syphilis symptoms eventually disappear completely but the disease continues and can cause severe problems in later years.

While abstinence from sexual contact is the only 100% effective prevention, using condoms is also effective. The treatment of gonorrhoea and syphilis is with antibiotics. The different sexually transmitted diseases each require specific antibiotics.

HIV & AIDS Infection with the human immunodeficiency virus (HIV) may develop into acquired immune deficiency syndrome (AIDS), which is a fatal disease. Exposure to blood, blood products or bodily fluids may put the individual at risk.

Apart from abstinence from sexual contact, the most effective preventative is always to practise safe sex using condoms. It's impossible to detect the HIV-positive status of an otherwise healthy-looking person without a blood test.

HIV/AIDS can also be spread through infected blood transfusions, but in Ireland these are safe. It can be spread by dirty needles: vaccinations, acupuncture, tattooing and ear or nose piercing can be potentially as dangerous as intravenous drug use if the equipment isn't clean. Fear of HIV infection should never preclude treatment for serious medical conditions.

WOMEN TRAVELLERS

Women travellers will probably find Ireland a blissfully relaxing experience, with little risk of hassle on the street or anywhere else. Nonetheless, you still need to take elementary safety precautions. Walking alone at night, especially in certain parts of Dublin, is probably unwise. Even though hitching in Ireland is safer than hitching pretty much anywhere else in Europe, it isn't recommended.

One or two hostel owners let the side down when it comes to bothering female guests. Keep your ears pinned to the ground and heed any warnings that come your way. Should you have serious problems, be sure to report them to the local tourist authorities... and to us!

There's little need to worry about what you wear in Ireland, and the climate is hardly conducive to controversial topless sunbathing. Finding contraception is not the problem it once was, although anyone on the pill should bring adequate supplies.

GAY & LESBIAN TRAVELLERS

Surprisingly for such an overwhelmingly Catholic country, Irish laws on homosexuality are among the most liberal and progressive in Europe. There is a common age of consent of 17, and neither gays nor lesbians (in the Republic) are excluded from the armed forces. Despite its dogma on the matter, the Catholic Church has maintained a silent neutrality on gay and lesbian issues.

Dublin, and to a lesser extent Belfast, Cork, Galway, Waterford and Limerick, have openly gay and lesbian communities, but elsewhere the scene is quiet. The monthly *Gay Community News* (W www .gcn.ie) is a free publication of the National Lesbian and Gay Federation (☎ 01-671 9076, e gcn@eircom.net), 2 Scarlett Row, Temple Bar, Dublin. The Web sites W www .gayireland.com, W www.gaire.com, W www .channelqueer.com, W www.irishmuffin .com and W www.glyni.org.uk are all online resources for the gay and lesbian community. Information is also available from the following organisations:

Outhouse (☎ 01-873 4932, e info@outhouse.ie, W www.outhouse.ie) 105 Capel St, Dublin. A gay, lesbian and transgender community centre.
Northern Ireland Gay Rights Association (NIGRA; ☎ 028-9066 4111) PO Box 44, Belfast

The following helplines can be called from anywhere in Ireland:

Gay Switchboard Dublin (☎ 01-872 1055) 8pm to 10pm Sunday to Friday and 3.30pm to 6pm Saturday
Lesbian Line Dublin (☎ 01-872 9911) 7pm to 9pm Thursday
Lesbian Line Belfast (☎ 028-9023 8668) 7.30pm to 10pm Thursday

Mensline Belfast (☎ 028-9032 2023) 7.30pm to 10.30pm Monday to Wednesday

On a negative note, in 2001 there was a substantial outbreak of syphilis among gay and bisexual men in Dublin. Gay organisations have strongly advised that care be taken so as to contain its spread. The Gay Men's Health Project (☎ 01-660 2189) offers practical advice on protection and treatment in case of infection.

DISABLED TRAVELLERS

If you have a physical disability, get in touch with your national support organisation (preferably the travel officer if there is one) and ask about your intended visit to Ireland. They often have libraries devoted to travel and can put you in touch with travel agencies who specialise in tours for the disabled.

Guesthouses, hotels and sights in Ireland are gradually being adapted for people with disabilities. Bord Fáilte's annual accommodation guide, *Be Our Guest*, indicates which places are wheelchair accessible. The NITB publishes *Accessible Accommodation in Northern Ireland*. Your travel agency may have access to the most recent details via Gulliver (see Tourist Offices earlier in this chapter) about facilities available for disabled people.

Public transportation can be a nightmare: if you're using a wheelchair, forget about getting a bus. Trains are accessible with help. In theory, if you call ahead, an employee of Iarnród Éireann (Irish Rail) will arrange to meet you at the station and accompany you to the train.

Further information on access for disabled travellers is available in the Republic from ☎ 1800 350150. Comhairle (The Access Service; ☎ 874 7503, W www.comhairle .ie), 44 North Great George St, Dublin, is an agency charged with supporting the rights of the disabled in the Republic. In Northern Ireland you can contact Disability Action (☎ 028-9066 1252), Unit 22, Stockman's Way, Belfast. Travellers to Northern Ireland can also check the Web site of Everybody's Hotel Directory (see Accommodation later in this chapter).

SENIOR TRAVELLERS

Senior citizens are entitled to many discounts in Europe on things such as public transport and museum admission fees, provided they show proof of their age. The minimum qualifying age is usually 60 to 65 for men and 55 to 65 for women. In your home country, a lower age may already entitle you to all sorts of interesting travel packages and discounts (on car hire, for instance) through organisations and travel agencies that cater for senior travellers. Start hunting at your local senior citizens' advice bureau.

Car rental companies usually won't rent to drivers aged over 70 or 75.

TRAVEL WITH CHILDREN

Successful travel with young children requires effort, but can be done. Try not to overdo things and consider using some sort of self-catering accommodation as a base. This frees you from the limited opening hours of restaurants and hotels, and gives you more flexibility. That said, Ireland is one of the more child-friendly countries in Europe, with provisions often made for children in hotels and restaurants. They're welcome in B&Bs, though you need to check on facilities when you book. Children are allowed in pubs (but not to consume alcohol) until 7pm or 8pm, and in smaller towns this restriction is treated with customary Irish flexibility.

You can often buy a family ticket for admission to attractions, and family passes are available on public transport. Special events aimed specifically at children occur during the year; check in the events guides published by the tourist boards. Include children in the planning process: if they've helped to work out where you'll be going, they'll be more interested when they get there. Include a range of activities – for example, balance a visit to Trinity College, Dublin, with one to the National Wax Museum. Other good sites for children in Dublin include The Ark, Dublin Zoo and Fort Lucan.

For further general information see Lonely Planet's *Travel with Children* by Cathy Lanigan.

DANGERS & ANNOYANCES

Ireland is safer than most countries in Europe but normal precautions should be observed. In Dublin, drug-related crime is quite common and the city has its fair share of pickpockets and thieves waiting to relieve the unwary of unwatched bags. See Dangers & Annoyances in the Dublin chapter for more details.

Don't leave valuables in view inside parked cars. Dublin is particularly notorious for car break-ins, and foreign-registered and rental cars are prime targets (though the latter no longer have any markings to identify them as such). Insurance policies often don't cover losses from cars. Cyclists should lock their bicycles securely and be cautious about leaving bags on the bike, particularly in larger towns or more touristy locations.

The police in the Republic are called by their Irish name of Garda Síochána, or just *garda* for one police officer and *gardaí* (pronounced gar-**dee** or, commonly, gar-**thee**) for more than one. In Northern Ireland the police were called the Royal Ulster Constabulary (RUC), but in 2001 their name changed to the Police Service of Northern Ireland.

The Troubles

Obviously, there's a certain degree of violence due to the Troubles in Northern Ireland, but it's unusual to come across any personally, and if the peace process continues violence should diminish. Still, it's probably best to ensure your visit to Northern Ireland doesn't coincide with the climax of the Orange marching season on 12 July. Many Northern Irish, both Protestant and Catholic, leave the province for a few days either side of that date.

If you confine yourself to the Antrim coast you may well never see the British army, but in Derry or South Armagh, on the other hand, its presence is more obvious. Tourists are treated with courtesy by the security forces, but you may be asked for some form of identification. Don't leave a bag unattended: apart from the risk of theft it could be the subject of a security alert.

A British accent can be a help or a hindrance, depending on who you speak to.

Racism

Racially, the Irish people are very homogeneous and in the past it was mainly the Traveller (Tinker) community that was the butt of intolerance. Today, that intolerance extends to other minority groups, especially those with different coloured skin.

In rural areas, where non-Caucasians are few, they are unlikely to experience anything more than a naive curiosity. In cities, however, especially Dublin with its large concentration of black students and asylum seekers, abuse and physical assaults are on the increase (see the boxed text 'Racism' in the Dublin chapter). Refugees from Eastern Europe, particularly those that can't speak English, are also subject to abuse. The widely proclaimed strength of the Irish economy has attracted illegal immigrants, whose presence (though small in number) has fanned racial intolerance.

EMERGENCIES

The emergency phone number throughout Ireland is ☎ 999. You can also dial ☎ 112 in the Republic. After dialling, specify whether you want the police (gardaí), an ambulance, fire service, coastal rescue, or mountain and cave rescue.

LEGAL MATTERS

If you need legal assistance contact the Legal Aid Board (☎ 01-240 0900), St Stephen's Green House, Dublin. It has a number of local law centres listed in the phone book.

Drugs

Importing illegal drugs is prohibited and could result in imprisonment. The possession of small quantities of marijuana attracts a fine or warning, but harder drugs are treated more seriously.

Drinking

The legal drinking age is 18 and you may need a photo ID to prove your age. Although public drunkenness is illegal, the police grant enormous leeway. If matters get out of hand, a police officer will usually give you a verbal caution before sending you on your way. Fighting is treated a little more harshly: if you're involved in a fight you may spend a night in a cell, to 'cool off'.

BUSINESS HOURS

Offices open 9am to 5pm on Monday to Friday. Shops open 9am to 5.30pm or 6pm, Monday to Saturday. On Thursday and/or Friday shops stay open later. Many also open on Sunday, typically from noon to 6pm. From October to April, tourist offices and attractions are usually open fewer hours or fewer days per week, or shut completely.

Outside the cities, shops and businesses often close for one afternoon in the week. It varies from region to region. In small towns most shops are also likely to close for an hour or so at lunchtime.

In Northern Ireland many tourist attractions close on Sunday morning, rarely opening until around 2pm, well after church finishing time.

For bank hours see Exchanging Money in the Money section earlier in this chapter; for post office hours see the Post & Communications section earlier in this chapter.

Pub Hours

After years of pressure, pub hours in the Republic were finally extended in 2000, but to many they remain too short and too confusing. All pubs are legally allowed to open from 10.30am Monday to Saturday and from noon on Sunday, but most pubs don't open their doors until noon daily. Closing hours differ depending on the day: 11.30pm Monday to Wednesday, 12.30am Thursday to Saturday and 11pm on Sunday. In addition, there's 30 minutes' worth of 'drinking up' time allowed. To make matters more complicated, many pubs have obtained legal bar extensions, which extends their opening hours to 2.30am on certain days. The only days when pubs will definitely be closed are Christmas Day and Good Friday.

In the North pubs can open whenever they wish but can only sell alcohol between 11.30am and 11pm Monday to Saturday and 12.30pm and 10pm on Sunday. Late licences are sometimes granted to pubs that provide food or entertainment; these licences allow pubs to remain open until 1am on weekdays and to midnight on Sunday.

PUBLIC HOLIDAYS & SPECIAL EVENTS

Northern and Southern public holidays (bank holidays) don't always coincide, which can have a bearing on the availability of accommodation in border resorts such as Newcastle.

Public holidays in the Republic (IR), Northern Ireland (NI) or both are:

New Year's Day 1 January
St Patrick's Day 17 March
Easter Monday varies
May Holiday 1 May
Spring Bank Holiday (NI) Last Monday in May
June Holiday (IR) First Monday in June
Orangeman's Day (NI) 12 July
August Holiday (IR) First Monday in August
August Holiday (NI) Last Monday in August
October Holiday (IR) Last Monday in October
Christmas Day 25 December
St Stephen's Day (Boxing Day) 26 December

St Patrick's Day, St Stephen's Day and May Day holidays are taken on the following Monday should they fall on a weekend. In the South, banks and many shops, pubs and offices close on Good Friday even though it isn't an official public holiday. In the North, most shops open on Good Friday but close the following Tuesday.

Following is a list of major annual events and festivals held around the island. Local tourist offices will have additional information. Also, the Association of Irish Festival Events (AOIFE) maintains a useful Web site at [W] www.aoifeonline.com; [W] www .art.ie is worth perusing too. Most sporting events are mentioned later in this chapter, under Spectator Sports.

January

Dublin International Theatre Symposium (☎ 01-608 2461, [W] www.dublintheatresympo sium.com) Overseas theatre companies converge on Dublin for a week in early January.
Unfringed (☎ 061-319 866) A theatre festival staged in various venues within Limerick, in late January.

Yeats Winter School (☎ 071-42693, **W** www
.yeats-sligo.com) A weekend of reading, lectures and a tour of Yeats country, in late January. There's also a summer program on offer, in late July.

February

All Ireland Dancing Championships (☎ 01-475 2220, **W** www.irishdancing.org/allireland.html) Irish dancers vie for places in April's worldwide event. It takes place in early February in a different city each year.

Dublin Toy and Train Fair (☎ 01-284 9199) A collectibles fair held four times a year. The first show is in mid-February.

Newtownabbey Arts Festival (☎ 028-9034 0000, **W** www.newtownabbey.gov.uk/whatson/ whatson1.htm) From visual arts to brass bands, this festival is held over two weeks in mid-February.

Newtownstewart Drama Festival (☎ 028-8166 2079) Over a week of theatre in the North in late February.

March

Belfast Literary Festival (☎ 028-9024 2338, **W** www.crescentarts.org/betweenthelines) A celebration of writing: readings, lectures and workshops presented by local and international authors. It's held in late March.

Bridge House Irish Festival (☎ 0506-22000) An indoor festival of Irish music, song and dance at the Bridge House Hotel, Tullamore, County Offaly, held over a week in mid-March.

Dublin Boat Show (☎ 01-490 0600, **W** www
.irishboatshow.ie) A panoply of watercraft on display, held in early to mid-March.

Dublin Film Festival (☎ 01-679 2937, **W** www
.dublinfilmfestival.com) A wide array of international films, screened in venues across Dublin. It's held in late March or April.

Irish International Antiques and Fine Arts Fair (☎ 01-670 2186) Ireland's largest antiques fair, held annually in Dublin, in mid-March.

Irish National Surfing Championships (☎ 096-49428) See Ireland's best master the mighty Atlantic at Bundoran in County Donegal, mid-March.

Limerick International Band Festival (☎ 061-410777, **W** www.shannon-dev.ie/bandfest) Brass and concert bands from around the world march the streets of Limerick in mid-March.

St Patrick's Day (☎ 01-676 3205, **W** www
.stpatricksday.ie) The streets of Dublin reverberate to a cacophony of parades, fireworks and lightshows for three days around 17 March. Over 250,000 attend. Cork, Armagh and Belfast also have parades; elsewhere festivities are less ostentatious.

April

Easter Parades Many small towns host an Easter parade. Ask the local tourist office for details.

Pan Celtic International Festival (☎ 066-718 0050, **W** www.panceltic.com) A week-long event celebrating aspects of Celtic culture in Tralee, County Kerry, in late April.

Samhlaíocht (☎ 066-712 9934, **W** www.samhla iocht.com) A festival of the arts held in Tralee, County Kerry, in mid-April.

World Irish Dancing Championships (☎ 01-475 2220) Four thousand dancers from all over the globe compete in early April. The location varies from year to year.

May

Balmoral Show (☎ 028-9066 5225, **W** www
.balmoralshow.co.uk) Large agricultural fair held in Belfast in mid-May.

Bantry Mussel Fair (☎ 027-50360, **W** www
.bantrymusselfair.ie) Mussels and music with picturesque Bantry Bay as a backdrop in mid-May.

Belfast Summerfest (☎ 028-9027 0342, **W** www
.belfastcity.gov.uk) Open-air music, sporting events and a carnival kick off the summer season in Belfast; it runs throughout May.

Belfast City Marathon (☎ 028-9027 0345, **W** www.belfastcity.gov.uk/marathon) Over 6000 people participate in this run, held in early May.

Cathedral Quarter Arts Festival (☎ 028-9023 2403, **W** www.cqaf.com) Most of the performing arts are represented during this 11-day event held in early May.

Cat Laughs Comedy Festival (☎ 056-63837, **W** www.thecatlaughs.com) A much-acclaimed gathering of world-class comics in Kilkenny, held from late May into June.

Cork International Choral Festival (☎ 021-430 8308, **W** www.corkchoral.ie) A welcoming and sociable four-day program of choral music and competition.

Fleadh Nua (☎ 01-280 0295, **W** www.comhaltas
.com/fleadh/nua.htm) Irish music and dancing at Ennis, County Clare, in late May.

Portrush Raft Race Weekend (☎ 028-7034 7234, **W** www.dataflo.co.uk/portrushraftrace) Three days of nautical activities in late May.

Writers' Week Listowel (☎ 068-21074, **W** www
.writersweek.ie) An established literary festival with an emphasis on creative workshops, held late May to early June.

June

Bloomsday (☎ 01-878 8547, **W** www.jamesjoyce
.ie) A re-enactment of the journey made round

Dublin by James Joyce's character Leopold Bloom, from Joyce's novel *Ulysses*. It's held on 16 June. Various readings and dramatisations of Joyce's work take place around town (see the boxed text 'Bloomsday' in the Dublin chapter).

Castlebar International Four Days Walks (☎ 094-24102, W www.castlebar4dayswalks .com) An event comprised of group rambles through Mayo's splendid scenery, enabling you to meet other walkers. It's held from the end of June to the beginning of July.

Enniskillen Air Show (☎ 028-6632 8282) Featuring an aerobatics display and pleasure flights, mid-June.

Holywood International Jazz Festival (☎ 028-9076 8563, W www.ulsterjazzevents.org.uk) A three-day affair in County Down held in early June.

Lough Derg Pilgrimage (☎ 072-61518, W www .loughderg.org) A three-day Catholic penitential pilgrimage involving a boat trip to a small island in Lough Derg; it's undertaken from 1 June to 15 August.

July

Galway Arts Festival (☎ 091-509700, W www .galwayartsfestival.ie) The Republic's largest all-round arts event is held in late July. It covers literature, music and the visual arts; it also features street performances and activities for children.

Galway Film Fleadh (☎ 091-751655, W www .galwayfilmfleadh.com) A major film festival with lots of filmmakers negotiating deals with studios. It's held in mid-July.

Reek Sunday (☎ 098-64114, W www.croagh -patrick.com/mountain.html) On the last Sunday in July there's a mass pilgrimage to the top of Mayo's Croagh Patrick.

August

Connemara Pony Show (☎ 095-21863) This mid-August event is dedicated to showcasing the hardy, indigenous Connemara pony.

Kerrygold Horse Show (☎ 01-668 0866, W www.rds.ie/kerrygold) This venerable five-day Dublin showjumping exhibition is a society affair, as much about people-watching as it is about horses. It's held in the second week of August.

Féile an Phobail (☎ 028-9028 4028, W www .feilebelfast.com) This Belfast extravaganza, held in early August, bills itself as Europe's largest community festival. It combines performing arts, sporting events and a carnival.

Kilkenny Arts Festival (☎ 056-52175, W www .kilkennyarts.ie) A week of music, performance and visual arts. Kilkenny's medieval charm adds to the experience. It's held in mid-August.

Puck Fair (☎ 066-976 2366, W www.puckfair .ie) This street festival, held in little Killorglin from 10 to 12 August, has its roots in the 17th century. There's a busking competition, lots of drinking, livestock roam the streets and, to top it off, a goat is crowned king of the festivities.

Rose of Tralee (☎ 066-712 1322, W www.rose oftralee.ie) This late-August festival centres on a beauty contest in which the winner takes the honorary title 'Rose of Tralee', recalling the heroine of a fanciful local tale from the 19th century.

September

Appalachian & Bluegrass Music Festival (☎ 028-8224 3292, W www.folkpark.com) The sight of a Kentuckian plucking on a banjo in Omagh may look out of place, but this is an entertaining and friendly three-day event featuring top-class musicians from home and abroad. It's held in the second week of September.

Galway International Oyster Festival (☎ 091-527282, W www.galwayoysterfest.com) This four-day event, held at the end of September, rather dubiously encourages combining large helpings of shellfish and beer with much music and merriment. Still, it seems to work, as it's been going for nearly 50 years. Watch out for the oyster-shucking competition.

International Sheepdog Trials (☎ 028-4461 0854) Clever dogs from Ireland and the British Isles wow spectators from all around the world. It's held in mid-September.

Lisdoonvarna Matchmaking Festival (☎ 065-707 4005, W www.matchmakerireland.com) 'Europe's biggest singles event' takes place in County Clare on weekends throughout September, with much dancing and carousing. If you haven't found your perfect partner come October, there's no hope for you.

Waterford International Festival of Light Opera (☎ 051-874402, W www.waterfordfestival .com) Somewhat misleadingly named, this late-September event is all over the road, staging anything from grand operas to Gilbert & Sullivan and even *Jesus Christ Superstar*. The fringe events are fun too.

October

Ballinasloe Horse Fair (☎ 090-543453) One of Europe's ancient horse fairs, this Galway event was an impressive trading ground until the arrival of the internal combustion engine. It's held in early October.

Belfast Festival at Queen's (☎ 028-9066 5577, W www.belfastfestival.com) Over 100,000 attend Ireland's largest arts festival, which promises (and delivers) a bold and eclectic mix of entertainment. A large fringe festival adds to the fun. The show is on for two weeks from late October.

Cork Jazz Festival (☎ 01-676 5342, Ⓦ www.corkjazzfestival.com) Top names in jazz attract music lovers worldwide in late October.

Dublin Theatre Festival (☎ 01-677 8439, Ⓦ www.eircomtheatrefestival.com) This two-week event in early October features new Irish and world cinema, and fringe shows.

Gourmet Festival (☎ 021-477 4026, Ⓦ www.kinsale.ie/gfest.htm) Great food and wine comes to the harbour town of Kinsale, County Cork, in mid-October. Each year sees a different cuisine theme. Membership required.

Cork Film Festival (☎ 021-427 1711, Ⓦ www.corkfilmfest.org) A long-running and respected film festival with a remit to raise the profile of Irish cinema and bring the best in international cinema to Irish shores. It's held mid- to late October.

Wexford Festival Opera (☎ 053-22144, Ⓦ www.wexfordopera.com) This prestigious event is to the opera world what Cannes is to the film industry (a fortnight away at an exotic seaside resort). Legends have performed here – book well ahead to avoid disappointment. It runs over two weeks from late October.

December
Christmas This is a quiet affair in the countryside, though on 26 December the ancient practice of Wren Boys is re-enacted, most notably in Dingle, County Kerry, when groups of children dress up and go about singing hymns.

ACTIVITIES
Although Ireland is expensive, many activities not only open up some of the most beautiful and fascinating corners of the island but are also within the reach of the tightest budget. A walk or cycle ride in the countryside will almost certainly be a highlight – as well as the cheapest part – of an Irish holiday. For those who have the money, other activities such as golf or fishing are available as part of holiday packages that include accommodation and transportation.

Most activities are well organised and have clubs and associations (some of which are listed here) that can give visitors invaluable information and sometimes substantial discounts. Many clubs have national or international affiliations, so check before leaving home.

The tourist board puts out a wide selection of information sheets and brochures and these can be a starting point for further research.

Walking
There are many superb walks in Ireland and walking has become increasingly popular since the early 1980s, when the Wicklow Way, the country's first designated long-distance path, was established. There are now over 30 'waymarked ways', varying in length from the 26km Cavan Way to the mammoth 900km Ulster Way. The path network is growing all the time, with an aim to link them all up eventually. Civilisation is never far away so it's generally easy to follow walks that connect with public transport and link hostels, B&Bs and villages.

The countryside can look deceptively gentle but, especially in the hills or on the open moors, the weather can turn nasty very quickly at any time of year. Although Ireland has a relatively mild climate there is one aspect of the weather that will affect the walker: rain. As well as getting you wet and cold, it renders the ground underfoot slippery, and low clouds in the hills make navigation problematic. If you're in upland areas it's vital to be well equipped: carry (and know how to use) a compass, good maps and/or a walking guidebook. This is important, as even though Ireland's ways are well marked (look for a yellow arrow with a walking figure), signs are sometimes missing or obscured.

Always leave details of your route with someone trustworthy and let them know when you should be back. Never walk alone in isolated areas.

The ways mainly follow old, disused roads, 'boreens' (small lanes or roadways) and forest trails. Ireland has a tradition of relatively free access to open country, often through privately owned land, but the growth in the number of walkers and the carelessness of a few have made some farmers less obliging (see Responsible Tourism earlier in this chapter).

Information The maintenance and development of the ways is administered in the

Republic by the National Waymarked Ways Advisory Committee (☎ 01-240 7717, W www.irishwaymarkedways.ie), Irish Sports Council, 21 Fitzwilliam Square, Dublin, and in the North by the Countryside Access and Activities Network (☎ 028-9038 1222), House of Sport, Upper Malone Rd, Belfast.

Call ☎ 999 for mountain rescue.

Guides & Maps Lonely Planet's *Walking in Ireland* contains in-depth route descriptions and maps of dozens of walking trails (including those mentioned below), plus lots of practical information on accommodation, food and public transport. Another useful guide is Michael Fewer's *Irish Long-Distance Walks*. *Best Irish Walks* by Joss Lynam is a collection of 76 short walks around the country. Regional and individual trail walking guidebooks are also available. A visit to a good bookshop such as Eason & Son in Dublin is recommended.

Tourist boards have free information and maps on popular walks, but if you're planning more than one day's walking it's worth investing in one of the route maps available. EastWest Mapping (☎/fax 054-77835, e eastwest@eircom.net) has good maps of long-distance walks in the Republic and the North.

Tim Robinson of Folding Landscapes (☎ 095-35886), Roundstone, County Galway, produces superbly detailed maps of the Burren, the Aran Islands and Connemara. His and Joss Lynam's *Mountains of Connemara: A Hill Walker's Guide* contains a useful detailed map.

For further details of maps for Ireland see the Maps section under Planning earlier in the chapter.

Organised Walks If you don't have a travelling companion one option you could consider is joining an organised walking group.

Go Ireland (☎ 066-976 2094, e goireland@fexco.ie, W www.goireland.fexco.ie), Old Orchard House, Killorglin, County Kerry, offers walking tours of the west, Donegal, Antrim and Fermanagh.

South West Walks Ireland (☎ 066-712 8733, e swwi@iol.ie, W www.southwestwalksireland.com), 40 Ashe St, Tralee, County Kerry, provides a series of guided and self-guided walking programs around the country, including the North.

British-based Joyce's Ireland (☎ 01275-474797, e joyce@joycesireland.co.uk, W www.joycesireland.com), 25 Dundry Lane, Bristol, offers walking tours for groups of up to 14 people, taking in both the Republic and the North. These tours have the advantage that your luggage is carried by minibus. Individual walks take from a couple of a hours to a full day.

Beara Way This moderately easy, 196km walk forms a loop round the delightful Beara Peninsula in West Cork. The peninsula is relatively unused to mass tourism and makes a pleasant contrast with the Iveragh Peninsula to the north.

Part of the walk, between Castletownbere and Glengarriff, follows the route taken by Donal O'Sullivan and his band after the English took his castle following an 11-day siege in 1602. At Glengarriff, O'Sullivan met up with other families and set out on a journey north, hoping to reunite with other remaining pockets of Gaelic resistance. Of the thousand men who set out that winter, only 30 completed the trek.

The Beara Way mostly follows old roads and tracks and rarely rises above 340m. There's no official start or finish point and the route can be walked in either direction. It could easily be reduced to seven days by skipping Bere and Dursey Islands, and if you start at Castletownbere you could reach Kenmare in five days or less.

Burren Way This 35km walk traverses the Burren limestone plateau in County Clare. It presents a strange, unique landscape to the walker. There's very little soil and few trees but a surprising abundance of flora. The way stretches between Ballyvaughan, on the northern coast of County Clare, and Liscannor to the south-west, taking in the village of Doolin, famous as a traditional-music centre. The trail south of Doolin to the dramatic Cliffs of Moher is a highlight of the route. From the cliffs a new path is being developed inland towards Liscannor (though some maps may still show the old route along the cliffs, which has been closed).

The best time for this walk is late spring or early summer. The route is pretty dry, but walking boots are useful as the limestone can be sharp.

Cavan Way In the north-west of County Cavan the villages of Blacklion and Dowra are the ends of the 26km Cavan Way. The way runs in a north-eastwards or south-westwards direction past a number of Stone Age monuments – court cairns, ring forts and tombs – and this area is said to be one of the last strongholds of Druidism. At the midpoint is the Shannon Pot, a pool on the boulder-strewn slopes of the Cuilcagh Mountains and the source of the River Shannon, which from there flows into Lough Allen. The Shannon Pot divides the walk into two parts: from Blacklion it is mainly hill walking; from Shannon Pot to Dowra it's mainly by road. The highest point on the walk is Giant's Grave (260m).

Dowra links up with the Leitrim Way, which runs between Manorhamilton and Drumshanbo. Blacklion is also on the Ulster Way.

Dingle Way This 168km walk in County Kerry loops round one of the most beautiful peninsulas in the country. It takes eight days to complete, beginning and ending in Tralee, with an average daily distance of 21km. The first three days offer the easiest walk but the first day, from Tralee to Camp, is the least interesting; it could be skipped by taking the bus to Camp and starting from there.

East Munster Way This 70km walk travels through forest open moorland, along small country roads and a river towpath. It's clearly laid out with black markers bearing yellow arrows, and could be managed in three days, starting from Carrick-on-Suir in County Tipperary and finishing at Clogheen in County Waterford. The first day takes

you to Clonmel, the second to Newcastle and the last to Clogheen.

Kerry Way The 214km Kerry Way is the Republic's longest waymarked footpath and is usually walked anticlockwise. It starts and ends in Killarney and stays inland for the first three days, winding through the spectacular Macgillycuddy's Reeks and past 1041m Mount Carrantuohil, Ireland's highest mountain, before continuing around the coast through Cahirciveen, Waterville, Caherdaniel, Sneem and Kenmare.

You could complete the walk in about 10 days, provided you're up to walking a good 20km a day. With less time it's worth walking the first three days, as far as Glenbeigh, from where a bus or a lift could return you to Killarney.

Accommodation isn't a problem, but you need to book in July and August. In contrast, places to eat aren't common, so consider carrying your own food.

Mourne Trail The Mourne Trail is actually the south-eastern section of the Ulster Way, south of Belfast, and runs from Newry, round the Mourne Mountains, to the seaside resort of Newcastle and then on to Strangford, where you can take a ferry across to Portaferry and continue north to Newtownards. From Newry to Strangford is a distance of 106km, which could probably be managed in four or five days.

There's gorgeous mountain, forest and coastal scenery along the way and, once you've left Newry, not much in the way of built-up towns to spoil the views. Provided you're reasonably fit and well shod, this is not an especially difficult route to walk, although it does climb as high as 559m at Slievemoughanmore, the highest point on the Ulster Way.

Slieve Bloom Way Close to the geographical centre of Ireland, the Slieve Bloom Way is a 77km waymarked trail through Counties Offaly and Laois, which does a complete circuit of the Slieve Bloom Mountains taking in most major points of interest. The trail follows tracks, forest firebreaks and old roads, and crosses the Mountrath–Kinnitty and Mountrath–Clonaslee roads. Its highest point is at Glendine Gap (460m). The recommended starting point is the car park at Glenbarrow, 5km from Rosenallis.

Camping in state forests is forbidden, but there's plenty of open space outside the forest for tents; otherwise, accommodation en route is almost nonexistent. There is no public transport to the area, although buses do stop in the nearby towns of Mountrath and Rosenallis.

South Leinster Way The tiny village of Kildavin in County Carlow, just south-west of Clonegal on the slopes of Mount Leinster, is the northern starting point of the 100km South Leinster Way, which winds through Counties Carlow and Kilkenny. It follows remote mountain roads and river towpaths through the medieval villages of Borris, Graiguenamanagh, Inistioge, Mullinavat and Piltown to the finish post at Carrick-on-Suir just inside the Tipperary border. The southerly section is not as scenic as the rest, but the low hills have their own charm and on a sunny day they offer fine views south over the Suir Valley and Waterford Harbour.

The way leads in a generally south-westwards direction but could easily be done the opposite way. It should take four or five days, depending on whether you stop over in Graiguenamanagh.

The route is marked so you should have no difficulty finding your way. Much of the trail is above 500m and the weather can change quickly. Good walking boots, outdoor gear and emergency supplies are essential.

Ulster Way: North-Eastern Section The Ulster Way makes a circuit round the six counties of Northern Ireland and Donegal. In total the footpath covers just over 900km, so walking all of it might take five weeks. However, it can easily be broken down into smaller sections that could more realistically be attempted during a short stay. The scenery along the way varies enormously, encompassing dramatic coastal views, gentler lakeside country and the mountainous inland terrain of the Mourne Mountains.

Some of the most spectacular scenery lies along the north-eastern section, which follows the Glens of Antrim and then the glorious Causeway Coastline, a Unesco World Heritage Site. The 165km north-eastern section begins unpromisingly in Belfast's western suburbs, heads north-eastwards to meet the coast at Glenarm, then follows the coast round to the Giant's Causeway; this can be completed in six or seven days. The stretch of coast immediately surrounding the Giant's Causeway is likely to be busy, especially in high summer, when you should book accommodation well ahead.

Walking this stretch of coast shouldn't be beyond most averagely fit and sensibly equipped people, but rockfalls along the coast can occasionally obstruct stretches of it. While some stretches of this walk can seem wonderfully wild, you're never going to be that far from civilisation.

Ulster Way: Donegal Section The main Ulster Way crosses into Donegal at the small pilgrimage town of Pettigo on Lough Erne, but then circles straight back to Rosscor in Northern Ireland. A spur – also confusingly called the Ulster Way – cuts north across the central moorlands of Donegal to Falcarragh on the northern coast. In all, if you follow the spur, this stretch of walk is 111km long, which means it can be walked in four or five days. Bear in mind, however, that much of central Donegal is bleak, boggy terrain where walking can be tough going, especially if the weather's bad – which it often is! Although the walking-man symbol sometimes appears on markers, in general you'll be looking out for white-painted posts which simply tell you that you're heading in the right direction.

This stretch of the Ulster Way is intended for wilderness lovers. Some of the scenery en route is truly magnificent, as you pass the Blue Stack and Derryveagh Mountains and Mount Errigal (752m), Donegal's highest peak. The route also skirts the glorious Glenveagh National Park, where you might want to divert and break your journey. There are few dramatic historic remains to distract you, but plenty of minor prehistoric burial sites en route.

Wicklow Way Opened in 1982, the popular 132km Wicklow Way was Ireland's first long-distance trail. Despite its name it actually starts in southern Dublin and ends in Clonegal in County Carlow, although most of the way is through Wicklow. From its beginnings in Marlay Park, Rathfarnham, in southern Dublin, the trail quickly enters a mountain wilderness (the highest point is White Hill at 633m). Forest walks, sheep paths, bog roads and mountain passes join up to provide a spectacular walk, which passes by Glencree, Powerscourt, Djouce Mountain,

Luggala, Lough Dan, Glenmacnass, Glendalough, Glenmalure and Aghavannagh.

Especially south of Laragh, some sections are desolate, with much of the trail above 500m. The weather can change quickly, so good walking boots, outdoor gear and emergency supplies are essential. There are many worthwhile detours: up Glenmacnass to the waterfall or up to the summit of Lugnaquilla Mountain, for example.

For the entire trail, allow eight to 10 days, plus time for diversions. It's easy to pick up sections and it can be done in either direction, though most walkers start in Dublin. Breaking the journey at Laragh, just under halfway, would let you visit the monastic site

Tracing Your Ancestors

Many visitors come to Ireland purely to track down their Irish roots. Success in this activity is more likely if you have managed to obtain some basic facts about your Irish ancestors before leaving home. The name of your ancestor who left Ireland and his or her approximate date of birth is essential, but it's also helpful to know the ancestor's county and parish of origin in Ireland, their religious denomination, and their parent's and spouse's names.

Good starting points for research in Ireland are the National Library (☎ 01-603 0200, W www.nli.ie), Kildare St, Dublin; the National Archives (☎ 01-407 2300, W www.nationalarchives .ie/genealogy.html), Bishop St, Dublin; and the Public Record Office of Northern Ireland (☎ 028-9025 5905, W http://proni.nics.gov.uk), 66 Balmoral Ave, Belfast. The Web sites of these facilities contain links to a wealth of online resources dedicated to helping you trace your Irish past. They also have details of local research centres throughout Ireland, which are useful if you have narrowed down your research to a particular county.

Other helpful resources include the General Register Office (☎ 01-635 4000, W www.groireland .ie), Joyce House, 8–11 Lombard St East, Dublin, and the General Register Office Northern Ireland (☎ 028-9025 2000, W www.groni.gov.uk), Oxford House, 49/55 Chichester St, Belfast. These agencies hold records of births, deaths and marriages in Ireland.

There are also numerous agencies and individuals that will do the research for you for a fee. For information on these, contact the Association of Professional Genealogists in Ireland (APGI), c/o The Honorary Secretary, 30 Harlech Crescent, Clonskeagh, Dublin; in the North also contact the Association of Ulster Genealogists and Record Agents (AUGRA), c/o The Honorary Secretary, Glen Cottage, Glenmachan Rd, Belfast.

Dozens of books are available on Irish genealogy. Tony McCarthy's *Irish Roots Guide* is a good introduction to the subject, and John Grenham's *Tracing Your Irish Ancestors* is an excellent comprehensive guide. North Americans in particular benefit from *A Genealogists Guide to Discovering Your Irish Ancestors* by Dwight Radford and Kyle Betit. Also handy is Bord Fáilte's booklet *Tracing Your Ancestors in Ireland*.

The magazine *Irish Roots* contains up-to-date information on genealogical resources and provides advice and information on constructing family trees. It's published in Ireland by Belgrave Publications (☎ 021-450 0067, e irishrts@iol.ie), Belgrave Ave, Cork.

at Glendalough and do some local walks. Because of the way's popularity, walking outside the busy June to August period is advisable. Camping is possible along the route, but you'll need to ask permission from local farmers. In peak season you should book accommodation in advance. If you're hostelling you'll need to carry food with you.

Cycling

Many visitors explore Ireland by bicycle. Although the most interesting areas can be hilly, some roads have poor surfaces and the weather is often wet, it's a great place for bicycle touring. The facilities are good, distances are relatively short, roads off the main highways have relatively little traffic and the scenery is beautiful – and you're never too far from a pub. If you intend to cycle in the west, the prevailing winds mean it's easier to cycle from south to north.

You can either bring your own bike or rent one in Ireland. Ferries transport bicycles for free or a small fee, and airlines will usually accept them as part of your 20kg luggage allowance. When buying your ticket, check with the ferry company or airline about any regulations or restrictions on the transportation of bicycles.

Bicycles can be transported by bus provided there's enough room in the luggage compartment; the charge varies. By train the cost varies from €2.50 to €7.50 for a one-way journey depending on the distance. Bicycles are not allowed on certain train routes, including the Dublin Area Rapid Transit (DART); check with Iarnród Éireann.

Typical bicycle rental costs are €9 to €16 per day or €40 to €65 per week plus a deposit of around €65, which is refunded when the bicycle is returned. Bags and other equipment can also be rented. Several dealers have outlets around the country; the dealers and their head offices are:

Irish Cycle Hire (☎ 041-685 3772, fax 685 3809, e irch@iol.ie, w www.irishcyclehire.com) Unit 6, Enterprise Centre, Ardee, County Louth
Raleigh Ireland (☎ 01-626 1333, e raleigh@iol.ie, w www.iol.ie/raleigh) Raleigh House, Kylemore Rd, Dublin – Ireland's biggest rental dealer, with many locations

Rent-a-Bike Ireland (☎ 061-416983, e emerald alp@eircom.net, w www.irelandrentabike.com) 1 Patrick St, Limerick, County Limerick

There are also many local independent outlets. Regional and national tour operators organise cycling holidays and the tourist boards can supply you with a list of them.

Irish Cycling Safaris (☎ 01-260 0749, e ics@kerna.ie, w www.cyclingsafaris.com), Belfield House, University College Dublin, organises tours for groups of cyclists in the south-west, the south-east and Connemara, with bikes, guides, a van that carries luggage, and B&B accommodation. Go Ireland (see Organised Walks earlier in this chapter) provides cycling tours of the west and Donegal.

Numerous tourist-office publications on cycling exist and there are a number of books and guides.

South-West Most of western Cork is ideal cycling territory. One recommended route is west from Cork town to Kinsale, then on through Timoleague, Butlerstown, Clonakilty, Rosscarbery and down to Baltimore and Clear Island. Another route is down the Mizen Head Peninsula (starting from Skibbereen, where you can hire bikes), looping around the village of Toormore to take in the southern and northern coasts. A third route would be a circular one of the Sheep's Head Peninsula, starting and finishing in Bantry.

In County Kerry, a wonderful tour would be around the starkly beautiful Beara Peninsula from either Kenmare, Glengarriff or Bantry, taking in the spectacular Healy Pass either down from Lauragh to Adrigole (good brakes are absolutely essential) or with a herculean slog in the other direction. Killarney makes a good base for cycling trips into (but not *around*, unless you want car and coach fumes in your lungs) the Iveragh Peninsula, where many sights are accessible only by bike or on foot. Examples of two such tours are the 30km ride via the Gap of Dunloe and the 80km trip via Lake Acoose and Moll's Gap.

In County Clare the Burren region is good mountain-biking territory.

North-West The Lough Gill tour in Yeats Country outside Sligo town lends itself to cycling. There are also many historic and prehistoric sites – and places associated with Yeats – in easy cycling distance of Sligo town, where you can hire bikes.

Achill Island in County Mayo has largely flat roads and so is ideal for cycling. Bikes can be hired at Achill Sound and returned there after cycling west to Keel, turning north up to Dugort and then back south on another road. There are also bikes for hire in Keel.

In County Galway, Clifden is the best base for cycling tours of the superb scenery of Connemara.

In County Donegal you can follow the coast road west of Donegal town via Killybegs to Malinmore. North of Killybegs, past Ardara to Dunfanaghy, the coast is magnificent. There are superb cycling tours around Bloody Foreland and Horn Head. The peninsula that extends west from Ardara and separates Loughros More Bay from Loughros Beg Bay is well worth cycling too. North-east of Donegal town the loop around Lough Eske is a pleasant shorter trip on roads surrounded by the Blue Stack Mountains.

North-East In County Down, Bangor is a good base from which to cycle the reasonably flat Ards Peninsula: you could follow the coast road south via Donaghadee to Portaferry, from where the A2 heads back north, skirting Strangford Lough. Alternatively, Newcastle is a good spot from which to explore the valley routes through the Mourne Mountains in south County Down.

In Antrim the scenic route along the coast north from Belfast to the Giant's Causeway passes through the foothills of the Antrim Mountains. From Enniskillen in Fermanagh you can hire bikes to visit ancient religious sites and antiquities, following roads along the shores of Lower Lough Erne to Belleek on the Donegal border and back.

South-East Just south of Dublin, the varied scenery of County Wicklow – moors, bogs, mountains, lakes, valleys and forests – provides some beautiful but strenuous cycling. From Wicklow town south to Wexford town the weather is warmer and the landscape flatter.

In County Wexford the relatively flat Hook Peninsula – out to the lighthouse at the tip of the head and back along the western side to Duncannon – is a good area to explore. Between County Wexford and County Waterford, by taking the Ballyhack to Passage East ferry you avoid the longer route north via New Ross. In the west of County Waterford the route through the Knockmealdown Mountains offers magnificent views.

Tipperary and Kilkenny have rich, rolling farmland interspersed with ancient monuments, such as the Rock of Cashel, and fine architectural remains. From Kilkenny town there's a beautiful cycling excursion to Kilfane, Jerpoint Abbey, Inistioge and Kells.

Centre In Westmeath, from Athlone north into County Longford, east of Lough Ree, is Goldsmith Country (named after the 18th-century poet, playwright and novelist Oliver Goldsmith), which has gentle terrain ideal for visiting by bike. A cycle tour of the drumlins (rounded hills formed by retreating glaciers) and lakes of Cavan, Monaghan and southern Leitrim along the quiet country roads is very pleasant.

Fishing

Ireland is regarded as one of Europe's premier fishing destinations, with nearly 14,500km of rivers, thousands of lakes and miles of unspoilt coastline. Freshwater game fish include salmon, sea trout and brown trout. Some managed fisheries also stock rainbow trout. Ireland's varying coastal water temperatures (warm Gulf Stream waters off the southern and western coasts, and cold waters in the north and east) support a wide range of marine species.

Ireland is justly famous for its coarse fishing, covering bream, pike, perch, roach, rudd, tench, carp and eels. Apart from some specialist angling on private waters, coarse fishing is generally free with the landowner's consent, although some of the fisheries boards have a requirement for a mandatory share certificate. Killing of pike over 6lb in weight is prohibited and anglers are limited to a quota of one pike. Killing of coarse fish is frowned upon; anglers are encouraged to return coarse fish alive. Many of the lakes and rivers are equipped with fishing stands to improve access, and the regional fisheries boards provide detailed information on access and fishing.

The great western lakes of Corrib, Mask and Conn provide a well developed angling infrastructure for fly-fishermen, with plenty of lakeshore B&Bs, good sturdy boats and knowledgeable boatmen to cater for visiting anglers. These lakes can be dangerous, as they tend to be littered with hidden rocks and shoals; visit first with a local boatman.

While Ireland is a land of opportunity for the angler, intensive agriculture and the growth of towns have brought about a general reduction in water quality in many areas, markedly so in some areas. Fish kills are a feature of the news during warm summer months, and some world-renowned fisheries have been lost in recent years due to water quality issues.

Information Bord Fáilte and the Northern Ireland Tourist Board (NITB) produce several information leaflets on fishing. Bord Fáilte also publishes *The Angler's Guide* annually, which lists accommodation, major fishing events and charter boat operators. Three good books are *Game Angling Guide*, *Coarse Angling Guide* and *Sea Angling Guide* from the Central Fisheries Board, published by Gill & Macmillan. They're full of practical information and details of the permits and licences required.

Licensing Fishing in the Republic is managed and promoted by regional fisheries boards. A state rod licence is required to fish for salmon or sea trout, costing €4 for one day, €13 for three weeks and €32 for a year. These licences are available from the local tackle shop or direct from the Central Fisheries Board (☎ 01-837 9206, Ⓦ www.cfb .ie), Balnagowan House, Mobhi Boreen, Mobhi Rd, Dublin.

Many of the premier rivers are hired out to fishing clubs by the fisheries boards. In such cases, day tickets are usually available

to visiting anglers at reasonable rates for both salmon and trout.

It's not necessary to have a licence for brown trout, rainbow trout or coarse fish, nor is it required for general sea angling. However, there is a system of share certificates (issued to help raise funds for maintaining stocks and keeping rivers clean) for trout and coarse fishing, which you purchase beforehand; in most regions payment is voluntary. The certificates cost about €16 for a year, €6.50 for three weeks or €4 for three days. The Central Fisheries Board will have details.

In the North, you need a rod licence (coarse/game fishing £7.40/9.60 for eight days), which is obtainable from the Foyle Fisheries Commission (☎ 028-7144 2100), 8 Victoria Rd, Derry, for the Foyle area, and from the Fisheries Conservancy Board (☎ 028-3833 4666), 1 Mahon Rd, Portadown, County Armagh, for all other regions. You also require a permit from the owner, which is usually the Department of Agriculture, Fisheries Division, Annexe 5, Castle Grounds, Stormont, Belfast. Call ☎ 028-9052 3491 and ask for the fisheries division. For game fishing it charges £11.65/23.50 for one/eight days; coarse fishing costs £6.80/11.90.

Water Sports
Ireland's more than 3100km of coastline, its rivers and its numerous lakes provide plenty of opportunities for a range of water sports.

Swimming & Surfing Climate and water temperatures are good reasons why Ireland isn't the first place you'd think of for swimming or surfing. On the other hand, it has some magnificent coastline and some great sandy beaches. Sadly, a number of Irish beaches suffer from pollution, but the cleaner, safer ones have been awarded the EU Blue Flag. You can get a list of these from the government agency An Taisce (☎ 01-454 1786, Ⓦ www.antaisce.org), Tailors' Hall, Back Lane, Dublin, or online at Ⓦ www.blueflag.org. Surfers should check Ⓦ www.surfingireland.net or Ⓦ www.vic torkilo.com for beach reports and forecasts.

The best months for surfing in Ireland are September and October, when the swells are highest. The water is also warmest in September because of the Gulf Stream. Following is a selection of Ireland's major surfing spots.

South-West & West Barleycove Beach on the Mizen Head Peninsula is Cork's only surfing beach but it isn't crowded. In Kerry, at Caherdaniel on the Iveragh Peninsula it's possible to hire equipment. The broad, empty beaches around Castlegregory on Castlegregory Peninsula are also decent spots. At Inch on the Dingle Peninsula the waves average 1m to 3m. Spanish Point near Miltown Malby and Lahinch in western Clare are also very good.

North-West & North Easky in County Sligo's west is highly regarded by surfers but by international standards it's uncrowded. Achill Island in County Mayo has surfing beaches, and Bundoran, Tullan Strand and Rossnowlagh are good sites in County Donegal. Portrush to Castlerock on the northern coast in Northern Ireland is a hugely popular surfing area. You can hire equipment in Portrush.

South-East In County Wexford, equipment is available for hire at Rosslare Strand. In County Waterford, Ballinacourty, Dunmore East and Tramore are all worth considering. Equipment and advice are available in Dunmore East.

Scuba Diving Ireland has some of the best scuba diving in Europe, almost entirely off the western coast among its offshore islands and rocks. The country's small size makes it easy to visit different sites. The best period for diving is roughly March to October. Visibility averages over 12m but can increase to 30m on good days. A number of centres around the country offer equipment and training; many of these are listed in the relevant sections in this guide. For more details about scuba diving in Ireland contact Comhairle Fó-Thuinn (CFT), The Irish Underwater Council (☎ 01-284 4601, fax 284 4602, Ⓔ scubairl@indigo.ie, Ⓦ www.scuba ireland.com), 78a Patrick St, Dun Laoghaire, County Dublin. The council is Ireland's diving regulatory body and publishes the dive magazine *SubSea*.

South-West Bantry Bay and Dunmanus Bay in County Cork are good sites. The area is largely virgin territory – a major draw with divers. In Bantry Bay you can dive to the wreck of the French frigate *La Surveillante*, and about 15km from Kinsale is the wreck of the *Lusitania*, sunk in WWI. Other good diving centres in Cork are the waters off Baltimore and Schull, and around Clear and Sherkin Islands.

The Iveragh Peninsula in Kerry has two main bases: Valentia Island and Caherdaniel. Other good Kerry diving spots are the Blasket Islands in Dingle Bay and Ballinskelligs.

West & North In County Clare, Kilkee, Ballyreen (near Lisdoonvarna), Doolin and Fanore are all popular diving centres, as are Achill Island and Clare Island (in Clew Bay) in County Mayo. County Galway offers plenty of opportunities too, particularly along the Connemara coastline and around the Aran Islands. In south-western Donegal, Donegal Bay and the waters off Malinmore are prime sites.

JANE SMITH

Ireland offers excellent diving opportunities.

East & South-East From Dun Laoghaire scuba divers head for the waters around Dalkey Island and Muglands. In County Wexford, the waters off Hook Head provide good diving opportunities.

Sailing There is a long history of sailing in Ireland and the country has over 120 yacht and sailing clubs, including the Royal Cork Yacht Club at Crosshaven, which, established in 1720, is the world's oldest. The most popular areas for sailing are the south-western coast, especially between Cork Harbour and the Dingle Peninsula; the Kerry coastline; the coast of Antrim; along the sheltered coast north and south of Dublin; and some of the larger lakes such as Lough Derg, Lough Erne and Lough Gill.

Ireland has a number of professional training schools catering for people of varying degrees of expertise. They operate under the auspices of the Irish Association for Sail Training (☎ 01-605 1621, W www .irishmarinefederation.com), Irish Marine Federation, Confederation House, 84–86 Lower Baggot St, Dublin. For more information contact the Irish Sailing Association (☎ 01-280 0239, fax 280 7558, e info@ sailing.ie, W www.sailing.ie), 3 Park Rd, Dun Laoghaire, County Dublin. This is the national body governing the sport. The association publishes a monthly magazine, *Ireland Afloat*. A recommended publication is the *Irish Cruising Club Sailing Directions*, available from booksellers. It contains details of port facilities, harbour plans and coast and tidal information.

Windsurfing The windsurfer has plenty of locations to indulge in this popular sport. Even the Grand Canal in Dublin is used by windsurfers. The western coast is the most challenging but is also less crowded. The bay at Rosslare in County Wexford is ideal for windsurfing and you can obtain equipment and tuition there from the Rosslare Windsurfing Centre (☎ 053-32101). The Irish Sailing Association (see the Sailing section above) is the sport's governing authority and has details of other centres offering tuition.

Canoeing There are many opportunities for canoeing and it's a great way to travel round the country. Ireland's indented coastline makes it ideal for exploring by canoe. The Liffey Descent in September is a major international competition. The type of canoeing in Ireland and degree of difficulty varies from gentle paddling to white-water canoeing and canoe surfing. The best time for white water is winter, when the heavier rainfall swells the rivers. Adventure centres around the country run courses and organise canoeing trips.

Information on facilities, locations and conditions can be obtained from the Irish Canoe Union (☎ 01-450 9838, fax 460 4795, e office@irishcanoeunion.com, W www .irishcanoeunion.com), House of Sport, Long Mile Rd, Walkinstown, Dublin; it also runs training courses.

Water-Skiing There are water-ski clubs all over Ireland offering tuition, equipment and boats. Bord Fáilte provides the names of some clubs, but a full list and other details are available from the Irish Water Ski Federation (☎ 028-9260 3117), 11 Highfields Ct, Lisburn.

Bird-Watching

The variety and size of the flocks that visit or breed in Ireland make it of particular interest to bird-watchers. It's also home to some rare and endangered species. For a description of some birds found in Ireland see Birds in the Flora & Fauna section of the Facts about Ireland chapter.

There are more than 70 reserves and sanctuaries in Ireland, but some aren't open to visitors and others are privately owned so you'll need permission from the proprietors before entering. It's illegal to interfere with wild birds, their nests and eggs.

Information can be obtained from the tourist boards and the following:

BirdWatch Ireland (☎ 01-280 4322, fax 284 4407, e bird@indigo.ie, W www.birdwatchireland .ie) Ruttledge House, 8 Longford Place, Monkstown, County Dublin
National Parks and Wildlife Service (☎ 01-661 3111) Dúchas, 51 St Stephen's Green, Dublin

Royal Society for the Protection of Birds
(RSPB; ☎ 028-9049 1547, W www.rspb.org.uk)
Belvoir Park Forest, Belfast

Some useful publications on bird-watching
are *Where to Watch Birds in Ireland* by
Clive Hutchinson, *Birds of Ireland* by G
D'Arcy, the *Complete Guide to Ireland's
Birds* by E Dempsey & M O'Cleary, and
Dominic Couzens' *Collins Birds of Britain
and Ireland*. A Web site that's worth a look
is W www.birdsireland.com.

South-West Clear Island in County Cork
is one of the best places in Europe for viewing Manx shearwater and other sea birds.
On the Skellig Islands there are colonies of
storm petrel, gannet and kittiwake.

North On the north-eastern cliffs of Tory
Island, Donegal, you can see colonies of
puffin; Rathlin Island in Antrim has
thousands of sea birds. Birds such as the
brent goose abound on the shores and mudflats of Strangford Lough in Derry.

East & South-East There are several bird-
watching sites near Dublin. North Bull
Island in Clontarf is a wildlife sanctuary
where many migratory birds pause in winter. Dalkey Island also has plenty of bird
life; Ireland's Eye and Lambay Island off
Howth are important sea bird sanctuaries.

County Wexford is one of the main areas
in Ireland for bird-watching. As well as the
Wexford Wildfowl Reserve on the North
Slobs, where thousands of migrating birds
make their winter home, there's the Saltee
Islands, one of Europe's most important
bird sanctuaries, plus the Hook Peninsula,
Lady's Island and Tacumshin.

Centre The shores of Lough Erne in Fermanagh and Lough Ree in Westmeath are
ideal for bird-watching. Castle Caldwell
Forest Park in Fermanagh is the main breeding ground of the common scoter duck.

Golf

There are nearly 400 golf courses in Ireland,
often in beautiful settings. They range from

illustrious, expensive ones at Killarney, Portmarnock near Dublin and Royal County
Down, to more modest places such as the one
at Castletownbere on the Beara Peninsula.

Bord Fáilte and the NITB produce information leaflets, plus brochures on customised golfing holidays with descriptions
of courses and local accommodation. You
could also try contacting the Golfing
Union of Ireland (☎ 01-269 4111, fax 269
5368, e gui@iol.ie, W www.gui.ie), Glencar House, 81 Eglington Rd, Donnybrook,
Dublin, or the Irish Ladies Golf Union
(☎ 01-269 6244), 1 Clonskeagh Square,
Clonskeagh Rd, Dublin.

Green fees, usually based on a per-day
rather than a per-round basis, start from
around €20 on weekdays (more at the
weekend), but top-notch places charge up to
€160. Courses are tested for their level of
difficulty; many are playable year round.

It's always advisable to book in advance.
Most clubs give members priority in booking
tee-off times. It's usually easier to book a tee-
off time on a public course. At the weekend,
on public holidays and days when the
weather is good it's often busy on all courses.
You should also check whether there's a
dress code and if the course has golf clubs for
hire (not all do) if you don't have your own.

Hang Gliding & Paragliding

Some of the finest hang-gliding and paraglid-
ing is found at Mount Leinster in Carlow,
Great Sugar Loaf Mountain in Wicklow,
Benone/Magillan Beach in Derry and Achill
Island in Mayo. The Irish Hang Gliding and
Paragliding Association (W www.ihpa.ie)
maintain an email list on their Web site,
enabling you to get in touch with local pilots.
For information on Northern Ireland check
the Ulster Hang Gliding and Paragliding
Club's Web site at W www.uhpc.f9.co.uk.

Rock Climbing

Ireland's mountain ranges aren't high –
Mount Carrantuohil in Kerry's MacGillycuddy's Reeks is the tallest mountain in
Ireland at only 1041m – but they're often
beautiful and offer some excellent climbing
possibilities.

Adventure centres around the country run courses and organise climbing trips. For further information contact the Mountaineering Council of Ireland (☎ 01-450 7376, fax 450 2805, Ⓦ www.mountaineering.ie), House of Sport, Long Mile Rd, Dublin, which also publishes climbing guides and the quarterly magazine *Irish Mountain Log*. Also check out Ⓦ www.climbing.ie.

South-West The highest mountains are in the south-west. County Cork has a number of easy climbs, including Mount Gabriel (407m) on Mizen Head Peninsula, Seefin (528m) on Sheep's Head Peninsula and Sugarloaf Mountain (574m) on the Beara Peninsula; Hungry Hill (686m), also on the Beara Peninsula, is more demanding. The Iveragh Peninsula in County Kerry, with the MacGillycuddy's Reeks, has lots of mountains just waiting to be climbed.

West & North-West In Galway, Clifden makes a good base for climbing in Connemara, and in Clare there's excellent rock climbing at Ballyreen near Fanore. Knocknarea (328m) outside Sligo town is an easy climb, and so, too, is Croagh Patrick (765m) in western Mayo, although it takes a lot longer. Some of the highest cliffs in Europe are on Achill Island in Mayo. Mount Errigal (752m) in Donegal is popular with climbers when the weather allows.

North-East & East The Mourne Mountains in County Down, Northern Ireland, have steep, craggy granite peaks, including Eagle Mountain, Pigeon Rock Mountain and Slieve Donard, which, at 848m, is the highest peak in the range. You can base yourself in nearby Newcastle. At the northern end of Lough Tay in the Wicklow Mountains are some spectacular cliffs popular with rock climbers. Also popular are the large crags in Glendalough, at the western end of the valley not far from the Upper Lake.

Horse Riding
Not surprisingly this is a popular pastime and there are dozens of centres throughout Ireland offering horses or ponies for riding along beaches, country lanes, mountain forest trails and over farmland. Possibilit range from hiring a horse for an hour (from €14) to fully packaged, residential equestrian holidays; in some places you can even combine it with English-language tuition. Bord Fáilte and the NITB have full details.

A recommended outfit is Canadian-based Hidden Trails (☎ 604-323 1141, Ⓦ www .hiddentrails.com), 202–380 West 1st Ave, Vancouver, British Columbia V5Y 3T7. It organises a variety of rides all across Ireland.

The wooded valleys and heathery mountains of northern County Waterford are good for horse riding, as are the Wicklow Mountains. Kildare is an equestrian paradise. Other areas include the Dingle Peninsula and Killarney National Park in Kerry, Connemara in Galway, around Bundoran and the Finn Valley in Donegal, and near Clonakilty in Cork.

For details on holidays in horse-drawn caravans see the Accommodation section later in this chapter.

COURSES
Irish Language
With the revival of the Irish language there is a growing number of courses in the language and culture, particularly in the Gaeltacht (Irish-speaking areas).

University College Galway runs intensive one/two-week courses costing €195/ 320 plus accommodation; contact the Irish Language Centre (☎ 091-595101) or Áras Mháirtín Uí Chadhain, University College Galway, Galway City. They also run intensive month-long courses. In Glencolmcille, Donegal, weekend and week-long courses in Irish and Irish culture, combined with outdoor activities, are provided from late March to October by Oideas Gael (☎ 073-30248, fax 30348, ⒠ oidsgael@iol.ie) at the Foras Cultúir Uladh (Ulster Cultural Foundation). Language courses cost from €65/140 for three-day/week-long courses; week-long cultural courses cost from €90 to €120. Accommodation can also be arranged costing €80 per person per week or €160 with breakfast and dinner.

Contact Bord Fáilte for information on other courses.

English Language

Given Ireland's significant contribution to English literature it's probably not surprising that it has become a centre for the learning of English, particularly for people from other Catholic countries, mainly Spain, Italy, France and Portugal.

Bord Fáilte publishes a list of schools that have been recognised by the Department of Education for teaching English as a foreign language. Some schools run summer programs and provide specialised courses (such as for business people); the schools can arrange accommodation and organise sporting and cultural activities.

There are English-language schools in other parts of the country but most are in and around Dublin. Some of the approved schools in Dublin are:

Centre of English Studies (☎ 01-671 4233, ⓦ www.cesireland.ie) 31 Dame St, Dublin
Dublin School of English (☎ 01-677 3322, ⓦ www.dse.ie) 10–12 Westmoreland St, Dublin
English Language Institute (☎ 01-475 2965, ⓦ www.englishlanguage.com) 99 St Stephen's Green, Dublin
Language Centre of Ireland (☎ 01-671 6266, ⓦ www.lci.ie) 45 Kildare St, Dublin

WORK

Ireland's economic upturn and the fall in unemployment mean that finding casual work has become easier. Lowly paid seasonal work is available in the tourist industry, usually in restaurants and pubs in cities such as Dublin, Belfast and Cork. Hostel notice boards sometimes advertise casual work and hostels themselves sometimes employ travellers to staff reception or clean rooms.

Without skills, though, it's difficult to find a job that pays sufficiently well to enable you to save money. You're almost certainly better off saving in your country of origin.

Sometimes volunteer work is available in return for bed and board, for example from the Burren Conservation Trust (see Fanore in the County Clare chapter).

Citizens of other EU countries can work legally in Ireland. If you don't come from an EU country but do have an Irish parent or grandparent, it's fairly easy to obtain Irish citizenship without necessarily renouncing your own nationality, and this opens the door to employment throughout the EU. Obtaining citizenship isn't an overnight procedure, so enquire about the process at an Irish embassy or consulate in your own country.

To work in the North, citizens of Commonwealth countries aged 17 to 27 can apply for a Working Holiday Entry Certificate that allows them to spend two years in the UK and to take work that's 'incidental' to a holiday.

Commonwealth citizens with a UK-born parent may be eligible for a Certificate of Entitlement to the Right of Abode, which entitles them to live and work in the UK free of immigration control. Commonwealth citizens with a UK-born grandparent, or a grandparent born before 31 March 1922 in what's now the Republic, may qualify for a UK Ancestry Employment Certificate, allowing them to work full time for up to four years in the UK.

Visiting full-time US students aged 18 and over can get a six-month work permit for Ireland and the UK through Council Exchanges (☎ 888 268 6245, ⓦ www.council exchanges.org/us), 633 3rd Ave, New York, NY 10017.

ACCOMMODATION

Bord Fáilte produces a range of annual publications listing B&Bs, hotels, camp sites and other accommodation, but they far from exhaust the possibilities. There are many places that aren't 'tourist board approved' but are in no way inferior to the approved places. The NITB publishes its own *Where to Stay* accommodation guide (£4.99). Gulliver, a joint venture of Bord Fáilte and the NITB, is a computerised accommodation reservation system (see Tourist Offices earlier in this chapter for details). Branches of both tourist offices will book local accommodation for a fee of €1.27, or €2.54 if the accommodation is in another town; it can be worth it to avoid the inconvenience of calling around, especially in high summer.

Everybody's Hotel Directory (ⓦ www .everybody.co.uk) is an Internet directory listing accommodation suitable for disabled (and able-bodied) travellers in the UK, including Northern Ireland.

Camping & Caravanning

Camping and caravan parks aren't as common in Ireland as they are in Britain or on the continent, but there are still plenty of them around Ireland. Camping barns, converted farm buildings providing basic shelter for up to a dozen people, are starting to crop up in parts of Ireland. Some hostels have camping space for tents and usually offer the use of the kitchen and shower facilities, which often makes them better value than the main camp sites. At commercial parks, tent sites typically cost €5 to €12 and many have coin-operated showers. Parks usually have different rates depending on the type of tent (a two-person tent as opposed to a family tent being the usual distinction) and whether you arrive by bike or car. Sites for caravans cost around €9 to €13.

Free tent camping may be available if you ask permission from the landowner. Around the touristy parts of County Kerry and Cork, farmers may ask for a couple of euros, but it shouldn't be too difficult to find one who'll let you camp for nothing.

An alternative to normal caravanning is to hire a horse-drawn caravan with which to wander the countryside. In high season you can hire one for around €750 a week. Contact Bord Fáilte for a list of operators. You can also get details online at W http://horsedrawn.in-ireland.net.

Hostels

The prices quoted in this book for hostel accommodation are for high season and for those aged over 18 (An Óige uses the terms senior and junior, where senior refers to those aged over 18). A dorm bed in high season – June to September – generally costs €10 to €19, except for in the more expensive Galway and Dublin hostels.

If you're travelling on a tight budget, the numerous hostels – both official and independent – offer cheap accommodation and are also great centres for meeting fellow travellers. From May to September and on public holidays, hostels can be heavily booked, but so is everything else.

An Óige and HINI are the two associations that belong to Hostelling International

(HI). You must be a member to stay in one of their hostels. For information on how to join, see Hostel Cards in the Visas & Documents section earlier in this chapter. An Óige and HINI hostels have changed a lot for the better. They now operate a fax-a-bed-ahead facility. Bookings can be made by credit card at many of the larger hostels. Some hostels have family and smaller rooms, and these days you can take a car to a hostel. An Óige has 32 hostels scattered around the South and HINI has eight in the North. To use a hostel you must have or rent a sleeping sheet.

The contact details of the hostel associations are:

An Óige (☎ 01-830 4555, fax 830 5808, ⓔ mail box@anoige.ie, W www.irelandyha.org) 61 Mountjoy St, Dublin
HINI (☎ 028-9031 5435, fax 9043 9699, W www.hini.org.uk) 22–32 Donegall Rd, Belfast

Ireland has seen independent hostels, with no membership requirements, pop up like toadstools after rain. They emphasise their easy-going ambience and lack of rules but, while most have no curfew, some don't allow you access to your room for part of the day. Not all are of a high standard: some are cold in winter, stuffy in summer and often cramped, with up to 20 people in a room sleeping on flimsy metal bunk beds. Also, as a result of recent pressures on the Irish government to find housing for large numbers of refugees and asylum seekers, some independent hostels have (almost overnight, and sometimes without advance notice) stopped catering for travellers and have become instead boarding houses for refugees.

The following associations do their best to offer reliable accommodation:

Independent Hostel Owners of Ireland (IHI; ☎ 073-30130, fax 30339, W www.holidayhound .com/ihi) Dooey Hostel, Glencolmcille, County Donegal
Independent Holiday Hostels of Ireland (IHH; ☎ 01-836 4700, fax 836 4710, ⓔ ihh@iol.ie, W www.hostels-ireland.com) 57 Lower Gardiner St, Dublin. A cooperative group with dozens of hostels in both the North and South.

Hostelworld.com (W www.hostelworld.com) An online hostel booking agency.

B&Bs

It sometimes seems as if every other house in Ireland is a B&B: you'll stumble upon them in the most unusual and remote locations.

The typical cost is €24 to €32 per person per night, and you rarely pay less or more than that, except in the big towns, where some luxurious B&Bs can cost €55 or more per person.

Sadly, most B&Bs, like hotels, charge a 'single supplement' for individual travellers. B&Bs are usually small, with two to four rooms, so from April to September they can fill up quickly. Outside big cities, most B&Bs accept cash only.

Hotels

Hotels range from the local pub to medieval castles. It's often possible to negotiate better deals than the published rates, especially out of season. Ask if any discounts are given and try to think of a reason why you merit one. Out of the main holiday season, hotels often have special deals for certain days of the week, but these are usually quite flexible and can often be extended to whatever days you want. Payment for a night's stay usually includes breakfast.

Self-Catering

Self-catering accommodation is often on a weekly basis and usually means an apartment or house where you look after yourself. The rates vary from one region and season to another. A smart cottage in Schull, County Cork, in August can cost €800 a week, sleeping six people, while the equivalent in Banagher, County Offaly, in April is about €250. Bord Fáilte publish a guide to registered self-catering accommodation that contains photos and descriptions.

Other Accommodation

During summer, there's accommodation in Dublin at Trinity College and University College (see Student Accommodation in the Places to Stay section of the Dublin chapter), and in Belfast at Queen's University

(see Hostels in the Places to Stay section of the Belfast chapter).

Guesthouses are often just like larger, more expensive B&Bs, but sometimes they're more like small hotels, with a restaurant and sitting room, and a telephone and TV in the rooms. Farmhouse accommodation usually means a B&B on a farm; they're sometimes excellent value and you may get a chance to see how the farm works. Country houses are rural B&Bs, normally costing a fair bit more and in a rather grander-than-usual house.

Another option is to hire a boat, which you can live aboard while cruising Ireland's inland waterways. One company offering boats for hire on the Shannon–Erne Waterway is Emerald Star (☎ 078-20234, fax 21433, W www.emeraldstar.ie), The Marina, Carrick-on-Shannon, County Leitrim. Lists of operators are available from the tourist boards.

FOOD
Local Food

Irish cooking once had a poor reputation, but things have improved enormously and now you can generally eat very well. Readily available high-quality produce, the influence of international cuisines brought over by immigrants, a growing awareness of healthy eating, the culinary experiences of the Irish abroad and the higher expectations of Ireland's numerous visitors have combined to produce what is called by some 'new Irish cuisine'. Of course, if you want meat or fish cooked until it's dried and shrivelled and vegetables turned to mush, there are still enough places that can perform the feat.

Irish meals are usually meat based, with beef, lamb and pork common options. Seafood, long neglected, is finding a place on the table in Irish homes. It's widely available in restaurants and is often excellent, especially in the west. Oysters, trout and salmon are delicious, particularly if they're direct from the sea or river rather than a fish farm.

Local cheeses (once mainly limited to an orange version of cheddar) are also widely available. Notable are cheeses from Clare and West Cork, particularly Gubbeen, a soft cheese from Schull, and the spicy Mileens.

Dublin's brie-like Dunbarra and Tipperary's Cashel Blue and Cooleeny cheeses are all worth trying.

Irish bread has a wonderful reputation and can be very good, particularly in Belfast, but, unfortunately, there's a tendency to rely on the infamous white sliced bread (*arán* in Irish). Irish scones are a delight – tea and scones is a great snack at any time of day – that even pubs often offer.

Traditional foods include:

Bacon and Cabbage Slices of boiled bacon or gammon with boiled cabbage on the side.

Barm Brack A spicy, cake-like bread, traditionally served at Halloween with a ring hidden inside (careful!).

Blaa Sausage rolls from Waterford.

Black and White Pudding Like meatloaf but sausage-shaped, cut into discs and fried.

Boxty A potato pancake, becoming rarer on menus.

Carrigeen A seaweed dish.

Champ A Northern-Irish dish of potatoes mashed with spring onions (scallions).

Coddle A Dublin dish of semi-thick stew made with sausages, bacon, onions and potatoes.

Colcannon Mashed potato, cabbage and onion fried in butter and milk.

Crubeens A Cork dish of pigs' trotters.

Dulse A dried seaweed that's sold salted and ready to eat, mainly in Ballycastle, County Antrim.

Guinness Cake A popular fruitcake flavoured with Guinness.

Irish Stew This quintessential Irish dish is a stew of mutton, potatoes and onions, flavoured with parsley and thyme and simmered slowly.

Soda Bread This bread, white and brown (also known as wheaten), is made from flour and buttermilk and found throughout the country.

Yellowman A hard, chewy toffee made in County Antrim.

Restaurants

Many Irish people (more so in rural areas) eat their main meal of the day at lunchtime. Every town has at least one hotel, pub or restaurant offering three-course lunches costing around €6.50. A similar meal in the evening may be at least double the cost.

The last decade has seen a huge increase in restaurants of every type and price range. Outside the principal centres the main alternatives to Irish food are provided by Italian and Chinese restaurants. But in cities such as Dublin, Belfast and Cork you'll also find a cosmopolitan range of cuisines, including French, Indian, Middle Eastern and Mexican. The result has been a huge change in attitudes to city dining. What was regarded as a luxury, experienced only on special occasions, is becoming almost a daily habit.

Fast Food

Fast food ranges from traditional fish and chips – fish and chip shops are called 'chippers' – to burgers, pizzas, kebabs and tacos. Pubs are often good places to eat, particularly at lunchtime, when a bowl of soup (usually vegetable) and some good bread can make a fine, economical meal.

Vegetarian

There are some superb vegetarian places, but you'll have to hunt for them. Hotels and restaurants often feature a vegetarian dish on their menus, though they can sometimes be bland and unimaginative. At more expensive restaurants it's a good idea to inform them in advance that you want a vegetarian meal. For vegetarians, staying at a B&B can be a bad deal: the best excuse for the high prices charged by most is the huge breakfast. The vegetarian alternative is usually just cornflakes and toast, but the charge is the same. Some are happy to serve baked beans on toast if you ask.

Publications

There are several specialist food and restaurant guides to Ireland. Bridgestone's *100 Best Restaurants in Ireland* by Sally & John McKenna is a practical, independent guide. Egon Ronay has a guide to Ireland, and recommended restaurants display an Egon Ronay plaque.

Bord Fáilte has its own publication, *Dining in Ireland*, but proprietors simply pay for their entry and submit their own write-up. The NITB publishes *Where to Eat*, which lists everything from the very expensive to the local Chinese takeaway.

DRINKS
Nonalcoholic Drinks

The Irish drink lots of tea, which is usually served in a small teapot with milk in a separate jug. Coffee is available in nearly all pubs, costing from €0.80 to €1.50, but don't expect a smile if you order one at 11pm on a busy night. If you ask for cream with your coffee, cream is what you'll get – a big dollop of it. Pubs and hotels also serve soft drinks and brand-named fizzy drinks (called 'minerals'), but to judge by the prices you might think they were deliberately discouraging customers from drinking them.

Alcoholic Drinks

'Stout' usually means Guinness, the famous black beer of Dublin, although in Cork it can mean Murphy's or Beamish. Originating in Britain, stout (also called 'porter' because of its popularity with porters at Covent Garden Market in London) was promoted by the Guinness family and soon gained an enduring stranglehold on the Irish tastebuds.

If you don't develop a taste for stout (and you should at least try), a wide variety of lager beers are available, including Irish Harp (brewed by Guinness) and many locally brewed 'imports' such as Budweiser, Foster's or Heineken. For British-style bitter try Smithwick's (the 'w' isn't pronounced) or Caffrey's. Simply asking for a Guinness or a Harp will get you a pint (570ml; €2.80 to €3.50 in a pub). If you want a half-pint (€1.40 to €1.75) ask for a 'glass' or a 'half'.

The Irish were pioneers in the development of distilling whiskey (distilled three times and spelled with an 'e' as opposed to twice-distilled Scotch whisky). Bushmills in County Antrim is the world's oldest legal distillery (1608). When ordering a whiskey, the Irish never ask for a Scotch (though Scotch whisky is available): they use the brand name of an Irish whiskey instead: Jameson's, Paddy's, Power's, Bushmills or whatever. It may seem expensive but the Irish measure is generous, by law.

Irish coffee is something you'll see on sale in hotels and restaurants, but it's not a traditional drink. It's a modern phenomenon and was considered novel when served to the first transatlantic passengers arriving at Shannon Airport (though some say it was really invented in San Francisco). It's a mixture of hot coffee and whiskey topped with cream.

ENTERTAINMENT

For information on annual festivals and events see Public Holidays & Special Events earlier in this chapter.

Pubs, Bars & Clubs

Listening to traditional music while nursing a pint of Guinness is the most popular form of entertainment in Ireland. If someone invites you to visit a particular pub for its 'good crack' (*craic* in Irish), don't think you've just found the local dope dealer. *Craic* is Irish for a good time – convivial company, sparkling conversation and rousing music.

In cities such as Dublin, Belfast and Cork old-style pubs are being replaced by sleek, modern bars whose main feature is a 250W stereo system. The nightclub scene in Dublin and Belfast is booming, with clubs offering different themes for different nights and partying well into the early hours.

These days many pubs and bars have satellite TV and you can go and watch the latest big – and not so big – sporting events.

Cinemas

Larger towns and cities have multiscreen cinemas, but only Dublin, Belfast and Cork have art-house cinemas showing alternative or foreign films. Belfast also has an IMAX cinema. Rural areas benefit from the Irish Film Board's travelling cinema, which boasts plush seating, air conditioning and a surround sound system.

Theatre

Theatre is popular all over Ireland. Dublin, particularly, is renowned for its excellent theatres and there's always a broad range of plays and shows on. Most famous is the Abbey Theatre (W www.abbeytheatre.ie), founded by WB Yeats, Lady Gregory and other writers and artists behind the Anglo-Irish literary revival. The Gate Theatre (W www.gate-theatre.ie) is a smaller company but puts on a remarkable variety of new and unusual work. Both the Gaiety (W www.gaietytheatre.net) and Olympia Theatres are beautifully preserved old showhouses that host a mix of plays, pantomimes and shows. Belfast has a range of theatres, most notably the Grand Opera House (W www.goh.co.uk). Most major towns have at least one theatre and, in the summer, companies tour the country.

Classical Music & Opera

The majority of classical music groups and opera companies are based in Dublin, though Belfast and Cork are also important centres. Main venues for performances are Dublin's National Concert Hall (W www .nch.ie), Belfast's Waterfront Hall (W www .waterfront.co.uk) and Grand Opera House, and the Cork Opera House. The most prestigious operatic event of the year is the Wexford Festival Opera in October (see the Wexford chapter for more details).

SPECTATOR SPORTS
Gaelic Football & Hurling

Ireland has two native games with a large, enthusiastic following – Gaelic football and hurling.

Gaelic football is a fast and exciting spectacle. The ball is round like a soccer ball and the players can pass it in any direction by kicking or punching it. The goalposts are similar to rugby posts, and a goal, worth three points, is scored by putting the ball below the bar, while a single point is awarded when the ball goes over the bar. Gaelic football is popular throughout Ireland.

Hurling is a ball-and-stick game something like hockey, but much faster and more physical. Visitors are often taken aback by the crash of players wielding what look like ferocious clubs, but injuries are infrequent. The goalposts and scoring method are the same as Gaelic football, but the leather ball or *sliotar* is the size of a baseball. A player can pick up the ball on their stick and run with it for a certain distance. Players can handle the ball briefly and pass it by palming it. The players' broad wooden sticks are called hurleys. Women's hurling is called camogie.

Hurling has an ancient history and is mentioned in many old Irish tales. The mythical Celtic hero Cúchulainn was a legendary exponent of the game. Today hurling is played on a standard field, but in the olden days the game might have been played across country between two towns or villages, the aim being to get the ball to a certain spot or goal.

Gaelic football and hurling are played nationwide by a network of town and country clubs and under the auspices of the Gaelic Athletic Association, or GAA (W www.gaa .ie). The most important competitions are played at county level, and the county winners out of each of the sport's four provinces come together in the autumn for the All-Ireland Finals, the climax of Ireland's sporting year. The Gaelic football and hurling finals are both played in September at Dublin's Croke Park.

Football & Rugby

Football (soccer) and rugby enjoy considerable support all over the country, particularly around Dublin; football is very popular in Northern Ireland.

The international rugby team consists of players from the North and the Republic and has a tremendous following. The highlights of the rugby year are the international matches played against England, Scotland, Wales, France and Italy in the Six Nations championship between January and March. Home matches are played at Lansdowne Rd Stadium, Dublin. See W www.irfu.ie for more details.

The North and the Republic field separate international football teams and both, though particularly the Republic's, have had a good record in competitions. International matches

JANE SMITH

The fast, physical game of hurling

are played at the Lansdowne Rd Stadium, Dublin, and Windsor Park, Belfast.

Many home players from the North and South play professional football in Britain and the most successful have the status of pop or movie stars. English clubs Arsenal, Liverpool and Manchester United, and Scottish clubs Celtic and Rangers have strong followings in Ireland.

Both North (W www.irishfa.com) and South (W www.fai.ie) have their own professional football league.

Road Bowling

The object of this sport is to throw a cast-iron ball along a public road (normally one with little traffic) for a designated distance, usually one or two kilometres. The person who does it in the least number of throws is the winner. The main centres are Cork and Armagh and competitions take place throughout the year, attracting considerable crowds.

Handball

Handball is another Irish sport with ancient origins and is also governed by the GAA. It is different from Olympic handball in that it is played by two individuals or two pairs who use their hands to strike a ball against a forecourt wall, rather like squash.

Athletics

Athletics is popular and the Republic has produced a few international stars, particularly in middle- and long-distance events. Cork athlete Sonia O'Sullivan consistently leads in women's long-distance track events worldwide, and Catherina McKiernan is one of the world's top marathon runners. In Ireland, the main athletic meets are held at Morton Stadium, Dublin. The Dublin Marathon is run on the last Monday in October.

Boxing

Boxing has traditionally had a strong working-class following. Irish boxers have often won Olympic medals or world championships. Barry McGuigan and Steve Collins, both now retired, were world champions in their day; Michael Carruth won the world welterweight title in 1998. Dublin's National Stadium is a popular venue. See W www.irishboxingnews.com for current information on the sport.

Horse Racing

Horses have played a big role in Irish life over the centuries and the country has produced a large number of internationally successful race horses.

A total of 27 racecourses dot the country, including Leopardstown in County Dublin, Fairyhouse in County Meath, and Naas, Punchestown and the Curragh in County Kildare. Major annual races include the Irish Grand National (Fairyhouse, April), Irish Derby (the Curragh, June) and Irish Leger (the Curragh, September). For more information on events contact the Irish Horseracing Authority (☎ 01-289 2888, W www.iha.ie), Leopardstown Racecourse, Foxrock, Dublin.

Greyhound Racing

With fixtures year round, greyhound racing has a strong following in Ireland. There are 20 tracks across the country, administered by the Irish Greyhound Board (☎ 061-316788, W www.igb.ie), 104 Henry St, Limerick.

Golf

Golf is enormously popular in Ireland and there are many fine golf courses. The annual Irish Open takes place in June or July and the Irish Women's Open in September. For details of venues, contact the Golfing Union of Ireland (☎ 01-269 4111, e gui@iol.ie, W www.gui.ie), 81 Eglinton Rd, Donnybrook, Dublin. Players to watch out for include Paul McGinley, Darren Clarke and Pádraig Harrington.

Cycling

Cycling is a popular spectator sport and events held annually include the Des Hanlon Memorial Race at Carlow (March or April), and the gruelling Milk Rás (May), which sometimes approaches 700 miles in length. 1998 saw Ireland host the first section of the Tour de France. Current Irish cyclists include Ciaran Power, Aidan Duff and Tommy Evans. For information on events try W www.irishcycling.com.

Snooker

Snooker has a cult following in Ireland. The Irish Masters takes place in Dublin in March. Top players are Fergal O'Brien and Ken Doherty, who is the only player in the sport to have ever won both the amateur and professional world championships.

SHOPPING

Online shoppers can visit W www.celtic links.com for a wide selection of Irish goods.

Clothing

First made by Aran Island women for their husbands to wear in the harsh local climate, the famous Aran sweater is sold throughout Ireland, though it's found most in County Galway. The hand-knitted variety costs significantly more than its machine-manufactured counterpart.

County Donegal is famous for its tweeds – Magee & Company (☎ 073-31100, W www .mageeshop.com), The Diamond, Donegal Town, has a large selection. Tweed can be purchased in lengths or finished as jackets, skirts or caps. Counties Wicklow and Dublin also produce tweed.

Irish linen is of high quality and comes in the form of everything from blouses to handkerchiefs, with the main centres in the North. Irish lace is another fine product, at its best in Limerick, or Carrickmacross in County Monaghan. The Irish produce some high-quality outdoor-activities gear – they do have plenty of experience with wet and cold weather, after all. Hand-woven shawls and woollen blankets also make lovely presents.

Crystal

Waterford Crystal (☎ 051-73311, W www .waterfordwedgwood.com), Kilbarry, Waterford, makes world-famous crystal that is available throughout Ireland, although the company has reduced its workforce in Waterford and moved some business overseas. Their main competitor is Cavan Crystal (☎ 049-433 1800, W www.cavancrystal

design.com), Dublin Rd, Cavan. Smaller manufacturers of crystal produce fine work and at more attractive prices. In the North, Tyrone Crystal (☎ 028-8772 5335, W www .tyronecrystal.com), Killybrackey, Dungannon, hosts factory tours.

Food & Drink

Irish whiskey isn't just spelled differently: it also has its own distinctive taste. The big names are Paddy's, Jameson's, Power's, Bushmills and Tullamore Dew, and they're not always readily available in other parts of the world. Two well established Irish liqueurs are Irish Mist and Bailey's Irish Cream. Bailey's now also produce Irish coffee in a bottle, ready mixed.

Some excellent handmade cheeses are worth considering as a gift to take home. See the Food section earlier in this chapter for cheese suggestions.

Pottery

All over the country there are small potteries turning out unusual and attractive work. The village of Belleek in County Fermanagh, which straddles the Northern Ireland border with Donegal, produces delicate bone china. In the South the area around Dingle in County Kerry has superb pottery. Enniscorthy in County Wexford, and Kilkenny and Thomastown in County Kilkenny also stand out in this regard. Generally, throughout West Cork and Kerry there are countless small workshops that open in the summer with their stocks of pottery and other craftwork. Stephen Pearce pottery, from Carrigaline in Cork, is available in gift shops all over Ireland.

Other Items

Other possibilities include Irish music; jewellery, especially Claddagh rings (see the boxed text 'Claddagh' in the Galway chapter), enamel work and baskets woven of willow or rush. Connemara marble is a natural green stone found in the west of Ireland; it is often fashioned into Celtic designs.

Getting There & Away

The Web site of the Irish Tourist Board (W www.irishtouristboard.com) has information on getting to Ireland from a number of countries. However you travel, be sure to take out travel insurance (see Travel Insurance in the Visas & Documents section of the Facts for the Visitor chapter).

AIR
Airports & Airlines
Dublin Airport (☎ 01-814 1111, W www.dublinairport.com, code DUB) is the Republic's major international airport. Shannon (☎ 061-712000, W www.shannonairport.com, code SNN), near Limerick, and Cork (☎ 021-431 3131, W www.corkairport.com, code ORK) also have sizable international facilities. There are scheduled nonstop flights from Britain, continental Europe and North America to Dublin and Shannon, and good nonstop connections from Britain and continental Europe to Cork. Other airports in the Republic with nonstop scheduled services from Britain are Kerry Airport (☎ 066-976 4350, code KIR) near Killarney, Waterford Airport (☎ 051-875589, code WAT) and Knock International Airport (☎ 094-67222, W www.knockinternationalairport.ie, code NOC).

Galway (☎ 091-755569, W www.galwayairport.com, code GWY), Sligo (☎ 071-68280, W www.sligoairport.com, code SXL) and Donegal (☎ 075-48284, W www.donegalairport.ie, code CFN) are all airports served by connecting domestic flights from Dublin.

Aer Lingus (W www.aerlingus.com) is the Irish national airline, with nonstop flights to Britain, continental Europe and the USA. Ryanair (W www.ryanair.com), the next-largest Irish airline, is a no-frills carrier with inexpensive services to Britain and continental Europe. Aer Árann (W www.aerarann.ie) is a small carrier that operates connecting flights from Dublin to various cities throughout Ireland; it also flies to Britain.

Northern Ireland's primary airport is

Belfast International Airport (☎ 028-9448 4848, W www.belfastairport.com, code BFS), 30km north-west of the city in Aldergrove. There are flights to Belfast International from Shannon in the Republic, Britain, continental Europe and the USA. Smaller but more convenient for the city centre is Belfast City Airport (☎ 028-9093 9093, W www.belfastcityairport.com, code BHD), which offers nonstop scheduled services to various British cities, as does Derry Airport (☎ 028-7181 0784, W www.derry.net/airport, code LDY).

Buying Tickets
Competition among airlines and agents is fierce, making air travel better value than ever before. But you have to research the options carefully in order to make sure you get the best deal. The Internet is an invaluable resource for checking air fares.

Full-time students and those aged under

26 (under 30 in some countries) have access to better deals than other travellers. You must show a document proving your date of birth or a valid International Student Identity Card (ISIC) when buying your ticket.

Generally, there's nothing to be gained by buying a ticket direct from the airline. Discounted tickets are released to selected travel agents and specialist discount agencies, and these are usually the cheapest deals going.

One exception to this rule is the expanding number of 'no-frills' carriers, which sell direct to travellers and charge extra (sometimes a lot extra) for on-board amenities. Unlike the 'full-service' airlines, no-frills carriers often make one-way tickets available at half the return fare; this makes it easy to plan an open-jaw itinerary, where you fly into one city and out of another.

The other exception is booking on the Internet, as many airlines, full-service and no-frills, offer some excellent fares to Web surfers. They may sell seats by auction or simply cut prices to reflect the reduced cost of electronic selling.

Many travel agencies have Web sites, which can make the Internet a quick and easy way to compare their prices. There is also an increasing number of agencies that operate only on the Internet. Online ticket sales work well if you are doing a simple one-way or return trip on specified dates. However, online fare generators are no substitute for a travel agent who knows all about special deals, has strategies for avoiding stopovers and can offer advice on everything from which airline has the best vegetarian food to the best travel insurance to bundle with your ticket.

You may find that the cheapest flights are being advertised by obscure agencies. Most such firms are honest and solvent, but there are some rogue fly-by-night outfits around. Paying by credit card can offer some protection since most card issuers will provide a refund if you don't get what you've paid for. Similar protection can be obtained by buying a ticket from a bonded agent, such as one covered by the Air Transport Organiser's Licence (ATOL) scheme in the UK. Should the ATOL agent go bust, the Civil Aviation Authority will guarantee a refund

or an alternative arrangement. Agents who only accept cash should hand over the tickets straight away and not tell you to 'come back tomorrow'. After you've made a booking or paid your deposit, call the airline to confirm that the booking was made. It's generally not advisable to send money (even cheques) through the post unless the agent is very well established – some travellers have reported being ripped off by fly-by-night mail-order ticket agents.

Think carefully before buying a ticket that is not easily refunded, as many travellers change their routes halfway through their trips. Be aware that no-frills tickets can be something of a lottery. In the case of delays or cancellations you won't be offered the same level of compensation that major carriers provide; check the terms of your ticket carefully before purchasing, and do not buy a no-frills ticket if you have inflexible travel plans.

Travellers with Special Needs

If they're warned early enough, airlines can often make special arrangements for travellers, such as providing wheelchair assistance at the airports or vegetarian meals on the flight. Children aged under two travel for 10% of the standard fare (or free on some airlines) as long as they don't occupy a seat, but they don't get a baggage allowance. 'Skycots', baby food and nappies should be provided by the airline if requested in advance. Children aged between two and 12 can usually occupy a seat for half to two-thirds of the full fare, and do get a baggage allowance.

The All Go Here Web site at **W** www .everybody.co.uk has a disability-friendly airline directory that provides information on the facilities offered by various airlines.

The UK

There is a dizzying array of flights on offer between Britain and Ireland. The London–Dublin air corridor alone is one of the busiest in the world. Here as well as on the London–Belfast route a handful of airlines compete for passengers, and enticingly low fares are often the result. Many other routes

Air Travel Glossary

Alliances Many of the world's leading airlines are now intimately involved with each other, sharing everything from reservations systems and check-in to aircraft and frequent-flyer schemes. Opponents say that alliances restrict competition. Whatever the arguments, there is no doubt that big alliances are the way of the future.

Courier Fares Businesses often need to send urgent documents or freight securely and quickly. Courier companies hire people to accompany the package through customs and, in return, offer a discount ticket which is sometimes a bargain. However, you may have to surrender all your baggage allowance and take only carry-on luggage.

Fares Airlines traditionally offer 1st class (coded F), business class (coded J) and economy class (coded Y) tickets. These days there are so many promotional and discounted fares available that few passengers pay full fare.

Lost Tickets If you lose your airline ticket, an airline will usually treat it like a travellers cheque and, after enquiries, issue you with another one. Legally, however, an airline is entitled to treat it like cash and if you lose it then it's gone forever. Take very good care of your tickets.

Onward Tickets An entry requirement for many countries is that you have a ticket out of the country. If you're unsure of your next move, the easiest solution is to buy the cheapest onward ticket to a neighbouring country or a ticket from a reliable airline which can later be refunded if you do not use it.

Open-Jaw Tickets These are return tickets where you fly out to one place but return from another. If available, this can save you backtracking to your arrival point.

Overbooking Since every flight has some passengers who fail to show up, airlines often book more passengers than they have seats. Usually excess passengers make up for the no-shows, but occasionally somebody gets 'bumped' onto the next available flight. Guess who it is most likely to be? The passengers who check in late. If you do get 'bumped', you are normally offered some form of compensation.

Reconfirmation Some airlines require you to reconfirm your flight at least 72 hours prior to departure. Check your travel documents to see if this is the case.

Restrictions Discounted tickets often have various restrictions on them – such as needing to be paid for in advance and incurring a penalty to be altered or cancelled. Others are restrictions on the minimum and maximum period you must be away.

Round-the-World Tickets RTW tickets give you a limited period (usually a year) in which to circumnavigate the globe. You can go anywhere the carrying airlines go, as long as you don't backtrack. The number of stopovers or total number of separate flights is decided before you set off and they usually cost a bit more than a basic return flight.

Ticketless Travel Airlines are gradually waking up to the realisation that paper tickets are unnecessary encumbrances. On simple one-way or return trips, reservations details can be held on computer and the passenger merely shows ID to claim their seat.

Transferred Tickets Airline tickets cannot be transferred from one person to another. Travellers sometimes try to sell the return half of their ticket, but officials can ask you to prove that you are the person named on the ticket. On an international flight, tickets are compared with passports.

tend to be competitive too, particularly from London to Cork or Shannon, and from Birmingham, Manchester or Glasgow to Dublin or Belfast. The proliferation of no-frills services in this market means that many of the best deals are now only available online, as discount airlines prefer to sell via the Internet in order to reduce overhead costs. Ireland's very own no-frills airline, Ryanair, keeps things interesting by frequently offering tickets for next to nothing (in such cases it's not unusual for airport taxes to exceed the base price of the ticket), but you have to be quick off the mark to pick up the best-priced deals as these fares sell out rapidly.

Advertisements for travel agencies and special fare offers appear in the travel pages of the weekend broadsheets, and in London's *Time Out*, the *Evening Standard* and the free magazine *TNT*.

For students or travellers aged under 26, popular travel agencies in Britain include STA Travel (☎ 0870 160 6070, W www.statravel.co.uk) and usit Campus (☎ 0870 240 1010, W www.usitcampus .co.uk). Both have branches throughout Britain. These agencies sell tickets to all travellers but cater especially for young people and students.

Other recommended travel agencies for all age groups include Bridge Travel (☎ 0870 727 5973, W www.bridgetravel .com), 55–59 High Rd, Broxbourne EN10 7DT; Bridge the World (☎ 0870 444 7474, W www.bridgetheworld.com), 4 Regent Place, Regent St, London W1R 5F; Flight Centre (☎ 0870 899 9888, W www.flight centre.co.uk); Global Village (☎ 0870 442 4844, W www.gvillage.co.uk), 57–9 Leather Lane, London EC1N 7TJ; and Trailfinders (☎ 020-7937 1234, W www.trailfinders .com), 215 Kensington High St, London W8 6BD. Tara Travel (☎ 020-8514 5141, W www.taratravel.com), 245 High Rd, Ilford IG1 1NE, specialises in travel to Ireland.

Online agents include W www.ebookers .com, W www.expedia.co.uk, W www .wannabeinireland.com and W www.travel ocity.co.uk. This last site specialises in

travel to Ireland. The Web site W www .priceline.co.uk acts as a clearing house for airlines looking to fill seats that often go empty. You set your own price for tickets; if the bid is accepted by the airline, you fly.

Often the best fares going are sold direct by airlines online, most notably by the no-frills carriers Ryanair, easyJet and Go. A list of airlines offering scheduled services between Britain and Ireland follows:

Aer Árann
☎ 0114-201 1998
W www.aerarann.ie
Aer Lingus
☎ 0845 973 7747
W www.aerlingus.com
Air Wales
☎ 0870 013 3151
W www.airwales.co.uk
British Airways
☎ 0845 773 3377
W www.britishairways.com
British European
☎ 0870 567 6676
W www.british-european.com
British Midland
☎ 0870 607 0555
W www.flybmi.com
easyJet
☎ 0870 600 0000
W www.easyjet.com
EuroCeltic
☎ 0870 040 0100
W www.euroceltic.com
Go
☎ 0870 607 6543
W www.go-fly.com
Luxair
☎ 01293-596633
W www.luxair.lu
Manx Airlines
☎ 0845 725 6256
W www.manx-airlines.com
Platinum Air
☎ 01253-400100
W www.blackpoolairport.com
Ryanair
☎ 0870 156 9569
W www.ryanair.com

To/From the Republic of Ireland On the busy London–Dublin route the best deals are with Ryanair (£40 to £180 return). Full-service airlines with several flights each per day on this route include Aer

Lingus, British Airways and British Midland. Return flight prices on these carriers range from £80 for advance-purchase tickets to £300 or more for fully flexible, refundable tickets. Many cheaper, limited-offer deals become available from time to time; these should be booked well in advance as low-priced seats are snapped up quickly.

Other destinations in the Republic served by nonstop flights from London are Cork, Shannon, Kerry, Knock and Waterford.

Most regional airports in Britain have flights to Dublin, and some also have services to Shannon, Cork or other places in the Republic. Fares between Birmingham, Manchester or Glasgow and Dublin are often comparable to London–Dublin fares, but less competitive routes can be much more expensive.

To/From Northern Ireland The London–Belfast corridor is where you'll find the best fares between Britain and Northern Ireland. British Airways, British European, British Midland, easyJet and Go all have nonstop flights on this route. Prices on the no-frills carriers easyJet and Go range from £50 to £175 return; prices on the full-service carriers start at £80 return for advance-purchase tickets and climb to £320 or more for fully flexible, refundable tickets. Keep an eye out for limited-offer low-priced seats.

Ryanair also operates some flights on the London–Derry route; cheap seats (from £39 one way) are sometimes available.

Because Scotland is Northern Ireland's next-door neighbour, fares tend to be affordable between Glasgow or Edinburgh and Belfast. Airlines flying these routes are British Airways, easyJet and Go.

Most regional airports in Britain have flights to Belfast.

Continental Europe

Dublin is connected with all major centres in Europe. Belfast also has good connections with the continent. In both cases, flights from Amsterdam, Brussels and Paris tend to offer the lowest fares. Frankfurt–Dublin is

also a competitive route. Shannon is served by flights from Brussels, Frankfurt, Paris and Moscow. There are flights to Cork from Amsterdam, Frankfurt and Paris.

In Germany, recommended agencies include STA Travel (☎ 01805 456422, W www.statravel.de) and usit Campus (☎ 01805 788336, W www.usitcampus.de). Both have branches throughout the country. Also check online at W www.justtravel.de and W www.expedia.de. Return fares range from €230 to €600 or more.

Popular travel agencies in France include usit Connections (☎ 08 25 08 25 25, W www.usitconnect.fr) and OTU Voyages (☎ 08 20 81 78 17, W www.otu.fr). Online agencies worth a look are W www.anyway.com, W www.travelprice.fr, and W www.govoyages.com. The national organisation of travel agents, SNAV, maintains a list of agents specialising in travel to particular destinations at W www.snav.org/recherche/decoup/form6.htm. Return fares cost from €150 to €500 or more.

While several major carriers offer convenient nonstop flights from Germany and France, prices can be high. An inexpensive alternative is to fly no-frills airlines Ryanair or Buzz (W www.buzzaway.com) to London, then pick up a cheap connecting flight onwards to Ireland. Both airlines have bargain fares from several cities in France and Germany. Ryanair also flies nonstop from Frankfurt to Shannon.

In Italy, try W www.travelprice.iol.it. CTS Viaggi (☎ 06 445 0141, W www.cts.it), Via Degli Ausoni 3, 00185 Rome, specialises in tickets for students and those aged under 26. Return flights on full-service airlines are expensive – often in the region of €500. Check with Ryanair for deals to Dublin; Go is a good bet for flights to Belfast. Travel on either airline requires a change in London.

Travellers from the Netherlands might want to try Kilroy Travels (☎ 020-524 5100, W www.kilroytravels.nl) or Air Fair (☎ 020-620 5121, W www.airfair.nl). Full-service carriers operate on the corridor from Amsterdam and Brussels to Dublin as well as other routes (return prices around €200).

Ryanair undercuts these with services from Brussels to Dublin and Shannon, and easy-Jet is a good choice with services on the Amsterdam–Belfast route.

Airlines with nonstop, scheduled flights from continental Europe to Ireland include:

Adria	W www.adria.si
Aer Lingus	W www.aerlingus.com
Aeroflot	W www.aeroflot.com
Aero Lloyd	W www.aerolloyd.de
Air France	W www.airfrance.com
Air Malta	W www.airmalta.com
Alitalia	W www.alitalia.com
Austrian Airlines	W www.aua.com
Cimber Air	W www.cimber.dk
CSA Czech Airlines	W www.csa.cz
easyJet	W www.easyjet.com
Finnair	W www.finnair.com
Iberia	W www.iberia.com
KLM	W www.klm.nl
Lufthansa	W www.lufthansa.com
Luxair	W www.luxair.lu
Maersk Air	W www.maersk-air.com
Malev Hungarian Airlines	W www.malev.hu
Ryanair	W www.ryanair.com
Scandinavian Airlines	W www.scandinavian.net
TAP Air Portugal	W www.tap.pt

The USA & Canada

In the USA discount travel agencies are known as consolidators. They sell cut-price tickets on scheduled carriers. Consolidators tend to be based in New York, San Francisco, Los Angeles and Chicago. Check the Sunday travel sections of the *New York Times*, *San Francisco Chronicle-Examiner*, *Los Angeles Times* or *Chicago Tribune* for the latest fares. The online guide W www.bestfares.com has leads on low-cost scheduled international flights but you must subscribe to view their selections. Courier fares can present a good deal for travelling across the Atlantic; visit W www.courier.org for more information. Now Voyagers Travel (☎ 212-431 1616, W www.nowvoyager travel.com) is one of the leading courier companies based in New York.

Students and those aged under 26 can get good deals through specialist travel agencies. Council Travel (☎ 800 226 8624, W www.counciltravel.com), America's largest student travel organisation, has around 60 offices in the USA. STA Travel (☎ 800 777 0112, W www.statravel.com) also has many branches in the USA. Popular online agents catering to all travellers are W www.flycheap.com, W www.expedia.com, W www.travelocity.com and W www.priceline.com. Ireland Consolidated (☎ 888 577 2900, W www.irelandair.com) specialises in arranging travel to Ireland.

Aer Lingus is the chief carrier between the USA and Ireland, with flights from New York, Boston, Baltimore, Chicago and Los Angeles to Shannon, Dublin and Belfast.

Other airlines operating nonstop flights from the USA to Ireland are American Airlines (from New York to Dublin and Shannon; ☎ 800 433 7300, W www.aa.com), Delta (from New York to Dublin and Shannon; ☎ 800 241 4141, W www.delta.com), Continental (from Newark to Dublin and Shannon; ☎ 800 231 0856, W www.continental.com) and Royal Jordanian (from Chicago and New York to Shannon; ☎ 800 223 0470, W www.rja.com.jo).

Return fares on nonstop services from the east coast to Ireland range from US$440 in the low season to US$740 or more during the high season; add US$150 to US$200 to this for return fares from Chicago and Los Angeles.

The heavy competition on transatlantic routes into London might make it often cheaper to fly to London and continue on to destinations in Ireland from there. In the low season, discount return fares from New York to London will be in the US$350 to US$650 range, in the high season US$600 to US$800. From the west coast, fares to London tend to cost around US$150 to US$200 more.

Travellers from Canada should check the travel sections of the *Globe & Mail*, *Toronto Star*, *Montreal Gazette* or *Vancouver Sun*. Travel CUTS (☎ 866-246 9762, W www.travelcuts.com) is Canada's national student travel agency and has offices in all major cities. There are no nonstop scheduled air services from Canada to Ireland, but affordable fares are available either by connecting to transatlantic gateways in the USA or by flying to London and then continuing from there on to Ireland.

Australia & New Zealand

There are no nonstop scheduled air services from Australia or New Zealand to Ireland; generally it's cheapest to fly to London or Amsterdam and then continue with a connecting flight to Ireland. There are several competing airlines and a wide variety of air fares. Round-the-World (RTW) tickets are often real bargains, and since Australia is pretty much on the other side of the world from Europe, these tickets are often cheaper than standard return fares.

Students and those aged under 26 are well served by the many offices of STA Travel (☎ 1300 360 960, W www.statravel.com .au). Flight Centre (☎ 131 131, W www .flightcentre.com) caters to all travellers. Shamrock Travel (☎ 03-9602 3700, W www .irishtravel.com.au), Level 9, 310 King St, Melbourne, Victoria 3000, specialises in arranging flights to Ireland.

The Saturday travel sections of the *Sydney Morning Herald* and Melbourne *Age* newspapers have many advertisements offering cheap fares. The *New Zealand Herald* has a travel section in which travel agencies advertise fares.

Excursion or Apex fares from Australia or New Zealand to most European destinations can have a return flight to Dublin tagged on at little or no extra cost. Return fares from Australia to Dublin range from around A$1700 in the low season up to A$3000 in the high season, but short-term special deals are often available.

From New Zealand, depending on which airline you choose, flights to Europe are generally via South-East Asia or the USA. Flight Centre (☎ 09-309 6171) has an office in Auckland at National Bank Towers; STA Travel (☎ 09-309 0458, W www.sta travel.co.nz) has its main office at 10 High St, Auckland. An RTW ticket may be cheaper than a return, which start from NZ$2200 in the low season and NZ$2700 in the high season.

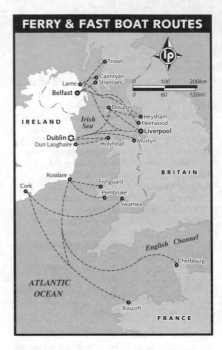

FERRY & FAST BOAT ROUTES

SEA

There are many ferry and fast boat services from Britain and France to Ireland. Competition from airlines has helped keep prices down. Travellers taking a car can bring up to four or five passengers along for free on some routes.

Throughout this section, the prices quoted are one-way fares for a single adult on foot/ up to five adults with a car.

The UK

Numerous services operate from ports in England, Scotland, Wales and the Isle of Man to the Republic and the North. It's wise to plan ahead because fares vary considerably, depending on the season, day of the week, time of day and length of stay. Some return fares don't cost much more than one way fares. Companies also provide special deals that are worth keeping an eye out for and offer reductions to ISIC card-holders and Hostelling International (HI) members.

OLIVER STREWE

OLIVER STREWE

OLIVER STREWE

OLIVER STREWE

OLIVER STREWE

Irish food will surprise and delight you, from fabulously fresh seafood and delicate speciality cheeses to hearty traditional dishes of coddle, colcannon and champ.

Ireland's outdoor activities open up some of the most beautiful and fascinating corners of the island. A walk or cycle ride in the countryside will almost certainly be a highlight of your visit.

The following is a list of shipping lines operating between Britain and Ireland.

Irish Ferries (☎ 0870 517 1717, W www.irish ferries.com) Corn Exchange Building, Ground Floor, Brunswick St, Liverpool L2 7TP. For ferry and fast boat services from Holyhead to Dublin, and ferry services from Pembroke to Rosslare.
Isle of Man Steam Packet Company (☎ 01624-661661, W www.steam-packet.com) Imperial Buildings, Douglas IM1 2BY. Ferry and fast boat services from Liverpool or Heysham to Dublin or Belfast, all via Douglas (on the Isle of Man).
Norse Merchant Ferries (☎ 0870 600 4321, W www.norsemerchant.com) Canada Dock, Liverpool L20 1DQ. Ferry services from Liverpool to Dublin or Belfast.
P&O Irish Sea (☎ 0870 242 4777, W www .poirishsea.com) Cairnryan DG9 8RF. Ferry and fast boat services from Cairnryan to Larne, and ferry services from Fleetwood to Larne and Liverpool or Mostyn to Dublin.
SeaCat (☎ 0870 552 3523, W www.seacat.co.uk) SeaCat Terminal, Donegall Quay, Belfast BT1 3AL. Fast boat services from Heysham or Troon to Belfast and Liverpool to Dublin.
Stena Line (☎ 0870 570 7070, W www.stenaline .com) Charter House, Park St, Ashford TN24 8EX. Ferry services from Holyhead to Dun Laoghaire and Stranraer to Belfast, also fast boat services from Holyhead to Dublin, from Fishguard to Rosslare, and from Stranraer to Belfast.
Swansea Cork Ferries (☎ 01792-456116, W www.swansea-cork.ie) Harbour Office, Kings Dock, Swansea SA1 1SF. Ferry services from Swansea to Cork.

To/From the Republic of Ireland The main routes from Britain to the Republic are:

Fishguard and Pembroke to Rosslare These popular, short ferry crossings take 3½ hours (from Fishguard) or four hours (from Pembroke) and cost around £25/190 during the peak season; at other times of the year the cost drops to as low as around £20/95. The fast boat crossing from Fishguard takes just over 1½ hours and costs around £30/200 during the peak season.
Holyhead to Dublin and Dun Laoghaire The ferry crossing takes just over three hours and costs around £20/185 during the peak season. The fast boat service from Holyhead to Dun Laoghaire takes a little over 1½ hours and costs £30/190 during the peak season.
Liverpool and Mostyn to Dublin The ferry service takes seven hours from Mostyn or 8½ hours from Liverpool and costs £30/140 during

the peak season. Cabins on overnight sailings cost more. The fast boat service takes four hours and costs up to £35/230 during the peak season.
Swansea to Cork The 10-hour crossing costs around £35/190 during the peak season. The ferry operates from mid-March to early November.

To/From Northern Ireland The main routes from Britain to the North are:

Heysham to Belfast This fast boat service takes four hours and costs £31/245.
Liverpool to Belfast The 8½-hour crossing costs £30/185 (including meals) during the day and £45/280 (including cabin and meals) at night.
Stranraer to Belfast The fast boat takes 1¾ hours and costs £30/254. The ferry takes 3¼ hours and costs £27/220.
Troon to Belfast This fast boat service takes 2½ hours and costs £26/233.
Cairnryan to Larne The fast boat takes one hour and costs £25/191. The ferry takes 1¾ hours and costs £21/171.
Fleetwood to Larne The eight-hour crossing costs £175 for a car with five adults; no foot passengers are carried.

France
Brittany Ferries (☎ 021-427 7801 in Ireland, 02 98 29 28 00 in France, W www .brittany-feries.com) operates a weekly service from Roscoff to Cork from early April to late September. The crossing takes 14 hours and costs up to €88/563 without accommodation.

Irish Ferries (☎ 053-33158 in Rosslare, 02 33 23 44 44 in Cherbourg, 02 98 61 17 17 in Roscoff, W www.irishferries.com) sails one to three times a week from Roscoff to Rosslare from late April to late September; the crossing time is 16 hours. Ferries from Cherbourg to Rosslare sail two to four times per week year round except in late January and all of February; crossing time is 17½ hours. Both services cost €107/575 without accommodation.

LAND & SEA
The low air fares from Britain make taking the bus or train hardly worth the hassle. On Bus Éireann there are frequent delays, and the train, unless you go from London, often involves difficult connections and hanging around late at night.

However, bus is the cheapest way to travel from Britain to Ireland. Bus Éireann and National Express operate Eurolines services direct from London and other UK centres to Dublin, Belfast and other cities in Ireland. For details in London contact Eurolines (☎ 0870 514 3219) or National Express (☎ 0870 580 8080); they share a Web site at Ⓦ www.gobycoach.com. The Eurolines service between London and Dublin takes about 12 hours and costs £35 to £55 return; fares are slightly higher from other cities in Britain. Eurolines services between London and Belfast take 13 to 16 hours and cost £60 return; the cost is about the same from other cities in Britain.

It's possible to combine a train and ferry ticket. The London–Dublin route takes eight to 10 hours via Holyhead and costs £75 return at peak times. Stena Line is currently offering a service between London Euston and Dublin. There are good rail links to most British ferry ports offering crossings to Ireland.

ORGANISED TOURS

Scores of companies offer general or special-interest tours of Ireland. See your travel agent, check the small ads in newspaper travel pages or contact Bord Fáilte (Irish Tourist Board) and the Northern Ireland Tourist Board (or the British Tourist Authority) for the names of operators. (See Tourist Offices in the Facts for the Visitor chapter for contact details of the tourist boards.)

In the USA there are a number of companies offering tours of Ireland. Check with your local travel agent for a rundown of available tours, or try CIE Tours International at Ⓦ www.cietours.com. Away.com (☎ 202-654 8000, Ⓦ www.away.com), 702 H St NW, Suite 200, Washington, DC 20001, is also worth checking, as it has a wide range of vacation packages available to suit various interests.

More expensive tours are operated by Abercrombie & Kent (☎ 800 323 7308, Ⓦ www.aandktours.com), 1520 Kensington Rd, Oak Brook, Illinois 60523; some tours include accommodation in castles and country houses. The company also organises activity-based tours or will help you prepare your own personal tour program.

Many of the bus, ferry and airline companies mentioned earlier also offer tour and accommodation packages.

Getting Around

On the map, travelling around Ireland looks simple enough – the distances are short and there's a network of roads and railways – but in practice there are a few problems. Towns or villages may not be connected by public transport and there are always a great many intriguing diversions to make. Public transport can be expensive (particularly train services), infrequent or both – and simply doesn't reach many of the interesting places. So having your own transport can be a major advantage and it's worth considering car rental for at least part of your trip. However, the proliferation of cars on the roads, the narrow streets in towns and villages and poor road signs in some places create their own difficulties. In fact, the dramatic increase in the number of cars on the road has resulted in extra delays travelling to and from urban centres at weekends and bank holidays.

If you opt not to drive, a mixture of buses, the occasional taxi, plenty of time, walking and sometimes hiring a bicycle will get you just about anywhere.

AIR

Ireland's size makes domestic flying unnecessary unless you're in a hurry, but there are flights between Dublin and Cork, Donegal, Galway, Kerry, Shannon, Sligo and Derry. There are also flights between Belfast and Shannon. Most flights within Ireland take 30 to 40 minutes.

Aer Rianta, the Republic's main airport authority (with responsibility for Dublin, Cork and Shannon Airports) publishes a guide to airport services and flight schedules. Its head office (☎ 01-844 4900, W www.aer-rianta.ie) is at Dublin Airport.

As well as handling international flights, Aer Lingus (W www.aerlingus.ie) is the main domestic airline. Its head office is at Dublin Airport and it has ticket offices in Dublin, Cork, Belfast and Shannon. For information and bookings call ☎ 01-886 8888 between 7.30am and 9.30pm; for flight information call ☎ 01-705 6705; or for information on their Belfast–Shannon route call their Belfast International Airport office on ☎ 028-9442 2888.

Another useful air service is the short flight across to the Aran Islands with Aer Árann (☎ 091-593034). See Getting There & Away under Aran Islands in the Galway chapter for details of fares and times. Aer Árann Express (☎ 1890 462726, 01-814 5240 in Dublin) operates reasonably priced flights to Kerry, Galway, Knock, Sligo and Donegal from Dublin.

BUS

Bus Éireann (☎ 01-836 6111, W www.bus eireann.ie), Busáras, Store St, Dublin, is the Republic's bus line with services throughout the South and to the North; you can book online.

All services are nonsmoking. Fares aren't much more than one-third of the regular train fares, and special deals are often available, for example cheaper midweek return tickets (see the boxed text 'Ferry, Bus & Train Discount Deals' later in this chapter). In winter the bus schedules are often drastically reduced and many routes simply disappear after September. The (free) national timetable is very useful but doesn't list fares.

Private buses compete with Bus Éireann in the Republic and sometimes run where the national buses are irregular or absent. The larger companies usually carry bikes for free but you should always check in advance. Most private companies are properly licensed and all passengers are insured, but if this is going to worry you then ask beforehand.

Ulsterbus (☎ 028-9033 3000), Milewater Rd, Belfast, is the service in the North; their call centre opens 7am to 11pm daily for timetable information. There are no private bus companies in the North.

Return fares are often the same as, or little more than, a one-way fare. Following are some sample one-way bus fares, travelling times, and their frequency from Monday to

Saturday (services are fewer or nonexistent on Sunday):

service	cost	duration (hours)	frequency (daily)
Belfast–Dublin	£10.50	3	7
Derry–Belfast	£7.50	1¾	10+
Derry–Galway	£16	6¼	4
Dublin–Cork	€17.15	4½	6
Dublin–Donegal	€12.70	4	5
Dublin–Rosslare	€12.70	3¼	9
Dublin–Tralee	€19.05	6	5
Dublin–Waterford	€8.90	2¾	7
Killarney–Cork	€12.70	2	5
Killarney–Waterford	€17.15	4	4

Local country buses can work out quite expensive, and services are usually infrequent. From Bantry in south-western Cork, for example, there's only one bus a week running the 26km journey to Kilcrohane, the last village on the Sheep's Head Peninsula, and the half-hour journey costs €5.10. Private buses on major routes may be cheaper than Bus Éireann. In County Donegal, Feda O'Donnell buses (☎ 075-48114), for example, charges less than €6.35 for any journey within the county; however, these journeys can be time-consuming.

TRAIN

Iarnród Éireann (Irish Rail; ☎ 01-836 3333, W www.irishrail.ie), Connolly Station, Amiens St, Dublin, operates trains in the Republic on routes that fan out from Dublin; make enquiries at Iarnród Travelcentre (☎ 01-836 6222), 35 Lower Abbey St, Dublin. Although trains get you to the major urban centres faster than buses, the train system is not as extensive: there's no north–south route along the western coast, no network in Donegal, no direct connections from Waterford to Cork or Killarney, and the Dublin–Belfast route (on the excellent Enterprise service) is the only direct train link between North and South. Distances, however, are short: the longest trip you can make by train from Dublin is 4½ hours to Tralee in County Kerry.

Regular one-way fares from Dublin include Belfast €26.65 (2¼ hours, eight daily), Cork €42.55 (3¼ hours, up to eight daily), Galway €20.30 (three hours 10 minutes, five daily) and Limerick €33.65 (2½ hours, up to 13 daily). Travelling by train on a one-way ticket is expensive, and it's worth considering a return ticket: a midweek return ticket is often about the same as a one-way fare. Both same-day return and one-way tickets from Dublin to Belfast cost €26.65. First-class tickets cost €5 to €10 more than the standard fare for a single journey.

Northern Ireland Railways (NIR; ☎ 028-9089 9411), Belfast Central Station, East Bridge St, Belfast, runs four routes from Belfast. One links with the system in the South via Newry to Dublin; the other three go east to Bangor, north-east to Larne and north-west to Derry via Coleraine, respectively.

As with buses, special fares are often available (for more information see the boxed text 'Ferry, Bus & Train Discount Deals' later in this chapter).

CAR & MOTORCYCLE

Ireland's new-found affluence means there are far more cars on the road than ever before, putting a strain on the country's national road system. The building of new roads and the upgrading of existing ones just cannot keep pace. Be prepared for delays, especially in popular tourist towns or busy commercial ones. AA Roadwatch provides traffic information in the Republic (☎ 1550 131 811). Unfortunately, there has also been a jump in the number of road accidents, testing the authorities' once lenient attitude to speeding and drink driving.

When you're travelling around Ireland, particularly the South, you'll need a good road map. Although Ireland is gradually shifting to the metric system, the imperial system is still widely used. In the North, speed-limit and distance signs are in miles. In the Republic, speed limits are usually shown in miles per hour, though in some areas they are in kilometres, and most car speedometers are in miles. The older white road signs give distances in miles, but the newer white signs and the green signs use kilometres. Brown signs with white lettering

TRAIN ROUTES

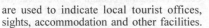

are used to indicate local tourist offices, sights, accommodation and other facilities.

On minor roads be prepared for potholes, especially in the South.

Petrol is considerably cheaper in the South than in the North. Unleaded petrol is available throughout the North and South. Most service stations accept payment by credit card, but some small, remote ones may take cash only.

Road Rules

A copy of Ireland's road rules is available from tourist offices. Driving in the Repub-

lic and the North is on the left and you should overtake only on the outside (to the right) of the vehicle ahead of you. Safety belts must be worn by the driver and all passengers. Children aged under 12 aren't allowed to sit on the front seats. Motorcyclists and their passengers must wear helmets.

When entering a roundabout, give way to approaching traffic already on the roundabout.

Speed limits in the North and South are generally the same as in Great Britain: 70mph (112km/h) on motorways, 60mph (96km/h) on other roads, and 30mph (48km/h) or as signposted in towns.

Never drink alcohol if you're planning to drive. Apart from the potential injury and loss of life, stiff fines, jail or other penalties could be incurred if you're caught driving under the influence. In the South the legal limit is 80mg of alcohol per 100ml of blood; in the North it's the same or 35mg on the breath (roughly two units of alcohol for a man and one for a woman).

Traffic offences (illegal parking, speeding etc) usually incur a fine, which you're normally allowed 30 days to pay.

On Ireland's major roads it's a common, but illegal, practice for vehicles to move over to the hard shoulder to allow overtaking (ie, speeding) vehicles to pass. On the quiet, narrow, winding rural roads it's advisable to stick to the speed limit, partly because of the danger of meeting tractors and head-on collisions, and partly because there may be a person walking or an animal grazing beside the road just around the next bend.

Parking

Double yellow lines painted on the kerbstones usually mean no parking at any time, and a single (or broken) yellow line warns of restrictions on parking times. The only way to establish the exact restrictions is to find the nearby sign that spells them out. Some cities also have red lines, which mean no stopping or parking. In Northern Ireland, kerbstones painted red, white and blue mean you're in a loyalist area; green, white and orange mean it's republican.

There are parking meters in Dublin, Belfast and most other cities. Usually parking in car parks or other specified areas is regulated by 'pay and display' tickets or disc parking (you have a disc, available from newsagents, which rotates to display the time you park your car).

In the North, some town centres have Control Zones (though these are gradually being withdrawn), where, for security reasons, cars absolutely must not be left unattended. Again, for security reasons, you can be fined for not locking your car.

When parking your car never leave valuables unattended or visible, especially in Dublin (see Dangers & Annoyances in the Dublin chapter for further parking warnings).

Rental

Car rental in Ireland is expensive, so you're often better off making arrangements in your home country with some sort of package deal. In July and August it's wise to book well ahead.

In the Republic typical weekly high-season rental rates with collision-damage waiver (CDW), insurance, value-added tax (VAT) and unlimited distance are around €275 for a small car (Ford Fiesta), €320 for a medium-sized car (Nissan Almera) and €405 for a larger car (Ford Mondeo). In the North, similar cars are marginally more expensive. Check that the attractive-looking posted price includes insurance (eg, for car theft and windscreen damage), CDW and VAT. If you're travelling from the Republic into Northern Ireland it's important to be sure that your insurance covers journeys to the North. Most cars are manual; automatic cars are available but they're more expensive to hire. There are often special deals and the longer you hire, the lower the relative daily rent. From October to May some companies discount all rates.

People aged under 21 aren't allowed to hire a car; for the majority of rental companies you have to be aged at least 23 and have had a valid driving licence for a minimum of one year. Your home-country licence is usually enough to hire a car for three months, though it's advisable to carry an international licence (see Driving Licence & Permits under Visas & Documents in the Facts for the Visitor chapter for more information). Some companies in the Republic won't rent to you if you're aged 74 or over; there's no upper age limit in the North.

The international rental companies Avis, Budget, Hertz and Thrifty, and the major local operators, Argus, Murray's European and Dan Dooley, have offices all over Ireland. There are many smaller, local operators, which often offer lower rates than the major companies.

Road Distances (km)

	Athlone	Belfast	Cork	Derry	Donegal	Dublin	Galway	Kilkenny	Killarney	Limerick	Rosslare Harbour	Shannon Airport	Sligo	Waterford	Wexford
Athlone	---														
Belfast	227	---													
Cork	219	424	---												
Derry	209	117	428	---											
Donegal	183	180	402	69	---										
Dublin	127	167	256	237	233	---									
Galway	93	306	209	272	204	212	---								
Kilkenny	116	284	148	335	309	114	172	---							
Killarney	232	436	87	441	407	304	193	198	---						
Limerick	121	323	105	328	296	193	104	113	111	---					
Rosslare Harbour	201	330	208	397	391	153	274	98	275	211	---				
Shannon Airport	133	346	128	351	282	218	93	135	135	25	234	---			
Sligo	117	206	336	135	66	214	138	245	343	232	325	218	---		
Waterford	164	333	126	383	357	163	220	48	193	129	82	152	293	---	
Wexford	184	309	187	378	372	135	253	80	254	190	19	213	307	61	---

Motorbikes and mopeds are not available for rent.

Motoring Clubs

The Automobile Association (AA; W www .aaireland.ie) has offices in Belfast (☎ 0870 950 0600 within Northern Ireland), Dublin (☎ 01-617 9950) and Cork (☎ 021-450 5155). The AA breakdown number in the Republic is ☎ 1800 667788; in the North it's ☎ 0800 887766. In the North, members of the Royal Automobile Club (RAC) can call ☎ 0800 029029 for information; its breakdown number is ☎ 0800 828282.

BICYCLE

Cycling is a popular, rewarding way to explore Ireland, both South and North. For information see under Activities in the Facts for the Visitor chapter.

HITCHING

Lonely Planet doesn't recommend hitching. It's never entirely safe in any country: the local nutter doesn't carry an identifying badge. Travellers who decide to hitch should understand that they are taking a small but potentially serious risk. People who choose to hitch are safer if they travel in pairs, travel in daylight hours and let someone know where they're planning to go. Women hitching on their own should be extremely careful when choosing lifts – if in doubt, don't. Many local women hitch alone without serious problems, but a tourist is likely to be more at risk.

That said, hitching in Ireland is generally easy. The major exceptions are heavily touristed areas, where there may be competition from other hitchers and cars are often full with families. In the Republic, though the number of people hitching has dwindled in recent years, there are usually a few – most likely tourists – on the roadside who use hitching as an everyday means of travel.

The usual hitching rules apply. Carry cardboard and a marker pen so you can make a sign showing where you're going. Try to look like a visitor and put your backpack out on view, ideally with a flag on it. Making yourself an obvious tourist is especially important in the North, and if the subject of the Troubles comes up in conversation it's probably best to exercise a bit of diplomatic caution. Cross-border roads are open and hitching between the Republic and the North presents few, if any, problems.

BOAT

There are many boat services to islands lying off the coast, including to the Aran and Skellig Islands to the west, the Saltee Islands to the south-east, and Tory and Rathlin Islands to the north. Ferries also operate across rivers, inlets and loughs. Some services provide useful short cuts, particularly for cyclists. These include the ferry across the River Suir from Ballyhack (County Wexford) to Passage East (County Waterford); from Carrigaloe, near Cobh, to Passage West, east of Cork town (both in County Cork); across the Shannon Estuary from Killimer (County Clare) to Tarbert (County Kerry); and from Strangford across to Portaferry on the Ards Peninsula (both in County Down).

The only ferry between the Republic and the North is the limited service across Carlingford Lough from Omeath on the Cooley Peninsula (County Louth) to Warrenpoint (County Down) in summer.

Cruises are very popular on the 258km-long Shannon-Erne Waterway – combining rivers, lakes and canals – from County Leitrim to Lough Erne in Northern Ireland. There is also a variety of cruises on other lakes and loughs.

If you ask at tourist offices about boat trips you won't always get the full information, because the offices don't recommend, or even mention, operators who aren't registered with them. Various boats from Portmagee, Ballinskelligs or Derrynane to the Skellig Islands off the Kerry coast, for instance, don't exist as far as official tourist lierature is concerned. Details of nontourist-board-affiliated boat trips are given under the relevant sections throughout this book.

LOCAL TRANSPORT

There are comprehensive local bus networks in Dublin (Bus Átha Cliath), Belfast (Citybus) and some other larger towns. The Dublin Area Rapid Transport (DART) line in Dublin is the only local train line. A new light rail system (Luas) is planned to begin operating in Dublin in the winter of 2002.

Taxis in Ireland tend to be expensive. There was a chronic shortage of taxis in Dublin until 2001, when 6000 new plates were allocated, making it now much easier to procure a taxi during peak periods. There are metered taxis in Belfast, Cork, Dublin, Galway and Limerick, but in other places you'll need to agree on the fare beforehand. If you book a taxi by telephone there may be a small pick-up charge. In Belfast and Derry there are share-taxi services operating rather like buses.

See Getting Around in specific chapters for more information.

ORGANISED TOURS

If your time is limited it might be worth considering an organised tour, though it's cheaper to see things independently and Ireland is small enough for you to get to even the most remote places within a few hours. Tours can be booked through travel agencies, tourist offices in the major cities, or directly through the tour companies themselves.

CIE Tours International (☎ 01-703 1888), 35 Lower Abbey St, Dublin, runs coach tours of the South and North departing from Dublin. The tours include accommodation, breakfast and dinner. Its four-day Taste of Ireland tour takes in Blarney, the Ring of Kerry, Killarney, the Cliffs of Moher and the region around the River Shannon (€349.25 in the high season). Its other coach tours are from four to 10 days in length.

Bus Éireann (☎ 01-836 6111), 59 Upper O'Connell St, Dublin, runs day tours to various parts of the South and the North (more frequently in summer), departing from Dublin's Busáras. Its seven-hour tour of Glendalough in Wicklow costs €25.40/12.70 per adult/child.

Ulsterbus Tours (☎ 028-9033 7004 from within the North) runs a large number of day trips throughout the North and the Republic. Call for information and bookings or visit the Ulsterbus Travel Centre (open 9am to 5.15pm Monday to Friday, 9am to noon on Saturday) in the Europa Bus Centre, Glengall St, Belfast.

Gray Line Tours (☎ 01-605 7705) in Dublin offers half-day, day and extended trips from Dublin to Newgrange, Glendalough, North Dublin and the Ring of Kerry.

Ferry, Bus & Train Discount Deals

Eurail passes (which make economic sense only if you intend to travel outside Ireland as well) are valid for train travel in the Republic of Ireland – but not in Northern Ireland – and entitle you to a reduction on Irish Ferries crossings between France (Cherbourg and Roscoff) and the Republic (Rosslare and Cork), but you must book ahead. The Eurail pass can be used only by non-Europeans who have been in Europe for less than six months.

Eurail passes can be bought within Europe, as long as your passport proves you've been there for less than six months. The outlets where you can do this are limited and the passes are more expensive than when bought outside Europe. Rail Europe (☎ 0870 584 8848), 179 Piccadilly, London W1V 0BA, is one such outlet. In the USA and Canada you can purchase passes over the phone on ☎ 1888 667 9734 and have them sent to your home by courier. Eurail's Web site is at ⓦ www.eurail.com.

If you've been in Europe for more than six months you're eligible for an **InterRail** pass (which, again, makes economic sense only if you intend to travel outside Ireland as well). The pass gives you a 50% reduction on train travel within Ireland and discounts on Irish Ferries and Stena Line connecting ferries. InterRail passes can be bought at most major train stations and student travel outlets.

For €10.20 in the South, £6 in the North, full-time students can have a **Travelsave** stamp affixed to their International Student Identity Card (ISIC). This gives up to 50% discount on Iarnród Éireann (Irish Rail) and Northern Ireland Railways (NIR), and 15% on Bus Éireann services for fares costing over €1.25. Holders of an EYC (or EuroFairstamp) can also have the Travelsave stamp attached to their card, which offers a 40% discount on trains only. The stamps are available from usit offices (see under Air in the Getting There & Away chapter for contact details). Iarnród Éireann's **Faircard** (€10.15) gives up to 50% reductions on any intercity journey to people aged under 26, while the **Weekender** (€6.35) gives up to 30% off (Friday to Tuesday) to people aged 26 and over.

There's a variety of unlimited-travel tickets for buses and trains, available to all ages, in the North and South. **Irish Rambler** tickets are available from Bus Éireann for bus-only travel within the Republic of Ireland. They cost €40.65 (for three days' travel out of eight consecutive days), €92.70 (eight days out of 15 consecutive days) or €133.35 (15 days out of 30 consecutive days). An Iarnród Éireann **Explorer** ticket offers unlimited train travel in the Republic (five days out of 15 consecutive days) for €91.45 or €114.15 to include Northern Ireland. For train and bus travel within the Republic, the **Irish Explorer Rail and Bus** ticket (€135.90) allows you eight days' travel out of 15 consecutive days.

In Northern Ireland, the **Freedom of Northern Ireland** pass allows unlimited travel on NIR, Ulsterbus and Citybus services for £11 for one day or £40 for seven consecutive days.

The **Irish Rover** ticket combines services on Bus Éireann and Ulsterbus. It costs €53.35 for three days, €118.10 for eight days and €184.15 for 15 days. The **Emerald Card** gives you unlimited travel throughout Ireland on all scheduled services of Iarnród Éireann, NIR, Bus Éireann, Dublinbus, Ulsterbus and Citybus. The card costs €157.50 for eight days or €271.80 for 15 days.

Children aged under 16 pay half-price for all these passes and for all normal tickets. Children aged under three travel for free on public transport.

You can buy the above passes after you arrive in Ireland at most major train and bus stations. Although they're good value, many of them make economic sense only if you're planning to travel around Ireland at the speed of light.

Over the Top and Into the West Tours (☎ 01-838 6128, toll-free 1800 424243, ⓦ www.celticbustours.com) offers daily historical and heritage tours of Wicklow and the Boyne Valley. Its three-day Into the West tour, with accommodation in quality guesthouses, takes in Connemara, the Burren and the Cliffs of Moher for €324; or there's its five-day Southern Exposure tour of Cork and Kerry which costs €470. It also runs mini tours that take only 14 people. Buses leave from outside the Dublin tourist office, on Suffolk St. You can also book online.

Paddywagon Tours (☎ 01-672 6007, e info@paddywagon.iol.ie) offers activity-filled three- and six-day tours all over Ireland with friendly tour guides. Accommodation is in IHH hostels. Its Jump On Jump Off tour of Ireland (€113) allows you to stay in any place en route for as long as you like and pick up a later bus.

Tir na nÓg (Land of Eternal Youth; ☎ 01-836 4684, fax 855 9059, e tnn@indigo.ie), 57 Lower Gardiner St, Dublin, offers three- to six-day backpacker tours to the west and north of Ireland costing upwards of €125. Buses take no more than 20 people and fill up fast, so book ahead. Nights are spent at IHH hostels along the way.

It's worth checking GoIreland.com (☎ 074-23800, W www.goireland.com), 104 Lower Main St, Letterkenny, County Donegal, for vacation packages, and the site at W www.12travel.ie. Both offer an array of tours to suit various interests.

For train enthusiasts, Railtours Ireland (☎ 01-856 0045), 58 Lower Gardiner St, Dublin, organises a series of one- and two-day train trips in association with Iarnród Éireann. A day trip from Dublin to Cork, Blarney Castle and Killarney costs €88.

See also Organised Walks under Walking, and Cycling, both under Activities in the Facts for the Visitor chapter.

The Republic of Ireland

HISTORY

This section covers 1921 onwards. For details of Irish history prior to this see History in the Facts about Ireland chapter.

The Irish Free State

The Irish Free State, as it was known until 1949, was established after the signing in December 1921 of the Anglo-Irish Treaty by the British government and an Irish delegation led by Michael Collins. Eamon de Valera had been elected president of the new self-proclaimed republic in August, but he remained in Dublin during negotiations. He wasn't consulted before the signing and was outraged when the delegates returned with what he and many other republicans regarded as a betrayal of the IRA's principles. Some would argue that because de Valera knew that what was on offer from the British would fall short of Irish expectations, he sent Collins to be the bearer of bad news. However, the treaty was ratified in the Dáil (Irish assembly or lower house) in January 1922. In June the country's first general election resulted in victory for the pro-treaty forces. Fighting broke out two weeks later.

The cause of dissatisfaction among republicans with the treaty was not only that the country was to be partitioned, with the six north-eastern counties remaining under British sovereignty, but that the rest of the island would remain part of the British Commonwealth and its Dáil members still had to swear allegiance to the Crown.

During the Civil War Collins was ambushed and shot dead in Cork by anti-treaty forces, and de Valera was imprisoned by the new Free State government, under Prime Minister William Cosgrave, which went so far as to execute 77 of its former comrades. The Civil War ground to an exhausted halt in 1923.

After boycotting the Dáil for a number of years, de Valera founded a new party, called Fianna Fáil (Warriors of Ireland), which won nearly half the seats in the 1927 election. De Valera and the other new teachta Dála (TDs; members of the Dáil) managed within weeks to enter the Dáil by the simple expedient of not taking the oath of allegiance to the Crown but signing in as if they had.

Fianna Fáil won a majority in the 1932 election and remained in power for 16 years. De Valera introduced a new constitution in 1937, doing away with the oath and claiming sovereignty over the six counties of the North. In 1938 the UK renounced its right to use certain Irish ports for military purposes, which it had been granted under the treaty. The South was therefore able to remain neutral in WWII. De Valera refused to pay land annuities, which had been agreed upon in the Anglo-Irish Treaty, to the British government. An economic war with Britain ensued, which severely crippled Irish agriculture and was resolved only shortly before the 1948 general election.

The Republic

Fianna Fáil lost the 1948 general election to Fine Gael – the direct descendants of the first Free State government – in coalition with the new republican Clann an Poblachta. The new government declared the Free State to be a republic at last. Ireland left the British Commonwealth in 1949. In 1955 it became a member of the United Nations.

When Sean Lamass came to power in 1959, as successor to de Valera, he sought to stem the continuing serious emigration by improving the country's economic prospects. By the mid-1960s his policies had been successful enough to reduce emigration to less than half what it had been in the mid-1950s, and many who had left began to return. He also introduced free secondary education.

In 1972 the Republic (along with Northern Ireland) became a member of the European Economic Community (EEC). At first, membership brought some measure of prosperity, but by the early 1980s Ireland was once more in economic difficulties and emigration figures rose again. By the early 1990s the Irish economy had begun to recover and is now one of the strongest in Europe.

The results of referenda in the 1980s on abortion and divorce left both illegal, but in another referendum on divorce in 1995 it was narrowly accepted, making Ireland the last nation in Europe to legalise it. While single mothers might still have a tough time in remote rural areas, in Dublin they're almost as commonplace as in London and no-one bats an eyelid.

Although the president's power is limited, the election of barrister Mary Robinson to the presidency in 1990 saw her modernise the institution and start to wield considerable informal influence over social policies. Her work contributed to a shift away from the traditionally conservative attitudes on issues such as divorce, abortion and gay rights. At the end of her popular term in 1997 she was appointed the United Nations high commissioner for human rights.

Robinson was succeeded as president by Mary McAleese, a Belfast-born Catholic nationalist and Queen's University law lecturer (who was unsuccessfully contested by

The Abortion Debate

The issue of abortion continues to tie Ireland in knots.

Prior to 1983 therapeutic abortions were legal and doctors could use their discretion as to whether or not a pregnancy was 'life-threatening' for a woman. Abortion for any other reason, including severe malformation or pregnancy due to rape, was, and still is, not permitted.

In 1983 the law was tightened and incorporated into the constitution, but in such woolly terms that things went on much as before, with one remarkable exception: women could no longer be given information about seeking abortions abroad. British phone books were duly removed from libraries, and British women's magazines were impounded or censored at the airports.

While trips to British abortion clinics continued unabated, Ireland held the moral high ground of protecting the unborn child at any cost – until 1992, when parents whose 14-year-old daughter had allegedly been raped by her friend's father took her to England for an abortion. When they contacted the *gardaí* (police) to ask if tissue from the foetus could be collected and used in the prosecution of the alleged rapist, they were issued with an injunction ordering them to bring the girl back, foetus intact, or face prosecution. All hell broke loose. The matter went to the High Court, which fudged the issue by saying that the girl could travel to the UK for an abortion since she was suicidal.

Anti-abortion campaigners demanded that the High Court prevent women leaving the country to seek abortions abroad, opening up the prospect of pregnancy tests at airports. Others interpreted the High Court ruling to mean that abortion had become legal if the woman was suicidal.

A referendum on the issue took place in 1992. A clear majority supported the right to travel abroad for an abortion, but the option of making abortion available to all women in Ireland wasn't offered.

Abortion is still illegal, but in 1995 a new law allowed doctors and pregnancy counselling services to give a pregnant woman the names and phone numbers of British abortion clinics, and now Irish women who travel to Britain for an abortion can do so without fear of any legal reprisals. However, Irish doctors and clinics are barred from making appointments or arrangements in Britain for their patients.

The contentious issue of abortion continues to be debated both in public and in medical circles. At the time of writing, Irish Medical Council members who voted against liberalising ethical guidelines on abortion threatened to take legal action against members in favour.

In June 2001 a floating abortion clinic, run by Dutch pro-choice foundation Women on Waves, docked in Dublin to much media attention. The all-female crew of doctors had planned to provide abortions, contraceptives and advice to Irish women in the customised vessel called *Aurora* 19km from the Irish coast – just outside territorial waters – but were challenged, ironically, by the Dutch government because they didn't have the necessary licence.

another female candidate, Dana, Ireland's first Eurovision Song Contest winner). Although more conservative than Robinson, McAleese was elected on a platform of continuing Robinson's work and has shown a similarly tolerant attitude on social issues. This was illustrated in 1999 by her high-profile visit to Outhouse, a gay, lesbian and transgender community centre in southern Dublin, and the following year by controversially receiving communion at a Church of Ireland service.

In 1994 Taoiseach (prime minister) Albert Reynolds, who had helped negotiate the first IRA cease-fire with Gerry Adams, was forced to resign. His resignation mainly resulted from the appointment of a president to the High Court, Harry Whelehan, who had been criticised for not tackling sexual scandals involving the Catholic Church more vigorously. Reynolds was succeeded by Fine Gael leader John Bruton, who came to power in coalition with the Labour Party and the Democratic Left. Bruton's government was the first to take office without a general election.

When it did face one in 1997 it was ousted by Fianna Fáil under Bertie Ahern, in partnership with the Progressive Democrats and a number of independents. Mary Harney became Ireland's first female tánaiste (deputy prime minister).

Bertie Ahern's government has been closely involved in the peace-making process in Northern Ireland. Among other things the 1998 Good Friday Agreement (see History in the Northern Ireland chapter) made provision for a North–South Ministerial Council, of which the Irish government would become a part, to deal with issues affecting the whole island. Another outcome of the search for a settlement in the North has been improved relations between the Republic and Britain, symbolised by the invitation from Bertie Ahern to British Prime Minister Tony Blair to address the Dáil.

GOVERNMENT & POLITICS

The Republic has a parliamentary system of government loosely based on the British model. The Oireachtas (Parliament) has a lower house known as the Dáil (pronounced dawl), which has 166 elected members who sit in Leinster House on Dublin's Kildare St. Dáil members are known as teachta Dála (TDs), the prime minister as taoiseach (roughly pronounced **tea**-shock) and the deputy prime minister as tánaiste. The Dáil has a relatively high percentage of female members.

The upper house is the Senate, or Seanad, and senators are nominated by the taoiseach or elected by university graduates and councillors from around the country. The Senate's functions are limited – senators debate on and pass legislation framed in the Dáil – but many critics claim it is merely a happy hunting ground for failed TDs.

The country's constitutional head of state is the president (An tUachtaran), who is elected by popular vote for a seven-year term and resides in Áras an Uachtaráin, in Phoenix Park, Dublin. The president has no executive power but does promulgate bills passed by the Dáil, appoint the taoiseach (on nomination from the Dáil) and government ministers (on the advice of the taoiseach), and is head of the defence forces.

The national flag is the tricolour of green, white and orange, the national symbol is the harp and the national anthem is *Amhrán na bhFiann* (The Soldier's Song).

The Republic's electoral system is proportional representation, a complex but fair system in which voters mark the electoral candidates in order of preference. As the first-preference votes are counted and candidates are elected, the voters' second and third choices are passed on to the various other candidates. Elections are held at least once every five years.

Political Parties

The two principal political parties are Fianna Fáil and Fine Gael, and third is the Labour Party with growing support for Sinn Féin and the Green Party.

Founded by Eamon de Valera and other notables, Fianna Fáil has been the driving force in Irish politics since the early years of the state. Fianna Fáil has normally won the greatest number of seats in general elections and has usually been either in government or barely out of it. It has always been a catch-all party, claiming to be the voice of the rural populace, urban workers and business community alike. Many of Ireland's most notable leaders have come from the party's ranks, including Eamon de Valera, Sean Lemass, Jack Lynch and, more recently, the colourful and wily Charles Haughey and Albert Reynolds. The current party leader is Bertie Ahern. Fianna Fáil has in the past usually taken a conservative line on social matters, particularly when it came to divorce, abortion and contraception.

Founded in 1933, Fine Gael, led by Michael Noonan, is the second-largest party and promotes enterprise. Its image has been clean cut, worthy, middle class and university educated.

Both parties see 'inclusive political talks' as the way forwards in the Republic's relations with the North.

Labour has been on the fringes of power for most of its existence, but has shared in various coalition governments with Fine Gael. The Labour Party, led by Ruairí Quinn, occupies the middle ground and attracts support from all classes of voters.

In 1985 a split in Fianna Fáil resulted in the formation of the Progressive Democrats, which is now led by Mary Harney, currently the tánaiste. Ironically, its two periods of power have been in coalition with Fianna Fáil. The left-wing Democratic Left merged with Labour in 1999.

Coalition has been a feature of most recent governments in the Republic, as the once mighty Fianna Fáil has found itself less able to muster the parliamentary majorities it used to command.

Unfortunately, Irish politics has been tarnished in recent years with a reputation for corruption and political scandals that has caused disillusionment among the electorate. In the late 1990s, the Moriarty Tribunal, set up to enquire into payments to politicians, revealed that former taoiseach Charles Haughey may have received as much as £2.5 million in cash gifts during his political career. Then the Flood Tribunal began uncovering irregularities and corruption in planning procedures at the local level.

These were among a series of political, financial and judicial scandals that plagued the Fianna Fáil government and led to the passing of the Ethics in Public Office Act.

ECONOMY

Ireland is in the middle of the greatest economic boom since independence and is experiencing one of the highest growth rates in the world. Dubbed the Celtic Tiger (an allusion to the once successful 'tiger' economies of Asia), the economy is healthy in almost every capacity, from record low interest rates to a negligible rate of inflation.

This success has been attributed to a variety of factors, including: the intelligent spending of EU funds (of which Ireland has been one of the biggest beneficiaries); the successful promotion of foreign investment through generous tax incentives, which has seen Ireland at the forefront of a number of key industries (such as information technology and pharmaceuticals); the explosion of the tourist industry, which has seen record numbers of visitors in the last decade; the high quality of education; and a reversal in the age-old trend of emigration – since 1995 more people have moved to Ireland than left; and the country's extremely low dependency rate, which means it has a greater proportion of people of working age than of those aged under 19 or over 64. Lastly, a new entrepreneurial class has emerged, consisting mostly of young graduates who have taken advantage of the favourable economic atmosphere to start up businesses, many of which have been very successful.

A striking feature of this boom is that the agricultural sector, which once dominated the economy, has had little to do with it. Yet it too is in a healthy state, despite setbacks caused in 2001 by the foot and mouth disease crisis. Ireland has one of the most efficient agricultural industries in the world and the debt burden of Irish farmers is very low.

Doubts persist, however, about the solidity of the economy. Ireland may be in the middle of a boom-and-bust cycle. Some economists argue that Ireland's dependence on transnational corporations, attracted by low corporate tax offered as an incentive, results in a fragile economy at the mercy of world trends. As EU countries get ever closer economically, it seems likely that Europe-wide rules on corporate tax will come into force, eliminating the tax packages that brought those transnational companies to Ireland's shores. The crash of the Asian tiger economies in the late 1990s also served as a warning of what could happen.

While many have benefited from the economic boom, and unemployment continues to fall, the gap between rich and poor has widened substantially. The relatively sudden level of growth has put Ireland's housing, healthcare and roads infrastructure under enormous pressure. Property prices, particularly in Dublin, have rocketed, making it increasingly difficult for those with even a decent income to buy property or to rent. Growing unrest among public sector workers in 2001 led to a number of strikes by teachers and transport workers. The country's wealth (the national income rose by 44% from 1994 to 1999) has yet to trickle down to many wage earners (wages are among the lowest in the EU) or the unemployed, who live on inner-city housing estates where drugs and crime are endemic.

Dublin

☎ 01 • pop 952,692

Dublin is one of Europe's most compelling capitals. If you've never visited, make plans to do so; if you have, you won't need us to tell you to return.

Why? Because Dublin is a city with soul, a place that has never lost sight of the fact that people are more fun than museums and that genuine human interaction is not the exclusive preserve of small villages and bored taxi drivers. If you want a city dripping with priceless works of art guarded by a 'Do Not Touch' sign, go to Rome. If you want a city that oozes style and confidence (but where the people would rather fall in front of a train than stop and chat) then Paris is for you. Sure, Dubliners will tell you, Dublin isn't the cleanest of cities, and apart from the beautiful Georgian squares and buildings nor is it architecturally all that memorable, but so what? Is an apartment block going to buy you a pint? Is an office building going to tell you a funny story and offer to show you around? Their advice is simple. Relax. Take it easy. Forget about the grimy streets, the eyesores on the skyline and have a good time.

But Dublin's mythical *craic*, or good time, isn't the only reason people stay. Ireland's economic revival has now become the stuff of European legend, but in Dublin that revival has literally transformed the city into a vibrant, cosmopolitan metropolis where there's work for anyone who wants it and plenty of money to be earned. All around you, it seems, Dubliners appear in a good mood, and it's not surprising considering that they've never had it so good.

Tourism, once a steady trickle of interested visitors, is now proportional to that of any of Europe's most visited cities. In summer, you can hardly walk down Grafton St – Dublin's main drag – for the sheer number of visitors who've come to sample the city's delights. New hotels, restaurants, bars and cafes are opening all the time and, on the surface at least, there appears to be no

Highlights

- Visit the National Museum's Treasury: it's free and it's fabulous

- Ponder one of Europe's most interesting repositories of religious books and other relics, Chester Beatty Library

- Take in Trinity College and the Book of Kells: a beautiful book amid an oasis of Elizabethan tranquillity

- Wander round Dublin's Georgian squares, particularly elegant St Stephen's Green and Merrion Square

- Take afternoon tea at the Shelbourne Hotel: you can't get more decadent for the price

- Get to the heart of Irish traditional music at Ceol

- Sup a pint of Guinness in John Mulligan's of Poolbeg St; a Dublin experience like few others

- Revel in the mayhem of St Patrick's Day, which lasts an entire bank holiday weekend!

end to the boom nor Dubliners' ability to enjoy it.

Inevitably, such dramatic change has also had a negative impact. In their eagerness to capture a larger share of the tourist market, many less-than-scrupulous developers offer lowest-common-denominator attractions to bring in the unquestioning visitor; restaurants will happily overcharge you for mediocre cuisine; and some city-centre hotels will tell you that the small box room barely large enough to fit you and your bags is actually a deluxe double. Temple Bar, Dublin's most popular quarter, is a perfect example of this paradox of prosperity: undoubtedly interesting and fun, it is also packed with terrible bars, bad restaurants and overpriced hotels.

Thankfully, there's much more to Dublin than the neatly packaged, sanitised version of the Dublin experience offered by Temple Bar. From the Georgian elegance of the city's southside to the up-and-coming areas of Smithfield north of the Liffey and farther afield, Dublin is a compelling, accessible city that will interest and entertain you.

HISTORY

Dublin celebrated its official millennium in 1988 but there were settlements here long before 988. The first early-Celtic habitation was on the banks of the River Liffey, giving rise to the city's Irish name, Baile Átha Cliath (Town of the Hurdle Ford), which comes from the ancient river crossing that can still be pinpointed today.

It wasn't until the Vikings turned up that Dublin became a permanent fixture. By the 9th century, raids from the north had become a fact of Irish life and some of the fierce Danes chose to stay rather than simply rape, pillage and depart. They intermarried with the Irish and established a vigorous trading port at the point where the River Poddle joined the Liffey in a black pool, in Irish a 'dubh linn'. Today there's little trace of the Poddle, which has been channelled underground and flows under St Patrick's Cathedral to dribble into the Liffey by the Capel St (or Grattan) Bridge. Anglo-Norman and then early-English Dublin were still centred on the black pool that gave the city its name.

The boom years came with the 18th century, the period of the Protestant Ascendancy, when, for a time, London was the only larger city in the British Empire. As the city expanded, the nouveaux riches abandoned medieval Dublin and moved north across the river to a new Dublin of stately squares surrounded by fine Georgian mansions.

The city's slums soon spread north in pursuit of the rich, who returned south to new homes in Merrion Square, Fitzwilliam Square and St Stephen's Green. In 1745 when James Fitzgerald, earl of Kildare, began building Leinster House, his magnificent mansion south of the Liffey, he was mocked for this foolish move away from the centre into the wilds. 'Where I go society will follow,' he confidently predicted, and was soon proved right. Today Leinster House is home to the Irish Parliament and is right in the centre of modern Dublin.

The Georgian boom years were followed by more trouble and unrest. The union with Britain in 1801, ending the separate Irish Parliament and returning power to London, spelled the end of Dublin's century of dramatic growth. Dublin entered the 20th century a downtrodden, dispirited place.

The 1916 Easter Rising caused considerable damage to parts of central Dublin, particularly along O'Connell St, where the General Post Office (GPO) was gutted. The continuing struggle between British forces and the IRA led to more damage, including the burning of the Custom House in 1921. A year later Ireland was independent, but then tumbled into the Civil War, which inflicted still more damage on the city, including the burning of the Four Courts in 1922 and a further bout of destruction for O'Connell St.

When peace finally came to Ireland, Dublin was exhausted – a shadow of its Georgian self. Until the 1970s it was a city in decay, but Ireland's becoming a member of what was then the European Economic Community (now the European Union) in 1972 held the prospect of better times to come. Today, Ireland's economic turnaround and cultural resurgence has completely transformed the city and gone a long way towards restoring its vitality.

Dublin's expansion has continued south to Dun Laoghaire and beyond, but the River Liffey remains a rough dividing line between southern 'haves' and northern 'have-nots', although that too is beginning to change as rising house prices lead to a gradual gentrification of the entire city centre.

ORIENTATION

Greater Dublin sprawls around the arc of Dublin Bay, bounded to the north by the hills at Howth and to the south by the Dalkey headland. Splitting the city in two is the unremarkable River Liffey, which traditionally also marks a psychological and social break between the poorer northside and the more affluent southside.

North of the River Liffey the important streets for visitors are O'Connell St and, just off it, Henry St, the major shopping thoroughfares. Most of the northside's B&Bs are on Gardiner St, which becomes rather run-down as it continues north. At the northern end of O'Connell St is Parnell Square. The main bus station, Busáras, and Connolly Station, one of the city's two main train stations, are near the southern end of Gardiner St.

Immediately south of the river, over O'Connell Bridge, is the Temple Bar area and the expanse of Trinity College. Nassau St, along the southern edge of the campus, and pedestrianised Grafton St are the main shopping streets. At the southern end of Grafton St is St Stephen's Green. About 2km west, beside the river, is Heuston Station, the city's other main train station.

The postcodes for central Dublin are Dublin 1, immediately north of the river and Dublin 2, immediately south. The posh Ballsbridge area south-east of the centre is Dublin 4. A handy tip for postcodes is to remember that even numbers apply to the southside and odd ones to the north.

Unless otherwise stated, all places mentioned in this chapter are on the Dublin map.

Maps

Lonely Planet's *Dublin City Map* has a complete index of all streets and sights, a Dublin Area Rapid Transport (DART) and

Finding Addresses

Finding addresses in Dublin can be complicated by the tendency for street names to change every few blocks and for streets to be subdivided into upper and lower or north and south parts, which in some cases are on two different sides of the city. It doesn't seem to matter if you put the definer in front of or behind the name – thus you can have Lower Baggot St or Baggot St Lower, South Anne St or Anne St South. Street numbering often runs up one side of a street and down the other, rather than having odd numbers on one side and even on the other. Also, the use of 'south' and 'north' usually means that the two streets are on opposite sides of the river, rather than running into one another. So, while South Great George's St is to be found off Dame St on the southern side, North Great George's St is on the northern side of the river, running parallel to Upper O'Connell St.

suburban rail plan and a unique walking tour of the city.

INFORMATION
Tourist Offices

Dublin's main tourist office is the Dublin Tourism Centre (Around Temple Bar map; ☎ 605 7700, ⓔ information@dublintourism .ie, Ⓦ www.visitdublin.com), located in (the now deconsecrated) St Andrew's Church, 2 Suffolk St. Here you'll find pretty much everything you'll need to kick-start your Dublin visit. There is a booking fee of €3.80 for all accommodation, €6.35 if it's self-catering. There is also a 10% deposit that is refunded through your hotel bill. The office opens 9am to 5.30pm Monday to Saturday, September to June; 8.30am to 6.30pm Monday to Saturday and 10.30am to 3pm Sunday, July and August.

There are also branches of Dublin Tourism at 14 O'Connell St (open 9am to 5pm Monday to Saturday), in the foyer of Bord Fáilte headquarters at Baggot St Bridge (Around St Stephen's Green map; open 9.30am to noon and 12.30pm to 5pm

Monday to Friday), at the new ferryport in Dun Laoghaire (Dun Laoghaire map; 10am to 6pm Monday to Saturday) and in the arrivals hall of Dublin airport (open 8am to 10pm daily).

The head office of Bord Fáilte (Around St Stephen's Green map; ☎ 1850 230330, ⓔ info@irishtouristboard.ie, ⓦ www.ireland .travel.com) is at Baggot St Bridge (entrance on Wilton Terrace). It provides information on the rest of the country. It opens 9am to 5.15pm Monday to Friday.

None of the tourist information offices in Dublin will provide information over the phone – they are exclusively walk-in services. The reason for this is that all telephone bookings and reservations are operated by Gulliver Info Res, a computerised information and reservation service that is available at all walk-in offices but, more impressively, from anywhere in the world. It provides up-to-date information on events, attractions and transport, and can also book accommodation. In Ireland, call ☎ 1800 668668; from Britain call ☎ 0800 6686 6866; from the rest of the world call ☎ 00 353 669 792083.

Money

The currency-exchange counter at Dublin Airport is in the baggage-collection area and opens for most flight arrivals; there is also an exchange desk on the departures floor.

There are numerous banks around the city centre with exchange facilities. The Bank of Ireland operates a bureau de change at 34 College Green (Around Temple Bar map) that opens 9am to 9pm Monday to Saturday, and 10am to 7pm on Sunday.

American Express (AmEx; Around Temple Bar map; ☎ 679 9000), 40 Nassau St, and Thomas Cook (Around Temple Bar map; ☎ 677 1721, 677 1307), 118 Grafton St, are next to the main and side entrances of Trinity College respectively. Thomas Cook opens 9am to 5.30pm Monday to Saturday, while AmEx opens 9am to 5pm Monday to Friday, and 9am to noon (the foreign-exchange desk stays open until 5pm) on Saturday. AmEx also has a desk in Dublin Tourism (St Andrew's Church branch).

Post & Communications

Dublin's famed GPO, on O'Connell St, north of the river, opens 8am to 8pm Monday to Saturday, and 10.30am to 6pm on Sunday and public holidays. Here you'll find the poste restante, a philatelic counter and a bank of telephones. South of the river the handy post office in South Anne St (Around St Stephen's Green map), just off Grafton St, is well patronised by foreign visitors and is used to dealing with their curious requests.

The cheapest place to make international phone calls in Dublin is at the Talk Shop (ⓔ info@talkshop.ie, ⓦ www.talkshop.ie), which has several branches spread throughout the city centre, including the Granary (Around Temple Bar map; ☎ 672 7212), 20 Temple Lane, and at 5 Upper O'Connell St (☎ 872 0200).

Internet Resources

A number of cafes and restaurants offer access to the Internet, including Central Cyber Café (Around St Stephen's Green St map; ☎ 677 8298, ⓔ info@centralcafe.ie), 6 Grafton St, which charges €6.35 per hour. Global Cyber Café (☎ 878 0295, ⓔ info@ globalcafe.ie) 8 Lower O'Connell St, charges the same.

Travel Agencies

AmEx and Thomas Cook both have offices in the centre of Dublin (see Money earlier in this section). The office of Union of Students in Ireland Travel (USIT; Around Temple Bar map; ☎ 602 1600), 19 Aston Quay, south of O'Connell Bridge, opens 9am to 6pm Monday to Friday (to 8pm on Thursday), and 10am to 5.30pm on Saturday.

Bookshops

Given Dublin's strong literary tradition it's not surprising that the city has some good bookshops.

Directly opposite Trinity College is the excellent Fred Hanna (Around Temple Bar map; ☎ 677 1255), 27–29 Nassau St. Nearby is the large, well stocked Hodges Figgis (Around St Stephen's Green map; ☎ 677 4754), 56–58 Dawson St, with a large selection of virtually every genre. Facing it is

Waterstone's (Around St Stephen's Green map; ☎ 679 1415), 7 Dawson St, which also carries a wide range of books. The Dublin Bookshop (Around St Stephen's Green map; ☎ 677 5568), 24 Grafton St, has a good Irish-interest section.

North of the Liffey, Eason's (☎ 873 3811), 40 O'Connell St, near the GPO, has a wide range of books and one of the biggest selections of magazines in Ireland. The Winding Stair (Around Temple Bar map; ☎ 873 3292), 40 Lower Ormond Quay, does new and second-hand books and has a cafe upstairs. There's a second branch of Waterstone's (☎ 878 1311) in the Jervis Street Centre.

A number of bookshops cater to special interests. Forbidden Planet (Around Temple Bar map; ☎ 671 0688), 5–6 Crampton Quay, is a wonderful science-fiction and comic-book specialist. The Sinn Féin Bookshop (☎ 872 7096) is at 44 Parnell Square West. An Siopa Leabhar (Around St Stephen's Green map; ☎ 478 3814), Harcourt St, just off St Stephen's Green, has books in Irish. The Irish Museum of Modern Art (IMMA; County Dublin map), at the Royal Hospital Kilmainham, and the National Gallery in Merrion Square both have bookshops offering a good range of art books and books on Ireland generally.

There is an excellent bookshop in the Dublin Writers' Museum, 18 Parnell Square North. The Library Book Shop at Trinity College has a wide selection of Irish-interest books, including, of course, various titles on the Book of Kells. For all kinds of official publications and maps, there's also the Dúchas bookshop (Around St Stephen's Green map; ☎ 661 3111), Sun Alliance House, Molesworth St.

You'll find a branch of Hughes & Hughes in Dublin airport and in the St Stephen's Green Shopping Centre (Around St Stephen's Green map; ☎ 478 3060).

Libraries
In keeping with Dublin's tradition as a literary capital, the city has plenty of libraries, both private and public. For information on public libraries, contact Dublin

Corporation (Around St Stephen's Green map; ☎ 661 9000), Cumberland House, Fenian St. The public library in the ILAC Centre (☎ 873 4333), Henry St, is well stocked with books and videos on virtually every subject.

Cultural Centres
Dublin has an international selection of cultural centres. The city is a popular centre for English-language instruction, particularly for students from Spain, Italy and France. The city's cultural centres, which are marked on the Around St Stephen's Green map unless stated otherwise, include:

Alliance Française (☎ 676 1732) 1 Kildare St
British Council (☎ 676 4088) Newmount House, 22–24 Lower Mount St
Goethe Institut (☎ 661 1155) 37 Merrion Square
Italian Cultural Institute (☎ 676 6662) 11 Fitzwilliam Square
Spanish Cultural Institute (off Dublin map; ☎ 668 2024) 58 Northumberland Rd

Laundry
Convenient laundries in north Dublin include Laundry Shop (☎ 872 3541), 191 Parnell St, off Parnell Square, and Laundrette (☎ 830 0340), 110 Lower Dorset St, near the Dublin International Youth Hostel.

Near Trinity College and Temple Bar is the cheerful All-Amcrican Laundrette Company (Around St Stephen's Green map; ☎ 677 2779), 40 South Great George St, which also has a handy notice board. South of the centre and just north of the Grand Canal is Powders Laundrette (off Around St Stephen's Green map; ☎ 478 2655), 42a South Richmond St.

If you're staying north-east of the centre at Clontarf there's the Clothes Line (off Dublin map; ☎ 833 8480), 53 Clontarf Rd. In Dun Laoghaire there's the Star Laundry (☎ 280 5074), 47 Upper George's St.

Prices start at about €6.50, increasing along with the size of your load.

Medical Services
The Eastern Regional Health Authority (ERHA; ☎ 679 0700, 1800 520520, **e** erha@

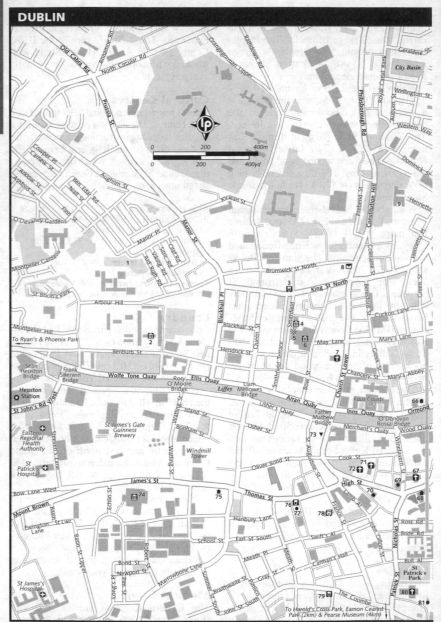

DUBLIN

DUBLIN

DUBLIN

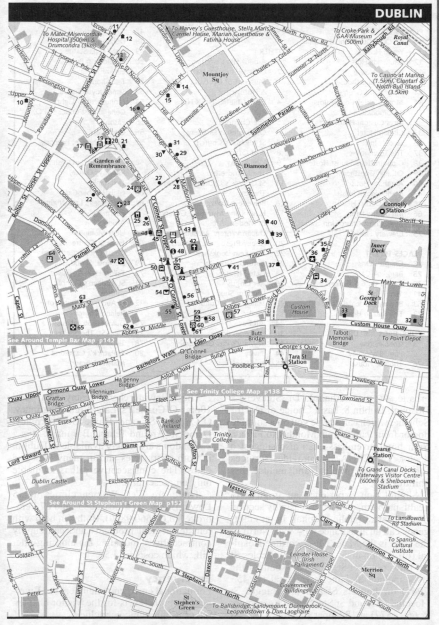

To Mater Misericordiae Hospital (500m) & Drumcondra (3km)

To Harvey's Guesthouse, Stella Maris, Carmel House, Marian Guesthouse & Fatima House

To Croke Park & GAA Museum (500m)

Royal Canal

William St

To Casino at Marino (1.5km), Clontarf & North Bull Island (3.5km)

Mountjoy Sq

North Circular Rd

Gardiner St Upper

Eccles St

Berkeley Rd

St Joseph's Pde

Dorset St Lower

Blessington St

Upper Dorset St

Paradise Pl

Temple St North

Frederick St North

Hardwicke St

Gardiner Pl

Charles St Great

Summer St North

Ballybough Rd

Portland Row

Snelie Pl

Gardiner Lane

Grenville St

Gardiner Lane

Summerhill Parade

Rutland St Lower

Bella St

Buckingham St

Gloucester Pl

Sean MacDermott St Lower

Diamond

Railway Rd

Corporation St

Foley St

Connolly Station

Sheriff St

Dominick St Upper

Bolton St

Dominick St Lower

King's Inns St

Parnell St

Garden of Remembrance

Parnell Sq West

Parnell Sq North

O'Connell St Upper

Thomas Lane

Marlborough St

Britain St

Moore St

Amiens St

Inner Dock

St George's Dock

Major St Lower

Memorial Rd

Custom House

Custom House Quay

Talbot Memorial Bridge

To Point Depot

Commons St

Jervis St

Capel St

Mary St

Henry St

Earl St North

Sackville Pl

Abbey St Lower

North Wall

Talbot St

Abbey St Middle

Abbey St Lower

O'Connell St Lower

Eden Quay

Butt Bridge

George's Quay

City Quay

See Around Temple Bar Map p142

Bachelors Walk

O'Connell Bridge

Burgh Quay

Tara St Station

Poolbeg St

Tara St

Dowlings Ct

Great Strand St

Ha'penny Bridge

Aston Quay

Quay Upper

Ormond Quay Lower

Millennium Bridge

Grattan Bridge

Wellington Quay

Temple Bar

Fleet St

See Trinity College Map p138

Townsend St

Sandwith St Lower

Essex Quay

Essex St East

Eustace St

Crow St

Anglesea St

Bank of Ireland

Trinity College

Pearse St

Pearse Station

Lord Edward St

Parliament St

Dame St

Suffolk St

To Grand Canal Docks, Waterways Visitor Centre (600m) & Shelbourne Stadium

Dublin Castle

Exchequer St

Nassau St

See Around St Stephen's Green Map p152

Lincoln Pl

Clare St

To Lansdowne Rd Stadium

Ship St Great

Golden La

Chancery La

Bride St

Peter Row

Peter St

Aungier St

Mercer St Lower

St Stephen's Green North

King St South

York St

Dawson St

Kildare St

Molesworth St

Leinster House (Irish Parliament)

Government Buildings

To Spanish Cultural Institute

Merrion Sq North

Merrion Sq

Merrion St Upper

St Stephen's Green

To Ballsbridge, Sandymount, Donnybrook, Leopardstown & Dun Laoghaire

Merrion Sq South

DUBLIN

PLACES TO STAY
10 An Óige Dublin International
    Youth Hostel
12 Caulfields Hotel
14 Lyndon House
15 Clifden Guesthouse
21 Hotel Saint George
31 Mount Eccles Court Budget
    Accomodation
32 Jurys Custom House Inn
33 Clarion Hotel
35 Jacob's Inn
37 The Townhouse
38 Globetrotter's Tourist Hostel
39 Othello Guesthouse
40 Abraham House
43 Marlborough Hostel
46 Royal Dublin Hotel
66 Inn on the Liffey
68 Jurys Christ Church Inn
75 Brewery Hostel

PLACES TO EAT
18 Chapter One
28 Bangkok Café
30 Cobalt Café & Gallery
41 101 Talbot
63 Bewley's Oriental Café
73 The Brazen Head

PUBS, BARS & CLUBS
3   Cobblestone
25 Parnell Mooney
76 Thomas House

79 Fallon's

OTHER
1   Arbour Hill Cemetery
2   Collins Barracks; National
    Museum of Decorative Arts
    & History
4   Ceol; Chief O'Neills Hotel &
    Pub
5   The Chimney
6   Old Jameson Distillery
7   St Michan's Church
8   Post Office
9   King's Inns
11 The Laundrette
13 St George's Church; Temple
    Theatre
16 Belvedere College
17 Hugh Lane Municipal Gallery
    of Modern Art
19 Dublin Writers' Museum
20 Abbey Presbyterian Church
22 Sinn Féin Bookshop
23 Rotunda Hospital
24 Gate Theatre
26 Aer Lingus
27 Laundry Shop
29 James Joyce Cultural
    Centre
34 Busáras
36 Police Station
42 St Mary's Pro-Cathedral
44 Savoy
45 Taxi Rank

47 ILAC Centre
48 Dublin Tourism
49 Anna Livia Statue
50 Dublin Bus; Bus
    Éireann
51 Talk Shop
52 James Joyce Statue
53 Monument of Light
54 General Post Office (GPO)
55 Eason's
56 Clery's & Co
57 Abbey Theatre; Peacock
    Theatre
58 Iarnród Éireann (Irish
    Railways Office)
59 Taxi Rank
60 Global Cyber Café
61 O'Connell's Late-Night
    Pharmacy
62 Arnott's
64 UGC Multiplex
65 Jervis St Centre
67 Christ Church Cathedral
69 Dublinia; Synod Hall
70 Tailors Hall; An Taisce
71 St Audoen's Catholic
    Church
72 St Audoen's Church of
    Ireland Church
74 Guinness Storehouse
77 Vicar St; The Shelter
78 Tivoli Theatre
80 St Patrick's Cathedral
81 Marsh's Library

erha.ie, W www.erha.ie), Dr Steevens's
Hospital, Dublin 8, has a Choice of Doctor
Scheme, which can advise you on a suitable
doctor from 9am to 5pm Monday to Friday.
Your hotel or embassy can also suggest a
doctor. The ERHA also provides services
for those with physical and mental disabilities.

Should you experience an immediate
health problem, contact the casualty section
of the nearest public hospital; in an emergency call an ambulance on ☎ 999. North of
the river is the Mater Misericordiae Hospital (off Dublin map; ☎ 830 1122), Eccles St
off Lower Dorset St. Hospitals south of the
river include St James's Hospital (☎ 453
7941) on James's St and the Baggot St
Hospital (Around St Stephen's Green map;
☎ 668 1577) at 18 Upper Baggot St.

The following chemists stay open until
10pm: O'Connell's Late Night Pharmacy,
O'Connell St; and Dame St Pharmacy,
Dame St (Around Temple Bar map).

Condoms are widely available in Dublin,
in both pharmacies and in many bars and
clubs. The contraceptive pill is available
only on prescription.

There are Well Women clinics at 35
Lower Liffey St (☎ 661 0083) and 67 Pembroke Rd (☎ 660 9860). Both can help with
female medical problems and can supply
contraceptives, including the morning-after
pill, which costs €34.50.

Emergency

For national emergency numbers see Emergencies in the Facts for the Visitor chapter.
Other useful numbers include:

Drugs Advisory and Treatment Centre (☎ 677 1122) Trinity Court, 30–31 Pearse St
Rape Crisis Centre (☎ 1800 778 888, 661 4911) 70 Lower Leeson St
The Samaritans (☎ 1850 609 090, 872 7700) This service is for people who are depressed or suicidal.

Dangers & Annoyances

Despite the fact that Dublin is one of Europe's safest capitals, in recent years its good reputation has been somewhat marred by an increase in petty crime, particularly pickpocketing, bag-snatching and car break-ins. So be sure to take the usual precautionary measures and you won't find yourself describing the contents of your bag/wallet/car to a jaded police officer. The most important of these is don't show off your valuables and don't leave anything in your car. The latter is particularly true for rental and foreign-registered vehicles, seen as an easy target by thieves. You should also bear in mind that insurance policies often don't cover losses from cars.

Certain parts of Dublin are unsafe after dark and visitors should avoid run-down, deserted-looking and poorly lit areas. Phoenix Park is not safe at night and you should not camp there. Unfortunately, some of the hostels are also in the rougher parts of north Dublin.

As in other parts of Europe, beggars, some of them alarmingly young, are commonplace. If you don't want to give them money but would like to do something to help the homeless and long-term unemployed, you could buy a copy of the magazine *The Big Issue* (€2.50), some of the proceeds of which go to them.

Like all big cities, Dublin is choking on traffic fumes. Smoking has not died the social death it has in other western countries: cinemas may be smoke-free zones but not even all the expensive restaurants have designated nonsmoking areas. Consequently, after a few days here you may feel your lungs need a burst of fresh air.

SOUTH OF THE LIFFEY

South Dublin has the fanciest shops, almost all the restaurants of note and a majority of

Racism

The influx of nonwhite, English-speaking immigrants and asylum seekers to Dublin has not been without its problems, especially for Africans and, to a lesser extent, Eastern Europeans. The irony is the vast majority of Dubliners deny that they have any racist feelings and that Ireland as a whole is not a racist country. That said, an overwhelming majority of blacks in Dublin have experienced some kind of racial harassment, especially taunting.

Racism *does* exist and *is* a problem. Thankfully, though, the more extreme kind of racism – punctuated by physical intimidation or violence – is infrequent and limited to a mindless minority whose heads are filled with stupid notions about immigrants 'stealing' Irish jobs – a fantasy concocted by reactionary bigots who have jumped onto the 'Ireland for the Irish' bandwagon. Still, there are enough right-minded Dubliners to ensure that in most cases sense and decency will prevail, and it is not unheard of for locals to rally to the side of the victim of racial abuse. If you do experience any problems, be sure to report them to the police.

the hotels, as well as most of the reminders of Dublin's early history and the finest Georgian squares and houses.

Trinity College

Ireland's premier university – and one of the city's most beautiful sights – was founded by Elizabeth I in 1592 on grounds confiscated from the Augustinian priory of All Hallows, which was dissolved in 1537. By providing an alternative to education on the continent, the queen hoped that the students would avoid being 'infected with popery'. The college is in the centre of Dublin, though at the time of its foundation it was outside the city walls. Archbishop Ussher, whose scientific feats included the precise dating of the act of creation to 4004 BC, was one of the college's founders.

Officially, the university's name is the University of Dublin, but Trinity College is its sole college. Until 1793 Trinity College

DUBLIN

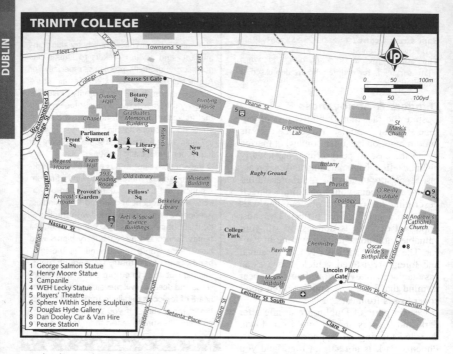

TRINITY COLLEGE

1 George Salmon Statue
2 Henry Moore Statue
3 Campanile
4 WEH Lecky Statue
5 Players' Theatre
6 Sphere Within Sphere Sculpture
7 Douglas Hyde Gallery
8 Dan Dooley Car & Van Hire
9 Pearse Station

remained completely Protestant apart from one short break. Even when the Protestants allowed Catholics in, the Catholic Church forbade it, a restriction that wasn't completely lifted until 1970. To this day Trinity College is still something of a centre of British and Protestant influence, even though the majority of its 9500 students are Catholic. Women were first admitted in 1903, earlier than at most British universities.

A good way to see the college is on an organised **walking tour** (*☎ 608 1724; €8.50; 10.15am-3.40pm Mon-Sat, last tour 3pm Sun mid-May-Sept*). They depart every 40 minutes from the main gate on College Green (the street in front of the college). The cost is good value since it includes the fee to see the Book of Kells.

Main Entrance Facing College Green, the Front Gate or Regent House entrance to the college grounds was built between 1752 and 1759 and is guarded by statues of the

poet Oliver Goldsmith (1730–74) and the orator Edmund Burke (1729–97).

Around the Campanile The open area reached from Regent House is divided into Front Square, Parliament Square and Library Square. The area is dominated by the 30m-high Campanile, designed by Edward Lanyon and erected between 1852 and 1853 on what was believed to be the centre of the monastery that preceded the college. To the left of the Campanile is a statue of George Salmon, college provost from 1888 to 1904, who fought bitterly to keep women out of the college. He carried out his threat to permit them 'over my dead body' by promptly dropping dead when the worst came to pass.

Chapel & Dining Hall Clockwise round Front Square from the Front Gate, the first building is the **chapel** (*☎ 608 1260, Front Square, Trinity College; free*), built from 1798 to plans made in 1777 by the architect

Sir William Chambers (1723–96) and, since 1972, open to all denominations. It's noted for its extremely fine plasterwork by Michael Stapleton, its Ionic columns and its painted, rather than stained-glass, windows. The main one is dedicated to Archbishop Ussher.

Next to the chapel is the dining hall *(Parliament Square; open to students only)*, originally designed in 1743 by Richard Cassels (aka Castle), but dismantled 15 years later because of problems caused by inadequate foundations. The replacement was completed in 1761 and may have retained some elements of the original design. It was extensively restored after a fire in 1984.

Graduates' Memorial Building & the Rubrics The 1892 Graduates' Memorial Building *(Botany Bay; closed to public)* forms the northern side of Library Square. Behind it are the tennis courts in the open area known as Botany Bay. The popular legend behind this name is that the unruly students housed around the square were suitable candidates for the British penal colony at Botany Bay in Australia.

At the eastern side of Library Square, the red-brick Rubrics Building dates from around 1690, making it the oldest building in the college. It was extensively altered in an 1894 restoration and then underwent major structural modifications in the 1970s.

Old Library To the south of the square is the Old Library *(☎ 608 2320, Library Square; admission part of Book of Kells tour)*, which was built in a rather severe style by Thomas Burgh between 1712 and 1732. The Old Library's 65m Long Room contains numerous unique ancient texts, and the **Book of Kells** (see the boxed text 'Book of Kells') is displayed in the Library Colonnades. Despite Ireland's independence, the Library Act of 1801 still entitles Trinity College Library, along with four libraries in Britain, to a free copy of every book published in the UK. Housing this bounty requires nearly another kilometre of shelving every year and the collection amounts to around three million books. Of course these cannot all be kept at the college library, so

there are now additional library storage facilities dotted around Dublin.

The **Long Room** *(☎ 608 2320, East Pavilion, Library Colonnades; adult/student €5.70/5.10, children under 12 free, includes admission to the Long Room & temporary exhibitions in the East Pavilion; open 9.30am-5pm Mon-Sat, noon-4.30pm Sun, from 9am June-Sept)* is mainly used for about 200,000 of the library's oldest volumes. Until 1892 the ground floor Colonnades was an open arcade, but it was enclosed at that time to increase the storage area. A previous attempt to increase the room's storage capacity had been made in 1853, when the Long Room ceiling was raised.

As well as the world-famous Book of Kells, on display is the so-called harp of Brian Ború, which was definitely not in use when the army of this early Irish hero defeated the Danes at the Battle of Clontarf in 1014. It does, however, date from around 1400, making it one of the oldest harps in Ireland.

Other exhibits in the Long Room include a rare copy of the Proclamation of the Irish Republic, which was read out by Pádraig Pearse at the beginning of the Easter Rising in 1916. The collection of 18th- and 19th-century marble busts around the walls features Jonathan Swift, Edmund Burke and Wolfe Tone, all former members of Trinity College.

The Long Room and Book of Kells exhibition gets packed out in high season. The Colonnades also houses a busy book and souvenir shop and a temporary exhibition hall.

1937 Reading Room, Exam Hall & Provost's House Continuing clockwise round the Campanile there's the 1937 Reading Room and the Public Theatre or Exam Hall, which dates from 1779 to 1791. Like the Chapel building it was the work of William Chambers and also has plasterwork by Michael Stapleton. The Exam Hall has an oak chandelier rescued from the Houses of Parliament (now the Bank of Ireland) across College Green and an organ said to have been salvaged from a Spanish ship in 1702, though evidence indicates otherwise.

Book of Kells

For visitors, Trinity College's prime attraction is the magnificent Book of Kells, an illuminated manuscript dating from around 800, making it one of the oldest books in the world. Although the book was brought to the college for safekeeping from the monastery at Kells in County Meath in 1654, it undoubtedly predates the monastery itself. It was probably produced by monks at St Colmcille's Monastery on the remote island of Iona, off the western coast of Scotland. When repeated Viking raids made their monastery untenable, the monks moved to the temporary safety of Kells in Ireland in 806, taking their masterpiece with them. In 1007, the book was stolen, then rediscovered three months later, buried in the ground. Some time before the dissolution of the monastery in 1535, the *cumdach* (metal shrine) was lost, possibly taken by looting Vikings who wouldn't have valued the text itself. About 30 of the beginning and ending folios have also disappeared.

St John the Eagle from the 8th-century Book of Kells

The Book of Kells contains the four gospels of the New Testament, written in Latin, as well as prefaces, summaries and other text. If it were merely words, the Book of Kells would simply be a very old book – it's the extensive and amazingly complex illustrations that make it so wonderful. The superbly decorated opening initials are only part of the story, for the book also has numerous smaller illustrations between the lines.

The 680-page book was rebound in four calfskin volumes in 1953. Two volumes are usually on display, one showing an illuminated page and the other showing text. The pages are turned over regularly, but you can acquire your own reproduction copy for a mere €22,000. If that's too steep, the library bookshop has various less expensive books, including *The Book of Kells*, a paperback with some attractive colour plates and text costing €16.50.

The Book of Kells is usually on display in the East Pavilion of the Library Colonnades, underneath the actual library. As well as the Book of Kells, the Book of Armagh (807) and the Book of Durrow (675) are also on display.

Behind the Exam Hall is the 1760 Provost's House, a particularly fine Georgian house where the provost, or college head, still resides. The house and its adjacent garden are not open to the public.

Berkeley Library To one side of the Old Library is Paul Koralek's 1967 Berkeley Library *(Fellow's Square; closed to public)*. This solid, square brutalist-style building has been hailed as the best example of modern architecture in Ireland, though it has to be admitted the competition isn't great. It's fronted by Arnaldo Pomodoro's 1982–3 sculpture *Sphere within Sphere*.

George Berkeley was born in Kilkenny in

1685, studied at Trinity when he was only 15 years old and went on to a distinguished career in many fields, but particularly in philosophy. His influence spread to the new English colonies in North America, where, among other things, he helped to found the University of Pennsylvania. Berkeley in California, and its namesake university, are named after him.

Arts & Social Science Building South of the Old Library is the 1978 Arts and Social Science Building, which backs on to Nassau St and forms the alternative entrance to the college. Like the Berkeley Library it was designed by Paul Koralek; it also houses the

Douglas Hyde Gallery of Modern Art
(☎ 608 1116; free; open 11am-6pm Mon-Wed
& Fri, to 7pm Thur, to 4.45pm Sat).

The Dublin Experience After the Book of
Kells the college's other big tourist attraction is the Dublin Experience (☎ 608 1688,
Arts & Social Science Building; adult/stu-
dent €4.20/3.50, €7/5.70 including Book of
Kells; hourly 10am-5pm mid-May-Oct). It's
a 45-minute audiovisual introduction to the
city. Shows take place at the back of the Arts
and Social Science Building.

Around New Square Behind the Rubrics
Building, at the eastern end of Library
Square, is New Square. The highly ornate
1853-7 **Museum Building** (☎ 608 1477,
New Square; free; open by prior arrangement only) has the skeletons of two enormous giant Irish deer just inside the entrance,
and the Geological Museum upstairs.

The 1734 Printing House, designed by
Richard Cassels to resemble a Doric temple
and now used for the microelectronics and
electrical engineering departments, is on the
northern side of New Square.

At the eastern end of the college grounds
are the rugby ground and College Park,
where cricket is played. There are a number
of science buildings here also. The Lincoln
Place Gate at this end is usually open and
makes a good entrance or exit from the college, especially if you're on a bicycle.

Bank of Ireland
The imposing Bank of Ireland building
(Around Temple Bar map; ☎ 671 1488, College Green; open 10am-4pm Mon-Wed &
Fri, to 5pm Thur), directly opposite Trinity
College, was originally built in 1729 to
house the Irish Parliament. When the Parliament voted itself out of existence by the
Act of Union in 1801, it became a building
without a role. It was sold in 1803 with instructions that the interior be altered to prevent its being used as a debating chamber in
the future. Consequently, the large central
House of Commons was remodelled but the
smaller chamber of the House of Lords survived. After independence the Irish govern-

ment chose to make Leinster House the new
parliamentary building and ignored the possibility of restoring this fine building to its
original use.

Over a long period of time, a string of
architects worked on the building, yet it
somehow manages to avoid looking like a
hotchpotch of styles. Edward Lovett Pearce
designed the circular central part, which
was constructed between 1729 and 1739,
and the eastern front was designed by James
Gandon in 1785. Other architects involved
in its construction were Robert Park and
Francis Johnston, who converted it from a
parliament building to a bank.

Inside, the banking mall occupies what
was once the House of Commons, but offers
little hint of its former role. The Irish House
of Lords is much more interesting, with
its Irish-oak woodwork, late-18th-century
Dublin crystal chandelier and 10kg silver-
gilt mace. The tapestries date from the
1730s and depict the 1689 Siege of Derry
and the Battle of the Boyne, the two great
Protestant victories over Catholic Ireland.

There are **tours** of the **House of Lords**
(free; 10.30am, 11.30am & 1.45pm Tues),
which also include an informal talk as much
about Ireland, and life in general, as the
building itself.

Around the Bank of Ireland
The area between the Bank and Trinity College (Around Temple Bar map), today a constant tangle of traffic and pedestrians, was
once a green swathe and is still known as
College Green. In front of the bank stands a
statue of Henry Grattan (1746–1820), a distinguished parliamentary orator.

The traffic island where College Green,
Westmoreland St and College St meet
houses public toilets (no longer in use) and
a **statue of the poet and composer Thomas
Moore** (1779–1852), which is renowned
because of James Joyce's comment in
Ulysses that standing atop a public urinal
wasn't a bad place for the man who penned
the poem The Meeting of the Waters.

The other end of College St, where it meets
Pearse St, has a 1986 sculpture known as the
Steyne. It's a copy of the steyne (the Viking

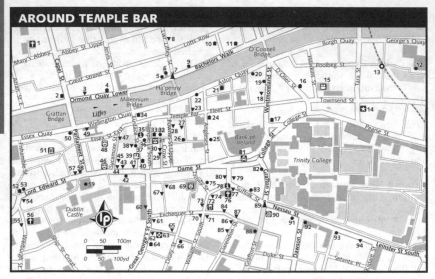

AROUND TEMPLE BAR

word for stone) erected on the riverbank in the 9th century to stop ships from grounding and removed in 1720.

Temple Bar

West of College Green and the Bank of Ireland, the maze of streets that make up Temple Bar (Around Temple Bar map) are sandwiched between Dame St and the river. One of the oldest areas of the city, Temple Bar's run-down buildings and cobbled streets were revitalised throughout the 1990s and it is now the most popular part of the city centre. Temple Bar has a number of interesting galleries and small museums, as well as a growing selection of trendy shops, but it is the area's pubs and restaurants that are its biggest draw, attracting tourists in their tens of thousands.

Frankly, Temple Bar has been ruined by the success it has had since it was first earmarked as the city's 'cultural quarter'. In an attempt to recreate a Left Bank atmosphere where artists' studios stood alongside cosy cafes and small boutiques selling ethnic artefacts, developers succumbed to the powerful financial draw and created an overly commercialised quarter full of over-

priced restaurants serving indifferent food, tacky souvenir shops aimed strictly at tourists and – with one or two exceptions – characterless bars. During the day, however, Temple Bar is pleasant enough; at night (especially at the weekend) it overflows with drunken locals and foreigners intent on renaming the area Temple Barf.

Dame St forms part of the southern boundary of Temple Bar and links new Dublin (centred around Trinity College and Grafton St) and old (stretching from Dublin Castle to encompass Christ Church and St Patrick's cathedrals). Along its route Dame St changes name to Cork Hill, Lord Edward St and Christchurch Place.

Information Temple Bar Information Centre (☎ 671 5717), 18 Eustace St, has information on the area and an exhibition on its development. It publishes the useful *Temple Bar Guide.* It opens 9am to 6pm Monday to Friday, year round, plus 11am to 4pm on Saturday and noon to 4pm on Sunday, June to August.

Exploring Temple Bar The western boundary of Temple Bar is formed by **Fishamble St,**

AROUND TEMPLE BAR

the oldest street in Dublin, dating back to Viking times – not that you'd know that to see it now. Christ Church Cathedral (see the entry later in this section for details), beside Fishamble St, dates from 1170, but there was an earlier Viking church on this site. Brass symbols in the pavement direct you towards a mosaic laid out to show the ground plan of the sort of Viking dwelling excavated here in 1980 and 1981. Another Viking area is being excavated closer to Parliament St.

Nearby is **Dublin's Viking Adventure** (☎ 679 6040, e viking@dublintourism.ie, *Essex St West; adult/student/family €7/5.40/ 19)* where there's an entertaining 40-minute tour of Viking Dublin, which was then known as Dyflin. You take a simulated ride on a

Viking ship and land at the village of Dyflin (complete with smells), which you then walk through. Actors play the roles of villagers and tell you about their way of life. It's not often you get to talk to exhibits in a museum.

In 1742 Handel conducted the first performance of his *Messiah* in the **Dublin Music Hall**, behind Kinlay House hotel on Lord Edward St, now part of a hotel that bears the composer's name. The Music Hall, which opened in 1741, was designed by Richard Cassels; the only reminder of it today is the entrance and the original door.

On **Parliament St**, which runs south from the river to the City Hall and Dublin Castle, the Sunlight Chambers beside the river has a beautiful **frieze** around the facade. Sunlight was a brand of soap manufactured by Lever Brothers, who were responsible for the late-19th-century building. The frieze shows the Lever Brothers' view of the world and soap: men make clothes dirty, women wash them!

Eustace St is an interesting road. Buildings on the street include the 1715 Presbyterian Meeting House, now **The Ark** (☎ 670 7788, 11a Eustace St), a children's cultural centre. The Dublin branch of the Society of United Irishmen, who sought parliamentary reform and equality for Catholics, was first convened in 1791 in the Eagle Tavern, now the Friends Meeting House. This should not be confused with the other Eagle Tavern, which is on Cork St.

Merchant's Arch leads to the **Ha'penny Bridge**. If you cross to the northern side of the Liffey, pause to look at the statue of two stout Dublin matrons sitting on a park bench with their shopping bags, dubbed **'the hags with the bags'**. The Stock Exchange lives on Anglesea St, in a building dating from 1878.

Dublin Castle

The centre of British power in Ireland and originally built on the orders of King John in 1204, Dublin Castle (Around Temple Bar map; ☎ 677 7129, Cork Hill, Dame St; adult/student & senior €4/3; open 10am-5pm Mon-Fri, 2pm-5pm Sat & Sun) is more palace than castle. Only the Record Tower, completed in 1258, survives from the original Norman castle. Parts of the castle's foundations remain and a visit to the excavations is the most interesting part of the castle tour. The moats, which are now completely covered by more modern developments, were once filled by the River Poddle. The castle is also home to one of Dublin's best museums, the Chester Beatty Library (see below).

Dublin Castle enjoyed a relatively quiet history despite a siege by Silken Thomas Fitzgerald in 1534, a fire that destroyed much of the castle in 1684, and the events of the 1916 Easter Rising. It was used as the official residence of the British viceroys of Ireland until the Viceregal Lodge was built in Phoenix Park. Earlier it had been used as a prison, though not always with great suc-

cess. Red Hugh O'Donnell, one of the last of the great Gaelic leaders, escaped from the Record Tower in 1591, was recaptured, and escaped again in 1592.

The castle, which tops Cork Hill, behind the City Hall, is still used for government business, and tours are often tailored round meetings and conferences or sometimes cancelled altogether, so it's wise to phone beforehand. The visitor centre in the southeastern corner of the Lower Yard has a gift shop and cafe.

Bedford Tower & Genealogical Office
The Bedford Tower and Genealogical Office are directly across the Upper Yard from the main entrance. In 1907 the collection known as the Irish Crown Jewels was stolen from the tower and never recovered. The Genealogical Office as an institution dates from 1552. Its present building dates from the 18th century.

The entranceway to the castle yard, beside the Bedford Tower, is topped by a statue of Justice which has always been a subject of mirth. She faces the castle and has her back to the city – seen as a sure indicator of how much justice the average Irish citizen could expect from the British. The scales of justice also had a distinct tendency to fill with rain and tilt in one direction or the other, rather than assuming the approved level position. Eventually a hole was drilled in the bottom of each pan so the rainwater could drain out.

Royal Chapel The Church of the Holy Trinity, previously known as the Royal Chapel, built in Gothic style by Francis Johnston between 1807 and 1814, is in the Lower Yard. Decorating the cold grey exterior are over 90 heads of various Irish personages and assorted saints carved out of Tullamore limestone. The interior is wildly exuberant, with fan vaulting alongside quadripartite vaulting, wooden galleries, stained glass and lots of lively looking sculpted angels.

Record Tower Rising over the chapel is the Record Tower, which was used as a storage facility for official records from 1579 until they were transferred to the Record Office in the Four Courts building in the

Originally built in 1204, Dublin Castle sits on top of Cork Hill.

Merrion Square's elegant doors

The gardens of St Patrick's Cathedral – said to be the earliest Christian site in Dublin

O'Connell St's historic GPO

Cross Sean Heuston Bridge to Dublin's grand Heuston Station

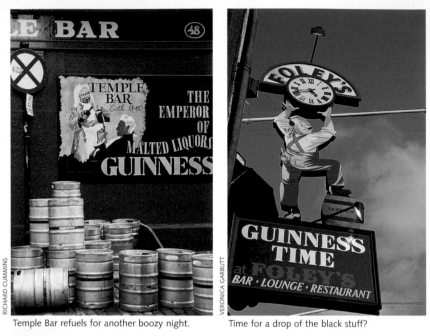

RICHARD CUMMINS

VERONICA GARBUTT

Temple Bar refuels for another boozy night.

Time for a drop of the black stuff?

DOUG McKINLAY

Keep an eye out for Irish patriot Robert Emmet, who apparently haunts Dublin's Brazen Head pub.

early 19th century. (When the Four Courts was burned out at the start of the Civil War in 1922, almost all these priceless records were destroyed.) Although the tower was rebuilt in 1813 it retains much of its original appearance, including the massive 5m-thick walls. It now houses the **Garda Síochána Museum** (☎ 668 9998; free; open 9.15am-5pm Mon-Fri), with exhibits dedicated to the history of the Irish police force.

Chester Beatty Library Reached from a separate entrance on Ship St and housed in the Clock Tower is the castle's newest attraction. The world-famous library and gallery (☎ 269 2386, W www.cbl.ie; free; open 10am-5pm Tues-Fri, 11am-5pm Sat & 1pm-5pm Sun; tours available 2.30pm Wed & Sat), houses the collection of mining engineer Sir Alfred Chester Beatty (1875–1968). The breathtaking collection includes over 20,000 manuscripts, rare books, miniature paintings, clay tablets, costumes and other objects spread across two floors. On the ground floor you'll find works of art from the Western, Islamic and East-Asian worlds, including perhaps the finest collection of Chinese jade books in the world. Also worth examining are the illuminated European texts.

The second floor is devoted to the major religions of the world – Judaism, Islam, Christianity, Hinduism and Buddhism. The collection of Qur'ans dating from the 9th to the 19th centuries (the library has over 270 of them) are considered by experts to be the best example of illuminated Islamic texts in the world. And it doesn't stop there. You'll also find some marvellous examples of ancient papyri, including the renowned Egyptian love poems from the 12th century, and some of the earliest illuminated gospels in the world, dating to around AD 200. The collection is rounded off with some exquisite scrolls and artwork from China, Japan, Tibet and South-East Asia.

City Hall & Municipal Buildings
Fronting Dublin Castle on Lord Edward St, the City Hall (*Around Temple Bar map*; ☎ 672 2204, W www.dublincorp.ie/cityhall; Cork Hill; adult/student & senior €3.80/ 1.25; open 10am-5.15pm Mon-Sat, 2pm-5pm Sun) was built by Thomas Cooley between 1769 and 1779 as the Royal Exchange and later became the offices of the Dublin Corporation. It stands on the site of the Lucas Coffee House and the Eagle Tavern, in which Dublin's infamous Hell Fire Club was established in 1735. Founded by Richard Parsons, earl of Rosse, it was one of a number of gentlemen's clubs in Dublin where less-than-gentlemanly conduct took place. It gained a reputation for debauchery and black magic, but there's no evidence that such things took place.

A brand new multi-media exhibition entitled 'The Story of the Capital' has opened in the basement. It traces the history of Dublin from its earliest beginnings up to 2000.

The 1781 Municipal Buildings, immediately west of the City Hall, were built by Thomas Ivory (1720–86), who was also responsible for the Genealogical Office in Dublin Castle.

Christ Church Cathedral
Christ Church Cathedral (*Church of the Holy Trinity*; ☎ 677 8099, e email@ccdub .ie, Christ Church Place; adult/student €2.50/1.25; open 9.45am-5.30pm) is just south of the river and west of the city centre and Temple Bar. Dublin's original Viking settlement stood between the cathedral and the river. This was also the centre of medieval Dublin, with Dublin Castle, the Tholsel (Town Hall; demolished in 1809) and the original Four Courts (demolished in 1796) all close by. Nearby, on Back Lane, is the only remaining guildhall in Dublin. The 1706 Tailors Hall was due for demolition in the 1960s but survived to become the office of An Taisce (National Trust for Ireland).

Originally built in wood by the Danes in 1038, the cathedral was subsequently rebuilt in stone from 1172, by Richard de Clare, earl of Pembroke (better known as Strongbow), the Anglo-Norman noble who invaded Ireland in 1170.

Through much of its history, Christ Church vied for supremacy with nearby St Patrick's Cathedral, but, like its neighbour, it fell on hard times in the 18th and 19th centuries and was virtually derelict by the time restoration took place. Earlier, the nave had been used as a market and the crypt had housed taverns. Today both Church of Ireland cathedrals are outsiders in a Catholic nation.

From the south-eastern entrance to the churchyard you walk past ruins of the chapter house, which dates from 1230. The entrance to the cathedral is at the south-western corner and as you enter you face the northern wall. This survived the collapse of its southern counterpart but has also suffered from subsiding foundations.

The southern aisle has a monument to the legendary Strongbow. The armoured figure on the tomb is unlikely to be of Strongbow (it's more probably the earl of Drogheda) but his internal organs may have been buried here. A popular legend relates that the half-figure beside the tomb is of Strongbow's son, who was cut in two by his father when his bravery in battle was suspect.

The southern transept contains the superb baroque tomb of the 19th earl of Kildare (died 1734). His grandson, Lord Edward Fitzgerald, was a member of the United Irishmen and died in the abortive 1798 Rising. The entrance to the Chapel of St Laurence is off the southern transept and contains two effigies, one of them reputed to be that of either Strongbow's wife or sister. Laurence O'Toole's embalmed heart was placed in the Chapel of St Laud.

An entrance just by the southern transept descends to the unusually large arched crypt, which dates back to the original Viking church. Curiosities in the crypt include a glass display case housing a mummified cat chasing a mummified mouse that were trapped inside an organ pipe in the 1860s! From the main entrance, a bridge, part of the 1871–78 restoration, leads to Dublinia (see the following section).

Dublinia
Inside what was once the Synod Hall attached to Christ Church Cathedral, the Medieval Trust has created Dublinia *(☎ 679 4611; adult/student €5/3.80; open 10am-5pm daily Apr-Sept; 11am-4pm Mon-Sat & 10am-4pm Sun Oct-Mar)*, a lively attempt to bring medieval Dublin to life. The ground floor has models of 10 episodes in Dublin's history that are explained through headsets as you walk around. On the 1st floor, finds from medieval excavations are displayed alongside a large model of the city. There are also models of the medieval quayside and of a cobbler's shop. On the top floor is the Medieval Fayre, a replica of a 12th-century fair outside the city gates. The displays include merchants' wares, a medicine stall, an armourer's pavilion, a medieval confessional booth and a bank. Finally you can climb neighbouring St Michael's Tower for views over the city to the Dublin Hills.

Your ticket gets you into Christ Church Cathedral free (via the link bridge).

St Patrick's Cathedral
St Patrick himself is said to have baptised converts at a well within the cathedral grounds, so the cathedral *(☎ 475 4817, Ⓦ www.stpatrickscathedral.ie, St Patrick's Close; bus No 50, 50A or 56A from Aston Quay or No 54 or 54A from Burgh Quay; adult/senior, student & child €4.50/3.20; open 9am-5pm Mon-Fri, 9am-6pm Sat, 9am-11am & 12.45pm-3pm & 4.15pm-6pm Sun Mar-Oct; 9am-5pm Mon-Sat, 10am-11am & 12.45pm-3pm Sun Nov-Feb; closed 24-26 Dec & 1 Jan)* stands on one of the earliest Christian sites in the city. Like Christ Church Cathedral it was built on unstable ground, with the subterranean River Poddle flowing under its foundations. Because of the high water table St Patrick's doesn't have a crypt.

Although a church stood on the Patrick St site from as early as the 5th century, the present building dates from 1190 or 1225 – opinions differ. Its current form dates mainly from some rather overenthusiastic restoration in 1864, which included the addition of the flying buttresses. St Patrick's Park, the expanse of green beside the cathedral, was a crowded slum until it was cleared and its residents evicted in the early 20th century.

Like Christ Church Cathedral, the building has suffered a rather dramatic history. A storm brought down the spire in 1316 and, soon after, the building was badly damaged in a fire. Another, more disastrous, fire followed

in 1362. This resulted in the addition of Archbishop Minot's west tower in 1370. In 1560
one of the first clocks in Dublin was added to
the 43m tower, and a 31m spire in 1749.
Oliver Cromwell, during his 1649 visit to Ireland, converted St Patrick's to a stable for his
army's horses, an indignity to which he also
subjected numerous other Irish churches.
Jonathan Swift was the dean of the cathedral
from 1713 to 1745, but prior to its restoration
it became very neglected.

Entering the cathedral from the south-
western porch you come almost immediately, on your right, to the graves of Swift
and Esther Johnson, or Stella, Swift's long-
term companion. On the wall nearby are
Swift's own Latin epitaphs to the two of
them, and a bust of him.

The huge, dusty Boyle Monument to the
left was erected in 1632 by Richard Boyle,
the earl of Cork, and is decorated with numerous painted figures of members of his
family. It stood beside the altar until, in 1633,
Thomas Wentworth, Dublin's viceroy and the
future earl of Strafford, had it shifted. Wentworth won this round in his bitter conflict
with the earl of Cork, but the latter had the
final say when he contributed to Wentworth's
impeachment and execution. The figure in
the centre on the bottom level is of the earl's
five-year-old son, Robert Boyle (1627–91),
who became a noted scientist. His contributions to physics include Boyle's Law, which
relates the pressure and volume of gases.

In the north-western corner of the church
is a cross on a stone slab, which once
marked the position of St Patrick's original
well. The southern transept was formerly a
separate chapterhouse.

During the cathedral's decay in the 18th
and 19th centuries the northern transept was
virtually a separate church. It now contains
memorials to the Royal Irish Regiments. The
Swift corner, in the northern transept, features Swift's pulpit, his chair and a book-
filled glass cabinet containing his death mask.

The Guinness family were noted contributors to the cathedral's restoration and a monument to Sir Benjamin Guinness' daughter
stands in the Chapel of St Stephen beneath a
window bearing the words 'I was thirsty and

ye gave me drink'! The chapel also has a
chair used by William of Orange at a service
in the cathedral after his victory at the Boyne.

In 2001 a new exhibition, 'Living Stones'
was inaugurated in the church. It features a
comprehensive view of the church's history
and symbolism, and also has sections on
Jonathan Swift and the important role of
music in St Patrick's. Admission to this is
included in the cathedral's admission price.

The cathedral's choir school dates back to
1432 and the choir took part in the first performance of Handel's *Messiah* in 1742. You
can hear the choir sing at 5.35pm Monday to
Friday. A real treat are the carols performed
around Christmas; call ☎ 453 9472 for details of how to obtain a hard-to-get ticket.

Marsh's Library

In St Patrick's Close, beside St Patrick's
Cathedral, is Marsh's Library (☎ 454 3511,
e marshlib@iol.ie, w www.kst.dit.ie/marsh,
St Patrick's Close; adult/senior & student
€2.50/1.25; open 10am-12.45pm & 2pm-
5pm Mon & Wed-Fri, 10.30am-12.45pm
Sat), founded in 1701 by Archbishop Nar-
cissus Marsh (1638–1713) and opened in
1707. It was designed by Sir William Robinson, who was also responsible for the Royal
Hospital, Kilmainham. The oldest public
library in the country, it contains 25,000
books dating from the 16th to early 18th
centuries, as well as maps, numerous manuscripts and a collection of incunabula, the
technical term for books printed before
1500. One of the oldest and finest books in
the collection is a volume of Cicero's *Letters
to His Friends* printed in Milan in 1472. The
manuscript collection includes one in Latin
dating back to 1400.

St Werburgh's Church

In Werburgh St, just south of Christ Church
Cathedral and beside Dublin Castle, St Werburgh's (Around Temple Bar map; ☎ 478
3710, Werburgh St; admission by donation;
open 10am-4pm Mon-Fri; phone or see the
caretaker at 8 Castle St to see inside) stands
on ancient foundations. Its early history, however, is unknown. It was rebuilt in 1662, in
1715 and again in 1759 (with some elegance)

after a fire in 1754. In 1810 the church's tall spire was ordered to be dismantled because authorities feared that rebels would use the vantage point to fire into Dublin Castle, but thankfully the order was not followed through. It is linked with the Fitzgerald family; Lord Edward Fitzgerald, a member of the United Irishmen who was a leader of the 1798 Rising, is interred in the vault. In what was an unfortunately frequent theme of Irish uprisings, compatriots betrayed him and he died from wounds received while being captured. Ironically, Major Henry Sirr, his captor, is buried in the graveyard. John Field (1782–1837), the pianist who invented the nocturne, was baptised here – he is buried in Moscow. In the porch you will notice two fire pumps which date from the time when Dublin's fire department was composed of church volunteers.

Werburgh St was also the location of Dublin's first theatre and Jonathan Swift was born just off the street at 7 Hoey's Court in 1667.

St Audoen's Churches

Lucky St Audoen has two churches to his name, both just west of Christ Church Cathedral. The smaller Church of Ireland church *(☎ 677 0088,* e *visits@ealga.ie, Cornmarket, High St; adult/senior/child €1.20/1.25/ 0.75; open 9.30am-4.45pm daily June-Sept)* is the only surviving medieval parish church in the city and easily one of Dublin's most beautiful places of worship. It was built between 1181 and 1212, though recent excavations unearthing a 9th-century burial slab suggest that it was built on top of an even older church. Its tower and door date from the 12th century and the aisle from the 15th century, but the church today is mainly a 19th-century restoration.

A recent restoration by Dúchas resulted in the addition of a visitors centre in the southern aisle, known as St Anne's Chapel. Here you will find a number of tombstones of leading members of Dublin society from the 16th to the 18th centuries. At the top of the chapel is the tower, which houses the three oldest bells in Ireland, dating from 1423. More bells were added in 1790, 1864 and 1880; the newer ones were recast in 1983, and the original bells were returned at the same time. Although the church's exhibits are hardly spectacular, the building itself is very beautiful and a genuine slice of medieval Dublin.

The church is entered from the north through an arch off High St. Part of the old city wall, this arch was built in 1240 and is the only surviving reminder of the city gates.

Joined onto the older Protestant St Audoen's is the newer and larger Catholic St Audoen's *(Cornmarket, High St; free),* a large church whose chief claim to local fame is Father Flash Kavanagh, who apparently used to read Mass at high speed so that his large congregation could head off to more absorbing Sunday pursuits, such as football matches.

National Museum

The National Museum *(Around St Stephen's Green map;* ☎ *677 7444,* e *marketing@ museum.ie, Kildare St; admission by donation; guided tours €1.25; open 10am-5pm Tues-Sat, 2pm-5pm Sun)* was designed by Sir Thomas Newenham Deane and completed in 1890. The star attraction is the Treasury, home to the finest collection of Bronze and Iron Age gold artefacts in the world and the world's most complete collection of medieval Celtic metalwork.

The centrepieces of the Treasury's unique collection are Ireland's most famous crafted artefacts, the **Ardagh Chalice** and the **Tara Brooch**. Measuring 17.8cm high and 24.2cm in diameter, the 12th-century Ardagh chalice is made of gold, silver, bronze, brass, copper and lead. Put simply, this is the finest exemplar of Celtic art ever found. The equally renowned Tara Brooch was crafted around AD 700 primarily in white bronze, but with traces of gold, silver, glass, copper, enamel and wire beading, and was used as a clasp for a cloak.

The Treasury includes many other stunning pieces, many of which are grouped together in 'hoards', after the manner in which they were found, usually uncovered by a farmer digging up a field or a bog. Be sure not to miss the Broighter and Mooghaun hoards.

Upstairs, Viking Age Dublin tells the story of Dublin's Viking era, with exhibits from the excavations at Wood Quay – the area between Christ Church Cathedral and the river, where Dublin City Council plonked its new headquarters. Other exhibits focus on the 1916 Easter Rising and the independence struggle between 1900 and 1921. Frequent short-term exhibitions are also held.

The National Museum's main annexe is at **Collins Barracks** (☎ 677 7444, Benburb St; free), off Ellis Quay, on the city's northern side. The former army barracks was completely renovated and opened in 1999 as the **National Museum of Decorative Arts & History**. Inside, you'll find artefacts ranging from silver, ceramic and glassware to weaponry, furniture and examples of folk life.

National Gallery

Opened in 1864, the National Gallery (Around St Stephen's Green map; ☎ 661 5133, W www.nationalgallery.ie, Merrion Square West; free; open 9.30am-5.30pm Mon-Wed & Fri-Sat, to 8.30pm Thur, noon-5.30pm Sun; free guided tours at 3pm Sat, 2pm, 3pm & 4pm Sun) looks out on Merrion Square. Its excellent collection is strong in Irish art, but there are also high-quality collections of every major school of European painting.

On the lawn in front of the gallery is a statue of the Irish railway magnate William Dargan, who organised the 1853 Dublin Industrial Exhibition at this spot; the profits from the exhibition were used to found the gallery. Nearby is a statue of George Bernard Shaw, a major benefactor of the gallery.

The gallery has three wings: the original Dargan Wing, the Milltown Rooms and the North Wing. The Dargan Wing's ground floor has the imposing Shaw Room, lined with full-length portraits and illuminated by a series of spectacular Waterford crystal chandeliers. Upstairs, a series of rooms is dedicated to the Italian early and high Renaissance, 16th-century northern Italian art and 17th- and 18th-century Italian art. Fra Angelico, Titian and Tintoretto are among the artists represented, but the highlight is undoubtedly Caravaggio's *The Taking of Christ*, which lay

undiscovered for over 60 years in a Jesuit house in Leeson St and was accidentally discovered by chief curator Sergio Benedetti.

The central Milltown Rooms were added between 1899 and 1903 to hold Russborough House's art collection, which was presented to the gallery in 1902. The ground floor displays the gallery's fine Irish collection plus a smaller British collection, with works by Reynolds, Hogarth, Gainsborough, Landseer and Turner. One highlight is the room at the back of the gallery displaying works by Jack B Yeats (1871–1957), younger brother of WB Yeats. Other rooms display specific periods and styles of Irish art, including one room of works by Irish artists painting in France.

Upstairs are works from Germany, the Netherlands and Spain. There are rooms full of works by Rembrandt and his circle and by the Spanish artists of Seville. The Spanish collection features works by El Greco, Goya and Picasso.

The North Wing was added only between 1964 and 1968 but has already undergone extensive refurbishment. It houses works by British and European artists.

The gallery also has an art reference library, a lecture theatre, a good bookshop and the deservedly popular *Fitzer's Café*.

Leinster House

The Dáil (Lower House) and Seanad (Upper House) of the Oireachtas na hÉireann (Irish Parliament) meet in Leinster House (Around St Stephen's Green map; ☎ 618 3000, 618 3271 for tour information, W www.irlgov.ie/oireachtas, Kildare St; observation gallery open when parliament in session, usually 2.30pm-8.30pm Tues, 10.30am-8.30pm Wed & 10.30am-5.30pm Thur Nov-May; free, pre-arranged guided tours available Mon-Fri when parliament in session). The entrance to Leinster House from Kildare St is flanked by the National Library and the National Museum. Originally built as Kildare House between 1745 and 1748 for the earl of Kildare, the building had its name changed when the earl also assumed the title of duke of Leinster in 1766. One of the members of the Fitzgerald family who held the title was Lord Edward

Fitzgerald, who died of wounds he received in the abortive 1798 Rising.

Leinster House's Kildare St frontage was designed by Richard Cassels to look like a town house, whereas the Merrion Square frontage was made to look like a country house. The lawn in front of the Merrion Square frontage was the site for William Dargan's 1853 Dublin Industrial Exhibition. There's a statue of him at the National Gallery end of the lawn. At the other end of the lawn is a statue of Prince Albert, Queen Victoria's consort. Queen Victoria herself was commemorated in massive form on the Kildare St side from 1908 until the statue was removed in 1948. The obelisk in front of the building is dedicated to Arthur Griffith, Michael Collins and Kevin O'Higgins, architects of independent Ireland.

The Dublin Society, later named the Royal Dublin Society, bought the building in 1814 but moved out in stages between 1922 and 1925, when the first government of independent Ireland decided to establish Parliament there.

The Seanad meets in the north-wing saloon, while the Dáil meets in a less interesting room that was originally a lecture theatre added to the original building in 1897. When Parliament is sitting, visitors are admitted to an observation gallery. You get an entry ticket from the Kildare St entrance on production of some identification. Bags can't be taken in, or notes or photographs taken. Parliament sits for 90 days a year, usually November to May.

Government Buildings

On Upper Merrion St, the domed Government Buildings *(Around St Stephen's Green map;* ☎ *662 4888,* W *www.irlgov.ie/ taoiseach, Upper Merrion St; free tours 10.30am-3.30pm Sat only, tickets from National Gallery ticket office* ☎ *661 5133)* were opened in 1911, in a rather heavy-handed Edwardian interpretation of the Georgian style. Each 40-minute tour takes about 15 people, so you may have to wait a while for a group to assemble. Tours can't be booked in advance, but on Saturday morning you can put your name down for one later in the

day. You get to see the Taoiseach's office, the cabinet room, the ceremonial staircase with a stunning stained-glass window designed by Evie Hone (1894–1955) for the 1939 New York Trade Fair, and innumerable fine examples of modern Irish arts and crafts.

Across the road at 24 Upper Merrion St, Mornington House is a Georgian mansion thought to be the birthplace of the duke of Wellington, who was somewhat ashamed of his Irish origins. It's possible that his actual birthplace was Trim in County Meath. The mansion is now part of the very posh Merrion Hotel.

National Library

Flanking the Kildare St entrance to Leinster House is the National Library *(Around St Stephen's Green map;* ☎ *603 0200,* W *www.nli.ie, Kildare St; free; open 10am-9pm Mon, 2pm-5pm Tues-Wed, 10am-5pm Thur-Fri, 10am-1pm Sat),* which was built between 1884 and 1890, at the same time and to a similar design as the National Museum, by Sir Thomas Newenham Deane and his son Sir Thomas Manly Deane. Leinster House, the library and museum were all part of the Royal Dublin Society (formed in 1731), which aimed to improve conditions for poor people and to promote the arts and sciences. The library's extensive collection has many valuable early manuscripts, first editions, maps and other items. The library's reading room featured in James Joyce's *Ulysses.* Temporary displays are often held in the entrance area.

On the second floor is the **Genealogical Office** *(*☎ *603 0200, National Library, Kildare St; open 10am-4.45pm Mon-Fri, 10am-12.30pm Sat)* where you can obtain information on how best to trace your Irish roots. It once conducted the trace for you (at a fee) but now simply points you in the right direction (for free).

Natural History Museum

The Natural History Museum *(Around St Stephen's Green map;* ☎ *677 7444, Merrion St; free; open 10am-5pm Tues-Sat, 2pm-5pm Sun)* has scarcely changed since 1857 when Scottish explorer Dr David Livingstone delivered the opening lecture. In the face of the city's newer high-tech museums, its Victorian charm has been beautifully preserved, making it one of Dublin's more interesting museums. Commonly referred to as the 'dead zoo', the museum's huge and well organised collection numbers about 2,000,000, roughly half of which are insects. That moth-eaten look often afflicting neglected stuffed-animal collections has been kept at bay and children are likely to find it fascinating.

On the ground floor, the collection of skeletons, stuffed animals and the like covers the full range of Irish fauna. It includes three skeletons of the Irish giant deer, which became extinct about 10,000 years ago. On the 1st and 2nd floors are fauna from around the world.

Grafton St & Around

Grafton St was the major traffic artery of south Dublin until it was turned into a pedestrian precinct in 1982. It's now Dublin's fanciest and most colourful shopping centre, with plenty of street life and the city's most entertaining buskers. The street is equally lively after dark, as some of Dublin's most interesting pubs are clustered around it.

Apart from fine shops, such as the Brown Thomas (Around Temple Bar map) department store, which opened in 1848, Grafton St also boasts **Bewley's Oriental Café** *(Around St Stephen's Green map; ☎ 677 6761, 78 Grafton St)*. This branch of the chain has memorabilia upstairs relating to the company's history.

Johnson's Court leads off Grafton St to the elegantly converted **Powerscourt Townhouse shopping centre** *(Around St Stephen's Green map; ☎ 679 4144, 59 South William St)*. Built between 1771 and 1774, this grand house has a balconied courtyard and, following its conversion in 1981, now shelters three levels of shops and restaurants. It was extensively restored between 1998 and 2000. The Powerscourt family's principal residence was Powerscourt House in County Wicklow and this city mansion was soon sold for commercial use. It survived that period in remarkably good condition and in its present incarnation forms a convenient link from Grafton St to the South City Market on South Great George St.

At the College Green end of Grafton St is the modern **statue of Molly Malone** (Around Temple Bar map) of song fame, rendered in such extreme deshabille that she's nicknamed 'the tart with the cart'.

Dublin Civic Museum

Located in the 18th-century Assembly House beside Powerscourt Townhouse shopping centre, Dublin Civic Museum *(Around St Stephen's Green map; ☎ 679 4260, 58 South William St; free; open 10am-6pm Tues-Sat, 11am-2pm Sun)* is a stone's throw from Grafton St. It has changing exhibitions relating to the history of the city. In particular, look out for the head from Nelson's Pillar on O'Connell St, which was toppled by the IRA in 1966. It's worth popping in just to see the architecture.

Mansion House

The Mansion House *(Around St Stephen's Green map; Dawson St; free; not open to the public)* was built in 1710 by Joshua Dawson, after whom the street is named. Only five years later the house was bought as a residence for the Lord Mayor of Dublin. The building's original brick Queen Anne style has all but disappeared behind a stucco facade tacked on in the Victorian era. The building was the site of the 1919 Declaration of Independence.

Next door is the **Royal Irish Academy** *(☎ 676 2570, 19 Dawson St; free; open 10.30am-5pm Mon-Fri)*, whose 18th-century library houses many important documents, including an extensive collection of manuscripts such as the *Táin Bó Cúailnge* (see the boxed text in the Counties Meath & Louth chapter). Also held there is the entire library of 18th-century poet Sir Thomas Moore.

St Stephen's Green & Around

On warm summer days the nine hectares of St Stephen's Green provide a popular lunchtime escape for office workers. The green was originally an expanse of open common land where public whippings, burnings and hangings took place. The green was enclosed

DUBLIN

AROUND ST STEPHEN'S GREEN

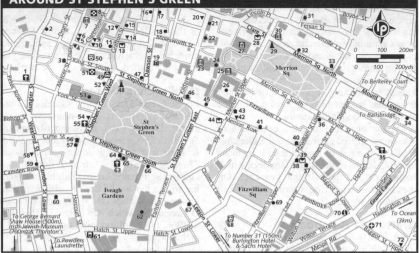

AROUND ST STEPHEN'S GREEN

PLACES TO STAY
3 Mercer Court
33 Merrion Square Manor
37 Latchford's
38 The Fitzwilliam
40 Longfield's
41 Georgian House; Ante Room
43 The Merrion; Restaurant Patrick Guilbaud
46 Méridien Shelbourne Hotel
56 Stephen's Green Hotel
60 Frankies Guesthouse
64 Staunton's on the Green
67 Clarion Stephen's Hall Hotel

PLACES TO EAT
4 Busy Feet & Coco Café
5 Café Metro
6 Velure
9 Rajdoot Tandoori
10 Café Mao
12 Bewley's Oriental Café
14 Gotham Café
20 Dail Bía
42 Cibo's
52 Peacock Alley (Fitzwilliam Hotel)
54 Shanahan's on the Green
58 Modern Green Bar

72 Langkawi

OTHER
1 Whitefriars Carmelite Church
2 All-American Laundrette Company
7 Dublin Civic Museum
8 Powerscourt Townhouse Shopping Centre
11 HMV
13 Post Office
15 Dublin Bookshop
16 Hodges Figgis
17 Waterstone's
18 Dúchas Bookshop
19 Mansion House
21 Alliance Française; Genealogical Office
22 National Library
23 National Museum
24 Leinster House (Irish Parliament)
25 Natural History Museum
26 Government Buildings
27 National Gallery; Fitzer's Café
28 Post Office
29 Oscar Wilde Statue
30 Oscar Wilde House
31 Dublin Corporation

32 Goethe Institut
34 British Council
35 St Stephen's Church
36 29 Lower Fitzwilliam St
39 Post Office
44 Post Office
45 Huguenot Cemetery
47 Aer Lingus
48 Fusiliers' Arch
49 Taxi Rank
50 Gaiety Theatre
51 St Stephen's Green Shopping Centre
53 Royal College of Surgeons
55 Unitarian Church
57 An Siopa Leabhar
59 Whelan's
61 The PoD; The Red Box
62 National Concert Hall
63 Catholic University Church
65 Newman House; The Commons
66 Iveagh House
68 Focus Theatre
69 Italian Cultural Institute
70 Bord Fáilte
71 Baggot St Hospital

by a fence in 1664 when the Dublin Corporation sold off the surrounding land for buildings. A stone wall replaced the fence in 1669 and trees and gravel paths soon followed within the park. By the end of that century restrictions were in force prohibiting buildings of less than two storeys or those constructed of mud and wattle around the green. At the same time, Grafton St, the main route to the green from what was then central Dublin, was upgraded from a 'foule and out of repaire' lane to a Crown causeway.

The fine Georgian buildings round the square date mainly from Dublin's mid-to-late-18th-century Georgian prime. At that time the northern side was known as the Beaux Walk and it's still one of Dublin society's most esteemed meeting places. Some further improvements were made in 1753, with seats being put in place, but in 1814 railings and locked gates were added and an annual fee of one guinea was charged to use the green. This private use continued until 1877 when Sir Arthur Edward Guinness, later Lord Ardilaun, pushed an act through Parliament to once again open the green to the public. He also financed the central park's gardens and ponds, which date from 1880.

The main entrance to the green is through Fusiliers' Arch at the north western corner. Modelled on the Arch of Titus in Rome, the arch commemorates the 212 soldiers of the Royal Dublin Fusiliers who died in the Boer War (1899–1902).

Across the road from the western side of the green are the 1863 Unitarian Church and the Royal College of Surgeons, the latter with one of the finest facades round St Stephen's Green. It was built in 1806 and extended from 1825 to 1827 to the design of William Murray. In the 1916 Easter Rising, the building was occupied by the colourful Countess Markievicz (1868–1927), an Irish nationalist married to a Polish count (for details see the boxed text 'Countess Markievicz' in the Facts about Ireland chapter). The columns still bear bullet marks.

Other notable buildings round the green include the imposing 1867 Méridien Shelbourne Hotel on the northern side, with statues of Nubian princesses and their ankle-fettered slave girls decorating the front. Just beyond the Shelbourne is a small Huguenot cemetery dating from 1693, when many French Huguenots fled here from persecution under Louis XIV.

At Nos 80–81 on the southern side of the green is **Iveagh House**, where the Guinness family once lived; today it is home to the Department of Foreign Affairs, the Irish Foreign Office. Designed by Richard Cassels in 1730, this was his first project in Dublin.

On the southern side is **Newman House** (☎ 475 7255, 85-86 St Stephen's Green; adult/child €3.80/2.50; open June-Aug as part of 40-minute tour: on the hour noon, 2pm-4pm Tues-Fri, 11am-1pm Sat, 2pm-4pm Sun), now part of University College, Dublin. These buildings have some of the finest plasterwork in the city. No 85 was built between 1736 and 1738 by Richard Cassels for Hugh Montgomery MP. The particularly fine plasterwork was by the Swiss stuccodores Paul and Philip Francini (also known as Paolo and Filippo Lafranchini) and can be best appreciated in the wonderfully detailed Apollo Room on the ground floor.

Richard Chapel Whaley MP took possession of No 85 in 1765 but decided to display his wealth by constructing a much grander home next door at No 86. Whaley's son Buck contrived to become an MP while still a teenager and also one of the more notorious members of Dublin's Hell Fire Club. He was also a noted gambler, once walking all the way to Jerusalem to win a bet.

The Catholic University of Ireland, predecessor of University College, Dublin, acquired the building in 1865, and then passed it to the Jesuits. Some of the plasterwork was a little too detailed for Jesuit tastes, however, so cover-ups were prescribed. On the ceiling of the upstairs saloon, previously naked female figures were clothed in what can best be described as furry swimsuits. One survived the restoration process.

The Catholic University named Newman House after its first rector, John Henry Newman. Gerard Manley Hopkins, professor of classics at the college from 1884 until his death in 1889, lived upstairs at No 86. It wasn't until some time after his death that his innovative, if rather depressing, poetry was published. His room is now preserved as it was during his residence. Among former students of the college are James Joyce; Pádraig Pearse, leader of the 1916 Easter Rising; and Eamon de Valera.

Next to Newman House is the **Catholic University Church**, or Newman Chapel, built between 1854 and 1856 with a colourful neo-Byzantine interior that attracted a great deal of criticism at the time. Today it's one of the most fashionable churches in Dublin for weddings.

One of Dublin's most beautiful parks is the landscaped **Iveagh Gardens** *(open dawn-dusk year round)*, directly behind Newman House and reached via Earlsfort Terrace or Clonmel St, just off Harcourt St. The imposing walls give the impression that they are private gardens, but they are one of the nicest places to relax on a summer's day or before a show in the National Concert Hall.

Harcourt St This elegant street, running from the south-western corner of the green, was laid out in 1775. Well known names associated with it include Edward Carson, who was born at No 4 in 1854. As the architect of Northern Irish unionism, he is perhaps not the most popular figure in Dublin's history, even though he sat in Westminster as the Trinity College representative (when the university was an electoral district). His reputation in Dublin was further damaged when he served as the prosecuting attorney during Oscar Wilde's trial for homosexuality. Bram Stoker, author of *Dracula*, lived at No 16, and George Bernard Shaw at No 61. For 99 years from 1859 to 1958 the Dublin to Bray train line used to terminate at Harcourt St Station, which is at the bottom of the road and now a giant bar called Odeon.

Merrion Square

Merrion Square (Around St Stephen's Green map), with its well kept Archbishop Ryan Park and elegant Georgian buildings, dates back to 1762. Round this square you can find some of the best of Dublin's Georgian entrances, with fine doors, peacock fanlights, ornate door knockers and more than a few foot scrapers where gentlemen removed mud from their shoes before venturing indoors.

Oscar Wilde spent much of his youth at 1 North Merrion Square. WB Yeats (1865–1939) lived at 52 Merrion Square East and later, between 1922 and 1928, at 82 Merrion Square South. George (AE) Russell (1867–1935), the 'poet, mystic, painter and cooperator', worked at No 84. Daniel O'Connell (1775–1847) was a resident of No 58 in his later years. The Austrian Erwin Schrödinger (1887–1961), co-winner of the 1933 Nobel Prize for physics, lived at No 65 between 1940 and 1956. Dublin seems to attract the writers of horror stories: Joseph Sheridan Le Fanu (1814–73), who penned the vampire classic *Carmilla*, was a resident of No 70.

The UK Embassy was at 39 Merrion Square East until it was burned out in 1972 in protest against Bloody Sunday in Derry, Northern Ireland. The Architectural Association is at 8 Merrion Square North, a few doors down from the Wilde residence.

The Leinster Lawn at the western end of the square has the 1791 Rutland Fountain and an 18m obelisk honouring the founders of independent Ireland.

Merrion Square hasn't always been merely graceful and affluent, however. During the Famine, soup kitchens were set up in the gardens, which were crowded with starving rural refugees.

Merrion Square East once continued into Lower Fitzwilliam St in the longest unbroken series of Georgian houses anywhere in Europe. In 1961 the Electricity Supply Board (ESB) knocked down 26 of the houses to build an office block.

At the south-eastern corner of Merrion Square the ESB had the decency to preserve one fine old Georgian house, **29 Lower Fitzwilliam St** *(☎ 702 6165,* e *numbertwentynine@mail.esb.ie, 29 Lower Fitzwilliam St; adult/student €3.20/1.25; open 10am-5pm Tues-Sat, 2pm-5pm Sun, closed 2 weeks before Christmas)*. It has been restored to give a good impression of genteel home life in Dublin between 1790 and 1820. A short film on its history is followed by a 30-minute guided tour in groups of nine or less.

Oscar Wilde House The first Georgian residence to be constructed on the square, 1 North Merrion Square, was built in 1762. Today it is owned by the American College Dublin, who have converted part of the house into a **museum** (☎ *662 0281*, **e** *pres ident@amcd.ie, 1 North Merrion Square; admission €2.50; open 10.15am-noon Mon, Wed & Thur)* devoted to Oscar Wilde.

In 1855 the surgeon Sir William Wilde and the poet Lady 'Speranza' Wilde moved here with their one-year-old son Oscar. They occupied the house until 1876. It is likely that Oscar's literary genius was first stimulated by the creative atmosphere of the house, where Lady Wilde hosted the city's most famous (and best frequented) literary salon.

Enthusiasts should check out the **Oscar Wilde statue** at the north-western corner of the square, as it is adorned with the witty one-liners for which Wilde became famous.

Upper Merrion St & Ely Place
Upper Merrion St (Around St Stephen's Green map), which runs south from Merrion Square to St Stephen's Green, was built around 1770. The duke of Wellington was probably born at 24 Upper Merrion St. On the other side of Merrion Row, Merrion St becomes Ely (pronounced e-lie) Place.

John Philpot Curran (1750–1817), a great advocate of Irish liberty, once lived at No 4, as did the novelist George Moore (1852–1933). The house at No 6 was the residence of the earl of Clare. Better known as Black Jack Fitzgibbon (1749–1802), he was a bitter opponent of Irish political aspirations and, in 1794 a mob attempted to storm the house. **Ely House** at No 8 is one of the city's best examples of a Georgian mansion. At one time the surgeon Sir Thornley Stoker (whose brother Bram Stoker wrote *Dracula*) lived here. Oliver St John Gogarty (1878–1957) lived for a time at No 25, but the art gallery of the Royal Hibernian Academy now occupies that position.

Fitzwilliam Square
South of Merrion Square and east of St Stephen's Green, the original and well kept Fitzwilliam Square (Around St Stephen's Green map) is a centre for the Dublin medical profession. Built between 1791 and 1825, it was the smallest and the last of Dublin's great Georgian squares. It's also the only square where the central garden is still the private domain of residents of the square. William Dargan (1799–1861), railway pioneer and founder of the National Gallery, lived at No 2, and Jack B Yeats (1871–1957) at No 18. Look out for the attractive 18th- and 19th-century coal-hole covers. The square is a night-time favourite for women practising the world's oldest profession.

Other South Dublin Churches
Next to the popular Avalon House backpackers hostel, the **Whitefriars Carmelite Church** *(Around St Stephen's Green map; ☎ 475 8821, 56 Aungier St; free; open 8am-6.30pm Mon & Wed-Fri, to 9.30pm Tues, 7pm Sat, 7.30pm Sun, 9.30am-1pm bank holidays)* stands on the site of the Whitefriars Carmelite monastery. The monastery was founded in 1278 but, like other monasteries, was suppressed by Henry VIII in 1537 and had all its lands and wealth seized by the Crown. Eventually the Carmelites returned to their former church and re-established it, dedicating the new building in 1827.

In the north-eastern corner of the church, the 16th-century Flemish oak statue of the Virgin and Child escaped destruction during the Reformation; it probably once belonged to St Mary's Abbey in north Dublin. The altar contains the remains of St Valentine, of St Valentine's Day fame, donated to the church in 1835 by Pope Gregory XVI.

Built in 1824 in Greek Revival style, **St Stephen's Church** *(Around St Stephen's Green map; ☎ 288 0663, Upper Mount St; free; open for services only 11am Sun & 11.30am Wed year round and 11am Fri July-Aug)*, complete with cupola, is at the far end of Upper Mount St from Merrion Square and has been converted into business units. Because of its appearance, it was nicknamed the 'peppercanister church'.

Other South Dublin Museums
Noted playwright George Bernard Shaw was born in Dublin in what is now home to

the **George Bernard Shaw House** *(Around St Stephen's Green map;* ☎ *475 0854, 33 Synge St; bus No 16, 19, 122 from Trinity College; adult/concession €5.10/3.80; open 10am-1pm & 2pm-5pm Mon-Sat, from 11am Sun Easter-Oct)* exhibition, just north of the Grand Canal. Note that it's possible to buy a combination ticket that also gives you access to the Dublin Writers' Museum and James Joyce Museum in Sandycove.

Located in an old synagogue, the **Irish-Jewish Museum** *(Around St Stephen's Green map;* ☎ *453 1797, 4 Walworth Rd; bus No 16, 19 & 122 from Trinity College; free; open 11am-3.30pm Tues, Thur & Sun May-Sept; 10.30am-2.30pm Sun only Oct-Apr)* was opened in 1985 by the then Israeli president, Chaim Herzog, who was actually born in Belfast. Dublin's small but culturally important Jewish population is remembered through photographs, paintings, certificates, books and other memorabilia.

NORTH OF THE LIFFEY

Though south Dublin has the lion's share of the city's tourist attractions, there are still many reasons to head across the Liffey.

Custom House

The Custom House, James Gandon's first great building, was constructed between 1781 and 1791 just past Eden Quay, in spite of opposition from city merchants and dock workers at the original Custom House, upriver in Temple Bar.

In 1921, during the independence struggle, the Custom House was set alight and completely gutted in a fire that burned for five days. The interior was later extensively redesigned, and a further major renovation took place between 1986 and 1988.

The glistening white building stretches for 114m along the Liffey. The best complete view is obtained from across the river, though a close-up inspection of its many fine details is also worthwhile. The building is topped by a copper dome with four clocks. Above that stands a 5m-high statue of Hope.

Beneath the dome is the **Custom House Visitor Centre** *(☎ 878 7660, Custom House Quay; admission €1.30; open from 10am-*12.30pm & 2pm-5.30pm daily mid-Mar-Sept; 10am-5pm Wed-Fri & 2pm-5pm Sun Nov-mid-March)*, which features a small museum on Gandon himself as well as the history of the building.

O'Connell St

O'Connell St is the major thoroughfare of north Dublin and probably the most important and imposing street in the city. It started life in the early 18th century as Drogheda St, named after Viscount Henry Moore, earl of Drogheda. There is still a Henry St, a Moore St and an Earl St nearby. The earl even managed to squeeze in an Of Lane! At that time, Capel St, farther to the west, was the main traffic route, and Drogheda St, lacking a bridge to connect it with south Dublin, was of little importance.

Dublin Corporation have announced a radical overhaul of the street. Over €45 million of public money as well as several hundred million euros of private investment will result in a new plaza in front of the GPO, wider footpaths, a new street linking O'Connell St with Moore St, a major shopping centre and a thorough re-appraisal of the street's building design.

The first project is the **Monument of Light** (aka the Millennium Spire), gracing the spot once occupied by Admiral Nelson. This 120m spire was originally planned to be constructed in time for New Year's Eve 1999, but it was delayed by objections; it wasn't finished until the end of 2001.

Nearby, a **James Joyce statue** stands nonchalantly outside Café Kylemore on the corner of pedestrianised North Earl St. Northside Dubliners commonly refer to it as the 'prick with the stick'. South of the former site of the column is a **fountain statue of Anna Livia**, Joyce's spirit of the Liffey – a 1988 addition to the streetscape.

Farther north is the **statue of Father Theobald Mathew** (1790–1856), the 'apostle of temperance' – a hopeless role in Ireland. This quixotic task, however, also resulted in a Liffey bridge bearing his name. The northern end of the street is completed by the imposing **statue of Charles Stewart Parnell** (1846–91), Home Rule advocate

The Name's the Game

It seems that Dubliners just aren't happy with the names given to the various statues, monuments and other assorted sights throughout the city, and in an effort to convey the deeper significance of what these sights represent, they are compelled to make up humorous rhyming names for them. Silly or not, they are often quite funny, perhaps a sign of how iconoclastic Dubliners really are.

Just next to the northern side of Ha'penny Bridge is a bronze sculpture of two women sitting on a bench with shopping bags at their feet – it's commonly known as 'the hags with the bags'.

At the end of Grafton St is a statue of a woman with a wheelbarrow loaded with cockles and mussels; she is Molly Malone, street vendor extraordinaire and the subject of Dublin's most famous song. But she is in such a serious state of deshabille that she is known as 'the tart with the cart'.

Not content with giving names to statues, Dubliners express their disapproval of buildings they consider ugly with rhyming names. Consequently, an unappealing apartment complex above The Oak bar on Dame St is 'the yoke on The Oak', and the rather box-like Waterways Visitor Centre in the docklands area is – you guessed it – 'the box on the docks'.

One of the funnier names was given to a well intentioned but ill-advised plan to place a luminous millennium clock in the Liffey underneath the Ha'penny Bridge. It would count down to the end of the century and people would see it from down the river; quite effective, you might think. But the problem was that you couldn't see the luminous numbers due to the dirt in the Liffey, and so 'the time in the slime' was removed.

Before Dublin's newest monument was even built (a 130m-high spire to replace Nelson's Pillar known as the Monument of Light) Dublin's wags had already taken to calling it 'the skewer by the sewer', 'the stiletto in the ghetto' and, in a macabre reference to the area's drug problem, 'the biggest needle in O'Connell St'.

Just across the street from the GPO on O'Connell St is a small statue of James Joyce, his head slightly cocked, his hand leaning on a walking stick. So how do Dubliners chose to remember their greatest writer? As 'the prick with the stick'. Joyce certainly loved his rhyming word play, so we're *almost* sure he would have smiled.

The best names of all are reserved for the Anna Livia statue on O'Connell St. Joyce enthusiasts will know that the author gave the Liffey a woman's personality and name, Anna Livia, and the statue of a woman lying in water was designed and built in tribute. The problem is that it's an ugly statue and the locals don't really like it, so 'the floozy in the Jacuzzi' and 'the hooer in the sewer' were coined. And it doesn't end there. Modern medicine has provided the latest name, which describes the small waterfall at the back of Anna Livia's head that drips water over her suggestively prone body 'Viagra Falls'.

and victim of Irish morality. Just to the west of O'Connell St is an energetic and colourful **open-air market** *(Moore St; open 8am-6pm Mon-Sat)*.

General Post Office

The GPO building *(☎ 705 7000,* **W** *www .anpost.ie, O'Connell St; open 8am-8pm Mon-Sat, 10am-6.30pm Sun & holidays)* on O'Connell St is an important landmark physically and historically. The building, designed by Francis Johnston and opened in

1818, was the focus for the 1916 Easter Rising when Pádraig Pearse, James Connolly and the other leaders read their proclamation from the front steps. In the subsequent siege the building was burned out. The facade is still pockmarked from the 1916 clash and from further damage wrought at the start of the Civil War in 1922. The GPO wasn't reopened until 1929. Its central role in the history of independent Ireland has made it a prime site for everything from official parades to personal protests.

Abbey Theatre

Opened in 1904, Abbey Theatre (☎ 878 7222, W www.abbeytheatre.ie, Lower Abbey St), on the corner of Marlborough and Lower Abbey Sts, is just north of the Liffey. Here the Irish National Theatre Society soon made a name not only for playwrights such as JM Synge and Sean O'Casey but also for Irish acting ability and theatrical presentation. The 1907 premiere of JM Synge's The Playboy of the Western World brought a storm of protest from theatregoers, and Sean O'Casey's The Plough and the Stars prompted a similar reaction in 1926. On the latter occasion WB Yeats himself came on stage after the performance to tick the audience off!

The original theatre burned down in 1951. It took 15 years to come up with a replacement and this dull building fails to live up to its famous name or the company's continuing reputation. Thankfully, plans are afoot to either completely refurbish the building or – more likely – to move it completely down to the Grand Canal Docks on the river's southern side. The smaller Peacock Theatre at the same location presents new and experimental works.

St Mary's Pro-Cathedral

On the corner of Marlborough and Cathedral Sts, just east of O'Connell St, is Dublin's most important Catholic church (☎ 874 5441, Marlborough St; free; open 8am-6.30pm). It was built between 1816 and 1825. Unfortunately, the cramped Marlborough St location makes it difficult to stand back far enough to admire the front with its six Doric columns, modelled on the Temple of Theseus in Athens.

The 1814 competition for the church's design was won by John Sweetman, a former owner of Sweetman's Brewery. And who organised the competition? Why William Sweetman, John Sweetman's brother. And did John Sweetman design it himself? Well, possibly not. He was living in Paris at the time and may have bought the plans from a French architect who designed the remarkably similar Notre Dame de Lorette in northern France. The only clue as to the church's architect is in the ledger, which lists the builder as 'Mr P'. And what does 'pro' mean? It's not clear, but it implies something like 'unofficial cathedral'.

You wouldn't know it now, but before Irish independence this area was once the busiest red-light district in Europe (thanks to the British garrison); it was known as Monto and featured in Joyce's Ulysses as Nighttown.

Parnell Square

The principal squares of north Dublin are poor relations of the great squares south of the Liffey, though they do have their points of interest. Parnell Square's northern side was built on land acquired in the mid-18th century by Dr Bartholomew Mosse, founder of the Rotunda Hospital, and was originally named Palace Row. The terrace was laid out in 1755 and Lord Charlemont bought the land for his home at No 22 in 1762. Charlemont's home was designed by Sir William Chambers, who also designed Lord Charlemont's extraordinary Casino at Marino (see later in the chapter). Today the building houses the Municipal Gallery of Modern Art. The street was completed in 1769 and the gardens were renamed Rutland Square in 1786, before acquiring their current name.

In 1966 the northern slice of the square was turned into a **Garden of Remembrance** for the 50th anniversary of the 1916 Easter Rising. Its centrepiece is a sculpture by Oisin Kelly depicting the myth of the children of Lir, who were turned into swans by their wicked stepmother.

There are some fine, though rather rundown, Georgian houses on the eastern side of the square. Oliver St John Gogarty, immortalised as Buck Mulligan in Joyce's Ulysses, was born at No 5 in 1878.

Rotunda Hospital In 1757, Dr Bartholomew Mosse opened the Rotunda Hospital, the first maternity hospital in Ireland or Britain. It was built at a time when Dublin's burgeoning urban population suffered horrific levels of infant mortality. The hospital shares its basic design with Leinster House because Richard Cassels reused the floorplan as an economy measure. To his Leinster House design Cassels added a three-storey tower, which Mosse had intended to use as a lookout to raise funds for the hospital's operation. The Rotunda Assembly Hall, now occupied by the Ambassador Cinema, was built as an adjunct to the hospital as another fundraiser. The Rotunda Chapel is over the main entrance of the hospital and was built in 1758 with superb coloured plasterwork by Bartholomew Cramillion.

The Rotunda Hospital still functions as a maternity hospital. The **Patrick Conway pub** *(Dublin's Pubs, Bars & Clubs map;* ☎ *873 2687, 70 Parnell St),* opposite the hospital, dates from 1745 and has been hosting expectant fathers since the day the hospital opened.

Gate Theatre In the south-eastern corner of Parnell Square is the Gate Theatre *(*☎ *874 4045, Parnell Square East),* opened in 1929 by Micheál MacLiammóir and Hilton Edwards (the actual building dates from 1784–86, when it was constructed as part of the Rotunda Hospital complex). MacLiammóir continued to act at his theatre until 1975, when he retired at the age of 76 after making his 1384th performance of the one-man show *The Importance of Being Oscar* (Oscar being Oscar Wilde, of course). The Gate Theatre was the stage for Orson Welles' first professional appearance and also featured James Mason early in his career.

Today it features a more exciting brand of theatre than its longtime rival, the Abbey, with a worthwhile mix of classic plays from Ireland and abroad, and more modern, experimental work.

Hugh Lane Municipal Gallery of Modern Art The Municipal Gallery of Modern Art *(*☎ *874 1903,* e *exhibitions@hughlane .ie,* w *www.hughlane.ie, 22 North Parnell Square; free to permanent collection, €6.35 to special exhibitions; open 9.30am-6pm Tues-Thur, 9.30am-5pm Fri-Sat, 11am-5pm Sun Sept-Mar; until 8pm Thur Apr-Aug)* has a fine collection of work by French Impressionists and by 20th-century Irish artists.

The gallery was founded in 1908 and moved to its present location in Charlemont House in 1933. The gallery was established by wealthy Sir Hugh Lane with no help from the government. He died in the 1915 sinking of the *Lusitania*, which was torpedoed off the southern coast of Ireland by a German U-boat. The lack of official funding was the subject of one of WB Yeats' most vitriolic poems *September 1913*. The Lane Bequest pictures, which formed the nucleus of the gallery, were the subject of a dispute over Lane's will between the gallery and the National Gallery in London. A settlement was finally reached in 1959, splitting the collection.

From November 1999 the gallery has displayed Manet's *Eva Gonzales*, Pissarro's *Printemps*, Berthe Morisot's *Jour d'Eté* and the most important painting of the collection, Renoir's *Les Parapluies*.

In June 2001 the gallery unveiled its most recent addition to its permanent collection, a recreation of Francis Bacon's London studio, complete with all of the painter's personal effects.

Dublin Writers' Museum This museum *(*☎ *872 2077, 18 North Parnell Square; adult/student/child €5.10/3.80/2.50, includes taped guides in English and other languages; open 10am-5.30pm Mon-Sat, from noon Sun),* celebrates the city's long and continuing history as a literary centre. The Gallery of Writers upstairs houses busts and portraits of some of Ireland's most famous writers; their letters, photographs and first editions are downstairs. The museum also has a bookshop and the *Chapter One* restaurant. Admission includes taped guides with readings from relevant texts in English and other languages. If you plan to visit the James Joyce Museum (see Sandycove in the Around Dublin section) and George Bernard Shaw House (see Other South Dublin Museums in the earlier South of the Liffey section), bear in mind that a combined ticket is cheaper than three separate ones.

While the museum concerns itself primarily with dead authors, next door at No 19 the Irish Writers' Centre provides a meeting and working place for their living successors.

DUBLIN

Great Denmark St

From the corner of Parnell Square, Great Denmark St runs north-east to Mountjoy Square, passing Belvedere House at No 6. The construction of this house began in 1775 and it has been used as the Jesuit **Belvedere College** (*6 Great Denmark St; closed to public*) since 1841. James Joyce was a student here between 1893 and 1898 and describes it in *A Portrait of the Artist as a Young Man*. The building is renowned for its magnificent plasterwork.

Mountjoy Square

Built between 1792 and 1818, Mountjoy Square was a fashionable and affluent centre at the height of the Protestant Ascendancy. Today it's a run-down symbol of north Dublin's urban decay, though redevelopment is beginning to happen.

Legends relate that this was where Brian Ború pitched his tent at the Battle of Clontarf in 1014. Residents of the square have included Sean O'Casey, who set his play *The Shadow of a Gunman* here, though he referred to it as Hilljoy Square. As a child James Joyce lived just off the square at 14 Fitzgibbon St.

St Mary's Abbey

Despite the intriguing history of St Mary's Abbey, there's little to see, and even finding the abbey is tricky: it's just west of Capel St in Meeting House Lane, which runs off a street named Mary's Abbey.

When the abbey was founded in 1139 by Benedictine monks this was a rural location, far from the temptations of city life. In 1147, it was taken over by the Cistercians. Until its suppression in the mid-16th century this was the most important monastery within English-controlled Ireland. The monastery's property was confiscated by Henry VIII in 1537; it turned out to be the most valuable in all of Ireland, at a total of £537 sterling. Mellifont Abbey, north of Dublin, came in second at £352 sterling, but no other Irish monastery was worth over £100 sterling.

By the end of the 16th century the abbey was virtually derelict. In 1676, stones from the abbey were used to construct Essex Bridge. Using it as a quarry soon removed all visible traces of the monastery and not until comparatively recently were the remaining fragments rediscovered.

The **chapter house** (*Around Temple Bar map;* ☎ *872 1490, Meeting House Lane; adult/student €1.25/0.60; open 10am-5pm Wed & Sun mid-June-mid-Sept*), where monks gathered after morning mass, is the only surviving part of the abbey. The floor level in the abbey is 2m below street level – a clear indication of the changes wrought over eight centuries.

James Joyce Cultural Centre

This house was were Denis Maginni taught dance in the front room early this century. Hardly remarkable, but the fact that he and his home featured several times in *Ulysses* led Joycean scholar and leading gay activist Senator David Norris to take over the house in 1982. He proceeded to restore the house and convert it into a centre for the study of Joyce and his books (☎ *878 8547,* e *joycean@iol.ie,* w *www.jamesjoyce.ie, 35 North Great George's St; adult/student €3.80/2.50; open 9.30am-5pm Mon-Sat, 12.30pm-5pm Sun; one-hour tours of north Dublin, adult/student €5.70/5.10, 2.15pm Mon-Sat*).

Visitors see the room were Maginni taught and a collection of pictures of the 17 different Dublin homes occupied by the nomadic Joyce family and the real individuals fictionalised in the books. Some of the fine plaster ceilings are restored originals, others careful reproductions of Michael Stapleton's designs. For information on James Joyce-related walking tours departing from the centre, see Walking Tours under Organised Tours later in the chapter.

St Michan's Church

Named after a Danish saint, St Michan's Church (☎ *872 4154, Lower Church St; adult/student/senior €2.50/1.90/0.65; open 10am-12.45pm & 2pm-4.45pm Mon-Fri, mornings only Sat*), near the Four Courts, was founded by Danes in 1095, though there's little trace of the original. The battlement tower dates from the 15th century, but otherwise the church was rebuilt in the late 17th century, considerably restored in the early 19th century and again after the Civil War, during which it had been damaged.

The church contains a 1724 organ which Handel may have played for the first performance of his *Messiah*. The organ case is distinguished by a fine oak carving of 17 entwined musical instruments on its front. A skull on the floor on one side of the altar is said to represent Oliver Cromwell. On the opposite side, a penitent's chair was where 'open and notoriously naughty livers' did public penance. But the church's main 'attraction' lies in the subterranean crypt, where bodies have been preserved to varying degrees, not by mummification but by the constant dry atmosphere. You can visit the church any time during opening hours, but you can see the crypt only as part of a tour. Tours are organised on an ad hoc basis depending on how many people are there.

Smithfield

Dublin's newest hotspot is the area in and around Smithfield Square, bordered to the east by Church St, to the west by Blackhall Place, to the north by North King St and to the south by Arran Quay. At the centre of this major development is the old hay, straw, cattle and horse Smithfield Market, which has now been replaced by a magnificent new civic space. The flagship of the Historic Area Rejuvenation Project (HARP) whose brief is to restore the north-west inner city, it features a pedestrianised square bordered on one side by 26m-high gas lighting masts, each with a 2m-high flame. The old cobblestones were removed, cleaned up and put back along with new granite slabs that give the whole square a thoroughly modern feel without sacrificing its traditional beauty.

Bordering the eastern side of the square are two of the city's best new museums: Ceol and, a little farther off, the Old Jameson Distillery. In keeping with its traditional past, the old **fruit and vegetable market** still plies a healthy wholesale trade on the square's western side. Although far from complete, Smithfield is expected to challenge the tourist attentions so far commanded by Temple Bar,

though developers are keen to avoid the kind of crass commercialism that has plagued the area south of the Liffey. Commercial interests, however, have not been entirely ignored and, in 2001, the first of many open-air concerts was held in Smithfield Square, featuring an impressive array of Irish and international artists headlined by the now-legendary Buena Vista Social Club.

Ceol This ultra-modern, interactive museum (☎ *817 3820,* ⓔ *info@ceol.ie,* ⓦ *www.ceol .ie, Smithfield Village; adult/student €6.35/ 5.10; open 10am-6pm Mon-Sat, 11am-6pm Sun)* in the Chief O'Neills complex is devoted entirely to *ceol* (music). The music in question is the Irish traditional kind. If that sounds a little limited, it is anything but.

The museum's interactive displays cover virtually every aspect of the entire tradition of Irish music both sung and instrumental from the Middle Ages, through the early attempts to catalogue the thousands of jigs, reels and hornpipes in the 18th century, and on to the explosion of the distinctly Irish sound on the international stage after WWII.

The wonderful audiovisuals detail the music's unique characteristics and sounds, with particular emphasis on the four main instruments: *uilleann* (elbow) pipes, fiddle, flute, and button accordion. Of particular interest is the room devoted to song, especially the *sean nós* style, an ancient form that involves the telling of a story through song punctuated by plenty of grace notes. There are many video performances by some of Ireland's best players. Kids will enjoy the game of musical twister, in which floor pads light up as a tune is played and the listener is invited to re-create the tune by standing on the pads.

The complex also includes a bar and a hotel (see Places to Stay and Trendy under Entertainment later in the chapter).

The Chimney As part of the ongoing development of the Smithfield area, an old distillery chimney (nicknamed 'the flue with the view'), built by Jameson's in 1895, has been converted into Dublin's first and only 360-degree observation tower (☎ *817 3820,*

Smithfield Village; adult/student €6.35/5.10).
A glass lift shuttles visitors to the top, where,
behind the safety of glass, you can see the entire city, the sea and the mountains to the
south. On a clear day, it makes for some nice
photo opportunities, but frankly Dublin's lack
of panoramic beauty (the city looks like a gigantic building site punctuated by green copper domes) makes the admission fee seem
rather excessive. You're better off seeing the
city from the Gravity Bar at the top of the
Guinness Storehouse (see Outside the Centre
later in this chapter): it's more expensive, but
at least you get to see the exhibits and enjoy
a lovely pint while you stare out the window.

Old Jameson Distillery
Where does Irish whiskey get its particular
colour and smooth bouquet from? While
most people have heard the term 'single
malt', how many can actually tell you what
it is? These are just some of the secrets you
can learn at the Old Jameson Distillery
(☎ 807 2355, Bow St; admission by tour
only, adult/student €6.30/3.80; available
every 30 minutes 10am-5.30pm), a museum
devoted to Irish whiskey just north of St
Michan's Church. It opened in 1997 after a
£7 million renovation of the old Jameson
distillery, which produced Ireland's best-
loved whiskey from 1791 until its closure in
1966 (when Jameson, along with the other
main Irish producers, united to form Irish
Distillers, with an ultra-modern distillery in
Midleton, County Cork).

The compulsory guided tour is well worth
it and kicks off with a short film, after which
visitors are led through a re-creation of the
old factory, where the guide explains the entire process of whiskey distilling from grain
to bottle. Visitors are then invited into the
Jameson Bar, where they are offered a complimentary glass of 'the hard stuff' (as it is
referred to in Dublin vernacular). The tour
finishes with a surprise competition, but
you'll have to visit to find out what it is!
There's also a restaurant on the premises.

King's Inns & Henrietta St
King's Inns, home of the Dublin legal profession, is on Constitution Hill and Henri-

etta St. This classical building (Henrietta St;
open only to members & their guests) by
James Gandon suffered many delays between its design in 1795 and its completion
in 1817. Several other architects lent a hand
along the way, including Francis Johnston,
who added the cupola.

Henrietta St, along the southern side of
the building, was Dublin's first Georgian
street and has buildings dating from 1720
but is unfortunately now in a state of disre-
pair. These early Georgian mansions were
large and varied in style. For a time Henrietta St rejoiced in the name Primate's Hill,
as the archbishop of Armagh and other high
church officials lived there. Luke Gardiner,
who was responsible for so much of the
early development of Georgian north Dublin, lived at 10 Henrietta St.

Arbour Hill Cemetery
West of the Old Jameson Distillery is a
small cemetery (Arbour Hill; free; open
9am-4.30pm Mon-Sat, 9.30am-noon Sun)
that is the final resting place of all 14 of the
executed leaders of the 1916 Easter Rising,
including Pádraig Pearse and James Connolly. The burial ground is plain, with the
14 names inscribed in stone. Beside the
graves is a cenotaph with the Easter Proclamation.

Four Courts
On Inns Quay beside the river the extensive
Four Courts (☎ 872 5555, Inn's Quay; free),
with its 130m-long facade was one of James
Gandon's (1743–1823) masterpieces. James
Gandon was 18th-century Dublin's pre-
eminent architect. The Custom House, King's
Inns and some elements of the Parliament
building (now the Bank of Ireland) are also
among his masterpieces. Construction on the
Four Courts began in 1786, soon engulfing
the Public Offices (built a short time previously at the western end of the same site),
and continued until 1802. By then it included
a Corinthian-columned central block connected to flanking wings with enclosed quad-
rangles. The ensemble is topped by a diverse
collection of statuary. The original four
courts – Exchequer, Common Pleas, King's

Bench and Chancery – branch off the central rotunda.

The 1224 Dominican Convent of St Saviour formerly stood on the site, but was replaced first by the King's Inns and then by the present building. The last Parliament of James II was held here in 1689. The Four Courts played a brief role in the 1916 Easter Rising, without suffering damage, but the events of 1922 were not so kind. When anti-Treaty forces seized the building and refused to leave, it was shelled from across the river. As the occupiers retreated, the building was set on fire and many irreplaceable early records were burned. This event sparked off the Civil War. The building wasn't restored until 1932.

Visitors are allowed to wander through, but not to enter courts or other restricted areas. In the lobby of the central rotunda you'll see bewigged barristers conferring and police officers handcuffed to their charges waiting to enter court.

Other North Dublin Churches
The soaring spire of **Abbey Presbyterian Church** *(Cnr Frederick St & North Parnell Square; free; open noon-7pm Sun only)* is a convenient landmark. Dating from 1864, the church was financed by the Scottish grocery and brewery magnate Alex Findlater and is often referred to as Findlater's Church.

St George's Church *(Hardwicke Place; closed to public)*, off Temple St, was built by Francis Johnston from 1802 in Greek Ionic style and has a 60m-high steeple modelled on that of St Martin-in-the-Fields in London. The church's bells were added in 1836. Although this was one of Johnston's finest works and the duke of Wellington was married here, the church is now used as a nightclub called the Temple Theatre (see Clubs under Entertainment later in the chapter).

Croke Park & GAA Museum
About 500m north-east of Mountjoy Square is the home of the Gaelic Athletic Association (GAA; the governing body of Ireland's national sports) and the country's largest stadium, Croke Park, where the All-Ireland finals are played in September (see Specta-

tor Sports later in this chapter). The history of Gaelic sports is the theme of a new museum *(☎ 855 8176, New Stand, Croke Park, Clonliffe Rd; bus No 3, 11, 11A, 16, 16A & 123 from O'Connell St; adult/student/child €3.80/2.55/1.90; open 9.30am-5pm daily May-Sept; 10am-5pm Tues-Sat & noon-4pm Sun Oct-Apr)* that is a must for sporting enthusiasts. You can also test your skills at both Gaelic football and hurling.

OUTSIDE THE CENTRE
There's still much more to see in Dublin. To the west are the Guinness Brewery in the colourful Liberties area, Kilmainham Jail and Phoenix Park. To the north and northeast are the Royal Canal, Prospect Cemetery, Botanic Gardens, the Casino at Marino and Clontarf. To the south and south east are the Grand Canal, Ballsbridge and the Royal Dublin Society Showground.

Guinness Brewery & Guinness Storehouse
West of St Audoen's churches, Thomas St metamorphoses into James's St in the area of Dublin known as the Liberties. Along James's St stretches the historic St James's Gate Guinness Brewery, where 2.5 million pints of stout are brewed daily. From its foundation by Arthur Guinness in 1759, the operation has expanded down to the Liffey and across both sides of the street. It covers 26 hectares and for a time was the largest brewery in the world. The oldest parts of the site are south of James's St; at one time there was a gate spanning the street.

The brewery is far more than just a place where beer is manufactured. It is an intrinsic part of Dublin's history and a key element of the city's identity. Accordingly, the quasi-mythical stature of Guinness is the central theme of the brewery's brand-new museum, the **Guinness Storehouse** *(☎ 408 4800, W www.guinnessstorehouse.com, St James's Gate; bus No 21A, 78 or 78A from Fleet St; adult/student €11.50/7.60; open 9.30am-7pm Mon-Sat, 11am-4.30pm Sun Apr-Sept; 9.30am-5pm Mon-Sat, 11am-5pm Sun Oct-Mar)*. It opened in December 2000 in place of the old – and much smaller –

DUBLIN

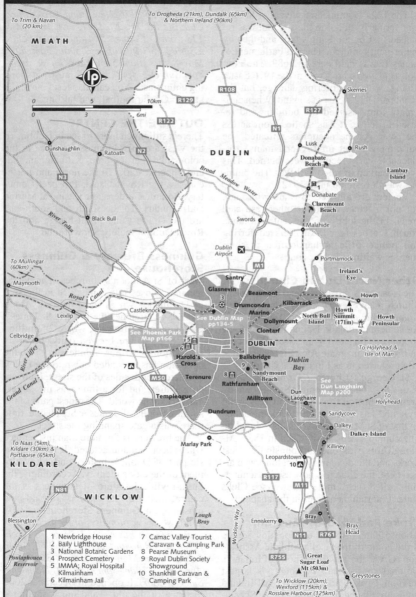

COUNTY DUBLIN

To Trim & Navan
(20 km)

To Drogheda (21km), Dundalk (65km)
& Northern Ireland (90km)

MEATH

R108

R129

R122

N1

0   5   10km
0   3   6mi

Dunshaughlin

Ratoath

N2

DUBLIN

Skerries

R127

Lusk   Rush

Donabate
Beach

N3

River Tolka

Black Bull

Broad Meadow Water

Portrane

Lambay
Island

Donabate

Claremount
Beach

To Mullingar
(60km)

Maynooth

Royal Canal

Leixlip

Celbridge

River Liffey

Swords

Dublin
Airport

M1

Malahide

Portmarnock

Ireland's
Eye

Howth

Santry

Glasnevin

Beaumont

Castleknock

Drumcondra

Kilbarrack

Sutton

Marino

North Bull
Island

Howth
Summit
(171m)

Howth
Peninsular

*See Dublin Map
pp134–5*

3

4

Dollymount

*See Phoenix Park
Map p166*

5

6

Clontarf

DUBLIN

Harold's
Cross

Ballsbridge

*Dublin
Bay*

To Holyhead &
Isle of Man

Grand Canal

7

9

Sandymount
Beach

*See Dun Laoghaire
Map p200*

M50

Terenure

8

Rathfarnham

Milltown

Dun
Laoghaire

To
Holyhead

N7

Templeogue

Dundrum

Sandycove

Dalkey

Dalkey Island

To Naas (5km),
Kildare (30km) &
Portlaoise (65km)

Marlay Park

Killiney

KILDARE

N81

Leopardstown

10

R117

M11

WICKLOW

Blessington

Lough
Bray

Wicklow Way

Enniskerry

Bray

Bray
Head

N11

R761

Poulaphouca
Reservoir

Great
Sugar Loaf
Mt (503m)

R755

Greystones

To Wicklow (20km),
Wexford (115km) &
Rosslare Harbour (125km)

1 Newbridge House	7 Camac Valley Tourist
2 Baily Lighthouse	Caravan & Camping Park
3 National Botanic Gardens	8 Pearse Museum
4 Prospect Cemetery	9 Royal Dublin Society
5 IMMA; Royal Hospital	Showground
Kilmainham	10 Shankhill Caravan &
6 Kilmainham Jail	Camping Park

Guinness Hop Store. It is the only part of the brewery that opens to visitors.

Undoubtedly, this is an impressive building. The exhibition, complete with all the latest interactive gadgets, is interesting enough, tracing the history of the brewery and giving a thumbnail sketch of how the beer is brewed. The main reason for coming here, however, is for the prize at the end of the visit: Dublin's most delicious pint of Guinness, served in the Gravity Bar at the top of the building and complete with a 360-degree panoramic view of Dublin.

Round the corner at No 1 Thomas St, a plaque marks the house where Arthur Guinness (1725–1803) lived. In a yard across the road stands St Patrick's Tower, Europe's tallest smock windmill, which was built around 1757.

IMMA & Royal Hospital Kilmainham

The Irish Museum of Modern Art *(IMMA; County Dublin map; ☎ 612 9900, Military Rd; bus No 24, 79 or 90 from Aston Quay; free; open 10am-5.30pm Tues-Sat, noon-5.30pm Sun)* at the old Royal Hospital Kilmainham is close to Kilmainham Jail. The permanent collection and regular temporary exhibitions display a range of 20th-century Irish and international art.

The Royal Hospital Kilmainham was built between 1680 and 1687 as a home for retired soldiers and continued to fill that role until after Irish independence. At the time of its construction, it was one of the finest buildings in Ireland and there was considerable muttering that it was altogether too good a place for its residents. The building was designed by William Robinson, whose other work included Marsh's Library near St Patrick's Cathedral.

In 2001, a new **heritage itinerary** *(adult/student €3.20/1.25; Tues-Sun June-Sept)*, run in conjunction with Dúchas, was launched to make the most of the building's treasures. Highlights include the Banqueting Hall and the stunning baroque chapel, which has papier-mâché ceilings and a set of exquisite Queen Anne gates. Also worth seeing are the fully restored formal gardens.

Free guided tours *(2.30pm Wed & Fri, 12.15pm Sun)* of the museum's exhibits include a new exhibition space in the restored Deputy Master's House at the north-eastern corner of the gardens. Tours for groups are held Tuesday to Friday (10am, 11.45am, 2.30pm and 4pm) but bookings must be made two weeks in advance. There's a good cafe and bookshop on the grounds.

Kilmainham Jail

Built between 1792 and 1795, Kilmainham Jail *(County Dublin map; ☎ 453 5984, Inchicore Rd; bus No 23, 51, 51A, 78 or 79 from Aston Quay; adult/student & child €4.50/1.90; open 9.30am-6pm daily Apr-Sept; 9.30am-5pm Mon-Fri & 10am-6pm Sun Oct-Mar; last admission 1 hour before closing),* is a solid, grey, threatening building. During each act of Ireland's long, painful path to independence, at least one part of the performance took place at the jail.

The uprisings of 1798, 1803, 1848, 1867 and 1916 ended with the leaders' confinement here. Robert Emmet, Thomas Francis Meagher, Charles Stewart Parnell and the 1916 Easter Rising leaders were all visitors, but it was the executions in 1916 that most deeply etched the jail's name into the Irish consciousness. Of the 15 executions that took place between 3 and 12 May after the rising, 14 were conducted here. As a finale, prisoners from the Civil War struggles were held here from 1922. The jail closed in 1924.

An excellent audiovisual introduction to the building is followed by a thought-provoking tour. Incongruously sitting outside in the yard is the *Asgard*, the ship that successfully ran the British blockade to deliver arms to nationalist forces in 1914. The tour finishes in the gloomy yard where the 1916 executions took place.

Phoenix Park

The 700-plus hectares of Phoenix Park (County Dublin map) make it one of the world's largest city parks, dwarfing Central Park in New York (a mere 337 hectares) and all the London parks – Hampstead Heath is only 324 hectares. There are gardens and lakes, a host of sporting facilities, the second-oldest public zoo in Europe, a visitor centre, a castle, the Garda Síochána (police) Headquarters, various government offices, the residences of the US ambassador and the Irish president, and even a herd of deer.

Lord Ormond turned this land into a park in 1671 but it wasn't opened to the public until 1747 by Lord Chesterfield. 'Phoenix' is actually a corruption of the Irish words for 'clear water', *fionn uisce.* The park played a crucial role in Irish history, as Lord Cavendish, the British chief secretary for Ireland, and his assistant were murdered outside what is now the Irish president's residence in 1882 by an Irish nationalist group called the National Invincibles. Lord Cavendish's home is now called Deerfield and is used as the US ambassador's residence.

Near the Parkgate St entrance to the park is the 63m-high Wellington Monument obelisk. This took from 1817 to 1861 to build, mainly because the duke of Wellington fell from public favour during its con-

struction. Nearby is the People's Garden, dating from 1864, and the bandstand in the Hollow. Behind the zoo, on the edge of the park, the Garda Síochána Headquarters has a small police museum.

In the centre of the park, the **Papal Cross** marks the site where Pope John Paul II preached to 1.25 million people in 1979. The **Phoenix Monument**, erected by Lord Chesterfield in 1747, looks very unphoenix-like and is often referred to as the Eagle Monument. The southern part of the park is given over to a large number of football and hurling pitches and, though they occupy about 200 acres, the area is known as Fifteen Acres. To the west, the rural-looking **Glen Pond** corner of the park is extremely attractive.

Back towards the Parkgate entrance is Magazine Fort, on Thomas' Hill. The fort took from 1734 to 1801 to build and never served any discernible purpose, although it was a target in the 1916 Easter Rising.

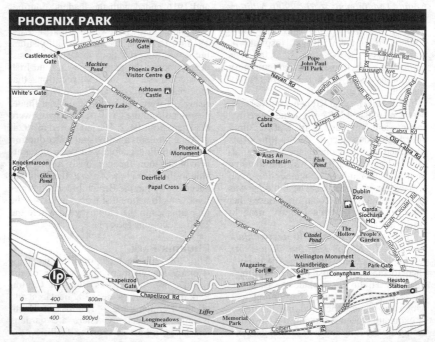

PHOENIX PARK

Dublin Zoo Established in 1830, 12-hectare Dublin Zoo (☎ 677 1425, Ⓦ www .dublinzoo.ie, Phoenix Park; bus No 10 from O'Connell St or 25 & 26 from Abbey St Middle; adult/child/family €8.90/5.30/ 27; open 9.30am-6pm Mon-Sat & 10.30am -6pm Sun May-Sept; 9.30am-4pm Mon-Fri, 9.30am-5pm Sat & 10.30am-5pm Sun Oct-Apr) is one of the oldest in the world, but is mainly of interest to children. It used to be a run-down zoo where depressed animals used to depress visitors, but a substantial facelift has ensured that while hardly a wildlife park, it's a much more pleasant place to stroll around in.

Áras an Uachtaráin The residence of the Irish president was built in 1751 and enlarged in 1782, then again in 1816, on the latter occasion by noted Irish architect Francis Johnston, who added the Ionic portico. From 1782 to 1922 it was the residence of the British viceroys or lord lieutenants. After independence it became the home of Ireland's governor-general until Ireland cut ties with the British Crown and created the office of president in 1937. The Phoenix Park Visitor Centre (see below) runs free one-hour tours of the house every Saturday between 10.30am and 4pm.

Phoenix Park Visitor Centre & Ashtown Castle The Phoenix Park Visitor Centre (☎ 677 0095, Ⓔ phoenixparkvisitor centre@ealga.ie, Phoenix Park; adult/student €2.50/1.25; open 9.30am-5pm Mar & Oct-Nov; to 6pm Apr-Sept; 9.30am-4.30pm Sat & Sun Nov-Mar; last admission 45 minutes before closing) is in what were the stables of the Papal Nuncio. A video outlines the history of the park and there are two floors of exhibits. Visitors are taken on a tour of neighbouring Ashtown Castle, a 17th-century tower house which had been concealed inside the Papal Nuncio until its demolition in 1986; box hedges pick out the ground plan of the old building.

The Royal Canal
Constructed from 1790, by which time the older Grand Canal was already past its

prime, the Royal Canal (off Dublin map), which encircles Dublin to the north, was a commercial failure – but its story is certainly colourful. It was founded by Long John Binns, a Grand Canal director who quit the board because of a supposed insult over his profession as a shoemaker. He established the Royal Canal principally for revenge but it never made money and actually became known as the Shoemaker's Canal. In 1840 the canal was sold to a railway company and tracks still run alongside much of the canal's route through the city.

The Royal Canal towpath makes a relaxing walk through the heart of the city. You can join it beside Newcomen Bridge at North Strand Rd, just north of Connolly Station, and follow it to the suburb of Clonsilla and beyond, over 10km away. The walk is particularly pleasant beyond Binns Bridge in Drumcondra. At the top of Blessington St, near the Dublin International Youth Hostel, a large pond, used when the canal also supplied drinking water to the city, attracts water birds.

National Botanic Gardens
Founded in 1795, the 19.5-hectare National Botanic Gardens (County Dublin map; ☎ 837 7596, Botanic Rd, Glasnevin; bus No 13, 13A or 19 from O'Connell St or bus No 34 or 34A from Middle Abbey St; free; open 9am-6pm Mon-Sat & 11am-6pm Sun Apr-Oct; 10am-4.30pm Mon-Sat & 11am-4.30pm Sun Nov-Mar) are directly north of the centre.

It is flanked to the north by the River Tolka. In the gardens is a series of curvilinear glasshouses dating from 1843 to 1869. The glasshouses were created by Richard Turner, who was also responsible for the glasshouse at Belfast Botanic Gardens and the Palm House in London's Kew Gardens. Within these Victorian masterpieces you will find the latest in botanical technology, including a series of computer-controlled climates reproducing environments of different parts of the world. The gardens also have a palm house. Among the pioneering botanical work conducted here was the first attempt to raise orchids from seed, back in

DUBLIN

1844. Pampas grass and the giant lily were first grown in Europe in these gardens.

Prospect Cemetery

Prospect or Glasnevin Cemetery *(County Dublin map;* ☎ *830 1133, Finglas Rd; bus No 40, 40A or 40B from Parnell St; free; always open),* north-west of the city centre, is the largest in Ireland. It was established in 1832 as a cemetery for Roman Catholics, who faced opposition when they conducted burials in the city's Protestant cemeteries. Many monuments and memorials have staunchly patriotic overtones, with numerous high crosses, shamrocks, harps and other Irish symbols. The single most imposing memorial is the colossal monument to Cardinal McCabe (1837–1921), archbishop of Dublin and primate of Ireland.

A modern replica of a round tower acts as a handy landmark for locating the tomb of Daniel O'Connell, who died in 1847 and was reinterred here in 1869, when the tower was completed. Charles Stewart Parnell's tomb is topped with a huge granite rock. Other notable people buried here include Sir Roger Casement, who was executed for treason by the British in 1916 and whose remains weren't returned to Ireland until 1964; the republican leader Michael Collins, who died in the Civil War; the docker and trade unionist Jim Larkin, a prime force in the 1913 general strike; and the poet Gerard Manley Hopkins.

There's also a poignant 'class' memorial to the men who have starved themselves to death for the cause of Irish freedom over the century, including 10 men in the 1981 H Block hunger strikes.

The most interesting parts of the cemetery are at the south-eastern Prospect Square end. The watchtowers were once used to keep watch for body snatchers. The cemetery is mentioned in *Ulysses* and there are several clues for Joyce enthusiasts to follow.

Casino at Marino

The Casino at Marino *(off Dublin map;* ☎ *833 1618, off Malahide Rd, Marino; bus No 20A, 20B, 27, 27B, 42, 42C or 123 from the city centre, DART to Clontarf Rd; adult/child & student €2.50/1.25; open by* guided tour only, 10am-5pm daily May & Oct; 9.30am-6pm daily June-Sept; noon-4pm Sun & Wed Feb-Mar & Nov; noon-5pm Sun & Thur Apr; closed Jan), just off Malahide Rd, north of the junction with Howth Rd, about 4km north-east of the city centre, is a casino only in the original Italian sense of the word. It's a pleasure house built for the earl of Charlemont in the grounds of Marino House in the mid-18th century. Although Marino House itself was demolished in the 1920s the casino survives as a wonderful folly.

Externally, the building, with its 12 Tuscan columns forming a temple-like facade and its huge entrance doorway, creates the expectation that inside it will be a simple single open space. But the interior is an extravagant convoluted maze: flights of fancy include chimneys for the central heating which are disguised as roof urns, downpipes hidden in columns, carved draperies, ornate fireplaces, beautiful parquet floors constructed of rare woods, and a spacious wine cellar. A variety of statuary adorns the outside but it's the amusing fakes that are most enjoyable. The towering front door is a sham and a much smaller panel opens to reveal the secret interior. The windows have blacked-out panels to hide the fact that the interior is a complex of rooms, not a single chamber.

In 1870 Marino House was sold to the government. The Marino estate followed in 1881 and the casino in 1930, though it was decrepit by then. Restoration is continuing and new planting helps to hide the surrounding houses.

Clontarf & North Bull Island

Clontarf, a bayside suburb 5km north-east of the centre, takes its name from *cluain tarbh* (bull's meadow). In 1014, Brian Ború defeated the Danes at the Battle of Clontarf, though the Irish hero was killed along with his son and grandson. The Normans later erected a castle here which was handed on to the Knights Templar in 1179, rebuilt in 1835 and later converted into a hotel.

The North Bull Wall, extending from Clontarf about 1km into Dublin Bay, was built in 1820 at the suggestion of Captain

William Bligh of HMS *Bounty* mutiny fame, in order to stop Dublin Harbour from silting up. Many birds migrate to North Bull Island from the Arctic in winter, and at times the bird population can reach 40,000. You reach the **interpretative centre** (☎ *833 8341, North Bull Island; free; open 10am-6pm daily*) on the island via the northern causeway, which is a good 1.5km to walk across. Bus Nos 30 and 32X run from Lower Abbey St to the start of the causeway on James Larkin Rd. The Royal Dublin and St Anne's golf courses are also on the island.

The Grand Canal

Built to connect Dublin with the River Shannon, the Grand Canal (off Dublin map) makes a graceful 6km loop round south Dublin. At its eastern end the canal forms a harbour connected with the Liffey at Ringsend. True Dubliners, it's said, are born within the confines of the Grand and Royal Canals. The canal hasn't been used commercially since 1960 but some stretches are attractive and enjoyable to stroll along. The canalside path also makes a fine bicycle ride.

Along the Canal The Grand Canal enters the Liffey at Ringsend, through locks that were built in 1796. The large Grand Canal Dock, flanked by Hanover and Charlotte Quays, is now used by windsurfers and canoeists. At the north-western corner of the dock is Misery Hill, once the site for the public execution of criminals. It was once the practice to bring the corpses of those already hung at Gallows Hill, near Upper Baggot St, to this spot, to be strung up for public display for anything from six to 12 months.

Upstream from the Grand Canal Dock is the **Waterways Visitor Centre** (☎ *677 7510,* e *waterwaysireland@ealga.ie, Grand Canal Quay; DART to Grand Canal Quay; adult/ child & student €2.50/1.25; open 9.30am-5.30pm June-Sept; 12.30pm-5.30pm Wed-Sun Oct & May*). It's run by Dúchas and houses an exhibition and interpretative centre on the construction and operation of Irish canals and waterways. The centre is part of an ongoing (and highly impressive) program of urban renewal that has transformed the area.

A **memorial to the 1916 Easter Rising** can be seen on the Mount St Bridge. A little farther south-west, Baggot St crosses the canal on the 1791 Macartney Bridge.

This lovely stretch of the canal with its grassy, tree-lined banks was a favourite haunt of the poet Patrick Kavanagh. Among his compositions is the hauntingly beautiful *On Raglan Road*, which Van Morrison put to music. One Kavanagh poem requested that he be commemorated by 'a canal bank seat for passers-by' and Kavanagh's friends obliged with a seat beside the lock on the southern side of the canal. A little farther along on the northern side you can sit down by Kavanagh himself, cast in bronze, comfortably lounging on a bench and watching his beloved canal.

Ballsbridge & Donnybrook

South-east of central Dublin, the suburb of Ballsbridge (County Dublin map) was principally laid out between 1830 and 1860. Many streets have British names with a distinctly military flavour. Many embassies, including the US embassy, are in Ballsbridge. It also has some of Dublin's most luxurious B&Bs and several top-end hotels. The main attractions are the Royal Dublin Society Showground and the **Lansdowne Rd rugby stadium**, though **Herbert Park** is also a favourite for sport, walking or just sitting around.

To the south of Ballsbridge is Donnybrook, at one time a village on the banks of the River Dodder. For centuries it was famous for the Donnybrook Fair, which was first held in 1204. By the 19th century it had become a 15-day event centred on horse dealing and was such a scene of drunkenness and sexual debauchery that the increasingly sedate residents of Donnybrook had it banned in 1855.

Royal Dublin Society Showground

The Royal Dublin Society (RDS) Showground *(County Dublin map; ☎ 668 9878, Merrion Rd, Ballsbridge; bus No 7 every 10 minutes from Trinity College),* about 15 minutes by bus from the city centre, is used for various exhibitions throughout the year. The society was founded in 1731 and had its headquarters in a number of well known Dublin buildings, including, from 1814 to 1925, Leinster House. The society was involved in the foundation of the National Museum, Library, Gallery and Botanic Gardens. The most important annual event at the showground is the August **Dublin Horse Show** *(☎ 668 0866 for tickets, Ballsbridge, postal address: Ticket Office, PO Box 121, Ballsbridge, Dublin 4; general admission €7.60, seating €8.90-15.25)*, which includes an international showjumping contest. Ask at the tourist office or consult a listings magazine for other events.

Pearse Museum

Pádraig Pearse was a leader of the 1916 Easter Rising and one of the first to be executed at Kilmainham Jail. St Enda's, the school he established with his brother Willie to further his ideas of Irish language and culture, is now a museum and memorial to the brothers.

The Pearse Museum *(off Dublin map; ☎ 493 4208, e visits@ealga.ie, St Enda's Park; bus No 16 from the city centre; free; open 10am-1pm & 2pm-5.30pm May-Aug; to 5pm Feb-Apr & Sept-Oct; to 4pm Nov-Jan)* is in St Enda's Park (sometimes known as Pearse Brothers Park), at the junction of Grange Rd and Taylor's Lane in Rathfarnham, about 4km south-west of the city centre.

ACTIVITIES
Beaches & Swimming

Dublin is hardly the sort of place to work on your suntan and even a hot Irish summer day is unlikely to raise the water temperature much above freezing. However, there are some pleasant beaches. Many Joyce fans feel compelled to take a dip in Forty Foot Pool at Dun Laoghaire (see Dun Laoghaire under Around Dublin later in the chapter). Sandy beaches near the centre of Dublin include Sutton (11km), Portmarnock (11km), Malahide (11km), Claremount (14km) and Donabate (21km). Although the beach at Sandymount is nothing special, it is only 5km south-east of central Dublin. Take bus No 3 from Fleet St.

There is a sad dearth of good quality

pools in and around Dublin, and only one recently opened Olympic-size pool – and that's closed to nonmembers. Most of the pools in Dublin are small, crowded and not quite hygienic. On the plus side, they don't charge very much for a 40-minute session, usually around €3.20 for adults and €2.20 for children. The best of the lot, at least in terms of convenience to the city centre, is the recently re-opened **Markievicz Leisure Centre** *(Around Temple Bar map; ☎ 672 9121, Townsend St; admission €4.50; open 7am-10pm Mon-Fri, 9am-6pm Sat, 10am-4pm Sun)*. For the admission price you can swim pretty much as long as you like.

ORGANISED TOURS

Many Dublin tours operate only during the summer months, but at that time you can take bus and walking tours.

Bus Tours

Bus Éireann You can book Bus Éireann tours directly at Busáras *(☎ 836 6111)*, through the Bus Éireann desks at the Dublin Bus office, 59 Upper O'Connell St, or at the Dublin Tourism office (Around Temple Bar map), St Andrews' Church, Suffolk St. The full-day tour to Glendalough runs from 10.30am, returning at 5.45pm, daily, April to October (adult/child €26/13); and runs Wednesday, Friday and Sunday only returning at 4.30pm November to March (adult/child €20.50/10.50). The Powerscourt House tour departs at 10am (returning at 5pm) on Tuesday only, June to September (adult/student/child €26/23/13). The Newgrange & the Boyne Valley tour departs at 10am and returns at 5.45pm daily except Friday, May to September and Thursday and Saturday only in April (adult/student/child €26/23/13); and 10am to 4.15pm Thursday and Saturday only, October to December (adult/student/child €20.50/18/10.50).

Dublin Bus Dublin Bus *(☎ 872 0000, w www.dublinbus.ie, 59 Upper O'Connell St)* tours can be booked at its office or at the Bus Éireann counter at Dublin Tourism in St Andrew's Church, Suffolk St. The Dublin City hop-on, hop-off tour operates every 15 minutes between 9.30am and 5pm, and every 30 minutes thereafter until 6.30pm daily, year round. The whole tour lasts around 1¼ hours but your ticket allows you to hop on and off as often as you wish at any of the 16 designated stops. You can rejoin the tour at any time throughout the day. The tour covers all of the city centre's major attractions, and while admission prices to the various sights is not included, your ticket gives you a limited discount at most of the places that charge admission – if you see everything, you'll save something close to €6.50. Tickets cost €10.20 (children half-price).

The very popular Ghost Bus tour runs at 8pm Tuesday to Friday and at 7pm and 9pm at the weekend, year round; it costs €19. The Coast & Castles tour, taking in the Botanic Gardens in Glasnevin, the Casino at Marino, Malahide and Howth, departs at 10am daily, year round and costs €15.50 (children €8).

The South Coast tour brings you to what is grandly dubbed the Irish Riviera – the stretch of coastline between Dun Laoghaire and Killiney. Departures are at 11am and 2pm daily, year round. The tour lasts approximately 3¾ hours and costs €15.50 (children €8).

Mary Gibbons Tours This company (☎ 283 9973) does full-day tours of Powerscourt and Glendalough, leaving from the Dublin Tourism office at 10.45am and returning between 5pm and 5.30pm on Thursday, Saturday and Sunday (€28). It also does a superb Newgrange & Boyne Valley tour that runs from 10.45am to 5.30pm or 6pm on Monday to Wednesday and Friday. It also leaves from the Dublin Tourism office and costs €28.

Wild Coach Tours The award-winning 'wild coach' tours run by Aran Tours (☎ 280 1899, ☒ www.wildcoachtours.com) run to Glendalough (including a short Dublin City tour) at 9.30am daily, returning at 5.30pm and cost €28/25.50 for adults/students & children. The Powerscourt afternoon tour is run from 1.30pm to 6pm daily, and costs €19/16.50. The half-day Castle Tour to Howth and Malahide, with visits to Malahide

Castle and a walk on Howth Head, depart at 9am and return at 1.15pm daily; it costs €19/16.50. All tours have a variety of pick-up points throughout the city; check the point nearest you when booking.

Bike Tours

Established in 2000, *Molly Malone Bike Tours* (☎ 086 604 2608, ☒ www.mollybikes .com) organises four-hour bike tours of the city centre for €21. They run at 11.30am and 4pm daily, May to August and 12.30pm daily from September to mid-October. Apart from providing bikes, they also have rain gear for anyone silly enough to be in Ireland without it. The tours are fairly gentle, with sightseeing stops every 400m and a 45-minute rest.

Walking Tours

Walking tours are a great way to explore this very walkable city. Two-hour *Dublin Footsteps Walking Tours* (☎ 496 0641) depart at 11am and 2.30pm daily from Bewley's Oriental Café, on Grafton St, and explore medieval Dublin or Georgian and literary Dublin. The tour costs €6.50, which includes a coffee or tea.

Historical Tours Run and managed by graduates of Trinity College, *historical tours* (☎ 845 0241) take two hours and depart from the front gates of Trinity College. The walks take place several times daily from mid-May to September and cost €7/5.

The highly recommended *1916 Easter Rising Walk* (☎ 676 2493) departs from the International bar on Wicklow St at 11.30am Monday to Saturday and 1pm on Sunday between April and September. It covers the parts of Dublin that were directly involved in the Easter Rising.

Literary Tours Ninety-minute walking tours of north Dublin, focusing on sites associated with James Joyce, depart from the *James Joyce Cultural Centre* (☎ 878 8547, 35 North Great George's St) at 11am and 2.30pm Monday to Saturday; outside the summer months phone to check departure times. The cost of a tour of the centre and the walk is €5.70.

Bloomsday

Six days after meeting her, the writer James Joyce had his first date with Nora Barnacle, the woman he was to marry, on 16 June 1904. Later, when he came to write his masterpiece *Ulysses*, which describes a single day in the life of Dubliner Leopold Bloom, the date he chose for this latter-day odyssey was 16 June 1904. Now Dublin duly celebrates Bloomsday on 16 June each year, with a range of entertainment, some serious, some less so, at venues all around the city. Serious Bloomsdayers don Edwardian costume for the day.

In general, events are designed to follow Bloom's progress round town. You can kick things off with breakfast either at the **James Joyce Cultural Centre** (☎ *878 8547, 35 North Great George St*) or at the **South Bank Restaurant** (☎ *280 8788, 1 Martello Terrace, Dun Laoghaire*). In both cases, the 'inner organs of beast and fowl' come accompanied by celebratory readings, a fact reflected in the prices.

In the morning, guided tours of Joycean sites usually leave from the GPO, on O'Connell St, and the James Joyce Cultural Centre.

James Joyce, one of Ireland's most revered authors

NICKY CAVEN

Lunchtime activity focuses on **Davy Byrne's** (*Around Temple Bar map; Duke St*), Joyce's 'moral pub', where Bloom paused to dine on a glass of Burgundy and a slice of Gorgonzola (€6.50 at today's prices). Street entertainers are likely to keep you amused as you eat.

In the afternoon, the guided walks are topped up with animated readings from *Ulysses* and Joyce's other books at appropriate sites and times: **Ormond Quay Hotel** (*Around Temple Bar map; Ormond Quay*) at 4pm and **Harrison's** (*Westmoreland St*) later in the day.

Should you have any energy left, you can spin things out to the early hours, perhaps in **Bewley's Oriental Café** (*Around St Stephen's Green map; 78 Grafton St*), where animated performances of Molly Bloom's closing (and at one time controversial) soliloquy take place.

Events also take place in the days leading up to and following Bloomsday. The best source of information about what's on in any particular year is likely to be the James Joyce Cultural Centre, although the free *Event Guide* also publishes outline details in advance. Popular events sell out quickly: advance booking, especially for the breakfast, is essential. You don't have to know anything about Joyce or his books to enjoy the day, although it certainly helps!

The 2¼-hour *Dublin Literary Pub Crawl* (☎ *454 0228*) starts at 7.30pm daily from April to October (with an extra tour at noon on Sunday) from the Duke pub on Duke St, just off Grafton St. The tours operates Thursday to Sunday only the rest of the year. The walk is great fun and costs €9/8 for adults/students, though Guinness consumption can quickly add a few pounds to that figure. The two actors who lead the tour put on a theatrical performance appropriate to the various places and pubs along the way; the pubs chosen vary from night to night. This award-winning tour is very popular, so be sure to get to the pub by 7pm to buy tickets.

Musical Walks The *Dublin Musical Pub Crawl* (☎ *478 0191*, ✉ *info@musicalpubcrawl.com*, 🖥 *www.musicalpubcrawl.com*) leaves from upstairs in Oliver St John Gogarty's pub, Temple Bar, at 7.30pm. It runs daily from April to October (Friday and Saturday only in November and February to March). The focus is on Irish traditional music: two musicians demonstrate the various styles and explain the music's history in a number of pubs in Temple Bar. The 2½-hour tours usually finish in Isolde's Tower pub, at the western end of Temple Bar. Tours cost €9/8 for adults/students & seniors.

In 2002 a new five-hour tour was launched

by these folks, called the Music & Comedy Coach, which is a nightly hop-on, hop-off tour of Dublin's pubs, clubs and restaurants. The on-board entertainment consists of local comics and musicians, and the tour brings you to the more off-the-beaten-track destinations, far from the madding tourists. The tours run 7pm to midnight daily, April to October. Tickets cost €15.50/10.50 for adults/students.

Macabre Tours In recent years there has been a growth of tours that focus on Dublin's more sinister past, both real and invented. Aside from the very popular ghost bus tour run by Dublin Bus (see above), there are a couple of good walking tours worth checking out.

The *Trapeze Theatre Company* (☎ 087 677 1512, W www.ghostwalk.cjb.com) runs the excellent Walk Macabre tour, which is as much a show as a walk through the spooky corners of Georgian Dublin. The tours usually run at 7.30pm by prior arrangement only (maximum 50 people), and depart from St Stephen's Green, in front of Planet Hollywood. It lasts 1¼ hours and costs €7.60.

A favourite tour with visitors to Dublin is the 1½-hour *Zozimus Experience* (☎ 661 8646, e info@zozimus.com, W www.zozimus .com), which leaves from the gates of Dublin Castle at around 9pm daily between May and October (7pm other months) on a tour of Dublin's superstitious and seedy medieval past. The costumed guide recounts stories of murders, great escapes and mythical events. The tour finishes with a macabre surprise that is not for the faint-hearted. Tours must be booked in advance and cost €8.

Carriage Tours

You can pick up a *horse and carriage* with a driver/commentator at the junction of Grafton St and St Stephen's Green. Half-hour tours cost up to €36 and the carriages can take four or five people. Tours of different lengths can be negotiated with the drivers.

SPECIAL EVENTS

For information on Dublin's special events, see Public Holidays & Special Events in the Facts for the Visitor chapter. For information on Bloomsday, 16 June, see the 'Bloomsday' boxed text.

PLACES TO STAY

Finding a place to stay in Dublin will be one of the more important decisions you'll make while you're here, as it will play a part in dictating the kind of time you'll have. If you're only here for the weekend, you'll want to stay as close to the city centre as possible – at the heart of the action. If you're planning a longer visit, the choice becomes less important, but it'll matter nonetheless. If you're lodging in the suburbs, you'll have to plan your excursions carefully. Public transport is slow, inefficient and, more importantly, virtually nonexistent after midnight. That leaves you relying on taxis that can be a nightmare to grab.

Like every other city in the world, the closer you stay to the centre, the more you'll pay, and in Dublin, that can be a lot. The city's renaissance as a tourist magnet has radically changed the accommodation map, with new hotels of varying quality springing up almost weekly. In the face of increased competition, many of Dublin's existing hotels, hostels and B&Bs have undergone a serious makeover, raising standards and improving services and amenities. The result is predictable. Sure, there's plenty more options for where to stay, but you'll pay for it. It is virtually impossible to get a really cheap room in Dublin anymore, and even the city's hostels, once the backbone of dirt-cheap accommodation, have substantially raised their prices. Basically, Dublin is one of Europe's more expensive cities to sleep in.

Another consequence of Dublin's popularity is that finding a bed is pretty tough in any price range, especially between April and September. If you can plan ahead and book your room, it will make life easier. The alternative is to go to one of the Dublin Tourism offices and ask them to book you a room. For €2.50 plus a 10% deposit on the cost of the first night, they'll find you somewhere to stay. Sometimes this may require a great deal of phoning around so it can be money well spent.

Accommodation prices vary according to season, reaching a peak during the main holiday periods and over public holidays. Prices quoted are those for the high season. You can usually get a bed in a hostel for €15 to €25. In a typical B&B the cost per person will be around €45 to €65. More expensive B&Bs or mid-range hotels cost around €57 to €82 per person. Dublin's top hotels cost upwards of €100 per person.

PLACES TO STAY – BUDGET
Camping
There's no convenient central camp site in Dublin. It is illegal (not to mention dangerous) to camp in Phoenix Park.

Shankill Caravan & Camping Park (County Dublin map; ☎ 282 0011, fax 282 0108, e shankillcaravan@eircom.net, Shankill) Bus No 46 from Eden Quay, DART to Shankill. Sites for 2 people €7.60-8.50. This camping ground, with excellent views of the mountains and top-class facilities, is 16km south of the centre on the N11 Wexford Rd.

Camac Valley Tourist Caravan & Camping Park (County Dublin map; ☎ 464 0644, fax 464 0643, e camacmorriscastle@eircom.net, Naas Rd, Clondalkin) Bus No 69 or 69X from city centre. Sites €5.10-5.80 per person. Only 35 minutes by bus from the city centre, this brand new camping ground is spread across several fields with an abundance of facilities.

Hostels
Since there are no conveniently central camp sites in Dublin, budget travellers usually head for one of Dublin's numerous hostels, one operated by An Óige (the Irish Youth Hostel Association), the others independently. They can be heavily booked from late April to late September, but then so is everything else.

An Óige (☎ 830 4555, fax 830 5808, e mailbox@anoige.ie, w www.irelandyha .org) has its office at 61 Mountjoy St, next to the Dublin International hostel; it opens 9.30am to 5.30pm Monday to Friday.

North of the Liffey There's a large number of hostels in the north of the city.

An Óige Dublin International Youth Hostel (☎ 830 1766, fax 830 1600, e dublin international@anoige.ie, 61 Mountjoy St) Dorms €12, private rooms €17 for members of Hostelling International (HI) & An Óige. This well equipped, 460-bed hostel is in a restored and converted old building. To stay here, you must have or hire a sleeping sheet. The hostel is in the run-down northern area of the city centre; security at the hostel is good but keep an eye on your bags in adjacent streets.

Marlborough Hostel (☎ 874 7629, fax 874 5172, e marlboro@internet-ireland.ie, 81-2 Marlborough St) Dorms/doubles from €11.50/12.70 per person. This hostel, next to the Pro-Cathedral, has a TV room, hot showers, lockers and a pleasant garden at the back. The price includes a continental breakfast. There's a good information board in the lobby.

Abbey Court Hostel (Around Temple Bar map; ☎ 878 0700, fax 878 0719, e info@ abbey-court.com, 29 Bachelor's Walk). Dorms/doubles from €15.50/23. For convenience you can't beat this hostel just next to O'Connell Bridge. All rooms are furnished handsomely and there are secure lockers throughout. Breakfast is included.

Litton Lane Hostel (Around Temple Bar map; ☎ 872 8389, fax 872 0039, e litton@ indigo.ie, 2-4 Litton Lane) Dorms €15.25-17.50, doubles €28-32. In a converted recording studio once used by Van Morrison and Sinead O'Connor, this new hostel is central, convenient and extremely comfortable.

Mount Eccles Court Budget Accommodation (☎ 873 0826, fax 878 3554, e info@ eccleshostel.com, 42 North Great George's St) Dorms €12-23, doubles €16.50-30.50. In a renovated Georgian townhouse on one of the northside's most beautiful streets, this place is a great choice if you can get a room. It's relatively new, so everything is still in pristine condition.

Jacob's Inn (☎ 855 5660, fax 855 5664, e jacobs@isaacs.ie, 21-28 Talbot Place) Dorms €12.70-24, doubles €22.30-35.50 per person. All rooms en suite. This hostel is located behind Busáras; there's a restaurant and self-catering kitchen on the premises. It's clean and modern with comfortable rooms and good amenities.

Globetrotter's Tourist Hostel (☎ 873 5893, fax 878 8787, e gtrotter@indigo.ie, 46-48 Lower Gardiner St) Dorms €19 including continental breakfast. With up to 12 people to some dorms there's bound to be a bit of disturbance, but this relaxed and welcoming hostel is a clean, modern place with good security. The breakfasts, in a pleasant dining room overlooking a garden, consist of a wide choice of cereals, juices and pastries.

Abraham House (☎ 855 0600, fax 855 0598, e stay@abraham-house.ie, 82-83 Lower Gardiner St) Dorms €12.70/20.30 in low/high season. Two large Georgian buildings have been joined to create this pleasant hostel at the heart of newly renovated Gardiner St. The dorms are large, airy and extremely well kept.

South of the Liffey There's plenty of hostel accommodation south of the Liffey.

Ashfield House (Around Temple Bar map; ☎ 679 7734, fax 679 0852, e ashfield@ indigo.ie, 19-20 D'Olier St) Dorms €14.60-23, doubles €18-38 per room. Just south of O'Connell Bridge, this relatively new hostel only has one dormitory, but its 25 other rooms include four-bed family rooms as well as doubles. A light continental breakfast is included.

Barnacles Temple Bar House (Around Temple Bar map; ☎ 671 6277, fax 671 6591, e tbh@barnacles.ie, 1 Cecilia St) Dorms/doubles €15.25/32 per person. The more expensive rooms in this place have en-suite bathrooms; self-catering facilities are available.

Brewery Hostel (☎ 453 8600, fax 453 8616, e breweryh@indigo.ie, 22-23 Thomas St) Bus No 68, 68A, 69A or 78A from Dame St. Dorms €12.70-20.50, doubles €19-32 per person. This small hostel, located virtually next door to the Guinness Brewery, has five bedrooms and seven dorms, all en suite. Breakfast is included.

Cobblestones Budget Accommodation (Around Temple Bar map; ☎ 677 5614, e cobblestones@ireland.com, 29 Eustace St) Rooms €15.25-17.80 per person with

breakfast, doubles €41-47. In the lively (and noisy) Temple Bar area, this hostel has no cooking facilities bar a microwave but guests get discounts in the adjoining pizza parlour.

Gogarty's Temple Bar Hostel (Around Temple Bar map; ☎ 671 1822, fax 671 7637, 18-21 Anglesea St) Dorms/doubles from €16.50/22. This popular hostel in the heart of Temple Bar has basic, clean dorms with comfortable wooden bunks. All rooms, including the dorms, are en suite. It's nearly always full so book in advance.

Kinlay House (Around Temple Bar map; ☎ 679 6644, fax 679 7437, e kinlay -dublin@usitworld.com, 2-12 Lord Edward St) Bus No 54A, 68A, 78A or 123. Bed in four-bed dorm €16.50, in better rooms €18.50-32. An institution among the city's hostels, Kinlay House is centrally located beside Christ Church Cathedral and Dublin Castle, but some rooms can suffer from traffic noise. It's big and well equipped, with cooking facilities and a cafe available. Continental breakfast is included.

Student Accommodation
From June to September you can stay in accommodation provided by the city's universities.

Trinity College (Around Temple Bar map; ☎ 608 1177, fax 671 1267, e reservations@tcd.ie, Accommodations Office, Trinity College) B&B €44-57.50 per person. Although it's expensive, the college sometimes has wonderfully positioned accommodation on campus. Rooms are only available from mid-June to the end of September, so be sure to book well in advance.

Mercer Court (Around St Stephen's Green map; ☎ 478 2179, fax 478 0873, e reservations@mercercourt.ie, Mercer St Lower) Doubles & twins €38.10-49.50, 5-bed self-catering apartment €750-876 per week. Owned and run by the Royal College of Surgeons, this is perhaps the best student accommodation option in the city: cheaper than Trinity but just as central, close to Grafton St and St Stephen's Green. The rooms are modern and up to hotel standard. They are available from late June to late September only.

PLACES TO STAY – MID-RANGE

B&Bs

If you're looking for budget accommodation, but want the kind of privacy you're unlikely to find in hostels, then a B&B is your best option. Traditionally the most popular kind of accommodation in Ireland, Dublin's B&Bs have undergone something of a renaissance in recent years, as demands for greater luxury and amenities have forced many B&B owners to renovate, upgrade and – inevitably – raise their prices. Today you'll find two kinds of B&B: the townhouse, the more traditional kind with two or three rooms in someone's home; and the guesthouse, a kind of upmarket, specialist B&B which is more expensive. Though still cheap in comparison to most of the city's hotels, it's unlikely that you'll find any kind of decent room a in townhouse for less than €25 and €40 in a guesthouse. What you're paying for is the kind of attentive service not usually found in hotels, as well as the convivial, more homely atmosphere.

Dublin's B&B street is Gardiner St, just east of O'Connell St. Virtually every house is a B&B, though some are better than others. Thankfully, the street's reputation for late-night danger has receded in the face of urban rejuvenation, though we still advise a modicum of caution at night, particularly on Upper Gardiner St past Mountjoy Square.

Farther out, you can find a better price and quality combination north of the centre at Clontarf or in the seaside suburbs of Dun Laoghaire or Howth. The Ballsbridge area, just south-east of the centre, offers quality and convenience, but you pay more for the combination. Other suburbs to try are Sandymount (immediately east of Ballsbridge) and Drumcondra (north of the centre toward the airport).

Gardiner St & Around There is a collection of places on Lower Gardiner St, near the bus and train stations, and another group on Upper Gardiner St, farther north near Mountjoy Square. Other B&Bs are in the streets around it.

Fatima House (off Dublin map; ☎ 874 5410, fax 878 1734, e hotels@indigo.ie, 17 Upper Gardiner St) Singles €23-38, doubles €24-37. One of the cheapest B&Bs on the street, its rooms are slightly shabby and its comforts a little bare. The owners are friendly and for the price you won't find much better.

Marian Guest House (off Dublin map; ☎ 874 4129, 21 Upper Gardiner St) Rooms from €25 per person, €3 supplement for single occupancy. This tiny guesthouse has six rooms, so the attention of the staff is excellent, even if the rooms are fairly basic. On the plus side, the breakfast is excellent.

Clifden Guesthouse (☎ 874 6364, fax 874 6122, e bnb@indigo.ie, W www.clifdenhouse.com, 32 Gardiner Place) Singles €38-76, doubles €32-70 per person. It's expensive, but it's a beautifully refurbished Georgian house with gorgeous rooms and plenty of amenities. A nice touch is the free parking, even after you've checked out!

Harvey's Guesthouse (off Dublin map; ☎ 874 8384, fax 874 5510, W www.harveys guesthouse.com, 11 Upper Gardiner St) Singles/doubles/quads with bathroom €45 /89/152.50. Spread across two attached houses, this guesthouse just north of Mountjoy Square has comfortable rooms with

---

Gay & Lesbian-Friendly B&Bs

Although most of the city's hotels wouldn't bat an eyelid if same-sex couples checked in, the same cannot be said of many of the city's B&Bs. There are, thankfully, a couple that actively pursue a gay clientele.

Frankies Guesthouse (Around St Stephen's Green map; ☎/fax 478 3087 e frankies guesthouse@ireland.com, 8 Camden Place) Singles/doubles from €44/77. This is a comfortable B&B with pleasant rooms equipped with TV and tea and coffee facilities.

Inn on the Liffey (☎ 677 0828, fax 872 4165, e innontheliffey@hotmail.com, 21 Upper Ormond Quay) Single/doubles/triples €57.50/82.50/121 Sun-Thurs, €63.50/95.50/ 140 Fri-Sat. This is a friendly, popular B&B on the northside quays. The rooms are clean and very tidy. Guests have free access to the sauna next door.

high ceilings and old-style wooden-frame beds.

Stella Maris (off Dublin map; ☎ 874 0835, e stellamaris@ireland.com, 13 Upper Gardiner St) Singles/doubles with bathroom €38/71. This pleasant little B&B has basic but comfortable rooms.

Carmel House (off Dublin map; ☎ 874 1639, fax 878 6903, 16 Upper Gardiner St) Singles €44-57, doubles €32-69 per person. Everything here is clean and pristine; the nine en-suite rooms are comfortable and relatively spacious.

Lyndon House (☎ 878 6950, fax 878 7420, e lyndonh@gofree.indigo.ie, 26 Gardiner Place) En-suite rooms from €90. This is a beautifully restored house, with comfortable rooms and extremely friendly service.

Othello Guesthouse (☎ 855 4271, fax 855 7460, 74 Lower Gardiner St) Singles/doubles from €45/84 with bathroom. This popular, tidy place has the usual facilities in all the bedrooms: tea and coffee facilities, TV and direct-dial phones.

Drumcondra About 30 minutes' walk (3km, five minutes by bus) east of Upper O'Connell St (along Dorset St), on the road to the airport, is the leafy suburb of Drumcondra (off Dublin map), a popular area for B&Bs. Most of the houses here are late-Victorian or Edwardian, and are generally extremely well kept and comfortable. As they're on the airport road, they tend to be full virtually throughout the year, so advance booking is definitely recommended. Buses No 3, 11, 11A, 16 or 36A from Trinity College/O'Connell St (€1.15) all stop along the Drumcondra Rd.

St Andrew's Guesthouse (☎ 837 4684, fax 857 0446, e andrew@dublinn.com, 1 Lambay Rd) Singles/doubles €51/90. This place has lovely en-suite rooms, with elegant period beds (all refurbished). It's located off the Drumcondra Rd, down Griffith Avenue and the third turn to the left. Bus No 36 or 36A stops along Griffith Avenue.

Griffith House (☎ 837 5030, fax 837 0343, e griffhse@indigo.ie, 125 Griffith Avenue) Doubles €63.50. This elegant house on a beautiful, tree-lined avenue has

four double rooms, three of them en suite. Each room is tastefully appointed, with large, comfortable beds and nice furniture. The house is strictly nonsmoking.

Tinode House (☎ 837 2277, fax 837 4477, e tinodehouse@eircom.net, 170 Upper Drumcondra Rd) Singles/doubles €63.50/70. This beautiful Edwardian house has four elegant bedrooms, all with bathrooms. The welcome is very friendly.

Ballsbridge & Donnybrook These B&Bs south-east of the centre are off the Dublin map. It's only a 10-minute bus ride from the city centre; bus Nos 5, 7, 7A, 8, 18 and 45 all stop in the area.

Ariel House (☎ 668 5512, fax 668 5845, e reservations@ariel-house.com, 52 Lansdowne Rd) Rooms €100.50. With 28 rooms, all en suite, this is hardly your average B&B, but not many B&Bs are listed Victorian homes that have been given top rating by Bord Fáilte. Recently restored to its 19th-century elegance, every room is individually decorated in period furniture, which lends the place an air of genuine luxury. If you have the dosh, this place beats almost any hotel – although solo travellers may be put off by the fact that you pay for the room, not the bed.

Glenogra House (☎ 668 3661, fax 668 3698, e gelongra@indigo.ie, 64 Merrion Rd) Singles/doubles €89/102. Almost directly opposite the Royal Dublin Showground, this tasteful Edwardian residence has 12 en-suite rooms, each decorated in a thoroughly modern style, with the usual amenities. It is strictly nonsmoking.

Guesthouses & Hotels

There is a hazy line dividing B&Bs, guesthouses and the mid-range hotels. Places in this mid-range bracket usually cost from €57 to €83 per person per night. Some of the small, central hotels in this category are among the most enjoyable places to stay in Dublin.

These mid-range places are a big jump up from the cheaper B&Bs in facilities and price but still cost a lot less than Dublin's expensive hotels. Another advantage is that breakfast is usually provided (it generally isn't in the top-notch hotels), with fruit, a choice of cereals, croissants, scones and other assorted delights to supplement the bacon and eggs.

North of the Liffey In this range you'll find some excellent places to stay north of the river.

Caulfields Hotel (☎ 878 0643, fax 878 1650, e caulfieldshotel@tinet.ie, 18-19 Dorset St) Singles/doubles €57.20/102. This small hotel is north of O'Connell St. The 20 rooms here are all very cosy. Some might say small, but for the price you won't get a city-centre location with anything much bigger. There's nightly traditional music in the bar downstairs. Prices include full Irish breakfasts and are higher at the weekend.

The Townhouse (☎ 878 8808, fax 878 8787, e info@townhouseofdublin.com, W www.townhouseofdublin.com, 47-48 Lower Gardiner St) Singles/doubles €67/102. This is one of our favourite places to stay in Dublin. Each of the rooms is decorated in a different style. It shares a dining room with the Globetrotter's Tourist Hostel next door. There is also a small Japanese garden. Prices include breakfast.

Hotel Saint George (☎ 874 5611, fax 874 5582, e hotels@indigo.ie, 7 Parnell Square East) Singles/doubles €70/121. Located at the top of O'Connell St, this recently opened hotel is inside a restored Georgian building, and it oozes elegance and class. The 36 rooms, all en suite, are surprisingly large, with simple but graceful furniture and large, comfortable beds. It's a little slice of Parisian style in Dublin.

Ormond Quay Hotel (Around Temple Bar; ☎ 872 1811, fax 872 1909, e ormondqh@indigo.ie, 7-11 Upper Ormond Quay) Singles/doubles with bathroom €108/142, less midweek. Beside the river, this hotel has a plaque outside noting its role in the sirens episode of *Ulysses*. The 60 rooms are clean and neat, even if the decor is a little loud. This hotel is openly gay-friendly (see also the 'Gay & Lesbian-Friendly B&Bs' boxed text earlier in this chapter).

Jurys Custom House Inn (☎ 607 5000, fax 829 0400, e customhouse_inn@jurys doyle.com, W www.doylehotels.ie, Custom House Quay) Rooms €82.50. The newest addition to the Jurys chain, this hotel has clean but small rooms decorated in a standard, unimaginative manner. It's a mid-range chain hotel, so you can't really expect more.

South of the Liffey As soon as you cross the Liffey, prices go up and what passes as a mid-range hotel here can often be considered a more expensive spot on the northside.

Aston Hotel (Around Temple Bar map; ☎ 677 9300, fax 677 9007, e stay@aston-hotel.com, 7-9 Aston Quay) Singles/doubles €89/178. The Aston, just off O'Connell Bridge, is a comfortable hotel with 27 rooms and all modern facilities, including cable TV and en-suite bathrooms.

Number 31 (off Around St Stephen's Green map; ☎ 676 5011, fax 676 2929, e number31@iol.ie, 31 Leeson Close) Rooms €60-115. Architect Sam Stephenson's (of Central Bank fame) former home has been converted into this lovely guesthouse just off St Stephen's Green. There are 19 tastefully appointed rooms.

Grafton Guesthouse (Around Temple Bar map; ☎ 679 2041, fax 677 9715, e grafton guesthouse@eircom.net, 26-27 South Great George's St) Singles/doubles with bathroom €63.50/114.50. Located in a Gothic-style building just off Dame St, this guesthouse has beautifully appointed rooms, even if they're a little cramped. It has no parking space.

Eliza Lodge (Around Temple Bar map; ☎ 671 8044, fax 671 8362, e info@dublin lodge.ie, 23-24 Wellington Quay) Singles/doubles €82.50/165. It's priced like a hotel, looks like a hotel, but it's still a guesthouse. Its 18 bedrooms are fabulous: comfortable, spacious and – due to its position right over the Millennium Bridge – with great views of the Liffey. It offers air-conditioning, TVs and, in the fancier rooms, Jacuzzis.

The Fitzwilliam (Around St Stephen's Green map; ☎ 660 0448, fax 676 7488, 41 Upper Fitzwilliam St) Singles/doubles €70/121. On the corner of Lower Baggot St, this place is central but is nevertheless quiet at night. There are 12 en-suite rooms in this small hotel.

Jurys Christ Church Inn (☎ *455 0000, fax 454 0012,* e *christchurch_inn@jurys doyle.com,* w *www.doylehotels.ie, Christchurch Place)* Rooms €82.50. This big hotel immediately opposite Christ Church Cathedral is, like its sister hotel at Custom House Quay (see above), big, basic and boring, but it's clean, tidy and cheap at the price. The location is excellent.

Latchford's (Around St Stephen's Green map; ☎ *676 0784, fax 662 2764,* e *latchfords@eircom.net,* w *www.latchfords-accomm.com, 99-100 Lower Baggot St)* Singles/doubles €88/138.50, less for week-long stays. Latchford's offers serviced rooms with self-catering facilities in an impressive Georgian house. There's an excellent bistro attached.

Merrion Square Manor (Around St Stephen's Green map; ☎ *662 8551, fax 662 8556,* e *merrionmanor@eircom.net, 31 Merrion Square North)* Singles/doubles €77/140. This is a real find and, for the price, there's nothing more central that is quite as nice. The 18 bedrooms are exquisitely decorated in a kind of nouveau Georgian style, a perfect marriage of 18th-century elegance and 21st-century convenience.

Staunton's on the Green (Around St Stephen's Green map; ☎ *478 2133, fax 478 2263,* e *hotels@indigo.ie, 83 St Stephen's Green)* Singles/doubles €95/178. Staunton's is in a Georgian house in an excellent position, and you're charged for it. The rooms, however, are very pleasant, with fine Georgian floor-to-ceiling windows and tasteful decor. Prices include breakfast.

Outside the Centre This hotel is within walking distance of the city centre.

Roxford Lodge Hotel (off Dublin map; ☎ *668 8572, fax 668 8158,* e *roxfordlodge@ eircom.net, 46 Northumberland Rd, Ballsbridge)* Singles/doubles €76/178. This elegant hotel has 20 bedrooms that are decorated to the highest standards. The real bonus, however, is that 15 rooms have Jacuzzis. You won't need us to tell you to make sure to ask for one when you book.

PLACES TO STAY – TOP END
North of the Liffey

Royal Dublin Hotel (☎ *873 3666, fax 873 3120,* e *enq@royaldublin.com, 40 Upper O'Connell St)* Singles/doubles €127/178. Perhaps its proximity to the Gresham – it's directly across the street – and the fact that it lives somewhat in the shadow of the more famous hotel makes this place a better option for those looking for a more relaxed ambience without sacrificing any of the high-class service.

Clarion Hotel (☎ *836 6404, fax 836 6522,* e *info@clarionhotelifsc.com, Custom House Quay)* Rooms €210. This hotel opened in 2001 in the Irish Financial Services Centre, right on Custom House Quay. Not surprisingly, it is geared almost exclusively to the business set. The cafe serves a pretty good selection of international fare, and there's also the San Vitae Health Club for guests.

Chief O'Neills Hotel (☎ *817 3838, fax 817 3839,* e *reservations@chiefoneills .com, Smithfield Village)* Doubles/suites €165/375. Part of the Smithfield Village complex that is home to Ceol, near the Old Jameson Distillery, this hotel has smallish but elegant rooms replete with extremely modern, minimalist furnishings. There are three very nice suites.

Morrisson Hotel (Around Temple Bar map; ☎ *878 2999, fax 878 3185, Lower Ormond Quay)* Rooms from €190.50. Dublin's only designer hotel (the interiors are the work of Irish fashion guru John Rocha) is as fabulous as it is expensive.

South of the Liffey

All of the following hotels are marked on the Around St Stephen's Green map unless stated otherwise.

Longfield's (☎ *676 1367, fax 676 1542,* e *lfields@indigo.ie, 9-10 Lower Fitzwilliam St)* Singles/doubles €115/178. This 26-room hotel between Merrion and Fitzwilliam Squares is a little slice of Georgian heaven.

Clarion Stephen's Hall Hotel (☎ *638 1111, fax 638 1122,* e *stephens@prem group.ie, 14-17 Lower Leeson St)* Singles/doubles €197/250 without breakfast. This hotel near the south-eastern corner of

St Stephen's Green has 37 rooms, all with bathroom.

Georgian House *(☎ 661 8832, fax 661 8834,* e *hotel@georgianhouse.ie, 18-22 Lower Baggot St)* Singles/doubles €140/ 242. Equally close to St Stephen's Green and Merrion Square, this is a fine old Georgian building that has recently been restored to pristine condition.

Méridien Shelbourne Hotel *(☎ 676 6471, fax 661 6006,* e *shelbourneinfo@ forte-hotels.com, 27 St Stephen's Green)* Singles/doubles from €267/362. This is indubitably the best address at which to meet in Dublin.

The Merrion *(☎ 603 0600, fax 603 0700,* e *info@merrionhotel.ie, Upper Merrion St)* Singles/doubles from €267/292, doubles in main house from €375. In time the Merrion may come to rival the Shelbourne as the city's most famous hotel. The rooms in the main house are nicer than the more sterile annexe at the back.

Stephen's Green Hotel *(☎ 607 3600, fax 661 5663,* e *stephensgreenres@ocallagh anhotels.ie, online reservations at* w *www .ocallaghanhotels.ie, St Stephen's Green)* Singles/doubles €356/381. You can't miss this stunning glass-fronted hotel on the southwestern corner of St Stephen's Green. Inside, the rooms do not disappoint: thoroughly contemporary, they all come equipped with modem lines and other electronic gadgetry such as satellite TV.

Westin Dublin *(Around Temple Bar map;* ☎ *604 0400,* e *reservations@westin.com,* w *www.westin.com, Westmoreland St)* Rooms from €280. Dublin's newest posh hotel opened in September 2001 directly opposite Trinity College, probably the best spot in town. Behind the Georgian facade is a hotel that is thoroughly contemporary with traditional touches.

Outside the Centre

Burlington *(off Around St Stephen's Green map;* ☎ *660 5222, fax 660 8496,* e *burling ton_hotel@jurysdoyle.com,* w *www.doyle hotels.ie, Upper Leeson St)* Singles/doubles without breakfast from €203/235. Ireland's largest hotel, the modern Burlington is 2.5km south of the centre, over the Grand Canal.

Sachs Hotel *(off Around St Stephen's Green map;* ☎ *668 0995, fax 668 6147, 19-29 Morehampton Rd)* Singles/doubles €115/190. This small but elegant and expensive place in the residential area of Ballsbridge has plenty of modern amenities but still retains its Georgian style.

Berkeley Court *(off Around St Stephen's Green map;* ☎ *660 1711, fax 661 7238,* e *berkeley_court@jurysdoyle.com, Lansdowne Rd)* Singles/doubles from €254/286. This hotel is south-east of the city centre in a quiet and relaxed location in Ballsbridge.

PLACES TO EAT
North of the Liffey

Dining possibilities here are more limited than the southside, consisting of a selection of cheap cafes, ubiquitous fast-food chains, and a small quantity of quality restaurants whose numbers are on the increase.

Bangkok Café *(☎ 878 6618, 106 Parnell St)* Mains around €10.50. Close to the Gate Theatre, the Bangkok Café may look a little rough around the edges but inside you'll find good Thai cuisine.

101 Talbot *(☎ 874 5011, 100-2 Talbot St)* Mains from €6.30. Open 5pm-11pm Mon, to 10pm Tues-Sat. Close to the river, 101 Talbot makes a brave attempt to bring good food north of the river. The prices are reasonable and the food moderately adventurous and well prepared. The emphasis is on Mediterranean and Middle Eastern cuisine.

Chapter One *(Dublin Writers' Museum;* ☎ *873 2266, 18 North Parnell Square)* Mains from €13. Open lunch & dinner Tues-Sun. The southside has all of Dublin's great restaurants... bar one. This fabulous spot in the basement of the Dublin Writers' Museum gives all the others a run for their money in its unerring pursuit of the best of classic French cuisine.

Cobalt Café & Gallery *(☎ 873 0313, 16 North Great George's St)* Mains €4-6.50. This splendid little cafe (the 'gallery' is little more than a few paintings on the wall) is our favourite on the northside. On the ground floor of an elegant Georgian building, it is bright and airy with a big fireplace to warm you up in the cold weather. The food is as good as the surroundings: nothing fancy, just big sandwiches stuffed with fresh produce.

Epicurean Food Hall (*Around Temple Bar map; Lower Liffey St*) Lunch €4-10. Open 9.30am-5.30pm Mon-Sat. This is a fabulous new food hall with a selection of takeaway counters offering French, Italian, Mexican, Japanese, Indian and Turkish dishes. There's a seating area in the middle of the hall.

Bewley's Oriental Café (☎ 677 6761, 40 Mary St) Breakfast €5. Open 7.30am-6pm Mon-Sat, to 7pm Thur. Bewley's is a Dublin institution, but the food certainly is not. This place is recommended more for its coffees and teas, as well as its ambience, than for its overcooked, underheated and overpriced fries.

Winding Stair Café (*Around Temple Bar map;* ☎ 873 3292, 40 Lower Ormond Quay) Lunch €5-10. Open 10.30am-6pm Mon-Sat. One of our favourite places in Dublin, the Winding Stair is a beautifully dusty old bookshop with a cafe spread across the second and third floors. It's perfect for reading while you eat and the vegetarian selections are pretty good.

Panem (*Around Temple Bar map;* ☎ 872 8510, 21 Lower Ormond Quay) Mains €6-9. Open 9am-5pm Mon-Fri, from 10am Sat. Pasta dishes and focaccia sandwiches are pretty good at this quayside cafe; on a nice day you can sit along the boardwalk and enjoy your lunch alfresco.

Temple Bar

All of the following places are on the Around Temple Bar map.

Restaurants The southside of the Liffey is packed with restaurants of all types.

Da Pino (☎ 671 9308, 38-40 Parliament St) Lunch €6.50. There are almost no cheap restaurants in Temple Bar; this is the exception. The lunch menu – offering a selection of delicious pizzas or a minute steak – is hard to beat.

Bad Ass Café (☎ 671 2596, 9-11 Crown Alley) Pizzas around €9. This popular pizza joint is a cheerful, bright warehouse-style

place south of Ha'penny Bridge. It offers reasonable pizzas in a convivial atmosphere and has pulleys to whip orders to the kitchen at busy times. Sinéad O'Connor once worked here as a waitress.

Il Baccaro (☎ 671 4597, Meeting House Square) Mains €6.50-10.50. At the southeastern corner of Meeting House Square (known as Diceman's Corner after a mime artist who used to perform on Grafton St) this Italian trattoria's rustic cuisine is very popular with Dublin's Italian community.

Osteria Antica Ar Vicoletto (☎ 670 8662, 5 Crow St) Mains less than €19. For a truly excellent Italian meal at reasonable prices, this place is hard to beat. The warm Gorgonzola salad is sublime and the spaghetti carbonara is as authentic as it gets.

Elephant & Castle (☎ 679 3121, 18 Temple Bar) Mains around €9. Open to 11.30pm Sun-Thur, to midnight Fri-Sat. Omelettes are a speciality at the popular, bustling but overpriced Elephant & Castle. This doesn't deter the fairly big queues that gather for Sunday brunch.

Gallagher's Boxty House (☎ 677 2762, 20-21 Temple Bar) Mains €8-11.50. A *boxty* resembles a stuffed pancake and tastes like a bland Indian *masala dosa*. Real Irish food is not something that's widely available in Dublin so it's worth trying this popular place.

Fans Cantonese Restaurant (☎ 679 4263, 60 Dame St) Mains from €9. Dame St's international mix of restaurants includes Chinese joints such as Fans. The menu is pretty standard – easy on the western palate with the more adventurous dishes reserved for their Chinese customers. Standard, but far from average.

Good World Restaurant (☎ 677 5373, 18 South Great George's St) Lunch €8.50-10.50. This restaurant has the best Chinese food in the area. It is popular with the Chinese community, who choose their dishes from a Chinese menu rather than the one presented to locals. Needless to say, the former has more exciting dishes than the latter.

Juice (☎ 475 7856, Castle House, 73 South Great George's St) Smoothies €3.20-4.50. A super-trendy vegetarian restaurant, Juice puts an imaginative, California-type spin on all kinds of dishes. The real treat is the selection of fruit smoothies, a delicious and healthy alternative to soft drinks.

Belgo (☎ *672 7555, 17-19 Sycamore St*) Lunch €6.50, dinner €25. The popular Belgo chain has finally come to Dublin, and brought its various cost saving specials along with it. Apart from *moules et frites*, they serve things like wild boar sausages and some really good seafood.

Dish (☎ *671 1248, 2 Crow St*) Set lunch €15.50. It's pretty pricey, but good, with a strong emphasis on organic produce and a constantly changing menu. This is the best restaurant of its price range in Temple Bar.

Eden (☎ *670 5372, Meeting House Square*) Meals from less than €25. Open noon-3pm and 6pm-10.30pm daily. Eden is the epitome of Temple Bar chic, with good, solid dishes served in minimalist surroundings. You can eat for less than €25 but it'll cost you more to eat well. It's very popular so book in advance.

The Mermaid Café (☎ *670 8236, 22 Dame St*) Meals around €32. Open lunch & dinner Mon-Fri, dinner only Sat & Sun. This place has a reputation as one of the better seafood restaurants in the city. The food is light and delicious, the surroundings bright and airy.

The Tea Rooms (☎ *670 7766, Clarence Hotel, 6-8 Wellington Quay*) Mains €11.50-22, set lunch €22. This is one of the trendiest restaurants in Dublin, but for once the food matches the hype.

Cafes Temple Bar has a number of excellent cafes.

Gruel (☎ *670 7119, 68a Dame St*) Breakfast €3.75, lunch €4.75. Open 7.30am-7.30pm Mon-Fri, 10.30am-5.30pm Sat. This is *the* best sandwich place in the city centre, with a menu of sublime sandwiches that changes daily.

Bewley's (☎ *677 6761, 11-12 Westmoreland St*) All-day breakfast €5. Open 7.30am-9pm Mon-Sat, 8.30am-9pm Sun. This is probably the most beautiful of all the Bewley's coffee houses, virtually untouched for over a century. Unfortunately, the food tastes like it too. Stick to a drink and a scone or cake.

Café Irie (☎ *672 5090, 11 Upper Fownes St*) From €3. It isn't – as the name suggests – even vaguely Jamaican (even if some of the dread-locked customers might wish it so), but at Café Irie the sandwiches, served on a variety of breads, are excellent, filling and cheap.

Queen of Tarts (☎ *670 7499, Cork Hill*) From €2.50. As the name suggests, this is a great place for pastries, both savoury and sweet. It's a tiny place with only a handful of tables, but it makes the Victorian atmosphere all that more intimate.

Simon's Place (☎ *679 7821, George's St Arcade, South Great George's St*) From €3.20. This is a great hangout joint, serving pretty big sandwiches and good coffee to a loyal clientele.

Guy Stuart (*George's St Arcade, Drury St*) 'Slow-food' exponents Jenny Guy and Lara Stuart opened this food stall in the George's St Arcade a couple of years ago to immediate success. The emphasis is on fresh Mediterranean produce and other delicacies to be savoured slowly and with relish, either in a sandwich or in their range of delicious soups.

Leo Burdock's (☎ *454 0306, 2 Werburgh St*) Meals €4-8. Open 5.30pm-11pm Mon-Sat. This place round the corner from Dublin Castle is reckoned to serve the best fish and chips in Ireland; not quite, but its great anyway.

Around Grafton St

Although pedestrianised Grafton St is devoid of restaurants (bar a selection of fast-food outlets), the streets around the city's No 1 shopping street offer plenty of options in all price ranges.

Restaurants The area around Grafton St has a top selection of restaurants.

Gotham Café (*Around St Stephen's Green map;* ☎ *679 5266, 8 South Anne St*) Pizza from €6.50. The trendy and popular Gotham Café serves a really good selection of pizzas.

Bewley's (*Around St Stephen's Green map;* ☎ *677 6761, 78 Grafton St*) Mains around €11.50. Open 7.15am-11.30pm Mon-Sat, 8.30am-10.30pm Sun. Apart from fast-food joints, Bewley's is the only place in which to eat on Grafton St proper. This is the flagship branch of the chain, and a recent renovation has converted it from an old-style cafe to a restaurant, with table service and fancier dishes than the other branches, though you can still get a lovely cup of coffee and a bun.

Trocadero (Around Temple Bar map; ☎ *677 5545, 3 St Andrew's St)* Mains around €13. Open until midnight Mon-Sat, to 11.30pm Sun. The Trocadero offers no culinary surprises, which is one reason why it's so popular. Simple food, straightforward preparation, large portions and late opening hours are its selling points.

Cedar Tree (Around Temple Bar map; ☎ *677 2121, 11a St Andrew's St)* Mains €8.90-15.50. This Lebanese restaurant has a good selection of vegetarian dishes.

Avoca Handweavers (Around Temple Bar map; ☎ *677 4215, 11-13 Suffolk St)* Mains around €9. On the top floor of this shop is an excellent cafe-restaurant that serves up wholesome Irish cuisine.

Aya (Around Temple Bar map; ☎ *677 1544, Clarendon St)* Mains €10.50-20. Attached to the swanky Brown Thomas department store, this relatively new Japanese restaurant is the best in the city centre. There's a revolving sushi bar where you can eat your fill for €25 Sunday to Tuesday between 6pm and 8pm (maximum 55 minutes) or, if you prefer, go a la carte from the great menu. There's an early bird special (up to 8pm) nightly for €16.50.

Café Mao (Around St Stephen's Green map; ☎ *670 4899, 2-3 Chatham Row)* From less than €10.50. Café Mao serves up interesting and varied Asian dishes. This is a popular lunch-time spot.

Imperial Chinese Restaurant (Around Temple Bar map; ☎ *677 2580, 12a Wicklow St)* Dim sum from €3.20 per dish. Open lunch & dinner daily. This long-established place is a favourite with the Chinese community and is noted for its lunch-time dim sum. These Chinese snacks are popular on Sunday, when the Imperial serves brunch Chinese-style in what is known as *yum cha*, or 'drink tea', the traditional accompaniment to dim sum.

The Odessa (Around Temple Bar map; ☎ *670 7634, 13 Dame Court)* Mains €13-20.50. Just off Exchequer St, this is a super-trendy restaurant where you can eat well in comfort and style. Sunday brunch is a favourite with the city's hip young things.

Rajdoot Tandoori (Around St Stephen's Green map; ☎ *679 4274, 26-28 Clarendon St)* Mains from €10.50, set lunch €11.50, set dinner €23. Visitors to India may remember Rajdoot as a popular brand of Indian motorcycle. In Dublin, however, the name is a byword for Indian cuisine at its very best, particularly the more aromatic flavours of North India.

Peacock Alley (Around St Stephen's Green map; ☎ *478 7015, Fitzwilliam Hotel, 109 St Stephen's Green)* Lunch/dinner around €25/50. This restaurant is owned by super-chef bad boy Conrad Gallagher, whose speciality is French provincial cuisine and getting himself into trouble with the law (he was recently accused of selling paintings belonging to the hotel without their permission).

Velure (Around St Stephen's Green map; ☎ *670 5585, 47 South William St)* 3-course meal about €38. Open lunch & dinner Tues-Sat & lunch Sun. Velure opened in June 1999 with a menu (and prices) fit to match those of the Clarence Hotel's Tea Rooms. If you plan on splashing out during your trip to Dublin, this is the place to do it. Reservations are advisable.

The Commons (Around St Stephen's Green map; ☎ *475 2597, Newman House, 85-86 St Stephen's Green)* 6-course 'tasting menu' €77. The food here is exquisite but pricey; it's advisable to book ahead.

Shanahan's on the Green (Around St Stephen's Green map; ☎ *407 0939, 119 St Stephen's Green)* Steak around €32. Dinner only Mon-Sat. Dublin's first top-range, American-style steakhouse has been rightfully lauded for the high quality of its steaks (vegetarians won't have much luck here), but you'll pay dearly for the privilege of being served one.

Cafes & Pubs Grafton St is the fast-food centre south of the Liffey. The area has office workers, students and tourists to feed and there are plenty of cafes and pubs to keep them happy at lunch-time.

Cornucopia *(Around Temple Bar map; ☎ 677 7583, 19 Wicklow St)* Mains around €5.50. Open to 8pm Mon-Wed & Fri, to 9pm Thur & lunch Sat. For those escaping the Irish cholesterol habit, Cornucopia is a popular wholefood cafe turning out healthy goodies. There's even a hot vegetarian breakfast as an alternative to muesli.

Munchies *(Around Temple Bar map; ☎ 604 0010, 2 South William St)* Meals €3-5.10. Now with a second branch in the city centre *(Around Temple Bar map ☎ 670 9476, Castlegate, Lord Edward St)*, Munchies is cleaning up on the lunch-time sandwich trade. They claim to produce the best sandwiches in Ireland. They're not *that* good but you won't be disappointed.

Nude *(Around Temple Bar map; ☎ 675 5577, 21 Suffolk St)* Wraps from €3.75. This ultra-cool place just off Grafton St has been a huge hit since it opened, serving tasty wraps with all kinds of Asian fillings. You can eat in or take away, but be sure to try one of their freshly squeezed fruit juices.

Harvey's Coffee House *(Around Temple Bar map; ☎ 677 1060, 14-15 Trinity St)* Around €6.50. Closed evenings. In the morning, you can fill up on bagels, scones and toast at this lovely little cafe near the tourist office. At lunch time they do big open sandwiches.

The Powerscourt Townhouse shopping centre (Around St Stephen's Green map) is stuffed with eating places and makes a great place for lunch.

Blazing Salads *(☎ 671 9552, top floor Powerscourt Townhouse shopping centre)* Lunch around €6.50. This popular vegetarian restaurant serves a variety of salads for €1 each.

Chompys' *(☎ 679 4552, 1st floor Powerscourt Townhouse shopping centre)* Snacks from €3.75. This place boasts bagels, pancakes and sandwiches for less than €6.50.

Lemon *(Around Temple Bar map; ☎ 672 9044, 66 South William St)* Pancakes from €3.20 Finally, a proper pancake joint in Dublin. And not one of those thick, American-style pancakes either, but the thin *crêpe* kind, which you can get with savoury or sweet fillings.

Alpha *(Around Temple Bar map; ☎ 677 0213, 37 Wicklow St)* Meals from €5.10. Celebrating its 101st birthday in 2001, the city centre's most traditional of Dublin restaurants has recently passed into Turkish ownership. Eager to maintain its proud tradition of serving solid lunches and dinners to the city's working community, the place has remained unchanged. Plans are afoot to open a second restaurant serving Turkish cuisine on the floor above. The atmosphere and friendliness of this place is one of a kind.

Kilkenny Kitchen *(Around Temple Bar map; ☎ 677 7066, 1st floor, 6 Nassau St)* Lunch from €6.50. Right opposite Trinity College, on the 1st floor of the Kilkenny Shop, this place serves generally excellent cafeteria-style food but at times the queues can be discouragingly long. There's a snack counter which, at peak times, can be somewhat faster.

Dail Bía *(Around St Stephen's Green map; ☎ 670 6079, 46 Kildare St)* Meals from €5. The name means 'parliament food' in Irish, and its appropriate: this basement cafe opposite the Dail has Irish-speaking staff and a bilingual menu, but you don't need to be an Irish speaker to enjoy its menu, which places a premium on health food.

Café Metro *(Around St Stephen's Green map; ☎ 679 4515, 43 South William St)* Sandwiches from €2.50, salads €6.50. This popular cafe on the corner of South William and Chatham Sts has the friendliest staff in town. The toasted sandwiches are good, but the real treats are the salads.

Busyfeet & Coco Café *(Around St Stephen's Green map; ☎ 671 9514, 41 South William St)* Lunch from €6.50. This recently opened cafe is one of the only places in town to serve a really good *chai*, a marvellous alternative to the stronger Irish tea and a good noncaffeine alternative to coffee.

There are several pubs with good food close to Grafton St.

Stag's Head *(Around Temple Bar map; ☎ 679 3701, 1 Dame Court)* Lunch €6.50. For a good pub lunch, we recommend the Stag's Head. Apart from being a popular drinking spot, this place turns out simple, well prepared, filling meals in elegant Victorian surroundings.

O'Neill's (Around Temple Bar map; ☎ *679 3671, 2 Suffolk St)* Lunch €8-9. The carvery lunch at this city-centre pub is rightfully renowned for its quality and size, attracting a loyal crowd daily.

The Brazen Head (☎ *679 5186, 20 Lower Bridge St)* Lunch around €8. This place, with a variety of menus offering everything from sandwiches to a carvery, is always packed at lunch time.

Modern Green Bar (Around St Stephen's Green map; ☎ *478 0583, 31 Wexford St)* Mains around €7.50. Food served noon-8pm daily. Only a couple of minutes' walk from St Stephen's Green, this relatively new bar serves a really good mix of pub grub, including pasta, Irish stew, curry, salads and the ubiquitous sandwiches. The portions are huge and the food delicious.

Merrion Row, Baggot St & Beyond

Merrion Row, leading south-east from St Stephen's Green, and its extension, Baggot St, have an eclectic selection of pubs and restaurants. All of these places are on or just off the Around St Stephen's Green map.

Cibo's (☎ *676 2050, 17a Lower Baggot St)* Mains from €10.50. Cibo's does pizza and pasta as well as more expensive Italian dishes.

The Ante Room (☎ *660 4716, 20 Lower Baggot St)* Mains around €14. Underneath the Georgian House guesthouse, The Ante Room is a seafood specialist with traditional Irish music on most summer nights.

Langkawi (☎ *668 2760, 46 Upper Baggot St)* Set lunch €14. Langkawi has reasonable, affordable Pacific Rim cuisine.

Ocean (☎ *668 8862, Charlotte Quay Dock)* Mains from €9. Fresh seafood is the mainstay at this trendy, minimalist eatery on the corner of Grand Canal Basin. We recommend the oysters followed by a crab salad.

Restaurant Patrick Guilbaud (☎ *676 4192, Merrion Hotel, 21 Upper Merrion St)* Gourmet dinner menu €102, set lunch €28. Open lunch & dinner Tues-Sat. With two Michelin stars on its résumé, this elegant

restaurant is perhaps one of the best restaurants in Ireland, and head chef Guillaume Le Brun does his best to ensure that it stays that way. If you eat here your stomach and credit card will know about it. There's nothing overpoweringly fancy; it's just good food, beautifully prepared and elegantly presented. Needless to say, reservations are essential.

Thornton's (☎ *454 9067, 1 Portobello Rd)* 6-course 'surprise' menu €75. Open dinner Tues-Sat, lunch Fri only. Kevin Thornton is probably the only chef in Dublin able to challenge Guilbaud's top-dog slot (see above), and he does so with a mouth-watering interpretation of new French cuisine. The service is faultless, if a little too formal.

Fitzer's Café (☎ *661 4496, The National Gallery, Merrion Square)* Mains €7-10.50. The National Gallery Fitzer's is the best branch of the Dublin chain. It's rather hidden away – you have to go through the gallery (admission is free) to find it – but the artistic interlude makes a pleasant introduction to this popular, if slightly pricier, restaurant. There's a *Fitzer's Take-Out (*☎ *660 0644, 24 Upper Baggot St)* not far away.

ENTERTAINMENT

Dublin is undoubtedly one of Europe's most vibrant entertainment capitals, with a plethora of options to satisfy (nearly) every desire. It has theatres, cinemas, nightclubs, concert halls, stadiums, horse racing and dog tracks, but the real centre of activity is still the pub – and in Dublin there are about 700 of them. A thriving nightlife (bars, cafes and clubs are packed virtually every night of the week) has made the city one of the most popular getaway destinations in Europe.

Dublin's 'party district' is undoubtedly Temple Bar, although its designation as the city's cultural quarter is somewhat of a misnomer, at least after sundown, when it turns into a northern Gomorrah with few rivals in Europe. The pubs and clubs are crammed, the music is loud, and the party goes on till the wee hours.

If 'Ibiza in the rain' isn't to your taste, do

The Perfect Pint of Guinness?

What makes a perfect pint of Guinness? This much-debated question has no complete, definitive answer, but we can offer a few indications, as gleaned from the experts themselves: Dubliners.

Everyone agrees that proximity to the St James's Gate Guinness Brewery is one requirement, for although a pint in Kuala Lumpur can still be a fine thing, Guinness at its best can be found only in Ireland. But not even that is a guarantee, for there are still some substandard pints to be had in Dublin. So, what is a good test?

The proper pour is an essential. First, you need a good, experienced bartender (preferably one who has served the required apprenticeship) who has ensured that the pipes are clean and free-flowing (there's nothing worse than dirty pipes). Once everything is in place, the pour can begin. The glass is tilted to about 45 degrees, then the tap is pulled forwards so that the liquid is poured against the back of the glass. When it is about three-quarters full, the glass is left to 'settle', which means that the heavier black liquid settles underneath the lighter, creamy head. After a few minutes, the pint is topped up by pushing the tap backwards, allowing only the black beer into the glass. When the pint is full, it is left to settle a second time, and then it's ready to drink. It isn't that difficult, but it takes time: as Guinness' advertising will tell you, 'It's worth waiting for'.

Now it is time to test the quality of the pint. When you're about halfway through, look at the sides of the glass: if there are rings of white foam round the inside (the thicker the better), you can

not despair: there's still plenty to do outside the confines of Temple Bar's cobbled streets. Most of the best old-fashioned pubs are outside the district, and in recent times Dubliners looking to discover a new trendy area have begun exploring the hitherto untapped resources of the northern side of the river, especially in and around the Smithfield area west of Capel St. Its cobbled streets and big, unused spaces have virtually guaranteed its role as the Temple Bar of the new millennium.

For entertainment information, pick up a copy of the weekly music review *Hot Press* (€2.50); the *Event Guide*, a bimonthly freebie available at many locations, including bars, cafes and hostels; or the fortnightly magazine *In Dublin* (€2.50). Wednesday's *Irish Times* (€1.25) has a pull-out entertainment section called *The Ticket* which has comprehensive listings of clubs and gigs.

Pubs

Since Irish life is closely tied up with pub culture, a visit to one of the many pubs spread throughout the city is an absolute must. Despite the challenges of 'Europeanisation' – the increase in cafes, clubs, restaurants and so on – pubs are still the hub of virtually all social activity in the city, a meeting point for friends and strangers alike, and where Dubliners are at their friendly and convivial best (and, it must be said, sometimes their drunken and incoherent worst!).

Extended opening hours mean that pubs now close at midnight Monday to Wednesday (last drinks served at 11.30pm), 1am Thursday to Saturday (last drinks at 12.30am) and 11.30pm on Sunday (last drinks 11pm). However, many also avail of late licences, which means they can serve up to around 1.45am. The listed pubs can be found on the Dublin's Pubs, Bars & Clubs map unless otherwise indicated.

Traditional Dublin is full of old-style, traditional establishments. Here are some of the best.

Flowing Tide (☎ 874 0842, 9 Lower Abbey St) Directly opposite the Abbey Theatre, this place attracts a great mix of theatregoers and northside locals. It's loud, full of chat and a great place to drink.

Patrick Conway (☎ 873 2687, 70 Parnell St) Although slightly out of the way, this place is a true gem of a pub. It has been operating since 1745, and no doubt new fathers

---

The Perfect Pint of Guinness?

be sure that the pint is a good one. First-time stout drinkers usually have difficulty with the bitter, heavy taste. If that is the case, have no fear: Guinness is most definitely an acquired taste. Practice does indeed make perfect!

Now that you know what to look for, where will you find the perfect pint of the 'black stuff', as it is referred to in Dublin? Most Dubliners agree that the pint served in the **Guinness Storehouse** is among the best served anywhere, despite Guinness' assurances that it is no different from that found in any pub.

Few will argue with the quality of the pint served in **John Mulligan's** of Poolbeg St, where the assorted regulars are considered experts on the subject. **Grogan's Castle Lounge** on South William St is another spot where the Guinness is top notch. **Kehoe's** of South Anne St has a lovely snug where you can enjoy an excellent pint. **Hartigan's**, just off St Stephen's Green on Lower Leeson St, might not look like much, but the Guinness is beyond reproach. All the above pubs are marked on the Dublin's Pubs, Bars & Clubs map.

A Guinness pilgrimage to **Kavanagh's** (off Dublin map), just behind the Glasnevin cemetery off DeCourcey Square, will be rewarded with a pint that is truly exceptional. The pub is commonly referred to as 'The Gravediggers' because it is the traditional drinking hole of the cemetery employees.

---

have been stopping in here for a celebratory pint since the day the Rotunda Maternity Hospital opened across the road in 1757.

Palace Bar (☎ 677 9290, 21 Fleet St) With its mirrors and wooden niches, Palace Bar is often said to be the perfect example of an old Dublin pub. It's within Temple Bar and is popular with journalists from the nearby *Irish Times*.

John Mulligan's (☎ 677 5582, 8 Poolbeg St) Just off Fleet St, outside the eastern boundary of Temple Bar, John Mulligan's is another pub that has scarcely changed over the years. It featured as the local in the film *My Left Foot* and is also popular with journalists from the nearby newspaper offices. Mulligan's was established in 1782 and has long been reputed to have the best Guinness in Ireland as well as a wonderfully varied collection of regulars.

Brogan's (☎ 679 9570, 75 Dame St) Only a couple of doors down from the Olympia Theatre, this is a wonderful old-style bar where conversation – not loud music – is king. The beer is also pretty good.

Stag's Head (☎ 679 3701, 1 Dame Court) At the intersection of Dame Court and Dame Lane, just off Dame St, the Stag's Head was built in 1770 and remodelled in 1895. It's sufficiently picturesque to have featured in a postage stamp series of Irish pubs.

The Long Hall (☎ 475 1590, 51 South Great George's St) Luxuriating in full Victorian splendour, this is one of the city's most beautiful and best-loved pubs. Check out the ornate carvings in the woodwork behind the bar and the elegant chandeliers. The bartenders are experts at their craft, an increasingly rare sight in Dublin these days.

Kehoe's (☎ 677 8312, 9 South Anne St) This is one of the most atmospheric pubs in the city centre and a real favourite with all kinds of Dubliners. It has a beautiful Victorian bar, a wonderful snug and plenty of other little nooks and crannies. Upstairs drinks are served in what was once the publican's living room. And it looks it!

Neary's (☎ 677 8596, 1 Chatham St) Neary's is a showy Victorian-era pub with a particularly fine frontage; it's popular with actors from the nearby Gaiety Theatre. The upstairs bar is one of the only spots in the city centre where you stand the chance of getting a seat on a Friday or Saturday night.

Grogan's Castle Lounge (☎ 677 9320, 15 South William St) This place is known simply as Grogan's (after the original owner), and is a city-centre institution. It

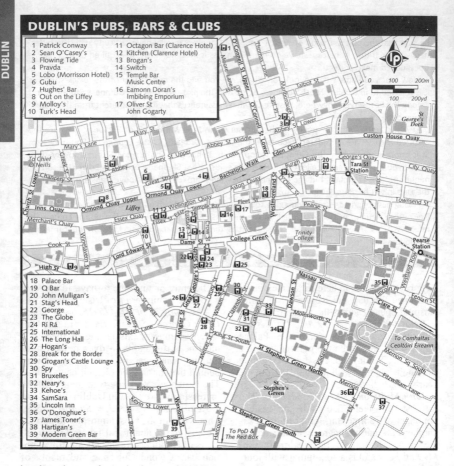

DUBLIN'S PUBS, BARS & CLUBS

1 Patrick Conway
2 Sean O'Casey's
3 Flowing Tide
4 Pravda
5 Lobo (Morrisson Hotel)
6 Gubu
7 Hughes' Bar
8 Out on the Liffey
9 Molloy's
10 Turk's Head
11 Octagon Bar (Clarence Hotel)
12 Kitchen (Clarence Hotel)
13 Brogan's
14 Switch
15 Temple Bar
   Music Centre
16 Eamonn Doran's
   Imbibing Emporium
17 Oliver St
   John Gogarty

18 Palace Bar
19 Q Bar
20 John Mulligan's
21 Stag's Head
22 George
23 The Globe
24 Rí Rá
25 International
26 The Long Hall
27 Hogan's
28 Break for the Border
29 Grogan's Castle Lounge
30 Spy
31 Bruxelles
32 Neary's
33 Kehoe's
34 SamSara
35 Lincoln Inn
36 O'Donoghue's
37 James Toner's
38 Hartigan's
39 Modern Green Bar

has long been a favourite haunt of Dublin's writers and painters as well as others from the bohemian, alternative set, most of whom seem to be waiting for the 'inevitable' moment when they are finally recognised as geniuses. An odd quirk of the pub is that drinks are marginally cheaper in the stone-floor bar than the carpeted lounge, even though they are served by the same bar!

James Toner's (☎ 676 3090, 139 Lower Baggot St) Toner's, with its stone floor, is almost a country pub in the heart of the city and the shelves and drawers are reminders that it once doubled as a grocery store. Not

that its suit-wearing business crowd would ever have shopped here…

Hartigan's (☎ 676 2280, 100 Lower Leeson St) This is about as spartan a bar as you'll find in the city and is the daytime home to some serious drinkers, who appreciate the quiet, no-frills surroundings. In the evening it's popular with students from the medical faculty of University College Dublin.

Lincoln Inn (☎ 676 2978, 19 Lincoln Place) What is it about medical students and dingy bars? If UCD students love Hartigan's (see above), then their Trinity equivalents flock to this pokey little hole at the back of the college. Don't be put off by the complete lack of decor: this is a wonderful little place with an ambience created entirely by its clientele.

Fallon's *(Dublin map; ☎ 454 2801, 129 The Coombe)* Just west of the city centre in the heart of medieval Dublin, this is a fabulously old-fashioned bar that has been serving a great pint of Guinness to a most discerning clientele since the end of the 17th century. Prize fighter Dan Donnelly, the only boxer ever to be knighted, was head bartender here for a while... in 1818.

Ryan's *(off Dublin map; ☎ 677 6097, 28 Parkgate St; bus No 23, 25, 26 from city centre)* Near Phoenix Park, this is one of only a handful of city pubs that has retained its Victorian decor virtually intact, complete with ornate bar and snugs. An institution among Dublin's public houses, this is truly worth the trip.

Music The following pubs are excellent venues for catching some traditional Irish and contemporary music.

Sean O'Casey's *(☎ 874 8675, 105 Marlborough St)* This place has a weekly menu of live rock and some Irish traditional music sessions.

For the best Irish traditional sessions in Dublin, two northside pubs are a must.

Hughes' Bar *(☎ 872 6540, 19 Chancery St)* This pub is directly behind the Four Courts and has nightly, if impromptu, sessions which often result in a closed door – that is, they go on long past official closing time. The pub is also a popular lunch-time spot with barristers working nearby.

Cobblestone *(Dublin map; ☎ 872 1799, North King St)* This pub is on the main square in Smithfield, the future hot spot of Dublin. The music sessions here are superb.

Chief O'Neills *(Dublin map; ☎ 817 3838, Smithfield Village)* In Smithfield, this pub is part of the complex that is home to Ceol. It is a great place for a drink and features nightly traditional sessions.

Oliver St John Gogarty *(☎ 671 1822, 58-59 Fleet St)* This pub is extremely popular with tourists, most of whom couldn't care less if the music is less than authentic.

International *(☎ 677 9250, 23 Wicklow St)* The International has live jazz and blues most nights.

Bruxelles *(☎ 677 5362, 7-8 Harry St)* This place has weekly live rock music, perhaps the only link the now-trendy pub has to its heavy metal past.

O'Donoghue's *(☎ 661 4303, 15 Merrion Row)* This, the most famous traditional music bar in Dublin, is where world-famous folk group the Dubliners started off in the 1960s. On summer evenings a young, international crowd spills out into the courtyard beside the pub.

Comhaltas Ceoltóiri Éireann *(off Dublin map; ☎ 280 0295, 35 Belgrave Square, Monkstown)* Serious aficionados of traditional music should make the trip towards Dun Laoghaire. The name (pronounced keol-tas quail-tori erin) means 'Fraternity of Traditional Musicians of Ireland'. It's here that you'll find the best Irish music and dancing in Dublin, with some of the country's top players. To get there, take bus No 7, 7A or 8 from Trinity College, get off before Monkstown village and follow the blue signs. Alternatively, you can take the DART; it's a five-minute walk inland (westwards, following the signs) from Seapoint Station.

Trendy These modern bars are Dublin's current hot spots.

Pravda *(☎ 874 0076, 35 Lower Liffey St)* Pravda, near the Ha'penny Bridge, is Russian in name only. It's a big place that is relaxed and easy-going. When it is full, however, the bouncers have been known to keep a careful eye on dress codes.

Lobo *(Morrisson Hotel; ☎ 878 2999, Lower Ormond Quay)* This is the northside's version of Temple Bar's Octagon Bar (see below), only far more difficult to get into if you don't look the part. If you haven't spent a fortune on your outfit (or look as though you have), forget it. If you get in, your prize is to spend an evening in the company of Dublin's well-to-do social climbers. We suggest you put this guide away before you try to gain access!

Octagon Bar *(☎ 670 9000, Clarence Hotel, 6-8 Wellington Quay)*. Temple Bar's

Gay & Lesbian Nightspots

The following venues can all be found on the Dublin's Pubs, Bars & Clubs map unless otherwise indicated. Nightly gay venues in Dublin include the multilevel, ever-throbbing **George** (*89 South Great George St*), the most popular place in town for drinking and cruising, especially when it hosts the Block disco on Friday and Saturday nights or bingo on Sunday night; and **Out on the Liffey** (*27 Upper Ormond Quay*), a 'harder' pub popular with the biker or butch set of both sexes.

Gubu (☎ *874 0710, Capel St*) is a relatively new bar owned by the same folks who own The Globe. Nicknamed 'gaybu', it is a stylish alternative to Out on the Liffey. It opens at 4pm daily.

Other places are gay, lesbian and/or mixed on certain nights of the week. Consult the *Gay Community News* monthly freebie – available through coffee shops around the city centre, Temple Bar Information Centre on Eustace St, or Condom Power (Around Temple Bar map) on Dame St – or the 'queer' pages of the fortnightly what's-on magazine *In Dublin*, for specific days and times.

There are plenty of clubs that run gay and lesbian nights. The scene is constantly changing, however, and while the nights mentioned below are pretty regular and steady, we recommend that you call ahead to confirm that they're still on.

Kitchen (☎ *677 6635, Clarence Hotel, 6-8 Wellington Quay*) Candy Club is a regular Monday gay and lesbian night that is pretty relaxed.

Switch (☎ *670 7655, 11 Eustace St*) Freedom, a Monday-night regular at one of Dublin's best clubs, sticks to a fun-but-safe formula of house anthems and disco classics.

The PoD (*Place of Dance; Around St Stephen's Green map;* ☎ *478 0166, 35 Harcourt St*) Friday night's HAM, aka Homo Action Movies, is one of Dublin's most enduring gay and lesbian nights – it's now all of five years old! The soundtrack is thumping house, uplifting and progressive.

Chief O'Neill's (*Dublin map;* ☎ *817 3838, fax 817 3839, Smithfield Village*) Libida – an excellent funk, Big Beat and Latin club – has had several homes over the last few years. At the time of writing it was based in Chief O'Neill's hotel on Saturday night, but check the *Gay Community News* to see if it has moved.

Molloy's (☎ *677 3207, 13 High St*) Near Christ Church Cathedral, this bar has lesbian-only night on Saturday called Stonewallz.

Rí Rá (☎ *677 4835, Dame Court*) '80s cheese and sleaze is the theme at Strictly Handbag, a long-running Monday night at one of Dublin's friendlier and easy-going clubs. It's not exclusively gay, but it is popular with the gay community.

Spy (☎ *677 0014, Powerscourt House, South William St*) This is one the hardest places to get in to unless you're dripping with glamour, but Sunday night's Hilton Edwards club (named after the gay co-founder of the Gate Theatre) requests only that you're gay and reasonably well dressed. It's cool, chic and, at the time of writing, the hottest ticket in town.

---

most chic watering hole is where you'll find Dublin's celebrities and their hangers-on. Drinks are marginally more expensive than elsewhere but judging by the clientele that have passed the bouncer's strict entry test this is hardly a concern.

Turk's Head (☎ *679 9701, 27-30 Parliament St*) This is one of the oddest – and so most interesting – bars in Temple Bar. Decorated in two completely different styles – one really gaudy, the other a recreation of LA circa 1930 – this place attracts a huge crowd nightly. It's very, very popular with tourists.

The Globe (☎ *671 1220, 11 South Great George's St*) The Globe is one of the first of the new breed of trendy pubs to open in the city. Still immensely popular, it is one of the few 'cool' pubs in town not to give a fig what you look like going in. Consequently, it is truly hip.

Hogan's (☎ *677 5904, 35 South Great George's St*) Once an old-style, traditional bar, Hogan's is now a gigantic boozer spread across two floors. A popular hangout for young professionals, it gets very full at the weekend with folks eager to take advantage of its late licence.

Q Bar (☎ 677 7835, O'Connell House, D'Olier St) Owned by the same folks who own Messrs Maguire (virtually next door), this is another huge place, only the style is much more modern, with plenty of chrome and velvet. There are DJs nightly, but you'll have to run the gauntlet of bouncers, who can be very selective about who they let in.

SamSara (☎ 671 7723, 35-36 Dawson St) A very new addition to the pub scene, this place is absolutely huge and themed to look like a huge Middle Eastern teahouse. The terminally trendy immediately flocked to it and have stayed.

Modern Green Bar (☎ 478 0583, 31 Wexford St) This is one of our favourite new bars in town. The decor is fairly simple, but it is highlighted by a series of beautiful digital photos tracing the flow of the Liffey from source to mouth. What people come here for, however, is the combination of great music (there are DJs nightly) and a convivial, friendly atmosphere that attracts both students and professionals alike. The all-day menu is also excellent (see Places to Eat).

Thomas House (Dublin map; ☎ 671 6987, 86 Thomas St) This place is a real dive, and so it is very popular with the alternative crowd, who love its total absence of decor and its great music.

Clubs

A few years ago, Dublin was awash with billboards that showed a sweaty, packed dance club with the words 'Open Your Windows Tokyo, Dublin's Having a Party' across the top. Much of Dublin's success as a tourist destination comes from the fact that the city has developed a reputation for being one of the party hotspots of Europe, despite the fact that nightclubs here close earlier than in any other European capital!

The seemingly endless list of 'what's on' is constantly changing, so check out the listings in *In Dublin* and *Event Guide*. The handy pocket guide *Dub Fly* is free and available in cafes and bars throughout the city centre. Most clubs open just after pubs close (11.30pm to midnight) and close at 2.30am or 3am. Admission to most costs between €5 and €8 on weekdays, rising to €13 at weekends. For gay and lesbian clubs, see the boxed text 'Gay & Lesbian Nightspots' earlier.

The listed clubs can be found on the Dublin's Pubs, Bars & Clubs map unless otherwise indicated.

The PoD (Place of Dance; Around St Stephen's Green map; ☎ 478 0166, 35 Harcourt St) Dublin's most renowned nightclub, this futuristic, metal-gothic cathedral of dance attracts a large weekend crowd of twentysomethings. To get past the notoriously difficult bouncers you'll really need to look the part. Sunday night is Odyssey, where the crowd goes mad to house music.

The Red Box (Around St Stephen's Green map; ☎ 478 0225, 35 Harcourt St) Located upstairs from the PoD, this is actually the coolest dance club in town. The floor is enormous and the willing crowds really fill it up. Look out for the big name international DJs that play here regularly.

Kitchen (☎ 677 6635, Clarence Hotel, 6-8 Wellington Quay) In Temple Bar, the U2-owned Kitchen is surprisingly laid back, considering its far-flung fame. The music is hard and fast (currently a mix of techno and house) and the back bar is usually patronised by celebrities and those eager to be seen.

Switch (☎ 670 7655, 11 Eustace St) Located beneath a pretty cheesy bar, this is one of our favourite nightclubs in town: it's small, sweaty and seriously hip, with a terrific selection of different dance beats mixed by excellent local DJs, helped along by international guests.

Eamonn Doran's Imbibing Emporium (☎ 679 9773, 3a Crown Alley) Open nightly. This is a large place with food, drink and music (mostly rock). Monday night, however, is Melting Pot, easily Dublin's best hip hop night.

Rí Rá (☎ 677 4835, Dame Court) Open nightly from 11.30pm. Rí Rá is one of the friendlier clubs in the city centre and is full nearly seven nights a week. Refreshingly, the bouncers here are friendly, funny and very fair. The emphasis here is on funk, both old and new, with ne'er a house beat to be heard.

Parnell Mooney *(Dublin map;* ☎ *873 1544, 71 Parnell St)* This late night bar at the top of O'Connell St is only worth going to on Wednesday, when it hosts the fabulous Firehouse Skank, Dublin's only hard reggae and dub night.

The Shelter *(Dublin map;* ☎ *454 5533, 58-59 Thomas St)* A 300-capacity venue attached to the larger Vicar St venue (see Music Venues below) has begun hosting a selection of club nights; the best of them is Velure on Saturday, with a compelling mix of funky soul, Latin and percussive house that has generated a die-hard, loyal following. If you get in before midnight it's free.

Temple Bar Music Centre *(*☎ *670 9202, Curved St)* There's something going on every night at the TBMC to suit every taste, from funk and disco to guitar-driven indie rock.

Temple Theatre *(Dublin map;* ☎ *874 5088, St George's Church, Hardwicke Place)* The sound of church bells has been replaced by the reverberations of loud house music at this northside club, formerly a church. Big-name international DJs often play here.

Break for the Border *(*☎ *478 0300, Lower Stephen St)* This huge country and western style eatery reverts to a nightclub once pubs close. It's good fun, if a little cheesy, and is renowned in Dublin as one of the biggest pick-up joints around.

Music Venues

Bookings can be made either directly at the venues or through HMV (Around St Stephen's Green map; ☎ 679 5334, 24-hour credit card bookings ☎ 456 9569), 65 Grafton St.

Classical Music & Opera Classical music concerts and opera take place in a number of city-centre venues.

National Concert Hall *(Around St Stephen's Green map;* ☎ *475 1572,* Ⓦ *www .nch.ie, Earlsfort Terrace)* Ireland's premier orchestral hall hosts a variety of concerts year round, including a series of lunch-time

concerts (€5.10) from 1.05pm-2pm Tuesday, June to September.

Bank of Ireland Arts Centre *(Around Temple Bar map;* ☎ *671 1488, Foster Place)* The arts centre hosts a regular Wednesday lunch-time recital beginning at 1.15pm (free) as well as an irregular evening program of concerts. Call for details.

Gaiety Theatre *(Around St Stephen's Green map;* ☎ *677 1717,* Ⓦ *www.gaiety theatre.net, King St South)* This popular Dublin theatre hosts, among other things, a program of classical concerts and opera.

Hugh Lane Municipal Gallery of Modern Art *(*☎ *874 1903, Charlemont House, Parnell Square)* From September to June the art gallery hosts up to 30 concerts of contemporary classical music at noon on Sunday.

Royal Dublin Showground Concert Hall *(County Dublin map;* ☎ *668 0866, Ballsbridge)* The huge hall of the RDS Showground hosts a rich program of classical music and opera throughout the year.

Rock & Pop The majority of these venues are on or just off the Dublin map unless otherwise indicated.

Point Depot *(*☎ *836 3633, East Link Bridge, North Wall Quay)* This is the premier indoor venue for all rock and pop acts playing in Dublin. Originally constructed as a rail terminus in 1878, it has a capacity of around 6000.

Vicar Street *(*☎ *454 5533,* Ⓦ *www.vicar street.com, 58-59 Thomas St)* Smaller performances take place at this new venue near Christ Church Cathedral. It has a capacity of 750 and offers a varied program of performers, with a strong emphasis on folk and jazz.

The Red Box *(Around St Stephen's Green map;* ☎ *478 0166, Harcourt St)* In the old Harcourt St station, this is the best venue for dance gigs, with top European dance bands and DJs strutting their stuff to crowds of groovy movers.

Temple Bar Music Centre *(Around Temple Bar map;* ☎ *670 0533, Curved St)* The centre hosts all kinds of gigs from Irish traditional to drum-and-bass.

Whelan's *(Around St Stephen's Green map;* ☎ *478 0766, 26 Wexford St,* Ⓦ *www*

.whelanslive.com) Gigs at Whelan's are mostly rock and folk.

Olympia Theatre (Around Temple Bar map; ☎ *677 7744, Dame St)* This pleasantly tatty place features everything from disco to country on Friday night. Midnight at the Olympia runs from midnight to 2am on Friday.

Cinemas

Dublin's cinemas are more heavily concentrated on the northern side of the Liffey. Admission prices are generally €4.50 for afternoon shows, rising to €7 in the evening.

UGC Multiplex (☎ *872 8400, Parnell Centre, Parnell St)* This seven-screen cinema has replaced many smaller cinemas.

Savoy (☎ *01874 6000, Upper O'Connell St)* The Savoy is a four-screen first-run cinema, and has late-night shows at the weekend.

Irish Film Centre (Around Temple Bar map; ☎ *679 5744, 6 Eustace St)* The Irish Film Centre has a couple of screens and shows classics and new independent films. The complex also has a bar, a cafe and a bookshop.

Screen (Around Temple Bar map; ☎ *671 4988, 2 Townsend St)* Between Trinity College and O'Connell Bridge, Screen shows fairly good art-house films on its three screens.

Theatre

Dublin's theatre scene is small but busy. Bookings can usually be made by quoting a credit card number over the phone, and the tickets can then be collected just before the performance.

Abbey Theatre (☎ *878 7222,* W *www .abbeytheatre.ie, Lower Abbey St)* The famous Abbey Theatre near the river is Ireland's national theatre. It puts on new Irish works as well as revivals of classic Irish works by writers such as WB Yeats, JM Synge, Sean O'Casey, Brendan Behan and Samuel Beckett. Tickets for evening performances can cost up to €23.50 except on Monday when they are cheaper. The smaller and less expensive *Peacock Theatre (*☎ *878 7222)* is part of the same complex.

Gate Theatre (☎ *874 4045,* W *www .gatetheatre.ie, 1 Cavendish Row)* Also to the north of the Liffey, the Gate Theatre specialises in international classics and older Irish works with a touch of comedy by playwrights such as Oscar Wilde, George Bernard Shaw and Oliver Goldsmith, although newer plays are sometimes staged too. Prices vary according to the what's on, but they're usually around €19.

Olympia Theatre (Around Temple Bar map; ☎ *677 7744, 72 Dame St)* This theatre specialises in light plays and, at Christmas time, panto.

Gaiety Theatre (Around St Stephen's Green map; ☎ *677 1717,* W *www.gaiety theatre.net, King St South)* Opened in 1871, Gaiety Theatre is used for modern plays and TV shows as well as musical comedies and revues.

Tivoli Theatre (☎ *454 4472, 135-136 Francis St)* Experimental and less-commercial performances take place here.

Andrew's Lane Theatre (Around Temple Bar map; ☎ *679 5720, 9-17 St Andrew's Lane)* This is a well established fringe theatre.

Project Arts Centre (Around Temple Bar map; ☎ *1850 260027,* W *www.project.ie, 39 East Essex St)* The centre puts on excellent productions of experimental plays by up-and-coming Irish and foreign writers.

Players' Theatre (Trinity College map; ☎ *677 2941 ext 1239, Regent House, Trinity College)* The Trinity College Players' Theatre hosts student productions throughout the academic year as well as the most prestigious plays from the Dublin Theatre Festival in October.

International (Around Temple Bar map; ☎ *677 9250, 23 Wicklow St)* This is one of several pubs that host theatrical performances.

The Ark (Around Temple Bar map; ☎ *670 7788, 11a Eustace St)* has a 150-seater venue that stages shows for kids aged between three and 13.

SPECTATOR SPORTS

All venues mentioned here are outside the area shown on the Dublin map.

Leopardstown Race Course (☎ 289 3607, Foxrock) The Irish love of horse racing can be observed about 10km south of the city centre in Foxrock. Special buses depart the city centre on race days: ring the race course for details.

Harold's Cross Park (☎ 497 1081, 151 Harold's Cross Rd) Bus No 16 or 16A. Greyhound racing takes place near Rathmines.

Shelbourne Stadium (☎ 668 3502, Bridge Town Rd, Ringsend) Bus No 3 from D'Olier St. This is also a greyhound track. For current information on horse and greyhound meetings call ☎ 1550 112218 (24 hours).

Lansdowne Rd Stadium (☎ 668 9300, Ballsbridge) DART: Lansdowne Rd Station. Rugby and international football matches take place here, near Ballsbridge. The rugby season is from September to April and the football season from August to May.

Croke Park Stadium (☎ 855 8176, Clonliffe Rd) Bus No 19 or 19A. Hurling and Gaelic football games are held from February to November here, at headquarters of the Gaelic Athletic Association, north of the Royal Canal in Drumcondra. Call ☎ 1550 112215 (24 hours) for the latest details.

SHOPPING

If it's made in Ireland, you can probably buy it in Dublin. Popular purchases include fine Irish knitwear such as the renowned Aran sweaters; jewellery with a Celtic influence, including Claddagh rings; books on Irish topics; crystal from Waterford, Galway, Tyrone and Tipperary; Irish coats of arms; china from Beleek; Royal Tara chinaware; and linen from Donegal. If you're interested in **antiques**, Francis St, south of Tivoli Theatre in the Liberties area, is the place to go.

Citizens of non-EU countries can reclaim the VAT (sales tax) paid on purchases made at stores displaying a cashback sticker; ask for details. For information on bookshops, see that entry in the Information section earlier in this chapter.

Department Stores & Shopping Centres

Dublin's main shopping street is on and around pedestrianised Grafton St and, on the northside, on and around Henry St, just off O'Connell St. Here you'll find the top department stores and shopping malls. Needless to say, Grafton St shops are posher and more expensive.

Arnott's (☎ 805 0400, 12 Henry St) Occupying a huge block with entrances on Henry, Liffey and Abbey Sts, this formerly mediocre department store has been completely overhauled and is now probably Dublin's best. It stocks virtually everything you could possibly want to buy, from garden furniture to high fashion, and everything is relatively affordable.

Clery's & Co (☎ 878 6000, O'Connell St) This graceful shop on O'Connell St is a Dublin classic. Recently restored to its elegant best, it caters to the more conservative Dublin shopper.

Brown Thomas (Around Temple Bar map; ☎ 605 6666, 92 Grafton St) This is Dublin's most expensive department store, suitably stocked to cater for the city's more moneyed shoppers. You'll find every top label represented here.

ILAC Centre (☎ 704 1460, Henry St) The ILAC Centre, off Henry St near O'Connell St, is a little dilapidated but still has some interesting outlets with goods at affordable prices.

Jervis St Centre (☎ 878 1323, Jervis St) Just north of Capel St Bridge, this is an ultramodern mall with dozens of outlets.

St Stephen's Green Shopping Centre (Around St Stephen's Green map; ☎ 478 0888, St Stephen's Green) Open 9am-6pm Sun-Fri, to 8pm Thur. Inside this flash shopping centre you'll find a diverse mixture of chain stores and individual shops.

Powerscourt Townhouse Shopping Centre (Around St Stephen's Green map; ☎ 679 4144, 59 South William St) The wonderful Powerscourt Townhouse Shopping Centre between South William St and Clarendon St, just to the west of Grafton St, is a big, modern shopping centre in a fine old building.

Designer Clothes

Temple Bar and the area around Grafton St are the best places for all kind of designer gear, both new and second-hand.

Eager Beaver *(Around Temple Bar map;* ☎ *677 3342, 17 Crown Alley)* Need a black suit for a wedding? A cricket jumper? Or a Victorian shirt, but don't want to spend a fortune? Then this is your place – it's a clothes hunter's paradise.

Harlequin *(Around Temple Bar map;* ☎ *671 0202, 13 Castle Market)* This is a wonderful store with a great selection of second-hand jeans, shirts and suits.

Jenny Vander *(Around Temple Bar map;* ☎ *677 0406, George's St Arcade)* Jenny Vander's selection of second-hand clothes is pretty wild. You can get a tarot card reading here too.

Hobo *(Around Temple Bar map;* ☎ *670 4869, 6-9 Trinity St)* This is an Irish designer store that sells clothes best described as 'clubber's clobber' – perfectly suited to the vast market of young people eager to look the part on the dance floor. The clothes are well made and quite snazzy.

Irish Crafts & Souvenirs

Avoca Handweavers *(Around Temple Bar map;* ☎ *677 4215, 11-13 Suffolk St)* This is the Dublin branch of Wicklow's famous craft shop – where you can find everything from woollen knits to hand-crafted gadgets.

The Kilkenny Shop *(Around Temple Bar map;* ☎ *677 7066, 6 Nassau St)* This shop has a wonderful selection of finely made Irish crafts, featuring clothing, glassware, pottery, jewellery, crystal and silver from some of Ireland's best designers.

Knobs & Knockers *(Around Temple Bar map;* ☎ *671 0288, 19 Nassau St)* This is where you'll find a Dublin doorknocker to grace your front door.

Irish Celtic Craftshop *(Around Temple Bar map;* ☎ *667 9912, 10-12 Lord Edward St)* This shop near Christ Church Cathedral specialises in well made, nontacky Irish crafts.

Dublin Woollen Company *(Around Temple Bar map;* ☎ *677 5014, 41 Lower Ormond Quay)* Near the Ha'penny Bridge, this is one of the major wool outlets in Dublin. It has a large collection of sweaters, cardigans, scarves, rugs, shawls and other woollen goods and runs a tax-free shopping scheme.

Claddagh Records *(Around Temple Bar map;* ☎ *677 0262, 2 Cecilia St)* This shop sells a wide range of Irish traditional and folk music.

Markets

George's St Arcade *(Around Temple Bar map; between South Great George St & Drury St)* This excellent covered market has some great second-hand-clothes stores.

Meeting House Square Market *(Around Temple Bar map; Meeting House Square)* This open-air market in Temple Bar takes place every weekend. You can buy all kinds of organic food and other delectable tidbits.

GETTING THERE & AWAY
Air

Dublin is Ireland's major international gateway airport, with direct flights from Europe, North America and Asia. See the Getting There & Away chapter for details on flights and fares.

Airline offices in Dublin include:

Aer Lingus (☎ 886 6705 for departures & arrivals, ☎ 886 8888 for reservations, @ bookings@ aerlingus.ie, **W** www.flyaerlingus.com) There are branches at: 40–41 Upper O'Connell St; 13 St Stephen's Green; Jury's Hotel, Ballsbridge; 12 Upper George's St, Dun Laoghaire
Aeroflot (☎ 844 6166, **W** www.aeroflot.org) Dublin Airport
Air Canada (☎ 1800 709900, **W** www .aircanada.ca) 7 Herbert St
Air France (☎ 844 5633, **W** www.airfrance .co.uk) Dublin Airport
Alitalia (☎ 677 5171, **W** www.alitalia.co.uk) 4–5 Dawson St
British Airways (☎ 1800 62 67 47, **W** www .britishairways.com) Dublin Airport
British Midland (☎ 407 3036, **W** www.flybmi .co.uk) Dublin Airport
Crossair (☎ 1890 200515, **W** www.crossair.ch) Dublin Airport
Delta Air Lines (☎ 1800 768080, **W** www .delta.com) 3 Dawson St
Finnair (☎ 844 6565, **W** www.finnair.co.uk) Dublin Airport
Iberia (☎ 407 3017, **W** www.iberia.com) 54 Dawson St
Lufthansa Airlines (☎ 844 5544, **W** www .lufthansa.co.uk) Dublin Airport

Manx Airlines (☎ 260 1588, W www.manx
-airlines.com) Dublin Airport
Qantas Airways (☎ 407 3278, W www.qantas
.com.au) Dublin Airport
Sabena (☎ 1890 200520, W www.sabena.com)
Dublin Airport
Scandinavian Airlines (SAS; ☎ 844 5888,
W www.scandinavian.net) Dublin Airport
Tyrolean Airways (☎ 608 0099, W www
.tyroleanairways.com) 140–142 Pembroke Rd

Bus

Busáras, at Store St, just north of the Custom
House and the Liffey, is Bus Éireann's central bus station. Information on buses is
available there from the Travel Centre
(☎ 836 6111, W www.buseireann.ie), 8.30am
to 7pm Monday to Saturday, and 9am to 7pm
on Sunday and public holidays.

For information on fares, frequencies and
durations to various destinations in the Republic and Northern Ireland, see Bus in the
Getting Around chapter.

Train

For general information contact Iarnród
Éireann Travel Centre (☎ 836 6222, W www
.irishrail.ie), 35 Lower Abbey St, which
opens 9am to 5pm Monday to Friday and
9am to 1pm on Saturday. Connolly Station
(☎ 836 3333), just north of the Liffey and
the city centre, is the station for Belfast,
Derry, Sligo and other points north. Heuston
Station (☎ 836 5421), just south of the Liffey and well west of the centre, is the station
for Cork, Galway, Killarney, Limerick,
Wexford, Waterford and other points west,
south and south-west. See Train in the Getting Around chapter for more information.

Boat

There are two direct services from Holyhead
on the north-western tip of Wales: one to
Dublin and the other to Dun Laoghaire, the
port on the southern side of Dublin Bay.
There are also services from Liverpool. A
new terminal is being built in Dublin and
should be operating by the time you read this.

You can also take advantage of bus/train
and ferry combinations in the UK. See Land
& Sea in the Getting There & Away chapter
for more information.

GETTING AROUND
To/From the Airport

Dublin Airport (County Dublin map; ☎ 814
1111) is 13km north of the centre and can be
reached by bus or taxi.

It has a left-luggage office (☎ 704 4633),
which opens 6am to 10pm daily (€3.20 per
item for 24 hours).

Bus Services The Airlink Express Coach
(☎ 872 0000, 873 4222), operated by
Dublin Bus, runs to/from Busáras (Dublin's
central bus station) costing €4.50 for adults
and €2.50 for children. It also runs to/from
Heuston and Connolly train stations for the
same price. Both journeys take about 30 to
40 minutes. Timetables are available at the
airport or in the city.

From the airport to Busáras, bus No 747
departs every 10 minutes between 5.45am
and 11.30pm, Monday to Saturday (every
20 minutes between 7.15am and 11.30pm
on Sunday). From Busáras, the service runs
every 10 minutes between 6.30am and
10.45pm Monday to Saturday (every 20
minutes between 7.30am and 11.10pm on
Sunday).

From the airport to Heuston Station, bus
No 748 departs every 15 minutes from
6.25am to 9.30pm Monday to Saturday (at
7am, 7.45am and every 25 minutes thereafter
until 10.05pm Sunday). From Heuston Station, buses run every 15 minutes between
7.10am and 10.20pm (7.50am, 8.40am and
every 25 minutes until 10.50pm). From
Connolly Station, buses also run every 15
minutes between 7.20am and 10.30pm Monday to Saturday, and every 25 minutes between 8.55am and 11pm on Sunday (first
departure at 8am).

Aircoach (☎ 844 7118, W www.aircoach
.ie) is a privately run service that operates
luxury air-conditioned coaches between the
airport and 15 locations throughout the city,
usually to cater for residents of the city's
biggest hotels, but they will pick up anyone.
From the airport, coaches run between 5am
and 11.30pm daily, and they stop at over a
dozen points throughout the city centre,
usually close to the bigger hotels (check the
Web site for exact locations). You will be

charged a flat rate of €5.10 per passenger (accompanied children free), irrespective of destination.

The alternative service is on the slower bus Nos 41 and 41A, which make a number of useful stops on the way, terminate on Eden Quay near O'Connell St and cost €1.40. The trip takes about an hour.

There are also direct buses between Dublin Airport and Belfast.

Taxi Services Taxis are subject to additional charges for baggage, extra passengers and 'unsociable hours'. However, a taxi usually costs about €16.50 between the airport and the centre, so between four people it's unlikely to be more expensive than the express bus. There's a supplementary charge of 80p from the airport to the city, but this charge doesn't apply from the city to the airport. Make sure the meter is switched on, as some Dublin Airport taxi drivers can be as unscrupulous as their brethren anywhere else in the world.

To/From the Ferry Terminals

Buses go to Busáras from the Dublin Ferryport terminal (☎ 855 2222), Alexandra Rd, after all ferry arrivals from Holyhead. Buses also run from Busáras to meet ferry departures. For the 9.45am ferry departure from Dublin, buses leave Busáras at 8.30am. For the 9.45pm departure, buses depart from Busáras at 8.30pm. For the 1am sailing to Liverpool, the bus departs Busáras at 11.45pm. All buses cost €2.50.

To travel between Dun Laoghaire's Carlisle terminal (☎ 280 1905) and Dublin, take bus No 46A to St Stephen's Green, or bus No 7, 7A or 8 to Burgh Quay, or take the DART (see Train later in this section) to Pearse station (for south Dublin) or Connolly station (for north Dublin).

Between Connolly & Heuston Stations

The 90 Raillink Bus runs between the two stations every 10 to 15 minutes at peak periods and costs €0.85. Connolly station is a short walk north of Busáras; Heuston is by the Liffey, on the western side of town.

Bus

Dublin Bus' (Bus Átha Cliath) information office (☎ 873 4222, W www.dublinbus.ie) at 59 Upper O'Connell St opens 9am to 5.30pm Monday to Friday and 9am to 2pm on Saturday. Free single-route timetables are available. The central bus station, or Busáras, is just north of the river, behind the Custom House, and has a left-luggage facility (€2.50 per day).

Buses run from around 6am (some start at 5.30am) to 11.30pm daily. Fares are calculated according to stages: one to three stages costs €0.85; four to seven costs €1.10; eight to 12 costs €1.35; and 13 to 23 costs €1.50. The city centre (Citizone) is within a 12-stage radius, so the maximum fare for travelling within the centre is €1.35.

You must tender exact change when boarding; if you give anything more you will be given a receipt for reimbursement, which you can only collect at the Dublin Bus main office.

One-day rambler passes cost €4.50 for the bus, or €6.60 for bus and rail. There are other bus passes for unlimited bus travel for three days (€8.25) and five days (€12.70). There are no discounts on these passes for students. Weekly bus passes cost €15.90 (students €12.70); weekly bus and rail passes cost €21.60 (plus €2.50 for an ID photo).

Nitelink late-night buses run from the College St, Westmoreland St and D'Olier St triangle. From Monday to Wednesday, there are usually only two departures, at 12.30am and 2am. From Thursday to Saturday, departures are at 12.30am, 2am and then every 20 minutes until 4.30am on the more popular routes and until 3.30am on the less frequented ones. Fares are €3.80 unless you're travelling to the far suburbs (places like Balbriggan in North County Dublin or Ashbourne in County Meath); then the fare is €5.70.

Train

The Dublin Area Rapid Transport (DART) provides quick train access to the coast as far north as Howth and as far south as Bray. Pearse Station is convenient for central

Dublin south of the Liffey, and Connolly Station for north of the Liffey. There are services every 10 to 20 minutes, sometimes even more frequently, from around 6.30am to midnight Monday to Saturday. Services are less frequent on Sunday. It takes about 30 minutes from Dublin to Bray to the south, or to Howth to the north. Dublin to Dun Laoghaire takes about 15 to 20 minutes. There are also Suburban Rail services north as far as Dundalk, inland to Mullingar and south past Bray to Arklow.

A one-way DART ticket from Dublin to Dun Laoghaire or Howth costs €1.50; to Bray it's €1.70. Within the DART region, a one-day, unlimited travel ticket costs €5.10 for an adult, €2.50 for a child or €8.90 for a family. A one-day ticket combining DART and Dublin Bus services costs €6.60 for an adult and €9.50 for a family (there is no child rate). A four-day pass allows you unlimited DART and bus travel for €12.70. A weekly rail and bus ticket costs €21.60 but requires an ID photo (€2.50).

Bicycles can't be taken on DART services, but they can be taken on the less frequent suburban train services, either in the guard's van or in a special compartment at the opposite end of the train from the engine. There's a €2.25 charge for transporting a bicycle up to 56km.

Heuston station has left-luggage lockers of three sizes, costing €1.90/3.20/5.10 for 24 hours. At Connolly station the facility costs €1.90 (backpacks €3.20).

Car

As in most cities, having a car in Dublin is as much a millstone as a convenience, though it can be useful for day trips outside the city.

There are parking meters around central Dublin and a large number of open and sheltered car parks. Parking illegally is not advised, especially as Dublin has introduced a clamping system, with a €95.50 charge for removal. However, you don't have to go far from the centre to find free roadside parking, especially in north Dublin. However, the gardaí warn visitors that it's safer to park in a supervised car park, since cars are often broken into even in broad daylight. Cars with foreign number plates, which may contain valuable personal effects, are a prime target. Rental cars are also targeted, but nowadays most have no external indication that they're owned by a rental company.

When you're booking accommodation check on parking facilities. Some B&Bs that claim to offer private parking, especially in the centre, may have a sharing arrangement with a nearby hotel to use its car park – provided the car park hasn't been filled by the hotel patrons' cars.

Rental See Car & Motorcycle in the Getting Around chapter for information on car rental. A number of rental companies have desks at the airport, and other operators are based close to the airport and deliver cars for airport collection. Some of the main rental companies in Dublin are:

Avis Rent-a-Car
(☎ 605 7555, W www.avis.com) 1 East Hanover St
(☎ 844 5204) Dublin Airport
Budget Rent-a-Car
(☎ 837 9802, W www.budgetcarrental.ie) 151 Lower Drumcondra Rd
(☎ 844 5150) Dublin Airport
Dan Dooley Car & Van Hire
(☎ 677 2723, W www.dan-dooley.ie) 42–43 Westland Row
(☎ 844 5156) Dublin Airport
Hertz Rent-a-Car
(☎ 660 2255, W www.hertz.com) 149 Upper Leeson St
(☎ 844 5466) Dublin Airport
Murrays Europcar
(☎ 614 2800, W www.europcar.com) Baggot St Bridge
(☎ 844 4179) Dublin Airport
Sixt Rent-a-Car
(☎ 862 2715, W www.icr.ie) Old Airport Rd, Santry
(☎ 844 4199) Dublin Airport
Windsor Thrifty
(☎ 1800 515800, W www.thrifty.ie) 125 Herberton Bridge, South Circular Rd
(☎ 840 0800) Dublin Airport

Taxi

Taxis in Dublin are expensive with a €2.40 minimum charge and €0.15 for one-ninth of a mile (or 40 seconds) thereafter. In addition there are a number of extra charges – €0.50 for each extra passenger, €0.50 for each piece of luggage, €2.50 for telephone bookings and €0.50 or €1 for unsociable hours (€0.50 from 8pm to midnight, 5am to 8am and all day Sunday; €1 from midnight to 5am and public holidays).

Taxis can be hailed on the street and are found at taxi ranks around the city, including on O'Connell St in north Dublin, College Green in front of Trinity College and St Stephen's Green at the end of Grafton St. There are numerous taxi companies that will dispatch taxis by radio. Try City Cabs (☎ 872 2688) or National Radio Cabs (☎ 677 2222). There aren't nearly enough taxis: queues at ranks can be frustratingly long, and even calling one by phone is often met with a negative response at busy times. Phone the Garda Carriage Office (☎ 475 5888) for complaints about taxis and queries regarding lost property.

Bicycle
Despite the shortage of cycle lanes and the traffic, Dublin isn't a bad place to get around by bicycle, as it is small enough and flat enough to make bike travel easy. Many visitors explore farther afield by bicycle, a popular activity in Ireland despite the often less-than-encouraging weather.

The hostels seem to offer secure bicycle parking areas, but if you're going to have a bike stolen anywhere in Ireland, Dublin is where it'll happen. Lock your bike up well. Surprisingly, considering how popular bicycles are in Dublin, there's a scarcity of suitable bike-parking facilities. Grafton St and Temple Bar are virtually devoid of places to lock a bike. Elsewhere, there are signs on many likely stretches of railing announcing that bikes must not be parked there. Nevertheless, there are some places, such as the Grafton St corner of St Stephen's Green.

Rental You can either bring your bike with you or rent one in Dublin, where basically you'll have a choice of two kinds of bike. Firstly there's the regular frame bike, either a racer or the all-terrain kind, which you can rent for around €13 per day or €50 per week. The more expensive high-spec aluminium bikes cost typically around €19 per day or €64 per week.

Raleigh Rent-a-Bike agencies can be found all over Ireland, north and south of the border. Contact them at Raleigh Ireland (☎ 626 1333), Raleigh House, Kylemore Rd, Dublin 10. Raleigh agencies in Dublin include the following:

C Harding for Bikes (☎ 873 2455) 30 Bachelor's Walk
Joe Daly (☎ 298 1485) Lower Main St, Dundrum
Hollingsworth Cycle (☎ 490 5094) 54 Templeogue Rd, Templeogue

Around Dublin

There are a number of seaside suburbs round the curve of Dublin Bay. Dun Laoghaire to the south and Howth to the north are historic ports and popular day trips from the city. Connected to central Dublin by the convenient DART train service, they also make interesting alternatives to staying in the city. Malahide with its castle, the imposing Anglo-Irish mansion of Newbridge House, and the village of Swords are other Dublin-area attractions.

DUN LAOGHAIRE
Dun Laoghaire (pronounced dun leary), only 13km south-east of central Dublin, is both a busy harbour with ferry connections to Britain and a popular resort. From 1821, when King George IV departed from here after a visit to Ireland, until Irish independence in 1922, the port was known as Kingstown. The fact that there are many B&Bs in Dun Laoghaire that are a bit cheaper than those in central Dublin, combined with the fast and frequent DART train connections, makes it easy to stay out here.

History
There was a coastal settlement on the site of Dun Laoghaire over 1000 years ago, but it was little more than a small fishing village until 1767, when the first pier was constructed. Dun Laoghaire grew more rapidly

DUBLIN

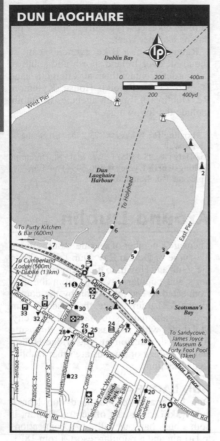

DUN LAOGHAIRE

PLACES TO STAY
17 Kingston Hotel
20 Annesgrove
21 Rosmeen House
23 Innisfree
30 Royal Marine Hotel

PLACES TO EAT
9 Brasserie Na Mara
27 Kaphian
32 GTI Café & Bistro
34 Fire Island

OTHER
1 Anemometer
2 Lifeboat Memorial
3 Bandstand
4 Compass Pointer
5 Carlisle (Mailboat) Pier
6 St Michael's (Car Ferry) Pier
7 Royal Irish Yacht Club
8 Ferry Terminal; Dublin Tourism
10 Dun Laoghaire DART Station
11 Dun Laoghaire & Rathdown Tourist Office
12 Pavilion Complex
13 Royal St George Yacht Club
14 King George IV Monument
15 National Yacht Club
16 Christ the King Sculpture
18 Oceantec
19 Sandycove & Glasthule DART Station
22 Police Station
24 National Maritime Museum
25 Post Office
26 Bank of Ireland
28 Aer Lingus
29 Dun Laoghaire Shopping Centre
31 Weir's
33 Dunphy's

after that, and the Sandycove Martello Tower was erected in the early 19th century, as there was great fear of an invasion from Napoleonic France.

Construction of the harbour was proposed in 1815 to provide a refuge for ships unable to reach the safety of Dublin Harbour in inclement weather. Originally, a single pier was proposed, but engineer John Rennie decided to build two massive piers enclosing a huge 100-hectare artificial harbour. Work began in 1817 and by 1823 the workforce comprised 1000 men. However, despite huge expenditure, the harbour wasn't com-

pleted until 1842, Carlisle Pier wasn't added until 1859 and parts of the West Pier stonework have never been finished. The total cost approached £1 million sterling, an astronomical figure in the mid-19th century.

Orientation & Information
Upper and Lower George's St, which runs parallel to the coast, is the main shopping street through Dun Laoghaire. The huge harbour is sheltered by the encircling arms of the East and West Piers. Sandycove with the James Joyce Museum and Forty Foot Pool is about 1km east of central Dun Laoghaire.

The Dun Laoghaire & Rathdown Tourist Office (☎ 205 4855) is at 8 Royal Marine Rd, about 100m from the ferry terminal. Just inside the terminal is an office of Dublin Tourism (☎ 1800 668668). A bureau de change, also in the terminal, opens for ferry arrivals and departures.

There is a branch of the Bank of Ireland at 101 Upper George's St, which has an ATM. It opens 10am to 4pm Monday to Wednesday and Friday (to 5pm Thursday). The post office, next door at No 102, opens 9am to 6pm Monday to Friday and 9am to 5.30pm on Saturday.

For the police dial ☎ 999, or ☎ 666 5000 for Dun Laoghaire's Garda station, 34–35 Corrig Avenue.

The Harbour

The 1290m East and 1548m West Piers, each ending at a lighthouse dating from the 1850s, have always been popular for walking (especially the East Pier), bird-watching and fishing (particularly from the end of the West Pier). You can also ride a bicycle out along the piers (bottom level only). In the 19th century the practice of 'scorching' – riding out along the pier at breakneck speed – became so prevalent that bicycles were banned for some time.

The East Pier has an 1890s bandstand and a memorial to Captain Boyd and the crew of the Dun Laoghaire lifeboat who were drowned in a rescue attempt. Near the end of the pier is the 1852 anemometer, one of the first of these wind-speed measuring devices to be installed anywhere in the world. The East Pier ends at the East Pier Battery with a lighthouse and a gun-saluting station, which is useful when visiting VIPs arrive by sea (which rarely happens nowadays, thanks to the aeroplane!).

The harbour has long been a popular yachting centre and the Royal Irish Yacht Club's building, dating from around 1850, was the first purpose-built yacht club in Ireland. The Royal St George Yacht Club's building dates from 1863 and that of the National Yacht Club from 1876. The world's first one-design sailing-boat class (a race in which all boats taking part are the same

type, so there's no need for handicaps) started life at Dun Laoghaire with a dinghy design known as Water Wag. A variety of specifically Dublin Bay one-design classes still race here, as do Mirrors and other popular small sailing boats.

Carlisle Pier, opened in 1859, is also known as the Mailboat Pier and was modified to handle drive-on, drive-off car ferries in 1970. With the completion of the new ferry terminal in 1995, the terminal here closed. There is talk of converting it into a museum, but at the moment it's just talk. St Michael's Pier, also known as the Car Ferry, was added in 1969. Over on the West Pier side of the harbour are two anchored lightships which have now been replaced by automatic buoys.

National Maritime Museum

This museum (☎ 280 0969, Haigh Terrace; closed for repairs) is housed in the Mariner's Church, built in 1837 'for the benefit of sailors in men-of-war, merchant ships, fishing boats and yachts'. The window in the chancel is a replica of the Five Sisters window at York Minster in England.

Exhibits include a French ship's longboat captured at Bantry in 1796 during Wolfe Tone's abortive invasion. The huge Great Baily Light Optic, driven by clockwork, came from the Baily Lighthouse on Howth Peninsula. It operated from 1902 until 1972, when it was replaced with an electrically powered lens. There's a model of the *Great Eastern* (1858), the early steam-powered vessel built by English engineer Isambard Kingdom Brunel. The boat proved a commercial failure as a passenger ship but successfully laid the first transatlantic telegraph cable between Ireland and North America. There are various items from the German submarine *U19*, which landed Sir Roger Casement in Kerry in 1916 (see Sandycove later in this section). These were donated 50 years after the event by the U-boat's captain, Raimund Weisbach.

Around the Town

Nothing remains of the *dún* (fort) that gave Dun Laoghaire its name, as it was totally destroyed during the construction of the train line. The train line from Dun Laoghaire to Dalkey was built along the route of an earlier line known as the Metals, which was used to bring stone for the harbour construction from the quarries at Dalkey Hill. By means of a pulley system, the laden trucks trundling down to the harbour pulled the empty ones back up to the quarry.

On the waterfront is a curious monument to King George IV to commemorate his visit in 1821. It consists of an obelisk balanced on four stone balls, one of which is missing as a result of an IRA bomb attack.

On the other side of Queen's Rd is the Christ the King sculpture, which was created in Paris in 1926, bought in 1949 and then put in storage until 1978 because the religious authorities decided they didn't really like it all that much.

Sandycove

Only 1km south of Dun Laoghaire is Sandycove, with a pretty little beach and the Martello tower that houses the James Joyce Museum. Sir Roger Casement, who attempted to organise a German-backed Irish freedom force during WWI, was born here in 1864. He was captured after being landed in County Kerry from a German U-boat and executed by the British as a traitor in 1916.

James Joyce Museum The Martello tower, which houses the museum (☎ 280 9265, Sandycove; adult/student/child €5 /4/3; open 10am-1pm & 2pm-5pm Mon-Sat, 2pm-6pm Sun April-Oct; by arrangement only Nov-Mar), is where the action begins in James Joyce's epic novel *Ulysses*. The museum was opened in 1962 by Sylvia Beach, the Paris-based publisher who first dared to put *Ulysses* into print, and has photographs, letters, documents, various editions of Joyce's work and two death masks of Joyce on display. Note that it's possible to buy a combination ticket that also gives you access to the Dublin Writers' Museum and George Bernard Shaw House.

A string of Martello towers was built around the coast of Ireland between 1804

and 1815 in case of invasion by Napoleon's forces. The granite tower stands 12m high with walls 2.5m thick and was copied from a tower at Cape Mortella in Corsica. Originally, the entrance to the tower led straight into what is now the 'upstairs'. Other tower sites included Dalkey Island, Killiney and Bray, south of Dun Laoghaire; and to the north, Howth and Ireland's Eye, the island off Howth. There are fine views from the tower. To the south-east you can see Dalkey Island with its signal tower and Killiney Hill with its obelisk. Howth Head is visible on the northern side of Dublin Bay. There's another Martello tower not far to the south near Bullock Harbour.

You can get to the tower by a 30-minute walk along the seafront from Dun Laoghaire Harbour, a 15-minute walk from Sandycove & Glasthule DART station or a five-minute walk from Sandycove Avenue West, served by bus No 8, which runs from Dublin through Dun Laoghaire.

Forty Foot Pool Below the Martello tower is the Forty Foot Pool, an open-air seawater bathing pool that took its name from the army regiment, the Fortieth Foot, that was stationed at the tower until the regiment was disbanded in 1904. At the close of the first chapter of *Ulysses*, Buck Mulligan heads off to the Forty Foot Pool for a morning swim. A morning wake-up here is still a Dun Laoghaire tradition, winter or summer. In fact, a winter dip isn't much braver than a summer one since the water temperature varies by only about 5°C, winter or summer. Basically, it's always bloody cold.

Originally nudist and for men only, pressure from female bathers eventually opened this public stretch of water to both sexes, despite strong opposition from the 'forty foot gentlemen'. They eventually compromised with the ruling that a 'togs must be worn' sign would now apply after 9am. Prior to that time nudity prevails and swimmers are still predominantly 'forty foot gentlemen'.

Activities

A series of walks in the area make up the signposted Dun Laoghaire Way. The *Her-*

itage Map of Dun Laoghaire, available from the tourist office and from bookshops, includes a map and notes on the seven separate walks.

Scuba divers head for the waters around Dalkey Island. **Oceantec** (☎ *280 1083, fax 284 3885, 10–11 Marine Terrace)*, a dive shop in Dun Laoghaire, hires out diving equipment at €38 per day (€30.50 per half-day). A one-hour local dive with a dive master costs €45.

Places to Stay

As a major ferry port, Dun Laoghaire has plenty of accommodation, especially B&Bs.

Rosmeen House (☎ *280 7613, 13 Rosmeen Gardens)* Singles/doubles €39/63.50. This is the best of the B&Bs on Rosmeen Rd, a lovely Spanish villa with elegant bedrooms that are supremely comfortable.

Annesgrove (☎ *280 9801, 28 Rosmeen Gardens)* Singles/doubles €32/72. This a pleasant and large suburban residence with well appointed bedrooms that come with the usual B&B perks, including tea and coffee facilities and TV.

Innisfree (☎ *280 5598, fax 280 3093, e djsmyth@clubi.ie, 31 Northumberland Avenue)* Singles with/without bathroom €29/36, doubles €45/50. Only a couple of minutes' walk from George's St, there is nothing spectacular about this B&B, but it is clean and neat. The bedrooms are tidy (if a little small) and the owners are gracious hosts.

Cumberland Lodge (☎ *280 9665, fax 284 3227, e cumberlandlodge@tinet.ie, 54 York Rd)* Singles €35-45, doubles €45-58. The four rooms in this fabulous Georgian house are all en suite, and each is spacious and very comfortable.

Other B&Bs can be found on nearby Mellifont and Corrig avenues.

Kingston Hotel (☎ *280 1810, fax 280 1237, e reserv@kingstonhotel.ie, Adelaide St)* Singles/doubles €82/115. A (long overdue) refurbishment has restored this fine hotel to its rightful position as one of Dun Laoghaire's best. The rooms are absolutely gorgeous and, for the money, better value than the town's top dog, the Royal Marine Hotel (see below).

Royal Marine Hotel (☎ *280 1911, fax 280 1089, e ryan@indigo.ie, Royal Marine Rd)* Rooms €229. Built in 1865, this is easily the best hotel in town. Sea-facing rooms have incredible views of much of Dublin Bay, while the general facilities are top class. It's very expensive, though: for the price, there's better (only not in Dun Laoghaire).

Places to Eat

Fire Island (☎ *280 5318, 107 Lower George's St)* Mains €14-20.50. Open from 5.30pm Tues-Sat. Owner/chef Tim Rooney was trained at the renowned cooking school at Ballymaloe House in County Cork, and it shows. The adventurous 'new Irish' cuisine is delicious.

Mao Café Bar (☎ *214 8090, Pavilion Complex)* Mains around €10.50. This is a branch of the popular restaurant in Dublin's city centre. The menu is 'Asian fusion', with European spins on Chinese and Thai dishes.

Brasserie Na Mara (☎ *280 6787, 1 Harbour Rd)* Mains €25.50. Near the harbour and next to the DART station, Brasserie Na Mara is the best restaurant in Dun Laoghaire and boasts an award-winning menu with an emphasis on seafood.

Kaphian (☎ *280 8337, 21 Upper George's St)* Breakfast €3.70-6.50, lunch around €7. Kaphian is a new cafe, with good sandwiches and nice coffee.

Kaffe Moka (☎ *284 6544, Pavilion Complex)* Snacks from €2.50. This is a branch of the popular chain. The coffee here is delicious and you can get virtually any caffeine concoction you can think of.

GTI Café & Bistro (☎ *284 6607, 59 Lower George's St)* Sandwiches €5-6.50. This place is brand new and the town is all the better for it. The sandwiches – Italian *panini*, Mexican wraps and American sandwiches – are extremely good.

Entertainment

Weir's (☎ *230 4654, 88 Lower George's St)* Despite a change in management, look and name (it used to be Cooney's), this town-centre pub is still one of the most popular in Dun Laoghaire.

Dunphy's (☎ 280 1668, 41 Lower George's St) At the southern end of town, this is one of the more traditional pubs in Dun Laoghaire, appealing to a mix of older drinkers and young swingers.

Purty Kitchen & Bar (☎ 284 3576, 2 Old Dunleary Rd) This place often has traditional Irish music or rock on Friday and Sunday. The rest of the week it's just a bar, frequented by the town's younger crowd.

Getting There & Away

See the introductory Getting There & Away chapter for details of the ferries between Dun Laoghaire and Holyhead in Wales.

Bus Nos 7, 7A and 8 from next to Trinity College cost €1.50 one way to Dun Laoghaire. The trip can take anywhere from 25 minutes to one hour depending on the traffic. The DART rail service takes you from Dublin to Dun Laoghaire in 15 to 20 minutes and also costs €1.50 one way.

DALKEY

One kilometre south of Sandycove is Dalkey (Deilginis), which has the remains of a number of old castles. On Castle St, the main street, two 16th-century castles face each other: Archibold's Castle and Goat Castle. Next to the latter is the ancient St Begnet's Church, dating from the 9th century. **Bulloch Castle** overlooking Bullock Harbour, north of town, was built by the monks of St Mary's Abbey in Dublin in the 12th century.

Goat Castle and St Begnet's Church have recently been converted into the **Dalkey Castle & Heritage Centre** (☎ 285 8366, Castle St; adult/student/child €4/3.50/2.50; open 9.30am-5pm Mon-Fri, 11am-5pm Sat & Sun, May-Oct; closed Mon-Fri Nov-Apr). Models, displays and exhibitions form a pretty interesting history of Dalkey and an insight into the area during medieval times. Worth paying close attention to are the different panels, written by author Hugh Leonard.

Dalkey has several holy wells, including **St Begnet's Holy Well** (Dalkey Island) next to the ruins of another church dedicated to St Begnet on the nine-hectare Dalkey Island, a few hundred metres offshore from Coliemore Harbour. Reputed to cure rheuma-

tism, the well is a popular destination for tourists and the faithful alike. To get there, you can rent a boat with a small outboard engine in Coliemore Harbour. To get one, simply show up (you can't book them in advance); they cost around €25 per hour.

To the south there are good views from the small park at Sorrento Point and from Killiney Hill. Dalkey Quarry is a popular site for rock climbers, and originally provided most of the granite for the gigantic piers at Dun Laoghaire Harbour. A number of rocky swimming pools are found along the Dalkey coast.

Dalkey is on the DART suburban train line, or, for a slower journey, you can catch bus No 8 from Burgh Quay in Dublin. Both cost €1.50.

HOWTH

The bulbous Howth Peninsula forms the northern end of Dublin Bay. Howth (Binn Éadair) town is only 15km from central Dublin and is easily reached by DART train or by simply following the Clontarf Rd out around the northern bay shoreline. En route you pass Clontarf, site of the pivotal clash between Celtic and Viking forces at the Battle of Clontarf in 1014. Farther along is North Bull Island, a wildlife sanctuary where many migratory birds pause in winter.

Howth is a popular excursion from Dublin and has developed as a residential suburb. It is a pretty little town built on steep streets running down to the waterfront. Although the harbour's role as a shipping port has long gone, Howth is now a major fishing centre and yachting harbour.

History

Howth's name (which rhymes with 'both') has Viking origins and comes from the Danish word 'hoved' (head). Howth Harbour dates from 1807 to 1809 and was at that time the main Dublin harbour for the packet boats from England. Howth Rd was built to ensure rapid transfer of incoming mail and dispatches from the harbour to the city. The replacement of sailing packets with steam packets in 1818 reduced the transit time from Holyhead to seven hours, but Howth's period of importance was short because, by 1813, the harbour was already showing signs of silting up. It was superseded by Dun Laoghaire in 1833. The most famous arrival to Howth was King George IV, who visited Ireland in 1821 and is chiefly remembered because he staggered off the boat in a highly inebriated state. He did manage to leave his footprint at the point where he stepped ashore on the West Pier.

In 1914 Robert Erskine Childers' yacht, *Asgard*, brought a cargo of 900 rifles into the port to arm the nationalists. During the Civil War, Childers was court-martialled by his former comrades and executed by firing squad for illegal possession of a revolver. The *Asgard* is now on display at Kilmainham Jail in Dublin.

St Mary's Abbey

St Mary's Abbey stands in ruins near the centre of Howth and was originally founded in 1042, supposedly by the Viking king Sitric, who also founded the original church on the site of Christ Church Cathedral in Dublin. St Mary's was amalgamated with the monastery on Ireland's Eye (see later) in 1235. Some parts of the ruins date from that time, but most of it was built in the 15th and 16th centuries. The tomb of Christopher St Lawrence (Lord Howth), in the south-eastern corner, dates from around 1470. You can walk around the abbey grounds, but to enter the abbey itself you need to obtain the key (instructions on where to get it are on the inside gate) from the caretaker.

Howth Castle

Howth Castle was acquired by the Norman noble Sir Almeric Tristram in 1177 and has remained in the family ever since, though the unbroken chain of male succession finally came to an end in 1909. The family name was changed to St Lawrence when Sir Almeric won a battle at St Lawrence's behest (or so he believed). Originally built in 1564, the St Lawrence family's Howth Castle has been much restored and rebuilt over the years, most recently in 1910 by the British architect Sir Edwin Lutyens.

A legend relates that in 1575 Grace O'Malley, the 'queen' of western Ireland, dropped in at the castle on her way back from a visit to England's Queen Elizabeth I. When the family claimed they were busy having dinner and refused her entry, she kidnapped the son and returned him only when Lord Howth promised that in future his doors would always be open at meal times. As a result, so it's claimed, for many years the castle extended an open invitation to hungry passers-by.

Despite Grace O'Malley's demands, the castle is no longer open, but you can visit the gardens in spring and summer and there's a popular golf course beyond the castle.

The castle gardens are noted for their rhododendrons, which bloom in May and June, for their azaleas and for a long stretch of 10m-high beech hedges planted back in 1710. The castle grounds also have the ruins of 16th-century Corr Castle and an ancient dolmen known as Aideen's Grave. It's said that Aideen died of a broken heart after her husband was killed at the Battle of Gavra near Tara in 184, but that's probably mere legend as the dolmen is thought to be much older.

To get to the castle, turn right out of the station, follow the road round then turn left at the sign for the Deer Park Hotel and National Transport Museum.

National Transport Museum

The somewhat ramshackle National Transport Museum (*☎ 848 0831, Howth Castle; adult/student €2.50/2; open 10am-5.30pm Mon-Fri Easter-Sept; 2pm-5pm Sat & Sun Oct-Easter*) has a range of exhibits, including double-decker buses, a bakery van, fire engines and trams, including a Hill of Howth electric tram that operated from 1901 to 1959. To reach the museum go through the castle gates and turn right just before the castle.

Around the Peninsula

The Summit (171m), to the south-east of the town, offers views across Dublin Bay to the Wicklow Mountains. From the Summit you can walk to the top of the Ben of Howth, which has a cairn said to mark a 2000-year-old Celtic royal grave. The 1814 Baily Light-house at the south-eastern corner is on the site of an old stone fort and can be reached by a dramatic cliff-top walk. There was an earlier hill-top beacon here in 1670.

Ireland's Eye

A short distance offshore from Howth is Ireland's Eye, a rocky sea-bird sanctuary with the ruins of a 6th-century monastery. There's a Martello tower at the north-western end of the island, where boats from Howth land, while the eastern end plummets into the sea in a spectacularly sheer rock face. As well as the sea birds overhead, you can see young birds on the ground during the nesting season. Seals can also be spotted around the island.

Doyle & Sons (☎ 831 4200) take boats out to the island from the East Pier of Howth Harbour during the summer, usually on weekend afternoons. The cost is €8.50 return. Don't wear shorts if you're planning to visit the monastery ruins because they're surrounded by a thicket of stinging nettles. And bring your rubbish back with you – far too many island visitors don't.

Farther north from Ireland's Eye is **Lambay Island,** an important sea-bird sanctuary that cannot be landed on.

Places to Stay

All of the B&Bs listed here are on Howth Hill, above the town. You can walk, but they are all served by bus No 31A from the port. The fare is €0.70.

Gleann-na-Smól (☎ 832 2936, fax 832 0516, e rickards@indigo.ie, Nashville Rd) Singles/doubles €38.50/53.50. This is a modern two-storey house with four en-suite bedrooms.

Hazelwood (☎/fax 839 1391, 2 Thormanby Woods, Thormanby Rd) €28 per person. This large, white bungalow has fabulous views of Ireland's Eye and the harbour. The rooms are quite nice, with colourful bedspreads. All are en suite.

Highfield (☎ 832 3936, Thormanby Rd) €32 per person. This is a fine Victorian house set back from the road. The rooms are beautifully decorated with a mix of antiques and modern comforts.

King Sitric (☎ 832 5235, fax 839 2442, e info@kingsitric.ie, Harbour Rd) Singles/doubles from €83/121. Howth's most famous restaurant (see Places to Eat below) has added eight marvellous rooms to its premises right on the port. Each is named after a lighthouse, and each is extremely well decorated to provide the maximum of comforts. All of the rooms have wonderful views of the port.

Deer Park Hotel (☎ 832 2624, fax 839 2405, e sales@deerpark.iol.ie, Howth Castle) Singles/doubles €102/153. Deer Park Hotel is by the golf course in the grounds of Howth Castle. The rooms are elegant and comfortable (as you would expect from a top-class hotel), but the hotel is a little too modern to give a genuine sense of the place's ambience. The views, on the other hand, are outstanding.

Places to Eat

If you want to buy food and prepare it yourself, Howth has fine seafood that you can buy fresh from the string of *seafood shops* on West Pier.

Maud's (☎ 839 5450, Harbour Rd) Sandwiches €5.10. Apart from some pretty good sandwiches, Maud's is known for its gorgeous ice creams.

El Paso (☎ 832 3334, Harbour Rd) Mains €9. This harbour-front restaurant serves up Tex-Mex cuisine in the evening Monday to Saturday and from 2pm on Sunday.

Porto Fino Ristorante (☎ 839 3054, Harbour Rd) Mains from €10. This place serves delicious Italian food.

Citrus (☎ 832 0200, Harbour Rd) Mains around €13. This is a fancy new place that serves up imaginative continental-style cuisine. For a harbourfront place, it has a surprising emphasis on meat dishes.

The Bloody Stream (☎ 839 0203, Harbour Rd) Seafood platter €14.60-17.50. Located directly below the DART station, this fine pub has a wonderful restaurant where you can eat two kinds of seafood platter, both delicious. In fine weather you can eat alfresco.

King Sitric (see Places to Stay) Mains €28, 5-course set dinner €44. Open noon-

11.30pm Mon-Sat. This place, near East Pier, is rightfully praised for its fine seafood. Try the excellent crab, which is always fresh. The wine list is superb and has won a number of domestic and international awards.

Getting There & Away
The easiest and quickest way to get to Howth from Dublin is on the DART train, which whisks you there in just over 20 minutes for a fare of €1.50. For the same fare, bus Nos 31 and 31A from Lower Abbey St in the city centre run as far as the Summit, 5km to the south-east of Howth.

MALAHIDE
Malahide (Mullach Ide) is 13km north of Dublin on the coast beyond Howth. It has virtually been swallowed by Dublin's northwards expansion, although it still has its own pretty marina. The well kept 101 hectares of the Malahide Demesne, which contains Malahide Castle, is the town's principal attraction. Talbot Botanic Gardens are next to the castle and the extensive Fry Model Railway is in the castle grounds.

Malahide Castle
Despite the vicissitudes of Irish history, the Talbot family managed to keep Malahide Castle *(☎ 846 2184, Malahide; adult/student/child/family €5.10/3.80/2.50/14, including the Fry Model Railway €8.90/6.70/3.80/22.25; open 10am-5pm Mon-Sat, 11am-6pm Sun & holidays Apr-Oct; 10am-5pm Mon-Fri, 2pm-5pm Sat & Sun & holidays Nov-Mar)* under its control from 1185 to 1976, apart from when Cromwell was in power (1649–60). It's now owned by Dublin County Council. The castle is the usual hotchpotch of additions and renovations. The oldest part is a three-storey, 12th-century tower house. The facade is flanked by circular towers, tacked on in 1765.

The castle is packed with furniture and paintings. Highlights include a 16th-century oak room with decorative carvings and the medieval Great Hall with family portraits, a minstrel's gallery and a painting of the Battle of the Boyne. Puck, the Talbot family ghost, is said to have last appeared in 1975.

The **parkland** *(free; open 10am-9pm Apr-Oct; to 5pm Nov-Mar)* around the castle is a good place for a picnic.

Fry Model Railway
Ireland's biggest model railway *(☎ 846 3779, Malahide Castle; adult/student/child/family €5.10/3.80/2.50/14, including Malahide Castle €8.90/6.70/3.80/22.25; open 10am-1pm & 2pm-5pm Mon-Sat, 2pm-6pm Sun & holidays Apr-Oct; 2pm-5pm Sat, Sun & holidays only other months)* at 240 sq metres, this model authentically displays much of Ireland's rail and public transport system, including the DART line and Irish Sea ferry services, in O-gauge (32mm track width). A separate room features model trains and other memorabilia. Unfortunately the operators suffer from the over-seriousness of some grown men with complicated toys; rather than let you simply look and admire, they herd you into the control room in groups for demonstrations.

Getting There & Away
Malahide is 13km north of Dublin. Bus No 42 (€1.50) from Talbot St takes about 45 minutes. The DART now stops in Malahide (€1.70), but be sure to get on the right train (it's marked at the front of the train) as the line splits at Howth Junction.

NEWBRIDGE HOUSE
North-east of Swords at Donabate is Newbridge House *(☎ 843 6534, Donabate; adult/student/child/family €5/3.80/2.50/14; open 10am-1pm & 2pm-5pm Mon-Sat, to 6pm Sun & holidays Apr-Sep, 2pm-5pm Sat, Sun & holidays only other months)*, a historic Georgian mansion with fine plasterwork, a private museum, an impressive kitchen and a large traditional **farm** *(adult/child/family €1.25/1/2.55)* with cows, pigs and chickens. In the stables is an astonishingly elaborate coach, built in 1790 for the Lord Chancellor. It was painted black for Queen Victoria's funeral and it wasn't until 1982 that the paint was scraped off to reveal the glittering masterpiece beneath. The size of the coach is almost as impressive as the decoration: the back wheels alone stand 1.65m high.

Donabate is 19km north of Dublin. Bus No 33B runs every 30 minutes (€2.20, one hour) from Eden Quay to Donabate village. You can also get there on the Suburban Rail service (€1.75, 30 minutes), which departs hourly from either Connolly or Pearse station in the city centre.

LUSK HERITAGE CENTRE

On the way to Skerries you'll spot the dominating turrets of Lusk church, now a heritage centre (*☎ 833 1618, Lusk; adult/child €1.25/0.50; open 10am-5pm Fri mid-June-mid-Sept only*) where a 9th-century round tower stands beside and joined to a medieval tower.

On the medieval tower's various floors are displays of medieval and later stone effigies from various churches in North County Dublin. The much less impressive 19th-century nave houses Willie Monks' dusty, somewhat forlorn collection of household and other items.

Bus No 33 from Eden Quay takes about an hour to get to Lusk (€3.50).

SKERRIES

The sleepy seaside resort of Skerries is 30km north of Dublin. St Patrick is said to have made his arrival in Ireland here at Red Island, now joined to the mainland. There's a good cliff walk south from Skerries to the bay of Loughshinny. At low tide you can walk to Shenick's, a small island off Skerries.

Skerries Watermill & Windmills Heritage Centre

This fully restored industrial mill (*☎ 849 5208, Skerries; adult/student/family €3.80/2.90/9.50; open 10.30am-6pm daily Apr-Sept; to 4.30pm daily Oct-Mar; closed 20 Dec-1 Jan*) comprises a watermill, five- and four-sail windmills, wetlands and a mill pond. Constructed in the 16th century for the Priory of Canons Regular of St Augustine, there has been a bakery on the site since 1840. It's a pretty interesting place, especially the part where you get to try your hand at grinding (which is far harder than you might think!). It is a five-minute walk from the Skerries train station (it is well signposted).

Getting There & Away

Bus No 33 (€3.50) departs from Eden Quay about every hour and takes approximately an hour to reach Skerries. Trains from Connolly station (€1.75) are less frequent but take around 30 minutes.

County Wicklow

Not all of Ireland's impressive landscapes are in the west of the country. Barely 16km south of Dublin, you can drive for an hour through wild and desolate scenery without seeing more than a handful of houses or people. The most beautiful parts of County Wicklow (Cill Mhantáin) fall within a broad north–south swathe running down the centre of the mountains, beginning at Glencree and ending near Avoca. The county's rolling granite hills are the source of Dublin's River Liffey. Glendalough has some of the country's best-preserved early-Christian remains.

Southern Wicklow was one of the last outposts of the Gaelic Irish; using remote valleys such as Glenmalure and the Glen of Imaal as hide-outs, families such as the O'Tooles and the O'Byrnes would sally forth to attack the English. Such was the Crown's concern that they built an access road from Dublin through the heart of the mountains to the bandits. Thanks to their efforts, the Military Rd still takes you through the finest Wicklow scenery.

In northern Wicklow, the Anglo-Irish gentry felt close enough to the safety of Dublin to build magnificent mansions such as those at Russborough near Blessington and Powerscourt near Enniskerry. The exquisite formal gardens of the latter are one of the county's biggest draws.

Wicklow is particularly known for its beautiful gardens, and during the Wicklow Gardens Festival in May and June many gardens not normally open to the public welcome visitors. For details contact Wicklow County Tourism (☎ 0404-66058, W www.wicklow.ie), St Manntan's House, Kilmantin Hill, Wicklow. It opens 9am to 5pm weekdays.

Wicklow's highways and main towns, many of them dormitories for Dublin, lie along the relatively narrow coastal strip leading south to Wexford. Heading south, there are pleasant seaside resorts and some fine beaches along the way.

For information on walking or cycling the

Highlights

- Walk the Wicklow Way, one of the finest hiking trails in Ireland
- Visit elegant Russborough House near Blessington, one of the most magnificent stately homes in Ireland
- Wander around Glendalough, the site of some of the best-preserved early-Christian remains in Ireland
- Spend a night in a *cillín*, or hermitage, in Glendalough – a haven for quiet contemplation
- Visit the gorgeous Italianate gardens and impressive waterfall at Powerscourt near Enniskerry

Wicklow Way, see Walking under Activities in the Facts for the Visitor chapter.

As well as the usual bus and train connections around County Wicklow, the award-winning 'wild coach' tours run by Aran Tours (see under Powerscourt and Glendalough later in this chapter) have earned rave reviews from participants and tourism authorities

209

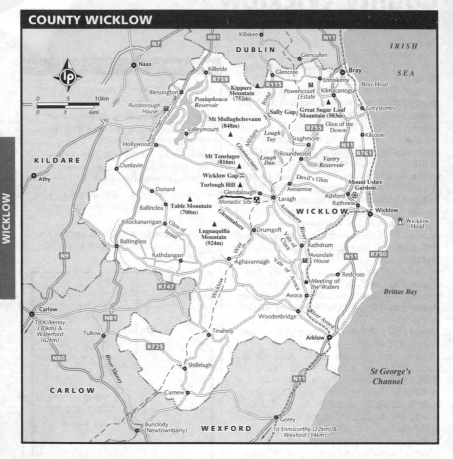

COUNTY WICKLOW

alike. The guides are all uniformly excellent, with plenty of energy and a terrific sense of humour that generates a kind of camaraderie uncommon to most tours.

Wicklow Mountains

From Killakee, a few kilometres north of Glencree, you can turn your back on Dublin and travel south for 30km across vast sweeps of heather-clad moors, bogs and mountains dotted with small corrie lakes along the Military Rd.

The Wicklow Mountains are a vast granite intrusion, a welling-up of hot igneous rock that solidified some 400 million years ago. The heat baked the overlying clays and sedimentary rocks, producing shiny mica schists that can be seen across the county. The soft metamorphosed rocks have weathered away over the millennia, exposing the granite, but significant traces remain, such as the cap of schist on top of Lugnaquilla Mountain.

The mountains were rounded and shaped during the Ice Ages, producing the smooth profiles you see today. While flattening the peaks, the ice also created deep valleys such as Glenmacnass, Glenmalure and Glendalough. Corrie lakes such as Lough Bray Upper and Lower were gouged out by ice at the head of glaciers.

Beginning on Dublin's southern fringes, the narrow Military Rd winds down to the remotest parts of Wicklow. The best place to join it is at Glencree from Enniskerry. It then runs south through the Sally Gap, Glenmacnass, Laragh, Glendalough and on to Glenmalure and Aghavannagh.

The British constructed the road early in the 19th century to get access to the Wicklow rebels who were holed up in the southern half of the county. It was a considerable feat of engineering, traversing open bog and barren mountainscapes for 50km.

Enniskerry makes a good starting point, and on the trip south you can divert east at the Sally Gap to look at Lough Tay and Lough Dan. Farther south you pass the great waterfall at Glenmacnass before dropping down into Laragh, with the magnificent monastic ruins of Glendalough nearby. Continue south through the valley of Glenmalure and, if you're fit enough, climb Lugnaquilla Mountain, Wicklow's highest peak.

ENNISKERRY
☎ 01 • pop 1275

Enniskerry, south of Dublin on the R117, owes its beginnings to the adjoining Powerscourt Estate. The landlord built this elegant, picturesque little village to accompany his impressive manor, the entrance to which is just south of the village square. Set round a small triangular green, the rows of cottages ooze quiet charm. A number of pleasant cafes make it a great place to unwind after a foray into the mountains.

Heading west up the hill takes you through some lovely scenery into Glencree and the hamlet of the same name, 10km up at the head of the valley and on the Military Rd.

Enniskerry is a popular day-trip destination for Dubliners, but the village has so far escaped the blight of modern urban development. Don't miss the small detour to Powerscourt Waterfall and the estate's gardens.

Places to Stay

Lacken House Hostel (☎ 286 4036, e mail box@anoige.ie, Knockree, Enniskerry) Dorms €9.50. This 58-bed An Óige hostel is situated in an old farmhouse with commanding views of Glencree. Accommodation can only be booked through the An Óige head office in Dublin (☎ 01-830 4555).

Cherbury (☎/fax 282 8679, Monastery, Enniskerry) En suite rooms €25.50 per person. Cherbury overlooks the valley in Monastery, 1km west of Enniskerry on the Dublin road.

Corner House (☎/fax 286 0149, Main St) Singles/doubles from €34.50/46. This place in Enniskerry has no en suites but the rooms are comfy.

Ferndale (☎/fax 286 3518, Ferndale, Enniskerry) Rooms from €25.50. Open Apr-Oct. Ferndale is a comfortable home with four well appointed rooms.

Powerscourt Arms (☎ 282 8903, fax 286 4909, Main St) En suite singles/doubles €47/89 including breakfast. This place is right in Enniskerry village facing the square. It has been recently renovated and its 12 rooms are comfortable and nicely decorated.

Summerhill House Hotel (☎ 286 7928, fax 286 7929, e res@summerhillhotel.iol .ie; off the N11) Rooms from €51 per person. This fabulous country mansion is about 700m south of town along the N11. It's elegant, comfortable and easily the best place to stay in town.

Places to Eat

Buttercups (☎ 286 9669, Enniskerry) Snacks from €3.80. Up the hill past the post office, this small deli and bread shop serves delicious takeaway food.

Poppies Country Cooking (☎ 282 8869, The Square) Lunch around €11.50. On the main square, this is the best place to eat in Enniskerry. It offers solid lunches (including several vegetarian options) and great cakes, all in a rustic atmosphere.

Johnnie Fox's (☎ 295 5647, Glencullen) Seafood platter €38. Three kilometres northwest of Enniskerry in Glencullen, this pub is renowned for its superb seafood. There's a great traditional music session nightly throughout the summer. Daniel O'Connell was a regular here and today it's a very popular tourist destination. Despite the crowds, it retains an authentic flavour.

Getting There & Away
Enniskerry is just 3km west of the N11. Dublin Bus (☎ 872 0000, 873 4222) No 44 (€1.65, every 20 minutes) takes about 1¼ hours to get to Enniskerry from Hawkins St in Dublin. Alternatively, you can take the DART train to Bray (€1.70) and get bus No 185 (€1.35, hourly) from the station, but the trip is longer and more expensive.

POWERSCOURT ESTATE
This 64 sq km estate, near Enniskerry, with its magnificent formal gardens, is a major tourist attraction (☎ 01-204 6000, W www .powerscourt.ie, Enniskerry; house & gardens adult/student/child €8/6.50/4, house only €3.50/2.50/2, gardens only €5.10/5.50/2.50; open 9.30am-5.30pm Feb-Oct; 9.30am-4.30pm Nov-Jan). The main entrance to the house and estate is 500m south of the square in Enniskerry.

Powerscourt House (built in 1743) was designed by Richard Cassels (aka Castle), who also designed Dublin's Leinster House and Russborough House near Blessington. Unfortunately, a disastrous fire gutted it in 1974 just before the house was to be opened to the public. Today it's owned by the Slazenger family.

The 20-hectare formal gardens were created in the 19th century, with Great Sugar Loaf Mountain providing a magnificent natural backdrop to the east.

Tickets come with a map laying out 40-minute and hour-long tours of the gardens. Don't miss the Japanese Gardens or the Pepperpot Tower, supposedly modelled on a three-inch version inside the house.

There is also a teashop, a garden centre and an outlet of the popular Avoca Handweavers shop, which has a range of fine Irish clothing.

A 7km walk takes you to a separate part of the estate that takes you to the 130m Powerscourt Waterfall (☎ 01-204 6000, Powerscourt Estate, Enniskerry; adult/student/child €3.50/2.50/2; open 9.30am-7pm, to dusk in win-

ter). It's the highest in Britain and Ireland, and is most impressive after heavy rain. You can also get to the falls by road following the signs from the estate.

Organised Tours
Aran Tours (☎ 01-280 1899, W www.wild coachtours.com) Adult/child €19/16.50. Departs 1.30pm & returns 6pm daily. Aran Tours runs an excellent tour to Powerscourt. There are several pick-up points throughout Dublin; check when booking for the one nearest you.

Mary Gibbons Tours (☎ 01-283 9973) €28. Departs 10.45am & returns 5pm-5.30pm Thur, Sat & Sun. Full-day tours of Powerscourt and Glendalough leave from the Dublin Tourism Centre at 2 Suffolk St (see the Dublin chapter).

There's also an excellent Guide Friday/Gray Line tour that includes Powerscourt gardens (for details see Organised Tours under Glendalough later in this chapter).

Getting There & Away
Getting to Powerscourt House under your own steam is not a problem (it's 500m from the town), but getting to the waterfall can be tricky. Alpine Coaches (☎ 01-286 2547) runs a shuttle service between the DART station in Bray, the waterfall and the house. There's plenty of visiting time and the whole deal costs €4.75 (admission fees extra). From the station, there are pick-ups at 11.05am, 11.30am, 12.30pm and 1.30pm daily, July to August (11.05am and 12.20pm only the rest of the year). The last departure from Powerscourt House is at 5.20pm daily.

GLENCREE
☎ 01
Just south of the border with Dublin and 10km west of Enniskerry is Glencree, a leafy hamlet set into the side of the valley of the same name which opens east to give a magnificent view down to Great Sugar Loaf Mountain and the sea.

The valley floor is home to the Glencree Oak Project, an ambitious plan to reforest part of Glencree with the native oak vegetation that once covered most of the country.

The village, such as it is, has a tiny shop and a hostel but no pub. A small grotto to the Virgin Mary, who is said to have appeared here in the 1980s, is set into the hillside. There's also a poignant German cemetery dedicated to servicemen who died in Ireland during WWI and WWII. Just south of the village, the former military barracks are now a retreat house and reconciliation centre for people of different religions from the Republic and the North.

Places to Stay

Stone House (☎ 286 4037, ⓔ *mailbox@ anoige.ie, Glencree)* Dorms €9.50. Located in a lovely old stone house, this An Óige hostel is clean and neat, if a little bare. It is closed between 10am and 5pm daily. It gets busy in summer so book ahead.

SALLY GAP

The Sally Gap is one of the two main east–west passes across the Wicklow Mountains. From the turn-off on the lower road (R755) between Roundwood and Kilmacanogue near Bray, the narrow road (R759) passes above the dark waters of Lough Tay and Lough Dan and the Luggala Estate. It then heads up to the Sally Gap crossroads, where it cuts across the Military Rd and heads north-west for Kilbride and the N81, following the young River Liffey, still only a stream. Just north of the Sally Gap crossroads is Kippure Mountain (752m) with its TV transmitter. The surrounding bogs have dark lines cut into them by turf-cutters.

LOUGH TAY & LOUGH DAN

Lough Tay lies like a spilled pint of Guinness at the bottom of a spectacular gash in the mountains, 5km south-east of the Sally Gap crossroads. The white sand – unique in these parts – surrounding the lake was imported at the turn of the 20th century from Florida. The lake is part of Luggala, a 2830-hectare private estate owned by Garech de Brun, a member of the Guinness family and the founder of Celtic Records. At the northern end of the lough sits Luggala House, overlooked by spectacular cliffs.

Luggala Estate covers almost all of the valley, as far down as Lough Dan, which nestles among lower hills to the south. Unfortunately, after many years of being a walker's and cyclist's paradise, the entire estate is now off-limits to visitors.

The road to the Sally Gap skirts the top of the valley on the eastern side and is crossed by the Wicklow Way walking trail, which continues south past Lough Dan. A good option is to walk part of the Wicklow Way to Lough Dan; from the highest point on the road this is about 4km. There's a lovely view of the cliffs and Lough Tay from among the trees on the valley floor.

ROUNDWOOD
☎ 01 • pop 440

At 238m above sea level, Roundwood is widely touted as Ireland's highest village, though it's hardly Mont Blanc. The village is essentially one long main street, which leads south to Glendalough and southern Wicklow. Otherwise, there isn't really much to the place. Turn-offs lead to Ashford to the east and the southern shore of Lough Dan to the west. Unfortunately, almost all Lough Dan's southern shoreline is private property and you can't get to the lake on this side. To the north is the turn-off to Bray.

There's a small tourist office (☎ 281 6557) on Main St with erratic opening hours, but usually 9am to 5pm Monday to Friday, June to September.

Roundwood's pubs are usually packed with tired walkers on weekend afternoons. There are shops, a post office and a thriving market held every Sunday afternoon, March to December, in the small hall on Main St.

North-west of the village you'll find some of the county's best scenery on the road to the Sally Gap, with a tremendous panorama over Lough Tay and the Luggala Estate.

Places to Stay

Roundwood Caravan & Camping Park (☎/*fax 281 8163, dicksonn@indigo.ie, Roundwood)* Hikers & cyclists including tent €9.50 per person, for 2 people €12. Open Easter-Sept. Within 500m of the village, this place has good facilities.

Ballinacor House *(☎ 281 8168, Round-wood)* Singles/doubles €23/41. This elegant and comfortable house on the outskirts of town comes recommended by readers.

Tochar House *(☎ 281 8247, Main St)* Dorms €15.25, singles/doubles €25.40/ 50.80. In the middle of Main St, the house has really comfy rooms, and a separate annexe where walkers and cyclists can bunk down for the night. The annexe has a bathroom, shower and tea and coffee facilities.

Coach House Inn *(☎ 281 8157, fax 281 8449,* e *thecoachhouse@eircom.net, Main St)* Singles/doubles €32/64 with breakfast. This elegant inn in the heart of town has comfortable if unspectacular rooms. The pub grub downstairs has been recommended by readers.

Getting There & Away
St Kevin's Bus Service (☎ 281 8119) passes through Roundwood (single/return €6.35/ 10.20, 1¼ hours) on its twice-daily run between Dublin and Glendalough; see Getting There & Away under Glendalough for more details.

GLENMACNASS
The most desolate section of the Military Rd runs through wild bogland between the Sally Gap crossroads and Laragh. Along the way you may catch glimpses of Lough Dan to the east and, until you reach the top of Glenmacnass Valley, not a single building breaks the sense of isolation.

The highest mountain to the west is Mt Mullaghcleevaun (848m), and River Glenmacnass flows south and tumbles over the edge of the mountain plateau in a great foaming cascade. There's a car park near the top of the waterfall. Be careful when walking on rocks near **Glenmacnass Waterfall** as a few people have slipped to their deaths. There are fine walks up Mt Mullaghcleevaun or in the hills to the east of the car park.

WICKLOW GAP
Between Mt Tonelagee (816m) to the north and Table Mountain (700m) to the southwest, the Wicklow Gap is the second major pass over the mountains. The eastern end of the road begins just to the north of Glendalough and climbs through some lovely scenery north-westwards up along the Glendassan Valley. It passes the remains of some old lead and zinc workings before meeting a side road which leads south and up Turlough Hill, the location of Ireland's only pumped storage power station.

A lake was created on the summit and a tunnel was bored down through the hill to the other lake at its base. The water is pumped to the top reservoir at times of low electricity demand and sent down through the turbines in the tunnel at times of high demand. You can walk up the hill to have a look over the top lake.

GLENDALOUGH
☎ 0404
Glendalough (Gleann dá Loch, 'Glen of the Two Lakes') is a magical place – an ancient monastic settlement tucked beside two dark lakes and overshadowed by the sheer walls of a deep valley. It's one of the most picturesque settings in Ireland and the site of one of the most significant ancient monastic settlements in the country.

Barely an hour from Dublin, Glendalough is extremely popular. Visit early or late in the day, or out of season, to avoid the coach-tour crowds and atmosphere-shattering school parties.

History
Glendalough's past and present status are thanks to St Kevin, an early-Christian bishop who established a monastery here in the 6th century. From rough beginnings as a hermitage on the southern side of the Upper Lake, accessible only by boat, his monastery began to attract followers. In time it became a monastic city catering to thousands of students and teachers.

The main sections of the monastery are thought to have been a few hundred metres west of the round tower, and it must have spread over a considerable area. Most of the present buildings date from between the 10th and 12th centuries. A famous son of Glendalough was St Laurence O'Toole, who studied here and then became abbot of

The Saint Who Lived in a Tree

Born around 498, St Kevin was a member of the royal house of Leinster and his name is derived from Cóemgen, meaning 'fair one' or 'well featured'. As a child he studied under the three holy men – Énna, Eoghan and Lochan – and supposedly went to Glendalough and lived in a tree. His closeness to animals became legendary: one story tells of a bird that trusted him so much she laid an egg in his hand! Later he lived as a hermit in the cave that became known as St Kevin's Bed. It was, however, impossible for him to escape the world completely: knowledge of his piety spread and people flocked to Glendalough to share his isolated existence. His monastic settlement spread from the Upper Lake to the site of the town whose remains we see today. St Kevin became abbot of the monastery in 570 and died in 617 or 618 – which would have made him around 120 years old! In the Middle Ages his shrine was so revered that seven pilgrimages to Glendalough were said to equal one to Rome.

JANE SMITH

WICKLOW

Glendalough in 1117 and archbishop of Dublin in 1161. Glendalough's remote location was still within reach of the Vikings, who sacked the monastery at least four times between 775 and 1071. The final blow came in 1398, when English forces from Dublin almost completely destroyed it. Efforts were made to rebuild and some life lingered on here as late as the 17th century, when, under renewed repression, the monastery finally died.

Geography

Glendalough Valley was carved out by a series of glaciers, the last one retreating around 12,000 years ago. There was once one long deep lake that was later divided into the two you see today by the delta of the River Poulanass from the southern slopes. The surrounding mountains are formed mostly of 400-million-year-old granite and schist, the remains of earlier sediments cooked by the welling-up granite. The granite has a number of mineral veins in it containing white quartz and ores of lead, silver and zinc. There were extensive mining operations here between 1800 and 1920, with as many as 2000 miners working the mines.

The remains of the mine buildings and poisonous grey tailings are clearly visible at the far end of the Upper Lake and on the surrounding slopes. Some of the shafts extended north for nearly 2km through the mountain into the Glendassan Valley; you can see the remains while driving through the Wicklow Gap.

Orientation & Information

At the valley entrance, before the Glendalough Hotel, is the **Glendalough Visitor Centre** (☎ 45325, 45352; adults/seniors/students & children €2.50/1.90/1.25; open 9am-5.15pm June-Aug; 9.30am-5.15pm Sept-mid-Oct & mid-Mar-May; 9.30am-4.15pm mid-Oct-mid-Mar). It has a high-quality 20-minute audiovisual presentation on the Irish monasteries.

At the Upper Lake a small information office (☎ 45425) has details of activities in the Wicklow Mountains National Park. It opens 10am to 6pm daily, May to August, and 10am to 6pm weekends only the rest of the year. There's usually someone on hand to help, but if you find it closed the staff may be out running guided walks. *Exploring the Glendalough Valley* (Dúchas, €1.30) is a good booklet on the trails in the area.

It's important to get your bearings in Glendalough as the ruins and sites are spread out all over the valley. Coming from Laragh you first see the visitor centre, then the Glendalough Hotel, which is beside the entrance to the main group of ruins and the round tower. The Lower Lake is a small dark

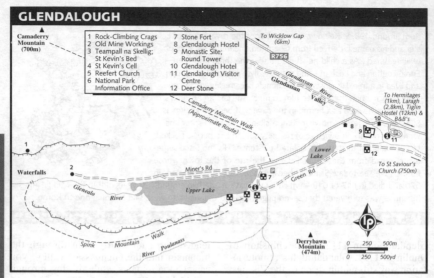

GLENDALOUGH

1 Rock-Climbing Crags	7 Stone Fort
2 Old Mine Workings	8 Glendalough Hostel
3 Teampall na Skellig;	9 Monastic Site;
St Kevin's Bed	Round Tower
4 St Kevin's Cell	10 Glendalough Hotel
5 Reefert Church	11 Glendalough Visitor
6 National Park	Centre
Information Office	12 Deer Stone

lake to the west, while farther west up the valley is the much bigger and more impressive Upper Lake, with a large car park (car/motorbikes €1.90/0.65) and more ruins nearby. Be sure to visit the Upper Lake and take one of the surrounding walks.

A model in the visitor centre should help you fix where everything is in relation to everything else.

Upper Lake Sites

The original site of St Kevin's settlement, **Teampall na Skellig**, is at the base of the cliffs towering over the southern side of the Upper Lake and accessible only by boat; unfortunately, there's no boat service to the site and you'll have to settle for looking at it across the lake. The terraced shelf has the reconstructed ruins of a church and early graveyard. Rough wattle huts once stood on the raised ground nearby. Scattered around are some early grave slabs and simple stone crosses.

Just east of here and 10m above the lake waters is a little 2m-deep cave called **St Kevin's Bed**, said to be where Kevin lived. The earliest human habitation of the cave was long before St Kevin's era. It may have

been the burial chamber of a Bronze Age chief or perhaps even a prehistoric mine – there's evidence that people lived in the valley for thousands of years before the monks arrived. In the green area just south of the car park is a large circular wall thought to be the remains of an early-Christian *caher* or stone fort.

Follow the lakeshore path south-west of the car park until you find the considerable remains of **Reefert Church** above the tiny River Poulanass. This is a small, rather plain, 11th-century, Romanesque nave-and-chancel church with some reassembled arches and walls. Traditionally, Reefert (King's Burial Place) was the burial site of the chiefs of the local O'Toole family. The surrounding graveyard contains a number of rough stone crosses and slabs, most made of shiny mica schist.

Climb the steps at the back of the churchyard and follow the path to the west and you'll find, at the top of a rise overlooking the lake, the scant remains of **St Kevin's Cell**, a small beehive hut. If you fancy the thought of living a 21st-century version of St Kevin's life (at least for a night, anyway), you can stay in one of the five hermitages that recently opened on the site; see Places to Stay for more details.

Lower Lake Sites

While the Upper Lake has the best scenery, the most fascinating buildings lie in the lower part of the valley east of the Lower Lake.

Just round the bend from the Glendalough Hotel is the stone arch of the **monastery gatehouse**, the only surviving example of a monastic entranceway in the country. Just inside the entrance is a large slab with an incised cross.

Beyond that lies a **graveyard**, which is still in use. The 10th-century **round tower** is 33m tall and 16m in circumference at the base. The upper storeys and conical roof were reconstructed in 1876. Near the tower, to the south-east, is the **Cathedral of St Peter and St Paul**, with a 10th-century nave. The chancel and sacristy date from the 12th century.

At the centre of the graveyard to the south of the round tower is the **Priest's House**. This odd building dates from 1170 but has been heavily reconstructed. It may have been the location of shrines of St Kevin. Later, during penal times, it became a burial site for local priests – hence the name. The 10th-century **St Mary's Church,** 140m south-west of the round tower, probably originally stood outside the walls of the monastery and belonged to local nuns. It has a lovely western doorway. A little to the east are the scant remains of **St Kieran's Church,** the smallest at Glendalough.

Glendalough's trademark is **St Kevin's Church** or Kitchen at the southern edge of the enclosure. This church, with a miniature round-tower-like belfry, protruding sacristy and steep stone roof, is a masterpiece. How it came to be known as a kitchen is a mystery as there's no indication that it was anything other than a church. The oldest parts of the building date from the 11th century – the structure has been remodelled since but it's still a classic early Irish church.

At the junction with Green Rd as you cross the river just south of these two churches is the Deer Stone in the middle of a group of rocks. Legend claims that, when St Kevin needed milk for two orphaned babies, a doe stood here waiting to be milked. The stone is actually a *bullaun,* used as a grinding stone for medicines or food. Many are thought to be prehistoric and they were widely regarded as having supernatural properties: women who bathed their faces with water from the hollow were supposed to keep their looks forever. The early churchmen brought them into their monasteries, perhaps hoping to inherit some of the stones' powers.

The road east leads to **St Saviour's Church,** with its detailed Romanesque carvings. To the west a nice woodland trail leads up the valley past the Lower Lake to the Upper Lake.

Walks

Numerous fine walks fan out from Glendalough. The first, easiest and most popular is the gentle but delightful half-hour walk along the northern shore of the Upper Lake to the lead and zinc mine workings, which date from 1800. The better route is along the lake shore rather than on the road, which runs 30m in from the shore. Continue on up the head of the valley if you wish.

Alternatively, you can go up **Spink Mountain**, the steep ridge with vertical cliffs running along the southern flanks of the Upper Lake. You can go part of the way and turn back, or complete a circuit of the Upper Lake by following the top of the cliff, eventually coming down by the mine workings and going back along the northern shore. The circuit takes about three hours.

The third option is a hike up **Camaderry Mountain** (700m), hidden behind the hills that flank the northern side of the valley. The walk starts on the road just 50m back towards Glendalough from the entrance to the Upper Lake car park. Head straight up the steep hill to the north and you come out on open mountains with sweeping views in all directions. You can then continue up Camaderry to the north-west or just follow the ridge west looking over the Upper Lake. To the top of Camaderry and back takes about four hours.

If you intend to go on a serious hike, make sure you take all the usual precautions,

WICKLOW

WICKLOW

Wicklow Mountains National Park

Most of Glendalough is contained within two nature reserves, owned and managed by Dúchas and legally protected by the Wildlife Act. The larger reserve, west of the Glendalough Visitor Centre, conserves the extensive heath and bog of the Glendalough Valley plus the Upper Lake and valley slopes on either side. The second reserve, Glendalough Wood Nature Reserve, conserves oak woods stretching from the Upper Lake as far as the Rathdrum road to the east.

Together with other state-owned land, the two reserves form the heart of the 20,000-hectare Wicklow Mountains National Park. The Liffey Head Bog, north-east of the Sally Gap, has recently been incorporated into the park, but there are plans to expand it further until it covers an area up to 30,000 hectares, basically most of the higher ground stretching the length of the Wicklow Mountains.

JANE SMITH

Wicklow is home to the rare hen harrier.

Most of Ireland's native mammal species can be found within the confines of the park. Large herds of deer roam on the open hill areas, though these were introduced in the 20th century after the native red deer population became extinct during the first half of the 18th century. The uplands are the preserve of foxes, badgers and hares. Red squirrels are usually found in the pine woodlands – look out for them around the Upper Lake.

The bird population of the park is plentiful. Birds of prey abound, the most common being peregrine falcons, merlins, kestrels, hawks and sparrow hawks. Hen harriers are a rarer sight, though they too live in the park. Moorland birds found in the area include meadow pipits and skylarks. Less common birds such as whinchats, ring ouzels and dippers can be spotted, as can red grouse, whose numbers are quickly disappearing in other parts of Ireland.

---

have the right equipment and tell someone where you're going and when you should be back. For Mountain Rescue ring ☎ 999. For more detailed information on walking in the area, check *Hill Walker's Wicklow*, *New Irish Walk Guides: East* and *New Irish Walk Guides: South East*, all by David Herman. For walking partners check at the hostels or go on an organised walk with the National Park information office (☎ 45425) or Tiglin Adventure Centre (☎ 40169) near Ashford.

Other Activities

At the western end of the valley beyond Upper Lake and the mine workings are a couple of large crags popular with rock climbers. The Mountaineering Council of Ireland publishes a guide to the routes, which is available from Joss Lynam (☎ 01-288 4672). **Laragh Trekking Centre** (see

Places to Stay later in this section) runs horse-riding excursions.

Organised Tours

Bus Éireann (☎ *01-836 6111*, **W** *www .buseireann.ie*) Adult/child €26/13 Apr-Oct, €20.50/10.50 Nov-Mar. Departs 10.30am & returns 5.45pm daily Apr-Oct, departs 10.30am & returns 4.30pm Wed, Fri & Sun Nov-Mar. Bus Éireann runs tours to Glendalough.

Aran Tours (☎ *01-280 1899*, **W** *www .wildcoachtours.com*) Adult/student & child €28/25.50. Departs 9.30am & returns 5.30pm daily. The best tour of Glendalough is Aran Tours' Wild Wicklow Tour, which also includes a short Dublin City tour and a visit to Avoca and the Sally Gap. It has a variety of pick-up points throughout Dublin; check the point nearest you when booking.

Guide Friday/Gray Line (☎ 01-670 8822, **W** *www.hoponhopoff.com)* Half-day tour €20.50, departs 10am & returns 2pm Sat May-Sept. Full-day tour €36, departs 10.30am & returns 5.30pm Sun May-Sept. The half-day tour is to Glendalough, while the full-day tour takes in Glendalough, Powerscourt and Russborough House. Reservations for both tours can be made through the Dublin Tourism Centre (☎ 01-605 7700), 2 Suffolk St, from where all tours depart.

Tir na nÓg Tours (☎ 1800 226242, 57 Lower Gardiner St, Dublin, **W** *www.tirna nogtours.com)* Adult/student/child €26/23/13. Daily full-day tours of Wicklow, which include Glendalough, the Sally Gap, Lough Tay, Laragh, Rathdrum and Avoca, depart from its offices at 9am and from the Dublin Tourism Centre at 9.30am.

Mary Gibbons Tours also runs a tour to Glendalough that includes a visit to Powerscourt; see under Powerscourt Estate earlier in this chapter for details.

Places to Stay

Hostels There are a couple of hostels in the area.

Glendalough Hostel (☎ 45342, fax 45690, **e** *glendaloughyh@ireland.com, The Lodge)* Dorms €15.50. This recently renovated An Óige hostel is near the round tower, set amid the deeply wooded glacial area that makes up the Glendalough valley.

Tiglin Hostel (☎/fax 49049, **e** *tiglin youthhostel@go.com, Devil's Glen State Forest, Tiglin, Ashford)* Dorms €9.50. About 10km north-east of Laragh via Annamoe, this 50-bed An Óige hostel is the first ever to be located in a state forest. Built in 1870, it was originally a farmhouse frequented by the playwright JM Synge. To book, call the hostel before 9am or after 5pm to catch the warden; otherwise, call the An Óige office (☎ 01-830 1766) in Dublin.

Hermitages For a truly a unique way to savour the atmosphere of Glendalough and for a real taste of the monastic life, you could stay in one of the recently opened hermitages.

Glendalough Cillíns (☎ 45140, 45777 for bookings, St Kevin's Parish Church, Glendalough) Huts €32. Known as *cillíns*, these hermitages were unveiled in 2001 with a view towards offering travellers the experience of contemplative solitude among the monastic ruins. The five cillíns are designed to provide one-person self-catering accommodation consisting of a bed, bathroom, small kitchen area and an open fire supplemented by a storage heating facility. Mobile phones, laptops, TVs and other electronic distractions are not quite forbidden, but there is no electricity.

The hermitages are in a field next to St Kevin's Parish Church, about 1km east of Glendalough on the R756 road to Laragh.

B&Bs & Hotels Most B&Bs are in or around Laragh, a village 3km east of Glendalough, or on the way there from Glendalough. There's also a good hotel.

Valeview (☎/fax 45292, **e** *lisa.mc@ oceanfree.net, Laragh)* Rooms from €24.50 per person. Farther down towards Glendalough, opposite the Trinity Church, Valeview has well kept rooms, a great view of the valley and, as well as the normal cooked breakfast, provides the option of yoghurt and fruit.

Carmel's (☎/fax 45297, **e** *carmels bandb@eircom.net, Annamoe)* Rooms with bathroom €25.40 per person. Open Mar-Oct. Carmel's is 5km north-east of Glendalough in Annamoe, on the main road to Roundwood. The rooms are fantastic, with large, comfortable beds and great views.

Derrybawn House (☎ 45134, fax 45109, Laragh) Singles/doubles from €51/70 including breakfast. This elegant place stands in wooded grounds about 2km south of Laragh on the road to Rathdrum.

Glendalough Hotel (☎ 45135, fax 45142, **e** *info@glendaloughhotel.ie, Glendalough)* Singles/doubles including breakfast €95.30/152.50. This hotel is next to the monastic ruins. Its 44 rooms have been thoroughly upgraded in the last couple of years to provide maximum comfort and not a small amount of luxury – which is adequately reflected in the prices.

WICKLOW

Places to Eat

At Glendalough itself there are surprisingly few places to eat.

Glendalough Hotel *(see Places to Stay)* 3-course lunch €15.20. The hotel has a huge restaurant that serves a very good lunch. There's also a limited bar menu, or a scone and tea for €2.30.

Otherwise, there's a **takeaway booth** in the Upper Lake car park. For anything else, you need to go into Laragh.

Wicklow Heather Restaurant *(☎ 45157, Main St, Laragh)* Mains around €8.50. Open around 5pm-8.30pm. This is about the best place for anything substantial. The trout (farmed locally) is excellent. During summer, villagers put out signs and serve tea and scones on the village green.

Getting There & Away

St Kevin's Bus Service (☎ 01-281 8119) runs to Glendalough from outside the Royal College of Surgeons, St Stephen's Green West, Dublin, at 11.30am and 6pm Monday to Saturday (11.30am and 7pm on Sunday) year round (single/return €5.10/14, 1½ hours). From Glendalough, the service to Dublin runs at 7.15am and 4.15pm Monday to Friday, 9.45am and 4.15pm Saturday, and 9.45am and 4.15pm Sunday.

GLENMALURE

Deep in the mountains, near the southern end of the Military Rd, is Glenmalure, a sombre and majestic blind valley overlooked on its western side by Lugnaquilla Mountain, Wicklow's highest peak at 924m, and flanked farther up by classic scree slopes of loose boulders. After coming over the mountains into Glenmalure you turn north-west at the Drumgoft bridge. From there it's about 6km up the road beside the Avonbeg River to a car park where trails lead off in various directions.

For a long time, Glenmalure was a stronghold of resistance to the English. Various clans, particularly the O'Byrnes, made forays up into the Pale, harassing the Crown's forces and loyal subjects. The most famous clan leader was Fiach MacHugh O'Byrne. In 1580 he defeated an army of 1000 English soldiers led by the lord deputy, Lord Grey de Wilton, at Glenmalure; over 800 men died in the battle and English control over Ireland was set back for decades. Fiach was captured in 1597 and his head impaled on the gates of Dublin Castle.

Near Drumgoft is Dwyer's or Cullen's Rock, which commemorates both the Glenmalure battle and Michael Dwyer, a 1798 Rising rebel who holed up here. Men were hanged from the rock during the Rising.

Walks

You can walk up Lugnaquilla Mountain or head up the blind Fraughan Rock Glen east of the car park. Alternatively, you can go straight up Glenmalure Valley passing the small, seasonal An Óige Glenmalure Hostel, after which the trail divides – heading north-east, the trail takes you over the hills to Glendalough, while going north-west brings you into the Glen of Imaal.

The head of Glenmalure and parts of the neighbouring Glen of Imaal are off-limits – it's military land, well posted with warning signs.

Places to Stay

These hostels make good bases for walking up Lugnaquilla.

Glenmalure Hostel *(☎ 01-830 4555, fax 830 5808, ℮ mailbox@anoige.ie, Glenmalure, Greenane)* Dorms €9.50. Open daily June-Aug, Sat only Sept-May. Once owned by Maud Gonne (WB Yeats' greatest inspiration) and the setting for JM Synge's play *Shadow of the Glen,* this small mountain hut has been converted into a 16-bed hostel. It has virtually no facilities save running water and beds, and is as close to the spartan living of the monastic monks as you're likely to get.

Aghavannagh House *(☎ 0402-36366, Aghavannagh)* This large An Óige hostel 14km south-west in a former barracks built at the time of the 1798 Rising (and used as a shooting lodge by Charles Stewart Parnell) was closed at the time of writing for renovation. It should reopen sometime during the summer of 2002; call the An Óige head office (☎ 01-830 4555) for details.

Western Wicklow

The western slopes of the Wicklow Mountains were less deeply glaciated than the eastern ones, and the landscape isn't as spectacular. From the Sally Gap crossroads to Kilbride, however, you pass the upper reaches of the River Liffey and some lovely wild scenery. Another picturesque trip passes over the Wicklow Gap from Glendalough.

Western Wicklow's most interesting features are the Poulaphouca Reservoir (also known as Blessington Lakes), nearby Russborough House and, farther south, the Glen of Imaal.

BLESSINGTON
☎ 045 • pop 1860
Blessington is 35km south-west of Dublin on the N81. Its main street is lined with solid 17th- and 18th-century town houses. There is nothing in town to detain the visitor, but it makes a good base for exploring the surrounding area.

Blessington owes its beginnings to an archbishop of Dublin, Michael Boyle, who designed it in the 1670s. Boyle's manor, Downshire House, was destroyed by fire in 1760, and the village was all but destroyed by rebels in 1798.

Blessington is near the shores of the Poulaphouca Reservoir, created in 1940 to drive the turbines of the local electricity supply board power station to the east of town and to supply Dublin with water.

Information
The tourist office (☎ 865850) is in the Blessington Business Centre, across the road from the Downshire House Hotel. It's usually open 10am to 6pm Monday to Saturday, June to August, but it basically depends on whether someone is there or not!

Places to Stay & Eat
Baltyboys Hostel (☎ 867266, fax 867032, e *mailbox@anoige.ie, Baltyboys, Blessington*) Dorms €8.90. Open Mar-Nov. On the peninsula opposite Russborough House,

this An Óige hostel is 5km from Blessington. Take the road south to Poulaphouca and turn east at Burgage Cross towards Valleymount. Dublin Bus No 65 stops in front of the hostel.

The Heathers (☎ 864554, e *theheathers@eircom.net, Poulaphouca, Blessington*) Singles/doubles €38/51 including breakfast. Overlooking the reservoir, this B&B is 7km south along the Baltinglass road and only 3km from Russborough House.

Haylands House (☎ 865183, e *haylandshouse@eircom.net, Dublin Rd*) Singles/doubles €30.50/51. This comfortable B&B is only 500m out of town on the main Dublin road.

Downshire House Hotel (☎ 865199, fax 865335, e *info@downshirehouse.com, Main St*) Rooms from €63.50 per person including breakfast. A family-run hotel, it is one of the prominent landmarks in town. Its 25 rooms are simply furnished but they're pleasant and very clean.

Rathsallagh House (☎ 403112, fax 403343, e *info@rathsallagh.com, Dunlavin*) Singles/doubles €108/140 including breakfast & dinner. More than a hotel, this is a superb country manor where luxury is commonplace and the food among the best you'll eat anywhere in Ireland. It's 20km south of Blessington.

Old Schoolhouse (☎ 891420, Main St) Mains €6.30-10. This new Italian restaurant has an excellent menu of pizzas, pasta dishes and grills.

Getting There & Away
Blessington has regular daily services by Dublin Bus (☎ 01-872 0000, 873 4222) No 65 from Eden Quay in Dublin (€3, 1½ hours, every 1½ hours). Bus Éireann (☎ 01-836 6111) express bus No 005 to and from Waterford stops in Blessington two or three-times daily; from Dublin it's pick-up only, from Waterford drop-off only.

RUSSBOROUGH HOUSE
Five kilometres south-west of Blessington is one of Ireland's finest stately homes, built for Joseph Leeson (1705–83), later the 1st earl of Milltown and later still Lord Russborough.

WICKLOW

Built between 1741 and 1751, Russborough House is a magnificent Palladian villa (☎ 045-865239, Blessington; adult/student/child €5/4/2.50; open 10.30am-5.30pm May-Sept; 10.30am-5.30pm Sun & bank holidays Apr & Oct). It was designed by Richard Cassels, at the height of his fame and ability (although he did not live to see it completed), with the help of another Irish architect, Francis Bindon.

At the front, the silver-grey granite central building is flanked by two elegant wings connected to the main block by curving, pillared colonnades.

Inside, the entrance hall features a floor of polished oak and a compartmental ceiling with a Doric frieze similar to the one designed by Cassels for Leinster House. The stunning black Kilkenny marble fireplace is another favourite touch of Cassels. From here, five doors with beautifully carved architraves lead to the impressive reception rooms.

The house was taken by Irish forces during the 1798 Rising and then by government forces, who only left in 1801 after a furious Lord Russborough challenged the commander of the British forces, Lord Tyrawley, to a duel 'with blunderbusses and slugs in a sawpit'.

The house remained in Leeson family hands until 1931. In 1952 it was sold to Sir Alfred Beit, nephew of another Sir Alfred Beit (co-founder of the de Beers diamond mining company). The elder Beit invested huge amounts of money to put together an impressive art collection, which on his death passed into the hands of his nephew, who brought them to Russborough House. The collection included works by Velázquez, Vermeer, Goya and Rubens. However, it has been the subject of some unwanted attention.

In 1974, an Englishwoman, Rose Dugdale, stole 16 of the paintings to help fund the IRA, but the paintings were soon recovered. In 1976, the house was transformed into a centre for the arts, but even the beefed-up security was not enough to stop the next robbery. In 1986, the notorious Dublin gangster Martin Cahill, better known as the General, broke into the estate and made off with

another haul of paintings. This time, however, the authorities were not so fortunate: they recovered only a part of the booty and even some of those had been badly damaged. A handful of the missing paintings eventually turned up in the Netherlands a few years ago, but some are still missing.

Twice bitten but thrice shy, Beit decided to hand over the most valuable paintings to the National Gallery in 1988. In return for the gift, the National Gallery often lends paintings to the collection as temporary exhibits.

But the story doesn't end there. In June 2001 a pair of thieves drove a jeep through the front doors and walked out with two paintings worth nearly €4 million, including a Gainsborough that had already been stolen – and recovered – twice before. At the time of writing the police were hot on their heels, but so far nothing has turned up.

The admission price includes a 45-minute tour of the house and all the important paintings. An additional 30-minute tour of the bedrooms upstairs containing more silver and furniture costs €3.20 (children free). This tour runs only at 2.15pm Monday to Saturday, but is pretty regular on Sunday.

The only organised tour of the house is run by Guide Friday/Gray Line (☎ 01-670 8822), which also includes a visit to Glendalough and Powerscourt Estate. It departs the Dublin Tourism Centre, 2 Suffolk St, at 10.30am, returning at 5.30pm, on Sunday only, June to September. It costs €36.

GLEN OF IMAAL

Seven kilometres south-east of Donard, the lovely Glen of Imaal is about the only scenery of consequence on the western flanks of the Wicklow Mountains. It's named after Mal, a brother of the 2nd-century king of Ireland, Cathal Mór. Unfortunately, the glen's north-eastern slopes are mostly cordoned off as an army firing range and for manoeuvres. Look out for red danger signs.

The area's most famous son was Michael Dwyer, who led rebel forces during the 1798 Rising and held out for five years in the local hills and glens. On the south-eastern side of the glen at Derrynamuck is a small whitewashed, thatched cottage where Dwyer and three friends were surrounded by 100 English soldiers. One of his companions, Samuel McAllister, ran out the front, drawing fire and meeting his death, while Dwyer escaped into the night. He was eventually deported in 1803 and jailed on Norfolk Island, off the eastern coast of Australia, but became chief constable of Liverpool near Sydney before he died in 1825. The cottage is now a small *folk museum* (☎ *01-647 3000, Derrynamuck; free; open 2pm-6pm daily mid-June–Sept)* on the Knockanarrigan–Rathdangan road.

Ballinclea Hostel (☎/*fax 045-404657,* **e** *mailbox@anoige.ie, Ballinclea)* Dorms €9.50. Open Mar-Nov. This 40-bed hostel is 5km south-east of Donard on the road to Knockanarrigan.

BALTINGLASS
☎ 0508 • pop 1065

Baltinglass, on the banks of the River Slaney, is in the far western corner of Wicklow. This small town grew up around the Cistercian **Abbey of Vallis Salutis**, founded in 1148 by Dermot MacMurrough as a satellite to Mellifont Monastery in County Louth. Some locals suggest MacMurrough was laid to rest here in 1171, though he is more probably buried near his base in Ferns, County Wexford. Records suggest that the Irish Parliament met in the abbey for three days in 1397. The ruined nave, with several simple Gothic arches and scant remnants of a cloister, lies 350m north of the town centre.

A stiff climb to the summit of Baltinglass Hill to the north-east brings you to **Rathcoran**, a large hill fort, and a Bronze Age cairn with several passage graves.

Bus Éireann buses (single/return €6.35/8.90, 1¼ hours) pass through Baltinglass between Dublin and Waterford and vice versa; from Busáras in Dublin, buses depart at 9am and 5.30pm Monday to Saturday, and at 11.30am, 4pm and 6pm on Sunday. From Baltinglass, departures are at 10.10am and 6.35pm Monday to Saturday, and 3.30pm and 7.23pm on Sunday. All buses stop in Main St.

The Coast

The main N11 from Dublin to Wexford passes to the west of Bray and then south through Wicklow. South of Kilmacanogue you see Great Sugar Loaf Mountain (503m) to the west and pass through a great glacial rift, the **Glen of the Downs**, carved out of an Ice Age lake by floodwaters. There's a forest walk up to a ruined tea house on top of the ridge to the east.

If you're travelling farther south, the coastal route through Greystones, Kilcoole and then along country lanes to Rathnew is preferable.

Worth seeing around Wicklow town are the Mt Usher Gardens near Ashford and the fine beaches of Brittas Bay, which stretch into County Wexford.

BRAY
☎ 01 • pop 25,252

Bray is a run-down dormitory town on the coast 19km south of Dublin. In 1854 the railway's arrival turned it into the 'Brighton' of Ireland, a bustling seaside resort with a long promenade fronted by a beach and backed by hotels and lodging houses, all nicely overshadowed by Bray Head to the south. James Joyce lived in Bray from 1889 to 1891. Unfortunately the seafront, which should be modern Bray's glory, is now home to cheap hotels, fast-food places, amusement arcades and endless parking space for DART train commuters. In short, Bray isn't very appealing. The other focal point is Main St, lined with shops and pubs.

Information

The tourist office (☎ 286 7128, 286 6796) is in the 19th-century courthouse beside the Royal Hotel at the bottom of Main St. It opens 9.30am to 5pm (to 4.30pm October to May) Monday to Saturday, year round. Enquire here about Finnegan Bray's (☎ 286 0061) half-day and full-day tours to Glendalough, Dublin and the 'Ballykissangel' of the popular TV soap, aka Avoca.

Excellent Dubray Books (☎ 286 9370), Main St, sells maps and walking guides.

Things to See & Do

The town's main attraction, housed in the tourist office, is the **heritage centre** (☎ *286 7128, Old Courthouse; adult/student €2.50/ 1.25; open 9am-5pm Mon-Fri & 10am-3pm Sat June-Aug; 9.30am-4.30pm Mon-Fri & 10am-3pm Sat Sept-May).* Spread across two floors, the permanent exhibition is titled 'From Strongbow to Steam' and covers the 1000-year history of Bray from the construction of the first castle in 1173 to the post-industrial age. The ground floor is designed to look like the banqueting hall of a medieval castle, while upstairs is devoted to the efforts of engineer William Dargan (1799–1867) to bring the railroad to Bray. Check for Sunday opening hours.

Like Sandycove, Bray has a **Martello Tower** (not open to the public), which is now a private residence owned by none other than U2's Bono. From Bray Head there are fine views southwards to Great Sugar Loaf Mountain, a prominent peak in the Wicklow Mountains. There's a fine 8km **cliff walk** around Bray Head to the pleasant coastal resort of Greystones farther south. Bray Head has many old smuggling caves and railway tunnels, including one that's 1.5km long. The inland rail route was an easier and more obvious choice, but the local earl didn't want the railway cutting through his land.

On the seafront in Bray is **National Sea-life** (☎ *286 6939,* **W** *www.sealife.com, Strand Rd; adult/child €7/5; open 9.30am-6pm Mon-Sat).* The old National Aquarium was taken over by a British company a couple of years ago and is now a much more pleasant place to visit, with a fairly big selection of different aquariums stocked with 70 different sea and freshwater species.

About 3km south of Bray on the Greystones road are **Kilruddery House & Gardens** (☎ *286 3405, Kilruddery; adult/child €6/4 house & gardens, €4/2 gardens only; open 1pm-5pm May, June & Sept).* Kilruddery has been home to the Brabazon family (earls of Meath) since 1618 and has one of the oldest gardens in Ireland. The house was designed in Elizabethan style by Richard Morrisson and his son William in 1820, but reduced to its present-day proportions by the 14th earl in 1953. Although the house itself is quite impressive, it is the orangery that truly captures the eye, full of light, plantlife and sculptures.

Places to Stay

If Dublin is full (highly probable over summer weekends) there are many B&Bs along Bray's sea-facing Strand Rd, just minutes from the DART station. At the northern end they tend to overlook car parks so it's worth continuing south towards Bray Head.

Sea Breeze House (☎/fax *286 8337, 1 Marine Terrace)* Rooms €50. Open Feb-Nov. Overlooking the sea, this is a pretty house with four fairly pleasant rooms, all en suite.

Moytura (☎ *282 9827,* **e** *braybandb@ eircom.net, Herbert Rd, at the junction with King Edward Rd)* Singles/doubles €32/50. This is a very nice house, with three pleasant en suite rooms.

Crofton Bray Head Inn (☎/fax *286 7182, Strand Rd)* Rooms from €30.50 per person including breakfast. In a 130-year-old building, this hotel is right on the seafront under Bray Head.

Royal Hotel (☎ *286 2935, fax 286 7373, Main St)* Singles/doubles €57/89. This modern place has a leisure centre with a pool, sauna and other watery amenities.

The Westbourne (☎ *286 2362, fax 286 8530, Quinsboro Rd)* Rooms from €38 per person. This is a smaller hotel, located above the Dusty Miller bar. Downstairs, the Tube nightclub opens from 11pm Thursday to Sunday.

Places to Eat

The Tree of Idleness (☎ *286 3498, The Seafront)* Mains from €13. This seafront restaurant with delicious Greek-Cypriot food is one attraction for which it's worth making the foray from Dublin. The suckling pig, filled with apple and apricot stuffing, is one of its most popular dishes.

The Porter House (☎ *286 0668, Strand Rd)* This popular pub claims to have Ireland's largest selection of beers from around the world.

Getting There & Away

Bus Dublin Bus No 45 (from Hawkins St) or No 84 (from Burgh Quay) serve Bray (single €1.50, one hour).

St Kevin's Bus Service (☎ 281 8119) runs buses daily from the town hall to Dublin at 8am and 5pm (single €1.65, one hour). From Dublin, buses leave at 11.30am and 6pm from in front of the Royal College of Surgeons, St Stephen's Green West.

Train Bray train station (☎ 236 3333) is 500m east of Main St just before the seafront. There are DART trains into Dublin and farther north to Howth every five minutes at peak times and every 20 or 30 minutes at quiet times (€1.50, 30 minutes).

The station is also on the main line from Dublin to Wexford and Rosslare Harbour, with up to five trains daily in each direction Monday to Saturday, four on Sunday.

Getting Around

Bray Sports Centre (☎ 286 3046), 8 Main St, is the Raleigh Rent-a-Bike dealer, with bikes costing €15.50 per day.

KILMACANOGUE

The biggest and best local craft shop is *Avoca Handweavers* (☎ 01-286 7466, Main St; open 9.30am-5.30pm daily). Set in a 19th-century arboretum in Kilmacanogue, 4km south of Bray on the N11, the showroom has a huge array of handmade crafts and garments. The splendid *cafe* serves excellent dishes, including beef and Guinness casserole, though vegetarians are very well catered for as well.

Bray tourist office's Wicklow Trail Sheet No 4 (€1.25) details a three-hour exploration of Great Sugar Loaf Mountain starting from Kilmacanogue.

Local bus No 145 from Bray sometimes stops in Kilmacanogue; check with the driver.

GREYSTONES TO WICKLOW

The resort of **Greystones**, 8km south of Bray, was once a charming fishing village, and the seafront around the little harbour is idyllic. In summer, the bay is dotted with dinghies and windsurfers. Sadly, the sur-

rounding countryside is vanishing beneath housing developments.

Ten kilometres south of Greystones on the N11 is **Ashford**, an unremarkable little town save for one attraction on its eastern outskirts, which draws horticulturists from all over the world. The eight-hectare **Mt Usher Gardens** (☎ 0404-40205, Ashford; adult/student & child €4.50/3.20; open 10.30am-5.30pm mid-Mar-Oct) are informally laid out around the River Vartry with rare plants from around the world. The gardens were first designed in 1868 by Dublin textile magnate Edward Walpole, with succeeding generations of the Walpole family working to maintain and expand the grounds. At the entrance you'll find craft shops, a bookshop and cafe. There are guided tours of the gardens (for groups only) costing €32.

Bus Éireann (☎ 01-836 6111) buses stop outside Ashford House 10-times daily between 8am and 8.30pm (one way €5.10, 50 minutes) on the Dublin–Rosslare Harbour route.

West of Ashford the road leads into the Wicklow Mountains through **Devil's Glen** (beginning 3km from Ashford), a beautiful wooded glen with a fine walking trail. **Tiglin Adventure Centre** (☎ 0404-40169), 3km farther west, runs courses in rock climbing and canoeing and also organises treks.

Tinakilly House Hotel (☎ 0404-69274, fax 67806, ☒ reservations@tinakilly.ie, Rathnew) Rooms from €104 per person including breakfast. This absolutely gorgeous Victorian Italianate manor house is just outside Rathnew, on the road towards Wicklow. It was built for Captain Robert Halpin (1836–94), who commanded the *Great Eastern*, which was famous for being the largest ship in the world and participated in the laying of the first transatlantic cable. There is a very good *restaurant* too; prices are high but the food is excellent.

WICKLOW

☎ 0404 • pop 6416

Wicklow town, 27km south of Bray, is not an exciting county town but does boast a fine big harbour, which hosts the start of the biennial Round Ireland Yacht Race. The sweep of beach and bay to the north and the bulge of Wicklow Head to the south are the area's best features.

While there's not much to see here, Wicklow makes a good base for exploring the surrounding area. Unfortunately, the layout is not very backpacker-friendly, with the bus stop and train station some distance from the hostel and the B&Bs, and from each other.

The helpful tourist office (☎ 69117, e wicklow@eircom.net) on Fitzwilliam Square opens 9.30am to 6pm Monday to Saturday, June to September; and 9am to 1pm and 2pm to 5pm on weekdays, October to May.

Wicklow's Historic Jail

Wicklow has an infamous jail (☎ 61599, Kilmantin Hill; adult/student including tour €5.35/3.05; open 10am-6pm daily, last admission 5pm). Its history is told through audiovisuals, figures, graphics and even actors at this new heritage centre housed in the prison where thousands of convicts were kept in inhumane conditions. The 1st floor has exhibits detailing the 1798 Rising in Wicklow and the consequences of the late 18th-century prison reforms, which for many prisoners resulted in transportation to the penal colonies in New South Wales. Their gruelling journey is outlined on a model of a convict ship, HMS *Hercules*, on the 2nd floor. The top floor is devoted to the story of the prisoners once they arrived in Australia. Tours take place every 10 minutes except between 1pm and 2pm.

Other Things to See & Do

The few remaining fragments of the **Black Castle** are on the shore at the southern end of town, with pleasant views up and down the coast. The castle was built by the Fitzgeralds from Wales in 1169 after they were granted land in the area by Strongbow. It used to be linked to the mainland by a drawbridge, and rumour has it that an escape tunnel ran from the sea cave underneath up into the town. At low tide you can swim or snorkel into the cave.

The walk along the cliffs to **Wicklow**

Head offers great views of the Wicklow Mountains. A string of **beaches** – Silver Strand, Brittas Bay and Maheramore – start 16km south of Wicklow; with high dunes, safe bathing and powdery sand, the beaches attract droves of Dubliners in good weather.

Special Events

Wicklow Regatta Festival – Ireland's longest established festival – is held every year for two weeks over July and August. The full program of events includes swimming, rowing, sailing and raft races, singing competitions, concerts and a Festival Queen Ball.

Places to Stay

Wicklow Bay Hostel (☎ 69213, 61174, fax 66456, e wicklowbayhostel@tinet.ie, Marine House) Dorms/doubles €10.20/25.50. This welcoming place may not boast the most scenic surroundings but there are fine views from the dorms, and it has a big, clean kitchen.

There's a clutch of B&Bs in and around Dunbur Hill and a few more uphill along St Patrick's Rd.

Bayview Hotel (☎ 67383, fax 67911, The Mall) Singles/doubles €38/76. Bayview is in the town centre. There's live traditional Irish music in the bar on Thursday night.

The Grand Hotel (☎ 67337, fax 69607, e grandhotel@tinet.ie, Abbey St) Singles/doubles from €61/91.50. This hotel is very comfortable, with large clean rooms and friendly staff.

Places to Eat

Hannah's (☎ 66264, Main St) Mains around €5.20. Hannah's will sort you out for breakfast, light lunches or afternoon tea.

The Old Forge (☎ 66778, Abbey Hill) Mains from €6.35. This place has a good choice of bar meals; in fine weather you can eat outside.

The Bakery Café and Restaurant (☎ 66770, Church St) 3-course set dinner €27. The cafe is a good spot for vegetarians, while the restaurant proper is a treat for gourmands, with a fine menu of mouth-watering food.

Getting There & Away

Up to two Bus Éireann (☎ 01-836 6111) buses leave daily from the Grand Hotel on Main St for Dublin (€5.85 one way, one hour) and for Rosslare Harbour. Three trains (☎ 01-836 6222) daily depart Dublin's Connolly station bound for Rosslare Harbour, stopping at Wicklow (single/return €10.20/ 12.70, 1¼ hours). The station is 10 minutes' walk north of the town centre.

Getting Around

Wicklow Cabs (☎ 66888), Main St, usually sends a few cabs to meet the evening trains from Dublin. The fare to anywhere in town is €4.50. The same company organises tours to local beauty spots, nightclubs and pubs.

Southern Wicklow

RATHDRUM

☎ 0404 • pop 1234

These days Rathdrum is little more than a few old houses and shops to the south of Glendalough and the Vale of Clara, the pleasant valley leading north to Laragh, but in the late 19th century it could have claimed to be the unofficial capital of Wicklow, with a healthy flannel industry and a poorhouse. The railway and fine aqueduct were built in 1861.

There's a small tourist office (☎ 46262) at 29 Main St, open 9am to 5.30pm Monday to Friday year round. It has leaflets and information on the town and surrounding area, including the Wicklow Way.

Avondale House

Two kilometres south of Rathdrum and in a marvellous 209-hectare estate is Avondale House (☎ 46111, Rathdrum; adult/concession €4.50/3.80; open 11am-6pm Mar-Oct; 11am-5pm Nov-Feb). It was the birthplace and family residence of 'Ireland's uncrowned king', Charles Stewart Parnell (1846–91), one of the leading figures of Irish history. The house was designed by James Wyatt in 1779 and features a stunning vermilion-coloured library, purported to be Parnell's favourite room, and a beautiful dining room.

From 1880 to 1890, Avondale became synonymous with the fight for Irish home rule, which was brilliantly led by Parnell until his shocking fall from grace. Another parliamentarian, Captain O'Shea, in a messy divorce suit named Parnell as correspondent – Parnell was indeed having an affair with O'Shea's wife, Kitty. Although Parnell married Kitty as soon as the divorce was granted, he was deemed 'unfit to lead' by the ultra-conservative church authorities and he retired in despair to Avondale.

After his death, there were deep divisions in Irish society as to the righteousness of the man, but there was no disagreement as to the level of his commitment to the home rule movement. It is perhaps ironic that the great 19th century hero of Irish independence was actually a Protestant landlord! You can visit the park during daylight hours year round.

Places to Stay

Most of Rathdrum's B&Bs are actually in the hamlet of Corballis, 1km along the road south to Avoca and Arklow.

Old Presbytery Hostel (☎ 46930, fax 46604, @ thehostel@hotmail.com, The Fairgreen, Rathdrum) Dorms/private rooms €11.50/25. You can also camp in the grounds of this IHH hostel, and there's a laundry.

Beechlawn (☎ 46474, fax 43389, @ caj@ tinet.ie, Corballis) Singles/doubles from €38/53.50. This four-room B&B is 500m south of Corballis on the Avoca road.

Avonbrae Guesthouse (☎/fax 46198, @ avonbrae@gofree.indigo.ie, Laragh Rd) Singles/doubles €38/61. The seven rooms at this charming guesthouse, about 500m north-west of Rathdrum on the road to Laragh, have fairly spartan furnishings, but they're neat and very comfortable.

Getting There & Away

The Bus Éireann (☎ 01-836 6111) Dublin–Wexford–Rosslare Harbour bus stops at Rathdrum twice daily (once on Sunday) in each direction (single/return €7.40/10.80, 1¾ hours). From Dublin, they depart at 9am and 5.30pm (2pm on Sunday). Three trains (☎ 01-836 6222) stop at Rathdrum daily in each direction between Dublin and Rosslare

WICKLOW

Harbour (single/return €10.20/12.70, 1½ hours).

VALE OF AVOCA

The Avonbeg and Avonmore Rivers come together to form the River Avoca at the **Meeting of the Waters**, a lovely spot made famous by Thomas Moore's 1808 poem of the same name.

The Vale of Avoca is a gentle, darkly wooded valley that is charming if hardly awe-inspiring. Unfortunately there's some badly scarred landscape north-west of Avoca village, the legacy of centuries of copper mining. The last mine closed in 1982. In the 18th century the valley was cut off from the outside world and had its own coinage, the cronbane.

The Meeting of the Waters is marked by a pub called *The Meetings* (☎ 0402-35226), which serves food all day and has music at the weekend year round. There are *ceilidhs* between 4pm and 6pm on Sunday, April to October. Buses to Avoca from Dublin stop at The Meetings, or you can walk from Avoca.

Avoca
☎ 0402 • pop 490

The tiny village of Avoca (Abhóca) shot to fame in 1996 when it was chosen as the location for the unexpectedly popular BBC TV series *Ballykissangel*. Frankly, the busloads of tourists hardly did the town's tranquil atmosphere any favours, but did bring in a lot of income. *Ballykissangel* was cancelled in 2000, so the film crews have gone, but reruns should guarantee that the town will remain popular for a while longer.

The focal point of the town and the series was Fitzgerald's, a suitably old-world pub by the river. While tucking into food here you can admire snapshots of the former stars on the walls. There's a seasonal tourist office (☎ 35022, e avocait@eircom.net) in the old courthouse (now the library).

Also in the village is *Avoca Handweavers* (☎ 35105, Main St), which has been going since 1723 and claims to be Ireland's oldest surviving business. You can look around the weaving sheds and then admire the pricey tweeds, throws and other fabrics in their

shop. The excellent *cafe* opens for lunches and teas.

Places to Stay

River Valley Park (☎ 41647, fax 41677, R754, Redcross) Tent site €11.50. This well equipped camp site is about 1km south of the village of Redcross, 7km north-east of Avoca on the R754 country road.

Koliba (☎/fax 32737, e koliba@eircom .net, Beech Rd) Rooms €25 per person. A thoroughly modern bungalow with comfortable, well appointed rooms, Koliba is a great choice in the area.

Sheepwalk House & Cottages (☎ 35189, fax 35789, w www.sheepwalk.com, Avoca). Rooms in main house €32-48.50 per person, cottages from €76 per person per week. Set in a glorious 1.5-hectare site overlooking the sea, this is our favourite place to stay in Avoca (even though it's 2km out of town) and we highly recommend it. The main house was built in 1727 – although it has been thoroughly restored (it received the top rating from Bord Fáilte). For two or more people, there are six self-catering cottages, complete with beamed ceilings and flagstone floors. Ask for one with an open fireplace. The *Ballykissangel* crew stayed here during filming.

Woodenbridge Hotel (☎ 35146, fax 35573, e wbhotel@iol.ie, Vale of Avoca) Singles/doubles from €45/89. Overlooking Woodenbridge Golf Course, 4km south of Avoca, this hotel dates from 1608 and is held to be Ireland's oldest hotel. Luckily, it has undergone several refurbishments since it first opened.

Getting There & Away

Bus Éireann bus No 133 from Dublin departs at 9am and 5.30pm daily (2pm on Sunday) and serves Avoca (single/return €7.90/12, two hours) via Bray, Wicklow and Rathdrum on its way to Arklow.

ARKLOW
☎ 0402 • pop 8519

Besides Bray, Arklow is probably County Wicklow's busiest town. A thriving commercial shopping centre with some light industry, it makes a reasonable base for exploring the Wicklow Mountains but is not particularly attractive in its own right.

Once a minor fishing village, Arklow became one of the country's busiest ports and a well known boat-building centre. Sir Francis Chichester's *Gypsy Moth IV* (now in Greenwich, London) and the Irish training vessel *Asgard II* were built here. In 1841 the port had 80 schooners working out of the harbour.

During the 1798 Rising, Arklow saw fierce fighting when some 20,000 of the rebels led by Father Michael Murphy tried to storm the town and were defeated by the better-equipped and better-trained British army. Murphy and 700 men died in the battle. A monument to them sits in front of St Mary and St Peter's church.

The tourist office (☎ 32484, W www.arklow.ie), in a Portakabin beside the courthouse, theoretically opens 9.30am to 1pm Monday to Saturday, June to September.

Arklow's seafaring past is explored in the small **maritime museum** (☎ 32868, St Mary's Rd; €3.20; open 10am-1pm & 2pm-5pm Mon-Sat May-Sept). Kids should enjoy the working model of the wheelhouse controls of a trawler.

Places to Stay & Eat
There are plenty of places to stay, especially on the southern side of town.

Valentia House (☎/fax 39200, e valentia house@esatclear.ie, Coolgreany Rd) Singles/doubles €35/63.50. The rooms in this house are decorated in a typically comfortable, simple fashion.

Royal Hotel (☎ 32524, fax 91091, Main St) Rooms from €45. The 11 rooms at this pleasant hotel are small but great value for money.

Kitty's (☎ 31669, Main St) Mains around €6.50. This pub-restaurant serves the usual selection of pub grub and other hot dishes, including a pretty good chicken and chips.

Getting There & Away
Bus Bus Éireann's express bus No 2 from Busáras in Dublin to Rosslare Harbour via Wicklow town serves Arklow 11-times daily (nine on Sunday), with departures from 7.30am (8.30am Sunday) to 8.30pm (single/return €8.90/13.35, 1½ hours). Alternatively, for the same price, you can get the slower (but more scenic) bus No 133, which also serves Avoca (2¼ hours). All buses stop outside the Chocolate Shop.

Train From Dublin, Irish Rail's South-Eastern Suburban line (☎ 01-836 6222) serves Arklow twice a day Monday to Friday and once on Saturday (single/return €10.20/12.70, 1½ hours). Intercity trains to Gorey and Rosslare Harbour stop in Arklow three times daily.

Counties Wexford & Waterford

The ferries arriving in Rosslare Harbour bring visitors to Counties Wexford and Waterford on their way to destinations farther afield, but there are places here to enjoy in their own right. The coastline offers superb beaches and possibilities for water sports while Mt Leinster in Wexford and the Comeragh Mountains in Waterford offer something entirely different. Both counties are rich in history, and the countryside, while lacking the rugged splendour of the island's west and south-west, has a beauty that surprises many visitors.

There's a short cut between Counties Wexford and Waterford by taking the Ballyhack to Passage East ferry, avoiding the longer route via New Ross.

County Wexford

County Wexford occupies the south-eastern corner of Ireland. The county is almost entirely flat, except near its western borders with Kilkenny and Carlow, where the Blackstairs Mountains rise to 796m at their highest point, Mt Leinster. There are some pleasant routes through these little-explored hills, particularly to the west of Enniscorthy and over the Scullogue Gap.

Wexford town is pleasant enough but retains few traces of its Viking past. To its north, a string of fine beaches runs along the coast towards County Wicklow. In the centre of County Wexford, Enniscorthy is an attractive town on the banks of the Slaney. Farther west, the River Barrow runs through New Ross, a good base for exploring the river's upper reaches.

On the southern coast is the fishing village of Kilmore Quay with its thatched cottages and, farther west, the flat and lonely Hook Peninsula, home to one of the world's oldest lighthouses.

The Wexford Coastal Walk (Slí Charman) follows the county's coastline for 221km from Ballyhack to Kilmichael Point.

Highlights

- Walk, cycle or drive along the lovely Hook Peninsula in County Wexford
- Learn about Wexford's rebel history at the 1798 Visitor Centre in Enniscorthy
- Relax and enjoy the views in the picture-perfect coastal town of Dunmore East in County Waterford
- Explore the Irish-speaking area of An Rinn

WEXFORD
☎ 053 • pop 15,862

Wexford (Loch Garman) vies with Waterford city for the position of principal settlement in the south-east. It was once a thriving port but over the centuries the slow-moving Slaney has deposited so much silt and mud in the estuary that the channel has become almost unusable. Now most commercial sea traffic goes through Waterford and all passenger traffic through Rosslare Harbour, 20km south-east.

Modern Wexford is renowned for its opera

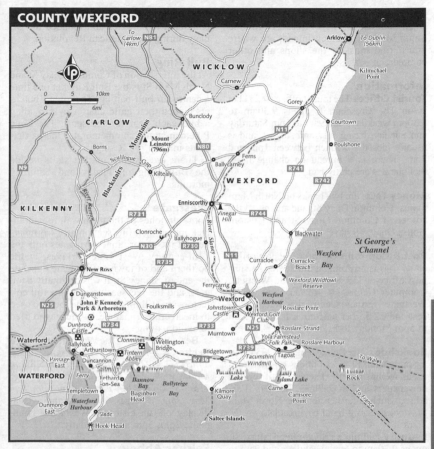

festival, a good time to visit provided you plan well ahead (see Special Events later in this section).

History

The Vikings arrived in the region around 850, attracted by its handy location near the mouth of the Slaney. The Viking name Waesfjord means 'harbour of mud flats' or 'sandy harbour'. The Normans captured the town just after their first landings in 1169, and traces of their fort can still be seen in the grounds of the Irish National Heritage Park north-west of town at Ferrycarrig.

Cromwell included Wexford in his Irish tour from 1649 to 1650. Three-quarters of the town's 2000 inhabitants were put to the sword, including all of the town's Franciscan friars – the standard treatment for towns that refused to surrender. After the massacre at Wexford, surrender became increasingly popular. During the 1798 Rising, rebels made a determined stand in Wexford town before they were defeated.

Orientation

From Wexford Bridge at the northern end of the town, the quays lead south-east along the waterfront, with the tourist office in the small kink called The Crescent. North and South Main St, a block inland, are where you'll find most of the shops and other commercial outlets.

Information

Tourist Offices The tourist office (☎ 23111) is on The Crescent. It opens 9.30am to 5.30pm weekdays and 9am to 5pm Saturday and Sunday during July and August, and is usually closed for lunch between 1pm and 2pm. There is a bureau de change here, though rates are pretty bad.

Money There are two banks on North Main St near Common Quay St, and another at the corner of Common Quay St and Custom House Quay; all have ATMs.

Post & Communications The post office (☎ 45314) is on Anne St and there is a sub-post office at 113 North Main St. Westgate Computer Centre (☎ 46291), next to the Westgate Heritage Centre, has Internet access for €2.55 per half-hour. It opens 9am to 5pm Monday to Friday.

Bookshops The Book Centre (☎ 23543) at 5 South Main St stocks books on Irish topics as well as a limited selection of foreign newspapers and magazines. Readers' Paradise, which is farther north on North Main St, stocks second-hand paperbacks.

Laundry Pádraig's Laundrette, 4 Mary St, opens 9.30am to 6pm weekdays and 9am to 9pm Saturday.

Medical Services For emergencies go to Wexford General Hospital (☎ 42233), 2.5km west of the centre on the N25.

Toilets There are public toilets near the tourist office and some more near St Iberius' Church.

The Crescent

As well as the Chamber of Commerce building, which houses the tourist office, The Crescent is home to a statue of Commodore John Barry. A local seaman born in 1745, he emigrated to America and founded the US navy during the American Revolution.

Bull Ring

At the intersection of Common Quay St and North Main St is the Bull Ring, at one time a centre for bull-baiting. The town's butchers gained their guild charter by providing a bull each year for the sport. The Lone Pikeman statue commemorates the participants in the 1798 Rising.

There are usually market stalls beside the Bull Ring on Friday and Saturday mornings.

Westgate

Some stretches of the town wall remain intact, including a fine section near Cornmarket. Of the six original town gates only the 14th-century West Gate survives, at the northern end of town on Westgate opposite the end of Slaney St. It was originally a toll gate, and the recesses used by the toll collectors are still intact, as is the lock-up used to incarcerate 'runagates' – those who tried to avoid paying.

Beside the gate is the **Westgate Heritage Centre** (*☎ 46506, 42611, Westgate; adult/ child €1.90/1.25; open 9.30am-5.30pm Mon-Sat & 2pm-6pm Sun July & Aug; 11am-5.30pm Mon-Fri & 2pm-6pm Sun May, June & Sept)*. Here, an audiovisual display tells the history of Wexford at 11am, noon, 2pm, 3pm and 4pm daily.

Selskar Abbey

Selskar Abbey was founded by Alexander de la Roche in 1190 after a crusade to the Holy Land. Its present ruinous state is a result of Cromwell's visit in 1649. Bascilla, the sister of Richard FitzGilbert de Clare (Strongbow), is supposed to have married Raymond le Gros, one of Henry II's brave lieutenants, in the abbey, and it is rumoured that Henry II did penance here for the murder of Thomas à Becket.

The ruins should be unlocked when the Westgate Heritage Centre is open. At other times, a key is available from the guardian at 9 Abbey St.

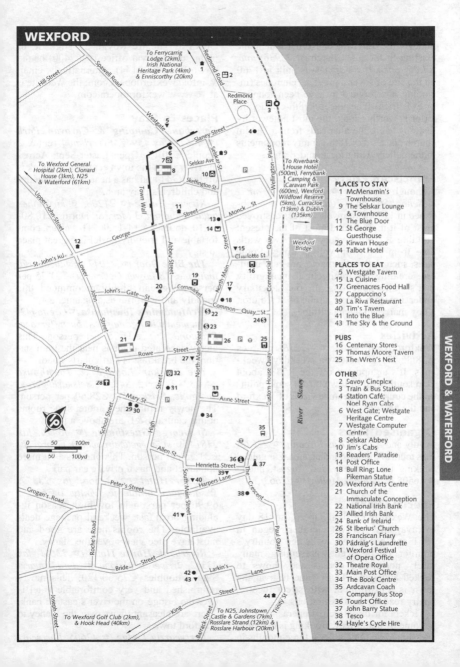

WEXFORD

To Ferrycarrig
Lodge (2km),
Irish National
Heritage Park (4km)
& Enniscorthy (20km)

Redmond
Place

To Wexford General
Hospital (2km), Clonard
House (3km), N25
& Waterford (61km)

To Riverbank
House Hotel
(500m), Ferrybank
Camping &
Caravan Park
(600m), Wexford
Wildfowl Reserve
(5km), Curracloe
(13km) & Dublin
(135km)

Wexford
Bridge

River Slaney

0   50   100m
0   50   100yd

To Wexford Golf Club (2km),
& Hook Head (40km)

To N25, Johnstown
Castle & Gardens (7km),
Rosslare Strand (12km) &
Rosslare Harbour (20km)

PLACES TO STAY
1 McMenamin's
   Townhouse
9 The Selskar Lounge
   & Townhouse
11 The Blue Door
12 St George
   Guesthouse
29 Kirwan House
44 Talbot Hotel

PLACES TO EAT
5 Westgate Tavern
15 La Cuisine
17 Greenacres Food Hall
27 Cappuccino's
39 La Riva Restaurant
40 Tim's Tavern
41 Into the Blue
43 The Sky & the Ground

PUBS
16 Centenary Stores
19 Thomas Moore Tavern
25 The Wren's Nest

OTHER
2 Savoy Cincplcx
3 Train & Bus Station
4 Station Café;
   Noel Ryan Cabs
6 West Gate; Westgate
   Heritage Centre
7 Westgate Computer
   Centre
8 Selskar Abbey
10 Jim's Cabs
13 Readers' Paradise
14 Post Office
18 Bull Ring; Lone
   Pikeman Statue
20 Wexford Arts Centre
21 Church of the
   Immaculate Conception
22 National Irish Bank
23 Allied Irish Bank
24 Bank of Ireland
26 St Iberius' Church
28 Franciscan Friary
30 Pádraig's Laundrette
31 Wexford Festival
   of Opera Office
32 Theatre Royal
33 Main Post Office
34 The Book Centre
35 Ardcavan Coach
   Company Bus Stop
36 Tourist Office
37 John Barry Statue
38 Tesco
42 Hayle's Cycle Hire

WEXFORD & WATERFORD

St Iberius' Church

South of the Bull Ring on North Main St, the existing St Iberius' Church (☎ 22936; tour €1.25; open 10am-5pm) was built in 1760 on the site of several previous churches (including one reputed to have been founded by St Patrick). The graceful 18th-century interior is worth a look, the most noteworthy features being the altar rails from a Dublin church and a set of 18th-century monuments in the gallery. Ring for a guided tour.

Franciscan Friary

Although the friary (☎ 22758, cnr Francis & School Sts; open 10am-5pm) was established in 1230, Cromwell's forces destroyed most of it in 1649 and most of the present building is 19th century. Only two walls date from pre-Cromwellian times. Some parts, such as the tabernacle, are very modern, creating an architectural incongruity that's quite appealing. In the sanctuary under a marble slab is a relic of St Adjutor, a boy martyr in ancient Rome.

Activities

Wexford Golf Club (☎ 42238) charges €28/32 for 18 holes on weekdays/weekends. It's signposted off the R733, about 2km south-west of town. From some points on the course you get nice views of Wexford and the harbour.

Organised Tours

In July and August, Bus Éireann (☎ 22522) runs tours of the surrounding area. For guided walking tours in July and August, phone ☎ 46505 or Thomas Molloy (☎ 22663).

Special Events

The Wexford Festival Opera, an 18-day extravaganza held in October, began in 1951 and has grown to be the country's premier opera event, presenting many rarely performed operas and shows to packed audiences. During the festival the town is transformed, with street theatre, poetry readings and exhibitions.

Tickets for the principal operas are hard to come by and pricey. Booking is essential and should be done at least three months in advance. Write to the Wexford Festival Opera at Theatre Royal, 27 High St, or phone the festival office (☎ 22400) or the box office (☎ 22144). Alternatively, email ⓔ info@wexfordopera.com; the Web site is at ⓦ www.wexfordopera.com.

Places to Stay

Ferrybank Camping & Caravan Park (☎ 42611, fax 45947, Ferrybank) Tent & 2 people €10.15. Open Easter-Sept. Across the river from the town centre, Ferrybank is off the R741 and has a heated pool, laundry and children's play area.

Kirwan House (☎ 21208, ⓔ kirwanhostel@eircom.net, 3 Mary St) Dorms €10.80-12.10, doubles €14-15.90. This clean, comfortable and friendly hostel is a great place to stay.

The Blue Door (☎ 21047, ⓔ bluedoor@indigo.ie, 18 Lower George St) €31.75 per person. We can highly recommend this friendly and well run establishment.

McMenamin's Townhouse (☎/fax 46442, ⓔ mcmem@indigo.ie, 3 Auburn Terrace, Redmond Rd) €31.75 per person. This nicely decorated place is near the train station; the breakfast is particularly good.

The Selskar Lounge & Townhouse (☎ 23349, fax 23843, ⓔ selskar@gofree.indigo.ie, Selskar St) €28.60 per person. The newly refurbished, motel-style rooms at this central B&B are above a pub.

St George Guesthouse (☎ 43474, fax 24814, ⓔ stgeorge@eircom.net, George St) €31.75 per person. This place is a bit more upmarket and has a private car park.

Talbot Hotel (☎ 22566, fax 23377, ⓔ sales@talbothotel.ie, Trinity St) €62.25/69.90 per person in low/high season including breakfast, weekend package deals available. The rooms here are good and most have nice views over the Slaney.

Riverbank House Hotel (☎ 23611, fax 23342, ⓔ river@indigo.ie, Wexford Estuary) Singles/doubles €75.60/120. This newly refurbished and very comfortable hotel is over the bridge on the river's eastern bank. There are pleasant views over the Slaney to Wexford town.

Ferrycarrig Lodge (☎ 42605, Ferrycar-

rig Rd) Singles/doubles from €32/50. This place on the banks of the Slaney is 2km to the north of Wexford and 10 minutes' walk from the Heritage Park.

Clonard House *(☎/fax 43141,* e *clonard house@indigo.ie, Clonard Great)* Singles/doubles €35/57 including breakfast. This 1780's farmhouse is 3km west of town off the N25 to Waterford.

Places to Eat

La Riva Restaurant *(☎ 24330, Crescent Quay, entrance on Henrietta St)* Mains €17-20. This casual but smart place has great views over the river. The menu is modern with French, Italian and Asian influences.

Tim's Tavern *(☎/fax 23861, 51 South Main St)* Mains €7.50 in the bar, €11-19 in the restaurant. This cosy pub-restaurant has a large menu and award-winning food. The portions are huge and all the traditional dishes are there, such as bacon and cabbage, Irish stew, and oysters and Guinness.

The Sky & the Ground *(☎ 21273, 112-113 South Main St)* Mains €14-19. Although meals are a little pricey here, the menu is interesting and rich. Crab and Guinness bisque costs €4.20.

La Cuisine *(☎ 24986, 80 North Main St)* Sandwiches & pies €1.50-2.50. This deli has good, reasonably priced food.

Cappuccino's *(☎ 23669, 25 North Main St)* €3.20-6.35. This place is a foodie's delight with great coffee as well as focaccia, baguettes, pasta and cakes. The Irish breakfast costs €5.

Westgate Tavern *(☎ 22086, Westgate)* Lunch & dinner €1.90-6.30. This casual pub serves soup, open sandwiches and more substantial meals.

Into the Blue *(☎ 22011, 80 South Main St)*. Lunch €2.50-5.70, set dinner menu €20-25 including a bottle of wine. Open 8am-5pm daily & 6.30pm-9.30pm Wed-Sat. Recommended by locals this place is both a deli and restaurant with sandwiches, salads and breakfasts to eat in or takeaway, as well as set three-course dinners.

There's a ***Tesco*** supermarket on The Crescent. You can put together a gourmet picnic at ***Greenacres Food Hall*** *(☎ 22975,*

North Main St) where you'll find a great selection of cheese, meats, olives and wine.

Entertainment

Pubs Even by Irish standards, Wexford has plenty of pubs, many of them strung along North and South Main Sts.

The Sky & the Ground *(see Places to Eat)* One of the most popular pubs in town, it has old-style decor and traditional music sessions most nights. It's a good family pub.

Thomas Moore Tavern *(☎ 24348, Cornmarket)* This is an atmospheric old pub.

The Wren's Nest *(☎ 22359, Custom House Quay)* This is the ideal place for a drink with a few friends.

Centenary Stores *(☎ 24424, Charlotte St)* For the 20–30 age group, this is the place, with traditional sessions on Wednesday night

Theatre & Cinemas Wexford has a number of venues dedicated to the arts.

Theatre Royal *(☎ 22144, 27 High St)* The Royal stages drama and opera.

Wexford Arts Centre *(☎ 23764, Cornmarket)* In the 18th-century Market House and Assembly Room, this centre caters for exhibitions, theatre, dance, music and film. It opens 10am to 6pm Monday to Saturday and in the evening for scheduled events.

Savoy Cineplex *(☎ 22321, The Square, Redmond Rd)* The three-screen Savoy is near the train station.

Getting There & Away

The N25 leads south-east from the quays and Trinity St to Rosslare Harbour. For Duncannon or Hook Head, turn west either at The Crescent along Harpers Lane or from Paul Quay along King St. For bus and train information to/from Wexford phone ☎ 33114 or 33162.

Bus Bus Éireann (☎ 22522) is based at the O'Hanrahan train station on Redmond Place. Buses run from Wexford to Rosslare Harbour (€3.35, 25 minutes, every 45 minutes Monday to Saturday, 10 on Sunday), Dublin (€10.15, 2¼ hours, 10 daily, eight on Sunday), Killarney (€20.35, 5½ hours, four daily, two on Sunday), Waterford (€9.80, one hour, nine daily, three on Sunday), Enniscorthy (€4.25, 25 minutes, hourly, seven on Sunday) and Cork (€15.90, 3½ hours, five daily, three on Sunday). Tickets are available from Station Café, 1a Redmond Square, across from the station.

JJ Kavanagh (☎ 0503-43081) operates a daily service to Carlow (€6.35) via Enniscorthy (€6.35) from Redmond Place at 7.20am but it doesn't operate during college holidays. Ardcavan Coach Company (☎ 22561) operates daily services to/from Dublin (€8.90); buses leave from The Crescent at 8am.

Train O'Hanrahan Station (☎ 22522) is at the northern end of town on Redmond Place. You can leave luggage there for €1.25 per item, per day.

Wexford is on the Dublin (€14.60, three hours) to Rosslare Harbour (€4.45, 30 minutes) line (via Enniscorthy and Wicklow) and is serviced by three trains daily in each direction.

Getting Around
Parking discs (€0.50 per hour) for street parking can be bought in most newsagents.

Noel Ryan Cabs & Minibus Hire (☎ 24056) is based at Station Café, 1a Redmond Square. You could also try Jim's Cabs (☎ 47108) on Selskar St. Most fares around the centre are €4.

At Hayle's Cycle Hire (☎ 22462), 108 South Main St, bikes cost €12.70 per day.

AROUND WEXFORD TOWN
Irish National Heritage Park
Four kilometres north-west of Wexford town on the N11 is the Irish National Heritage Park (☎ 053-20733, Ferrycarrig; adult/16-18 years/under 16s €6.35/3.80/3.20; open 9.30am-6.30pm daily Mar-Nov; last admission 5pm). It's an outdoor theme park that attempts to condense the country's entire history on one site.

Admission includes a 90-minute guided tour and takes in re-creations of a Mesolithic camp site, a Neolithic farmstead, a dolmen, a cist burial tomb, a stone circle, a *ráth* or ring fort, a monastery, a *crannóg* (lake settlement), a Viking shipyard, a motte and bailey, a Norman castle, a round tower and a couple of other smaller displays. A replica Viking longship is anchored on the Slaney outside the park.

A taxi to the park from Wexford should cost about €4.50.

Johnstown Castle & Gardens
Seven kilometres south-west of Wexford town on the way to Murntown, the former home of the Fitzgerald and Esmonde families is a splendid 19th-century castellated house overlooking a small lake and surrounded by 20 hectares of thickly wooded gardens.

The castle and its outbuildings now house an agricultural research centre, the headquarters of the Irish Environmental Protection Agency and an **agricultural museum** (☎ 053-42888, Wexford; adult/child €3.20/1.90; open 9.30am-5.30pm daily Apr-Nov). The main attraction is the collection of Irish country furniture. There's also a small Famine exhibition detailing with life before, during and after the potato blight. Other parts of the castle are used to host conferences.

The castle itself isn't open to the public, but the **gardens** (adult/child €3.80/0.65; open 9am-5.30pm daily) are.

Wexford Wildfowl Reserve
The North Slobs, a swathe of low-lying land reclaimed from the sea, lie 5km north-east of Wexford town. In winter, they are home to half the world's population of the Greenland white-fronted goose, numbering some 10,000 birds.

Wexford Wildfowl Reserve (☎ 053-23129, North Slob; free; guided tours on request; open 9am-6pm daily mid-Apr-Sept; 10am-5pm rest of year) was set up to protect the birds' feeding grounds. Alongside the usual visitor centre there's an observation tower and assorted hides.

Winter is also a good time to spot the brent goose from Arctic Canada, and throughout the year you'll see the mallard, pochard, godwit, mute and Bewick's swans, redshank, tern, coot, oystercatcher and many other species.

The reserve is on the Wexford to Dublin road; head north for 3.5km from Wexford until you see a signpost pointing to the right.

Curracloe Beach

Over 11km long, Curracloe is one of a string of magnificent beaches that line the coast north of Wexford town. Extensive dunes behind the beach provide some shelter, and you can pitch a tent if you're discreet. The opening scenes of the 1997 film *Saving Private Ryan* were filmed here. It's 13km north-east of Wexford off the Dublin road. **Curracloe House Equestrian Centre** (☎ 053-37583) offers trail rides along the beach year round.

Hotel Curracloe (☎ 053-37308, fax 37587, e *hotelcurracloe@eircom.net)* Singles €44-57, doubles €82-95. This place is good value but it's a long walk to the beach. There's live music at the weekend.

ROSSLARE STRAND

☎ 053

Rosslare Strand is about 8km north-west of Rosslare Harbour and 15km south-east of Wexford town. The long, golden beaches attract huge crowds in summer and there are also good walks north to Rosslare Point. The long, shallow bay is ideal for windsurfing. Boards, wetsuits and tuition are available from the **Rosslare Windsurfing Centre** (☎ 32101). **Rosslare Sailboard Centre** (☎ 32566) provides canoes and dinghies too. **Rosslare Golf Links** (☎ 32203) runs along the beach road; green fees are €32/44 for weekdays/weekends.

Places to Stay & Eat

Burrow Holiday Park (☎ 32190, fax 32256, e *burrowpk@iol.ie, Rosslare)* Tent sites €15-20. Just south of the village, this park has excellent facilities, including a laundry, games room and tennis courts. The fee takes no account of tent size or number of people.

Lyngfields B&B (☎ 32593, Tagoat) €25.40 per person. This place is signposted 3.2km from Rosslare on the road to Tagoat; it's good value for nice en-suite rooms.

Kelly's Resort Hotel (☎ 32114, fax 32222, Rosslare) Singles/doubles €67/127 including breakfast. With every sports and

Forth & Bargy Is Yola to Me

Faint remnants of a dialect called *Yola*, sometimes called 'Forth and Bargy', still survive in south-eastern County Wexford. Yola stands for 'ye olde language' and is a mixture of old French, English, Irish, Welsh and Flemish. Examples of the language would be to *curk*, meaning to sit on your thighs, or to be *hachee* or bad-tempered. A *chi o' whate* means a small amount of straw, while a *stouk* is a truculent woman. There is a story told of a local Yola speaker who had never left the valley where she was born. In the late 1960s she was brought to the top of the valley so that she could take a peek at the world beyond. She took one look and turned to go home, muttering that she didn't like what she saw!

leisure facility in the book, this hotel is popular with families. The three-course set menu costs €18 per person in the restaurant and there is a cafe for snacks.

The Oyster Restaurant (☎ 32439, Rosslare) Mains €10-18. Open 6pm-9pm Fri, 5pm-9pm Sat & Sun. This place, 100m from Kelly's, serves roasts, steaks and fish dishes.

Getting There & Away

Only the 9.30am bus from Rosslare Harbour to Wexford and the 5.45pm from Wexford to Rosslare Harbour stop at Rosslare Strand, Monday to Saturday (one hour). Trains on the mainline from Dublin to Rosslare Harbour (single/return €14.60/19.05, three hours 10 minutes) via Wexford (€4.45, 28 minutes) stop at Rosslare Strand three times a day. Trains to Waterford leave twice daily.

ROSSLARE HARBOUR

☎ 053 • pop 900

In the south-eastern corner of the country, Rosslare Harbour (Ros Láir) is a busy port with ferry connections to Wales and France. The harbour's surroundings are not particularly pretty or pedestrian-friendly and you might prefer to head straight on to Wexford. If you do need to stay there is plenty of accommodation in what is really a large village.

Orientation & Information

The ferry port is the main focus of the town. A road leading uphill from the harbour becomes the N25 and takes you to the B&Bs and hotels. A little further along this road is Kilrane where there are a few more B&Bs and a pub.

The tourist office (☎ 33232), on the N25 in Kilrane about 1.6km west of town, opens 11am to around 2pm daily, year round. There is a Bank of Ireland with an ATM and bureau de change on St Martin's Rd, which runs off the N25.

Yola Farmstead Folk Park

Just outside of Tagoat, on the N25, is an interesting folk park (☎ 32610, e yolafst@ iol.ie, Tagoat; adult/child €4.45/3.20; open 9.30am-5pm daily May-Oct; 9.30am-4.30pm Mon-Fri Mar-Apr & Nov). It's a reconstructed village from the 19th century with thatched cottages, a working windmill (one of the few left in the country) and a tiny church, all intended to give visitors an impression of what life was like in rural Ireland (albeit a sanitised version). There's the ubiquitous craft shop and a Heritage and Genealogy Centre where visitors can trace their roots.

Places to Stay & Eat

Most people arriving in Rosslare Harbour head straight out again. With the exception of one or two nice B&Bs, there's not much here except big unattractive hotels and bad food. If you find yourself stuck or just too tired to go any further there are plenty of places to stay.

An Óige Rosslare Harbour Hostel (☎ 33399, fax 33624, Goulding St) Dorms beds €8.90/11.45 in low/high season. This place is up the hill from the ferry terminal; take the flight of steps on the left as you leave the harbour and cut down beside Hotel Rosslare. It opens early or late for ferry arrivals and departures.

Clifford House (☎ 33226, e clifford house@eircom.ie, St Martin's Rd) €24/29 per person in low/high season. This place is situated in pleasant gardens with lovely views from most rooms.

St Martin's B&B (☎ 33133, St Martin's Rd) €24/29 per person in low/high season. The beautifully decorated rooms in this comfortable place are a better alternative to the overpriced hotels.

MacFadden's Bar & Restaurant (☎ 33590, Kilrane) Mains €10-13. This place, on the N25 about 2.4km from the harbour terminal, serves meals all day between noon and 9.15pm.

Getting There & Away

Bus The Bus Éireann service from Rosslare Harbour to Dublin (€11.45, three hours) runs six times a day and stops at Wexford (€3.20, 25 minutes). There are five buses a day (three on Sunday) to Waterford (€11.70, one hour 20 minutes) via Wexford and New Ross. Buses leave from Rosslare Europoort station.

Train Trains (☎ 33114) depart from Rosslare Europoort station, at the ferry terminal, for Wexford (€4.45, 28 minutes, three daily), Dublin (€19.05, three hours 10 minutes, three daily) and Waterford (€12.10, one hour 20 minutes, two daily except Sunday) via Rosslare Strand (€4.45, 10 minutes, five daily).

Car Budget (☎ 33318), Hertz (☎ 23511) and Murrays (☎ 33634) share a desk in the ferry terminal.

Boat Two ferry companies operate services to and from Rosslare Harbour and there's a convenient train and bus station by the ferry terminal.

Stena Line (☎ 33997) has four crossings a day, between 8.30am and 11pm, to Fishguard in Wales (3½ hours) on the Lynx catamaran. Fares range from €28 to €38 for foot passengers depending on the time of year, and €105 to €215 for a car plus driver. There are two crossings daily by the Superferry, which is €6 to €13 cheaper.

Irish Ferries (☎ 33158) has two daily sailings to Pembroke in Wales (3¾ hours) costing €100/230 in the low/high season. Irish Ferries sails three times a week to Cherbourg in France. From April to September there are also three sailings a week to Roscoff in

France, taking 16 to 24 hours. Foot passengers pay €57 to €108 for adults and €19 to €23 for children. Forget about taking the car unless you want to pay around €380. For more information see Sea in the Getting There & Away chapter.

SOUTH OF ROSSLARE HARBOUR

Nine kilometres south of Rosslare Harbour is **Carnsore Point**, where Ireland's first nuclear power station was to be built, had cost not killed it off. Carnsore Point was noted as the country's south-easternmost point on the map drawn by Ptolemy in the 2nd century. Offshore to the east is Tuskar Rock Lighthouse. The village of **Carne** has a few pretty, whitewashed, thatched cottages and a fine beach.

Lobster Pot (☎ 053-31110, Carne) Meals €3.20-7.50. This is an excellent pub and seafood restaurant that gets very crowded in summer. Their seafood chowder is one of the best on this planet.

Heading back up the road takes you past Lady's Island Lake in the middle of which is **Our Lady's Island**, site of an early Augustinian priory (you can still see a tower and graveyard) and still a centre of devotion and pilgrimage. Turning west brings you to **Tacumshin**, where in 1840 Nicholas Moran built the Tacumshin Windmill, one of Ireland's few thatched windmills. The key can be picked up from the shop where you park but you'll probably be charged to visit the windmill.

Bridgetown, 12km south-west of Wexford town, was the first part of Ireland to be colonised by the Anglo-Normans.

There's no public transport to this area.

KILMORE QUAY

☎ 053 • pop 400

A small fishing village on the eastern side of Ballyteige Bay, peaceful Kilmore Quay is noted for its lobsters and deep-sea fishing. The **Seafood Festival** in the second week of July involves all types of seafood tastings, music and dancing.

Lining the attractive main street up from the harbour are a fair number of pretty whitewashed thatched cottages. The harbour is the jumping-off point for the Saltee Islands, clearly visible out to sea. In the harbour the Guillemot Lightship houses a small **maritime museum** (☎ 21572; adult/child €2.55/1.25; open noon-6pm daily June-Aug; Sat & Sun in May & Sept).

Activities

There are some wrecks and great marine life around Kilmore Quay and the nearby Saltee Islands for divers to explore. Contact **Quay House** (see Places to Stay) or **Pier House Diving Centre** (☎ 29703) to hire gear.

To the north-west quite a good sandy beach stretches towards Cullenstown and there are some signposted **walking trails** behind the dunes.

Places to Stay & Eat

Killturk Hostel (☎ 29883, fax 29522, Grange) Dorms/twin rooms €12.70/17.15 including linen. This hostel, 2km out of Kilmore Quay along the R739, is a good place to stay. There is a low-priced cafe here.

Quay House (☎ 29988, fax 29808, ⓔ kil more@esatclear.ie) From €32 per person. This roomy B&B is the pick of the bunch.

The Haven (☎ 29979) €23-26 per person. This B&B is just off the main street near Quay House and has good views from some rooms.

Hotel Saltees (☎ 29601) €33/37/40 per person in Sept-Mar/Apr-June/July & Aug, single supplement €6.35. Rooms are nice here but you'll get better value elsewhere. There's a disco in the lounge on Saturday night.

Stella Maris Centre (☎ 29922) The centre has a coffee shop serving sandwiches and light meals for under €6.

Silver Fox Restaurant (☎ 29888) Starters €3.75-7.50, mains €13-19, early-bird 2-course dinner (5pm-7pm) €14. This is a highly recommended seafood restaurant and fills up nightly, even in winter, so booking is essential.

Wooden House Restaurant and Bar (☎ 29804) This place has traditional music sessions most nights.

Kehoe Pub & Parlour (☎ 29830) Another

popular pub in town; it has live bands at the weekend.

Getting There & Away

Public transport to Kilmore Quay is very limited. Viking Buses travel between Kilmore Quay and Wexford three-times daily. Bus Éireann has a service on Wednesday and Saturday from Wexford. For details, ask at the post office.

SALTEE ISLANDS

The Saltee Islands are 4km offshore from Kilmore Quay and feature some of the oldest rocks in Europe, dating back 2000 million years or more. Findings also suggest that the islands were inhabited by the pre-Celts as long ago as 3500 to 2000 BC.

In more recent times the haunt of privateers and smugglers, the Saltees now constitute one of Europe's most important bird sanctuaries, home to over 375 recorded species, principally the gannet, guillemot, cormorant, kittiwake, puffin and the Manx shearwater. The best time to visit is the spring and early-summer nesting season; once the chicks can fly, the birds leave. By early August it's eerily quiet.

The Saltees – nicknamed the 'graveyard of a thousand ships' – were touched by the 1798 Rising: it was here that two of the Wexford rebel leaders, Bagenal Harvey and Dr John Colclough, were found hiding before they were both brought to Wexford, hanged and beheaded.

The Saltees were bought in 1943 by Michael Neale, who then crowned himself Prince Michael, the 'First Prince of the Saltees'. He even erected a throne and obelisk in his own honour on the Great Saltee.

To book a crossing to the Saltees try local boatmen such as Dec Bates (☎ 053-29684, 087 252 9736), John Devereaux (☎ 053-29637, 087 292 6469) or Dick Hayes (☎ 053-29704, 087 254 9111). Boats leave from the harbour at Kilmore Quay most days in summer at about 10.30am and return at about 3pm, with more crossings according to numbers. Docking on the islands depends on the direction of the winds, and the operators will know the night before whether a landing

---

Baginbun Head

The Anglo-Normans first touched Irish soil at this spot in 1169. Joining forces with the far larger army of Dermot MacMurrough, they captured Wexford in the same year. Ramparts were built to fortify the headland at Baginbun until more Normans arrived in 1170 under Raymond le Gros. Shortly after he landed, 3000 Irish-Norse soldiers set out from Waterford city and attacked Baginbun, outnumbering the defenders seven to one.

Le Gros stampeded a herd of cattle onto them and then taught them a lesson in organised warfare. Seventy of Waterford's citizens and soldiers were captured, had their legs broken and were thrown over the cliffs to their death. So it was to be that:

At the creek of Baginbun,
Ireland was lost and won.

After the Norman leader Strongbow had landed at Passage East with another 1200 men, the Anglo-Normans gathered their forces and marched on to Waterford city, marking the start of more than 800 years of English involvement in Ireland.

---

is possible or not. It's a 30-minute crossing and the return fare is €15.25 if the boat is full, €63.50 if you're the only one. For more on the islands read *The Saltees, Islands of Birds and Legends* by Richard Roche & Oscar Merne (O'Brien Press).

HOOK PENINSULA & AROUND
☎ 051

The south-west of the county is dominated by the long, tapering finger of the Hook Peninsula, terminating at Hook Head. Cromwell's statement that Waterford town would fall 'by Hook or by Crooke' referred to the two possible landing points from which to take the area: here or at Crooke in County Waterford. In good weather, it's a fine journey out to the lighthouse at the tip of the head and back along the western side to Duncannon.

If you're feeling fit Wicklow's Lugnaquilla Mountain (924m) makes for excellent climbing.

Walpole's informal Mt Usher Gardens, Ashford

Steep walking on Glendalough's Spink Mountain

COLIN SHAW

You don't have to go far off the beaten track in County Waterford to find unspoiled, sleepy villages.

DOUG McKINLAY

Hook Head Lighthouse, County Wexford

DOUG McKINLAY

Etching crystal at the Waterford Crystal Factory

COLIN SHAW

One for the road?

The area between Kilmore Quay and Bannow, just east of the peninsula, is littered with Norman ruins. There's a good reason for this. Just south of Bannow Bay is **Baginbun Head** where the Anglo-Normans made their first landings in Ireland (see the boxed text 'Baginbun Head'). At Bannow Bay are the overgrown earthen ramparts built by the Normans when they first arrived. The stone **Martello tower** dates back to the early 1800s. The estuary here is rich in bird life such as brent geese, redshank, wigeon and teal.

Travelling back to the R733 towards Hook Peninsula you'll pass through **Wellington Bridge** where the Irish chapter of the Hell's Angels meet over the June bank-holiday weekend! In this town are the ruins of a **Norman village** which was known as Clonmines. Unfortunately the ruins are on private land and access is prohibited, but you will get a good view of them just south of the bridge as you come into town from the east. The redbrick chimney in a paddock by the roadside on the north side of the bridge is the remains of a **silver mine**. It was in operation from the 16th to the 19th century and supplied the Irish mint with silver.

On the way out to Hook is a 12th-century Cistercian abbey in a lovely rural setting near the village of Saltmills, **Tintern Abbey** (☎ 562650, Saltmills; adult/child €1.90/ 0.75 including guided tour; open 9.30am-6pm June-Sept). It was founded by William Marshall, earl of Pembroke, after he nearly perished at sea, and was named after another abbey in Wales where its first monks came from. To get there turn off the R734 at Saltmills where the sign for the abbey points along the road you're on. Also here is a three-way sign for **Tintern Trails**, 3km of walks around the abbey estate and surrounding area.

Continuing south towards the head, **Fethard-on-Sea** is the largest village in the area and home to the ruins of a 9th-century church and a 15th-century castle. Due to instability you can't wander through the ruins. There is a small tourist office in the main street (☎ 397502) which opens 9.30am to

5.30pm Monday to Friday in July and August.

The journey out to **Hook Head** is lovely, the land extremely flat with few houses interrupting the open space. On a clear day you can see across to the Blackstairs mountains to the north. About 2km from the head, turning left at a T-junction brings you down to the village of **Slade**, where a ruined castle dominates the harbour.

Farther south, Hook Head is crowned by Europe's, and possibly the world's, oldest **lighthouse** (☎ 397055; guided tours €4.45/ 2.55 9.30am-5.30pm daily Mar-Oct). It's said that monks lit a beacon on the head from the 5th century and that the first Viking invaders were so happy to have a guiding light that they left the monks alone. In the 12th century a more solid beacon was erected by Raymond le Gros; 800 years later it's largely the same structure you see today and was manned until 1996.

There are fine **walks** both sides of the head, a haunting and beautiful place in the evening. Be careful of the numerous blowholes on the western side of the peninsula. The rocks around the lighthouse are Carboniferous limestone, rich in fossil remains. If you search carefully, you may find 350-million-year-old shells and tiny disc-like pieces of crinoids, a type of starfish. Hook Head is also a good vantage point for **birdwatching**: over 200 species have been recorded passing through.

Coming back up the other side of the peninsula, about 5km from the lighthouse, is the enormous **Loftus Hall**, a privately owned, English-style mansion which looks desperately out of place here. The entire Hook Peninsula once formed part of the Loftus Estate.

Continue along the road towards Duncannon and you'll come across the ruins of a **medieval church** by the roadside. It's opposite the Templar's Inn (see Places to Eat). Here there is a 13th-century cross with a lamb engraving. This was known as the *Agnus Dei* and was associated with the Knights Templar who were given land around here by Henry II in 1172.

The village of **Duncannon** is a small

holiday resort with a wide, sandy Blue Flag beach and a good view over Waterford Harbour. To the west is **Duncannon Fort** (☎ 389454; adult/child €2.55/1.25; open 10am-5.30pm June-Sept). It's a star-shaped fortress built in 1586 on the site of an earlier Norman construction in defence from an attack by the Spanish Armada. The fort was used by the Irish army as a training base during WWI and, more recently, as a set for The Count of Monte Cristo starring Richard Harris and Guy Pearce.

Four kilometres north of Duncannon is **Ballyhack**, from where a ferry sails year round to Passage East in County Waterford (see Passage East later in this chapter). There's also a 15th-century **Knights Templar castle** (☎ 389468; open 9.30am-6.30pm daily June-Sept).

Dunbrody Abbey is a beautiful ruin on the western side of Hook Head, near the village of Campile and about 9km north of Duncannon. It was built around 1170 by Cistercian monks from Buildwas in Shropshire, England. Most of the structure survives and there is also a hedge maze. Nearby are the ruins of **Dunbrody Castle** (☎ 388603; adult/child/family €1.90/1.25/5; open 10am-7pm July & Aug; 10am-6pm Apr-June & Sept). It has a craft shop and small museum. There's an additional charge to visit the **maze** (adult/child/family €2.55/1.25/6.35).

Scuba Diving

Hook Head is popular with divers. The best spots are out from the inlet under the lighthouse or from the rocks at the south-western corner of the head. The underwater scenery is pleasant, with lots of caves, crevasses and gullies. It's a maximum of 15m deep. If it's too rough, try Churchtown, about 1km back from the point just before the road goes inland by the ruined church. Follow the path west to some gullies and coves. Otherwise, try the rocks south of Slade Harbour, a popular area.

The **Hook Sub-Aqua Club** (☎ 388302) in Slade provides dive-site information and a full range of facilities, including a compressor and storage. **Wexford Diving Centre and**

Dive Charters (☎ 053-39373), at Riverstown Farm, Murrintown, has similar facilities and offers diving charters. Tanks can be filled at Hotel Naomh Seosamh in Fethard-on-Sea (see Places to Stay), and in summer local dive groups often meet here.

Places to Stay

Most of the accommodation is in Fethard-on-Sea or Arthurstown, but there are a few B&Bs in more remote areas. Campers should stock up and head 12km south out to Hook Head, where there's free camping along the shore.

Fethard Camping & Caravan Park (☎ 397123, Fethard-on-Sea) Tent & 2 people €12.70. This park is at the northern end of Fethard-on-Sea.

Ocean Island Caravan Park (☎/fax 397148, Fethard-on-Sea) Tent & 2 people €12.70. This park is about 1km north of town and has a shop and games room.

Arthurstown Hostel (☎ 389411, Arthurstown) Dorms €9.50. The only hostel in the region is 1km south of Ballyhack on the western side of the peninsula.

Arthur's Rest (☎ 389192, Arthurstown) Singles/doubles €31.75/57.20. This B&B is in a nice spot near the harbour.

Hotel Naomh Seosamh (☎ 397129, Fethard-on-Sea) From €25 per person including breakfast. On the main street, this small hotel is nicely decorated and is popular at the weekend.

Dunbrody Country House Hotel (☎ 389600, fax 389601, e dunbrody@ indigo.ie, w www.dunbrodyhouse.com, Arthurstown) €95-160 per person May-Oct, €75-95 per person Nov-Apr including breakfast. This award-winning, luxurious hotel is set in eight hectares of stunning grounds.

Places to Eat

Fethard-on-Sea's hotels and pubs are the peninsula's principal eating spots.

The Vine Cottage (☎ 397133, Saltmills). On the road to Tintern Abbey, this pub is a nice place for a beer and a snack.

The Village Kitchen (☎ 397460, Fethard-on-Sea) €2.40-7.50. This is a small coffee shop with sandwiches and light meals.

Templar's Inn (☎ *397162, Templetown*)
€2.35-6.30. This popular inn specialises in
seafood and gets very crowded at lunchtimes, so get there early.

*Dunbrody Country House Hotel (see
Places to Stay)* Mains €16-24. This superb
restaurant boasts award-winning chefs and
wonderful reviews.

Getting There & Away

Bus services are virtually nonexistent to this
part of Wexford. On Monday and Thursday,
Bus Éireann buses running from Wexford to
Waterford will drop you in Fethard-on-Sea.
They leave Wexford town at 2.50pm; return
services leave Fethard-on-Sea at 11.26am.
At least one bus daily runs from New Ross
to Duncannon.

If you're travelling on to Waterford, it's
well worth taking the 10-minute crossing on
the Ballyhack to Passage East ferry. It'll
save you a long drive northwards via New
Ross. For details on fares and times see Passage East in the County Waterford section
later in this chapter.

NEW ROSS

☎ 051 • pop 6147

New Ross (Rhos Mhic Triúin), 34km west of
Wexford town on the River Barrow, was developed as a port town by the Normans in the
12th century. It was given its name to distin-
guish it from Old Ross, which was a large
settlement to the east. Today it advertises itself as the 'Norman gateway to the Barrow
Valley', but you'd have to look fairly hard to
find any trace of its Norman past. It's not an
especially pretty town, with large oil-storage
tanks and old warehouses looming over the
riverbanks, but the eastern bank is better than
the western one, with some steep, narrow
streets and St Mary's Church.

New Ross was the scene of fierce fighting
during the 1798 Rising when a group of
rebels under Bagenal Harvey and John Kelly
tried to take the town. They were repelled by
the defending garrison, leaving 3000 people
dead and much of the town in ruins.

A tourist office (☎ 421857) operates from
the refurbished grain-store building at 22
The Quay. It opens 9am to 1pm and 2pm to

6pm Monday to Saturday, and 11am to 4pm
Sunday, June to August.

Things to See

The roofless ruin on Church Lane is **St
Mary's Church**, which was founded by Isabella of Leinster and her husband, William,
in the 13th century. It's one of the largest medieval churches in Ireland. The church key is
available from the caretaker across the road.

The **SS Dunbrody Famine Ship** (☎ *425239,
adult/child €5.70/3.20; open 9am-6pm daily
Apr-Sept; noon-5pm Oct-Mar*) is a full-scale
reconstruction of SS *Dunbrody*, built in 1845
and used to ferry emigrants escaping the ravages of the Famine to the USA. On board is
a visitor centre which features a short film detailing the history of the original ship as well
as the construction of the new one. There's
also a database of Irish emigration to America from 1820 to 1920. The plan is for the SS
Dunbrody to make a return voyage to Boston,
but this is on hold until funding can be found.

Places to Stay

MacMurrough Farm Hostel (☎ *421383,
MacMurrough*) Dorms €10.15, doubles &
twins €25.40. This hostel, 3km north-east
of town, sleeps only 17 people. Bikes are
available for hire.

Riversdale House (☎ *422515, fax
422800, Lower William St*) Singles/doubles
€37/50. Open Apr-Nov. Only five minutes'
walk from the centre, this place has pleasant gardens and a personal touch.

Clarion Brandon House Hotel (☎ *421703,
fax 421567,* ✉ *brandonhouse@eircom.ie*)
Singles €76-89, doubles €115-140. At the
top end of the scale, this hotel provides comfort and elegance and offers packages for
stays of two nights or more with evening
meals.

Getting There & Away

Bus Éireann (☎ 053-22522) has a service between Waterford (€4.70, 20 minutes, three
daily) and Dublin (€8.90, three hours) via
New Ross and Enniscorthy. Buses also run
seven times a day (three on Sunday) to Rosslare Harbour (€9, one hour) via Wexford
(€7.35, 40 minutes). At least one bus daily

goes to Duncannon on the Hook Peninsula. Buses depart from Ryan Brothers on the quay.

AROUND NEW ROSS

Five kilometres south of New Ross, **Dunganstown** was the birthplace of Patrick Kennedy, grandfather of John F Kennedy. Patrick left Ireland for the USA in 1858 and JFK visited the town during his presidency. The original Kennedy house no longer exists, but there's a small cottage belonging to the Ryan family, who are direct descendants, and a small plaque marks the spot. Nearby is **Kennedy Homestead** (☎ 051-388264, Dunganstown; adult/child €3.20/1.90; open 10am-5.30pm daily May-Sept). This visitor centre celebrates five generations of the Irish-American dynasty. It also features photographs of the Kennedys in the USA.

A couple of kilometres to the south is the **John F Kennedy Park and Arboretum** (☎ 051-388171, New Ross; adult/child/family €2.55/1.25/6.35; open 10am-8pm May-Aug; 10am-6.30pm Apr & Sept; 10am-5pm Oct-Mar). It covers 252 hectares of woodlands and gardens with more than 4500 species of trees and shrubs. Funded by some prominent Irish-Americans, the park was opened by Eamon de Valera in 1968 in memory of the late US president. There is a small visitor centre, tearooms and a picnic area.

Slieve Coillte Hill, opposite the park entrance, offers a splendid view of the surrounding countryside and the Saltee Islands.

ENNISCORTHY
☎ 054 • pop 7640

Enniscorthy (Inis Coirthaidh) is an attractive hilly town on the banks of the Slaney in the heart of County Wexford, 20km north of Wexford town. It was the site of some of the fiercest fighting of the 1798 Rising when rebels captured the town and castle and set up camp nearby at Vinegar Hill. A visitor centre tells the story brilliantly.

Information

The tourist office (☎ 34699), in the Castle and County Museum, opens 10am to 1pm and 2pm to 5.30pm Monday to Saturday, mid-June to August, and 2pm to 5.30pm Sunday and bank holidays the rest of the year. It has a free Enniscorthy Town Trail map.

There is a Bank of Ireland on Abbey Square. The main post office has a bureau de change and is at the bottom of Castle Hill on Abbey Square. Internet access is available from Café del Mar (☎ 38531), Castle Hill, at €1.25 for 12 minutes, and for hostel guests at Platform 1 (see Places to Stay) at €1.25 for 10 minutes.

Enniscorthy Castle & Wexford County Museum

Enniscorthy has an impressive Norman castle (☎ 35926, e wexmus@iol.ie, Castle St; adult/child €3.80/0.65; open 10am-1pm & 2pm-6pm Mon-Sat, 2pm-5.30pm Sun June-Sept; 2pm-5.30pm Oct-Nov & Feb-May; 2pm-5.30pm Sun Dec & Jan). A fine stout building with drum towers at the corners, it dates back to 1205 and was a private residence until 1951. Queen Elizabeth I rewarded the poet Edmund Spenser for the many flattering things he said about her in his epic *The Faerie Queene* by awarding him the lease on the castle, but he sold it on to a local landlord, Edward Sinnott, whose grandson then sold it on to Sir Henry Wallop in 1580.

It was attacked by Cromwell in 1649, and during the 1798 Rising rebels took control of the town and used the castle as a prison. Today it houses Wexford County Museum, a mish-mash of bits and pieces, which is sorely in need of an overhaul. The first floor mainly covers 20th-century history and includes some interesting artefacts from the 1916 Easter Rising, as well as the 1798 Rising. On the top floor, among cobwebs, chipped paint and inches of dust, you'll find exhibits on local sports, agriculture and maritime history.

1798 Visitor Centre

The castle was overtaken as the town's most important attraction in 1998 by the opening of this interpretive centre (☎ 37596, fax 37198, e 98com@iol.ie, Mill Park Rd; adult/child €5.10/3.20; open 9.30am-6pm Mon-Sat, 11am-6pm Sun, last admission 5pm). It commemorates the bicentennial of

Wexford's abortive uprising against British rule in Ireland. Little is left to the imagination, with rich interactive displays and audiovisuals highlighting the circumstances and events surrounding the rebellion, as well as the fate of the rebels, most of whom were butchered with impunity by Crown forces. It's an excellent museum – it has been heralded as Ireland's best – and well worth the admission cost. From Abbey Square walk along Mill Park Rd for about five minutes and then take the first right after the school.

St Aidan's Cathedral

This impressive Roman Catholic cathedral was built in 1846 and designed by Augustus Pugin, who had a passion for late-13th- and early-14th-century Gothic church architecture. The son of a French immigrant, he was also responsible for designing the Houses of Parliament in London.

Vinegar Hill

Just 2km south-east of the town, this was where a group of rebels set up camp during the 1798 Rising after having captured the town. After 30 days on the hill they were forced to withdraw by royal forces. There is a memorial to the uprising and great views of the Slaney and surrounding countryside. To get there follow the sign from Templeshannon on the eastern side of the river that says 'Vinegar Hill 2km', not the sign that mentions the golf course and Country House as well. It should take you about 30 minutes.

Activities

Green fees are €25/34 weekdays/weekends at **Enniscorthy Golf Club** (☎ 33191, New Ross Rd), 2.4km south-west of town.

Slaney Canoe Hire (☎ 34526) charge €63.50 per day for their top-of-the-range, Canadian-made canoes. Just call ahead and they'll bring the canoe to a place on the riverbank that suits you.

One-hour guided walks of the town in English and French can be booked at **Castlehill Crafts & Tours** (☎ 36800, fax 36628, Castle Hill) next to Café del Mar. It costs €3.80 but there must be a minimum of five people.

There's plenty of good **fishing** in the Slaney. Go to **Cullens** (☎ 33478, 14 Templeshannon) for tackle hire and permits.

Special Events

Enniscorthy holds its Strawberry Fair in late June/early July when pubs extend their hours and strawberries and cream are laid on heavily. For exact dates and details phone ☎ 21688.

The Blackstairs Blues Festival (☎ 35364), over a weekend in September, attracts a number of international artists and appreciators.

Places to Stay

Platform 1 (☎ 37766, fax 37769, e plat@ indigo.ie, Railway Square) Dorms €10.15/ 12.70, singles & twins €17.80/20.35 per person in low/high season. We can highly recommend this clean, roomy and well run hostel. There is a pool room and TV lounge, and staff will help you find your way around town.

PJ Murphy's (☎ 33522, 9 Main St) Singles/doubles from €22.90/40.65. Rooms, located above the bar, are small but comfortable enough for the price.

Old Bridge House (☎ 34222, e obhouse@ indigo.ie, Slaney St) €23 per person. This small place is well situated overlooking the river, though rooms are basic.

Castle Hill House (☎ 37147, 2 Castle Hill) €25 per person. This is the pick of places to stay with nicely decorated rooms, a homely atmosphere and friendly, helpful hosts.

Lemongrove House (☎ 36115, Blackstoops) Singles/doubles €31.75/55.90. An elegant country house, it's 1km north of town on the N11. Rates usually drop a little in winter

Treacy's Hotel (☎ 37798, fax 37733, e info@treacyshotel.com, Templeshannon) Singles €44-57, doubles €89-100. Just over Enniscorthy Bridge from the town centre, rooms here are somewhat overpriced for what you get but it's friendly and offers good service.

Murphy Flood's Hotel (☎/fax 33413, Main St) Singles/doubles €44.50/76.25 including breakfast. This hotel is conveniently close to Market Square.

Places to Eat
De Olde Bridge (☎ *33917, 2 Templeshannon)* Snacks €2.50-3.80, meals €5.70-7.50. Open 8.30am-6pm daily. This is the place to go for sandwiches, pasta or curries.

The Cozy Kitchen (☎ *36488, 11 Rafter St)* Meals €4.80-6.30. Open 9am-6pm Mon-Sat. This popular deli and restaurant serves healthy meals and vegetarian dishes.

Galo Chargrill Restaurant (☎ *38077, 19 Main St)* Open noon-3pm & 6pm-11pm Tues-Sun. Great smells emanate from this place where you can also get pasta and vegetarian dishes.

Self-caterers could try *Pettitt's Supermarket* on Duffey Hill.

Entertainment
There are plenty of pubs in Enniscorthy. Most of those directed at a younger crowd are on the eastern side of the river, especially along Templeshannon.

Antique Tavern (☎ *33428, 14 Slaney St)* This tiny, half-timbered tavern is a nice place for beer (but not for 'footpads, thimblemen or three-card tricksters').

The White House (☎ *33096, Templeshannon)* The small and inviting White House is within stumbling distance of the hostel. There's live music every weekend during summer and on Sundays only the rest of the year.

The Old House (☎ *36086, 6 Templeshannon)* Live music can be heard here during the week and there's a disco at the weekend.

The Tavern (☎ *33016, 5 Templeshannon)* This cosy pub with an open fire is not as wild as The Old House next door.

Slaney Plaza (☎ *37066, Templeshannon)* There are daily screenings at this cinema. Tickets cost €5.10.

Shopping
The Enniscorthy area has been well known as a centre of pottery since the 17th century. The tourist office has a free pottery trail guide.

Forestwood (☎ *051-424844, Clonroche)* and *Carley's Bridge Potteries* (☎ *33512, Enniscorthy)*, which dates back to 1694, are both on the road to New Ross.

Badger Hill Pottery (☎ *35060, Enniscor-*

thy) is farther along the same road and *Kiltrea Bridge Pottery* (☎ *35107, Enniscorthy)* is north-west of the town centre.

Getting There & Away
Bus Bus Éireann buses stop on Templeshannon Quay on the eastern bank of the river outside the Bus Stop Shop. There are about nine buses daily (roughly every two hours) to Dublin (€10.15, two hours), Wexford (€4.25, one hour) and Rosslare Harbour (€6.75, one hour).

Train The train station (☎ 33488) is on the eastern bank of the river. Enniscorthy is on the Dublin (€14.60, 2½ hours) to Rosslare Harbour (€8.90, one hour) line which goes via Wexford (€5.70, 30 minutes). Three trains run daily in each direction.

FERNS
☎ 054 • pop 1000
Ferns is 7km north-east of Enniscorthy. Most traffic whizzes south for Wexford and Rosslare Harbour, but this sleepy little village was once the administrative capital of Leinster and an important diocese for several hundred years. It was the base of the MacMurrough kings of Leinster, in particular Dermot MacMurrough, who brought the Normans to Ireland and died here in 1171 (see The Norman Conquest under History in the Facts about Ireland chapter). Places to stay are disappointing here and, as you really only need an hour or so to take in the sights, you'd be better off using nearby Enniscorthy as a base.

Ferns Castle
Dating back to around 1220, the remains of this castle *(free; open year round)* at the north-western end of the village are thought to stand on the site of Dermot MacMurrough's old fortress. A couple of walls and part of the moat survive, with good views available from the top of the one complete tower. To the left of the door at the top is a murder hole through which oil or arrows could be dropped onto attackers below. Parliamentarians under Sir Charles Coote destroyed the castle and put most of the local population to death in 1649.

Other Things to See

At the eastern end of the main street is **St Edan's Cathedral** which was built in the early Gothic style in 1817. The remains of a high cross near the entrance are said to mark the grave of Dermot MacMurrough. The graveyard here also marks the burial place of Father Redmond who supposedly saved the life of a young French student, one Napoleon Bonaparte.

Other antiquities include the remains of **St Mary's Abbey**, founded by Dermot Mac-Murrough in 1158, just south-east of the cathedral, and **Ferns Cathedral** just behind it. The latter was built by Normans in the 13th century but was burnt down in 1577 by a local chieftain.

At the top of the main street (the western end) is the modern **St Aidan's Cathedral** and a little further along you'll find the remains of **Ferns Castle**.

Getting There & Away

Ferns is on the Bus Éireann Dublin–Rosslare Harbour route via Wexford and Enniscorthy. Buses run nine times a day. Buses from Dublin to Waterford also stop in Ferns three times a day.

MT LEINSTER

Bunclody, on the border with County Carlow 16km north-west of Ferns, is a good base from which to climb Mt Leinster. At 796m it's the highest mountain in the Blackstairs. If you want to drive to the top, take the Borris road out of Ferns for 8km, turn right at the sign for the South Leinster Scenic Drive, and continue to the radio mast at the top. The last few kilometres are on narrow, exposed roads with steep fall-offs, so drive slowly and watch out for sheep. If the weather is good you should be able to see parts of counties Waterford Carlow, Kilkenny and Wicklow.

Mt Leinster is also home to some of Ireland's best hang-gliding. **The Mt Leinster Hang-Gliding Club** (☎ *01-455 6437*) runs day courses for around €150. For **guided walks** in the Blackstairs Mountains you could contact **Brian Gilsenan** (☎ *054-77828*).

County Waterford

Wedged into Ireland's south-eastern corner, County Waterford combines the low farmland and sandy coastlines typical of County Wexford with the more rugged landscape common in County Cork. While Waterford city can only be described as ugly, the attractive coastal towns of Dunmore East, Tramore and Dungarvan have great character. It's well worth diverting away from the coast for a drive through the Nire Valley, which sits between the Comeragh and Monavullagh Mountains and further west to the historical towns of Lismore and Cappoquin on the River Blackwater.

South of Dungarvan, in the county's south west, the area between An Rinn and Ardmore is a Gaeltacht – Irish-speaking – area with its own special heritage and culture.

WATERFORD

☎ 051 • pop 44,155

Waterford (Port Láirge) is first and foremost a commercial city and port. The River Suir's estuary is deep enough to allow large modern ships right up to the city's quays and the port is still one of Ireland's busiest. Sadly, this means the northern bank of the river is marred by industrial development.

Waterford is Ireland's oldest city and has been inhabited since 914. Some parts of Waterford feel almost medieval, with narrow alleyways leading off many of the larger streets. Reginald's Tower marks the city's Viking heart and there are some attractive Georgian houses and commercial buildings. On the whole, though, Waterford is an ugly, dirty place with little of interest outside its heritage sites. The quays are little more than one long parking lot with a bus station. An apparent, large number of aimless, bored youths makes some parts of the centre feel unsafe at night.

The hand-blown Waterford crystal made here is one of Ireland's most famous exports.

History

In the 8th century Vikings settled at a riverside site called Port Láirge, which they

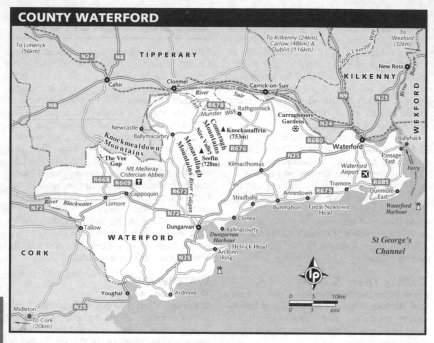

COUNTY WATERFORD

renamed Vadrafjord. Recent excavations suggest the city was founded in 914 and quickly became a booming trading post. In their efforts to consolidate their presence, the Vikings adopted a ferocity in dealing with the natives which made it the most powerful – and feared – settlement in the country. All the local tribes paid them a tribute, known in Irish as the Airgead Sróine (nose money): if you didn't pay it, they cut off your nose!

Waterford's strategic importance ensured that its fortunes were closely linked to those of the island as a whole. In 1170 an Irish-Viking army was defeated in battle by the newly arrived Anglo-Normans: 70 prominent citizens were thrown to their deaths off Baginbun Head. Later that year the city was besieged by Strongbow, who overcame a desperate defence.

In 1210 King John extended the original Viking city walls and Waterford became Ireland's most powerful city and an important trading centre. In the 15th century it resisted the forces of two pretenders to the English Crown, Lambert Simnel and Perkin Warbeck, thus earning the motto *Urbs intacta manet Waterfordia* (Waterford city remains unconquered).

The town defied Cromwell in 1649 but in 1650 his forces returned and the city finally surrendered. Although it escaped the customary slaughter, much damage was done and the population declined: Catholics were either exiled to the west or shipped as slaves to the Caribbean.

Orientation

Waterford lies on the tidal reach of the River Suir, 16km from the coast. The main shopping street runs directly south from the Suir, beginning as Barronstrand St and changing names as it runs south to become Broad St, Michael St and John St before intersecting with Parnell St. This runs north-east back up to the river, becoming The Mall on the way.

Most of the sights and shopping areas lie within this triangle.

Information

Tourist Offices The tourist office (☎ 875 788, fax 877388) is in The Granary on Merchant's Quay. It opens 9am to 6pm Monday to Saturday, 11am to 5pm Sunday, from April to September; and 9am to 1pm and 2pm to 5pm weekdays the rest of the year.

Money There are a number of banks along The Quay. Ulsterbank has an ATM and a bureau de change.

Post & Communications The post office is on Parade Quay and there is a smaller post office on O'Connell St. In Parnell Court, off Parnell St, you can send and receive email at Voyager Internet Café (☎ 843843) from 11am to 11pm daily.

Bookshops The excellent Book Centre on Barronstrand St has three floors and sells books (including some foreign papers and magazines) and records; there's also a cafe. Gladstone's on Gladstone St sells second-hand paperbacks.

Laundry Duds 'n' Suds, 6 Parnell St, is a laundrette with a rudimentary cafe. It opens 8.30am to 8pm Monday to Saturday.

Medical Services Waterford Regional Hospital (☎ 873321) is on St John's Hill, 2.5km south-east of the town centre.

Toilets You'll find public toilets on Merchant's Quay, near the bus station, and more further down near the Clocktower.

Reginald's Tower

The most interesting relic of the walls is Reginald's Tower at the northern end of the Mall, built by the Normans in the 12th century on the site of a Viking wooden tower. With walls 3m to 4m thick, it was the city's key fortification.

Over the years the tower has served as a mint, an arsenal and a prison. Many of Waterford's royal visitors stayed in this 'safe house', including Richard II, Henry II and James II, who took a last look at Ireland from the tower before departing to exile in France.

The **tower museum** (☎ 873501, The Quay; adult/child €1.90/1.25; open 10am-5pm Mon-Fri, 2pm-6pm Sat & Sun Easter-Oct) has several exhibits, including artefacts connected to one of Waterford's most famous sons, Thomas Francis Meagher (1823–67). Meagher was a Young Ireland leader captured for his part in the 1848 Rising and shipped to a penal colony in Australia. From there he escaped to the USA, where he eventually became governor of Montana.

Behind the tower, a section of the **old wall** is incorporated into Reginald's bar and restaurant. The two arches were sallyports, to let boats 'sally forth' onto the inlet, which used to flow right by the wall.

The Mall

The Mall is a wide 18th-century street running back from the river and built on reclaimed land which, until 1735, was a tidal inlet running alongside the walls. The **City Hall** was built in 1788 by local architect John Roberts. A remarkable Waterford glass chandelier hangs in the council's meeting room (there's a replica in Philadelphia's Independence Hall in the USA). The City Hall houses Waterford's **Municipal Art Gallery** but access is only via sporadic guided tours (for details phone ☎ 873501, extension 489).

Also built by John Roberts, the **Theatre Royal** is Ireland's finest intact 18th-century theatre.

The austere **Bishop's Palace** was begun in 1741 after a stretch of the wall was demolished. One of Ireland's finest town houses, it was designed by Richard Cassels (or Castle), who was also responsible for Powerscourt House in County Wicklow, Westport House in County Mayo, and Dublin's Leinster House and Rotunda Hospital. It now acts as the city engineering offices.

Waterford Treasures

The Granary, which is also home to the tourist office, houses this exhibition (☎ 304500; adult/child €5.10/2.55; open 9.30am-9pm June-Aug; 9.30am-6pm Sept

WATERFORD

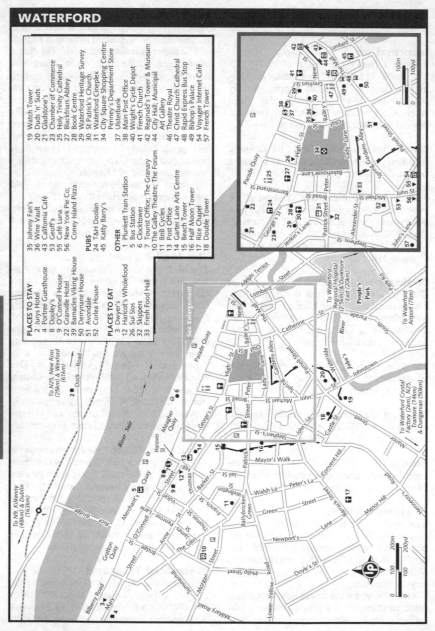

PLACES TO STAY
2 Jurys Hotel
4 Portree Guesthouse
8 Dooley's
9 O'Connell House
22 Granville Hotel
39 Barnacles Viking House
50 Derrynane House
51 Avondale
52 Corlea House

PLACES TO EAT
3 Dwyer's
12 Haricot's Wholefood
26 Sul Sios
32 Skippers
33 Fresh Food Hall

35 Johnny Fan's
36 Wine Vault
43 California Café
53 Geoff's
55 Café Luna
56 New York Pie Co;
     Coney Island Pizza

PUBS
24 T&H Doolan
45 Katty Barry's

OTHER
1 Plunkett Train Station
5 Bus Station
6 Clocktower
7 Tourist Office; The Granary
10 The Galley Theatre; The Forum
11 BnB Cycles
13 Post Office
14 Garter Lane Arts Centre
15 Beach Tower
16 Half Moon Tower
17 Rice Chapel
18 Double Tower

19 Watch Tower
20 Duds 'n' Suds
21 Gladstone's
23 Chamber of Commerce
25 Holy Trinity Cathedral
27 Blackfriars Abbey
28 Book Centre
29 Waterford Heritage Survey
30 St Patrick's Church
31 Waterford Cineplex
34 City Square Shopping Centre;
     Penney's Department Store
37 Ulsterbank
38 Main Post Office
40 Wright's Cycle Depot
41 French Church
42 Reginald's Tower & Museum
44 City Hall; Municipal
     Art Gallery
46 Theatre Royal
47 Christ Church Cathedral
48 Rapid Express Bus Stop
49 Bishop's Palace
54 Voyager Internet Café
57 French Tower

& *May; 10am-5pm rest of year).* It was once a grain store that has been superbly converted into a museum, with plenty of sleek metal and glass to give it a futuristic look. The exhibits are equally fascinating, with a comprehensive collection of local treasures from the last 1000 years, including Viking artefacts. Audiovisual displays and interactive presentations of Waterford's heritage are expertly put together.

Christ Church Cathedral
Behind City Hall is Europe's only neoclassical Georgian cathedral, Christ Church Cathedral *(☎ 874119, Cathedral Square; admission by donation).* It was designed by John Roberts and stands on the site of an 11th-century Viking church. When the medieval cathedral was demolished, a remarkable collection of 15th-century Italian priests' vestments was uncovered.

Don't miss the tomb of James Rice, seven times lord mayor of Waterford, who died in 1469 and is depicted in a state of decay with worms and frogs crawling out of his body. The cathedral also houses several Bibles written in Irish.

There is usually someone there to guide you around the place if you wish.

French Church
The ruins of a French Church built in 1240 by Franciscan monks (Grey Friars) are on Greyfriars St. It became a hospital after the dissolution of the monasteries and was then occupied by French Huguenot refugees between 1693 and 1815. One of its last leading doctors was TF Meagher's father, Thomas Meagher Senior, mayor of Waterford. You can pick up the church key across the road at 5 Greyfriars St.

Other Buildings
The ruins and square tower of the Dominican **Blackfriars Abbey** on Arundel Square date back to 1226. Nearby on Barronstrand St the Catholic **Holy Trinity Cathedral** was built between 1792 and 1796 by John Roberts, who also designed the Protestant Christ Church Cathedral. The sumptuous interior boasts a fine carved pulpit, painted pillars with Corinthian capitals and lovely Waterford crystal chandeliers.

Near Patrick St is the old city wall's **Half Moon Tower. St Patrick's Church** on Jenkin's Lane is an 18th-century Catholic chapel which managed to survive the savage suppression of Catholicism at that time. At the top of Jenkin's Lane is the **Beach Tower**, another remnant of the old city wall.

The **Chamber of Commerce** building on George's St was originally built as a town house by John Roberts and has a magnificent staircase.

Edmund Ignatius Rice, founder of the Christian Brothers, established his first school at Mt Sion on Barrack St, where the **Rice Chapel** is a delightful combination of red brick and stained glass, with Rice's tomb in pride of place awaiting the likely canonisation of its occupant. If you phone ☎ 874390 you can also arrange to see an audiovisual presentation on Rice's life and works.

Waterford Crystal Factory
The first Waterford glass factory was established at the western end of the riverside quays in 1783, but closed in 1851 as a result of punitive taxes imposed on the raw materials by the British government. The business wasn't revived until 1947, and the existing factory opened in 1971. Today, it employs 1600 people, among them highly skilled glass blowers, cutters and engravers who take from eight to 10 years to learn their craft. The glass is a heavy lead (over 30%) crystal made from red lead, silica sand and potash.

The visitor centre *(☎ 373311, Cork Rd; adult/child €5.70/free; open 8.30am-4pm Apr-Oct)* is 2km south of the centre. Between April and October you can guide yourself around the plant, with staff on hand to explain things. During the rest of the year there are free guided tours every 20 minutes between 9am and 4pm (every 10 minutes in July and August).

In summer you can buy a ticket in advance from the tourist office to avoid long queues at the factory. Afterwards you can part with large amounts of money in the Crystal Gallery and then have lunch or tea in the *cafe.*

Genealogical Centre

If you have ancestors from the Waterford area, the Genealogical Centre at the **Waterford Heritage Survey** (☎ *876123, Jenkin's Lane; open 9am-1.15pm & 1.45pm-5pm Mon-Fri May-Oct)* may have all the details you need to complete the family tree.

Organised Tours

One-hour **guided walking tours** (☎ *873711, 851043)* depart from the Granville Hotel on Meagher Quay at noon and 2pm or from The Granary at 11.45am and 1.45pm daily, March to October (€5.10).

The *Galley Cruising Restaurant* (☎ *421723)* operates two-hour cruises between Easter and September. The lunch cruise leaves at noon and costs €17.80, the 3pm afternoon tea cruise costs €10.15 and the dinner cruise leaves at 7pm and costs €32. Prices are lower if you go without food and beverages.

Special Events

Waterford's Light Opera Festival takes place in September and October. It's cheaper and more easily accessible than the more famous Wexford Festival Opera but booking is still advisable. For more details contact the Theatre Royal (☎ 874402), The Mall, Waterford.

Places to Stay

The frequency of buses to Tramore (see later in this chapter) means you can stay there and commute into Waterford if you can't find anything here that takes your fancy.

Hostels & B&Bs For a city with such a huge amount of tourist traffic, Waterford is disappointingly lacking in good, central B&Bs. Wherever you stay in the centre, traffic noise can be a problem.

Barnacles Viking House (☎ *853827, fax 871730,* e *viking@barnacles.iol.ie, Coffee House Lane, Greyfriars, The Quay)* Dorms €10.15/12.70, doubles with private bathroom €19.70/22.25 in low/high season, including breakfast. This rather soulless, modern hostel is in the city's old quarter. The door is locked from noon to 3pm.

Avondale (☎ *852267, 2 Parnell St)* Singles/doubles €44.50/63.50. This place advertises itself as a luxury town house.

Portree Guesthouse (☎ *874574, Mary St)* Singles/doubles from €35.60/58.45. An attractive Georgian house in a quiet part of town, this B&B is one of the best in the centre.

O'Connell House (☎ *874175, 3 O'Connell St)* €25.40 per person. This place is very good value.

Derrynane House (☎ *875179, 19 The Mall)* Singles/doubles €21.60/43.20, with bathroom €1.25 extra. Accommodation in this lovely late-Georgian house is basic but rooms are clean and spacious.

Corlea House (☎ *875764, 2 New St)* Singles/doubles €25/43 including breakfast. Although basic, this B&B offers very good value for the centre and is close to some good cafes and bars.

Hotels There are a number of reasonable hotels to choose from.

Granville Hotel (☎ *305555, fax 305566,* e *stay@granville-hotel.ie, Meagher Quay)* Singles/doubles from €89/140. This classy place is well located near the Granary.

Dooley's (☎ *873531, fax 870262,* e *hotel@ dooleys-hotel.ie, Merchant's Quay)* Singles/doubles €76/140. Dooley's offers reasonable value for money with its attractive, spacious rooms.

Jurys Hotel (☎ *832111, fax 832863,* e *waterford-hotel@jurysdoyle.com, Dock Rd, Ferrybank)* Singles/doubles from €82/108. You'll be pleased to know that this place, on the other side of the river, is much better on the inside. There are some great views of Waterford town and port from up here.

Places to Eat

Restaurants Waterford has several decent restaurants.

Johnny Fan's (☎ *879535, High St)* Mains €12-22, 'happy hour' 3-course dinner (5pm-6.45pm) €16.45. Though not cheap, this is an excellent Chinese restaurant.

Wine Vault (☎ *853444, High St)* Light meals €5.70-9.50. This place is good value for money. A sample from the menu is escallop of beef with spinach on home-made bread with a warm potato salad for €8.25.

Dwyer's (☎ 77478, 8 Mary St) Mains €20-23, early-bird 3-course menu (6pm-7pm) €22.25. This is one of the best restaurants in town, serving modern Irish cuisine.

Cafes & Fast Food The city's cafes offer the best value eating in the city. The most interesting places are on Michael St and John St.

California Café (☎ 855525, 8 The Mall) Meals €4.75-5.40. This casual place is licensed and serves typical Tex-Mex, southwest and LA-style dishes.

Geoff's (☎ 874787, 9 John St) Light meals €2.50-7. Geoff's is always full of people, which is a good sign. *Panini*, sandwiches and Mexican-influenced meals are the main fare here.

Café Luna (☎ 843439, 53 John St) Light meals & snacks €5-10. Open until 3am Thur-Sun. This rather groovy place is popular with students and serves great coffee.

Haricot's Wholefood (☎ 841299, 11 O'Connell St) Meals €7-9, lunch specials €5.70. Open 10am-8pm Mon-Fri & 10am-5.45pm Sat. This licensed place serves vegetarian dishes. Oak-smoked haddock pie with potato salad costs €8.85.

Suí Síos (☎ 841063, 54 High St) Light meals €5-7. A pleasant little cafe, it serves salads, sandwiches, breakfasts and great coffee.

Coney Island Pizza (☎ 850200, 14 John St) Pizzas €7.10-11.40. This place has free delivery.

New York Pie Co. (☎ 304204, 17 John St) Pies €2-5.40. Open noon-3am Wed-Sat, 5pm-3am Sun. This place has every kind of pie and hot dog you can imagine.

Skippers (☎ 872942, 46 Patrick St) Snacks €1.60-4.30. This fish and chip shop has a burger menu too.

Fresh Food Hall (☎ 870865, 37 Michael St) This place is a deli serving a variety of sandwiches and snacks.

Entertainment

Pubs Waterford's nightlife relies heavily on the presence of students from all over the country who attend the local technical college. Weekends are the big nights, when many pubs feature live music and clubs stay open till around 4am. Most clubs are concentrated around the intersection of Parnell St, John St and John's Lane.

Katty Barry's (☎ 855095, Mall Lane) This small, dark and friendly place is rumoured to serve the best Guinness in the area.

T&H Doolan (☎ 872764, 31 George's St) The venerable T&H Doolan incorporates a remnant of the 1000-year-old city wall. Sinead O'Connor played here before she hit the big time and there is still live music most nights.

Geoff's (see Places to Eat) Geoff's, one of the city's hippest bars, is situated where John St becomes Michael St.

Theatre & Cinemas There are plenty of opportunities for exploring the arts in Waterford.

Garter Lane Arts Centre (☎ 855038, 22a O'Connell St) Open 10am-6pm Mon-Sat. This theatre, in an 18th-century building, stages films, exhibitions, poetry readings and plays.

The Galley Theatre (☎ 871111, The Glen) Located in The Forum, this place puts on plays most nights.

City Hall (☎ 875788, The Mall) The 90-minute Waterford Show here combines music, dancing and wine in a program about the city's history. It takes place at 8.45pm on Thursday, Friday and Sunday from May to September. Tickets cost €8.90 and can be booked at the tourist office, Waterford Crystal Factory or City Hall.

Waterford Cineplex (☎ 74595, Patrick St) This five-screen cinema shows first-run films.

Getting There & Away

Air Waterford Airport (☎ 875589) is 7km south of the city at Killowen. Euroceltic Airways (reservations ☎ 875020) has two daily flights to London's Luton airport from €87 one way.

Bus The Bus Éireann station (☎ 879000) is on the waterfront at Merchant's Quay. There are plenty of buses daily to Dublin (€10.15), Cork (€12.70), Wexford (€9.80), Killarney (€17.15) and Dungarvan (€7.35).

Rapid Express Coaches (☎ 872149), at Parnell Court on Parnell St, runs a service between Waterford and Dublin via Dungarvan and Carlow (€10.15, at least eight daily).

Suirway (☎ 382209) has four buses daily from Monday to Saturday to Dunmore East (€2.30, 30 minutes) and Passage East (€2.15, 30 minutes). They depart from the waterfront next to the Bus Éireann station. Look for the red and white buses.

Train From Plunkett train station (☎ 873401) on the northern side of the river, there are five services a day to Dublin (€17.15, three hours) via Kilkenny (€10.15, 45 minutes), Limerick (€22.90, three hours, two daily) and Rosslare Harbour (€12.10, one hour 20 minutes, two daily). Trains to Cork (€22.90, three to five hours, four daily) go via Limerick Junction. You can leave luggage at the station for €1.25 per item per 24 hours.

Getting Around

There is no bus service to the airport. A taxi (☎ 877773) will cost around €12.70.

Disc parking (€0.65 per hour) is in operation in the centre and there are paid car parks along the quays and at The Glen, just west of the centre.

There are taxi ranks at Plunkett train station and outside Penney's department store at City Square Shopping Centre.

Wright's Cycle Depot (☎ 874411), on Henrietta St, is a Raleigh Rent-a-Bike outlet. Bike hire costs €12.70/50 per day/week. BnB Cycles (☎ 870356), 22 Ballybricken Green, also hires out bikes.

PASSAGE EAST

Eleven kilometres east of Waterford city on the coast road is Passage East, with its little harbour and thatched cottages at the foot of low hills. The Passage East to Ballyhack ferry makes a useful short cut between Counties Waterford and Wexford. The ferry company (☎ 051-382480) operates a continuous service from 7am to 10pm, April to September, and 7.20am to 8pm the rest of

the year. On Sunday and public holidays, the first sailings are at 9.30am. The 10-minute crossing costs €5.60/8.25 one way/return for a car, €1.25/1.90 for pedestrians, and €2.55/3.20 for cyclists. Return tickets are valid for an unlimited time.

Just south of the village is **Crooke**, with the remains of the Geneva Barracks nearby. Built in the 18th century as part of a settlement for Swiss refugees, the buildings were turned into barracks after the plan fell through. It was here that a young rebel of the 1798 Rising came to confess his sins to a priest who turned out to be an army officer in disguise. The lad was arrested and subsequently hanged, a story immortalised in the song *Croppy Boy*.

Suirway (☎ 051-382422) runs two buses daily Monday to Friday and four on Saturday to Passage East from Waterford city (€2.15, 30 minutes).

DUNMORE EAST

☎ 051 • pop 1500

Dunmore East (Dún Mór), a fishing village strung out along a coastline of red sandstone cliffs and discreet coves, is a really lovely spot. The main street is lined with thatched cottages and the larger buildings, such as the Haven Hotel, were once homes of wealthy merchant families who called the village home during the early 19th century.

The harbour is overlooked by an unusual **Doric lighthouse** built in 1823. At this time the town was a station for the steam packets which carried the mail between England and the south of Ireland.

There's a good view of Hook Head lighthouse across the water in County Wexford. The noisy birds nesting in the cliffs around the harbour are kittiwake. The most popular **beaches** are Counsellor's Beach, facing south and set among the cliffs, and Ladies Cove, in the village. As it's only 20km from Waterford city, it's a popular getaway for day-trippers so it gets very busy during summer and at the weekend throughout the year.

Activities

The **Dunmore East Adventure Centre** (☎ 383783) hires out equipment for windsurfing, canoeing, surfing and snorkelling. Short courses in most of these sports are also available.

If you're interested in going **fishing** for sharks or exploring old wrecks off the coast contact **Dunmore East Angling Charters** (☎ 383397, 087 268 2794).

Dunmore East Golf Club (☎ 383151) is on a cliff top overlooking the town and Waterford Harbour. Green fees are €12.70-19 and club hire is €7.60.

Places to Stay

Creaden View (☎ 383339, Harbour Rd) Singles/doubles €32/50. This is an excellent B&B but make sure you get a room with a view.

Church Villa (☎ 383390, fax 383023, e churchvilla@eircom.net) Singles/doubles €32/50. This is one of a row of cottages near The Ship (see Places to Eat). Rooms are cosy and spotless.

Ocean View (☎ 383695) €25 per person. This is next door to Church Villa and is very similar in standard.

Haven Hotel (☎ 383150, fax 383488, Harbour Rd) Singles/doubles €57/89 including breakfast. This impressive-looking Victorian mansion is overpriced for the pokey, ordinary rooms, though the lounge bar is nice.

Ocean Hotel (☎ 383136, fax 383576, Harbour Rd) From €38-45 per person. A slightly tatty hotel, it seems a bit out of place in the main street.

Candlelight Inn (☎ 383215, fax 383289, Harbour Rd) €32/44 per person Nov-Mar/Apr-Oct. This place caters mainly for families and tries hard to please with its pool room, pizza bar, swimming pool, disco and live entertainment, though the rooms are in need of some sprucing up.

Places to Eat

The Bay Café (☎ 383900, Harbour Rd) Snacks & meals €1-7.50. Open 9am-6pm daily. This place serves sandwiches and more filling meals including burgers, lasagne and pies.

The Ship (☎ 383141, 383144, Harbour Rd) Mains €17-20. Open for lunch daily

June-Aug, Tues-Sat Apr-Oct, Sunday lunch only the rest of the year; open for dinner daily Apr-Oct, Tues-Sat Nov-Mar. This bar and restaurant serves fantastic seafood in casual surrounds.

Strand Inn (☎ 383174, Ladies Cove) Dinner around €25. Open 12.30pm-2.30pm & 7pm-10pm Overlooking Ladies Cove, this inn specialises in seafood. The bar food is more than adequate if you don't want to spend too much.

Anchor Bar (☎ 383133, Ladies Cove) Bar meals €6.35-10.15. This place is popular with groups of friends and young families. There is live music most weekends.

Power's Bar (☎ 383318, Dock Rd) This is a nice, intimate place for a drink.

Getting There & Away

Suirway (☎ 382422) runs four buses daily Monday to Saturday from Waterford to Dunmore East (€2.30, 30 minutes).

TRAMORE

☎ 051 • pop 6536

The busiest of County Waterford's seaside resorts, Tramore (Trá Mhór) is 14km south of Waterford. A delightful 5km beach is backed with 30m-high dunes at its eastern end. Tramore itself is fairly tacky, with amusement arcades and fast-food outlets running along the seafront and a monstrous water park plonked in the middle of town.

The tourist office (☎ 381572), Railway Square, is in the old railway station which ran to Waterford city from 1853 to 1960. The tourist office opens 9.30am to 5.30pm Monday to Saturday from June to August. It has a brochure detailing two walks in and around town, and another detailing a 35km drive that takes in megalithic tombs (dolmens) and standing stones in the area.

Things to See & Do

Standing on the shore, the bay is hemmed in by **Great Newtown Head** to the south-west and **Brownstown Head** to the north-east, with their standing pillars and the **Iron Man**, a huge painted iron figure of an 18th-century sailor in white breeches and blue jacket with his arm pointing seawards as a warning to approaching ships. The pillars were erected by Lloyds of London in 1816 after 360 lives were lost when a boat mistook Tramore Bay for Waterford Harbour and was wrecked.

One of Tramore's biggest attractions is the very expensive **Splashworld** 'where you can enjoy tropical temperatures all year round' *(☎ 390176, Railway Square; adult/child €7.60/6.10; open 9am-8pm Mon-Fri, 10am-7pm Sat & Sun, reduced hours Nov-Feb).*

Places to Stay
Fitzmaurice's Caravan Park (☎ 381968, Tramore) Tent & 2 people €14/16.50 in low/high season. This park, 300m from the beach on the Waterford side of town, hires out caravans by the week or night, depending on availability. There is a bus stop right out the front.

Cliff House (☎ 381497, e hilary@cliffhouse.ie, 14 Cliff Rd) €29.20 per person. The house has some great views but it's a long walk to the centre.

West Cliffe (☎ 381365, 5 Newtown) From €25-28 per person. This place also has nice views and is closer to the centre than Cliff House.

The Gallery (☎ 390460, Church Rd) €21.60 per person. This is one of the cheapest options around; all the rooms are en suite.

O'Shea's Hotel (☎ 381246, fax 390144, Strand St) Doubles €47-57/35-38 per person May-Aug/Sept-Apr, single supplement €12-25. Despite the outrageous single occupancy supplement, O'Shea's is a rather attractive hotel with good views but rooms vary in size and comfort.

Majestic Hotel (☎ 381761, fax 381766, e info@majestic-hotel.ie, Railway Square) Singles €57-76, doubles €89-120. This rather grand hotel is opposite the bus stop. Seaview rooms will cost you an extra €12.70.

Places to Eat
Unless you're happy to live on fast food, Tramore doesn't offer a lot in the way of good eating.

Apicus (☎ 390955) Starters €3.80-5.70, mains €7-14. Open 6pm-10pm Thur-Sun. This cosy Italian restaurant serves pizzas, pasta and meat dishes.

Rocketts Seahorse Tavern (☎ 386091, Main St) Bar meals €7-10. This is an award-winning pub.

Getting There & Away
Bus Éireann (☎ 873401) runs over 20 buses daily from Waterford to Tramore (€1.90, 30 minutes). Rapid Express buses also serve Tramore from Waterford. The bus stop is outside the tourist office near Splashworld.

DUNGARVAN
☎ 058 • pop 7175
Thanks to the recent dredging and development of the harbour, Dungarvan (Dún Garbhán) is a picturesque port and market town with an attractive centre and lively waterfront. Surrounded by patchwork hills, it sits on the wide bay where the River Colligan meets the sea and derives its name from St Garvan who founded a monastery here in the 7th century. A castle was built here by the Anglo-Normans in the 12th century but much of the town's buildings date from the early 19th century when the duke of Devonshire began a program of rebuilding.

Modern Dungarvan is now the administrative centre of Waterford. Abbeyside, in the north-east of town, was the birthplace of Ernest Walton, whose work on nuclear fission won the Nobel Prize for physics in 1951.

Dungarvan has some great restaurants and makes a convenient base for exploring western County Waterford, the Ring Peninsula and the mountainous north.

Orientation & Information
Dungarvan is easily navigated on foot. The town's main shopping area is the neatly laid out Grattan Square on the southern side of the river. Main St (also called O'Connell St) runs along one side of it. Parnell St, which comes off the square towards the harbour, is also called Lower Main St.

The very helpful tourist office (☎ 41741, e tiodgar@indigo.ie) is in the Council building on TF Meagher St next to the post office. It opens 9am to 9pm Monday to Saturday and 9am to 5pm Sunday in July and August, and 9am to 6pm Monday to Saturday the rest of the year. It has a free town trail and map.

The post office is on TF Meagher St and most of the banks are on Grattan Square. Free, 15-minute Internet access is available at the library (☎ 41231) on The Quay but it's wise to book ahead.

Things to See

By the quays, **King John's Castle**, erected in 1185, is just a collection of rotting walls, but scaffolding present at the time of writing suggests it may be more than that in the future.

Dungarvan Museum (☎ 45960, St Augustine St; free; open 10am-4.45pm Mon-Fri) is small but nicely presented and well worth a visit. It covers the town's maritime history with relics from shipwrecks. It also includes local Famine history, newspaper clippings and titbits from the last two centuries and focuses on local personalities and their achievements. Look for the pink and grey building with the coat of arms.

The solitary **Augustinian Abbey** on the other side of the bridge overlooks Dungarvan harbour. It dates mainly from the 19th century but incorporates features from the original 13th-century building, including a well preserved tower and nave. The original abbey was destroyed during the Cromwellian occupation of the town.

The **Old Market House** (☎ 48944, Lower Main St; free; open afternoons Tues-Sat) is home to an arts centre and hosts regular exhibitions.

As you leave Dungarvan on the R672 to travel west, you'll pass a **monument** to the greyhound Master McGrath, which won the Waterloo Cup three times in the 1860s.

Special Events

Over the early May bank-holiday weekend, 17 Dungarvan pubs and two hotels play host to the Féile na nDéise, a lively traditional music and dance festival that attracts around 200 musicians. For more information phone ☎ 42998.

Places to Stay

Although there are a number of B&Bs on the other side of the bridge from the centre, they are a bit of a walk from the sites.

Dungarvan Holiday Hostel (☎ 44340, fax 36294, Youghal Rd) Dorms/doubles €11.45/12.70 per person. Opposite the garda station on the N25, this place is not in an attractive part of town but is just under 10 minutes' walk to the centre.

Amron (☎/fax 43337, Mitchell St) €19-25 per person. It's close to the centre and just a few minutes' walk to the harbour.

Casey's Townhouse (☎ 44912, 8 Emmet Terrace) Singles/doubles €32/50. We can highly recommend this comfortable B&B. The breakfasts are great too.

Alwin House (☎ 45994, fax 42355, e alwin@cablesurf.com, 1 South Terrace) Singles/doubles €35/57. This beautiful home has only one single room.

Lawlor's Hotel (☎ 41122, fax 41000, e info@lawlors-hotel.ie, TF Meagher St) Singles/doubles €67/106 June-Sept, €60/92 Apr-May, €38/76 the rest of the year, including breakfast. This tastefully decorated old-world hotel is just off Grattan Square.

Places to Eat

An Bialann (☎ 42825, 31 Grattan Square) Lunch specials €5.70. This popular place serves healthy home-cooked food.

JR's Hamburger Restaurant (☎ 42769, 71 O'Connell St) Snacks €3.20-6.35. Open noon-1am, till 3am at the weekend. This is an award-winning fast-food joint.

The Mill (☎ 45488, Davitts Quay) Mains €14-19. Open 5pm-9.45pm daily, lunch June-Aug. This is one of the two great restaurants in town. Cajun and Louisiana cuisine are specialities.

The Tannery (☎ 45420, Quay St) Starters €5-9.50, lunch mains €5.70-10.80, dinner mains €17-22. This is the other top restaurant in town and is highly recommended by locals. Dishes are modern Irish with some French and Asian influences.

Entertainment

Moorings (☎ 41461, Davitt's Quay) This place overlooking the harbour is nice for a drink but don't bother with the accommodation on offer.

The Anchor Bar (☎ 41249, The Quay) A little further along on the harbour front, this

The Barber of Kilmacthomas

In 1650, when Oliver Cromwell and his army prepared to take Waterford city, they were delayed by flooding of the River Mahon and were forced to camp outside the town of Kilmacthomas (between Waterford and Dungarvan). Ever conscious of his appearance, Cromwell ordered that the local barber be brought to him so that he could get a decent shave. The barber duly arrived and was preparing his razor when Cromwell warned him that a cut would cost the barber his life. Undeterred, he proceeded to shave his belligerent customer cleanly and without drawing blood.

Later, when recounting the story to the locals, the barber was asked whether Cromwell's threat had made him nervous. 'Well, look at it this way', he is said to have answered, 'I was holding the razor to his neck!' Apocryphal or not, the story guaranteed the barber a free pint in his local pub for the rest of his days.

bar is open only in the evening and often features traditional music.

Bean A'Leanna (☎ 44882, 86 O'Connell St) This traditional pub has music sessions Thursday to Sunday and set dancing classes on Monday night.

Getting There & Away

Bus Éireann (☎ 051-873401) has five buses a day (four on Sunday) to Dublin (€11.45, 3½ hours) via Waterford (€7, one hour) and 10 buses a day (six on Sunday) to Cork (€10.15, one hour 40 minutes) via Waterford from the stop on Davitt's Quay.

RING PENINSULA
☎ 058

An Rinn, 12km south of Dungarvan on Helvick Head, is one of the most famous Gaeltacht areas in Ireland. It's rugged and unspoilt – the real Ireland. All the road signs are in Irish and the drive from Dungarvan is stunning. At the small harbour in Helvick Head is a **monument** to the crew of *Erin's Hope* who died when it sank near here in 1867. Nearby is an interesting house, sitting

on rocks right over the water, that was once a monastery. You can look down on its roof from high spots in the town.

Colaiste na Rinne (☎ 46128), the 100-year-old Irish language college on the Helvick Head road, runs summer language courses for children (10–18 years old). It also runs *ceilidhs* of traditional music and dance, most nights during the summer.

Criostal na Rinne (☎ 42127) is a crystal workshop and showroom in Helvick Head. You can have items inscribed. It opens year round from 9am to 6pm Monday to Friday and 10am to 6pm Sunday, though hours do vary.

Places to Stay & Eat
Leaba & Bricfeasta B&B and Ceol na Mara Hostel (☎ 46425, An Rinn) Dorms €10.80, singles/doubles €24 per person. Open Mar-Oct. This place sits high above the town.

Helvick View (☎ 46297, Helvick Head road) €21.60 per person. This B&B offers basic accommodation and stunning views of Dungarvan Bay and the surrounding countryside.

An Carn (☎/fax 46611, Rath na mBininneach, An Rinn) Singles/doubles €38/63.50. Open mid-Mar-mid-Dec. Situated high on a hill in a large old home, this restaurant and B&B opens for dinner Thursday to Saturday.

Getting There & Away
The limited bus service runs from Waterford at 1.45pm on Saturday. This becomes a daily service during July and August.

ARDMORE
☎ 024 • pop 330

South of Helvick Head the coast road veers inland and, after 23km, brings you back to the sea at Ardmore, famous for its 12th-century round tower. It is claimed locally that St Declan set up shop here between 350 and 420, well before St Patrick arrived from Britain to convert the heathens. Now Ardmore is a popular seaside resort with a Blue Flag beach. Don't be put off by the ugly sprawl of caravan parks that spoil the coastal view to the east: this is a pleasant little place, as long as you like things nice and quiet.

Information

The locally run tourist office (☎ 94444) is in a white sandcastle-shaped building on the seafront. It opens 11am to 4pm daily May to September and it has a bureau de change. A town walk leaflet is available here or from Dungarvan's tourist office.

St Declan's Church & Oratory

In a striking position on a hill above the town, the ruins of St Declan's Church and a fine slender round tower stand on the site of St Declan's original monastery. The 29m-high round tower dates back to the 12th century.

The outer western gable wall of the 13th-century church features some stone carvings retrieved from an older 9th-century church and placed here. They show the Archangel Michael weighing souls, the adoration of the Magi, Adam and Eve, and a clear depiction of the judgement of Solomon. Inside the church are two ogham stones, one of them with the longest inscription of any known ogham stone in Ireland. The site was leased to Sir Walter Raleigh in 1591, after the dissolution of the monasteries and, in 1642, the building was occupied by Royalist troops.

The smaller building in the compound is the 8th-century St Declan's Oratory, or Beannachán, which is said to be the resting place of St Declan. The roof and upper parts of the walls were restored in the 18th century. The depression in the floor is due to worshippers removing earth from the grave site – it was supposed to protect from disease.

St Declan's Well

Overlooking the sea, St Declan's Well is beyond the Cliff House Hotel to the south of town. Pilgrims once washed in it. Beside it are the ruins of Dysert Church. A fine 5km cliff walk leads from the well; a free map is available from the tourist office or from the Cliff House Hotel. On the way you'll pass the wreck of a crane ship which was blown ashore in 1987 on its way from Liverpool to Malta.

At the southern end of the beach is **St Declan's Stone**, said to have arrived from Wales across the sea borne by a glacial boulder. Crawling under it on St Declan's Day (24 July) is said to cure rheumatism and bring spiritual benefits.

St Declan's Way

This 94km walk mostly traces an old pilgrimage way from Ardmore to the Rock of Cashel in Tipperary. A map guide (€5.70), which also shows circular routes taking in parts of it, is available from the tourist office.

Places to Stay & Eat

Ardmore Beach Hostel (☎ 94501, Main St) Dorms €10.80, family rooms at a discount. This hostel is in an old stone house near the seafront. Ask at the Cup & Saucer Restaurant opposite.

Round Tower Hotel (☎ 94494, fax 94254, e rth@tinet.ie) €41.30/34.30 per person May-Sept/Oct-Apr. Mains €10-14, set menu €19. This B&B and restaurant is in the village.

Paddy Mac's (☎ 94166, Main St) Bar food €4-7. This place offers good pub snacks and lunches such as roasts, jacket potatoes and open sandwiches.

Getting There & Away

There are three buses daily (one on Sunday) from Cork (€9.30, 1¾ hours) to Ardmore. There are two daily to Waterford via Dungarvan in July and August (otherwise it's a Friday and Saturday only service). Buses stop outside O'Reilly's pub on Main St.

NORTHERN COUNTY WATERFORD

Some of the most scenic parts of County Waterford are in the north around **Ballymacarbry** and in the **Nire Valley**, which runs between the Comeragh and Monavullagh Mountains. The hills form the easternmost extension of a great mass of red sandstone from the Devonian period, some 370 million years ago, which underlies most of Cork and Kerry's scenery. While not as rugged as the west of Ireland, the mountain scenery here has a stark beauty of its own and doesn't attract much tourist traffic. Take care driving through here as stock and wide tractors wander onto the roads.

Things to See
Driving from Waterford to Ballymacarbry you can take in **Curraghmore Gardens** (☎ 051-387102, Portlaw; admission to gardens & shell grotto by guided tour, €3.80 per person; open 2pm-5pm Thur). It's 14km north-west of Waterford city. The fine Georgian house dates from the 18th century but the estate has been home to the Marquis of Waterford since the 12th century. You can visit the gardens but the house opens only to groups by prior arrangement.

Activities
The **East Munster Way** walking trail covers some 70km between Carrick-on-Suir in County Tipperary and the northern slopes of the Knockmealdown Mountains. Access to the route is at Fourmilewater, a few kilometres north-west of Ballymacarbry. For more details see Walking under Activities in the Facts for the Visitor chapter.

For an excellent **guided walk** of the area covering archaeology, geology, flora and fauna, contact **Michael Desmond** (☎ 052-36238, e hiking@indigo.ie). Six-hour walks take place on Saturdays and a reasonable degree of fitness is required. Otherwise make sure you're around for the Comeragh Mountain Walking Festival (☎ 052-36239), which takes place on the second weekend in October. There's a number of guided walks varying in difficulty and length and all the local pubs have plenty of traditional music each night.

The lovely wooded valleys and heathery mountains are good for pony trekking. **Melody's Riding Stables** (☎ 052-36147, Ballymacarbry, behind Melody's pub), open Easter to October, has trail rides costing €25 for two hours, €38 for three hours and €70 for a day's ride, including lunch.

From March to September the Nire and Suir Rivers provide great opportunities for **fishing**. Permits can be arranged through Hanora's Cottage (see Places to Stay).

Places to Stay
Powers the Pot (☎ 052-23085, fax 23893, Harneys Cross) Tent & 2 people €10.15. Open May-Oct. This is a charming camp site, signposted off the road between Rathgormuck and Clonmel, about 5km east of Clonmel. There's a bar here with an open fire and meals are served.

Hanora's Cottage (☎ 052-36134, Nire Valley) Standard rooms €57-63, superior rooms €70-82 per person, including breakfast. In the Nire Valley, this remote luxury B&B provides absolute solitude. There is an excellent restaurant too, and special B&B and dinner rates are available. From the main Dungarvan–Clonmel road (R672), head to Ballymacarbry then turn east off the N72 to Nire Church.

Old School House (☎ 052-36963, Ballymacarbry) €23-25 per person. This small B&B is on the R672, 1km south of Melody's pub.

Getting There & Away
There's a Tuesday only bus service from Dungarvan at 2pm, and two buses from Clonmel on Friday at 1.20pm and 5.35pm.

CAPPOQUIN
☎ 058 • pop 1000
The small market town of Cappoquin is overlooked by the Knockmealdown Mountains. The River Blackwater takes an abrupt turn southwards near the town and the Blackwater Valley to the west is picturesque. The valley is where traces of the earliest Irish peoples have been found – Mesolithic microliths (small stone blades) from around 9000 years ago have been discovered.

There's excellent coarse and game **fishing** locally, and **Glenshelane Park**, just outside the town, offers some lovely forest walks and picnic spots. Salmon-fishing permits are available from Titelines (☎ 54152) tackle shop on the main street.

The stunning **Mt Melleray Cistercian Abbey** (☎ 54404; free; open year round) is just over 6km to the north of town and is signposted from the centre. The abbey was founded in 1832 by a group of Irish monks who had been expelled from a monastery near Melleray in Brittany, France. A fully functioning monastery, Mt Melleray opens to visitors seeking quiet reflection and to those who wish to see something of the daily routine. There's no charge for a bed in the guesthouse, but it would be bad manners not to make a donation.

Cappoquin House (☎ 54004; adult/child €6.35/3.20; open Apr-July) is a Georgian mansion (built 1779) and gardens overlooking town and the River Blackwater. It's the private residence of the Keane family who've lived here for 200 years. The entrance to the house is in the centre of town – take the road for the monastery and look for a set of huge black iron gates just a few metres up on your left.

Getting There & Away
One bus a day (except Sunday) leaves Dungarvan for Cappoquin at 9.30pm and returns to Dungarvan at 7am (15 minutes). There are two buses a week from Waterford (one hour 10 minutes) via Dungarvan leaving at 8.30am Friday and 5.30pm Sunday. There's also one bus a week leaving Cork (one hour 20 minutes) at 4.30pm on Friday. Buses stop outside Morrissey's pub. For details contact Waterford bus station (☎ 051-873401).

LISMORE
☎ 058 • pop 750
Lismore is a small town beautifully situated on the River Blackwater at the foot of the Knockmealdown Mountains. The river rolls on east and then south to Youghal and the sea.

Although most of the buildings in the town date from the early 19th century, Lismore was the location of a great monastic university first founded by St Cartach, or Carthage, in the 7th century. In the 8th century the monastery became a famous centre of learning under St Colman. From the 10th century on it was sacked many times by the Vikings but hung on as the religious capital of Deise (Deices). Until the 17th century, the remains of eight churches could still be seen.

Lady Louisa's Walk follows the banks of the Blackwater from the town centre for about a quarter of a mile.

Information
Lismore has a tourist office (☎ 54975) in the Lismore Heritage Centre, based in the old courthouse on Main St in the town centre. It has a bureau de change. It opens daily April to October and stocks a free town walk map. Guided tours of the town take place at 11.30am and 3pm daily. Alternatively, for €1.25 you can buy *A Walking Tour of Lismore*, which describes all the local sights.

St Carthage's Cathedral
This striking cathedral was built in 1633 but stands on the site of another church built in the early 13th century. The spire and ceilings were added in the early 19th century. Inside are some noteworthy tombs, including a MacGrath family crypt dating from 1557, and the small chapel of St Colmcille.

Lismore Castle
From the Cappoquin road there are fine glimpses of majestic Lismore Castle overlooking the river. At night-time it's lit up like a Christmas tree and looks stunning. The original castle was erected by Prince John, lord of Ireland, in 1185. It was the local bishop's residence until 1589, when it was presented to Sir Walter Raleigh along with around 200 sq km of the surrounding countryside. He later sold it to the earl of Cork, Richard Boyle, whose 14th child, Robert Boyle (1627–91), was born here and is credited with being the first methodical modern scientist.

Lismore Castle passed to the duke of Devonshire in 1753, and the 6th duke of Devonshire built the current structure in the early 19th century. It does incorporate small sections of the earlier buildings, however. During rebuilding, the 15th-century *Book of Lismore* and the Lismore Crozier (both now in the National Museum in Dublin) were discovered. The book not only documents the lives of a number of Irish saints, but also holds an account of the voyages of Marco Polo. A more recent castle occupant was Adele Astaire, sister of the famous Fred.

The castle is closed to day-trippers but can be rented by seriously rich groups for functions. You can visit the three hectares of the dual-level **gardens** *(☎ 54424; adult/child €3.80/1.90; open 1.45pm-4.45pm daily Easter-Sept)*. The lower level is a stunning flower garden while the upper level is a formal garden in an Elizabethan layout.

Lismore Heritage Centre

In the old courthouse is Lismore Heritage Centre *(☎ 54975, fax 53009, Main St; adult/child €3.80/3.20; open 9.30am-5.30pm Mon-Sat (till 6pm June-Aug), noon-5.30pm Sun; closed weekends Oct-Apr)*. Every half-hour there is an audiovisual presentation that takes you through local history, from the arrival of St Carthage in 636 to the present day. It also tells the story of the Book of Lismore, discovered in the castle in 1814.

Places to Stay & Eat

There's no official camp site nearby but you could ask local farmers if you can camp in their fields.

Beechcroft *(☎ 54273, Deerpark Rd)* Singles/doubles with bathroom from €24/48, without from €21/43. This is a comfortable place with a nice garden. It's in a high part of town and there are pleasant views of the surrounding countryside.

Lismore Hotel *(☎ 54304, fax 53068, Main St)* €50-57 per person. There's nothing special about the rooms here – not for their price – but some of them have good views of the castle. In the 1840s this was a favourite lodging place of William Makepeace Thackeray.

Madden's Bar *(☎ 54148, East Main St)* Serving decent lunches in summer, this place has pictures of Fred Astaire on his visits to the town to see his sister when she lived at Lismore Castle.

Getting There & Away

One bus a day (except Sunday) leaves Dungarvan for Lismore via Cappoquin at 9.30pm and returns to Dungarvan at 6.55am (20 minutes). There are two buses a week from Waterford (one hour 20 minutes) via Dungarvan leaving at 8.30am Friday and 5.30pm Sunday. Buses stop outside O'Dowd's pub on West St. For details contact Waterford bus station *(☎ 051-873401)*.

County Cork

Ireland's biggest county, County Cork (Corcaigh) has everything that makes Ireland so attractive – a case could be made for arriving here before Dublin. Cork city is still engagingly small but it bustles with visitors and students year round. The northern part of the county is renowned for fishing, while the main tourist trail heads down to Kinsale, Ireland's gourmet capital, and west through the historic towns of Clonakilty and Skibbereen to the peninsulas jutting into the Atlantic. These underpopulated extremities are rich in history and nature, and offer wonderful scenery for walkers, climbers and cyclists. The county's best-known attraction is the Blarney Stone, but just drifting through western Cork will probably be more memorable.

Cork

☎ 021 • pop 179,970

The Republic's second-largest city is a pleasant place in which to while away a day or so. The city has some fine Georgian buildings; Grand Parade and South Mall boast the finest architecture. The pubs are lively and the food is excellent.

The city's population is growing rapidly as people take up employment in the new service industries. Students keep the place buzzing with events and entertainment.

HISTORY

The city dates back to the 7th century, surviving Cromwell's visit only to fall to William of Orange in 1690. In the 18th century it was an important commercial centre with a major butter market. A century later the Famine reduced Cork to a sorry place from where many disillusioned, dispossessed emigrants bade farewell to their homeland. The nearby port of Cobh remained the major departure point until 1970.

Cork played a key role in Ireland's struggle for independence. Thomas MacCurtain, a mayor of the city, was killed by the Black and

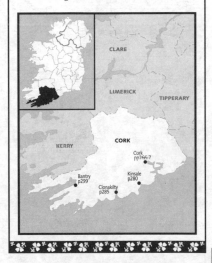

Highlights

- Taste the gastronomic treats of Kinsale
- Go walking and bird-watching on remote Clear Island
- Don't miss Mizen Head Peninsula – the most unpopulated and stunning part of Cork's coastline
- Visit Bantry House for its eclectic collection of art and beautiful gardens
- Climb Hungry Hill on the Beara Peninsula for some great views

Tans in 1920. His successor, Terence MacSwiney, died in London's Brixton prison after 75 days on hunger strike. The Black and Tans were at their most brutal in Cork and much of the town was burned down during the Anglo-Irish War. Cork was also a centre for the Civil War that followed independence.

ORIENTATION

The city centre is an island between two channels of the River Lee. The curve of St Patrick's St is the centre of the main shopping

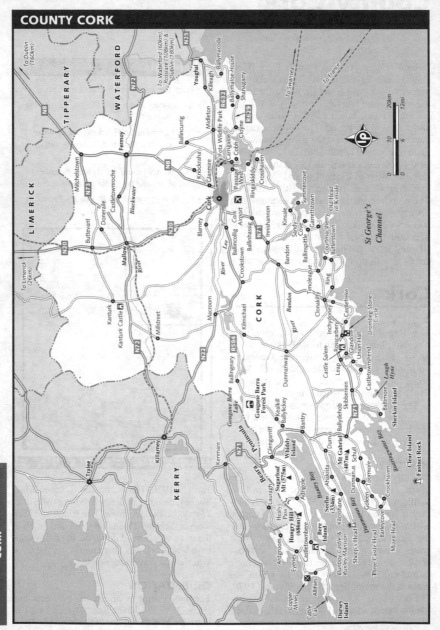

COUNTY CORK

Walking Tour of Cork

This tour starts at the eastern end of South Mall, across the river from the grey **City Hall**. On a visit to Ireland in 1963, President John F Kennedy gave an address from the steps of the City Hall. He had returned as a conquering hero to the land his great-grandfather had left, and the city came to a standstill as a massive crowd turned out to welcome him.

Walk west along the river until you reach **Holy Trinity Church**, designed by the Pain brothers in 1834 for Father Theobald Matthew, the 'Apostle of Temperance'. He led an effective, but short-lived, crusade against 'the demon drink', which resulted in a reduction in the production of whiskey by more than half in the early 1840s.

Take the turning to the right just before the church, which brings you out on South Mall. Across the road to the right you'll see the **Imperial Hotel**, dating back to 1816, where Michael Collins, commander-in-chief of the Irish Free State army, slept before setting out on a journey that would end in ambush and his death on 22 August 1922. When he arrived at the Imperial the two sentries in the lobby were asleep and Collins knocked their heads together in irritation.

Walk west along South Mall until you reach a small monument to the victims of the Hiroshima and Nagasaki atomic bombs on your left. A few steps farther and you'll reach the ornate **Nationalist Monument**, erected in memory of the Irish patriots who died between the 1798 and 1867 Risings.

Turn right along Grand Parade, with the tourist office on your right and three 18th century bow fronted houses on your left. Between Oliver Plunkett and Washington Sts is the small Bishop Lucey Park on the left. Cross the park to the old church in the right, end corner, which now houses the Cork Archive Centre. Adjoining it is the **Triskel Arts Centre**, an important arts venue (see the later Entertainment section).

Turn left down South Main St. Just before the Tudor-style **Beamish & Crawford brewery** turn left again down Tuckey St and go to the end, where, on the left, a bollard bears testimony to the days when Grand Parade was an open canal and boats moored by the quayside.

Head south along Grand Parade, past the Nationalist Monument again. From there, turn left along South Mall then right onto the single-arched **Parliament Bridge**, built by the British in 1806 to commemorate the union of the British and Irish Parliaments five years previously. Cross the bridge and turn right along Sullivan's Quay. To your right you'll see **South Gate Bridge** (1713), which marks the site of the medieval entrance to the city.

Continue straight ahead along French Quay and Bishop St to **St Finbarr's Cathedral**. From there it's a short walk west to the entrance of **University College Cork** (UCC), where you'll find the gorgeous **Honan Chapel**, built in 1915. The stained-glass windows and elaborate mosaic floors are well worth a look. Also near here is the **Greek Revival portico** originally built for Cork County Jail.

Bus No 8 will ferry you back into the town centre from the main gate of UCC.

---

precinct, with restaurants and trendy shops crammed into the pedestrianised streets of the Huguenot Quarter to the north. From the centre, Washington St (which becomes Lancaster Quay and Western Rd) leads south-west to the university, Killarney and western Cork.

Over the river and to the north-east are Kent Train Station and several cheap B&Bs. In this district MacCurtain St is the main thoroughfare. The Shandon area, west of here up on a hillside, cherishes some interesting old buildings but is otherwise rather rundown.

INFORMATION
Tourist Offices

The tourist office (☎ 427 3251), Grand Parade, opens 9.30am to 5.30pm Monday to Friday and 9.30am to 4pm Saturday year round, with extended hours in July and August. It's mainly a souvenir shop with little information about Cork city itself – none that's free anyway.

From June to September you'll be better off visiting the Cork City Information Booth in St Patrick's St on the corner of Winthrop

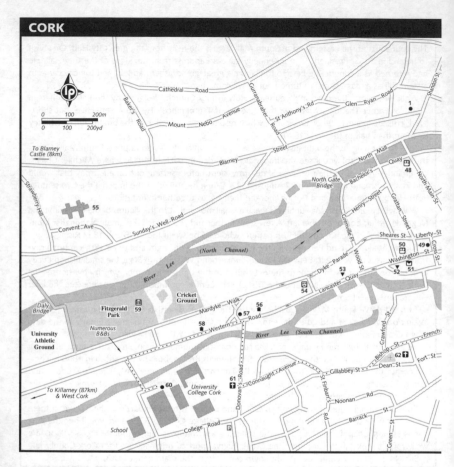

CORK

St; it has a lot of city information and its leaflets and maps are free.

Money
The Bank of Ireland and Allied Irish Bank, both on St Patrick's St, have ATMs and currency-exchange facilities.

Post & Communications
The main post office is on Pembroke St, just off Oliver Plunkett St. There are smaller post offices on MacCurtain and Washington Sts.

At Webworkhouse (☎ 427 3090), 8a Winthrop St, Internet access costs €6.35 per hour. For the same price there's also Internet access at i dot café (☎ 427 3544) in the Gate Multiplex cinema on North Main St.

Bookshops
Liam Ruiséal Teo (☎ 427 0981), 49–50 Oliver Plunkett St, has an extensive range of new books. The Shelf (☎ 431 2264), 12 George's Quay, has second-hand books and opens 9.30am to 5.45pm Monday to Friday. Waterstone's runs between St Patrick's and Paul Sts. Vibes & Scribes, 3 Bridge St, has a great selection of second-hand books,

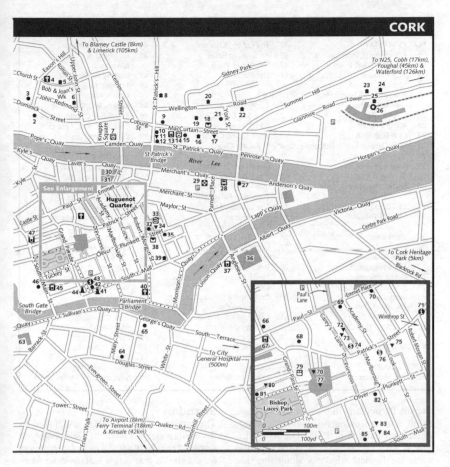

CORK

---

records and CDs. For lovers of blood-and-gore literature there's also Mainly Murder at 2a Paul St.

Laundry

The Laundrette, 14 MacCurtain St, is next to the Everyman Palace Theatre; Clifton Laundrette, Western Rd, is opposite the gates of University College Cork (UCC).

Emergency

City General Hospital (☎ 431 1656), 6 Infirmary Rd, is about 1km south-east of the centre, just south of the river.

THINGS TO SEE
St Finbarr's Cathedral

Dramatically lit at night, this imposing Protestant cathedral (☎ 496 3387; €2.50 donation requested; open 10am-5.30pm daily Apr-Sept; 10am-12.45pm & 2pm-5pm daily Oct-Mar) was designed by the Victorian architect William Burges, who was also responsible for Cardiff Castle and Castell Coch in Wales. He beat 67 other entrants in a competition to design a new cathedral to replace the crumbling old one. Work was completed in 1879. The finished building has three spires and a High Victorian

CORK

PLACES TO STAY
5   Kinlay House Shandon
6   Shandon Court Hotel
8   Acorn House
16 Metropole Hotel
19 Isaac's Hostel; Isaac's Hotel;
    Greene's Restaurant
20 D'Arcy's B&B
22 Auburn House
23 Clon Ross B&B
24 Aaron House Tourist Hostel
25 Tara House
39 Imperial Hotel
56 Garnish House
58 Brazier's Westpoint House

PLACES TO EAT
11 Taste of Thailand
17 Luciano's
34 Valparaiso
52 Pi
53 Café Paradiso
72 The Strasbourg Goose
73 Café Mexicana
75 Ambassador Chinese
    Restaurant
77 English Market
78 The Oyster Tavern
80 The Yumi Yuki Club
83 Clancy's
84 Wild Ways

PUBS & CLUBS
13 The Shelbourne

37 The Lobby; Charlie's
45 An Spailpín Fánac
47 The Other Place
67 The Roundy

OTHER
1   Cycle Scene
2   Shandon Craft Centre; Cork
    Butter Museum
3   Firkin Crane Centre
4   St Anne's Church
7   Cork Arts Theatre
9   The Living Tradition
10 Vibes & Scribes
12 Irish Ferries Office
14 Everyman Palace Theatre
15 The Laundrette
18 Post Office
21 Tents & Leisure
26 Kent Train Station
27 Union Chandlery &
    Hillwalkers
28 Bus Station
29 Merchant's Quay Shopping
    Centre
30 Cork Opera House; The Half
    Moon Theatre
31 Crawford Municipal Art
    Gallery
32 P Cashel
33 Webworkhouse
35 Pro-Musica
36 City Hall
38 Main Post Office

40 Holy Trinity Church
41 Hiroshima & Nagasaki
    Monument
42 Brittany Ferries Office
43 Tourist Office; Stena Line
    Office; Budget
44 Nationalist Monument
46 Beamish & Crawford Brewery
48 Gate Multiplex; i dot café
49 Courthouse
50 Kino
51 Post Office
54 UCC Granary Theatre
55 Cork City Gaol; National
    Radio Museum
57 Clifton Laundrette
59 Cork Public Museum
60 Greek Revival Portico
61 Honan Chapel
62 St Finbarr's Cathedral
63 Elizabeth Fort
64 The Red Abbey
65 The Shelf
66 The Great Outdoors
68 Waterstone's
69 Mainly Murder
70 Avis
71 Cork City Information Booth
74 Allied Irish Bank
76 Bank of Ireland
79 Capitol Cineplex
81 Triskel Arts Centre
82 Liam Ruiséal Teo
85 Swansea Cork Ferries Office

interior. Particularly impressive are the huge pulpit and the colourful chancel ceiling, which was painted in 1935. The rose window at the western end depicts the Creation while the highest windows along the side walls show the signs of the zodiac.

Inside you'll also see a cannonball that was shot from Elizabeth Fort during the siege of Cork in 1690 and lodged in the original cathedral's spire. It wasn't discovered until 1865 when the medieval building was demolished.

The Red Abbey

This Augustinian priory, founded in the 14th century, is the oldest building in Cork. All that can be seen now are the ruins of a tower. It's on the corner of Mary and Douglas Sts.

Shandon

The northern side of Cork is dominated by the curious stepped tower of 18th-century **St Anne's Church** (☎ 450 5906, John Redmond St; admission free; open 9.30am-5pm Mon-Sat), which was built on the site of a medieval church that was destroyed in 1690. Two of the church walls are faced with limestone and two with sandstone. Inside is a small collection of 17th-century Bibles and other books including the letters of poet John Donne. The salmon-shaped weathervane was apparently chosen because the local monks reserved for themselves the right to fish for salmon in the river. If you want to climb the tower and ring the church bells you'll have to pay €4.45/ 3.80 per adult/child.

Nearby is the expensive **Shandon Craft Centre** in what was once part of the Cork

Butter Exchange. There's not much to see here but a few shops selling the usual Irish souvenirs. Next door is the **Cork Butter Museum** (☎ 430 0600, *Shandon; adult/child €3.20/2.55; open 10am-1pm & 2pm-5pm Mon-Sat May-Sept; by arrangement only Oct-Apr*). Exports from here went to Europe, India, South America and Australia. The exhibition covers dairying in Ireland, the butter trade and butter manufacturing throughout history.

Cork Public Museum

At the time of writing this rather old-fashioned museum (☎ 427 0679, *Fitzgerald Park; admission free Mon-Fri, €2.54/1.27 Sun; open 11am-1pm & 2.15pm-6pm Mon-Fri, 3pm-5pm Sun, except bank-holiday weekends June-Aug; 2.15pm-5pm the rest of the year*) was about to undergo a €1.8 million extension. This means that many of the artefacts in storage – mostly devoted to Cork's role in the fight for independence, as well as archaeology – will be able to be exhibited. The museum is in pretty Fitzgerald Park, north of Western Rd.

Take bus No 8 to the main gates of UCC and follow the brown sign pointing to the museum.

Crawford Municipal Art Gallery

Crawford Municipal Art Gallery (☎ 427 3377, *Emmet Place; admission free; open 10am-5pm Mon-Sat*) is in a building that was built in 1724 as the Customs House and became the Cork School of Art in 1884. It now houses an excellent permanent collection, featuring works by Irish artists such as Jack Yeats and Seán Keating, as well as works of the British Newlyn and St Ives schools.

Beamish & Crawford Brewery

This brewery (☎ 491 1100, *South Main St; guided tour €3.80/3.20*) runs guided tours at 10.30am and noon every Thursday from May to September, and at 11am from October to April. The tour ends with a tasting.

Cork City Gaol

The jail (☎ 430 5022, *Convent Ave, Sunday's Well; adult/child €4.45/2.55; open 9.30am-6pm daily Mar-Oct; 10am-5pm daily Nov-Feb; last admission 1 hour before closing*), west of the city, received its first prisoners in 1824 and its last in 1923. The 35-minute taped tour, which guides you around the restored and refurnished cells, is very moving and probably more interesting than the 20-minute audiovisual display on the prison's history. Upstairs is the **National Radio Museum** (same admission price as the jail) where, alongside collections of beautiful old radios, you can hear the story of Gugliemo Marconi's conquest of the airwaves.

Take bus No 8 from the bus station to the stop outside UCC, then walk north across Fitzgerald Park and over Daly Bridge. Turn right up the hill along Sunday's Well Rd, left along Convent Ave and you'll see the brown signpost to the jail.

Cork Heritage Park

Cork Heritage Park (☎ 435 8854, *Bessberro, Blackrock; adult/child €4.45/1.90; open 10.30am-5.30pm daily Apr-Sept; by appointment only Oct-Mar*) is a collection of maritime and other exhibits in landscaped gardens 5km east of the city. You can walk or take Bus No 2.

ORGANISED TOURS

Between June and September, *Arrange Unlimited* (☎ 429 3873, ⓔ arrange@iol.ie) organises walking tours on request.

Bus Éireann (☎ 450 8188) operates a three-hour open-top bus tour of Cork city and Blarney Castle from June to August (€7.60/3.80), departing from the bus station at 10.30am and 2.45pm daily.

Between late May and September, *Guide Friday* (☎ 01-676 5377) runs open-top hop-on, hop-off daily bus tours around Cork city from Grand Parade opposite the tourist office. Tickets cost €10.80/3.20.

SPECIAL EVENTS

The Cork International Jazz Festival and the International Film Festival both take place in October. Tickets for both can sell out quickly. Programs are available from Cork Opera House (see under Entertainment for details). The International Choral and Folk

Dance Festival runs from late April to early May in the City Hall and other venues.

The Leinster/Munster Literary Festival takes the form of writing workshops, readings, seminars and exhibitions during March in various towns all over Cork county. It attracts around 50 local and overseas writers. For details contact Munster Literary Centre (☎ 431 2955), 26 Sullivan's Quay.

PLACES TO STAY
Hostels

Isaac's Hostel (☎ 450 8388, fax 450 6355, e corkhostel@isaacs.ie, 48 MacCurtain St) Dorms from €10.80, 4-bed dorms €16.50 per person. This big place is very popular and fills up quickly. It has 24-hour dorm access.

Aaron House Tourist Hostel (☎ 455 1566, 455 2477, Glanmire Rd Lower) Dorms €9.50, twin rooms €12.70 per person. This place is very basic but is the cheapest hostel in town.

Kinlay House Shandon (☎ 450 8966, fax 450 6927, e kinlay.cork@usitworld.com, Bob & Joan's Walk) Dorms €11.45, twin rooms €33, includes light breakfast. This friendly hostel is in the old Shandon district immediately behind St Anne's Church. Internet access costs €1.90 for 15 minutes and the laundry service is €5 per load.

B&Bs

B&B prices vary greatly, as does the quality, so it's worth shopping around if you have the time. Glanmire Rd Lower near the train station, has the cheapest places.

Tara House (☎ 450 0294, 52 Glanmire Rd Lower) Rooms without bathroom €25.40 per person. The rooms here are small but clean and cheap.

Clon Ross B&B (☎ 450 2602, 85 Glanmire Rd Lower) Singles/doubles €35.55/55.90. This friendly place is opposite the train station.

The central B&Bs tend to be a bit pricey and the more affordable ones are generally pretty awful. Here are a few we can recommend.

Auburn House (☎ 450 8555, 3 Garfield Terrace, Wellington Rd) Singles/doubles €27.95/48.30, en suite €34.30/55.90. This tasteful and comfortable B&B has a more intimate atmosphere than most around here.

Acorn House (☎ 450 2474, e info@acornhouse-cork.com, 14 St Patrick's Hill) Rooms €31.75 per person. This is one of the best value places in the centre. You get spacious rooms, great breakfasts and one of the best showers you'll have in the country.

D'Arcy's B&B (☎ 450 4658, fax 450 2791, e accommodation@darcysguesthouse.com, 7 Sidney Place, Wellington Rd) Rooms with/without bathroom €31.75/38.10 per person. This beautiful old house has large rooms – the ones on the top floor have fantastic views of the city.

On the opposite side of town, along Western Rd near UCC, there are plenty of B&Bs, all of which have their own car park. All are relatively expensive considering their distance from the centre. Here's the pick of the bunch. ✗ ✗ ✗ *Very accommoda*

Garnish House (☎ 427 5011, fax 427 3872, e garnish@iol.ie, Western Rd) Rooms Nov-Feb/Mar-Oct €38.10/44.50 per person. This luxury B&B has lovely rooms, though they are quite small, and great breakfasts. *June 11– 15, 2013*

Brazier's Westpoint House (☎ 427 5526, fax 427 4091, e westpoint@eircom.net, Western Rd) Singles/doubles €38/64. This place has decent rooms and is reasonably priced.

Hotels

Metropole Hotel (☎ 450 8122, fax 450 6450, e ryan@indigo.ie, MacCurtain St) Singles/doubles €108/152. Originally a temperance hotel, the Metropole is still somewhat drab but offers good deals for two nights or more with dinner.

Isaac's Hotel (☎ 450 0011, fax 450 6355, e cork@isaacs.ie, 48 MacCurtain St) Singles/doubles €73/101 Mar-Oct, €70/89 Nov-Feb. Attached to the hostel of the same name, Rooms here have floor boards and some have small sitting rooms. Those at the front are quite noisy.

Imperial Hotel (☎ 427 4040, fax 427 5375, South Mall) Rooms from €100. This hotel has been recently refurbished in an elaborate Greco-Roman style.

CORK

Shandon Court Hotel (☎ *455 1793, fax 455 1665,* ✉ *qualshan@indigo.ie, cnr Upper John St & John Redmond St)* Rooms €35-57 per person. Rates vary from month to month at this unexciting but comfortable hotel in the historical area of Shandon.

PLACES TO EAT
Restaurants

Cork has dozens of wonderful restaurants to choose from. A few of our favourites are listed here. Some restaurants offer early-bird menus (order before 7pm) so you can enjoy top-end food at greatly reduced prices.

Greene's Restaurant (☎ *455 2279, Isaac's Hotel, MacCurtain St)* Bar meals €3.75-5, starters €5.50-8.25, mains €19-21, 3-course early-bird (5.45pm 7pm) menu €16.50. The menu at this superb restaurant and bar often includes interesting dishes such as ostrich and venison. A sample from the bar menu: grilled Cajun goat's cheese with a spicy tomato sauce on brown bread, €5.

Taste of Thailand (☎ *450 5404, 8 Bridge St)* Starters €3.75-6, curries €12-15. According to some locals this is the best Thai food in Cork.

Valparaiso (☎ *427 5488, 115 Oliver Plunkett St)* Starters €3.75-6.65, mains €13.35-18.50. Open 5pm-11pm. This atmospheric Spanish restaurant has live music and tapas on Tuesday night for €14 per person.

Clancy's (☎ *427 6097, 15-16 Princess St)* Bar meals from €5.75, restaurant mains from €10. This place boasts an award-winning chef and a great early-bird special: order at 5.30pm and pay €6.75, order at 6.15pm and pay €7.80, plus you get a free glass of beer or wine.

Pi (☎ *422 2860, Courthouse Chambers, Washington St)* Pizzas €7.35-10.15, a la carte €16.50-21.30. This modern, funky restaurant has received a number of write-ups in local papers. The a la carte menu is a bit pricey but pizzas, *bruschetti*, *panini* and *calzone* are more affordable.

The Yumi Yuki Club (☎ *427 5777, Triskel Arts Centre, Tobin St)* Sushi, noodle & meat dishes €5-12, 2-course early-bird special (4pm-6pm) €8.25. This tiny Japanese restaurant doubles as a jazz club.

Café Mexicana (☎ *427 6433, Carey's Lane)* Dishes €4.45-11.45. This place has all the usual Mexican fare and about half a dozen different ways of serving nachos.

Ambassador Chinese Restaurant (☎ *427 3261, 3 Cook St)* Starters €4-8, mains €14-20. Open for dinner only. This comfortable place is acknowledged as the best Chinese restaurant in town.

Cafes & Pubs

Luciano's (☎ *455 9838, MacCurtain St)* Meals €1.25-10. Open noon-1.30am Mon-Sat & 4pm-1.30am Sun. This pizzeria and fast-food joint is perfect for those post-pub munchies. Besides pizza there's lasagne, curries, burgers and toasted sandwiches.

Wild Ways (☎ *427 2199, 21 Princess St)* Meals €1.90-3.70. Open 8am-5.30pm Mon-Sat. This organic sandwich shop also has a selection of home-made soups.

The Oyster Tavern (☎ *427 2716, 4 Market Lane)* Bar meals €5.70. This large, traditional pub at the English Market has a great selection of beer on tap and has won various tourism awards. The food is more modern than traditional. *Excellent ★★★★*

✗***Café Paradiso*** (☎ *427 7939, 16 Lancaster Quay)* Lunch/dinner mains €10.80/17.80. Open noon-3pm & 6.30pm-10.30pm. This cafe offers delicious dishes for vegetarians and is popular with students. *June 11/2013*

The Strasbourg Goose (☎ *427 9534, 17-18 French Church St)* Snacks & light meals €3.20-8.25, 4-course lunch €14.60. This reasonably priced and licensed cafe serves soup, toasted sandwiches, salads and delicious light meals.

Self-Catering

If you're self-catering or want to put together a picnic, head straight for the ***English Market***, off the western end of St Patrick's St (access from Grand Parade too). There's great local and imported produce here, such as cheeses, paté, terrines, smoked fish, bread, olives and wine. It opens 9am to 5.30pm Monday to Saturday.

[handwritten margin note: Comfortable for singles. Excellent service.]

CORK

ENTERTAINMENT

For information about what's on in Cork pick up a copy of *thelist.ie*, available from the tourist office, newsagents, some clothes and record shops, hostels and a few B&Bs. It's also available online at **W** www.thelist.ie.

Pubs

Cork's cultural rivalry with Dublin extends to drink. Locally brewed Murphy's is the stout of choice here, or there's Beamish, which is often cheaper.

The Shelbourne (☎ 450 9615, 16-17 MacCurtain St) This place attracts a young crowd and gets going at night.

An Spailpín Fánac (☎ 427 7949, South Main St) The Beamish ought to be good since this dark, old pub is opposite the Beamish & Crawford Brewery. It's 'probably the oldest pub in Ireland' according to the tourist board pub guide.

The Lobby (☎ 431 9307, 1 Union Quay) This dingy-looking pub has live music most nights.

Charlie's (☎ 496 5272, 2 Union Quay) Like The Lobby next door, this place has live music most nights.

Clubs

Cork is full of interesting clubs and bars that go well into the wee hours. Many are hidden away in quiet lanes above shops and restaurants. Door charges range from free to €10. For information on gay and lesbian clubs you could try Gay Information Cork (☎ 427 1087), which opens 7pm to 9pm Wednesday and 3pm to 5pm Saturday, or check in *thelist.ie*.

The Half Moon Theatre (☎ 427 0022, behind Cork Opera House) This place has live music as well as DJs and opens its doors at 11.30pm each night.

The Roundy (☎ 427 7682, 1 Castle St) This groovy cafe-bar features DJs upstairs from Tuesday to Sunday, a live band on Monday and the occasional film night on Wednesday.

The Other Place (☎ 427 8470, upstairs 8 South Main St) This gay and lesbian club is also a cafe and bookshop. Admission is free before 10pm.

The Yumi Yuki Club (see Places to Eat) This restaurant also features either live bands (mainly jazz) or DJs each night except Monday.

Theatre & Cinemas

Cork prides itself on its cultural pursuits.

Cork Opera House (☎ 427 0022, Emmet Place) This is the top mainstream theatre.

Cork Arts Theatre (☎ 450 8398, Knapps Square) This theatre, north of the river, is more adventurous.

UCC Granary Theatre (☎ 490 4272, box office 490 4275, Mardyke St) It presents various plays throughout the university terms; tickets cost €5.

Everyman Palace Theatre (☎ 450 1673, MacCurtain St) There's a range of musical and dramatic productions here most nights of the week. Tickets cost around €11.50.

The downbeat *Kino* (☎ 427 1571, Washington St West) and the *Triskel Arts Centre* (☎ 427 2022, Tobin St) show art-house films. While *Gate Multiplex* (☎ 427 9595, North Main St) and *Capitol Cineplex* (☎ 427 8777, Grand Parade) show mainstream films.

Firkin Crane Centre (☎ 450 7487, Eason's Hill, Shandon) Near St Anne's Church, Shandon, this centre has mid-week sessions of traditional dancing in the summer and is a venue for national and international dance companies.

SHOPPING

There's some great shopping to be had in Cork. The little streets and lanes north of St Patrick's St are the most interesting. Try Paul's Lane for antiques.

The Living Tradition (☎ 450 2564, 40 MacCurtain St) Open 9.30am-5.30pm Mon-Sat. If you're keen on traditional music look in here. The shop sells a wide range of tapes, CDs and music publications.

Tents & Leisure (☎ 450 0702, York St) Just off MacCurtain St, this place sells and hires out tents.

Union Chandlery & Hillwalkers (☎ 427 1643, 10 Clontarf St) has camping and trekking gear as well as a range of trekking guides.

Walking the Beara Way you'll come to Eyeries, a cluster of brightly coloured houses.

Inviting pubs abound in County Cork.

Union Hall, Cork, is renowned for its fishing.

Take in the views of rugged Clear Island while keeping an eye out for its famous sea bird colonies

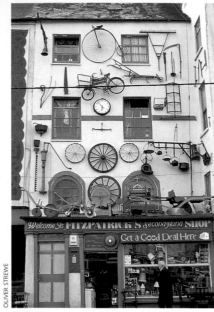

Cork's famous magnetic second-hand shop

Towering Blarney Castle dates from 1446.

Casting a line in Cork's River Blackwater

Getting the 'gift of the gab', Blarney

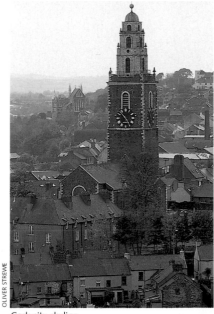

Cork city skyline

The Great Outdoors (cnr Paul & Corn-market Sts) This is a camping, trekking and winter sports store.

P Cashel (13 Winthrop St) This disorganised but interesting shop is home to an eclectic assortment of antiques and junk – from phrenology heads to spiky tortoises.

Pro-Musica (☎ 427 1659, 20 Oliver Plunkett St) This place sells musical instruments, including traditional Irish ones, as well as sheet music for all tastes.

GETTING THERE & AWAY
Air
Cork Airport (☎ 431 3131) is 8km south of the city on the N27. Airlines servicing the airport are British Airways, Ryan Air, Aer Lingus, Aer Arann and Jersey European (for details see the Getting There & Away chapter). There are direct flights to Dublin, London, Manchester, Exeter, Jersey, Paris, Rennes and Amsterdam. Other overseas flights go via Dublin.

Bus
Bus Éireann (☎ 450 8188) operates from the bus station on the corner of Merchant's Quay and Parnell Place. You can get to most places from Cork, including Dublin (€16.50, 4¼ hours, six daily), Killarney (€11.95, two hours, eight daily), Waterford (€12.70, 2¼ hours, seven to eight daily) and Kilkenny (€12.70, three hours, four daily).

Train
Kent Train Station (☎ 450 4777) is north of the River Lee on Glanmire Rd Lower. It has left luggage lockers costing €1.25 per item per 24 hours.

There's a direct train connection to Dublin (€44.50, three hours, nine daily) and Limerick (€17.80, 1½ hours, eight daily). There's a service to Tralee (€22.90, 2¼ hours) via Killarney (€22.90, 1½ hours) five times a day. There's also a rather circuitous route to Waterford (€22.90, three to five hours) via Limerick Junction and Tipperary once a day.

An hourly service south-east to Cobh stops at Fota, enabling you to take in the Fota Wildlife Park and Cobh Heritage Centre (see the following Around Cork City section) on a round trip.

Boat
Regular ferries link Cork with the UK and France. Brittany Ferries (☎ 427 7801), 42 Grand Parade, run to Roscoff at 3.30pm every Saturday from March to September. This crossing takes 14 hours.

Swansea Cork Ferries (☎ 427 6000), 52 South Mall (also an office at the ferry terminal), operate four times a week for €30.50 to €43.20 one way, depending on the month you travel. The crossing between Cork and Swansea takes 10 hours.

For more details see Sea in the Getting There & Away chapter.

GETTING AROUND
To/From the Airport
The airport is 8km south of the city centre on the South City Link Rd. It takes about 20 minutes to get there by car. Bus Éireann No 226 runs between the airport and the bus station on Parnell Place and into the city centre.

To/From the Ferry Terminal
The ferry terminal is at Ringaskiddy, about 15 minutes by car south-east from the city centre along the N28. Bus Éireann runs a fairly frequent daily service to the terminal; the journey takes about 45 minutes.

Bus
Most places you'll need to get to are within easy walking distance of the centre. If you're staying a long time it might be worth considering a weekly ticket. You'll need a photo to obtain it.

Car
Budget (☎ 427 4755) has a desk at the tourist office as well as at the airport (☎ 431 4000). Avis (☎ 428 1111) is on Emmet Place, opposite the Crawford Municipal Art Gallery.

Parking Parking coupons (€0.75 per hour) are obtainable from the tourist office and some newsagents. They must be displayed inside the car window to park virtually

CORK

anywhere in the city centre. Alternatively, use the big car park behind Merchant's Quay Shopping Centre, or park for free in the Shandon area, north of Pope's Quay.

Taxi
Try Shandon Cabs (☎ 450 2255) or Cork Taxi Co-op (☎ 427 2222).

Bicycle
For bicycle hire try Cycle Scene (☎ 430 1183), 396 Blarney St, where hire costs €12.70/50 per day/week.

Around Cork City

BLARNEY CASTLE
Even the most untouristy visitor will probably feel compelled to kiss the **Blarney Stone** and get the gift of the gab or, as an 18th-century French consul put it, 'gain the privilege of telling lies for seven years'. It was Queen Elizabeth I, exasperated with Lord Blarney's ability to talk endlessly without ever actually agreeing to her demands, who invented the term.

Dating from 1446, the castle (☎ 021-438 5252, Blarney; adult/child €4.45/1.25; open 9am-6.30pm Mon-Sat & 9.30am-5.30pm Sun May & Sept; 9am-7pm Mon-Sat & 9.30am-5.30pm Sun June-Aug; 9am-6pm (or sundown) Mon-Sat & 9.30am-5pm (or sundown) Sun Oct-Apr; last admission 30 minutes before closing) is a tower house built on solid limestone in wonderful grounds; remember to pack a picnic.

Bending over backwards to kiss the sacred rock requires a head for heights. You're unlikely to fall since there's a grill and someone there to hold you. The stone is at the top of the castle; the long spiral staircases are narrow, steep and uneven so be careful. Other than signs for the name of each room, there's not a great deal of explanation of what each part of the castle was used for and who lived here. In our opinion thc admission price warrants a little more.

Your enjoyment of your visit to Blarney will probably be in inverse proportion to the number of coach tours there at the time.

Getting there at opening time is one way to beat the crowds. Blarney is 8km north-west of Cork and buses run there regularly from Cork bus station (€2.25, 30 minutes).

PASSAGE WEST
If you're travelling from west to eastern Cork and want to avoid going through Cork city it's worth knowing about the Ferry Link (☎ 021-481 1223), which connects Passage West and Glenbrook with Carrigaloe daily between 7am and 12.10am. The crossing takes five minutes. One-way fares are €3.20 for a car and €1.25 for pedestrians; bikes travel free.

FOTA WILDLIFE PARK
Fota Wildlife Park (☎ 021-481 2678, Carrigtwohill; adult/child €6.60/3.95; open 10am-6pm Mon-Sat & 11am-6pm Sun mid-March-Oct; 10am-4pm Mon-Sat & 11am-4pm Sun Nov-mid-March), a kind of zoo without cages, is 10km east of Cork. It spreads itself over 70 acres and is ideal for children. Giraffes, ostriches, monkeys, kangaroos and penguins wander freely, and lemurs invade the coffee shop. Cheetahs may not have space to hit full speed here but they're bred and exported to countries from where they originated. Look out for the glorious white and brown scimitar-horned onyx, believed to be extinct in the wild.

The *coffee shop* is pretty ordinary so it might be worth bringing a picnic. A 'gravy train' runs a circuit round the park every 15 minutes (€0.65).

With time on your hands it's worth strolling down to look at the graceful exterior of the 18th-century **Fota House**, once one of Ireland's grandest houses but now sadly neglected, and the 150-year-old **arboretum**, both towards the station end of the park.

Since cars must be left outside and visitors walk around the park, it's probably easier to take the hourly Cork to Fota train (€2.80 return, 15 minutes) which goes on to Cobh.

COBH
☎ 021 • pop 8460
Picturesque Cobh (pronounced cove) was for many years the port of Cork and has al-

The Irish Diaspora

About half the people born in Ireland since 1820 have emigrated, but the story of Irish emigration goes back much further than that, and continued, albeit on a smaller scale, until very recently.

Between 1652 and 1653, Oliver Cromwell expelled around 30,000 soldiers and had thousands of civilians transported. The West Indies was a favourite destination because, once there, they could be sold as slaves. After the Treaty of Limerick was signed in 1691, another 20,000 men and their families fled to France.

In the 18th century emigration to North America began, especially from Ulster, where Presbyterians were weary of being treated as second-class citizens. Between 1791 and 1853, 39,000 convicts were transported to Australia from Cobh for crimes ranging from theft to murder. Between 1848 and 1850, 4000 orphaned girls were sent to Australia from the workhouses to provide mates for the men.

The most dramatic and tragic period of emigration was precipitated by the Potato Famine of 1845–51, which accelerated an already well established process. During that period more than a million people left and, between 1855 and 1914, another four million Irish people emigrated for a new life, mostly in the USA and Britain.

Once a man or woman – and women often outnumbered men in their determination to leave – had decided to book their transatlantic passage it was understood that they were unlikely ever to return; hence the 'American Wake', a farewell party recognised as marking a final parting between emigrants and their families and friends.

Accurate figures are difficult to come by but today tens of millions of people around the world are of Irish origin. In North America approximately 40 million claim an Irish connection, with the biggest concentration of those being in New York, Boston and Philadelphia. Some of these people feel their roots strongly, a few even contributing financially to the nationalist paramilitaries in Northern Ireland. About one-third of Australia's 19 million or so people also have an Irish connection.

Ireland's improved economic circumstances have staunched the flow of emigrants and since the early 1990s there has been net immigration. Many of these immigrants have been the returning children of the diaspora.

ways had a strong connection with Atlantic crossings. In 1838 the *Sirius* was the first steamship to cross the Atlantic, sailing from Cobh. The *Titanic* made its last stop here before its fateful Atlantic crossing in 1912, and when the *Lusitania* was sunk off the coast of Kinsale in 1915, it was here that many of the survivors were brought and the victims buried.

In the British era it was known as Queenstown because it was where Queen Victoria arrived in 1849 on her first visit to Ireland. The world's first yacht club, the Royal Cork Yacht Club, was founded here in 1720, but now operates from Crosshaven on the other side of Cork Harbour.

The surrounding industry makes Cobh's outlook a bit grim though the brightly coloured buildings contribute to the aesthetic appeal of the town and the spectacular cathedral makes a visit a must.

Orientation
Cobh is on Great Island, which fills much of Cork Harbour, and is joined to the mainland by a causeway. It faces Haulbowline Island (once the base of the Irish Naval Service) and Spike Island (the greener of the islands; it houses a prison).

Information
The old yacht club building now houses a small tourist office (☎ 481 3301) and arts centre, open 9.30am to 5.30pm Monday to Friday and 11.30am to 5.30pm Saturday and Sunday, March to September; and 2.30pm to 5.30pm daily, October to February. They have a good (free) town map.

CORK

There's a cybercafe at Atlantic Inn (☎ 481 1489) on West Beach; it costs €2.55 for 15 minutes.

Guided walks lasting 1½ hours leave from the Commodore Hotel (see Places to Stay) at 11am daily (€6). There's a 'ghost walk' at 8.30pm on Tuesday, Thursday and Saturday from Pillars Bar on Westbourne Place. It takes 1¼ hours and costs €6.35. Ask at the tourist office for details on both these walks or phone ☎ 481 5211 (e info@titanic-trail.com).

St Colman's Cathedral

Cobh is dominated by this massive but comparatively new cathedral (☎ 481 3222, Cathedral Place; admission by donation; mass times 8am & 10am Mon-Fri; 6pm Sat; 8am, 10am, noon & 7pm Sun) standing on a huge platform above the town. Construction of the French Gothic-style cathedral began in 1868 but wasn't completed until 1915. The Irish communities in Australia and the USA contributed much of the construction cost. The cathedral is noted for its 47-bell carillon, the largest in Ireland; the biggest bell weighs 3440kg. St Colman (522–604) is the patron saint of the local diocese of Cloyne. A leaflet on the main features inside is available at the entrance.

Cobh Heritage Centre

Part of Cobh train station has been converted to house the impressive Cobh Heritage Centre (☎ 481 3591, Old Railway Station; adult/child €5/2.50, free for under-eights; open 10am-6pm daily, last admission 5pm). The 'Queenstown Story', which tells of the mass emigration following the Famine, the era of the great liners and the tragedies of the Titanic and Lusitania, is well worth a visit. The Blarney Woollen Mills, also housed in the centre, is supposed to 'capture the essence of the great Irish shopping experience' but it's just an excuse to sell knitwear and souvenirs to tourists at inflated prices.

Cobh Museum

A small history museum (☎ 481 4240, High Rd; adult/child €1.25/0.65; open 11am-1pm & 2pm-6pm Mon-Sat, 3pm-6pm Sun Easter-

Oct) is housed in the 19th-century Scottish Presbyterian church that overlooks the train station. There are model ships as well as paintings, photographs and some artefacts from 18th- and 19th-century Cobh.

Activities

Early June to September, **Marine Transport Services** (☎ 481 1485) organises three one-hour **harbour cruises** each day costing €3.80/2.50. The tourist office has details.

Fota Island Golf Club (☎ 488 3700) is 5km from Cobh on the R624. It is stunning and simply reeks of money so if you can afford the €50–80 green fees, you should play a round.

Places to Stay

Don't be too easily seduced by the B&Bs on the waterfront. They tend to be overpriced at around €28–32 per person.

Beechmount Tourist Hostel (☎ 481 2177, e skids@indigo.ie, John O'Connell St) Dorms €8.90. This place opens year round apart from a week over Christmas.

Westbourne House (☎ 481 1391, 12 Westbourne Place) Rooms €19 per person without bathroom. This is the cheapest B&B around and is conveniently located close to the tourist office, train station and heritage centre.

Ardeen (☎ 481 1803, 3 Harbour Hill) Rooms €23-25 per person. This place has nice views from the front rooms and is a couple of minutes' walk from the cathedral and Main St.

Ard Na Laoi (☎ 481 2742, 15 Westbourne Place) Rooms €25 per person. There are no single rooms here but there are triples.

Bellavista (☎ 481 2450, fax 481 2215, e bellavis@indigo.ie, Bishop's Rd) Singles/doubles €50.80/88.95. This luxury B&B has great views and an attractive conservatory where guests have breakfast.

Water's Edge Hotel (☎ 481 5566, fax 481 2011, e watersedge@eircom.net, next to the tourist office) Singles/doubles from €70/88, executive suites €127/200. This new hotel offers excellent accommodation in spacious and attractive rooms which are, as the name suggests, on the water's edge.

Commodore Hotel (☎ 481 1277, fax 481 1672, Westbourne Place) Singles/doubles €61/100, €71/115 July & Aug. Although this place has a certain old-world charm, it's not a patch on the Water's Edge.

Places to Eat

There's not a lot in the way of eateries in Cobh, especially if you find yourself here out of summer. The one or two pubs that serve dinner off-season usually close the kitchen at 7pm. We suggest you eat a big lunch.

The Beacon (☎ 481 4855, 22 East Beach) Early-bird menu (in before 7pm) & Sunday lunch €13.90 per couple. Open 4.30pm-9.30pm Mon-Sat, 12.30pm-3pm & 5pm-7pm Sun. This place is one of the few worth trying and is recommended by the locals.

The Peninsula (☎ 481 3345, 13 Midleton St) Starters €3.55-4.80, mains €7.50-10.40. This Chinese restaurant offers a 3-course set menu for €10 from 5pm-8pm Monday to Thursday.

Jacob's Ladder (at the Water's Edge Hotel, see Places to Stay). Lunch €6.30-11.40, dinner €15.20-20.25. This modern and tastefully decorated place is situated right on the water with some great views out to Cobh Harbour. You'll need to book ahead. The menu includes such delights as baked cod with coriander mash and herb cream.

Getting There & Away

Cobh is 24km south-east of Cork, off the main N25 Cork to Rosslare road. Hourly trains connect Cobh with Cork (€3, 30 minutes). Alternatively, between June and September you can take a passenger cruiser which leaves Cobh for Passage West at 3.15pm and costs €7/4.45.

Getting Around

All of Cobh's sites are within easy walking distance. If you need a cab try Harbour Cabs on ☎ 481 4444.

JAMESON HERITAGE CENTRE

This distillery (☎ 021-461 3594, Midleton; adult/concession €5.70/2.50; open 10am-

Ballymaloe House

This cooking school, guesthouse and restaurant (☎ 021-465 2531, fax 465 2021, e res@ballymaloe.ie, Shanagarry) is 12km south-east of Midleton on the R629 between Shanagarry and Cloyne. To have a degree from this prestigious cooking school is the equivalent of going to the Cordon Bleu in Paris – it's a chef's ticket to the world. On your travels you might catch *A Year at Ballymaloe*, a cooking program on Ireland's national TV station, RTE1.

The food at the guesthouse restaurant can be described as modern Irish and the five-course set menu is around €45 per person. For starters you might have Ballycotton fish mousse with saffron beurre blanc, and for the main course, roast peppered duck with lemon served with a white spring vegetable purée. Accommodation is in a vine-covered manor house where each room is decorated differently. It's expensive, with singles costing €100 to €115 and doubles at €170 to €190.

6pm daily Mar-Oct; noon-3pm Mon-Fri Nov-Feb) is about 20km east of Cork. Whiskey has been distilled here since the early 19th century, and the old works were opened to the public after a new distillery was opened. Twenty-four million bottles of whiskey are produced at this new plant each year. There's a tourist office (☎ 461 3702) which opens 9.30am (11.30am on Sunday) to 1pm and 2.15pm to 5.30pm daily.

Forty-five-minute guided tours start with a film show and continue with a walkabout that reveals the whole whiskey-making process. The tour ends in the bar, where two lucky volunteers get to compare assorted Irish whiskeys with Scotch and Bourbon. Everyone gets a free tipple and there's a *cafe* for snacks and lunches.

Between March and October there are regular daily tours between 10am and 6pm. During the rest of the year there are tours at noon and 3pm on weekdays.

There are eight buses a day (six on Sunday) from Cork bus station (€4.25, 25 minutes).

CORK

YOUGHAL

☎ 024 • pop 5940

Youghal (Eochaill; pronounced yawl) is a historically interesting town where the River Blackwater meets the sea. Unfortunately the town itself is grimy and noisy in parts, mostly thanks to the trucks and buses that thunder through narrow Main St all day long. At the time of writing many shops and businesses were closing down, which gave the town a decaying feeling. Although Youghal is worth visiting, a half-day trip is all you'll need.

Sir Walter Raleigh was town mayor here from 1588 to 1589 and, tradition has it, he planted the first potatoes here after bringing them back from the New World. The town was Captain Ahab's port in John Huston's *Moby Dick*.

Orientation & Information

The old Clock Gate at the southern end of North Main St is Youghal's major landmark. There's no tourist office but there's an information point (☎ 20170) at Market House, Market Square. The free leaflet Youghal Town Trail is available from here.

Ninety-minute guided tours of the town costing €4.45 leave from the tourist information point at 11am Monday to Saturday from June to August.

Things to See

Heading from south to north, some of the town's sights are detailed here.

Fox's Lane Folk Museum *(☎ 20170; open 10am-1pm & 2pm-6pm Tues-Sat July & Aug; call ☎ 291145 Sept-June)*, signposted down an alley between The Mall and South Main St, displays over 400 bygones and a Victorian kitchen.

The curious **Clock Gate** bridges Main St. In 1777 the present building, a combination of clock tower and jail, replaced the medieval Trinity Gate, a key part of the town's fortifications. In 1798 several members of the rebellious United Irishmen were hanged from its walls.

The **Red House**, on North Main St, was designed in 1706 by the Dutch architect Leuventhen with typically Dutch characteristics, such as the cornerstones positioned under the triangular gable. Its name comes from its red bricks. A few doors farther up the street are **Alms Houses** built in 1610 by Richard Boyle, the local lord, to house ex-soldiers.

Across the road stands the 15th-century **Tynte's Castle**. Originally it had a defensive riverfront position but as the Blackwater silted up and changed course it was left high and dry. In 1584 the castle was confiscated and given to Sir Robert Tynte, who married the widow of the English poet Edmund Spenser. Today it's semi-derelict.

Built in 1220, **St Mary's Collegiate Church** *(e friendsofstmarys@eircom.net, off Emmet Place; admission free)* incorporates elements of an earlier Danish church dating back to the 11th century. In the late 16th century the earl of Desmond housed his troops here, leading to the destruction of the old chancel roof. Inside there's a monument to Richard Boyle, who bought Raleigh's Irish estates and became the first earl of Cork. It shows him with his wife and all 16 of his children (those who died as infants are shown lying down). Look out, too, for a monument to Catherine, widow of the 11th earl of Desmond, who supposedly died in 1614, aged 140! This is one of the oldest churches still in use in Ireland. At other times it's usually locked; phone ☎ 91076 for the key. The churchyard is bounded by a fine stretch of the town wall and one of the remaining turrets. The walls date back at least as far as the 13th century and remained in use until the 17th century. Services are on Sunday at 11.30am and Wednesday at 10.30am.

Beside the church, **Myrtle Grove** is an interesting house which retains some 16th-century features. Local history relates that it was home to Sir Walter Raleigh, who made the mistake of smoking tobacco in front of a servant who had never seen such a thing and, accordingly, threw a bucket of water over him to douse the fire. The weather vane depicts the famous story of Raleigh, Elizabeth I, the puddle and the cloak.

Places to Stay

Sonas Caravan Park (☎ 98132, Ballymacoda) Tent & 2 people €11.45, showers

€1.25. Open May-mid-Sept. This park is about 15km south of Youghal, on the seashore. To get there, take the road off the N25 (west of town) to the village of Ballymacoda, then head west through the village.

Roseville (☎ 92571, New Catherine St) Rooms €24-25 per person. Rooms in this lovely house are very good value and you get a choice of breakfast dishes.

Aherne's Guesthouse & Restaurant (☎ 92424, fax 93633, ⓔ ahernes@eircom .net, 163 North Main St) Singles/doubles from €101/140. This luxury B&B offers 12 spacious en suite rooms.

Places to Eat

Coffee Pot (☎ 92523, 77 North Main St) Meals €4.15-9.50. For light lunches, try this basic but good-value coffee shop in the middle of town for open sandwiches, burgers and mixed grills.

The Olde Porter House (☎ 92445, Main St) Bar food €6.35-8.90. This pub also has live entertainment most nights.

The Tower Restaurant (☎ 91869, Main St) Light meals & snacks €3.10-5.40; 3-course set menu €15.90. This BYO bistro serves sandwiches as well as hot meals.

Aherne's Guesthouse & Restaurant (see Places to Stay) Bar meals €8.90-12.70, restaurant meals €23.50-29.20. This award-winning place serves wonderful seafood dishes as well as traditional bar food.

Getting There & Away

There are frequent Bus Éireann buses to Cork (€7.35, 1¼ hours, 13 daily) and Waterford (€11.45, every two hours).

Western Cork

KINSALE
☎ 021 • pop 3960
Kinsale (Cionn tSáile) has a picture-postcard prettiness though it's blighted by traffic jams in summer (as well as on Sunday and public holidays throughout the year). The crowds are drawn not just by the scenery and historic buildings but by the fact that Kinsale is the undisputed gourmet cap-

ital of Ireland. The Old Head of Kinsale juts out into the Atlantic, about 15km south-west of town. It's now taken over by a very exclusive golf course and access is restricted.

History

In September 1601, a Spanish fleet anchored at Kinsale was besieged by the English. The Irish army marched the length of the country to attack the English but were defeated in battle outside Kinsale on Christmas Eve. For the Catholics of Kinsale, the immediate consequence was that they were banned from the town. It was another 100 years before they were allowed to return. Historians now cite 1601 as the beginning of the end of Gaelic Ireland.

After 1601 the town developed as a ship-building port. In the early 18th century Alexander Selkirk left Kinsale Harbour on a voyage that left him stranded on a desert island, providing Daniel Defoe with the idea for *Robinson Crusoe*.

Orientation & Information

Most of Kinsale can be covered quite easily on foot. Most of the hotels and restaurants ring the harbour, but some are out at Scilly, a peninsula to the south-east. A path continues from there to Summercove and Charles Fort. To the south-west, Duggan Bridge links Castlepark Marina and the scant ruins of James Fort to Pier Rd.

The tourist office (☎ 477 2234), on the harbourfront close to the bus stop, opens 9.15am to 1pm and 2.15pm to 5.30pm Monday to Saturday, March to October, plus on Sunday in July and August. They have a walking map detailing five walks in and around Kinsale lasting from one to two hours. It's also available from some shops and B&Bs.

There is an Allied Irish Bank with ATM on Pearse St. Kinsale Laundrette (☎ 477 2205) is on Main St and opens 9am to 6.30pm Monday to Friday. Kinsale Bookshop (☎ 477 4244), at 8 Main St, has a large selection of children's books. The post office is on Pearse St. Finishing Services (☎ 477 3571), at 71 Main St, has Internet access from 9am to 5pm Monday to Friday.

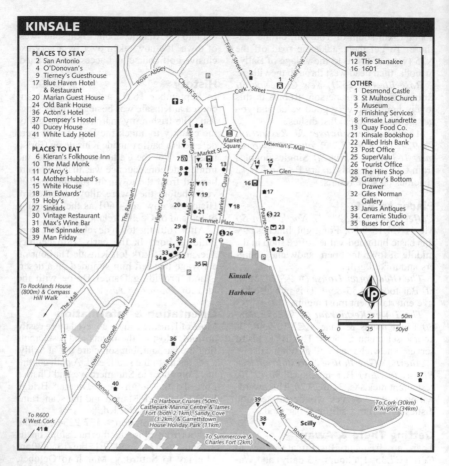

KINSALE

PLACES TO STAY
2 San Antonio
4 O'Donovan's
9 Tierney's Guesthouse
17 Blue Haven Hotel & Restaurant
20 Marian Guest House
24 Old Bank House
36 Acton's Hotel
37 Dempsey's Hostel
40 Ducey House
41 White Lady Hotel

PLACES TO EAT
6 Kieran's Folkhouse Inn
10 The Mad Monk
11 D'Arcy's
14 Mother Hubbard's
15 White House
18 Jim Edwards'
19 Hoby's
27 Sinéads
30 Vintage Restaurant
31 Max's Wine Bar
38 The Spinnaker
39 Man Friday

PUBS
12 The Shanakee
16 1601

OTHER
1 Desmond Castle
3 St Multose Church
5 Museum
7 Finishing Services
8 Kinsale Laundrette
13 Quay Food Co.
21 Kinsale Bookshop
22 Allied Irish Bank
23 Post Office
25 SuperValu
26 Tourist Office
28 The Hire Shop
32 Granny's Bottom Drawer
32 Giles Norman Gallery
33 Janus Antiques
34 Ceramic Studio
35 Buses for Cork

Market Square

Newman's Mall

The Glen

Emmet Place

Kinsale Harbour

To Rocklands House (800m) & Compass Hill Walk

To R600 & West Cork

To Harbour Cruises (50m), Castlepark Marina Centre & James Fort (both 2.1km), Sandy Cove (3.2km) & Garrettstown House Holiday Park (11km)

To Summercove & Charles Fort (2km)

To Cork (30km) & Airport (34km)

Scilly

0   25   50m
0   25   50yd

Museum

The small museum (☎ 477 7930, *Market Square; adult/child €2.55/1.25; open 10.30 am-5.30pm Mon-Sat & 2.30pm-5.30pm Sun Apr-Oct*), in the 17th-century courthouse displays, exhibits relating to the 1915 sinking of the *Lusitania*.

Desmond Castle

This early 16th-century tower house (☎ 477 4855, *Cork St; adult/child €2.55/1.25; open 10am-6pm mid-Apr-early Oct; closed Monday except public holidays; last admission 45 minutes before closing*) was occupied by

the Spanish in 1601. Since then it has served as a prison for French and American captives and as a workhouse during the Famine. In the care of Dúchas (see Useful Organisations in the Facts for the Visitor chapter for details), it now houses a small museum on the history of wine.

St Multose Church

St Multose is the patron saint of Kinsale and this Church of Ireland church (☎ 477 2220 *for the rectory*) is one of Ireland's oldest. It was built around 1190 by the Normans on the site of a 6th-century church. Apparently

CORK

it was here that Prince Rupert proclaimed Charles II as king of England. Not much of the interior is original but the exterior is brilliantly preserved and the graveyard has some interesting large family tombs. A guide is available for €1.25 at the entrance.

Charles Fort

In Summercove, 2km east of Kinsale, stand the huge ruins of 17th-century Charles Fort (☎ 477 2263; adult/senior/student/family €3.20/2.20/1.25/7.60; open 10am-6pm daily mid-Mar-Oct; Sat & Sun only Nov-mid-Mar; last admission 5.15pm). It's one of the best-preserved star forts in Europe. Now a Dúchas site, it was built in the 1670s and remained in use until 1921, when much of the fort was destroyed as the British withdrew. Although it protected the town from sea attacks, it was William of Orange who attacked it from the land after the Battle of the Boyne in 1690. Most of the ruins you see inside date from the 18th and 19th centuries.

Even those not thrilled by military history will enjoy the harbour views from the huge walls. If you follow the signposted Scilly Walk you'll have similar views all the way.

Activities

One-hour guided walking tours leave from outside the tourist office at 11.15am daily (☎ 477 2873). There's a nice one-hour walk around Compass Hill (head south-west towards Rocklands House) that gives you lovely views out to Kinsale Harbour.

Castlepark Marina Centre (☎ 477 4959) organises deep-sea fishing (€38 plus €6.35 rod hire) and scuba-diving trips and tuition. They will also ferry you across the harbour (€1.25) to catch the cruise boats from Denis Quay. Hostel accommodation is also available here (see Places to Stay later in this section).

For harbour cruises to Charles Fort, James Cove and up the Bandon River phone Kinsale Harbour Cruises (☎ 477 3188, 087 227 2319). Boats leave seven times a day during summer, five times a day at the weekend the rest of the year, from Denis Quay on Pier Rd, at the southern end of town. It costs €6.35/3.80 for adult/concession.

Fishing tackle can be hired at The Hire Shop (☎ 477 4884, 18 Main St) for about €10.15 per day.

The Kinsale School of Languages (☎/fax 477 4545, e info@kinsaleschool.com) at Sandy Cove, 3km west of town, has Irish language courses for beginners.

Special Events

The first Kinsale Arts Festival (☎ 477 4959) was held in 1998 and continues each September. Local and international artists and performers descend on the town for 10 days of various events.

The four-day Gourmet Festival held during the first weekend in October is organised by the restaurants that make up the Good Food Circle of Kinsale. Membership for the four days costs €250 and includes admission to various events such as tastings, some meals, a harbour cruise and a 10% discount in the restaurants. Tickets to some events are available on the day. For details and bookings contact Peter Barry (☎ 477 4026), Scilly, Kinsale.

Places to Stay

Kinsale offers few accommodation bargains, particularly if you're travelling alone. You may prefer to make a day trip from Cork.

Camping & Hostels There are a couple of options for camping around Kinsale and a hostel not far from the town centre.

Garrettstown House Holiday Park (☎/fax 477 8156, Kinsale) Tent & 2 people €14. Open May-Sept. This is the closest camp site to Kinsale. It's not actually in Garrettstown itself but is 1.3km south-west of Ballinspittle (11km south-west of Kinsale) on the R600.

Castlepark Marina Centre (☎ 477 4959, Castlepark Marina) Dorms €11.45, doubles €28, including breakfast. This clean, modern hostel near James Fort is about 1km south of Kinsale over Duggan Bridge. From June to September ferries run on the hour after 8am from Denis Quay at the southern end of Pier Rd; at other times of year call the owner, Eddie McCarthy, and he may be able to collect you. There's a small beach immediately behind the hostel, an on-site *cafe* and The Dock pub next door.

Dempsey's Hostel (☎ *477 2124, Eastern Rd*) Dorms €8.90, doubles €24, linen hire €1.25. Open year round. This is an uphill walk from the centre and closer to town than the Castlepark Marina Centre. It's in a noisy location, behind the Texaco garage on the Cork road, but the traffic noise is muted inside.

B&Bs There are lots of B&Bs in and around Kinsale, but many close from November to March and some have doubles only. Be aware that many B&Bs above shops in the centre have pokey rooms and are a bit pricey.

Marian Guest House (☎ *477 4253, 62 Main St*) En suite rooms €15-19 per person. This is the cheapest B&B in town as long as you don't mind tiny rooms and the family dog.

O'Donovan's (☎ *477 2428,* e *odonovans _bb@iolfree.ie, Guardwell*) Singles/doubles from €35/50. This place is centrally located and very good value. It has a strict non-smoking policy.

Tierney's Guesthouse (☎ *477 2205, fax 477 4363, 70 Main St*) Doubles without/with bathroom €44.50/56.50. This is one of the nicest places in the centre.

Ducey House (☎ *477 4592, Denis Quay*) Rooms from €28 per person. This gorgeously decorated 18th-century townhouse has a very laid back atmosphere. Try to stay in 'Isabella's Room' and enjoy the huge bathroom.

San Antonio (☎ *477 2341, 1 Friar's St*) Rooms €26.70 per person. This friendly place has great views over Kinsale from the front rooms and, like O'Donovan's, is very good value.

Rocklands House (☎ *477 2609, Compass Hill*) B&B & self-catering cottage from €38-44 per person. This home in nice gardens is about 15 minutes walk from the town centre. The more expensive rooms have nice views.

Hotels There are a number of hotels close to the town centre.

White Lady Hotel (☎ *477 2737, fax 477 4641,* e *wlady@indigo.ie, Lower O'Connell St*) Singles/doubles €76/89. This is a nice hotel but a bit pricey for singles.

Blue Haven Hotel & Restaurant (☎ *477 2209, fax 477 4268,* e *bluhaven@iol.ie, 3 Pearse St*) Standard/superior rooms €178/215. This place is very pricey but it does have special deals throughout the year.

Old Bank House (☎ *477 4075, fax 477 4296,* e *oldbank@indigo.ie, 11 Pearse St*) Rooms €150-230. This is a well run, elegant establishment and is a particular favourite of visiting golfers.

Acton's Hotel (☎ *477 2135, fax 477 2231,* e *info@actonshotelkinsale.com, Pier Rd*), Singles/doubles €82.50/115 Nov-Feb, €115/150 the rest of the year. Rooms at the front of this huge hotel have nice views but it's not good value compared to some of the lovely B&Bs around.

Places to Eat

Restaurants The food in Kinsale really is worthy of its reputation. Your mouth will water just reading some of the menus pinned up in restaurant windows. Some of the more upmarket places serve affordable lunches and early-bird menus.

Max's Wine Bar (☎ *477 3677, Main St*) Mains €14-20, 3-course early-bird menu €16. This is one of the favoured places of locals. If you're on a bit of a budget at least try to have lunch here when Cashel blue cheese and pine kernel tart with a warm pear salad will only set you back €7.50.

Vintage Restaurant (☎ *477 2502, 50 Main St*) Starters €8.90-15.90, mains €25-27. One of the most expensive places in town, this restaurant remains one of the best and most interesting.

Hoby's (☎ *477 2200, 5 Main St*) Mains €11.40-19.70, 3-course dinner €20.20. Hoby's is small with a modern interior, subtle lighting and excellent service.

D'Arcy's (☎ *477 3990, 2 Main St*) Starters €3.20-8.25, mains €10.80-17.75, lunch €6-12.60. This traditional Irish restaurant is good value. The lunch menu is the same as the dinner menu but cheaper.

Blue Haven Restaurant (see *Places to Stay*) Starters €5.70-10.80, mains €8.90-

10.80. This restaurant has a nice outdoor area and is cheaper than most restaurants in the centre.

The Spinnaker (☎ *477 2098, Scilly)* Starters €5-8.80, mains €14.60-18.90. Open 6pm-10pm. As the name suggests, this is a cosy, nautical-themed, seafood restaurant. You'll need to book as it's quite popular.

Man Friday (☎ *477 2260, Scilly)* Starters €6.30-8.80, mains €17.50-21.50. Although there are some great views over to Kinsale, not all tables have an aspect, so book ahead to get the table you want. A sample from the menu: roast free-range duckling with a nectarine and brandy sauce, €19.

Cafes & Pubs You'll find the standard of pub food pretty high in Kinsale due to the competition from restaurants and cafes.

Mother Hubbard's (☎ *477 2440, Market St)* Snacks & light meals €2.50-6.30. This is a great place for breakfast and inexpensive meals such as toasted sandwiches, chip butties and salads.

Sinéads (☎ *477 2333, Pier Rd)* Meals €3.80-10.80. This licensed cafe has seating upstairs with nice views over the harbour. Gourmet baguettes and tapas are some of the things on offer.

White House (☎ *477 2125, Pearse St)* Snacks & meals €3.75-9.50. In central Kinsale this popular pub is the oldest in town and offers good-value bar food, including all the traditional fare.

The Mad Monk (☎ *477 4609, 1 Main St)* Meals €6.30-12.65. This is definitely a place for meat eaters with plenty of burgers, steaks and mixed grills. Meals have names such as 'Friar Tuck's Beef Burger' and 'Sister Ursula's Bit on the Side'.

Kieran's Folkhouse Inn (☎ *477 2382, Guardwell)* Light meals & snacks €4.45-7, mains €5.70-8.90. This multi-award-winning Spanish-themed pub serves reasonably priced grub. Don't bother with the accommodation here – it's a bit expensive for what you get.

Jim Edwards' (☎ *477 2541, Market Quay)* Bar meals €3.50-13.30, restaurant meals €14-17.80. This is one of the best pubs for seafood.

Self-Catering Those making their own meals should go to the ***SuperValu*** supermarket on Pearse St and maybe the ***Quay Food Co.*** (see Shopping) for some luxuries.

Entertainment

Kinsale has a lively pub scene and live music is easy to find in summer.

1601 (☎ *477 2529, Pearse St)* This place is always crowded and you can read up on the finer details of the battle while you wait to be served.

The Mad Monk *(see Places to Eat)* It gets very lively as the day progresses and traditional music sessions take you well into the wee hours.

The Shanakee *(An Seanachai;* ☎ *477 7077, Main St)* This huge pub doubles as a disco and has live music nightly.

The nightclub at the ***White Lady Hotel*** *(see Places to Stay)* is popular with the younger crowd on Friday, Saturday and Sunday nights. ***Bacchus*** *(attached to Kieran's Folkhouse Inn, see Places to Eat)*, opens at the weekend and features live music.

Shopping

There's some great shopping in Kinsale, especially for high-quality linen, antiques, ceramics and crystalware.

Ceramic Studio (☎ *477 7021, 42 Main St)* This workshop and studio sells original, modern designs.

Janus Antiques (☎ *477 4342, 44 Main St)* Next door, this place sells stunning 17th- to 19th-century French antiques as well as some rather pricey homewares.

Giles Norman Gallery (☎ *477 4373, 45 Main St)* This photographic gallery has hundreds of black-and-white scenes of Ireland. Prices range from €20 to €635 or more.

Granny's Bottom Drawer (☎ *477 4839, 53 Main St)* It has a nice selection of exquisite Irish linen, damask and nightwear.

Quay Food Co. (☎ *477 4000, Market Quay)* This deli sells local and imported cheeses, charcuterie, olives and coffee.

Getting There & Away

Bus Éireann buses connect Kinsale with Cork (€5, 45 minutes, 10 daily). The bus stops at

CORK

the Esso garage on Pier Rd near the tourist office. Phone ☎ 450 8188 for bus information.

Getting Around

You can hire bikes for €10.15 per day from The Hire Shop (☎ 477 4884) at 18 Main St. Kinsale Cabs can be contacted on ☎ 477 2642. The fare to the Castlepark Marina Centre is about €4.

KINSALE TO CLONAKILTY

Following the quays west out of Kinsale, the main R600 road passes through Ballinspittle and sleepy **Timoleague** where you'll find the ruins of a Franciscan friary. From here you can continue on the R600 to Clonakilty but we recommend you divert along the R601 to picturesque **Courtmacsherry** which stretches itself out along an inlet of mudflats in Courtmacsherry Bay.

CLONAKILTY

☎ 023 • pop 2950

This very friendly town has a lot going for it. The expansive sandy bay is great for swimming as is the beach at nearby Inchydoney Island but watch for the dangerous riptide; when lifeguards are on duty a red warning flag indicates danger.

It's easy to see why tourism is really starting to hit stride. There are plenty of places to stay and some great eating. It's also a good place to poke around for antiques, second-hand books and jewellery. For those who like live music, traditional or otherwise, Clonakilty is the place for you. You can hear live bands or traditional sessions every night of the week throughout the year.

Michael Collins was born nearby and went to school in Clonakilty, a fact of which the community is very proud.

History

Clonakilty received its first charter in 1292 but was refounded in the early 17th century by the 1st earl of Cork. He settled it with 100 English families and planned a Protestant town from which Catholics would be excluded. His plan failed: Clonakilty is now very Irish and very Catholic – the Presbyterian chapel has been turned into a post office.

From the mid-18th to mid-19th century over 10,000 people worked in the town's linen industry. Houlihan & Sons bakery by the public water pump was once a linen hall, and the fire station stands on the site of the old linen market. What was once a corn mill driven by the nearby river has been pleasingly converted into a library.

Orientation

Roads converge on Asna Square, dominated by a statue commemorating local men who died at the Battle of Big Cross during the 1798 Rising. Also in the square is the small Kilty Stone, which gave Clonakilty its name. At Inchydoney Island, about 4km from the centre, there are some great beaches.

Information

The friendly and helpful tourist office (☎ 33226), Ashe St, opens 9am to 7pm daily June to August; 9.30am to 5.30pm Monday to Friday and 9.30am to 5pm Saturday the rest of the year. A good map of the town and its surrounds is available for free from here and from many hotels and B&Bs.

The Allied Irish Bank on the corner of Pearse and Bridge Sts has an ATM. The post office is in the old Presbyterian chapel on Bridge St. For Internet access go to Hi-Tech (☎ 34557), 10–12 Asna St, where it costs €1.90 for 15 minutes.

The Old Mill Library (☎ 34275), on Kent St, opens 10.30am-6pm Tuesday to Saturday. The Wash Basket (☎ 34821) is a laundrette on Spiller's Lane. There are public toilets on the corner of Rossa and Kent Sts.

The *Historical Walk of Clonakilty and its Sea-Front* booklet (€3.20) includes a clearly illustrated map of the town and is available from Kerr's Bookshop on Ashe St. Clonakilty Bookshop on Pearse St stocks second-hand books. Spiller's Lane, off Bridge St, shelters a cluster of antique and craft shops.

Things to See & Do

The impressive **Church of the Immaculate Conception** *(cnr Bridge & Oliver Plunkett Sts)* was built in the 1870s and has some lovely mosaic work.

CORK

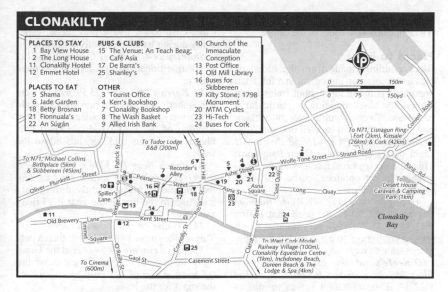

CLONAKILTY

PLACES TO STAY
1 Bay View House
2 The Long House
11 Clonakilty Hostel
12 Emmet Hotel

PLACES TO EAT
5 Shama
6 Jade Garden
18 Betty Brosnan
21 Fionnuala's
22 An Súgán

PUBS & CLUBS
15 The Venue; An Teach Beag; Café Asia
17 De Barra's
25 Shanley's

OTHER
3 Tourist Office
4 Kerr's Bookshop
7 Clonakilty Bookshop
8 The Wash Basket
9 Allied Irish Bank

10 Church of the Immaculate Conception
13 Post Office
14 Old Mill Library
16 Buses for Skibbereen
19 Kilty Stone; 1798 Monument
20 MTM Cycles
23 Hi-Tech
24 Buses for Cork

West Cork Model Railway Village
(☎ 33224, Inchydoney Rd; adult/child
€5.10/3.80; open 11am-5pm daily Feb-
Oct) features not only a working replica of
the West Cork Railway as it was during
WWII, but superb miniature models of the
main towns in western Cork as they were in
the 1940s: Clonakilty, Dunmanway, Kinsale
and Bandon.

Clonakilty Equestrian Centre (☎ 33533)
charges €32 per person for a two-hour
beach ride. They also do shorter rides for
beginners.

Places to Stay

Desert House Caravan & Camping Park
(☎ 33331, fax 33048, Coast Rd) Tent & 2
people €6.35, B&B €21.60/24.15 per person without/with bathroom. Open Easter &
May-Sept. This park, 1km east of town on
the road to Ring, overlooks the river and
offers camping as well as B&B.

Clonakilty Hostel (☎ 33525, fax 35673,
Old Brewery Lane) Beds in 6-bed dorms
€10.15, doubles €25.40. These prices go
up a bit in July and August. This brightly
painted hostel is in a quiet cul-de-sac off
Emmet Square. There is a small kitchen and

dining room, and the hostel offers access for
disabled people.

The Long House (☎ 33011, 15 Wolfe
Tone St) Rooms €19 per person with shared
bathroom. This small, clean but basic place
is the best value B&B in the town centre.

Bay View House (☎ 33539, Old Timoleague Rd) Singles/doubles from €31/53.
Just outside town near the roundabout, this
frilly place has some nice views over the
inlet and serves great breakfasts.

Tudor Lodge (☎ 33046, e tudorlodge1@
eircom.net, MacCurtain Hill) Singles/dou-
bles €31.75/50.80. This attractive B&B sits
on top of MacCurtain Hill and has great
views over the town.

Emmet Hotel (☎ 33394, fax 35058,
Emmet Square) Singles/doubles €57/100.
This picturesque Georgian place was refur-
bished in 1998.

The Lodge & Spa (☎ 33143, fax 352
29, e reservations@inchydoneyisland.com,
Inchydoney Island) Singles €130-150, doubles €200-260 plus 10% service. This place
overlooking some beautiful beaches offers
absolute five-star luxury. You can incorporate
some thalassotherapy (seawater) spas, beauty
treatments and massage with your stay. The

CORK

restaurant here is superb (see Places to Eat). It's signposted 4km south of the centre.

Places to Eat

Black pudding (made from the blood of pigs and a common ingredient in a full Irish breakfast) is found throughout Ireland, but Clonakilty black pudding is particularly renowned. Even if you're not into black pudding, you can still eat well in Clonakilty.

Betty Brosnan (☎ *34011, 58 Pearse St*) Light meals €2.85-5.40. Open 9am-6pm. This cafe serves breakfast as well as sandwiches, jacket potatoes, curry with rice, sausages and chips.

An Súgán (☎ *33498, 41 Wolfe Tone St*) Bar meals €6.30-11.30, restaurant mains €11.45-15.25. This is a very popular lunch spot so you'll need to get in early for a table at that time of day.

O'Keefe's (*at the Emmet Hotel, see Places to Stay*) Starters €3.80-7.55, mains €12-18. This restaurant serves up dishes with Asian and Mediterranean influences. A sample from the menu includes Thai fried salmon on a bed of pak choy poached in coconut milk.

Café Asia (☎ *33419, Recorder's Alley*) Open 12.30pm-11.30pm. This place, next to The Venue nightclub (see Entertainment), advertises itself as a fusion-food bar.

Jade Garden (☎ *34576, MacCurtain Hill*) Starters €2.50-4.45; mains €5.70-8.90. This restaurant is more traditional farmhouse than Chinese in its decor but is comfortable nonetheless.

Shama (☎ *36945, 12 Ashe St*) Starters €3.20-4.45, mains €7-8.25. Open 5pm-midnight Mon-Wed & 5pm-2am Thur-Sun. Good for late-night, post-pub munchies, this Pakistani and Indian restaurant serves biryani, kofti, balti and thali dishes.

Fionnuala's (☎ *34355, 30 Ashe St*) Antipasti €3.75-5, pasta €8.80-13.90, pizza €8.80. This Italian place also serves good coffee.

The Lodge & Spa (*see Places to Stay*) This restaurant boasts an award-winning chef and costs €45 per person for four courses. Book a table early to watch the sun set over the ocean as you dine.

Entertainment

Clonakilty has a lively pub scene, especially during its 10-day festival in July.

Shanley's (☎ *33790, 11 Connolly St*) This small, traditional pub has live music most nights.

De Barra's (☎ *33381, 55 Pearse St*) This atmospheric pub has live music every night of the week; on Friday you can catch Noel Redding of the Jimi Hendrix Experience. Photos of famous rock legends adorn the walls.

An Teach Beag (☎ *33883, 5 Recorder's Alley*) This pub, with a nice beer garden, has traditional music nightly during July and August; the rest of the year it's Friday and Saturday nights.

The Venue (☎ *33419, Recorder's Alley*) This is place more of a nightclub than a pub.

There is a *cinema* (☎ *34141*) at the Quality Hotel just out of town. To get there turn right at the end of O'Reilly St and follow the signs for the hotel.

Getting There & Away

There are two buses daily to Cork (€8.50, 1¼ hours) and Skibbereen (€5.85, 40 minutes). Buses stop on Pearse St coming from Cork and on the coast road going to Cork.

Getting Around

MTM Cycles (☎ 33584), 33 Ashe St, hires out bikes for €8.90/50 per day/week. A nice bike ride is to Dureen Beach, 13km south of town.

AROUND CLONAKILTY
Lisnagun Ring Fort

Of over 30,000 ring forts scattered across Ireland, Lisnagun (Lios na gCon) is the only one that has been reconstructed to give some impression of life in a 10th-century defended farmstead (*adult/child €2.55/1.25; open 9am-5pm Mon-Fri, 10am-5pm Sat & Sun*). It is complete with a souterrain (underground chamber) and a central hut thatched by someone who would have been paid only in food for his months' labours.

In theory the fort keeps regular hours. In practice, if there's no-one there to collect the admission fee you'll get to see only the circular ditch and the encircling wooden palisade.

To get there take the turning at the roundabout at the end of Strand Rd signposted to Bay View House B&B. Follow this road uphill for 2km until you reach a T-junction. Turn right and about 100 yards along you'll see cast iron farm gates on your right. Go through the gates and keep walking straight ahead until you come to a crossroads with a cowshed. Take the track to the left and walk downhill until you reach a minor road. Turn right and the fort is on the left, near the Clonakilty Agricultural College.

Michael Collins Birthplace

Dúchas manages a small memorial centre to Michael Collins, who was born near Clonakilty in 1890. The old house where he was born and lived for about 10 years has been repaired but little remains of the newer house his family later built beside it, where Collins lived until he emigrated to London in 1906. This was burned down by the Black and Tans in 1921. Despite the meagre remains, the place generates a sense of respect for a man who would have been heartbroken at the consequences of the treaty he signed in 1921.

The birthplace site is signposted on the N71, 5km west of Clonakilty.

ROSSCARBERY TO SKIBBEREEN

You can get from Rosscarbery to Skibbereen along the main N71 via Leap, but far more enjoyable is the longer route that winds south-west from the end of the causeway at Rosscarbery, taking in the picturesque villages of Glandore and Union Hall as well as some stunning coastal scenery.

Rosscarbery

☎ 023 • pop 455

Set back from the main N71, Rosscarbery (Ros O'gCairbre) is little more than a village at the head of a landlocked inlet of Rosscarbery Bay with a quiet central square. O'Donovan Rossa, founder of the Fenians, was born here in 1831. The shallow estuary beside the causeway is wonderful for watching wading birds, especially golden plover, in winter.

St Fachtna's Cathedral dates back to the 12th century and has an elaborately carved western doorway as well as an impressive statue of Lord Carbery (1763–1842) in slashed doublet and hose.

Rosscarbery Riding Centre (☎ 48232) organises **pony trekking**. It's signposted opposite the turn-off for Owinhincha Beach. The Warren is a small **swimming beach**, one mile south-east of town. The turn-off is at the eastern end of the causeway. Also here is a small **pitch and putt course** (☎ 48203) costing €2.55 per round, but you will need your own clubs. To reach Rosscarbery's centre coming from Clonakilty, turn right at the end of the causeway just before the unmissable Celtic Ross Hotel.

Getting There & Away There's one bus a day from Cork (leaving at 9am) to Rosscarbery (€9.80, 1½ hours) via Clonakilty. This service continues to Baltimore, Schull and Skibbereen (€3.75, 25 minutes).

Castle Salem

The most surprising aspect of this 15th-century castle (☎ 023-48381, Rosscarbery; adult/family €2.55/6.35; call ahead for guided tour; open daily year round), originally called Benduff Castle, is the entrance. In the 17th century, a house was built onto one of the 3m-thick castle walls, and at the top of its carpeted staircase an ordinary-looking door opens onto the 1st floor of the castle. Otherwise the castle is slowly crumbling away.

Cromwell gave it to an English soldier, Major Apollo Morris, who later became a Quaker. He renamed it Shalom, Hebrew for peace, which was corrupted into Salem. An old Quaker churchyard is behind the wall on the right immediately after entering the grounds. William Penn (founder of Pennsylvania) is said to have visited Morris in the house.

Castle Salem is signposted off the N71 Skibbereen road west of Rosscarbery. The entrance is through a farmyard. Accommodation is available in the 17-century house attached to the castle (see Places to Stay later).

CORK

Drombeg Stone Circle

Of the many stone circles in western Cork, this particular group of 17 stones, dating from around 100 BC and excavated in 1957, is particularly impressive, not least because of its stunning setting. On the south-western side a horizontal stone (the axial stone), with ancient markings carved on it, faces two taller stones (portal stones) on the north-eastern side. The axis of these two stones and the recumbent one is aligned to sunset on the winter solstice (21 December).

Travelling from Clonakilty, the N71 crosses a causeway at Rosscarbery. Just past the end of the causeway, beside the Orchard B&B, a road is signposted off to the left for Glandore, Coppinger's Court and assorted B&Bs. Some way along this road the stones are signposted to the left and a rough road continues to a small car park; from there a path leads to the circle.

Glandore & Union Hall

☎ 028

The exquisite fishing villages of Glandore (Cuan Dor) and Union Hall burst into life in summer when well-off boating folk arrive, something that would surely have dismayed William Thompson (1785–1833), who established a commune in Glandore as a model for his socialist philosophy. Marx refers to him in *Das Kapital*.

Union Hall, accessible from Glandore via a narrow road bridge over the estuary, was named after the 1800 Act of Union, which abolished the separate Irish Parliament. Its equally unfortunate Irish name, Bréantrá, means 'foul beach'. The author Jonathan Swift came here in 1723 to grieve over the death of his friend Vanessa.

Ceim Hill Museum This small museum *(☎ 36280, Union Hall; adult/child €2.55/1.25; open 10am-7pm daily year round)* is run by Teresa O'Mahony, who practises folk medicine in her ancient farmhouse. It's recommended for its wonderful mixture of eccentricity and genuine artefacts, not to mention the spectacular views from the winding track. The museum is signposted off the road to Castletownsend from Union Hall.

Places to Stay There are a couple of pleasant options in the area.

Meadow Camping Park (☎ 33280, e the_meadow@oceanfree.net, Rosscarbery road, Glandore) Tent site €11.50-12.70. Open mid-Mar-Sept. This park is 2km east of Glandore on the R597 to Rosscarbery.

Maria's Schoolhouse (☎/fax 33002, e mariasschoolhouse@eircom.net, Cahergal, Union Hall) Beds in 10-bed dorm €10.15, private rooms with en suite facilities €38-45. If prizes were being handed out for hostels then this would have to be the frontrunner. A stunning conversion of a 19th-century school building, it has comfortable and cheerful dorms. Maria cooks dinners on request for €19 per person (vegetarians catered for) and the buffet breakfast costs €6.35. The hostel also organises sea-kayaking trips exploring the coastline close by. To get there turn right after crossing the causeway into Union Hall and continue through the village following the sign for Skibbereen. It's signposted at the edge of town about 1km from the centre.

Newtown Lodge (☎ 48007, Rosscarbery) Rooms €25 per person. This pleasant B&B is on the other side of the N71 from the centre and is signposted.

Bay View House (☎ 33115, Glandore) Singles/doubles €31.75/50.80, €38/64 July & Aug. This newly refurbished place has the best views in the area; ask for Room 1 or 3.

Seascape B&B (☎ 33920, Union Hall) Rooms €24 per person. We can highly recommend this attractive B&B, which has huge rooms, great views and is excellent value. Look for the large stone house on the water's edge.

Ardagh House (☎/fax 33571, Union Hall) Singles/doubles €32.40/50.75. This place is also located on the waterfront and has an elegant seafood restaurant (open for dinner only from April to October).

Castle Salem (☎ 48381, fax 48388, e mdaly@unison.ie, w www.castlesalem.com, Rosscarbery) B&B €20-25 per person. Open Feb-Nov. Service and hospitality is excellent here. You can stay in a 17th-century house on the estate; ask for the bed that Penn slept in.

Places to Eat You'll be lucky to find anywhere serving food in Union Hall or Glandore from November to March, except at the weekend. If you find yourself in such a situation head to Kikshaw's pub in Leap, 3km from Union Hall.

Pilgrim's Rest (☎ 48063, 6 South Square, Rosscarbery) Breakfast €6.30, light meals & snacks €3.75-8.25. This laid-back, licensed cafe doubles as a bookshop.

O'Callaghan Walshe's Seafood Restaurant (☎ 48125, The Square, Rosscarbery) Starters €7.55-12, mains €20.25-27.30. Open 6.30pm-9.15pm Wed-Sun; Fri & Sat only Nov-Feb. This pricey restaurant serves excellent seafood and generous portions.

The Rectory (☎ 33072, Glandore) Open 7pm-9.30pm Easter-Sept. This fine-dining restaurant is in a manor house on the R597 between Glandore and Union Hall. It has lovely views across gardens and Glandore Harbour.

Getting There & Away Although buses do not pass through these two villages, they do stop in nearby Leap (3km north) and most hostel and B&B owners will pick you up from here if you pre-arrange it.

SKIBBEREEN
☎ 028 • pop 1926

Traffic-blighted Skibbereen (Sciobairín) owes its existence to Algerians who raided nearby Baltimore in 1631. The frightened English settlers moved north-east, establishing two settlements that grew into Skibbereen. For a long time the town was associated with its Protestant founders but during the Famine years it became known for the sufferings of the local Catholic peasantry. The repercussions were long-lasting: nearly half the local population emigrated in the first half of the 20th century.

Today the town prospers from its Friday market (12.30pm to 2.30pm) and a steady influx of tourists on the western Cork trail. The town attracts lots of younger visitors on a tight budget and as a result you can get good value for money in Skibbereen.

For three days in July Skibbereen hosts a traditional music festival when the streets and pubs come alive with music day and night. For more information contact ⓔ skibbereen fleadh@hotmail.com.

Orientation

The main landmark is a statue, dedicated to the heroes of the many Irish rebellions against the British, which stands at the junction of three roads. Market St heads south past the post office to Lough Hyne and Baltimore. The main shopping street, Main St, leads to a junction with Ilen St, which heads west over the river to Ballydehob and Bantry. North St heads towards the main Cork road.

Information

The tourist office (☎ 21766) is on North St and opens 9.15am to 1pm and 2.15pm to 5.30pm weekdays October to May; 9am to 6pm Monday to Saturday June and September; and 9am to 7pm daily July and August. *The Skibbereen Trail* takes you on a historical walking tour of the town and is available from the tourist office, newsagents and the Heritage Centre on Upper Bridge St for €1.25.

There is an Allied Irish Bank with ATM on Bridge St. For Internet access go to coffee.pot.com (☎ 087 244 2550) at the Regal petrol station on the R596 at the eastern edge of town. It opens 10.30am to 7pm Monday to Friday and 11am to 6pm at the weekend. Fifteen minutes costs €1.90.

Hourihane's Laundrette is in an alleyway off Bridge St near where it bends to the right in the direction of Schull. It opens 10am to 10pm daily. There's also West Cork Dry Cleaners (☎ 21627) at 49 Bridge St, opposite Eldon Hotel.

The Heritage Centre

Built on the site of the town's old gasworks, this place (☎ 40900, Old Gasworks Bldg, Upper Bridge St; adult/child €3.80/1.90; open 10am-6pm Tues-Sat, last admission 5.15pm) houses two exhibitions. The main one is very informative and covers the Famine with particular emphasis on the local experience through audiovisual and interactive displays. Skibbereen was particularly

CORK

hard hit and you can hear first-hand experiences spoken through actors (even Jeremy Irons gets in on the act).

The second, smaller exhibition tells the story of nearby Lough Hyne, the first marine nature reserve in Ireland, through a 15-minute film and photographs.

West Cork Arts Centre

This place is on North St, next to the church (☎ 22090; admission free; open 10am-6pm Mon-Sat). It hosts 13 art exhibitions each year with a focus on local artists, and in summer it often stages something theatrical or musical. The notice board at the entrance provides useful information about what's on.

Abbeystrewery Cemetery

This cemetery, 1km east of the centre on the N71 to Schull, is home to mass graves of 8000 to 10,000 people who died during the Famine.

Activities

If you are interested in learning about traditional music, dance and song, contact the **West Cork School of Traditional Music** (☎ 087 244 2550) or ask at coffee.pot.com (see Information earlier).

Places to Stay

Hideaway Camping & Caravan Park (☎ 33280 or 22254, e the_hideaway@ocean free.net, R596) Tent & 2 people €11.45-12.70. Open late Apr-mid-Sept. This park is 1km south-east of town on the road to Castletownsend.

Russagh Mill Hostel & Adventure Centre (☎ 22451, Skibbereen) Tent & 2 people €8.90-10, dorms €10-12.70, private rooms €30-35. This place is 1.5km south-east of town on the R596. It was once a corn mill and much of the old machinery is still lying around. The owner is an experienced mountaineer and canoeist. For between €10 and €13 you can join in a day's **kayaking, rock climbing** (up the side of the hostel building) or whatever may be going on. It's a popular place with families and children.

Bridge House (☎ 21273, Bridge St) Singles/doubles €23/45 without bathroom. This

friendly B&B is easily the best place to stay in town. The lavish Victorian-style decor is quite seductive and there is a spa bath in the bathroom.

Lenroy House (☎ 22751, 10 North St) En suites from €23-25 per person. This place, opposite the West Cork Arts Centre, offers good value for money.

Eldon Hotel (☎ 22000, fax 22191, e welcome@eldon-hotel.ie, Bridge St) Rooms €35-38 per person Oct-Apr, €45 per person May-Sept, including breakfast. Each room in this 19th-century hotel has been individually decorated and, although quite small, they are very comfortable. It's rumoured that this is where Michael Collins spent his last night before being killed.

Places to Eat

O'Donovan Cafe (☎ 22537, 12 Bridge St) Snacks & sandwiches €2.55-4.45. This wholefood cafe serves soups, terrines, sandwiches and rolls. Vegetarians are well catered for.

King's Palace (☎ 21301, 31 Bridge St) Starters €2.80-4.45, mains €4.80-12.60. Open noon-2pm Wed-Sun & 5pm-midnight daily. This Chinese restaurant has a huge menu which includes European dishes as well.

Kalbo's Bistro (☎ 21515, 48 North St) Snacks €3.20-5, dinner mains €10.80-17.15. Open for lunch and dinner, this modern place serves delicious soup, sandwiches, salads and a selection of main meals that includes a couple of vegetarian options.

Self-caterers should go to **Fields Supermarket** on Bridge St near the Market St corner.

Getting There & Away

Bus Éireann buses run four-times daily (three on Saturday and Sunday) to Cork (€11.70, one hour 50 minutes), and three-times daily (one only on Sunday) to Schull (€4.25, 30 minutes) from outside the Eldon Hotel on Main St.

Getting Around

Bicycles can be hired from Roycroft's Cycles (☎ 21235) on Ilen St opposite the West

Cork Hotel; this building acted as a soup kitchen during the Famine. Wheel Escapes operates a drop-off and pick-up bike-hire service for €8.90 per day with helmet, lock and tool bag; ask at the tourist office for details.

BALTIMORE
☎ 028 • pop 260

Just 13km down the River Ilen from Skibbereen, the population of picturesque Baltimore swells enormously during the summer months as sailing folk, anglers, divers and visitors to Sherkin and Clear Islands flock in. The harbour is dominated by the remains of the Dún na Sead (Fort of the Jewels), one of nine castles built in the area by the O'Driscoll clan, as well as the unusual beacon. Make sure you take a stroll to the Beacon at sunset for some beautiful views of outlying islands.

Information
The small tourist office (☎ 21766) at the harbour opens May to September but lots of useful information is pinned up on a board outside in low season. Staff can also arrange accommodation on both Clear and Sherkin Islands.

Activities
There's some great **diving** to be had on the reefs around Fastnet Rock and a number of nearby shipwrecks. **Aquaventures Dive Centre** (*see The Stone House under Places to Stay*) charges €51 for one dive with gear rental, €32 if you have your own wetsuit and fins, and €22 without rental.

The **Baltimore Sailing School** (☎ 20141) provides sailing courses from May to September for both beginners and advanced sailors.

For **deep-sea fishing** trips phone **Michael Walsh** (☎ 20352, 21675) or call in at **Algiers Inn Angling Centre** (☎ 20145, Main St). You could also try **Nick Dent** (☎ 21709).

You can hire fishing tackle from Cotter's Grocery Store on the harbour.

Atlantic Sea Kayaking (☎ 20511) has sea-kayaking expeditions from here or from Schull (see later in this chapter). Day or overnight trips (camping on nearby islands) are available.

Special Events
Over the third weekend of May, Baltimore stages a seafood festival: jazz bands perform and mussels and prawns are on offer in the pubs. Contact the tourist office for more details.

Places to Stay
Rolf's Hostel (☎/fax 20289, Baltimore Hill) Dorms €11.40-12.70, doubles €34. Set in a large garden on the edge of town, this pleasant and friendly hostel has a cafe and offers bike hire and a laundry service.

Casey's of Baltimore (☎ 20197, fax 20509, ⓔ caseys@eircom.net, Skibbereen road) Rooms €49.50 per person Oct-May, €59 per person June-Sept. This place has large rooms with great views and elegant, simple decor.

The Stone House (☎/fax 20511, ⓔ aqua vent@aquaventures.ie, Lifeboat Rd) Rooms €28-32 per person with a €7.60 surcharge for singles June-Aug. Rooms sleep one to four people and if you want to go diving there are special packages available to guests (see Activities earlier).

Fastnet House (☎/fax 20515, ⓔ fastnet house@eircom.net, Main St) Singles/doubles €38/57, €23 per person Nov-Feb. This early 19th-century house offers nice rooms near the harbour.

Places to Eat
Casey's of Baltimore (see Places to Stay) Mains €8.25-9.50. You can get breakfast, lunch and dinner here along with great views over the bay. The fish is always fresh and there are different specials each day.

Café Art (see Rolf's Hostel under Places to Stay) Baguettes €3.80-5, light meals €6.30-9.50, mains €12-16.50. One of the best places to eat without busting the budget is attached to Rolf's Hostel in a cafe that doubles as an art gallery. Dishes are mainly European and the smells emanating from here are wonderful.

Declan McCarthy's Bar (☎ 20263, The Square) Bar food €5.70-10.15, restaurant mains €11.45-17.70. This is the place for

CORK

traditional Irish food, even though the Beatles decor is not particularly Irish.

Chez Youen *(☎ 20136, The Quay)* Set menus €23.50-31. Open nightly in summer, Thur-Sun the rest of the year. This restaurant overlooking the harbour serves good French-style seafood. A sample from the menu: melon with port for starters followed by poached salmon with fennel sauce.

Island Cottage Restaurant *(☎ 38102, Heir Island)* This place on nearby Heir Island is highly recommended by locals and is only open in summer. You will need to book well ahead. Call ☎ 39153 or 22001 for details of boats to Heir Island.

Getting There & Away
From Monday to Saturday there's one bus a day to Baltimore from Skibbereen with an extra service on Fridays and during July and August (€2.80, 20 minutes).

From June to mid-September a boat leaves Baltimore for Schull via Heir Island at 10am, 1.45pm and 4.40pm, returning from Schull at 11.30am, 3pm and 5.40pm; call ☎ 39153 for details. A single crossing costs €7.60; bikes are free.

CLEAR ISLAND
☎ 028 • pop 150
Rugged Clear Island (Oileán Cléire), also called Cape Clear, is the second-most-southerly point of Ireland after Fastnet Rock, 6km to the south-west. Clear Island is also an Irish-speaking (Gaeltacht) area, with one shop, a few B&Bs and three pubs. It's a place for walking, exploring archaeological ruins and bird-watching: the island is probably the best place in Europe for viewing Manx shearwater and other sea birds. Each year at the beginning of September the island hosts a week-long storytelling festival (see the boxed text 'Cape Clear Island Storytelling Festival').

A number of books have been written about the ecology of the island: *The Natural History of Cape Clear*, edited by JTR Sharrock is available in most bookshops in western Cork. *Cape Clear Magic* was written by an American expat, Chuck Kruger, who founded the storytelling festival. This book explains his fascination for the island and why he has made this remote place his home for the last nine years.

The island has its own Web site at Ⓦ www.oileán-chleire.ie/index.htm.

Orientation & Information
The island is 5km long and just over 1.5km wide at its broadest point. It narrows in the middle where an isthmus divides the northern and southern harbours. There's a tourist information post (☎ 39100) beyond the pier, next to the coffee shop. It opens 4pm to 6pm daily, July and August. If it's closed the coffee shop stocks a useful *Walkers' Guide* (€2.55) as well as a useful pamphlet titled *Oileán Chléire – An Island for All Seasons* which includes a map of the island and a listing of all the activities and accommodation you'll find here.

You'll find public toilets down at the harbour.

Things to See
The small **heritage centre** *(open 2pm-5.30pm daily June-Aug)* has exhibits on the island's history and culture. There are fine views looking north across the water to the Mizen Head Peninsula. From here it's a short walk downhill to the shop and pubs.

The ruins of **Dunamore Castle**, the stronghold of the O'Driscoll clan, can be seen perched on a rock on the north-western side of the island (follow the track from the harbour).

Bird-Watching
The white-fronted, two-storey **bird observatory** is by the harbour. Turn right at the end of the pier and it's 100m along. It's worth calling in to ask about any planned bird-watching trips.

Clear Island is famous for large movements of sea birds, especially in July and August, when Manx shearwater, gannet, fulmar and kittiwake regularly fly past the island's southern end. The guillemot is the only notable sea bird that breeds on the island; the others live on the westerly Kerry rocks and fly past each morning heading for the Celtic and Irish Seas. In the evening they

Cape Clear Island Storytelling Festival

The brainchild of an American expat writer who moved to the island in the early 1990s, the Cape Clear Island Storytelling Festival brings hundreds of people to Cape Clear from all reaches of the globe to celebrate writing and exchange stories and experiences. Activities such as boat trips to Fastnet lighthouse, bird-watching, archaeological and nature walks take place throughout festival. It's helped to boost the island's economy enormously and attracts sponsors from big businesses in Ireland.

The festival usually takes place over three days at the beginning of September. Tickets cost €38 for adults and €25 for children under 16. You should book tickets and accommodation well ahead – the festival is getting more and more popular each year and there's only space for 300. For more information contact Christine Sawyer on ☎ 028-39116 or e storytelling@ireland.com. The Web site is w http://indigo.ie/~stories.

return and the sight is equally amazing: in summer up to 35,000 shearwater can fly past in an hour, just skimming the surface of the water.

The best place from which to view the birds is Blananarragaun, the south-western tip of the island. To reach it from the pier, head up to the shop and turn right, following the sign for the camp site. When the road ends, head due south to the end of the spur of land. For a guided bird-watching tour contact the adventure centre at Cape Clear Island Hostel (see Places to Stay).

Other Activities

Cape Clear Island Hostel (see Places to Stay) houses an **adventure centre** that arranges a number of outdoor activities, including kayaking, diving, fishing and whale or dolphin watching. For guided walks covering historical, archaeological or ecological aspects of the island phone ☎ 39157 (during summer).

For trips to Fastnet or **bird-watching boat trips** phone ☎ 39153.

Irish language courses are run by Ciaran and Mary O'Driscoll from time to time. Ask at Ciarán Danny Mike's (see Places to Eat) or phone ☎ 39153 for details.

And if there's anything you need to know about **goat husbandry** contact the resident goat farmer on ☎ 39126. He makes goat ice-cream and cheese, available for tastings.

Places to Stay

Don't expect too much from the accommo-

dation here. It's all pretty basic, as it ought to be. The *camp site* (☎ 39119) costs €3.80 per person per night and opens June-Sept.

Cape Clear Island Hostel (☎ 39198, fax 39144, South Harbour) €8.90 per person. Open Mar-mid-Oct. An Óige's fairly basic hostel is in the large white building at the south harbour.

Cluain Mara (☎ 39153, 39172) Rooms €21/23 per person with/without bathroom. B&B is available year round here; evening meals cost €12.70. It is signposted but not so easy to find – ask at the last of the three pubs or at the coffee shop.

Ard Na Gaoithe (☎ 39160, The Glen) Rooms €23 per person. This place is an uphill walk from the south harbour but is a nice place to stay. If you haven't booked ahead check if the proprietor, Eileen, is in the coffee shop before trudging up there. Evening meals are available in summer.

Self-catering cottages are available. Ask at the coffee shop or Ciarán Danny Mike's (see Places to Stay).

Places to Eat

In summer there's a *chip van* at the north harbour.

Siopa Beag (☎ 39145, North Harbour) This coffee shop and grocery store has a few supplies for self-caterers.

Chistin Cléire (☎ 39145) Open Easter-Oct. Near the pier, this is the only restaurant; it serves light meals.

Ciarán Danny Mike's (☎ 39172) Bar meals around €6.35-11.45. This is the only

CORK

place serving pub food year round. The helpings are enormous.

The Night Jar *(☎ 39102, North Harbour)* Open June-Aug. This bar opens seasonally and serves lunches from midday.

Getting There & Away
Boats leave Schull pier for Clear Island once a day in June and September, three times a day in July and August. The one-way/return fare is €7.65/11.45. Call Kieran Molloy on ☎ 28278 for more details.

The boat from Baltimore (☎ 39119) takes 45 minutes to cover the 11km journey and it's a stunning trip on a clear day, retracing the route the Algerians took through the harbour when they launched their attack in 1631. From Baltimore boats leave at 2.15pm and 7pm daily (plus noon and 5pm on Sunday in June), June to September. Coming back they leave Clear Island at 9am and 6pm Monday to Saturday, and 11am, 1pm, 4pm and 6pm (noon and 6pm only in September) on Sunday. The return fare is €10.15/18; bikes travel free.

Mizen Head Peninsula

From Skibbereen the road winds west to Ballydehob. Expats from Britain and northern Europe are scattered across western Cork. While Kinsale attracts the well heeled, the less economically advantaged – or blow-ins as they are semi-affectionately called – have discovered the land around Ballydehob. They help breathe new life into the area, as many local young people leave to look for work elsewhere.

From Ballydehob the road goes west to Schull, with Mt Gabriel (407m) identifiable by the two tracking spheres, part of an air-and-sea monitoring system, perched on the summit.

From the top of Mt Gabriel (which can be reached by road) and most high ground on the peninsula, there are views of the Fastnet lighthouse on a rock 11km off the coast. The first lighthouse was built in 1854 but

was replaced in 1906 by a sturdier one, which is now fully automated.

The next stop west is Goleen, a small village on the way to Crookhaven, Barleycove and Three Castle Head. Returning from Mizen Head you can take the spectacular coastal road that traces Dunmanus Bay for most of the way to Durrus. At Durrus, one road heads for Bantry while the other turns west to the Sheep's Head Peninsula.

For more insight into this beautiful and fascinating part of Ireland read *The North Side of the Mizen* by Patrick McCarthy and Richard Hawkes. It delves into the history, customs and legends of the area.

SCHULL
☎ 028 • pop 650

A small, laid-back fishing village between the foot of Mt Gabriel and a picturesque harbour, Schull (pronounced skull) gets as touristy as anywhere on the Ring of Kerry from June to September, but relapses into tranquillity during the rest of the year. For some Irish people, civilised Ireland ends here and they are surprised that people want to venture into or live in the wilds farther south.

Schull hosts a number of sailing events during the year which attract visitors from far and wide.

Orientation & Information
Schull's shops and hotels are strung along one long main street that runs parallel with the harbour. Halfway along, a road to the left leads to the planetarium and hostel. Continuing straight along the main street will take you to Goleen on the R592.

The Allied Irish Bank branch at the top of Main St has an ATM and bureau de change. The Laundry Basket (☎ 086 847 0555) on Main St opens 9am to 6pm daily during summer and 9.30am to 5pm Monday to Saturday the rest of the year.

Schull Planetarium
In the grounds of Schull Community College, the Republic's only planetarium *(☎ 28552, Colla Rd; adult/child €4.45/ 2.55; open 3pm-5pm Sun May & Sept; 3pm-*

5pm Tues & Sat, 7pm-9pm Thur June; 2pm-5pm Tues-Sat, 7pm-9pm Mon & Thur July & Aug) has an 8-metre dome and a video and slide show. There's a star show most days, which is included in the admission price.

The planetarium is at the Goleen end of the village on the Colla road, just past Schull Backpackers' Lodge. You can also reach it by walking along the Foreshore Path from the pier.

Other Things to See
If you would like to visit a local cheese-making farm, contact either **Gubbeen Cheese** (☎ 28231) or **West Cork Natural Cheeses** (☎ 28593) for directions.

Activities
There's a challenging walk up **Mt Gabriel** from Schull, making a round trip of about 14km. The mountain was once mined for copper and there are Bronze Age remains as well as 19th-century mine shafts and chimneys. Less active people could try the short Foreshore Path from the pier out to Roaringwater Bay and the many nearby islands.

The very hilly and interesting **Coosheen Golf Links** (☎ 28182, *Coosheen)* offers superb views over Schull Harbour and out to Long Island. It costs €15.25 for 18 holes and €12.70 for club hire, although it's members only on Saturday afternoon and Sunday morning. The course is signposted 2.2km from Schull off the R592 to Ballydehob.

Schull Watersports Centre (☎ 28554, *The Pier)* rents out windsurfing equipment for €19 per half day and snorkelling gear for €6.35 per day. Diving trips can also be arranged. It opens 9.30am-12.30pm and 2pm-4.30pm Monday and Wednesday to Saturday.

Atlantic Sea Kayaking (☎ 28554) has sea kayaking expeditions from here or from Baltimore. Day or overnight trips (camping on nearby islands) are available.

For a fishing trip contact **Rooster Deep Sea Angling** (☎ 086 824 0642). You can also go **pony trekking** from *Colla House Hotel* (☎ 28105).

Places to Stay
Schull Backpackers' Lodge (☎/fax 28681, e schullbackpackers@tinet.ie, Colla Rd) Dorms €10.15, singles €15.25, doubles €30.50/35.60 for shared bath/en suite. This timber lodge is in a quiet, forested location. Camping is sometimes possible.

Twelve Arch Hostel (☎/fax 37232, e info @12archhostel.ie, Palm Grove, Church Rd, Ballydehob) Dorms €8.90/10.15 in low/high season, double en suites €30, camping €3.80 per person including a hot shower. Open year round. If you find yourself out of luck in Schull try this very clean and comfortable hostel in nearby Ballydehob. Its en suite rooms are better than some B&Bs. Laundry facilities are available. The twice-daily Clonakilty to Schull bus stops in Ballydehob.

Schull Central (☎ 28227, Main St) Singles/doubles €28/45. This friendly place has comfortable clean rooms. Rates go down a little in winter.

Adele's (☎ 28459, Main St) B&B €25.40 per person. If you're having trouble finding a single room it's worth asking here.

Glencairn (☎ 28007, Ardmanagh Drive) Singles/doubles from €29/45.75. This place has three doubles and one single room. It's only 100m from Main St.

East End Hotel (☎ 28101, fax 28012, e eastendhotel@eircom.net, Main St) Singles/doubles €47/89 May-Sept, from €38/63.50 the rest of the year. This hotel is at the Ballydehob end of Main St and has a pub with open fires.

Places to Eat
You'll find that most places offer local produce such as Gubbeen cheese and oak-smoked bacon on their menus. Self-caterers can try the two **supermarkets** on the main street.

The Courtyard (☎ 28390, Main St) Snacks & light meals €3.20-9.50. This delicatessen and coffee shop sells a wide range of local cheeses and meats. Behind the deli is **The Courtyard Bar** where you are just as likely to see people sipping tea as downing a pint of Guinness.

Organic Oasis (☎ 27886, Main St)

CORK

Although there's nowhere to sit down here you can buy wholefoods to takeaway, as well as alternative remedies.

Waterside Inn *(☎ 28203, Main St)* Bar food €2.30-10, restaurant mains €16.45-21. This casual pub serves what is probably the best seafood chowder in Ireland (€4.80).

Adele's *(see Places to Stay)* Main dishes around €12. To sample locally baked bread with coffee there's nowhere better than Adele's. At night it reopens as a restaurant serving modern dishes and organic produce.

Getting There & Away
Buses leave Skibbereen at 1.05pm and travel to Schull (€4.25, 30 minutes). Boats for Clear Island and Sherkin Island leave from the pier. See the Baltimore Getting There & Away section for details of the Schull to Baltimore boat service.

Getting Around
For bus and taxi services around the Mizen phone Betty Johnson's Bus Hire on ☎ 28410 or 087 265 6078.

Bikes can be hired from Schull Backpackers' Lodge (see Places to Stay) or from Cotter's Yard (☎ 28889, after hours and Sunday ☎ 35185), Main St, for €10.10 per day. Wheel Escapes operates a drop-off and pick-up bike hire service for €8.90 per day with helmet, lock and tool bag. Contact Mizen Tourism in Goleen or the tourist office in Skibbereen for details.

WEST OF SCHULL TO MIZEN HEAD
☎ 028
If you are driving or cycling take the coastal route from Schull to Goleen as there are some great views out to Clear Island and Fastnet lighthouse on a clear day. The landscape gets very interesting and rocky around the hamlet of Toormore. From Goleen roads run out to Mizen Head and to the picturesque harbour village of Crookhaven.

By the roadside, between Schull and Goleen, is a Stone Age **altar wedge tomb**, one of 12 on the Mizen Peninsula. There are no signs but look for a small parking area surrounded by a low stone wall, exactly 7.2km from the centre of Schull.

Goleen
Mizen Tourism (☎ 35225, fax 35422) in Goleen at the eastern end of town opens year round. There's plenty of free information here on local sights and activities as well as bureau de change and Internet access.

If you fancy exploring the rugged landscape around here there are 13km **guided walks** between Goleen and Schull for €6.35 per person including tea. Ask at the tourist office.

If you hanker after artistic creativity it's worth coming to Goleen just to visit **The Ewe Art Centre** *(☎ 35492,* e *courses@theewe .com,* w *www.theewe.com, Goleen; one week's accommodation & three days' tuition €197 per person, nonparticipating residents €159 per person; open Easter-Oct)*, a magical artists' hideaway with pretty gardens and stunning views. Sheena and Kurt offer one-week creative escapes to let you try your hand at pottery and other handicrafts such as puppet making, tiles and decorating and sculpture. Shorter courses are also available as well as nonresidential ones. Nonartists may be content to check out the small shop where Sheena's colourful work is on display. Look for a blue house tucked into the hillside. It's signposted to the right as you enter Goleen from Schull.

Places to Stay & Eat There are several options in and around Goleen.

Altar Restaurant *(☎ 35254, Toormore)* Singles/doubles €31.75/50.80 with breakfast. Lunch €7.60-10.15, 3-course set dinner €31.75. Open lunch & dinner daily, weekends only Oct-Mar. This white-washed, slate-floored restaurant is on the R591, about 8km west of Schull. At lunchtime you can sample dishes such as oysters in stout. The Altar also has a couple of well equipped rooms. There are remains of a megalithic tomb on the hillside beside the restaurant.

Heron's Cove *(☎ 35225, fax 35422,* e *suehill@tinet.ie, Goleen)* Singles €31.75, doubles €49-63. Restaurant mains €16-20. This picture-perfect and peaceful B&B overlooks a small inlet, surrounded by fuschias. It's marvellous value for money with spacious rooms, friendly staff and hotel-standard facilities. Room 3 is particularly nice. The restaurant specialises in seafood dishes; it opens for lunch and dinner May to October, dinner only the rest of the year.

Fortview House (*☎/fax 35324, Gurtyowen, Toormore*) Rooms €35 per person. This remote B&B is on the road that turns off the R592 for Durrus (near the Altar Restaurant), about 1km north-east of Goleen.

The Green Kettle (*☎ 35033, Main St*) Lunch & snacks €2.70-5.70, dinner €12-16.50. This homely cafe serves cream teas, fish and chips, and toasted sandwiches during the day and more substantial meals for dinner.

Getting There & Away There's one bus a day that goes to Goleen from Skibbereen (€6.75, one hour five minutes) via Schull, leaving Skibbereen at 7.45pm. In the other direction buses leave Goleen at 7.45am and 5.30pm (5.30pm only on Sunday). Buses go no further down the peninsula than Goleen.

Crookhaven

The anymore-laid-back-and-it-would-be-in-a-coma Crookhaven was built on the far side of a spur of land that runs eastwards from the mainland, enclosing a harbour. Crookhaven was once very important as the most westerly harbour along the coast. Mail from America was collected here and it was a busy port for sailing and fishing ships from all over the world.

On the other side of the harbour you'll see the remains of a stone quarry that closed in 1939. Today the village still attracts sailors and there are some nice swimming beaches nearby.

Galley-Cove House (*☎/fax 35137, e galleycovehouse@hotmail.com*) Singles/doubles €38/57. This friendly, modern home is half a kilometre south-west of town on the main road. There are some lovely views out to the Atlantic Ocean and Fastnet lighthouse from here.

The Turning Point (*☎/fax 35520*) Singles/doubles €38/57. Open year round. This lovely B&B has a sauna for guests and is

nicely situated on a high point in Crookhaven for great views out to Clear Island.

O'Sullivan's Bar (*☎ 35319*) Snacks €2.55-5. This waterfront bar serves sandwiches and soup year round.

Crookhaven Inn (*☎ 35309*) Open Apr-Oct. This small, intimate bar next to the sailing club serves dishes such as steak-and-stout pie.

Brow Head

This is the most southerly point on the Irish mainland and well worth the walk there. As you leave Crookhaven you will notice a turn-off to the left marked 'Brow Head'. We suggest you leave your car at the bottom of the hill. The track is very rough and narrow and there's nowhere to pull over should you meet a tractor coming the other way. After about 1km the road ends. Continue on a walking track to Brow Head where you'll see an observation tower. This is the place from where Gugliemo Marconi transmitted his first message (to Cornwall) and received a reply.

Barleycove

This is western Cork's most splendid beach and, because a smaller beach nearer the camp site attracts holidaymakers, Barleycove itself is never crowded. The sand dunes here were thrown up by a tidal wave that hit the coast after an earthquake in Lisbon in 1755. The beach is a great place for children, with long stretches of sand and a safe sandy area where a stream flows down to the sea. Access to the beach is via a boardwalk and pontoon bridge to protect the surrounding wetlands.

Mizen Head

Mizen Head Visitor Centre (*☎ 35115, Mizen Head; adult/concession €4.45/3.50, under-12s €2.50, under-fives admission free; open 10.30am-5pm daily mid-Mar-May & Oct; 10am-6pm daily June-Sept; 11am-4pm Sat & Sun Nov-mid-Mar*) is located in the Keeper's House and Engine Room of the Mizen Head Fog Signal Station, which was completed in 1909 and became automated in 1993. It complements Fastnet lighthouse and gives extra protection to Atlantic-bound

CORK

ships. Propped up on a small island, it's connected to the mainland by a superb suspension bridge that gives exciting views of the nearby rock formations. The bridge was built in its entirety elsewhere and lifted into position here by cables.

You can see how the keeper lived and how the lighthouse worked both before and after automation. The exhibition also covers the ecology and geology of the Mizen Head; there is a *cafe* and the obligatory souvenir shop.

On a clear day the vision out of the windows will enthral you. Look out for gannets swirling and diving above the rocks. In July and August you can see whales from Mizen Head, and seals can often be seen from the bridge throughout the year, when the waters are calm.

NORTHSIDE OF THE PENINSULA

Although there's not as much to see on this side of the peninsula, it's well worth driving along the coast road as you get some wonderful views out to Sheep's Head Peninsula and beyond to the magnificent Beara Peninsula.

Three Castle Head

A prime reason for making the journey to Three Castle Head, at the north-western tip of the peninsula, is to visit 13th-century **Mizen Castle** on the headland. According to the *Annals of Innisfallen* it was built in 1217 and was once a stronghold of the O'Mahoney clan. Today it's a lonely ruin by the side of a supposedly haunted lake, with a sheer drop to the sea behind it.

Durrus & Around

The coastal road on the northern side of the peninsula takes you past the ruins of another **medieval castle** at Dunmanus.

In Durrus (Dúras) you could drop into **Kilvarock Garden** (*☎ 027-61111; adult/child €3.80/2.55; open 2.30pm-5.30pm Sat & Sun, other times by appointment*).

Dunbeacon Campsite (*☎/fax 027-61246)* Camping per adult/child €3.20/1.25. Open year round. This park is about 5.5km south-west of Durrus on the R591.

Blairs Cove House (*☎ 027-61127, Durrus)* Singles/doubles €115/190, €76/140 Nov-Feb. Set dinner in the mainly seafood restaurant costs €39 per person. This luxury oasis, 2km south-west of Durrus, is set in acres of gardens with wonderful views over Dunmanus Bay to the Sheep's Head and Beara peninsulas. The restaurant opens for dinner only, Monday to Saturday during July and August.

BANTRY
☎ 027 • pop 2936

Bantry (Beanntraí) narrowly missed fame in the late 18th century thanks to storms that prevented a French fleet landing to join the United Irishmen's rebellion. A local Englishman, Richard White, was rewarded with a peerage for trying to alert the British military in Cork. His grand home is open to the public and this, along with an exhibition devoted to the events of 1796, is now the town's main attraction.

Before Irish independence, Bantry Bay was a major anchorage for the British navy and, after WWII, Spanish trawlers were regular visitors. The bay's deep waters were also exploited by Gulf Oil, who built an oil terminal on Whiddy Island, bringing unexpected prosperity.

The island is close to Bantry Harbour and can be seen from the Cork road when entering town. In 1979, 51 lives were lost when fire broke out at the terminal. The disused storage tanks are still visible as you approach Bantry from Glengarriff or Kilochrane.

Orientation & Information

The two main roads into Bantry converge on the large Wolfe Tone Square, now mostly a free car park. A small market is held here on Friday and some of the region's many expats, who are known as 'blow-ins' or 'hippies' to the locals, come in to sell their wares.

The tourist office (*☎ 63084*), in the old courthouse at the eastern end of Wolf Tone Square, opens 9.15am to 5.30pm Monday to Saturday, May to September, and 10am to 6pm on Sunday, July and August. The post office is on Blackrock Rd and there's an Allied Irish Bank with ATM on New St.

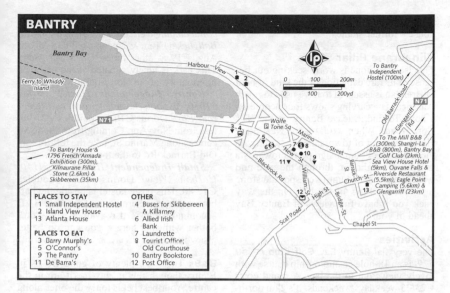

BANTRY

Bantry Bay

Harbour View

Ferry to Whiddy Island

To Bantry Independent Hostel (100m)

N71

0   100   200m
0   100   200yd

Glengarriff Rd

Old Barrack Road

N71

Wolfe Tone Sq

Marina

Street

To The Mill B&B (300m), Shangri-La B&B (800m), Bantry Bay Golf Club (2km), Sea View House Hotel (5km), Ouvane Falls & Riverside Restaurant (5.5km), Eagle Point Camping (5.6km) & Glengarriff (23km)

To Bantry House & 1796 French Armada Exhibition (300m), Kilnaurane Pillar Stone (2.6km) & Skibbereen (35km)

Blackrock Rd

New St

William St

Barrack St

Church St

Bridge St

High St

Scart Road

Chapel St

PLACES TO STAY
1 Small Independent Hostel
2 Island View House
13 Atlanta House

PLACES TO EAT
3 Barry Murphy's
5 O'Connor's
9 The Pantry
11 De Barra's

OTHER
4 Buses for Skibbereen & Killarney
6 Allied Irish Bank
7 Laundrette
8 Tourist Office; Old Courthouse
10 Bantry Bookstore
12 Post Office

Bantry Bookstore (☎ 50064), New St, opens daily and has a stock of some local-interest and second-hand books. The laundrette (☎ 51403) is next to the tourist office but the entrance is on New St.

Bantry House & Gardens

Striking Bantry House (☎ 50047, Bantry Bay; admission €7.60, gardens only €2.55, children free; open 9am-6pm daily, extended hours July & Aug) is superbly situated overlooking the bay and set within acres of gardens. It was bought in 1739 by Richard White who was made Lord Bantry by the English in 1797.

Parts of the house date back to the mid-18th century, but the fine sea-facing northern front was added in 1840. Despite its air of fading gentility, the interior is noted for its French and Flemish tapestries and the eclectic collection of art and objets assembled by the 2nd earl of Bantry during his overseas peregrinations between 1820 and 1850.

But the gardens of Bantry House are its greatest glory and feature in the closing scenes of the film *Moll Flanders*. A vast lawn sweeps down towards the sea from the

front of the house and the formal Italian garden at the back has an enormous stairway offering spectacular views over the house and Bantry Bay. Come in May to see the ring of wisteria beautifully in bloom around the fountain.

The house is about 1km south-west of the centre on the N71.

It's possible to stay in one wing of the house (see Places to Stay).

1796 French Armada Exhibition Centre

Considering how Lord Bantry obtained his title it's ironic that the grounds of the house now harbour an exhibition (☎ 51796; adult €3.80, children free; open 10am-6pm daily Mar-Oct) recording the sorry saga of the attempted landing of the French Armada frigate *La Surveillante*. It was scuttled by the crew in 1796 and today lies 100 feet down in the bay. It was discovered in 1981 after sonar equipment was used in a salvage attempt of an exploded tanker. The exhibition includes a detailed history of the time, an exhibition about the salvage mission and a few artefacts rescued from the frigate. The centre is run independently of

CORK

Bantry House even though it's in the house's former stables.

Kilnaurane Pillar Stone

This isolated stone is worth seeking out because of its rare depiction of the kind of boat St Brendan is assumed to have used to reach America. The carving shows four people on a boat. To find it, leave Bantry on the N71 Cork road. When you reach Westlodge Hotel, 2km out of town, take the turning on the left. After 800m a sign points towards a gate on the right. Go through the gate and walk straight ahead until you spot the stone just over the brow of the hill. On the way back you'll have fine views of Bantry Bay ahead of you.

Activities

The very flat **Bantry Bay Golf Club** (☎ 50 579) is an 18-hole championship course with lovely views out to the bay. A round costs €23/25 weekdays/weekends. It's 2km northeast of town on the N71 to Killarney.

Organised Tours

George Plant Minibus Tours (☎ 50654, 086 239 8123) operates day trips to Mizen Head Peninsula on Tuesday and Thursday (€10.15), the Beara Peninsula on Monday, Friday and Saturday (€12.70) and to Kenmare and Gougane Barra Forest Park on Wednesday (€12.70).

You can reach Whiddy Island by boat (☎ 50310); it leaves from the pier daily between May and September (return €5.10).

Special Events

In the second week of May, Bantry holds a mussel fair with various musical events and free mussels distributed around the pubs.

The week-long West Cork Chamber Music Festival is held at Bantry House at the end of June and beginning of July. The house closes to the public during this time, although the garden, craft shop and tearoom remain open.

Places to Stay

Camping & Hostels The camp site and hostels are situated in and around Bantry.

Eagle Point Camping (☎ 50630, **e** eagle pointcamping@eircom.net, Glengarriff Rd, Ballylickey) Tent & 2 people €20.35 July & Aug, €19 at other times. Open May-Sept. This park is nicely situated at the end of a promontory, about 6km from town.

Bantry Independent Hostel (☎/fax 51050, **e** bantryhostel@eircom.net, Reenrour East) Dorms €10.15, doubles €22.90, less from Nov-Apr. Coming from the town centre along Marino St, take the left fork up Old Barrack Rd to the top of the hill.

Small Independent Hostel (☎ 51140, Harbour View) Dorms €8.90, doubles €17.80. This basic hostel is beside the harbour on the northern bank of the bay. B&B accommodation is also available but don't bother with that here – you can do better elsewhere.

B&Bs There are plenty of good B&Bs in Bantry though few of any merit are in the centre. Your best bet is to try the ones along Glengarriff Rd.

Island View House (☎ 50257, Harbour View) Rooms without en suite €19 per person. You can't do better than this place for good value. Rooms are basic but clean and comfortable with nice views.

Atlanta House (☎ 50237, Church St) Rooms €25 per person. This place offers the best value and quality in the centre.

The Mill (☎ 50278, Glengarriff Rd) Singles/doubles €31.75/57.20. This friendly place had just opened for business at the time of writing so everything should be fresh and new. A laundry service is available.

Shangri-La (☎ 50244, Glengarriff Rd) Singles/doubles from €31.75/50.80. This popular place is run by a charming couple who have created a very homely atmosphere. Breakfast is terrific. The only complaint is that rooms on the road side can be noisy.

Hotels There are a couple of good hotels to choose from.

Bantry House (see Bantry House & Gardens) Singles €108-120, doubles €190-216, including breakfast. Dinner €31.75. Romantics will jump at the chance to stay here. You get the use of the magnificent library and the gardens to yourself after the crowds have gone home.

Sea View House Hotel (☎ 50073, fax 51555, ℮ seaviewhousehotel@eircom.net, Ballylickey) Singles/doubles from €82/152 May-Sept, €70/100 the rest of the year. This four-star country house is on the N71 5km north-east of Bantry. If you reach a sharp bend where the road to Macroom is signposted, you've passed it.

Ouvane Falls & Riverside Restaurant (☎ 50056, Glengarriff Rd, Ballylickey) Singles €32, doubles €57-64. For the views it offers and the standard of rooms you can't beat this place, situated on a small inlet of Glengarriff Harbour. The restaurant serves lunch and dinner and there is live music in the lounge bar at the weekend.

Places to Eat

The Pantry (☎ 52181, New St) Snacks & light meals €2.35-7.55. Best of the few cafes, it's situated up a flight of stairs near Vickery's Inn. Alongside the usual salads, soups and sandwiches, you can get chicken burritos here.

Barry Murphy's (☎ 50900, The Quay) Sandwiches & light meals €2-6.30. Unexciting but good-value pub grub is available here.

De Barra's (New St) Mains €12.65-18.40. Open from 6.30pm Tues-Sat. The dishes here have a strong French influence; there is also a kids' menu.

O'Connor's (☎ 50221, Wolfe Tone Square) Mains €13.85-20.20. This is an acclaimed seafood restaurant where mussels are a speciality.

Getting There & Away

Bus Éireann has a service to Killarney (€11.70, 2¼ hours) via Glengarriff and Kenmare. The private Berehaven bus (☎ 70007) links Castletownbere with Bantry via Glengarriff. It leaves from the fire station in Wolfe Tone Square at noon and 5.50pm on Monday, and 3.45pm on Tuesday, Friday and Saturday.

Getting Around

Bikes can be hired at The Mill (see Places to Stay) for €8.90 per day.

Sheep's Head Peninsula

The least visited of Cork's three peninsulas, Sheep's Head Peninsula nevertheless has a charm of its own. There are no substantial antiquities but a loop road runs close to the sea along most of its length; there are wonderful seascapes to appreciate and country walks where other visitors will be few.

The second turning on the right after leaving Bantry southwards for Cork is the beginning of **Goat's Path Scenic Route**, which runs along the northern side of the peninsula. The southern part of the loop road begins farther along the main Cork road, just past the Esso garage. This road also follows part of the 88km **Sheep's Head Way**, a trail that traces the peninsula's coastline. At the eastern end of this road, near Durrus, there is a **memorial** to those who died just off the coast here in an Air India crash in 1985. You will get some fine views of both Mizen Head and the Beara Peninsula by taking the R591 from Kilcrohane up Mt Seefin and down again towards Bantry.

Ahakista (Atha an Chiste) consists of a couple of pubs and a few houses stretched out along the R591. An ancient stone circle is signposted at the southern end of Ahakista where the road bends to the left. Access is via a short pathway.

The peninsula's other village is Kilcrohane, 6km to the south-west beside a fine beach.

WALKING

A walk to the summit of **Seefin** (334m) begins at the top of Goat's Path, about 2km north of Kilcrohane. Across the road from the walk's start is a rather forlorn imitation of Michelangelo's *Pietà*, erected by an American with local family roots. Although there's no obvious path, it isn't difficult to aim for the summit and reach it in less than 45 minutes. There are fine views from the top, and not many people make the climb.

There's also a good three-hour walk from the top of the Goat's Path. Standing near the

Pietà and facing Bantry Bay, locate an old road about 100m to the right, recognisable by a low slate wall on the sea-facing side. Follow this remote track until it joins a surfaced road that heads out farther west along the peninsula and eventually crosses to the southern side where the main road leads back to Kilcrohane. A left turn at the village church would bring you back to the start of the walk at the top of the Goat's Path.

You can also walk part or all of the **Sheep Head's Way**, which begins at Turning Table, Tooreen, near Kilcrohane, and circles the peninsula via Sheep's Head, Bantry and Durrus.

GETTING THERE & AWAY

On Saturdays only a bus leaves Bantry at 10am and 2.20pm for Ahakista and Kilcrohane. Bantry to Ahakista takes 30 minutes. They depart Kilcrohane at 10.40am and 3.15pm.

Beara Peninsula (Ring of Beara)

The appeal of the Beara Peninsula (Mor Choaird Bheara) lies in its startling natural beauty, best experienced by climbing the hills and cycling the roads. It's on a grander scale than the Sheep's Head Peninsula to the south and occupies parts of both Cork and Kerry. The Beara is a harsh, rocky landscape with intermittent patches of lush greenery. It makes wonderful walking country and is littered with prehistoric rocks, stone circles, standing stones and old tombs.

The 196km **Beara Way** is a well signposted walk linking Glengarriff with Kenmare (in Kerry) via Castletownbere, Bere Island, Dursey Island and the northside of the peninsula. The Beara Tourism and Development Association (☎ 027-70054) is located in the Square in Castletownbere. If you haven't picked up walking maps and guides already you will find them here. For more details see Walking under Activities in the Facts for the Visitor chapter.

ORIENTATION & INFORMATION

A small northern part of the peninsula lies in Kerry but is dealt with here for the convenience of people travelling the Ring of Beara. Castletownbere in Cork or Kenmare in Kerry would make good bases for exploring the peninsula. Small official tourist offices are open in Castletownbere and Glengarriff in July and August.

In theory you could drive the 137km around the coast in one day, but at the price of missing a great deal. In particular you would miss the spectacular **Healy Pass**, which cuts across the peninsula to join Adrigole in Cork with Lauragh in Kerry.

The route described below assumes you are starting out from Glengarriff and working your way round the peninsula clockwise to Kenmare.

GLENGARRIFF

☎ 027 • pop 245

A long, thin village, Glengarriff (An Gleann Garbh) is strung out along the main western Cork to Killarney road. It's marked by the Eccles Hotel at the eastern end. At the western end the road divides, with one branch leading to Kenmare and the other to the Beara Peninsula. Its sheltered position at the head of Bantry Bay, together with the influence of the Gulf Stream, gives it a particularly mild climate, and the local flora is lush and sometimes exotic. The best place to explore this unique vegetation is Bamboo Park (see later in this section).

During the second half of the 19th century, Glengarriff became a popular retreat for prosperous Victorians, who would sail from England to Ireland then take the train to Bantry, from where a paddle steamer chugged over to Glengarriff. By 1850 the road to Kenmare had been blasted through the mountains and the link with Killarney was established.

A major attraction is the Italianate garden on nearby Garinish Island, although it's pleasant just walking in the crassly named Blue Pool Amenity Area, which rings the coast in the middle of the village. From the shore here you might be lucky enough to see seals loitering on the large rocks in the bay.

Information
The Bord Fáilte tourist office (☎ 63084) opens only in July and August and is inconveniently positioned in the Eccles Hotel car park. You'd do better to call into the privately run version in the shop in the village centre beside the Blue Pool Ferries terminal. It opens 10am to 1pm and 2pm to 6pm Monday to Saturday, June to August. The small Allied Irish Bank on the main street has a bureau de change but no ATM.

Bamboo Park
This unusual place (☎ 63570; adult/child €3.80/1.25; open 9am-7pm daily Apr-Oct) has been able to flourish due to the unique climactic conditions of Glengarrif. Twelve hectares of exotic gardens include palm trees, bamboo, ferns and woodlands. It extends from the main road near the Eccles Hotel down to a small beach. Lining the waterfront are 13 ivy-covered stone pillars, the origin of which remains unexplained.

Garinish Island
In the early 20th century the English architect Harold Peto created an Italianate garden (☎ 63040; adult/senior/child €3.20/2.20/1.25; open 10am-4.30pm Mon-Sat, 1pm-6.30pm Sun Mar & Oct; 10am-5.30pm Mon-Sat, 12pm-6.30pm Sun Apr-June & Sept; 9.30am-6.30pm Mon-Sat, 11am-6.30pm Sun July & Aug; last admission one hour before closing) on Garinish (Ilnacullin) island. He planted exotic plants never before seen in Ireland, and they continue to flourish, providing a blaze of colour in a landscape usually dominated by greens and browns. There are panoramic views from the top of the 19th-century Martello tower, built to watch out for a possible Napoleonic invasion. The gardens are run by Dúchas.

Two ferry companies serve the island about every 20 minutes from 9am to 5.30pm Monday to Saturday and 1pm-6pm Sunday. Harbour Queen Ferries (☎ 63116) leave from a pier on the other side of the road from the Eccles Hotel, while the Blue Pool Ferries (☎ 63333) terminal is in the centre of the village, near the Quills Woollen Market. The crossing takes 10 minutes (adult return €6.35, children aged over 10 years €3.20, children under 10 free) and you'll probably see colonies of seals basking on rocks on your way there.

Glengarriff Woods
These 300-hectare oak and pine woods were owned by the White family of Bantry House in the 18th century. After the government took over in the 1950s the range of trees was expanded. The thick tree cover maintains humid conditions that allow ferns and mosses to flourish. Look out especially for tiny white flowers on red stems rising from rosettes of leaves: these are rare kidney saxifrage.

The woodlands and bogs are also home to the Kerry slug, the 'aristocrat of slugs', found only here and in parts of Kerry and the Iberian Peninsula. It's coffee-coloured with cream spots.

To get to the woods, leave Glengarriff on the N71 Kenmare road. The entrance is about 1km along on the left. A sign, just inside the gate, points across a footbridge to Lady Bantry's Lookout. It's a short, steep climb which brings you out on top of the world.

Activities
Ocean Discovery Diving Centre (☎ 60290) in Adrigole charges €76.25 for two dives with full equipment hire. For deep-sea fishing trips contact Harbour Queen Ferries (☎ 63116).

Special Events
The Caha Walking Festival (☎ 63555) is a hill-walking festival that takes place over three days in May. Walks vary according to ability; some are guided. Book your accommodation ahead if you plan to come at this time.

Places to Stay
Dowlings Camping & Caravan Park (☎/fax 63154, Castletownbere Rd) Tent & 2 people from €11.45. Open Easter-Oct. One kilometre west of Glengarriff on the Castletownbere road, this park has a games room, a licensed bar and traditional music from June to August.

CORK

Murphy's Village Hostel (☎/fax 63555, ⓔ *murphyshostel@eircom.net, The Village)* Dorms €9.50-10.80, twin rooms €29. Open year round. This well run hostel is in the centre of Glengarriff, between the Blue Pool Ferries terminal and Casey's Hotel.

B&Bs line the road out to Bantry. There are some cheaper alternatives in the village centre.

Maureen's B&B (☎ 63201, main street) Singles/doubles €25/45; €4.45 less without breakfast. This small place doubles as a craft shop.

Cottage Bar & Restaurant (☎ 63226, fax 63532, ⓔ *glengarriffcottage@eircom.ie, main street)* Singles/doubles €25/43; This place is next door to Maureen's and has a great evening meal deal for guests: €10 with a free glass of wine.

River Lodge B&B (☎ 63043, Castletownbere Rd) Singles/doubles €31.75/50.80. This large, graceful home with pleasant gardens is at the western edge of town on the road to Castletownbere.

Eccles Hotel (☎ 63003, fax 63319, ⓔ *eccleshotel@iol.ie, Glengarriff Harbour)* Singles/doubles from €70/115 Apr-Sept, €50/76 the rest of the year. This recently refurbished hotel boasts past literary guests such as Thackeray, Yeats and Shaw but is very much a coach-tour stop-off now. Rooms vary in size; some are small and not worth the asking price, especially when guests are charged €12.70 extra for a seaview room.

Casey's Hotel (☎ 63010, fax 63072, main street) Singles/doubles €48/84 June-Aug, €40/68 the rest of the year. This hotel is right in the village centre and close to pubs and cafes. The restaurant here is exceptional (see Places to Eat).

Places to Eat

Rainbow Restaurant (☎ 63440, main street) Mains €8.90-17.15, kids' meals €4.45. A variety of dishes can be enjoyed here including sirloin steak with black pepper sauce, prawn and chicken stir-fry, and Bantry Bay mussels with white wine.

Johnny Barry's (☎ 63315, main street) Bar food €2.30-8.25. This pub near the post office offers great seafood meals.

Blue Loo (☎ 63167, main street) Snacks €2.30-3.50. Try this place for cheap sandwiches.

Casey's Hotel (see Places to Stay) Bar food €2.50-8.90, restaurant starters €3.20-7.55, mains €13.90-19.40. Open 6.30pm-10pm nightly. The bar serves traditional meals such as beef-and-Guinness pie while the restaurant is the best place in town for a slap-up meal.

Getting There & Away

A bus travels twice a day between Bantry and Glengarriff (€3, 15 minutes) then onto Kenmare and Killarney. Coming from Bantry it stops outside the post office; going back to Bantry it stops by the phone boxes across the road. The private Berehaven bus (☎ 70007) departs for Bantry daily and on Thursday continues on to Cork.

Getting Around

Jem Creations (☎ 63113), where the road divides for Castletownbere, rents out bicycles for €10.15/57 per day/week.

SUGARLOAF MOUNTAIN

As you head out of Glengarriff towards Castletownbere the landscape becomes very rocky and weird. After 8km look out for a turning on the right; it's 500m after a disused school, opposite a blue Community Alert Area sign. Follow this road for 1.5km and leave your bicycle or car near the single two-storey house (with pine trees behind it) or near the bungalow just past it. Sugarloaf Mountain (575m) is best approached by walking up behind the houses and crossing an old road. A steady approach up the side of the mountain would bring you to the triangulation point at the summit in about an hour. The official turn-off for the mountain is 13km from Glengarriff where there is also a sign for two standing stones.

There are excellent views from the top: the Caha Mountains to the north, Hungry Hill to the west, Garinish Island to the east and Bantry Bay spread out to the south. On the way up, look out for the insectivorous great butterwort around the old road, in May and June.

HUNGRY HILL

Hungry Hill (686m), made famous by Daphne du Maurier in her book of the same name is the highest point on the peninsula. A sign points to one route to the top, 7km west of Adrigole. A longer but more comfortable ascent begins by ignoring this sign, carrying along the road, and turning right just past a church on the right side of the road. This road goes north until blocked by a wire sheep gate. A vehicle could be left just before this or taken past for another kilometre or so. The overgrown road eventually stops near some lakes and, from here, keeping the lakes to the left, you head up the eastern ridge and climb the summit from the northern side.

A quicker descent can be made by following the stream down the south-western side to some farmhouses and a road that connects with the one where you began. The whole journey will take at least five hours but the rockscapes are fabulous and the views of western Cork from the top are tremendous. Less arduous would be a walk to the end of the road and a picnic by the lakes.

Hungry Hill Lodge (☎ 60228, Adrigole) Dorms €12.70, doubles €31-38. This small, simple hostel sits on the cycle route, about 150m after the T-junction on the Castletownbere road west of Adrigole village. There is space for tents and bike hire is available.

CASTLETOWNBERE & AROUND

☎ 027 • pop 1000

Castletownbere (Baile Chais Bhéara) is home to Ireland's second-largest fishing fleet and when its full name – Castletownbere-haven – is used, it shares with Newtown-mountkennedy, in County Wicklow, the proud claim of having the country's longest place name. The main town on the peninsula, it originally developed out of the copper-mining industry at Allihies and remains little touched by tourism.

Castletownbere is little more than one traffic-choked street with the Bere Island ferry and the harbour in the east and the main square given over to a fire station, garage, car park and fishing supplier. Tourist information (☎ 70344) is available in July and August from what amounts to a garden shed squeezed in next to the fire station. Otherwise there are supermarkets, a post office with a limited bureau de change, an Allied Irish Bank branch with an ATM and a string of pubs. O'Shea's Laundrette (☎ 70966) on Main St opens 9am to 6pm Monday to Saturday.

Dunboy Castle & Puxley Mansion

About 3km south-west of Castletownbere you come to a sign to Dunboy Castle (☎ 70044, Castletownbere; admission €0.65 per person, €2.55 per car; open year round). In a beautiful setting, little now remains of the 13th-century castle, the fortress of the O'Sullivan clan, who ruled supreme for three centuries before succumbing to the English in 1602.

Don't make the mistake of thinking the grand ruins you come to first are the magnificent remains of a Gaelic stronghold. This is Puxley Mansion, bearing testimony to the vast wealth generated by the copper mines on the Puxley family estate. Daphne du Maurier tells the story of the Puxley family in *Hungry Hill*. The house was built in the Romanesque style in the 19th century and was burned down by the IRA in 1921, but enough remains to show the extravagance of style. Check out the Italian marble of the columns, still standing in what was once the grand hallway.

If you don't mind roughing it, it's possible to camp in the grounds of Dunboy Castle for €2.50 per person. Ask at the house on the right after passing the main gate.

On a good day you're much better off walking down. When the gate's not staffed put the admission fee in the box.

Derreena Taggart Stone Circle

This stone circle is close to the roadside, about 1km from Castletownbere, and is signposted at the western end of town. At the edge of town on the way out, you will notice a solitary standing stone on a mound next to a cream-coloured house with a brown roof.

CORK

Dzogchen Beara Retreat Centre

This remote Buddhist meditation and training centre (☎ 73032, fax 73177, Garranes, Allihies) is about 8km south-west of Castletownbere on top of Black Ball Head. The solitude, not to mention the stunning views, is magical. Visitors are welcome to attend sessions but you should call first. The retreat offers regular seminars and study groups. Accommodation is available in self-catering cottages or the hostel.

Activities

The exposed and rugged **Berehaven Golf Club** (☎ 70700) is 5km east of the centre and costs €19 for a round.

Places to Stay

Berehaven Camper & Amenity Park (☎ 70700, Berehaven) Tent & 2 people €8.90. This place is at the golf club and has tennis courts, a games room, a sauna and a 12-hole minigolf course.

Beara Hostel (☎ 70184, R572) Dorms €10.15, doubles €24-26, camping €8.90 including use of hostel's facilities. This hostel is on the R572 just past the sign for Dunboy Castle, 2.5km-west of Castletownbere. Some doubles are in pleasant wooden chalets.

Harbour Lodge Budget Accommodation (☎/fax 71043, Castletownbere) Singles €19-25, doubles €25/38 shared bath/en suite. This place, just behind Main St, feels much like a hostel although there are no dorms. The rooms are perfectly adequate and good value.

Rodeen B&B (☎ 70158, Castletownbere) Rooms €32 per person. About 2km east of the centre, this place has ocean views and serves evening meals.

Ford Rí Hotel (☎ 70379, fax 70506, The Harbour) Singles/doubles €50/89 Apr-Oct, €38/64 Nov-Mar. This hotel is on the other side of the harbour from Main St and looks out over the town.

Places to Eat

Seafood is the call of the day here. It's abundant and relatively cheap.

Cronin's Hideaway (☎ 70386, Main St) Takeaway €0.90-2.80. Open 12.30pm-1.45pm & 5pm-12.30am Mon-Sat, 12.30pm-

midnight Sunday. Here it's the usual take-away fare – fish and chips, burgers and sandwiches.

Niki's (☎ 70625, Main St) Mains €12-17. This seafood cafe/restaurant has dishes with Eastern and Caribbean influences.

Murphy's Restaurant (☎ 70244, Main St) Meals €5-9.50. This is the place for hearty, budget meals such as mixed grills, curried prawns with rice and burgers. The seafood platter is only €8.90 and kids' meals cost €4.45.

Mariner Restaurant & Wine Bar (☎ 71111, Main St) Snacks & light meals €2.50-7.60, mains €15-21. Open 10am-3pm & 5.30pm-9.30pm Tues-Sat, reduced hours Nov-Feb. This popular place serves baguettes, soup, chilli, baked potatoes, seafood and steaks.

Getting There & Away

Buses run from Cork (€14, three hours 20 minutes) twice daily via Bantry, Glengarriff (€5.85, 45 minutes) and Adrigole. In July and August there's also one bus daily, Monday to Saturday, to Killarney via Eyeries, Ardgroom, Lauragh and Kenmare.

Getting Around

Bikes can be hired from the SuperValu supermarket (☎ 70020) on the eastern side of town near the ferry. It opens 8am to 9pm daily (open 9am Sunday); hire costs €8.90 per day.

BERE ISLAND
☎ 027 • pop 210

Bere Island lies just 1 mile off the port of Castletownbere. Due to its deep anchorage, this island was used as a base for the British navy. The 21km section of the **Beara Way** is the best reason for visiting the island. There are a couple of pubs and small shops but tourist accommodation is limited.

Murphy's Ferry Service (☎ 75014, 087 238 6095) runs ferries at 8am, 10am, 11.30am, 1pm, 3pm, 5pm, 7pm and 8.30pm from the Pontoon Pier, about 6km east of Castletownbere off the R572, to Rerrin on the eastern side of the island. The crossing takes 15 to 20 minutes.

CORK

The Bere Island Car Ferry (☎ 75009) leaves from Castletownbere Quay opposite the SuperValu supermarket and runs to the western side of the island. Ferries leave seven times a day (five on Sunday) from the end of June to September, five times a day (three on Sunday) the rest of the year. It costs €5 return for a foot passenger and €19 for a car with two passengers.

DURSEY ISLAND
☎ 027 • pop 60

At the end of the peninsula is Dursey Island, just 6.5km long by 1.5km wide and 250m offshore. Ireland's only cable car connects the inhabitants and their cattle with the mainland, swaying precariously 100 feet above Dursey Sound. Three hundred people sought refuge here in 1602 when Dunboy Castle was under siege by the English; they were slaughtered and thrown into the sea. In the 9th century the Vikings used the island as a staging post for villagers they had kidnapped before selling them as slaves to Scandinavia and Spain. Now the island is a wild bird and whale sanctuary, and dolphins can sometimes be seen swimming in the waters around it.

The cable car (€3.20 return) crosses between 9am and 11am, 2.30pm and 5pm, and 7pm and 8pm, Monday to Saturday. Note that cattle get precedence over humans in the queue for the ride! The two Sunday-morning crossings are timed to get people to mass at Cahermore or Allihies, but there are also crossings at 7pm and 11pm. From June to August there are also Sunday crossings between 4pm and 5pm.

Although there's no accommodation on the island it's easy to find somewhere to camp. The Beara Way loops round the island for 11km, and the signal tower is an obvious destination for a shorter walk. Bikes are not allowed on the cable car.

ALLIHIES & THE COPPER MINES
Copper was discovered in 1810. While mining quickly brought wealth to the Puxley family, who owned the land, it brought low wages and dangerous, unhealthy working conditions for the workforce, which at one time numbered 1300 men, women and children. Experienced Cornish miners were brought into the area, and the ruins of their stone cottages remain. As late as the 1930s, over 30,000 tonnes of pure copper were being exported annually, but by 1962 the last mine was closed.

In Allihies (Na hAilichí), a small tourist information kiosk, beside the church, opens in the peak season. Allihies is served by the privately run Berehaven bus company. Call ☎ 027-70007 for information.

NORTHSIDE OF THE BEARA
After leaving Allihies, look back almost immediately and you'll be able to see the Bull, Cow and Calf Rocks off Dursey Head. Heading north and east from Allihies, a 23km coastal road with hedges of fuchsia and rhododendron twists and turns all the way to **Eyeries**, a cluster of brightly coloured houses overlooking Coulagh Bay. The town is also home to Milleens cheese, which you will no doubt see all over Ireland.

Nearby, at Ballycrovane, is Ireland's tallest ogham stone at 5.18m high. Unfortunately the stone is on private land and unsignposted. If you're driving or cycling watch out for grazing sheep wandering onto the road. The coast road eventually rejoins the main road at the small village of **Ardgroom** (Ard Dhór).

As you head east towards Lauragh look for signs pointing right to the Ardgroom **stone circle**, a beautifully located Bronze Age monument, the most striking in a valley littered with reminders of prehistory. The ground can be boggy so be careful after rain.

Although **Lauragh** (Laith Reach), northeast of Ardgroom, is actually in Kerry, it's included here for the convenience of people travelling the Ring of Beara. Lauragh is home to the century-old **Derreen Gardens** (☎ 064-83103, Derreen, Lauragh; adult/child €3.80/1.90; open 10am-6pm daily Apr-Sept), planted by the 5th Lord Lansdowne around the turn of the 20th century. An abundance of interesting plants thrive here, including spectacular New Zealand tree ferns and red cedars, normally found in rainforests.

CORK

From Lauragh, a serpentine road travels 11km south across **Healy Pass**, offering spectacular views of the rocky inland scenery. About 1km west of Lauragh along the R572, is a road to **Glanmore Lake**. The scenery along here is stunning. In the middle of the lake on a tiny island are the remains of an old hermitage.

Walking

The walk to Glanmore Lake is well worth doing if the weather is good – the road gets very boggy otherwise. Follow the road then take the first turning to the right and stay on it until it ends by a couple of farms, the first of which has a stone circle in its back yard. From the end of the road, a path continues across a stream and into the valley until it reaches the remains of some stone dwellings. This undemanding walk will take you less than an hour from the stone circle.

A more exhilarating walk is to head up behind the house with the stone circle, crossing a sheep fence and keeping to the right of the stream. A stiff climb leads to a hanging valley with mountains on both sides. Head right to climb the shorter summit of **Cummeennahillan** (361m), which affords tremendous views. From there you can walk along the mountain ridge then down through holly woods and invasive rhododendrons through another farm to the Glanmore Lake road. This longer trek takes at least a couple of hours.

Places to Stay

Creveen Lodge Caravan & Camping Park (☎ 064-83131, Healy Pass road) €8.90 per car plus €1.25 per adult, €0.65 per child aged under 12 & €4.75 per hiker or cyclist. Open Easter-end Oct. This park is 1.5km south-east of Lauragh on the R574.

Glanmore Lake Hostel (☎ 064-83181, Glanmore Lake) Dorms €8.90 June-Aug, €6.35 at other times. Open Easter-Sept. This remote An Óige hostel is in an old schoolhouse 5.6km from Lauragh. Take the road for Glanmore Lake and just keep going.

Josie's Lakeview House (☎ 064-83155, Glanmore Lake) B&B €25 per person. This peaceful place has some of the most spectacular views in Ireland. The rooms are small but comfortable and evening meals are available (except Tuesday). It's 4.5km from Lauragh along the road to Glanmore Lake.

Getting There & Away

The bus service is very limited. Running between Killarney and Castletownbere, it operates only in July and August, and stops in Lauragh once daily, Monday to Saturday.

Northern Cork

The chief reasons for visiting northern Cork are the fishing and the golf. A few distinguished country houses with fine gardens are open to the public for evening meals and short stays, but this is not budget travellers' country.

MALLOW & AROUND

pop 7770

Much bigger than Fermoy, Mallow (Mala) is a prosperous, picturesque town in the Blackwater Valley that caters for fishing, golfing and horse racing. Nineteenth-century visitors to its spa christened it the 'Bath of Ireland', although these days the comparison would seem pretty far-fetched. Today it's a sugar manufacturing and agricultural centre.

The tourist office (☎ 022-42222), on Bridge St near the castle, opens 9.30am to 1pm and 2pm to 5pm on weekdays, March to October, plus on Saturday and at lunchtime, June to August.

At Buttevant, 20km north of Mallow on the N20, are the ruins of a 13th-century **Franciscan abbey**. From Mallow to Killarney the landscape is fairly nondescript, although you might want to divert to see the well preserved remains of 17th-century **Kanturk Castle** – it's said that the mortar was mixed with the blood of the builders who were forced to work on its construction. The English, however, objected to an Irish chief building such a massive mansion and didn't allow it to be roofed.

Assolas Country House (☎ 029-50015, fax 50795, e assolas@eircom.net, Kanturk) Singles/doubles from €89/152, including breakfast; dinner €38 per person. Open mid-Mar-Oct. This is a peaceful, 17th-century family home surrounded by beautiful gardens. The restaurant has won many good-food awards and most of the produce is home-grown. It's off the N72, 13km west of Mallow.

Buses run hourly every day between Mallow and Cork (€6.35, 35 minutes) and trains run every two hours (€7, 25 minutes). For Kanturk you really need your own transport.

MICHAEL COLLINS AMBUSH SITE

In 1922 Michael Collins, commander-in-chief of the army of the new Provisional Government that had just won independence from Britain, was assassinated at Beal-na-Blath, near Macroom. He was on a tour of western Cork and was recognised by anti-Treaty forces, who were meeting secretly nearby. In the evening they ambushed his car and Collins was shot dead. Apparently Collins ignored advice to drive on after the first shots were fired, choosing instead to make a fight of it.

The site of the ambush is marked by a stone memorial with a Gaelic inscription. Each year, a commemorative service is held on the anniversary of the killing (22 August).

Follow the N22 west from Cork then after about 20km take the left turn (R590) to Crookstown. From there turn right onto the R585 to Beal-na-Blath. The ambush site is on the left after 4km.

GOUGANE BARRA FOREST PARK

This is the most picturesque part of inland Cork. The source of the River Lee is a mountain lake fed by numerous silver streams. St Finbarr, the founder and patron saint of Cork, came here in the 6th century and established a monastery. He had a her-

NICKY CAVEN

Michael Collins, signatory of the 1921 Treaty

mitage on the island in **Gougane Barra Lake** (Lough an Ghugain), which is now approached by a short causeway. The small, modern chapel on the island has fine stained-glass representations of obscure Celtic saints.

A road runs through the park in a loop and a signboard map shows the meandering paths and nature trails leading off it. It's worth heading for Bealick's summit for the fine views.

Getting There & Away

In July and August there's a Saturday-only bus service that leaves Macroom at 8am and passes by the Gougane Barra Forest Park. George Plant Minibus Tours (☎ 022-50654, 086 239 8123) operates day trips to the Gougane Barra Forest Park from Bantry on Wednesday (€12.70).

Driving down from Cork to Bantry along the N22 and R584 you'll see a signpost for the park after Ballingeary. Returning to the main road afterwards and continuing west, you'll pass over the Pass of Keimaneigh and emerge on the N71 at Ballylickey, midway between the Beara Peninsula and the Sheep's Head Peninsula.

CORK

County Kerry

Kerry has some of Ireland's most wild and rugged terrain and is home to the country's highest mountain, Carrauntoohil, at 1039m. The town of Killarney bursts at the seams with tourists all year round while the Ring of Kerry is chock-a-block with tour coaches throughout summer, but the rest of the county is big enough for visitors to escape the crowds. The tourist hype detracts little from the landscape's wild splendour. Countless opportunities exist for long and short walks, easy and hard climbs and bike rides where your only companions will be the birds, the odd sheep and a few like-minded travellers. Especially beautiful is Dingle Peninsula, though the Iveragh Peninsula to the south (the Ring of Kerry) has even more opportunities for open-air activities. To the north of the county the landscape becomes flatter as it stretches towards the River Shannon which separates County Kerry from County Clare.

Killarney & Around

KILLARNEY
☎ 064 • pop 12,011

Killarney (Cill Airne) is synonymous with tourism. There's more registered accommodation here than anywhere else outside Dublin and the shops around the tourist office do a fine line in leprechaun-adorned T-shirts, mugs, towels – you name it. Coachloads of tourists arrive here en masse throughout the year. Those who prefer things a little more sedate should consider using Kenmare as a base.

The town has its own form of environmentally friendly transport – the horse-drawn jaunting car – which also gives it its distinctive aroma of dung.

History
Killarney and the surrounding valley has been inhabited since the Bronze Age when copper was mined at Ross Island. At that time Cashel in County Kilkenny was the

Highlights

- Walk or cycle in beautiful Killarney National Park
- Cycle or drive through the stunning Ballaghbeama Gap, avoiding the ritualised Ring of Kerry
- Take a boat trip to Skellig Michael, with its astonishing 7th-century monastery
- Swim with Fungie the dolphin in Dingle
- Take your time in the superb Blasket Centre museum and cultural centre on the Dingle Peninsula

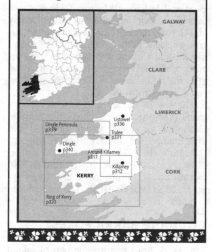

power base of Ireland and Killarney was a subkingdom. It became a stronghold of the O'Donoghue clan. In the 7th century a monastery was founded by St Finian on Inisfallen Island and Killarney became a focus for Christianity in the region.

It wasn't until the 18th century that the town was developed as a centre for tourism by Lord Kenmare. A century later it continued to be visited by royals and dignitaries from around Europe, including Queen Victoria.

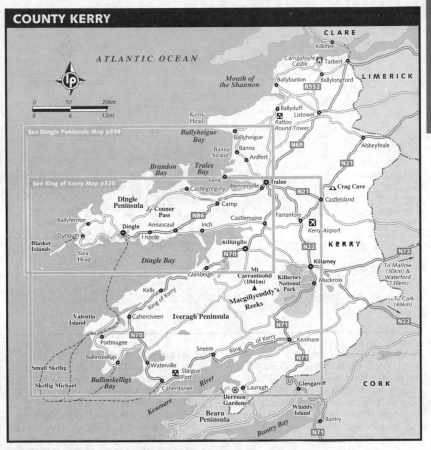

COUNTY KERRY

Orientation
The centre of Killarney is focused on the T-junction where New St meets High and Main Sts. As it heads south, High St becomes Main St then swings around to the left into East Ave Rd where all the large hotels are. The National Park is to the south, while the bus and train stations are to the east of the centre.

Information
Tourist Office Killarney's busy but efficient tourist office (☎ 31633), in a new building on the corner of Beech Rd, opens 9am to 6pm (to 8pm in July and August) Monday to Saturday and 10am to 6pm on Sunday, May to October; and 9.15am to 5.30pm Monday to Saturday the rest of the year. *Where Killarney* (€1.90) is a good monthly 'what's on' guide. You may find it in your B&B or hostel, in bookshops or at the tourist office.

Money Many banks have either a bureau de change or an ATM or both; there's a branch of American Express (☎ 35722) on East Avenue Rd.

Post & Communications The post office is on New St. Internet access is available at

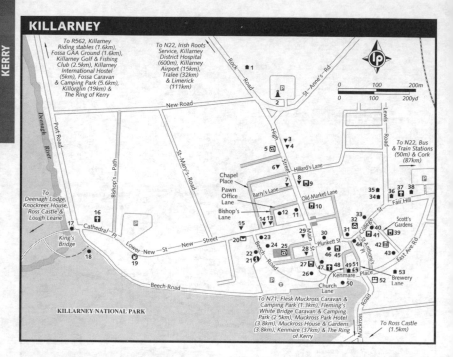

KILLARNEY

To R562, Killarney
Riding stables (1.6km),
Fossa GAA Ground (1.6km),
Killarney Golf & Fishing
Club (2.5km), Killarney
International Hostel
(5km), Fossa Caravan
& Camping Park (5.6km),
Killorglin (19km) &
The Ring of Kerry

To N22, Irish Roots
Service, Killarney
District Hospital
(600m), Killarney
Airport (15km),
Tralee (32km)
& Limerick
(111km)

To N22, Bus
& Train Stations
(50m) & Cork
(87km)

To
Deenagh Lodge,
Knockreer House,
Ross Castle &
Lough Leane

KILLARNEY NATIONAL PARK

To N71, Flesk Muckross Caravan &
Camping Park (1.3km), Fleming's
White Bridge Caravan & Camping
Park (2.5km), Muckross Park Hotel
(3.8km), Muckross House & Gardens
(3.8km), Kenmare (37km) & The Ring
of Kerry

To Ross Castle
(1.5km)

Compustore Internet cafe (☎ 37255), which is upstairs in the Inisfallen Mall on Main St and opens 10am to 6pm Monday to Saturday. There's also WEB-Talk (☎ 37033), 53 High St, which offers cheap phone calls abroad and opens 10am to 9pm Monday to Saturday and 2pm to 8pm on Sunday. Both charge €2.55 for 20 minutes or €5.10 for one hour.

Cultural Centres The Irish Roots Services (☎/fax 33506, Tralee Rd, ⓔ info@irish rootsservices.com) can help you trace your Irish ancestors and relatives.

Left Luggage There's a left luggage office at the bus station (☎ 37509) costing €1.60 per bag per 12 hours. It opens from 7.30am to 6.30pm daily. Ask at the coffee shop in the station.

Emergency Killarney District Hospital (☎ 31076) is in St Margaret's Rd, just north-west of the centre.

St Mary's Cathedral
Built between 1842 and 1855, this cruci-form cathedral, at the western end of New St in Cathedral Place, was designed by the architect Augustus Pugin and is a superb example of neo-Gothic revival architecture.

In the 1840s the cathedral was used as a hospital, and during the Famine it acted as a refuge for the destitute – the huge tree on the front lawn marks the mass grave of those who died.

Museum of Irish Transport
This is an interesting museum (☎ 32638, Scotts Gardens, East Ave Rd; adult/child €3.80/1.90; open 10am-6pm daily Mar-Oct; 11am-4pm daily Nov-Feb). Its collection of shiny old cars, bicycles and assorted odds and ends includes an 1844 Meteor Starley Tricycle found in a shop's unsold stock in 1961, and a 1910 Wolseley that was used by Countess Markievicz and WB Yeats.

KILLARNEY

Killarney Model Railway

Next to the tourist office is Killarney Model Railway (☎ *34000, Beech Rd; adult/child €3.80/1.25; open 10.30am-6pm daily mid-Mar-Oct & Dec)*. If this is your thing you'll find 90 sq m of model trains (one of Europe's largest sets, apparently) and a miniature model of Europe.

Other Things to See

At the northern end of High St is a **memorial** to Famine victims erected by the Republican Graves Association in 1972. Curiously, the inscription reads: 'This memorial will not be unveiled until Ireland is free.'

On Fair Hill is a **Franciscan friary**, built in the 1860s, displaying an ornate Flemish-style altarpiece and some impressive tile work. It has stained-glass work by Harry Clarke.

If you would like to watch some **Gaelic football** and you're in town for the season, head for the Fossa GAA ground on the N72, 1.6km west of the centre.

Activities

You can fish for trout and salmon in the Rivers Flesk and Laune and in the lakes in Killarney National Park. The small lakes around the southern side of Killarney towards Kenmare also have trout, although there's no coarse fishing locally. Permits, licences, equipment and information are available from **O'Neill's** (☎ *31970, 6 Plunkett St)*.

Killarney Riding Stables (☎ *31686, Ballydowney, Killarney)*, 1.6km west of the centre on the R562, has one/two/three-hour rides (costing €19.05/31.75/44.45) as well as four- and six-day rides for more experienced riders (packages with B&B cost from €392).

Killarney Golf & Fishing Club (☎ *31034,* Ⓦ *www.killarney-golf.com)* is 2.5km west of town on the N72. The course hugs Lough Leane and has great views of the mountains. Green fees are €63.55 per person, students €31.75.

Places to Stay

Camping There are several camp sites not far from town.

Flesk Muckross Caravan & Camping Park (☎ *31704, fax 35439, Muckross Rd)* Tent & car €8.55. This place, about 1.3km out of town on the N71 to Kenmare, is not particularly attractive but it's close to town and has many on-site facilities including a bureau de change, grocery shop and bike rental.

Fossa Caravan & Camping Park (☎ 31497, fax 34459, e fossaholidays@ eircom.net, Fossa) Tent & 2 people €10.80. This facility is 5.6km west of town on the N72 Killorglin road. There are plenty of trees and views out to the MacGillycuddy Reeks.

Fleming's White Bridge Caravan & Camping Park (☎ 31590, fax 37474, Ballycasheen Rd) Tent & 2 people €10.15. To get to this small caravan park with its many flower beds, head south out of town along Muckross Rd and turn left at Woodlawn. It's about 2km along this road.

Hostels Some places will pick you up from the bus or train stations. Even though there are so many hostels, you'd be well advised to book ahead in the summer.

Killarney International Hostel (☎ 31240, fax 34300, e anoige@killarney.iol.ie, Aghadoe House) Dorms €10.15-12.05, doubles €30.50. In a striking 18th-century manor house overlooking lakes and forests, this An Óige hostel is 5km west of the centre off the N72 to Kilorglin. A complimentary bus service runs to/from the train station and staff can arrange packed lunches, tours to the National Park and bike hire (€7.60 per day).

Súgán Hostel (☎ 33104, Lewis Rd) Dorms/doubles €11.45/28. This central and intimate hostel (with one double room) is run by Pa Sugrue who knows how to have a good time and has a wealth of information on what's on around town.

Killarney Railway Hostel (☎ 35299, fax 32197, Park Rd) Dorms/doubles €10.80/ 31.75. This well equipped IHH hostel is on the eastern side of the Franciscan friary. Guests can take advantage of discounted tours of the Ring of Kerry (€12.70), Dingle Peninsula (€15.90) and Gap of Dunloe (€15.25), as well as lake cruises (€7.60 per hour) and bike hire (€7.60 per day).

B&Bs & Hotels There are dozens, if not hundreds, of B&Bs and guesthouses in Kil-

larney. That said, finding a room can be tricky from June to August, in which case it might be better to let the tourist office find one for you for a €1.25 fee. New Rd, Rock Rd and Muckross Rd are good places to start looking. There are some luxury hotels too.

Fairview Guesthouse (☎/fax 34164, Lewis Rd). Singles €38.10, doubles €63.50-76.20 May-Sept, singles €35.55, doubles €54.65-57.15 Oct-Apr. This well run guesthouse has good amenities and tries hard to please.

Rathmore House (☎ 32829, Rock Rd) Singles €31.75, doubles €50.80-63.50. This comfortable B&B with good breakfasts and parking for guests is only a five-minute walk from the centre.

Ross Hotel (☎ 31855, fax 31139, e ross@ kph.iol.ie, Kenmare Place) Singles/doubles €86.40/122 May-Sept, €71.15/91.50 Oct-Apr. This attractive hotel is right in the town centre.

Killarney Park Hotel (☎ 35555, fax 35266, e info@killarneyparkhotel.ie, Kenmare Place) Singles/doubles €209.65/317.65 May-Oct, €158.85/216 Nov-Apr. This is a seriously nice hotel with great facilities (including an indoor pool and spa, snooker room and library). If you want to savour some of the luxury without getting into too much debt, opt for a meal in the hotel restaurant (around €42).

Killarney Royal Hotel (☎ 31853, fax 34001, e royalhot@iol.ie, College St) Singles €133.40-177.90, doubles €127.05-190.60. This central hotel has spacious rooms and five-star facilities.

Muckross Park Hotel (☎ 31938, fax 31965, Muckross Rd) Singles/doubles €116.90/177.90 May-Sept, €90.20/124.50 Oct-Apr. If you want to get away from frenetic Killarney, this luxurious hotel in an 18th-century building makes a pleasant choice, so long as your pockets are deep enough. It's across the road from the entrance to Muckross House, about 4km from Killarney.

Places to Eat

More-expensive restaurants tend to hug the northern end of High St. For cheaper eats, head down to Main St or turn down New St. Self-caterers should go to *Tesco* supermarket on Beech Rd.

Restaurants Killarney has a variety of restaurants.

Gaby's (☎ 32519, 27 High St) Starters €5-12, mains €22-36. This award-winning and very expensive seafood restaurant is rather posh: dress up.

The Blue Door (☎ 33755, 57 High St) Meals & snacks €3.50-10. If you just can't decide what you want, this place serves Thai, Spanish, Italian, Irish, Cajun and Mexican dishes.

Sceilig (☎ 33062, High St) Meals around €5.70. For a hearty Irish stew or roast chicken with ham, this cosy restaurant with a woody interior is the place to go.

The Flesk (☎ 31128, 14 Main St) Mains €11.40-22.20. The popular and upmarket Flesk has an extensive menu – with dishes such as a roast half of duckling with walnut stuffing and orange and brandy sauce. There's an early-bird special of €3.80 off each main course between 5.30pm and 6.45pm.

Fast Food & Cafes There are plenty of places for a snack or light meal.

The Bean House (☎ 37877, 8 High St) Sandwiches & baguettes €2.35-3.15. Coffee nuts can choose between a dozen or so ways of having their fix here.

Brícín (☎ 34902, 26 High St) Lunch around €7. This cafe and craft shop opens for lunch only and has a great selection of cakes and tarts.

Ma Reilly's (☎ 39220, 20 New St) Meals €3.15-9.50. Good cheap food is to be found here, including seafood chowder and special kids' meals.

Busy B's (☎ 31972, 15 New St) Snacks & meals €2.50-8. Open 7am-midnight Mon-Wed, 7am-3am Fri & Sat. Breakfast is offered all day at this casual eatery, along with sandwiches, burgers, fish and chips, and baked potatoes.

Teo's (☎ 36344, 13 New St) Lunch €5.50-7.50, dinner €9.20-11.30. Serving mainly Italian dishes and pizzas, this cafe

also has a three-course set dinner for €25.35.

Mac's Ice-cream Parlour (☎ 35213, 6 Main St) The ice-cream sold here – around 30 flavours – is made on the premises.

Entertainment

Many Killarney pubs have live music. At some it's traditional and often impromptu while at others it's very tourist oriented. Some pubs don't admit anyone aged under 21.

Courtney's (☎ 32689, Plunkett St) Traditional music sessions here are well worth it.

The Laurels Singing Pub and Wine Bar (☎ 31149, Main St) If you're one to avoid loud coach parties attempting traditional Irish dance, the Laurels isn't for you, but if the mood takes you you'll find something on here every night of the week. Doors open at 8.30pm and entertainment begins at 9.15pm.

O'Connor's (☎ 30200, 7 High St) This place has a bit of everything – traditional music, stand-up comedy, readings and pub theatre. Entertainment starts at around 9.15pm each night.

Killarney Grand (☎ 31159, Main St) There's traditional music nightly here from 9pm to 11pm, at which time it becomes a nightclub with live bands until 1am. The occasional set-dancing night creeps in too.

The Crypt (☎ 31038, College St) Admission €5.10. This club plays mainly drum and bass. It opens nightly.

Scott's Gardens Hotel (☎ 31060, between College St & East Avenue Rd) Scott's has traditional music from Thursday to Sunday night and every night during July and August. Things get going at around 9pm.

Shopping

A good look around town will reveal a few worthwhile shops in Killarney though you will need to sift through those selling shamrocks, Guinness souvenirs and bad quality linen.

Variety Sounds (☎ 35755, 7 College St) Here you'll find traditional music, instruments, sheet music and learn-to-play books.

Aran Sweater Market (☎ 39756, Plunkett

St) This place offers the biggest range of Aran sweaters in town.

O'Neills (☎ *31970, 6 Plunkett St)* Camping and trekking gear can be found here.

Memories (☎ *34447, 74 High St)* Head here for a selection of good quality Irish linen and lace.

Getting There & Away

Air Kerry Airport (☎ 066-64644) is at Farranfore, about 15km north of Killarney off the N22. There are direct Aer Lingus flights to Dublin, and Manx Airlines flights to Luton and Manchester. It's also possible to fly direct from London Stansted to Kerry Airport; call Ryanair in Dublin (☎ 01-609 7800) for details.

Bus Bus Éireann (☎ 34777, 30011) operates from next to the train station, with regular links to Tralee (€5.85, 35 minutes, hourly), Cork (€11.95, one hour 35 minutes, hourly), Dublin (€19.05, six hours, four daily), Galway (€19.05, two hours 10 minutes, four daily), Limerick (€12.45, two hours 10 minutes, four daily), Waterford (€17.15, 4½ hours, hourly) and Rosslare Harbour (€20.30, two daily).

From late May to mid-September, the Ring of Kerry has its own service, departing Killarney at 8.30am and 1.30pm for Killorglin, Caherciveen, Waterville, Caherdaniel, Sneem and back to Killarney.

Train Killarney's train station (☎ 31067) is next to the bus station on Park Rd, just east of the centre. Five trains a day go to Cork (€22.90, two hours 10 minutes) and Tralee (€7, 45 minutes). Take the train to Mallow to change for Dublin, Waterford and Limerick.

Getting Around

To/From the Airport There's no bus service from the airport to town. A taxi will cost about €12.70.

Car You should avoid driving in the centre as it gets very crowded. Disc parking costs €0.65 per hour. If you want to hire a car to explore the Ring of Kerry there's an Avis desk (☎ 36655) at the tourist office on Beech Rd, Budget (☎ 34341) is in Kenmare

St next to the Amex office and Hertz (☎ 34126) is in Plunkett St.

Bicycle Bicycles are ideal for exploring the scattered sights of the Killarney area, many of which are accessible only by bike or on foot. Several places hire bikes at €8.90/44.50 per day/week including pannier bags, tool kit and maps. There's O'Sullivan's Bike Hire (☎ 31282), with one shop on Bishop's Lane and another opposite the TIC. Killarney Rent-a-Bike (☎ 32578) is in Old Market Lane alongside the Laurels pub.

Jaunting Car If you're not on two wheels, Killarney's traditional transport is the horse-drawn jaunting car, which comes with a driver known as a *jarvey*. The pickup point is on Kenmare Place just past the town hall but they also congregate in the N71 car park opposite Muckross House and at the Gap of Dunloe. Trips cost €15.25 to €44.45, depending on distance; the traps officially carry four people.

AROUND KILLARNEY
Killarney National Park

Killarney's 10,236-hectare National Park extends to the south-west of town, with two pedestrian entrances immediately opposite St Mary's Cathedral and others (for drivers) off the N71.

Enclosed within the park are beautiful Lough Leane (the Lower Lake or 'Lake of Learning'), Muckross Lake and the Upper Lake, as well as the Mangerton, Torc, Shehy and Purple Mountains. Areas of oak and yew woodland stretch for miles. This is wonderful walking and biking country, although there are also specific sights to see. A herd of red deer lives in the park and many species of bird can be spotted. In 1982 the park was designated a Unesco Biosphere Reserve.

An adventurous 30km cycle tour of the park (best undertaken on a dry day) is marked on the Around Killarney map.

Knockreer House & Gardens Near the St Mary's Cathedral entrance to the park stands Knockreer House, surrounded by lovely gardens. The original 19th-century

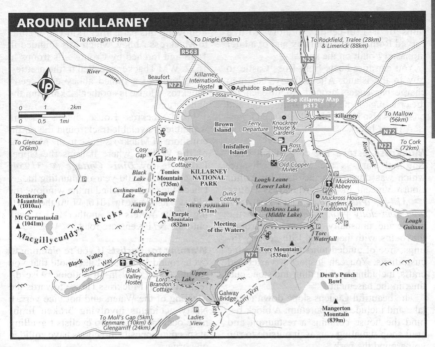

AROUND KILLARNEY

To Killorglin (19km)
To Dingle (58km)
To Rockfield, Tralee (28km) & Limerick (88km)
R563
N22
River Laune
Beaufort
N72
Killarney International Hostel
Fossa
Aghadoe
Ballydowney
See Killarney Map p312
To Mallow (56km)
Killarney
N72
To Cork (72km)
To Glencar (26km)
Cosy Gap
Brown Island
Ferry Departure
Knockreer House & Gardens
Ross Castle
River Flesk
N22
Kate Kearney's Cottage
Black Lake
Tomies Mountain (735m)
KILLARNEY NATIONAL PARK
Inisfallen Island
Old Copper Mines
Lough Leane (Lower Lake)
Muckross Abbey
Beenkeragh Mountain (1010m)
Cushnavalley Lake
Gap of Dunloe
Dinis Cottage
Muckross House, Gardens & Traditional Farms
Mt Carrantuohil (1041m)
Auger Lake
Purple Mountain (832m)
Sheliy Mountain (571m)
Muckross Lake (Middle Lake)
Lough Guitane
Macgillycuddy's Reeks
Meeting of the Waters
Black Valley
Gearhameen
Kerry Way
N71
Torc Mountain (535m)
Torc Waterfall
Black Valley Hostel
Lord Brandon's Cottage
Upper Lake
Kerry Way
Devil's Punch Bowl
Galway Bridge
To Moll's Gap (5km), Kenmare (10km) & Glengarriff (24km)
Ladies View
Kerry Way
Mangerton Mountain (839m)

0   1   2km
0   0.5   1mi

building burned down and the present incarnation dates from the 1950s. The house isn't open to the public, but you can walk around the gardens and there are great views across the valley and lakes to the mountains. To get to the house from the St Mary's Cathedral entrance, follow the path immediately to your right uphill for about 500m (even though the sign says it's only 250m).

Ross Castle Restored by Dúchas, Ross Castle dates back to the 14th century, when it was a residence of the O'Donoghues (☎ 35851, Ross Rd; adult/child €3.80/1.60; open 9am-6.30pm daily June-Aug; 10am-6pm daily May & Sept; 10am-5pm Tues-Sun Oct). It was the last place in Munster to succumb to Cromwell's forces under the command of Ludlow.

According to prophecy, the castle would be captured only from the water, so in 1652 Ludlow had floating batteries brought upriver from Castlemaine, then transported overland before being launched onto the lake. Seeing the prophecy about to be fulfilled, the defenders, having resisted the English siege from the land for months, surrendered promptly.

It's a 2.4km walk from the St Mary's Cathedral pedestrian park entrance to Ross Castle. If you're driving from Killarney, turn right opposite the Esso garage at the start of Muckross Rd, just past the roundabout. The castle is at the end of the road near the car park. There's a path leading through the woods from the castle to Muckross House.

Inisfallen Island The first monastery on the island is said to have been founded by St Finian the Leper in the 7th century. The island's fame dates from the early 13th century when the *Annals of Inisfallen* were written here. The annals, now in the Bodleian Library, Oxford, England, remain a vital source of information on early

Munster history. On the island, there are ruins of a 12th-century oratory with a carved Romanesque doorway and of a later monastery built on the site.

You can hire boats from Ross Castle to row to the island. Alternatively, boatmen charge passengers around €6.30 each for the crossing. Some Gap of Dunloe boat and bus tours also stop at the island (see Organised Tours later).

Muckross Estate The core of Killarney National Park is the Muckross Estate, which was donated to the state by Arthur Bourn Vincent in 1932. **Muckross House** (☎ 31440, adult/child €5.10/2.05; open 9am-6pm daily year round) opens to the public and, unusually, you can walk around the rooms, with their faded 19th-century fittings, free of guided tours or overintrusive custodians. You can inspect a variety of crafts, including bookbinding and stone cutting, in the basement.

The beautiful gardens slope down to the lake and include an arboretum. A block behind the house contains a restaurant and craft shop. Jaunting cars wait outside to run you around the park.

Immediately east of Muckross House are the **Muckross Traditional Farms** (☎ 35571; adult/child €5.10/2.05, combined ticket with Muckross House €7.60/3.50; open 10am-7pm daily June-Sept; 1pm-6pm daily May; 1pm-6pm Sat, Sun & public holidays 21 Mar-Apr & Oct). These are reproduction Kerry farmhouses of the 1930s complete with chickens, pigs, cattle and horses. You can walk round the circuit or save your legs and use the 'vintage coach' that shuttles between the buildings.

Muckross House is 5km from town on the N71 Kenmare road. Vehicle access is about 1km beyond the Muckross Park Hotel. During the summer a tourist bus leaves for the house at 1.45pm from outside O'Connor's pub in Killarney, returning at 5.15pm (return €6.35). The house is also included in some day tours of Killarney.

If you're walking or cycling to Muckross there's a cycle track alongside the Kenmare road for most of the first 2km. A path then

turns right into Killarney National Park. Following this path, after 1km you'll come to **Muckross Abbey**, which was founded in 1448 and torched by Cromwell's troops in 1652. WM Thackeray called it 'the prettiest little bijou of a ruined abbey ever seen'. Muckross House is another 1.5km from the abbey ruins.

From Muckross House, there's a 3.7km walkable or cyclable track round the northern shore of Muckross Lake to the **Meeting of the Waters**, where it joins the Upper Lake. Nearby *Dinis Cottage* (☎ 31954) serves teas in a 200-year-old hunting lodge. Check the graffiti etched in the window: the oldest dates back to 1816. From the Meeting of the Waters it's another 1.5km back onto the N71 Kenmare road.

Warning for Cyclists If you're planning to cycle round Muckross Lake, note that you should do so only in an anticlockwise direction (from Muckross House towards the Meeting of the Waters and not vice versa). Nasty accidents involving broken limbs have occurred when two cyclists travelling at speed in opposite directions have collided on corners.

Gap of Dunloe Technically the Gap of Dunloe is outside the National Park but, as most people start or end their visit to it in the park, details are included here. In high summer, the Gap is Killarney tourism at its worst. Every day cars and buses disgorge countless visitors at Kate Kearney's Cottage, who then proceed on a one-hour horse-and-trap ride through the Gap; no cars are allowed in summer. You could also walk through the narrow gorge to the Black Valley Hostel at the other end, but don't do this in summer if you want to be alone.

The best way to see the Gap is to hire a bike from Killarney and cycle to Ross Castle, then take the boat across the lakes to Lord Brandon's Cottage and cycle through the Gap and back into town via the N72 and a path through the golf course (including bike hire about €19).

The boat ride alone justifies the trip. It lasts 1½ hours and passes through all three lakes, with lovely views of the surrounding mountains and of the Meeting of the Waters and Ladies View, which was much enjoyed by Queen Victoria's ladies-in-waiting, who gave it its name. Lunches and teas are available at the 19th-century *Kate Kearney's Cottage* (☎ *44146)* and *Lord Brandon's Cottage*.

Organised Tours

Guided two-hour **walks** of the National Park (☎ 44339, 087 639 4362) leave at 11am daily from the Shell petrol station on Lower New St in Killarney (adult/child €6.35/3.15).

A number of Killarney companies run daily day trips by bus around the Ring of Kerry, the Gap of Dunloe and Dingle Peninsula, costing around €18.50, €21 and €19.50, respectively. Tours last from 10.30am until around 5.30pm. Half-day tours, taking in Aghadoe, Ross Castle, Muckross House and Torc Waterfall, also operate daily, as do bike tours and lake cruises. Some companies you might try are *O'Connor Tours* (☎ *30200, 7 High St)*, *Dero's Tours* (☎ *31251, 22 Main St)*, *Corcoran's* (☎ *36666, 8 College St)* and *Cronin's Tours* (☎ *31521, College St)*. However, unless you're really pushed for time these are too rushed a way to do justice to the scenery.

Destination Killarney (☎ *32638, Scott's Gardens)* and *Killarney Watercoach Cruises* (☎ *31068)* operate hour-long lake cruises with commentary from Ross Castle five times a day (around €6.35). A number of private boat owners offer lake trips for the same price from near Ross Castle but you won't find them around during winter.

Killarney to Kenmare

The N71 links Killarney to Kenmare, with spectacular lake and mountain scenery along the way. Two kilometres south of the entrance to Muckross House a path leads 200m to the pretty **Torc Waterfall**. After another 8km on the N71 you come to **Ladies View**, with fine views along Upper Lake. There's another good viewpoint 5km farther along at **Moll's Gap**.

Ring of Kerry

The Ring of Kerry, the 179km road circuit round the Iveragh Peninsula, is one of Ireland's premier tourist attractions. Although it can be 'done' in a day by car or bus, or three days by bike, the more time you take the more you'll enjoy it. The stretch of road between Waterville and Caherdaniel in the south-west of the peninsula is reason enough for coming here. The Ballaghbeama Gap cuts across the peninsula's central highlands with some spectacular views and remarkably little traffic: it's perfect for a long cycle. See Walking under Activities in the Facts for the Visitor chapter for details of the 214km Kerry Way, which starts and ends in Killarney. It is marked on the Ring of Kerry map.

Tour buses approach the Ring in an anticlockwise direction. In high season it's hard to know which is more unpleasant – driving round behind them or travelling in the opposite direction and meeting them on blind corners. Note that petrol gets more expensive the farther west you go: fill up before setting out. Also, things get much quieter at the western end of the Iveragh Peninsula, when you leave the Ring of Kerry for the Skellig Ring.

An 80km cycle tour via Lough Acoose and Moll's Gap is marked on the Ring of Kerry map.

GETTING AROUND

Late May to mid-September Bus Éireann operates a Ring of Kerry bus service. Buses leave Killarney at 8.30am and 1.30pm Monday to Saturday, and 9.40am (July and August only) and 12.45pm (May to September only) on Sunday. They stop at Killorglin, Glenbeigh, Kells, Caherciveen, Waterville, Caherdaniel and Sneem before returning to Killarney via Moll's Gap. For more details ring Killarney bus station (☎ 064-34777).

KILLORGLIN
☎ 066 • pop 3266
Travelling anticlockwise from Killarney, the first town on the Ring is Killorglin (Cill Orglan), which is famed for its annual Puck Fair

KERRY

RING OF KERRY

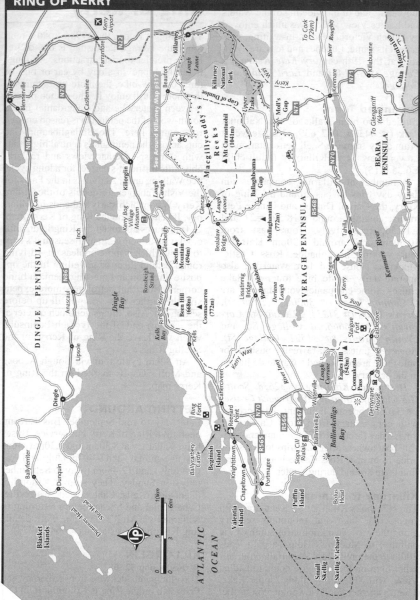

Festival. Although there's not a great deal to see here, it's a pleasant town with a nice setting on the River Laune – the eight-arched bridge over the river was built in 1885 – and there are some excellent places to stay and eat, and plenty of busy pubs with live music.

Mid-Kerry Tourism has its office (☎ 976 1451) in a stone booth beside the unclearly marked roundabout from which one of the roads leads to Glenbeigh. It opens 9am to 5.30pm Monday to Saturday year round and 11am to 3pm on Sunday during the summer.

Puck Fair Festival

This rumbustious three-day celebration takes place during the second weekend in August. It is based round the custom of installing a billy goat (a puck), its horns festooned in ribbons, on a pedestal in the town centre and leaving it there while everyone takes advantage of the special licensing hours. Pubs stay open till 3am, although it often seems that they simply serve for three days nonstop. Accommodation is hard to come by if you haven't booked in advance.

The Fishery

The Fishery is a salmon smokery (☎ 976 1106) on the other side of the river from the centre – turn left over the bridge. You can see how salmon are smoked and buy it fresh. Orders of any size can be delivered to anywhere in Europe and the USA.

Places to Stay

West's Holiday Park (☎ 976 1240, fax 976 1833, Killarney Rd) Tent & 2 people €8.95, showers €0.65. Open Easter-Oct. This small, family-oriented park is just under 2km from the bridge in Killorglin on the road to Killarney. It has a pool, tennis court and children's play area.

Laune Valley Farm Hostel (☎ 976 1488, Banshagh) Beds in 4/6-bed dorm €11.45/ 10.15, double rooms €26.70-35.55. This IHH property, 1.8km from the bridge on the N70 to Tralee, comes complete with satellite TV.

The River's Edge (☎/fax 976 1750, ⓔ coffeya@tinet.ie, The Bridge) Singles/ doubles €38.10/50.80, minisuites €38.10/

63.55. We highly recommend this friendly B&B which has a great spot overlooking the river. Both the minisuites – decorated in a Mediterranean villa style – and the standard rooms are extremely comfortable.

O'Grady's (☎ 976 2012, fax 064-33685, Canberra House, Upper Bridge St) Singles/ doubles €35.55/45.75. Ask for one of the rooms at the back of this pleasant B&B as they are much quieter.

Places to Eat

Bunkers Bar & Coffee Shop (☎ 976 1381, Iveragh Rd) Starters €3.20-5, mains €8.50-15. This combined pub-restaurant-takeaway is not the most attractive of places but the menu is huge and the prices reasonable.

Da Vinci (☎ 976 1055, Old School Rd) Pasta & pizza €9-10. This Italian bistro is tastefully decorated with subtle lighting.

Kerry's Vintage Inn (☎ 976 2337, Upper Bridge St) Meals €4.50-10. This pleasant little pub serves above-average pub grub, including all the traditional dishes.

Harmony (☎ 976 2588, Mill Rd) Mains €9.50-13. This Chinese restaurant had just opened at the time of writing but was already acclaimed by locals. It serves all the usual Cantonese dishes.

Nick's Restaurant (☎ 976 1219, Lower Bridge St) Starters €3.70-9.50, mains €14.60-21.40. We're told that people come from miles away and stay in Killorglin just to eat here. Inside it's cosy and feels like a cellar; the wine list is well chosen.

Bianconi (☎ 976 1146, Annadale Rd) Mains €14-21.50. This is a fine-dining restaurant with an award-winning French chef. Dishes include turbot fillet in seaweed with cucumber ribbons.

Entertainment

Clifford's Tavern (☎ 976 1539, Upper Bridge St) This traditional bar with an open fireplace has room to move, unlike most places in Killorglin, and there are traditional music sessions on Friday and Saturday nights.

Old Forge (☎ 976 1231, The Square) At the top of Bridge St, this place has traditional music during the week and a disco and live bands at the weekend.

KERRY

The Kerry Bog Pony

This unique breed of pony has existed in Kerry since before the 17th century. Its ancestor was probably originally imported from Asturias, Spain. There were once large herds of these small ponies, then known as Hobbies, which, because of their strength, toughness and easy maintenance, were used to bring turf from the bogs and seaweed to farms.

However, their numbers declined rapidly when many were taken (back) to Spain to serve as pack animals, and food, for the British army during the Peninsular Wars against Napoleon at the start of the 19th century. This decline was accelerated by changes in agricultural equipment and practices that necessitated the use of stronger, taller ponies and horses. By the early 20th century they were thought to be extinct.

Enter John Mulvihill, who runs the Kerry Bog Village Museum and is a breeder of ponies and horses. He discovered a small group of ponies but, although he recognised their rare quality, didn't know that they were Kerry Bog ponies until they had undergone blood typing and DNA testing. Following an intensive breeding program and the creation of the Kerry Bog Pony Society to protect them, there are now about 200. They were designated a rare breed in 1994 and today are used for riding and trekking.

JANE SMITH

The Laune Bar *(Lower Bridge St)* Just around the corner from The River's Edge B&B, this is not an attractive bar but Thursday night traditional sessions really get going.

Getting Around
Bikes can be hired from O'Shea's Cycle Centre (☎ 976 1919), Lower Bridge St, for €9.50/50.80 per day/week.

KERRY BOG VILLAGE MUSEUM
On the N70 between Killorglin and Glenbeigh and worth a quick stop is the Kerry Bog Village Museum (☎ 066-976 9184; *adult/child €3.15/1.90; open 9am-7pm daily Mar-Oct; on request Nov-Feb).* It recreates the buildings of a 19th-century bog village, with the homes of the turfcutter, the blacksmith, thatcher and labourer, and a dairy. Admission includes €0.65 off an Irish coffee at the Red Fox pub next door. Some Kerry Bog ponies are in a field behind the museum.

Red Fox *(☎ 976 9288, Glenbeigh)* Meals €5-7.50. This pub is a real tourist trap but serves good pub food ('turfcutter's delight' is a steak burger) and puts on live-music

weekends. There's a useful notice board, and a phone, just inside the porch.

CAHERCIVEEN
☎ 066 • pop 1300
As late as 1815, Caherciveen (Cathair Saidhthin), also spelled Cahersiveen, had only five houses, but it's now one of the larger settlements along the Ring, even if it remains more or less one long street.

Daniel O'Connell, 'The Great Liberator', was born near here. The ruins of his home can be seen to the left of the new bridge as you come into town from Kells.

The tourist office (☎ 947 2589), in The Barracks, opens 10am to 6pm Monday to Saturday and 1pm to 6pm on Sunday, May to September; and 9.30am to 5.30pm weekdays the rest of the year. It sells an *O'Connell Heritage Trail* leaflet (€1.25). The 6.5km trail takes about 2½ hours.

The Barracks
This heritage centre is superbly situated in what was once an intimidating Royal Irish Constabulary (RIC) barracks (☎ 947 2777; *adult/child €3.80/1.90; open 10am-6pm*

Mon-Sat & 1pm-6pm Sun May-Sept; 10am-5pm Mon-Fri Oct-Apr). The building was burned down in 1922 by anti-Treaty forces, but was reconstructed to its present remarkable state, looking not unlike some kind of castle for a film set. The story goes that the plans for this building got mixed up with ones intended for India; when you see it you might believe this particular piece of blarney.

The exhibits feature information on Daniel O'Connell, the Fenian Rising and other subjects of local and national interest. To get there, coming from the Kells end of town, turn right at the junction of Bridge and Church Sts.

Ballycarbery Castle & Ring Forts

Continue past The Barracks and over the bridge for 2.4km for the ruins of Ballycarbery Castle. Unfortunately, the castle is on private land and the only access is via the beach at the end of the road when the tide's out.

Along the same road are two stone ring forts. Leacanabuaile is the smaller one and dates from the 9th century. Cahergall, the larger, dates from the 10th century and has stairways on the inside walls, a beehive hut and the remains of a house. It's accessible by foot. Leave your car in the parking area next to a stone wall and walk up the pathway.

Special Events

The Caherciveen Celtic International Music Festival takes place over the bank holiday weekend in August. Phone John O'Connor on ☎ 947 3262 for more information.

Places to Stay

Mannix Point Camping & Caravan Park (☎ 947 2806, fax 947 2028, Mannix Point) Tent site €5.10 per person. Open mid-Mar-Sept. A well run but windy place, it's a 15-minute walk west of town, signposted off the N70. Rates include showers.

Sive Hostel (☎ 947 2717, e sivehostel@ oceanfree.net, 15 East End) Dorms €10.15-11.45, doubles €24.15-26.70. This IHH property is at the eastern end of the long main street. It has three double rooms. Boat trips to the Skellig Islands can be arranged here.

O'Shea's B&B (☎ 947 2402, Church St) Singles/doubles €31.75/48.30. This attractive B&B is just a short stroll from the Barracks.

Caherciveen Park Hotel (☎ 947 2543, fax 947 2893, Valentia Rd) Singles/doubles €50.80/88.95 June-Aug, €38.10/63.50 Sept-May. This hotel is more like a B&B, though some rooms are quite spacious.

Places to Eat

Helen Shine Coffee Shop (☎ 947 2056, Main St) Meals €2.50-2.90. This place serves soup, sandwiches and basic meals.

Cráineen's Bar (☎ 947 2168, Main St) Bar snacks €2-4.50. Food here consists mainly of sandwiches. There's traditional music some nights.

The Seahorse Restaurant (☎ 947 2153, Main St) Meals €14-19. Open for dinner only. With its own fish shop out front, this seafood restaurant has both traditional and Asian-influenced dishes.

The Fertha (☎ 947 2023, 20 Main St) Bar food €7-9. This large pub serves roasts, poached salmon and curry among other things. The bar is a nice place to stop for a drink and on Friday night local bands play to a laid-back crowd.

The Red Rose (☎ 947 2293, 24 Church St) Lunch €5-10, dinner €11.40-16.50. A little bit of everything is available here, including Thai soup, Italian pasta and Spanish chicken.

Getting There & Away

As well as the regular Ring of Kerry bus service, from April to October there is a ferry service (☎ 947 6141) to Knightstown on Valentia Island from Reenard Point, 5km west of Caherciveen. The 10-minute crossing costs €5.10 for a car (pedestrians and cyclists €3.80). It operates 7.30am to 10.30pm Monday to Saturday, and 8.30am to 10.30pm on Sunday.

VALENTIA ISLAND
☎ 066

Valentia Island (Oileán Dairbhru) may be only 11km long and 3km wide but it doesn't feel like an island, especially if you come by road. It's a low-key place; a day or half-day trip is all you'll need.

Valentia was chosen as the site for the first transatlantic telegraph cable, and when the connection was made in 1858 it put Caherciveen in direct contact with New York even though it had no connection with Dublin! The link worked for 27 days before failing, but went back into action some years later. The telegraph station was in operation until 1966.

In 1992 the **fossilised footprints** of a marine creature dating back around 365 million years were discovered on some rocks near the lighthouse at the north-western point of the island. The discovery of this tetrapod footprint was the first of its kind in Europe.

The Skellig Experience

Immediately across the bridge from Portmagee you'll see a construction that looks something like a bomb shelter. This is The Skellig Experience (☎ 947 6306; adult/child €4.45/2.20; open 10am-6pm daily Easter-Oct; 10am-5pm Oct-mid-Nov) and it contains exhibitions on the life and times of the Skellig Michael monks, the history of the lighthouses on Skellig Michael, and the wildlife. If you're planning a trip to the Skelligs it's worth coming here for background information. If the weather's bad this may be as close as you get to the islands.

Getting There & Away

Most visitors reach Valentia Island via the bridge from Portmagee. From April to October, pedestrians, cyclists and motorists can also cross by ferry from Reenard Point near Caherciveen to the pier at Knightstown (see Getting There & Away under Cahirciveen earlier).

SKELLIG ISLANDS

A boat trip to the two Skellig Islands (Oileáin na Scealaga), 12km out in the Atlantic Ocean, is one of the highlights of a trip to Ireland. The crossing can be rough and there are no toilets or shelter on Skellig Michael, the only island you may land on. Bring stout shoes, something to eat and drink, warm clothing and something waterproof to protect you from the boat's spray.

Bird-Watching

If you can't get to the Galapagos then a trip to the Skelligs offers a taste of the peculiar pleasure of spying on nesting sea birds. From the boat, look out for diminutive storm petrels, black birds that dart over the water like swallows, and for yellow-headed gannets with a wingspan of 107cm. Kittiwakes – lemon-beaked seagulls with black-tipped wings – are easy to see and hear around the covered walkway of Skellig Michael just after stepping off the boat. They winter at sea but then come in their thousands to breed between March and August. Farther up the rock you'll see snub-nosed fulmar, black-and-white guillemot and razorbill. Look out, also, for the delightful puffins with their multicoloured beaks and waddling gait. Puffins lay one egg at the end of a burrow in May and parent birds can be seen guarding their nests. Puffins stay only until the first week or two of August.

Skellig Michael

The 217m-high jagged rock of Skellig Michael (Archangel Michael's Rock), the larger of the two islands and a Unesco World Heritage Site, looks like the last place on earth that anyone would try to land, let alone establish a community. Yet early-Christian monks survived here from the 6th until the 12th or 13th century. They were influenced by the Coptic Church founded by St Anthony in the deserts of Egypt and Libya, and their desire for solitude led them to this remote, westernmost corner of Europe.

The monastic buildings are perched on a saddle in the rock, some 150m above sea level, and are reached by 600 steps cut into the rock face. The astounding 6th-century oratories and beehive cells vary in size, the largest cell having a floor space of 4.5m by 3.6m. The projecting stones on the outside have more than one possible explanation: steps to reach the top and release chimney stones, or maybe holding places for turf that covered the exterior. Some cells have interior rows of stones, and the guides who live on the rock from mid-May to September will provide a possible explanation for these as well. They'll also point out the cistern in the rock for storing rainwater.

Little is known about the life of the monastery, but there are records of Viking raids in 812 and 823. Monks were killed or taken away but the community recovered and carried on. Legend even says that one of these raiders, Olaf Tryggvesson, was converted by the monks and became Norway's first Christian ruler. In the 11th century a rectangular oratory was added to the site, but although it was expanded in the 12th century the monks abandoned the rock around this time, perhaps because of more than usually ferocious Atlantic storms.

After the introduction of the Gregorian calendar in 1582, Skellig Michael became a popular spot for weddings. Marriages were forbidden during Lent, but since Skellig used the old Julian calendar a trip over to the islands allowed those unable to wait for Easter to tie the knot.

In the 1820s two lighthouses were built on Skellig Michael, together with the road that runs round the base.

You're asked to do your picnicking on the way up to the monastery, or at Christ's Saddle just before the last flight of steps, rather than among the ruins. This is to keep sandwich-loving birds and their droppings away from the monument.

Warning A notice on the island warns of 'an element of danger' in visiting Skellig Michael. Although you could fall on the rocks or stone steps, the biggest element of danger seems attached to getting off the boat at the island. Make sure your shoes have a good grip.

Small Skellig

Small Skellig is a bird sanctuary and you cannot land on it. While Skellig Michael looks like two triangles linked by a spur, Small Skellig is longer, lower and much craggier. From a distance it looks as if someone had battered it with a feather pillow that burst. Close up you realise you're looking at a colony of 20,000 pairs of breeding gannets, the second largest breeding colony in the world. Most boats circle

the island so you can see them. Check beforehand if the boat will pause to look for basking seals.

Getting There & Away

Because of concerns for the fragility of Skellig Michael there are limits on how many people can visit on the same day. Nineteen boats are licensed to carry no more than 12 passengers each, so there should never be more than 250 people there at any one time. Because of these limits it's wise to book ahead in July and August, always bearing in mind that if the weather's bad the boats may not sail. Trips usually start around Easter but high seas and bad weather can put them off until May.

You can depart from either Portmagee (and even Caherciveen), Ballinskelligs or Derrynane. The boat owners try to restrict you to two hours on the island, which is the bare minimum, on a good day, to see the monastery, look at the birds and have a picnic. The crossing from Portmagee takes about 90 minutes, from Ballinskelligs about 60 minutes (return around €32 from both places).

Some operators to try include: Owen Walsh (☎ 066-947 6327, 947 6115), Michael O'Sullivan (☎ 066-947 4255), Des Lavelle (☎ 066-947 6124) and Sean and Sheila O'Shea (☎ 066-947 5129). Most pubs and B&Bs in the area will point you in the right direction anyway.

WATERVILLE
☎ 066 • pop 500
The popular beach resort of Waterville (An Coireán) is a triangle of pubs, restaurants and shops on a narrow bit of land between Ballinskelligs Bay and Lough Currane. Charlie Chaplin was probably the town's most famous visitor; there's a statue of him on the foreshore and photographs of him in the Butler Arms Hotel.

Waterville has one of the world's most exclusive **golf courses**, which brings a number of famous faces to town from time to time.

For a pleasant 13km drive or a challenging walk from Waterville take the turn-off for

Lough Currane, 0.8km east of Waterville (where the roadsign includes 'Lakelands Farm Guesthouse' and 'Lake Rise B&B'). Sheep, mountains, water, lush greenery and waterfalls make for some of Ireland's most 'Irish' scenery. Drivers should note that the road is narrow and there are not many places to turn.

Activities

Waterville Golf Links (☎ 947 4102) charges a ridiculous €127 a round (€63.50 before 8am and off-season) but it is one of the most stunning links courses in the world and attracts serious golfers from all over.

There are lots of **angling** possibilities around Waterville. Lough Currane has free fishing for sea trout while the Inny River is a breeding ground for wild salmon and trout. Sea angling takes in mackerel, pollack and shark. The **Tadhg O'Sullivan** (☎ 947 4433, Main St) tackle shop has information.

Places to Stay

Clifford's B&B (☎/fax 947 4283, Main St) Rooms €22.85-25.40 per person. This is the first B&B you pass if you are coming from Caherdaniel and is a five-minute walk to pubs and restaurants. It has unmarred views from rooms at the front.

Butler Arms Hotel (☎ 947 4144, fax 947 4520, e butarms@iol.ie, Main St) Rooms €89 per person mid-May-Sept, €71.80 Oct-mid-May. This 1940s hotel is the most upmarket hotel in town and was having a bit of a facelift at the time of writing.

Scariff Inn (☎ 947 5143, fax 947 5425, e scarriff@aol.com, Caherdaniel) Singles/doubles €38.10/58.45. Meals €8-11. Restaurant open for lunch & dinner Apr-Sept. About 5km south of Waterville on the N70 on the Coomakesta Pass, this B&B and **restaurant** boasts 'Ireland's best-known view' (fog permitting) from its Vista Bar – it really is stunning.

The Smuggler's Inn (☎ 947 4330, fax 947 4422, Cliff Rd) Singles/doubles €48.30/68.60 May-Sept, €44.45/63.50 Oct-Apr. Across from the golf course above a long, sandy beach, this B&B and restaurant (see Places to Eat) is popular with

golfers. The rooms are in need of a bit of a facelift, however.

Places to Eat

The Sheilin (☎ 947 4231, Top Cross) Mains €14-20, early-bird 2-course menu (6pm-7.30pm) €17.65. Open for dinner only. This restaurant specialises in seafood.

The Smuggler's Inn (see Places to Stay) Bar food €8-14, restaurant mains €19-25. Open for lunch and dinner. This attractive restaurant, with a nautical theme, has floor-to-ceiling glass windows for some great views across Ballinskelligs Bay.

SKELLIG RING

The Skellig Ring, a Gaeltacht or Irish-speaking area, is a scenic route that links Waterville with Portmagee via Ballinskelligs (Baile an Sceilg). It's signposted as you leave and is an enjoyable cycle route; however, there are lots of small unmarked roads, making it easy to get lost. For a great view of the Skellig Islands, don't pass up the coin-operated telescope by the roadside, just north of the Skellig Chocolate Factory.

Siopa Cill Rialaig Art Gallery

This remote gallery, en route to Ballinskelligs, contains work by local and international artists and writers (☎ 066-947 9324, e cillrialaig@easatclear.ie, Ballinskelligs; open 11am-5pm daily). It is home to the Cill Rialaig Project which seeks to provide an international retreat for artists, writers and composers. Cheap accommodation and free studio space are available to genuine artists who are then asked to donate a piece of work to the gallery. Those wishing to apply need to send a CV with pictures of their work and details of any exhibitions.

To reach the gallery, look for the stone buildings on the R566 with the cone-shaped, thatched roofs.

Ballinskelligs Monastery & Bay

The exact relationship between this monastery and the one on Skellig Michael isn't clear. It was probably founded after the monks left Skellig in the 12th or 13th century. The sea is gradually wearing away the ruins and it's the sort of place that children like to explore. Continue past the post office in Ballinskelligs down to Ballinskelligs Bay and walk to the remains from there. At the western end of this beautiful Blue Flag beach are the last remnants of a 16th-century castle stronghold of the McCarthys. Turn left at the junction after the post office for the castle.

Skellig Chocolate Factory

Just when you were least expecting it, by the roadside on the R565, in the middle of nowhere, there looms a small chocolate factory (☎ 066-947 9119, Skellig Ring; free; open 8.30am-8.30pm daily). Tastings are available though coach parties stop here and things can get very clogged up.

Places to Stay & Eat

Ballinskelligs Hostel (☎ 066-947 9229, Prior House) Open Easter-Sept. Dorms €7.60-8.90. This An Óige hostel, with its bright external mural, is reached by turning right at the small junction after passing the post office. There's a small grocery shop next door.

Behind the post office, **Ballinskelligs Inn** (☎ 066-947 9104) serves food and has accommodation Easter to September (B&B around €26 per person).

CAHERDANIEL
☎ 066

Pretty Caherdaniel is tightly wedged into the foothills of Eagle Hill. It consists of just a couple of streets but boasts a particularly important historic house, a couple of sandy beaches by the harbour and a choice of hostels.

Derrynane National Historic Park

Having grown rich on smuggling with France and Spain, the O'Connells bought **Derrynane House** and the surrounding parkland (☎ 947 5113, Derrynane; adult/child €2.55/1.25; open 9am-6pm Mon-Sat & 11am-7pm Sun May-Sept; 1pm-5pm Tues-Sun Apr & Oct; 1pm-5pm Sat & Sun Nov-Mar; last admission 45 minutes before closing). They evaded official restrictions

on the purchase of land by Catholics with the help of a cooperative Protestant.

The house is largely furnished with items relating to Daniel O'Connell, the campaigner for Catholic emancipation. Most amazing of all is the restored triumphal chariot in which O'Connell rode around Dublin after his release from prison in 1844.

There is a walking track through the surrounding wetlands from where you can spot wild pheasant and other birds. The grounds also include a sandy beach and **Abbey Island**, which can usually be reached on foot across the sand. The **chapel**, which O'Connell added to Derrynane House in 1844, is a copy of the ruined one on Abbey Island.

Look out for an **ogham stone** on the left of the road leading down to the house.

Activities

Caherdaniel competes with Valentia Island as the **diving** base for the Iveragh Peninsula. Two companies offer courses and equipment hire: **Derrynane Diving School** (☎ 947 5110) and **Skellig Aquatics Dive Centre** (☎ 947 5277). The latter, opposite Caherdaniel Village Hostel, can also arrange abseiling, rock climbing and hill walking. Contact **Derrynane Sea Sports** (☎ 947 5266) for canoeing, windsurfing and water-skiing.

Places to Stay & Eat

Glenbeg Caravan & Camping Park (☎ 947 5182) Tent & 2 people €10.80. Open mid-Apr-early Oct. This place is situated on a small, sandy beach from where you get wonderful views out to the Kenmare River and across to the Beara Peninsula. It's 2.5km east of town on the N70.

Caherdaniel Village Hostel (☎ 947 5227) Dorms €10.15, twins & doubles €26.70. This IHH property is in an interesting building in the congested main street.

The Olde Forge (☎ 947 5140) Singles/doubles €31.75/48.30. A pleasant B&B with good views, it is 1.2km east of Caherdaniel on the N70.

Dunbree House (☎ 947 5317) Rooms €21.60 per person. This tiny place is opposite the Blind Piper and has two double rooms with shared bathroom only.

The Blind Piper (☎ *947 5126*) Bar food €4-12. This atmospheric pub and restaurant has outdoor seating in summer and opens for meals year round.

STAIGUE FORT

This 2000-year-old fort is one of Ireland's finest dry-stone buildings. Its 5m-high circular wall up to 4m thick is surrounded by a large bank and ditch, rather like at Grianán of Ailéach in County Donegal, although this fort hasn't been so thoroughly restored.

The fort probably dates from the 3rd or 4th century. Despite having sweeping views down to the coast it can't be seen from the sea. It may have been a communal place of refuge, or a royal residence as the sophisticated staircases incorporated into the walls suggest.

It's near the village of Castlecove, about 4km off the N70, reached by a potholed country lane which narrows as it climbs to the site. In summer the road becomes the scene of absurd traffic jams! A sign by the gate demands €0.65 for access to the land (for what it calls 'trespass') even though the fort is owned by Dúchas. A small metal honesty box is nearby to put the money in.

KENMARE

☎ 064 • pop 1150

At the point where the Finnihy, Roughty and Sheen Rivers empty into Kenmare River, the pocket-sized town of Kenmare (Neidín) is ablaze with vivid yellow, green, red and blue buildings. Outside the summer months it's a sleepy place but, for those with their own transport, Kenmare makes a much more pleasant alternative to Killarney as a base for visiting the Rings of Kerry and Beara.

Orientation & Information

In the 18th century Kenmare was laid out on an X-plan, with a triangular market square in the centre and Fair Green nestling in its upper V. To the south, Henry and Main Sts are the primary shopping and eating/drinking thoroughfares, with Shelbourne St joining them up at the southern end. Ken-

mare River stretches out to the south-west, with glorious views of the Caha Mountains.

The tourist office (☎ 41233), in the Square, opens 9.15am to 5.30pm Easter to October (till 7pm during July and August). Pick up a free heritage-trail leaflet showing places of historic interest. The post office at the top of Henry St is also a good place for local walking maps and guides when the tourist office is closed. It also has Internet access but it's very expensive at €2.55 for 10 minutes. Kenmare has its own Web site at Ⓦ www.neidin.net.

The Allied Irish Bank, on the corner of Main and Henry Sts, has an ATM and bureau de change. You'll find public toilets opposite the Holy Cross Church in Old Killarney Rd.

Kenmare Heritage Centre

Behind the tourist office is Kenmare Heritage Centre (☎ *41233, adult/child €2.55/ 1.25; open 9.15am-7pm Mon-Sat July & Aug; 9.15am-5.30pm Mon-Sat Easter-June & Sept*). It recounts the history of the town from its founding as Neidín by William Petty-Fitzmaurice in 1670. Particularly interesting is the information about the Kenmare Poor Clare Convent (still standing behind Holy Cross Church), which was founded in 1862 and provided local women with work as needlepoint lacemakers. Samples of their work are on display here and more can be seen upstairs in **Kenmare Lace and Design Centre**. Also interesting in the heritage centre is the story of Margaret Anna Cusack (1829–99), the Nun of Kenmare and an early advocate of women's rights who was eventually hounded out of Kenmare as a political agitator, then renounced Catholicism in favour of Protestantism and died, embittered, in Leamington, England.

Other Things to See

South-west along Market St and Pound Lane is the Bronze Age **Druid Circle**, the largest stone circle in south-west Ireland, with 15 stones ringing a boulder dolmen. Sadly, the land nearby has been used to dump rubbish. The €1.25 admission fee is a bit cheeky and the circle can be seen from the road anyway.

Our Lady's Well is a holy well in a small, pretty flower garden. To get there walk down Bridge St, which runs beside the tourist office and through the car park to the modern, whitewashed church. The well is in the far corner of the car park.

Holy Cross Church in Old Killarney Rd was built in 1864 and boasts a splendid wooden roof with 14 angels carved from Bavarian wood. The mosaics on the arches in the aisles and around the stained-glass window over the altar are another feature.

Next to the car park, opposite the church, is the early-19th-century Hutchin's Folly Tower, allegedly built by an American who settled in Kenmare after peace was negotiated with America in 1783.

Activities

Kenmare Golf Club (☎ 41291) charges €25.40 for 18 holes (€38.10 on Sunday) and €9.50 for club hire. The entrance is on the R569 to Cork, about 100m from the top of Main St.

You can hire snorkelling and diving gear from Kenmare Bay Diving (☎ 42238) in nearby Bonane. The three-hour beginner's diving program costs €31.75.

Seafari River Cruises (☎ 83171) depart from Kenmare Pier around Kenmare Bay on whale, dolphin and seal watching trips. The company also rents out sailing, canoeing and windsurfing equipment.

Beach and mountain rides are offered by Hazelwood Riding Stables (☎ 41420), 3.2km south-west of Kenmare on the R571 to Lauragh, as well as lessons for children and beginners.

Kenmare is ringed with lovely scenery and short walks can be made along the river or into the hills. The Kerry Way passes through Kenmare (see Walking under Activities in the Facts for the Visitor chapter for details).

Special Events

During the last week of May, the town hosts the Kenmare Walking Festival when people can undertake a series of walks of varying difficulty around town. To join in you must register at a booth in the Square 30 minutes before the walk departs. For more

information phone ☎ 41682 or email [e] walking@kenmare.com. During the festival two-day classes in mountain skills, costing around €65, are also organised; if you want to take part call ☎ 066-69244. Accommodation in town is hard to come by during the festival, so be sure to book ahead.

Places to Stay

Camping & Hostels It's possible to camp not far from town.

Ring of Kerry Caravan & Camping Park (☎ 41648, fax 41631, Kenmare) Tent & car €11.45. Open Apr-Sept. This camp site is 5km west of town on the Sneem road and has lovely views of the Caha Mountains.

Fáilte Hostel (☎ 12333, fax 12466, cnr Shelbourne & Henry Sts) Dorms €10.80, twin rooms €21.60-24.15. With a good kitchen and sitting room, this is a pleasant IHH hostel.

Finnegan's Corner Hostel (☎ 41083, Shelbourne St) Dorms €10.80. On the opposite corner to Fáilte Hostel, above Finnegan's Cycle Centre, this hostel has a laundry and kitchen, plus a car park at the back.

B&Bs & Hotels There are plenty of B&Bs in town though the ones in the centre tend to be quite upmarket with prices to match; a 10-minute walk north will reveal some cheaper options.

Rose Cottage (☎ 41330, The Square) Singles/doubles €38.10/63.50 June-Aug, €31.75/50.80 Sept-May. Beside Fair Green, this was where the original Poor Clare nuns stayed when they arrived in Kenmare in 1861.

Hawthorn House (☎ 41035, fax 41932, Shelbourne St) Singles €25.40-35.55, doubles €50.80-63.50 depending on room size. This well located place has lovely rooms; it's one of the nicest places in the centre.

The Wander Inn (☎ 42700, [e] wanderinn@eircom.net, 2 Henry St) Singles/doubles €38.10/63.50 Mar-Oct, €31.75/50.80 Nov-Feb. Rooms here are tastefully decorated and some are quite spacious.

Ard Na Mara (☎ 41399, Pier Rd) Singles/doubles €31.75/50.80. This 1950s-style house is about three minutes' walk from the centre on the way to the pier and has great views over Kenmare Bay. Book well ahead for a single room in July and August.

Ashberry Lodge (☎ *42720, Sneem Rd*) Singles/doubles €31.75/57.15 Mar-Oct, €25.40 per person Nov-Feb. Eight minutes' walk from the centre on the N70 to Sneem, this good-value B&B has pleasant rooms and views of the Caha Mountains.

The Lodge (☎ *41512, fax 42724,* e *the lodgekenmare@eircom.net, Kilgarvan Rd*) Singles/doubles €88.95/101.65 late June-early Sept, €76.25/88.95 early Sept-late June. This luxurious manor house has large rooms and is good value considering the quality.

Places to Eat
Kenmare is a gourmet's delight with plenty of reasonably priced restaurants and cafes with innovative menus. Self-caterers should try Hallissey's supermarket in the Square.

Restaurants There are many restaurants to choose from in Kenmare. Here are a few of our favourites.

The Coachman's Restaurant and Inn (☎ *41311, Henry St*) Mains €11-12. With a continental-style decor, this place serves good-value, basic meals such as Irish stew, chicken curry, escalope of Kerry lamb and baked salmon. Unexciting but well priced single/double rooms cost up to €38.10/45.75.

Mulcahy's Restaurant (☎ *42383, 16 Henry St*) Starters €5-8, mains €18-19.50. This modern place serves interesting dishes that could be described as modern Irish – for instance, roast quail with black pudding, seasonal vegetables and a game and chocolate sauce.

The Horseshoe (☎ *41553, 3 Main St*) Starters €3-9, mains €11-20. Recommended by locals, the house speciality is barbecued spare ribs.

An Leath Phingin (☎ *41559, 35 Main St*) Starters €4-8, mains €11.50-17.50. Although you wouldn't know from its name, this is an Italian restaurant serving homely country cooking. Try the home-made pork sausages flavoured with fennel seeds.

D'Arcy's (☎ *41589, Main St*) Starters €6-

8, mains €15-22. Reputedly the best restaurant in town, this place opens for dinner only.

Cafes There are several cafes in Henry St.

O'Leary's Sandwich Bar and Café (*Henry St*) Sandwiches & cakes €2-3. Open 8am-6pm Mon-Fri & 9am-6pm Sat. Here you can get freshly made bagels and sandwiches as well as doughnuts, scones and muffins for less than you'd pay in the trendier cafes in town.

Jam (☎ *42144, Henry St*) Sandwiches €2.50-4.80. This modern coffee shop and bakery also has great salads.

Purple Heather Bistro (☎ *41016, Henry St*) Lunch & snacks €3-12. This relaxed and cosy bar/bistro has a choice of vegetarian meals and a delicious Guinness fruit cake.

Shopping
Kenmare is a good place to shop for real Irish crafts although it has its fair share of leprechaunery and prices are fairly high.

Nostalgia (☎ *41389, 27 Henry St*) This Irish linen shop has some gorgeous antique linen and lace though it's very pricey.

PF Kelly (☎ *42590, 18 Henry St*) You'll find some beautiful modern jewellery here. The salt servers by the West Cork designer Marika O'Sullivan are stunning. It also takes commissions.

Kenmare Bookshop (☎ *41578, Shelbourne St*) Everything Irish, including maps and guides, is stocked here.

Noel & Holland (☎ *42464, 3 Bridge St*) This second-hand bookshop sells some rare editions.

Getting There & Away
As well as the main Ring of Kerry bus service, there's a bus to Killarney (45 minutes) where you can change for Tralee, and a twice-daily bus to Skibbereen (two hours 25 minutes) via Glengarriff and Bantry. Every Friday afternoon a bus goes to Lauragh, Ardgroom and Castletownbere. Buses stop outside Roughty Bar on Main St.

Getting Around
Finnegan's Cycle Centre (☎ 41083), below Finnegan's Corner Hostel on Shelbourne St,

is the Raleigh Rent-a-Bike dealer, with bikes costing €10.15/63.50 per day/week.

Northern Kerry

The northern Kerry landscape is somewhat ordinary and many travellers rush through to County Clare via the Tarbert ferry. However, there are some places of historical interest and the coastal strip is popular with Irish holiday-makers.

TRALEE
☎ 066 • pop 19,950

Tralee (Trá Lí), at the start of the Dingle Peninsula, has enough attractions to occupy half a day but otherwise it's an unattractive town and you may be better off using more appealing Listowel as a base in Northern Kerry.

Founded by the Normans in 1216, Tralee has a long history of rebellion. In the 16th century the last ruling earl of the Desmonds was captured and executed. His head was sent to Elizabeth I, who had it displayed on London Bridge. His property was given to Sir Edward Denny. The Desmond castle once stood at the junction of Denny St and The Mall. Any trace of medieval Tralee that survived the Desmond Wars was razed in the Cromwellian period.

The Rose of Tralee festival (see the boxed text) is in the last week of August.

Orientation

Tralee is a fairly small town and you'll find most things you need along The Mall and its continuation, Castle St. Wide, elegant Denny St and Day Place are the oldest parts of town with buildings from the 18th century. Ashe St is home to the Courthouse, a solemn, fortress-like building. The tourist office is at the southern end of Denny St. The bus and train stations are a five-minute walk north-east of the town centre.

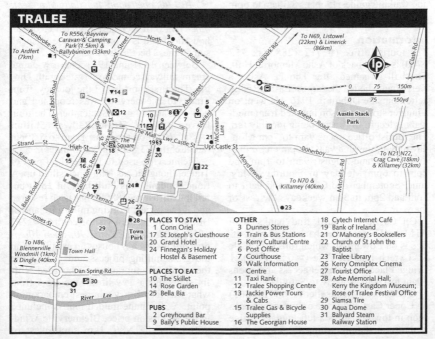

TRALEE

PLACES TO STAY
1 Conn Oriel
17 St Joseph's Guesthouse
20 Grand Hotel
24 Finnegan's Holiday Hostel & Basement

PLACES TO EAT
10 The Skillet
14 Rose Garden
25 Bella Bia

PUBS
2 Greyhound Bar
9 Baily's Public House

OTHER
3 Dunnes Stores
4 Train & Bus Stations
5 Kerry Cultural Centre
6 Post Office
7 Courthouse
8 Walk Information Centre
11 Taxi Rank
12 Tralee Shopping Centre
13 Jackie Power Tours & Cabs
15 Tralee Gas & Bicycle Supplies
16 The Georgian House
18 Cytech Internet Café
19 Bank of Ireland
21 O'Mahoney's Booksellers
22 Church of St John the Baptist
23 Tralee Library
26 Kerry Omniplex Cinema
27 Tourist Office
28 Ashe Memorial Hall; Kerry the Kingdom Museum; Rose of Tralee Festival Office
29 Siamsa Tíre
30 Aqua Dome
31 Ballyard Steam Railway Station

The Rose of Tralee

Every August Tralee comes into its own when it hosts the famous Rose of Tralee festival. Although the idea of a beauty contest is outdated in most people's minds, the title of the 'Rose' is still very much coveted in Ireland. Contestants must be Irish by birth or ancestry, which is why many past winners have been American or Australian for instance. During the five days of the festival, the town's pubs, theatres and restaurants feature events and live music well into the evening.

The Rose of Tralee Festival Office (☎ 066-712 1322, fax 712 3227, e info@rose oftralee.ie, w www.roseoftralee.ie) is in Ashe Memorial Hall on Ivy Terrace in the centre.

The Walk Information Centre (☎ 712 8733), 40 Ashe St, is the HQ of South-West Walks Ireland and has a lot of useful maps and walking guides. It opens 8.30am to 6pm Monday to Saturday.

Information
The tourist office (☎ 712 1288, fax 712 1700) is at the back of Ashe Memorial Hall. The hall is named after Thomas Ashe, a Kerryman who led the largest Easter Rising action outside Dublin in 1916. He went on a hunger strike in prison but died from medical neglect in 1917 after being forcibly fed. The tourist office opens 9am to 7pm Monday to Saturday and 9am to 6pm on Sunday during July and August; 9am to 1pm and 2pm to 6pm Monday to Saturday, May, June, September and October; and 9am to 1pm and 2pm to 5pm weekdays the rest of the year.

On Castle St you'll find banks with ATMs and bureaux de change. The post office is on Edward St, which runs off Castle St. Cytech Internet Café (☎ 714 4472), 1 Bridge Place, has Internet access and opens 10am to 10pm Monday to Saturday.

O'Mahony's Booksellers (☎ 712 2266) on Upper Castle St is the only decent bookshop in town. There's a left luggage office at the train station costing €2.55 per item

for 24 hours, and you'll find public toilets off Russell St.

Kerry the Kingdom Museum
Also in the Ashe Memorial Hall but entered round the corner from the tourist office is this museum (☎ 712 7777, Ivy Terrace; adult/child €7.60/3.80; open 10am-6pm daily mid-Mar-Oct; 10am-5pm Nov & Dec). It gives a concise history of Ireland – with an emphasis on Kerry. Also here is the Geraldine Experience, a multimedia presentation that includes a ride around the re-creation of a walled town from 1450. Children love it and a commentary in eight languages is available.

Other Things to See & Do
The **Georgian House** was built by Justice Robert Day, a member of Tralee's upper class and a local political figure in the 1790s. He was the son of Maurice Day, who was the Knight of Kerry. Today the house is a **visitor centre** (☎ 712 6995, 3 Day Place; adult/child €5.10/1.90; open noon-4pm daily May-Sept; call ☎ 087 264 7195 for an appointment at other times). It recreates a typical Georgian household and is a pleasant place to spend some time. There's also a tearoom.

Between 1891 and 1953 a narrow-gauge **steam railway** connected Tralee with Dingle. The first short leg of the journey, from Tralee to Blennerville, was reopened and now operates May to September. The train leaves **Ballyard Steam Railway Station** (☎ 712 1064) on the hour, 11am to 5.30pm (adult/child €3.80/1.90, 20 minutes).

Blennerville used to be the chief port of Tralee, though it has long since silted up. A flour **windmill** was built here in 1800 but fell into disuse by 1880. It has been restored and is the largest working mill in Ireland or Britain. The modern **visitor centre** (☎ 712 1064; adult/child €3.80/1.90; open 10am-6pm daily Apr-Oct) houses an exhibition on the grain milling process and one on the thousands of emigrants who boarded 'coffin ships' for a new life in the USA from what was then Kerry's largest embarkation point. A 30-minute guided tour is included in the admission price. Blennerville Windmill is on the N86, 1km south-west of

Tralee. One way to get there is by the steam railway.

The Roman Catholic **Church of St John the Baptist** (☎ 712 2522, Castle St), with its 61m spire, was built in the mid-19th century in the neo-Gothic style. Some artefacts from an earlier chapel dating from 1780 remain, including the water font and gables that now sit in the transepts of the present-day church.

On the south-western outskirts, in an impressive building, is the **Aqua Dome** (☎ 712 8899; adult/child €7.60/6.35; open 10am-10pm daily June-Aug; phone for other times as they vary). It has water slides, wave pools, saunas, minigolf, the lot, but you pay through the nose to use them.

Organised Tours
Jackie Power Tours and Cabs (☎ 712 9444, 2 Lower Rock St) can arrange minibus tours to Dingle and Slea Head, the Ring of Kerry and around Northern Kerry.

Places to Stay
Central accommodation is mostly in expensive hotels or above pubs where rooms tend to be very smoky. For B&Bs your best bet is Pembroke St where there are a few well priced places only a few minutes' walk from the centre. Most B&Bs raise their prices by €5 or €6 during the Rose of Tralee festival.

Bayview Caravan & Camping Park (☎ 712 6140, Killeen) Tent & 2 people €12.70. Open year round. This small park, 1.5km north of the centre on the R556, has special offers such as stay for three nights, pay for two.

Finnegan's Holiday Hostel (☎/fax 712 7610, ℮ imptralee@indigo.ie, 17 Denny St) Dorms €10.80-12.05, doubles €31.75. This Georgian hostel is well positioned in the nicest street in town. Cooking and lounge facilities here are exceptionally good.

St Joseph's Guesthouse (☎ 712 1174, fax 712 1254, 2 Staughton's Row) Singles/doubles €29.20/50.80. This place offers a good single rate for such a central location though the bedrooms aren't of the same standard as the elegant rooms in the rest of the house.

Conn Oriel (☎ 712 5359, ℮ connoriel@

dol.ie, 6 Pembroke Square) Singles/doubles €31.75/48.30. Only 200m from the centre, this place is a much better option than the pokey and noisy central B&Bs.

Grand Hotel (☎ 712 1499, fax 712 2877, ℮ info@grandhoteltralee.com, Denny St) Singles €57.15-63.50, doubles €96.55-114.35. This friendly hotel is going for the old-world feel, with lots of dark reproduction furniture.

Places to Eat
It's not hard finding somewhere reasonable for lunch or a snack. In the evening, however, you're better off sticking to pubs for meals. For self-caterers there's Dunnes Stores on North Circular Rd.

The Skillet (☎ 712 4561, Barrack Lane) Meals €10-15. This place serves mainly seafood and steaks and is good value. It's also open for breakfast and afternoon tea.

Rose Garden (☎ 712 9393, Lower Rock St) Mains €8-14, early-bird 3-course dinner (5pm-7pm) €13.85. This is your best bet for Chinese. Prices are €2.50 to €4 less at the takeaway counter next door.

Finnegan's Basement (☎ 712 7610, 17 Denny St) Starters €3-7.50, mains €12-21. This restaurant and wine bar, with its stone walls and gingham tablecloths, serves international cuisine. It's downstairs from Finnegan's Holiday Hostel.

Bella Bia (☎ 714 4896, Ivy Terrace) Pizza & pasta €8-14, mains €14-19. This Italian restaurant opens for lunch and dinner and serves good food in modern surrounds.

Entertainment
Castle St is thick with pubs, many of them with live entertainment of one kind or another.

Baily's Public House (☎ 712 1527, Ashe St) This dark and labyrinth-like pub is lively and friendly and our favourite drinking haunt in town. There are traditional sessions most nights, and local musicians performing original material.

Greyhound Bar (☎ 712 6668, Pembroke St) This place has slate and wood floors and a long bar to sit at. It has jazz in summer in the beer garden.

Siamsa Tíre (☎ 712 3055, **e** *siamsatire@ eircom.net, Ivy Terrace)* At this venue (pronounced shee-am-sah tee-reh) the National Folk Theatre of Ireland re-creates aspects of Gaelic culture through song, dance, drama and mime. There are three to five shows a week May to September and tickets cost around €15.

Kerry Cultural Centre (☎ 712 6381, Edward St) Musical evenings, some with traditional song and dance, are put on about once a week. If there's an entry fee it's usually around €6.

Getting There & Away

The Bus Éireann station (☎ 712 3566) is next to the train station on John Joe Sheehy Rd on the north-eastern edge of the centre. Daily buses connect Tralee with Dublin (€19.05, hourly; change at Limerick) via Listowel (€5.10, 30 minutes, seven daily). Bus No 40 runs daily every hour to Waterford (€19.05, 5½ hours) via Killarney (€5.85, 2½ hours) and Cork (€12.70, five hours).

From the train station (☎ 712 3522) there's a service five times a day to Cork (€22.90, two hours 10 minutes) via Killarney (€7, 45 minutes). Trains to Dublin depart four times a day (four hours). Change at Limerick Junction for Limerick.

Getting Around

There's a taxi rank on The Mall, or you could try Kerry Cabs (☎ 712 7000) or Jackie Power Tours and Cabs (☎ 712 9444). Tralee Gas and Bicycle Supplies (☎ 712 2018), Strand St, rents out bikes for €8.90/ 44.45 per day/week plus €50.80 deposit.

AROUND TRALEE
Crag Cave

Crag Cave was discovered only in 1983 when problems with water pollution led to a search for the source of the local river (☎ 714 1244, Castleisland; adult/child €5.10/3.15; open 10am-6pm July & Aug; 10am-5.30pm daily mid-Mar-June & Sept-Nov). Although the cave entrance had been known for years the system had never been explored until then. The 4km-long cave

opened to the public in 1989; admission is by a 30-minute guided tour.

To get there, take the N21 to Castleisland from Tralee and the cave is signposted to the left – from here it's only 4km along a minor road. In July and August there's at least one bus a day Monday to Saturday between Tralee and Castlemaine, which stops in Castleisland.

Ardfert
☎ 066

Ardfert (Ard Fhearta) lies about 7km northwest of Tralee on the Ballyheigue road. Most of **Ardfert Cathedral** (☎ 713 4711; adult/child €1.90/0.75; open 9.30am-6pm daily Apr-Sept & Oct bank holiday weekend), which is owned by Dúchas, dates back to the 13th century. Additions were made in the 15th and 17th centuries. Set into one of the interior walls is an effigy popularly said to be of St Brendan the Navigator, who was educated in Ardfert and founded a monastery here. There are ruins of two other churches – 12th-century Templenahoe and the 15th-century Templenagriffin – in the grounds, and there's a small visitor centre with an exhibition on the cathedral's history. The continuing work on shoring up the cathedral will take many years and access to the interior is by guided tour only.

Turning right in front of the cathedral and going 500m down the road brings you to the extensive remains of a **Franciscan friary**, dating from the 13th century but with 15th-century cloisters.

In July and August, Bus Éireann No 274 between Tralee and Ballyheigue stops in Ardfert at least once daily.

RATTOO ROUND TOWER

Kerry's only complete round tower has six floors and is in fine condition. The top windows face the four points of the compass to act as lookouts for raiders, suggesting that this was a wealthy monastic site in the 9th and 10th centuries. Nothing else remains from that era on this site. To the east are the ruins of a 15th-century church.

The tower is visible from the main road before entering the small town of Ballyduff from the south. The turning is signposted. There's no access to the tower, only to the graveyard next door.

BALLYBUNION
☎ 068 • pop 1400

In June 1834 a longstanding feud between two Ballybunion (Baile an Bhuinneánaigh) families culminated in a brawl on the beach involving over 3000 combatants. During the summer the beach is still crowded, but mainly with Irish holiday-makers, who have made Ballybunion a popular seaside resort. From October to April, however, the town is completely lifeless and you'll be lucky to find a place to stay let alone anywhere to eat.

Tourist information is available from a small seasonal tourist office (☎ 27711) on Main St. There's little to see except the ruins of Ballybunion Castle overlooking the beach, where there are opportunities for **swimming** and **surfing** and some **caves** to explore.

Many tourists come here to play golf at the famous **Ballybunion Golf Course** (☎ 27146), which hosted the 2000 Irish Open. It costs €95.30 for a round on the old course or €50.80 on the newer Cashen course, plus €31.75 for club hire.

If you decide to stay in summer make sure you book well ahead, like about a year. The following places are usually open May to September.

The Astor (☎ 27888, Sandhill Rd) Singles/doubles €31.75/45.75. This luxury B&B has great views and is better value than most other places in town.

The Old Course B&B (☎/fax 27171, **e** oldcourse@eircom.net, Golf Links Rd) Singles/doubles €44.45/63.50. This cheerfully decorated place overlooks the golf course and is a five-minute walk from the centre. Singles are only available if there are plenty of rooms free (not likely in summer).

Regular Bus Éireann buses connect Ballybunion with Tralee and Listowel.

LISTOWEL
☎ 068 • pop 3656

Listowel (Lios Tuathail), home of the Kerry butter factory, is 15km south of Tarbert, from where a ferry crosses the Shannon

Estuary to County Clare. It's an attractive and tidy Georgian town with a large park and the scenic River Feale running along the southern side of the centre. While the main attraction in Listowel is the annual Writers' Week (see Special Events), there are a few things to see and no doubt the cultured and relaxed atmosphere, not to mention the great food, will entice you to spend a night or two here. It makes a much more pleasant alternative to Tralee as a base to explore Northern Kerry.

Orientation & Information

The town centres on the Square, in the middle of which is St John's Theatre and Arts Centre, previously St John's Church, which houses the tourist office (☎ 22590). It opens 10am to 1pm and 2pm to 6pm Monday to Saturday, June to September; and 9.30am to 1pm and 2pm to 6pm weekdays, October to April. Church and William Sts, north from the Square, are where you'll find most pubs and restaurants, while a short walk down Bridge Rd to the south will take you to the river and Childers Park.

There's a Bank of Ireland with an ATM and bureau de change in the Square. The post office is at the northern end of William St. Surprisingly for a town credited with spawning 360 books by more than 60 writers, McGuire's Bookshop, at the top of Church St, is the only decent bookshop. A number of titles by local writers are also available from the bookshop at the Kerry Literary and Cultural Centre.

Moloney's Laundrette (☎ 21263) on Bridge Rd opens 9.30am to 6.30pm Monday to Saturday, and you'll find public toilets off Market St.

Things to See

Not surprisingly Listowel is home to the **Kerry Literary and Cultural Centre**. Inside is the Writers' Exhibition (☎ 22212, **w** www .seanchai-klcc.com, 24 The Square/ child €5.10/2.55; open 10am-6pm daily Mar-Oct). This consists of a visual presentation about historical and literary Northern Kerry and an exhibition on local writers. You get to listen to a *seanchaí* (pronounced

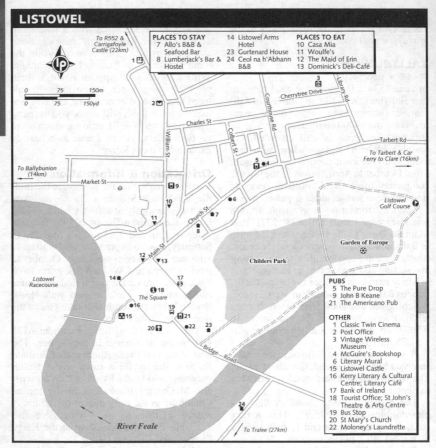

LISTOWEL

PLACES TO STAY		14 Listowel Arms Hotel	PLACES TO EAT
7 Allo's B&B & Seafood Bar		23 Gurtenard House	10 Casa Mia
8 Lumberjack's Bar & Hostel		24 Ceol na h'Abhann B&B	11 Woulfe's
			12 The Maid of Erin
			13 Dominick's Deli-Café

PUBS
5 The Pure Drop
9 John B Keane
21 The Americano Pub

OTHER
1 Classic Twin Cinema
2 Post Office
3 Vintage Wireless Museum
4 McGuire's Bookshop
6 Literary Mural
15 Listowel Castle
16 Kerry Literary & Cultural Centre; Literary Café
17 Bank of Ireland
18 Tourist Office; St John's Theatre & Arts Centre
19 Bus Stop
20 St Mary's Church
22 Moloney's Laundrette

shan-a-key; storyteller). Every Tuesday and Thursday in July and August the centre puts on a *Seisún-Cois na Feile* – a performance of traditional song, music, dance and folklore (adult/child €6.35/3.80).

St Mary's Church in the Square was built in 1829 in the neo-Gothic style. It has some lovely mosaic work over the altar and a vaulted roof with timber beams.

Twelfth-century **Listowel Castle**, behind the Kerry Literary and Cultural Centre, was once the stronghold of the Fitzmaurice family, the Anglo-Norman lords of Kerry. The Dúchas-owned castle was the last in Ireland to hold out against the Elizabethan attacks during the Desmond revolt. Now it's just a ruined tower but is undergoing conservation work (at the time of writing it was covered in scaffolding) and should be open to visitors by summer 2003.

Activities

Listowel Golf Course (☎ 21592), on the banks of the River Feale, is about 2km west of the centre off the N69 to Tarbert. You can also walk through Childers Park and the 'Garden of Europe' to get there. It costs €19.05 for 18 holes.

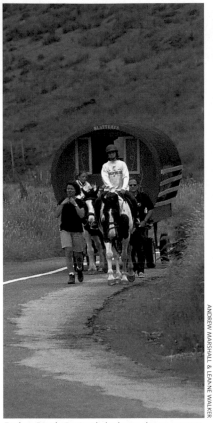

Explore Dingle Peninsula by horse-drawn caravan

ANDREW MARSHALL & LEANNE WALKER

Waterville's bog cotton fields, County Kerry

RICHARD CUMMINS

Sea thrift blooming in Tralee Bay, County Kerry

COLIN SHAW

The wild splendour of Kerry's coast is a magnet for visitors to Ireland year round.

RICHARD MILLS

RICHARD CUMMINS

RICHARD MILLS

Primeval forest, Killarney

Peat being stacked for drying in County Kerry

EOIN CLARKE

Sea birds are the only inhabitants of mountainous Great Blasket Island, County Kerry.

RICHARD MILLS

Skellig Michael's astounding monastic site is perched on the rock some 150m above sea level.

The River Feale provides many opportunities for **angling** year round. Contact the **North Kerry Anglers Association** (☎ *21504, 6 The Square*) for a permit.

Special Events
Writers' Week takes place each May. Details are available from Writers' Week, PO Box 147, Listowel, or call ☎ 21074. Readings, poetry, music, drama, seminars, storytelling and many other events are held at various places around town. John B Keane is probably the most famous writer associated with Listowel and usually features in Writers' Week. Bryan MacMahon, a short-story writer, is another local literary talent. On Church St there's a **mural** depicting these and other well known local writers.

The other big event of the year are the **Listowel horse races** in late September. The racetrack is just west of the town.

Places to Stay
Lumberjack's Bar & Hostel (☎ *22689, 19 Church St*) Beds in 4-bed dorm €11.45. This friendly place is only a couple of minutes' walk from the town centre.

Allo's (☎/*fax 22880, 41-43 Church St*) Singles/doubles €44.45/101.65. This luxury town house offers lovely rooms but has only one single room. The bar downstairs is a cross between a traditional Irish pub and a 1930s bar.

Gurtenard House (☎/*fax 21137, Bridge Rd*) Rooms €24.15 per person. This big, beautiful and peaceful 200-year-old house has large, beautifully decorated rooms, and no TV.

Ceol na h'Abhann B&B (☎/*fax 21345, Tralee Rd*) Singles €31.75-35.55, doubles €50.80. This picturesque, thatched-roof house on the riverbank with tall trees all around is the nicest spot in town. It's on the other side of the river from the centre; head down Bridge Rd and turn right over the bridge.

Listowel Arms Hotel (☎ *21500, fax 22524, The Square*) Singles/doubles €63.50/88.95. This well run, Georgian-style hotel has big rooms and a relaxed ambience. Some rooms have a view of the town and others a view of the river and racetrack. Rates can be higher in the summer.

Places to Eat
Listowel has some wonderful restaurants, cafes and pubs, and the prices are very reasonable too.

Dominick's Deli-Café (☎ *23988, cnr The Square & Main St*) Lunch €2-6. This cheap and popular lunch and breakfast spot serves a daily soup special and makes fresh sandwiches.

Literary Café (☎ *22212, Kerry Literary & Cultural Centre, 24 The Square*) Lunch €3-6. This modern and trendy cafe is *the* place for lunch with friends. It serves sandwiches, salads and specials such as poached salmon or loin of pork for a very reasonable €6.30.

The Maid of Erin (☎ *21321, Main St*) Lunch €3-5.50. This spacious pub with wooden floors and literary quotes on the walls serves sandwiches and large gourmet baguettes. The facade of the building features some plasterwork depicting Mother Ireland by Pat McAuliffe (1846–1921). You'll see more work by him on shop fronts around the centre.

Casa Mia (☎ *23467, 11 William St*) Pasta €8-9.50, mains €11-17.50. This small Italian bistro, bedecked with Chianti bottles and bright orange table cloths, is very popular.

Woulfe's (☎ *21083, 17 Lower William St*) Meals around €10. Open for lunch and dinner. This casual and intimate pub has a wonderful menu with a bit of everything.

Allo's Seafood Bar (see *Places to Stay*) Lunch €7.50-10, dinner €22-23.50. Lunch is just as good and much more affordable than dinner at this multi-award winning pub and restaurant. Try the steamed Fenit crab claws in garlic butter (€9.85 at lunch-time).

Entertainment
Listowel has a number of great pubs, most with live music and traditional sessions during the week.

The Pure Drop (☎ *23001, Church St*) This pub is well known by locals and has live music at the weekend and pub theatre on Wednesday in July and August, starting at 9.30pm. It's also highly recommended

KERRY

Walking the Dingle Peninsula

The 168km circular Dingle Way walking trail could be started in Tralee. It passes through Dingle and Dunquin, returning to Tralee via Castlegregory. The whole walk takes eight days but the last four days, from Dunquin to Tralee, are by far the best in terms of scenery. The section between Tralee and Camp is, according to a few readers, quite difficult and not suitable for children.

If you prefer to go with a group and your pockets are deep enough, you could join a Wild Ireland (☎ 066-976 0211) guided walking tour of Dingle Peninsula. The eight-day walk costs €393, which includes airport transfers to the Dingle Peninsula from Shannon, Cork or Kerry airports, accommodation and all meals.

JANE SMITH

A number of walking guides are available from the tourist office in Dingle and from the tourist office or Walk Information Centre in Tralee. Two you might find useful are *The Dingle Peninsula – 16 Walks Through its Heritage* by Maurice Sheehy (€3.90) and *The Dingle Way Companion* by Tony O'Callaghan (€7). Both have plenty of maps and a lot of detail.

---

for its lunch-time sandwiches and salads (€2.50-5).

The Americano Pub *(☎ 23930, The Square)* As the name suggests this place is all-American with live music on Saturday and Sunday nights covering country and western, blues, and rock and roll.

John B Keane *(37 William St)* Owned by the writer of the same name, this small, unassuming bar features pub theatre every Tuesday and Thursday at 9.15pm.

St John's Theatre and Arts Centre *(☎ 22566, The Square)* The centre hosts drama, music and dance events year round.

Getting There & Away

Buses run daily to Tralee (€5.10, 30 minutes, every two hours) and Limerick (€11.70, one hour 35 minutes, four daily, one on Sunday). In July and August there are three buses daily to Ballybunion. Buses from Cork to the Cliffs of Moher and Galway also stop in Listowel three times a day (twice on Sunday). The bus stop is on the northern side of the Square.

AROUND LISTOWEL
Carrigafoyle Castle

The peaceful location of this five-storey castle, perched above the Shannon Estuary, is very attractive. Built in the channel between the mainland and Carrig Island, its name comes from *Carragain Phoill* (Rock of the Hole). It was probably built at the end

of the 15th century by the O'Connors, who ruled most of northern Kerry. It was besieged by the English in 1580, was retaken by O'Connor but fell again to the English under George Carew in 1600, during the suppression of O'Neill's rebellion, and was finally destroyed by Cromwell's forces in 1649. You can climb the spiral staircase to the top for a good view of the estuary.

You really need a car to get here. The castle is 2km west of the village of Ballylongford (Bea Atha Longphuirb), which is rarely accessible by bus from Listowel.

Tarbert

Tarbert is 16km north of Listowel on the N69. Shannon Ferry Limited (☎ 065-905 3124) runs a 20-minute car ferry between Tarbert and Killimer in County Clare from 7.30am (9.30am on Sunday) to 9.30pm daily (passengers/cars €3.15/12.70 one way). It's useful if you want to avoid travelling through congested Limerick city. The ferry dock is 2.2km west of Tarbert and is clearly signposted. (See under Killimer in the County Clare chapter for more details.)

If you have a bit of time to spare before you catch your ferry you should visit the **Tarbert Bridewell Jail and Courthouse** *(☎ 36500; adult/child €5.10/2.55; open 10am-6pm daily Apr-Oct)*. The exhibition features models and displays on the social and political conditions of the 19th century.

AUDIO CONNOR PASS FOR DRIVING

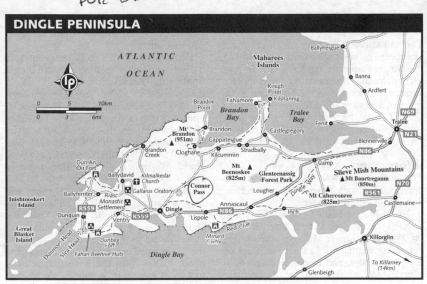

DINGLE PENINSULA

From the jail you can take the **John F Leslie Woodland Walk**, a 3.8km walk along Tarbert Bay towards the mouth of the Shannon.

Bus Éireann No 13 runs to Tarbert from Tralee (€7.35, 55 minutes) via Listowel (15 minutes) once a day.

Dingle Peninsula

Less touristy and arguably more stunning than the Ring of Kerry, the Dingle Peninsula is the Ireland of *Ryan's Daughter* and *Far and Away*, with an extraordinary number of ring forts, high crosses and other ancient monuments.

Dingle is the main town. Ferries run from Dunquin to the now-deserted Blasket Islands, off the tip of the peninsula. A touring route, the Slea Head Drive, heads west from Dingle to Slea Head, Dunquin, Ballyferriter, Brandon Creek and back to Dingle. You could drive it in a day but it's worth taking your time and staying overnight en route.

An unusual way to get around the peninsula is by horse-drawn caravan. This is only possible between March and September and

prices range from €317 to €635 per week. Ask at Dingle's tourist office for more details or phone David Slattery on ☎ 066-718240.

ORGANISED TOURS

A number of Dingle-based companies operate tours of the peninsula.

O'Connors (☎ 087 248 8008) Bus tours of Slea Head depart from the tourist office in Dingle at 11am daily.

Moran's Slea Head Tours (☎ 066-915 1155, 087 275 3333, Moran's Garage). €10.15 per person. Buses leave from the pier in Dingle at 10am and 2pm daily.

Sciúird (☎ 066-915 1606, 915 1937, Fios Feasa) €10.15 per person. Sciuird has 2½-hour archaeological tours departing from Dingle at 10.30am and 5pm daily. These tours explore the remains of house sites, defensive forts, monastic sites and burial chambers.

Kirrary (see Places to Stay in Dingle) organises archaeological tours to Slea Head (€10.15).

Dingle nature walks, led by a botanist, take 2½ hours in groups of six or seven. Book at the tourist office in Dingle and pack your own refreshments.

DINGLE

☎ 066 • pop 1536

The attractive little port of Dingle (An Daingean) makes a good base for exploring the Dingle Peninsula and has a famous resident dolphin. What saves it from complete surrender to tourism is the continued existence of a large resident fishing fleet. At the time of writing, a small stretch of the quay was knee-deep in bulldozers paving the way for a new tourism complex.

Information

The tourist office (☎ 915 1188), by the pier, opens 9.15am to 5.30pm Monday to Saturday, mid-April to October.

The banks on Main St have ATMs and bureaux de change. Dingle Internet Café (☎ 915 2478), Lower Main St, offers Internet access costing €2.55 for 15 minutes or €7.60 per hour, and opens 10am to 6pm Monday to Saturday and 2pm to 6pm on Sunday.

Fungie the Dolphin

In the winter of 1984 fisherfolk began to notice a solitary bottlenose dolphin that followed their vessels, jumped about in the water and sometimes leaped over their boats. Fungie the dolphin is now an international celebrity.

Boats leave the pier all year round for a one-hour dolphin-spotting trip; call **Dingle Boatmen's Association** (☎ 915 2626; adult/child €8.90/3.80 – free if Fungie doesn't show, but he usually does). The association also runs a daily two-hour boat trip, leaving at 8am, for those who want to swim with Fungie (adult/child €12.70/6.35 plus €17.80 to hire wetsuit) but you need to book ahead. Wetsuits and snorkelling gear can also be hired from **Flannery's** (☎ 915 1967, Cooleen) and from **Dingle Marine and Leisure Centre** (☎ 915 1066, Strand St).

You can usually see Fungie from the shore, although you won't be nearly as close. To get to the best viewing spot take the Tralee road and turn right down a lane about 1.5km from the Esso garage. The turning is easy to miss so look for a set of whitish gateposts beside the lane. At the end of the lane is a tiny parking space (remember that the farmer needs access to his fields). Walk along the sea wall towards the old tower and you'll come to the harbour mouth.

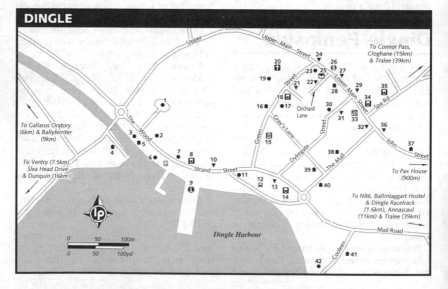

Dingle Oceanworld

Opposite Dingle Harbour is this aquarium (☎ 915 2111, Dingle Harbour; adult/child €7/4.10; open 9.30am-9pm daily July & Aug; 9.30am-6pm Mon-Sat & 10am-5.30pm Sun May, June & Sept; 9.30am-5pm Mon-Sat & 10am-5pm Sun Oct-Apr). It concentrates on showing off the fish and other sealife from the local area including sharks and turtles. There's a walk-through tunnel, a touch pool, a shark tank and a display of tropical fish and corals. The admission price is a little high though.

Other Things to See & Do

Next to St Mary's Church in Green St is the **Trinity Tree**, an unusual three-trunked tree, representing the Holy Trinity, which has been carved with biblical characters. It looks like something out of a fairy tale.

Every August the **Dingle Races** bring crowds from far and wide. The racetrack is opposite Ballintaggart Hostel, about 1.5km east of town on the N86.

The **Dingle Regatta**, a race in the harbour in traditional Irish *currach* canoes, is held in early to mid-August.

Activities

Hidden Ireland Tours (☎ 915 1868) provides organised **walking** programs including half-day walks in the beautiful countryside west of Dingle and full-day hikes up Mt Brandon.

Snorkelling and **scuba diving** in Dingle Bay and around the Blasket Islands can be arranged at **Dingle Marina Diving Centre** (☎ 915 2422) on the waterfront, near the harbour.

Ask at the tourist office for details of **sea fishing** trips, or call ☎ 915 1163. **Dingle Marine and Leisure Centre** (☎ 915 1066, Strand St) hires out fishing tackle.

If you would like to go **rock climbing** or **horse riding** contact **Mountain Man** (☎ 915 2400, Strand St). It also hires out bikes and arranges walking and archaeological tours. **Long's Trekking Centre** (☎ 915 9034) in Ventry has guided horse rides of the area costing €15.90 per hour or €76.25 for the day including lunch.

Places to Stay

Camping & Hostels Dingle has lots of hostel accommodation, but it's still advisable to book if you plan to stay in summer.

Ballintaggart Hostel (☎ 915 1454, fax 915 2207, e info@dingleaccommodation.com, Racecourse Rd) Tent site €5.10 per person, dorms €10.15-12.70, twin & double rooms €35.55. About 1.5km east of Dingle on the N86 is this popular hostel. Accommodation is in a spacious early-19th-century house and there's a free shuttle service to/from town, plus coin-operated Internet access.

The Sleeping Giant (☎ 915 2666, Green St) Beds in 6-bed dorm €10.15, singles/

doubles €17.80/33. Open Apr-Nov. This cute house is right in the centre and very good value, but book ahead as there's not much room.

Lovett's *(☎ 915 1903, Cooleen)* Twins & triples €14 per person. Lovett's is a small family house in a quiet street, about 150m from the main roundabout.

B&Bs & Hotels There are plenty of B&Bs in the centre though they can be a bit pricey in summer. The nearby fish processing plant can make the smell unbearable at the B&Bs along the harbour front.

Sráid Eoin House *(☎ 915 1409, fax 915 2156, John St)* Singles/doubles €38.10/50.80. Never mind the 1980s decor, this family home is probably the best value B&B in the centre.

Blackberry Lodge *(☎ 915 2604, The Mall)* Singles/doubles with bathroom €31.75/44.50 June-Aug, €25.40/35.55 Sept-May. This clean place, with wooden floors and pine furniture, is also very good value.

Kirrary *(☎ 915 1606, Avondale)* Rooms €25.40 per person. The chatty owners of this family home will make you feel very welcome. Bike hire is available, and three-hour archaeological tours to Slea Head cost €10.15 per person.

The Captain's House *(☎ 915 1531, fax 915 1079, e captigh@eircom.net, The Mall)* Singles/doubles €44.45/76.25. This lovely big house has an eclectic mix of furniture and one of the biggest cats we've ever seen.

Ocean View B&B *(☎ 915 1659, 133 The Wood)* Singles/doubles €20.35/35.55 including continental breakfast, €21.60/38.10 including cooked breakfast. Though this place has no en-suite rooms, it's very good value and rooms at the back have pleasant views of the harbour.

Pax House *(☎ 915 1518, fax 915 1650, Upper John St)* Singles/doubles €50.80/88.95. This large and flamboyantly decorated guesthouse has superb views of Dingle Harbour and out to the Iveragh Peninsula. It's been highly recommended by a number of readers and is about 1.5km east of the centre. There's just one single room.

Milltown House *(☎ 915 1372, fax 915* *1095, e milltown@indigo.ie, Milltown)* Singles €63.50, doubles €76.25-82.60. This luxury B&B, on the other side of the harbour from the centre, is where Robert Mitchum stayed during the making of *Ryan's Daughter* in 1969. Rooms overlook the harbour and the town, or the golf course behind. Breakfasts are a real treat here.

Benner's Hotel *(☎ 915 1638, fax 915 1412, e benners@eircom.net, Main St)* Singles/doubles €114.35/177.80 July & Aug, from €76.25/114.35 Apr-June, Sept & Oct, €69.90/101.65 Nov-Mar. Benner's, in a Georgian house, is elegantly furnished and adequately luxurious for the price.

Places to Eat

Dingle has plenty of interesting and varied places to eat. Here are a few that we can recommend.

Restaurants You'll find a number of restaurants around Main and John Sts.

Global Village Restaurant *(☎ 915 2325, Main St)* Open Wed-Sun. This international restaurant features dishes from a number of different countries including Ireland, Thailand, Greece, India, Mexico and New Zealand.

The Mystic Celt *(☎ 915 2117, Main St)* Mains €14-22.80. This place offers traditional Celtic cuisine such as beef and Guinness pie, and Irish stew. You can also take cooking classes here for €44.45 per person; call for details.

The Half Door *(☎ 915 1600, John St)* Mains €16.25-23.50, early-bird menu (6pm-7pm) €27.30. There's a great atmosphere at this seafood restaurant. Chicken, duck and beef dishes are available too.

Old Smokehouse *(☎ 915 1061, cnr Main St & The Mall)* Mains €13-17.80. This unpretentious eatery has a small but varied menu, with dishes such as Toulouse sausages; there's outdoor seating in summer.

El Toro *(☎ 915 1820, Green St)* Pizza & pasta €7.30-11.40, seafood €14-21. At this seafood restaurant you'll also find homemade pasta and gourmet pizzas.

Armada *(☎ 915 1505, Strand St)* Mains €11-17.80. This seafood and grill restaurant is recommended by locals as one of the best eateries in town.

Cafes & Pubs Dingle has some good cafes.

Scribes Rest (Orchard Lane). Lunch around €6.30, dinner €9.50-17.80. Cafe open 9am-5pm daily, restaurant open 6pm-10pm Thur-Sat. This cafe and restaurant serves such lunches as pizza, chicken satay and chicken and mushroom pie. Dinners include fish, meat and pasta dishes and salads.

The Dingle Gourmet Store (☎ 915 0988, Main St) Snacks & light meals €5-9.50. Open 10am-6pm daily. This tiny place serves gourmet snacks and sandwiches. It's very popular, so get there early for lunch.

Greary's (☎ 915 9024, Holyground) Meals €5.70-10.80. Open for breakfast, lunch and dinner. This good-value cafe has an attractive stone-wall interior and its dishes include burgers, vegetable lasagne and baked potatoes.

An Café Liteártha (☎ 915 2204, Dykegate Lane) Snacks €2.50-5. This relaxing place is a bookshop with a small, quiet and inexpensive cafe at the back.

Entertainment
Many pubs have live music, but a few in town are particularly worth checking out.

O'Flaherty's (☎ 915 1983, Strand St) This open-plan bar, with beer barrels for tables, has traditional sessions every night in summer, while spontaneous sessions can occur at any time out of season.

Dick Mack's (☎ 915 1960, Green St) With a shoe repair shop on one side and a drinks counter on the other, this old-style pub is always crowded, though some complain it's become too touristy.

Maire de Barra (☎ 915 1215, Strand St) Popular with a young crowd, this place has live bands most weekends.

An Droisead Beag (Small Bridge Bar; ☎ 915 1723, Lower Main St) This pub is by the bridge and has traditional music from 9pm nightly.

An Conair (☎ 915 2011, Spa Rd) An Conair has set dancing nights and a beer garden at the back.

Shopping
Brian de Staic (☎ 915 1298, The Wood) This local jewellery designer can carve your name in Ogham script on the piece you choose.

Lisbeth Mulcahy (☎ 915 1688, Green St) At this gallery and shop, local artist Lisbeth Mulcahy weaves beautiful rugs, scarves and wall hangings on a 150-year-old loom. Also sold here are superb ceramics by her husband who has a workshop west of Dingle (see Louis Mulcahy Pottery under Dunquin later in this chapter).

Green Lane Gallery (☎ 915 2018, Green St) Here you'll find an interesting (but expensive) collection of paintings and sculpture, many by local artists.

The Craft Village (The Wood) The Craft Village is a group of workshops churning out linen, pottery, woodwork, leatherwear and clothes.

Getting There & Away
Bus Éireann buses stop outside the car park behind the SuperValu store. Buses for Dingle leave Tralee (☎ 712 3566) at 11am, 2pm, 4.15pm and 6pm Monday to Saturday, plus 9am from late May to mid-September and 8.10pm from June to September (€7.85). At least five buses a day Monday to Saturday depart Killarney for Dingle (€11.70).

An infrequent bus service links Dingle to Ventry, Slea Head, Dunquin and Ballyferriter.

Getting Around
Dingle is easily navigated on foot. For a taxi call Dingle Co-op Cabs (☎ 915 1000); it can also give private tours of the peninsula.

There are several bike rental places, including Paddy's Bike Hire (☎ 915 2311), Dykegate St, which charges €7.60/35.55 per day/week, and Foxy John's (☎ 915 1316), Main St, charging €6.35/31.75 per day/week.

NORTHSIDE OF THE PENINSULA
☎ 066
There are two routes from Tralee to Dingle, though they both follow the same road out of Tralee past the Blennerville Windmill. Near the village of Camp a right fork heads off to the Connor Pass, while the N86 via

Annascaul takes you to Dingle quicker. The Connor Pass route is much more beautiful and panoramic. At Kilcummin a road to the west heads to the relatively little-visited villages of Cloghane and Brandon and on to Brandon Point, with fine views of Brandon Bay.

Castlegregory

A small, traffic-congested village, Castlegregory (Caislean an Ghriare) once rivalled Tralee as a bustling metropolis. It has a seasonal visitor centre on Tailor's Row and a couple of hostels. A sand-strewn road heads north on a spit of land between Tralee and Brandon Bays to Rough Point. It's very pretty and would be more so were it not for the caravans and bungalows marring the views. The broad, empty beaches around Castlegregory are perfect for surfing.

Beyond Rough Point are the **Maharees Islands**. Illauntannig is the largest of these and is the site of a 6th-century monastery. Remains of the settlement include a stone cross, a church and beehive huts. Two small adjoining islands can be reached by foot from Illauntannig at low tide. The islands are privately owned and used to graze cows but trips (taking about 10 minutes) can be arranged through Castle House, or Harbour House in conjunction with a **scuba diving** trip (for both see Places to Stay later). Some say this area makes for some of the best diving in Europe due to the complete absence of pollution.

About 8km east of Castlegregory is the turn-off for **Glenteenassig Forest Park**, which makes for some scenic drives or walks through an area of forest and mountain lakes.

Cloghane

Cloghane (An Clochán), on the southwestern edge of Brandon Bay, has a wonderful stretch of beach and is a good starting point for a climb up Mt Brandon.

Cloghane has an information centre (☎ 713 8277), open June to August, where you can buy the *Cloghane and Brandon Walking Guide* (€3.80) with details of all the trails you'll see signposted. Those interested in the region's many archaeological sites should ask

about guided walks or buy *Loch a'Dúin Archaeological and Nature Trail* (€3.80).

Immediately opposite the information centre, **St Brendan's Church** has a stained-glass window showing the Gallarus Oratory and Ardfert Cathedral. About 2.7km north of Cloghane, in a white school building, is a **Heritage & Craft Centre** (☎ 713 8137) that displays old photographs and artefacts from the area from the last two centuries.

Dingle Peninsula Cheese *(Stradbally; open 11am-5.30pm Mon-Thur & 11am-3pm Sun)* is a farmhouse dairy which opens to visitors for tasting and purchasing. It's 7km east of Cloghane or, from the other direction, 2.5km west of Stradbally.

Mt Brandon

At 951m, Mt Brandon (Cnoc Bhréannain) is Ireland's second-highest mountain. Allow at least five hours for the climb, and make sure there's no danger of a mist descending, as the top is frequently shrouded in cloud. During the walk keep an eye on the weather for signs of change for the worse and be prepared to cut the walk short. Take a compass with you – if you do get caught in mist you'll need it to make your way down. The traditional way up the mountain is the Saint's Rd, which starts at Kilmalkedar Church (see under West of Dingle later) although much of this path has become overgrown and is difficult to stick to, so you might want to begin a little further along at Ballinloghig. A more demanding approach starts from the east just beyond Cloghane and is clearly signposted.

The ruins of **St Brendan's Oratory** mark the summit. The legend is that the navigator saint climbed the mountain with his seafaring monks before they set out in their curraghs for the journey to Greenland and America.

Connor Pass & Around

At 456m, the Connor (or Conor) Pass is the highest in Ireland and offers spectacular views of Dingle Harbour to the south and Mt Brandon to the north. On a foggy day you'll see nothing but the road just in front of you. There's a car park near the summit. Take the path up behind it to see the peninsula spread out below you.

Places to Stay

Anchor Caravan Park (☎ 713 9157, Castle-gregory) Tent & 2 people €8.90-10.15. Open Easter-Sept. The park is on the R560 just east of Castlegregory.

Euro Hostel (☎ 713 9133, Strand St, Castlegregory) Dorms/doubles €8.90/17.80. This small hostel is above Fitzgerald's Bar at the junction of the road to Rough Point in town.

Connors Guesthouse (☎ 713 8113, fax 713 8270, e oconnorsguesthouse@tinet.ie, Cloghane) Tent site €6.35 per person, rooms €24.15 per person including breakfast, singles €27.95 July & Aug. Rooms here have been newly refurbished and the pub downstairs serves evening meals. Camping is in a field behind the pub and you can use the B&B showers.

Castle House (☎ 713 9183, e caia leanti@unison.ie, Castlegregory) Singles/doubles €31.75/50.80. On the R560 at the northern edge of town, this elegant family home has big rooms and the owner can arrange trips to the Maharees Islands.

Harbour House (☎ 713 9292, fax 713 9557, e dive@iol.ie, Scraggane Pier, near Kilshannig) Singles/doubles €31.75/45.75 including breakfast. This B&B and dive centre is at the end of the road that leads to Rough Point, about 5km north of Castlegregory. It provides diving instruction (PADI) and takes divers to the waters around the Maharees Islands.

Crutchs Hillville House Hotel (☎ 713 8118, fax 713 8159, e macshome@iol.ie, Connor Pass Rd) Rooms around €44.45 per person including breakfast. 4-course dinner €27.95. This bright, airy and inviting place is 6km east of Cloghane on the road to Castlegregory. Rooms are large and peaceful and some have four-poster beds.

Getting There & Away

A year-round bus service leaves Tralee for Castlegregory on Friday only at 8.55am and 2pm and returns at 10.35am only. In July and early August there are also two services daily on Wednesday, leaving Tralee at 10.20am and 4.15pm, and returning at 11.05am and 5pm. Friday only, bus No 273 leaves Tralee at 8.55am and 2pm for Cloghane (one hour 10 minutes). Returning, it leaves at 10.05am and 3.10pm.

TRALEE TO DINGLE VIA ANNASCAUL

For drivers this route has little to recommend it other than being faster than the Connor Pass route. By bike it's less demanding. On foot the journey constitutes the first three days of the Dingle Way.

The main reason to pause in Annascaul (Abhainn an Scáil), also spelled Anascaul, is to visit the **South Pole Inn** (☎ 066-915 7388, *Main St*) by the river on your way to or from Dingle. It commemorates villager Tom Crean (1877–1938), who went to the South Pole with Robert Falcon Scott and Ernest Shackleton. You can study the memorabilia and read up on his expeditions while tucking into your lunch.

A **walking trail** begins at the South Pole Inn and heads 14km north to Ballyduff Bridge near Kilcummin and Brandon Bay.

CASTLEMAINE TO DINGLE

The quickest route between Killarney and Dingle is by way of Killorglin and Castlemaine. At Castlemaine (Caisleán na Mainge; birthplace of the Australian outlaw, the Wild Colonial Boy) the R561 heads west to Dingle, soon meeting the coast and passing Inch on the way to joining the main Tralee road to Dingle. Apart from the odd pub or two there's little provision for food, so bring your own.

At least two Bus Éireann buses between Tralee and Dingle stop at Lispole daily. From late May to mid-September they also stop at Castlemaine and Inch and continue to Killarney.

Mt Caherconree

About 11km west of Castlemaine is the turn-off for Mt Caherconree, one of the higher mountains on the peninsula at 825m. The road ends at Camp on the northern side of the peninsula; about 4km along is an Iron Age promontory fort that may have been built by Cúror MacDáine, king of Munster. Whichever direction you come, there are stunning views from this narrow, exposed and high (even a little scary) road.

Inch

The main attraction at Inch (Inse) is the 6km-long **sand spit** that runs into Dingle Bay – a location for *Ryan's Daughter* and the film of *The Playboy of the Western World*. The sand dunes were once home to Stone Age and Iron Age settlements, and graves and shell-middens can be found if you look hard. In the 18th century, looters used to mislead ships onto the beach with lanterns then proceed to plunder the cargo.

Cars are allowed on the beach, but be very careful because vehicles regularly get stuck in the wet sand. Bring your gear for **surfing** waves, which average 1 to 3m. ***Sammy's Store*** (☎ *066-915 8118*), at the car park for the beach, has some tourist information and refreshments.

Lispole

The road from Inch to tiny Lispole (Lios Póil) passes through Annascaul. Between Annascaul junction and Lispole look out for a turning on the left to the 15th-century **Minard Castle**, a single keep on a low cliff looking out to sea. It has been in a dangerous condition since its destruction by Cromwellian forces in the 17th century. Children should not be left unsupervised. The roads around here are very confusing and it's easy to get lost.

If you have time you might want to stop at the **Freshwater Experience** (☎ *066-915 1042, Lispole; adult/child €3.80/2.55; open 9.30am-6pm Mon-Sat & 11am-6pm Sun July & Aug; 9.30am-5pm Mon-Sat & 11am-5pm Sun Easter-June, Sept & Oct)*. On the N86, this is a wildfowl and otter sanctuary with an archaeological park featuring models of an ancient ogham stone, a stone circle, a wedge tomb and a *crannóg* (artificial island), but it may really only be of interest to kids.

Camping is possible in the field opposite Inch Beach (€5.10 for a tent and two people). Ask at Sammy's Store.

Phoenix Café & Vegetarian Hostel (☎/*fax 066-976 6284, Shanahill East, Castle-*

maine) Tent site €5.70 per person, dorms €11.45, doubles with/without bathroom €40.65/35.55. Breakfast or lunch €5.70, 3-course dinner €19.05. About 6km west of Castlemaine on the R561 is this brightly painted, laid-back place. The owners, will pick you up from Castlemaine or, if you call ahead to arrange it, from Tralee or Killarney airports for €1.25 per mile. The hostel is strictly vegetarian, and vegans are catered for too. If you wish to eat at the cafe only, it's advisable to book.

Caherbla House (☎ *066-915 8120,* ℮ *caherbla@eircom.net, Inch)* Rooms from €24.15-25.40 per person. This B&B is close to the beach and has nice views of the Inch promontory and the Iveragh Peninsula.

WEST OF DINGLE
☎ 066

The area west of Dingle takes in the Slea Head Drive – a beautiful stretch of road – and has the greatest concentration of ancient sites in Kerry, if not in the whole of Ireland. To do the sites justice you should use one of the specialist guides on sale in the An Café Liteártha cafe/bookshop or the tourist office in Dingle town. The sites listed in this book are among the most interesting and easiest to find.

This part of the peninsula is a Gaeltacht, or Irish-speaking, area. The landscape is dramatic, except when it's hidden in mist, and there are striking views of the Blasket Islands from Slea Head. The sandy beach nearby, Coumenole, is lovely to walk along but, like most in the area, is treacherous for swimming.

Tourism came late to Dingle but the area is handling it well, avoiding the tackiness of Killarney and the Ring of Kerry. In 1971, David Lean filmed *Ryan's Daughter* here. Much of it was shot near Dunquin, and the ruins of the film's schoolhouse can still be found. The path down to the Blasket Island ferry was also used in the film. Film buffs should inquire at Kruger's pub in Dunquin.

Orientation

If you cross the bridge west of Dingle and take the first right, where there's a clutter of signs (mostly in Gaelic), you come to a Y-junction after 5km. To the right are Kilmalkedar Church and Brandon Creek, from where you could return to Dingle on a circular route. To the left are the Gallarus Oratory and the Riasc site, from which you can reach Ballyferriter and Dunquin. This road continues down the coast and back to Dingle. Continuing straight on after the bridge will take you to Slea Head and Dunbeg Fort.

Kilmalkedar Church
This 12th-century church was once part of a complex of religious buildings. The characteristic Romanesque doorway has a tympanum with a head on one side and a mythical beast on the other. There is an ogham stone, pierced by a hole, in the grounds. About 50m away is a two-storey building known as **St Brendan's House**, which is believed to have been the residence of the medieval clergy. The road connecting these two ruins is the beginning of the **Saint's Rd**, the traditional approach to Mt Brandon (see earlier in this chapter). The church is 1.7km southeast of Murreagh village on the R559 to Dingle.

Ballyferriter
Continue towards Slea Head and you'll come to the small village of Ballyferriter (Baile an Fheirtearaigh), named after Piaras Ferriter, a poet and soldier who emerged as a local leader in the 1641 rebellion and was the last Kerry commander to submit to Cromwell's army.

There is the small **Dingle Peninsula Museum** (Músaem Chorca Dhuibhne; ☎ 915 6333; adult/child €1.90/1.25; open 9.30am-5pm daily Easter & June-Sept). It has displays on the ecology and geology of the Dingle Peninsula.

During the 1580 rebellion in Munster, **Dún an Óir Fort** (Fort of Gold) was held by an international brigade of Italians, Spaniards and Basques. On 17 November, English troops under Lord Grey attacked the fort and the people inside surrendered. 'Then putt I in certeyn bandes who streight fell to execution. There were 600 slayne,' said the poet Edmund Spenser, who was secretary to Lord Grey. The remains of the fort are scant but the views are lovely.

To reach the fort head west from Ballyferriter and after 1km turn right at a brown sign to Dún an Óir Hotel. After a further 1.5km, take the right fork at a Y-junction and go straight on, ignoring side tracks, until you come to a T-junction. Turn right and after roughly 300m you'll see a signpost to the fort along a wretchedly surfaced road: do your car's suspension a favour and walk it.

Faoileán Pottery Studio (☎ 915 6294, Ballyferriter West) is about 1.5km west of Ballyferriter and offers residential pottery courses, or two-hour basic courses at 2pm and 4pm on Monday and Wednesday, June to August.

Gallarus Oratory
Simple but stunning, this superb dry-stone oratory is in perfect condition, apart from a slight sagging in the roof, and has withstood the assault of the elements for some 1200 years. Traces of mortar suggest that the interior and exterior walls may have been plastered. Shaped like an upturned boat, it has a doorway on the western side and a small round-headed window on the eastern side. Inside the doorway are two projecting stones with holes that once supported the door.

The oratory is signposted off the R559 about 3km north-east of Ballyferriter. It's half a kilometre down the road on the left. A bus leaves Dingle at 9am and drops off at Gallarus 10 minutes later on Tuesday and Friday only. From Gallarus it picks up for Dingle at 1.25pm. There is a charge for parking close to the oratory – an outrageous €1.25 per person – so we suggest you just park a little further away.

Riasc Monastic Settlement
The remains of this 5th- or 6th-century monastic settlement are impressive. Excavations have revealed, among other finds, the foundations of an oratory first built with wood and later stone, a kiln for drying corn and a cemetery. Most interesting is a pillar with beautiful Celtic designs. The ruins are signposted off the R559, 1.5km north-east of Ballyferriter.

Dunquin

If Ballyferriter is small, it does at least have a centre, unlike scattered Dunquin (Dún Chaion), from where you catch a boat to the Blasket Islands. It's on the Slea Head Drive.

One of the best exhibitions you'll see in Ireland and which should not be missed is the wonderful **Blasket Centre** *(Ionad an Bhlascaoid Mhóir;* ☎ *915 6444, Dunquin; adult/child €3.15/1.25; open 10am-7pm daily July & Aug; 10am-6pm daily St Patrick's weekend-June)*. This Dúchas-operated centre celebrates the lost lifestyle of the Blasket Islanders, and the Irish language and culture. The building is an architectural splendour and cost €5 million to build, most of it provided by the EU. There's a cafe with Blasket Island views and a small bookshop.

One of the most interesting potteries on the peninsula is **Louis Mulcahy Pottery** *(☎ 915 6229, Clogher, Ballyferriter; open 10am-5.30pm Mon-Sat & 11am-5.30pm Sun)*. Some pieces are as tall as the potter himself and have been sold or given to such people as Bill Clinton and the Pope. Purchases can be delivered overseas from the shop. The pottery is on the road just north of Dunquin.

Slea Head & Dunmore Head

Slea Head offers some of the Dingle Peninsula's best views, good walks and fine beaches, and is thoroughly popular with coach parties.

Dunmore Head is the most westerly point on the Irish mainland and the site of the wreckage in 1588 of two Spanish Armada ships.

The road between Dunquin and Slea Head is dotted with **beehive huts**, **forts**, **inscribed stones** and **church sites**. The **Fahan huts** are accessible from two points and you'll see signs pointing the way from the road.

Prehistoric **Dunbeg Fort**, on a cliff-top promontory, has a sheer drop to the Atlantic and four outer walls of stone. Inside are the remains of a house and a beehive hut as well as an underground passage. The fort is 8km south of Dunquin on the R559; the entrance is opposite a large stone house with a stone roof.

To visit these sights you'll be charged €1.25, steep given that there's no 'presentation' (they just sit and take your money) and other sites on the peninsula are free.

Ventry

The small village of Ventry (Ceann Trá) is next to a wide sandy bay. Between Ventry and Dunbeg Fort, on the R559, is **The Celtic & Prehistoric Museum** *(☎ 915 9941, adult/ child €3.80/2.55; open 10am-5pm Apr-Sept; call for opening hours out of season)*. It has a collection of fossils including a woolly mammoth skull with 3m tusks, and artefacts from the Bronze Age, Celtic and Viking periods. It's small but well set up and makes a nice stopoff.

Activities

Ceann Sibéal Golf Club *(☎ 915 6255)*, Ballyferriter, is a wild and windy links course and costs €44.45, plus €15.90 club hire from June to August (€31.75 the rest of the year). It's signposted from the R559.

Irish language courses are available at **An Portán B&B** *(see Places to Stay)* in Ballyferriter, which offers course, accommodation and food packages. A one-week course with/without accommodation and meals costs €444.70/209.65. You could also try **Oidhreacht Chorca Dhuibhne** *(☎ 915 6100)* in Ballyferriter.

Places to Stay

Free camping is possible near Ferriter's Cove but there are no facilities.

Oratory House Camping (Campáil Teach An Aragail; ☎ *915 5143, fax 915 5504,* e *tp@iol.ie, Gallarus)* Tent & 2 people €10.15. Open May-late Sept. Europe's most westerly campsite is 300m from the Gallarus Oratory.

Dunquin Hostel (☎ 915 6121, fax 915 6355, Dunquin) Dorms €6.35-8.90. Open year round. This An Óige hostel is conveniently close to the Blasket Centre and not too far from the ferry departure point for Great Blasket Island.

Slea Head Farm (☎ 915 6120, w *www .sleaheadfarm.com, Slea Head)* Singles/ doubles with shared bathroom €33/55.90.

Literary Island

Great Blasket Island has a great literary tradition that is responsible for around 40 published titles. It all began when a visiting English scholar encouraged an islander to write down his memoirs in the 1930s. This roused the interest of other scholars who visited the island to learn more about the remote community. They in turn encouraged more islanders to write about their experiences and language. Lyrical stories of many islanders' lives survive and are available at the Blasket Centre in Dunquin or at An Café Liteártha or the tourist office in Dingle. Some of the many diaries and scribbles, still in manuscript form, can also be seen at the Blasket Centre.

One of the best books to come from out of the island is the English translation of Thomas O'Crohan's *The Islandman*. Maurice O'Sullivan's *Twenty Years A-Growing*, the translation of Peig Sayers' *Peig* and *An Old Woman's Reflections*, and Pádraig Tyers' *Blasket Memories* are also well worth reading. *The Blasket Islands – Next Parish America* by Joan and Ray Stagles is a history of the Blaskets by two Americans who first visited in 1966 and were fascinated by the place. These books have inspired many great authors to write about the island and its people, including Dylan Thomas and John Millington Synge.

On the R559 between Dunbeg Fort and Dunquin, south of Dunmore Head, this basic B&B has some of the best views in Ireland. It's perched on a cliff high above the sea and is not for those who are prone to vertigo.

An Portán B&B (☎ 915 6212, fax 915 6222, e donn@tinet.ie, W www.anportan .com, Dunquin) Singles/doubles €31.75/ 50.80. Lunch from €7-15, dinner €13-22. Restaurant open Easter-Sept. This place has been recommended by a number of readers. It has good views out to the Blasket Islands and a restaurant serving traditional and modern Irish cuisine. It's possible to take a one-week Irish language course – see Activities.

Ferriter's Cove (☎ 915 6295, Ballyferriter) Singles €31.75, doubles €45.75-48.30. This bright and airy B&B has wooden floors and large rooms. Follow the signs to the golf club and you'll see it on your left.

Getting There & Away

Year round, Monday and Thursday only, a bus operates from Dingle to Dunquin via Ventry, Slea Head and Ballyferriter. Late June to mid-September a bus leaves Dingle at 12.30pm and 3.10pm Monday to Saturday. For more details phone Bus Éireann in Tralee (☎ 066-712 3566).

BLASKET ISLANDS

The Blasket Islands (Na Blascaodaí), 5km out into the Atlantic, are the most westerly islands in Europe. At 6km by 1.2km, Great Blasket (An Blascaod Mór) is the largest and most visited and is mountainous enough for strenuous walks, including a good one detailed in Kevin Corcoran's *Kerry Walks*. All of the Blaskets were inhabited at one time or another and there is evidence of Great Blasket being inhabited in the Iron Age and early-Christian times. The last islanders left for the mainland in 1953 after the government and the remaining inhabitants agreed that it was no longer feasible to live in such remote and harsh conditions.

Two and three-hour **cruises** (€19.05 per person) around the islands can be booked through the Dingle tourist office (☎ 915 1188) or direct with Blasket Island Tours (☎ 086 875 9692).

There's no accommodation on the islands but camping is free. A *cafe* on Great Blasket Island serves snacks and campers can arrange to have cooked meals.

Getting There & Away

Weather permitting, boats operate Easter to September (adult/child €12.70/6.35 return, 20 minutes). Boats leave Dunquin on the hour 10am to 3pm and return on the half-hour. The last boat from Great Blasket leaves at 3.30pm.

Counties Limerick & Tipperary

While they don't have the dramatic scenery of neighbouring Cork, Kerry, Clare and Galway, both County Limerick and County Tipperary have places of interest that invite you to pause rather than merely pass through. Limerick city makes an obvious base for visiting Lough Gur and the village of Adare, while County Tipperary boasts the Rock of Cashel as well as the pleasant towns of Cahir, Carrick-on-Suir and smaller Fethard.

County Limerick

In 1690, the Siege of Limerick played centre stage in the struggle between Ireland and England, to which the imposing remains of the city's castle bear testimony. As well as the historic interest and amenities of Limerick city itself, the fascinating historic and prehistoric sites south of the city make ideal bicycle excursions. The nearby village of Adare is one of the prettiest in Ireland, in striking contrast with proletarian Limerick city.

LIMERICK
☎ 061 • pop 52,000

Despite its setting on the River Shannon, having a name to put pens in motion and its status as one of Ireland's largest cities, Limerick (Luimneach) was once regarded as pretty dismal. Today, it's shedding both its grim 'Stab City' image (it used to have a reputation for violence) and its reputation for squalor so poignantly painted by Frank McCourt in *Angela's Ashes*. With urban regeneration continuing apace and a number of attractions, including the excellent Hunt Museum and some fine Georgian architecture to match Dublin's, Limerick is a place of interest in its own right. There are plenty of places to eat and the city has an energetic music scene. It's also a good base for exploring the sights of nearby southern Clare, such as Bunratty Castle.

Highlights

- Visit the Hunt Museum, with its excellent collection of Irish art and antiquities, in Limerick city
- Explore Lough Gur and its remarkable Stone Age remains, south of Limerick city
- Discover the spectacular Rock of Cashel in County Tipperary, best visited in early morning or late afternoon

History

The Vikings first reached Limerick in the 10th century. From then on they fought over the town with the native Irish until Brian Ború's forces defeated the Norsemen at the Battle of Clontarf in 1014. Throughout the Middle Ages the Irish clustered to the south of the Abbey River in Irishtown and the English to the north in Englishtown.

In 1690, Limerick acquired heroic status in the ongoing saga of the English occupation of Ireland. After the Battle of the Boyne, the defeated Jacobite forces withdrew west behind the famously strong walls of Limerick town. Surrender seemed

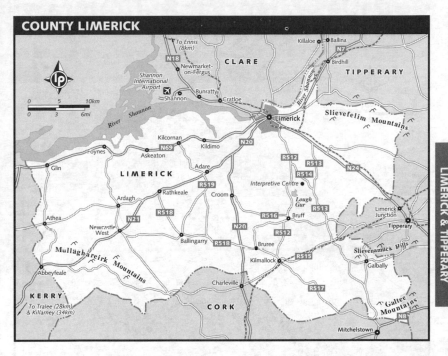

COUNTY LIMERICK

inevitable, but the Irish Jacobite leader Patrick Sarsfield escaped with 600 men and launched a surprise attack on the English supply train. Cannons, mortars and 200 wagons of ammunition were destroyed. Sarsfield and his followers returned undetected to Limerick.

Months of bombardment followed and eventually Sarsfield sued for peace. The terms of the Treaty of Limerick were agreed and Sarsfield and 14,000 soldiers were allowed to leave the city for France. The treaty guaranteed religious freedom for Catholics, but the English reneged on it and enforced fierce anti-Catholic legislation, an act of betrayal that came to symbolise the injustice of British rule.

The new town of Limerick developed and prospered in the 18th century after the old town walls were demolished. However, by the early 20th century that prosperity had passed and in 1919 there was a general strike in protest against British military rule. A Strike Committee took charge of running essential services and for one week the city of Limerick operated outside all legal structures. The Strike Committee even issued its own banknotes, becoming known as the Limerick Soviet.

Limerick has revived considerably in recent years and, although there are still pockets of poverty, a lot of redevelopment is taking place and many of the old Georgian houses to the south are being restored.

Orientation

The main street through town changes name from Rutland St to Patrick St, O'Connell St, The Crescent and Quinlan St as it runs south. Most things of interest are clustered to the north on King's Island (the oldest part of Limerick and once part of Englishtown), to the south around The Crescent and Pery Square (the city's notable Georgian area), and along the riverbanks. The train and bus station lies south-east, off Parnell St.

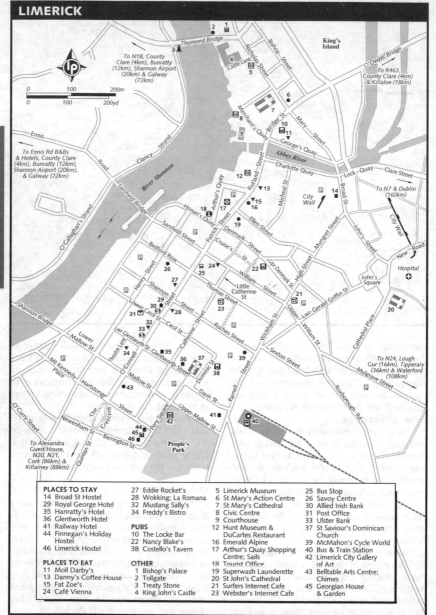

LIMERICK

To N18, County Clare (4km), Bunratty (12km), Shannon Airport (20km) & Galway (72km)

To Ennis Rd B&Bs & Hotels, County Clare (4km), Bunratty (12km), Shannon Airport (20km), & Galway (72km)

To R463, County Clare (4km) & Killaloe (18km)

To N7 & Dublin (160km)

To N24, Lough Gur (16km), Tipperary (36km) & Waterford (108km)

To Alexandra Guest House, N20, N21, Cork (86km) & Killarney (88km)

King's Island

Thomond Bridge
O'Dwyer Bridge
River Shannon
Abbey River
Charlotte Quay
Lock Quay
Clare Street
City Wall
City Wall
New Road
Hospital
John's Square
People's Park

PLACES TO STAY
14 Broad St Hostel
29 Royal George Hotel
35 Hanratty's Hotel
36 Glentworth Hotel
41 Railway Hotel
44 Finnegan's Holiday Hostel
46 Limerick Hostel

PLACES TO EAT
11 Moll Darby's
13 Danny's Coffee House
15 Fat Zoe's
24 Café Vienna

27 Eddie Rocket's
28 Wokking; La Romana
32 Mustang Sally's
34 Freddy's Bistro

PUBS
10 The Locke Bar
22 Nancy Blake's
38 Costello's Tavern

OTHER
1 Bishop's Palace
2 Tollgate
3 Treaty Stone
4 King John's Castle

5 Limerick Museum
6 St Mary's Action Centre
7 St Mary's Cathedral
8 Civic Centre
9 Courthouse
12 Hunt Museum & DuCartes Restaurant
16 Emerald Alpine
17 Arthur's Quay Shopping Centre; Sails
18 Tourist Office
19 Superwash Launderette
20 St John's Cathedral
21 Surfers Internet Cafe
23 Webster's Internet Cafe

25 Bus Stop
26 Savoy Centre
30 Allied Irish Bank
31 Post Office
33 Ulster Bank
37 St Saviour's Dominican Church
39 McMahon's Cycle World
40 Bus & Train Station
42 Limerick City Gallery of Art
43 Belltable Arts Centre; Chimes
45 Georgian House & Garden

Information

The tourist office (☎ 317522), on Arthur's Quay near the river, opens 9am to 7pm Monday to Friday, 9am to 6pm Saturday and Sunday during July and August; 9.30am to 1pm and 2pm to 5.30pm Monday to Saturday, May, June, September and October; and 9.30am to 1pm and 2pm to 5.30pm weekdays and 9.30am to 1pm on Saturday, November to April.

The post office is on Lower Cecil St, while the banks on O'Connell St have ATMs and bureaux de change.

Limerick has two central Internet cafes. Websters! (☎ 312066), 44 Thomas St, opens 9am to 9pm Monday to Saturday and 1pm to 9pm on Sunday. Surfers (☎ 440122), 1 Upper William St, opens 10.30am to 9pm Monday to Saturday and 12.30pm to 9pm on Sunday. Both charge €1.90 per 15 minutes.

Parking discs are available from most newsagents.

For washing your smalls there's Superwash Launderette at 19 Ellen St.

St Mary's Cathedral

The oldest building in the city is the restored cathedral (☎ 310293, Merchant's Quay; admission by donation €1.90; open 9am-1pm & 2.30pm-5pm Mon Sat June Sept; 9am 1pm Mon-Sat Oct-May). It was founded in 1172 by Donal Mór O'Brien, king of Munster. The original Romanesque western doorway and clerestory survive, but the chancel and chapels were added in the 15th century. There are grand tombs, memorial stones and splendid black-oak misericords (support ledges for choristers) dating from around 1489, carved with pictures of animals and other figures. The graveyard boasts many 18th-century tombstones.

King John's Castle

In order to guard and administer the rich Shannon region King John of England had this castle (☎ 411201, Castle St; adult/child €5.60/3.45; open 9.30am-6pm daily July-Aug; 9.30am-5.30pm daily Apr-June & Sept-Oct; 10.30am-4.30pm daily Nov-Mar; last admission one hour before closing) built between 1200 and 1212, on the site of an earlier fortification. The new cannon technology necessitated stronger defences than ever before and the castle became the most formidable bastion of English power in the west of Ireland.

But whoever described the modern interpretive centre in the middle as a 'crossbarred horror' hit the nail square on the head – interesting it may be, beautiful it isn't. After watching a five-minute slide-show on the castle's history and an excellent short film dramatising the last siege of the castle in 1690–91 you can descend to inspect the remains of mines and countermines dug by besiegers and besieged. Also here are the remains of a Viking settlement that predates the Norman settlement. In the courtyard stand replicas of medieval weapons of siege warfare.

Opposite the castle on the other side of the river, the **Treaty Stone** marks the spot on the riverbank where the Treaty of Limerick was signed. But before you cross the bridge look out for the 18th-century **Bishop's Palace** and the ancient **toll gate**.

Limerick Museum

This small museum (☎ 417826, Castle Lane; free; open 10am-1pm & 2.15pm-5pm Tues Sat), in purpose-designed premises beside King John's Castle, houses a collection recounting the history of the city. Exhibits include Bronze and Stone Age artefacts, the civic sword and the city charters of Charles I, and the walls are packed with paintings and prints.

Hunt Museum

The private collection of John and Gertrude Hunt forms this wonderful museum (☎ 312833, Rutland St; adult/child €5.35/2.55; open 10am-5pm Mon-Sat & 2pm-5pm Sun year round). Housed in the Palladian Custom House on the banks of the river, it contains probably the finest collection of Bronze Age, Celtic and medieval treasures outside Dublin. Look out in particular for a marvellous 17th-century statue of Apollo draped with the tools of assorted trades; for an extraordinary self-portrait of the artist Robert Fagan and his half-naked wife; and

Limerick & *Angela's Ashes*

Rarely does a city become so overwhelmingly associated with one book as Limerick has with Frank McCourt's *Angela's Ashes*, published in 1996, and for which McCourt subsequently won the prestigious Pulitzer Prize. It's a sometimes harrowing, sometimes humorous recollection of his family's desperate poverty in 1930s and 1940s Limerick (though the story begins in Brooklyn, New York, where he and his brother Malachy were born; the adults they meet in Limerick often refer to them as little 'Yanks').

Although Limerick has changed considerably since that time, much still remains. And a trip to the city will give you a chance to see some of the buildings and visit some of the locales where Frank spent the greater part of his childhood – from Windmill St where his grandmother found the first home in Limerick for Angela and her family, to the St Vincent de Paul Society where Angela went to beg for food and clothing, and to the Carnegie Free Library (now the city art gallery) from which his dad used to bring books home for the children to read. See Organised Tours for details of walking tours of these and other parts of Limerick associated with *Angela's Ashes*.

MARTIN HARRIS

for a Syracusan coin thought to have been one of the '30 pieces of silver' paid to Judas to betray Christ.

Limerick City Gallery of Art
In the heart of Georgian Limerick, beside People's Park, lies the Limerick City Gallery of Art (☎ 310633, *Carnegie Building, Pery Square; free; open 10am-6pm Mon-Fri, 10am-7pm Thur & 10am-1pm Sat*). It has an excellent permanent collection, which includes work by artists Jack B Yeats and Sean Keating, as well as temporary exhibitions.

Georgian House & Garden
The magnificent Georgian House (☎ 314130, *2 Pery Square; adult/child €2.55/1.25; open 9.30am-4.30pm Mon-Fri*) is a superb example of Georgian townhouse architecture. Designed by architect James Pain, and one of six in this terrace dating from 1838, it has been meticulously restored over several years. About 75% of its features are original, while the rest have been carefully replicated. Both the garden and the rear coach house have also been restored and the latter hosts exhibitions.

Organised Tours
From June to August walking tours depart and return to the tourist office on Arthur's

Quay. There's both a historical tour (departing at 11am and 2.30pm weekdays) and a two-hour tour (departing 2.30pm daily) of Limerick locations mentioned in Frank McCourt's *Angela's Ashes* (see the boxed text above). Both tours cost adult/child €5.10/2.55. For information contact **St Mary's Action Centre** (☎/*fax 318106*, e *smidp@iol.ie*, w *www.iol.ie/~smidp/*) at 44 Nicholas St.

Late June to September, Bus Éireann (☎ 313333) operates open-top bus tours of the city costing €6.35/3.15 per person.

Places to Stay
Hostels There are several good hostels in Limerick.

Limerick Hostel (☎/*fax 314672, 1 Pery Square*) Adult/child €10.80/9.55. This large, rambling An Óige hostel, in Limerick's Georgian heart, is a short walk from the bus and train station. It has 66 beds, accepts credit cards and hires out bikes.

Finnegan's Holiday Hostel (☎/*fax 310 308, 6 Pery Square*) Dorms €12.70. Part of the same terrace of Georgian houses as Limerick Hostel, this Independent Holidays Hostel (IHH) still retains some of the original features. It's hostel policy to provide a safe environment for women and one of the dorms, which range in size from six to 22 beds, is for women only.

Broad St Hostel (☎ *317222,* e *broad streethostel@tinet.ie, Broad St)* Dorms €13.30, singles/doubles from €19/43.20. About a 15-minute walk north of the bus and train station, Broad St is a secure, spotless hostel. Rates include continental breakfast and bed linen.

B&Bs Alexandra Terrace on O'Connell Ave just south of the centre has several B&Bs. Otherwise, Ennis Rd, in the north-west towards Shannon, is lined with B&Bs for several kilometres.

Alexandra Guest House (☎ *318472, 6 Alexandra Terrace, O'Connell Ave)* Rooms €25.50 per person. This is a comfortable three-storey, red-brick Victorian house.

St Anthony's (☎ *45607, 8 Coolraine Terrace, Ennis Rd)* Singles/doubles €22.25/47. Open Apr-Oct. Within walking distance (about 1km) of the centre, this nonsmoking B&B has three cosy rooms, one with shower.

Glen Eagles (☎/fax *455521, 12 Vereke Gardens, Ennis Rd)* Singles/doubles with shower €31.75/50.80. Open Mar-Oct. There are four comfortably furnished rooms in this friendly B&B, in a quiet cul-de-sac about 500m from the centre.

Hotels Most of the big hotels along Ennis Rd are unnecessarily expensive for the average traveller.

Railway Hotel (☎ *413653, fax 419762, Parnell St)* Singles/doubles €56.40/96.80. This rambling old hotel opposite the station has adequate facilities including a bar and restaurant, even if the water for the shower does take a while to heat up.

Royal George Hotel (☎ *414566, fax 317171, O'Connell St)* Singles/doubles €57/75.60. The renovated Royal George is comfortable and central and has a good restaurant, but can be noisy at night.

Glentworth Hotel (☎ *413822, fax 413073, Glentworth St)* Singles/doubles €69.30/113.40. The building is Victorian, but inside the decor is very modern with marble-tile floors and steel rails.

Hanratty's Hotel (☎ *410999, fax 411077,*

5 Glentworth St) Singles/doubles €44.10/ 69.30. In contrast to the Glentworth, Hanratty's, the oldest hotel in Limerick, retains its endearing old-world character.

Woodfield House Hotel (☎ *453022, fax 326755, Ennis Rd)* Rooms €54-62.90 per person. Just 1km from town, this is a comfortable, three-star hotel with a very good restaurant.

Places to Eat

Restaurants You can choose from a number of restaurants in town.

Freddy's Bistro (☎ *418749, Theatre Lane)* Mains €18.90-21.45. Open 6.30pm till late Tues-Sat. Tucked away between Lower Mallow and Lower Glentworth Sts, this restaurant in a former coach house serves top-notch Irish cuisine with the emphasis on seafood.

La Romana (☎ *314994, 36 O'Connell St)* Pasta €8.80-10.65, pizza €7.25-8.80. Open 5pm-11pm. Opposite the Royal George Hotel, La Romana serves delicious Italian meals and has an extensive wine list (mostly from Italy).

Fat Zoe's (☎ *314717, Rutland St)* Pasta €7.25-12, pizza €11.30. Across from the Hunt Museum, in the 19th-century Commercial Buildings, this popular eatery offers tasty dishes in a dimly lit setting.

DuCartes (☎ *312662, Hunt Museum, Rutland St)* Meals €4.45-10.75. Open 10am-5pm Mon-Sat & 2pm-5pm Sun. This classy restaurant serves modern Irish cuisine and is a popular lunch stop. It has a nonsmoking area. Arrive early for the tables with river views.

Mustang Sally's (☎ *400417, 103 O'Connell St)* Mains €13.25-19.55. Open 5pm till late daily. As well as Mexican food this bright Tex-Mex joint serves steak, chicken and seafood. Below it, on the ground floor, is **The Sports Bar**, where you can wash the food down with a good pint of Guinness.

Moll Darby's (☎ *411511, George's Quay)* Pizza €7.60-11.40, mains €15.15-18.90. This popular, relaxed bistro, in a good spot beside the river, serves delicious fish, game, poultry and vegetarian meals and tasty, crispy pizzas.

Fast Food & Cafes Limerick has plenty of places for a quick snack or meal.

Sails (☎ 416622, 1st floor, Arthur's Quay Shopping Centre, Patrick St) Meals €6-7.60. A busy pit stop for shoppers, Sails offers tasty, cheap eats including bangers and mash. There's also a deli counter for takeaway food.

Wokking (☎ 312444, 37 O'Connell St) Meals €5.70-9.45. Opposite the Royal George Hotel, this place, with a sit-in counter and takeaway service, offers good, reasonably priced Chinese food.

Eddie Rocket's (☎ 314700, 115 O'Connell St) Mains €5-6.30. This US-style diner dishes up good burgers and hot dogs and comes complete with working jukeboxes.

Danny's Coffee House (☎ 400694, 5 Rutland St) Mains €5.10-6.30. Danny's is a stylish, friendly place where tea and coffee comes in big mugs and there's a good selection of pastries.

Café Vienna (☎ 411720, 67 William St) Mains €4.95-6.25. Popular at lunchtime, this large, self-service place is OK for soups, sandwiches, salads and light meals. There's also a deli section for takeaway food.

Chimes (☎ 319866, Belltable Arts Centre, 69 O'Connell St) Mains €5.10-7.60. In the basement of the arts centre, the cafe positively buzzes when the art crowd and office workers come in to refuel.

Entertainment

Limerick has a vibrant music scene and you'll find something happening somewhere every night whether it's traditional, jazz or rock.

Nancy Blake's (☎ 416443, Upper Denmark St) Popular with the student community, there's music nightly at this dimly lit, atmospheric pub with its sawdust-strewn wood floor.

Costello's Tavern (☎ 418250, 4 Dominic St) Costello's is a large, cavernous, friendly pub with traditional music on weekend nights and a good pint of Guinness.

The Locke Bar (☎ 413733, George's Quay) This bar is popular with young locals, and there's traditional music on Sunday,

Monday and Tuesday nights. Its outdoor tables beside the river are immensely busy on mild evenings.

Belltable Arts Centre (☎ 319866, 69 O'Connell St) The excellent arts centre plays hosts to visiting musicians, singers and travelling theatre companies, and has a small art gallery.

Savoy Centre (☎ 311900, Bedford Row) Off Henry St, the Savoy houses an eight-screen cinema; also here is *Termites* nightclub, where you can dance Saturday night away from 11pm.

Getting There & Away

Air Shannon Airport (☎ 712000), in County Clare, handles both domestic and international flights.

Bus Bus Éireann services operate from the bus and train station (☎ 313333), a short walk south of the centre. There are regular connections to Dublin (€13.35 one way, one hour 15 minutes), Tralee (€12.20, two hours), Cork (€12.20, one hour 50 minutes), Galway, Killarney, Rosslare, Donegal, Sligo, Shannon, Derry and most other centres. You can be dropped at the bus stop on O'Connell St.

Train There are regular trains to all the main towns: eight trains daily to Dublin; two daily to Rosslare Harbour, Cahir and Tipperary; and one to Cork. Other routes involve changing at Limerick Junction, 20km south-east of Limerick. Phone Colbert station (☎ 315555) for details.

Getting Around

Regular buses connect Limerick bus and train station with Shannon Airport (€4.70 one way). The airport is 24km north-west of Limerick, about 30 minutes by car.

As Limerick is quite small you can easily get around on foot or by bike. To walk across town from St Mary's Cathedral to the train station takes about 15 minutes.

Bikes can be hired at Emerald Alpine (☎ 416983), 1 Patrick St, for €15.25/63.55 per day/week, plus €15.25 if returning outside Limerick. McMahons Cycle World

(☎ 415202), 30 Roches St, is part of the national Raleigh Rent-a-Bike scheme.

AROUND LIMERICK

A few places south of Limerick could be taken in by car in a day or covered by bike over a few days. The R512 road to Lough Gur continues through the village of Bruff to the historic town of Kilmallock. From there, it's a short journey to the pretty village of Bruree, former home of Eamon de Valera. From Bruree a country road leads to Bruff and the R512 back to Limerick.

Lough Gur

The area around this small horseshoe-shaped lake is of great archaeological significance. Numerous Stone Age sites are scattered around the lake. Coming from the city on the R512, the first is the 4000-year-old **Grange Stone Circle**, just past the village of Grange to the left of the road. With its 113 stones it's the largest in Ireland. One kilometre farther along the road a left turn goes up towards Lough Gur. Farther down the R512, 100m past a ruined 15th-century church, there's a **wedge tomb** on the other side of the road.

Another 2km along the R514, in a thatched replica of a Neolithic hut, is an interpretive centre *(☎ 061-360788, Lough Gur; adult/concession €3.15/1.90; open 10am-6pm daily early May-late Sept)*. Here you can see a 12-minute slide presentation on the prehistoric remains. There's also a small **museum** with a few Neolithic artefacts and a replica of the Lough Gur shield that's now in the National Museum in Dublin (although the Lough Gur finds in the Hunt Museum in Limerick are more impressive). The 700 BC shield is 72cm in diameter with six circles of raised bosses designed to weaken the impact of an enemy's sword.

The lake, to which you can walk from the centre, is set in pleasant parkland, perfect for picnics; look out for the burial mounds, standing stones, ancient enclosures and other remains dotted around. To get there, leave Limerick on the N24 road south to Waterford. Look for a sign to Lough Gur indicating a right turn at the roundabout outside town. This takes you onto the R512.

Kilmallock

☎ 063 • pop 1500

On the River Lubach 26km south of Limerick, Kilmallock was Ireland's third-largest town in the Middle Ages, after Dublin and Kilkenny. It developed around an abbey founded in the 7th century by St Mocheallóg. From the 14th to the 17th centuries it was the seat of the earls of Desmond, in an important defensive position. In the mid-18th century it had a brief flurry of renewed importance with the coming of the railway, then sank back into the sleepy state it's in today.

Coming into Kilmallock from Limerick, the first place you'll see (to your left) on the main street is a **medieval stone mansion** – one of 30 or so that once housed the town's prosperous merchants and landowners. A little farther along is the four-storey **King's Castle**, a 15th-century tower house with the street pavement running through it. Across the road a lane leads down to the tiny **Kilmallock Museum** *(☎ 91300, Sheares St; free; open 1.30pm-5.30pm Mon-Fri, 2pm-5pm Sat & Sun)*. It houses a ramshackle local collection and a model of the town in 1597.

Beyond the museum and across the River Lubach are the ruins of the 13th-century **Dominican priory**, with an attractive 13th-century east window and a tower and south window added in the 15th century. Kilmallock surrendered to Cromwell's forces in 1648 and the priory was sacked and partly destroyed.

Returning to the main street, head back towards Limerick then turn left into Orr St, which runs down to the 13th-century **Collegiate Church**. This has a round tower, which probably belonged to an earlier, pre-Norman monastery on the site. The impressively carved door on the southern side of the nave dates from the 15th century.

Farther along the main street, turn left into Wolfe Tone St. Just before the bridge you'll see a plaque marking the house where the Irish poet Aindrias Mac Craith died in 1795. Across the road, one of the pretty, single-storey **cottages** (the fifth one from the bridge) leaves its door open so you can peek in and see what a three-roomed dwelling once looked like.

On the other side of the main street in Emmet Place is **Blossom Gate**, the one surviving gate of the original medieval town wall, traces of which can be seen nearby.

Deebert House (☎ 98106, fax 82002, Kilmallock) Singles/doubles €32.40/48.30. Open Mar-Nov. This B&B is in a fine Georgian house with a carefully manicured front garden. The bedrooms are nonsmoking and organic produce is used in the preparation of meals. To find it go down Wolfe Tone St, turn right after the bridge and head up the hill.

Up to four Bus Éireann buses run each day Monday to Saturday from Limerick.

Bruree
☎ 063 • pop 265

As a child, Eamon de Valera lived in a small cottage in Bruree (Brú Rí) and attended a Christian Brothers school in the nearby town of Charleville. The **cottage** where he spent his formative years is open to the public, although there's little in it apart from some period furnishing and fittings. At the Kilmallock end of the village a sign points to the cottage, just over 1km down the road. The key to the house is available from the next house, 250m farther up the road on the right-hand side.

In the National School attended by de Valera, off Main St by the bridge, is the **De Valera Museum and Bruree Heritage Centre** *(☎ 90900, Water St; adult/child €3.80/1.25; open 10am-5pm Tues-Fri, 2pm-5pm Sat & Sun)*. It contains items associated with his life, as well as information on local history.

Buses between Limerick and Charleville stop in Bruree twice a day Monday to Saturday. Bruree is off the Limerick–Cork road (N20) and on the R518 from Kilmallock.

ADARE & AROUND
☎ 061 • pop 900

This pretty 19th-century village 16km south-west of Limerick is tourist Ireland at its most sanitised. The charming thatched cottages that comprise part of the village were created by the 3rd earl of Dunraven in the 1820s; nowadays they're mostly craft shops or restaurants. Coach tours generally stop in Adare (Áth Dara), which means high prices for food and accommodation.

Information
The helpful tourist office (☎ 396255), in Adare Heritage Centre, Main St, opens 8.30am to 7pm weekdays, 9am to 6pm weekends July and August; 9am to 7pm weekdays, 9am to 6pm weekends June and September; 9am to 6pm daily in October; and 9am to 1pm and 2pm to 5pm Monday to Saturday, March to May and in November and December.

The Allied Irish Bank nearby has an ATM and bureau de change. Traffic congestion can be bad at times. There's a free car park behind the heritage centre.

Adare Heritage Centre
In the centre of the village is a surprisingly good heritage centre *(☎ 396666, Main St; adult/concession €3.80/2.55; open 9am-5pm Mon-Sat & 10am-5pm Sun Mar-Dec)*. It uses models and a short audiovisual presentation to help you make sense of the ruins scattered about; the model showing the village in 1500 is particularly worth a look.

Desmond Castle
Dating back to around 1200, this photogenic ruined castle was partly rebuilt in the following century and besieged by English forces in 1580. When Cromwell's army took possession in 1657, it had already lost its strategic importance. Restoration work is continuing; when it's complete you should be able to view the castle, in the grounds of Adare Manor golf course, without risking your life on the busy main road.

Adare Manor
When the earl of Dunraven decided to create a new mansion in 1832 he enlisted the architectural help of James Pain and AC Pugin, who came up with quirky details such as 52 chimneys and 365 windows. The building work it offered is said to have helped the village survive the Famine rather better than some others. Nowadays the house is an exclusive hotel (see Places to Stay) surrounded by golf courses. Most of the year you can walk around its lovely grounds, but in summer there's usually someone at the gate to control the number of visitors.

Religious Houses

At the time of the dissolution of the monasteries in 1539, Adare had three flourishing religious houses, the remains of which can still be seen. In the village itself, next to the heritage centre, the dramatic tower and southern wall of the **Church of the Most Holy Trinity** are the remains of a 13th-century Trinitarian monastery (the only one in Ireland) which was restored by the 1st earl of Dunraven and is now the Catholic church. There's a restored 14th-century **dovecote** which used to belong to the monastery down the side turning next to the church.

The ruins of a **Franciscan friary** founded by the earl of Kildare in 1464 stand in the middle of Adare Manor golf course beside the River Maigue south of the village. Ask at the clubhouse for permission to visit but you'll have to walk all the way to the 15th tee. Look out for a well preserved sedilia (set of seats for priests) in the southern wall of the chancel.

South of the village, on the N21 north of Adare Manor, the Church of Ireland parish church was once the **Augustinian friary**, founded in 1316. It was also known as the Black Abbey. The tower was added in the 15th century and the church was restored in 1807 by the 1st earl of Dunraven.

Celtic Park & Gardens

About 8km north-west of Adare there's an interesting collection of re-created 'Celtic' structures (plus a few originals) on the site of an original Celtic settlement, at Celtic Park (☎ 394243, Kilcornan; adult/child €4.45/free; open 9.30am-6pm daily Mar-Oct). There's also an extensive rose garden and tearoom.

Castle Matrix

Legend has it that Ireland's first potato was grown in the grounds of this carefully restored and still-lived-in 15th-century Norman tower (☎ 069-64284, Rathkeale; admission by donation, includes guided tour; open 10.30am-6.30pm Sat-Thur May-Sept). It's notable for its extensive collection of books, artefacts and *objets d'art*. The enjoyable tours given by the owner last about an

hour, but opening hours are flexible and it's a good idea to call the day before. The castle is 13km south-west of Adare on the N21.

Organised Tours

July to September a costumed guide leads daily 30-minute, historical walking tours (☎ 396666) of Adare.

Special Events

International artists come to perform at the Adare Music Festival (☎ 415799), held over St Patrick's weekend in March.

Places to Stay

There are lots of B&Bs in and around the village but single travellers are in for an expensive time: better to stay in Limerick and commute.

Elm House (☎ 396306, Clounanna Rd, Mondellihy) Singles/doubles €31.75/45.70. This cosy B&B, 1km north of town, is in a restored 19th-century home and has three rooms, one with shower.

Riversdale (☎ 396751, Station Rd) Singles/doubles €38.10/63.55. This modern, two-storey home is a short walk from the centre and has substantial reductions for children.

Dunraven Arms (☎ 396633, fax 396541, Main St) Rooms €113.64 per person. With its comfy old-world charm, the Dunraven Arms is a positive snip compared to Adare Manor.

Adare Manor (☎ 396566, fax 396124, ✉ info@adaremanor.ie, Rathkeale Rd) Rooms €317.45 per person. In extensive grounds beside the River Maigue this luxurious hotel comes complete with indoor pool, gym, sauna – and golf course.

Places to Eat

Seán Collins (☎ 396400, Main St) Sandwiches €2.15, meals €6.95. This down-to-earth pub serves simple food all day plus reasonable meals at lunchtime.

Lena's Bar (☎ 396114, Main St) Snacks & meals €3.80-7.60. This is a large pub serving filling snacks and sandwiches all day.

Dovecot (☎ 396255, Adare Heritage Centre, Main St) Sandwiches €2.50, meals

€7.50-8.80. Open same hours as the heritage centre. This clean, airy cafeteria serves traditional meals such as Irish stew and shepherd's pie at lunchtime, and snacks the rest of the day.

Wild Geese (☎ 396451, *Main St*) Mains €10.20. Open 6.30pm-10pm Tues-Sat. Wild Geese is an award-winning restaurant serving delicious, contemporary cuisine in a Victorian setting.

Blue Door (☎ 396481, *Main St*) Mains €13.25-21. Open 11am-2.30pm & 6.30pm-9.30pm Mon-Fri, 11am-9.30pm Sat, 11am-3.30pm Sun. This cosy, thatched cottage restaurant serves delicious food. The path up to it is through a well kept rose garden and in fine weather you can eat at the tables outside.

Oak Room Restaurant (☎ 396566, fax 396124, Adare Manor, Rathkeale Rd) Starters €18.30, mains €30-36, plus service charge. This is luxury dining: oak-panelled walls, chandeliers, great views and excellent food.

Entertainment
Bill Chawke Lounge Bar (☎ 396160, *Main St*) There's traditional music every Thursday night and a sing-along on Friday night.

Seán Collins (☎ 396400, *Main St*) This traditional pub has Irish music on Tuesday and Sunday nights year round.

Getting There & Away
The five daily Dublin–Tralee buses call at Limerick and then Adare (return to Limerick €4.85). For times contact Limerick bus station (☎ 061-313333).

County Tipperary

County Tipperary occupies a fair chunk of Ireland's southern midlands and boasts the sort of limey, fertile soil that farmers dream of. Consequently, Tipperary is at the heart of Irish farming. The county is mostly flat in the centre, with hills intruding over the borders from other counties. The River Suir cuts through the county's heart and every major town lies on the banks of the Suir or one of its tributaries. Some towns have

---

It's a Long Way...

No WWI movie would be complete without some British private singing:

It's a long way to Tipperary,
It's a long way to go.
It's a long way to Tipperary,
To the sweetest girl I know…

It was written as a marching song by Englishman Jack Judge in 1912. He had never set foot in Ireland and the word 'Tipperary' was chosen only for its sound.

---

active animal fairs or marts, especially Tipperary town, which, incidentally, isn't the major settlement: Clonmel is far larger, while Carrick-on-Suir, Thurles and Nenagh also have bigger populations.

TIPPERARY
☎ 062 • pop 4770
Despite its evocative name and association with 'that' song, Tipperary (Tiobrad Árann), originally an Anglo-Norman settlement, is an unremarkable working town.

The tourist office (☎ 51457), in the Excel Centre (the town's art and cultural centre) on Mitchell St, opens 9.30am to 5.30pm Monday to Saturday year round. To get there head north from Main St along St Michael's St and take the first turning right. The post office is on Davis St north off Main St.

Things to See
Midway along Main St there's a **statue of Charles T Kickham** (1828–82), a local novelist (author of *Knocknagow*) and Young Irelander. The foyer of the **Sean Treacy Memorial Swimming Pool**, at the eastern end of Main St, houses two display cabinets, with letters, photographs and artefacts relating to the old IRA and the War of Independence (1919–21); Sean Treacy led the war's very first engagement in a quarry a few kilometres north of the town. It's free, but for die-hard enthusiasts only. A lively

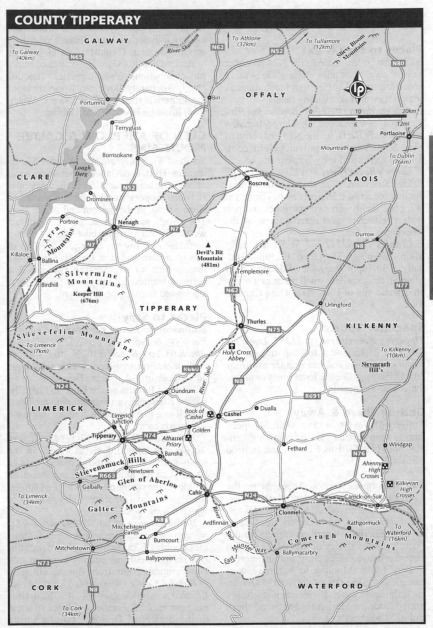

cattle mart is held at the eastern end of Main St on Wednesday and Friday.

Places to Stay & Eat

B&Bs can be found along the N24 on either side of town. Most pubs along Main St serve breakfast, tea and coffee, and lunch; in peak season they also do evening meals.

Ach na Sheen (☎ 51298, Bansha Rd) Singles/doubles €29.20/50.80. A large, friendly, purpose-built B&B, on the N24 just south of Main St, Ach na Sheen provides clean, comfortable rooms and tasty breakfasts.

Lacey's Royal Hotel (☎ 51204, fax 33596, Bridge St) Rooms with shared bathroom including breakfast €38 per person. The Royal is a good family-run two-star hotel and pub with a restaurant, and entertainment at the weekend.

Cranley's (☎ 33917, 7 St Michael's St) Mains €6.60-15.75. Open 12.30pm-3pm daily, 6.30-10pm Tues-Sat. Hidden just off Main St, this excellent small restaurant offers an eclectic mix of Irish, Italian and Chinese food.

Spectator Sports

Tipperary Racecourse (☎ 51357, Limerick Rd) One of Ireland's leading tracks, it's 3km out of town and has regular meetings during the year. See the local press or phone the course for details.

Getting There & Away

Rafferty Travel (☎ 51555), Main St, opens 9am to 6pm Monday to Saturday and handles bookings for Bus Éireann and Iarnród Éireann.

Bus Most buses stop on Abbey St by the river, except for the Rosslare Harbour service, which stops outside Rafferty Travel. Bus Éireann runs up to seven buses daily on the Limerick–Waterford express route. There's also one a day on weekdays in each direction between Tipperary and Shannon in County Clare. Monday to Saturday, Kavanagh's (☎ 51563) runs services to Dublin via Cahir and Cashel. Buses leave at 7.45am from outside the Marian Hall at the northern end of St Michael's St.

Train To get to the station head south along Bridge St. Tipperary is on the Waterford–Limerick Junction line. There's one daily service to Cahir, Clonmel, Carrick-on-Suir, Waterford and Rosslare Harbour, and multiple connections from Limerick Junction (☎ 51406), barely 3km from Tipperary along the Limerick road, to Cork, Kerry, Waterford, Rosslare Harbour and Dublin.

GLEN OF AHERLOW & GALTEE MOUNTAINS

South of Tipperary are the splendid Slievenamuck Hills and Galtee Mountains, separated by the gently beautiful Glen of Aherlow. Between Tipperary and Cahir is Bansha (An Bháinseach), at the eastern end of the glen. The village marks the start of a 20km trip west to Galbally, an easy **bike ride**. It's a wonderful area for low-key **hiking**, with plenty of country accommodation. Cahir is a good base from which to explore the Galtees. The **scenic drive** through the Glen of Aherlow is signposted from Tipperary town.

Places to Stay

Ballinacourty House Caravan & Camping Park (☎ 062-56000, fax 56230, Glen of Aherlow) Tent & car €10.79, hikers & cyclists including tent €5.08, plus €1.27 per adult. Open mid-Apr-Sept. This scenic oasis, 10km from Bansha on the R663 to Galbally, has excellent caravan and camping facilities, as well as a fine garden, restaurant, wine bar and tennis court.

Ballydavid Wood (☎ 062-54148, Glen of Aherlow) Adult/child €10.16/7.62. In the south-eastern corner of the glen, this An Óige hostel is an old hunting lodge in a beautiful setting on the northern slopes of the Galtees. It's 3km off the Tipperary–Cahir road, from which it's signposted.

Bansha House (☎ 062-54194, fax 54215, e banshahouse@eircom.net, Bansha) Singles/doubles €38.09/68.56. This delightful B&B is in a Georgian country house in spacious grounds 200m from Bansha village.

Bansha Castle (☎ 062-54187, fax 54294, Bansha) Singles/doubles €44.45/76.20. Dinner from €22.85. Former residence of some of the Butlers of Ormond, Bansha Castle provides comfortable accommodation in a lovely, restored 19th-century mansion.

Getting There & Away

Bus Éireann express bus No 55 from Limerick to Waterford via Tipperary town stops at Bansha five-times daily. Contact Rafferty Travel (☎ 062-51555) in Tipperary town.

CASHEL

☎ 062 • pop 2345

Cashel (Caiseal Mumhan) is a prosperous market town with a staggering tourist drawcard in the Rock of Cashel. Unfortunately, it's on the main Dublin–Cork road and traffic rolls through at all hours. The good news is that the ruins you've come to admire are well away from the traffic and that Main St doesn't feel swamped by tourism.

Information

The town hall in the main street contains Cashel's tourist office (☎ 61333), which opens 9.30am to 5.30pm Monday to Friday, and 9am to 1pm on Saturday. The post office is at the bottom of Main St. The Allied Irish Bank and Bank of Ireland on Main St have ATMs.

Rock of Cashel

This is one of Ireland's most spectacular archaeological sites (☎ 61437; adult/child €4.45/1.90; open 9am-7.30pm daily mid-June-mid-Sept; 9.30am-5.30pm daily mid-Mar-mid-June; 9.30am-4.30pm daily mid-Sept-mid-Mar; final admission 45 minutes before closing). On the outskirts of Cashel a huge lump of limestone bristling with ancient fortifications rises up from the centre of a grassy plain. Mighty stone walls encircle a complete round tower, a roofless abbey and the finest 12th-century Romanesque chapel in the country. For over a thousand years, the Rock of Cashel was a symbol of power, the base of kings and churchmen who ruled over the region and large swathes of the country.

The word 'cashel' is an anglicised version of the Irish word *caiseal*, meaning 'fortress', and it's easy to imagine that the site developed in territory hostile to the Church.

From the Dublin road, the Rock is concealed by smaller hills until the last minute. There are two parking spaces for disabled visitors on the Rock itself; everyone else should use the car park at the foot (€1.90). The site is busy, especially in July and August, so go first thing in the morning or in late afternoon.

History In the 4th century, the Rock of Cashel was chosen as a base by the Eóghanachta clan from Wales, who went on to conquer much of Munster and become kings of the region. For some 400 years it rivalled Tara as a centre of power in Ireland.

The clan's links with the Church started early: St Patrick came and converted its leader, Aengus, in the 5th century in a ceremony in which St Patrick accidentally stabbed Aengus in the foot with his crozier. Thinking this a painful initiation rite, the king bore the pain with fortitude. The Rock thereafter also became known as St Patrick's Rock.

In the 10th century the clan lost possession of the Rock to the O'Brien, or Dál gCais, tribe under Brian Ború's leadership. In 1101, King Muircheartach O'Brien presented the Rock to the Church, a move designed to curry favour with the powerful bishops and to stop the Eóghanachta ever regaining the Rock, as they could never ask the Church to return such a present. So the Eóghanachta, by now the MacCarthys, moved to Cork. As a sign of goodwill Cormac MacCarthy built Cormac's Chapel in 1127 before leaving. This chapel proved to be too small. A new cathedral was built in 1169 but was replaced in the 13th century.

In 1647, the Rock fell to a Cromwellian army under Lord Inchiquin which sacked and burned its way to the top. Early in the 18th century the Protestant Church took it over for 20 years, but this was the last time the Rock was officially used as a place of worship. The abbey roof collapsed only in the late 18th or early 19th century.

Hall of the Vicars Choral The entrance to the Rock is through this 15th-century house, which contains the ticket office. A

20-minute audiovisual presentation runs every half-hour, detailing the Rock's history (there are French, German and Italian showings as well as English). The exhibits downstairs include some very rare silverware, Bronze Age axes and **St Patrick's Cross**, a badly worn 12th-century crutched cross with a crucifixion scene on one face, animals on the other. Tradition held that the kings of Cashel and Munster – including Brian Ború – were inaugurated at the base of the cross. A replica stands outside, in the castle courtyard. The kitchen and dining hall upstairs contain some period furniture, tapestries and paintings.

The Cathedral This 13th-century Gothic structure overshadows the other ruins. Entry is through a small porch facing the Hall of the Vicars Choral. The cathedral's western end is formed by the **Archbishop's Residence**, a 15th-century, four-storey castle which had its great hall built over the nave. Soaring above the centre of the cathedral is a huge, square tower with a turret on the south-western corner.

Scattered throughout are monuments, panels from 16th-century altar tombs and coats of arms of the Butlers. On the northern side of the choir is the recess tomb of Archbishop Hamilton. Opposite this is the tomb of Miler Mac Grath, who died in 1621. Miler was Catholic bishop of Down and Connor until 1569, when he switched to the Protestant faith and ordained himself Protestant archbishop of Cashel with Elizabeth I's blessing. Her forces were busy at the time torturing and executing his rival, the Catholic Archbishop Dermot O'Hurley.

Round Tower On the north-eastern corner of the cathedral is the sandstone 11th- or 12th-century round tower, the earliest building on the Rock. It's 28m tall and the doorway is 3.5m above the ground – perhaps for structural rather than defensive reasons.

Cormac's Chapel This is the Rock of Cashel's *pièce de résistance*, standing completely intact to the south of the cathedral. Built from 1127, Cormac's Chapel is small,

solid, stone roofed and cruciform shaped, with an unusual square tower on either side. Compared with other churches of the same era, the chapel is sophisticated in design and displays influences from Britain and the Continent – including the square towers.

Outside are impressive Romanesque arches, richly carved. Above the north door (opposite the entrance) in the minute courtyard adjoining the cathedral is a carving of a Norman helmeted figure firing an arrow at a huge lion which has just killed two animals.

The chapel's interior is dark, its windows either blocked up – perhaps to shield the murals from light – or in the constant shadow of the cathedral. The barrel-vaulted nave is only 12m long, with a fine archway into the east chancel boasting many finely carved heads and capitals. The southern tower leads to a stone-roofed vault or croft above the nave. Inside the main door to the chapel, on the left, is the sarcophagus said to house King Cormac, dating from between 1125 and 1150. The deeply cut, interlacing design is highly developed, with motifs more commonly found on metalwork from earlier centuries.

Outside, restoration work on the external masonry is visible. Inside, in the chancel, the carvings and ancient frescoes have been restored as much as possible, though little remains of the frescoes.

Hore Abbey

The extensive ruins of 13th-century Hore Abbey are set in farmland less than 1km north of the base of the Rock. It was the last daughter house – a religious house affiliated to the main monastery – of the Mellifont Cistercians and was a gift from a 13th-century archbishop who expelled the Benedictine monks after dreaming that they planned to murder him. A pleasant walk (signposted) from the Rock leads to the abbey, passing O'Brien's Holiday Lodge (see Places to Stay) on the way.

Cashel Folk Village

A thatched yellow building houses this small but interesting museum *(Dominic St; adult/concession €2.55/0.65; open 9.30am-7.30pm daily)*. It incorporates old buildings and shop fronts from around the town. Of particular interest are the model penal chapel where priests might have said mass in the days when by doing so they risked imprisonment, the slate-fronted republican museum room, and a traditional Romany caravan which was home to a family of 16 until 1986. Read some of the folk remedies: shamrock and dogfern paste to cure lumbago, garlic in the shoe to ward off rheumatism and a cow dung poultice for ulcers and blood poisoning.

Other Things to See

Around town there are a number of ruins which are sometimes overlooked. To get your bearings it's worth calling into the small **Cashel Heritage Centre** (☎ *61333, Town Hall, Main St; free; open 9.30am-5.30pm Mon-Fri & 9am-1pm Sat)*. Attached to the tourist office, it has an interpretive display and a model showing what Cashel looked like in the 1640s.

The first right-hand turn after leaving the Rock leads onto Dominic St, with its small **St Dominic's Friary** ruin from 1243, which, unlike Hore Abbey, has been engulfed by the town. It was closed at the time of writing but can be viewed from the outside. Up John St, from directly opposite the Cashel Palace Hotel, is the **GPA Bolton Library** (☎ *61944, John St; adult/child €1.90/0.65; open 9.30am-5.30pm daily mid-Mar-mid-Oct; 9.30am-5.30pm Mon-Fri mid-Oct-mid-Mar)*. GPA stands for Guinness Peat Aviation. This small building, once a chapter house in the grounds of the graceful, 18th-century Protestant cathedral, is now home to valuable manuscripts and first editions.

Cashel Palace Hotel (see Places to Stay) is a lovely, red-brick Queen Anne residence built by Edward Lovett Pearce (architect of the Bank of Ireland in College Green, Dublin) for Archbishop Bolton in 1730.

Places to Stay

Hostels Cashel has two good hostels.

O'Brien's Holiday Lodge (☎ *61003, fax 62797, Dundrum Rd)* Dorms/private rooms €12.70/19 per person, camping €6.35. This IHH hostel, in a converted coach house north-west of town, is friendly and well equipped, with views of the Rock and Hore Abbey to die for. Beds are in clean, spacious rooms.

Cashel Holiday Hostel (☎ *62330, fax 62445, 6 John St)* Dorms/private rooms €11.45-12.70/15.90 per person. In a quiet, three-storey Georgian terrace off Main St, this IHH hostel gets good reports from travellers. It has a recreation room, kitchen and laundry.

B&Bs Dominic St, on the way from Main St to the Rock, has several quiet B&Bs with views of the Rock.

Rockville House (☎ *61760, Dominic St)* Singles/doubles €32.40/48.30. This large, two-storey place is the closest Dominic St B&B to the Rock; it has six en-suite rooms and a rear car park.

Abbey House (☎*/fax 61104, 1 Dominic St)* Singles/doubles €38.10/50.80. Opposite St Dominic's Friary, this small, cream-coloured bungalow offers good facilities and evening meals but fills up quickly.

Maryville (☎*/fax 61098, Bank Place)* Singles/doubles from €38.10/55.90. The rear entrance is beside St Dominic's Friary (it also has an entrance on Main St). More like a small hotel, Maryville is friendly and has comfortable beds, but adjoining walls are thin and the shared showers are small.

Ashmore House (☎ *61286, fax 62789,* ⓔ *ashmorehouse@eircom.net, 16 John St)* Singles/doubles €34.30/63.50. The rooms in this Georgian terraced house are as carefully maintained as the flowers in the boxes on the front window ledges.

Rosguill House (☎ *62699, fax 61507, Dualla Rd)* Singles/doubles €44.50/63.55. Open May-late Oct. This place, 1km from Cashel on the R691, has Rock views, nonsmoking bedrooms and exceptionally good breakfasts.

Hotels For a historic setting you could stay at a castle or a palace.

Kearney's Castle Hotel (☎ *61044, Main St)* Singles/doubles with bathroom including breakfast from €38/57. The hotel is in a 15th-century square tower once known as Quirke's Castle, and the sparsely decorated interior has retained its medieval feel.

Cashel Palace Hotel (☎ 62707, fax 61521, Ⓦ www.cashel-palace.ie, Main St) Singles/doubles €132.50/195.30. This exquisite hotel, built in 1732 as an archbishop's palace, has an unbeatable view of the Rock to which it is joined by a private footpath. The sad news is that, given its room rates, you're talking dreamland for most travellers.

Places to Eat

Despite the number of tourists flowing through, the Cashel eating scene is, with a few exceptions, fairly basic. Cashel Irish Blue cheese is actually made at Beechmount in Fethard, 15km to the east, but you can still buy chunks of it in the tourist office.

Coffee Shop (☎ 61680, 7 Main St) Meals under €6.50. For tea and coffee, breakfast or a light lunch the best place is above the Bakehouse Bakery across from the tourist office. It's cafeteria style and is packed at lunchtimes. Specials include Cashel blue cheese quiche.

Hannigan's (☎ 61737, Ladyswell St) Mains €7.75-16.35. For good traditional food such as roast beef try this atmospheric old pub opposite Pasta Milano. It gets very busy at lunchtime when locals comes to dine.

Pasta Milano (☎ 62729, Ladyswell St) Pizza €7.50-13.20, pasta €9.45-15.75. Open noon-midnight daily. If you look out over Cashel from the Rock, you can't miss the bright orange exterior of this excellent Italian restaurant. It has a 10% service charge.

The Spearman Restaurant (☎ 61143, 97 Main St) Starters €3.80-6.65, mains €11.40-20.80. Behind the town hall building, this cosy and highly regarded restaurant serves a selection of delicious meals including grilled lemon sole and pepper steak in mushroom sauce.

Chez Hans (☎ 61177, Dominic St) Starters €4-9, mains €17-26. Open 6pm-10pm Tues-Sat. This restaurant, in a converted Wesleyan chapel close to the Rock, is the best in town. The terrific food includes several vegetarian options.

Entertainment

The pubs, as well as Brú Ború, lay on music especially in summer.

Brú Ború (☎ 61122, St Patrick's Rock) Admission €10.15. Open from 9pm Tues-Sat mid-June-mid-Sept. Just below the Rock, Brú Ború is a centre for traditional Irish music, song, dance and storytelling. There's craic galore plus an optional pre-show banquet.

Hannigan's (☎ 61737, Ladyswell St) Hannigan's pulls a good pint and presents regular traditional music sessions.

Davern's (☎ 61121, 20 Main St) This local is popular for its craic and live music at the weekend.

Getting There & Away

Bus Éireann runs six express buses daily between Dublin and Cork via Cahir and Fermoy. Late June to August there are an extra four buses daily to Cahir, which has the closest train station. There's also one bus daily on the Cork–Athlone route via Thurles, Roscrea and Birr. Rafferty Travel (☎ 62121), 102 Main St, handles Bus Éireann tickets and inquiries.

Kavanagh's (☎ 51563) has one bus daily to Dublin, leaving Cashel at 8.30am. From Dublin, it leaves George's Quay near Tara St Station at 6pm. It also does a twice-daily run between Cashel and Clonmel, departing from Cashel at noon and 6.35pm.

The nearest train stations are at Cahir and Thurles.

Getting Around

McInerney's (☎ 61225) on Main St hires out bicycles (€8.82 per day) as do the two hostels. Cahir and Fethard are both within cycling distance.

ATHASSEL PRIORY

Athassel Priory sits peacefully on the western bank of the River Suir 8km south-west of Cashel. This extensive, long-abandoned Norman monastery was built around 1200 by William de Burgh, who wanted it to be one of the richest and most important in the country. The native Irish, in the guise of the earl of Desmond and the O'Briens, burned the priory and its accompanying town in 1319 and again in 1329. What's left today are the remains of a gatehouse, gateway, surrounding walls and the cloisters or arched passageways where monks would walk in prayer, as well as some foundations of various other monastic buildings, including the chapter house.

To get there take the N74 to the village of Golden, then head south for 2km to the priory.

CAHIR
☎ 052 ● pop 2235

Cahir (An Cathair; pronounced care) is 15km south of Cashel, at the eastern tip of the Galtees and on the banks of the River Suir. Dominated by its spectacular castle, Cahir is on the main Dublin–Cork road, ensuring constant heavy traffic. St Declan's Way passes through town.

Orientation & Information

Buses stop in Castle St near a large car park (€0.65 for two hours) between the tourist office and the castle. East of Castle St, the square is ringed with shops, pubs and cafes. The post office is north of the square in Church St.

The tourist office (☎ 41453) opens 9am to 6pm Monday to Saturday, April to September, and also 11am to 5pm on Sunday during July and August. Ask for its free leaflet showing walking routes around Cahir Park.

Cahir Castle

Cahir's most noteworthy feature is the great 13th- and 15th-century castle (☎ 41011, Castle St; adult/child €2.53/1.26, open 9am-7.30pm daily mid-June-mid-Sept; 9.30am-5.30pm daily mid-Mar-mid-June & mid-Sept-mid-Oct; 9.30am-4.30pm daily mid-Oct-mid-Mar). One of Ireland's largest, the castle was founded by Conor O'Brien in 1142 and passed to the Butler family in 1375. Its occupants surrendered to Cromwell in 1650 without a struggle – memories of the battering the place had suffered at the hands of the earl of Essex and his meagre two cannons in 1599 were still fresh. Consequently the castle is remarkably intact. It was also extensively restored in the 1840s and again in the 1960s, when it came into state ownership.

The castle, run by Dúchas, sits on a rocky

island in the River Suir. It consists of three wards (yards) surrounded by a thick fortifying curtain wall, with the main structural towers and halls around the innermost ward. Entry is along the sloping barbican running parallel to the inner-ward wall, and then through the reception area. This opens into the small middle ward, overshadowed by the large gatehouse and keep to the right. Go through this gatehouse, under the reconstructed and fully functioning portcullis, to reach the inner ward. Its buildings are sparsely furnished, although there are small exhibitions on arms, Irish castles and Irish women in Tudor times. Don't miss the 10,000-year-old antlers of a giant Irish deer in the banqueting hall.

Beside the north-eastern tower, the small **well tower** offers the best vantage point over the river (marred, unfortunately, by the ugly grain silo). The tower spirals down to the river and once provided a vital water supply for any extended siege.

The large garden-like outer ward has a **19th-century cottage** at the far end. This houses a short audiovisual show on other local sites of historic interest.

Afterwards, cross the bridge beside the castle and follow the road for five minutes until you come to the ruins of 13th-century **Cahir Abbey**, on Abbey St.

Swiss Cottage

A pleasant riverside path from behind the car park wanders 2km south to Cahir Park and the Swiss Cottage (☎ 41144, Cahir Park; adult/child €2.55/1.25; open 10am-6pm daily May-Sept; 10am-1pm & 2pm-5pm Tues-Sun Apr; 10am-1pm & 2pm-4.30pm Tues-Sun late Mar & Oct-Nov). The Swiss Cottage, also run by Dúchas, is an exquisite thatched cottage ornée, the best in Ireland, surrounded by roses, lavender and honeysuckle. It was designed by Regency architect John Nash as a place of retreat for Richard Butler, 12th Baron Caher, and his wife. In accordance with contemporary French ideas, the cottage was supposed to look as if it had sprung fully formed from the earth; straight lines and symmetry were abhorred and your guide will point out all the tricks used to make it seem more 'natural'. The 30-minute (compulsory) guided tours are thoroughly enjoyable.

John Nash was also responsible for **St Paul's Church** (1820), whose graceful spire is visible from Cahir Bridge in the town centre.

Places to Stay
The Apple Caravan and Camping Park (☎ *41459, fax 42774, Moorstown*) Adult/child including tent €5.40/2.85. Open May-Sept. This quiet camp site is on a fruit farm on the N24 between Cahir (6km) and Clonmel (9km).

Lisakyle Hostel (☎ *41963, Church St*) Dorms/private rooms €10.15/11.45 per person. There is simple accommodation in this IHH hostel, 2km south of town on a back road to Ardfinnan past the Swiss Cottage. In Cahir, the house opposite the post office in Church St, handles enquiries and arranges lifts to the hostel.

Kilcoran Farm Hostel (☎ *41906, Cahir*) Private rooms €12.70 per person. This secluded hostel is 6km west of Cahir, signposted off the N8 Mitchelstown road at the Top petrol station, from which it's 1km. It's on an organic farm, has free showers, kitchen facilities and donkey rides for kids.

Ballydavid Wood (☎ *062-54148, Glen of Aherlow*) This, the nearest An Óige hostel, is 10km away (see Glen of Aherlow & Galtee Mountains earlier).

The Rectory (☎ *41406, fax 41365, Cashel Rd*) Rooms €25.40 per person. Open May-Sept. In a lovely, old-world Georgian house about 1km from the centre, this B&B has five rooms, one with private bathroom.

Ashling (☎ *41601, Cashel Rd*) Singles/doubles €38.10/50.80. Close to The Rectory, this smaller, nonsmoking place is set in pleasant gardens and has three en-suite rooms.

Carrigeen Castle (☎/*fax 41370, Cork Rd*) Singles/doubles €35.55/45.85. As well as viewing a castle you can also spend the night in one. Now a B&B, this 16th-century castle and former prison 1km from the centre, is often mistaken for Cahir Castle.

Kilcoran Lodge Hotel (☎ *41288, fax 41994, Cork Rd*) Rooms €38.10-57.15 per person. Amenities at this pink-coloured, three-star hotel, 6km along the Cork road, include a pool and health club.

Places to Eat
Coffee Pot Restaurant (☎ *41728, 2 Castle St*) Snacks €4.45-6.25, meals €6.25-8.80. Open 8.30am-9pm daily. Opposite Cahir Castle car park and above a souvenir shop, this cafe is popular with tourists as well as locals. There are views of the castle and it serves breakfast all day.

Galtee Inn (☎ *41247, The Square*) Dishes €6.95. Just along from Kay's, this pub is good for inexpensive lunches. The menu includes beef curry and tagliatelle bolognese as well as more traditional offerings.

Roma Café (*Church St*) Dishes €3.80-6.30. Just off the Square, this standard eatery serves pizzas as well as burgers and sandwiches and also has a takeaway section.

Getting There & Away
Bus Cahir is on several Bus Éireann (☎ 062-51555) express routes, including Dublin-Cork, Limerick-Waterford, Galway-Waterford, Kilkenny-Cork and Cork-Athlone. There are six buses daily to Cashel (15 minutes). Buses stop near the Coffee Pot Restaurant.

Kavanagh's (☎ 062-51563) buses travel Monday to Saturday between Tipperary town, Cashel and Dublin via Cahir.

Train Monday to Saturday, the Cork-Rosslare Harbour train stops once a day at Cahir, while the Dublin-Clonmel train stops twice. Contact Thurles train station (☎ 0504-21733) for details.

MITCHELSTOWN CAVES
The Galtee Mountains are mainly sandstone, but along the southern side runs a narrow band of limestone that is home to the Mitchelstown Caves (☎ 052-67246, Burncourt; adult/concession €4.45/1.90; open 10am-6pm daily year round). They're near Burncourt, 16km south-west of Cahir and signposted on the N8 to Mitchelstown (Baile Mhistéala). Far superior to Kilkenny's Dunmore Caves and yet less developed for

The Rock of Cashel, County Tipperary, was the Munster seat of power for over a thousand years.

Adare's Dunraven Arms oozes old-world charm.

Intricate stone detail from the Rock of Cashel

Quirky Adare Manor, County Limerick

This graceful bridge spans the River Nore at Bennettsbridge, County Kilkenny.

Jerpoint Abbey's fine Celtic stone carvings

Elaborate stonework decorating Kilkenny Castle

Originally a wooden structure built in 1172 by Strongbow, Kilkenny Castle is a 'must' for visitors.

tourists, these caves are among the most extensive in the country.

In 1833, Michael Condon was quarrying limestone when he lost his crowbar down a crack in the rock. His efforts to retrieve it opened up the system now called the New Caves. Another cave system nearby – called the Old Caves – was already known to have been used in prehistoric times. Although the Old Caves contain the system's largest chamber, the New Caves form the basis of the tour. Exploration begins through Condon's original opening. Internal temperatures are fairly constant at around 13°C. Underground, there are nearly 2km of passages and spectacular chambers full of textbook formations, inventively labelled from classical and biblical sources.

Call at English's farmhouse opposite the car park for tickets and a tour guide (a tour requires a minimum of two people).

Places to Stay

Mountain Lodge Hostel (☎ *052-67277, Burncourt*) Adult/child €9.53/6.98. Open Mar-Sept. This An Óige hostel, in a former shooting lodge, lies 6km north of the caves and is a handy base for exploring the Galtee Mountains. It's north off the main Mitchelstown–Cahir road.

Getting There & Away

Daily Bus Éireann (☎ 062-51555) express buses from Dublin to Cork or Athlone drop off at the Mountain Lodge Hostel.

CLONMEL

☎ 052 • pop 15,200

Clonmel (Cluain Meala, 'Meadows of Honey') is Tipperary's largest, liveliest, most cosmopolitan town. It's the home of Bulmer's cider; if you're coming from Carrick-on-Suir watch for their orchards alongside the road. Laurence Sterne (1713–68), author of *A Sentimental Journey* and *Tristram Shandy*, was a native of the town.

At the age of 16, Charles Bianconi (1786–1875) was sent from Italy to Ireland by his father in an attempt to break Charles' liaison with a young woman. In 1815, Bianconi set up a coach service between Clonmel

and Cahir, and the company quickly grew to become a nationwide passenger and mail carrier. For putting Clonmel on the map, Bianconi was twice elected mayor. The company's former headquarters is now Hearn's Hotel on Parnell St – Hearn was Bianconi's assistant.

Orientation & Information

Clonmel's heart lies on the northern bank of the Suir. Set back from the quays and running parallel to the river, the main street runs east–west, starting off as Parnell St and becoming Mitchell St and O'Connell St before passing under West Gate and becoming Irishtown and Abbey Rd. Running north off this long thoroughfare is Gladstone St, with lots of shops and pubs.

The tourist office (☎ 22960), Sarsfield St, opens 9.30am to 6pm Monday to Saturday, May to September, and 9.30am to 5pm Monday to Friday the rest of the year. The post office is on Emmet St, which runs north off Mitchell St.

Clonmel Library (☎ 24545), Market Place, has free Internet access 10am-5.30pm Monday and Tuesday, 10am to 8.30pm Wednesday and Thursday, and 10am to 5pm Friday and Saturday. At Circles snooker hall (☎ 23315), Market St, you can surf the Internet 11am to 11pm daily for €5.70 per hour.

Walking Tour

Clonmel has some interesting old buildings. A good starting point is **Hearn's Hotel**, the former headquarters of Bianconi's coach business. South of Parnell St in Nelson St is the refurbished **County Courthouse** designed by Richard Morrison in 1802. It was here that the Young Irelanders of 1848, including Thomas Francis Meagher, were tried and sentenced to transportation to Australia.

West along Mitchell St (past the pistachio-coloured town hall with its statue commemorating the 1798 Rising) and south down Abbey St is the **Franciscan friary**. The 15th-century tower is surrounded by newer work dating only from 1848 and 1884. Inside, near the door, is a 1533 Butler tomb depicting a knight and his lady. There's some fine modern stained glass, especially in St Anthony's Chapel to the north.

Back up on Mitchell St at the junction with Sarsfield St is the **Main Guard**, a Butler courthouse from 1674, based on a design by Christopher Wren. It's undergoing major restoration. Turn south down Bridge St and cross the river, following the road round until it opens out at **Lady Blessington's Bath**, a picturesque stretch of the river, excellent for picnicking.

Return to O'Connell St. Spanning the far end is the **West Gate**, an 1831 reconstruction of an earlier town gate.

Just before the arch is Wolfe Tone St, which heads north past **White Memorial Theatre**, once the Wesleyan chapel, to **Old St Mary's Church**, built in 1204 by William de Burgh and boasting a fine octagonal tower. To the northern and western sides are overgrown stretches of the 14th-century town wall.

On the other side of West Gate is **Irishtown**, named after those native Irish who worked inside the town but were forbidden to live within its walls.

A modern, custom-made building houses the Tipperary South Riding County Museum (☎ 25399, The Borstal, Market Place; free; open 10am-5pm Mon-Fri, 10am-1pm & 2pm-5pm Sat). It has interesting displays on the history of County Tipperary from Neolithic times up to today and hosts regular temporary exhibitions.

Places to Stay

Camping There's a good camp site south of Clonmel.

Power's the Pot Caravan & Camping Park (☎ 23085, fax 23893, Harney's Cross, Clonmel) Tent, car & 2 people €10.15, hikers & cyclists including tent €5.70 per person. This park has a Clonmel address even though it's 9km south-east in County Waterford on the northern slopes of the Comeragh Mountains. To get there, cross south over the river in Clonmel and then follow the road to Rathgormuck. The park has a thatched restaurant and is a good base for walking.

First Bloody Sunday

Among the exhibits owned by the Tipperary South Riding County Museum is the shirt worn by Michael Hogan, who was captain of the Tipperary Gaelic Football team in Croke Park when they played Dublin in November 1920. In retaliation for the deaths of 14 British army intelligence officers, the British police auxiliaries (Black and Tans) opened fire on the crowd and players during a match, killing Hogan and 13 others. This was the first of several Bloody Sundays.

B&Bs & Hotels Many B&Bs are on Marlfield Rd, due west of Irishtown and Abbey Rd.

Benuala (☎ 22158, Marlfield Rd) Rooms €21.60-24.15 per person. A nonsmoking B&B, Benuala has comfortable rooms, does good breakfasts and accepts credit cards.

Hillcourt (☎ 21029, Marlfield Rd) Rooms €25.40 per person. Hillcourt is a pleasant bungalow with five en-suite rooms, a garden for guests' use and a large reduction for children.

Hearn's Hotel (☎ 21611, fax 21135, Parnell St) Rooms €31.75-44.45 per person. Rooms have modern facilities including colour TV and direct-dial telephone, but Bianconi's former coaching house retains much of its historical charm.

Amberville (☎ 21470, Glenconnor Rd) Singles/doubles €32.40/48.25. North off Western Rd beside St Luke's Hospital, this B&B is about 500m from the centre. It has five homely rooms (three en-suite) and accepts credit cards.

Clonmel Arms Hotel (☎ 21233, fax 21526, ℯ theclonmelarms@eircom.net, Sarsfield St) Rooms €44.45-88.95 per person. This fine hotel towards the river has 31 well appointed rooms, a good restaurant (see Places to Eat) and a bar.

Places to Eat

Niamh's (☎ 25698, Mitchell St) Meals €6.95. Open 9am-5.45pm Mon-Fri & 9am-5pm Sat. Niamh's is a cosy, relaxed deli-cum-cafe offering jams, breads, cakes, hot lunchtime meals and a range of coffees.

Angela's (☎ 26899, *Abbey St*) Meals €5.80-6.80. Open 9am-5.30pm Mon-Fri & 9am-5pm Sat. Interesting framed photos line the wall at Angela's which dishes up imaginative hot meals such as salmon bake with ginger chilli, as well as filling baguettes and great coffee.

Tierney's Pub (☎ 24467, *13 O'Connell St*) Snacks €5-6.30, mains €11.30-21. Winner of several awards, its extensive menu includes a good selection of fish dishes and some vegetarian options.

Mulcahy's (*see Places to Eat*) Bar food €4.45-7.50, restaurant mains €11.30-18.85. This vast pub offers inexpensive meals at its self-service carvery while its restaurant, *East Lane Cafe*, offers a mix of Irish and international cuisine.

Catalpa (☎ 26821, *Sarsfield St*) Pasta & pizza €6-7.25, mains €9.80-16.35. Open 12.30pm-2.30pm & 6.30pm-11pm daily. Catalpa's is a delightful, candlelit basement restaurant serving traditional Italian food plus a selection of steak dishes for the carnivore.

Clonmel Arms Hotel (☎ 21233, *Sarsfield St*) Mains €11.30-16.34. Food served 12.30pm-9.30pm daily. The hotel's opulent *Paddock Bar* is one of the best places in town for good-value pub meals. It has a variety of dishes from chicken curry to smoked salmon.

Entertainment
Many bars have local bands and Irish music.

Mulcahy's (☎ 25054, *47 Gladstone St*) Mulcahy's hosts Irish music in its bar on Wednesday, Friday and Sunday, while for clubbers there's *Danno's* nightclub Thursday to Sunday nights.

Clonmel Arms Hotel (☎ 21233, *Sarsfield St*) Here, the *Paddock Bar* has live music on Thursday, Friday and Sunday nights, while its *Club Millennium* is a Friday and Saturday nightclub (it opens at 11pm).

Lonergan's (☎ 21250, *35-36 O'Connell St*) There's traditional Irish music every Monday night at this fine old pub.

South Tipperary Arts Centre (☎ 27877,

Nelson St) This place, off Parnell St, has a program of art exhibitions, plays and films.

Spectator Sports
North of town is the horse-racing course *Powerstown Park Racecourse* (☎ 21422, *Powerstown Park, Clonmel*). It has 13 meetings a year; call for details of fixtures.

Getting There & Away
Bus Bus Éireann (☎ 051-79000) has two buses daily to Cork, up to six to Dublin, and numerous services to Waterford, Limerick and Kilkenny. Tickets can be bought at Rafferty Travel (☎ 22622), 45 Gladstone St, or at the train station where the buses stop. Kavanagh's (☎ 062-51563) has twice-daily buses between Cashel and Clonmel.

Train The train station (☎ 21982) is on Prior Park Rd. Head north along Gladstone St, past the Oakville Shopping Centre and it's just after the Statoil service station. Clonmel is on the Cork–Rosslare Harbour line, with one train a day Monday to Saturday. Dublin–Clonmel trains run twice a day Monday to Saturday via Limerick Junction.

AROUND CLONMEL
Directly south of Clonmel are the **Comeragh Mountains** over the border in County Waterford. There's a fine scenic route south to Ballymacarbry and the Nire Valley. Instead of coming back the same way you can do a circle, heading down to Ballymacarbry from the east and heading back up to Clonmel from the western side. For more details, see Northern County Waterford in the Counties Wexford and Waterford chapter.

The **East Munster Way** (see Walking under Activities in the Facts for the Visitor chapter) passes through Clonmel following the old towpath along the River Suir. At Sir Thomas Bridge the trail cuts south away from the river and into the Comeraghs to Harney's Crossroads before rejoining the River Suir again at Kilsheelan Bridge, from where it follows the towpath all the way to Carrick-on-Suir. From Clonmel, you can take shorter walks along parts of the trail using the same towpath.

The main road between Clonmel and Carrick-on-Suir follows the river through some lovely countryside dotted with ruined 16th- and 17th-century tower houses and roofless medieval churches.

FETHARD
☎ 052 • pop 980

Sleepy Fethard (Fiodh Ard), 14km north of Clonmel on the River Clashawley, is one of the best examples of a medieval walled town. It's sprinkled with medieval ruins, but hasn't caught on to the potential of tourism, making it a pleasant place for those seeking peace and quiet.

Things to See
The single most striking survivor from medieval times is **Holy Trinity Church** (☎ 26643, Main St; free; open by appointment), off Main St through a cast-iron gateway. The church dates from the 13th century and boasts a sturdy tower that looks as if it was built to defend the church, although the clergy probably lived in it. Surrounding the churchyard is a stretch of reconstructed **medieval wall** complete with 15th-century turrets. Unfortunately, to get into the churchyard you must collect a key from Whyte's supermarket in Main St. Close to the church in Main St is the 17th-century **town hall**, with some fine coats of arms mounted on the facade.

The greatest concentration of medieval remains (some of which have been incorporated into later buildings) are south of the church at the end of Watergate St. Beside Castle Inn are the ruins of several fortified 17th-century **tower houses**. Better still you can see the entire length of the **town wall** dating from the 15th or 16th centuries, although parts are even older. Near Watergate Bridge a **sheila-na-gig** is set into a section of the wall. East along Abbey St is the 14th-century **Augustinian friary**, now a Catholic church and with some fine, medieval stained glass.

Places to Stay & Eat
The Gateway (☎ 31701, Rocklow Rd) Singles/doubles with bathroom & TV €27.95/50.80. This is a small, whitewashed B&B with four rooms, near the ruined 15th-century North Gate.

PJ Lonergan's (☎ 31447, Market Square) Mains €6.65-7.50. At the eastern end of Main St, this is an authentic old pub, with a relaxing atmosphere and well prepared meals such as roast beef.

Getting There & Away
There's no public transport to Fethard but it would make a pleasant cycle ride from Cashel, 15km to the west.

CARRICK-ON-SUIR
☎ 051 • pop 5170

The market town of Carrick-on-Suir (Carraig na Siúire), 20km east of Clonmel, grew to considerable importance through the brewing and wool industries during the Middle Ages. For a long time, the seven-arched 15th-century bridge was the first crossing point on the river for the 40km from the Suir's mouth at Waterford Harbour. In the 18th century, the population was 11,000, more than twice what it is today. Compared to Clonmel, Carrick-on-Suir is quiet and unsophisticated, perhaps because the N24 bypasses the town centre. The town is surrounded by rich green farmland, with the Comeragh Mountains in the distance.

Most places make a fuss of their famous offspring only after their demise, but Carrick-on-Suir was quick to honour Sean Kelly, one of the world's greatest cyclists of the late 1980s. The town square bears his name, as does the sports centre.

From Carrick-on-Suir the **East Munster Way** winds west to Clonmel before heading south into Waterford. For more details see Walking under Activities in the Facts for the Visitor chapter.

Orientation & Information
Few streets have signs on them, but you can orient yourself using the street map on Main St near the Allied Irish Bank.

Off Main St through a cast-iron gate, an old church houses the tourist office (☎ 640200), open 9am to 1pm and 2pm to 5pm Monday to Saturday, and 2pm to 5pm on Sunday, March to October. Part of the tourist office is a small **heritage centre** *(adult/child €2.55/1.90)* which opens the same hours. It has a display on local history, but makes little attempt to contextualise its ragbag of exhibits.

Ormond Castle

Carrick-on-Suir was once the property of the Butlers, the earls of Ormond, who built the castle on the banks of the river in the 14th century *(☎ 640787, Castle St; adult/child €2.55/1.25; open 9.30am-6.30pm daily mid-June-early Sept)*. Anne Boleyn, the second of Henry VIII's six wives, may have been born here, though other castles also claim this distinction. She was the great-granddaughter of the 7th earl of Ormond. The Elizabethan mansion next to the castle was built by the 10th earl of Ormond, Black Tom Butler, in anticipation of a visit by his cousin, Queen Elizabeth I, who unfortunately never got round to seeing the result of all his efforts.

Some rooms have fine 16th-century stuccowork, especially the Long Gallery with its depictions of Elizabeth and the Butler coat of arms. Considering the turmoil of the period, it's interesting to note the house's almost complete lack of defences. Indeed, this Dúchas-owned castle is Ireland's only example of the sort of Tudor manor house common in more settled England.

Places to Stay

***Carrick-on-Suir Caravan and Camping Park** (☎ 640461, Kilkenny Rd Ballyrichard)* Tent & car €7.60, hikers & cyclists including tent €4.45 per person. Open Mar-Oct. This small park with 12 tent pitches is only a few minutes' walk from the centre.

***Fatima House** (☎ 640298, John St)* Rooms with bathroom €27.95 per person. This agreeable, two-storey B&B has six rooms and is about 500m west of the Greenside bus stop.

***Carraig Hotel** (☎ 641455, fax 641604, Main St)* Rooms €50.80-57.15 per person. This hotel is central with direct-dial telephones and tea and coffee facilities in its 14 bright, clean rooms.

***The Bell and Salmon Arms** (☎ 645555, fax 641293, Main St)* Singles/doubles

€41.60/69.30. This comfortable hotel has well appointed, spacious rooms and a popular bar.

Places to Eat

There are few good eateries in town, though most of the Main St pubs offer reasonably priced lunches.

Carraig Hotel** (see Places to Stay)* Pasta €6.95-8.20, mains €10.20-17. Pub grub is available in the hotel's bar while its elegant ***Galleway's Bistro is one of Carrrick's best restaurants, with seafood and steak dishes featuring on its menu.

***The Weir** (☎ 640205, 3 Bridge St)* Snacks €2.50-3.80, mains around €6.50. Open 8am-7pm. Near Sean Kelly Square, this pleasant, narrow cafe serves breakfasts, snacks and hot lunches in big portions.

Getting There & Away

Bus Buses stop at Greenside, the park beside the N24 road. Follow New St north from Main St, then turn right.

Bus Éireann (☎ 879000) has extensive buses to Carrick-on-Suir. Bus No 55 between Limerick and Waterford serves Tipperary town, Cahir, Clonmel and Carrick-on-Suir up to seven-times daily, with connections to Galway and Rosslare Harbour. Bus No 7 from Clonmel to Dublin via Carrick-on-Suir and Kilkenny stops up to six-times daily, with connections to Cork.

Train The station is north of Greenside, off Cregg Rd. There's one train a day Monday to Saturday on the Cork–Rosslare Harbour line via Limerick Junction and Waterford. Contact Thurles train station (☎ 0504-21733) for details.

AHENNY & KILKIERAN HIGH CROSSES

Roughly 5km and 8km north of Carrick-on-Suir and signposted off the road to Windgap are the two groups of high crosses at Ahenny and Kilkieran.

At Ahenny the two impressive crosses are both 4m tall and date from the 8th century. Unusually, they're almost exclusively covered in an interlacing design in high relief.

The more typical religious scenes appear only on the base. The crosses are said to represent the transition from the older abstract designs of high crosses to the pictorial scenes found on many later crosses.

Another odd feature are the removable capstones, sometimes known as mitres (bishops' hats). Legend has it that these caps can cure migraine headaches if placed on the sufferer's head. Given the size of the stones, the victim would have more than migraine to worry about!

About 2km nearer Carrick-on-Suir are the three Kilkieran crosses. The western cross is similar to those in Ahenny: 4m tall, richly decorated and with mitre intact. The second is extremely plain.

The most interesting is the needle-like Long Shaft Cross, in a shape unique in Ireland. At the far end of the cemetery is **St Kieran's Well**, whose waters are also said to cure headaches.

THURLES & AROUND
☎ 0504 • pop 6600

Thurles (Durlas), a large market town 22km north of Cashel, was founded by the Butlers in the 13th century. Little of note has been built since and Liberty Square, the town square, is little more than an ugly car park. The tourist information desk (☎ 23579) is part of the Lár na Páirce museum on Slievenamon Rd south off Liberty Square; it opens 10am to 5pm Monday to Saturday year round.

Holy Cross Abbey

Six kilometres south-west of Thurles beside the River Suir is the picturesque Cistercian Holy Cross Abbey (*free; open 9am-8pm daily, West Range open 10am-6pm Mon-Sat & 11am-6pm Sun mid-Apr-Oct*). The abbey was in ruins until the early 1970s, but the cloisters and chapels were restored and now form a living church again. Founded in 1168, it got its name from the relic of the cross on which Christ was crucified that was held in a shrine here (it's now in the Ursuline Convent in Blackrock, Cork). The buildings you see today, however, date from the 15th century, when the abbey was largely remodelled.

A Relic of the True Cross

Holy Cross Abbey was once home to a relic of the True Cross, a splinter of wood said to be from Jesus' cross. It was kept in a golden shrine studded with precious stones and attracted pilgrims from all over Ireland to the abbey from its foundation in 1168. The splinter was said to have been presented by Pope Pascal II to the king of Munster, Murtagh O'Brien, in 1110. It was the only cross relic in the country and was passed on to the nuns of the Ursuline Convent in Blackrock, Cork, in the 19th century, where it remains.

The ground plan is typically Cistercian: a fine cruciform church with a square tower and cloisters to the east. Inside the church, look out for the small fleurs-de-lis and other symbols carved on the old stone pillars, the individual trademarks of the stonemasons. There's also a fine sedilia in the chancel and a medieval fresco showing a hunting scene.

In the restored West Range there's a tourist office, exhibition area and shop. Holy Cross Abbey is on the R660 signposted from Thurles and Cashel.

Other Things to See

In Thurles there survive the ruins of two square tower houses: 15th-century **Barry's Castle** by the bridge and **Black Castle** at the opposite end of Liberty Square, behind the shops. A tiny, incongruous **bird sanctuary**, which you view from the bridge, sits on an island in the middle of the River Suir.

In Liberty Square is **Hayes Hotel**. Here, as every Irish schoolchild learns, the Gaelic Athletic Association (GAA) was founded in 1884 to foster the pursuit of Irish sports and pastimes, particularly Gaelic football and hurling, which it continues to oversee. Over the years, the GAA has been the most successful of the Gaelic revivalist groups. An interesting museum (and shop) of Gaelic games is **Lár na Páirce** (*☎ 23579, Slievenamon Rd; adult/child €3.80/1.90; open 10am-5pm Mon-Sat*). It has a 20-minute video of game highlights.

Getting There & Away

Bus Éireann (☎ 061-418855) bus No 71 stops at Thurles once daily between Cork and Athlone, with connections to Cahir, Roscrea and Carrick-on-Suir.

Dublin–Limerick trains stop in Thurles (☎ 21733) up to 15-times daily; Dublin–Cork trains stop up to five-times daily.

ROSCREA

☎ 0505 • pop 4170

For somewhere to break your journey between Dublin and Limerick, the medium-sized town of Roscrea (Ros Cré) is more inviting than Nenagh. On the eastern edge of the county, it can be used as a base for exploring the Slieve Bloom Mountains to the north-east. Although the main Limerick–Dublin road cuts through the town, the wide streets are better able to cope with the traffic than those in smaller towns.

Roscrea owes its beginnings to a 5th-century monk, St Crónán, who set up a way station for the travelling poor. Most of the historical structures are on or near the main street, Castle St.

Tourist information is available from Roscrea Castle (see later).

Things to See

Coming into the town centre from the Dublin side, the main road passes through the remains of **St Crónán's second monastery**. To the right you see a truncated **round tower** while on the other side is what's left of the western gable of 12th-century **St Crónán's Church** with its finely worked stone Romanesque doorway. The rest of the church was torn down in 1812, with some of the stones used to build the present church. A 12th-century **high cross** once stood in the churchyard but was removed for restoration and will be housed in a proposed interpretive centre.

The site of St Crónán's first monastery is almost 2km east of town and south of the main Dublin road. The Book of Dímma, a 7th-century illuminated manuscript that originated here, can now be seen in Trinity College, Dublin.

In the centre of town is the Dúchas-restored, 13th-century **Roscrea Castle**, with the substantial remains of a gatehouse, walls and towers. Inside the courtyard stands austere **Damer House**, the Queen Anne-style residence of the Damer family, which houses **Roscrea Heritage Centre** (☎ 21850, Castle St; adult/concession €3.15/1.25; open 10am-6pm daily Apr-Oct). This contains several interesting exhibitions, including one on the medieval monasteries of the midlands and another on early-20th-century farming life.

At the southern end of The Mall, in Rosemary Square, is Roscrea's answer to Brussels' Mannequin Pis, a **fountain** with four cherubs pouring water out of urns. Nearby, Abbey St has considerable remains of a 15th-century **Franciscan friary**.

Places to Stay & Eat

Grant's Hotel (☎ 23300, fax 23209, Castle St) Singles/doubles €51/88.20. Grant's, opposite the castle, is a fully restored, elegant and comfortable former coaching inn; the Irish tricolour is proudly displayed above the entrance.

La Seranata (☎ 22431, The Mall) Pizza & pasta €6.30-8. Open noon-10pm daily. This cosy old-world restaurant, just off Castle St beside the river, serves good Italian food and houses a small art gallery.

Getting There & Away

Up to 13 Bus Éireann (☎ 01-836 6111) express buses stop at Roscrea between Dublin (two hours) and Limerick (one hour). There are also daily buses to Sligo, Carrick-on-Shannon, Athlone, Thurles, Cahir, Cork and Shannon.

Two Dublin–Limerick trains stop at Roscrea twice a day Monday to Saturday, and once on Sunday. For details ring ☎ 21823.

NENAGH & AROUND

☎ 067 • pop 5645

Nenagh (An tAonach) is a busy, rather dreary town on the main Dublin–Limerick road and blighted by heavy traffic. Most street names are in Gaelic.

The tourist office (☎ 31610), on Connolly St (Sraid ui Chonghaile), the Silvermines road, opens 9.30am to 1pm and 2pm to 5.30pm Monday to Saturday, May to early September. The Bank of Ireland and Allied Irish Bank on Connolly St have ATMs.

Things to See

In the early 13th century **Nenagh Castle** was the seat of the first Butler of Ireland, Theobald fitzWalter, and it remained in the family's possession for 400 years. The fitzWalters changed their name to Butler and in the late 14th century moved their principal seat of power to Kilkenny Castle. All that remains of their castle at Nenagh is a striking circular **donjon** or tower, dating from 1217. It's over 30m tall; the final 8m was added by the bishop of Killaloe in 1860. There's no public access.

Across the road is a Doric courthouse and beside it the Convent of Mercy, originally a prison. Within the convent's grounds is **Nenagh Heritage Centre** (☎ 32633, Kickham St; adult/child €2.55/1.25; open 9.30am-5pm Mon-Fri & 2.30pm-5pm Sun Mar-early Oct). The centre is in two parts; the most interesting is the Gatehouse Gaol, where 17 men were hanged between 1842 and 1858. You can inspect the cells of the condemned and read about their crimes, before gazing on their last drop. Along the driveway is the octagonal Governor's House, which contains a genealogy centre and good mock-ups of an old country schoolroom, a pub/shop, a kitchen and dairy.

Getting There & Away

Bus Buses to Nenagh stop in Banba Square near the courthouse; some also stop at the train station. Bus Éireann express buses between Dublin and Limerick stop in Nenagh up to 14-times daily. A less frequent daily service runs from Tralee to Roscrea, Athlone and Carrick-on-Shannon via Nenagh. In July and August, the Galway–Rosslare Harbour bus also stops at Nenagh.

Rapid Express Coaches (☎ 26266), Ballinamona, runs three to four buses daily to Dublin via Roscrea, Portlaoise and Kildare, leaving from outside Slattery's clothing store in Pearse St.

Train The station (☎ 31232) is on the Thurles side of town. Dublin–Limerick trains stop here twice a day Monday to Saturday (one on Sunday).

LOUGH DERG

The 130-sq-km Lough Derg, a popular boating and fishing area, marks the border between Counties Tipperary and Clare and extends north into Galway. The **Lough Derg Way** begins in Limerick city and ends at the pretty village of Dromineer in Tipperary.

If you're heading north-east from Limerick city towards Nenagh it's more enjoyable to take the scenic route from Birdhill along the River Shannon to Ballina and then follow the road between the eastern edge of Lough Derg and the Arra Mountains rather than to follow the N7 all the way. Ballina is joined by the Shannon Bridge to the heritage town of **Killaloe** in County Clare (see Killaloe & Around in the County Clare chapter).

County Kilkenny

The verdant farming county of Kilkenny is peppered with solid stone walls and medieval ruins. The Normans liked this part of Ireland and settled here in large numbers, leaving their stamp on Kilkenny city, Ireland's most enchanting medieval settlement. The county's most attractive areas are along the Rivers Nore and Barrow, on which there are some delightful villages such as Inistioge and Graiguenamanagh. Jerpoint Abbey and Kells Priory are two of the country's finest medieval monastic settlements.

Since medieval times, Kilkenny's history has been inextricably linked with the fortunes of one Anglo-Norman family, the Butlers, earls of Ormond. After arriving in 1171, they made the region their own, promoting first the Norman cause and then that of the English royal household. They were based in Kilkenny city.

Walking the stretch of the South Leinster Way that crosses southern Kilkenny offers an opportunity to see rural Ireland at its prettiest.

Kilkenny

☎ 056 • pop 18,696

The first thing you should know about Kilkenny is that it's a city. Not a large town, but a city proper, although with less than 20,000 inhabitants you could be forgiven for thinking otherwise. The next thing you should know – although you'll discover it pretty much as soon as you arrive – is that Kilkenny is the most attractive city in Ireland. Far removed from the urban mayhem of Dublin and Cork, Kilkenny's medieval character is still very much alive, most notably in the city's narrow winding streets and old-fashioned shop fronts.

Although much of the city's charm owes a huge debt to its medieval past, when Kilkenny was a powerful seat of political power, the modern city is a vibrant cultural centre, renowned throughout Ireland for its devotion to the arts. Buskers and street

Highlights

- Spend time in medieval Kilkenny, the most beautiful city in Ireland
- Visit Jerpoint Abbey and Kells Priory, two of Ireland's finest medieval monastic settlements
- Explore the Rivers Nore and Barrow, by which you'll find charming villages such as Inistioge
- Take in the Kilkenny Arts Festival, one of Ireland's most important cultural gatherings
- Enjoy the Cat Laughs Comedy Festival, one of the top festivals in the country

artists are a perennial feature, and the streets are also lined with some of the best pubs, cafes, restaurants and shops in this part of the country.

Overlooking everything is the town's splendid medieval cathedral, named after St Canice (Cainneach, or Kenneth), who founded a monastery here in the 6th century; hence the city's Irish name, Cill Chainnigh,

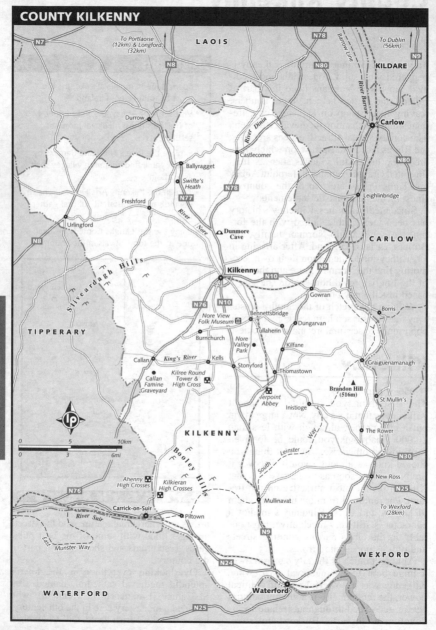

COUNTY KILKENNY

LAOIS

To Portlaoise
(12km) & Longford
(32km)

N7

N8

To Dublin
(56km)

N9

KILDARE

Barrow Line

River Barrow

N78

N80

Durrow

River Dinin

Carlow

Castlecomer

Ballyragget

N80

Swifte's
Heath

N78

Leighlinbridge

Freshford

N77

Urlingford

River Nore

Dunmore
Cave

CARLOW

N8

Silveardagh Hills

Kilkenny

N10

N9

Gowran

Borris

N76

N10

TIPPERARY

Nore View
Folk Museum

Bennettsbridge

Dungarvan

Tullaherin

Burnchurch

Nore
Valley
Park

Kilfane

King's River

Callan

Kells

Stonyford

Thomastown

Graiguenamanagh

Callan Famine
Graveyard

Kilree Round
Tower &
High Cross

Brandon Hill
(516m)

St Mullin's

Jerpoint
Abbey

Inistioge

The Rower

KILKENNY

Leinster Way

N30

Booley Hills

South

New Ross

N25

Ahenny
High Crosses

Kilkieran
High Crosses

Mullinavat

To Wexford
(28km)

Carrick-on-Suir

Piltown

N25

River Suir

N9

East
Munster Way

N24

WEXFORD

WATERFORD

Waterford

N25

0   5   10km
0   3   6mi

or monastery of Canice. The town's other 'must-see' attraction is the mighty castle, which sits majestically on a sweep in the Nore. Kilkenny is sometimes called the 'marble city' because of the local black limestone seen to most striking effect in the cathedral.

HISTORY

In the 5th century, St Kieran is said to have visited Kilkenny and, on the site of the present Kilkenny Castle, challenged the chieftains of Ossory to accept the Christian faith. St Canice established his monastery here in the 6th century. Kilkenny consolidated its importance in the 13th century under William Marshall, the earl of Pembroke and son-in-law of the Anglo-Norman conqueror Strongbow. Kilkenny Castle was built to secure a crossing point on the Nore.

During the Middle Ages, Kilkenny was intermittently the unofficial capital of Ireland, with its own Anglo-Norman Parliament. In 1366 the Parliament passed the so-called Statutes of Kilkenny, a set of Draconian laws aimed at preventing the assimilation of the increasingly assertive Anglo-Normans into Irish society. Anglo-Normans were prohibited from marrying the native Irish, taking part in Irish sports, speaking or dressing like the Irish or playing any Irish music. Any breach of the law resulted in the confiscation of Anglo-Norman property and death to the native Irish: Ireland's own version of apartheid.

Although the laws remained theoretically in force for over 200 years, they were never enforced with any great effectiveness and did little to halt the absorption of the Anglo-Normans into Irish culture.

During the 1640s, Kilkenny sided with the Catholic royalists in the English Civil War. The 1641 Confederation of Kilkenny, an uneasy alliance of native Irish and Anglo-Normans, aimed to bring about the return of land and power to Catholics. After Charles I's execution, Cromwell besieged Kilkenny for five days, destroying much of the southern wall of the castle before Ormond surrendered. The defeat signalled a permanent end to Kilkenny's political influence over Irish affairs.

ORIENTATION

At the junction of several major highways, Kilkenny straddles the Nore, which flows through much of the county. St Canice's Cathedral sits on the northern bank of the River Bregagh (a tributary of the Nore) to the north of the town centre outside the town walls. Kilkenny's main thoroughfare runs south-east from the cathedral, past St Canice's Place to Irishtown (where the common folk were once concentrated, outside the town walls) then over the bridge, eventually becoming Parliament St, which then splits into two. Kilkenny Castle is on the banks of the Nore and dominates the town's southern side.

INFORMATION

The tourist office (☎ 51500, W www.ireland .travel.ie) is in the lovely stone Shee Alms House on Rose Inn St. The office sells excellent guides to the town and walking maps of the county for €0.50 per sheet. It also runs an efficient accommodation booking system costing €1.30 (€2.55 for anywhere outside the county) plus 10% of the cost of the accommodation, which is deducted when you pay the hotel or B&B. It opens 9am to 6pm Monday to Saturday, April to October (to 7pm Monday to Saturday and 11am to 5pm on Sunday during July and August); 9am to 5pm Monday to Friday the rest of the year.

For information on local events, check out the weekly *Kilkenny People* newspaper or tune into Radio Kilkenny, which broadcasts from 7am to 2am on 96.6 FM. The Kilkenny Tourist Hostel (see Places to Stay later in this section) has an excellent notice board for events around town that is updated daily.

The Kilkenny Book Centre (☎ 62117, W www.kilkennybookcentre.com), 10 High St, stocks a range of books and maps on Ireland. It opens 9am to 6pm Monday to Saturday (and 2pm to 6pm Sunday during July and August only).

There is a branch of the Allied Irish Bank at 3 High St. It has an ATM. You can change money at the bank or in the tourist office.

Celtel (☎ 20303), 26 Rose Inn St, is Kilkenny's best Internet cafe. It opens 8am to

10pm daily, and charges a whopping €3.80 for 30 minutes (nowhere else is cheaper), but students get a 20% discount (you'll need to show a student card). Webtalk (☎ 50066), next door at 25 Rose Inn St, charges the same; it opens 10am to 9pm Monday to Saturday, and 2pm to 8pm on Sunday.

St Luke's Hospital (☎ 51133) is on Freshford Rd, about 5km north of Kilkenny city. There is a branch of Boots the Chemist (☎ 71222) at 36–38 High St. If you need the police, whose station is on Dominic St, dial ☎ 999 or 22222.

KILKENNY CASTLE

The first structure on this strategic site overlooking the Nore was a wooden tower built in 1172 by Richard de Clare, the Anglo-Norman conqueror of Ireland better known as Strongbow. Twenty years later his son-in-law, William Marshall, erected a stone castle with four towers, three of which still survive. The castle (☎ 21450; adult/student €4.50/1.90; open 10am-7pm daily June-Sept; 10.30am-12.45pm & 2pm-5pm Tues-Sat, 11am-12.45pm & 2pm-5pm Sun Oct-Mar; 10am-5pm daily Apr & May) was bought by the powerful Butler family in 1391 and their descendants continued to live there until 1935. Maintaining such a structure became an enormous financial strain and most of the furnishings were finally sold at auction. The castle was handed over to the city in 1967 for the princely sum of £50 and is now administered by Dúchas.

Work continues to restore the castle to its Victorian splendour and many of the rooms have only recently been opened to the public. The Long Gallery (the wing of the castle nearest the river), with its vividly painted ceiling mixing Celtic and Pre-Raphaelite motifs with portraits of the Butler family members over the centuries, is particularly splendid and forms the focus of the 40-minute guided tour.

The castle is also home to the Butler Gallery, one of the country's most important art galleries outside Dublin. There are art exhibitions throughout the year. In the basement, the castle kitchen houses a popular summertime restaurant (see Places to Eat later in this section).

Twenty hectares of parkland (free; open 10am-8.30pm daily in summer) extend to the south-east, with a Celtic-cross-shaped rose garden, a fountain to the northern end and a children's playground to the south.

ST CANICE'S CATHEDRAL

The approach to the cathedral on foot from Parliament St leads you over Irishtown Bridge and up St Canice's Steps, which date from 1614; the wall at the top contains fragmentary medieval carvings. Around the cathedral (☎ 64971, ⓔ stcanicecathedral@ eircom.net, St Canice's Place; admission by donation; open 9am-1pm & 2pm-6pm Mon-Sat & 2pm-6pm Sun Easter-Sept; 10am-1pm & 2pm-4pm Mon-Sat & 2pm-4pm Sun Oct-Easter) are a graveyard, a round tower and an 18th-century bishop's palace. Although the present cathedral was built between 1202 and 1285, it has a much longer history.

This site may well have pre-Christian significance. Legend has it that the first monastery was built here by St Canice, Kilkenny's patron saint, who moved here from Aghaboe, County Laois, in the 6th century. There are records of a wooden church on the site which was burned down in 1087. The 30m-high round tower (adult/student €1.90/1.30; open 9am-1pm & 2pm-6pm Mon-Sat, 2pm-6pm Sun year round), which is beside the church, is the oldest structure within the cathedral grounds and was built sometime between 700 and 1000 on the site of an earlier Christian cemetery. Apart from missing its crown, the round tower is in excellent condition, and you can admire the fine view from the top. It's a tight squeeze and you'll need both hands to climb the steep ladders.

St Canice's was built in early English Gothic style but then suffered a catalogue of catastrophes and resurrections. The first disaster, when the bell tower collapsed in 1332, is connected with the story of Kilkenny's legendary witch, Dame Alice Kyteler (see the boxed text 'The Witch of Kilkenny'). In 1650, Cromwell's forces defaced and damaged the church, even using it to stable their horses. Repairs began in

Kilkenny 381

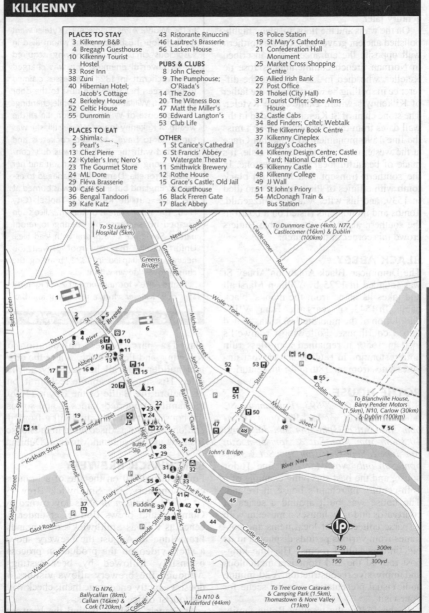

KILKENNY

PLACES TO STAY
- 3 Kilkenny B&B
- 4 Bregagh Guesthouse
- 10 Kilkenny Tourist Hostel
- 33 Rose Inn
- 38 Zuni
- 40 Hibernian Hotel; Jacob's Cottage
- 42 Berkeley House
- 52 Celtic House
- 55 Dunromin

PLACES TO EAT
- 2 Shimla
- 5 Pearl's
- 13 Chez Pierre
- 22 Kyteler's Inn; Nero's
- 23 The Gourmet Store
- 24 ML Dore
- 29 Fléva Brasserie
- 30 Café Sol
- 36 Bengal Tandoori
- 39 Kafe Katz
- 43 Ristorante Rinuccini
- 46 Lautrec's Brasserie
- 56 Lacken House

PUBS & CLUBS
- 8 John Cleere
- 9 The Pumphouse; O'Riada's
- 14 The Zoo
- 20 The Witness Box
- 47 Matt the Miller's
- 50 Edward Langton's
- 53 Club Life

OTHER
- 1 St Canice's Cathedral
- 6 St Francis' Abbey
- 7 Watergate Theatre
- 11 Smithwick Brewery
- 12 Rothe House
- 15 Grace's Castle; Old Jail & Courthouse
- 16 Black Freren Gate
- 17 Black Abbey
- 18 Police Station
- 19 St Mary's Cathedral
- 21 Confederation Hall Monument
- 25 Market Cross Shopping Centre
- 26 Allied Irish Bank
- 27 Post Office
- 28 Tholsel (City Hall)
- 31 Tourist Office; Shee Alms House
- 32 Castle Cabs
- 34 Bed Finders; Celtel; Webtalk
- 35 The Kilkenny Book Centre
- 37 Kilkenny Cineplex
- 41 Buggy's Coaches
- 44 Kilkenny Design Centre; Castle Yard; National Craft Centre
- 45 Kilkenny Castle
- 48 Kilkenny College
- 49 JJ Wall
- 51 St John's Priory
- 54 McDonagh Train & Bus Station

1661, but there was still much to be done a century later.

On the walls and the floor are many highly polished ancient **graveslabs**. On the northern wall opposite the entrance a slab inscribed in Norman French commemorates Jose de Keteller, who died in 1280; despite the difference in spelling he was probably the father of Kilkenny's witch, Dame Alice Kyteler. The stone chair of St Kieran embedded in the wall dates from the 13th century. Don't miss the fine 1596 monument to Honorina Grace at the western end of the southern aisle. It's made of beautiful local black limestone. In the southern transept is a beautiful **black tomb** with effigies of Piers Butler, who died in 1539, and his wife, Margaret Fitzgerald. Tombs and monuments (listed on a board in the southern aisle) to other notable Butlers crowd this corner of the church.

BLACK ABBEY

The Dominican Black Abbey on Abbey St was founded in 1225 by William Marshall and takes its name from the monks' black habits. In 1543, six years after Henry VIII's dissolution of the monasteries, it was turned into a courthouse. Following Cromwell's visit in 1650, it remained a roofless ruin until restoration in 1866. Much of what survives dates from the 18th and 19th centuries.

ROTHE HOUSE

Rothe House (☎ 22893, Parliament St; adult/concession €2.55/1.90; open 10am-6pm Mon-Sat & 3pm-5pm Sun July-Aug; 10.30am-5pm Mon-Sat & 3pm-5pm Sun Apr-June & Sept-Oct; 1pm-5pm Sat & 3pm-5pm Sun only Nov-Mar) is a fine Tudor house, and the best surviving example of a 16th-century merchant's house in Ireland. The house was built around a series of courtyards and now houses a museum with a sparse collection of local items and costumes from various periods displayed in its old timber-vaulted rooms. The fine king-post roof of the 2nd floor is a meticulous and impressive reconstruction. A 20-minute audiovisual presentation sets the scene for your visit.

In the 1640s, the wealthy Rothe family

The Witch of Kilkenny

In the Middle Ages, Dame Alice Kyteler went through four husbands, all of whom died in suspicious circumstances. Having acquired some powerful enemies, she was charged with witchcraft in 1324. Witnesses claimed to have seen her sweeping dust to the door of her son, William Outlawe, while chanting: 'To the house of William, my son, lie all the wealth of Kilkenny town.' Worse still, she was supposed to have sacrificed cockerels and consorted with the devil. She was duly convicted, along with her sister, her son and her maid, Petronella. Dame Alice managed to escape to England but Petronella was burned at the stake outside Kilkenny's Tholsel (City Hall). The sister's fate is unknown. Alice's son escaped his sentence by offering to reroof part of St Canice's Cathedral with lead tiles. Unfortunately, the new roof proved too heavy and collapsed in 1332, bringing the church tower down with it.

Dame Alice's former home at 27 St Kieran's St is now Kyteler's Inn, a restaurant and bar.

played a part in the Confederation of Kilkenny, and Peter Rothe, son of the original builder, had all his property confiscated. His sister was able to reclaim it, but just before the Battle of the Boyne (1690) the family supported James II and so lost the house permanently. In 1850 a Confederation banner was discovered in the house. It's now in the National Museum, Dublin.

SMITHWICK BREWERY

Founded in 1710 on the site of a Franciscan monastery, the Smithwick Brewery (☎ 21014, Parliament St) is now owned by Guinness and brews Budweiser under licence as well as Smithwick's own brands. From June to August the brewery shows a short video on the production process, ostensibly followed by beer tastings. Although the brewery allows visitors, it doesn't exactly encourage them; check with the tourist office for details.

St Francis' Abbey, behind the brewery,

was founded by William Marshall in 1232 but desecrated by Cromwell in 1650. The monks were reputed to be expert brewers.

NATIONAL CRAFT GALLERY

Recently opened in Castle Yard is the National Craft Gallery (☎ 61804, W www .craftscouncil-of-ireland.ie, Castle Yard; free; open 10am-6pm daily Apr-Dec; closed Sun rest of year). This new gallery funded by the Crafts Council of Ireland showcases contemporary Irish crafts. Its high-quality exhibitions highlight the diversity and imagination of crafts in Ireland, with a special emphasis on ceramics.

OTHER THINGS TO SEE

Stretches of the old Norman city walls can still be traced, but **Black Freren Gate** on Abbey St is the only gate still standing.

Shee Alms House, on Rose Inn St, was built in 1582 by local benefactor Sir Richard Shee and his wife to provide help for the poor. It continued as a hospital until 1740 but now houses the tourist office. The **Tholsel**, or City Hall, on High St was built in 1761 on the spot where Dame Alice Kyteler's maid, Petronella, was burned at the stake in 1324 (see the boxed text 'The Witch of Kilkenny'). Just north of the Tholsel is the **Butter Slip**, a narrow alleyway built in 1616 to connect High St with Low Lane (now St Kieran's St) and once lined with the stalls of butter sellers.

On the corner of Parliament St and the road leading down to Bateman's Quay, a **monument** beside the Bank of Ireland marks the site of the Confederation Hall, where the national Parliament met from 1642 to 1649. Nearby is **Grace's Castle**, originally built in 1210 but lost to the family and converted into a prison in 1568 and then in 1794 into a courthouse, which it remains today. Rebels from the 1798 Rising were executed here. People taking part in one of Tynan's Tours (see Organised Tours) get to see inside the cells.

Across the river stand the ruins of **St John's Priory**, which was founded in 1200 and was noted for its many beautiful windows until Cromwell's visit. Nearby, **Kilkenny College**, on John St, dates from 1666. Its students included Jonathan Swift and the philosopher George Berkeley, but it now houses Kilkenny's county hall.

ORGANISED TOURS

Tynan Tours (☎ 65929, 087 265 1745, e info@tynantours.com) Adult/concession €4.50/3.80. Tynan Tours conducts hourlong walking tours of the town six-times daily (four on Sunday) March to October, starting from the tourist office. Three tours per day Tuesday to Saturday are scheduled for the rest of the year.

The Kilkenny Tour, run by Tynan Tours, is a hop-on, hop-off, open-top-bus tour of the town that departs from Kilkenny Castle every half-hour between 10am and 5pm. Tickets cost €7.60/3.80.

JJ Kavanagh & Sons (☎ 31106, e info@ jjkavanagh.ie, W www.jjkavanagh.ie) runs open-top-bus tours of Kilkenny (€10.20), departing from the Parade at 6.30am, 8.30am, 11am, 2.40pm and 5.45pm Monday to Saturday (1.50pm and 6.20pm Sunday), mid-May to mid-September. It also does tours of Kilkenny from Dublin (€24.20 including the transfer from Dublin and Kilkenny city tour), departing from in front of the Gresham Hotel on O'Connell St, Dublin, at 10am, 1pm and 5.45pm Monday to Saturday and 5.45pm and 9pm on Sunday, also mid-May to mid-September.

Buggy's Coaches (☎ 41264) runs tours of the Nore Valley upon request; they cost around €6.50 per person.

SPECIAL EVENTS

Kilkenny is rightly known as the festival capital of Ireland, with several world-class festivals throughout the year that attract thousands of people. The most important of all, established in 1973, is the Kilkenny Arts Festival (☎ 52175, e kaw@iol.ie). Over 10 activity-packed days in late August, the city plays host to theatre, music, literature, visual arts and children's events, and other outdoor activities. Accommodation at this time is like gold dust, and you're seriously advised to book far in advance.

But that's not nearly the half of it. Other festivals throughout the year include:

Cat Laughs Comedy Festival (☎ 63207) June bank-holiday weekend. For details see Public Holidays and Special Events in the Facts for the Visitor chapter.

Confederation of Kilkenny Festival (☎ 51500) June. This festival commemorates Kilkenny's days as the Irish capital.

Kilkenny Rhythm & Roots (☎ 51500) May bank-holiday weekend. Over 30 different venues participate in hosting Ireland's biggest music festival.

Kilkenny International Air Rally (☎ 21483) End of June. This impressive air display takes place at Kilkenny Airport.

Ultimate Frisbee Tournament (☎ 51500 or ⓔ iancud@hotmail.com) Mid-June. This is an excellent weekend of booze, lunacy and ultimate Frisbee.

PLACES TO STAY
Camping
Tree Grove Caravan & Camping Park (☎ 70302, fax 21512, Danville House, New Ross Rd) Tent & 2 people €10.20. This small park is 1.5km south of Kilkenny.

Nore Valley Caravan & Camping Park (☎ 27229, Annamult) This park is about 11km away, near Bennettsbridge; see under Central Kilkenny later in this chapter for details.

Hostels
Kilkenny Tourist Hostel (☎ 63541, fax 23397, ⓔ kilkennyhostel@eircom.net, 35 Parliament St) Dorms/doubles/quads €13/33/58.50, €1.30 more May-Sept. This IHH hostel is friendly, clean and central. It has a kitchen and laundry (€3.80) and guests can get a shiatsu massage (€15.25) on Sunday and Monday mornings.

Foulksrath Castle (☎ 67144, fax 67144, ⓔ mailbox@anoige.ie, Ballyragget) Dorms/rooms €7.50/9.50. This An Óige hostel is beautifully sited in a 16th-century Norman castle 13km north of Kilkenny in Jenkinstown, near Ballyragget. From June to September, it serves reasonably priced meals. For details of how to get there by bus, see Getting There & Away later in this section.

B&Bs
There are plenty of B&Bs but accommodation can still be hard to find at the weekend

and during festival times. Bed Finders (☎ 70088), 23 Rose Inn St, can help you find somewhere to stay without charging a fee.

Rose Inn (☎ 70061, 9 Rose Inn St) Dorms/rooms from €13/19 per person. This charming little spot opposite the tourist office has a six-bed dorm and rooms with four-poster beds. It's central, cheap and cheerful.

Bregagh Guesthouse (☎ 22315, Dean St) Singles/doubles €32/63.50. Also central is this very pleasant place near St Canice's Cathedral.

Kilkenny B&B (☎ 64040, ⓔ kilkenny bandb@eircom.net, Dean St) Singles/doubles €45/63.50. You can't miss this place on Dean St; it's the only house painted royal blue with yellow railings. It's comfortable but the owners are sticklers on breakfast times: you must show up between 8.30am and 9.30am.

Celtic House (☎/fax 62249, 18 Michael St) Singles/doubles €32.50/57. This is a beautifully decorated house near the train station with modern, airy rooms, all en suite. Ask for a room with a view of the castle.

Dunromin (☎ 61387, fax 70736, ⓔ valtom @oceanfree.net, Dublin Rd) Singles/doubles €32/51. Breakfast at this lovely, 19th-century house about 500m from the centre of town is top-notch.

Lacken House (☎ 61085, fax 62435, ⓔ info@lackenhouse.ie, Dublin Rd) Rooms from €45 per person including breakfast & 4-course dinner. Open Apr-Oct. This B&B just out of town is highly rated; its restaurant is excellent (see Places to Eat).

Hotels
Berkeley House (☎ 64848, fax 64829, ⓔ berkeleyhouse@eircom.net, 5 Lower Patrick St) Singles/doubles €57/95.50. This Georgian place has a distinct air of faded glory, though it's pretty comfortable.

Ristorante Rinuccini (☎ 61575, fax 51288, ⓔ info@rinuccini.com, ⓦ www .rinuccini.com, 1 The Parade) Singles/doubles €51/102 with breakfast. Better known as a restaurant (see Places to Eat), this is a plush, modern guesthouse with gorgeous Italian furnishings. Breakfast is served in the bedrooms only.

Zuni (☎ 23999, fax 56400, ⓔ info@

zuni.ie, W *www.zuni.ie, 26 Patrick St)* Singles/doubles €70/114.50. Situated in a 1902 building that once served as a playhouse, Zuni has an ultra-modern, minimalist design, with lots of clean lines, muted lighting and not a flower in sight. See also Places to Eat.

Hibernian Hotel (☎ *71888, fax 71877,* e *info@hibernian.iol.ie,* W *www.thehiber nian.com, 1 Ormonde St)* Rooms from €88. Located in a Victorian building that once housed a bank, this hotel is the best of Kilkenny's top spots, with plenty of charm, character and comfort.

PLACES TO EAT
Restaurants
Ristorante Rinuccini (see Places to Stay) Mains around €13. This cellar restaurant is fairly upmarket and has delicious pasta dishes, all freshly prepared.

Lautrec's Brasserie (☎ *62720, 9 St Kieran's St)* Set dinner €14. Open to 1am. Near Kyteler's Inn, this late-night restaurant serves an eclectic range of Italian and Mexican dishes.

Fléva Brasserie (☎ *70021, 84 High St)* Mains around €16. The menu here, near the Tholsel, is very 'new world cuisine', with everything from eggs Florentine to Thai chicken.

Pearl's (☎ *23322, 10 Irishtown)* Mains around €14. Pearl's serves excellent Chinese dishes that are well worth the price. The ambience is very relaxed.

Bengal Tandoori (☎ *64722, Pudding Lane)* Sun brunch €14. Locals flock to this place for the eat-as-much-as-you-like Sunday brunch (1pm to 5pm). Otherwise, it has the usual selection of Indian dishes, with a particular emphasis on hotter Bengali dishes.

Shimla (☎ *23788, 6 Dean St)* Mains from €8.90. Opposite Bregagh Guesthouse, this is an excellent Indian restaurant with an extensive menu.

Zuni (☎ *23999, 26 Patrick St)* Dinner from €32. Asian fusion is the theme of this busy, trendy restaurant. The food is simply delicious.

Edward Langton's (☎ *21728, 69 John St)* Lunch around €6, set dinner €23.50, a la carte dishes €16-18. Dinner to 11pm.

North-east of the river, this pub has an award-winning restaurant. Lunches such as roast beef will cost a reasonable €6.35, and sandwiches start at €4.45 including chips.

Jacob's Cottage (Hibernian Hotel; ☎ *71888, 1 Ormonde St)* Mains from €15.25. This fine restaurant in the Hibernian Hotel is very popular with locals, who come for the well presented and imaginative Irish cuisine.

Kyteler's Inn (☎ *21604, 27 St Kieran's St)* Meals from €8.90. Dame Kyteler's old house is one of the tourist magnets in town and while the food at this pub is not great, it is very popular.

Lacken House (☎ *61085, Dublin Rd)* Dinner from €28. Widely regarded as the best local restaurant, this place is just out of town. See also Places to Stay.

Cafes
Kilkenny Castle Kitchen (☎ *21450, Kilkenny Castle)* Mains from €3.80. In summer this is a good place for lunch or for delicious, if pricey, cakes; you don't have to pay the castle admission charge to eat here.

Kilkenny Design Centre (☎ *22118, Castle Yard)* Lunch around €10. Open 9am-5pm daily. The restaurant upstairs here is excellent for snacks or lunch but attracts large coach parties.

Café Sol (☎ *64987, William St)* Lunch around €8.90, dinner around €32. This is an excellent choice for lunch, with the sort of colour scheme to evoke the sunny Med rather than wet and windy Kilkenny.

Kafe Katz (☎ *56688, 3 Ormonde St)* Mains from €3.80. This is a small, bright and airy spot, with outdoor seating in summer, that serves a wide range of sandwiches and *panini*.

The Gourmet Store (☎ *71727, 56 High St)* Sandwiches from €2.50. This speciality food store has terrific takeaway sandwiches, all packed with mouth-watering ingredients.

Chez Pierre (☎ *64655, 17 Parliament St)* Mains from €5.10. Open 10am-5pm daily. This cheery French cafe serves delicious home-made classics such as *croque monsieur* and *tartines*.

ML Dore (☎ *63374, 65 High St)* Mains

from €7.60. Open to 10pm. This cafe favours over-the-top kitsch decor as a backing for a good choice of lunch and dinner dishes.

ENTERTAINMENT
Pubs

With more than 65 licensed pubs in the city (roughly around one for every 300 inhabitants!), there's no shortage of places to have a pint and a bit of a laugh.

The Pumphouse (☎ 63924, 26 Parliament St) This pub offers rock and pop, as well as traditional music on Tuesday and Wednesday.

O'Riada's (27 Parliament St) This is a great old bar whose only acknowledgement of the 20th century is in the use of electricity. It's our favourite pub in town.

John Cleere (☎ 62573, 22 Parliament St) This pub stages regular, year-round productions of plays, revues, poetry readings and anything else that's going. Monday night is traditional Irish music and folk night. Spontaneous sessions can happen at any time.

The Witness Box (☎ 64337, 13 Parliament St) Here you'll find live music six nights a week, including traditional sessions on Tuesday and Wednesday and rock bands at the weekend.

Matt the Miller's (☎ 61696, 1 John St) Just across the river, this is another popular pub in which to hang out.

Nightclubs

The Zoo (☎ 70555, 40 Parliament St) Admission €9. In a basement a few doors up from Kilkenny Tourist Hostel, this club has weekend discos from 11.30pm until 3am. The music is pure rave, with pumping techno and hard house. On other nights it hosts comedy shows.

Nero's (☎ 21064, 25 St Kieran's St) Admission €8. Next door to Kyteler's Inn, Nero's is a big and popular dance club spread across two floors featuring the latest dance music until 3am Thursday to Sunday.

Edward Langton's (☎ 21728, 69 John St) Admission €8. Over the river, this is the most popular club in town, with a disco on Tuesday and Saturday nights. The music is

fairly safe, usually chart hits and dance anthems.

Club Life (Club House Hotel; ☎ 21994, Patrick St) Admission €7.50. Starting around 8.30pm on Tuesday night in July and August, there's live musical entertainment of the more touristy type here.

Theatre & Cinemas

Watergate Theatre (☎ 61674, Parliament St) This theatre hosts drama, comedy and musical performances by both professional and amateur groups.

The *John Cleere* (see Pubs earlier for details) stages various productions.

Kilkenny Cineplex (☎ 23111, Fair Green, Gaol Rd) This is Kilkenny's only multiplex cinema, with four screens showing the latest releases.

About 15km south of Kilkenny, just outside the hamlet of Callan, is a disused **quarry** that has been turned into an amphitheatre with superb acoustics. It is planned to stage drama, pageants, music and choral recitals here but nothing yet has happened; contact the Kilkenny tourist office for the current schedule.

SHOPPING

All shops open from 9am to 6pm Monday to Saturday; some stay open until 9pm on Thursday.

Kilkenny Design Centre (☎ 61804, Castle Yard) Across The Parade from Kilkenny Castle are the elegant former Castle Stables (1760), which have been tastefully converted into the Kilkenny Design Centre. There's an outstanding collection of Irish goods and crafts for sale. Behind the shop through the arched gateway is Castle Yard, lined with the studios of various local craftspeople. The newly established National Craft Gallery (see earlier in this chapter) is also here.

Rudolf Helzel Gold & Silversmiths (☎ 21497, 10 Patrick St) This fine jewellers sells attractive contemporary designs.

GETTING THERE & AWAY
Bus

Bus Éireann (☎ 64933) operates out of McDonagh train station and provides services to and from Dublin: six a day Monday to Saturday, and five on Sunday (single/return €8.90/10.20, two hours). There are three buses daily (two on Sunday) to and from Cork town (single/return €14/21, three hours), although you usually have to change buses in Cahir. Two buses daily (except Sunday) also pass through Kilkenny en route from Dublin to Waterford.

On the Waterford–Longford route, one bus daily passes through in each direction (Waterford single/return €6.35/12.70, Longford €4/4.80, one hour). In July and August, one bus a day Monday to Saturday links Kilkenny with Galway and Waterford. On Thursday there's also a bus between New Ross and Kilkenny, leaving from New Ross at 10am and from Kilkenny at 1.15pm.

JJ Kavanagh & Sons (☎ 31106) runs five buses daily between Kilkenny and Cashel via Kells and Fethard, and buses to Carlow, Portlaoise and Thurles. These buses stop on The Parade.

Buggy's Coaches (☎ 41264) runs a service to Foulksrath Castle (and the An Óige hostel), Ballyragget, Dunmore Cave and Castlecomer. Buses (€1.90, 20 minutes) leave The Parade at 11.30am and 5.30pm Monday to Saturday; they leave from the hostel at 8.25am and 3pm. Some JJ Kavanagh & Sons buses also pass near the hostel.

Train
McDonagh train station (☎ 22024) is on Dublin Rd, north-east of the town centre via John St. Four trains daily (five on Friday) link Dublin (Heuston Station) with Waterford via Kilkenny (single/return €15.90/20.50, just under two hours). For details of departure times phone ☎ 01-836 6222.

GETTING AROUND
JJ Wall (☎ 21236), 86 Maudlin St, rents out bikes at €15.25 per day, plus a deposit of €38. The circuit round Kells, Inistioge, Jerpoint Abbey and Kilfane makes a fine day's ride.

Barry Pender Motors (☎ 65777), 1.5km out on Dublin Rd, offers car rental for a steep €76 per day (cheaper in the off-season, when some cars are available for €47).

Castle Cabs (☎ 61188), 1 Rose Inn St, has taxis available 24 hours a day. Its small fleet also includes an eight-seater cab, and it offers a left-luggage service (€1.30 per bag per day).

Central Kilkenny

The most scenic parts of this area, taking in some of the Nore and Barrow Valleys, are from Graiguenamanagh in the east, down to The Rower and then north-west on the road to Inistioge, Thomastown, Kells and Callan near the Tipperary border.

BENNETTSBRIDGE
☎ 056 • pop 601

Bennettsbridge, on the Nore, has two of Ireland's most renowned potteries and an official camping ground. In a big mill by the river is *Nicholas Mosse Pottery* (☎ 27105, **W** www.nicholasmosse.com; open 10am-6pm Mon-Sat year round, 2pm-6pm Sun July & Aug). It turns out handmade spongeware – creamy-brown pottery covered with sponged patterns – and there's a lovely *cafe* upstairs offering reasonably priced fare, including scones from €2.

Almost 2km north of Bennettsbridge on the R700 road to Kilkenny you'll find *Stoneware Jackson Pottery* (☎ 27175, **W** www.stonewarejackson.com, Ballyreddin; open 10am-6pm Mon-Sat). It produces a wide variety of chunky pottery.

Another good pottery shop is *The Bridge* (☎ 27077, **W** www.bridgepottery.com, Chapel St; open 10am-6pm Mon-Sat, noon-6pm Sun).

On the other side of the Nore is *Dyed in the Wool* (☎ 27684, **W** www.dyedinthewool.ie, Bennettsbridge; open 10am-6pm Mon-Fri, noon-6pm Sat & Sun). This knitwear factory sells its wares in some of Ireland's best design stores. Here you can buy things at source, minus the mark-up of the retail outlets.

Two kilometres south of Bennettsbridge on the Waterford road is **Nore Valley Park** (☎ 27229, Annamult; adult/child €2.55/2; open 9am-7pm Mon-Sat Easter-mid-Sept).

This is an open farm aimed at kids: they can bottle feed lambs and goats, cuddle rabbits, play in a fort and jump on a straw bounce. There's a tearoom and picnic area.

A couple of kilometres west of Bennettsbridge, near the hamlet of Danesfort, is the **Nore View Folk Museum** (☎ *27749, Danesfort Rd; free; open 10am-6pm daily June-Sept; 2.30pm-5.30pm daily rest of year*). It's a privately owned folk museum displaying local items of interest, including old farming tools and other bric-a-brac.

Nore Valley Camping & Caravan Park (☎ *27229, Annamult*) Camping for hikers & cyclists €6.50 per person. Open Easter-Oct. This park is on a farm. If you're coming into Bennettsbridge from Kilkenny along the R700, turn right just before the bridge and the park is signposted.

KELLS

Only 13km south of Kilkenny, Kells is not to be confused with its namesake in County Meath. This is a treat of a hamlet, nestling beside a fine stone bridge on the King's River, a tributary of the Nore. In Kells Priory, the village has one of Ireland's most impressive and romantic monastic sites.

Every Saturday at 8pm from June to September, there is a barbecue at *Shirley's* (☎ *056-28302*) in the middle of the village. For €10.20 you can eat your fill and enjoy the traditional music.

Kells Priory

The earliest remains of the magnificent Kells Priory date from the late 12th century, while the bulk of the present ruins dates from the 15th century. In a sea of rich farmland, a protective wall, carefully restored, connects seven dwelling towers. Inside the walls are the remains of an Augustinian abbey and the foundations of some chapels and houses. It's unusually well fortified for a monastery and the heavy curtain walls hint at a troubled history. Indeed, within a single century from 1250, the abbey was twice fought over and burned down by squabbling warlords.

Extraordinarily there's no charge for visiting and no set opening hours, provided you don't mind braving the sheep in the surrounding fields. The ruins are 800m east of Kells on the Stonyford road.

Kilree Round Tower & High Cross

Two kilometres south of Kells (signposted from the priory car park) there's a 29m-high round tower and a simple early high cross, which is said to mark the grave of a 9th-century Irish high king, Niall Caille. He's supposed to have drowned in the King's River at Callan some time in the 840s while attempting to save a servant, and his body washed up near Kells. His final resting place lies beyond the church grounds because he wasn't a Christian.

Callan Famine Graveyard

Ten kilometres west of Kilree, and signposted off the main road 2km south of Callan, is a cemetery where the local victims of the Great Famine are buried. It isn't much to look at, but it is a poignant reminder of the anonymity of starvation: the victims here have no names.

THOMASTOWN & AROUND
☎ 056 • pop 1581

Thomastown is a small market town nicely situated by the Nore. Unfortunately it's also on the main Dublin to Waterford road (N9) and the traffic can be horrific. However, most people ignore this aspect of the town and concentrate on its many drinking establishments.

Named after Welsh mercenary Thomas de Cantwell, Thomastown has some fragments of a medieval wall and the partly ruined 13th-century **Church of St Mary**. **Mullin's Castle** down by the bridge is the sole survivor of the 14 castles that were originally here.

On the outskirts of Thomastown is **Mount Juliet** (☎ *73000, fax 73019,* e *info@ mountjuliet.ie*), a stately home built in the early 19th century by the earl of Carrick and named in honour of his wife Juliet. Today it is one of the country's most elegant country hotels, nestled in over 1500 acres of parkland, which also include a championship golf course designed by none other than Jack Nicklaus. Naturally, it is one of Europe's top-ranked courses. You can walk into the grounds at any time, but you're looking at the better part of €260 to spend the night.

At the edge of town, there's a craft shop at *Grennan Mill Craft School (☎ 24557, Waterford road; open 9am-5pm Mon-Sat).*

Jerpoint Abbey

One and a half kilometres south-west of Thomastown is Jerpoint Abbey *(☎ 24623, Waterford road; adult/concession €2.50/ 1.90; open 9.30am-6.30pm daily June-mid-Sept; 10am-1pm & 2pm-5pm (to 4pm in 2nd half of Nov) Wed-Mon mid-Sept-Nov & Mar-May).* Established by a king of Ossory in the 12th century, and now one of Ireland's finest Cistercian ruins, it has been partially restored. The fine tower and cloister are late 14th or early 15th century. Fragments of the cloister are particularly interesting, with a series of often amusing figures carved on the pillars. There are also stone carvings on the church walls and in the tombs of members of the Butler and Walshe families. Faint traces of a 15th- or 16th-century painting remain on the northern wall of the church. This chancel area also contains a tomb thought to be that of Felix O'Dullany, Jerpoint's first abbot and bishop of Ossory, who died in 1202.

According to local legend, St Nicholas (or Santa Claus) is buried near the abbey. While retreating in the Crusades, the knights of Jerpoint removed his body from Myra in modern day Turkey and reburied him in the Church of St Nicholas to the west of the abbey. The grave is marked by a broken slab decorated with a carving of a monk.

A few kilometres from Jerpoint Abbey, in the town of Stonyford, and housed in an old stone-walled farm building is the nationally renowned **Jerpoint Glass Studio** *(☎ 24350, near Mount Juliet entrance; open 9am-6pm Mon-Fri, 10am-6pm Sat & noon-6pm Sun year round).* Many of the pieces produced here are extremely beautiful. You can watch glass blowers at work 9am to 5pm weekdays (to 2pm on Friday).

Abbey House (☎ 24166, fax 24192, Jerpoint Abbey) Singles/doubles from €32/51. If you want to stay at Jerpoint Abbey, this attractive Georgian house is opposite the entrance.

Kilfane

Three kilometres north of Thomastown on the Dublin road, the village of Kilfane has a small, ruined **13th-century church** and **Norman tower**, 50m off the road and signposted. The church has a remarkable stone carving of Thomas de Cantwell called the Cantwell Fada or Long Cantwell. It depicts a tall, thin knight in detailed chain-mail armour brandishing a shield decorated with the Cantwell coat of arms.

Another 2km north along the N9 brings you to the **Kilfane Glen and Waterfall** *(☎ 24558, off the N9; adult/concession €5.10/3.80; open 11am-6pm daily July & Aug; 2pm-6pm Sun Apr, June & Sept).* This is a Romantic-period garden with a *cottage ornée* (an elaborately decorated cottage). The top part of the garden is replete with works of art by Irish artists.

Getting There & Away

Bus Éireann (☎ 64933) operates six buses daily (five on Sunday) between Dublin and Waterford with stops at Gowran, Thomastown and Mullinavat. One service daily links Waterford with Longford via Thomastown, Kilkenny, Carlow, Tullamore and Athlone. On Thursday there's also one service from New Ross, leaving at 10am. Buses stop outside O'Keeffe's supermarket on Main St. From Kilkenny, the fare to Thomastown is single/return €5.85/7.

Thomastown is on the main Dublin–Waterford train line with the same service as Kilkenny. It's about 15 minutes from Kilkenny, 25 minutes from Waterford and two hours from Dublin. The train station is 1km west of town past Kavanagh's supermarket.

INISTIOGE
☎ 056 • pop 270

Inistioge (in-ish-**teeg**) is a delightful little village with a 10-arched stone bridge spanning the Nore and a picturesque tree-lined square with many of its original shop and pub fronts. Somewhere so inviting could hardly

KILKENNY

hope to escape the Hollywood sleuths: Inistioge's film credits include *Widow's Peak* (1993), *Circle of Friends* (1994) and *Where the Sun Is King* (1996). Inistioge is also on the South Leinster Way (see Walking under Activities in the Facts for the Visitor chapter for details).

One kilometre south, on Mt Alto, is **Woodstock Park**. The hike up is well worth the effort for the panorama of the valley below and the demesne itself. The 18th-century house was one of the finest in the county but was destroyed during the Civil War in 1922. The elevated garden and forest are now a state park with picnic areas and trails. For another fine walk, follow the riverbank and climb any of the surrounding hills. At the bottom of the hill that leads to Woodstock Park is a **pottery** which produces lovely work in light pastel colours. The Inistioge Walking Group (☎ 58995) usually meets on the last Sunday of the month at noon in the town square for walks of Woodstock Park. Call for details.

The Motte Restaurant (☎ 58655, Plas Newydd Lodge) Set dinner €30. This beautiful country restaurant has a carefully prepared menu that features all the skills and expertise of the best of Irish cuisine.

Getting There & Away

On Thursday only, a single bus runs between New Ross and Kilkenny, calling at Inistioge on the way. It leaves New Ross at 10am and returns from Inistioge at 1.50pm.

GRAIGUENAMANAGH
☎ 0503 • pop 1374

Graiguenamanagh (**greg**-na-mana) is a small market town on a lovely stretch of the River Barrow, 23km south-east of Kilkenny at the foot of Brandon Hill (516m). There's no public transport but it is on the South Leinster Way.

Duiske Abbey

Dating back to 1204, Duiske Abbey *(☎24238; open 10am-5pm Mon-Fri year round, 2pm-5pm Sat & Sun June-Aug)* was once Ireland's largest Cistercian abbey. Today it has been completely restored and

its pleasantly simple, whitewashed interior is in everyday use. Its name comes from the Irish Dubh Uisce (Black Water), a tributary of the Barrow.

Inside the abbey to the right of the main entrance is the Knight of Duiske, a 14th-century, high-relief carving of a knight in chain mail who's reaching for his sword. On the floor nearby a glass panel reveals some of the original 13th-century floor tiles, which are now 2m below the present floor level.

In the grounds stand two early high crosses, brought here for protection in the last century. The smaller Ballyogan Cross has panels on the eastern side depicting the crucifixion, Adam and Eve, Abraham's sacrifice of Isaac, and David playing the harp. The western side shows the massacre of the innocents.

Around the corner the **Abbey Centre** houses a small exhibition of Christian art, plus pictures of the abbey in its unrestored state.

Opposite the abbey, *Café Duiske (☎ 24988, Abbey St)* serves meals such as lasagne (€5.10).

GOWRAN
☎ 056 • pop 476

The village of Gowran, 12km east of Kilkenny, is famous for its **racecourse** and 13th-century **St Mary's Church** *(☎ 21668)*, which has some fine carvings and Butler-family tombs. There's usually someone around to let you in if it's closed (which it usually is).

Gowran is on the Dublin to Waterford express bus route, with six services daily (five on Sunday) in each direction. To and from Kilkenny, the fare is €4/4.85 single/return.

Southern Kilkenny

Much of southern Kilkenny is sparsely populated, with gentle hills separating the valleys of the Rivers Nore, Barrow and Suir. Carrick-on-Suir in Tipperary and Waterford town are within easy reach.

Southern Kilkenny is crossed by the **South Leinster Way**, which runs from Carrick-on-

Suir, through Piltown, Mullinavat, Inistioge, Graiguenamanagh and then on to Borris in County Carlow. See Walking under Activities in the Facts for the Visitor chapter for more details.

MULLINAVAT

☎ 051 • pop 275

Twelve kilometres north of Waterford on the Kilkenny road (N9), Mullinavat makes an agreeable spot to spend a relaxing day or two.

Tory View (☎/fax 895513, on the N9) Rooms with/without bathroom €25.50/20.50 per person. Two kilometres south of the village, this place offers B&B in smallish rooms. Evening meals are available.

Rising Sun (☎ 898173, Main St) En suite singles/doubles €38/63.50 including breakfast. This is a beautiful 17th-century stone building with an upstairs restaurant – but it's a bit pricey.

Express buses between Dublin and Waterford call at Mullinavat six-times daily (five on Sunday), stopping outside Mulhearn's on Main St. One service daily links Mullinavat with Longford via Thomastown, Carlow, Tullamore and Athlone. In July and August there's also one request service daily linking Mullinavat with Galway via Kilkenny, Thurles and Nenagh. The fare from Kilkenny is €8.90/12.70 single/return.

Northern Kilkenny

CASTLECOMER & AROUND

☎ 056 • pop 1380

An attractive town 18km north of Kilkenny, Castlecomer is on the River Dinin, which flows across the Castlecomer Plateau. The town became a centre for anthracite mining after the fuel was discovered nearby in 1636; the mines closed for good only in the mid-1960s. The anthracite was widely regarded as being Europe's best, containing very little sulphur and producing almost no smoke.

Castlecomer saw action in the 1798 Rising when the Fenian rebels, led by Father John Murphy, captured it en route from Wexford to the midlands. There's little to do here, but the tree-lined square and neat town houses are thoroughly pleasing.

Things to See

Eight kilometres west of Castlecomer is **Ballyragget**, with an almost intact square tower in the 16th-century **Butler Castle** *(closed to the public).*

Almost 2km south of Ballyragget is **Swifte's Heath**, home to Jonathan Swift during his school years in Kilkenny.

Places to Stay & Eat

Foulksrath Castle (☎ 67144, fax 67144, e mailbox@anoige.ie, Ballyragget) Dorms/rooms €7/9.50. Near Ballyragget, this is now a busy An Óige hostel with a superb setting. For more details see Places to Stay under Kilkenny earlier in this chapter.

Avalon Inn (☎ 41302, fax 41963, The Square) Singles/doubles €29/63.50. In Castlecomer, this flower-covered pub/guesthouse on the square near the bridge is in the old mine offices.

Getting There & Away

Castlecomer is on Bus Éireann's (☎ 64933) route between Cork, Kilkenny and Dublin and is served by up to four buses a day Monday to Saturday (three on Sunday). Buses stop outside Houlihan's. The fare from Castlecomer to Kilkenny is single/return €3.40/4.60; to Dublin it's €8.90/10.20. JJ Kavanagh & Sons (☎ 31555) runs buses twice daily between Clonmel, Kilkenny, Castlecomer, Athy and Dublin (Gresham Hotel); from Castlecomer the journey to Dublin takes 1¼ hours. Buggy's Coaches (☎ 41264) runs a service from Kilkenny to Castlecomer; four buses leave in each direction Monday to Saturday (€1.90, 25 minutes).

DUNMORE CAVE

Ten kilometres north of Kilkenny on the Castlecomer road (N78) is Dunmore Cave *(☎ 056-67726, adult/concession €2.55/1.90; open 9.30am-7pm daily mid-June-mid-Sept; 10am-5pm daily mid-Mar-mid-June & mid-Sept-Oct; 10am-5pm Sat & Sun Nov-mid-Mar)*. It is a large cave divided into three

KILKENNY

pàrts, with many limestone formations. According to sources, marauding Vikings killed 1000 people at two ring forts near Dunmore Cave in 928. When survivors hid in the caverns the Vikings tried to smoke them out by lighting fires at the entrance. It's thought that they then dragged off the men as slaves and left the women and children to suffocate. Excavations in 1973 uncovered the skeletons of at least 44 people, mostly women and children. They also found coins dating from the 920s but none from a later date. One theory suggests that the coins were dropped by the Vikings (who often carried them in their armpits, secured with wax) while enthusias-

tically engaged in the slaughter. However, there are few marks of violence on the skeletons, which lends weight to the theory that suffocation was the cause of death.

The cave is well lit and spacious. After a steep descent you enter imaginatively named caverns full of stalactites, stalagmites and columns, including the 7m Market Cross, Europe's largest freestanding stalagmite. It's damp and cold, so a sweater is advised. The compulsory guided tours are worthwhile.

Buggy's Coaches (☎ 056-41264) runs four buses a day Monday to Saturday (return €3.80) from The Parade in Kilkenny, dropping you off 1km from the cave.

Central South

The four counties of Kildare, Carlow, Laois and Offaly make up a large portion of the Irish midlands. Sites of interest include the Rock of Dunamase near Portlaoise, Moone High Cross in Kildare, Kildare town's cathedral, Browne's Hill Dolmen just outside Carlow town, Rosse Estate and Observatory in Birr and, most impressive of all, Clonmacnoise on the banks of the River Shannon, probably Ireland's most important monastic site.

County Kildare

Kildare (Cill Dara), to the west and southwest of Dublin, is mostly rich green farmland in the south, with the extensive Bog of Allen peatland hogging the north-western corner. A limestone plain underlies the pasture and bog. It is one of the most prosperous counties in Ireland and, in a recent survey, the county with the fastest-growing population apart from Dublin. One main reason is that Kildare is one of the most important breeding and training grounds for racehorses in the world. More than any other county, Kildare is synonymous with the multi-million-pound bloodstock industry – partly because Irish law levies no taxes on stud fees (thanks to former prime minister and horse-owner Charles J Haughey) – and Kildare town is twinned with another famous horse-breeding centre, Lexington-Fayette in Kentucky, USA. The county is dotted with private stud farms for champion thoroughbreds.

The main towns are dominated by traffic, a problem that should be alleviated as the local councils finish building bypasses round them. Nearly all the country's main road and train arteries cross the county, as do the 18th-century Grand and Royal Canals, which are now enjoying a new lease of life. The River Barrow marks the county's western border, while the Curragh forms a great sweep of unfenced countryside to the south.

GRAND & ROYAL CANALS

The Grand and Royal Canals were built in the 18th century to revolutionise goods and passenger transport but, as the railways superseded them during the 19th century, the

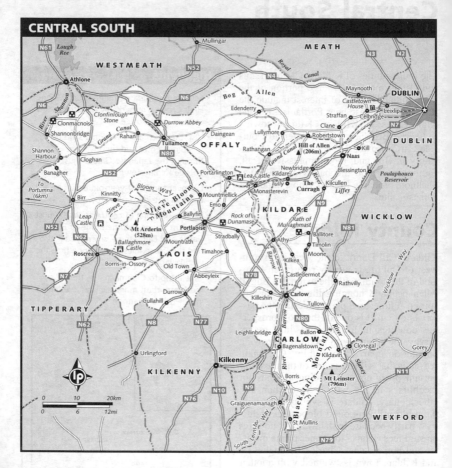

CENTRAL SOUTH

canals fell into disuse. Today they're owned by Dúchas and offer a pleasant way of drifting across the country.

Grand Canal

The Grand Canal was first commissioned in 1715 by an Act of Parliament, but a lack of funds delayed its construction and the first cargo barges only started to operate between Dublin and Sallins in 1779. It carried passengers until 1852 and goods until 1960. The canal threads its way from Dublin through County Kildare to Robertstown. From there one branch heads west through Tullamore to join the River Shannon at Shannon Harbour in County Offaly, while the other turns south to join the River Barrow at Athy, providing passage to New Ross in County Wexford and to Waterford town.

Besides the many finely crafted locks and tiny lock cottages, you will come across treasures such as the seven-arched Leinster Aqueduct, 5km north of Naas near the village of Sallins, where the canal crosses the River Liffey. Farther south of Robertstown, sections of the River Barrow are particularly lovely.

Royal Canal

The Royal Canal follows Kildare's northern border and also wends its way to the River Shannon, joining it farther north at Cloondara (or Clondra) in County Longford above Lough Ree. However, it's only navigable between Blanchardstown in County Dublin and Mullingar in County Westmeath. It was never a profitable enterprise, but its history is a colourful one. It was founded by Long John Binns, a director of the Grand Canal Company who quit the board over a supposed insult about him being a shoemaker. He established the Royal Canal in 1790 but it never made money as it duplicated the purpose of the earlier canal. The duke of Leinster backed the project on condition that it was routed by his house near Maynooth. Sadly, the canal has not aged gracefully. Restoration work aims to link the Dublin-city section with the River Liffey and to improve the section west of Mullingar. The Royal Canal should be fully navigable early in the new millennium.

Barges & Boats

Boating facilities are available only on the Grand Canal.

Lowtown Cruisers (☎ 045-860427, Robertstown) Six-berth narrowboats €571 per week Sept, €952 per week July & Aug. River Shannon narrowboats can be hired from Lowtown Marina, which is 13km west of Naas, 1km west along the northern bank of the canal over the bridge from Robertstown.

Grand Canal Hotel (☎ 045-870005, Robertstown) Trips on the hour 2pm-6pm Sun. Adult/concession €4.50/3.20. The *Eustace*, a refurbished canal barge, departs for 45-minute trips from the Grand Canal Hotel. During the summer there are also day trips from Robertstown.

Walking the Towpaths

The canal towpaths are ideal for walkers, and Robertstown makes a good starting point for many canal walks. Three *Canal Bank Walks* leaflets, which detail a 45km trail along the Grand Canal from Edenderry to Celbridge, can be picked up at tourist offices. For more

information call **County Kildare Youth and Sports** *(☎ 045-879502)*.

Robertstown is also at the hub of the Kildare Way and River Barrow towpath trails, the latter stretching all the way to St Mullins, 95km south in County Carlow. From there it's possible to connect with the South Leinster Way at Graiguenamanagh or the southern end of the Wicklow Way at Clonegal, north of Mt Leinster.

MAYNOOTH & AROUND
☎ 01 • pop 8528

Twenty-four kilometres west of Dublin on the N4, Maynooth (Maigh Nuad) has a tree-lined main street with stone-fronted houses and shops and the Royal Canal passing to the south of the centre. Main St runs east–west. Leinster St runs south off Main St to the canal and the train station (accessed via a couple of footbridges over the canal).

St Patrick's College

St Patrick's College and Seminary *(☎ 628 5222, Main St)*, also called Maynooth College, at the western end of town, has been turning out Catholic priests since 1795 and became a college of the National University in 1910. Ironically, the seminary was founded by the English, alarmed at the prospect of Irish priests studying in France and picking up ideas about revolution and republicanism.

The college has 5500 students. Over the last two centuries it has trained more than 11,000 Catholic priests, but now has fewer seminarians than ever before, a reflection of the Catholic Church's waning importance. At present about 300 men are studying for the priesthood.

You enter the college via Georgian Stoyte House, which has fine plastered ceilings. Beyond that is St Joseph's Square laid out as a rose garden. Across the square is St Patrick's House, a fine Victorian Gothic building, with the College Chapel looming at one end; this is the world's largest choir chapel, with stalls for more than 450 choristers. Through St Patrick's House is the delightful Bicentennial Garden, with lily ponds and imitation standing stones.

There is a small **visitor centre** *(☎ 708*

3576, St Patrick's College, Main St; tours adult/concession €3.80/1.90; open 11am-5pm Mon-Fri & 2pm-6pm Sat & Sun May-Sept). It shows a video on the College's history and stocks a leaflet for guiding yourself around the buildings. There is also a small science museum *(adult €1.30; open 3pm-5pm Tues & Thur & 2pm-6pm Sun May-Sept).*

Maynooth Castle

The ruined gatehouse, keep and great hall of the 13th-century castle stand by the entrance to St Patrick's College. The key can be picked up from 1 Parsons St in return for a deposit.

The castle was one of the homes of the Fitzgeralds (the other was at Kilkea; see Naas to Carlow later in this section). After the 1536 rebellion led by Silken Thomas Fitzgerald, the English besieged the castle, whose garrison surrendered after being promised leniency. Then, in what became ironically known as the Pardon of Maynooth, Thomas and his men were summarily executed. The castle was dismantled in Cromwellian times when the Fitzgeralds moved to Kilkea Castle.

Canoeing

The town of **Leixlip** on the River Liffey between Maynooth and Dublin is an important canoeing centre. It's the starting point of the Irish Sprint Canoe Championships and annual 28km International Liffey Descent Race, when the Electricity Supply Board releases 30 million tonnes of water from the Poulaphouca Reservoir in County Wicklow to bring the river up to flood level. Canoes can be hired from **Kilcullen Canoe and Outdoor Pursuits Club** *(☎ 045-812 408),* 10km south-west of Naas.

Places to Stay

Curraghchase House (☎/fax 628 5726, ⒺⒸ curragh@tinet.ie, Moyglare Rd) Singles/doubles €38/57. This pleasant B&B is 1km west of town on the R148.

Windgate Lodge (☎ 627 3415, Barberstown, Straffan) Singles/doubles with bathroom and breakfast from €38/63.50. This lodge is 2km farther south in Barberstown.

Glenroyal Hotel & Leisure Club (☎/fax

629 0909, Ⓔ hotel@glenroyal.ie, Straffan Rd) Singles/doubles from €67/85. This multifacility hotel (a 20m pool and a fitness club are on the premises) is about 1.5km south of town along the R406.

Moyglare Manor (☎ 628 6351, fax 628 5405, Ⓔ moyglare@iol.ie, R157) Singles/doubles including breakfast €140/229. If your trunkload of cash is weighing you down, stay at this lovely Georgian manor, 3.5km to the north. It's one of Ireland's best country houses, with a fine restaurant and stunning bedrooms.

Places to Eat

Kehoe's Delicatessen (☎ 628 6533, Main St) Snacks from €1.90. This place is very popular for light lunches such as soup and toasted sandwiches.

Mandarin (☎ 629 2265, 1 Main St) Mains around €10. At the bottom of Main St, this is the town's only worthwhile Chinese restaurant.

Getting There & Away

Bus Nos 67 and 67A (☎ 872 0000) leave D'Olier St in Dublin for Maynooth (€1.50, one hour, about every half-hour).

Maynooth is linked to Dublin by the Western Suburban line (☎ 836 6222) and is on the main Dublin–Sligo line, with regular trains in each direction (single/return €2.20/4.20, 40 minutes, about every hour).

CELBRIDGE

☎ 01 • pop 12,289

Celbridge, 6.5km south-east of Maynooth on the River Liffey, wouldn't have a lot going for it were it not home to the magnificent Palladian Castletown House.

Castletown House

This is a huge Irish mansion *(☎ 628 8252, Celbridge; adult/child & student €3.80/1.60; open 10am-6pm Mon-Fri & 1pm-6pm Sat & Sun June-Sept; 10am-5pm Mon-Fri & 1pm-5pm Sun Oct; 2pm-5pm Sun only Nov-Dec; 1pm-5pm Sun only Apr-May).* With its tree-lined avenue from the village (continue straight ahead after entering the gate), it's said to be Ireland's largest private house. It was built between 1722 and 1732 for William Conolly, who started life as the son of a pub owner and rose to become speaker of the Irish House of Commons. He financed Castletown House from a fortune amassed as a land agent in the aftermath of the Battle of the Boyne.

Castletown was designed by Alessandro Galilei, and continued by Edward Lovett Pearce (creator of the Bank of Ireland building on College Green, Dublin). The style is, inevitably, Palladian: there is hardly a big house built in Ireland in the 18th century that wasn't influenced by the style of Italian architect Andrea Palladio (1508–80), though the Irish version was certainly added to by the likes of Richard Cassels (Castle), James Gandon and Lovett Pearce. The house remained with the Conolly family until 1965, when it was bought by the Guinness family, who ran it in conjunction with the Irish Georgian Society. In 1979 the Castletown Federation took it over and it is now cared for by Dúchas, who touched the place up with a €6.25 million restoration of the property.

Many of the magnificent rooms were decorated well after the building had been finished. The Italian Francini brothers did the plasterwork in the hall and above the main staircase.

Castletown has two follies, commissioned by William Conolly's wife, Lady Louisa, to provide employment for the poor. The **obelisk**, designed by Richard Cassels, can be seen from the Long Gallery at the back of the house. The even more curious **Wonderful Barn**, lying north-east on private property just outside Leixlip, dates from 1743. It consists of four domes one on top of another and scaled by a spiral staircase.

Castletown is 21km west of Dublin on the N4. Bus Nos 67 and 67A leave D'Olier St in Dublin about every hour for Celbridge (single/return €2.25/3.80, about one hour); the bus stops at the house gates.

Celbridge Abbey

At the other end of Main St from Castletown House, and beside the River Liffey, is Celbridge Abbey (☎ 627 5508, Clane Rd; admission to grounds adult/concession €3.20/1.90; grounds open 10am-6pm Mon-Sat & noon-6pm Sun). It was built in the 1690s by Bartholomew van Homrigh, a Dutch merchant who became Lord Mayor of Dublin. His daughter, Vanessa, was a close friend of Jonathan Swift, whose visits to her at the abbey she marked by preparing a bower and planting laurel trees.

The abbey is now owned by the St John of God Brothers but the picturesque grounds are open to the public. Facilities include a model railway, river walks, picnic areas and a cafe.

Places to Stay

Springfield (☎ 627 3248, fax 627 3123, on the R405, Celbridge) Rooms from €55 per person. This is a fabulous Georgian home about 2km south of Celbridge. The four bedrooms are simply stunning, while the 1km running track will keep joggers happy.

Getting There & Away

Bus Nos 67 and 67A go from D'Olier St in Dublin to Celbridge (single/return €2.25/3.80, about one hour, roughly hourly).

STRAFFAN

For one crazy weekend in September 2005, golf fans throughout the world will know the name of this village south-west of Celbridge on the road to Clane, as the nearby **K Club** (Kildare Hotel & Country Club; ☎ 01-601 7300) will host the Ryder Cup, the biennial tournament that sees the best US golfers play the best of the Europeans. Designed by Arnold Palmer, this is one of the best golf courses in Ireland and has been the home of the European Open since 1995. For €165 you can play a round; during the winter season (October to March) temporary greens are in play, so you're better off playing during the summer. Be sure to book in advance.

Tiger Woods and the other golfers probably won't have time, but you can visit the **Straffan Steam Museum** (☎ 01-627 3155, Straffan; adult/concession €3.80/2.50; open 2pm-6pm Tues-Sat June-Aug; 2.30pm-5.30pm Sun only Apr, May & Sept). Housed in the former church of St Jude in Lodge Park, the museum contains several working steam engines and displays on the history of

CENTRAL SOUTH

steam power. There's also an 18th-century walled garden.

At the **Straffan Butterfly Farm** (☎ 01-627 1109, Ovidstown; adult/concession €3.80/ 2.50; open noon-5.30pm daily May-late Aug) in Ovidstown, you can see butterflies flying freely in a tropical greenhouse, as well as stick insects, bird-eating spiders and reptiles safely behind glass.

Kildare Hotel & Country Club (☎ 01-601 7200, fax 601 7299, ℮ hotel@kclub.ie, Ⓦ www.kclub.ie, Straffan) Singles/doubles from €355/432. This fabulous Georgian estate has been restored and converted into one of the best hotels in Europe. At these prices, need we say more?

Bus Éireann (☎ 01-836 6111) runs five services daily (one on Sunday) from Dublin to Straffan.

BOG OF ALLEN
The Bog of Allen is Ireland's best-known raised bog, a huge expanse of peat that once covered much of the midlands. The bog stretches like a brown desert through Offaly, Laois and Kildare, but like other raised bogs it's rapidly being reduced to potting compost and fuel. For details of the Bord na Móna Bog Rail Tour, see Shannonbridge under County Offaly later in this chapter. (See also the boxed text 'Ireland's Disappearing Bogs' in the Facts about Ireland chapter.)

RATHANGAN
☎ 045 • pop 1190
The sleepy Victorian village of Rathangan, surrounded by the Bog of Allen, is on the Grand Canal 20km west of Naas but well off the beaten track. For information on coarse fishing and boat hire contact John Conway (☎ 524331) at the Carasli Caravan and Camping Park.

In a converted farm in Lullymore on the R414 9km north-east of Rathangan is **Peatland World** (☎ 860133, Lullymore; adult/student €4.50/3.80; open 9.30am-6pm Mon-Fri year round & 2pm-6pm Sun Apr-Oct). This interpretative centre has displays covering flora, fauna, fuel, conservation and archaeological finds, as well as a video presentation and trails through parts of the bog.

About 1km south of Peatland World is the **Lullymore Heritage & Discovery Park** (☎ 870238, Lullymore; adult/child €4.50/ 2.50; open 9am-6pm Mon-Fri & noon-6pm Sat & Sun Apr-Oct; 9am-4.30pm Mon-Fri Nov-Mar). Here you'll find a reconstructed Mesolithic village, a Neolithic farm and an exhibition on early Christian history, as well as a miniature golf course. There's also a children's playground.

Milorka (☎ 524544, Portarlington Rd) Rooms including breakfast €32 per person. This place is 1km along the Portarlington road in Kilnantogue. Rooms are excellent, and evening meals are available.

HILL OF ALLEN
The Hill of Allen rises above the flatlands of Kildare, which gradually change from green to the desolate brown of the Bog of Allen. Nine kilometres north-west of Newbridge and marked today by a folly, the hill has been a strategic spot through the centuries due to its commanding views in all directions.

The Iron Age fortifications are said to mark the home of Fionn McCumhaill, the leader of the Fianna, a mythical band of warriors who feature in many tales of ancient Ireland.

ROBERTSTOWN
Tiny Robertstown might have had all passing traffic diverted for the past 100 years. It's 12km north-west of Naas, Kildare's uninspiring county town, and its old buildings overlook the Grand Canal, which is spanned by a stone bridge. On summer Sundays, the refurbished barge, Eustace, offers short cruises (☎ 045-870005). (See Barges & Boats under Grand & Royal Canals earlier in this chapter.)

NEWBRIDGE & THE CURRAGH
☎ 045 • pop 12,970
The town of Newbridge (Droichead Nua) is the gateway to the Curragh. At around 20 sq km, it is one of the country's largest pieces of unfenced fertile land. In the past, it was known for its large internment camp which housed prisoners during times of crisis – the War of Independence, Civil War and WWII.

All that remains is the large military barracks, used by the Irish army.

Today, however, the Curragh is better known for its **racecourse** (☎ 441205), which was built in the 19th century; during the Civil War, interned soldiers watched the crowds gather on race days from behind the wire fencing! The wide open spaces that surround the racecourse are used by horse trainers to exercise their thoroughbred charges.

The N7 highway runs through the Curragh between Newbridge and Kildare town. The No 126 Dublin–Kildare bus service stops in Newbridge and at Curragh Camp. You might want to pause to visit the **Newbridge Cutlery Visitor Centre**.

KILDARE
☎ 045 • pop 4278

Kildare is a small cathedral and market town 24km south-west of Naas. Its busy triangular square with pubs on each side makes a pleasant change from the county's other nondescript urban centres, although when it's wet it is an awfully dreary place.

In Market House in the centre of the square, the county's main tourist office (☎ 522696) is, unfortunately, a bit of a disaster. Nominally open from June to September, it suffers from a lack of funding and staffing. At the time of writing it was closed; whether this sorry state of affairs will be remedied is anyone's guess.

St Brigid's Cathedral

One of the country's best-loved saints, St Brigid is remembered by St Brigid's Cross, a simply constructed four-pointed cross woven from reeds and found in many homes and gift shops. In the 5th century she founded a religious centre, unusual in that it was shared by nuns and monks, who were separated by screens in church. A fire, tended only by virgins over the age of 30, was kept burning perpetually in a fire temple, out of bounds to males. It survived until the dissolution of the monasteries in 1537. The restored fire pit can be seen in the grounds of the 13th-century Protestant St Brigid's Cathedral (☎ 045-521352, Market Square; free; open 10am-1pm & 2pm-5pm Mon-Sat & 2pm-5pm Sun May-Oct), whose solid presence looms over Kildare square.

Inside the cathedral, there is a fine stained-glass window facing west that depicts the three main saints of Ireland: Patrick, Brigid and Colmcille. The most important monument in the church is the tomb of Walter Wellesley, bishop of Kildare from 1529 to his death 10 years later. The tomb disappeared soon after his death and was found again only in 1971, when it was restored and placed in the cathedral.

The 10th-century round tower in the grounds is Ireland's second highest at 32.9m. Its original conical top has been replaced with an unusual Norman battlement. In the graveyard are buried members of the Fitzgerald family, earls and dukes of Kildare.

Provided the guardian is around, you can also climb to the top of the round tower on payment of €3.20.

Irish National Stud & Japanese Gardens

Three kilometres south of the centre in the village of Tully is the Irish National Stud (☎ 045-521251, W www.irish-national-stud.ie, Tully; admission including Japanese Gardens adult/student & senior/child €7.60/5.70/3.80; open 9.30am-6pm daily mid-Feb-mid-Nov). It was set up in 1900 by Colonel Hall Walker (of Johnnie Walker whiskey fame, later Lord Wavertree), who gave it to the Crown in 1915. The site was chosen because the mineral rich River Tully is especially good for bone formation. Walker was remarkably successful with his horses, although his breeding techniques were notably eccentric: when a foal was born, he drew up its horoscope and used this to decide whether to keep it. The stallion boxes were built with lantern roofs that were opened to reveal the moon and the stars, thus influencing the horses' fortunes. In the hands of the Irish government since 1943, the stud's purpose is to breed high-quality stallions to mate with mares from all over the world.

On the hour every hour there are guided tours of the stud, which let you see the intensive-care unit for newborn foals and learn about the horse that likes to listen to the radio and the horse with the straw allergy. Afterwards you can walk through the various stables, paddocks and meadows, or pop into the foaling unit and watch a 10-minute video on the birth of a foal. Better still, if you visit in spring or early summer, you might be able to watch a foal being born. Its most famous tenant is 19-year-old Indian Ridge, who covers 75 mares a season for €44,000 *each*. Not surprisingly, he's insured for over €12.5 million.

The small but interesting **Irish Horse Museum** examines the role horses have played in Irish life over the centuries and includes the impressively big skeleton of Arkle, who won the prestigious Cheltenham Gold Cup race in Britain for three years running in the 1960s.

Next door are the delightful Japanese Gardens *(☎ 045-521617; see National Stud for details)*, created between 1906 and 1910 by Colonel Hall Walker. Laid out by master gardeners Tassa Eida and his son Minoru (and 40 other nameless workers!), they are considered by experts to be the best of their kind in Europe. Although not entirely oriental in style (they include such western trees as Scots pine), they were created in accordance with the strict rules of Japanese gardening.

The gardens chart the journey from birth to death through 20 landmarks, including the Tunnel of Ignorance (No 3, which represents a child's lack of knowledge), the Hill of Ambition (No 13) and a series of bridges signifying – among other things – engagement (No 8) and marriage (No 9). Finally, you pass through the Gateway to Eternity (No 20), beyond which lies not everlasting life but a Buddhist sand garden. Despite the incongruity of its setting, the garden is a wonderful place to go for a stroll…provided it isn't raining.

The large visitor centre houses a cafe, a shop and a children's play area.

If you walk from Kildare look out for the ruins of the 12th-century **Black Abbey** on the left. Shortly afterwards a turn on the right leads to **St Brigid's Well**. It's probably sacrilegious to say so but this quiet spot would make a great place for a picnic.

Places to Stay

Fremont *(☎ 521604, Tully Rd)* Singles/doubles without bathroom €29/45. This place is in town, about 500m south of the town square.

Mount Ruadhan *(☎ 521637 Old Rd, Southgreen)* Rooms with/without bathroom €25.50/23 per person. This pleasant bungalow surrounded by a landscaped garden is 2km south of Kildare – you'll find a signpost at the town's only traffic lights – on the road to the National Stud.

Silken Thomas *(☎ 522389, The Square)* Singles/doubles €25.50/45. This small guesthouse above the popular pub is nothing fancy, but it's central and a very convenient place to put your head down for the night.

St Mary's *(☎ 521243, Maddenstown)* Rooms with/without bathroom including breakfast from €25.50/23 per person. This B&B is near the National Stud.

Curragh Lodge Hotel *(☎ 522144, fax 521247, on the N7)* Rooms including breakfast €45-63.50 per person. About 800m south of Market Square on the main Dublin road, this charming hotel has elegant, comfortable rooms.

Martinstown House *(☎ 441269, fax 441208, The Curragh)* Rooms from €82.50 per person. This 200-year-old country manor built in the 'strawberry hill' Gothic style on the edge of the Curragh flatlands, with elegant rooms and a terrific, easy-going atmosphere.

Places to Eat

You needn't move far from Kildare's main square for a meal.

Silken Thomas *(☎ 522698, The Square)* Meals around €11.50. This popular pub, partly converted from a cinema, has reasonable food in an old-world atmosphere. Upstairs, the Geraldine Hall puts on local plays.

Boland's Pub *(☎ 521263, The Square)* Mains around €5. Across the square, this pub serves dishes such as steak-and-mushroom pie.

Getting There & Away

The main N7 highway from Dublin to western Ireland passes through Kildare. Bus

Éireann serves Kildare from Dublin (return €10.80, one hour), with 14 buses a day weekdays, 13 on Saturday and eight on Sunday. One service a day stops at the National Stud and Japanese Gardens; it departs from Busáras, Dublin's central bus station, at 9am and returns at 3.45pm. On Sunday, there are two services, departing Dublin at 10am and noon, and returning at 3pm and 5.30pm.

The Arrow train (☎ 836 3333) runs the 55km trip from Heuston station (single/return €10.20/10.80, 30 minutes, about every 35 minutes).

NAAS TO CARLOW

The 48km stretch of the N9 between Naas and Carlow town offers several interesting side trips.

Kilcullen

The tiny village of Kilcullen is on the River Liffey, 12km east of Kildare town. Nearby at **Old Kilcullen**, the scant remains of a high cross and round tower are all that remain of an early-Christian settlement.

On the edge of the Curragh, 4km north-west of Kilcullen on the western side of the L19, **Donnelly's Hollow** was the scene of numerous victories of Dan Donnelly (1788–1820), Ireland's greatest bare-knuckle fighter of the 19th century. It's said he had a reach so long that he could touch his knees without having to stoop. An obelisk at the centre of the hollow details his glorious career.

Back in Kilcullen his mummified arm can be seen in **The Hideout** (☎ 045-482121, Main St), a famous and wildly eccentric pub.

For some truly good country cuisine, try *Berney's Bar & Restaurant* (☎ 045-481260, Main St), although the 'country' in question is more France than Ireland. There is a set five-course dinner for €45.

JJ Kavanagh & Sons buses (☎ 056-31106 in Kilkenny, ☎ 01-679 1549 in Dublin, W www.jjkavanagh.ie) serve Kilcullen (single/return €5.10/6.35, 50 minutes, four times a day Monday to Saturday (two on Sunday) on their way from Dublin to Clonmel.

Ballitore & Timolin

During the 18th and 19th centuries, Ballitore was a Quaker settlement. One of the settlers was Abraham Shackleton, an ancestor of the Antarctic explorer Ernest, who was born nearby in Kilkea House.

Housed in an old schoolhouse is the **Quaker Museum** (☎ 0507-431109, Main St; admission by donation; open 11am-6pm Tues-Fri & 11am-1pm Sat year round, depending on presence of caretaker). Its most famous student was the political philosopher Edmund Burke (1729–97).

You can see a functioning water mill and a display covering the history of milling and baking at the **Crookstown Mill and Heritage Centre** (☎ 0507-23222, Ballitore; adult/concession €3.20/1.90; open 10am-7pm or 8pm daily Apr-Sept). It also has a coffee shop and a new craft shop.

Two kilometres west is the **Rath of Mullaghmast**, an Iron Age hill fort where Daniel O'Connell, champion of Catholic emancipation, held one of his 'monster rallies' in 1843.

Two kilometres south of Ballitore and just north of Moone, the village of Timolin is home to the **Irish Pewter Mill and Craft Centre** (☎ 0507-24164, Main St; open 9.30am-5pm Mon-Sat year round).

Griesemount (☎ 0507-23158, fax 40687, ℮ griesemount@eircom.net, Ballitore) Singles/doubles including breakfast from €38/64. Open mid-Feb-mid-Nov. This small Georgian house just off the N9 road to Carlow has four beautiful, large rooms that come highly recommended. The atmosphere is cosy and very relaxed.

Moone

The barely noticeable village of Moone is just south of Timolin. One kilometre west in an early-Christian monastic churchyard is the magnificent **Moone High Cross**. This 8th- or 9th-century masterpiece is slender and, at 6m, remarkably tall. The numerous crisply carved panels display biblical scenes.

Moone High Cross Inn (☎ 0502-24112, fax 24992, Bolton Hill) Singles/doubles including breakfast €45/63.50. Closed Jan. This 18th-century inn is a delightful bar and

From Kilkea to the Antarctic

Sir Ernest Shackleton (1874–1922) may not have been the first man to reach the South Pole but he is widely recognised to be one of the greatest – and bravest – polar explorers of them all. He was born in Kilkea, a descendant of the founder of the Quaker school in Ballitore (see Ballitore & Timolin earlier in this chapter), but financial hardships forced a move to London in 1884. At 16 he joined the Mercantile Marine as an apprentice, and in 1901 he got his first taste of polar adventure when he joined Robert Falcon Scott's first Antarctic expedition. In 1909 he became the first explorer to publicly declare his intention to reach the South Pole, leading his own expedition which was forced to turn back only 97 nautical miles from his goal. Despite his failure, Shackleton's fame was established.

MARTIN HARRIS

Following the success of Roald Amundsen and Robert Scott in reaching the South Pole in 1911–12 (with Scott dying tragically on the way back), Shackleton's name was added to the pantheon of exploring greats as a result of his 1914–16 Imperial Trans-Antarctic Expedition, better known as the *Endurance* expedition (after his ship). His goal was to cross the entire continent on foot, but on 19 January 1915 he awoke to find that his ship was ice-bound in the Weddell Sea, thousands of miles from terra firma. In October, Shackleton and his 27 companions were forced to abandon the ship because it had been crushed, and for the next six months he and his men lived on the floating ice pack, surviving entirely on seals and penguins. Eventually they launched three lifeboats, and after a nightmarish six-day journey they landed on Elephant Island, near the Palmer Peninsula in Antarctica.

With the mission to cross the continent now abandoned, Shackleton embarked on what has been called the greatest small-boat journey in maritime history. Along with five of his men, they set off in one of the boats for South Georgia Island, nearly 1500km away. They arrived 16 days later, at which time Shackleton arranged for the rescue of the others left on Elephant Island. The magnificent example of his leadership under such terrible conditions assured his place in history, with Jameson Boyd Adams, one of the men on the expedition, declaring that he was 'the greatest leader that ever came on God's earth, bar none'. Shackleton died on 5 January 1922 as he had lived, on board the *Quest*, a small expedition vessel off the coast of South Georgia Island.

guesthouse about 100m west of the N9, 1km south of Moone village. It does hefty pub food including a great Irish stew.

Kilkea Castle

This 12th-century castle, completely restored in the 19th century, is 5km north-west of Castledermot on the Athy road and was once the second home of the Maynooth Fitzgeralds. The castle grounds are supposed to be haunted by the son of Silken Thomas, Gerald the Wizard Earl, who rises every seven years from the Rath of Mullaghmast to free Ireland from its enemies, a neat trick given that the Wizard Earl was buried in London.

Although the castle is now an exclusive hotel (☎ 0503-45156, fax 45187, W www .kilkeacastle.ie, Castledermot; singles/doubles from €152/203) you can still have a drink in the bar and pick up a booklet on the building's history. It is Ireland's oldest continuously inhabited castle. Among its oddities is an **Evil Eye Stone** set high up on the exterior wall at the back of the castle. Thought to date from the 13th or 14th century, this is a depiction of various animal, half-human and birdlike figures erotically entwined. The castle has formal gardens and a forest park.

Castledermot

Castledermot's ruined **Franciscan friary** is right by the road at the southern end of town on Abbey St. It dates from the mid-13th century and the key is available from the adjacent cottage.

A little farther north on Main St and back from the road is a **churchyard**, the site of a monastery founded originally by St Diarmuid in 812. Two fine 9th- or 10th-century granite high crosses stand beside the remains of a round tower 20m high and topped with a medieval battlement, and a 12th-century Romanesque church doorway.

Places to Stay & Eat There are a couple of options nearby.

Doyle's Schoolhouse Inn (*☎/fax 0503-44282, Main St, Castledermot*) Singles/doubles €32/70. Set dinner €35. This small, intimate inn is consistently rated as one of Ireland's best restaurants. Reservations for dinner (where only a set menu is available) are essential.

De Lacy Restaurant (*☎ 0503-45156, Kilkea Castle*) Set lunch €23.50, set dinner €38. If you fancy eating mouth-watering cuisine in a real 12th-century castle (the views over the gardens are fabulous), then this is the spot.

ATHY

☎ 0507 • pop 5306

Athy is located at the junction of the River Barrow and the Grand Canal near the Laois border. The name Athy (Áth Í; pronounced a-**thigh**) dates from the 2nd century AD, when a Celt by the name of Ae was slain in a battle between clans from Munster and Leinster at a ford (*áth*) over the River Barrow, which was henceforth known as Áth Ae, the ford of Ae. The town itself, however, was not founded until the 12th century, when the Norman baron Robert de St Michael built a castle (since demolished) at the ford, around which grew up a French-speaking settlement. During the 14th century Athy became an important garrison town, a last line of defence against the encroachment of the Irish who threatened the Pale. In 1417 Sir John Talbot built a tower to house the garrison, which is today a private house and known as **White's Castle**.

At a time when so many Irish towns have succumbed to the lustre of crass commercialism, Athy has retained the feel of a genuine country town, with a pleasant if somewhat dilapidated old square. Apart from the sturdy sight of White's Castle, the town's most notable landmark is the modern Catholic Church, housing the Stations of the Cross by noted Irish artist George Campbell and a crucifix designed by local artist Brid Ní Rinn.

The town hall houses a tourist office and **heritage centre** (*☎ 33075; Town Hall, Emily Square; adult/concession/child €2.55/1.90/ 1.30; open 10am-1pm & 2pm-5pm Mon-Sat & 2pm-5pm Sun Apr-Sept; 10am-1pm & 2pm-5pm Mon-Fri Oct-Mar*). Athy's history is pretty well covered, including the 1798 Rising, Potato Famine and WWI, which saw 2000 men from the town enlist in the British Army There is also a fascinating exhibit on Sir Ernest Shackleton, born 9km south-east of Athy in Kilkea (see the boxed text 'From Kilkea to the Antarctic').

There's coarse, salmon and trout **fishing** on the Grand Canal and the River Barrow. For information check with Kane's pub (*☎ 31434*).

Places to Stay & Eat

Forest Farm (*☎/fax 31231, e forestfarm@ eircom.net, Dublin Rd*) Singles/doubles around €23/48.50. This is a small country farmhouse surrounded by a working farm about 5km south of Athy.

Ballindrum Farm (*☎/fax 26294, e ballin drumfarm@eircom.net, Ballindrum*) Singles/doubles with bathroom €32/51. This modern farmhouse is 9km from Athy, in Ballindrum.

Leinster Arms (*☎ 32040, Leinster St*) Mains around €7.60. This place on the corner of Emily Square has a guesthouse upstairs, but at the time of writing the rooms were being renovated – they should be complete by the time you read this.

Castle Inn (*☎ 31427, 33 Leinster St*) Snacks from €2.50. For cheap-and-cheerful pub food, try here: it has a selection of sandwiches and the usual hot dishes.

Tonlegee House (*☎/fax 31473, w ton legeehouse.com, Kilkenny Rd*) Singles/ doubles €70/102. Dinner about €38.50.

Everyone seems to agree that this elegant country house about 2km south of town is one of the finest country homes in Ireland, with a restaurant to match. It's expensive, but worth it.

Getting There & Away
Bus Éireann (☎ 01-836 6111) has seven buses a day (five on Sunday) that serve Athy (single/return €7.60/8.90, just over one hour from Dublin) on the Dublin–Cork route and vice versa. JJ Kavanagh & Sons (☎ 056-31106 in Kilkenny, ☎ 01-679 1549 in Dublin) runs four buses a day (two on Sunday) between Dublin (from outside the Gresham Hotel on O'Connell St) and Clonmel, stopping in Athy (single/return €3.80/7.60, 1¼-hours).

County Carlow

Carlow (Ceatharlach), Ireland's second-smallest county, has the scenic Blackstairs Mountains to the east, the Killeshin Hills to the west, and sections of the Rivers Barrow and Slaney, with quietly picturesque villages such as Rathvilly, Leighlinbridge and Borris. The Dublin–Carlow town route via south-western Wicklow runs through some wild and lightly populated country. The rest of Carlow is mainly undulating farmland where you will quite often see sugar beet awaiting collection by the roadside. Browne's Hill Dolmen, the county's most interesting archaeological feature, is just outside Carlow town.

CARLOW
☎ 0503 • pop 11,721
Its strategic location on the River Barrow, on the border with the Pale, made Carlow a frontier town for many centuries. Today, the county capital is a busy market and industrial centre serving a large rural area. It was the first town outside Dublin to have electric street lighting, from power generated downstream at Milford. Railway pioneer William Dargan, who founded the National Gallery in Dublin, was born here. Although most visitors come to inspect Browne's Hill

Dolmen on the outskirts, the town itself makes for some interesting walking, with a number of buildings worth checking out.

Orientation & Information
Dublin St is the city's principal north–south axis, with Tullow St, the main shopping street, running off it at a right angle. The tourist office (☎ 31554), in Kennedy Ave, opens 9am to 1pm and 2pm to 5pm weekdays (and 10am to 1pm and 2pm to 5.30pm on Saturday, June to August). The post office is on the corner of Kennedy Ave and Dublin St.

Walking Tour
Start your walk at the **Carlow Courthouse**, at the northern end of Dublin St. Designed by William Vitruvius Morrisson in 1830, this elegant building based on the Parthenon in Athens is considered to be one of the finest courthouses in the country – and Carlow only got it through a mix-up in the plans, with the building originally intended for Cork. On its steps is a cannon taken from the Russians during the Crimean War.

Cross Dublin Rd and walk south-east down College St to **St Patrick's College** *(closed to the public)*, Ireland's first post-penal seminary. Opened in 1793, it is thought to be the longest seminary in continuous use in the world. Just beside the college is the 1833 **Cathedral of the Assumption**, which has an elaborate pulpit and some fine stained-glass windows. John Hogan's statue of Bishop Doyle, better known as JKL (James of Kildare and Leighin) for his work as a supporter of Catholic emancipation, includes a woman who represents Ireland rising up against her oppressors.

At the bottom of College St, turn right into Tullow St, the town's principal shopping thoroughfare. At the end of the first lane to your left is a small square at the centre of which is a statue known as the **Liberty Tree**. Designed by John Behan to commemorate the 1798 Rising, this bronze piece (that doesn't really look like a tree) stands in the middle of a fountain.

Walk back to Tullow St and turn left.

CARLOW

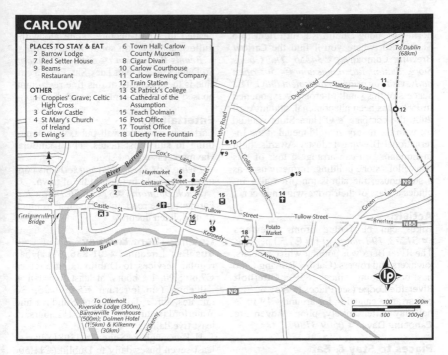

PLACES TO STAY & EAT
2 Barrow Lodge
7 Red Setter House
9 Beams Restaurant

OTHER
1 Croppies' Grave; Celtic High Cross
3 Carlow Castle
4 St Mary's Church of Ireland
5 Ewing's
6 Town Hall; Carlow County Museum
8 Cigar Divan
10 Carlow Courthouse
11 Carlow Brewing Company
12 Train Station
13 St Patrick's College
14 Cathedral of the Assumption
15 Teach Dolmain
16 Post Office
17 Tourist Office
18 Liberty Tree Fountain

Tullow St then becomes Castle St, and on your right you'll see **St Mary's Church**. Inside this Church of Ireland church, built in 1727 (the tower and spire were added in 1834), are a number of statues by Richard Morrisson.

Continue down Castle St to **Carlow Castle**, built by William de Marshall in the 13th century on the site of an earlier Norman motte-and-bailey fort. Officials once had to be paid danger money to live here among the native Irish. The castle survived Cromwell's attentions and would be largely intact if a certain Dr Middleton hadn't decided to convert it into an asylum. In order to remodel the interior, he set charges at its base and in so doing reduced the once mighty castle to a single wall flanked by two towers. Spanning the Barrow is the **Graiguecullen Bridge**, an attractive five-arched stone structure that was originally constructed in 1569 but widened in 1815. It is thought to be the oldest and lowest bridge over this particular river.

Cross the bridge and turn right, walking north along Chapel St until you reach a tall Celtic **high cross** built to mark the **Croppies' Grave**, where 640 United Irish rebels were buried following the bloodiest fighting of the whole 1798 Rising. The name 'croppie' came from the insurgents' habit of cropping their hair to indicate their allegiance to the rebel side.

Recross the bridge, turn left and walk east along Centaur St. Just past Haymarket is the **town hall**, which houses the small **Carlow County Museum** (☎ 40730, Centaur St; adult/concession €1.30/0.65; open 11am-5pm Tues-Fri, 2pm-5pm Sat & Sun). It has some interesting displays on the town's history.

Farther east down Centaur St and on your left is a gorgeous little shop called the **Cigar Divan** with a Victorian shop front. It dates from the late 19th century, when Turkish cigarettes were all the rage, and it is still one of the town's nicer curiosities.

At Dublin St, turn left and retrace your

CENTRAL SOUTH

steps back to the courthouse. About 500m north-east along Dublin Rd, turn right into Station Rd, where you'll find the **Carlow Brewing Company** (*☎ 34356, The Goods Store, Station Rd; admission €4.50; open daily, visits by prior arrangement only)*. The success of this small microbrewery, opened in 1998, has been phenomenal, and in April 2000 the company's O'Hara Stout walked off with the first prize gold medal at the International Brewing Industry Awards, held in London. You can arrange a tour of this marvellous stone building, formerly used as a storehouse; the admission price also includes a glass of their prize-winning beer.

Activities
Bikes can be rented from **Colemans** (*☎ 31273, 19 Dublin St)* for €7.50 per day. The River Barrow is popular with canoeists, kayakers and rowers (Carlow Rowing Club has been going since 1859). **Otterholt Riverside Lodge** (see Places to Stay & Eat) can arrange canoeing for around €19 for a half-day. Alternatively, phone **Adventure Canoeing Days** (*☎ 0509-31307)*.

Places to Stay & Eat
Otterholt Riverside Lodge (*☎ 30404, fax 35106, Kilkenny Rd)* Dorms/doubles €13/16.50 per person. This IHH hostel has one 10-bed dorm and a couple of private rooms, as well as delightful gardens.

Red Setter House (*☎ 41848, 14 Dublin St)* Singles/doubles from €30.50/56. This is a spotless, central B&B with a range of rooms, some with shower, some without.

Barrow Lodge (*☎ 41173, The Quay)* Singles/doubles €32.50/56. This lodge has a pleasant riverside setting.

Barrowville Townhouse (*☎ 43324, fax 41953, Kilkenny Rd)* Singles/doubles including breakfast €37/58.50. Only 500m south of the town centre, this is an attractive 18th-century town house that has been meticulously restored and converted into a top-class B&B.

Dolmen Hotel (*☎ 42002, fax 42375, e reservations@dolmenhotel.ie, Kilkenny Rd)* Rooms from €50 per person. This is a modern hotel with all the trimmings, including a substantial activities centre. It's nestled in a half-hectare estate along the Tullow, about 1.5km south of the town.

Beams Restaurant (*☎ 31824, 59 Dublin St)* Dinner €32. Open Tues-Sat. French cuisine is the speciality at this fine restaurant, housed in an 18th-century coach house.

Entertainment
Carlow has wall-to-wall pubs, with something to suit most tastes. The triangular Haymarket is a good spot.

Ewing's (*☎ 31138, Haymarket)* This popular pub is right in the middle of town.

Teach Dolmain (*☎ 31235, 76 Tullow Rd)* Farther up the road, this place makes much of its dolmen decor.

Getting There & Away
Bus Bus Éireann (*☎ 01-836 6111)* has regular services to Dublin (single/return €7.60/8.90, 1½ hours, at least five daily), Kilkenny (single/return €5.60/6.35, 30 minutes, three daily except Sunday) and Waterford (return only €7.60, 1½ hours, at least five daily).

JJ Kavanagh & Sons (*☎ 43081)* has at least seven buses daily to Dublin (€11.50/16.50) and Waterford (€7.60/8.90). There is also a twice-daily service to Kilkenny (€3.80/7.60, 45 minutes). The twice-daily service to Portlaoise (€4.85, one hour) also stops in Athy (€3.80 each way, 30 minutes). There is also a service between Carlow and Newbridge (€4.85, one hour 40 minutes), that stops in Kildare (€4.50, 1¼ hours) and the Curragh (€4.85, one hour 25 minutes). This service only runs during college terms (September to June).

Train The station (*☎ 31633)* is on Station Rd to the north-east of town. Carlow is on the Dublin to Kilkenny and Waterford line with at least four trains daily in each direction (three on Sunday). A day return to Dublin or Waterford costs €7.60.

AROUND CARLOW TOWN
Browne's Hill Dolmen
This 5000-year-old granite monster is believed to have the largest capstone in Europe,

weighing well over 100 tonnes. When complete, the structure would have been covered with a mound of earth. The dolmen is 3km east of town on the R726 Hacketstown road; a path leads round the field to the dolmen. There's no public transport but you could cycle.

BORRIS
☎ 0503 • pop 584
Sixteen kilometres south of Leighlinbridge, the Georgian village of Borris is overlooked by a disused railway viaduct with 16 arches. **Borris House** is the residence of the Mac-Murrough Kavanaghs, descendants of the ancient kings of Leinster, and is still in the family's possession.

A most remarkable MacMurrough Kavanagh was Arthur (1831–89), who was born with only rudimentary limbs yet learned to ride and shoot and later became an MP. Visits to the castle are by appointment only. The entrance is at the northern end of town near the White House pub.

Borris is a starting point for the Mt Leinster Scenic Drive (which can also be walked) and is also on the South Leinster Way. Alternatively, there's a lovely 10km walk along a towpath beside the River Barrow to picturesque Graiguenamanagh, just inside County Kilkenny.

Breen's (☎ 73231, Main St) Singles/doubles including breakfast €22/38. This basic place is in the middle of town.

Lorum Old Rectory (☎ 75282, fax 75455, ☑ lorum@lorum.com, Kilgreaney) Singles/doubles from €51/70. Dinner €35. Closed for dinner Sun. Halfway between Borris and Bagenalstown, this historic country house is overlooked by the Blackstairs Mountains.

Foley's (☎ 24641) operates one bus daily (except Sunday) to Borris from Kilkenny, leaving at 5.30pm (€4.50, one hour).

MT LEINSTER
At 796m, Mt Leinster offers some of Ireland's finest hang-gliding. It's also worth the hike up for the panoramic views over Counties Carlow, Wexford and Wicklow. To get there from Borris, follow the Mt Leinster

Scenic Drive signposts 13km towards Bunclody in County Wexford (see Mt Leinster in the Counties Wexford & Waterford chapter for details). It takes a good two hours on foot or 20 minutes by car.

SOUTH LEINSTER WAY
South-west of Clonegal, on the northern slopes of Mt Leinster, is the tiny village of **Kildavin**, the starting point of the South Leinster Way. For details see Walking under Activities in the Facts for the Visitor chapter.

County Laois

Laois (pronounced leash) is the only inland county surrounded on all sides by counties that do not touch the coast. For most visitors it's somewhere to whip through en route to Limerick or Cork, with a fairly uninteresting landscape of raised bogs and poor farms. Yet with time to linger you'll find some pleasant country towns and the unspoiled Slieve Bloom Mountains.

PORTLAOISE
☎ 0502 • pop 3531
Although founded by the O'Mores just before the 16th-century Plantation, Portlaoise is mostly modern, and only the courthouse by Richard Morrison on the corner of Main and Church Sts is notable. Bristling with wire fencing at the eastern end of town is a maximum-security prison, Portlaoise's main claim to fame for many people. There's very little to keep you here, and the completion of a bypass means you can skip it altogether.

To the west lie the Slieve Bloom Mountains, while to the east is the one historic site worth a special detour, the impressive Rock of Dunamase on the Stradbally road (see later in the chapter).

Information
The tourist office (☎ 21178), in the shopping-centre car park beside the bypass on James Fintan Lawlor Ave, has lots of information on the county. To get there from Main St, cut through the lane beside

Dowling's cafe. It opens 10am to 6pm Monday to Saturday, May to September.

Places to Stay & Eat

O'Loughlin's (☎ *21305, fax 60883,* ℯ *oloughlins@eircom.net, Main St)* Rooms from €38 per person. This hotel has a bar, restaurant and nightclub *(Club 23; open Thur-Sat only)* downstairs.

The Kitchen & Foodhall (☎ *62061, Hyand's Square)* Set lunch €7. This is a wonderful restaurant and food shop with a terrific atmosphere. If for some reason you're stuck in town, this place will cheer you up.

Getting There & Away

Portlaoise is on one of the busiest main roads in the country, at the junction of the N8 and N7. Bus Éireann (☎ 01-836 6111) runs 14 buses daily that pass through Portlaoise (single/return €8.90/13.35, 1½ hours) from Dublin on their way to Cashel, Cork, Limerick and Kerry. It is also on the Waterford, Kilkenny, Carlow, Athlone and Longford route. JJ Kavanagh & Sons private bus company (☎ 056-31106) runs two buses daily to Carlow (€4.85, one hour).

Just one hour from Dublin on the main line to Tipperary, Cork, Limerick and Tralee, Portlaoise is serviced by nine daily trains from Dublin alone (single/return €14.60/15.25). The station (☎ 21303), on Railway St, is a five-minute walk north of the town centre.

ROCK OF DUNAMASE

Six kilometres east of Portlaoise along the Stradbally road is a dramatic fractured limestone hill covered with the remains of fortifications. It may not be Cashel, but the surrounding countryside is so flat that the summit offers fine views of the Timahoe round tower to the south, the Slieve Blooms to the north and – on a clear day – the Wicklow Mountains to the east.

It seems that the site was known outside Ireland as long ago as 500 BC. The Egyptian astronomer Ptolemy wrote of a place called Dunum, and it is held here that what he was writing of was Dun Masc, the Celtic name for Dunamase. Little was left of the original fortifications after a sacking by the Vikings in 845. The slopes of Dunamase can be treacherous, particularly on the northern side, and these natural barriers would have complicated any assault on its defenders.

Dunamase was later given away by Dermot MacMurrough, king of Leinster, as part of his daughter Aoife's dowry when in 1170 she married Strongbow, the Norman invader of Ireland. Dunamase was then reinforced by William Marshall, Strongbow's successor.

The local clan, the O'Mores, captured the rock from the English towards the end of the 14th century and held it until it was retaken by Charles Coote in 1641. He was a leading Parliamentarian and one of Cromwell's most able leaders in Ireland. Recaptured five years later by Catholic forces, it was finally wrecked by Cromwell's henchmen in 1650.

The earth embankments 500m to the east of the rock are known as Cromwell's lines, although they're actually the remains of an Iron Age two-ringed fort. The main ruins consist of a badly shattered 12th- or 13th-century castle on the summit (best seen from the northern side) surrounded by an outer wall of which little remains. You enter the complex through the twin-towered gateway, which leads to the outer bailey and fortified courtyard to the south-east.

JJ Kavanagh & Sons (☎ 056-31106) two daily Portlaoise to Carlow buses pass by the rock. Otherwise, it's a good hour's walk from Portlaoise town centre.

EMO COURT & DEMESNE

Thirteen kilometres north-east of Portlaoise is the former country seat of the 1st earl of Portarlington, Emo Court (☎ *0502-26573, Emo; adult/concession €1.90/1.30, grounds free; open for guided tours 10am-6pm daily mid-June-mid-Sept; grounds open during daylight hours).* The rather unusual house, restored by Dúchas, with its prominent green dome was designed by James Gandon (architect of Dublin's Custom House) in 1790 and served as a Jesuit novitiate for many years. The estate offers long walks through forests and by Emo Lake, and is littered with Greek statues. From the Emo village gate it's a 2km walk along the drive to the house.

South of Emo village off the main Port-laoise road is the elegantly simple **St John's Church** *(Coolbanagher; free; open 10am-6pm daily)*, also designed by Gandon in 1786.

Emo is just off the main Portlaoise–Dublin road, and has daily buses in both directions.

STRADBALLY

The village of Stradbally (or Strathbally), 10km south-east of Portlaoise, was once a seat of the mighty O'More clan. Most of the present buildings date from the 17th century.

The clan was the force behind the Franciscan friary established here in 1447. The O'Mores were the holders of the Book of Leinster, a manuscript compiled between 1151 and 1224 to record all the knowledge of Aéd Crúamthainn, scribe to the high kings of Ireland. The book is now in Trinity College Library, Dublin.

Stradbally Steam Museum & Narrow Gauge Railway

At the southern end of town, this museum *(☎ 0502-25444, Stradbally)* has a collection of fire engines, steam tractors and steam-rollers, lovingly restored by the Irish Steam Preservation Society. Unfortunately, the museum is currently closed for renovation and there is no date set for its reopening.

The 1895 Guinness Brewery steam locomotive in the village is used six times annually for a day trip to Dublin. During the three-day Steam Rally in early August the 40 hectares of Cosby Hall are taken over by steam-operated machines and vintage cars.

Getting There & Away

JJ Kavanagh & Sons (☎ 056-31106) runs three buses a day Monday to Saturday from Portlaoise to Kilkenny via Stradbally (€2.50, 15 minutes). Stradbally is also on Bus Éireann's (☎ 01-836 6111) twice-daily Waterford–Longford service, which also passes through Kilkenny, Carlow, Portlaoise and Athlone.

PORTARLINGTON
☎ 0502 • pop 3320

Portarlington (Cúil an tSúdaire) grew up under the influence of French Huguenot and German settlers introduced by Lord Arlington, who was granted land here after the Cromwellian wars. Some of the finer 18th-century buildings are a result of the efforts of Henry Dawson, earl of Portarlington, to improve the town. Unfortunately, many are terribly neglected.

The 1851 **St Paul's Church** *(free; open 7am-7pm daily)* on the site of the original 17th-century French church, was built for the Huguenots, some of whose tombstones stand in a corner of the churchyard. The power station's large **cooling tower** is a local landmark. Built in 1936, it was the first in Ireland to use peat to generate electricity.

Portarlington is on the main train lines between Dublin and Galway, Limerick, Tralee and Cork, with hourly trains daily in both directions. For details contact Portlaoise train station (☎ 0502-21303). There are no bus services.

LEA CASTLE

On the banks of the River Barrow 4km east of Portarlington, this ivy-clad 13th-century ruin was the stronghold of Maurice Fitzgerald, 2nd baron of Offaly. It consists of a fairly intact towered keep with two outer walls running down to the Barrow and a twin-towered gatehouse. It was burned in 1315 by Edward Bruce, the brother of Robert the Bruce of Scotland, when he came to Ireland at the invitation of Irish chieftains to create trouble for the Anglo-Normans. Crowned high king of Ireland, Edward Bruce hassled the forces loyal to England until he was killed in 1318 at the Battle of Faughart near Dundalk. His remains are said to be buried in a churchyard at Faughart, 4km from Castleroche.

In the 16th century Silken Thomas sought refuge here after his failed 1534 rebellion against Henry VIII. In 1650 the castle was blown up by Cromwell's forces, fresh from their success at Dunamase.

In the early morning and evening the ruins can be tranquil and evocative. Access is through a farmyard half a kilometre to the north off the main Monasterevin road (R420).

MOUNTMELLICK
☎ 0502 • pop 2325

Mountmellick is a faded market town with many Georgian houses, 10km north of Portlaoise on the River Owenass. Its fortunes rose with Quaker settlers who produced linen, which was exported by barge on a branch of the Grand Canal, which runs away to the east. Something of a boom town in the late 18th and early 19th centuries, it was home to Ireland's first sugar-beet factory, built in 1851. There's a display on Quaker life and Mountmellick embroidery at the small **heritage centre** (☎ 24525, Cod's Mill, Portlaoise Rd; open 10am-5pm Mon-Fri year round, 2pm-6pm Sat & Sun June-Sept).

Mountmellick is on Bus Éireann's (☎ 01-836 6111) twice-daily Waterford–Longford route. There's also a daily (except Sunday) service to and from Dublin (€8.90/13.35, two hours) via Naas, Newbridge and Kildare.

MOUNTRATH & AROUND
☎ 0502 • pop 1298

Like so many other Irish settlements, Mountrath is associated with St Patrick and St Brigid, who are supposed to have established religious houses here, although no trace of either remains. Much of the town and surrounding land belonged to Sir Charles Coote, an ardent supporter of Cromwell during and after the wars of the 1640s. Mountrath's glory days were in the 17th and 18th centuries, when it prospered from the linen industry.

St Fintan's Tree

Three kilometres east on the Portlaoise road, there are scant remains of the 6th-century monastery of St Fintan at Clonenagh. St Fintan's Tree is a large sycamore with a water-filled groove in one of its lower branches. Supposedly this never dries out, and the tree has long been a place of pilgrimage. The coins embedded in the trunk are offerings by pilgrims who attribute healing powers to the water.

Ballyfin House

Eight kilometres north of Mountrath off the Mountmellick road is Ballyfin House, built by Sir Charles Henry Coote in 1850 to the designs of Richard Morrison. Overlooking a small lake in quiet, rolling countryside, it has been described as Ireland's finest 19th-century house. Inside, some of the ornamentation is completely over the top. Sir Charles reckoned all good houses should have a lake, and the one in front is artificial.

An intriguing piece of contemporary aristocratic eccentricity was megalithomania, or a passion for building imitation Stone Age monuments. Ballyfin has an excellent example in the form of a rough stone shelter hidden among the trees on the far side of the fence to the right of the avenue, about 200m short of the house.

Places to Stay & Eat

Conlán House (☎/fax 32727, ℮ conlan house@oceanfree.net, Burke's Cross, Killanure) Rooms with bathroom €32 per person. This place, 7km west of town on the edge of the Slieve Blooms, has three comfortable rooms.

Phelan's Restaurant (Main St) Snacks from €2.50. By the square, Phelan's serves reasonable burgers and chips.

Roundwood House (☎ 32120, fax 32711, ℮ roundwood@eircom.net, Slieve Blooms Rd) Singles/doubles including breakfast €60/120. Dinner €35.50. This Palladian mansion, 5km outside Mountrath, is one of the finest country houses in Ireland and has wonderful original furnishings and superb service without a hint of pretension. For the quality of the place, the prices are decent and the dinner is excellent.

Getting There & Away

Mountrath is on the main Bus Éireann (☎ 01-836 6111) Dublin–Limerick route, with up to four buses daily in each direction.

SLIEVE BLOOM MOUNTAINS

One of the best reasons for visiting Laois is to explore the Slieve (pronounced shleeve) Bloom Mountains. Their name means Mountains of Bladhma, after a Celtic warrior who used the mountains as a refuge. Not as splendid as their cousins in Wicklow and the west, the Slieve Blooms stand out for their relative absence of visitors. They boast moorlands, pine forests and hidden valleys.

The highest point is Mt Arderin (528m) south of the Glendine Gap on the Offaly border. On a clear day it's possible to see the highest points of all four of the ancient provinces of Ireland. East is Lugnaquilla in Leinster, west is Nephin in Connaught, north is Slieve Donard in Ulster, and south-west is Carrantuohil in Munster.

Mountrath to the south and lovely **Kinnitty** to the north of the hills make good bases (see earlier for the former and under County Offaly later for the latter). **Glenbarrow**, south-west of Rosenallis, has a gentle walk by the River Barrow, which has its source just a few kilometres farther up in the hills. There are some waterfalls, a large moraine on the northern side of the river and unusual local plants, including orchids, butterwort and blue fleabane. Other spots worth checking out are **Glendine Park** near the Glendine Gap, and the **Cut** mountain pass. The road north of the mountains from Mountmellick to Birr via Clonaslee and Kinnitty is particularly scenic.

Slieve Bloom Way

The Slieve Bloom Way is a 77km signposted trail which does a complete circuit of the mountains, taking in most major points of interest. See Walking under Activities in the Facts for the Visitor chapter for details.

WESTERN LAOIS

South of the Slieve Bloom Mountains, **Borris-in-Ossory** on the N7, once known as the Gate of Munster, was a major coaching stop in the 18th century before the railways developed. It's on the Bus Éireann express Dublin–Limerick route, with four buses daily (three on Sunday) in each direction.

About 3km farther west on the same road is **Ballaghmore Castle** (☎ 0505-21453, off the N7, Ballaghmore; adult/concession €3.80/2.50; open 10am-5.30pm daily year round). The square tower fortress dating from 1480 has been faithfully restored. Those with good eyesight might spot the **sheila-na-gig** in the southern wall.

ABBEYLEIX
☎ 0502 • pop 1259

Abbeyleix (pronounced abbey-**leeks**), 14km south of Portlaoise, is as well tended a country town as you will find. It grew up around a 12th-century Cistercian monastery in nearby Old Town, though the only traces of this are two ancient monuments. In the 18th century the local landowner, Viscount de Vesci, moved the town centre to its present location and supervised the layout of tree-lined streets and neat town houses. During the Famine, de Vesci proved a kinder landlord than many and the fountain obelisk in the square was erected as a thank you from his tenants.

De Vesci's mansion, **Abbeyleix House**, was erected in 1773 from a design by James Wyatt. It's 2km south-west of town on the Rathdowney road, but is not open to the public.

The old National School building at the northern end of town is now the **Heritage House** (☎ 31653, on the N8; adult/student/child €2.50/1.90/1.30; open 10am-6pm Mon-Sat & 1pm-6pm Sun Mar-Oct; 9am-5pm Mon-Fri Nov-Feb). It details the town's history and contains some examples of the Turkish-influenced carpets woven in Abbeyleix from 1904 to 1913 – including carpets woven for the Titanic. A *coffee shop* in the basement serves breakfast until noon and light lunches.

Places to Stay & Eat

Preston House (☎/fax 31432, Main St) Doubles including breakfast €66. You can stay at this creeper-clad place in what were once the assembly rooms. There's also a great country-style cafe with some excellent vegetarian choices.

Hibernian Hotel (☎ 31252, fax 31888, Main St) Rooms including breakfast from €32 per person. This striking greystone building has well appointed, comfortable rooms.

Entertainment

Morrissey's (☎ 31233, Main St) This is a marvellous old pub-shop that used to act as a travel agency and undertaker's as well.

Drinkers down their pints around an old-fashioned stovepipe, or perch on stools at a sloping counter.

Getting There & Away

Abbeyleix is on an express Bus Éireann (☎ 01-836 6111) route between Dublin (single/return €10.80/16.50, one hour 40 minutes, every two hours) and Cork.

JJ Kavanagh & Sons (☎ 056-31106) runs a bus Monday to Saturday between Portlaoise, Abbeyleix, Durrow, Cullahill and Urlingford. From Portlaoise, buses depart at 11.30am and 5.30pm (€2.30, 20 minutes); from Urlingford, buses depart at 7.45am and 2pm (€3.30, 1¼ hours).

TIMAHOE

Tiny Timahoe is just a handful of houses around a grassy square, 10km north-east of Abbeyleix on a minor road (R426). South of the village seven roads converge on a 30m-tall **round tower** with a slight tilt, all that remains of a 12th-century monastery. The tower has a beautifully worked Romanesque entrance.

DURROW

In Durrow, about 10km south of Abbeyleix, neat rows of houses surround a manicured green with the imposing gateway to the 1716 **Castle Durrow**, a large Palladian villa, on the western side. Unfortunately, the castle is privately owned and not open to the public.

Castle Arms Hotel (☎ 0502-36117, fax 36566, The Square) Rooms €32 per person including breakfast. This place on the square provides entertainment on most weekends throughout the year.

KILLESHIN CHURCH

Killeshin Church is a mere 5km from Carlow town. Killeshin used to be one of the biggest towns in Laois and had one of the finest round towers in the country. A local farmer is said to have destroyed it in the 18th century in case it collapsed and killed his livestock. The shattered **11th-century church** has a steeply arched Romanesque doorway.

County Offaly

Offaly has the typical flat, boggy landscape of central Ireland, exemplified by the extensive Bog of Allen and Boora Bog between Ferbane and Kilcormac. The Bog of Allen is an enormous brown expanse that stretches over into Kildare and which – along with many other bogs – is being mined by the huge machines of the Bord na Móna (Irish Turf Board) for potting compost and fuel briquettes (for details of the Bord na Móna Bog Rail Tour see Shannonbridge later in this chapter). However, some of Offaly's bogs, such as Clara Bog, are remarkably untouched and are recognised internationally for their plant and animal life.

The mighty River Shannon forms part of Offaly's border with Galway, while the Grand Canal also threads its way through the county. Offaly shares the Slieve Bloom Mountains with County Laois. The county is also home to the extensive monastic ruins of Clonmacnoise, one of Ireland's 'must see' attractions.

BIRR

☎ 0509 • pop 3355

On the River Camcor, a small tributary of the Shannon, Birr owes its existence to the expansive demesne of Birr Castle and its owners, the earls of Rosse, the first of whom personally supervised the construction of the town. Although for much of the 20th century Birr was something of a rural backwater, today it is a vibrant urban hub that has made the most of its Georgian heritage. Many traditional shop fronts along Connaught and Main Sts have been cleaned up and restored to their former beauty, and while there is a slight tendency to indulge in the 'faux-Georgian' look, the overall effect remains intact and Birr is one of the most pleasant stopovers in the whole region.

History

After starting out as a 6th-century monastic site founded by St Brendan of Birr, the town acquired an Anglo-Norman castle in 1208, which was the home of the O'Carrolls.

During the Plantation of 1620, the castle and estate were given to Sir Laurence Parsons, who laid out streets, established a glass factory and issued decrees that anyone who 'cast dunge rubbidge filth or sweepings in the forestreet' was to be fined four pennies.

Later, the Parsons became earls of Rosse. The present earl and his wife still live on the estate, which has remained in the family for 14 generations.

Orientation & Information

All the main roads converge on Emmet Square, where a statue of the duke of Cumberland (victor of the Battle of Culloden, Scotland) stood on the central column until 1925. In one corner, Dooly's Hotel, dating from 1747, was once a coaching inn on the busy route to the west. The post office is in the north-western corner of Emmet Square.

The tourist office (☎ 20110), Main St, is about 300m from Emmet Square; just follow the signpost. It opens 9.30am to 5.30pm daily, May to mid-September only. There were plans to move it Crotty's Church on Castle St but at the time of writing nothing had happened.

Also worth checking out is the Ely O'Carroll Tourism Office (☎ 20923, W www.ely ocarroll.com) in the Small Business Centre on Brendan St. Sponsored by the Shannon Redevelopment Programme, it opens 10am to 5pm Monday to Friday year round and provides excellent information on the town and the region.

The two finest streets of Georgian houses are tree-lined Oxmantown Mall, connecting Rosse Row and Emmet Square, and John's Mall.

Birr Castle & Demesne

Most visitors to Birr come to see the castle and grounds (W www.birrcastle.com, adult/student/child €5.10/4.05/3.15; demesne open 9am-6pm daily year round). Most of the present structure dates from around 1620, when Sir Laurence Parsons was granted the estate. A later Laurence presided over alterations in the early 19th century, which left the castle almost exactly as you see it today. In 1820 the castle was fortified again after a

local Protestant woman, Mrs Legge, convinced her brethren that the Catholics were going to rise up and kill them in their beds.

The demesne, which runs north from the castle, consists of 50 hectares of magnificent gardens set around a large artificial lake. The formal gardens, about 500m east of the castle itself, hold over 1000 species of shrubs and trees from all over the world, including a collection from the Himalayas and China, brought back from the 6th earl's 1935 honeymoon in Peking. Here you'll also find the world's tallest box hedges, planted in the 1780s and now standing some 12m high.

About 100m west of the castle, spanning the Camcor, is a suspension bridge built in 1820, making it the oldest wrought iron bridge of its kind in Ireland.

The Rosse Telescope & Historic Science Centre Housed inside the Exhibition Pavilion, just north of the castle, is a huge telescope built by William Parsons (1800–67), the 3rd earl of Rosse, in 1845. Built using local engineering and materials, and with a reflector that is 183cm in diameter, the 'leviathan of Parsonstown' was until 1915 the largest in the world, attracting all manner of scientists and astronomers. The instrument was used to map the moon's surface, and made innumerable discoveries, including the spiral galaxies. Demonstrations are held three-times daily.

To make the most of the family's scientific pedigree, the Rosses recently opened a new historic science centre (admission included in the castle ticket; open 9am-6pm daily year round). It is in the restored Stable Block (built in the 1850s), just inside the main entrance to the demesne. The exhibits catalogue the fairly impressive family inventions over the last two centuries, including a lunar heat machine invented by the 4th earl, Laurence Parsons, and a steam turbine invented by his brother, Charles Rosse.

Other Things to See & Do

The tourist office has a free leaflet covering a town trail with 10 stops at Birr's most important landmarks. John's Mall has John Henry Foley's statue of the 3rd earl of Rosse and a Russian cannon from the Crimean War. Nearby is the **Birr Stone**, a megalithic stone found in an early-Christian monastery and said to have marked the centre of Ireland. Some fine Victorian houses built between 1870 and 1878 are on the side of the square opposite the Birr Heritage Centre. This was closed at the time of writing but the Civic Trust was hoping to reopen it.

South-west of Emmet Square are the remains of **Old St Brendan's Church**, reputedly the site of St Brendan's 6th-century settlement.

A fine **riverside walk** runs east along the River Camcor from Oxmantown Bridge near the Catholic church to Elmgrove Bridge.

Birr Outdoor Education Centre (☎ 20029, Roscrea Rd), offers courses in walking, sailing, canoeing and rock-climbing in the nearby Slieve Blooms.

Places to Stay

Farmhouses & B&Bs As well as the usual B&Bs, it is possible to stay at farmhouses in the area.

Minnock's Farmhouse (☎ 20591, fax 21684, e minnocksfarm@eircom.net, Roscrea Rd) Rooms with bathroom from €23.50 per person. About 1km south of town near the entrance to the castle, this award-winning farmhouse is an excellent choice, with comfortable rooms in a lovely rural environment.

Ring Farmhouse (☎/fax 20976, e ring farm@gofree.indigo.ie, The Ring, Roscrea Rd) Rooms from €24.50 per person. This working farm only 2km south of town, just off the main Roscrea road, offers comfortable accommodation in a warm family setting.

Walcot B&B (☎ 21247, fax 20625, e walcot@hotmail.com, Oxmantown Mall) Singles/doubles €45/63.50. This charming Georgian town house in the centre of town has four elegant bedrooms and a lovely private garden.

The Maltings Guesthouse (☎/fax 21345, Castle St) En suite singles/doubles from €45/63. Nestled on the river right by the castle, this is a terrific option, with tastefully decorated rooms and a good restaurant downstairs.

The Stables Guesthouse (☎ 20263, fax 21677, e cboyd@indigo.ie, Oxmantown Mall) Rooms with bathroom from €32 per person. Better known as a restaurant, this place has spacious, airy rooms.

Hotels There are some lovely hotels to choose from here.

Spinner's Townhouse (☎/fax 21673, e spinners@indigo.ie, w www.spinners -townhouse.com, Castle St) Rooms from €29 per person. Open Mar-Nov. The best place in town is this charming hotel, a stone's throw from the castle gates. Its 14 rooms, all carefully decorated with locally made furniture and woven linen, are set around a fabulous courtyard garden that is great for reading and relaxing.

County Arms Hotel (☎ 20791, fax 21234, e countyarmshotel@eircom.net, Railway Rd) Rooms from €46 per person including breakfast. This friendly place with well equipped rooms is within walking distance of the town centre on Railway Rd, which becomes the road to Roscrea.

Dooly's Hotel (☎ 20032, fax 21332, e doolyshotel@esatclear.ie, w www.doolys hotel.com, Emmet Square) Rooms from €45 per person including breakfast. Built in 1747 as a coaching lodge, Dooly's has 18 comfortable rooms decorated in an 18th-century style (but with 21st-century conveniences).

Tullanisk House (☎ 20572, 1850 215815, fax 21783, e tullanisk@printworks.net, Birr Estate) Rooms €45-76 per person, single-room supplement €10.20. This 18th-century Georgian lodge is 2km out on the Banagher road, in an 320-hectare park studded with deer. The spacious rooms and vaulted corridors are decorated with antiques, books and a music library. The owners are big fans of holistic treatment, and courses are run regularly.

Self-Catering This is a good option if you'd like to stay and explore the area for longer.

Croghan Lodge (☎ 20023, fax 21583, e rossea@gofree.indigo.ie, Birr Castle Demesne) From €350 per week. This lovely cottage on the castle grounds has been fully restored and completely refitted with all modern conveniences. There are two bedrooms (it sleeps four in total). Although weekly rentals are preferred, shorter periods are also possible.

Places to Eat
Birr's growing reputation as an elegant town is in part due to its fine restaurants, all of which promote the best of new Irish cuisine.

Dooly's Hotel (see Places to Stay) has three different dining options. There's an excellent cafeteria-style coffee shop (open 8.30am to 10pm; mains from €4); filling and delicious pub lunches are available at the Coach House Lounge (open 12.30pm to 3pm; mains from €6.50); while the award-winning Emmet Room restaurant at the front of the hotel serves both Irish and international cuisine (mains around €10)

Spinner's Bistro (☎ 21673, Castle St) Lunch around €10, dinner around €25. This is one the town's busiest restaurants, with a great reputation for good food and wine; in warm weather, eating in the courtyard garden is a real treat.

Riverbank (☎ 21528, Riverstown) Mains around €10. Situated along the banks of the River Brosna about 2km south-west of Birr, this wonderful restaurant has earned plenty of rave reviews for its superb, freshly prepared dishes.

County Arms Hotel (see Places to Stay) Dinner around €25. Good bar lunches and fine dinners in the evenings are served here. The garden is a source of many of the fresh vegetables.

The Stables (see Places to Stay) Set dinner around €25. Celebrated for its cuisine and character, The Stables attracts diners from all over the county.

The Maltings Restaurant (see Places to Stay) Lunch around €12, dinner €25. This is another good choice, with a fine selection of carefully prepared Irish dishes.

Tullanisk House (see Places to Stay) Set dinner €38. This place blends old-English and Asian influences.

The Thatch (☎ 20682, Crinkill) Set lunch €15.50. Only 2km south-east of Birr in tiny Crinkill, this gorgeous thatched pub is a real find. In 1999 it won the All-Ireland Pub of the Year award, not only for its classic, country look but for its superb Irish cuisine.

Entertainment
Craughwell's (☎ 21839, Castle St) Craughwell's is great for a fine traditional session on Friday night and impromptu sing-along sessions on Saturday.

Kelly's (☎ 20175, Green St) This is a locals' haunt, just off the square towards the castle.

Foster's (☎ 20088, Connaught St) At the back of Dooly's Hotel, this is an old-style pub which gets a good crowd at the weekend and usually has music.

Palace Bar (☎ 20374, O'Connell St) This bar often has live bands at the weekend, but is best for a quiet drink.

Market House Tavern (☎ 20180, Market Square) This is Birr's most modern bar, and so it's popular with the younger crowd.

County Arms Hotel (see Places to Stay) The bar in the hotel regularly hosts an excellent traditional session.

Melba's Nite Club (☎ 20032, Emmet Square) In the basement of Dooly's Hotel, this is the town's only nightclub. With lots of flashing lights and a soundtrack straight out of the Top 40, it's a bit of fun.

Getting There & Away
Birr is on the Dublin–Portumna route, which also serves Tullamore and Maynooth. Bus Éireann (☎ 01-836 6111) services depart Dublin at 9.45am and 3.45pm Monday to Saturday (single/return €10.20/14, 3¼ hours); you'll have to change buses in Roscrea. There's a direct service from Dublin, which runs at 4pm on weekdays only (2¼ hours). On Sunday, buses depart Dublin at 12.30pm and 3.45pm – you'll need to change as Roscrea. Check with the bus station in Athlone (☎ 0902-72651) for times of buses leaving Birr.

Kearn's Coaches (☎ 22244 for a recorded schedule) runs daily services from Dublin and Tullamore through Birr to Portumna (in Galway). Three buses a day pass through Birr on Sunday, Monday and Friday; two a day on Saturday; and one a day Tuesday to Thursday. Up to two buses daily go from Portumna to

Birr and Dublin (one way from Birr €7.60). All buses stop in Emmet Square.

LEAP CASTLE

South-east of Birr between Kinnitty and Roscrea (in Tipperary) are the remains of Leap Castle, in one of the few areas of Offaly rich in pre-Christian ring forts and burial mounds. It was originally an O'Carroll family residence, keeping guard over a crucial route between Munster and Leinster, and was renowned for a 'smelly ghost'; indeed it was said by locals to be one of the most haunted castles in Europe. It was destroyed in 1922 during the Civil War. Today it hosts occasional Irish music sessions with Sean Ryan, arguably the best tin-whistle player in Ireland.

KINNITTY

It's a lovely journey from Birr to the hamlet of Kinnitty, a jumping-off point for the Slieve Bloom Mountains. There's also a good trip over the hills to Mountrath (County Laois), and a pleasant drive around the northern flanks of the hills between Kinnitty and Mountmellick (also in County Laois).

Places to Stay

Kinnitty is well known for its superb castle hotel, but there's other, cheaper accommodation available.

Ardmore House (☎ 0509-37009, e *ardmorehouse@eircom.net, The Walk)* Rooms including breakfast from €25 per person. This is a lovely stone house set in off the main road, about 200m from Kinnitty. Brass beds, turf fires and home-made brown bread are the order of the day.

Kinnitty Castle (☎ 0509-37318, fax 37284, e *kinnittycastle@eircom.net, Kinnitty)* Singles/doubles from €152/305. Three kilometres south-east of town, this former O'Carroll residence is one of Ireland's most renowned castles. Now a luxury hotel, it is popular for celebrity weddings, especially from Britain.

BANAGHER & AROUND
☎ 0509 • pop 1414

While a post office clerk in the quiet riverside town of Banagher in 1841, Anthony

Trollope (1815–82) wrote his first novel, *The Macdermots of Ballycloran*. Charlotte Brontë (1816–55) honeymooned here, and her husband, the Reverend Arthur Bell Nicholls, stayed on after she died in England. Cuba Ave is named after local boy George Frazer, who became governor of that island.

There is a tourist information desk (☎ 51458) in Crank House on Main St, and some pleasant pubs and restaurants.

Things to See & Do

About 3km south of Banagher and 10km north-west of Birr, in Lusmagh near the confluence of the Rivers Little Brosna and Shannon, is **Cloghan Castle** (☎ *51650, Banagher; minimum €32 per tour; open for tours by prior arrangement only)*. The well preserved Norman keep has an adjoining 19th-century house and protective walls. Cloghan Castle has been in use for nearly 800 years. The first castle was a McCoghlan stronghold, which was later taken over by the mighty O'Carroll clan, and over the course of its history the castle has seen more than its fair share of bloodshed. The present owner has brought together a very interesting and varied assortment of antiques. Pride of place in the main hall goes to the enormous antlers of an Irish elk. At the end of the hour-long tour, visitors can examine Cromwellian armaments in the rustic dining room and marvel at just how heavy the breastplates were. There's no bus service, but the owners will collect people from Crank House by arrangement.

Twenty kilometres south of the castle is **Emmell Castle** (☎ *0506-52566)*, also owned by the Thompsons, which can be rented by the week.

Seven kilometres north-east of Banagher is **Cloghan**, where all six roads out of town lead into wide tracts of peat. Five kilometres from Cloghan, on the road north-westwards to Shannonbridge, 16th-century **Clonony Castle's** four-storey square tower is enclosed by an overgrown castellated wall. Stories that Henry VIII's second wife, Anne Boleyn, was born here are unlikely to be true, but her cousins Elizabeth and Mary Boleyn are buried beside the ruins.

Eight kilometres south of Banagher on

the County Galway side of the border is the delightful **Meelick Church**, one of the oldest still in use in Ireland.

You can hire canoes for trips on the River Shannon or Grand Canal from **Shannon Adventure Canoeing Holidays** (☎ *51411, 21 Cuba Ave*).

Places to Stay & Eat

Crank House Hostel (☎ *51458, fax 51798, Main St*) Beds in 2- & 4-bed rooms €10.15 per person. Open year round. This excellent IHH is the only hostel in the region. Crank House also contains the tourist information desk, an exhibition room for local artists and the office of Crann (☎ *51718*), set up to restore some of the deciduous trees that once covered much of Ireland. At the back is *Alma's Traditional Irish Coffee Shop*, open until 6pm daily.

Ashling (☎ *51228, Cuba Ave*) Singles/doubles with bathroom €28/45. This is a good, basic spot to spend the night.

Hayes B&B (☎ *51360*, e *elyocarroll@tinet.ie, Main St*) Singles/doubles with bathroom from €28/46. This is a fairly comfortable house.

The Vine House (☎ *51463, Main St*) Mains from €8.50. This pub and restaurant is a popular stop with people cruising the Shannon, who come for the good food and pleasant ambience.

Entertainment

JJ Hough's (☎ *51893, Main St*) In the evening you could do worse than head for this pretty, vine-draped 'singing pub'.

Getting There & Away

Kearn's Coaches (☎ *22244*) includes Banagher on its daily Portumna–Dublin service.

SHANNONBRIDGE

☎ 0905 • pop 266

At otherwise unremarkable Shannonbridge a narrow bridge crosses the river into County Roscommon. Look for the 19th-century **fort**, on the western bank just up from the bridge, where heavy artillery was placed to bombard Napoleon lest he was cheeky enough to try to invade via the river.

Bord na Móna Bog Rail Tour on Clonmacnoise & West Offaly Railway, Blackwater Railway (☎ *74114*) Adult/student/child €5/3.75/3.20. Trips leave on the hour 10am-5pm daily Apr-Oct. Just south of Shannonbridge, this 45-minute tour takes you through the Blackwater section of the Bog of Allen on the narrow-gauge line which used to transport the peat. A green-and-yellow diesel locomotive pulls one carriage at an average speed of 24km/h across 9km of bog rail (only a tiny section of the nearly 1200km of railway in the area). During the trip, you'll be told about the bog landscape and its special flora, which has remained unchanged for thousands of years.

The journey begins near the Bord na Móna Blackwater (Uisce Dubh in Irish) peat-fired power station, which is visible for miles around. Tickets are available from the coffee shop.

CLONMACNOISE

This is Ireland's most important monastic site (☎ *0905-74195, Shannonbridge; adult/student/child €3.80/2.55/1.60; open 9am-6pm daily mid-Mar-mid-Sept; 10am-5pm daily mid-Sept-mid-Mar*). It is superbly placed, overlooking the River Shannon from a ridge, and consists of a walled field containing numerous early churches, high crosses, round towers and graves in remarkably good condition. The site is surrounded by marshy ground and fields known as the Shannon Callows. These are home to many wild plants and are one of the last refuges of the seriously endangered corncrake (see the boxed text 'The Corncrake Crisis' in the County Donegal chapter).

History

Of the several monastic sites that dot the edges of this section of the Shannon, this is by far the most spectacular, ranking alongside Glendalough in Wicklow as the country's most important. Roughly translated, Clonmacnoise (Cluain Mhic Nóis) means 'Meadow of the Sons of Nós'. The glacial ridge called the Esker Riada (Highway of the Kings) on which it stands was once one of the principal cross-country routes between

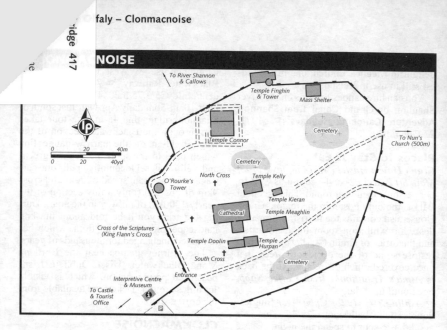

Leinster and Connaught. St Ciarán, the son of a chariot-maker, is said to have founded the monastery in 548 and died only seven months later after building the first church with the assistance of Diarmuid, the high king of Tara.

The monastery's beginning was humble as only eight followers of Ciarán had set out with him, but it soon became an unrivalled bastion of Irish religion, literature and art. Between the 7th and 12th centuries monks from all over Europe came to study and pray here. Clonmacnoise was one of the reasons Ireland became known as the 'island of saints and scholars' while much of Europe languished in the Dark Ages. Such was its importance that the high kings of Connaught and Tara were brought here for burial; many lie in the cathedral, or the Church of Kings, among them the last high king of Tara, Rory O'Connor, who died in 1198.

Most of the remains date from the 10th to 12th centuries; earlier buildings of wood, clay and wattle have long since disappeared. The monks would have lived in small huts scattered in and around the monastery, which would probably have been surrounded by a ditch or rampart of earth. It was recorded that

there were 106 houses and 13 churches here in 1179, when the site was ravaged by fire. These scattered Irish sites contrast with the strict layout and planning of monasteries elsewhere in Europe.

The river became a deadly conduit when Viking raiders used it to penetrate into the heart of Ireland. Clonmacnoise was pillaged repeatedly between 830 and 1165 (records suggest on at least eight occasions). The Vikings were not the only ones guilty of attacks: the monastery was burned at least 12 times between 720 and 1205, and attacked 27 times by native Irish forces between 830 and 1165. After the 12th century, it fell into decline and by the 15th century it was home to a bishop of only minor importance. The end came in 1552 when it was plundered by the English regiment based in Athlone: 'Not a bell, large or small, or an image, or an altar, or a book, or a gem, or even glass in a window, was left which was not carried away.'

Among the treasures that survived the continued onslaught are the crozier of the abbots of Clonmacnoise in the National Museum, Dublin, and the 12th-century *Leabhar na hUidhre* (The Book of the Dun Cow), now in the Royal Irish Academy in Dublin.

Information
Dúchas provides a museum, an on-site interpretive centre and coffee shop. The tourist office (☎ 0905-74134) in the car park opens April to September.

Visiting early or late will help you avoid the crowds. The 20-minute audiovisual show provides a good introduction to the site.

High Crosses
In the compound are three replicas of 9th-century high crosses (the originals are now in the museum for protection). The sandstone **Cross of the Scriptures** is the most richly decorated and has unique upwards-tilted arms. Its western face depicts the crucifixion, soldiers guarding Jesus' tomb and the arrest of Jesus. On the eastern face are scenes of St Ciaran and King Diarmuid placing the corner stone of the cathedral. It's also known as King Flann's Cross because a rough inscription on the base is said to attribute it to him. He died in 916.

Nearer the river the **North Cross** dates from around 800. Only the shaft remains, adorned by lions, rich spirals and a single figure, thought to be the Celtic god Cerrunnos or Carnunas, who sits in a Buddha-like position. The two-headed snake is associated with him. The richly decorated **South Cross** has more carvings, including the crucifixion on the western face.

Cathedral
The biggest building at Clonmacnoise, the cathedral, or MacDermot's Church, was built in the 12th century but incorporates part of a 10th-century church. Its most interesting feature is the intricate 15th-century Gothic doorway with carvings of St Francis, St Patrick and St Dominic and a badly worn Latin inscription which, roughly translated, says: 'This doorway was erected for the eternal glory of God.'

The door is also known as the Whispering Door because a whisper carries from one side of it to the other. It's said that lepers would come here to confess because the door's acoustics would let the priest hear their confession from a safe distance.

The last high kings of Tara – Turlough Mór

MATT KING

The Cross of the Scriptures, Clonmacnoise

O'Connor (died 1156) and his son Ruairí or Rory (died 1198) – are said to be buried near the altar.

Temples
The small churches are called temples, a derivation of the Irish word *teampall* (church). Past the scant foundations of **Temple Kelly** (1167) is the tiny **Temple Kieran**, less than 4m long and 2.5m wide. Also known as St Ciarán's Church, it's believed to be the burial place of St Ciarán, the site's founder. His hand was kept here as a relic until the 16th century, but is now lost. The remarkable crozier of the abbots and a chalice are supposed to have been discovered here in the 19th century.

The floor level in Temple Kieran is lower than outside because local farmers have for centuries been taking clay from the church to place in the four corners of their fields, where it's said to protect crops against an eelworm parasite and cattle against redwater disease. The floor was covered in slabs to stop further digging but even today handfuls of clay are removed from outside the church in the early spring.

Near the temple's south-western corner is a *bullaun* (an ancient grinding stone), supposedly used for making medicines for the monastery's hospital. Today the rainwater that collects in it is supposed to cure warts.

CENTRAL SOUTH

Continuing round the compound you come to the 12th-century **Temple Meaghlin**, with its attractive windows, and the twin structures of **Temple Hurpan** and **Temple Doolin**. Doolin is named after Edmund Dowling, who repaired it in 1689 and made it the family crypt. At the same time he may have restored Temple Hurpan, which is also known as Claffey's Church.

Round Towers

Overlooking the River Shannon is the truncated O'Rourke's Tower, a 20m-high tower named after the high king of Connaught, Fergal O'Rourke (died 964). The top of the tower is said to have been blown apart by lightning in 1135, but the tower was used until 1552.

Temple Finghin and its round tower are on the northern boundary of the site, also overlooking the Shannon. The quaint building, also known as MacCarthy's Church and Tower, appears in most photographs of Clonmacnoise and dates from around 1160 to 1170. It has some fine Romanesque carvings and the unusual miniature tower's cone roof has stones set in a herringbone pattern. This is the only Irish round tower roof that has never been altered. Most such towers were used by monks for protection when their monasteries were attacked, but this one was probably used as a bell tower as the doorway is at ground level.

Other Remains

Still used by Church of Ireland parishioners on the last Sunday of the summer months, **Temple Connor** is a little, roofed church. Beyond the site's boundary wall, 500m east through the modern graveyard, is the secluded **Nun's Church** with wonderful Romanesque arches; it's well worth seeking out. West of the church is a **cairn** said to mark the burial place of a servant of St Ciarán who was supposedly refused burial in the monastery graveyard after losing the saint's dun cow.

On the ridge near the car park is a motte with the oddly shaped ruins of a 13th-century **castle**. John de Grey, bishop of Norwich, is said to have had it built to watch over the Shannon.

Museum

The three beehive-like structures near the entrance are a museum echoing the design of the early monastic dwellings. It contains the originals of the three principal high crosses and various artefacts uncovered during excavation, including silver pins, beaded glass and an ogham stone.

The museum also contains many of Clonmacnoise's 8th- to 12th-century graveslabs, the largest collection of early-Christian graveslabs in Europe. Many are in remarkable condition with inscriptions clearly visible, often starting with '*oroit do*' or '*ar*', meaning 'a prayer for'.

Places to Stay

Glebe Touring Caravan & Camping Park (☎ 0902-30277, Clonfanlough) Sites €11.50. Open Easter-mid-Sept. This caravan park on the edge of the village of Clonfanlough, 5km east of Clonmacnoise, is in a beautiful rural setting. Amenities include a modern shower and toilet block, TV and games room, laundry, baby-changing room and kitchen.

Kajon House (☎/fax 0905-74191, Creevagh) Rooms including breakfast with/without bathroom €25.50/20.50 per person. Open Feb-Oct. This bungalow is on the road signposted to Tullamore, about 1.5km from the ruins.

Meadowview (☎ 0905-74257, Clonmacnoise) Rooms including breakfast from €28 per person. Open Apr-Sept. This pleasant B&B is only 1km from the entrance to the ruins.

Getting There & Away

Clonmacnoise is 7km north of Shannonbridge and about 24km south of Athlone. From Dublin, Bus Éireann (☎ 01-836 6111) runs buses only as far as Athlone (single/return €9.30/14, two hours, hourly), but Paddy Kavanagh (☎ 0902-74839, 087 240 7706) runs a minibus to Clonmacnoise from Athlone (return €12.70), departing Athlone Castle at 11am and returning at 2pm. To visit both Clonmacnoise and the West Offaly Railway (see Shannonbridge earlier in this chapter) costs €19.

There are river cruises to Clonmacnoise

from Athlone in County Westmeath; see River Cruises under Athlone in the Central North chapter for details.

TULLAMORE
☎ 0506 • pop 9221

Tullamore (Tulach Mór), Offaly's county town 80km due west of Dublin on the Grand Canal, is pleasant enough to while away a few hours, with Charleville Forest Castle the main attraction.

You may be familiar with the name from the whiskey that was produced here; it is thought that Tullamore Dew is the easiest of Irish whiskies to drink by virtue of its smooth bouquet and gentle flavour. The town likes to advertise its whiskey-making tradition, despite the fact that the distillery has long since moved to Clonmel, County Tipperary.

Founded in 1750 by the Bury family of Limerick, Tullamore soon superseded Philipstown (now Daingean) as the county capital. In 1785 a hot-air balloon crashed and started a fire that consumed hundreds of homes!

Information
The tourist office (☎ 52617), on Bury Quay between the defunct Irish Mist factory and the canal, opens Monday to Friday, June to September. The post office faces O'Connor Square, which is little more than a car park.

Charleville Forest Castle
Sitting in a large estate to the west of the town centre is the great neo-Gothic structure of Charleville Forest Castle (☎ 21279; 30-minute tour booked in advance adult/child €4.45/2.55). What some call a 'Gothic fantasy castle', due to its spires and turrets, was the family seat of the Burys, who in 1798 commissioned the design from Francis Johnston, one of Ireland's most famous architects.

From the entrance on Charleville Rd, south of town on the road to Limerick, there's a rough 1.5km lane (take the right fork after you enter the gate) to the castle itself which is popular with joggers. (Tullamore Harriers is one of Ireland's premier running clubs.) The present owners of the castle intend to restore the property and turn it into a classy hotel.

Tours must be booked in advance; if you haven't booked, your best hope of tagging onto a tour is 11am to 5pm Wednesday to Sunday, June to September, or at the weekend only during April and May. The castle grounds are also worth exploring.

Tullamore Dew Heritage Centre
In the same building as the tourist office is the heritage centre (☎ 25015, W www.tullamore-dew.org, Bury Quay; adult/student/child €4.50/3.50/2.90; open 9am-6pm Mon-Sat & noon-5pm Sun May-Sept; 10am-5pm Mon-Sat & noon-5pm Sun Oct-Apr). It tells the story of Tullamore Dew whiskey and the importance of the distillery in the town's development. At the end of your visit, you get to sample a glass of this fine liquor.

Cruises
Celtic Canal Cruisers (☎ 21861) Boats for 2 people in the low season €530, for 9 people in July up to €1610. You can cruise west to the River Shannon, joining it at Shannon Harbour, or east to Edenderry, Laytown and down into the Grand Canal and River Barrow systems.

Places to Stay & Eat
High House (☎ 51358, Main St) Rooms from €35.50 per person. With comfortable rooms, High House is the more preferable of the two hotels on the main street, though neither is ideal because of the noise of traffic roaring through.

Tullamore Court Hotel (☎ 46666, fax 46677, O'Moore St) Singles/doubles €121/204. Incredibly expensive for the town, this hotel is about as modern and amenity-stocked as Tullamore is ever likely to get; guests have free access to the leisure centre and swimming pool.

Bridge House Inn (☎ 45916, Bridge St) This inn seems to be the most popular place to eat. It has a familiar mix of grills and steaks.

Getting There & Away
Bus The Bus Éireann (☎ 21431) stop is at the train station, south of town on Western Relief Rd off Charleville Rd. From Tullamore there

is one bus daily each way on the route between Dublin (single/return €10.20/14, 1¾ hours) and Portumna (€8.90/13.35, one hour), and one daily on the route between Waterford (€13/19, 3½ hours) and Longford (€10.20/14, 1½ hours). Kearn's Coaches (☎ 0509-22244) runs services from Tullamore on its Dublin–Portumna route: three buses a day on Monday, Friday and Sunday, two on Saturday and one a day Tuesday and Wednesday.

Train There are eight trains a day Monday to Saturday (five on Sunday) to Dublin (single/return €12.10/20.35, one hour) and Galway (€20.95/29.20, 2½ hours).

DURROW ABBEY

St Colmcille (also known as St Columba) founded a monastery at Durrow Abbey in the 6th century, and the monastery's scriptorium later produced the Book of Durrow, a Latin gospel. The book was kept here for over 800 years until the dissolution of the monasteries, when it fell into the hands of a local farmer. The book's bright illustrations survived being immersed in his cattle's drinking water to ward off evil spirits. In 1661 the local bishop gave it to Trinity College, Dublin, where it can be seen today.

The Book of Durrow fared better than the rest of the monastery, which was damaged in 1186 by Hugh de Lacy. He literally lost his head in the process when a local man took exception to his using the monastery stones to build a castle on the mound nearby.

Today, the site's only prominent structures are a Georgian mansion and a derelict 19th-century Protestant church. Some high kings of Tara are said to have been buried here.

The remains include St Colmcille's Well to the north-east of the church and a 10th-century high cross. The eastern face of the cross shows King David, Abraham's sacrifice of Isaac and the Last Judgement, while the western face shows soldiers guarding Jesus' tomb and the crucifixion.

Durrow Abbey is 7km north of Tullamore down a long lane west off the N52 Kilbeggan road.

EDENDERRY
☎ 0405 • pop 3591

On the River Boyne bordering County Kildare and the Bog of Allen, Edenderry is 16km north-east of Daingean. Although it sprang to life with the arrival of the Grand Canal in 1802, Edenberry goes back to the 14th century and the de Berminghams, whose ruined **Carrickoris Castle** is 7km north of town on Carrick Hill. The name Edenderry came from the oak woods that once blanketed the hills around the town. The local O'Connor family used to harry the English and retreat into the bogs that cover the region. The post office is on the oddly named JKL St (named after Bishop Doyle, better known as JKL – James of Kildare and Leighin).

Three kilometres north-west on the Rhode road is the scanty monastic site of **Monasteroris**. It was built for the Franciscans by John de Bermingham in 1325 to ease his conscience over his father's massacre of 32 local chieftains 20 years earlier in Carrickoris Castle.

There's a pleasant **walk** from the imposing town hall along the canal out to the Downshire Bridge.

Places to Stay & Eat

Auburn Lodge (☎ 31319, @ auburnlodge@ eircom.net, Colonel Perry St) Rooms €25 per person. This cosy guesthouse is in the middle of town.

The Coffee Shop (☎ 32426, O'Connell Square) Breakfast €4.50. This restaurant serves plain, dependable food.

Getting There & Away

Bus Éireann (☎ 01-836 6111) has a service to Dublin (€7.40/10.80, 1½ hours) every half-hour Monday to Friday (11 on Saturday, six on Sunday). A single daily bus goes to and from Tullamore, Banagher and Birr.

County Clare

Clare (An Clár) may not receive the attention of Kerry or Galway, but it does have its own special attractions. It's almost a peninsula, with the Shannon Estuary cutting deep into its southern border and Galway Bay on its northern side. Wedged between Kerry and Galway, Clare's land is mostly poor, with a large sweep of limestone rock in the north of the county forming the unique, fascinating Burren region. The landscape of the Burren contains countless monuments, castles and rare flowers, and there are some wonderful walks. The county has some spectacular scenery, particularly around the Cliffs of Moher.

Many of Clare's towns and villages have resisted the commercialisation and 'prettification' of more heavily touristed places in Ireland. Ennis, Clare's county town, retains its charming narrow streets, while villages such as Ennistymon have many old shops, and pubs that host traditional music sessions on summer evenings. Two villages have become magnets for particular types of visitors. Doolin attracts music lovers and backpackers, while genteel Ballyvaughan is a weekend seaside retreat for the more well heeled.

The county has some 250 castles in various stages of preservation: Knappogue near Quin and the famous tower house at Bunratty are fine examples. As for activities, there's scuba diving at Kilkee, Doolin and Fanore, excellent rock climbing at Ballyreen near Fanore, and caving is possible all over the Burren.

The shortest route to Clare if you're travelling north up the coast is via the car ferry from Tarbert in County Kerry to Killimer.

Ennis & Around

ENNIS
☎ 065 • pop 15,300

Ennis (Inis), Clare's principal town, is a busy market centre and one of the Republic's larger towns. It lies on the banks of the River Fergus, which runs east then south into the

Shannon Estuary. The town's medieval origins are visible in its narrow streets, and there are many old shops and pubs. The most important historical site is Ennis Friary, founded in the 13th century by the O'Briens, kings of Thomond, who also built a castle in Ennis in the 13th century. Much of the wooden town was destroyed by fire in 1249

CLARE

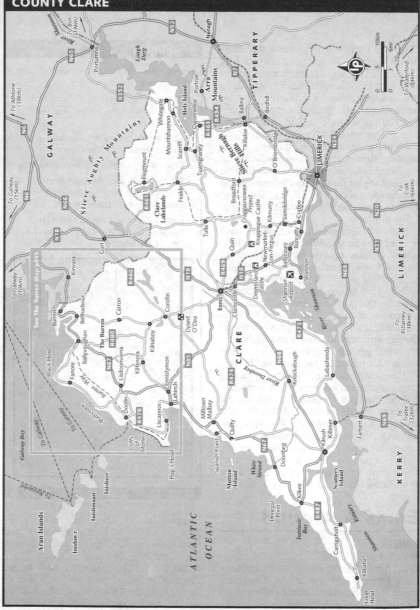

COUNTY CLARE

and again in 1306, when it was razed by one of the O'Briens.

In the town centre is a memorial to Daniel O'Connell, whose election to the British Parliament by a huge majority in 1828 forced Britain to lift its bar on Catholic MPs and led to the Act of Catholic Emancipation a year later.

Eamon de Valera was teachta Dála (TD; member of the Irish Parliament) for Clare from 1917 to 1959. There's a bronze statue of him near the courthouse.

Orientation

The old town centre is on O'Connell Square, and the principal streets – O'Connell St, High St (becoming Parnell St), Bank Place and Abbey St – radiate from there. The large but not particularly attractive cathedral (1843) is at the southern end of O'Connell St.

Information

The excellent tourist office (☎ 682 8366), on Arthur's Row, opens 9.30am to 6.30pm daily, June to September; 9.30am to 1pm and 2pm to 5.30pm Monday to Saturday, April to May and October; and 9.30am to 1pm and 2pm to 5.30pm Monday to Friday, November to March.

You can change money at the Bank of Ireland (which also has an ATM) and Ulster Bank, both on O'Connell Square.

The post office is on Bank Place, northwest of O'Connell Square. De Valera Library (☎ 682 1616), on Harmony Row, offers free Internet access 10am to 5.30pm Monday, Wednesday and Thursday; 10am to 8pm Tuesday and Friday; and 10am to 2pm on Saturday.

Ennis Bookshop (☎ 682 9000), 13 Abbey St, is good for maps and books of local interest.

Ennis Friary

Just north of O'Connell Square is Ennis Friary (☎ 682 9100, Abbey St; adult/concession €1.30/0.50; open 10am-6pm daily June-mid-Sept; 10am-5pm Tues-Sun mid-May & mid-Sept-Oct). It was founded by Donnchadh Cairbreach O'Brien, king of Thomond, some time between 1240 and 1249, though a lot of the present structure was completed in the 14th century. Partly restored, it has a graceful five-section window dating from the late 13th century and a McMahon tomb (1460) with alabaster panels depicting scenes from the Passion, including the entombment of Christ. At the height of its fame in the 15th century, the friary was one of Ireland's great centres of learning, with over 300 monks in residence. They were expelled in 1692.

Being a Dúchas site, Ennis Friary offers the usual informative guided tours in season.

Clare Museum

Close to the tourist office is this modern museum (☎ 682 3382, Arthur's Row; adults/children €3.80/1.90; open 9.30am-6.30pm daily June-Sept; 9.30am-1pm & 2pm-5.30pm Mon-Sat Apr-May & Oct; 9.30am-1pm & 2pm-5.30pm Mon-Fri Nov-Mar). The 'Riches of Clare' exhibition tells the story of Clare from 6000 years ago to the present day using original artefacts and audiovisual presentations. It also relates the development of the submarine by Clare-born JP Holland.

Special Events

Fleadh Nua (☎ 684 2988, e ceoltrad@ eircom.net), a lively traditional music festival with singing, dancing and workshops, takes place in late May.

Places to Stay

Abbey Tourist Hostel (☎ 682 2620, Harmony Row) Dorms/private rooms €12.50/ 19 per person including light breakfast. Open year round. Most dorms at this pleasant hostel, close to the centre, have four beds. There are clean showers (towels provided) and, as well as the free breakfast, guests can prepare their own food in the kitchen.

Aín Karem (☎ 682 0024, 7 Tulla Rd) Singles/doubles €28/44. North-east of the centre, Aín Karem is in a comfortable two-storey house; buses stop outside.

Ardlee House (☎ 682 0256, Clare Rd) Singles/doubles with bathroom €34/46. Ardlee is a pleasant bungalow that has

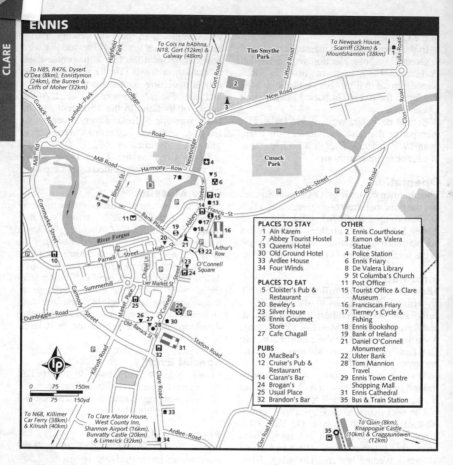

ENNIS

To Cois na hAbhna,
N18, Gort (12km) &
Galway (48km)

To Newpark House,
Scarriff (32km) &
Mountshannon (38km)

Tim Smythe
Park

To N85, R476, Dysert
O'Dea (8km), Ennistymon
(24km), the Burren &
Cliffs of Moher (32km)

Cusack
Park

River Fergus

Arthur's
Row

O'Connell
Square

To N68,
Killimer
Car Ferry (38km)
& Kilrush (40km)

To Clare Manor House,
West County Inn,
Shannon Airport (16km),
Bunratty Castle (20km)
& Limerick (32km)

To Quin (8km),
Knappogue Castle
(10km) & Craggaunowen
(12km)

0   75   150m
0   75   150yd

PLACES TO STAY	OTHER
1 Ain Karem	2 Ennis Courthouse
7 Abbey Tourist Hostel	3 Eamon de Valera
13 Queens Hotel	Statue
30 Old Ground Hotel	4 Police Station
33 Ardlee House	6 Ennis Friary
34 Four Winds	8 De Valera Library
	9 St Columba's Church
PLACES TO EAT	11 Post Office
5 Cloister's Pub &	15 Tourist Office & Clare
Restaurant	Museum
20 Bewley's	16 Franciscan Friary
23 Silver House	17 Tierney's Cycle &
26 Ennis Gourmet	Fishing
Store	18 Ennis Bookshop
27 Cafe Chagall	19 Bank of Ireland
	21 Daniel O'Connell
PUBS	Monument
10 MacBeal's	22 Ulster Bank
12 Cruise's Pub &	28 Tom Mannion
Restaurant	Travel
14 Ciaran's Bar	29 Ennis Town Centre
24 Brogan's	Shopping Mall
25 Usual Place	31 Ennis Cathedral
32 Brandon's Bar	35 Bus & Train Station

comfortably furnished rooms and a rear car park.

Four Winds (☎ 682 9831, Clare Rd) Singles/doubles with bathroom €38.10/55.90. Open mid-Mar–mid-Oct. This B&B has five rooms and a garden; it accepts credit cards.

Clare Manor House (☎/fax 682 0701, Clare Rd) Nonsmoking rooms with bathroom & TV €23.95 per person. This semi-Tudor-style property, about 1.5km south of the centre, has six well appointed rooms.

Newpark House (☎ 682 1233, e newparkhouse.ennis@eircom.net, Tulla Rd) Singles/doubles from €44/64. Open Easter–Oct.

This beautiful country manor dating from 1650 is 2km north of Ennis. To get there go along the Scarriff road (R352) and turn right at the Roselevan Arms. It is finely furnished and has excellent, home-cooked breakfasts.

Old Ground Hotel (☎ 682 8127, fax 682 8112, O'Connell St) Rooms €44.50-76.20 per person. This lovely old hotel with a modern rear extension provides 83 deluxe rooms in the centre of town.

Queens Hotel (☎ 682 8963, fax 682 8628, Abbey St) Rooms €44.50-76.20 per person. This is a comfortable 30-room hotel.

West County Hotel (☎ 682 8421, fax 682

3759, Clare Rd) Rooms €31.75-82.55 person. Just south of Ennis, this large hotel has spacious rooms, a play centre for children and a leisure centre that includes no less than three pools.

Places to Eat

Cruise's Pub and Restaurant (☎ 684 1800, Abbey St) Mains €6.95-13.25. Bar food 3.30pm-9pm, restaurant 6pm-9pm. Built in 1658, this place is full of old-world character and is excellent for a drink and a meal.

Brogan's (☎ 682 9859, O'Connell St) Lunch mains €6-12, dinner mains €10-21. Here you can eat good pub food in cosy snugs in the front dining area.

Brandon's Bar (☎ 682 8133, O'Connell St) Mains €6-7. Food served 12.30pm-4pm. Brandon's is an authentic old pub, serving reasonably priced, honest fare like roast beef or Irish stew.

Old Ground Hotel (☎ 682 8127, O'Connell St) Mains €6.30-11.35. Rock-solid Irish fare (cabbage and piles of spuds etc), with some French influence, is served at tables in the bar of this grand old hotel.

Silver House (☎ 682 9491, O'Connell St) Lunch mains around €7.30. A good choice for rice and noodles, it has an extensive evening menu but offers better value at lunch-time.

Cloister's Pub and Restaurant (☎ 682 9521, Abbey St) Mains around €17.50, 4-course dinner €22.60. Food served noon-10pm. Here the emphasis is on the food rather than the drink; it serves superior meat and fish dishes, and a good-value four-course dinner.

Ennis Gourmet Store (☎ 684 3314, Old Barrack St) Sandwiches €3.15-4.40, salads around €5.65. This is a tiny but excellent cafe-delicatessen; try the local cheeses or the home-made jams.

Cafe Chagall (Old Barrack St) Panini & salads €4.90-5.55. Here you can get good coffee and a delicious panini filled with organic cheeses, browse the second-hand books and see the display of colourful paintings on the walls.

Bewley's (☎ 684 0461, Bank Place) Sandwiches around €3.15, meals around €6.60.

This branch of the Dublin institution has a cosy dining area at street level and a large, busy self-service area upstairs.

JD's Coffee House (☎ 684 1630, Merchant's Square) Mains €3.70-6.95. Open 7.30am-6pm Mon-Sat. Friendly JD's serves breakfast till noon including a massive 'mega breakfast', and has a good selection of sandwiches, baguettes and cakes.

Entertainment

As the capital of a renowned music county, Ennis is not short of good music pubs.

Cruise's Pub and Restaurant (see Places to Eat) Cruise's congenial bar is one of the best places for traditional music, with sessions nightly from 9.30pm.

Ciaran's Bar (☎ 684 0180, Francis St) This small, cosy place is popular with the local football crowd and has Irish music on Friday evening.

Brandon's Bar (see Places to Eat) Brandon's has live music several nights a week from traditional Irish to blues to glam rock; also here is the Bordwalk nightclub for late-night drinking and dancing.

MacBeal's (☎ 682 0211, Cornmarket St) This big pub attracts a mixed crowd with its jazz, blues and retro music and its weekend nightclub.

Usual Place (☎ 682 0515, Upper Market Place) This attractive, old-style local in an ancient stone building is good for a quiet tipple.

Cois na hAbhna (☎ 682 0996, Gort Rd) At this low, pentagonal music hall, 1.5km north of town along the N18, a *ceilidh* (a session of traditional music and dancing) is held 8.30pm to 11pm on Wednesday night, year round (€2.50). There's an *oiche ceilidh* (music night) from 9.30pm to 11.30pm most Saturdays (€6). Its shop has a good selection of tapes, books and records for sale.

Shopping

On Saturday, there is a *market* at the Market Place. For general shopping, use the huge *Ennis Town Centre* mall, which contains Dunnes supermarket and can be entered halfway down O'Connell St.

Getting There & Away

Bus The Bus Éireann depot (☎ 682 4177) is at the train station. Buses run from Ennis to Limerick (40 minutes) up to 16 times a day Monday to Saturday (15 on Sunday). There are 12 direct buses to Dublin (four hours) Monday to Saturday (10 on Sunday), 14 daily to Galway (two hours), 12 to Cork (three hours) and up to seven a day (four on Sunday) to Shannon Airport (30 minutes).

Train From Ennis station (☎ 684 0444), direct trains for Dublin (three hours) via Limerick leave twice a day Monday to Saturday (once a day on Sunday). There are frequent trains between Dublin and Limerick, 37km south-east of Ennis; check with Limerick train station (☎ 061-313333).

Getting Around

For a taxi call Burren Taxis (☎ 682 3456) or pick one up at the taxi stands at the train station and beside the Daniel O'Connell Monument.

Tierney's Cycles and Fishing (☎ 682 9433), 17 Abbey St, has well maintained mountain bikes costing €15.20/50.40 per day/week, which includes a helmet, lock and repair kit. Tom Mannion Travel (☎ 682 4211), 71 O'Connell St, can fix you up with anything from a car to a motor home.

AROUND ENNIS

North of Ennis is the early-Christian site of Dysert O'Dea; to the south-east are several fine castles.

Getting Around

Local and express buses cover most areas around Ennis, but their frequency varies; many buses run only May to September (some only July and August) and on certain days. Before making plans confirm times and destinations with Ennis bus station (☎ 065-682 4177).

You can pick up the express bus service between Galway and Limerick in Ennis (up to 14 times daily) to get to Clarecastle, Newmarket-on-Fergus and Bunratty, but many stops on the route are 'request only'. Bus No 334 also operates daily to Limerick

via Clarecastle, Newmarket-on-Fergus and sometimes Bunratty. On weekdays an infrequent service goes north-west to Ennistymon, then south along the coast to Kilkee.

Dysert O'Dea

On the Corofin road (R476) 9km north of Ennis is Dysert O'Dea, the site where St Tola founded a monastery in the 8th century. The church and high cross, the White Cross of St Tola, date from the 12th or 13th centuries. The cross depicts Daniel in the lions' den on one side and a crucified Christ above a bishop carved in relief. Look for carvings of animal and human heads in a semicircle on the southern doorway of the Romanesque church. There are also the remains of a 12m-high round tower.

In 1318, the O'Briens, who were kings of Thomond, and the Norman de Clares of Bunratty fought a pitched battle nearby, which the O'Briens won, thus postponing the Anglo-Norman conquest of Clare for some two centuries. The 15th-century O'Dea Castle nearby houses the **Clare Archaeology Centre** (☎ *065-683 7401, Corofin; adult/concession €4.50/2.25; open 10am-6pm daily May-Sept*). A 3km history trail around the castle passes some two dozen ancient monuments – from ring forts and high crosses to an ancient cooking site.

South of Dysert O'Dea off the N18 is **Dromore Wood** (☎ *065-683 7166, Ruan; free; visitor centre open 10am-6pm daily mid-June-mid-Sept, wood open daylight hours year round*). This Dúchas nature reserve encompasses some 400 hectares as well as the ruins of the 17th-century O'Brien Castle, two ring forts and the site of Kilakee church.

Getting There & Away In July and August, Bus Éireann (☎ 065-682 4177) runs one bus a day Monday to Friday from Limerick (20 minutes), which leaves Ennis for Corofin and Ennistymon at 2.10pm, passing Dysert O'Dea en route. The rest of the year, a bus departs Ennis on the same route at 3pm on weekdays and at 3.50pm on Saturday.

Quin

☎ 065 • pop 150

Quin (Chuinche), a tiny village 10km south-east of Ennis, was the site of the Great Clare Find of 1854, the most important discovery of prehistoric goldwork in Ireland. Sadly, few of the several hundred torcs, gorgets and other pieces, discovered by labourers working on the Limerick–Ennis railway, made it to the National Museum in Dublin: most were sold and melted down. The source of this and much of ancient Ireland's gold may have been the Wicklow Mountains.

Quin Abbey This is a Franciscan friary *(☎ 684 4084, Quin; free; open 10.30am-6pm Mon-Fri & 11.30am-5pm Sat & Sun May-Oct; call for viewing at other times)*. It was founded in 1433 using part of the walls of an older de Clare castle built in 1280. Despite many periods of persecution, Franciscan monks lived here until the 19th century. The last friar, Father Hogan, who died in 1820, is buried in one corner. The impressively named Fireballs McNamara, a notorious duellist and member of the region's ruling family, is also buried here. An elegant belfry rises above the main body of the abbey, and you can climb the narrow spiral staircase to look down on the fine cloister and surrounding countryside.

Beside the friary is the 13th-century Gothic **Church of St Finghin**.

Knappogue Castle

Three kilometres south-east of Quin is Knappogue Castle *(☎ 061-368103, Quin; adult/child €3.80/2.15; open 9.30am-4pm daily Apr-Oct)*. It was built in 1467 by the McNamaras, who held sway over a large part of Clare from the 5th to mid-15th centuries and built 42 castles in the region. Knappogue's huge walls are intact, and it has a fine collection of period furniture and fireplaces.

When Oliver Cromwell came to Ireland from England in 1649, he used Knappogue as a base while in the area, which is one of the reasons it was spared from destruction. The McNamara family regained the castle after the Restoration in 1660.

There's a small souvenir shop in the courtyard. Knappogue also hosts medieval banquets (☎ 061-360788); see Medieval Banquets under Bunratty in the Eastern and South-Eastern Clare section later in this chapter. Knappogue, unlike Bunratty, lays on knives and forks.

Craggaunowen Project

For a sense of Irish history visit the Craggaunowen Project *(☎ 061-367178, Quin; adult/child €6.30/3.80, family of up to 6 children €15.75; open 10am-9pm daily May-Aug; 10am-5pm daily Apr & Sept-Oct)*. Six kilometres south-east of Quin, it includes re-created ancient farms, dwellings such as a *crannóg* (artificial island) and a ring fort, plus real artefacts including a 2000 year old oak road, and related items such as Tim Severin's leather boat the *Brendan*, in which he crossed the Atlantic in 1976–77. Craggaunowen Castle is a small, well preserved McNamara fortified house. With lots of animals, some rare, this is a good place to bring kids.

The Craggaunowen Project also has a pleasant little cafe. Cullaun Lake nearby is a popular boating and picnic spot with forest trails.

Dromoland Castle

North of Newmarket-on-Fergus is Dromoland Castle *(☎ 061-368144, Newmarket-on-Fergus; rooms €185-417 per person)*. This magnificent building, constructed in 1826, is today one of Ireland's finest hotels. It sits in 220 hectares of vast, beautiful gardens by the River Fergus and has an 18-hole golf course. Inside, oak panels and silken fabrics adorn virtually every bit of wall space. A room in the hotel is beyond most travellers' budgets, but you can venture in for a drink at the bar.

Mooghaun Ring Fort In Dromoland's demesne are the remains of one of Europe's largest Iron Age hill forts: three circular earthen banks enclosing some 13 hectares. The fort's occupants may have been the owners of the huge gold hoard uncovered nearby in Quin in 1854. Access to the fort is

CLARE

through Dromoland Forest, signposted off the Newmarket–Dromoland road (N18).

Eastern & South-Eastern Clare

Clare's eastern boundary is formed by the River Shannon and long, narrow Lough Derg, which stretches some 48km from Portumna in County Galway, to just south of Killaloe. The road between the two towns swings west of the lake through some gentle countryside and picturesque hamlets, such as Mountshannon. From the high ground there are panoramic views across the lake to the Silvermine Mountains in Tipperary. Eastern Clare is fishing and shooting country, and the villages on the western shores of Lough Derg are favoured by hunters.

South-eastern Clare is visually unremarkable compared with the county's Atlantic coastline or the lakeside scenery north of Killaloe. Most people pass through quickly, taking in diversions such as Bunratty Castle or Cratloe's ancient oak woods. Some 24km west of Limerick is Shannon Airport.

SHANNON AIRPORT
☎ 061

Shannon, Ireland's second-largest airport, sits in the apparent wilderness of south-eastern Clare. It used to be a vital fuelling stop on the transatlantic air route, as piston-engined planes barely had enough range to make it across the ocean. If you fly into Shannon (Sionainn), the extensive runways and numerous departure gates will remind you of its successful past. Large-scale redevelopment to upgrade the airport is now taking place.

It's said that Irish coffee (a healthy slug of whiskey in a strong coffee topped with cream) was invented at Shannon Airport for early transatlantic passengers.

The world's first duty-free shop opened at Shannon in 1947; today, duty free is only available to those flying beyond the EU.

Information
The tourist office (☎ 471664), in the arrivals hall, opens 6am to 6pm daily; next door is the Aer Rianta (☎ 712000) desk for airport and flight information.

The Bank of Ireland (☎ 471100) opens from the first flight (about 6.30am) to 5.30pm. In Shannon Town Centre – an enclosed shopping mall in the dreary town of Shannon – there are two banks (Ulster Bank and Allied Irish Bank) and a post office.

Places to Stay
There's plenty of accommodation 5km from the airport in Shannon, Ireland's only 'new town'.

Moloney's B&B (☎ *364185, 21 Coill Mhara St)* Doubles €21.60-24.15 per person. Moloney's is a nonsmoking house with four rooms only 400m from Shannon Town Centre down a quiet cul-de-sac.

Avalon (☎/fax *362032, 11 Ballycastlemore Hill)* Singles/doubles €40.85/48.25. A spacious bungalow, it has three comfy rooms (two en suite) and views of the River Shannon.

Oak Wood Arms Hotel (☎ *361500, fax 361414, Airport Rd)* Rooms €50.80-62.20 per person. The hotel has lots of charm with its traditionally furnished rooms, oak panelling and brass fittings.

Shannon Great Southern Hotel (☎ *471 122, fax 471982, Shannon Airport)* Rooms €127 per person. This stylish hotel with 115 en-suite rooms and gym is directly in front of the airport terminal.

Places to Eat
Shannon Knights Inn (☎ *361045, Shannon Town Centre)* Meals under €8. It's worth going into town for this large pub, which serves reasonably priced bar food.

Café 2000 (☎ *361992, Shannon Town Centre)* Snacks under €6.50. Open 8am-5pm Mon-Fri, 8am-3pm Sat. This is a surprisingly stylish cafe, offering hearty snacks and good coffee.

Getting There & Away
Air For general inquiries, call the airport authority, Aer Rianta (☎ 712000). Airlines

with direct flights to Shannon include: Aer Lingus (☎ 715400), Aeroflot (☎ 715400), British Airways (☎ 472344), Delta Air Lines (☎ 471200), Servisair (☎ 472344) and Virgin Atlantic (☎ 704470).

Bus There are six Bus Éireann buses daily to Ennis (four on Sunday). The ticket office (☎ 474311) in the airport opens at 7am, the first bus leaves at 8am and the one-way fare is €4.40. There are also services to major centres including: Limerick (40 minutes, eight daily, seven on Sunday), Galway (two hours, up to five daily, one on Sunday) and Dublin (three hours 20 minutes, three daily).

Taxi A taxi to the centre of Limerick or Ennis costs about €24, with possible extra charges for luggage or 'unsociable hours'.

BUNRATTY
☎ 061

The castle at Bunratty (Bun Raite), which overlooks the Shannon Estuary, is in excellent condition and well worth a look, but it's a prime tourist attraction and is besieged by coach tours April to September. With an attached folk park and Durty Nelly's 'auld Oirish' pub nearby, the area is as close as you'll get to a medieval Irish Disneyland. Go early in the day.

A small visitor information office (☎ 364321) in Bunratty Village Mills, opposite the castle, opens 9am to 5.30pm on weekdays, year round; plus 9am to 5.30pm at the weekend, mid-May to September. It has a bureau de change and beside it is an ATM.

Bunratty Castle & Folk Park
The Vikings built a fortified settlement at this spot, a former island surrounded by a moat. Then came the Normans, and Thomas de Clare built the first stone structure on the site in the 1270s.

The present castle (☎ 361511, Bunratty; adult/child €6.50/4 including folk park, families €18.90; open 9am-4.45pm daily June-Aug; 9.30am-4.15pm daily Sept-May) is the fourth or fifth incarnation to occupy the location beside the River Ratty. It was built in the early 1400s by the energetic McNamara

family, but fell shortly thereafter to the O'Briens, kings of Thomond, in whose possession it remained until the 17th century. Admiral Penn, father of William Penn, the Quaker founder of the US state of Pennsylvania and the city of Philadelphia, resided here for a short time.

A complete restoration was carried out in modern times, and today the castle's magnificent Great Hall holds a fine collection of 14th- to 18th-century furniture, paintings and wall hangings.

Medieval Banquets The Great Hall hosts 'medieval banquets' (☎ 360788), replete with comely maidens playing the harp, court jesters cracking corny jokes, and food à la Middle Ages (a pale imitation) served by wenches and washed down with mead, a kind of honey wine. You eat with your fingers. A seat at the banquet table will set you back €41.60, and they're heavily booked with coach parties. The whole thing is stage Irish but taken in spirit can be quite fun.

The banquets at Knappogue and Dunguaire castles (the latter in Galway) are generally smaller, quieter and often more pleasant. All run two banquets at 5.30pm and 8.45pm daily subject to demand. Bunratty's runs year round, Knappogue's from May to October and Dunguaire's from May to September.

Bunratty Folk Park The folk park (open 9am-6.30pm daily June-Aug; 9.30am-6.30pm daily Sept-May) is a reconstructed traditional Irish village, with cottages, a forge and working blacksmith, weavers weaving and buttermakers making butter. There's a complete village street with post office, pub and small cafe, some of them transplanted from the site of Shannon Airport.

The **Shannon Ceilí** (bookings ☎ 360788; €37 per person; 5.30pm-8.45pm daily May-Oct; open subject to demand Nov-Apr) is held in a barn in the folk park, serving up music, dancing, wine, Irish stew, apple pie and soda bread. It's meant to demonstrate how the peasants passed their time while the gentry gorged themselves in the safety of their castles.

Places to Eat

Muses (☎ *364082, Bunratty House Mews)* Mains €18.80-22.55. In the cellar of a fine Georgian house, Muses is the best and most expensive restaurant in the area. The food, with mostly Irish ingredients, is top class. To get there head up the lane past Fitzpatrick Bunratty Shamrock Hotel.

Durty Nelly's (☎ *364861, beside Bunratty Castle)* Mains €15.10-22.70. This old-world pub serves good bar food and houses two fine restaurants: *Oyster (open noon-10.30pm daily),* downstairs, and *Loft (open 6pm-10.30pm Mon-Sat).*

Kathleen's Irish Pub (*at Bunratty Castle Hotel;* ☎ *364116)* Mains €7.60-15.20. This efficient pub serves a variety of tasty food from traditional Irish stew to pepperoni pizza.

Blarney Woollen Mills (☎ *364321, Bunratty Village Mills)* Mains €6.25-10. On the 1st floor of this store opposite the castle, there's a cafeteria-style restaurant serving snacks and light meals to weary shoppers.

Entertainment

Durty Noel's (see Places to Eat) Built in 1620, the atmosphere at Durty Nelly's is laid on by the shovel load. A peat fire burns in front of rough wooden chairs and benches. It can be good fun, and the pub attracts a local crowd as well as tourists. There's music most evenings.

Mac's Bar (☎ *361511, Bunratty Folk Park)* Mac's has Irish music on Wednesday, Friday, Saturday and Sunday evenings, June to September; at the weekend only the rest of the year. It's accessible even after the park is closed.

Kathleen's Irish Pub (at Bunratty Castle Hotel; ☎ *364116)* Kathleen's is a large, old Irish bar that hosts traditional music sessions nightly, mainly for the guests in the hotel.

Shopping

Avoca Cottage (☎ *364029, Bunratty)* Situated across the river from Durty Nelly's, it has a good selection of tweeds, crafts and woollen suits, plus Waterford crystal and Belleek pottery.

Blarney Woollen Mills (☎ *364321, Bunratty Village Mills)* This store stocks every conceivable Irish jumper (sweater), Irish linen and Tipperary crystal.

Ballycasey Craft and Design Centre (☎ *362105, Ballycasey)* This centre is home to weavers, silversmiths, leatherworkers and potters. Follow the N18 north-west from Bunratty, then take the left fork toward Shannon; Ballycasey is on the left shortly after the fork.

Getting There & Away

Up to eight Bus Éireann buses run directly from Limerick to Bunratty stopping outside the Fitzpatrick Bunratty Shamrock Hotel. Bunratty is also served by up to 17 daily buses (10 on Sunday) on the Shannon Airport–Limerick route. Contact Limerick bus station (☎ 313333) for times.

Buses travelling south through Bunratty leave Ennis daily from 10.12am onwards. Contact Ennis bus station (☎ 065-682 4177) for more details.

CRATLOE
☎ 061 • pop 100

Cratloe, 3km east of Bunratty just north of the main Limerick road (N18), is a picturesque village overlooking the Shannon Estuary. Nearby are hills covered in oak trees – a rare sight in Ireland today, although such forests once blanketed the island. The oak roof beams of Westminster Hall in London are said to be from Cratloe. To reach the woods, go along the Kilmurry road from Cratloe, under a railway bridge and turn right. There are some fine **walks** in the area and views over the estuary from Gallows Hill and Woodcock Hill.

Off the N18 is **Cratloe Woods House** (☎ *327028, Cratloe; adult/concession €3.15/ 1.90; open 2pm-6pm Mon-Sat June-mid-Sept).* This rare 17th-century longhouse is still lived in. Admission includes an excellent guided tour.

The Cratloe area has a fair selection of guesthouses.

Cratloe Heights (☎ *357253, Ballymorris, Cratloe)* Rooms €21.60-25.40 per person. Open May-Oct. This B&B has three non-smoking rooms, one with a private bathroom.

Cratloe Lodge (☎ *357168, Cratloe)*

Did someone call a taxi?

Early-Christian ruins, Clonmacnoise, Co Offaly

Cross of the Scriptures, Clonmacnoise, Co Offaly

The Burren's extraordinary limestone landscape

5000-year-old Poulnabrone Dolmen, the Burren

One of Ireland's most spectacular sights, the Cliffs of Moher, County Clare, reach up to 203m in height.

Singles/doubles €29/45.40. Cratloe Lodge is in a quiet location just off the N18 with a pub opposite. Maura and Tom, the owners, will give you a warm welcome.

While there's no bus service directly to Cratloe, plenty of buses pass through Bunratty about 3km to the west. It's a pleasant walk from there.

KILLALOE & AROUND
☎ 061 • pop 970

Killaloe (Cill Dalua) is one of the principal crossings on the River Shannon, and a fine old 13-arched bridge spans the river. Across the river and in County Tipperary, **Ballina** is Killaloe's other half and some of the better pubs and restaurants are found there. From Killaloe, the Shannon is navigable all the way north to Lough Key in County Sligo, and in summer the town is jammed with weekend sailors.

The town has a fine setting, with the Slieve Bernagh Hills rising abruptly to the west, the Arra Mountains to the east and Lough Derg at its doorstep. It's also on the 180km East Clare Way.

Orientation & Information
The narrow street running from the river on the Killaloe side is Bridge St, which turns right, becoming Main St. The tourist office (☎ 376866), in The Lock House beside Shannon Bridge in Killaloe, opens 10am to 6pm daily, May to mid-September. Below, in the same building, free Internet access is available in Killaloe Library (☎ 376062), open 10am to 1.30pm and 2.30pm to 5.30pm Monday, Tuesday and Thursday; 10am to 5.30pm and 6.30pm to 8pm Wednesday and Friday; and 10am to 2pm on Saturday.

Things to See & Do
Also known as St Flannan's Cathedral, **Killaloe Cathedral** (☎ 376687, Limerick Rd) dates from the early 13th century and was built by the O'Brien family on top of an earlier 6th-century church. There are some magnificent carvings inside around the Romanesque southern doorway, which dates from an older chapel. Next to the doorway is early-Christian **Thorgrim's Stone**, unusual

in that it bears both the old Scandinavian runic and Irish ogham scripts. It's the shaft of a stone cross and could have been carved by a converted Viking doing penance for his past sins. The runic script reads: 'Thórgrímr carved this cross.' The translation of the ogham is: 'A blessing on Thórgrímr.' In the cathedral grounds is **St Flannan's Oratory**, of 12th-century Romanesque design.

Next to the tourist office is the **Killaloe Heritage Centre** (☎ 376866, The Lock House, Bridge St; adult/child €1.90/1.30; open 10am-6pm daily May-Sept). Its exhibits deal with local history and the cathedral.

For all your fishing needs go to **TJ's Angling Centre** (☎ 376009, Main St, Ballina).

Places to Stay & Eat
There are lots of B&Bs in the area, but it's a popular getaway spot so call ahead.

Kincora House (☎ 376149, fax 375251, Church St, Killaloe) Singles/doubles €38.10/ 63.50. Run by Ursula Quirke, this central, friendly B&B is just a few doors up from the cathedral.

Simply Delicious (☎ 375335, Main St, Ballina) Mains €6.30-7.60. Local people throng to this cafe near the bridge, which opens for breakfast and serves sandwiches, snacks and hearty lunches.

Molly's Bar and Restaurant (☎ 376632, Main St, Ballina) Mains €8.85-19. This restaurant by the river seats 56, is fully licensed and dishes up good food in a friendly atmosphere.

Gooser's Bar and Eating House (☎ 376792, Main St, Ballina) Restaurant mains €18.25-35. This thatched pub has some of the best food in town; its restaurant at the back is fine though expensive. Similar but cheaper food is available in the bar.

Entertainment
The pubs usually provide some kind of music during the week. As well as Molly's and Gooser's (see Places to Stay & Eat) there are a couple of others worth mentioning.

Crotty's Bar (☎ 376965, Main St, Killaloe) Situated at the end of a courtyard behind the Crotty grocery store, this authentic local pub provides traditional music some weekends.

CLARE

Anchor Inn (☎ 376108, Bridge St, Killaloe) The friendly Anchor Inn presents set dancing on Wednesday night, and a younger crowd turns up for the disco at the weekend.

Getting There & Away
There are five Bus Éireann (☎ 313333) buses a day Monday to Saturday from Limerick to Killaloe (45 minutes). The bus stop is outside the cathedral.

KILLALOE TO MOUNTSHANNON
The journey north on either side of Lough Derg to Mountshannon, or Portroe in Tipperary, is very scenic. To get to Mountshannon from Killaloe take the Scarriff (An Scairbh) road.

About 1.5km north of Killaloe, **BealBorú** is an earthen mound or fort said to have been Kincora, the palace of the famous Irish king Brian Ború, who defeated the Vikings at the Battle of Clontarf in 1014. Traces of Bronze Age settlement have been found. With its commanding view over Lough Derg, this was obviously a site of strategic importance.

About 3km north of Killaloe is the **University of Limerick Activity Centre** (☎ 061-376622, fax 375137, ⓔ ul.activity@iol.ie, ⓦ www.ul.ie/~sports/activity.html, Two Mile Gate). Here individuals and groups can learn kayaking, canoeing, sailing and windsurfing. A weekend training course costs about €100.

About 4.5km north of Killaloe is Cragliath Hill, which has another fort, **Griananlaghna**, named after Brian Ború's great grandfather, King Lachtna.

Places to Stay & Eat
Lough Derg Holiday Park (☎ 061-376329, fax 376777, ⓦ www.loughderg.net, Scarriff Rd, Killaloe) Tent & car €10.15 plus adult/child €3.15/1.90, hikers & cyclists including tent €6.35 per person. This park, 5km north of Killaloe on the R463, is scenically positioned on the lake shore. There are 24 tent sites and it has its own activity centre.

Lantern House (☎ 061-923034, fax 923 139, Ogonnelloe, Killaloe) Rooms €31.75 per person. In the village of Ogonnelloe (Tuath Ó gConnaille), this delightful guest-house on a hill has great views of the lake. Its restaurant serves simple, wholesome food, but only opens 6pm to 9pm so it's wise to book.

Kincora Hall (☎ 061-376000, fax 376665, Killaloe) Singles/doubles €95.25/114.25. This lovely 31-room hotel is about 1km north of Killaloe. The rooms are spacious and tastefully furnished, the food in its restaurant is good and there's a bar on the premises.

MOUNTSHANNON & AROUND
☎ 061 • pop 200
Mountshannon (Baile Uí Bheoláin), on the south-western shores of Lough Derg, is an attractive 18th-century village. The small stone harbour is usually busy with fishing boats and is the main port for trips to Holy Island, one of Clare's finest early-Christian settlements.

Holy Island
Lying 2km offshore from Mountshannon, Holy Island (Inis Cealtra) is the site of a monastic settlement thought to have been founded by St Cáimín in the 7th century. On the island you'll see a round tower that is over 27m tall (though missing its top storey). You'll also find four old chapels, a hermit's cell and some early-Christian gravestones dating from the 7th to 13th centuries. One of the chapels has an elegant Romanesque arch. Inside the chapel is an inscription in old Irish, which translates as: 'Pray for Tornog, who made this cross.'

The Vikings treated this monastery roughly in the 9th century, but under the subsequent protection of Brian Ború and others it flourished. The Holy Well was once the focus for a lively festival that was banned in the 1830s because a lot of, well, nonreligious behaviour was creeping in.

Ireland Line Cruises (☎ 375011, Killaloe) Adult/child €6.30/4.40. Late Apr-Oct. You can take a cruise around the island from Mountshannon. Trips can also be arranged from Mountshannon through the **East Clare Heritage Centre** (☎ 921351, 921615, Tuamgraney), about 10km southwest on the R352.

Places to Stay

Lakeside Caravan & Camping Park (☎ 927225, fax 937336, W www.lakeside ireland.com, Mountshannon) Tent & car €11.45 plus adult/child €1.25/0.65, hikers & cyclists including tent €6.35 per person. Open May-Sept. This spacious park is in a great spot beside the lake. It also hires out boats and equipment for **windsurfing**, **rowing** and **sailing**. From Mountshannon, head north along the Portumna road (R352) for 2km and take the first turning on the right.

Derg Lodge (☎ 927180, fax 927180, Whitegate Rd, Mountshannon) Singles/doubles €22.85/40.65. This pleasant four-room B&B, within walking distance of the town, also has bikes for hire.

Oak House (☎/fax 927185, Mountshannon) Singles/doubles €32.40/48.25. A delightful country house, 6km north of the village. It has a lovely garden and overlooks the lake.

Mountshannon Hotel (☎ 927162, fax 927272, e mountshannonhotel@tinet.ie, Main St, Mountshannon) Rooms €44.45 per person. This charming 14-room hotel is right in the village with full facilities and a decent restaurant.

Places to Eat

An Cupán Caife (The Coffee Cup; ☎ 927275, Main St) Mains around €8.70. Open 10am-9pm daily Mar-Nov. This cosy, licensed (and BYO wine) bistro serves good, homely food.

Cois na hAbhna (☎ 927189, Main St) Mains €6.30-10.50. An atmospheric pub, it serves good bar food all day (and an a la carte menu from 7pm to 10pm). There's traditional Irish music and dance on Wednesday night, and other entertainment at the weekend.

Getting There & Away

On weekdays, Bus Éireann (☎ 313333) bus No 345 from Limerick to Killaloe continues to Scarriff (8km south-west of Mountshannon). On Saturday only, bus No 346 from Limerick (departing at 1.15pm) to Whitegate via Scarriff runs to Mountshannon (one hour 25 minutes). Buses stop outside Keane's on the main street.

NORTH TO GALWAY

North of Mountshannon, the R352 follows Lough Derg to Portumna in Galway. Inland is an area known as the **Clare Lakelands**, based around Feakle, where numerous lakes offer good coarse fishing.

South-Western & Western Clare

Loop Head at the county's south-western tip is a big wedge splitting the mighty waves of the Atlantic Ocean. The coast between Loop Head and Kilkee has some outstanding cliff scenery. North of Kilkee, a popular seaside resort, the road (N67) moves inland, but there are some worthwhile detours to the lonely coast and beaches where Spanish Armada ships were wrecked over 400 years ago. Kilkee, White Strand, Spanish Point and Lahinch all have good beaches.

North and north-west of Ennis are a number of small villages, including Corofin and Ennistymon. These are both at the southern limits of the outstanding Burren region, and nearby are Hag's Head (a superb walk with excellent views) and the Cliffs of Moher, one of Ireland's most spectacular natural features. From there the road dips downhill towards Doolin, a well-known rest stop for backpackers and a centre of Irish music.

This region is great for cycling and two signposted routes are the Loop Head Cycleway and West Clare Cycleway.

GETTING THERE & AWAY

There are infrequent local bus services to the coastal towns and villages; some buses run from Limerick, while others are on express routes from Galway or Tralee. Services are more frequent May to September. Phone the bus station at Ennis (☎ 065-682 4177) or Limerick (☎ 061-313333) for exact times and fares.

Bus Éireann express bus No 15 terminates

in Ennis or Ennistymon. It runs through Doolin, Lisdoonvarna, Lahinch, Miltown Malbay, Kilkee and Kilrush. The Killarney–Galway bus No 50 stops in Ballyvaughan, Lisdoonvarna, Doolin, the Cliffs of Moher, Lahinch, Miltown Malbay, Doonbeg, Kilkee and Kilrush. Bus No 333 travels between Limerick, Ennis, Ennistymon, Lahinch, Quilty, Doonbeg, Kilkee and Kilrush.

Bus No 336 between Kilkee and Limerick travels via Kilrush and Ennis four times a day Monday to Saturday (three on Sunday). Late May to September, bus No 337 runs three-times daily (once on Sunday) between Limerick and Lisdoonvarna, passing through Ennis, Ennistymon, Lahinch, Liscannor, the Cliffs of Moher and Doolin en route. The rest of the year it goes once daily only.

KILLIMER
☎ 065 • pop 150

Killimer is a nondescript village, close to the Shannon Estuary and Moneypoint, Ireland's largest power station. At 915 megawatts, Moneypoint is capable of supplying 40% of the country's needs and burns two million tonnes of coal a year.

The Colleen Bawn (White Girl) was a woman called Eileen Hanly who was murdered in 1819 and thrown into the Shannon by her husband, John Scanlon. Her body washed ashore and was buried in Killimer graveyard. Scanlon was hanged. The story has inspired novels, plays, songs and operas. Unfortunately, her tombstone was carried away by souvenir hunters.

Getting There & Away

Shannon Ferry Limited (☎ 905 3124, W www.shannonferries.com) runs a 20-minute car ferry from Killimer, across the Shannon Estuary, to Tarbert in County Kerry, on the hour, year round, and on the half-hour June to September (one-way/return bikes & foot passengers €3.15/5.10, cars €12.70/19.05, motorcyclists €7.60/10.15). April to September, the schedule is from 7am (9am on Sunday) to 9pm; during the rest of the year sailings are 7am (10am on Sunday) to 7pm. From Tarbert schedules begin and finish 30 minutes later. You pay on board.

KILRUSH
☎ 065 • pop 2750

This small town with its pretty, pastel-painted centre overlooks the Shannon Estuary and the hills of Kerry to the south. Kilrush (Cill Rois) has the western coast's biggest marina, at Kilrush Creek; it has a Web site at W www.kilrushcreekmarina.ie.

Kilrush's tourist office (☎ 905 1577), in the town hall on Market Square, opens 10am to 1pm and 2pm to 6pm Monday to Saturday, late May to August. On Frances St, the main street, you'll find an Allied Irish Bank (with an ATM) and the post office. The Internet Bureau (☎ 905 1061), at the bottom of Frances St, offers Internet access for €3.80 per 30 minutes.

Things to See & Do

Situated in the town hall is the **Kilrush Heritage Centre** (☎ 905 1596, Market Square; adult/concession €2.50/1.30; open 10am-6pm Mon-Fri & noon-4pm Sat & Sun June-Aug). It has an exhibition on the history of the region and an audiovisual presentation on the Famine entitled 'Kilrush in Landlord Times'.

If you're interested in stained glass, **St Senan's Catholic church**, in Toler St, contains eight detailed examples by well known artisan Harry Clarke. East of town is **Kilrush Wood**, which has some fine old trees and a picnic area.

An exhibition on the history and wildlife of Scattery Island is housed in the Dúchas-run **Scattery Island Visitor Centre** (☎ 905 2144, Merchant's Quay; free; open 10am-6pm daily mid-June-mid-Sept).

Near the marina is **Kilrush Creek Adventure Centre** (☎ 905 2855, fax 905 2597, W www.kcac.nav.to, Kilrush Creek; half/full day €25/38). It offers a range of activities including archery, windsurfing, kayaking and sailing, plus accommodation (see Kilrush Creek Lodge under Places to Stay & Eat).

Weather permitting, **Scattery Island Ferries** (☎ 905 1237, Cappa, Kilrush) runs boats from Kilrush Marina to see bottle-nose dolphins in the Shannon Estuary (€11.40, two to three hours).

Places to Stay & Eat

There are plenty of B&Bs in the Kilrush area.

Katie O'Connors Holiday Hostel (☎ 905 1133, fax 905 2386, e cwglynn@eircom .net, Frances St) Dorms/double rooms €11.40/23.95. Open mid-Mar-Dec. This 18th-century, IHH property, above the Keltic Korner grocery store, houses 28 guests in snug lodgings.

Kilrush Creek Lodge (☎ 905 2595, fax 905 2597, Kilrush Creek) Dorms/singles/ doubles from €12.60/25.20/37.80 including breakfast. Part of the adventure centre, the lodge has spacious rooms, a laundry, a kitchen and two TV lounges.

Dolphins Pass (☎ 905 1822, Aylevarroo, Kilrush) Singles/doubles €32.40/48.25. Open Apr-Oct. Watch the sunset or the dolphins at this relaxed beachside B&B, 3km west of Kilrush.

Coffey's (☎ 905 1104, Market Square) Sandwiches €2.50, pizzas €4.75-9.15. This inexpensive cafe serves breakfasts all day, decent sandwiches and pizzas, plus fish and chips from its busy takeaway section.

Getting There & Around

For information on buses to and from Kilrush, see Getting There & Away under South Western & Western Clare earlier in this chapter.

You can hire bikes at Gleeson's Cycles (☎ 905 1127), Henry St, for €10.15/44.50 per day/week plus deposit.

SCATTERY ISLAND

This uninhabited, windswept, treeless island, 2.5km south-west of Cappa pier, is the site of a Christian settlement founded by St Senan in the 6th century. Its 36m-high **round tower** is one of the tallest and best preserved in Ireland, and the entrance is at ground level instead of the usual position high above the foundation. There are remains of five **medieval churches**, including a 9th-century cathedral.

To build his monastery, St Senan had to rid the island of a monster. The Irish name for the island is Inis Cathaigh, Cathach being the sea serpent who had made his lair on the island. With the help of archangel Raphael, Senan banished the monster and also excluded all women. A local, apparently very friendly, virgin named Cannera wanted to join Senan, provoking much speculation about how he withstood the temptation.

> Legend hints that had the maid,
> Until morning's light delayed,
> And given the saint one rosy smile,
> She'd ne'er have left his lonely isle.

Scattery was a beautiful but unfortunate site for a monastery, as it was all too easy for the Vikings to sail up the estuary and pillage the place, which they did repeatedly in the 9th and 10th centuries. They occupied the island for 100 years until 970, when they were dislodged by Brian Ború.

Getting There & Away

The harbour at Cappa village near Kilrush is where you catch the boat to Scattery Island. To get there turn left at the bottom of Frances St in Kilrush and follow the road for 2km.

During the summer, Scattery Island Ferries (☎ 065-905 1237) runs boats from Cappa pier to the island (return €5.70, 20 minutes). There's no strict timetable as the trips are subject to demand and weather conditions. You can buy tickets at the small kiosk on Merchant's Quay.

KILKEE

☎ 065 • pop 1330

During the summer, Kilkee's wide semicircular bay is thronged with day-trippers and holiday-makers mainly from Clare and Limerick. Kilkee (Cill Chaoi) first became popular in Victorian times when rich Limerick families built seaside retreats here. Today, Kilkee is a little too fat with guesthouses, amusement arcades and takeaways, though recent development has seen the resort town become a tad more gentrified.

Information

The seasonal tourist office (☎ 905 6112), on O'Connell St, is just up to the left from the seafront. It opens 10am to 1pm and 2pm to 6pm daily, June to mid-September. On

O'Curry St, the main street, the Bank of Ireland and Allied Irish Bank both have ATMs. The post office is on Circular Rd, off the western end of O'Curry St.

Things to See & Do

Many visitors come for the fine sheltered **beach** and the **Pollock Holes**, natural swimming pools in the Duggerna Rocks to the south of the beach. **St George's Head** to the north has good cliff walks and scenery, while south of the bay the **Duggerna Rocks** form an unusual natural amphitheatre. Farther south is a huge **sea cave**. These sights can be reached by driving to Kilkee's West End area and following the coastal path.

Kilkee is a well known **diving** centre. There are shore dives from the Duggerna Rocks fringing the western side of the bay, or boat dives on the Black Rocks farther out. Right at the tip of the Duggerna Rocks is the small inlet of Myles Creek, out from which there's excellent underwater scenery. **Kilkee Diving and Watersports Centre** (☎ 905 6707, ℮ kilkee@iol.ie, George's Head, Kilkee) by the harbour has tanks and other equipment for hire and runs PADI courses (€445 over two weekends).

Places to Stay

Camping & Hostels There are several options for campers around here.

Cunningham's Holiday Park (☎ 905 6430 July-Aug, otherwise ☎ 061-451009, fax 327877, ℮ cunninghams@eircom.net, Kilkee) Tent & car €12.70, hikers & cyclists including tent €5.10 per person. Open June-early Sept. Coming from Kilrush, turn left after the roundabout. Cunningham's is a few minutes' walk from the town and beach.

Green Acres Caravan & Camping Park (☎ 905 7011, Doonaha, Kilkee) Family tent & car €11.45, hikers & cyclists including tent €5.10 per person. This is a small, peaceful park beside the Shannon 6km south of Kilkee on the R487.

Kilkee Hostel (☎/fax 905 6209, O'Curry St) Dorms €11.45. Open Mar-Oct. This IHH property is clean, well run and only 50m from the seafront. It rents out bikes and has a well equipped kitchen, a laundry room and a small coffee shop.

B&Bs & Hotels There are countless guesthouses in Kilkee, though usually a little more expensive than in other areas. There are some good B&Bs at the West End. At busy times you may have to take whatever the tourist office can get you. There are also plenty of hotels in Kilkee, but for the extra money you don't get much extra luxury.

Bayview (☎ 905 6058, O'Connell St) Singles/doubles €33/53.30. Bayview is a large, bright guesthouse with good views of the bay and a substantial reduction for children.

Harbour Lodge (☎ 905 6090, 6 Marine Parade) Singles/doubles €32.40/50.80. This B&B is a charming, one-storey terraced house offering cosy rooms, a dining room overlooking the harbour, a good breakfast selection and a cup of tea or coffee when you arrive.

Stella Maris Hotel (☎ 905 6455, fax 906 0006, O'Connell St) Rooms €31.75-50.80. This tastefully furnished, family-run hotel has comfy rooms, open peat fires and a dining room with views of the bay.

Places to Eat

Side Tracks (☎ 905 6098, Erin St) Lunch mains €6.25. This popular local serves inexpensive lunchtime bar meals such as beef and chicken burgers, while in the evening there's a la carte dining in its steak and seafood restaurant.

Old Bistro (☎ 905 6898, O'Curry St) Mains €12-17. It's hard to miss this place with its boldly painted black, yellow and red frontage. Inside, the menu features fresh local seafood as well as meat and vegetarian choices. In the evening it can get crowded so come early or book ahead.

Pantry (☎ 905 6576, O'Curry St) Lunch mains €5.70-6.95, dinner mains €10.75-13.25. There are plenty of fast-food outlets, but this busy cafe stands out for its delicious home-cooking and reasonable prices.

Entertainment

Myle's Creek (☎ 905 6670, O'Curry St) Kilkee's trendiest spot; the pub is on the band circuit and attracts many of Ireland's best young rock and alternative groups.

Mary O'Mara's (☎ 905 6286, O'Curry St) An atmospheric old pub, O'Mara's pours a good pint and presents traditional music and sing-alongs several nights a week.

Getting There & Away

For information on buses to and from Kilkee, see Getting There & Away under South-Western & Western Clare earlier in this chapter.

KILKEE TO LOOP HEAD

The land from Kilkee south to Loop Head is poor and flat, but the cliff scenery is spectacular: the coast is peppered with sea stacks, arches and wave-sculpted rocks. It's a glorious day's bike ride down to the head and back. Better still, if you have the energy, is the 24km cliff walk between Loop Head and Kilkee. The cliffs compare with the more famous Cliffs of Moher to the north and are much less visited.

Intrinsic Bay

About 3km south of Kilkee is Intrinsic Bay, named after the ship wrecked here in 1856 en route to America. The summit shadowing the bay is Lookout Hill. To the north are Diamond Rock and **Bishop's Island**, the latter a remarkable pillar of rock with a medieval oratory perched on the summit. The oratory is attributed to the 6th-century St Senan, who also built the settlement on Scattery Island (see earlier in this chapter). Later, a selfish bishop supposedly lived here while his people starved in a famine; when the gap to the mainland widened in a storm, the bishop himself starved to death.

Kilbaha

At the end of the R487, 7km east of Loop Head, Kilbaha's tiny church, about 500m inland from the village towards Loop Head, contains an unusual relic of more repressive times. The **Little Ark** is a small, mobile, wooden altar used by Catholics in the 1850s. In order for the priest to celebrate mass, the altar was wheeled below the high-tide mark, where it was outside the jurisdiction of the

local Protestant landlord. A stained-glass window above the church door depicts the ark in use. Father Michael Meehan, the courageous local priest who had the ark built, is buried in the church.

There's a **Submerged Forest**, a collection of 5000-year-old tree stumps (probably pine) on the shore east of Rinvella Bay, near Kilbaha. They were originally preserved in a peat bog, which was washed away as the sea level rose, leaving the stumps visible.

Keating's (☎ 905 8009, Main St) This simple, friendly local claims to be the closest pub on the Irish mainland to New York.

Carrigaholt

☎ 065 • pop 100

On 15 September 1588, seven tattered ships of the Spanish Armada took shelter off Carrigaholt (Carraig an Chabaltaigh), a tiny village inside the mouth of the Shannon Estuary. One, probably the *Annunciada*, was torched and abandoned, sinking somewhere out in the estuary. Today, Carrigaholt has a safe beach and the substantial remains of a 15th-century McMahon castle with a square keep overlooking the water.

To view resident bottle-nose dolphins (there are about 120 pods in the Shannon Estuary), head for **Dolphinwatch** (☎ 905 8156, 088 258 4711, ⓦ www.dolphinwatch.ie, Carrigaholt; adult/child €12.60/7.60). Opposite the post office, Dolphinwatch runs two-hour trips in the estuary from May to October.

Long Dock (☎ 905 8106, West St) Snacks €6.25, mains €12.65-18.95. Open 11.30am till late daily Easter-Sept. This cosy pub-cum-restaurant is the best place to eat. It serves inexpensive bar food, seafood dinners and has Irish music at the weekend.

Morrissey's Village Pub (☎ 905 8041, West St) Morrissey's has traditional music plus set and line dancing at the weekend.

Loop Head

On a clear day, Loop Head (Ceann Léime), Clare's southernmost point, has magnificent views south to the Dingle Peninsula crowned by Mt Brandon (953m), and north to the Aran Islands and Galway Bay. There are

Cúchulainn's Leap

The 'Loop' in Loop Head is a corruption of the word 'leap'. Legend has it that the Celtic warrior Cúchulainn was being chased all over Ireland by the formidable Mal. Cornered on this headland, he leapt onto a sea stack and, when she tried to follow him, Mal fell to her death. The sea turned crimson and her body washed ashore at various points along the coast, giving Hag's Head and Malbay their names. Some say the headland resembles a seated woman looking out over the Atlantic. West of the lighthouse you'll find the sea stack in question; the gap is known as Cúchulainn's Leap.

bracing walks in the area and a long hike running along the cliffs to Kilkee.

KILKEE TO ENNISTYMON

North of Kilkee, the 'real' west of Ireland begins to assert itself. The N67 runs inland for some 32km until it reaches Quilty. Take the occasional lane to the west and search out unfrequented places such as **White Strand**, north of Doonbeg. **Ballard Bay** is 8km north of Doonbeg, where an old telegraph tower looks over some fine cliffs. **Donegal Point** has the remains of a promontory fort. There's good **fishing** all along the coast, and safe **beaches** at Seafield, Lough Donnell and Quilty.

Getting There & Away

From May to September Bus Éireann's express Killarney–Galway bus No 50 stops three times a day (twice on Sunday) at Doonbeg, Miltown Malbay and Lahinch. From Monday to Saturday, the rest of the year, bus No 333 connects Doonbeg, Quilty, Spanish Point, Miltown Malbay and Lahinch. Contact Ennis bus station (☎ 065-682 4177) for times and fares.

Doonbeg

☎ 065 • pop 1200

Doonbeg (An Dún Beag) is a tiny fishing village about halfway between Kilkee and Quilty. Near the mouth of the River Doonbeg,

another Armada ship, the *San Esteban*, was wrecked on 20 September 1588. The survivors were later executed at Spanish Point. **White Strand** (Trá Ban) is a quiet beach, 2km long and backed by dunes. There are two **ruined castles**: Doonmore is on White Strand, while Doonbeg is in the village by the river.

Places to Stay & Eat For campers the side roads around Doonbeg are good places to pitch a tent and watch the sun go down.

An Tinteán (The Hearth; ☎ *905 5036, fax 905 5344, Main St)* Rooms with bathroom €25.40 per person. This is a friendly B&B with a turf fire and fine rooms in the centre of the village.

San Esteban (☎*/fax 905 5105, Rhynagonaught)* Rooms with bathroom €25.40 per person. San Esteban is a cosy cottage in a peaceful location 1km from Doonbeg, signposted from the north of the village.

Olde Kitchen Restaurant (☎ *905 5039, Main St)* Mains €6.25-10. This restaurant serves hearty steaks and seafood in the Igoe Inn, which provides music each Monday night.

Quilty

☎ 065 • pop 300

The small village of Quilty (Coillte), on a particularly bleak stretch of coast, is a centre for seaweed production. Kelp and other plants are collected, dried on the stone walls and sent for processing. The resulting alginates are used in toothpaste, beer, agar and certain cosmetics.

One of the most powerful ships of the Spanish Armada, the *San Marcos*, was wrecked off nearby Mutton Island in September 1588. It had taken a terrible battering, and only four of its 1000-strong crew survived.

Quilty has a good **beach**, and boats are available for **deep-sea angling** for bass and flatfish.

Clonmore Lodge (☎ *708 7020, fax 708 7270, Kilkee Rd)* Singles/doubles with bathroom €31.75/55.85. Open Mar-early Nov. This rural B&B is on a working farm that overlooks the ocean some 3km south of the village.

Spanish Point

Spanish Point (Rinn na Spáinneach) gets its name from the execution of 60 Spanish Armada survivors on Cnoc na Crocaire (Hill of the Gallows) nearby. They had swum ashore, only to be executed by Boetius Clancy, the sheriff of Clare, and Turlough O'Brien, the local chief loyal to the English Crown. At the great, rock-strewn beach you can **fish** for bass, and when the waves are running there's good **surfing**.

Miltown Malbay

☎ 065 • pop 615

Like Kilkee, Miltown Malbay was a resort favoured by well-to-do Victorians, though the town isn't actually on the sea: the beach is 2km south at Spanish Point. Miltown Malbay has a thriving music scene and every year hosts a **Willie Clancy Irish Music Festival** (*☎ 708 4148*) as a tribute to one of Ireland's greatest pipers. The festival usually occurs during the first week in July, when the town is overrun with wandering minstrels, the pubs are packed, and Guinness is consumed by the bucket load. You can also find music in the surrounding villages.

Ocean View Restaurant (*☎ 708 4649, Main St*) Mains €8.85-15.25. Open daily from 11am. It serves mainly steaks and chicken plus salads and sandwiches, in a low-key atmosphere. It adjoins O'Loughlin's Bar, which has traditional music and sing-along nights.

O'Friel's Bar (*☎ 708 4275, The Square*) Just off the southern end of Main St, O'Friel's is an authentic, old-style pub with a coal fire and – unlike so many pubs these days – no TV. Once home to Willie Clancy himself, it has traditional sessions on Saturday and Sunday night.

Lahinch

☎ 065 • pop 550

Lahinch (Leacht Uí Chonchubhair) is the archetypal seaside resort – full of fast-food joints and amusement arcades – but with the addition of a world class golf course. The town sits on protected Liscannor Bay with a fine beach. In 1943, a US bomber flying off

course landed on the beach, and the 12 airmen were repatriated to Allied forces through Northern Ireland. Lahinch is very busy in the summer: you may prefer to move on to Ennistymon, Liscannor or Doolin.

The tourist office, Lahinch Fáilte (*☎ 708 2082, W www.lahinchfailte.com*), on Kettle St (which is off the northern end of Main St), opens 9am to 8pm daily, May to October, and 9am to 5pm the rest of the year. Surprisingly, there are no banks, though you can change money at the post office and there's an ATM outside the tourist office.

The **surfing** can be good at any time of year and surfboards and wet suits can be rented on the seafront from **Lahinch Surf Shop** (*☎ 708 1543*). For those who like to swim in warmer water there's the **Lahinch Seaworld Leisure Centre** (*☎ 708 1900, The Promenade; adult/child €4.45/3.15; open 10am-8pm*). The **Willie Daly Riding Centre** (*☎ 707 1385, Ballingaddy*), between Lahinch and Ennistymon, has pony trekking (€16 for 2½ hours); it's signposted from the north of the town.

Places to Stay & Eat There are a number of decent options in Lahinch.

Lahinch Caravan & Camping Park (*☎ 708 1424, fax 708 1194, Lahinch*) Tent site €8.90. Open May-Sept. Close to the beach and only 200m south of the village, this is a peaceful park with full amenities.

Lahinch Hostel (*☎ 708 1040, fax 905 6209, Church St*) Dorms/private rooms €11.35/12 per person. A pleasant IHH property in the town centre, it's close to the beachfront and has laundry facilities.

Mrs O'Brien's Kitchen (*☎ 708 1020, Main St*) Mains €8.25-9.85. This is a lively but smoky cafe-cum-bar that serves up tasty, decent-sized meals. It has a good vegetarian selection and on weekend nights you can eat and drink to the accompaniment of traditional music.

Mr Eamon's (*☎ 708 1050, fax 708 1810, Kettle St*) Mains €16.45-19. Open noon-9.30pm Mon-Sat & noon-9pm Sun Mar-Jan. Mr Eamon's is a small, inviting place with a deserved reputation for fine food. It specialises in seafood – fresh from Liscannor

CLARE

Bay – but it also does steak and vegetarian dishes.

ENNISTYMON
☎ 065 • pop 920

The moderately attractive little town of Ennistymon (Inis Díomáin) is 3km inland from Lahinch on the banks of the River Cullenagh. The town started out as a settlement round a castle built by Turlough O'Brien in 1588. It's essentially one long main street – which divides into Old Town, Church and Main Sts; the river runs directly below and parallel to it.

The economic boom doesn't seem to have reached here, with its many closed shop fronts, though the library (☎ 707 1245), behind the square, does have the latest computer technology offering free Internet access. It opens 10am to 5.30pm Monday, Tuesday and Thursday, 10am to 5.30pm and 6.30pm to 8pm Wednesday and Friday, and 10am to 2pm on Saturday). The Bank of Ireland, in Parliament St, has a bureau de change and ATM.

The bridge over the River Inagh is just above the 200m rapids known as the **Cascades**, which are impressive when the river is high. There's trout and salmon fishing here. The Cascades are just down the lane under the archway. It's a pleasant stroll around here in the evening. When the Cullenagh is in flood, though, the waters can rise almost to the houses.

Places to Stay & Eat
Station House (☎ 707 1149, fax 707 1709, Ennis Rd) Rooms with bathroom €24.15 per person. About 500m south of the centre, Station House is a solid, two-storey, non-smoking B&B with comfortable rooms and a private car park.

Falls Hotel (☎ 707 1004, fax 707 1367, e falls@iol.ie, Ennistymon) Rooms €44.45-63.50. This large, relaxed hotel is in an old country house in 20 hectares of wooded gardens close to the town centre.

Fitzpatrick's Coffee House (☎ 707 1600, Parliament St) Breakfast €4.45, lunch €6.35. Next to the supermarket and frequented by locals, Fitzpatrick's serves good,

solid fare like roast beef as well as sandwiches and salads.

Byrne's Restaurant (☎ 707 1080, Main St) Mains €17-21. Open 12.30pm-3pm & 6.30pm-9.30pm Tues-Sat. This elegant restaurant has views of the falls and serves good-quality, modern-Irish cuisine.

Entertainment
Cooley's House (☎ 707 1712, Main St) This is a charming old pub with a low ceiling and traditional sessions on Wednesday evening and most nights in summer.

Eugene's (Main St) Eugene's is a cosy place for a drink and has music on weekend nights.

Getting There & Away
Bus Éireann bus No 15 between Limerick and Lisdoonvarna stops at Ennistymon in front of Aherne's on Church St. Contact the bus station in Ennis (☎ 682 4177) or Limerick (☎ 061-313333) for details.

LISCANNOR & AROUND
☎ 065 • pop 250

This small fishing village offers a fine view over Liscannor Bay and Lahinch as the road (R478) heads north to the Cliffs of Moher and Doolin. Liscannor (Lios Ceannúir) has given its name to a paving stone with ripples on the surface. The stone is widely used locally for floors, walls and even roofs.

John Philip Holland (1840–1914), the inventor of the submarine, was born in Liscannor. He emigrated to the USA in 1873, and he hoped his invention would be used to sink British warships.

Things to See & Do
On the way north to the Cliffs of Moher and close to Murphy's Arch Bar is the **Holy Well of St Brigid** – look for the tall, stone column topped with an urn nearby. The well's significance probably predates Christian times, as its Irish name suggests a connection with a pre-Christian god, Crom Dubh.

People from all over Clare and the Aran Islands come to pray and drink the healing waters. There is a collection of discarded religious memorabilia in a grotto nearby. The pilgrimage to the well takes place in July, particularly on the last weekend of the month, and there can be up to 400 people there on the Sunday.

Clahane Beach to the west of Liscannor is good and safe. A 'lost city' and church known as Kilstephen are supposed to sit on an underwater reef in Liscannor Bay. The Celtic hero Conan is buried on **Slieve Callan** to the south. He is said to lie with the key to the lost church.

The ruined square **castle** on the point just north of Liscannor was built by the O'Connor family.

Places to Stay & Eat
Liscannor Village Hostel (☎ 708 1550, fax 708 1417, Liscannor) Dorms €12.60. Open Apr-Oct. This IHH property, at the eastern end of the village behind the Conch Shell restaurant, is a big, well run place but could be cleaner.

Sea Haven (☎ 708 1385, fax 708 1474, Liscannor) Singles/doubles €32.40/48.15. Coming from Lahinch, this B&B is just before the village clearly visible on the hill to the right. It's clean, comfortably furnished and has good, firm beds.

Moher Lodge Farmhouse (☎ 708 1269, fax 708 1589, ⓔ moherlodge@eircom.net, Liscannor) Rooms €27.95 per person. Open Apr-Oct. There are superb views from this friendly B&B, which is 3km north-west of Liscannor, close to the Cliffs of Moher.

Vaughans Anchor Inn (☎ 708 1548, ⓦ www.vaughansanchorinn.com, Main St) Mains €8.20-25.40. Tasty, inexpensive meals using fresh seafood from Liscannor Bay are on offer here. The dining room is at the rear while the front bar has a warm, open fire.

Conch Shell (☎ 708 1888, ⓦ www.the conchshellrestaurant.com, Main St) Mains €17-21. Open for dinner Wed-Mon mid-June-mid-Oct; Thur-Sat mid-Oct-mid-June. The menu at this upmarket, upstairs restaurant overlooking the bay features delicious, fresh seafood but it also offers meat and vegetarian dishes.

Entertainment
Joseph McHugh's (☎ 708 1163, Main St) This is as genuine an old Irish pub as you'll find anywhere, down to the groceries and other oddments piled on the shelves. Here the *craic* (crack) starts early, and there's music on Tuesday night.

Vaughans Anchor Inn (see Places to Stay & Eat) Vaughans doesn't have the atmosphere of Joseph McHugh's, but does dish up music most nights during the summer.

Getting There & Away
From May to September, Bus Éireann's Killarney–Galway express bus No 50 stops at Liscannor. Bus No 337 between Limerick and Lisdoonvarna stops daily year round. Contact the bus station at Ennis (☎ 682 4177) or Limerick (☎ 061-313333) for times and fares.

HAG'S HEAD
Hag's Head forms the southern end of the Cliffs of Moher and is an excellent place from which to view the cliffs. The 8km **Hag's Head Walk** from the Cliffs of Moher car park is superb and well worth the effort but the winds can get very blustery so be careful. The return trip takes about three hours.

To get to the head from Liscannor, go just over 5km towards the Cliffs of Moher until, about 500m past the Moher Lodge, you spot a rough, potholed track on the left. You can drive a short distance to the brow of the hill; then you have to walk along the path out towards the point. There's a huge sea arch at the tip and another visible to the north. At the head a signal tower was erected in case Napoleon tried to attack on the western coast. The tower is built on the site of an ancient promontory fort called Mothair, which has given its name to the famous cliffs to the north.

CLIFFS OF MOHER
One of Ireland's most spectacular sights, the heavily touristed Cliffs of Moher (Aillte an Mothair, or Ailltreacha Mothair) rise from Hag's Head and reach their highest

point (203m) just north of O'Brien's Tower, before slowly descending farther north again. On a clear day the views are tremendous: the Aran Islands stand etched on the waters of Galway Bay, and beyond lie the hills of Connemara in western Galway.

From the cliff edge you can just hear the booming far below as the waves crash and gnaw at the soft shale and sandstone. Sections of the cliff often give way, and they're generally so unstable that few birds or plants make them their home. With a due-west exposure, sunset is the best time to visit – many of the tourist buses will have left by then too.

Information

There's a bureau de change, a small cafe and a gift shop full of souvenirs at the visitor centre (☎ 065-708 1171; open 9am-8pm daily July & Aug; 9am-7pm June; 9am-6.30pm May & Sept; 9.30am-6pm Apr; 9.30am-5pm Oct-Mar). Be warned: the cliffs are one of the most popular attractions in Ireland, and coaches roll up ceaselessly during the day. The car park costs an excessive €2.50.

Things to See & Do

From the car park, there's a bracing walk to Hag's Head (see earlier). Part of the Hag's Head Walk was walled off with Liscannor stone by the eccentric local landlord Cornelius O'Brien (1801–57), who built the lookout tower, **O'Brien's Tower** (adult/child €2.50/0.75; open 9am-7.30pm daily Apr-Oct), to impress lady visitors. You can climb up and use the telescope. The **sea stack** – covered with seabirds and their guano – just below the tower is called Breanan Mór and is itself over 70m high.

The cliffs just north of Moher are known as **Aill na Searrach** (Cliff of the Foals) because a group of young fairy horses are supposed to have leapt into the sea at this point. There's a precipitous and dangerous path to the base of these cliffs, suitable only for the fittest of walkers and in dry weather. The beginning of the path is signposted about 2km north of the Cliffs of Moher car park. You can also reach this path by following the cliff-top path north from O'Brien's Tower, as if walking to Doolin.

Getting There & Away

Bus Éireann's Limerick–Lisdoonvarna bus No 337 stops daily at the Cliffs of Moher, as does the express bus from Galway to Kilrush. Contact Ennis bus station (☎ 065-682 4177) for times and fares. See also Organised Tours under Galway in the County Galway chapter.

The Burren

The Burren region, between Corofin in northern Clare and Kinvara in County Galway, and stretching to the Atlantic coast, is an extraordinary, unique place – an ancient sea bed forced up by geological forces.

Boireann is the Irish for 'rocky country', and when you see the kilometres of polished limestone stretching in every direction you'll know why one of Cromwell's generals was moved to exclaim that there was 'neither water enough to drown a man, nor a tree to hang him, nor soil enough to bury him'.

Along the coast are a few settlements, including Doolin, a popular Irish-music centre with some wonderful caves nearby, and Ballyvaughan, an attractive little village on the southern coast of Galway Bay. This area has a lot of historical sites, notably Corcomroe Abbey and the churches of Oughtmama near Bellharbour. The deeply indented coastline has plenty of wildlife and some fine walks.

INFORMATION

The nearest information point is the Cliffs of Moher Visitor Centre (☎ 065-708 1171). A must if you intend spending some time in the Burren is Tim Robinson's *The Burren* (€5.70) map and guide, available in many shops, which shows almost every object and place of interest. *Book of the Burren* (€15.10), published by Tír Eolas, is a delightful introduction to its ecosystems, history and folklore.

ARCHAEOLOGY

The Burren's bare limestone hills were once lightly wooded and covered in soil. Towards the end of the Stone Age, about 6000 years ago, the first farmers arrived in the area. They began to clear the woodlands

THE BURREN

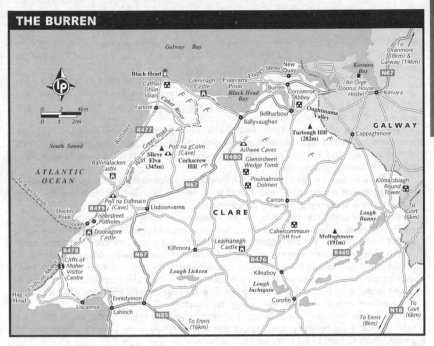

Galway Bay

To Oranmore (8km) & Galway (14km)

Black Head

Cathair Dhún Iórais

Fanore

Gleninagh Castle

Finavarra Point

Flaggy Shore

New Quay

Black Head Bay

Burren

Kinvara Bay

Corcomroe Abbey

An Óige Doorus House Hostel?

Kinvara

Caher River

R477

Green Road

Burren Way

Ballyreen

South Sound

Poll na gColm (Cave)

Slieve Elva (345m)

Corkscrew Hill

Ballinalacken Castle

Bellharbour

Ballyvaughan

Oughtmama Valley

Turlough Hill (282m)

GALWAY

Cappaghmore

ATLANTIC OCEAN

To Aran Islands

Poll na Eidhnain (Cave)

Doolin Point

Doolin

Fisherstreet Potholes

Doonagore Castle

R479

Lisdoonvarna

Aillwee Caves

R480

Gleninsheen Wedge Tomb

Poulnabrone Dolmen

N67

Carron

CLARE

Kilmacduagh Round Tower

To Gort (6km)

Lough Bunny

R478

Cliffs of Moher Visitor Centre

Kilfenora

N67

Leamanegh Castle

Lough Lickeen

Kilnaboy

Cahercommaun Cliff Fort

R476

Mullaghmore (191m)

R460

To Gort (6km)

Hag's Head

Cliffs of Moher

Liscannor

Ennistymon

Lahinch

N85

To Ennis (16km)

Lough Inchiquin

Corofin

To Ennis (8km)

N18

To Gort (6km)

0   2   4km
0   1   2mi

and use the upland regions for grazing. Over the centuries, the soil was eroded and the huge mass of limestone we see today began to emerge.

Despite its desolation, the Burren supported quite large numbers of people in ancient times and has over 2500 historic sites. Chief among them is the 5000-year-old Poulnabrone Dolmen, one of Ireland's finest ancient monuments.

There are around 70 megalithic tombs erected by the Burren's first settlers. Many of these tombs are wedge-shaped graves, stone boxes tapering both in height and width and about the size of a large double bed. The dead were placed inside, and the whole structure was covered in earth and stones. Gleninsheen, south of Aillwee Caves, is a good example.

Ring forts dot the Burren in prodigious numbers. There are almost 500, including Iron Age stone forts such as Cahercommaun near Carron.

In later times, many castles in the area were built by the region's ruling families, and these include Leamanegh Castle near Kilfenora, Ballinalacken Castle near Doolin and Gleninagh Castle on the Black Head road.

Unfortunately many ring forts and stone walls have been bulldozed into extinction.

FLORA & FAUNA

Soil may be scarce here, but the small amount that gathers in the cracks is limey, well drained and rich in nutrients. This, together with the soft Atlantic climate, supports an extraordinary mix of Mediterranean, Arctic and Alpine plants. Of Ireland's native wildflowers 75% are found here.

The Burren is a stronghold of Ireland's most elusive mammal, the weasel-like pine marten. They're rarely seen, although there are certainly some living near Gleninagh Castle and up the Caher Valley. Badgers, foxes and even stoats are common throughout the

Geology of the Burren

The Burren is the most extensive limestone region, or karst (after the original Karst in Slovenia), in Ireland or Britain. It consists almost entirely of limestone, except for a cap of mud and shale that sits on the higher regions, from Lisdoonvarna north to Slieve Elva.

During the Carboniferous period 350 million years ago, this whole area was the bottom of a warm and shallow sea. The remains of coral and shells fell to the sea bed, and coastal rivers dumped sand and silt on top of these lime deposits. Time and pressure turned the layers to stone, with limestone below and shale and sandstone above.

Massive rumblings in the earth's crust some 270 million years ago buckled the edges of Europe and forced the sea bed above sea level, at the same time bending and fracturing the stone sheets to form long, deep cracks. Wind, rain and ice have since removed most of the overlying shale, leaving these mountains of limestone.

The difference between the areas of porous limestone and nonporous shale is acute. Shale country is a depressing dull green, covered in acid bogs, marshes and reeds. On limestone the soil is sparse, water disappears and grey rock predominates.

Being slightly acidic, rainwater dissolves the limestone, widening the vertical cracks known as grikes. (The horizontal slabs are called clints.) Springs, rivers and even lakes (such as the turloughs around Corofin) appear and disappear. The water follows weak points (sinkholes) in the rock, carving out underground rivers and caverns. The calcium bicarbonate from the dripping water below creates stalactites (the ones that hang down) and stalagmites (the ones that shoot up). When these underground caverns collapse – which they do periodically – they form a depression. Rainwater is caught on top of the shale and eventually drains off at the edges into the limestone, which it erodes. A ring of caves appears along the shale-limestone boundary.

The southern boundary of the Burren is roughly where the limestone dips under the shale between Doolin and Lough Inchiquin. Underneath the limestone of the Burren is a huge mass of granite, which surfaces to the north-west in Connemara.

During numerous ice ages, glaciers scoured the hills, rounding the edges and sometimes polishing the rock to a shiny finish. The glaciers also dumped a thin layer of rock and soil over the region. Huge boulders were carried by the ice, incongruous aliens on a sea of flat rock. Seen all over the Burren, these 'glacial erratics' are often a visibly different type of rock.

The only surface river in the Burren is the Caher River, which flows down the Caher River Valley (the so-called Khyber Pass) before meeting the sea at Fanore. The valley is lined with glacial sediments, which stop the water from leaking away.

region. Otters and seals live along the shores around Bellharbour, New Quay and Finavarra Point.

The estuaries along this northern coast are rich in bird life and frequently attract brent geese during the winter. More than 28 of Ireland's 33 species of butterfly are found here, including one endemic species, the Burren green.

Unfortunately, modern farming and EU 'land-improvement' grants have had their effect on the Burren: weedkillers and fertilisers encourage grass and little else.

WALKING

'Green roads' are the old highways of the Burren, crossing hills and valleys to some of the remotest corners of the region. Unpaved, many were built during the Famine as part of relief work, while some date back possibly thousands of years. They're now used mostly by hikers and the occasional farmer. Many are signposted.

Particularly good walks are the green road from Ballinalacken Castle to Fanore, which forms part of the Burren Way, and the climb up Black Head to the Iron Age fort called

Cathair Dhún Iorais. The Burren Way (see Walking under Activities in the Facts for the Visitor chapter) runs down through the Burren from Ballyvaughan to Doolin and then south to the Cliffs of Moher.

Guided nature, history, archaeology and wilderness walks are available through **Burren Hill Walks** (☎ 065-707 7168) based at Corkscrew Hill, Ballyvaughan, or **South-West Walks Ireland** (☎ 066-712 8733) in Tralee, County Kerry.

CAVING

Serious caving isn't for the faint-hearted. If you fancy trying it, take a course or at least find an experienced guide. Tim Robinson's *The Burren* map and guide has most of the cave entrances marked on it; more serious spelunkers should consult *The Caves of County Clare* by CA Self.

GETTING THERE & AWAY

For precise times and other details of buses to the Burren area, ring the bus stations in Ennis (☎ 065-682 4177), Limerick (☎ 061-313333) or Galway (☎ 091-562000).

Various buses pass through the Burren. From Limerick bus No 337 runs three times daily (once on Sunday) from late May to September, once daily the rest of the year. It connects with Ennis, Ennistymon, Lahinch, Liscannor, the Cliffs of Moher, Doolin and Lisdoonvarna. Express bus No 50 connects Galway with Ballyvaughan, Lisdoonvarna, Lahinch, Kilkee and Tralee. It runs three times daily (once on Sunday) from late May to late September. From Galway to Kinvara, Ballyvaughan, Black Head, Fanore, Lisdoonvarna and Doolin, bus No 423 runs three-times daily (once on Sunday) from late May to late September. The rest of the year it runs once a day, Monday to Saturday.

See also Organised Tours under Galway in the County Galway chapter.

GETTING AROUND

The best way to see the Burren is on foot (see Walking earlier in this section) or by cycling; good mountain bikes are available in Doolin from Aille River Hostel (☎ 065-707 4260) and Paddy's Doolin Hostel (☎ 065-707 4006), or from Burke's Garage (☎ 707 4022) in Lisdoonvarna. You can easily ride a mountain bike along the green roads.

DOOLIN
☎ 065 • pop 200

Doolin – or Fisherstreet on some maps – stretches for several kilometres along the road. Despite its remoteness and somewhat desolate surroundings it has some of the best music pubs in the west, a couple of decent restaurants and cafes, and plenty of good hostels and guesthouses. It's also an excellent base for the Burren, which lies just to the north. There are ferries to the Aran Islands (see Aran Islands in the County Galway chapter), and the Cliffs of Moher begin a few kilometres south.

Doolin is extremely popular among backpackers and music lovers, and at night the pubs are filled with a cosmopolitan crowd. In the high season it can be difficult to get a bed, so try to book ahead. The place is particularly popular with German aficionados of traditional Irish music, who flock with all the zeal of medieval pilgrims to visit what was once the base of the Kellys, a popular German-Irish music family.

Orientation & Information

Doolin is made up of three parts. Coming from the north along the R479 you first hit St Catherine's Catholic church on the left, then after less than 1km the upper village of the Roadford area, with a shop, restaurant and cafes, hostels, two pubs and the Doolin post office. Then there's a slightly bigger gap before reaching Fisherstreet, the lower village, which has the popular Paddy's Doolin Hostel, more shops and O'Connor's pub. It's another 1.5km to the harbour and the ferry to the Aran Islands.

There are no banks in Doolin, but a mobile bank visits on Thursday. You can change money and travellers cheques in Roadford at the post office, and in Fisherstreet at Paddy's Doolin Hostel.

Places to Stay

Camping & Hostels Budget travellers are well catered for here. All but the Aille River

Hostel remain open year round, and they're all IHH affiliated.

Nagles Doolin Caravan & Camping Park (☎ 707 4458, fax 707 4936, Doolin) Tent site €5.10 plus adult/child €2.55/1.25. Open Apr-Sept. The camp site, with views of the Cliffs of Moher, has full facilities and is only 100m from the harbour.

O'Connors Riverside Camping & Caravan Park (☎ 707 4314, fax 707 4498, Roadford, Doolin) Tent site €6.35. Open May-Sept. On a farm beside the Aille River, in the upper village, it has showers, toilets and a quiet, scenic location.

Paddy's Doolin Hostel (☎ 707 4006, fax 707 4421, e doolinhostel@tinet.ie, Fisherstreet, Doolin) Dorms/private rooms €10.70-11.35/€15.15 per person. More commonly known as Paddy Moloney's, this friendly hostel is in the lower village. Paddy's can get busy, so book ahead. Across the road from Paddy's, **Fisherstreet House** is usually reserved for groups.

Aille River Hostel (☎ 707 4260, e ailleriver@esatclear.ie, Roadford, Doolin) Dorms/doubles €9.45/22.70. Open mid-Mar-Dec. The hostel is in a charming converted, 17th-century farmhouse with turf fires, hot showers and free laundry. It's in a picturesque spot by the river in the upper village.

Rainbow Hostel (☎ 707 4415, e rainbowhostel@eircom.net, Roadford, Doolin) Dorms/private rooms €10.10/10.70-12.60 per person. Near McGann's pub in the upper village, this 16-bed bungalow has an open turf fire in its lounge. Bus Éireann buses stop outside.

Flanagan's Village Hostel (☎ 707 4564, Roadford, Doolin) Dorms/private rooms €10.10/13.25 per person. Just down the hill from the church, this is a modern hostel with six-bed dorms and a lounge with comfy armchairs.

B&Bs & Hotels Doolin has a wide range of pleasant accommodation.

Doolin House (☎ 707 4259, Roadford, Doolin) Rooms €23 per person. In the upper village past the post office and McGann's pub, this excellent two-storey B&B has good views from its upstairs rooms.

Killilagh House (☎ 707 4392, e killilagh house@esatclear.ie, Roadford, Doolin) Rooms €25-32 per person. Across from Doolin Café, this is a friendly place with clean, bright bedrooms and a comfortable lounge.

Atlantic View (☎ 707 4189, Doolin) Rooms €31.50 per person. Owned by the same people who operate the ferries, this is the closest B&B to the harbour. It has been completely renovated, with light, airy rooms and panoramic views of the cliffs and ocean.

Island View House (☎ 707 4346, fax 707 4844, Doolin) Singles/doubles €38.10/48.30. Open Apr-Oct. Three kilometres from Doolin on the Lisdoonvarna road via Garrahy's Cross, this welcoming B&B offers tea and scones on arrival, and has firm beds and substantially reduced rates for children.

Moloney's Horseshoe Farmhouse (☎ 707 4006, fax 707 4421, Fisherstreet, Doolin) Singles/doubles with bathroom €54.65/59.70. Open mid-Mar-Oct. Moloney's is near Paddy's Doolin Hostel and owned by the same family. It has four rooms, is nonsmoking and accepts credit cards.

Aran View House (☎ 707 4061, fax 707 4540, Coast Rd, Doolin) En suite rooms €44.50-64 per person. Open May-Sept. This is a welcoming Georgian hotel north of town past St Catherine's church. Set in 40 hectares of land, it has commanding views and spacious rooms.

Places to Eat

Given its size and remote location, Doolin has a remarkable number of top-notch restaurants.

Doolin Café (☎ 707 4795, Roadford, Doolin) Mains €5-8.90. Opposite the post office, this cafe serves delicious vegetarian dishes.

O'Connor's (☎ 707 4168, Fisherstreet, Doolin) Mains €7.60-15.25. O'Connor's attracts tourists by the coachload for its music and ample servings of solid Irish pub grub like beef in Guinness stew.

McGann's (☎ 707 4133, Roadford, Doolin) Mains €7.50-13.90. McGann's is quieter and less formal than O'Connors, but the food is similar and just as good. Order at the bar then find a seat at one of the wooden tables near the open fire.

Flagship Restaurant (☎ 707 4688, Roadford, Doolin) Mains €6.50-13.95. Open 10am-6pm Tues-Sun Easter-Sept. This restaurant, in the Doolin Craft Gallery 1km from the upper village along the Lisdoonvarna road (turn just before St Catherine's Church), serves delicious home-cooked snacks and light meals. Hillary Clinton once dined (and shopped) here.

Bruach na hAille (☎ 707 4120, Roadford, Doolin) Mains €11.35-19. Open 6pm-9pm daily mid-Mar-Oct. If you feel like splashing out try this genteel old cottage restaurant next to McGann's pub. The imaginative menu is mostly seafood with some vegetarian choices, and its early-bird three-course meal (6pm to 7.30pm) is great value at €12.75.

Lazy Lobster (☎ 707 4390, Roadford, Doolin) Mains €12.95-22. Open 6.30pm-10pm daily. The Lazy Lobster, near the post office, serves fresh Doolin lobster (depending on availability). The creative, Asian-influenced menu also includes such dishes as salmon marinated in vodka.

Entertainment
Doolin is renowned for Irish music, and you can hear it almost every night in summer and at the weekend in winter.

O'Connor's (see Places to Eat) This Doolin pub packs in the tourists and has a great atmosphere when the traditional music, singing and drinking are all in full swing.

McGann's (see Places to Eat) McGann's has a friendly atmosphere, good music and *craic*, and photographs of the singing Kellys on the walls.

MacDiarmada's (☎ 707 4700, Roadford, Doolin) Also known as MacDermott's, this pub is frequented by locals and reportedly has some of the village's best traditional music.

Aran View House (see Places to Stay) The bar at this hotel provides a pleasant escape from the tumult in the village.

Getting There & Away
Bus Buses stop outside the post office in Roadford, Paddy's Doolin Hostel in Fisherstreet, and the Rainbow Hostel near Mc-Gann's pub. There are buses between Doolin and Ennis, Limerick, Galway and Dublin. For contact details, see Getting There & Away under The Burren earlier in this chapter.

Boat Doolin is the ferry departure point to the Aran Islands (see Aran Islands in the County Galway chapter). These are operated daily, Easter to September, by Doolin Ferries (☎ 707 4455, fax 707 4417, W www.doolin ferries.com), The Pier, Doolin. When the pier kiosk is closed contact the Atlantic View B&B (☎ 707 4189).

It takes around 30 minutes to cover the 8km to Inisheer, the smallest and closest of the three Aran Islands (return €19). There are around seven sailings daily from June to August, beginning at 10am. The last ferry returns from Inisheer at 5.30pm.

From June to August the first ferry to Inishmór, the largest island, leaves Doolin Harbour at 10am and the last ferry from Inishmór departs at 4pm (return €25.20, 50 minutes).

From June to August the first ferry to Inishmaan leaves at 10am and the last ferry back to Doolin leaves at 4.30pm (return €22.70, 40 minutes).

Getting Around
The Paddy's Doolin and Aille River hostels hire out bikes for €8.80/44.10 per day/week.

AROUND DOOLIN
Doonagore Castle
If you follow the coastal road (R478) for about 3km south of Doolin you'll come to Doonagore Castle, a restored 15th-century tower with a surrounding walled enclosure (or *bawn*). There's a lovely view from here over Doolin and the Aran Islands, especially at sunset.

Ballinalacken Castle
Five kilometres north of Doolin en route to Fanore is Ballinalacken Castle. Sitting astride a small cliff, this 15th-century O'Brien tower house is in excellent repair. However, it's privately owned and you may only climb the tower and enjoy the amazing view as a guest at the nearby hotel (Ballinalacken Castle Country House & Restaurant; ☎/fax 065-707

4025, [e] ballinalackencastle@eircom.net, Coast Rd, Doolin; rooms around €55 per person).

Just beside the gateway to the castle and hotel, a minor road leads inland up into the Burren. After about 1km, it meets one of the Burren's ancient green roads, and in good weather this route up to Fanore makes for a lovely walk. It also forms part of the Burren Way (see Walking under Activities in the Facts for the Visitor chapter).

Caving

The Doolin area is very popular with spelunkers. The British seem particularly fond of this sport and use Doolin as a base, spending their days crawling blindly through dirty holes and their nights crawling blindly through Doolin's pubs. The **Fisherstreet Potholes** are nearby, and **Poll na gColm**, 5km north-east of Lisdoonvarna, is Ireland's longest cave, with over 12km of mapped passageways.

A few hundred metres south of Ballinalacken Castle, you'll see some low cliffs on the eastern (or inland) side across a field. These hide the entrance to **Poll na Eidhnain** (or Poll na Ionáin), a cave that, after a difficult and mucky passage, widens to a chamber containing a 6m stalactite said to be the longest in Western Europe. The cavern is difficult to get to, and the farmer is not keen on trespassers, so ask permission first.

The rocks to the north of Doolin Harbour are honeycombed with an unusual system of undersea caves called the **Green Holes of Doolin**. They're the longest known undersea caves in temperate waters. Non-divers can look into Hell, a large gash in the rocks, north of the harbour and about 50m from the sea. The gash is about 6m wide, and the heaving water at the bottom leads to a maze of submarine passages.

LISDOONVARNA

☎ 065 • pop 650

Lisdoonvarna (Lios Dún Bhearna), often just called 'Lisdoon', is well known for its mineral springs, which people have been visiting for centuries to imbibe and bathe in. The town also used to be the centre for *basadóiri*

(matchmakers) who, for the appropriate fee, would fix a person up with a mate. Most aspiring swains would hit town in September, after the hay was in. Today, genuine matchmaking is a little thin on the ground, but the Lisdoonvarna Matchmaking Festival (☎ 707 4405, fax 707 4406), held in late September/early October, is still a great excuse for drinking, merrymaking and music in the pubs. With all those singles events, a few romances must blossom.

Orientation & Information

Lisdoonvarna is essentially a one-street town with a square in the centre from where you turn west for Doolin and the coast. The town has plenty of shops, pubs, B&Bs and smart hotels with good restaurants, but no bank or ATM. You can, however, change money at the post office on Main St to the north. Lisdoonvarna Laundrette (☎ 707 4577), at the rear of the car park facing the Imperial Hotel, opens 10am to 6pm, Monday to Saturday.

Spa Wells Health Centre

At the southern end of town is Ireland's only working spa (☎ 707 4023, Main St; sulphur bath €23; open 10am-6pm daily June-Sept). It has a sulphur spring, a Victorian pump house, massage room, sauna and mineral baths, all in an agreeable, wooded setting. The iron, sulphur, magnesium and iodine in the water are supposed to be good for rheumatic and glandular complaints, so if you have a spot of hyperthyroidism or ankylotic spondylitis, this is the place for you. You can drink the water, but it's not a pleasant experience.

Burren Smokehouse Visitor Centre

If you've ever wanted to know more about the 'ancient Irish tradition of oak-smoking Atlantic salmon', the video at the visitor centre (☎ 707 4432, Doolin Rd; free; open 9am-7pm daily) should answer your questions. Smoked salmon in all its guises is on sale, with free samples, and local tourist information is available. The centre is just west of Lisdoonvarna on the Doolin road (N67).

Places to Stay & Eat

There are lots of B&Bs and some of the cheaper ones are in the centre. Lisdoonvarna has about a dozen hotels, all charging around €50 to €65 for singles and €55 to €95 for doubles, depending on the season.

O'Loughlin's (☎ 707 4038, Main St) Singles/doubles €24/40. O'Loughlin's is an unpretentious, friendly B&B with clean rooms and rear car park.

Imperial Hotel (☎ 707 4042, fax 707 4428, Main St) Rooms €38 per person. 3-course dinner €19. Among the best, this yellow and blue, 100-room hotel is central, and its long, light and airy restaurant (open from 6pm) offers a wide selection of dishes including vegetarian.

Carrigann Hotel (☎ 707 4036, fax 707 4567, Doolin Rd) Rooms €50 per person. Carrigan Hotel, opposite Burren Smokehouse, is a small, peaceful hotel set in a landscaped garden and with its own restaurant.

Sheedy's Restaurant (☎ 707 4026, fax 707 4555, Liscannor Rd) Mains €15-24. Inside Sheedy's Spa View Hotel, this stylish restaurant dishes up excellent, modern Irish food and service in equal proportions.

Irish Arms (Main St) Meals €7.50. This pub, next to the post office, wears its colours openly: the Irish tricolour hangs over the front and Glasgow Celtic football club memorabilia lines the interior. The food is of the fish and chips variety, but is filling and tasty.

Getting There & Around

For bus services, see Getting There & Away under The Burren earlier in this chapter. Burke's Garage (☎ 707 4022), just off the square, has bikes for hire for €8.80/44.10 per day/week.

BALLYREEN

A deserted stretch of rocky coast about 6km south of Fanore, Ballyreen is a lovely spot and a good place to camp. There's a cliff called **Ailladie**, which boasts some of Ireland's finest rock climbing. For scuba divers, a barely visible track leads to a small inlet that has some excellent underwater scenery on the left, dropping quickly to a depth of about 20m, with vertical walls and gullies covered in jewel anemones.

Offshore after heavy rain you may see currents of brown water coming through the clear surface water. These are resurgences: fresh water flooding from an undersea cave. On land, Ice Age glaciers have polished the limestone to a gloss. The incongruous stones and boulders were dumped here by glaciers. There's no bus to Ballyreen.

FANORE

☎ 065 • pop 150

Fanore (Fanóir), 5km south of Black Head, is less a village and more a stretch of coast, with a shop, a pub, and a few houses scattered along the main road (R477). It has a fine sandy beach with an extensive backdrop of dunes. It's the only **safe beach** between Lahinch and Ballyvaughan. The remains of a Stone Age settlement were discovered near the small river that runs down through the dunes. Along the road south of the beach are a scattering of 10th- and 11th-century **church ruins**.

The only shop in the area is a small grocery store/post office/newsagent/fishing-tackle shop next to the Admiral's Rest Seafood Restaurant (see later).

Things to See & Do

Just behind Fanore Beach, a road goes inland and up the Caher River Valley, or **Khyber Pass**. This is the only surface river in the Burren. The first few kilometres are very pleasant, and there are foxes, badgers and pine martens in the area, though you'll be lucky to spot any.

John McNamara at the **Admiral's Rest Seafood Restaurant** (☎ *707 6105*, ✉ *jdmna @iol.ie, Fanore*), the home of the Burren Conservation Trust, organises a Burren Wildlife Weekend once a year in May. The trust also does historical research of some of the offshore islands. It has a **nature reserve** about 5km south of Fanore in the Caher River Valley. Volunteers are given free accommodation (and sometimes free food) at the Admiral's Rest in exchange for working at the reserve. Contact John for details.

Fanore has a couple of lovely **walks**. On

the coast road about 400m south of the beach, a small road goes inland. After about 3km, it meets an old green road that can be followed south to Ballinalacken Castle and is part of the Burren Way. Alternatively, you can park at the Admiral's Rest Seafood Restaurant and go straight up through the fields to the green road. On top of this hill are two caves. **Poll Dubh** is a relatively easy cave for amateurs to explore, with delicate stalactites on view. The other, **Poll Mor**, is home to badgers, foxes, hares and rabbits.

There's a well preserved **ring fort** and souterrain on top of a hill at the southern end of Fanore and about 1km inland.

Places to Stay & Eat
Admiral's Rest Seafood Restaurant (☎ 707 6105, ✉ jdmna@iol.ie, Fanore) Rooms including breakfast €19 per person. Dinner €6.35-27.75. This restaurant-cum-B&B is at the southern end of Fanore. Rooms are clean and tidy and you dine 'a la Fred Flintstone' at stone tables in the restaurant, which only uses wild fish and fresh lobster, the latter being its speciality. If you stay a week or more you get a free boat ride on Galway Bay.

Entertainment
O'Donohue's (☎ 707 6104, Fanore) This pub, 4km south of the beach, is a friendly place, with music on Saturday night. It hosts some of the sessions for the Lisdoonvarna Matchmaker Festival in September. There are no other bars along this stretch of coast.

Getting There & Away
For information on bus services, see Getting There & Away under The Burren earlier in this chapter.

BLACK HEAD & CATHAIR DHÚN IORAIS
Black Head, Clare's north-westernmost point, is a bleak but imposing mountain of limestone dropping swiftly into the sea. The head has an unstaffed lighthouse and good shore **angling** for sea bass and cod. If you're lucky, you may see dolphins.

There's a great hike up the head to the large Iron Age stone fort, Cathair Dhún Iorais (Fort

of Irghus). The views across Galway Bay and the Aran Islands are exceptional, especially with the steep walls of the fort as a backdrop. Inland, the hills rise to 318m and farther back is Slieve Elva (345m), capped with shale. Some of the intervening summits are marked with Bronze Age cairns. On your way up to the fort you cross an old green road.

BALLYVAUGHAN & AROUND
☎ 065 • pop 260
Ballyvaughan (Baile Uí Bheacháin) is a small, pretty fishing village on a quiet corner of Galway Bay that attracts well heeled visitors. Its attractive pubs, restaurants and places to stay make it a good base for visiting the northern part of the Burren.

Just west of the village, past the holiday cottages, is the quay and Monk's Bar. The harbour was built in 1829 at a time when boats traded with the Aran Islands and Galway, often bringing in turf – a scarce commodity in this area.

Ballyvaughan is a T-junction. Going south and inland on the N67 brings you to the centre of the Burren, Aillwee Caves, Poulnabrone Dolmen and Lisdoonvarna. Turning west leads you to the magnificent coast road (R477), Black Head and south towards Doolin. Going north-east on the N67, you reach Kinvara and County Galway.

Information
There are no banks in Ballyvaughan, but you can change money on Main St in the post office or at the Whitethorn Craft and Visitor Centre, 3km north-east of Ballyvaughan on the way to Kinvara.

Burren Exposure
At the Whitethorn Craft and Visitor Centre, 3km north-east of town on the N67, is the Burren Exposure *(☎ 707 7277, Kinvara Rd; adult/child €4.45/2.50; open 10am-5pm daily Easter-Sept)*. It has an interesting series of audiovisual presentations on the history, geology, flora and fauna of the region.

Corkscrew Hill
Six kilometres south of Ballyvaughan on the Lisdoonvarna road is a series of severe

bends up Corkscrew Hill. The road was built as part of a Famine-relief scheme in the 1840s. From the top there are spectacular views of the northern Burren and Galway Bay, with Aillwee Mountain and the caves on the right and Cappanawalla Hill on the left, and with the partially restored 16th-century Newtown Castle, erstwhile residence of the O'Lochlains, at its base. From here, the route to Lisdoonvarna is through boggy, fairly boring countryside.

Gleninagh Castle

Down a narrow leafy lane and just off the coast road about 6km west of Ballyvaughan is Gleninagh, another 16th-century O'Lochlain castle (the O'Lochlains were chieftains in this region). The castle was inhabited as late as 1840. In front of the castle is a holy well still in use, and the ruins of a medieval church. To the east you may find a small horseshoe-shaped mound of earth: a *fulacht fiadh* (cooking place) dating from the Bronze Age.

Places to Stay

You can *camp* in many of the fields around Ballyvaughan or along the coast just beyond the harbour. There are no hostels in Ballyvaughan; the closest is *Johnston's Independent Hostel* in Kinvara, County Galway (see the County Galway chapter). There are many guesthouses out around Doorus and New Quay – they all get busy in season, so book ahead.

Stonepark House (☎ 707 7056, *Bishops Quarter*) Singles/doubles €25.40/43.20. Open Apr-Sept. Stonepark is a small (three rooms) but neat B&B in a peaceful location just over 1km along the Kinvara road.

Rusheen Lodge (☎ 707 7092, *fax 707 7152,* e *rusheenl@iol.ie, Lisdoonvarna Rd*) Rooms around €45 per person. This particularly good B&B, a little over 1km south on the N67, isn't cheap, but the rooms and breakfasts are top class.

Hyland's Hotel (☎ 707 7037, *fax 707 7131, Main St*) Rooms with bathroom around €59 per person. Open Apr-Dec. This 19-room, family-run place in the heart of Ballyvaughan is an old but refurbished

hotel with spacious rooms and modern facilities.

Places to Eat

Most bars in town serve food.

Tea Junction Café (☎ 707 7289, *Main St*) Meals €3.80-5.70. This cafe in the centre where the three roads into the village converge, serves a top-notch, filling breakfast and good meals (including vegetarian) all day.

Whitethorn Craft and Visitor Centre (☎ 707 7044, *Kinvara Rd*) Mains €8.20. This place has a friendly coffee-shop-cum-restaurant where you can enjoy the view out over the bay while you eat. It has a small bar.

O'Brien's (☎ 707 7003, *Main St*) Mains €7.90-15.75. A few doors down from Hyland's Hotel, this is a relaxed, informal pub and restaurant, which does a good line in seafood too. Sandwiches are available during the day until 6pm.

Monk's Bar (☎ 707 7059, *Main St*) Mains €8.20-15.15. A popular place on the harbour, Monk's Bar has a large seafood selection as well as some old stand-bys like Irish stew. Try the melt-in-your-mouth mussels in garlic butter.

Entertainment

O'Brien's (see Places to Eat) The centre of the floor is set aside for dancing Thursday to Sunday nights to more contemporary music.

Monk's Bar (see Places to Eat) Visitors delight in Monk's traditional music sessions on Tuesday and from Friday to Sunday in summer, and there's plenty of floor space for dancing.

Ólólainn (Main St) This tiny place (pronounced o-**loch**-lain), on the left as you head down to the harbour, is a lovely old country pub. Sip your Guinness in the front bar or enjoy the intimacy of one of the snugs in the back.

Getting There & Away

For information on bus services see Getting There & Away under The Burren earlier in this chapter. The Spar supermarket is the Bus Éireann agent.

CENTRAL BURREN

The road through the heart of the Burren – the R480 – runs south from Ballyvaughan to Leamanegh Castle, where it joins the R476 which runs south-east to Corofin, and north-west to Kilfenora. Travelling south from Ballyvaughan (on the N67), turn east before Corkscrew Hill at the Aillwee Caves sign. The road goes past Gleninsheen Wedge Tomb, Poulnabrone Dolmen and into some really desolate scenery.

Aillwee Caves

A good place to spend a rainy afternoon or to take children is the extensive limestone Aillwee Caves system (☎ 065-707 7036, Ballyvaughan; adult/concession €6.30/3.50, families from €17.65; open 10am-6.30pm daily July-Aug; 10am-5.30pm daily Sept-June). The main passage penetrates for 600m into the mountain, widening into larger caverns, one with its own waterfall. The caves were carved out by water some two million years ago. Near the entrance are the remains of a brown bear, extinct in Ireland for over 10,000 years.

Aillwee was discovered in 1944 by a local farmer, and today has a discreetly designed outer building with an excellent cafe. The delicatessen here makes its own cheese. Behind the cave entrance there is a relatively easy scramble up Aillwee Mountain (300m), with fine views from the summit. You can only go into the cave as part of a guided tour; the last tour departs at 5.30pm (6.30pm in summer). Try to visit early in the day before the crowds arrive.

Gleninsheen Wedge Tomb

This tomb is known in folklore as the Druid's Altar, though the druids lived a long time after this was built. The tomb is beside the R480 just south of Aillwee Caves. It's thought to date from 4000 to 5000 years ago and, like most of the other tombs in the Burren, it's on high ground.

A magnificent gold torc was found nearby in 1930 by a boy hunting rabbits. It was in a crack in the limestone and at first the boy thought it was part of a coffin. Dating from around 700 BC, the torc is reckoned to be one of the finest pieces of prehistoric Irish craftwork and is now on display at the National Museum in Dublin.

Poulnabrone Dolmen

Poulnabrone Dolmen is one of Ireland's most photographed ancient monuments – the one you see on all the postcards. The dolmen is a three-legged tomb, sitting in a sea of limestone without a house in sight, 8km south of Aillwee and signposted from the R480.

Poulnabrone was built over 5000 years ago. It was excavated in 1989, and the remains of more than 25 people were found among pieces of pottery and jewellery. Radiocarbon dating suggests that they were buried between 3800 and 3200 BC. When the dead were originally entombed here, the whole structure was covered in a mound of earth, which has since worn away. The Irish *poll na bró* means 'hole of the grinding stone', and the capstone weighs five tonnes.

At quiet times of day, this can be a truly lovely spot. Try to visit early in the morning or at sunset for good photographs. Sadly, though, some unthinking travellers have used small rocks scattered around to build their own miniature cairns and dolmens, threatening not only the magic of the place but also its delicate ecosystem. Local people are then left with the job of repairing the damage.

Carron & Cahercommaun Cliff Fort

Near the tiny village of Carron (Carran on some maps; An Carn in Gaelic), a few kilometres east of the R480, is the remote **Burren Perfumery and Floral Centre** (☎ 065-708 9102, Carron; free; open 9am-6pm daily). It uses wildflowers of the Burren to produce its scents, and it's the only handicraft perfumery in Ireland. There's a free audiovisual presentation on the flora of the Burren.

Three kilometres south of Carron and perched on the edge of an inland cliff is the great stone fort of Cahercommaun. It was inhabited in the 8th and 9th centuries by people who hunted deer and grew a small amount of grain. There are the remains of a souterrain leading from the fort to the outer cliff face. To get there, go south from Carron and take a left turn for Kilnaboy. After 1.5km a path on the left leads up to the fort.

East of Carron

If you turn east at Carron, you have two options. The first is to turn north after about 3km, which takes you on a magnificent drive through a valley to Cappaghmore in County Galway. If you continue east from Carron you come close to the lovely **Mt Mullaghmore** (191m). Later, just over the Galway border on the main road to Gort (R460), is **Kilmacduagh**, a monastic site with a splendid round tower.

LEAMANEGH CASTLE

Leamanegh is a fine castle-cum-fortified-house 8km north west of Corofin on the Kilfenora road. Its name (pronounced **lay-um-on-ay**) comes from the Irish for 'deer's leap' or 'horse's leap'. If you look carefully, you'll see that there are two parts joined together. The five-storey tower house on the right was built around 1480 by the O'Briens and is more solid and better defended than the main house, which Conor O'Brien added in 1640. This has four storeys, and its most appealing features are the largely intact stone window frames. The whole building was originally surrounded by a high wall.

Just above the tower-house entrance is a vertical shaft or 'murder hole'. If this was the 15th century and you were an uninvited guest, all manner of unspeakable things might have been dropped on you from here, including boiling oil, tar, arrows, dead animals – or anything else that came to hand.

Today, the castle is on private property and no public access is allowed.

KILFENORA

☎ 065 • pop 200

The tiny, windswept village of Kilfenora (Cill Fhionnúrach) lies on the southern fringes of the Burren, 8km south-east of Lisdoonvarna. Most visitors come to savour the traditional music in its pubs and to see the monastic remains, high crosses and diminutive 12th-century cathedral.

Maire Rua McMahon

Conor O'Brien was killed in 1651 while fighting for the royalists against Cromwell. His wife, the notorious Maire Rua McMahon, reportedly refused to accept his body back into Leamanegh Castle. After his death, she offered to marry one of Cromwell's soldiers to ensure that her son Donough didn't lose his inheritance. Marry Maire did, but she and her son still lost the estate. Despite this setback, Maire and her new husband, John Cooper, stayed together. They regained their property in 1675, but later records show she was tried – and acquitted – for Cooper's subsequent murder. She died in 1686.

Burren Centre

At the time of research the centre (☎ 708 8030, Main St), which houses information on the Burren, was closed and being completely rebuilt. Call to see whether it has reopened.

Kilfenora Cathedral

The pope has the honour of also being the bishop of the diocese of Kilfenora and Killaloe; in the past the ruined 12th-century cathedral was an important place of pilgrimage. St Fachan (or Fachtna) founded the monastery here in the 6th century, and it later became the seat of Kilfenora diocese, the smallest in the country.

The cathedral is the smallest you're ever likely to see. Only the ruined structure and nave of the more recent Protestant church are actually part of the cathedral. The chancel has two primitive carved figures on top of two tombs. One is a bishop (note the mitre), and it must be said that neither was a very handsome gentleman. The theory goes that after the Black Death in the 14th century there was a general decline in craft skills across the continent, and these poor carvings may be examples of this.

High Crosses

Kilfenora is best known for its high crosses, three in the churchyard and a large

12th-century example in the field about 100m to the west.

The most interesting one is the 800-year-old **Doorty Cross**, standing prominently to the west of the church's front door. It differs significantly from the standard Irish high cross in that it's without the usual pierced disc or wheel. It was lying broken in two until the 1950s, when it was re-erected.

The eastern face of the cross is the better preserved. One interpretation of the carvings has Christ on top ordering two figures in the middle to destroy the devil/bird at the bottom, which is misbehaving; another is that it portrays St Patrick. The western face is much less clear. Christ still appears to be on top, this time surrounded by birds. Directly underneath are delicate designs and a man on horseback holding the ends of the patterns. Some say it's Christ's entry into Jerusalem. One theory suggests the cross may commemorate Kilfenora being made the diocesan seat in the 12th century.

Places to Stay & Eat

Mrs Mary Murphy (☎ 708 8040, Main St) Singles/doubles €25.40/43.20. Open mid-Feb-Nov. This welcoming, central B&B has three en-suite rooms and filling breakfasts.

Lakeside Lodge (☎ 707 1710, fax 707 1182, Lickeen, Kilfenora) Singles/doubles €30.50/48.30. Open mid-Mar-Oct. About 4km south-west along the Ennistymon road beside Lickeen Lough, this pleasant, four-bedroomed property is on a working farm. It's nonsmoking and there are bikes for hire.

Linnane's (☎ 708 8157, Main St) Snacks under €4. This pub is fine if you're just after soup or a sandwich.

Vaughan's Pub (☎ 708 8004, Main St) Mains €6.95-9.45. Food served noon-9pm. Local produce, including North Clare cheese and organic meat, is used in the preparation of Vaughan's good-value, traditional Irish menu.

Entertainment

Several pubs put on traditional music throughout the year.

Linnane's (☎ 708 8157, Main St) Framed photos of past performers line the wall at this old pub which has traditional Irish music and the occasional British folk singer on Wednesday, Saturday and Sunday.

Vaughan's Pub (☎ 708 8004, Main St) The attached barn is the scene for set dancing on Thursday and Sunday nights and regular Irish music sessions.

COROFIN & AROUND
☎ 065 • pop 200
Corofin (Cora Finne), also spelled Corrofin, is a small village on the southern fringes of the Burren. Commonly found in the area are turloughs (from the Irish *turlach*), small lakes that often disappear during dry summers. O'Brien castles abound in this boggy countryside: two of them are on the shores of nearby Lough Inchiquin.

Corofin is home to the interesting **Clare Heritage Centre** (☎ 683 7955, e clare heritage@eircom.net, Church St; adult/concession €2.50/1.30; open 10am-5pm daily mid-June-Sept). It has a display covering the period around the Potato Famine. Over 250,000 people lived in Clare before the Potato Famine; today the county's population stands at about 91,000 – a drop of some 64%. In a separate building nearby the **genealogical centre** (open 9am-5.30pm Mon-Fri year round) has facilities for people researching their Clare ancestry. Contact the heritage centre for more information.

About 4km north-west of Corofin, on the road to Leamanegh Castle and Kilfenora (R476), look for the small town of **Kilnaboy**. The ruined church here is well worth seeking out for the sheila-na-gig over the doorway.

Places to Stay & Eat

There are plenty of B&Bs in Corofin and the surrounding area – many of them are in Kilnaboy along the road to Kilfenora.

Lakefield Lodge (☎ 683 7675, fax 683 7299, Ennis Rd) En-suite singles/doubles €33/44.30. Open Mar-Nov. Lakefield Lodge is a bright, spotless B&B, and accepts credit cards.

Shamrock and Heather (☎ 683 7061, Station Rd) Singles/doubles €29.85/44.30. Open Mar-Oct. The comfortable rooms in this bungalow have full facilities, and there are reduced rates for children.

Corofin Arms (☎ *683 7373, Main St*) Mains €10-14.50. Good, inexpensive bar food (sandwiches, baguettes, salads) is served during the day, and there's a la carte dining in the evening (6pm-9.30pm).

Bofey Quinn's (☎ *683 7321, Main St*) Mains €7.50-13.25. Restaurant open noon-9.30pm. At this well regarded pub you'll find simple delicious meals such as Irish stew and pasta plus more substantial steak and seafood offerings.

Getting There & Away

Bus Éireann bus No 333 from Kilkee or Doonbeg to Ennis and Limerick stops in Corofin on Monday only. Check with the Ennis bus station (☎ 065-682 4177) for times.

NORTHERN BURREN

Low farmland stretches south from County Galway until it meets the bluff limestone hills of the Burren. The Burren begins west of Kinvara and Doorus in County Galway, where the road forks, going inland to Carron or along the coast to Ballyvaughan.

From Oranmore in County Galway to Ballyvaughan, the coastline wriggles along small inlets and peninsulas; some, such as Finavarra Point and New Quay, are worth a detour.

Inland near Bellharbour is the largely intact Corcomroe Abbey, while the three ancient churches of Oughtmama lie up a quiet side valley. Galway Bay forms the backdrop to some outstanding scenery: bare stone hills shining in the sun, with small hamlets and rich patches of green wherever there's soil.

Getting There & Away

Late May to late September, Bus Éireann bus No 50 between Galway and Cork passes through Kinvara and Ballyvaughan up to four-times daily. Bus No 423 between Galway and Doolin also stops in those two places; there are up to three buses daily, May to September, and one bus a day Monday to Saturday the rest of the year. Check the details with the bus station at Galway (☎ 091-562000) or Ennis (☎ 065-682 4177).

New Quay & the Flaggy Shore

New Quay (Ceibh Nua), on the **Finavarra Peninsula**, is about 2km off the main Kinvara to Ballyvaughan road (N67). There are a few thatched cottages on the peninsula and also the ruins of a 17th-century mansion.

It's worth stopping at *Linnane's Bar* (☎ *065-707 8120, New Quay*), a modest pub next to Ireland's largest oyster farm, for its delicious fresh seafood. Mains cost around €6 to €15.

The Flaggy Shore, west of New Quay, is a particularly fine stretch of coastline. Layers of limestone march boldly into the sea and, behind the coastal path, swans parade gently on **Lough Muirí**. There are otters in the area. On the way out to **Finavarra Point** (continue on the road past Linnane's Bar) you pass **Mt Vernon Lodge**, once the summer home of Lady Gregory, playwright and friend of WB Yeats. She was prominent in the Anglo-Irish literary revival.

On Finavarra Point is one of the western coast's few **Martello towers**, built in the early 1800s to warn Galway in case Napoleon sneaked into Ireland through the back door. The road loops back and joins the main road beside a small lake rich in bird life, including duck, moorhen and heron.

Bellharbour

Bellharbour (Beulaclugga) is no more than a crossroads with some thatched holiday cottages and a pub, about 8km east of Ballyvaughan. There's an excellent **walk** along an old green road that begins behind the modern Church of St Patrick, 1km north up the hill from the Y-junction at Bellharbour, and threads north along Abbey Hill.

Inland from here are the ruins of Corcomroe Abbey, the valley and churches of Oughtmama, and the interior road that takes you through the heart of the Burren.

Wildlife A sighting of seals along the coast west of Bellharbour is almost guaranteed. Go about 1km along the Ballyvaughan road until you spot a large farm shed on the right then follow the path down to the shore. This inlet is also thick with birds, and winter

The Legend of Corcomroe

In 1317, the Battle of Corcomroe was fought very near Corcomroe Abbey between two O'Brien clans trying to win control of Clare. Legend has it that one of the chieftains, Donough, was passing by Lough Rask on his way to battle when he saw a witch washing a pile of bleeding limbs in the water. The witch told Donough that her name was Bronach Boirne and that the corpses would be those of his soldiers if he insisted on going into battle. To make matters worse, Donough's own head was in the pile.

Donough's men tried to capture the elusive witch, but she flew up in the air and rained curses on them. To reassure his men, Donough told them that Bronach was the lover of his arch rival, Dermot O'Brien, and her warnings merely a ploy to frighten them off. Unfortunately for Donough, by that night he and most of his army were lying dead in the abbey.

Incidentally, on nearby Moneen Mountain is a pass called Mam Catha (Pass of the Battle), which could refer to the route taken by Donough and his army. Dermot, the victor, later defeated de Clare of Bunratty, halting the spread of Anglo-Norman influence in Clare for a couple of hundred years.

visitors include brent geese from northern Canada.

Corcomroe Abbey Corcomroe, a former Cistercian abbey 1km inland from Bellharbour, lies in a small, tranquil valley surrounded by low hills. It was founded in 1194 by Donal Mór O'Brien. His grandson, Conor O'Brien (died 1267), king of Thomond, occupies the tomb in the northern wall, and there's a crude carving of him below an effigy of a staring bishop armed with a crosier. Some fine Romanesque carvings are scattered throughout the abbey.

Oughtmama Valley Oughtmama is a lonely, deserted valley hiding some small, ancient churches. To get there turn inland at Bellharbour, left at the Y-junction, and go up to a clump of trees and a house on the right. A rough track from there leads east up a blind valley to the churches. St Colman Mac-Duagh, who also built churches on the Aran Islands, founded the monastery here in the 6th century. The churches were built in the 12th century by monks in search of solitude. It's a hardy walk up **Turlough Hill** behind the chapels, but the views are tremendous. Near the summit are the remains of a hill fort.

County Galway

County Galway is one of the highlights of any visit to Ireland. Stretching westwards from Ballinasloe in the midlands, through the wilds of Connemara, to the craggy Atlantic coastline beyond Clifden, Galway has just about everything packed into its 5940 sq km. It's the second-largest county in Ireland, after Cork, and the city of Galway is the western coast's liveliest, most populous settlement.

Galway's neighbour to the south is County Clare, and the Burren limestone region peters out near Kinvara, a picturesque little coastal town just within the Galway border. The limestone emerges out to sea in a long, grey reef that forms the three Aran Islands. These are famous for their folklore, bleak but evocative scenery, Irish speakers and woollen sweaters.

Galway's landscape is extremely varied. Lough Corrib cuts off the rugged coastal region from the largely flat interior that makes up the bulk of the county.

Galway

☎ 091 • pop 57,000

Galway city is a delight, with its narrow streets, old stone and wooden shop fronts, good restaurants and busy pubs. It's also the administrative capital of the county and home to the local government, University College Galway and a regional college east of town. There's a ferry to the Aran Islands from the docks, although you're better off travelling farther west along the Connemara coast and taking a boat from Rossaveal.

In marked contrast to most of the depopulated western coast, Galway is one of Europe's fastest-growing, increasingly cosmopolitan cities; it ranks fourth in size in the Republic, after Dublin, Cork and Limerick. Large factories and a bustling energy underlie its relative economic security.

Galway has always attracted a bohemian crowd of musicians, artists, intellectuals and young people – a mix that's partly due

Highlights

- Enjoy the lively nightlife and festivals of Galway city
- Journey through the wonderfully scenic Lough Inagh Valley in Connemara
- Watch the bird life and enjoy the tranquillity of Inishbofin Island
- Get in touch with nature by walking the glens of Connemara National Park
- Walk or cycle the ruggedly beautiful Sky Road near Clifden in Connemara
- Visit Inishmór, the largest of the Aran Islands, and explore magical Dun Aengus perched on its southern cliffs
- Cycle round the timeless Aran Islands of Inishmaan and Inisheer

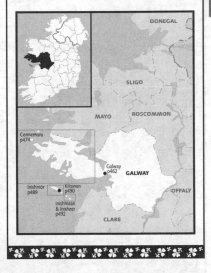

to the presence of the university. The main attractions for the traveller are the nightlife and pubs, where talk and drink flow with equal force. The city is a major Gaelic centre and Irish is widely understood. The Druid Theatre is one of the best in Ireland,

GALWAY

GALWAY

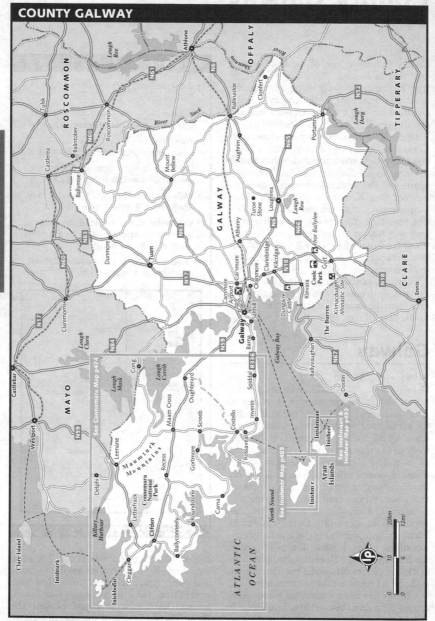

COUNTY GALWAY

and the city hosts a hugely popular arts festival every summer. The place goes wild during Galway Race Week in the last week of July. If you haven't booked, accommodation is difficult to find at these times.

While the city centre deserves its accolades, the approaches and suburbs don't. Coming from the east, you pass huge modern hotels, barren housing developments and the ugly regional college. The coastal road west through the beach resort of Salthill and on to Spiddal is one of the worst examples of ribbon development in the country. Only after Spiddal do the bungalows start to thin out.

HISTORY

Galway grew from a small fishing village in the Claddagh area at the mouth of the River Corrib to become an important walled town when the Anglo-Normans under Richard de Burgo (also spelled de Burgh or Burke) captured territory from the local O'Flahertys in 1232. The Irish word for 'outsiders' or 'foreigners' is *gaill*, which may be the origin of the city's name in Irish, Gaillimh. The town walls were built by the Anglo-Normans from around 1270.

Galway became something of an outpost in the 'wild west'. In 1396, Richard II granted a charter to the city, effectively transferring power from the de Burgos to 14 merchant families or 'tribes'. This led to the name 'City of the Tribes', by which Galway is still known. These powerful families were mostly English or Norman in origin, and clashes with the leading Irish families of Connemara were frequent. At one time the city's western gate bore the prayer and warning: 'From the fury of the O'Flahertys, good Lord deliver us.' To ensure the ferocity was kept outside, the city fathers warned in the early 16th century that no uninvited 'O' or 'Mac' should show his face on Galway's streets.

English power throughout the region waxed and waned, but the city maintained its independent status under the ruling merchant families, who were mostly loyal to the English Crown. Galway's relative isolation encouraged a huge trade in wine, spices, fish and salt with Portugal and Spain. At one point the city rivalled Bristol and London in the volume of goods passing through its docks.

For a long while Galway prospered. A massive fire in 1473 destroyed much of the town but created space for a new street layout, and many solid stone buildings were erected in the 15th and 16th centuries.

It's said that Christopher Columbus tarried in Galway to hear Mass and pray at the Collegiate Church of St Nicholas of Myra. This Galway side-trip supposedly occurred either because one of the crew was a Galway man or because Columbus wished to investigate tales of St Brendan's earlier voyage to the Americas from here.

Galway's faithful support of the English Crown led to its downfall with the arrival of Cromwell. The city was besieged in 1651 and fell in April 1652. Cromwell's forces under Charles Coote wreaked their usual havoc, and Galway's long period of decline began. In 1691 the city chose the wrong side again, and William of Orange's forces added to the destruction. The important trade with Spain was almost at an end and, with Dublin and Waterford taking most of the sea traffic, Galway stagnated until its revival in modern times.

ORIENTATION

Galway's tightly packed town centre lies on both sides of the River Corrib, which connects Lough Corrib with the sea, though Eyre Square and most of the main shopping areas are on the river's eastern bank. There are three main bridges; the northernmost, Salmon Weir Bridge, looks over a salmon trap and is overshadowed by Galway Cathedral.

From Eyre Square, the meandering main shopping street starts as Williamsgate St, becomes William St and then Shop St, before splitting into Mainguard St and High St. Just east of Eyre Square is the combined bus and train station, north of which is the tourist office.

South and east of Wolfe Tone Bridge is the historic, but totally redeveloped, district of Claddagh; to the west is the beach resort of Salthill, a fairly popular area for accommodation and restaurants.

GALWAY

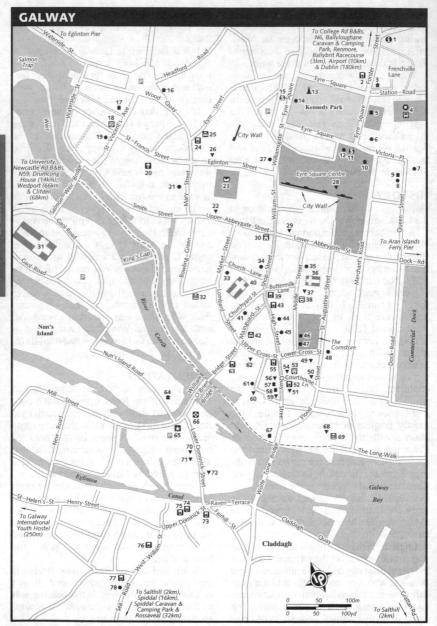

GALWAY

To Eglinton Pier

Waterside St

Salmon Trap

Weir

To University, Newcastle Rd B&Bs, N59, Drumcong House (14km), Westport (66km) & Clifden (68km)

Salmon Weir Bridge

Gaol Road

31

Gaol Road

King's Gap

Nun's Island

River Corrib

Nun's Island Road

Headford Road

Wood Quay

17

18

19

St-Vincent's-Ave

St-Francis Street

St-Vincent's Ave

16

25

24

26

20

21

22

Mary Street

Smith Street

23

Eglinton Street

City Wall

Eyre Street

15

14

Kennedy Park

Eyre Square

Williamgate St

William St

13

Eyre Square Centre

28

City Wall

To College Rd B&Bs, N6, Ballyloughane Caravan & Camping Park, Renmore, Ballybrit Racecourse (3km), Airport (10km) & Dublin (180km)

Forster Street

1

2

3

Station Road

Frenchville Lane

5

4

6

Victoria Pl

12 11

10

7

9

8

Queen Street

To Aran Islands Ferry Pier

Dock Rd

Merchant's Road

Commercial Dock

Upper Abbeygate Street

Lower-Abbeygate St

29

30

Bowling-Green

Market Street

Lombard Street

Church Lane

Shop Street

34

33

40

32

Churchyard St

Mainguard St

High Street

Buttermilk Lane

Middle Street

Cross Street

35

36

37

38

39

43

41

42

44

45

46

47

The Cornstore

48

St-Augustine-Street

Upper-Cross-St

Lower-Cross-St

62

63

61

60

55

56

57

58

59

54

53

49

50

51

52

Courthouse Ln

Flood Street

64

William Street

O'Brien Bridge

Bridge-Street

Mill Street

New Road

Eglinton

66

65

70

71

72

Lower-Dominick-Street

67

68

69

The Long Walk

Wolfe Tone Bridge

St-Helen's-St

Henry Street

Canal

75 74

73

Upper-Dominick-St

Fairhill St

Raven Terrace

Claddagh Quay

Galway Bay

Claddagh

To Galway International Youth Hostel (250m)

76

West-William-St

77

78

Sea Road

To Salthill (2km), Spiddal (16km), Spiddal Caravan & Camping Park & Rossaveal (32km)

Galway Bay

0   50   100m

0   50   100yd

To Salthill (2km)

Grattan Rd

GALWAY

PLACES TO STAY
3 Galway Hostel
5 Great Southern Hotel
9 Celtic Tourist Hostel
10 Kinlay House; Celnet
   e.centre; usit
16 Wood Quay Hostel
17 Salmon Weir Hostel
57 Barnacle's Quay Street House
58 Spanish Arch Hotel
64 St Martin's B&B
67 Jury's Galway Inn

PLACES TO EAT
22 Couch Potatas
26 Conlon's Restaurant
28 Sails
29 Food for Thought
37 Aideen's Brasserie Eleven
49 Mocha Beans
50 Cactus Jacks
51 Fat Freddy's
54 Druid Lane Restaurant
56 Pierre's
59 McDonagh's
60 Kirwan's Lane Creative
   Cuisine
62 Busker Brownes
68 Scoosi
70 Pasta Paradiso
71 Left Bank Café
72 Le Graal

PUBS
2 An Púcán
24 McSwiggan's
39 Taaffe's Bar
43 The King's Head
52 The Quays
55 Seáan Ua Neáhtain
63 The Lisheen Bar
73 Monroe's Tavern
74 Roísín Dubh
75 Taylor's Bar
76 The Blue Note
77 The Crane Bar

OTHER
1 Ireland West Tourism Office
4 Bus & Train Station
6 Island Ferries Ticket Office
7 Island Ferries Information
   Office
8 Celtic Cycles
11 Bank of Ireland
12 Eyre Square Centre Entrance
13 Pádraic O'Conaire's Statue
14 Browne's Doorway
15 Bank of Ireland
18 Town Hall Theatre
19 Town Hall
20 Franciscan Abbey
21 The Bubbles Inn
23 Post Office
25 Corrib & Apollo Taxis

27 Stephen Faller
30 Lynch's Castle; Allied Irish
   Bank
31 Galway Cathedral
32 Nora Barnacle House
33 Lynch Memorial Window
34 Eason's Bookshop
35 Mulligan Records
36 Augustinian Church
38 An Taibhdhearc na Gaillimhe
   (Galway Theatre)
40 Collegiate Church of St
   Nicholas of Myra
41 Hawkins House
   Bookshop
42 Galway Taxis
44 Old Malt Shopping Arcade;
   net@access Cyber Cafe;
   Olde Malte Laundrette
45 Kenny's Bookshop
46 Charlie Byrne's Bookshop
47 River Deep Mountain
   High
48 Mayoralty House
53 Druid Theatre
61 Design Concourse
   Ireland
65 Police Station
66 Bridge Mills
69 Spanish Arch; Galway City
   Museum
78 The Laundrette

GALWAY

Available in bookshops is *Medieval Galway*, a guide and map published by Tír Eolas.

INFORMATION
Tourist Offices
The big Ireland West Tourism office (☎ 563081) on Forster St, north of Eyre Square, opens 9am to 5.45pm Monday to Saturday in May; 9am to 6.45pm Monday to Saturday in June; 8.30am to 7.45pm daily in July and August; and 9am to 5.45pm weekdays, 9am to noon Saturday, the rest of the year. It's busy at the height of the season and there may be delays of an hour or more in making accommodation bookings.

There's a seasonal tourist office (☎ 563 081) in Salthill open June to September. Head towards the seafront along Salthill Rd until you come to a roundabout at the promenade. Turn left and you'll see the office.

Money
Irish banks each have several branches in the city centre. There's a Bank of Ireland on Eyre Square, while the branch at 43 Eyre Square next to the entrance to the Eyre Square Centre also has a bureau de change. A branch of the Allied Irish Bank is in Lynch's Castle on Shop St. The banks open 10am to 4pm weekdays (to 5pm on Thursday) and have ATMs. The main tourist office also changes money, as does the post office.

Post & Communications
The post office on Eglinton St opens 9am to 5.30pm Monday to Saturday.

To get on the Internet there's net@ccess Cyber Cafe (☎ 569772), in the Old Malt shopping arcade, where you can surf 10am to 9pm weekdays, 10am to 7pm Saturday and noon to 6pm Sunday for €6.30 per hour.

Downstairs, at Kinlay House hostel, Celtel e.centre (☎ 566620), Merchant's Rd, opens 8am to 10pm daily and charges €6.30 for the first hour then €2.50 for each subsequent hour.

Travel Agencies

The usit office (☎ 565177) is at Kinlay House, Merchant's Rd.

Bookshops

Hawkins House (☎ 567507), 14 Churchyard St, opposite the Collegiate Church of St Nicholas of Myra, has a wide selection of books. Charlie Byrne's (☎ 561766), in the Cornstore on Middle St has a huge collection of second-hand and discounted books. Eason's (☎ 562284), on Shop St, is a general bookshop and newsagents, while Kenny's Bookshop (☎ 562739), High St, is one of the leading antiquarian bookshops in Ireland, with maps, prints and an art gallery.

Laundry

The central Olde Malte Laundrette, in the Old Malt shopping arcade off High St, opens 8.30am to 6pm Monday to Saturday. Otherwise, there's The Laundrette on Sea Rd and The Bubbles Inn, 19 Mary St.

EYRE SQUARE

The square is the focal point of the eastern part of the city centre, though it shows no great imagination in its design and layout. The eastern side of the square is taken up almost entirely by the Great Southern Hotel, a large, grey, limestone pile. In the centre of the square is **Kennedy Park**, named after US President John F Kennedy who visited Galway in 1963; a stone tablet in the square marks the occasion.

On the western side of the square is **Browne's Doorway** (1627), a fragment from the home of one of the city's merchant rulers. Behind Browne's Doorway is a curious, rusted, metal sculpture supposed to evoke the sails of a *húicéir* (hooker), a traditional Galway vessel. It was designed by Eamon O'Doherty and erected during the city's quincentennial in 1984. To the north is a controversial statue of the Galway-born writer Pádraic O'Conaire (1883–1928), a noted hell-raiser.

COLLEGIATE CHURCH OF ST NICHOLAS OF MYRA

This Protestant church with its curious pyramidal spire dates from 1320 *(☎ 564648, Market St; €1.25 donation requested; open 9am-5.45pm Mon-Sat & 1pm-5pm Sun Apr-Sept; 10am-4pm Mon-Sat & 1pm-5pm Sun Oct-Mar)*. It's not only Galway's most important monument but also the largest medieval parish church in Ireland still in use. Although it has been rebuilt and enlarged over the centuries, much of the original form has been retained. After Cromwell's victory, the church suffered the usual indignity of being used as a stable. Much harm was done – look for the damaged stonework – but at least it survived; 14 other Galway churches were razed to the ground. The church has numerous finely worked stone tombs and memorials. The two church bells date from 1590 and 1630.

Parts of the floor are paved with gravestones from the 16th to 18th centuries, and the Lynch Aisle holds the tombs of the powerful Lynch family. A large block tomb in one corner is said to be the grave of James Lynch, a mayor of Galway in the late 15th century who condemned his son, Walter, to death for killing a young Spanish visitor. None of the townsfolk would act as executioner. The mayor was so dedicated to upholding justice that he personally acted as hangman, after which he went into seclusion – or so the story goes. A stone plaque, complete with skull and crossbones beneath it, on the **Lynch Memorial Window**, outside on Market St north of the church, tells the tale and claims to be the spot where the gallows stood.

At the end of the southern transept is the empty frame that once held an icon of the Virgin Mary. It was supposedly taken to Gyor in western Hungary (where it's still an object of veneration) in the 17th century by an Irish bishop sent packing by Cromwell.

NORA BARNACLE HOUSE

Across the road from Lynch's Memorial Window is Bowling Green. The small terraced

Looking across to the grey, quartzite peaks of the Maumturk Mountains, County Galway

Lough Corrib cuts through the flat interior of County Galway before emptying into Galway Bay.

The *chevaux de frise* – a defensive forest of sharp stone spikes – of magical Dún Aengus, Inishmór

RICHARD CUMMINS

Galway's imposing cathedral

OLIVER STREWE

'Get your own Aran sweater.'

DOUG McKINLAY

The annual horse fair at Ballinasloe attracts horse buyers and sellers and merrymakers alike.

RICHARD MILLS

Connemara's wild and barren coastline is a maze of rocky islands, inlets and sparkling white beaches.

house at No 8 was once the home of Nora Barnacle (1884–1951), companion and, later, wife to James Joyce. He first visited the house in 1909 and again several times during the summer of 1912. The house is now a small museum dedicated to the couple (☎ 564743, 8 Bowling Green; admission €1.25; open 10am-5pm daily mid-May-mid-Sept).

LYNCH'S CASTLE

On the corner of Shop and Upper Abbeygate Sts, parts of the old stone town house called Lynch's Castle (now a branch of the Allied Irish Bank) date back to the 14th century. Most of the present building, claimed by some to be the finest town castle in Ireland, dates from around 1600, however. The Lynch family were the most powerful of the 14 ruling Galway 'tribes', and members of the family held the position of mayor no less than 80 times between 1480 and 1650.

Lynch's Castle has numerous fine stone features on its facade, including the coats of arms of Henry VII, the Lynches and the Fitzgeralds of Kildare, as well as gargoyles, which are unusual in Ireland.

THE SPANISH ARCH

A 1651 drawing of Galway clearly shows its extensive city walls. But since the visits of Cromwell in 1652 and William of Orange in 1691, and the subsequent centuries of neglect, the walls have almost completely disappeared. Near the river, east of Wolfe Tone Bridge, the Spanish Arch (1584) appears to have been an extension of the walls through which ships unloaded their goods – often wine and brandy from Spain.

The small, rundown **Galway City Museum** (☎ 567641, Spanish Parade; adult/child €1.25/0.65; open 10am-1pm & 2pm-5pm Mon-Sat) is by the arch. There are lots of exhibits but there's no cohesive narrative to them.

GALWAY CATHEDRAL

From the Spanish Arch, a pleasant riverside path runs upriver and across the Salmon Weir Bridge to the second church in town dedicated to St Nicholas (☎ 563577, Gaol Rd; admission by donation; open 8am-6pm daily). The cathedral's full name is rather a mouthful: the Catholic Cathedral of Our Lady Assumed into Heaven and St Nicholas. It's a huge, imposing structure, dedicated by the late Cardinal Richard Cushing of Boston in 1965. The exterior design isn't to everyone's taste and critics vie for the most caustic descriptions. The interior, however, with its high, curved arches and central dome, has a certain, simple, solid elegance.

SALMON WEIR

Salmon Weir Bridge crosses the Corrib just east of the cathedral. Upstream is the great weir where the waters of the Corrib cascade down one of their final descents before reaching the sea in Galway Bay. The weir controls the water levels above it, and when the salmon are running you can often see shoals of them waiting in the clear waters before making the rush upstream.

The earliest records of Galway include references to the de Burgo family owning the fisheries on the town's weirs. Today they're owned by the Central Fisheries Board. The salmon and sea trout seasons are usually February to September, but most fish pass through the weir during May and June. To obtain fishing permits and to book a time you must write to The Manager, Galway Fisheries (☎ 562388), Nun's Island, Galway.

SALTHILL

Within walking distance of the city is Salthill (Bóthar na Trá), an old-fashioned seaside resort. The beaches are often packed in hot weather but are not particularly good. **Leisure World**, in Salthill Park, has three covered pools and a giant waterslide (☎ 521455, Rockbarton Rd; adult/child €4.80/3.30; open 8am-10pm daily).

Next to the seasonal tourist office is the **Galway Atlantaquaria** (National Aquarium of Ireland; ☎ 581500, Seapoint Promenade; adult/child €6.30/3.80; open 10am-5pm Wed-Sun). Here you can see interesting displays and live presentations on underwater life.

GALWAY

ORGANISED TOURS

O'Neachtain Tours (☎ 553188, Spiddal) Adult/student/child €18.90/16.40/11.35. 9.45am from the Galway tourist office, 10am from the Salthill tourist office, returning at 5pm. Spiddal-based O'Neachtain Tours runs daily, year-round coach tours to Connemara or the Burren and Cliffs of Moher.

Lally Coaches (☎ 562905, Spiddal) Adult/student/child €18.90/16.40/11.35. 9.45am from the Salthill tourist office, 10.10am from the Galway tourist office. The company operates similar tours of Connemara and the Burren.

Corrib Princess (☎ 592447, Furbo Hill, Furbo) Adult/child €7.55/3.80. 2.30pm & 4.30pm daily (plus 12.30pm in July & Aug) May-Sept. Cruises, lasting 1½ hours, on the River Corrib and Lough Corrib are available. The boat departs from Eglinton Pier, at the northern end of Waterside St, upriver from the Salmon Weir. You can book at the tourist office.

SPECIAL EVENTS

Galway has an amazing number of events throughout the year. The following are just some of the highlights.

The well established Cúirt Poetry and Literature Festival (☎ 565886) takes place in April and grows in importance each year.

The Galway Film Fleadh (☎ 751655), in early July, is one of the biggest film festivals in the country. The city parties with a vengeance at the Galway Arts Festival (☎ 583800) in late July; the whole town turns out for this two-week extravaganza of theatre, music, art, comedy and a parade.

Late July/early August is Galway Race Week (☎ 753870), as much an event off the course as it is on it; the racecourse, 3km east of the city centre at Ballybrit, hosts a traditional Irish fair. Established in 1954, the Galway International Oyster Festival (☎ 527282) is held during the third week of September accompanied by lots of partying (see also Clarinbridge & Kilcolgan later).

PLACES TO STAY

The city has a huge variety of accommodation, but you may still have difficulty finding a bed in July and August. There's more accommodation in Salthill, a couple of kilometres to the south-west.

Camping

Ballyloughane Caravan & Camping Park (☎ 755338, fax 752029, Ballyloughane Beach, Renmore) Car & small tent €3.80 plus €5.10 per adult, hikers & cyclists including tent €5.70 per person. Open Apr-Sept. This peaceful, secure camp site is off the Dublin road (N6) 5km from Galway. Its beachside location gives it good views across the bay.

Along the coast road 18km west of Galway city is *Spiddal Caravan & Camping Park* (see Places to Stay under Spiddal to Roundstone later in this chapter).

Hostels

Legions of hostels dot Galway, several of which are extremely central. Most open year round except for a few days over Christmas.

Galway Hostel (☎ 566959, Frenchville Lane) Dorms €12.60, rooms with bathroom €18.90 per person. The corridors may be narrow in this old building and some of the rooms cramped, but the showers are clean and it's close to the station.

Kinlay House (☎ 565244, fax 565245, Merchant's Rd) Dorms €13.85-17.65 per person including breakfast, rooms €20.15-22.70 per person. This modern, bright place has spacious, well equipped rooms. The four flights of stairs to the reception can leave you a bit breathless if you're carrying a backpack.

Celtic Tourist Hostel (☎ 566606, Queen St) Dorms/rooms €15.10/21.40 per person. It has a large self-catering kitchen, clean showers and dorms and rents out bikes. Smoking is only allowed in the common room next to the reception.

Barnacle's Quay Street House (☎/fax 568 644, 10 Quay St) Dorms €12.70-19.05, doubles €23.50 per person. Surrounded by pubs, restaurants and cafes, this hostel is at the heart of the action.

Wood Quay Hostel (☎ 562618, 23-24 Wood Quay) Dorms €12.60. This independent hostel in St Anne's House, just north of the city centre, has a decent kitchen and eating area but cramped washrooms.

Salmon Weir Hostel (☎ 561133, St Vincent's Ave) Dorms €11.35-12.65, doubles €35.30. Around the corner from Wood Quay, this is a clean, medium-sized hostel with a 3am curfew for late-night revellers. All bathrooms are shared.

Galway International Youth Hostel (☎ 527411, fax 528710, St Mary's College, St Mary's Rd) Dorms €12.70. Open late June-late Aug. Take bus No 1 from Eyre Square, or, if you're walking, follow Upper Dominick St through the name changes of Henry St and St Helen's St, then turn left (south) onto St Mary's Rd. Here you'll come to An Óige's huge, 120-bed hostel in a boys' school – a good way to make use of the large rooms during the summer break.

B&Bs

There aren't many B&Bs in the city centre, but there are lots in the surrounding suburbs, some a short walk away.

St Martin's B&B (☎ 568286, 2 Nun's Island Rd) Rooms €25.20 per person. This B&B is delightfully situated right on the Corrib. The home cooking, comfortable rooms, friendliness of the owners and proximity to the sights, restaurants and pubs in the centre put it above everything else.

There are plenty of places less than 10 minutes' walk away from the centre on Newcastle Rd, which runs parallel to the river to the west.

Villa Nova (☎ 524849, 40 Lower Newcastle Rd) Singles/doubles from €32.40/50.80. Villa Nova is another friendly place in a quiet spot off the main road. All its four rooms are en suite.

North of the city, Forster St and College Rd, again about 10 minutes' walk from the centre, also have lots of B&Bs.

Copper Beech House (☎/fax 569544, 26 College Rd) Singles/doubles €31.50/50.40. This modern guesthouse has well equipped rooms all with showers.

Salthill and adjacent Renmore are good hunting grounds for B&Bs; Upper and Lower Salthill Rds are lined with places.

Devondell (☎ 528306, 47 Devon Park, Lower Salthill Rd) Singles/doubles €32.40/63.60. It's worth staying here for the breakfasts alone, but it's also nice to be greeted with tea and scones, especially after a long journey.

Roncalli House (☎ 584159, 24 Whitestrand Ave, Lower Salthill Rd) Rooms €25.20 per person. This pleasant place has been recommended by readers, and the occasional celebrity has been known to stay here.

Mandalay by the Sea (☎ 524177, fax 529952, 10 Gentian Hill, Blake's Hill) Singles/doubles €35.55/55.85. About 3.5km from the city past Salthill, this two-storey, balconied house offers views of Galway Bay and a touch of opulence minus the price tag.

Clare Villa (☎ 522520, 38 Threadneedle Rd) Singles/doubles €38.10/57.15. Open Feb-Oct. There are six clean, comfy rooms, all with showers, at this modern property near the beach.

Bayview (☎ 526008, 20 Seamount) Singles/doubles €38.10/63.15. Open Apr-Oct. Off Threadneedle Rd close to the beach, Bayview is a nonsmoking house with three en-suite rooms. Bus No 1 stops nearby.

Hotels

Jury's Galway Inn (☎ 566444, fax 568415, Quay St) Rooms €91.40 per person. Overlooking the Corrib and Wolfe Tone Bridge, this 128-room residence has all the comforts of a modern hotel.

Great Southern Hotel (☎ 564041, fax 566704, Eyre Square) Rooms €135.85 per person. This sumptuous, 114-room, 19th-century hotel takes up the complete eastern side of Eyre Square. Facilities include a pool, steam room and sauna.

Spanish Arch Hotel (☎ 569600, fax 569191, Quay St) Rooms €163.80 per person. It may be smaller than the others, but this 20-room hotel makes up for it with period charm and proximity to shops, restaurants and pubs.

PLACES TO EAT
Restaurants

The Quay St area is awash with restaurants, but finding a quiet one can be difficult.

Cactus Jacks (☎ 563838, Courthouse

GALWAY

Lane) Mains €7.50-14.50. Beside the Druid Theatre, this excellent, licensed Tex-Mex place also offers Cajun and vegetarian food.

Fat Freddy's (☎ 567279, The Halls, Quay St) Mains €7-9.50. Popular Fat Freddy's brings a touch of the Mediterranean to Galway with its tasty pasta and pizzas, chequered tablecloths and candles in wine bottles.

Aideen's Brasserie Eleven (☎ 561610, 19 Middle St) Mains €11.50-22.70. Open 12.30pm-7.30pm daily. This Italian-style brasserie combines friendly service with fresh produce and caters for people with special dietary requirements including vegetarians.

McDonagh's (☎ 565001, 22 Quay St) Mains €7.50-9.50. A Galway fixture for years, McDonagh's is excellent for seafood; be sure to try the 'wild' local mussels. Queues spill out into the street at night.

Druid Lane Restaurant (☎ 563015, 9 Quay St) Mains €14-18.80. An intimate, tastefully decorated restaurant on two levels, it has a nonsmoking area downstairs. The dishes from the imaginative, modern Irish menu are beautifully presented and there's an extensive wine list.

Pierre's (☎ 566066, 8 Quay St) Mains €12.50-18.30. This is a popular French-style restaurant with pre-theatre (6pm-7pm) three-course meals for €17.50.

Le Graal (☎ 567614, 13 Lower Dominick St) Dishes €2.50-5. Open 6pm-12.30am daily. On the other side of the Corrib, this charming tapas restaurant serves tasty Spanish nibbles and a choice of wine from around the world. It also offers salsa classes on Tuesday.

Scoosi (☎ 568010, Spanish Parade) Dishes €6-15. Fine Italian food is on offer at this upbeat eatery near the river. It's a large restaurant but still fills up in the evening.

Kirwan's Lane Creative Cuisine (☎ 568266, Kirwan's Lane) Mains €21.40-24.60. Open from 6pm Mon-Sat. Kirwan's Lane may be the oldest street in the city but this restaurant, with its modern Irish cuisine, could happily sit in the most stylish areas of New York or London.

Drimcong House (☎ 555115, Moycullen) 5-course dinner €25.20-34. Open 6.30pm-10.30pm Tues-Sat. One of the best restaurants in the country, Drimcong House can't be recommended highly enough. It has a very reasonable (for its price bracket) set menu including vegetarian choices. In summer you need to book well ahead. It's 14km along the Clifden road (N59).

Cafes

Busker Brownes (☎ 563377, Upper Cross St) Mains €7-18.90. In historic Slate House dating from 1615, this popular, almost 24-hour cafe-bar serves excellent seafood.

Food for Thought (☎ 565845, Lower Abbeygate St) Sandwiches €4.40, baked potatoes €1.90-5. This busy place does a good line in vegetarian and wholefood sandwiches and delicious desserts.

Mocha Beans (☎ 565919, 2 Lower Cross St) Coffee from €0.65. A good spot for a caffeine fix, Mocha Beans delivers a smorgasbord of coffees, plus smoothies, shakes and juices.

Couch Potatas (☎ 561664, 40 Upper Abbeygate St) Potato meals under €8. Open noon-9pm daily. This makes a very appropriate and popular place for a bite to eat in this tuber-devouring land.

Conlon's Restaurant (☎ 562268, Eglinton St) Fish and chips €5.60-7, mains €11.30-23.95. Nobody does fish and chips better than Conlon's; the more expensive menu items include wild salmon and smoked mackerel.

Sails (☎ 568275, Eyre Square Centre) Sandwiches €3.75, mains €6.30. This popular self-service restaurant is on the lower level of the Eyre Square Centre next to the enclosed 12th-century Shoemaker Tower.

There are fewer choices on the other side of the river.

Left Bank Café (☎ 567791, 49 Lower Dominick St) Mains €6.95. Open 8am-7pm daily. This bohemian cafe does a good line in sandwiches and snacks as well as reasonably priced, filling meals.

Pasta Paradiso (☎ 563666, 51 Lower Dominick St) Pasta €7.25-9, pizza €6.25-21. A bright, busy Italian eatery, its delicious pasta is specially brought direct from Italy.

ENTERTAINMENT

The *Galway Edge* includes listings of what's on in Galway and the surrounding area. Published on Thursday, it is available free from the tourist office and other venues around town. Check the *Galway Advertiser*, the community newspaper, too. Also available free around town, *thelist.ie* contains weekly news on events, music, theatre, pubs and clubs.

Pubs

There's always a lot going on in Galway's pubs.

Seáan Ua Neáhtain (☎ 568820, 17 Upper Cross St) This cosy, 19th-century pub has a truly fabulous atmosphere and can attract a somewhat flamboyant crowd.

The King's Head (☎ 566630, 15 High St) The King's Head has a narrow frontage, but inside it stretches way back to a small stage – where musicians perform rock music most nights and traditional music on Wednesday night.

Taaffe's Bar (☎ 564066, 19 Shop St) A traditional, enormously popular bar with Irish music nightly at 5pm and 9pm.

McSwiggan's (☎ 568917, 3 Eyre St) Entering here is like entering a labyrinth, it has so many bars on so many different levels, but the pints and the food are good.

The Quays (☎ 568347, Quay St) The Quays is full of bric-a-brac and draws a lively crowd. There's music most nights from traditional to pop.

The Lisheen Bar (☎ 563804, 5 Bridge St) This is one of Galway's best venues for traditional and folk music, which takes places nightly and on Sunday afternoon.

There are some flashier but less atmospheric pubs around Eyre Square.

An Púcán (☎ 561528, 11 Forster St) This pub, just off the square, has folk music and ballads most nights and is great for a singalong.

There are also some great pubs west of the Corrib.

Monroe's Tavern (☎ 583397, Upper Dominick St) Monroe's is a choice spot for traditional music and ballads, and the only pub in the city to offer set dancing (Tuesday).

Róisín Dubh (Black Rose; ☎ 586540, Upper Dominick St) This wonderful old pile is good for traditional music on Monday and Tuesday nights, and alternative music at the weekend.

Taylor's Bar (☎ 587239, Upper Dominick St) Next to Róisín Dubh, this is a similarly venerable establishment with live traditional music on Tuesday, Thursday and Sunday nights.

The Blue Note (☎ 589116, 3 West William St) Here, a young crowd gyrates each night to the latest dance music played by guest DJs.

The Crane Bar (☎ 587419, 2 Sea Rd) The Crane is another old pub where the traditional music flies most nights and attracts a friendly, local crowd.

Theatre

Galway has three good theatres.

Druid Theatre (☎ 568617, Courthouse Lane) This long-established theatre is famed for its experimental works by young Irish playwrights.

Town Hall Theatre (☎ 569777, Courthouse Square) Just off St Vincent's Ave, this theatre is more middle-of-the-road with Broadway or West End shows and visiting singers.

An Taibhdhearc na Gaillimhe (Galway Theatre; ☎ 562024, Middle St) The most important theatre in Galway – but not of much interest to most travellers – is the Galway Theatre, which stages plays in Irish.

SHOPPING

The big *Eyre Square Centre*, south-east of Eyre Square, cunningly incorporates a reconstructed stretch of the medieval city wall. The other central shopping centres are *Bridge Mills*, in an old mill building by the river at the western end of William O'Brien Bridge, and *The Cornstore* on Middle St.

Stephen Faller (☎ 561226, Williamsgate St) The purchase of choice for most visitors to Galway is a Claddagh ring in silver or gold (see the boxed text 'Claddagh' on the next page). Buy them here or at one of the other jewellery shops in the town centre.

Design Concourse Ireland (☎ 566927,

Claddagh

If you ever go across the sea to Ireland
Then maybe at the closing of your day
You can sit and watch the moon rise over
  Claddagh
And see the sun go down on Galway Bay

Arthur Colahan, *Galway Bay*, 1947

A romantic icon in the hearts and songs of Irish-Americans for generations, Claddagh village was once Galway's main commercial fishing centre – up to 3000 people and 300 boats were based here at one stage. Strictly speaking, the district begins at the southern end of Wolfe Tone Bridge. Among the boats were the traditional Galway sailing vessels with pitched black hulls and rust-coloured sails known as *púcáin* and *gleoitoige*, today collectively called Galway hookers.

Claddagh used to have its own costume and dialect, as well as its own king. Although the traditional Claddagh of thatched roofs, Irish speakers and fishing boats disappeared in the 1930s, you'll still see many people wearing Claddagh rings. The rings depict a crowned heart nestling between two outstretched hands; it signifies friendship (the hands), loyalty (the crown) and love (the heart). If the heart points towards the hand, the wearer is taken or married; towards the fingertip means that he or she is looking for a partner. It has been the wedding ring used throughout much of Connaught since the mid-18th century and is enjoying a renaissance today, judging from the well stocked jewellery-shop windows.

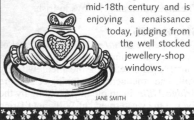

JANE SMITH

Kirwan's Lane) The Design Concourse Ireland is a wonderful place to look around: it displays (and sells) the cutting edge in Irish design – from furniture and tableware to high fashion in Donegal tweed (no less) – from all 32 counties.

River Deep, Mountain High (☎ 563968, Middle St) This is one of the better places for outdoor clothing and equipment.

Mulligan Records (☎ 564961, 5 Middle St) If you're an aficionado of traditional Irish music go to this record store; it does mail order.

Royal Tara China (☎ 751301, Mervue) Just outside town, the china factory is worth a look. Take the Dublin road (N6) then turn at the first left after the Galway Ryan Hotel.

Galway Irish Crystal Heritage Centre (☎ 757311, Merlin Park) The heritage centre, a bit farther along the N6, will meet all your needs in the stemware department.

Connemara Marble Industries (☎ 555 102, Moycullen) This factory, 13km northwest of Galway on the N59, is great if you're interested in how the local marble is worked.

GETTING THERE & AWAY
Air
Carnmore Airport (☎ 755569) is 10km east of the city. Aer Arann and Aer Lingus together have five flights daily to Dublin.

Bus
From the bus station (☎ 562000), behind the Great Southern Hotel on Eyre Square, there are frequent Bus Éireann services to all major cities in the Republic and the North. The one-way fare to Dublin (3¾ hours) costs €11.35.

For details of buses to Rossaveal (for the Aran Islands) see Getting There & Away under Aran Islands later in this chapter.

A lot of private companies are also represented.

Feda Ódonaill Coaches (☎ 761656) runs from Galway via Sligo to Donegal Town and onto Crolly, County Donegal (5½ hours, twice daily Monday to Saturday, three on Sunday). Buses depart from in front of Galway Cathedral, except the last bus on Sunday (8pm), which leaves from Eyre Square.

Bus Nestor (☎ 797144) runs four to six buses daily to Dublin via Dublin Airport. The first bus leaves from outside the Imperial Hotel, Eyre Square, at 7.15am (7.55am on Sunday), the last at 5.30pm (6pm on Friday and Sunday).

Michael Nee Coaches (☎ 095-51082)

runs three services daily (four on Friday) between Forster St Bus Park and Clifden (1½ hours) from June to September.

Walsh Coaches (☎ 098-35165) operates a bus from Eyre Square to Westport (four hours) at 5.10pm on Sunday. McNulty Coaches (☎ 097-81086) leave Eyre Square for Belmullet (five hours) via Westport and Newport at 4pm, 5.30pm and 6pm on Friday.

Train

From Ceannt train station (☎ 564222), behind the Great Southern Hotel on Eyre Square, there are up to five trains daily to/from Dublin (one way from €20.15, 2½ hours). Connections with other train routes can be made at Athlone (one hour).

GETTING AROUND
To/From the Airport

A bus runs once daily Monday to Saturday between the airport and Galway bus station (€3.15). It leaves the airport at 1.25pm, and leaves the bus station at 12.50pm. A taxi to/from the airport costs about €15.

Bus

You can walk to almost everything in Galway and even out to Salthill, but there are regular buses from Eyre Square. Bus No 1 runs from Eyre Square to Salthill and sometimes onto Blackrock; bus No 2 goes from Knocknacarra and Blackrock through Eyre Square to Renmore; bus No 3 runs between Eyre Square and Castlepark; and bus No 4 goes to Newcastle.

Car

Drivers will need parking discs to park on the street; these are available from the tourist office and newsagents. The car park just over William O'Brien Bridge is next to the police station, so it should be safe.

Bicycle

Most hostels, including Kinlay House and Salmon Weir Hostel, rent out bikes. At Celtic Cycles (☎ 566606), on Queen St next to Celtic Tourist Hostel, bikes cost €12.60/50.40 per day/week. If the shop is closed, call at the hostel.

Taxi

Galway Taxis (☎ 561111) is on Mainguard St; Corrib & Apollo Taxis (☎ 564444) is on Eyre St north of Eglinton St. There's also a couple of big taxi ranks in the city centre on Eyre Square and by the train station.

South of Galway City

Many visitors pass through the small part of Galway south of the city on their way to or from the spectacular limestone Burren region in County Clare. But there are many places worth visiting in the area, including the tranquil monastic settlement and round tower at Kilmacduagh.

CLARINBRIDGE & KILCOLGAN
☎ 091 • pop 500

Some 16km south of Galway, Clarinbridge (Droichead an Chláirín) and Kilcolgan (Cill Choglán) are the focus of Galway's famous Clarinbridge Oyster Festival, held during the second weekend of September and precursor to the Galway International Oyster Festival.

Paddy Burke's Oyster Inn (☎ 796107, Clarinbridge) Oysters €20.15/10.10 per dozen/half-dozen, mains €9.15-13.80. Open 12.30pm-10pm daily. This old-fashioned, thatched inn by the bridge is famous for its long association with the festival and for its seafood, though it does cater for other tastes including vegetarian.

Moran's Oyster Cottage (☎ 976113, The Weir, Kilcolgan) Oysters €20.15/10.10 per dozen/half-dozen, mains €8.60-16.15. A little farther south, signposted off the road in Kilcolgan near the post office, is this wonderful thatched pub and restaurant overlooking narrow Dunbulcaun Bay, where the famous Galway oysters are reared. During the festival, the world oyster-opening championships are held here.

Getting There & Away

Clarinbridge is on the main Galway–Gort–Ennis–Limerick road (N18) and is served by numerous Bus Éireann buses from Galway. Kilcolgan is also on the N18; Moran's Oyster Cottage is about 1.5km to the west.

KINVARA & AROUND
☎ 091 • pop 430

Kinvara (Cinn Mhara) is a delightful, peaceful village, tucked away on the southeastern corner of Galway Bay. A small stone harbour is home to a number of Galway hookers (traditional sailing boats) and there are some lively pubs.

Dunguaire Castle

Dunguaire Castle, north of Kinvara on the shore, was erected around 1520 by the O'Hynes (☎ 637108, 061-360788 in Shannon, Kinvara; adult/child €3.50/1.90; open 9.30am-5.30pm daily mid-Apr-Sept). It later passed into the hands of Oliver St John Gogarty (1878–1957), poet, writer, surgeon, Irish Free State senator and 'the wildest wit in Dublin'. The castle is supposedly built on the site of the 6th-century royal palace of Guaire Aidhne, the king of Connaught.

The castle is in excellent condition and the displays on each floor are dedicated to a particular period in its history, right down to the last mildly eccentric owner, who lived here during the 1960s. It has a gift shop and guided tours, as well as medieval banquets held at 5.30pm and 8.45pm daily, May to September. The banquets are on a more intimate scale than those at Bunratty Castle near Shannon in County Clare, and slightly cheaper at €37.80 per person.

Just south of Dunguaire is a bare **stone arch**, the only remains of an older castle.

Special Events

On the May bank holiday weekend, Kinvara hosts the Fleadh na gCuach (Cuckoo Festival), a music festival. Galway's hookers are celebrated in the second weekend in August during the Cruinniú na mBáid (Gathering of the Boats) festival.

Places to Stay & Eat

Johnston's Independent Hostel (☎ 637164, Main St) Dorms €10.10. Open July & Aug. Johnston's is a quaint, medium-sized hostel

(24 beds) up the hill from the harbour. Showers and laundry cost extra.

Doorus House (☎/fax 637512, Doorus, Kinvara) Seniors/juniors €10.15/7.60. The An Óige hostel is 6km north-west, signposted off the main road to Ballyvaughan (N67). The building was once owned by Count Floribund de Basterot, who entertained here such notables as WB Yeats, Lady Augusta Gregory, Douglas Hyde and Guy de Maupassant. Yeats and Lady Gregory are said to have first mooted the idea of the Abbey Theatre in Dublin while visiting Doorus House. It's a good base for exploring the Burren.

Burren View (☎ 637142, fax 0905-44474, Doorus, Kinvara) Singles/doubles €32.40/48.25. Open Easter-Oct. About 6km northwest of Kinvara, it's in a scenic spot on a peninsula with views of Galway Bay and the Burren. You can go swimming at the nearby Blue Flag beach.

Clareview (☎/fax 637170, Kinvara) Singles/doubles €33.65/50.80. Open Mar-Oct. Clareview is a large, modern farmhouse about 3km east of Kinvara on the R347. Its five rooms are all en suite and dinner is available.

Rosaleen's (☎ 637503, Main St) Mains €9.15-17.60. There's a bit of a Mexican flavour to Rosaleen's, where the menu includes vegetable enchiladas along with roast chicken and pan-fried cod. Filling, tasty sandwiches and desserts are also on offer.

Getting There & Away

Late May to late September, Bus Éireann's Galway–Killarney bus No 50 stops in Kinvara three to four-times daily Monday to Saturday, and twice on Sunday.

Bus No 423 serves the Burren coast once daily, running via Kinvara between Ballyvaughan, Black Head, Fanore, Lisdoonvarna and Doolin.

For more details contact Galway bus station (☎ 091-562000).

GORT & AROUND
☎ 091 • pop 1090

About 37km south-east of Galway is a 16th-century Norman tower known as **Thoor**

Ballylee (☎ *631436, Peterswell; adult/child €5.05/2.50; open 10am-6pm daily Easter-Sept)*. It was the summer home of WB Yeats from 1922, and the inspiration for one of his best-known works, *The Tower*. The restored tower contains his furnishings and fittings and you can see an audiovisual presentation on his life. From Gort take the Loughrea road (N66) for about 3km, then follow the sign.

About 5km north of Gort is the Dúchas-run **Coole Park** (*Cúil; ☎ 631804, Gort; adult/concession €2.55/1.25; open 9.30am-6.30pm Tues-Sun Easter-mid-June; 10am-5pm daily mid-June-Aug & Sept)*. It was the home of Lady Augusta Gregory, co-founder of the Abbey Theatre and a patron of Yeats. An exhibition focuses on the literary importance of the house and the flora and fauna of the surrounding nature reserve.

Five kilometres south-west of Gort is the extensive monastic site of **Kilmacduagh**. Beside a small lake is a well preserved round tower, the remains of a small, 14th-century cathedral (Teampall Mór MacDuagh), an oratory dedicated to St John the Baptist, and various other little chapels. The original monastery is thought to have been founded by St Colman MacDuagh at the beginning of the 7th century. St MacDuagh founded the monastery under the patronage of King Guaire Aidhne of Connaught, who gave his name to Dunguaire Castle in Kinvara. Such was the monastery's importance that it became the focus for a new diocese in the 12th century. The 34m-high round tower leans some 60cm from the perpendicular and the doorway is 8m above ground level. There are fine views over the Burren from here and you can visit any time.

There are regular buses from Galway to Gort.

Connemara

Connemara (Conamara) is the wonderfully wild, barren region north-west of Galway city. It's a stunning patchwork of bogs, lonely valleys, pale grey mountains and small lakes that shimmer when the sun shines. Its devotees – Irish, French, Americans, Germans – buy up remote cottages as holiday homes or spend a small fortune on a week's holiday in a castle hotel during the salmon-fishing season.

Connemara isn't a distinct geographical region like the Burren. At its heart are the Maumturk Mountains and the grey, quartzite peaks of the Twelve Bens (or Pins), which offer some tremendous hill walking. They look south over a plain dotted with lakes and run southwards into the sea around Carna and Roundstone in a maze of rocky islands, tortuous inlets and sparkling white beaches. The coastal road west of Spiddal (R336) eventually enters this maze, and it's well worth losing yourself for a day or two around Carraroc; the Garumna, Lettermullen and Lettermore Islands; Roundstone; and Ballyconneely Bay. Pink granite is the predominant rock in this lower country, while the mountains and northern part of the region are made of a mixture of quartzite, gneiss, schist and greenish marble.

However, the best scenery is in the middle of the region. The journey from Maam Cross north-west to Leenane (R336) or north-east to Cong (R345) takes you through Joyce Country, a stunning mountainous region. The trip north along Lough Inagh Valley past the Twelve Bens and around Kylemore Lake is difficult to surpass.

One of the most important Gaeltacht (Irish-speaking) areas in the country begins just west of Galway city around Barna and stretches westwards through Spiddal and Inverin, and along much of the coast as far as Cashel. Ireland's national Irish-language radio station, Radio na Gaeltachta, is based at Costello and does much to sustain the language. The Irish-language weekly newspaper *Foinse* (Source) is published in Spiddal.

Heading west from Galway you have two options: the coast road (R336) through Salthill, Barna and Spiddal, or the inland route (N59) through Oughterard, which leads directly to the heart of Connemara.

If you intend any detailed exploration, the excellent *Connemara: Introduction and Gazetteer* (€15.10) by Tim Robinson is a must. *Connemara: A Hill Walker's Guide* by Robinson and Joss Lynam is also invaluable.

GALWAY

CONNEMARA

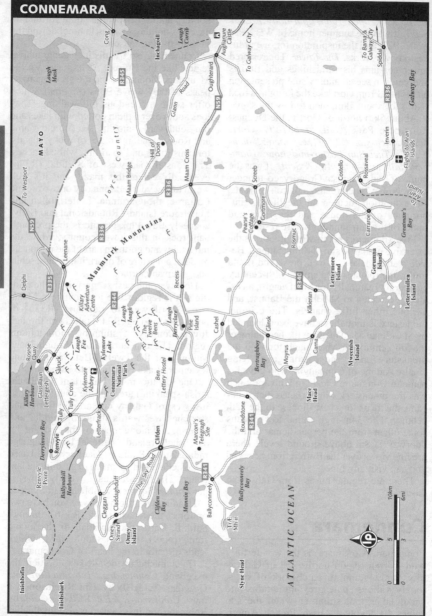

GETTING THERE & AWAY

There are numerous Bus Éireann services running to most parts of Connemara. Many of them originate in Galway, so check with the bus station (☎ 091-562000) there for times and fares. Services can be sporadic, and many operate May to September only or July and August only.

Bus Nos 61 and 419 run between Galway, Oughterard, Maam Cross, Recess, Roundstone, Ballyconneely and on to Clifden five-times daily (twice on Sunday), late June to August. Bus No 61 also continues from Clifden to Kylemore, Leenane and Westport; at other times of the year it runs only once daily from Galway to Clifden via Maam Cross and Leenane, but doesn't make all the above stops.

Galway, Cong, Leenane and Clifden are connected by the infrequent bus No 420, Monday to Saturday. Bus No 424 runs between Galway, Spiddal, Inverin, Rossaveal, Carraroe and the Lettermore and Lettermullen Islands five-times daily (once on Sunday). Bus No 416 runs once daily Monday to Saturday, year round, between Galway, Oughterard, Maam Cross, Rosmuc, Recess, Glinsk, Carna and Moyrus.

Many road signs in this area are in Irish only. See the Place Names Appendix at the back of this book for English-language equivalents.

SPIDDAL

☎ 091 • pop 300

Just 17km west of Galway, Spiddal (An Spidéal) is a lively little roadside settlement geared to tourism with some good pubs. Some houses are among the finest in Ireland, partly because of grants from the Irish government to encourage people to continue living in the area and to speak Gaelic. At the Galway City end of the village is the Irish-language *Coláiste Chonnacht (Connaught College;* ☎ *553383, Spiddal),* founded in 1910, and *Standún (*☎ *553108, Spiddal; open 9.30am-6.30pm Mon-Sat Mar-Dec),* a long-standing, massive craft shop with a currency exchange and pleasant tearoom.

Nearby is the large *An Ceardlann (Spiddal Craft Centre;* ☎ *553376; open 9am-6pm* *Mon-Sat, 2pm-6pm Sun),* a collection of craftshops, in front of which is a good **beach**, which gets crowded during summer.

If you're looking for open landscapes and wild coastlines, leave Spiddal behind and head west towards Roundstone.

SPIDDAL TO ROUNDSTONE

A few kilometres west of Spiddal, the scenery starts to become more dramatic. Before Costello (Casla), you'll notice signs for Rossaveal (Ros a' Mhíl), the main departure point for ferries to the Aran Islands (see Getting There & Away under Aran Islands later in this chapter). Past Costello it's well worth turning west off the main road for **Carraroe** (An Cheathrú Rua) and into a maze of rugged islands, all connected to the mainland, and inlets. Carraroe is famous for its fine beaches, including the Coral Strand, which is composed entirely of shell and coral fragments. Equally well known is University College Galway's **Irish Language Centre** *(Áras Mháirtín Uí Chadhain;* ☎ *091-595101, An Cheathrú Rua).* It offers one/two-week courses in the Irish language for €190.45/317.45; with accommodation from €133.30 per week; with room and board from €304.75.

Lettermore, **Gorumna** and **Lettermullen** Islands are low and bleak, with a handful of farmers eking out an existence from tiny, rocky fields. Fish farming is big business, and there are salmon cages floating in some of the bays.

From **Screeb** (Scriob) you can head north to Maam Cross or continue along the coast. Near Gortmore, about 5km west of Screeb along the R340, is the Dúchas-run **Pearse's Cottage** *(*☎ *091-574292, Ros Muc; adult/ concession €1.25/0.50; open 10am-6pm daily Easter & mid-June-mid-Sept).* Pádraig Pearse (1879–1916), one of the leaders of the Gaelic revival, founded the bilingual School of St Enda (Scoil Éanna) in Dublin in 1908. He was the least political of the 1916 rebels, being heavily imbued with an almost religious need for blood sacrifice, but nevertheless was the commander-in-chief of the insurgents and named president of the provisional government. After the revolt he was executed by the British. He wrote some of his short stories and plays in this cottage, which is also called by its Irish name, Teach an Phiarsaigh.

Continuing along the R340 brings you to **Carna**, a small fishing village with a marine biology research station nearby. From Carna there are some good walks out to **Mweenish Island** or north to Moyrus and out to **Mace Head**. Back on the R340, it's a lovely journey north to **Cashel** (An Caiseal) and south again on the R341 to Roundstone.

Places to Stay

Spiddal Caravan & Camping Park (☎ 091-553372, fax 553976, Spiddal) Car & tent €11.45, cyclists/hikers €4.45. Open mid-Mar-Oct. This camp site is on the R336 18km west of Galway and about 1.5km west of Spiddal village. It's also signposted in Irish as Pairc Saoire an Spidéil and has a riverside setting. Its modern facilities include a toilet block, laundry and free showers.

Plenty of B&Bs line the road between Spiddal and Roundstone.

Col Mar-House (☎/fax 091-553247, Salahoona, Spiddal) Singles/doubles €32.40/48.25. This relaxed country home surrounded by woods and gardens has been recommended by readers and is only 1.5km west of Spiddal.

Hotel Carraroe (☎ 091-595116, fax 595187, Carraroe) Rooms €57.15 per person. Also called Óstán An Cheathrú Rua, this congenial, 25-room hotel is now part of the Best Western chain.

Some exclusive hotels are tucked away out here; they're also good places to stop for a sandwich, drink or meal if you can rise to their prices.

Ballynahinch Castle Hotel (☎ 095-31006, fax 31085, Recess) Rooms €72.65-139.70 per person. This lovely hotel south-west of Recess was formerly the home of Humanity Dick (1754–1834), a local landlord, MP and one of the chief forces behind the Royal Society for the Prevention of Cruelty to Animals (RSPCA). Ballynahinch Castle is well worth a visit even just for a drink in the bar and a scout around the delightful grounds.

Zetland Country House Hotel (☎ 095-

31111, fax 31117, Cashel Bay) Rooms €77.45-92.70 per person. This secluded, 19th-century manor has panoramic views and is in a tranquil setting overlooking Cashel Bay. Facilities include an excellent seafood restaurant and a tennis court.

Cashel House Hotel (☎ 095-31001, fax 31077, Cashel) Rooms €84.30-121.40 per person. At the head of Cashel Bay, this 32-room hotel surrounded by 17 hectares of woodland and gardens also has a stable of Connemara ponies; riding lessons are available.

ROUNDSTONE

☎ 095 • pop 240

The small fishing village of Roundstone (Cloch na Rón), 16km south-west of Recess on a western extension of Bertraghboy Bay, consists essentially of one main street of tall houses, shops and a couple of pubs overlooking the water. The small harbour is home to lobster boats and many a *cúrach* (currach), the featherweight rowing boat of black tar on hide or canvas laid over a wicker frame.

Just south of the centre is a **craft complex**, in Michael Killeen Park, with various small factory shops selling everything from teapots to sweaters. One of the more interesting shops is *Roundstone Musical Instruments* (☎ 35808; open 9am-9pm daily July-Sept; 9am-7pm daily Mar-June & Oct; 9am-7pm Mon-Sat Nov-Feb). It makes and sells the *bodhrán*, the goatskin drum beloved of traditional Irish musicians, as well as tin whistles, harps and Irish flutes. Farther south and off the road to Ballyconneely (R341) are the magnificent **white beaches** of Gurteen (or Gorteen) Bay and Dog's Bay.

Looming behind the neat stone harbour is **Mt Errisbeg** (298m); it's the only significant hill along this section of coastline. There's a pleasant walk from Roundstone to the top: follow the small road past O'Dowd's pub in the centre of the village. From the summit there are wonderful views across the bay to the distant humps of the Twelve Bens.

Places to Stay

Gurteen Beach Caravan & Camping Park (☎ 35882, Roundstone) Hikers & cyclists

€8.80 per person. This peaceful camp site is in a great spot 2km west of town near the beach, and has full facilities.

St Joseph's (☎/fax 35865, Main St) Singles/doubles €38.10/49.50. Mrs Lowry's excellent, central B&B offers a warm welcome and good views over the harbour.

Roundstone House Hotel (☎ 35864, fax 35944, Main St) Rooms €49.50 per person. It's almost worth coming to Roundstone just to stay at this friendly 13-room place. In summer it serves an excellent evening meal and there are good views over the bay to Connemara.

Places to Eat
Several pubs serve food.

Beola Restaurant (☎ 35871, Main St) Mains €11.30-23.90. Open 6pm-9pm daily Easter-mid-Oct. This attractive restaurant provides good service and well presented food. Its imaginative menu, specialising in fresh seafood, includes fresh fillet of monkfish in a lemon and soy sauce.

O'Dowd's (☎ 35809, Main St) Mains €10.10-19.60. O'Dowd's, an authentic old Irish pub, dishes up tasty food in its cosy bar and in the restaurant. It has an extensive menu of pasta, fish, meat and vegetarian dishes, and views over the harbour.

ROUNDSTONE TO CLIFDEN
Some 12km west of Roundstone is **Ballyconneely**. If you detour south off the R341 from there towards the Connemara Golf Club, you pass the ruins of **Bunowen Castle** before reaching the shore at **Trá Mhóir** (great beach), a lovely expanse of white sand. Back on the R341, as it curves north toward Clifden it passes the fine beach at **Mannin Bay**.

CLIFDEN
☎ 095 • pop 920
Clifden (An Clochán), the capital of Connemara, is some 80km west of Galway at the head of narrow Clifden Bay. Astride the Owenglin River, the tightly packed houses and the needle-sharp spires of the town's churches are shadowed by the steep Twelve Bens to the east. A landlord, John D'Arcy, was the main force behind the establishment

of the town around 1812, but the Famine ruined the family, and their estate along The Sky Road is now deserted. Today, the town is clearly geared to tourism.

Information
The tourist office (☎ 21163) is on Galway Rd, the extension of Market St. It opens 9.45am to 5.45pm Monday to Saturday, noon to 4pm Sunday, in July and August; 9.30am to 5.30pm Monday to Saturday May, June and September; and 10am to 4.55pm Monday to Saturday in April.

There's an Allied Irish Bank branch on Market Square and a Bank of Ireland branch just down from the square; both have ATMs. The post office is on Main St, while Internet access is available from the Two Dog Cafe (☎ 22186), on Church Hill just off the square past the Alcock & Brown Hotel, for €7.55 per hour.

You can take your laundry to the Shamrock Washeteria on Market Square opposite the Allied Irish Bank.

Activities
There are superb **walking** and **cycling** possibilities. All you need to plan your tour of the area is Map 31 in the OS Discovery Series. Heading directly west from Clifden, **The Sky Road** takes you on a loop out to a town known as Kingston and back to Clifden through some rugged, stunningly beautiful coastal scenery. The round trip of about 12km can easily be walked or cycled.

The **Connemara Walking Centre** *(☎ 213 79, Island House, Market St)*, near Market Square, runs guided walking trips exploring local sites of historical, geographical and natural interest. A day's walk costs €18.90; longer walks are available. The centre also sells maps.

Errislannan Riding Centre *(☎ 21134, Ballyconneely Rd)*, about 3.5km south on the R341, has Connemara ponies for hire (€25.20 per hour) for riding along the beach and up into the hills. Lessons are available.

Places to Stay
Clifden Town Hostel (☎ 21076, 21642, Market St) Dorms €10.10-12.60, private

Alcock & Brown

MARTIN HARRIS

Derrygimlagh Bog, 6km south of Clifden, is the site of Marconi's former wireless station and where the aviator Captain John Alcock and his navigator Lieutenant Arthur Brown landed after their historic transatlantic flight.

On 15 June 1919 Alcock and Brown flew a Vickers Vimy over 3000km from Newfoundland in Canada to Ireland, landing in the bog near Clifden. This first successful flight across the Atlantic took six hours and 12 minutes, with the aircraft travelling at an average speed of over 190km/h.

A 'wing' monument to Alcock and Brown was erected on a hill, from which there's a walking trail to the site of the landing.

rooms €15.10 per person. A friendly establishment, this central IHH property has 34 beds in bright spick-and-span rooms.

Brookside Hostel (☎ 21812, Fairgreen) Dorms €11.35, private rooms €12.60 per person. Open Mar-Oct. The Owenglin River trickles past this IHH hostel in a quiet spot off the bottom of Market St.

Even though the Clifden area is awash with B&Bs, accommodation here tends to be pricey.

Kingstown House (☎ 21470, fax 21530, Bridge St) Rooms €22.85-25.30 per person. Kingstown House is a large, hospitable guesthouse in the town centre; there are eight rooms, most with attached bathroom.

Many B&Bs are to the south on the Ballyconneely road (R341).

Mallmore House (☎ 21460, Ballycon-

neely Rd) Rooms €26.65 per person. Open Mar-Oct. A restored Georgian manor house in 14 hectares of woodland about 2km from town, Mallmore is elegantly decorated and furnished. The super breakfasts include pancakes and smoked salmon.

Barry's Hotel (☎ 21287, fax 21499, Main St) Rooms €31.75-57.15 per person. Open mid-March-Nov. Barry's is a small, family-run hotel with comfortable rooms and traditional music in its bar.

Alcock & Brown Hotel (☎ 21206, fax 21842, Market Square) Rooms €44.45-55.90. The building is a rather ugly, concrete-and-glass bunker but the interior is fine and you're greeted by a large open fire in the lobby.

Foyle's (☎ 21801, fax 21458, Main St) Rooms €44.45-65.40 per person. Open June-Aug. Clifden's oldest hotel, Foyle's has 28 en-suite rooms with all mod cons.

Places to Eat

For inexpensive meals the pubs offer the best choice.

O'Grady's Seafood Restaurant (☎ 214 50, Market St) Mains €15.75-18.85. Open 12.30pm-2.30pm & 6pm-10pm daily Apr-Oct. O'Grady's is one of the best seafood restaurants in western Galway and even catches its own fish. The menu is cheaper at lunch-time.

Fogerty's (☎ 21427, Market St) Mains €10.70-18.30. Open 12.30pm-2.30pm & 6pm-10pm. Fogerty's, in a thatched stone house, is also worth trying. Along with traditional Irish dishes you get Mexican, Thai and Italian choices, all served in old-world elegance.

D'Arcy Inn (☎ 21146, Main St) Mains €6.30-8.80. Good, honest meals are available at this pub, with the emphasis on seafood and friendly service. There's live music and poetry readings every Thursday.

EJ Kings (☎ 21330, Market Square) Mains €6.25-11.30. A busy old pub, EJ Kings serves soups, salads and traditional food like Irish stew at reasonable prices; it has a more formal, pricier restaurant upstairs.

Cullen's (☎ 21983, Market St) Mains €6.20-14.50. Good for sandwiches and snacks during the day, Cullen's becomes a full-blown restaurant in the evening. Try to save room for the home-cooked rhubarb pie.

Getting There & Away

The bus stops are on Market St near Cullen's and the library. For information phone the bus station in Galway (☎ 091-562000). Buses run between Galway, Clifden and Westport via Oughterard and Maam Cross or via Cong and Leenane. For more details, see the Getting There & Away section at the start of the Connemara section.

Michael Nee Coaches (☎ 51082) run between Clifden (from the square) and Galway three-times daily, June to September. During the same period there are two buses daily to Cleggan (twice weekly from October to May), from where the ferry sails to Inishbofin and Inishturk islands.

Getting Around

A one-way traffic system operates in the town centre. John Mannion (☎ 21160, 21155), on Railway View off Main St, is a Raleigh agent and hires out bicycles for €7.50/44.10 per day/week.

CLIFDEN TO CLEGGAN

The deeply indented coastline north of Clifden brings you to the tiny village of Claddaghduff (An Cladach Dubh), which is signposted off the road to Cleggan. Turning west here down by the Catholic church you come out on **Omey Strand**, and at low tide you can drive or walk across the sand to **Omey Island**, a low islet of rock, grass and sand with a few houses for the island's population of 20. During the summer, horse races are held on Omey Strand.

CLEGGAN

☎ 095 • pop 250

Cleggan (An Cloiggean) is a small fishing village 16km north-west of Clifden, which visitors pass through en route to Inishbofin Island. The village has a post office but no bank.

Harbour House (☎ *44702*, e *harbour .house@oceanfree.net, Cleggan*) Singles/ doubles €32.40/48.25. Harbour House is a

rather chic, two-storey property, with spacious rooms and good breakfasts.

Getting There & Away

See Clifden and the introductory Getting There & Away entry to this Connemara section for information on buses. Cleggan is the departure point for boats to Inishbofin Island. Boats also leave here for Inishturk Island (see that section in the Counties Mayo & Sligo chapter).

INISHBOFIN ISLAND

☎ 095 • pop 200

Inishbofin Island, some 9km out in the Atlantic from Cleggan, is a haven of tranquillity. It's compact – 6km long by 3km wide – and the highest point is a mere 86m above sea level. It consists of some of the oldest rocks in Ireland, and the amazing **bird life** includes corncrakes, choughs, corn buntings and a variety of sea birds. Good sheltered beaches, open grassland, quiet lanes and a strong sense of isolation make Inishbofin special. Just off the northern beach is **Lough Bó Finne**, from which the island gets its name. *Bó finne* means 'white cow'.

History

Inishbofin's historical figure of note was St Colman, who at one stage was a bishop in England. He fell out with the English Church in 664 over its adoption of a new calendar, and exiled himself to Inishbofin, where he set up a monastery. North-east of the harbour is a small 13th-century **church** and **hollowed stone**, or *bullaun*, said to occupy the site of Colman's original monastery.

Grace O'Malley, the famous pirate queen who was based on Clare Island, used Inishbofin as a base in the 16th century.

Cromwell's forces captured Inishbofin in 1652 and built a star-shaped prison for priests and clerics. Many died or were killed; one bishop was reputedly chained to Bishop's Rock near the harbour and drowned as the tide came in.

Information

Inishbofin's small post office has a grocery shop as well as a currency-exchange facility.

Legend of Inishbofin Island

According to legend, Inishbofin Island was once permanently enveloped in a thick blanket of fog. One day some fishermen came upon the island and lit a fire near the lake – immediately the mist began to clear. Emerging from the mist was a woman with a long stick driving a white cow (bó finne) in front of her. She hit the white cow with the stick, turning it to stone. Irritated at such behaviour, the fishermen grabbed the stick and struck her, upon which she also turned to stone.

Until the late 19th century, two white stones stood by the lake: the 'remains' of the cow and its owner. No-one knows what happened to the stick.

Pubs and hotels will usually change travellers cheques. For walking tours of Inishbofin, contact the **Connemara Walking Centre** (☎ 21379) in Clifden.

Places to Stay & Eat

You can pitch a tent on most unfenced ground, but not on or near the beaches.

Inishbofin Island Hostel (☎/fax 45855, Insishbofin) Dorms €9.45-10.10, rooms €13.85 per person. Open Apr-Oct. A fine IHH hostel, 500m up from the harbour, it offers panoramic views and *camping* (€5.05).

Doonmore Hotel (☎/fax 45804, Inishbofin) Rooms €31.75-38.10 per person. Open mid-Apr-mid-Oct. In a choice location close to the harbour, Doonmore has comfortable, unpretentious rooms in both its modern extension and the original building. Dinner in its nonsmoking dining room, where seafood is the speciality, costs around €25.

Day's Hotel (☎ 45809, fax 45803, Inishbofin) Rooms €38.10-50.80 per person. Open Apr-Oct. This modest, comfortable hotel has turf fires and a dining room looking out over the harbour. The food (mains €14-20) is creative, with excellent fresh fish.

Day's Bar (☎ 45829, Inishbofin) Dishes €5-12. Adjoining Day's Hotel, this welcoming bar supplies ample pub grub and a lively atmosphere.

Getting There & Away

King's Ferries (☎ 44642, 21520) runs the MVs *Island Discovery* and *The Queen* to Inishbofin from Cleggan at 11.30am and 6.45pm daily, April to October, with additional sailings in July and August. The fare is €15.10 return (bikes go free) and the trip takes 45 minutes. You can buy the tickets at the Mace supermarket in Cleggan.

Inishbofin Ferries (☎ 45903, 45806 or 45831) operates the MV *Galway Bay*, also twice daily, April to October, with an extra daily sailing June to August. The fare is €12.60 return. Alternatively, you can take its smaller, more interesting *Dún Aengus* mailboat. Buy your ticket from the kiosk on the pier in Cleggan or from the Spar supermarket.

If you're lucky you'll see dolphins following the ferries.

Getting Around

Inishbofin Cycle Hire (☎ 45833), at the pier, hires out bicycles for €6.30/9.45 per day/24 hours; you're also given a free cycling map of the island.

LETTERFRACK

☎ 095 • pop 150

Letterfrack (Leitir Fraic), founded by the Quakers in the mid-19th century, is some 15km north-east of Clifden on the N59. It lies at the head of Ballynakill Harbour, but the sea is visible only from west of the crossroads and from the entrance to Connemara National Park. The village is barely more than a crossroads with a few pubs and B&Bs.

Old Monastery Hostel (☎ 41132, fax 41680, Letterfrack) Dorms/private rooms €10.10/15.10 per person. Open year round. This hostel is recommended for its free breakfast, friendliness, and optional vegetarian evening meal (from €7.55). There are also bikes for hire and *camping* (€6.30) is possible, so it's worth considering as a base for visiting Connemara National Park, literally next door.

Pangur Ban (☎ 41243, Letterfrack) Mains €13.50-17.50. Open 6pm-9pm daily. Worth a splurge, this lovely, thatched cottage restaurant, 100m west of the crossroads, serves terrific food and runs a cookery school. Dishes include venison cooked in Guinness.

In July and August, Bus Éireann (☎ 091-562000) buses run from Clifden once daily Monday to Saturday; the rest of the year they operate twice a week.

CONNEMARA NATIONAL PARK

Connemara National Park, managed by Dúchas, covers 2000 hectares of bog, mountain and heath south-east of Letterfrack. The headquarters and visitor centre are housed in pleasant old buildings just south of the crossroads in Letterfrack (☎ 095-41054, Letterfrack; park admission adult/child €2.55/1.25; centre open 9.30am-6.30pm daily July & Aug; 10am-6.30pm daily June; 10am-5.30pm daily Apr, May & Sept-mid-Oct).

The centre gives an insight into the park's flora, fauna and geology, as well as showing maps and various trails. Bog biology and the video Man and the Landscape are interesting, so wandering around is not a waste of time. It has an indoor eating area and rudimentary kitchen facilities for walkers.

The park encloses a number of the Twelve Bens, including Bencullagh, Benbrack and Benbaun. The heart of the park is Gleann Mór (Big Glen), through which flows the River Polladirk. There's fine walking up the glen and over the surrounding mountains. There are two- to three-hour guided nature walks on Monday, Wednesday and Friday in July and August, leaving the centre at 10.30am. Bring good boots and rainwear. There are also short, self-guided walks and, if the Bens look too daunting, you can hike up Diamond Hill nearby.

NORTH OF LETTERFRACK

There's some fine scenery along the coast north of Letterfrack, especially from Tully Cross east to Lettergesh and Salruck.

North of Letterfrack you first come to Tully Cross (Tulac na Croise), which has a line of neat, thatched holiday cottages and some nice little pubs.

Just short of Salruck is Glassillaun Beach, a breathtaking expanse of pure white sand. There are other fine beaches, at Gur-teen and at Lettergesh, where the beach horse-racing sequences for John Ford's 1952 film The Quiet Man were shot.

Things to See & Do

There are fine walks all along the coast and around Renvyle Point to Derryinver Bay. There's an excellent hill walk, which takes four to five hours each way, from the post office at Lettergesh up Binn Chuanna and Maolchnoc and then down to Lough Fee.

Focusing on the sea and marine life is Oceans Alive (☎ 095-43473, Letterfrack; adult/child €4.75/3.15; open 10am-7.30pm daily May-Aug, 10am-5pm daily Sept-Apr). This is an interesting if pricey aquarium and museum complex at Derryinver Bay on the Renvyle Peninsula. From Letterfrack head north; the centre is signposted to the left before you reach Tully Cross.

For sea trips or deep-sea angling on the MV Queen of Connemara, contact John or Phil Mongan at Oceans Alive.

On Glassillaun Beach to the north-east is Scuba Dive West (☎ 095-43922, e scuba divewest@eircom.net, Letterfrack), offering courses and diving on the surrounding coast and islands (full-day dive €56.70 with instructor and equipment).

Places to Stay

Renvyle Beach Caravan & Camping (☎ 095-43462, fax 43894, Renvyle) Tent site €5.10 per person. Open Easter-Sept. This camp site, 1.5km west of Tully Cross, is in a beautiful location with direct access to the sandy beach.

Connemara Caravan & Camping Park (☎ 095-43406, Lettergesh, Renvyle) Tent site €6.05 per person. Open May-Sept. In a 1.6-hectare park, the camp site has all mod cons plus the chance to see dolphins from the nearby beach.

Killary Harbour Hostel (☎ 095-43417, Rosroe Quay, Renvyle) Seniors/juniors €10.15/7.60. Open Mar-Sept. Set in wonderful scenery, this An Óige property is 13km north-east of Tully Cross on Rosroe Quay, 8km off the N59. The Austrian philosopher Ludwig Wittgenstein (1889–1951) stayed here for seven months in 1948. Some food and supplies are available at the hostel, but the nearest shop is 5km away in Lettergesh, so stock up in advance. There's a fine hike from the hostel along an old road by the fjord to Leenane.

Sunnymeade *(☎ 095-43491, fax 43491, Tully, Renvyle)* Singles/doubles €32.40/ 48.25. With sweeping views of the Atlantic, Sunnymeade is a down-to-earth, welcoming B&B.

Renvyle House Hotel *(☎ 095-43511, fax 43515, Renvyle)* €50.80-95.25 per person. This 56-room converted country house was once owned by the poet Oliver St John Gogarty and is the best place in the area to have a drink or snack or relax after a walk. Staying here would destroy most travellers' budgets but there are special rates throughout the year.

Getting There & Away
Bus Éireann (☎ 091-562000) bus No 420 runs Monday to Saturday year round between Galway and Clifden, calling at Cong, Leenane, Salruck, Lettergesh, Tully Church, Kylemore, Letterfrack, Cleggan and Claddaghduff en route.

KILLARY HARBOUR & AROUND
Mussel rafts dot long, narrow Killary Harbour, which looks like a fjord but may not actually have been glaciated. It's 16km long and over 45m deep in the centre, and has a superb anchorage. **Mt Mweelrea** (819m) towers over its northern shores. From Leenane at the south-eastern end of the harbour, the road runs west for about 2km along the southern shore before veering inland. However, you can continue **walking** along the shore to Rosroe Quay on an old road.

The well run **Killary Adventure Centre** *(☎ 095-43411, fax 095-42314, e adventure@killary.com, Leenane)*, 3km west of Leenane on the N59, offers activities in just about every adventure (and other) sport you can think of – including canoeing, sea kayaking, sailing, rock climbing and archery, to name just a few. Prices for a day range from €75 to €245 depending on the activity. Accommodation starts from €13.85

in a dorm. It also has a restaurant and bar with a great view of Killary Harbour.

From Nancy's Point, about 2km west of Leenane, **Sea Cruise Connemara** *(☎ 091-566736, 1800 415151; adult/child €13.85/ 7.55; four-times daily Apr-Oct)* offers 1½-hour cruises of Killary Harbour aboard the catamaran *Connemara Lady*.

There is magnificent scenery around the northern side of Killary Harbour, and up the R335 to Delphi (the turn-off is to the left shortly after Leenane) and into the Doolough Valley in County Mayo, one of the most ruggedly scenic valleys in the country (see the Counties Mayo & Sligo chapter).

LEENANE
☎ 095 • pop 50
Leenane (also spelled Leenaun) makes a convenient, scenic stopover on the way north, and the road north-west to Louisburgh (in Mayo) via Delphi is startlingly beautiful. Leenane's name in Irish, An Líonán, means 'ravine', referring to the way the sea edges its way into narrow Killary Harbour.

The village boasts both a cinematic and literary connection. It was the location for *The Field* (1989), based on John B Keane's poignant play about a tenant farmer's ill-fated plans to pass on a rented piece of land to his son. The dance and pub scenes were filmed in the village and the church scene at nearby Aasleagh. The village's name made it onto the literary map with the success in London and New York of Martin McDonagh's play *The Beauty Queen of Leenane*.

There's no bank or ATM, but the post office changes foreign currency.

Things to See & Do
The **Leenane Cultural Centre** *(☎ 42323, Leenane; adult/concession €2.50/1.25; open 9am-6pm daily Apr-Sept)*, over the bridge from the centre, focuses on the development of the woollen industry. It gives demonstrations of carding, spinning and weaving, with a 13-minute video every half-hour setting the historical and social context. You can visit the adjacent field to see the different breeds of sheep used in

Ireland. Locally made woollen garments are on sale, and there's a pleasant coffee shop.

There are several excellent walks from Leenane, including one to **Aasleagh Waterfall** (Eas Liath), about 3km away on the north-eastern side of Killary Harbour.

Places to Stay & Eat

Several B&Bs line the road from the west into Leenane.

Killary House (☎ 42254, Leenane) From €27 per person. In a converted farmhouse just a few minutes' walk from the village, its front rooms have views of the bay, while the rear ones look up to the hills behind. Note the low height of the bedroom doors.

Blackberry Cafe (☎ 42240, Leenane) Mains €14.50-18. Mostly serving fresh seafood, this is a surprisingly stylish restaurant given the remoteness of the location.

Gaynor's (Leenane) Snacks under €7. Offering sandwiches and snacks, Gaynor's is a traditional Irish pub where the farmers and other locals come for a quiet drink and to catch up on each other's news.

Village Grill (☎ 42253, Leenane) Breakfast €5.70, snacks €3.80-10.75. The Village Grill is a good choice for filling sandwiches, snacks and meals.

OUGHTERARD

☎ 091 • pop 750

The small town of Oughterard (Uachtar Árd), 27km along the main road from Galway to Clifden, calls itself the 'Gateway to Connemara'. And sure enough, immediately west of town, the countryside opens up to sweeping panoramas of lakes, mountain and bog that get more spectacular the farther west you travel.

Oughterard itself is a pleasant little town and one of Ireland's principal angling centres. It has a number of good cafes, pubs and restaurants as well as some fairly exclusive country-house establishments hidden in the surrounding countryside.

The focus of the anglers' attention is Lough Corrib (see the following section), just north of town. Nearby attractions include Aughanure Castle to the south-east and the lovely drive along the Glann Rd by Lough Corrib to a vantage point overlooking the Hill of Doon.

Information

The extremely helpful, locally run tourist office (☎ 552808) in Main St offers Internet access at €4.70 per hour. It opens 9am-6pm weekdays, 10am-5pm Saturday and Sunday, May to September; and 9am to 5pm weekdays October to April.

The Bank of Ireland, Main St, has an ATM and bureau de change. You can also change money at Fuschia Crafts, Main St. The post office is at the eastern end of Main St next to the Mace supermarket.

Aughanure Castle

Three kilometres east of Oughterard and off the main Galway road (N59) is the 16th-century O'Flaherty fortress, Aughanure Castle *(☎ 552214, Oughterard; adult/concession €2.55/1.25; open 10am-6pm daily June-early Sept; 10am-6pm Sat & Sun early Sept-Oct)*. The clan controlled the region for hundreds of years after they fought off the Normans, and the 'fighting O'Flahertys' were constantly at odds with the forces of Galway. The six-storey tower house stands on a rocky outcrop overlooking Lough Corrib and has been extensively restored. Surrounding the castle are the remains of an unusual double bawn or perimeter fortification. Underneath the castle, the lake washes through a number of natural caverns and caves.

Places to Stay

Canrawer House Hostel (☎ 552388, Station Rd) Dorms/rooms €10.15/15.25 per person. This modern, purpose-built hostel is at the Clifden end of town, just over 1km south along the Galway road. It has a large, airy kitchen and, if you've ever wanted to learn to fish, the owner will take you on an organised trip.

There are legions of B&Bs around Oughterard, but not many right in town.

Jolly Lodger (☎ 552682, Main St) Singles/doubles €25.20/40.30. Though modernised, this two-storey, greystone town house retains many of its original features. The breakfasts are excellent.

Western Way (*☎ 552475, Camp St*) Singles/doubles €35.55/48.25. Open Mar-Oct. This small, relaxed B&B, just down from Market Square, has three rooms (two en suite) and accepts credit cards.

Waterfall Lodge (*☎ 552168, Glann Rd*) Singles/doubles €38.10/63.45. If you prefer a country setting try this tastefully furnished period home in a picturesque, wooded garden. It's a nonsmoking B&B, and all rooms are en suite.

Corrib House Hotel (*☎ 552329, fax 552522, Bridge St*) Rooms €33-47 per person. This is a comfortable old hotel with 27 en-suite rooms and a good restaurant.

Currarevagh House (*☎ 552312, fax 552731, Oughterard*) Rooms €68.60-88.90 per person. Open Apr-late Oct. It's difficult to think of a more romantic place than this 19th-century mansion on the shore of Lough Corrib just outside Oughterard. It's renowned for its exquisite evening meals and quality accommodation.

Places to Eat

Le Blason (*☎ 557111, Bridge St*) Mains €16-20. Open 7pm-10pm daily, noon-2.30pm Sat & Sun. The elegant Le Blason, on the river near the bridge, combines French cuisine with the finest Irish produce. Save room for the *crème brûlée*.

Corrib House Hotel (*☎ 552329, Bridge St*) Mains €10-15. The service here is friendly and efficient and the menu is a creative mix of steak, poultry and fish dishes – baked cod in a cumin and coriander crust, for example.

O'Fatharta (*☎ 552692, Main St*) Mains €10.70-18.90. Open in the morning for tea, coffee and snacks, this cosy restaurant serves savoury meals and delicious desserts at lunch-time and in the evening. Seafood features prominently but meat-eaters and vegetarians are well catered for.

The pubs are best for inexpensive food.

Boat Inn (*☎ 552196, Market Square*) Sandwiches €2.50, mains around €6.25. For good bar food, try this place. As well as a wide choice of sandwiches, there's fish, roast of the day and tasty desserts. It also has a more expensive restaurant.

Keogh's Bar (*☎ 552222, Market Square*) Soup & sandwiches under €6. Keogh's is the place to come for filling, simple soup and sandwiches.

Entertainment

Many of the pubs in the area have music.

Keogh's Bar (*see Places to Eat*) Keogh's has something for almost everyone: there's a TV, pool table and Internet terminal in the rear, grocery shop at the front and traditional music at the weekend (more frequently in summer).

Power's Bar (*☎ 557047, Market Square*) This intimate, thatched pub, opposite Keogh's, serves a good pint and has live music at the weekend.

Getting There & Away

From Oughterard you can catch boats to Inchagoill Island (see the Lough Corrib section).

LOUGH CORRIB

The Republic's largest lake, Lough Corrib is over 48km long and covers some 200 sq km. It virtually cuts off western Galway from the rest of the country and encompasses over 360 islands. On the largest one, Inchagoill, there's a monastic settlement that visitors can get to from Oughterard or Cong.

Lough Corrib is world famous for its salmon, sea trout and brown trout, and the area attracts legions of anglers from all over the world in season. The highlight of the **fishing** year is the mayfly season, when zillions of the small lacy bugs hatch over a few days (usually in May) and drive the fish and anglers into a frenzy. The hooks are baited with live flies, which join their cousins dancing on the surface of the lake. The main run of salmon doesn't begin until June. The owner of Canrawer House Hostel in Oughterard (see earlier) is a good contact for information and boat hire; you can buy fishing supplies from **Thomas Tuck** (*☎ 091-552335, Main St, Oughterard*).

Inchagoill Island

The largest island on Lough Corrib and some 7km north-west of Oughterard, Inchagoill is a lonely place hiding many ancient remains. Most fascinating is an obelisk called **Lia Luguaedon Mac Menueh** (Stone of Luguaedon, Son of Menueh) marking a burial site. It stands about 75cm tall near the Saints' Church, and some people claim that the Latin writing on the stone is the oldest Christian inscription in Europe – apart from those in the catacombs in Rome. It's certainly the oldest Latin inscription in Ireland.

Teampall Phádraig (St Patrick's Church) is a small oratory of a very early design with some later additions. The prettiest church is the Romanesque **Teampall na Naoimh** (Saints' Church), probably built in the 9th or 10th century. There are carvings around the arched doorway.

The island can be reached by boat from Oughterard (or Cong in County Mayo). **Corrib Cruises** (☎ 092-46029, Cong, County Mayo) sails from Oughterard to Inchagoill Island (adult/child €12.60/6.40) and on to Cong (€15.10/7.55) April to October. Departures are at 10am, 11am, 2.45pm and 5pm.

MAAM CROSS

West of Oughterard, **Maam Cross** (Crois Mám) is the first settlement along the Clifden road (N59). By the turn-off for Leenane, *Peacocke's* (☎ 091-552306, fax 552216, Maam Cross) is a huge tourist complex complete with hotel, bar, shops, restaurant and petrol station. There's also a replica Irish cottage from *The Quiet Man* film with models of the actors inside.

From Maam Cross the trip north to Leenane is lovely, but if you have only one run through the region it's better to stay on the Clifden road and turn north onto the R344 into the Lough Inagh Valley instead. It's also a pleasant journey south towards **Screeb** and the coast.

RECESS & AROUND
☎ 095

Recess (Straith Salach), on the N59 between Clifden and Maam Cross, is nothing more than a few houses and *Joyce's Craft Shop* (☎ 34604). Turning north about 2km west of here brings you onto the R344, which will take you through the wonderful Lough

Inagh Valley. If you continue along the main road towards Clifden instead, there are some marvellous views over **Lough Derryclare** and **Pine Island**. The grassy lay-by (about 2km west of the R341 turning to Roundstone) overlooking the island is an excellent place to camp. About 1km west of here off the Clifden road is a dead-end road heading north into a great valley enclosed by a ring of six of the **Twelve Bens**. It's a beautiful drive up this road, and there's a challenging circuit hike of the six peaks.

Ben Lettery Hostel (☎/fax 51136, Ballinafad, Recess) Seniors/juniors €10.15/7.60. Open Easter-Sept. This An Óige hostel, on the main Clifden road, is an excellent base to explore the Twelve Bens and makes a good starting or finishing point for the walk mentioned previously. The hostel is 8km west of Recess and 13km east of Clifden.

Lough Inagh Valley

The journey north along the Lough Inagh Valley is one of the most scenic in the country. There are two fine approaches up valleys from the south, starting on either side of Recess, and the long sweep of Derryclare and Inagh Loughs accompanies you for most of the way. On the western side are the brooding Twelve Bens, while just beyond the valley on the northern side is the picturesque drive beside Kylemore Lake.

Lough Inagh Lodge (☎ 34706, fax 34708, Recess) Rooms €76.80-104.75 per person. About 7km up the Inagh Valley is the atmospheric, Victorian, Lough Inagh Lodge, an upmarket country-house hotel. It's a worthwhile place to stop for a snack, particularly in good weather. The location is magnificent and there's a path in front of the lodge down to the lake.

Towards the northern end of the valley, a track leads off the road west up a blind valley, which is also well worth exploring.

Kylemore Abbey & Lake

About 17km north-east of Clifden and just outside the northern end of the Lough Inagh Valley is the almost equally scenic **Kylemore Lake** and its accompanying abbey. The road skirts the northern shore of the lake, winding through overhanging trees, with magnificent views across the silent lake. South of the lake are the Twelve Bens and Connemara National Park, while the mountains behind the abbey are **Dúchruach** (530m) and **Binn Fhraoigh** (545m).

The lake passes under the road and extends to the north, where you will see the castellated towers of the 19th-century neo-Gothic **Kylemore Abbey** among the trees (☎ *41146, Connemara; adult/concession €4.40/2.90; open 9am-5pm daily Mar-Oct; 10am-4pm daily Nov-Feb)*. The abbey was built for a wealthy English businessman, Mitchell Henry, after he had spent his honeymoon in Connemara and had fallen in love with the region. During WWI, a group of Benedictine nuns left Ypres in Belgium and eventually set up in Kylemore, turning the place into an abbey.

Today, the nuns run an exclusive convent boarding school here and some sections of the abbey are open to the public. There's also a craft shop and tearoom.

You can walk up behind the abbey to a statue overlooking Kylemore Lake. A short walk beside the lake from the abbey leads to the restored neo-Gothic **Memorial Church** (1868).

Aran Islands

The same stretch of limestone that created County Clare's Burren region surfaces in the middle of Galway Bay to form the three Aran Islands (Oileáin Árainn): Inishmór, Inishmaan and Inisheer. The islands are like one long, undulating reef, with no significant hills or mountains – although, on the western side of Inishmór and Inishmaan, the land rises high enough to create some very dramatic cliffs over the Atlantic. As in the Burren, the limestone and, below that, the older bluestone create a spectacular moonscape: sheets of grey and grey-blue rock with flowers and grass bursting from the cracks.

Even the smallest patches of rocky land are bordered by stone walls. Over the centuries, tonnes of seaweed were brought up from the beaches, mixed with sand and laid out on the bare rock to start walls. The walls may be hundreds or even thousands of years old, so have respect for them and replace any stones you dislodge. On Inishmaan and Inisheer many of the walls are up to eye level, and it's a joy to walk for hours along the sandy lanes between them. The odd-looking seaweed you will see drying atop the stone walls on the islands is sea rod collected at low tide. It's sent to the mainland, where it's used in the production of cosmetics.

The islands are a major tourist attraction, with quick, convenient travel connections to the mainland, a plethora of accommodation, and a veritable armada of bicycles to hire. Inishmór – the largest of the three – is exceedingly busy during the summer, with armies of day-trippers and shuttle buses all over the island. At the busiest times, the 100 or so licensed vehicles on Inishmór get locked in traffic jams in the lanes! In spite of this you'll still get a genuine hello or wave of the arm from a local farmer.

If you have the time, try to get to the smaller islands, particularly Inishmaan – the least visited – and allow yourself a few days for exploration. Inisheer is the smallest and closest to land, just 8km from Doolin, in County Clare.

You can change money on the islands but banking facilities are limited and there are no ATMs.

HISTORY
The islands have some of the most ancient pre-Christian and Christian remains in Ireland. Farming was once much easier to pursue here than on the densely forested mainland. The most significant ruins on the islands are massive Iron Age stone forts, such as Dún Aengus on Inishmór and Dún Chonchúir on Inishmaan. Almost nothing is known about the people who built these structures, partly because their iron implements quickly rusted away. In folklore, the forts are said to have been built by the Firbolgs, a Celtic tribe who invaded Ireland from Europe in prehistoric times.

Christianity reached the islands remarkably quickly, and some of the earliest monastic settlements were founded by St Enda

(Éanna) in the 5th century. Any remains you see today are later, from the 8th century onwards. Enda appears to have been an Irish chief who converted to Christianity and spent some time studying in Rome before seeking out a suitably remote spot for his monastery. Many great monks studied under him, including Colmcille (or Columba), who went on to found the monastery on Iona in Scotland.

From the 14th century, control of the islands was disputed by two Gaelic families, the O'Briens and the O'Flahertys. During the reign of Elizabeth I, the English took control, and in Cromwell's times a garrison was stationed here.

As Galway's importance waned, so too did that of the islands. They became a quiet and windy backwater. The islands' isolation allowed Irish culture to survive when it had all but disappeared elsewhere. Irish is still very much the native tongue, and until around the 1930s people wore traditional Aran dress: bright-red skirts and black shawls for women, baggy woollen trousers and waistcoats with a colourful belt (or crios) for men. The classic cream sweater knitted in complex patterns originated here. You may still see old people wearing some elements of traditional dress, particularly on Inishmaan. The other Aran trademark is the currach (rowing boat).

BOOKS & MAPS
The elemental nature of life on the islands has always attracted writers and artists. The dramatist John Millington Synge (1871–1909) spent a lot of time on the islands, and his play Riders to the Sea (1905) is set on Inishmaan. His book The Aran Islands (1907) is the classic account of life here and is readily available in paperback. The American Robert Flaherty came to the islands in 1934 to shoot Man of Aran, a dramatic account of daily life. It became a classic and there are regular screenings of it in Kilronan on Inishmór. The islands have produced their own talent, particularly the writer Liam O'Flaherty (1896–1984) from Inishmór. O'Flaherty, who wandered around North and South America before returning to Ire-

land in 1921 and fighting in the Civil War, wrote several outstanding novels, including Famine.

The mapmaker Tim Robinson has written a wonderful, though not easily accessible, two-volume account of his explorations on Aran called Stones of Aran: Pilgrimage and Stones of Aran: Labyrinthe. His The Aran Islands: A Map and Guide (€6.30, or €12.60 with a companion guide) is superb. Two other excellent publications in paperback are The Book of Aran, edited by Anne Korf and published by Tír Eolas (€20), consisting of articles by 17 specialists covering diverse aspects of the islands' culture, and Aran Reader (Lilliput Press, €12.60), edited by Breandán & Ruairí O hEither, with essays on the islands' history, geography and culture by various scholars.

GETTING THERE & AWAY
Air
If time is important or seasickness on the often rough Atlantic a concern, you can fly to the islands with Aer Árann (☎ 091-593034, fax 593238). The mainland departure point is Connemara regional airport at Minna, near Inverin (Indreabhán), about 35km west of Galway. A connecting bus from outside the Galway and Salthill tourist offices costs €3.15 one way. The return flight to the islands costs €44.10/36.55/25.20 for adults/students/children (aged 12 and under). Flights operate to all three islands four times daily (hourly in summer) and take less than 10 minutes.

Boat
Only one big ferry line makes the run to the islands daily year round. Island Ferries' services from Rossaveal, about 40km west of Galway, are popular because the crossing is quick (about 40 minutes) and there are frequent sailings. To Inishmór, ferries operate three-times daily April to October (with extra sailings in July and August), twice daily November to March. To Inisheer and Inismaan they run once daily May to September. Fares cost €18.90/10.10 (students €15.10) return.

The return Galway–Rossaveal bus trip

costs €5.05/3.80/2.50 and leaves the Island Ferries Galway ticket office (☎ 091-568903, ⓦ www.aranislandferries.com), off Victoria Place, 90 minutes before the scheduled departure. If you have a car you can leave it free in the car park near the Island Ferries Rossaveal office (☎ 091-561767).

Doolin Ferries (☎ 065-707 4189, 707 4455) operates a daily service (April to September) from Doolin to Inisheer and (June to August) to Inishmaan and Inishmór. It's only 8km to Inisheer, taking about 30 minutes and costing €18.90 return. See Doolin in the County Clare chapter for more details.

O'Brien Shipping (☎ 091-567676), affiliated with Doolin Ferries, operates a cargo boat service from Galway city docks that takes passengers to the islands daily at 10am, June to September (three times weekly the rest of the year). The fare is €15.10 return. O'Brien Shipping has a desk in the Galway tourist office in summer.

GETTING AROUND
The islands of Inisheer and Inishmaan are small enough to explore on foot, but to see larger Inishmór, bikes are the way to go. You can also arrange transport on Inishmór with any of the small tour vans or pony traps (see Getting Around under Inishmór later in the chapter).

Inter-island services are run by Island Ferries (☎ 091-561767). From May to September, according to demand, one to four Rossaveal–Inishmór boats daily continue to Inishmaan and Inisheer, but from October to March there are only about three a week.

INISHMÓR
☎ 099 • pop 900
Inishmór (Big Island), or just Árainn in Irish, the largest of the three islands, slopes upwards from its comparatively sheltered northern shores to the southern edge, then plunges straight into the tumultuous Atlantic Ocean. After climbing the hill west of Kilronan, the island's capital, all you can see are rock, stone walls and boulders, scattered buildings and the odd patch of deep-green grass and potato plants.

Orientation
Inishmór is 14.5km long and a maximum 4km wide, running north-west to south-east. All ferries and boats arrive and depart from Kilronan (Cill Rónáin) on Cill Éinne Bay on the south-eastern side of the island. The airstrip is 2km farther south-east, on the other side of the bay, and faces Kilronan. One principal road runs the length of the island, with many smaller lanes and paths of packed dirt and stone leading off it.

Information
The small tourist office (☎ 61263), on the waterfront west of the ferry pier in Kilronan, opens 10am to 1pm and 2pm to 5pm daily, April to mid-September. The Bank of Ireland north of the village centre opens Wednesday only (10am to 12.30pm and 1.30pm to 3pm), but the post office nearby, the Ionad Árann (Aran Heritage Centre) and some shops change money.

Things to See
You'll get a better appreciation of your trip if you first visit **Ionad Árann** *(☎ 61355, Kilronan; adult/child €3.15/1.90; open 10am-7pm daily June-Aug; 11am-4pm daily Apr, May, Sept & Oct)*. Just off the main road leading out of Kilronan, it offers a useful introduction to the geology, wildlife, history and culture of the three islands. The admission fee includes a viewing of Robert Flaherty's 1934 film, *Man of Aran* screened here three times daily. The centre also has a coffee shop.

Inishmór has three impressive stone forts, probably about 2000 years old.

Two-thirds of the way down the island from Kilronan and perched on the edge of the sheer southern cliff is one of the most amazing archaeological sites in the country, **Dún Aengus** *(Dún Aonghasa; ☎ 61008; adult/child €1.25/0.50; open 10am-6pm daily Mar-Oct; 11am-5pm daily Nov-Feb)*. It has a remarkable *chevaux de frise*, a defensive forest of sharp stone spikes around the exterior of the fort to help stop any would-be attackers. Dún Aengus is a magical place and shouldn't be missed: you won't forget the sight and sound of wild swells pounding the cliff face. Try to go at a quieter time, such as

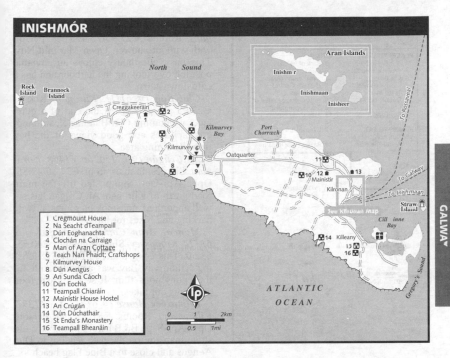

INISHMÓR

North Sound

Rock Island

Brannock Island

Creggakeeráin

Kilmurvey Bay

Port Chorrúch

Oatquarter

Kilmurvey

Mainistir

Kilronan

See Kilronan Map

Straw Island

Cill inne Bay

Killeany

ATLANTIC OCEAN

Gregory's Sound

Aran Islands

Inishmór

Inishmaan

Inisheer

To Rossaveal

To Galway

To Inishmaan

GALWAY

1 Cregmount House
2 Na Seacht dTeampaill
3 Dún Eoghanachta
4 Clochán na Carraige
5 Man of Aran Cottage
6 Teach Nan Phaidt; Craftshops
7 Kilmurvey House
8 Dún Aengus
9 An Sunda Cáoch
10 Dún Eochla
11 Teampall Chiaráin
12 Mainistir House Hostel
13 An Crúgán
14 Dún Dúchathair
15 St Enda's Monastery
16 Teampall Bheanáin

0 1 2km
0 0.5 1mi

late evening, when there are fewer visitors. Be *very* careful when approaching the cliffs. There are no guard rails and the winds can be strong: tourists have been blown off and killed on the rock shelf below.

Halfway between Kilronan and Dún Aengus is the smaller **Dún Eochla**, a perfectly circular ring fort. Directly south of Kilronan and dramatically perched on a promontory is **Dún Dúchathair**, surrounded on three sides by cliffs.

The ruins of numerous stone churches trace the island's monastic history. The small **Teampall Chiaráin** (Church of St Kieran), with a high cross in the churchyard, is near Kilronan. To the south-east, near Cill Éinne Bay, is the early-Christian **Teampall Bheanáin** (Church of St Benen). Past Kilmurvey is the perfect **Clochán na Carraige**, an early-Christian stone hut that stands 2.5m tall, and the ruins of various small early-Christian remains known rather inaccurately as the **Na Seacht dTeampaill** (Seven

Churches), consisting of a couple of ruined churches, monastic houses and some fragments of a high cross from the 8th or 9th century. To the south is **Dún Eoghanachta**, another circular fort. Near the airstrip are the sunken remains of a church said to be the site of **St Enda's Monastery** in the 5th century.

There's a fine beach at **Kilmurvey**, west of Kilronan, and it's pleasant to stay here away from the 'bustle' of Kilronan. Before the beach, in the sheltered little bay of **Port Chorrúch**, up to 50 grey seals make their home, sunning and feeding in the shallows.

Places to Stay

Hostels There are several hostels on the island.

Kilronan Hostel (☎ 61255, fax 61313, e kilronanhostel@ireland.com, Kilronan) Dorms €12.60 per person including breakfast. This clean, friendly hostel is a short walk from the pier. The floors have been insulated so although the hostel's above Tí Joe Mac's

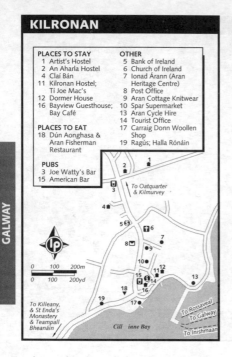

KILRONAN

PLACES TO STAY
1 Artist's Hostel
2 An Aharla Hostel
4 Claí Bán
11 Kilronan Hostel;
   Tí Joe Mac's
12 Dormer House
16 Bayview Guesthouse;
   Bay Café

PLACES TO EAT
18 Dún Aonghasa &
   Aran Fisherman
   Restaurant

PUBS
3 Joe Watty's Bar
15 American Bar

OTHER
5 Bank of Ireland
6 Church of Ireland
7 Ionad Árann (Aran
   Heritage Centre)
8 Post Office
9 Aran Cottage Knitwear
10 Spar Supermarket
13 Aran Cycle Hire
14 Tourist Office
17 Carraig Donn Woollen
   Shop
19 Ragús; Halla Rónáin

To Oatquarter
& Kilmurvey

0   100   200m
0   100   200yd

To Killeany,
& St Enda's
Monastery
& Teampall
Bheanáin

To Rossaveal
To Galway

Cill inne Bay

To Inishmaan

pub, you hear very little noise. It also hires out bikes.

An Aharla Hostel (☎ 61305, Kilronan) Dorms €8.80. There are two four-bed dorms in this laid-back former farmhouse, quietly positioned not far from Joe Watty's Bar.

Artist's Hostel (☎ 61456, Kilronan) Dorms €8.80. Close to An Aharla, this small property has good ocean views and a complimentary light breakfast.

Mainistir House Hostel (☎ 61169, fax 61351, Mainistir) Dorms/rooms €10.70/ 12.60 per person. Breakfast, bed linen and free pick-up are included in the rates at this appealing 60-bed hostel on the main road north of Kilronan. It has a large kitchen, and there are bicycles for hire.

B&Bs Here are some B&Bs we recommend.

Dormer House (☎ 61125, Kilronan) Rooms €22.70-25.20 per person. Dormer House is a large, clean, reasonably priced B&B behind Tí Joe Mac's.

Bayview Guesthouse (☎ 61260, Kilronan) Rooms €27.95/25.40 per person with/without shower. Open Mar-mid-Nov. This busy guesthouse enjoys an enviable position overlooking the harbour and has a cafe downstairs.

Claí Bán (☎ 61111, Kilronan) Rooms €23.95 per person. At the end of a quiet lane, welcoming Claí Bán has clean, modern facilities and good views of the bay from its dining area.

An Crúgán (☎ 61150, fax 61468, Kilronan) Singles/doubles from €37.80/42.85. Open Apr-Oct. Signposted off the main road north of Kilronan, An Crúgán has six well appointed, nonsmoking rooms, private parking and bikes for hire.

Man of Aran Cottage (☎ 61301, fax 61324, Kilmurvey) Singles/doubles €40.65/ 63.50. This cosy, thatched B&B overlooking Kilmurvey Bay was actually built for the eponymous film. It serves great food and rents out bikes.

Kilmurvey House (☎ 61218, fax 61397, Kilmurvey) Rooms €31.75 per person. Open Apr-Sept. B&B here is in a lovely, old stone mansion on the path leading to Dún Aengus and close to a Blue Flag beach.

Cregmount House (☎ 61139, Creggakeerain) Singles/doubles €33/53.30. Open Apr-Nov. At the north-western end of the island, 9km from Kilronan, Cregmount House is a pleasant, three-room, nonsmoking B&B with views across Galway Bay.

Places to Eat

Dún Aonghasa & Aran Fisherman Restaurant (☎ 61104, Kilronan) Mains €7-20. The restaurant has an extensive menu in which fish features prominently, but there are also pizzas and sandwiches on offer. Outside, there's a patio with tables for fine days.

Man of Aran Cottage (see Places to Stay) Sandwiches from €2.50, set dinner €21.60. This idyllic place serves fresh fish and flavoursome organic vegetables and herbs, which the owners grow in their garden. It offers soup, sandwiches and sweets during the day, and full dinners in the evening.

Mainistir House Hostel (see Places to

Stay) Buffet dinner €10.10. Mainistir House serves great-value organic, largely vegetarian buffet dinners at 8pm (7pm in winter); it's wise to book ahead.

Bay Café *(☎ 61260, Kilronan)* Under €6. Open 8.30am-9.30pm daily mid-Mar-Oct. The Bay Café, at the Bayview Guesthouse, is a relaxing self-service place good for a coffee or snack while you're waiting for the ferry.

Teach Nan Phaidt *(☎ 61330, Kilmurvey)* Soups €3.15, sandwiches €2.50-6.30. This thatched property, at the turn-off to Dún Aengus fort, is a convenient pit stop for walkers and cyclists. There are several craft shops nearby.

An Sunda Cáoch *(The Blind Sound; ☎ 61218, Kilmurvey)* Soups €3.15, sandwiches €2.50-6.30. An Sunda Cáoch, at the start of the path to Dún Aengus, serves filling, home-made soups and sandwiches and great cakes.

Entertainment

There's music in most Kilronan pubs at night.

Joe Watty's Bar *(Kilronan)* For Irish music and *craic* at its best, visit this old pub just north of Kilronan.

American Bar *(An Américéan Béar; ☎ 61130, Kilronan)* The American Bar attracts a mixed, convivial crowd and presents live traditional, folk and rock music.

Ragús *(☎ 61104, Halla Rónáin, Kilronan)* Admission €7.55. Ragús is an exciting one-hour show of traditional Irish dance, music and song performed daily in the Halla Rónáin at 2.45pm, 5pm and 9pm.

Shopping

A hand-knitted Aran sweater is top of many people's shopping lists when visiting the islands. In Kilronan, either **Aran Cottage Knitwear** *(☎ 61117)*, on the road towards Kilmurvey, or **Carraig Donn Woollen Shop** *(☎ 61123)*, near the old pier, can accommodate.

Getting Around

Near the pier Aran Cycle Hire (☎ 61132) hires out good bikes costing €6.30 per day.

You can also bring your own bicycle on the ferry.

Numerous minibuses greet tourists as they disgorge from the ferry. They offer 2½-hour tours of the island's principal sights for €6.30. However, walking and cycling will give you more of a sense of the place.

Pony traps with a driver are available for a return trip between Kilronan and Dún Aengus costing €25.20 to €31.50 (for up to four people).

INISHMAAN
☎ 099 • pop 300

Although Inishmaan (Inis Meáin; Middle Island) is the least visited of the Aran Islands, it's well worth the effort of getting there. Martin McDonagh's play *The Cripple of Inishmaan* may have put the island's name on the world map, but the locals aren't hellbent on attracting tourists, so visitor facilities are limited.

Inishmaan is about 5km long by 3km wide. The fields are bordered by high stone walls, and it's a delight to wander along these small lanes or along the cliffs to take in some of the tranquillity that attracted the playwright JM Synge and the nationalist Pádraig Pearse.

Orientation & Information

Inishmaan's main settlement is An Córa, whose buildings spread out along the road that runs east–west across the centre of the island. The principal boat landing stage is on the eastern side of the island, while the airstrip is in the north-eastern corner. In An Córa, the helpful Inishmaan Island Co-operative (☎ 73010), north-west of the pier and post office, dispenses tourist information.

Things to See

The chief archaeological site is **Dún Chonchúir**, a massive oval-shaped stone fort built on a high point and offering good views of the island on a fine day. It's similar to Dún Aengus on Inishmór, but is built inland overlooking a limestone valley. Chonchúir is said to have been a brother of Aengus. Dún Chonchúir's age is a bit of a puzzle: it's thought to have been built

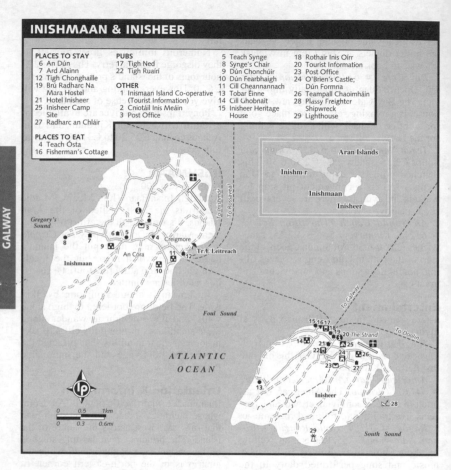

INISHMAAN & INISHEER

PLACES TO STAY
6 An Dún
7 Ard Alainn
12 Tigh Chonghaille
19 Brú Radharc Na
   Mara Hostel
21 Hotel Inisheer
25 Inisheer Camp
   Site
27 Radharc an Chláir

PLACES TO EAT
4 Teach Ósta
16 Fisherman's Cottage

PUBS
17 Tigh Ned
22 Tigh Ruairí

OTHER
1 Inismaan Island Co-operative
   (Tourist Information)
2 Cniotáil Inis Meáin
3 Post Office

5 Teach Synge
8 Synge's Chair
9 Dún Chonchúir
10 Dún Fearbhaigh
11 Cill Cheannannach
13 Tobar Éinne
14 Cill Ghobnait
15 Inisheer Heritage
   House

18 Rothair Inis Oírr
20 Tourist Information
23 Post Office
24 O'Brien's Castle;
   Dún Formna
26 Teampall Chaoimháin
28 Plassy Freighter
   Shipwreck
29 Lighthouse

sometime between the 1st and 7th centuries.

Teach Synge, a thatched cottage on the road just before you head up to the fort, is where the writer JM Synge spent his summers between 1898 and 1902.

Cill Cheannannach is a rough 8th- or 9th-century church south of the pier. The well preserved stone fort **Dún Fearbhaigh**, a short distance west, dates from about the same time.

Synge's Chair is to the west of the island near the end of a path that leads to a sheer cliff overlooking Gregory's Sound. It's a sheltered spot where JM Synge spent much time in reflection.

In the east of the island, about 500m north of the boat landing stage, is **Trá Leitreach**, a safe, sheltered beach.

Places to Stay & Eat

Most B&Bs serve evening meals, mostly using organically grown food, costing from around €19.

Ard Alainn (☎/fax 73027, Inishmaan) Rooms €21.60 per person. Open May-Sept. Ard Alainn, signposted just over 2km from the pier, has five simple rooms all with shared bathroom. Mrs Faherty's breakfasts will keep you going all day.

An Dún (*☎/fax 73047, Inishmaan*) Singles/doubles €38.10/63.50. Opposite the entrance to Dún Chonchúir, An Dún has four comfortable, nonsmoking rooms all with bathroom, and bikes for hire. It serves reasonably priced omelettes and pasta dishes in its restaurant (mains €4.50-9.50).

Tigh Chonghaille (*☎/fax 73085, Inishmaan*) Singles/doubles €34.30/58.40. Just up to the right of the pier, Tigh Chonghaille has six spacious rooms. It serves seafood in its restaurant (mains €7.50-16.35).

Teach Ósta (*☎ 73003, Inishmaan*) Mains €6.50-11.50. This terrific little bar, the island's only pub, hums with life on summer evenings and supplies snacks, sandwiches, soups and seafood platters.

Shopping
The knitwear factory *Cniotáil Inis Meáin* (*☎ 73009, Inishmaan*) exports fine woollen garments to some of the world's most exclusive shops, but sells them much cheaper here from its factory shop.

INISHEER
☎ 099 • pop 300

Only 8km off the coast from Doolin in County Clare, Inisheer (Inis Oírr; Eastern Island) is the smallest of the three Aran Islands. The view from the ferry is of a sheltered white beach backed by modern bungalows – few traditional thatched cottages and buildings survive – overlooked by a squat, stone 15th-century castle. To the south there's a maze of fields with barely a building in sight. The island has a timelessness about it, and a summer stroll through its sandy lanes is hard to beat. Despite a regular ferry service and proximity to the mainland, the absence of major archaeological sites and tourist amenities keeps the number of visitors down, making Inisheer rather special.

Information
In July and August a small wooden kiosk at the harbour provides tourist information 10am to 6pm daily. At other times you

can contact the nearby Inisheer Island Co-operative (*☎ 75008*) for assistance. The post office, south of the pier, changes money.

Things to See & Do
Most sights are in the north of the island. The 15th-century O'Brien's Castle (Caislea'n Uí Bhriain) overlooks the beach and harbour. It was built within the remains of a ring fort called Dún Formna dating from as early as the 1st century. Nearby is an 18th-century signal tower. On the Strand (An Trá) is the 10th-century Teampall Chaoimháin (Church of St Kevin), with some gravestones and shells from an ancient kitchen midden (dumping ground). West of the beach and pier, Inisheer Heritage House (*☎ 75021, Inisheer; admission €0.65; open 2pm-4pm daily July Aug*) is a typical stone-built thatched cottage with some interesting old photographs. It has a craft shop and cafe.

Cill Ghobnait (Church of St Gobnait), south-west of Inisheer Heritage House, is a small 8th- or 9th-century church named after Gobnait, who fled here from Clare trying to escape an enemy who was pursuing her. A 2km walk south-west of the church leads to the Tobar Éinne (Well of St Enda).

The best parts of Inisheer are uninhabited and the signposted 10.5km Inisheer Way is a recommended walk. The eastern road to the lighthouse is more popular, but the coast around the western side is wilder. On the eastern shore is the rusting hulk of the *Plassy*, a freighter wrecked in 1960 and thrown high up onto the rocks. The uninhabited lighthouse (1857) on the island's southern tip, with its neat enclosure, is off limits.

Places to Stay & Eat
Inisheer Camp Site (*☎ 75008, Inisheer*) Sites €3.15 with shower. Open May-Sept. This is a basic camp site overlooking the windswept Strand.

Brú Radharc Na Mara Hostel (*☎/fax 75024, Inisheer*) Dorms €10.10-11.35, rooms €13.85-14.50 per person. This spotless IHH hostel near the pier has ocean views, bikes for hire and continental or Irish breakfast.

GALWAY

Radharc an Chláir (☎/fax 75019, Inisheer) Singles/doubles €27.95/48.25. A pleasant nonsmoking B&B near O'Brien Castle, it also has bike hire and evening meals (€17.80).

Hotel Inisheer (Óstán Inis Oírr; ☎ 75020, Inisheer) Singles/doubles €37/63. Open Apr-Sept. This modern hotel, just up from the Strand, has homely en-suite rooms, and serves hearty meals in its bar and restaurant.

Fisherman's Cottage (☎ 75073, Inisheer) Mains €11.35-16.40. Cosy Fisherman's Cottage, near the pier, specialises in tasty, fresh seafood accompanied by organically grown vegetables.

Entertainment

Tigh Ned (☎ 75004, Inisheer) A mixed crowd comes to this welcoming, unpretentious place for its lively traditional music.

Tigh Ruaírí (☎ 75020, Inisheer) Tigh Ruaírí is an atmospheric and friendly old hostelry that also presents live music sessions.

Getting Around

Bikes are available for hire from Rothair Inis Oírr (☎ 75033, Inisheer) for €6.30 per day. Some B&Bs also hire out bicycles (see Places to Stay).

Eastern Galway

Separated from the wild, bleak landscape of Connemara and the county's western coast by Lough Corrib, this region is markedly different. Eastern Galway is relatively flat, and its underlying limestone has given it a well-drained, fertile soil. This is the largest section of the county, but it lacks areas of significant interest. Country towns such as Ballinasloe, Loughrea and Tuam serve relatively prosperous farming regions.

GETTING THERE & AWAY

Bus Éireann (☎ 091-562000) express buses from Galway serve Ballinasloe and Loughrea; local bus No 427 connects Galway, Ballinasloe and Loughrea with Portumna.

BALLINASLOE & AROUND

☎ 0905 • pop 5790

The biggest town in eastern Galway, Ballinasloe (Béal Átha na Sluaighe), is on the main Dublin–Galway road (N6). The town is pleasant enough, but there's no real reason to stay, except possibly over the eight days at the start of October when **Ballinasloe Horse Fair** attracts horse buyers and sellers and merrymakers.

Historically, Ballinasloe was a strategic crossing point over the River Suck. In the early 12th century, Turlough O'Connor, king of Connaught, built a castle to guard the river crossing, and this became the nucleus of the town's development.

Around 6km south-west of town on the N6, Aughrim was the site of a crucial victory by William of Orange over the Catholic forces of James II in 1691, the bloodiest battle ever fought on Irish soil. The **Battle of Aughrim Visitor Centre** *(☎ 73939, Aughrim; adult/child €3.80/1.90; open 10am-6pm Tues-Sat early June-early Sept)* helps put it into perspective within the framework of 17th-century European national and dynastic conflict. Signposts from the interpretive centre indicate the actual battle site.

Hyne's Hostel (☎ 73734, Ballinasloe) Dorms/rooms €11.35/12.60 per person. Open year round. Close to the centre, this IHH property only has 12 beds, so book ahead in summer or when the horse fair is on. It rents out bikes and can arrange pick-up.

CLONFERT CATHEDRAL

Around 21km south-east of Ballinasloe, off the R256, is the tiny 12th-century cathedral at Clonfert. It's on the site of a monastery said to have been founded in 563 by St Brendan the Navigator, which was ravaged by Vikings in 844 and 1179. The remarkable six-arched Romanesque doorway, with its human and animal heads, dates from the 1160s, but much of the limestone carvings were badly restored in the 19th century.

LOUGHREA & AROUND

☎ 091 • pop 3360

Loughrea (Baile Locha Riach) is a large, busy market town 26km south-east of Galway. It gets its name from the little lake at the southern end of town. Not to be confused with St Brendan's Church on Church St, which is now a library, **St Brendan's Catholic Cathedral** (☎ *841212, Barrack St; free; self-guided audio tours available from presbytery 10am-11am, 11.30am-1pm, 2pm-5.30pm Mon-Fri)*, dating from 1903, is renowned for its Celtic-revival stained glass, furnishings and marble columns. Loughrea has Ireland's only functioning medieval **moat**, which runs from the lake at Fair Green near the cathedral to the River Loughrea north of town.

Near Bullaun, 7km north of Loughrea, is the remarkable **Turoe Stone**, a phallic standing stone covered in delicate La Tène-style relief carvings. It dates from between 300 BC and AD 100. There are similarly carved stones in Brittany associated with La Tène Celts (late Iron Age). The stone wasn't set here originally, but was found at an Iron Age fort a few kilometres away.

PORTUMNA
☎ 0509 • pop 985

In the south-eastern corner of the county, the lakeside town of Portumna is an attractive place and a popular base for boating and fishing on **Lough Derg**. Dúchas-run **Portumna Castle** (☎ *41658, Castle Ave; adult/child €1.90/0.75; open 10am-6pm daily Apr-Oct)* was built in 1618 by Richard de Burgo (or Burke) and boasts a formal, geometrically laid-out garden of some pretension.

Counties Mayo & Sligo

Despite the fact that Mayo and Sligo share a history of rural poverty and are equally remote and underpopulated, County Sligo – the smaller of the two – is better known to most travellers, thanks largely to the evocative poetry of WB Yeats. However, the qualities of landscape and sense of place that inspired Yeats belong equally to both Mayo and Sligo. And, apart from a small number of towns, both counties are ideal for anyone wishing to escape the well worn tourist trail.

County Mayo

Mayo (Maigh Eo) has an identity that distinguishes it from other parts of Ireland on several different levels: a haunting, introspective landscape; a Connaught accent with its own inflection; and a people far removed from cosmopolitan Dublin or touristy Killarney.

The county was particularly hard hit by the Famine, and the woeful refrain 'County Mayo, God help us!' – still used among older Irish at home and abroad – probably dates from this sad time. In the 20th century Mayo's history was marked by massive emigration and, apart from a few small industries, a chronic lack of employment. More recently, the county's infrastructure has been modernised and its industry, agriculture and services are being developed.

CONG
☎ 092 • pop 200
Blink your eyes while passing through the small town of Cong (Conga) and you won't see much, but there's a great deal hidden beyond that ordinary main street. In 1951 American director John Ford came here with John Wayne and Maureen O'Hara to film *The Quiet Man*, and there are still many reminders of that momentous event. True fans of the film will want to buy *Complete Guide to the Quiet Man Locations* by Lisa Collins.

Cong is just east of the border with County Galway and 1km north of Lough Corrib.

Highlights

- Explore ruggedly remote Achill Island off the coast of western Mayo
- Cycle or drive from Louisburgh to Leenane (County Galway) through the wildly beautiful Doolough Valley
- Visit Céide Fields in northern Mayo, one of the most extensive Stone Age excavations in Europe
- Wander along the Hollow, the long, wide sandy beach at Enniscrone
- Discover County Sligo's varied scenery, which inspired WB Yeats
- Take in the panoramic but spooky Carrowkeel Passage Tomb Cemetery in the Bricklieve Mountains
- Wander around the religious remains of uninhabited Inishmurray Island

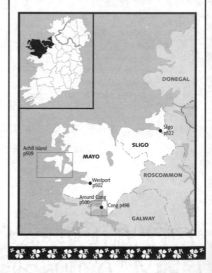

Information
The tourist office (☎ 46542), on Abbey St in the old courthouse building opposite Cong Abbey, opens 10am to 6pm daily, March to

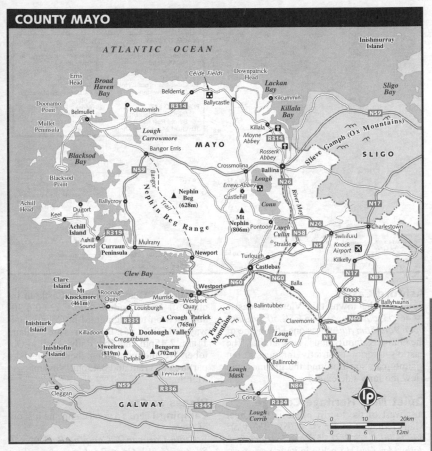

COUNTY MAYO

ATLANTIC OCEAN

Inishmurray Island

Erris Head

Broad Haven Bay

Céide Fields

Downpatrick Head

Lackan Bay

Sligo Bay

Doonamo Point

Belmullet

Belderrig

Ballycastle

Kilcummin

Killala Bay

Pollatomish

Killala

N59

Mullet Peninsula

Lough Carrowmore

Moyne Abbey

R314

Slieve Gamph (Ox Mountains)

Bangor Erris

MAYO

Rosserk Abbey

SLIGO

Blacksod Bay

Crossmolina

Ballina

Lough

N26

Blacksod Point

Nephin Beg (628m)

Errew Abbey

Castlehill

River Moy

Achill Head

Ballycroy

Conn

N17

Keel

Dugort

Mt Nephin (806m)

Pontoon

Lough Cullin

N58

Swinford

Charlestown

Achill Island

R319

Ashill Sound

Curraun Peninsula

Mulrany

Newport

Turlough

Straide

N26

N5

Knock Airport

Kilkelly

Castlebar

N60

Clew Bay

Westport

N60

Balla

N17

N83

Clare Island

Mt Knockmore (461m)

Roonagh Quay

Murrisk

Westport Quay

Knock

R323

Ballyhaunis

Louisburgh

Croagh Patrick (765m)

Ballintubber

Claremorris

N60

Inishturk Island

R335

Killadoon

Doolough Valley

Partry Mountains

Lough Carra

N17

Inishbofin Island

Cregganbaun

Mweelrea (819m)

Bengorm (702m)

Delphi

Lough Mask

Ballinrobe

Leenaue

Cleggan

N59

R336

GALWAY

R345

Cong

R334

Lough Corrib

N84

0   10   20km
0   6   12mi

December. Get a copy of the *Heritage Trail* brochure to explore the town and discover the fascinating history of the 1123 Cong Cross, now in the National Museum in Dublin. The local booklets *The Glory of Cong* and *Cong: Walks, Sights, Stories* have more information. A self-guided tour using *The Quiet Man* map takes in locations from the film.

There are no banks but you can change money at the post office on Main St.

Cong Abbey

Founded by Turlough Mór O'Connor, high king of Ireland and king of Connaught in 1120, this ruinous Augustinian abbey occupies the site of an earlier 6th-century abbey. It has a carved doorway on the northern side and fine windows and decorated medieval stonework in the **Chapter House**. West of the abbey on a small island in the nearby river stands the **Monk's Fishing House**, where a bell was rung every time a fish was caught. The concrete 1960s-style Catholic church, beside the abbey, is an eyesore built with utter disregard for its surroundings. The small **O'Duffy's Cross**, at the junction of Main and Abbey Sts, is the reconstructed remains of a 14th-century high cross.

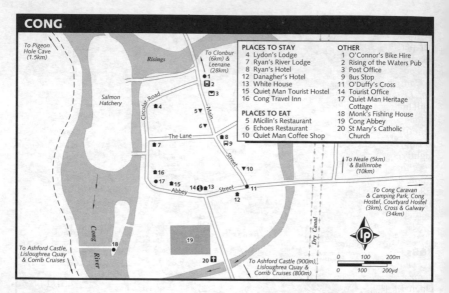

CONG

PLACES TO STAY
4 Lydon's Lodge
7 Ryan's River Lodge
8 Ryan's Hotel
12 Danagher's Hotel
13 White House
15 Quiet Man Tourist Hostel
16 Cong Travel Inn

PLACES TO EAT
5 Micilín's Restaurant
6 Echoes Restaurant
10 Quiet Man Coffee Shop

OTHER
1 O'Connor's Bike Hire
2 Rising of the Waters Pub
3 Post Office
9 Bus Stop
11 O'Duffy's Cross
14 Tourist Office
17 Quiet Man Heritage Cottage
18 Monk's Fishing House
19 Cong Abbey
20 St Mary's Catholic Church

Ashford Castle

South of the town, this Victorian castle (☎ 46003; adult/concession €5/2.50; grounds open 9am-5pm daily) was once the home of the Guinness family and is now a hotel. The castle's interior is strictly for guests, but visitors can stroll around the grounds and view the fairy-tale exterior.

Quiet Man Heritage Cottage

Just west of the tourist office is the Quiet Man Heritage Cottage (☎ 46089, Abbey St; adult/child €3.50/1.25; open 10am-5pm daily Mar-Oct). In a life-imitating-art exercise so twisted it begs a map, it attempts to re-create the exact set John Ford used to film many of the interior shots of The Quiet Man in Hollywood. Of course, original cottages such as this one – and their interiors – were his inspiration but, hey, they want real Hollywood. The cottage also contains the **Cong Archaeological and Historical Exhibition**, which rather ambitiously attempts to trace the story of Cong and its surrounds from 7000 BC to the 19th century in a very small space.

Cruises

Corrib Cruises (☎ 46029, Cong) sales from Lisloughrea Quay at Ashford Castle to In-chagoill Island (adult/child €12.60/6.30) and then on to Oughterard in County Galway (€15.12/7.55). Departures are at 10am, 11am, 2.45pm and 5pm daily, April to October. Weather permitting, there are also departures at 11am and 2.45pm, November to March.

Places to Stay

Camping There's a good camp site just out of town.

Cong Caravan & Camping Park (☎ 460 89, fax 46448, Quay Rd, Lisloughrey) Tent site €8.25, plus adult/child €1.90/1.60. This pleasant camp site is 2km east of town, off the Galway road (R346), close to the shore of Lough Corrib. It has a laundrette, boat and bike rental, and a shop.

Hostels Cong has a number of hostels to offer.

Cong Travel Inn (☎ 46310, fax 46116, Abbey St) Rooms €15.75 per person. This hostel provides excellent-value, modern, clean rooms with shower and tea and coffee facilities. There's also a separate, self-catering communal kitchen.

MAYO & SLIGO

Quiet Man Tourist Hostel (☎ 46089, Abbey St) Dorms/private rooms €9.45/11.40 per person. Don't let its position opposite the abbey cemetery put you off staying at this cosy, spick-and-span place.

Cong Hostel (☎ 46089, fax 46448, Quay Rd, Lisloughrey) Dorms €9.50. Affiliated with both An Óige and IHH, this large, congenial hostel next to the camp site offers the benefits of modern facilities and proximity to Lough Corrib. It screens *The Quiet Man* nightly in the hostel picture theatre.

Courtyard Hostel (☎/fax 46203, Garracloon Lodge, Cross) Dorms/private rooms €8.80/€12.60 per person, tent site €3.80. This quiet, secluded hostel is in converted stables 3km east of Cong in the village of Cross; call ahead for a free pick-up.

B&Bs Central B&Bs include the following.

Lydon's Lodge (☎ 46053, fax 46523, Circular Rd) Rooms €31.75-38.90 per person. Open Mar-Oct. Lydon's Lodge is a comfortable, rustic establishment that caters mainly for anglers.

White House (☎ 46358, Abbey St) En suite singles/doubles €31.50/45.40. Open Mar-Oct. The children's toys in the lobby let you know immediately that this is someone's home. It has light, airy bedrooms.

Ryan's River Lodge (☎/fax 46057, The Lane) Rooms with shower €25.40 per person. Open Mar-Sept. This homely property has four comfy rooms and a pleasant garden to relax in. It accepts credit cards.

Hotels There are several attractive hotels in Cong.

Ryan's Hotel (☎ 46243, fax 46634, Main St) Rooms €36.80-53.35 per person. Ryan's has a charming, old-world interior and an enviable riverside location.

Danagher's Hotel (☎ 46028, Abbey St) Singles/doubles €44.10/75.60. Danagher's, near the town's main junction, is an old-style, 11-room hotel.

Places to Eat

Some eateries open from May to September or October only.

Echoes (☎ 46059, Main St) Starters €3.15-8.80, mains €12.60-22.70. Consider unleashing your credit card at Echoes, a brash, award-winning restaurant that uses produce from its own butchery and deli.

Micilín's Restaurant (☎ 46655, Main St) Mains €10-19. More demure than its neighbour a few doors away, cosy Micilín's makes a good alternative to Echoes.

Danagher's Hotel (☎ 46028, Abbey St) Mains €6.30-12. Danagher's Hotel has a fine old bar, a basic eating area and a fancier restaurant.

Quiet Man Coffee Shop (☎ 46034, Main St) Snacks under €6. This pleasant coffee shop does appetising, home-made sandwiches, snacks, scones and pies.

Getting There & Away

Monday to Saturday Bus Éireann (☎ 096-71800) bus No 51 from Galway to Ballina stops at Ashford Castle gates in the early afternoon, while bus No 420 between Galway and Clifden stops outside Ryan's Hotel in the early evening.

If you're travelling by car or bike farther into County Mayo, eschew the main N84 to Castlebar and take the longer, but much more attractive, route west to Leenane (starting with the R345) and north to Westport via Delphi.

Getting Around

There are enough interesting sites close to Cong to make a bike worth having. They can be hired from O'Connor's (☎ 46008), Main St, for €12.60/50.40 per day/week. (O'Connor's is the combined Esso station, Spar supermarket and craft shop next to the Rising of the Waters pub.)

AROUND CONG

There's a surprising amount to see and do around Cong, including a collection of caves, a canal that never functioned, a stone circle and a curious folly. The limestone strata of the Cong area accounts for the numerous caves, for the failure of the canal and for the local phenomenon known as 'the rising of the waters', where water from Lough Mask to the north percolates through the limestone and emerges from the ground

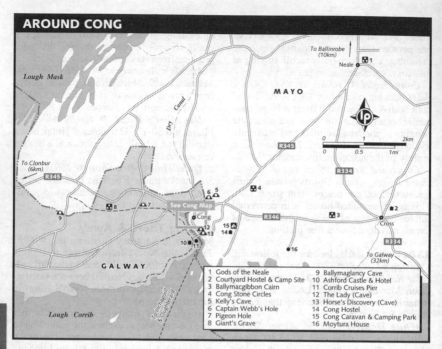

AROUND CONG

To Ballinrobe
(10km)

To Clonbur
(6km)

MAYO

Lough Mask

R345

R345

R334

R334

R345

6 5

4

8 7

R346

3

2

See Cong Map

Cong

12

15

13 14

2km

1mi

10

11

16

GALWAY

To Galway
(32km)

To Inchagoill
& Oughterard

Lough Corrib

1	Gods of the Neale	9	Ballymaglancy Cave
2	Courtyard Hostel & Camp Site	10	Ashford Castle & Hotel
3	Ballymacgibbon Cairn	11	Corrib Cruises Pier
4	Cong Stone Circles	12	The Lady (Cave)
5	Kelly's Cave	13	Horse's Discovery (Cave)
6	Captain Webb's Hole	14	Cong Hostel
7	Pigeon Hole	15	Cong Caravan & Camping Park
8	Giant's Grave	16	Moytura House

at Cong before flowing down to Lough Corrib.

Caves

The Cong area is peppered with caves, many of them only a short walk from the village.

Pigeon Hole is about 1.5km west of Cong and can be reached by road or by the walking track from across the river. Stone steps lead down into the cave, which is sometimes very wet. From the Pigeon Hole, take the R345 west towards Clonbur, passing the Giant's Grave turn-off, and go onto a lane that turns south about 5km from Cong. A stream flows into the extensive **Ballymaglancy Cave**, which is off the road to the right. The cave has stalactites and stalagmites.

Two other caves are north-east of Cong, near the road to Cross (R346). **Captain Webb's Hole** is just outside Cong, a short distance beyond the dry canal and behind the school grounds. It's actually a deep, water-filled hole in the ground where, two

centuries ago, a local villain is said to have hurled a succession of local women. Another 200m from Cong, a wide path leads to **Kelly's Cave**, which is usually locked up; the key is kept at the Quiet Man Coffee Shop (a small deposit may be required). **The Lady** and **Horse's Discovery** are two other caves beside a road to the castle.

The Dry Canal

Lough Mask is about 10m higher than Lough Corrib, and in the mid-18th century it was decided to cut a canal between the two. The project started in 1848, using labourers who were desperate for work due to the deprivations of the Famine years. In 1854, when construction was nearing completion, the economic basis for the canal was already in question as railways rapidly spread across the country. Then a greater problem was discovered – the canal wasn't watertight. The porous limestone simply soaked up any water that flowed into it.

Although various schemes for sealing the canal bed were considered, the whole expensive project was abandoned in 1858. The dry canal runs north–south to the east of Cong.

Circles & Graves

The stone slabs of the megalithic burial chamber known as the **Giant's Grave** can be visited easily between the Pigeon Hole and Ballymaglancy Cave. A path leads into the forest south of the R345 road to Clonbur, about 2km from Cong. About 100m from the road take the turn-off to the left; the grave is off that path to the right.

There are several stone circles in the area, including the excellent **Cong Stone Circles** about 1.5km north-east of Cong just east off the Neale road (R345). About 3.5km east of Cong, north off the Cross road (R346), is **Ballymacgibbon Cairn**, supposedly the site of a legendary Celtic battle. **Moytura House**, near the shores of Lough Corrib, takes its name from this battle and was a childhood home of Oscar Wilde.

Neale

The village of Neale, 6km north-east of Cong, has some interesting sites. If you take the turn-off at the northern end of the village, the curious stone known as the **Gods of the Neale** is about 200m east of the main road, just inside the walls of Neale Park. The slab, originally found in a nearby cave, is carved with figures of a human, animal and reptile in low relief and is dated 1757.

Inchagoill Island

In the centre of Lough Corrib is the island of Inchagoill (see Lough Corrib under Connemara in the County Galway chapter). The island can be reached by boat from the jetty next to Ashford Castle (see Cruises under Cong earlier) and from Oughterard in County Galway.

WESTPORT

☎ 098 • pop 4250

The prosperous heritage town of Westport (Cathair na Mairt) is on the River Carrow-

beg and the shores of Clew Bay in the southern half of County Mayo. It didn't acquire its postcard prettiness gradually, like many other small Irish towns – it was designed that way. The Mall, with the river running along the centre, is as picturesque a main street as you'll find anywhere. The present Westport House was built on the site of an O'Malley castle, which was once surrounded by about 60 hovels and the original settlement of Westport. These were moved when the house was planned, and the Brownes, who came here from Sussex during the reign of Elizabeth I, even had the course of the river altered to make the Mall a grand approach to the gates of the house. This wasn't entirely successful, as the Mall is still subject to occasional flooding.

Orientation & Information

Westport consists of two parts: the town proper and Westport Quay on the bay, just outside town on the road to Louisburgh (R335). The tourist office (☎ 25711), in James St, opens 9am to 5.45pm daily in July and August; 9am to 5.45pm Monday to Saturday April to June and September; and 9am to 12.45pm and 2pm to 5.15pm on weekdays the rest of the year.

P Dunning (☎ 25161), on the corner of The Octagon and James St, is a cyberpub offering Internet access 11am to 9pm daily at €7.60 per hour. The Allied Irish Bank, Shop St, and the Bank of Ireland, on the North Mall near the post office, have ATMs and bureaux de change. The Bookshop (☎ 26816), Bridge St, has a good selection of OS maps and books on Ireland.

For information about fishing, inquire at Hewetson (☎ 26018), Bridge St.

Westport House

The present house dates from 1730 (☎ 25430, **W** www.westporthouse.ie, Quay Rd; adult/child including animal park €15.10/9.55, families (up to 6 children) €49; house open 11.30am-5.30pm Mon-Fri, 1.30pm-5.30pm Sat & Sun July-late Aug; 1.30pm-5.30pm daily June & late Aug-early Sept; 2pm-5pm Sun late Apr-May & early Sept-late Sept; animal park open

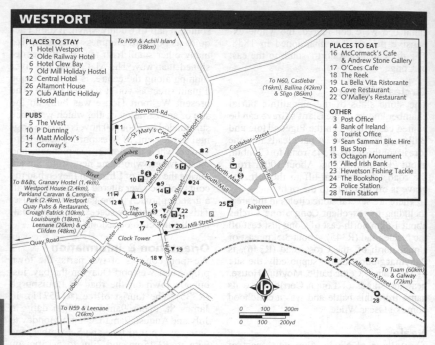

WESTPORT

To N59 & Achill Island (38km)

To N60, Castlebar (16km), Ballina (42km) & Sligo (86km)

Newport Rd
St Mary's Cres
Newport St
Castlebar Street
Distillery Road
North Mall
South Mall
James Street
Bridge Street
Shop St
Mill Street
Fairgreen
Mill Street
Peter St
The Octagon
Clock Tower
Quay Road
Tober Hill Rd
John's Row
High St
Altamount Street

To B&Bs, Granary Hostel (1.4km), Westport House (2.4km), Parkland Caravan & Camping Park (2.4km), Westport Quay Pubs & Restaurants, Croagh Patrick (10km), Louisburgh (18km), Leenane (26km) & Clifden (48km)

To Tuam (60km) & Galway (72km)

To N59 & Leenane (26km)

0   100   200m
0   100   200yd

PLACES TO STAY
1   Hotel Westport
2   Olde Railway Hotel
6   Hotel Clew Bay
7   Old Mill Holiday Hostel
12 Central Hotel
26 Altamont House
27 Club Atlantic Holiday Hostel

PUBS
5   The West
10 P Dunning
14 Matt Molloy's
21 Conway's

PLACES TO EAT
16 McCormack's Cafe & Andrew Stone Gallery
17 O'Cees Cafe
18 The Reek
19 La Bella Vita Ristorante
20 Cove Restaurant
22 O'Malley's Restaurant

OTHER
3   Post Office
4   Bank of Ireland
8   Tourist Office
9   Sean Samman Bike Hire
11 Bus Stop
13 Octagon Monument
15 Allied Irish Bank
23 Hewetson Fishing Tackle
24 The Bookshop
25 Police Station
28 Train Station

MAYO & SLIGO

same hours but only June-early Sept). Commercialisation is pushed to the hilt here, from a fake 'dungeon' to tacky souvenirs for sale in the 'Gifte Shoppe'. Consider a visit only if your itinerary doesn't include an Irish stately home elsewhere.

To reach Westport House, head out of town west on Quay Rd towards Croagh Patrick and Louisburgh. After about 1km, just before you get to Westport Quay, there's a road to the right which leads to the entrance to the grounds.

The Octagon Monument
This memorial was erected in 1845 in honour of an eminently forgettable local banker, whose statue stood upon an octagonal podium at the top of the column. During the Civil War, troops decapitated the statue, and it was later removed. In 1990 a Roman-looking statue of St Patrick complete with serpent-entwined staff replaced the unfortunate capitalist.

Clew Bay Heritage Centre
This heritage centre (☎ 26852, The Quay; adult/child €2.55/1.25; open 10am-5pm Mon-Fri & 3pm-5pm Sun July & Aug; 10am-5pm Mon-Fri June & Sept; 10am-2pm Mon-Fri Apr, May & Oct) is down on the pier in Westport Quay. It has an interesting collection of local artefacts and documents, including the spinning wheel presented by the people of Ballina to Maud Gonne, the dynamic political rebel who was married briefly to Major John MacBride and was the object of Yeats' adoration. The centre provides a genealogical service too.

Places to Stay
Camping & Hostels Westport has several good budget options.

Parkland Caravan & Camping Park (☎ 27766, fax 25206, **e** camping@west porthouse.ie, Westport House, Quay Rd) Tent, car & 2 people €19.70, hikers & cyclists €16.50 per tent. Open mid-May-early

Sept. Part of the Westport House estate, this large camp site is scenically sited in woodland between the river and Clew Bay.

Old Mill Holiday Hostel (☎ *27045, fax 28640, Barrack Yard)* Dorms €8.80, private rooms €11.35-12.60 per person. Next to the tourist office off James St, this charming old IHH hostel has a large kitchen-lounge and clean, comfy, single-sex and mixed dorms. Enter through the arch.

Club Atlantic Holiday Hostel (☎ *26644, fax 26241, Altamount St)* Dorms €10.10, singles €16.50-20.30, doubles €25.40-40.65. Open Mar-Oct. This super An Óige/IHH hostel, near the train station and within walking distance of the town centre, has a games room, Internet access and a three-hectare conservation area. Bike hire is available. Although there's an enormous eat-in kitchen, you can order breakfast for €3.15.

Granary Hostel (☎ *25903, Quay Rd)* Dorms €9.45. Open Apr-Sept. What this simple hostel in a converted grainstore lacks in facilities it makes up for in character. At the back there's a conservatory and a big garden to hang out your washing, and there's a convenient supermarket across the road. The hostel is in Westport Quay, near the Westport House entrance.

B&Bs The tourist office books rooms in the town's plentiful supply of B&Bs but, if you should arrive late, Altamount St has a few of the cheaper ones and they're close to the train station. Another group of B&Bs lines Quay Rd between the two parts of town.

Altamont House (☎ *25226, Altamount St)* Rooms €25.40 per person. Open Mar-Oct. Close to the train station, this unpretentious B&B has clean rooms and a neat rear garden.

Adare House (☎ *26102, fax 26202, Quay Rd)* Singles/doubles €32.40/48.30. This modern, two-storey home has six rooms (four with bathroom) and good firm beds.

Hotels There are some attractive hotels in town.

Hotel Clew Bay (☎ *25438, fax 25783, James St)* Rooms €41.30-63.55 per person. Hotel Clew Bay has 28 finely furnished

rooms and simply drips with old-world charm.

Central Hotel (☎ *25027, fax 26316, The Octagon)* Rooms €44.45-57.15. This beautiful old hotel has been fully refurbished and is a short walk from restaurants and pubs.

Olde Railway Hotel (☎ *25166, fax 25090, The Mall)* Rooms €44.45-88.95 per person. This 15-room Victorian showcase hotel is where the English novelist Thackeray chose to stay on his tour around Ireland in the 19th century.

Places to Eat

Quay Cottage (☎ *26412, The Harbour)* Mains €16-22.50. Open 6pm-10pm daily. Hidden down the side road leading to Westport House estate, Quay Cottage is a delightful, cosy restaurant with a nautical theme. The menu mainly features seafood but are a few meat and vegetarian dishes.

The Towers (☎ *26534, The Harbour)* Mains €7.50-12.50. This Tudoresque pub has several cosy bar rooms, a bistro and a beer garden. It serves fresh, traditional food all day and specialises in seafood. Its 'Atlantic platter' is a medley of every seafood item on the menu.

La Bella Vita Ristorante (☎ *26679, High St)* Pasta €8.25-13.90, mains €14-19. This cosy Italian restaurant, in a three-storey town house, offers a wide range of pasta dishes as well as steak, chicken and vegetarian choices.

The Reek (☎ *28955, High St)* Mains €8-13. Open Tues-Sun. A little up the hill from the centre, this is a relaxing place for lunch or a snack or you can just linger over a coffee on the sofa. The desserts are good.

O'Malley's (☎ *25101, Bridge St)* Mains €9.45-19. This immensely popular pub has an incredible array of dishes culled from many different cuisines, including Thai, Indian, Sri Lankan, Mexican and Italian.

McCormack's *(Bridge St)* Mains €5.50-8. If this bright, upstairs cafe is busy you can always check out the paintings in the Andrew Stone Gallery across the landing.

O'Cee's *(The Octagon)* Meals €4.75-6.30. Open 8.30am-7pm Mon-Sat & 10am-6pm Sun. O'Cee's is a popular cafeteria-style eatery that attracts a shopping-weary crowd from the adjoining supermarket.

Entertainment

Matt Molloy's (☎ 26655, Bridge St) This is a great old pub with wooden floors, a warm fire in the back and bric-a-brac everywhere. It's owned by Matt Molloy of the Chieftains and can get overcrowded when Irish music sessions are on. Sometimes there's an admission charge to hear well known performers.

Conway's (☎ 26145, Bridge St) With its dark-wood walls, smoke-stained ceiling and friendly banter, Conway's exudes old-world charm by the bucket-load. The back room, like Molloy's, can get packed on traditional music nights.

The West (☎ 28984, Bridge St) The West, on the corner of South Mall, is another popular, smoke-filled old pub attracting a mixed crowd. It has music sessions on Sunday.

P Dunning (☎ 25161, The Octagon) Locals flock here during the week to watch big sporting events on the TV, and there's traditional music on weekend nights. Tables are put out on the pavement on fine days.

Getting There & Away

Bus Éireann (☎ 096-71800) buses running Monday to Saturday to/from The Octagon in Westport include: two to Achill (one on Sunday), up to four to Ballina (two on Sunday), two to Belfast (bus No 66), up to seven to Cork (two on Sunday), up to eight to Galway (four on Sunday), and two to Sligo (one on Sunday). For Shannon Airport and Limerick, change in Galway.

The train station (☎ 25253) is on Altamount St within easy walking distance of the town centre. There are three daily connections (four on Sunday) to Dublin (3½ hours) via Athlone.

Getting Around

For a cab call Moran's Executive Taxis (☎ 25539). Sean Sammon Bike Hire (☎ 25020), James St, hires out bikes for €7.60 per day, or you can hire one from the Club Atlantic Holiday Hostel (see Places to Stay), which also provides a trilingual pamphlet with seven suggested itineraries.

AROUND WESTPORT
Croagh Patrick

Croagh Patrick (also known as 'the Reek') towers to the south-west of Westport. From the top of this mountain St Patrick performed his snake-expulsion act – Ireland has been free of venomous serpents ever since. Climbing the 765m holy mountain is an act of penance for thousands of pilgrims on the last Sunday of July (Reek Sunday). The truly contrite make the trek along Tóchar Phádraig (Patrick's Causeway), the original 40km route from Ballintubber Abbey, and ascend the mountain barefoot.

The trail for less contrite folk begins beside Campbell's pub in the village of **Murrisk** (Muraisc), west of Westport. There's a sign (between the pub and the car park) pointing the way, and there's no mistaking the route. At the start of the path is a new information centre (☎ 098-64114) open 11am to 5pm daily. If the weather is clear, the 1½- to two-hour climb to the small church at the top gives fine views year round.

Opposite the car park is the **National Famine Memorial**, a metal sculpture of a three-masted sailing ship covered in skeletons, commemorating the Potato Famine. Following the path down past the memorial brings you to the remains of **Murrisk Abbey** founded by the O'Malleys in 1547.

Louisburgh & Around
☎ 098 • pop 500

Louisburgh (Cluain Cearbán) got its name from the 1st marquess of Sligo, who laid it out and had a relative fighting against the French at the Battle of Louisburgh in Canada. The town is home to the **Granuaile Visitors Centre** (☎ 25711, 66341, Church St; adult/child €3.15/1.60; open 10am-6pm Mon-Sat June-Sept). The centre, in a disused church, is dedicated to the life and times of Grace O'Malley (1530–1603), the pirate queen and the most famous of the O'Malley clan. It also includes an exhibition on the Famine and the terrible privations it caused.

There are some excellent **beaches** in the vicinity: Old Head Beach (which has a Blue Flag) and the Silver Strand are particularly sandy and safe and are suitable for **surfing** and other water sports.

Old Head Forest Caravan & Camping Park (*☎ 087 648 6885, fax 01-280 1206, Old Head, Louisburgh*). Family tent €10.15, hikers & cyclists €6.35. Open June-Sept. This medium-sized camping park is about 4km from Louisburgh, just off the main road to Westport, and a short walk from the Blue Flag beach.

Bus Éireann (☎ 096-71800) bus No 450 links Westport and Louisburgh via Murrisk up to three times a day, Monday to Saturday.

Killadoon

Killadoon is a small village of scattered houses on the coast. It's reached by a narrow coastal road heading south from Louisburgh or by turning west off the R335 at Cregganbaun. Its main attractions are the panoramic ocean views and long sandy beaches.

On Thursday only, Bus Éireann (☎ 096-71800) bus No 450 from Westport and Louisburgh continues to Killadoon up to three times daily.

Doolough Valley

There are two roads connecting Westport and Leenane (County Galway), but the one nearest the coast (the R335) via Louisburgh and Delphi travels through the stunning Doolough Valley. It's wildly beautiful, not least because of the lonely expanse of **Doo Lough** (Dark Lake) with the **Mweelrea Mountains** behind. At the southern end of the lake **Bengorm** rises to 702m. The landscape changes from baize green and sparkling wet stone to a forbidding grey as shadows envelop everything when cloudbanks spread in from the Atlantic.

During the Potato Famine, the valley was the scene of tragedy when some 600 men, women and children walked from Louisburgh to Delphi Lodge hoping that the landlord would offer them food. Help was flatly refused and, on the return journey, around 400 perished through hunger and exposure. There's a memorial to the unfortunate souls along the road.

DELPHI
☎ 095

The Brownes of Westport, originally Catholic, converted to Protestantism to avoid the constraints of the penal laws, thus allowing one family member to be ennobled as the marquess of Sligo at the time of union with Britain in 1801. The 2nd marquess, a friend of Byron, gave the unlikely name of Delphi to his fishing lodge on the border of Galway and Mayo. He had travelled in central Greece and returned home convinced that his starkly beautiful territory strongly resembled the area around Delphi. The closest settlement of size is Leenane in Galway.

Delphi Lodge (*☎ 42211, fax 42296, Leenane*) Singles/doubles €114.30/152.50. Today, this remote Georgian lodge caters mostly for well-to-do anglers who fish in the peaceful local waters; permits are available.

Mountain Lodge & Spa (*☎ 42987, 42208, fax 42303, ẽ delphigy@iol.ie, ẉ www.delphiescape.com, Leenane*) Singles/doubles from €151/277 including meals & choice of 25 activities per night. This beautifully isolated lodge provides a range of organised outdoor activities and a health spa program.

CLARE ISLAND
☎ 098 • pop 150

Clare Island, at the mouth of Clew Bay, is 5km from the nearest mainland point, Roonagh Quay. Bay View Hotel (☎ 26307), near the harbour, has tourist information.

The mountainous island rises up to **Mt Knockmore** (461m), which is the highest point and dominates the landscape. The island has the ruins of the Cistercian **Clare Island Abbey** (circa 1460) and **Granuaile's Castle**, both associated with the piratical Grace O'Malley. The tower castle was her stronghold, although it was altered considerably when the coastguard took it over in 1831. Grace is said to be buried in the small abbey, which contains a stone with her family motto: 'Invincible on land and sea.'

The island has safe, sandy beaches and is perfect for **walking** and **climbing** on a clear day. It is also one of the dwindling number of places where you can find **choughs**,

---

Grace O'Malley

Grace O'Malley (1530–1603), also called Granuaile and the daughter of a Connaught chief, established her own fleet and commanded her own army. From her Clare Island base she controlled the Clew Bay area and attacked the ships of those who had submitted to the English. In 1566 she married Richard Burke, a neighbouring clan chief (her first husband, Donal O'Flaherty, had died years earlier), and her power grew to such an extent that the merchants of Galway pleaded with the English governor to do something about her.

In 1574 her castle (Carrigahowley Castle, now called Rockfleet Castle, near Newport) was besieged, but she turned the siege into a rout of the English and sent them packing. In 1577 she was held in prison but, mysteriously, managed to get herself released on a promise of good behaviour. Over the next few years she craftily entered a number of alliances, both with and against the English.

In 1593 she travelled to London and was granted a pardon after meeting Elizabeth I, who offered to make her a countess. Grace declined, for she already considered herself the queen of Connaught.

Back in Ireland she appeared to be working for the English, but it seems likely that she was still fiercely independent. In the final recorded reference to her, in the English State Papers of 1601, an English captain tells of meeting one of her pirate ships, captained by one of her sons, on its way to plunder a merchant ship.

---

which look like blackbirds but have red beaks.

Places to Stay & Eat

Cois Abhainn (☎ 26216) Rooms from €22.85 per person. A good getaway, Mary O'Malley's B&B is 5km from the harbour in the remote south-west corner, but you can arrange a pick-up.

Bay View Hotel (☎ 26307, fax 26002) Singles/doubles €31.50/56.70. Open June-Sept. Set beside the harbour, this efficient hotel attracts sea anglers, divers and sailing folk.

Clare Island Lighthouse (☎ 45120, fax 45122) Singles/doubles €88.95/152.45. In the island's north this unusual hotel dates from 1806 and has all the comforts one would expect for the price.

If you're just going for the day to the harbour it's best to take your own food, though pub grub is available at the Bay View Hotel, and B&Bs do evening meals for guests and nonguests (from €15.25).

Getting There & Away

Clare Island Ferries (☎ 28288, 087 414853) and O'Malley's Ferries (☎ 25045, 087 232 1785) make the 25-minute trip from Roonagh Quay, 8km west of Louisburgh (adult/child €12.60/6.30 return). There are eight sailings daily in July and August, and from three to five daily in May, June and September; for the October–April schedule call the operators.

INISHTURK ISLAND

☎ 098 • pop 98

Inishturk Island lies about 12km off Mayo's western coast. Evidence of pre-Christian life has been found, but it's believed that the ancestors of many of today's inhabitants were driven here in Cromwell's time. The island doesn't receive many tourists, despite the two **sandy beaches** on its eastern side, wonderful **flora and fauna** and a rugged, hilly landscape ideal for **walking**.

B&B is available at a few places.

Teach Abhainn (☎ 45110, fax 45778, Inishturk) Singles/doubles €25.40/40.65. Open year round. On a working farm about 1.5km from the harbour, this B&B has seven comfortable rooms all with shared bathroom, and serves filling home-cooked meals using organic produce (dinner €17.80).

Ocean View House (☎ 45520, fax 45655, Inishturk) Singles/doubles €25.40/45.70 per person. Open year round. Ocean View, close to the harbour, has six neat rooms (three with bathroom). Organic food is also used in its meals (dinner €19).

Helen and John Heane (☎ 45541) operate ferries from Cleggan in County Galway and from Roonagh Quay. The *Caher Star* sails from Cleggan pier at 11am and 6pm Tuesday to Thursday, from Roonagh Quay at 11am and 6.30pm Friday to Monday (adult/ child €18.90/9.45 return).

NEWPORT
☎ 098 • pop 520

The small 18th-century town of Newport (Baile Uí Fhiacháin), on the River Newport about 12km north of Westport, is a popular base for fishing in the nearby loughs and Clew Bay.

The tourist office (☎ 41822), on Main St opposite the Angler's Rest pub, opens weekdays June to September. The post office, with a bureau de change, is on the other side of the river. There are no banks.

From 1892 to 1936, the Great Western Railway ran a line from Westport to Achill Sound. It was later pedestrianised and now offers an interesting walk across the viaduct that dominates Newport, with views of the river. Newport is also at one end of the Bangor Trail (see Bangor Erris later in this chapter).

Places to Stay & Eat

Debille House (☎ 41145, fax 41777, Main St) Singles/doubles €31.75/50.80. Open June-Sept. This is a rather stately, three-storey, stone town house in the town centre with a garden for guests' use.

Newport House (☎ 41222, fax 41613, Main St) Singles/doubles €125/210. Genteel Newport House is the poshest place in these parts. Dinner in its nonsmoking restaurant costs a stiff €40, but the snug little bar is worth a visit any time.

The Village Bakery (☎ 42949, Main St) Lunch €4.50-5.70. The bakery, below Debille House, sells wonderful fresh cakes, pies and tarts as well as quiches and hot soups at lunch-time.

Getting There & Away

A Bus Éireann (☎ 096-71800) service links Achill Island and Westport via Newport once a day, Monday to Saturday, year round.

In July and August, bus No 66 from Achill Sound to Belfast stops at Newport and goes on through Ballina, Sligo and Enniskillen. The bus stop is outside Debille House.

NEWPORT TO ACHILL ISLAND
Burrishoole Abbey

Founded in 1486 by the Dominicans, what remains of the abbey is a solid tower and the eastern window of the cloisters. It's beside the river that drains Lough Furnace into the sea. About 2.5km north-west of Newport on the Newport–Achill road, a sign points the way, and it's 1km down to the left.

Rockfleet Castle

Formerly known as Carrigahowley, this 15th-century tower house has a strong association with Grace O'Malley (see the boxed text on the previous page). After the death of her first husband, Grace married Richard Burke – on the condition that at the end of the first year either party could summarily dissolve the marriage. When the year was over she shut herself up in her fortified castle and announced the divorce as he approached. True or not, the castle, at the head of the inlet, does look impregnable. Grace O'Malley is supposed to have lived out the rest of her years here, and in 1574 she successfully repulsed an English force besieging the castle.

To get here, turn south at the sign about 5km west of Newport on the Achill road.

Mulrany & Curraun Peninsula

The village of Mulrany (An Mhala Raithní, also called Mallaranny or Mulranny) stands on the isthmus between Clew Bay, with its (supposed) 365 islands, and Bellacagher Bay and boasts a lovely, wide Blue Flag beach. To get to it, either take the footpath opposite the defunct Mulrany Bay Hotel, a huge cream-and-chocolate pile on the N59, or the one starting beside the Top service station.

Places to Stay

Traenlaur Lodge (☎ 098-41358, Lough Feeagh, Newport) Seniors/juniors €9.55/7. A former fishing lodge with its own small harbour on Lough Feeagh, this An Óige hostel is 8km from Newport and signposted

MAYO & SLIGO

on the road to Achill. It's a great place to relax especially if you're walking the Western Way or Bangor Trail which meet here.

Achill seems the obvious destination if you're travelling from Newport, but the wild Curraun Peninsula, joined to Achill Island by a bridge, has a B&B where you can get away from it all.

Teach Mweewillin (☎ 098-45134, fax 45225, Curraun, Achill) Singles/doubles from €29.85/48.25. Open May-Sept. The B&B sits on a hillside in the remote southwest corner of the peninsula with views across to Achill Island. The bedrooms are nonsmoking, and Mrs Cannon provides evening meals on request.

ACHILL ISLAND
☎ 098 • pop 3500

Joined to the mainland (the Curraun Peninsula) by a bridge, Achill (An Caol) combines views, bogland and mountains on just one island. At 147 sq km, it's the largest off the Irish coast. For most of the 20th century Achill was forgotten by tourists and – many islanders would assert – the Dublin government. The amount of arable land is limited, and there are few employment opportunities to keep young people around. Slievemore Deserted Village is the most dramatic evidence of the process of decay that affected remote rural Ireland. Today, however, tourists are returning and with them new 'deserted villages' are being built – neat, white, identical holiday cottages that remain empty for nine months of the year.

The village of Keel is the island's main centre of activity.

Information

The helpful, locally run tourist office (☎ 47353), in a portable cabin beside the Esso service station in Cashel, opens 9am to 5pm weekdays year round (with extended hours in July and August). Bord Fáilte (☎ 45384), in a cabin at the other side of the same service station, opens in July and August only.

Most villages have a post office and O'Malley's Spar supermarket in Keel doubles as a post office and changes money. There are no banks on the island but mobile banks visit the various villages (the tourist office's *A Visitor's Guide* has the times) and there's a Bank of Ireland ATM at the craft shop beside Sweeney's supermarket.

Slievemore Deserted Village

Different explanations have been given for the abandonment of Slievemore some time in the middle of the 19th century. The 'booley houses' here were the summer residences of cattle grazers. Years of famine may have forced them to seek a living nearer the sea: the inhabitants, it seems, moved permanently down to the coast at Dooagh.

Dooagh

This village is where Don Allum, the first person to row across the Atlantic Ocean in *both* directions, landed in September 1982 in his 6m-long plywood boat, the *QE3*, after 77 days at sea. The Pub (that's its name) has photos and other memorabilia of the feat, and there's a small memorial opposite.

Beaches

Achill has some lovely beaches that are often all but deserted even in fine weather. Those at Keel, Keem and Dugort (Doogort on some maps) are Blue Flag beaches, and the ones at Dooega, Dooagh and Dooniver are just as sandy.

Activities

The island is perfect for **walking** and even the highest point (Mt Slievemore, 672m) presents no problems. It can be climbed from behind the deserted village, and from the top there are terrific views of Blacksod Bay. A longer climb would take in Mt Croaghaun (668m), Achill Head and a walk atop some of the highest cliffs in Europe. The walk is covered in *New Irish Walk Guides: West and North* (Gill & Macmillan) by Tony Whilde and Patrick Simms.

Sea-angling gear is sold by **O'Malley's Island Sports** (☎ 43125, Keel), which also arranges boat hire. With its clear, clean waters Achill is a good **diving** spot and **Dol-Fin Divers** (☎ 45473, Achill Sound) offers training and equipment hire.

Other activities include **windsurfing**,

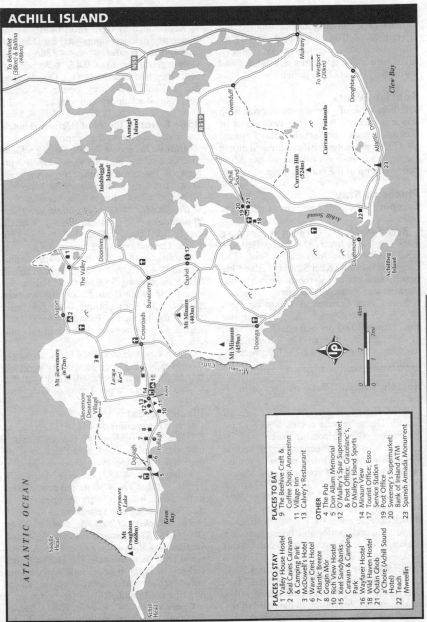

ACHILL ISLAND

To Belmullet
(38km) & Ballina
(48km)

N59

Mulrany

To Westport
(20km)

Clew Bay

Dooghbeg

Curraun Peninsula

Atlantic Drive

Owenduff

R319

Curraun Hill
(524m)

Achill
Sound

Annagh
Island

Inishbiggle
Island

Achill Sound

19 20
21
18

22

23

Cloghmore

Achillbeg
Island

The Valley

Dooniver

Cashel

17

Dugort

Mt Slievemore
(671m)

3

Loaca
Keel

Crossroads

Bunacurry

Mt Minaun
(405m)

Mt Minaun
(459m)

Minaun Cliffs

Doocga

Slievemore
Deserted
Village

16
9 13 14
12 11
15
10

Keel

ATLANTIC OCEAN

7 8
6
5
4

Dooagh

Pollagh

Corrymore
Lake

Keem Bay

Mt Croaghaun
(668m)

Saddle
Head

Achill
Head

4km
2mi

0   1   2

MAYO & SLIGO

PLACES TO STAY
1 Valley House Hostel
2 Seal Caves Caravan
   & Camping Park
3 McDowell's Hotel
6 Wave Crest Hotel
7 Atlantic Breeze
8 Grogin Mór
10 Rich View Hostel
15 Keel Sandybanks
   Caravan & Camping
   Park
16 Wayfarer Hostel
18 Wild Haven Hostel
21 Óstán Ghob
   a'Choire (Achill Sound
   Hotel)
22 Teach
   Mweellin

PLACES TO EAT
9 The Beehive Craft &
   Coffee Shop; Annexeinn
11 Village Inn
13 Calvey's Restaurant

OTHER
4 The Pub
5 Don Allum Memorial
12 O'Malley's Spar Supermarket
   & Post Office; Gracelanc's,
   O'Malleys Island Sports
14 Minaun View
17 Tourist Office; Esso
   Service Station
19 Post Office
20 Sweeney's Supermarket;
   Bank of Ireland ATM
23 Spanish Armada Monument

hang-gliding from the top of Mt Minaun (403m), **rock climbing** and **surfing**. Richie O'Hara at **McDowell's Hotel** (☎ 43148, *Slievemore Rd*), south-west of Dugort, gives instruction and hires out canoes and surfboards (€12.70 per hour).

Special Events

The best time of year for traditional Irish music and dance is the first two weeks of August, when the Scoil Acla Festival (☎ 47306) promotes Irish culture and music through a number of workshops. Most bands end up in the pubs at night.

Places to Stay

Camping Beachside camp sites include the following.

Keel Sandybanks Caravan & Camping Park (☎ 43211, fax 32351, Keel) Tent site €8.25. Open late May-early Sept. The camp site is beside Keel Strand, a Blue Flag beach, and has a TV room, laundry, hot showers and a campers' kitchen.

Seal Caves Caravan & Camping Park (☎ 43262, The Strand, Dugort) Tent site €8.25, plus €0.65 per person. On the north of the island in a sheltered bay, Seal Caves has great views and two Blue Flag beaches nearby.

Hostels The island has a number of inviting hostels.

Wild Haven Hostel (☎ 45392, Achill Sound) Dorms/private rooms €9.45/12.60 per person. This welcoming hostel, with its own bar, is over the bridge on the left behind the parish church. Breakfast and evening meals are available if you order in advance.

Rich View Hostel (☎ 43462, Keel) Dorms/private rooms €8.90/12.70 per person. Shay, the friendly live-in owner-manager is very knowledgeable about the island. Facilities at this relaxed and comfortable house include a cooker, fridge, showers and second-hand books in the common room.

Valley House Hostel (☎ 47204, fax 47334, The Valley) Dorms €8.20. Open mid-Mar-Oct. Lovely sandy beaches are within walking distance of this hostel, in the north of the island, with views of Mt Slievemore. It also

has a licensed bar. To get there, take the road to Keel and turn right (north-east) at the Bunacurry junction signposted for Dugort.

Wayfarer Hostel (☎/fax 43266, Keel) Dorms/private rooms €9.45/10.70 per person. Open mid-Mar-early Oct. Overlooking the bay, this two-storey house has clean, neat rooms, a laundry and lounge.

B&Bs & Hotels Plenty of B&Bs and hotels are scattered around the island.

Atlantic Breeze (☎ 43189, Pollagh, Keel) Singles/doubles €27.80/42.90. Open Apr-Sept. A three-room property with great views from its conservatory, it hires out bikes and offers a babysitting service.

Grogin Mór (☎ 43385, Pollagh, Keel) Singles/doubles €35.55/48.25. This is a small, comfy B&B close to Keel that also hires out bikes. The bedrooms are nonsmoking.

Óstán Ghob a'Choire (Achill Sound Hotel; ☎ 45245, fax 45621, Achill Sound) Singles/doubles €35.25/60.45. This modern, brash establishment, on the western side of Achill Sound bridge, is the first hotel you come to on the island. It hosts Irish nights, sing-alongs and dancing in July and August.

Wave Crest Hotel (☎ 43115, Dooagh) Rooms €24.15-33 per person. By contrast, this is a charmingly faded, cordial place, whose bar serves a good drop of Guinness.

Places to Eat

Calvey's Restaurant (☎ 43158, Keel) Mains €5-16.50. Open Mon-Sat. Calvey's serves up fresh local seafood, and meat from its own attached butchery.

Village Inn (☎ 43214, Keel) Mains €7-15.50. You can enjoy soup and sandwiches in the small front bar with its open fire, or dine in the adjoining restaurant.

The Beehive Craft & Coffee Shop (☎ 43134, Keel) Snacks under €7. Open 10.45am-5.45pm daily Easter-Oct. A combined craft shop and cafe, the Beehive specialises in home-made soups served with brown scones and a mouth-watering selection of baked goodies.

Graceland's (☎ 43147, Keel) Meals €2.90-6.30. No prizes for guessing the favourite singer of the owner of this large, bright, self-service cafe offering filling soups, sandwiches and seafood salads.

If you're camping or hostelling, stock up at **Sweeney's** supermarket, just across the bridge as you enter Achill, or at **O'Malley's Spar** supermarket in Keel. Nearly all the hotels serve lunch or dinner to nonguests.

Entertainment
From May to September most pubs and hotels have music.

Annexe Inn (☎ 43268, Keel) The Annexe is the best for traditional music, with sessions most nights in July and August, and weekends the rest of the year.

Minaun View (Keel) You'd expect to hear rebel or folk songs at this friendly Republican pub, but the music of choice is country.

Getting There & Away
A Bus Éireann (☎ 096-71800) bus runs across the island from Dooagh, taking in Keel, Dugort, Dooega and Achill Sound before crossing to Mulrany, Newport, Westport and finally Ballina Monday to Saturday year round. Check the schedule with the tourist office as it changes daily. In July and August bus No 66 runs from Dooagh to Keel, Achill Sound, Westport, Sligo, Enniskillen and eventually Belfast. It leaves Dooagh at 7.30am and Achill Sound 20 minutes later. Coming from Westport, the bus leaves at 5.45pm.

Getting Around
Bikes can be hired from a number of places around the island including O'Malley's Island Sports (☎ 43125), the Raleigh Rent-a-Bike agent in Keel.

BANGOR ERRIS
☎ 097 • pop 250
The main reason for visiting this village is to begin or end the 48km **Bangor Trail**, which connects Bangor (Bain Gear), as it's called, and Newport. This extraordinary walk takes you through the bleakest, most remote landscape found anywhere in Ireland. A useful guide is *County Mayo: The Bangor Trail* (€7.60) by Joe McDermott

and Robert Chapman, available in Keohane's Bookshop in Ballina and elsewhere. Unfortunately, you'll need more than one of the 1:50,000 OS maps to cover the trail.

Hillcrest House (☎ 83494, Main St) Singles/doubles €31.75/50.80. Mrs Cosgrove greets you with afternoon tea when you arrive at this carefully tended, well appointed bungalow B&B.

Kitty's Tavern (aka Kiltane Tavern; ☎ 83034, Main St) Mains under €7. Opposite Hillcrest House, Kitty's serves pub food all day and has fresh and smoked local wild salmon for sale.

See Getting There & Away under Mullet Peninsula for bus transport information.

MULLET PENINSULA
☎ 097
Probably the least visited corner of Ireland, this strange, sparsely populated and remote region is exposed to the ravages of the Atlantic on its western side, while its eastern coast forms part of the sheltered Blacksod Bay. The flat peninsula, 30km in length, rarely rises more than 30m above sea level, and the boggy land offers a poor livelihood. The peninsula is Irish speaking and Belmullet is the main settlement.

Information
In Belmullet, Erris Tourist Information Centre (☎ 81500), Barrack St, opens 9.30am to 4.30pm weekdays, Easter to September. The Ulster Bank (Banc Uladh), Main St, and the Bank of Ireland, Carter Square by the roundabout, both have ATMs. The post office is at the western end of Main St, opposite the Údarás na Gaeltachta (Gaeltacht Authority; ☎ 82382) and library, which has a small exhibition on the peninsula.

Belmullet
Belmullet (Béal an Mhuirthead), a functional, laid-back town, was founded in 1825 by the local landlord William Carter who built it to an unimaginative plan – one main street with side roads at right angles. Carter also designed a canal joining Broad Haven Bay with Trawmore and Blacksod Bay to the south, and a bridge now crosses the narrow channel.

MAYO & SLIGO

Blacksod Point & Around

The road south from Belmullet loops round the tip of the peninsula to rejoin itself at Aghleam. Near the point are the remains of an old church, and the view across the bay takes in the spot where *La Rata Santa Maria Encoronada*, part of the 1588 Spanish Armada, came in and was later burned by its captain. It sank beneath the waters of Blacksod Bay where it remains today.

The road to Blacksod Point passes Elly Bay on the eastern coast, which has a pleasant beach and is a favourite haunt of birdwatchers. Farther south it passes sandy Mullaghroe Beach. In the early years of the 20th century, a whaling station operated at Ardelly Point, just north of the beach.

Doonamo Point

Built on a spit of land and defended by water on three sides, this typical promontory fort is the main point of interest north of Belmullet. There are other forts farther north at Doonaneanir and Portnafrankach near Erris Head, but this one is the most accessible.

Places to Stay & Eat

The usual run of bungalow B&Bs lines the main road approaching Belmullet.

Mill House (☎ *81181, American St)* Singles/doubles €30.50/48.25. Open June-Aug. Near Carter Square, this good-value B&B provides cosy rooms and bicycle hire.

Western Strands Hotel (☎ *81096, Main St)* Singles/doubles €31.50/50.40. Decent digs and reasonable food are available at this central, old-style and busy pub.

Square Meal Restaurant (☎ *20984, Carter Square)* Mains €5.35-11. Open 9am-6pm Mon-Sat & 11am-4pm Sun. This smoothly polished restaurant lives up to its name serving substantial, honest food on pine-wood tables.

Appetiser Café (☎ *82222, Main St)* Meals €5.35-12. Near the roundabout, this cosy wee place offers tasty soup, salads and sandwiches, as well as meals.

Getting There & Away

Monday to Saturday a Bus Éireann bus runs once daily (twice daily in July and August) from Ballina to Bangor Erris (one hour) and Belmullet (1½ hours) then south to Blacksod Point. Contact Ballina bus station (☎ 096-71800) for the schedule.

McNulty's Coaches (☎ 81086), with an office on Chapel St down past the post office in Belmullet, runs a service four times weekly to Castlebar.

Getting Around

In Belmullet, you can hire bikes from Walsh's Garage (☎ 82260), Chapel St, opposite the McNulty's Coaches office.

POLLATOMISH
☎ 097 • pop 150

Pollatomish (Poll an Tómais), also spelled Pullathomas, is a lovely little village some 16km east of Belmullet, signposted on the road to Ballycastle (R314). There's a pleasant sandy beach nearby and walks up to Benwee Head from where there are terrific views.

Kilcommon Lodge Hostel (☎*/fax 84621, Pollatomish)* Dorms €9.45. Open year round. This small, 20-bed IHH property is a delight, with clean dorms, evening meals and a peat fire in the common room.

BALLYCASTLE & AROUND
☎ 096 • pop 200

The Ballycastle (Baile an Chaisil) area boasts some of the oldest, most extensive Stone Age excavations in Europe, and some beautiful coastal scenery. The pretty village consists of one sloping street. Tourist information is available from the craft shop at the Ballycastle Resource Centre on Main St.

Céide Fields

Over 5000 years ago there was a wheat-and-barley-farming community with domesticated cattle and sheep at Céide Fields (Achaidh Chéide). The growth of the bog led to the decline and eventual end of the community, and their stone walls and farm buildings disappeared into the bog. Perhaps the farmers, gradually diminishing the soil's fertility, contributed to the growth of the bog, or maybe the wet climate made it inevitable. Whatever the cause, the farms lay buried for thousands of years, but have now been excavated and opened to the public as the oldest enclosed landscape in Europe and the most extensive Stone Age monument in the world.

It's worth visiting the **Interpretive Centre** (☎ 43325, Ballycastle; adult/child €3.15/ 1.25; open 9.30am-6.30pm daily June-Aug; 9.30am-5.30pm daily Sept; 10am-5pm daily mid-Mar-May & Oct; 10am-4.30pm daily Nov). Run by Dúchas in a modern glass pyramid overlooking the site, it incorporates an exhibition court and audiovisual room detailing aspects of the site's architecture, botany and geology. There's also a tearoom and, across the road, a panoramic viewing platform.

Céide Fields is 8km west of Ballycastle on the main R314 road.

Downpatrick Head

North-east of Ballycastle, Downpatrick Head has a fenced-off blowhole that occasionally shoots up plumes of water. The rock stack just off the shore is called **Dun Briste**.

Places to Stay & Eat

Céide House (☎ 43105, Main St) Rooms €26 per person. This pub offers inexpensive accommodation in the middle of the village, though the music may at times be loud.

Sunatrai (☎ 43040, Killala Rd) Singles/doubles €31.75/43.20. Open mid-June-mid-Aug. Its ample breakfasts and scenic location make this a good choice. The owners also speak French.

Mary's Cottage Kitchen (☎ 43361, Main St) Meals €4.70-8.25. At the lower end of Main St, this greystone cottage bakery serves tasty sandwiches, light meals and ambrosial apple and rhubarb pies.

Getting There & Away

Bus Éireann (☎ 71800) bus No 445 runs between Ballina and Ballycastle once or twice a day, Monday to Saturday, stopping outside Katie Mac's pub.

KILLALA & AROUND

☎ 096 • pop 710

Though the town itself is rather nondescript, Killala (Cill Alaidh or Cill Ála) has a scenic setting on Killala Bay and important historical connections.

It's claimed that St Patrick founded Killala, and the Church of Ireland cathedral is supposedly built on the site of the first Christian church, where St Patrick installed Muiredach as the town's first bishop. The 25m round tower is evidence of the role the town played in early Church history; it was struck by lightning in 1800 and the cap is a later reconstruction.

On 22 August 1798, over 1000 troops under the command of General Humbert landed in Killala Bay, the plan being that Irish peasants would rise in rebellion and help Napoleon in his war against the British. At first there were dramatic successes, with Killala, Ballina and Castlebar falling. On 8 September, however, Humbert was defeated by Cornwallis at Ballinamuck in County Longford. The best account of Humbert's arrival in Killala was written by the Protestant Bishop Stock. He was put under house arrest by the French, and his *Narrative* is available in some bookshops in Ballina and Castlebar.

Information

Tourist information is available 9.30am to 5.30pm daily, July to September, from the community centre (☎ 32166) as you enter Killala on the Ballina road (R314). There are no banks or ATMs, but there's a post office in the centre.

Rathfran Abbey

The Dominicans came here in 1274 and built a friary, but only some ruins remain. In 1590 the friary was closed down and burned by the English, but the monks stayed in the community until the 18th century.

Take the R314 road that heads north out of Killala and, after 5km and crossing the Cloonaghmore River, turn right. After another 2km turn right at the crossroads.

Breastagh Ogham Stone

The stone is 2.5m high, but the ogham script is not easy to read. It's in a field by the left side of the R314 just past the crossroads with the turning for Rathfran Abbey (not the earlier crossroads, which has a sign for both the stone and the abbey). Cross the ditch just where the sign points to the stone.

Kilcummin & Lackan Bay

Kilcummin, at the head of Killala Bay, is where General Humbert's army landed in 1798. A right turn off the main R314 is signposted for Kilcummin. On the R314 just after the turning to Lackan Bay a sculpture of a French revolutionary soldier helping a prostrate Irish peasant marks the place where the first French soldier died on Irish soil. Lackan Bay itself is wonderfully sandy and ideal for young children.

Places to Stay & Eat

The better places to stay are found outside Killala town.

Beach View (☎ 32023, Ross, Killala) Singles/doubles €32.40/48.25. Beach View is 3km from Killala, signposted off the R314 northbound to Ballycastle, and a short walk from Ross Strand. It has good hot showers and clean rooms that look onto a large rear garden.

Chez Nous (☎ 32056, Ross, Killala) Singles/doubles €27.95/45.70. Close to Beach View, this B&B is equally clean and comfortable.

When it comes to food there's not a great deal of choice.

Anchor Inn (Ballycastle Rd) Meals €2.90-15.25. This casual pub is one of the best places in town for good-value, honest meals – from sausages and chips to sirloin steak (with chips).

Getting There & Away

The Ballina–Ballycastle bus, which runs once or twice a day Monday to Saturday, stops outside McGregor's newsagent's. Ring Bus Éireann (☎ 71800) for details.

BALLINA & AROUND

☎ 096 • pop 8200

The largest town in the county, Ballina (Béal an Átha; pronounced balli-**nagh**) is renowned for its fishing and is a good base for exploring northern Mayo and the North Mayo Sculpture Trail. The tourist office can give you information on interesting walks near the town.

Ballina is an unattractive Connaught town, with some decent pubs and fine restaurants. Its most famous progeny is Mary Robinson, the much-loved former president of Ireland.

Information

The tourist office (☎ 70848), Cathedral Rd, beside St Muredach's Cathedral across the River Moy from the centre, opens 10am to 1pm and 2pm to 5.30pm Monday to Saturday, mid-April to September. Several banks line Pearse St, including the Ulster Bank and Bank of Ireland, both with ATMs and bureaux de change. The post office is at the top of O'Rahilly St, the southern extension of Pearse St.

Keohane's Bookshop (☎/fax 21475), Tone St, has a decent selection of maps and walking guides. Opposite is Jiffy Cleaners laundrette, though it's not self-service.

Rosserk Abbey

Close to the River Rosserk, a tributary of the Moy, this Franciscan abbey dates from the mid-15th century. It's remarkably well preserved, and there's an interesting carved piscina (a perforated stone basin for carrying away the water used in rinsing the chalices) in the chancel. Like Rathfran Abbey near Killala, Rosserk was burned down by Richard Bingham, the English governor of Connaught, in the 16th century.

To get there, leave Ballina on the R314 for Killala and after 6.5km turn right at the sign and take the first left at the next crossroads. Continue for another kilometre, then turn right at the next sign for the abbey.

Moyne Abbey

Established by the Franciscans around the same time as Rosserk, this abbey was also burned down by Richard Bingham in the 16th century. Perhaps he did a better job on this one, as it is in worse condition than its neighbour.

After leaving Rosserk Abbey go back to the main road and continue north for another 3km until you can see the abbey on the right across a field. After returning across the field, continue north-west for 1.5km until the main R314 is reached. Turn right for Killala or left for Ballina.

North Mayo Sculpture Trail

This trail of 15 outdoor sculptures essentially follows the R314 from Ballina (Point A; *Guest Space* by Peter Hynes) to Blacksod Point (Point O; *Deirble's Twist* by Michael Bulfin). The project was inaugurated to mark 5000 years of Mayo history, and leading sculptors from eight countries were commissioned to create works of art reflecting the beauty and wilderness of the northern Mayo countryside.

The *North Mayo Sculpture Trail* is a 60-page book detailing each sculpture with notes on the location, artist, sculpture, history, flora and fauna. It's available from tourist offices and bookshops. The trail is called Tír Sáile in Gaelic. It's about 90km and is walkable.

Fishing

The **River Moy** is one of the most prolific salmon rivers in Europe and a leaflet listing the fisheries and contacts for permits is available from the tourist office. You can see the scaly critters jumping in the Ridge (salmon pool), with otters and grey seals in famished pursuit. The season runs from February to September, but the best fishing is June to August.

Lough Conn, south-west of Ballina, is an important brown trout fishery, and there's no shortage of places with boats and ghillies (guides) available round the lake. Pontoon is a good base for trout fishing in both Lough Conn and **Lough Cullin** to the south, and again there are plenty of places hiring boats and dispensing advice. The daily rate for hiring a motor boat is around €40.

For licences, permits and supplies contact **Ridge Pool Tackle Shop** (☎ 72656, Cathedral Rd, Ballina).

Special Events

The two-week Ballina Street Festival (☎ 70905), one of the best outdoor parties in the country, takes place in early July. Heritage Day is when shop fronts – and Ballina

townsfolk – take on a 19th-century look during the festival.

Places to Stay

Ballina has plenty of B&Bs.

Belleek Caravan & Camping Park (☎ 71533, ⓔ lenahan@indigo.ie, Ballina) Family tent €8.90, hikers, cyclists & motorcyclists €5.70. This well equipped park with 16 tent pitches is 2.5km from Ballina about 300m off the Killala road.

Adara House (☎ 71112, Station Rd) Singles/doubles €29.20/50.80. Open Jan-Oct. Close to the centre, this B&B has four cosy rooms (three with bathroom) and accepts credit cards.

Bartra House Hotel (☎ 22200, fax 22111, Pearse St) Rooms with bathroom €44.45 per person. This central, 24-room, old-style hotel also has a restaurant and bar.

Downhill House Hotel (☎ 73444, fax 73411, Sligo Rd) Rooms €63.50-77.45 per person. North of the centre on the Sligo road (N59), Downhill House is Ballina's poshest hotel and comes complete with swimming pool, Jacuzzi and sauna.

Places to Eat

Murphy Bros (☎ 22702, Clare St) Bar food €7.60-18.90, restaurant mains €12.70-21.40. Lunch 12.30pm-2.30pm, dinner 5pm-8.30pm. Salmon – poached, grilled, baked or smoked – is the speciality of Ballina and you can try it at this excellent old pub-restaurant, north of the tourist office.

Tullios (☎ 21890, Pearse St) Pasta €8.25-10.80, meat mains €12.70-16.50. Good for just a coffee or a full meal, Tullios is a stylish bar-restaurant with a peat fire, sand-coloured walls and marble-topped bar.

Dillons (☎ 72230, Dillon Terrace) Pasta €10.15-10.80, baked potatoes €7.25. You enter this old stone building through an archway at the northern end of Pearse St. Its mainly Irish menu is complemented by Mexican and Italian dishes, and there's traditional music on Wednesday night.

Padraic's (☎ 22383, Tone St) Meals €6.25-13. If you're suffering withdrawal symptoms from the 'full Irish' then Padraic's

MAYO & SLIGO

can satisfy – its breakfasts include black and white pudding and waffles.

Entertainment

Ballina counts some 60 pubs, and many have traditional music sessions on Wednesday and Friday evenings. Among the best are the following.

An Bolg Buí (The Yellow Belly; ☎ 22561, Tolan St) By the bridge, this dark, intimate, wood-panelled pub has traditional and folk music every Wednesday night.

The Garden Inn (☎ 70969, Garden St) One of the best places for traditional music, the Garden Inn welcomes all-comers to take part in the sessions.

Broken Jug (☎ 73097, O'Rahilly St) High, solid wooden doors lead into this cavernous pub, furbished in stone and wood, where young people come to drink and dance at its nightclub.

Getting There & Away

From the bus station (☎ 71800), on Kevin Barry St south-west of the centre, Bus Éireann buses go west to Achill Island, east to Sligo, to the North (Belfast, Enniskillen, Derry) and south to Limerick, Shannon and Cork.

Barton Transport (☎ 01-628 6026) buses leave Dublin for Ballina from Cook St on Friday at 5.30pm and 5.45pm. They return to Dublin on Sunday at 5pm and 5.30pm from the Burmah service station on Foxford Rd.

The train station (☎ 71800) is on Station Rd, the southern extension of Kevin Barry St. The Westport–Dublin train stops at Ballina up to three-times daily. Connections to other routes can be made at Athlone.

Getting Around

Bicycles can be hired from Michael Hopkins (☎ 21609), on Pearse St across from Dunnes Stores, for €8.85/37.80 per day/week.

CROSSMOLINA & AROUND
☎ 096 • pop 350

The small undistinguished town of Crossmolina (Crois Mhaoiliona), 13km west of Ballina, sits near the northern shores of

Lough Conn. There's a small seasonal tourist office off the main street, and a Bank of Ireland (no ATM) opposite Hiney's pub.

North Mayo Family History Research & Heritage Centre

It's well worth setting aside a few hours for the heritage centre (☎ 31809, e normayo@iol.ie, Castlebar Rd; museum adult/child €3.80/1.25, garden €5.10/1.25, combined ticket €7.60/1.25; open 9am-4pm Mon-Fri, 2pm-6pm Sat & Sun June & Sept; 9am-4pm Mon-Fri Oct-May, July & Aug). Just over 3km south towards Castlehill, the centre houses a collection of old farm machinery and domestic implements, has woodland walks, an ornamental and organic garden and a tearoom.

If you have a family connection with northern Mayo, it'll do an initial assessment for €63; if this looks promising your full family record is researched (€190 to €254, less the initial assessment fee).

Errew Abbey

The abbey, beside Lough Conn, is the remains of a house for Augustinian monks built around 1250 on the site of an earlier 7th-century church. As with other abbeys in Mayo, the monks wisely chose to live close to where they could fish, and the location of Errew Abbey is particularly picturesque.

To get there, take the Castlebar road south, and 1km past the heritage centre turn left at the sign and keep going for another 5km. The entrance is next to a farm.

Activities

Crossmolina serves as a quiet retreat for anyone wishing to fish in **Lough Conn** or explore the lakes and scenery around **Mt Nephin** (806m). The mountain takes under two hours to climb and is described, along with other walks in Mayo, in *New Irish Walk Guides: West and North* (Gill & Macmillan) by Tony Whilde and Patrick Simms.

Places to Stay & Eat

Lake View House (☎ 31296, Ballina Rd) Singles/doubles with bathroom €32.40/48.25. Open Apr-Oct. Close to the town centre, this aptly named B&B has six spick-and-span rooms, and bikes available for hire.

Enniscoe House *(☎ 31112, fax 31773, Castlehill)* Singles/doubles €96.60/167.70. A great getaway, this 18th-century home next to the heritage centre is off the main road and secluded by woodland. Dinner costs €35.55.

Hiney's *(☎ 31202, Main St)* Meals €6.25-6.60. Though you wouldn't know it from the tacky doorway with the thatched cover, Hiney's is a great old pub where food, served all day, comes in huge helpings.

The Tea Room *(Main St)* Soup €1.75, sandwiches €1.65-2. Customers from the attached supermarket drop into this inexpensive tearoom for refreshment before lugging their shopping home.

Getting There & Away
There are regular Bus Éireann *(☎ 71800)* buses to Ballina and Castlebar. The bus stop is outside Hiney's.

CASTLEBAR & AROUND
☎ 094 • pop 7650
Though it's the county town, Castlebar (Caisleán an Bharraigh) has far less appeal to travellers than Westport or even Ballina. Its old shops have been replaced by more modern stores, and there's little to evoke its past, but the town does have a place in history.

Here in 1798 General Humbert's army of French revolutionary soldiers and dispossessed Irish peasants encountered the numerically stronger British forces under the command of General Lake. The defeat of the British and their ignominious cavalry retreat became known as the Castlebar Races.

The large, attractive village green, known as The Mall, was once the cricket ground of the Lucan family, who own a significant amount of property in the area. The notorious Lord Lucan disappeared after the murder of his children's nanny in London in 1974, and hasn't been heard of since.

Orientation & Information
The main thoroughfare changes its name from Ellison St to Main St to Thomas St as you head north. The Mall is to the east.

The tourist office *(☎ 21207)*, Linenhall St, opens 9.30am to 1pm and 2pm to 5.30pm, late May to early September. To get there, turn left (west) at the northern end of Main St, by the bridge.

The Allied Irish Bank, Main St, and Bank of Ireland, Ellison St, have ATMs and bureaux de change. Una's Laundrette *(☎ 24100)* is in New Antrim St, round the corner from the tourist office.

Turlough Round Tower
The 9th-century tower stands next to a ruined 18th-century church and a graveyard that is still in use. The tower is about 5km north-east of Castlebar on the N5 road.

Michael Davitt Memorial Museum
The museum *(☎ 31022, Straide; adult/child €3.15/1.25; open 10am-6pm daily year round)* houses a small collection of material relating to the life of Michael Davitt (1846–1906), a Fenian and founding member of the Irish National Land League, who is buried in the nearby churchyard. There's also a short video about the man.

Take the N5 east and turn left (north-east) onto the N58 to Straide (Strade on some maps). It's 16km from Castlebar.

Ballintubber Abbey
The only church in Ireland that was founded by an Irish king and is still in use, Ballintubber Abbey *(☎ 30934, Ballintubber; free; open 9am-midnight daily)* was set up in 1216 next to the site of an earlier church founded by St Patrick after he came down from Croagh Patrick. It's one of the most impressive church buildings in Ireland and well worth a visit.

Features of the church include the 15th-century western doorway and 13th-century windows on the right side of the nave. The nave roof was erected in 1965 and is an Irish-oak reproduction of the timber one burned down by Cromwell's soldiers in 1653.

Take the N84 south towards Galway and after about 13km turn left at the Campus service station; the abbey is 2km along this road.

Places to Stay & Eat

Castlebar has plenty of accommodation should you decide to stay.

Green Bay B&B *(☎ 21572, The Mall)* Rooms with shower €23.30-28.35 per person. Ideally positioned, this reasonably priced, lemon-yellow B&B on one corner of The Mall is hard to miss.

Daly's Hotel *(☎ 21961, fax 22783, The Mall)* Singles/doubles €44.45/58.40. Daly's is Castlebar's oldest hotel, with lots of character, expansive rooms and a warm, pleasant bar that serves up decent meals costing €7 to €15.

Oriental *(☎ 23810, Main St)* Mains €8.25-11.35. Open for lunch 12.30pm-2.30pm Mon-Sat & 1pm-2.30pm Sun, for dinner 5.30pm-12.30am Sun-Thur & 5.30pm-1am Fri-Sat. The extended hours of this reasonably priced Chinese restaurant mean that you can still get a good meal even if you arrive late in town.

Samuel's Harvest *(☎ 27797, New Antrim St)* Meals under €7. Open 9am-6pm Mon-Sat. This cafe bakes its own bread and provides freshly prepared food using local produce. The breakfasts are big and the desserts hard to resist.

Gavin's Bakery *(☎ 24300, Main St)* Food under €6. This bakery is good for sandwiches and cakes but also offers cooked breakfasts and soups.

Getting There & Away

Bus Éireann (☎ 096-71800) bus No 21 connecting Westport (20 minutes) and Dublin (4½ hours) stops outside Flannelly's pub in Market St three-times daily (once on Sunday) in each direction. Monday to Saturday bus No 51 runs four-times daily (twice Sunday) south to Shannon and Cork and north to Ballina. In July and August only, bus No 69 north-east to Sligo (2¼ hours) operates once a day, Monday to Saturday.

McNulty's Coaches (☎ 097-81086), based in Belmullet, runs a service from Castlebar to Belmullet at 5.30pm Monday to Wednesday and Friday, returning the next day at 8.15am.

The Westport–Dublin (3¼ hours) train stops at Castlebar up to four-times daily. The station is just out of town on the N84

towards Ballinrobe. For times call ☎ 098-25253.

Getting Around

Taxis can be hired by ringing Ralph's Taxis (☎ 088 256 8220).

You can rent bikes from Bike World (☎ 25220), New Antrim St, and Tommy Robinson's service station (☎ 21355), in Spencer St south of The Mall. The latter charges €12.70/50.80 per day/week and organises cycle tours of the area.

KNOCK

☎ 094 • pop 440

The once undistinguished village of Knock (Cnoc Mhuire), at the junction of the N17 and the R323, has been famous for over a century as the site of visions and miracles: Catholic Ireland's answer to Lourdes or Fatima.

The Knock Marian Shrine consists of several churches and shrines, including the modern basilica and the Church of the Apparition. North of the latter are shops, restaurants and the tourist office (☎ 88193), which opens 10am to 5pm daily, May to September. There's a Bank of Ireland nearby with an ATM, but it only opens 10.15am to 12.15pm on Monday and Thursday, May to October (Monday only the rest of the year).

Church of the Apparition

One wet evening in August 1879, two young Knock women were struck by the sight of Mary, Joseph and St John the Evangelist standing in light against the southern gable of the local church. Others were called to witness the apparition, and a Church investigation quickly confirmed it as a bona fide miracle. Other miracles followed as the sick and disabled claimed amazing recoveries after visiting the church. Another Church commission upheld Knock's status in 1936. Today, the Knock industry continues, and dutiful worshippers are always found praying at the chapel built to enclose the scene of the apparition. Above the altar is a sculptural representation of what people saw. Near the church is the modern **Basilica of Our Lady, Queen of Ireland**, which can accommodate 12,000 people.

Accompanying the fervent, almost medieval piety of the pilgrims is a display of commercial exuberance that can seem unspeakably tacky. Wall thermometers, shake-up snow domes and plastic holy-water bottles shaped like the Virgin are easy to mock. But remember that people spend much of their savings to come here and, for many of the Catholic faithful, Knock is as sacred a place as the Wailing Wall in Jerusalem is to Jews, Mecca to Muslims or the Ganges to Hindus. Knock was visited by Pope Paul VI in 1974, Pope John Paul II in 1979 (the centenary of the apparition) and Mother Teresa in 1993.

Knock Folk Museum
In a building near the basilica is this small museum (☎ 88100; adult/concession €3.80/ 2.55; open 10am-6pm daily May-Oct). It's one of the better museums of its type and serves as an ideal introduction to the Knock phenomenon. There's plenty of attractively presented material on the apparition and subsequent Church commissions of inquiry, including photographs of the crutches left behind by grateful pilgrims. The museum also houses an extensive collection of craft tools, costumes and various artefacts relating to rural life in the west of Ireland.

Places to Stay
Knock Caravan & Camping Park (☎ 88100, fax 88295, Claremorris Rd) Tent site €8.90. Open Mar-Oct. This fully serviced, sheltered camp site is only a five-minute walk south of the shrine.

Aishling House (☎ 88558, Ballyhaunis Rd) Rooms with/without shower €24.15/ 21.60 per person. Mrs Coyne makes guests welcome at this roomy B&B close to the shrine.

Knock International Hotel (☎ 88466, Main St) Rooms €32 per person. Though a humbler establishment than its name might suggest, this modest 10-room hotel is clean and comfortable.

Getting There & Away
Knock Airport (☎ 67222), 15km north by the N17 near Charlestown, has daily Aer Lingus connections with Dublin, and direct flights to the UK. Bus Éireann (☎ 096-71800) bus No 21 connects Knock with Westport, Castlebar, Athlone and Dublin three-times daily (once on Sunday). There are also regular direct connections with Sligo, Ballina, Galway and Cork.

County Sligo

Despite its small size, County Sligo (Sligeach) provides a rich variety of scenery and numerous prehistoric sites. Its closest association, however, is with the poet and dramatist William Butler Yeats (1865–1939). Though he was educated in Dublin and London, his poetry is inextricably linked with the county of his mother's family. He visited Sligo frequently, becoming a close friend of the Gore-Booths, who lived at Lissadell. There are many reminders of Yeats' presence in the county town of Sligo and in the rolling green hills around it.

SLIGO
☎ 071 • pop 17,800
Sligo town is a busy port and commercial centre on the banks of the Garavogue River as it flows into Sligo Bay, with the twin mountains of Knocknarea and Benbulben looming in the distance.

Outside the Ulster Bank on Stephen St is the interesting **sculptural portrayal of Yeats** that has his poetry inscribed all over it. Hard to find are two famous lines from *Easter 1916*:

> All changed, changed utterly:
> A terrible beauty is born…

The poem pays homage to the executed rebels of the Easter Rising, including Sean MacBride, who was married to Maud Gonne. Yeats' unrequited love for Maud Gonne underlies many of his greatest poems. Politics divided them: while she remained a rebel and a socialist all her life, Yeats ended up alarmingly close to fascism.

Information
The modern North-West Regional Tourism

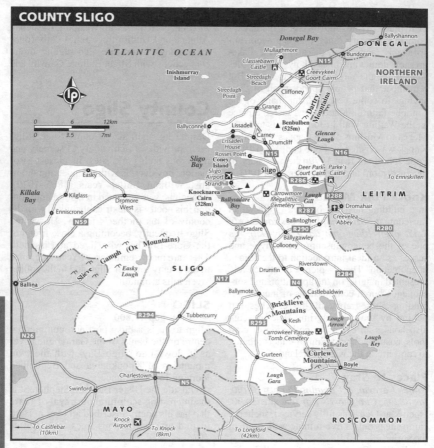

COUNTY SLIGO

office (☎ 61201) is south of the centre on Temple St. It opens 9am to 8pm weekdays and 9am to 5pm on Saturday during July and August; 9am to 5pm weekdays and 9am to 1pm on Saturday April to June; and 9am to 5pm or 6pm weekdays the rest of the year. There's also a smaller, branch office at the Yeats Building.

Ulster Bank, the Bank of Ireland and the Allied Irish Bank, all with ATMs and bureaux de change, have branches on Stephen St.

The post office is on Wine St.

Free Internet access is available at Sligo County Library (☎ 47190), Bridge St, 10am to 12.45pm and 2pm to 4.45pm Monday to Friday. Bring some ID. It's also available in a branch library at Sligo County Museum.

You can leave your laundry at Pam's Laundrette (☎ 44861), Johnston Court, off O'Connell St, which opens 9am to 7pm Monday to Saturday.

Visit Keohane's Bookshop (☎ 42597), Castle St, for maps and books by and about Yeats. The Winding Stair Bookshop (☎ 41244), on the corner of Lower Knox St, is named after one of Yeats' best-known works and has Irish-interest books and a cafe.

Sligo County Museum

Although there is other material, the main appeal is the Yeats room at the museum (☎ 42212, Stephen St; free; open 10.30am-12.30pm & 2.30pm-4.30pm Mon-Sat June-Sept; 10.30am-12.30pm Mon-Sat Apr, May & Oct). Here there are photographs, letters and newspaper cuttings connected with the poet WB Yeats, and drawings by Jack B Yeats, his brother. The room across the hall contains an apron dress worn by Countess Constance Markievicz (a member of the Gore-Booth family) while interned in Britain after the 1916 Rising.

Model Arts & Niland Gallery

The gallery (☎ 41405, Stephen St; free; open 10am-5.30pm Tues-Sat) is housed in magnificent new premises with lots of space to show off its fascinating collection. It has a selection of over 200 paintings by Irish artists such as Charles Lamb; Sean Keating; Jack B Yeats, who said he never did a painting without putting a thought of Sligo into it; and Anne Yeats, WB's daughter.

Sligo Abbey

The town's founder, Maurice FitzGerald, established the abbey around 1250 for the Dominicans, but it burned down in the 15th century and was rebuilt (☎ 46406, Abbey St; adult/child €1.90/0.75; open 10am-6pm daily Apr-Oct). It was put to the torch once again in 1641, and ruins are all that remain. The oldest parts of the abbey are the choir, the 15th-century eastern window and the altar.

The abbey is a Dúchas site. If it's locked, a key is available from the caretaker, Tom Loughlin, at 6 Charlotte St.

The Courthouse

The Victorian architecture of the courthouse on Teeling St is very unusual for Ireland, and it stands out as a reminder of the other power that once ruled this land. The exterior is extravagantly Gothic and modelled on the Law Courts in London. Inside, the building still functions as a working courthouse, and on a busy day the foyer takes the overspill from the small public gallery.

Yeats Building

On the corner of Lower Knox and O'Connell Sts, near Hyde Bridge, the Yeats Building is the centre for the Yeats International Summer School (☎ 42693), a two-week international gathering of scholars at the start of August each year. The rest of the year it houses the **Sligo Art Gallery** (☎ 45847, Lower Knox St; free; open 10am-5pm Mon-Sat), with travelling exhibitions and paintings often up for sale. The building also has a small tourist office.

Special Events

The 10-day Sligo Arts Festival (☎ 69802, e artsfestival@tinet.ie) takes place from late May to early June.

Places to Stay

Camping There's a camp site just outside Sligo.

Gateway Caravan & Camping Park (☎/fax 45618, e gateway@oceanfree.net, Ballinode) Tent & car €12.70 plus €0.65 per adult, hikers & cyclists €6.35 per person including tent. There are 10 tent pitches at this camp site 3km north-east of Sligo on the N16. Facilities include free showers and a campers' kitchen. Local buses stop outside the park.

Hostels You can choose from a number of hostels in town.

White House Hostel (☎ 45160, fax 44456, Markievicz Rd) Dorms €9.45. This three-storey hostel's central location makes it a good choice; it's within walking distance of sights, restaurants, pubs and shops.

Yeats County Hostel (☎ 46876, 12 Lord Edward St) Dorms €8.80. This place is close to the bus and train stations, but can fill up quickly so it's a good idea to book ahead.

Harbour House (☎/fax 71547, e harbour house@eircom.net, Finisklin Rd) Dorms €12.70-17.80, private rooms €15.25-17.80 per person. About 1km north-west of the centre, this IHH-affiliated hostel is about as close to luxury as a budget traveller can get. It's wheelchair accessible, meals and bike hire are available and it accepts credit cards.

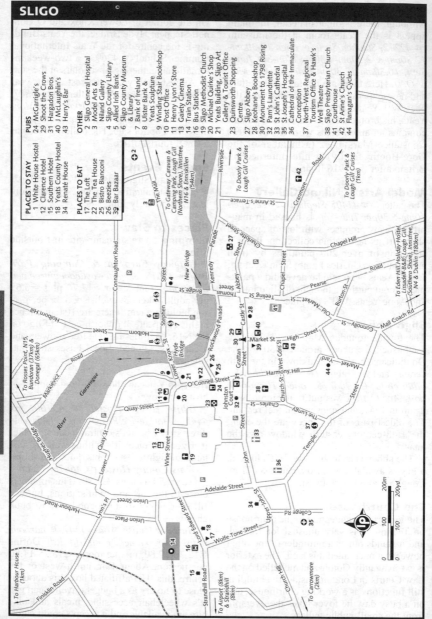

SLIGO

PLACES TO STAY
1 White House Hostel
12 Clarence Hotel
15 Southern Hotel
18 Yeats County Hostel
34 Renaté House

PLACES TO EAT
17 The Loft
22 The Tea House
25 Bistro Bianconi
26 Beezies
39 Bar Bazaar

PUBS
24 McGarrigle's
29 Shoot the Crows
31 Hargadon Bros
40 J McLaughlin's
43 Harry's Bar

OTHER
2 Sligo General Hospital
3 Model Arts &
    Niland Gallery
4 Sligo County Library
5 Allied Irish Bank
6 Sligo County Museum
    & Library
7 Bank of Ireland
8 Ulster Bank &
    Yeats Sculpture
9 Winding Stair Bookshop
10 Post Office
11 Henry Lyon's Store
13 Gaiety Cinema
14 Train Station
16 Bus Station
19 Sligo Methodist Church
20 Michael Quirke's Shop
21 Yeats Building, Sligo Art
    Gallery & Tourist Office
23 Quinsworth Shopping
    Centre
27 Sligo Abbey
28 Keohane's Bookshop
30 Monument to 1798 Rising
32 Pam's Laundrette
33 St John's Cathedral
35 St Joseph's Hospital
36 Cathedral of the Immaculate
    Conception
37 North-West Regional
    Tourism Office & Hawk's
    Well Theatre
38 Sligo Presbyterian Church
41 Courthouse
42 St Anne's Church
44 Flanagan's Cycles

Eden Hill Holiday Hostel (☎/fax 43204, ⓔ *edenhill@iol.ie, Pearse Rd)* Dorms/private rooms €9.45/22.70. This IHH hostel, about 10 minutes' walk south-east of the centre on the Dublin road, accommodates 30 people in cosy but faded rooms.

B&Bs & Hotels The most central B&B is Renaté House; other B&Bs line the various approach roads into town.

Renaté House (☎ 62014, 9 Upper John St) Singles/doubles from €25.20/37.80. This clean, three-storey B&B has a prime central position close to all amenities. There are six rooms (four with en-suite bathroom), each with its own tea- and coffee-making facilities.

Lissadell (☎ 61937, Mail Couch Rd) Singles/doubles with bathroom €32.40/50.80. Lissadell is a nonsmoking B&B with three rooms about 10 minutes' walk south-east of the centre.

Clarence Hotel (☎ 42211, Wine St) Rooms with bathroom €38.10-59.70 per person. The Clarence is a small but striking, greystone hotel set back from the street, with finely furnished rooms.

Southern Hotel (☎ 62101, fax 60328, ⓦ *www.sligosouthernhotel.com, Strandhill Rd)* Singles/doubles €71.40/114.35. Beside the bus and train stations, this stately hotel has comfortable rooms and an open fire in the lobby to greet its guests.

Places to Eat
The Loft (☎ 46770, 17-19 Lord Edward St) Mains €10-16. One of the better eateries around, The Loft is opposite the train station and uses the railway as the theme for its decor. The menu is mostly made up of Mexican dishes, fish and burgers, with a small selection of vegetarian dishes.

Bistro Bianconi (☎ 41744, 44 O'Connell St) Mains €13.60-17.30. Open for lunch 12.30pm-2.30pm (June-Aug only), dinner 5.30pm-10pm. This friendly Italian bistro serves fresh pasta, and pizzas from its wood-fired oven.

The Tea House (☎ 43999, 34 O'Connell St) Mains €5.70-10.70. The menu offers a huge selection of meals and snacks. Although

it's a big place it's likely to be crowded, especially at lunchtime.

Beezies (☎ 43031, 45 O'Connell St) Meals €3-7. Beezies, a flashy, modern cafe-bar, entered down an alleyway off O'Connell St, serves good soups and sandwiches.

Bar Bazaar (☎ 44749, 34 Market St) Snacks around €3. For a caffeine fix try this tiny cafe, which has a range of good coffees and second-hand books for sale.

Entertainment
Hargadon Bros (☎ 70933, 4 O'Connell St) No place in Sligo can beat this one for atmosphere. While it doesn't have music, its dark wood interior is like a stage set, with snugs, nooks, crannies and 19th-century bar fixtures.

McGarrigle's (☎ 41667, O'Connell St) Cavernous McGarrigle's has dimly lit snugs downstairs and a good 'alternative music' bar upstairs.

J McLaughlin's (☎ 44209, 9 Market St) This wood-panelled, old-world pub presents traditional music every Tuesday night and the occasional photo exhibition.

Shoot the Crows (Castle St) This long, dark, narrow drinking establishment attracts a young, alternative clientele and has traditional music on Tuesday and Thursday nights.

Harry's Bar (High St) Serious drinking is best conducted at Harry's Bar, where there are lots of happy-hour offers and the cheapest pints in town.

Hawk's Well Theatre (☎ 61526, ⓦ *www.hawkswell.com, Temple St)* This well regarded theatre, attached to the tourist office, presents a varied program of concerts, dance and serious drama and is always worth checking out.

Gaiety Cinema (☎ 62651, Wine St) The four-screen cinema shows mainstream, first-release films at 6.30pm, 8.30pm, 8.45pm and 11pm daily.

Shopping
Michael Quirke (☎ 42640, Wine St) Come here for hand-crafted, contemporary wood sculptures. Examples of Michael's work, which depicts figures from Irish mythology,

MAYO & SLIGO

are displayed in the window, and during business hours you can see him sculpting.

Getting There & Away

Air From Sligo Airport (☎ 68280), Strandhill Rd, there are direct Aer Lingus flights to Dublin up to three-times daily.

Bus Bus Éireann (☎ 60066) bus No 23 runs four-times daily to Dublin (€12.20 one way, four hours). Bus No 64 provides a Galway–Sligo–Derry service up to five-times daily. The bus station is below the train station, west of the centre on Lord Edward St.

Feda Ódonaill Coaches (☎ 075-48114, 091-761656) runs a service between Crolly (in County Donegal) and Galway via Donegal and Sligo up to three-times daily. The buses arrive and depart from in front of Henry Lyon's Store on the corner of Wine and Quay Sts.

Train Trains leave the station (☎ 69888) three-times daily (four on Friday) for Dublin (€19.05 one way, 3¼ hours) via Boyle, Carrick-on-Shannon and Mullingar.

Getting Around

There's a bus service from the airport into town (€2.20), while a taxi costs about €12. Ace Cabs (☎ 44444) and Feehily's Taxis (☎ 43000) offer a 24-hour service. Bike hire, costing €12.60/50.40 per day/week, is available from Flanagan's Cycles (☎ 44477), Market Yard.

AROUND SLIGO TOWN
Rosses Point

The scene of a battle between two Irish warlords in 1257, Rosses Point (An Ros) is a picturesque seaside resort with a lovely Blue Flag beach. It's easily reached on a Sligo town bus.

Places to Stay & Eat B&Bs aren't difficult to find, although they can fill up quickly in season.

Greenlands Caravan & Camping Park (☎ 071-77113, Rosses Point) Tent site €8.25. Open Easter-mid-Sept. Greenlands, on the point next to the golf course, has 19 tent sites and access to two safe beaches.

Kilvarnet House (☎ 071-77202, Rosses Point) Singles/doubles with bathroom €32.40/50.80. Open Mar-Nov. Kilvarnet is a friendly B&B with four rooms and all mod cons. To get there follow the road up beside the post office.

Yeats Country Hotel (☎ 071-77211, fax 77203, Rosses Point) Rooms with bathroom €38-101 per person. This three-star hotel on the point mostly attracts golfers and families. It has spacious bedrooms and a leisure centre for guests.

Moorings Restaurant (☎ 071-77112, Rosses Point) Mains €12-18. Close to the Yeats Country Hotel and with views of the bay, Moorings specialises in fresh seafood served in elegant surroundings.

Carrowmore Megalithic Cemetery

Managed by Dúchas, Carrowmore's megalithic cemetery (☎ 61534, Carrowmore; adult/concession €1.90/0.75; open 9.30am-6.30pm daily May-Oct) has over 60 stone circles and passage tombs, making it one of the largest Stone Age cemeteries in Europe. Over the years, many of the stones have been removed – a survey in 1839 noted 23 more sites than now exist – and a complicating factor is that some of the best stones are on private land. The dolmens were the actual tombs and were probably covered with stones and earth, so it requires some imagination to picture what this 2.5km-wide area might once have looked like.

To get there, leave town by Church Hill and carry on south for 5km; the site is clearly signposted.

Cillard (☎ 071-68201, Carrowmore) Singles/doubles €30.50/50.80. Open May-Sept. Close to the cemetery, Cillard is a nonsmoking B&B on a working farm.

Knocknarea Cairn

About 2km north-west of Carrowmore is the hill-top cairn grave of Knocknarea. Around 1000 years younger than Carrowmore, the huge cairn (328m) is supposed to be the grave of the legendary Queen Maeve (Queen

Mab in Welsh and English folk tales). The 40,000 tonnes of stone have never been excavated, despite speculation that a tomb on the scale of the one at Newgrange in County Meath lies buried below.

Leave Sligo as for Carrowmore and a sign shows the way to Knocknarea. If you're leaving from the Carrowmore cemetery, continue down the road and turn right at the junction with a church. At the next crossroads (signposted Mescan Meadhbha Chambered Cairn) turn left, and leave your vehicle at the car park. From there it's a 30-minute walk to the summit and panoramic views.

Primrose Grange House (☎ *071-62005, Knocknarea)* Singles/doubles €35.55/57.15. Open Feb-Nov. This farmhouse B&B is just along the road that leads to the Knocknarea car park. It has six rooms, two with private bathroom.

Deer Park Court Cairn

Dating from around 3000 BC, the impressive court tomb (also called Magheraghanrush Court Cairn) stands on a wooded limestone hill with fine views of Lough Gill. The court area is in the centre of the tomb, with two burial chambers opening off at one end and another at the other end.

Take the N16 east from Sligo and turn off on the R286 for Parke's Castle. Almost immediately after joining this road turn left at the Y-junction onto a minor road signposted for Manorhamilton. Continue for about 3km, park in the car park, then follow the trail through the trees.

Strandhill

☎ 071 • pop 650

The long, sandy beach at Strandhill (An Leathras), 8km west of Sligo off the R292 airport road, is something of a **surfing** mecca, and at low tide you can walk across to Coney Island. The story goes that New York's Coney Island was named by a man from Rosses Point. There's also a golf course.

Strandhill Caravan & Camping Park (☎ *68120, Strandhill)* Tent site €8.25 plus €0.65 per person. Open Easter-mid-Sept. This camp site has 35 tent pitches and is ideally positioned beside the beach.

Strandhill Lodge & Hostel (☎ *68313, fax 68810, Shore Rd)* Dorms/private rooms €8.80/12.70 per person. Close to the beach, this large, two-storey house has an open fire in the lounge and there's a pub across the road.

Ocean View Hotel (☎ *68115, fax 68009, Main St)* Rooms €44-60 per person. This homely, mock-Tudor, three-star hotel is on the main road in the shadow of Knocknarea Cairn.

Getting There & Away

Bus Éireann (☎ 071-60066) buses run to Strandhill and Rosses Point, but there's no public transport to other places of interest in the area. A bicycle hired in Sligo would be the best way to get around. While it's possible to walk to both Carrowmore and Knocknarea from town, it's a long day's return trek.

SOUTH OF SLIGO TOWN
Collooney

☎ 071 • pop 200

Collooney (Cúil Mhuine) is about 15km south of Sligo on the N4. The **Teeling Monument**, at the village's northern end, commemorates the daring of Bartholomew Teeling. He was marching with Humbert's French-Irish army when it encountered stiff resistance from an English gunner. Teeling charged up to the gunner and killed him, thus allowing the army to march to eventual defeat at the Battle of Ballinamuck in Longford in September 1798. Although the French were treated as prisoners of war, Teeling and 500 other Irishmen were executed.

Now a three-star hotel, **Markree Castle** (☎ *67800, fax 67840, Collooney; rooms €73.65-82.55 per person)*, signposted off the main road on the left after leaving the village, has remained in the Cooper family since Cromwell's time. When Charles Kingsley stayed here in the 19th century he wrote that he cried over the misery inflicted on the local peasantry – at the same time exalting in the excitement of fishing for salmon in the estate's river. And it's said that Mrs Alexander wrote the hymn *All Things Bright and Beautiful* after her stay here.

MAYO & SLIGO

Ballymote

☎ 071 • pop 250

Near this small town, 11km south of Collooney and off the tourist trail, is ivy-covered **Ballymote Castle**, on the Tubbercurry road. The early-14th-century castle, contested among Irish chiefs before succumbing to the English in 1577, is now crumbling into obscurity. From here O'Donnell marched to disaster at the Battle of Kinsale in 1601.

The **Protestant church** is worth a glance, if only to read the plaque saying that the clock was paid for by the tenants of Ballymote Estate as a mark of respect for Sir Robert Gore-Booth of Lissadell. Unlike many similar tributes this one was genuine: Robert Gore-Booth mortgaged Lissadell House during the Famine to raise money for food for the starving. Constance Markievicz, his daughter, received a minute-long ovation from the local peasants here after her release from a British jail in June 1917.

Places to Stay & Eat There are a few reasonably priced B&Bs.

Hillcrest (☎ 83398, Emmet St) Rooms €25-48 per person. A modest terraced home, just up from the centre, it has only shared bathrooms but is a friendly place. Michael Collins is believed to have visited the house a week before his death.

Stonepark Restaurant (☎ 83372, Main St) Mains €5-16. Probably the town's best eatery, Stonepark opens for breakfast and has an a la carte menu in the evening (6pm to 9pm).

There are also several unpretentious pubs to choose from.

Carrowkeel Passage Tomb Cemetery

Situated on a hilltop in the Bricklieve Mountains overlooking Lough Arrow, this place is uplifting, with panoramic views on a clear day, and also a little spooky, given the 14 cairns, various dolmens and scattered remnants of other graves. The place has been dated to the late Stone Age (3000 to 2000 BC).

The site, west off the N4 road, is closer to Boyle in County Roscommon than Sligo town. If you're coming from the latter, turn right at the sign in the village of Castlebaldwin, then left at the fork as indicated. The site is about 2km uphill from the gateway. You can take an Athlone bus from Sligo and ask to be dropped off at Castlebaldwin.

Coopershill House (☎ 071-65108, fax 65466, Riverstown) Rooms €80 per person. Open Apr-Oct. Coopershill House is a handsome retreat for anyone wanting to relax in a Georgian family mansion. There are facilities for boating and fishing and an Irish meal with good wine and open log fires costs from €36.80. Riverstown, close to the Carrowkeel Passage Tomb Cemetery, is halfway between Sligo and Boyle.

Lough Arrow

The 8km-long Lough Arrow close to the Leitrim border is of interest to anglers, particularly for its brown trout (the season runs May to September). Windsurfing and sailing are allowed on the lake.

Arrow Lodge (☎ 079-66298, fax 66299, Kilmactranny) Singles/doubles with bathroom €44.45/68.60. Open Feb-Nov. A restored Victorian lodge in a woodland setting by the lake, it offers B&B in four rooms and caters mostly for anglers. Boat rental, guided services by Robert the owner and evening meals are available.

Tubbercurry

☎ 071 • pop 400

Quiet, off the beaten track Tubbercurry (Tobar an Choire), also spelled Tobercurry, comes alive around mid-July, when the weeklong **South Sligo Summer School** (☎ 85010) of music and dance takes place. On the second Wednesday in August, the town's big **fair day** is held. Nearly all the pubs have music.

Killoran's (☎ 85679, Main St) Mains €7-13. Open 8am-10pm Mon-Sat & 11am-8pm Sun. The first place to call in at is Killoran's, which functions as a combined restaurant/pub/touristoffice/takeaway/travel agent/off-licence.

Easky & Enniscrone

☎ 096 • pop 500 (combined)

The main route west to Mayo is pleasant

enough, but there's little to detain the visitor. Easky (Eascaigh) has the ruins of a 15th-century castle, and the **surfing**, possible year round, is highly regarded. For details contact the Easky Surfing and Information Centre (☎/fax 49020), on the main street, open 10am to 6pm weekdays.

Atlantic 'n' Riverside Caravan & Camping Park (☎ 49001, Easky) Tent site €5.10, plus €2.55 per adult. Open late Apr-Sept. The park, behind the information centre, is beside the Easky River and just a few minutes' walk from the ocean. Register at the post office.

At Enniscrone (Innis Crabhann) farther west, the sandy, 5km-long, Blue Flag beach known as the Hollow is one of the best in Ireland. Here you can take seaweed and steam baths at Kilcullen's Seaweed Baths (☎ 36238, Enniscrone; baths €10.10-12.70; open 10am-10pm daily July & Aug; 10am-9pm daily May-June & Sept-Oct; 10am-8pm daily Jan-Apr; 10am-8pm Sat & Sun Nov-Dec).

Atlantic Caravan & Camping Park (☎ 36132, fax 36980, Enniscrone) Tent site €6.35. Open Apr-Oct. The camp site is wonderfully located next to the beach and has 50 tent pitches.

Getting There & Away
Bus Éireann's (☎ 071-60066) Dublin–Sligo express bus No 23 and Galway–Derry express bus No 64 stop outside Quigley's in Collooney. Saturday only, Sligo–Castlerea bus No 460 stops at Collooney, Ballymote and Tubbercurry. Local bus No 475 runs from Sligo to Collooney, Monday to Saturday. From Easky and Enniscrone buses run four-times daily (once on Sunday) to Sligo and Ballina, and three-times daily (once Sunday) to Donegal.

The Dublin–Sligo train stops at Collooney and Ballymote three-times daily (four times on Friday). Call Sligo station (☎ 071-69888) for times.

LOUGH GILL
A round trip of 48km would take in most of this lough south-east of Sligo as well as Parke's Castle, which, though in County Leitrim, is included in this section. There are many legends associated with Lough Gill;

one that can be tested easily is the story that a silver bell from the abbey in Sligo was thrown into the lough and only those free from sin can hear its pealing. We're all ears.

Dooney Rock
There are good views of the lough and its islands from the top of Dooney Rock. Yeats immortalises the rock in *The Fiddler of Dooney*.

Leave Sligo heading south on the N4 and after 500m turn left at the sign to Lough Gill. Another left at the T-junction brings you onto the R287 and the Dooney Rock viewpoint.

Innisfree Island
If Yeats hadn't written *The Lake Isle of Innisfree*, this tiny island (Inis I raoigh) near the south-eastern shore wouldn't attract so many visitors, and it would probably have kept the air of tranquillity that so moved the poet:

> I will arise and go now, and go to Innisfree,
> And a small cabin build there, of clay and
>   wattles made;
> Nine bean rows will I have there, a hive for
>   the honey bee,
> And live alone in the bee-loud glade.

From the Dooney Rock car park turn left at the crossroads and after 3km turn left again for another 3km. A small road leads down to the lake.

Creevelea Abbey (County Leitrim)
The ruinous Creevelea Abbey was the last Franciscan friary founded in Ireland before the orders were suppressed. The columns in the cloister have some interesting carvings of St Francis, one displaying his stigmata and another one showing him in a pulpit with birds perched on a tree. The abbey was burned in 1590 by Richard Bingham, but restored by the monks before they were again ejected by Oliver Cromwell. They returned yet again and thatched the church roof, remaining until the end of the 17th century.

From Innisfree, return to the R287 and continue east until you see the sign for the abbey in the village of **Dromahair**.

MAYO & SLIGO

William Butler Yeats

NICKY CAVEN

The most celebrated of Irish poets, William Butler Yeats (1865–1939) was born in a suburb of Dublin. His mother was from Sligo, and Yeats spent a lot of time there as a child. At the age of nine he moved with his family to London, but six years later they returned to Ireland. His early interest in the occult led him to help found the Dublin Hermetic Society, and the budding poet became more and more interested in Irish mythology.

As his poetry became better known, he counted among his friends William Morris, George Bernard Shaw and Oscar Wilde. At the age of 37 he met the much younger James Joyce, who remarked that the meeting came too late for Joyce to help Yeats improve his writing! Yeats' most important encounter, though, was with Maud Gonne (1866–1953), whose nationalism and socialism provided a healthy balance to his predilection for mysticism and ill-defined romanticism. The story of their relationship has attracted a lot of speculation – especially about the sexual side – with Maud Gonne refusing to marry him. She took the title role in his one-act play *Cathleen Ni Houlihan* (1904), which has been credited with being the catalyst for the 1916 Easter Rising. Her husband, Sean MacBride, was one of those subsequently executed.

Yeats became a senator of the Irish Free State in 1922 and the following year received the Nobel Prize for Literature. In 1928 he moved to Italy where, in the following years, his flirtation with fascism sat uneasily alongside his stature as a poet of world renown.

Parke's Castle (County Leitrim)

The placid setting of Parke's Castle (☎ 071-64149, Fivemile Bourne; adult/concession €2.55/1.25; open 10am-6pm daily mid-March-Oct), with swans drifting by on Lough Gill, belies the fact that the early Plantation architecture was created out of an unwelcome English landlord's insecurity and fear. The carefully restored, three-storey castle forms part of one of the five sides of the *bawn*, which also has two rounded turrets at its corners. Try to join one of the guided tours after viewing the 20-minute video *Stone by Stone*, which gives a general introduction to the area's antiquities.

From Creevelea Abbey, continue east along the R287, turn left towards Dromahair and continue northwards. To return to Sligo from Parke's Castle turn west onto the R286.

Getting There & Away

Car & Bicycle Leave Sligo east via The Mall past the hospital, then turn right off the N16 onto the R286, which leads to the northern shore of Lough Gill and round to Innisfree. The southern route is less interesting until you reach Dooney Rock.

Boat *Wild Rose Water Bus* (☎ 071-64266, 0872 598869) 2-hr trip adult/child €10.10/5.05, 1-hr trip €7.60/3.80. There are cruises on Lough Gill from Doorly Park (a 30-minute walk east of Sligo town) twice daily, and five-times daily from Parke's Castle, mid-June to September (Sunday only in April, May and October).

NORTH OF SLIGO TOWN
Drumcliff & Benbulben

WB Yeats died in 1939 in Roquebrune, France, but his wishes were: 'If I die here, bury me up there on the mountain [the cemetery in Roquebrune], and then after a year or so, dig me up and bring me privately to Sligo.' True to his wishes, his body was interred in the churchyard at Drumcliff in 1948 – where his great-grandfather had been rector – although it was hardly a private affair, as the photographs in the Sligo County Museum make clear.

Yeats' grave is on the left near the Protestant church, and alongside Yeats is buried Georgie Hyde-Lees, whom he married in 1917, when she was 15 and he was 52. The epitaph is from his poem *Under Ben Bulben*:

Cast a cold eye
On life, on death.
Horseman, pass by!

In the 6th century, St Colmcille had chosen the same location for the foundation of a monastery. You can still see the remains of the **round tower**, damaged by lightning in 1936, on the main road near the churchyard. In the churchyard is an 11th-century **high cross**, whose eastern face depicts Christ in Glory, Daniel in the lions' den, Adam and Eve, and Cain's murder of Abel; on the western side, you can make out the presentation in the temple and the crucifixion.

Outside the churchyard is **Drumcliff Visitors Centre** (☎ 071-44956, Drumcliff; adult/child €2.55/1.90; open 9am-5pm Mon-Sat & 1pm-5pm Sun). It has a 15-minute, interactive audiovisual presentation on Yeats, St Colmcille and Drumcliff. The admission fee includes entry to the church.

To get there take the 8.45am bus from Sligo (arriving 9am) because the next one is at 4.15pm, which means you'll miss the two daily return buses that pass through Drumcliff at 12.45pm and 4.53pm (though there is a 3pm bus from Sligo to Drumcliff on Saturday only).

The limestone plateau of **Benbulben** (525m), the most westerly of the Dartry Mountains, is about 2km north-east of Drumcliff and dominates the landscape.

Glencar Lough

As well as **fishing**, the attraction of the lake is the beautiful **waterfall** signposted from the car park. Yeats refers to this picturesque spot in The Stolen Child. The surrounding countryside is best enjoyed by walking east along the road and taking the steep trail that heads north to the valley. From Drumcliff it's less than 5km to the lake, and there's also a bus service from Sligo. Ring Bus Éireann (☎ 071-60066) for details.

Lissadell House

Hidden in woodland lies Lissadell House (☎ 071-63150, Drumcliff; adult/concession €3.80/1.90; open 10.30am-12.30pm & 2pm-4.30pm Mon-Sat June-mid-Sept). It is the ancestral home of the Gore-Booth family, among whose members was Constance Markievicz (1868–1927), a friend of Yeats and a participant in the 1916 Easter Rising. The death penalty she received for her involvement was later withdrawn and, in 1918, she became the first woman elected to the British House of Commons. Like many Irish rebels who came after her, she refused to take her seat.

Constance's sister Eva was a poet, and Yeats' poem In Memory of Eva Gore-Booth and Con Markievicz is inscribed on a sign at the entrance to the house.

The light of evening, Lissadell,
Great windows, open to the south,
Two girls in silk kimonos...

Yeats visited Lissadell frequently and in 1894 wrote of the interior: 'Great sitting room as high as a church and all things in good taste.'

Lissadell has an informative, 45-minute guided tour. To get there, follow the N15 north from Sligo and turn west at Drumcliff, just past Yeats Tavern.

Mullaghmore

If you turn left at Cliffony, off the N15, the main road to Mullaghmore (An Mullach Mór) first passes **Streedagh Beach**, a grand crescent of sand that was the final resting place for many of the 1300 sailors who perished when three ships from the Spanish Armada were wrecked nearby.

The **beach** at Mullaghmore is also delightfully wide and safe. It was in this bay that the IRA assassinated Lord Mountbatten and members of his family in 1979. On the way to the Mullaghmore headland you pass **Classiebawn Castle**, built for Lord Palmerston in 1856 and later the home of Lord Mountbatten. The castle isn't open to the public, but the neo-Gothic pile can be viewed from the N15 and the R279 as you approach Mullaghmore.

Inishmurray Island

If access were easier to arrange, a visit to this uninhabited island would be a must. It contains the remains of **three churches**, beehive cells and **open-air altars**. The old monastery is surrounded by a stone wall with five separate entrances to the central area, which contains the churches and altars. The monastery was founded in the early 6th century by St Molaise, and a wooden statue of the saint that once stood in the main church is now in the National Museum in Dublin.

The monks on Inishmurray assembled some fascinating pagan relics. There's a collection of cursing stones; those who wanted to lay a curse did the Stations of the Cross in reverse, turning over the stones as they went along. There were also separate burial grounds for men and women and a strong belief that if a body was placed in the wrong ground it would move itself during the night.

Only 6km separates Inishmurray from the mainland, but there's no regular boat service and the lack of a harbour makes landing subject to the weather. Trips can be arranged through **Lomax Boats** (☎ *071-66124, Mullaghmore)* or **Joe McGowan** (☎ *071-66267, Streedagh Point)*.

Creevykeel Goort Cairn

North of Cliffony on the N15 is a well preserved, stone court tomb. Constructed around 2500 BC it has a wide, high front tapering away to a narrow end with an open central area. The unroofed court stands outside the front entrance. At some later stage, chambers were added to the western side of the cairn.

Places to Stay & Eat

Celtic Farm Hostel (☎*/fax 071-63337,*
Grange) Dorms/private rooms €10.10/12.70 per person. About 1km north of Grange, this 14-bed, nonsmoking hostel is a useful base for exploring northern Sligo and offers a free pick-up.

Benbulben Farm (☎ *071-63211, fax 73009, Barnaribbon, Drumcliff)* Singles/doubles €31.75/48.30. Open Apr-Sept. The biggest drawcard of this farmhouse B&B, 2km north of Drumcliff, is its elevated setting on the slopes of Benbulben.

Beach Hotel (☎ *071-66103, fax 66448,* ⓔ *beachhot@iol.ie, The Harbour, Mullaghmore)* Singles/doubles €92/108 in the high season. Close to a Blue Flag beach the hotel has a gym and pool and can arrange fishing trips. The *Fishes' Circle* restaurant here serves excellent, fresh seafood (mains €7.50-16.30).

Yeats Tavern (☎ *63117, Drumcliff)* Mains €8.20-16.50. Food served 12.15pm-9.45pm. The huge car park is indicative of the popularity of this pub on the main N15 road about 100m from Yeats' grave. The extensive menu falls into three main categories: seafood, steak and poultry.

Getting There & Away

There are regular Bus Éireann (☎ 071-60066) buses between Sligo, Drumcliff, Grange and Cliffony, as most buses to Donegal and Derry go along the N15. In Drumcliff the bus stop is near the church, in Grange it's outside Rooney's newsagents, and in Cliffony it's O'Donnell's Bar. The first bus leaves Sligo at 8.45am; the last bus from Cliffony is at 4.35pm.

Central North

Someone once described Ireland as a dull picture with a wonderful frame. Indeed, most visitors are attracted by the frame – the coast – and rarely venture inland to explore the picture. There is good reason for this, at least in part: the six counties of the central north (Cavan, Monaghan, Roscommon, Leitrim, Longford and Westmeath) have long been considered Ireland's less appealing counties, with comparatively little to distract the visitor. But while they may never lure the same hordes as the west or south, they do have a number of places of great interest, and the smaller number of visitors can make them that much more attractive.

Cavan, Monaghan and Donegal border Northern Ireland and, together with the six counties there, make up the province of Ulster. All border crossing points between the Republic and the North are now open, though you will occasionally have to pass through a garda checkpoint when crossing back into the Republic.

County Cavan

The low, undulating county of Cavan (An Cabhán) is barely a two-hour drive from Dublin and lies just south of the border with Northern Ireland. Cavan is dominated by lakes (it's said there is one for every day of the year), bogs and drumlins, which are small round hills deposited and shaped by retreating glaciers during the last Ice Age. In the far north-west of the county, the wild and barren Cuilcagh Mountains are the source of the River Shannon, at over 300km long the mightiest river in Ireland or Britain.

Cavan is famous for its potholed roads, which are often twisty and badly signposted. The roads seem to go over the drumlins, whereas in neighbouring Monaghan they go round them.

Cavan is in many ways a hard place, with a no-nonsense attitude to life that is born out of the inclement weather, difficult economic

circumstances and a people who have long been the butt of Irish humour as the most miserly in the country!

HISTORY

Archaeological evidence suggests that Cavan was inhabited as far back as Neolithic times. Magh Sleacht, a plain in the north-west of the county near the border

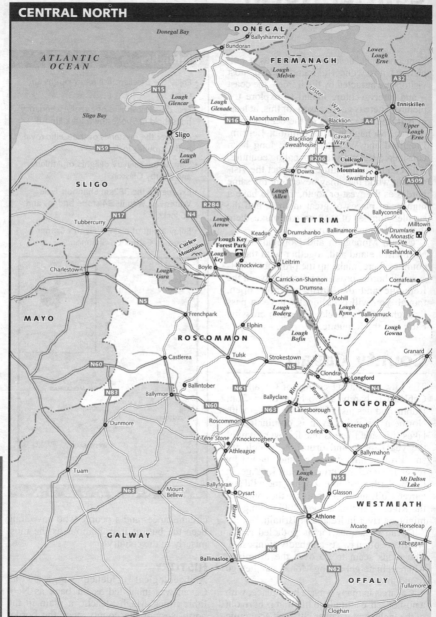

CENTRAL NORTH

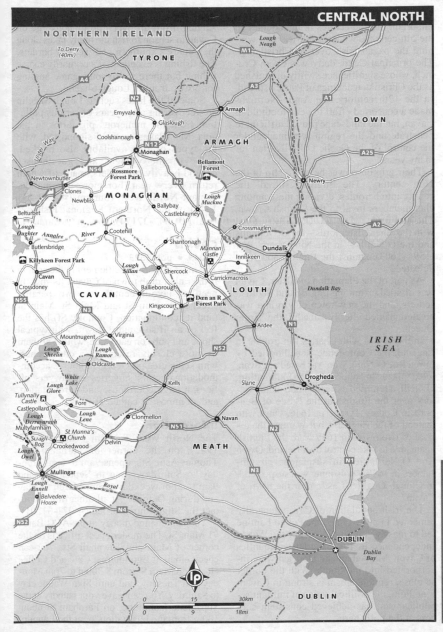

CENTRAL NORTH

NORTHERN IRELAND

To Derry (40mi)

Lough Neagh

TYRONE

A4

N2

Emyvale
Coolshannagh
Glaslough

Armagh

ARMAGH

DOWN

A3

A1

A25

N12

Monaghan

Bellamont Forest

N54

Rossmore Forest Park

Newtownbutler
Clones
Newbliss

MONAGHAN

Ballybay
Castleblayney

Lough Muckno

Newry

A2

Belturbet

Lough Oughter

Annalee River

Cootehill

Crossmaglen

Dundalk

Dundalk Bay

Butlersbridge

Shantonagh

Killykeen Forest Park

Lough Sillan

Shercock

Mannan Castle

Inniskeen

Cavan

Crossdoney

CAVAN

Ballieborough

Carrickmacross

LOUTH

N55

N3

Kingscourt

Dœn an R Forest Park

IRISH SEA

Mountnugent

Virginia

Ardee

N1

Lough Sheelin

Lough Ramor

N52

Oldcastle

White Lake

Kells

Slane

Drogheda

Lough Glore

Tullynally Castle

Fore

Lough Lene

Clonmellon

Navan

N2

Castlepollard

Lough Derravaragh

Multyfarnham

St Munna's Church

Delvin

N51

MEATH

N1

Scragh Bog

Crookedwood

Lough Owel

Mullingar

N3

Lough Ennell

Royal Canal

Belvedere House

N4

N52

N6

DUBLIN

Dublin Bay

DUBLIN

0   15   30km
0   9   18mi

village of Ballyconnell, was one of the most important druidic centres in the country in the 5th century, when St Patrick was winning the pagan Irish over to Christianity. The principal Celtic deity was Crom Cruaich, whose significance swiftly diminished as the Christian teachings of Patrick spread. In the 12th century, the Anglo-Normans made a concerted effort to get a foothold in Cavan, but the landscape proved difficult to penetrate and the region remained under the control of the Gaelic O'Reilly clan for many years.

Their grip on power began to slip in the 16th century. The English 'shired' the county into baronies, dividing these among clan members loyal to the English Crown. The end came when the O'Reillys joined with the other Ulster lords – the O'Donnells and the O'Neills – in the Nine Years' War (1594–1603) against the English and were defeated.

As part of the Plantation of Ulster, Cavan was divided up among English and Scottish settlers, and the new town of Virginia was created, named after Elizabeth I, the Virgin Queen.

In the 1640s, with Charles I in trouble in England, the Confederate Rebellion led by Owen Roe O'Neill, who was based at Cavan, took place in opposition to Plantation. O'Neill, a returned exile, had one major victory over the English at the Battle of Benburb in County Tyrone in 1646. Only with the end of the English Civil War and the arrival of Cromwell in 1649 were the English again able to take control over Ireland. Owen Roe O'Neill died in suspicious circumstances in 1649 – poisoning was suspected – in Clough Oughter Castle near the town of Cavan.

The Irish population of Cavan generally remained in poverty and the Potato Famine led to massive emigration. After the War of Independence in 1922, the Ulster counties of Cavan, Monaghan and Donegal were incorporated into the South. With the border so close, republicanism is strong in Cavan: Sinn Féin, the political voice of militant republicanism, has achieved consistent success at the polls here.

FISHING

Anglers from all over Europe converge on Cavan in season to fish the many lakes along the county's southern and western borders. The fishing is excellent; it's primarily coarse fishing but there's also some game angling for brown trout in Lough Sheelin.

Some of the lakes such as Lough Sheelin are recovering after years of serious pollution from the numerous pig farms in the area. Most lakes are well signposted, with the types of fish available also marked. Some of the villages and guesthouses depend heavily on anglers, many of whom return every year. For more information, contact North West Tourism (☎ 049-433 1942) or the Northern Regional Fisheries Board (☎ 049-37174), both in Cavan town.

CAVAN
☎ 049 • pop 5623

The most important settlement in the county is the rather drab town of Cavan. Its slightly peculiar layout centres on two parallel streets, Farnham St and Main St. Main St (and its continuation, Connolly St) has the feel of an Irish country town, with typical shops and pubs on each side, while Farnham St more closely resembles a city avenue, with some elegant Georgian houses accommodating doctors' surgeries and lawyers' offices, a large courthouse and garda station, and an imposing cathedral.

Information

The North West Tourism office (☎ 433 1942), on the corner of Farnham and Thomas Ashe Sts, opens 9am to 6pm Monday to Saturday, June to September, and 9am to 5pm weekdays from March to May and during October. At all other times, contact the Sligo tourist office (☎ 071-61201).

You can change money at the ACC Bank, 91 Main St. The modern post office is on the corner of Main and Townhall Sts. You can check email at Ego Internet Café and Coffee House on Main St from 8.30am to 7pm Monday and Tuesday, and until 8pm Wednesday to Saturday. You can leave your laundry at the Supaklene laundrette, on Farnham St about 100m from the bus station, or at the Laundry

Basket, at the southern end of Connolly St. The latter opens 10am to 6pm Monday to Saturday. There's also a small genealogical office (☎ 436 1094) in Cana House, signposted up the hill from the Presbyterian church on Farnham St. It opens 9.30am to 4.30pm Monday to Friday year round.

Things to See & Do

Cavan developed round a 13th-century Franciscan friary of which no traces remain. On the site of the friary in Abbey St is an 18th-century **Protestant church tower** that marks the grave of Owen Roe O'Neill, though it's not very impressive.

Two kilometres south-east of the town centre on the N3 is the **Cavan Crystal Factory** (☎ 133 1800, fax 133 11198, Dublin Rd; free; showroom open 9.30am-6pm Mon-Fri, 10am-5pm Sat & noon-5pm Sun). Cavan Crystal is Ireland's second-oldest crystal manufacturer. There's a visitor centre with an audiovisual display of crystal making, a showroom with Cavan crystal and local crafts on sale, and a restaurant and coffee shop. Factory tours will resume in 2002.

The **Cavan Equestrian Centre** (☎ 433 2017, fax 433 1400, Ballyhaise Rd), 1.5km north of town off the N3, is internationally recognised and is one of the largest centres in the country. Visitors can attend showjumping events most weekends, and horse auctions six times a year; ring for details.

Courses in **canoeing** are given by local Irish Canoe Union instructors on the River Erne. Check out the notice board in Louis Blessing's pub. The large **County Cavan Swimming and Leisure Complex** (☎ 436 2888, Drumalee; open 7.30am-10pm Mon-Fri, 11am-6pm Sat & Sun) just north-east of town has a swimming pool (adult/child from €3.80/2.30) and a number of other sporting facilities.

Places to Stay

Bridge Restaurant (☎ 433 1538, 5 Coleman Rd) Singles/doubles €29.20/50.80. Close to the bus station, this is the most central place with B&B-style accommodation. It offers spacious rooms; there's a €25 key deposit.

Oakdene (☎ 433 1698, 29 Cathedral Rd) Singles/doubles €31.75/50.80. This semi-detached house has four spotless rooms available.

Glendown (☎ 433 2257, 33 Cathedral Rd) Singles/doubles €31.75/50.80. Glendown is a friendly, comfortable home with all mod cons run by Tom and Eileen Flynn, and it's gay friendly.

There are some real gems farther out of town.

Lisnamandra Farmhouse (☎ 433 7196, fax 433 7196, Crossdoney) Singles/doubles with shower €31.75/48.25. Open Apr-Oct. This farmhouse is 7km south-west along the R198 to Crossdoney and well signposted on the left-hand side. You should book ahead. A full dinner can be arranged for about €18.

Farnham Arms Hotel (☎ 433 2577, fax 436 2606, Main St) Singles/doubles €53.35/89. This typical provincial hotel is almost opposite Market Square in the centre of town.

Hotel Kilmore (☎ 433 2288, fax 433 2458, Dublin Rd) Singles/doubles €66/104. This recently refurbished hotel is on the N3 just beyond the Cavan Crystal Factory.

Places to Eat

Ego Internet Café & Coffee House (☎ 437 3488, Convent Buildings, Main St) Mains €6.30. This is a friendly place with hot pitta sandwiches, home-made desserts and good coffee.

Melbourne Bakery (Main St) Mains €6.35. Halfway up Main St is this old-world canteen with Formica table tops and cream buns galore.

Mr Wong's Happy Valley Restaurant (Main St) Mains €8.25. For a Chinese takeaway, head here, where Main and Connolly Sts meet.

Farnham Arms Hotel (see Places to Stay) Mains €6.35. Open for lunch 12pm-6pm. The comfortable lounge here serves reliable carvery lunches, while the **Imperial** bar (☎ 437 3027) serves reasonable hot food (mains €7.60) and sandwiches in airy surroundings.

Kloisters (☎ 437 1485, Main St) Mains €13-20. Probably the best place in town,

Kloisters is in an old convent basement opposite the Melbourne Bakery and offers vegetarian dishes, steaks and seafood. The *Mustang Sally* bar, in the same building, serves decent bar food all day.

Entertainment

McGinnity's Corner Bar (☎ 433 1236, College St) McGinnity's has won a regional 'pub of the year' title and sometimes has music at the weekend.

The Imperial (☎ 437 3027, Main St) This cavernous, trendy bar with stylish mosaic decor has music from Wednesday to Sunday.

Black Horse Inn (☎ 433 2140, Main St) Near the post office, this is a popular place with young locals and has pool tables.

Louis Blessing's (☎ 433 1138, 92 Main St) You might come across Cavan's old timers at this rustic pub and grocery in a small courtyard off Main St.

An Sibín (The Speakeasy; ☎ 433 1064, 86 Main St) The most popular pub these days is the renovated Speakeasy, with wooden floors and real fires, on the corner of Townhall and Main Sts. It has live Irish music on Wednesday night.

Getting There & Away

The small bus station (☎ 433 1353) is at the southern end of Farnham St near the bridge and roundabout. The ticket office opens 7.30am to 8.30pm daily.

Cavan is on the Dublin–Donegal, Galway–Belfast and Athlone–Belfast bus routes. On weekdays there are five daily buses to Dublin (€8.90, two hours), three buses to Belfast (€15, three hours) two to Galway (€22.85, 3¾ hours) and four to Donegal (€12.20, 2¼ hours). Bus Éireann also has services running from Cavan through the county to Bawnboy, Ballyconnell, Belturbet, Virginia, Kells, Dunshaughlin, Navan and many other small towns, including Cootehill.

Wharton's (☎ 433 7114) runs private buses leaving the nearby Mallard's Hotel for Parnell Square in Dublin (€5.10 one way) at 7.30am Monday to Friday and 8am on Saturday.

Getting Around

Taxis can be ordered on ☎ 433 1172 or ☎ 433 2876.

AROUND CAVAN TOWN
Kilmore Cathedral

This modest Church of Ireland cathedral, built in 1860, is about 5km west on the R198 Crossdoney road to Killykeen Forest Park. On the western side of this relatively modern building is a fine 12th-century Romanesque doorway brought here from an Augustinian monastery on Trinity Island in Lough Oughter. If you look closely, you'll notice that some of the stones have not been replaced in the correct order. In the churchyard is the grave of Bishop William Bedell (1571–1642), who commissioned the first translation of the Old Testament into Irish; there's a copy of it on display in the chancel.

Killykeen Forest Park

On the shores of Lough Oughter, 12km north-west of Cavan, is this forest park (☎ 049-433 2541, fax 436 1044, e kill keen@coillte.ie; car/family €1.90/4.45; open year round). Lough Oughter has a tortuous outline, and the park has some fine walks, nature trails, fishing spots and good chalets for rent among its 243 hectares of trees and inlets. Many of the low wooded islands in the lake are likely to have been *crannógs* – fortified, artificial islands. Within the park to the north is the inaccessible **Clough Oughter Castle**, built in the 13th century by the O'Reillys on an island in the lake, and the place where the rebel leader Owen Roe O'Neill died in 1649. The best way to get near it is from the southeast, along a narrow road running north from the village of Garthrattan.

There are self-catering *chalets* on the shores of Lough Oughter that can be rented by the week for €241/254 for four/six people in the low season or €495/597 during the high season. Weekend rentals are also available.

Canadian-style **canoes** and other boats can be rented for a paddle on Lough Oughter or the Erne waterways, and there's coarse fishing, tennis and horse riding within the park.

Pighouse Folk Museum

From Crossdoney you'll see signposts for the Pighouse Folk Museum (☎ 049-433 7248, Corr House, Cornafean; adult/child €3.80/1.25; open by appointment). Its hodgepodge of artefacts dating from the 1700s is preserved in the original pighouse and barns. If you like rummaging through other people's attics, then you'll love this place. It's almost worth the trip just for the view the museum affords of the drumlins and valleys.

The museum opens by appointment, so phone ahead to see if Mrs Faris is going to be there. Unfortunately, it can only be reached by car.

Drumlane Monastic Site

One kilometre south of Milltown, north of Killeshandra on the R201 road to Belturbet, is Drumlane, a monastic site dating from the 6th century. (The small church and peculiar round tower were built later.) The monastery was founded by St Mogue, and the site's location between two small lakes – Drumlane and Derrybrick – and the surrounding hills is its most attractive feature.

Butlersbridge

Six kilometres north of Cavan is the pretty hamlet of Butlersbridge on the Annalee River. **Ballyhaise House** nearby was designed by Richard Cassels (aka Castle) and is worth a quick look for its fine brickwork. It's now an agricultural college.

Derragarra Inn (☎/fax 049-433 1003, Butlersbridge) Mains €7.60-16.50. An attractive ivy-clad, thatched pub by the Annalee River, it has good bar food available all day, a reasonably priced tourist menu and peat fires. The beer garden and live music at the weekend are a real draw.

Belturbet & Around

☎ 049 • pop 1248

On the River Erne 16km north-west of Cavan on the N3, Belturbet is an old-fashioned inland town that exudes a bleak charm. It is predominantly an angling centre with cruises available. *Emerald Star* (☎ 952 2933) has several cruisers for hire on the Shannon-Erne Waterway between Belturbet and Belleek

year round. A four-berth boat costs from €520 per week in the low season.

Hilltop Farm (☎/fax 952 2114, Kilduff) Singles/doubles €25.40/45.70. Hilltop Farm, 3km south on the road to Cavan, offers 10 rooms with B&B, and has facilities for anglers.

The Olde Post Inn (☎ 047-55555, fax 55111, Clover Hill) Singles/doubles €38.10/76.20. Mains €17-22. Restaurant open for dinner Tues-Sat & for lunch Sun. Situated 4km from Belturbet, this charming 200-year-old stone house originally housed the village post office and has nine comfortable rooms. It also has an excellent *restaurant* with modern Irish cuisine on offer.

Bus Éireann (☎ 433 1353) stops here four times daily (three times on Sunday) in each direction on the route between Cavan and Donegal (2¼ hours). The bus stop is outside O'Reilly's Garage. You can rent bicycles – and seek advice about cycling routes – from Padraig Fitzpatrick's (☎ 952 2866) on Bridge St. Bikes cost €12.70 per day.

Lough Sheelin

Lough Sheelin, 24km south of Cavan, is noted for its game angling, especially in May and June. The two main accommodation centres – at opposite ends of the 6km-long lough – are the villages of Finnea, just over the border in County Westmeath, and Mountnugent. There are several places in Mountnugent where you can stay and hire boats for fishing.

Ross House (☎/fax 049-434 0218, Mountnugent) Singles/doubles from €44.45/63.50. This beautiful period farmhouse in mature grounds on the lake's edge has a sauna, Jacuzzi, tennis, horse riding and boat hire to entice you. Evening meals are by arrangement.

Crover House Hotel (☎ 049-854 0206, fax 854 0356, Mountnugent) Singles/doubles from €57/101. Recently refurbished, this family-run hotel on the lakeshore has private gardens and boats for hire.

WESTERN CAVAN

Sometimes known as the Panhandle because of its long, narrow shape, western Cavan is dominated by the starkly beautiful, but little-visited, Cuilcagh Mountains. To the south-west, Magh Sleacht, which is the area around Kilnavert and Killycluggin, is supposed to have been a druidic centre dedicated to the deity Crom Cruaich. In the far north-western corner of the county, the road runs parallel to the Northern Irish border before dividing. The left fork heads west to Dowra and Blacklion, a desolate area with some interesting ancient sites. The right fork heads north to Swanlinbar and the border.

Getting There & Away

There are few buses serving this remote part of the county. The express Donegal–Dublin buses pass through Ballyconnell, Bawnboy and Swanlinbar four-times daily. Swanlinbar is also on the Athlone–Derry route, which runs once a day Monday to Saturday. The Galway–Belfast bus goes via Sligo and stops in Blacklion twice daily. Contact Bus Éireann in Cavan (☎ 049-433 1353) for more information.

Ballyconnell
☎ 049

Ballyconnell, 29km north-west of Cavan and 7km west of Belturbet, is the gateway to the Cavan Panhandle. There's not a lot in the village itself, but it's a good base from which to explore. Ballyconnell has lots of B&Bs, most of them situated on the Cavan road into town.

Sandville House (☎ 952 6297, e sandville@eircom.net, Ballyconnell) Dorms €9.50. Open Mar-Nov. The county's only hostel, this IHH property is 3km south-east of Ballyconnell, signposted off the Belturbet road (R200), in a peaceful, rural two-hectare setting. It has an area to pitch a tent and bikes for hire. The Dublin–Donegal bus stops at the Slieve Russell Hotel in Ballyconnell on request, and if you ring the hostel beforehand they can arrange to pick you up.

Woodford Lodge (☎ 952 6198, Ballyheady) Singles/doubles €25.40/44.45. This comfortable B&B 4km from town on Ballinamore road has facilities for anglers.

Snugborough House (☎ 952 6346, Ballyconnell) Singles/doubles with bathroom €31.75/50.80. An imposing neo-Georgian

house set off the road, 1km from town on the Swanlinbar road.

Slieve Russell Hotel (☎ 952 6444, fax 952 6046, e slieve-russell@quinn-hotels.com, Ballyconnell) Singles/doubles €120.65/203.20. About 2km south-east of Ballyconnell, this grandiose hotel is something of a legend. Built by a local millionaire, it features marble, fountains, restaurants, bars, nightclubs, a swimming pool and an 18-hole golf course.

Kilcorby Log Cabins (☎ 952 2869, fax 952 2698, e kilcorby@utvinternet.com, Ballyconnell) 5/6-bed cabin from €216 per weekend; €273/527 per week in low/high season. Anglers in particular may wish to hire one of these fully equipped cabins on Lough Oughter, in a secluded spot 4km south of Ballyconnell on the Cavan road. Boats can be hired on a daily basis.

Pólo D (☎ 952 6228, Ballyconnell) Lunch mains €6.35, dinner €17-20. Open for lunch & dinner Wed-Sat, lunch only Mon & Tues. This restaurant at the northern end of the main street is an old-world cottage. Sandwiches, salads and light snacks are served for lunch, while the more substantial evening meals include crispy duck and grilled salmon.

Dowra & Black Pig's Dyke

Dowra is on the upper reaches of the River Shannon, and between the river and Mt Slievenakilla (545m) to the east is a 5km section of the mysterious Black Pig's Dyke, an earthworks that wriggles wormlike across much of the region. It's thought to have been built as a fortification and frontier of Ulster as early as the 3rd century.

Melrose Inn (☎ 078-43025, Dowra) Singles/doubles €15.25/30.50. The nine renovated standard rooms over this pub are the hamlet's only accommodation.

Blacklion
☎ 072

Five kilometres south of Blacklion are the remains of a *cashel* (ring fort) with three large, circular embankments. Inside is a sweathouse, a stone hut that served as a type of Turkish bath or sauna and was used

The Sweathouse

Sweathouses, built of stone and with a small opening or doorway, were used to ease aches and pains, some of them alcohol-inflicted. Readers of Leon Uris' epic novel *Trinity* will remember the well used sweathouse in the fictional town of Ballyutogue.

A turf fire would be lit inside for several hours and when the sweathouse was sufficiently hot the fire was removed. The patient would then go inside and sit or lie on a pile of rushes or straw until they felt they had sweated enough. They would then emerge and take a dip in a nearby running stream.

mostly in the 19th century. Between Dowra and Blacklion there are the remains of quite a number of these curiosities.

MacNean House and Bistro (☎ 53022, 53404, Main St) Singles/doubles €33/58.40. This is one of the few B&Bs in or around Blacklion and it also provides a much-praised set dinner in the evening (€40.65) cooked by award-winning chef Neven Maguire.

The Galway–Belfast and Sligo–Belfast buses stop in Blacklion twice daily. In summer, the latter bus originates in Westport and stops in Blacklion once daily. The bus stop is in front of Maguire's pub.

The Cavan & Ulster Ways

Blacklion and Dowra are the ends of the 26km Cavan Way, and Blacklion is also on the Ulster Way. See Walking in the Facts for the Visitor chapter for details.

EASTERN CAVAN

Heading east from the town of Cavan you move into the heart of drumlin country. The history of foreign settlement has left its mark on the fabric and layout of the main towns.

Getting There & Away

Four or five daily Bus Éireann (☎ 049-433 1353) express buses on the Donegal–Dublin route pass through Virginia (three on Sunday), and there are also daily buses on the hour each hour between Cavan and Dublin.

Cootehill is on a Dundalk–Cavan route, and there are buses on Monday, Wednesday and Friday. One bus a day on weekdays during the school year (September to June) runs from Cootehill to Monaghan. A Dundalk–Cavan bus passes through Kingscourt on Tuesday and Thursday. There's also a Kingscourt–Navan–Dublin service, which has two buses a day Monday to Saturday and one on Sunday.

Virginia
☎ 049

On the shores of Lough Ramor in the southeastern corner of the county, the origins of Virginia (Achadh Lir) go back to the Plantation of Ulster in the early 17th century. Like the US state first settled in 1607, it was named after Elizabeth I, the Virgin Queen. Six kilometres north-west is **Cuilcagh House**, home of the Sheridan family, where Jonathan Swift is said to have come up with the idea for *Gulliver's Travels* while visiting in 1726. It is not open to the public. Like the rest of Cavan, the accent can be quite difficult to decipher; locals pronounce the town name **ver**-ginee!

Lough Ramor Camping & Caravan Park (☎ 854 7447, fax 854 8366, Ryefield) Tent site €7.60 plus adult/child €1.90/1.25. Open May-Oct. This small, basic camp site is 5km south of Virginia on the southern tip of Lough Ramor.

St Kyran's (☎ 854 7087, Dublin Rd) Singles/doubles with bathroom €32.40/50.80. Open Apr-Sept. On the lakeshore 1km from Virginia, this modern ranch-style house has nice lake views and good breakfasts.

White House (☎ 854 7515, Oldcastle Rd) Singles/doubles €31.75/50.80. This is a friendly, comfortable place 1km south-west along the R395 to Oldcastle.

Park Hotel (☎ 854 7235, 854 7203, e virginiapark@eircom.net, Virginia Park) Singles/doubles from €70/127. An 18th-century former hunting lodge overlooking a small lake, it has 40 rooms, a nine-hole golf course, walking trails and pleasure gardens. The restaurant serves good but pricey evening meals (full dinner €35) and bar snacks during the day.

Cootehill

Farther north, the small, neat market town of Cootehill (An Mhuinchille) is named after the Cootes, a Planter family who, after acquiring some confiscated land from the O'Reillys, were instrumental in founding the town in the 17th century. This colourful clan had many interesting members, including Sir Charles Coote, who was one of Cromwell's most ruthless and effective leaders, and Richard Coote (1636–1701), who first became governor of New York state, and then later New Hampshire and Massachusetts.

Maudabawn Cultural Centre (☎ 049-555 9504, e info@maudawn.com) runs popular three-day and week-long summer schools in Irish history, language, music and culture (€63.50 to €127 for a week-long course).

There are several dining and lodging options in the village.

Shercock

Shercock (Searcóg) is a pretty little village on the shores of Lough Sillan, 13km southeast of Cootehill. The lake is noted for its pike fishing.

Annesley Heights (☎ 042-966 9667, Carrickmacross Rd) Singles/doubles €31.75/ 50.80. Open year round. This modern B&B is east of town and has four large en-suite rooms. Angling facilities and a local tour guide are available.

Kingscourt
☎ 042

In the far east of County Cavan, Kingscourt (Dún an Rí) is a fairly drab village, though **St Mary's Catholic Church** has some superb 1940s stained-glass windows by the artist Evie Hone. The church has views of the surrounding region, and just to the northwest is 225-hectare **Dún an Rí Forest Park** (☎ 966 7320; car €3.80, free on foot; open Apr-Oct), with wooded walks, picnic spots and a famous wishing well.

Hilltown View (☎ 966 8559, Kells Rd) Singles/doubles €25.40/43.20. This is a modern, comfortable town house on the edge of town.

Cabra Castle (☎ 966 7030, fax 966 7039) Singles/doubles including breakfast €95.25/ 152.40. Cabra Castle, 3km out of Kingscourt

on the Carrickmacross road, is an imposing structure with 29 rooms in 36 hectares of parkland and its own nine-hole golf course, but it isn't cheap. It's worth trying for a snack or meal for lunch or the set dinner (€36.20).

County Monaghan

Few visitors ever pass through Monaghan (Muineachán), a landscape of neat round hills crisscrossed by unkempt hedgerows and scattered farms. The hills are drumlins, deposited by the glaciers of the last Ice Age in a belt stretching from Clew Bay in County Galway across the country to County Down. It's pleasant but never spectacular scenery. Walkers and cyclists may enjoy the peaceful country lanes if the weather is cooperative. Monaghan has fewer lakes than neighbouring Cavan, though the fishing is still good.

Patrick Kavanagh (1905–67), one of Ireland's most respected poets, was born in this county, in Inniskeen. *The Great Hunger*, a long poem that he wrote in 1942, and *Tarry Flynn*, a novel written in 1948, evoke the atmosphere and frequently grim reality of life for the poor farming community.

The barren terrain has restricted the development of large-scale mechanised farming but, despite this, Monaghan's farming cooperatives are among the most active and forward-looking in the country. Monaghan is noted for its lace, and this eye-straining craft continues in Clones and Carrickmacross, the centres of the industry since the early 19th century.

HISTORY

The earliest traces of humans in this region date back to before the Bronze Age. None of the sites here measure up to the magnificent monuments of County Meath, though the Tullyrain Ring Fort close to Shantonagh in the south of the county is worth a look, as are Mannor Castle near Carrickmacross and the crannóg in Convent Lake in Monaghan. Like Cavan, County Monaghan is lacking in religious remains despite its proximity to Armagh, the principal seat of St Patrick. The round tower and high cross in Clones in the west of the county are among the scant remains from this period of Irish history.

Unlike Cavan and much of Ulster, Monaghan was largely left alone during the Ulster Plantation. The transfer of Monaghan land to English hands came later – after the Cromwellian wars – and much of it was granted to soldiers and adventurers or bought by them from local chieftains (under pressure and often for a fraction of its true value). These new settlers levelled the forests and built numerous new towns and villages, each with their own Protestant church. The planning and architecture exemplified their tidy, no-frills approach to life. Disapproving of Irish pastoral farming methods, they introduced arable farming, and the linen industry later became very profitable.

Monaghan's historical ties with Ulster were severed by the partition of Ireland in 1922 and, though republicanism is quite strong, it's not as visible as you might expect. A number of towns have Sinn Féin bookshops and advice centres.

MONAGHAN
☎ 047 • pop 5842

The county town of Monaghan is 141km north-west of Dublin and just 8km south of the border with Northern Ireland. Though it has a population of less than 6000, it's the only town of any size in the county. Its design and buildings reflect the influence of the British newcomers of the 17th and 18th centuries and of the money generated by the linen industry in the 18th and 19th centuries; many of the town's important buildings are quite elegant limestone edifices. Other than the county museum, though, there isn't much to keep a visitor here beyond a day.

History

Nothing remains of the ruling MacMahons' 1462 friary or their earlier forts, but in Convent Lake, just behind St Louis Convent, there is a small, overgrown crannóg that served as the headquarters for the family around the 14th century.

After the turbulent wars of the 16th and 17th centuries, the town was settled by Scottish Calvinists, who built a castle using the rubble of the old friary, some fragments of which can be seen near the Diamond. The 19th-century profits from the linen trade transformed the town and brought many sturdy new buildings.

Orientation & Information

The principal streets of Monaghan form a roughly continuous arc, broken up by the town's three main squares – Church Square, the Diamond (the Ulster name for town squares) and Old Cross Square – where most of the sights and important buildings can be found. To the west of this arc at the top of Park St is Market Square. Here, the tourist office (☎ 81122), in the 1792 Market House on Market St, opens 9am to 5pm weekdays (until 6pm June to August), and 9am to 1pm on Saturday, April to October.

The post office is on Mill St, which runs between Hill St and North Rd. You can get your laundry done at Supreme Dry Cleaners on Park St just south of the tourist office.

There are two small lakes, Peter's Lake to the north of the Diamond and Convent Lake at the south-western corner of town. A one-way traffic system operates through the centre of town.

Monaghan County Museum & Gallery

Just north-west of the tourist office at the start of Hill St is this excellent museum, one of the best regional museums in Ireland (☎ 82928, 1-2 Hill St; free; open 10am-1pm & 2pm-5pm Tues-Fri, 11am-1pm & 2pm-5pm Sat year round). Taking up two Victorian houses, it includes exhibits from the Stone Age to modern times including local medieval crannóg artefacts, and it has displays on lace-making, the linen industries, the abandoned Ulster Canal and, of course, the border with the North. The museum's prized possession, though, is the **Cross of Clogher**, a bronze 13th- or 14th-century altar cross.

Local and national artists have occasional exhibits in the Art Gallery wing.

Other Things to See

At the top of Dawson St is **Church Square**, the first of the three squares, with an 1857 obelisk for one Colonel Dawson, who was killed in the Crimean War. Overlooking the square is a fine Doric 1830 **courthouse**, the former Hibernian Bank (1875) and the Gothic St Patrick's Church.

In the centre of town, the **Diamond** is the town's original marketplace, with a Victorian sandstone fountain presented to the town in 1875 in honour of the baron of Rossmore, a member of the area's former leading family. This spot was once occupied by the **Market Cross** (and sundial), which was moved to Old Cross Square at the end of Dublin St to accommodate the baron's memorial.

The birthplace of **Charles Gavan Duffy**, one of the leaders of the Young Ireland Movement and a founder of the *Nation* newspaper, is at 10 Dublin St. In the 1840s, the *Nation* set out to teach Irish people about their history and literature, as well as to present a non-sectarian view of Irish news. Later, Duffy moved to Australia, where he became a premier of Victoria. Nearby, the **Sinn Féin Advice Centre** has a display of republican literature.

South of the Ulster Canal on the Dublin road, the imposing **St Macartan's Catholic Cathedral** with its slender spire was designed by JJ McCarthy (responsible for the College Chapel in Maynooth, County Kildare) and is said to be his finest building, though some feel it has been marred by the later addition of incongruous Carrara-marble statues. It has good views of the surrounding area.

Convent Lake with its crannóg is at the bottom of Park St, over the canal. There are a few exhibits on the convent, crannóg and local history at **St Louis Convent Heritage Centre** (☎ 83529, Broad Rd; adult/concession €1.25/0.65; open 10am-noon & 2.30pm-4.30pm Mon, Tues, Thur & Fri, 2.30pm-4.30pm Sat & Sun). The annual **Harvest Time Jazz & Blues Festival** (☎ 82928) features international musicians and is held the first week in September.

Places to Stay

Ashleigh House (☎ 81227, 37 Dublin St) Singles/doubles with bathroom €31.75/56, without €25.40/50.80. This is a modern town house with 12 rooms in the town centre.

Willow House (☎ 71443, Tullybryan, Clones Rd) Singles/doubles €21.60/50.80. The friendly Mrs McCaffrey offers three spacious doubles and a standard single in her town house with a garden, 2km from the centre.

Glendrum House (☎ 82347, Drumbear) Singles/doubles €25.40/50.80. There are five comfortable rooms in this gay-friendly, modern home, 10 minutes' walk from the town centre (on the R188).

Lakeside Hotel (☎ 83599, fax 82291, Lakeside, North Rd) Singles/doubles €57.15/89. This recently refurbished Georgian hotel beside Peter's Lake is a five-minute walk from town on the Derry road.

Four Seasons Hotel (☎ 81888, fax 83131, Coolshannagh) Singles/doubles €54.60/104.15. Unconnected to the Four Seasons international chain, this large, modern hotel has good facilities including a swimming pool, sauna and gym. It's less than 1km from town on the N2.

Hillgrove Hotel (☎ 81288, fax 84951, Old Armagh Rd) Singles/doubles €67.30/114.30. This large, snazzy hotel with 44 modern bedrooms is located on the outskirts of town.

Places to Eat

Paramount (☎ 77333, 30 Market St) Mains €16-21. Open 6.30pm-10pm Wed-Mon. This classy, minimalist restaurant over Cooper's pub serves excellent seafood and steak.

Mediterraneo (☎ 82335, 58 Dublin St) Mains €8.50-15. This relaxed, airy bistro serves decent Italian staples.

Andy's Bar and Restaurant (☎ 82277, 12 Market St) Lunch around €6, set dinner €25.40. Open Tues-Sun. An award-winning restaurant facing the tourist office, it's one of the best places in town for food or a quiet drink by the fire.

Diva's (☎ 72707, 34 Market St) Mains €5.50-7.50. Open 9am-8pm Mon-Fri & 9am-6pm Sat. Diva's is a popular, colourful little cafe with a good selection of sandwiches, hot wraps and daily specials.

The Squealing Pig Bar and Restaurant (☎ 84562, The Diamond) Mains €10.50-15. Open 5pm-10.30pm Mon-Sat, bar food available noon-3pm Mon-Fri. Good solid traditional Irish food and steaks are served in this cosy new bar and restaurant.

Pizza D'Or (☎ 84777, Market Square) Pizza €6.30-9. Open 5pm-late Wed-Mon. Chef David O'Rourke's claim to fame is that he's the fastest pizza-flipper in the Republic! Sample his delicious spicy 'Pizza Hot' special (€8.75).

Hang Fung (Park St) Mains €8.25. Open 5pm-1am. This tiny takeaway is a favourite with the town's Chinese community.

Entertainment

An Poc Fada (☎ 72395, North Rd) A lively, traditional Irish bar that becomes packed in the late evening, especially on Wednesday and Sunday nights for the live rock music. Its name means Long Puck, an ancient hurling game still played around the Cooley mountains in County Louth.

McCaughey's (☎ 71754, 39 Park St) This is a real pub where gents still drink whiskey and red at the bar in the afternoon.

Terry's (☎ 81149, 6 Market St) With innocuous background music, this is a pleasant local bar for the over-30s.

Traynor's (☎ 82957, 30 Park St) Head here for traditional Irish music on Thursday nights.

Club Mexx (Four Seasons Hotel; see Places to Stay) Admission €6.35. Open Wed, Fri & Sat. The disco at this hotel seems to be the new hot-spot for Monaghan's revellers.

Getting There & Away

From the bus station (☎ 82377) on North Rd beside the former train station, there are numerous daily intercity services within the Republic and into the North. These include nine daily (six on Sunday) to Dublin (€9, two hours); six (four on Sunday) to Derry (€9.75, two hours) via Omagh; and five (two on Sunday) to Belfast (€9, two hours) and Armagh (40 minutes). There are also many local services to the nearby towns of Castleblayney, Ballybay, Carrickmacross and Ardee daily.

McConnon's private bus company (☎ 82020) runs two buses daily from Church Square (outside Ronaghan's chemist) to O'Connell St in Dublin (single €6.35), serving Castleblayney, Carrickmacross and Slane en route, and one bus daily to Clones.

Getting Around

The closest place to hire a bike is the local Raleigh dealer, Paddy McQuaid (☎ 88108), in Emyvale, about 12km north of Monaghan (€12.70/50.80 per day/week). He can deliver bikes to Monaghan town if necessary.

ROSSMORE FOREST PARK

This park (☎ 047-4331046; car €2.55 July & Aug, free on foot; open year round), 3km south-west of Monaghan on the Newbliss road (R189), was originally the home of the Rossmores, but only the buttresses to their castle's walls and the entrance stairway remain. Besides forest walks and picnic areas, the park has Californian sequoias, some of the tallest trees in Ireland. Other points of interest include the Rossmores' pet cemetery as well as Iron Age wedge and court tombs. A gold collar (or lunula) from 1800 BC was found here in the 1930s and taken to the National Museum in Dublin. Fishing in the lakes here is popular.

GLASLOUGH
☎ 047

Glaslough, 9km north-east of Monaghan, is a neat little village of cut-stone cottages set beside its namesake, Glaslough (Green Lake). To get there from Monaghan, take the N2 Omagh road north, turn east onto the N12 for about 2km then turn north onto the R185.

Beside the village is the 500-hectare demesne of **Castle Leslie**, a magnificent 19th-century Italianate mansion overlooking the lake. The castle's attractions include a toilet used by Mick Jagger. **Greystones Equestrian Centre** (☎ 88100, Castle Leslie) has some fine hacks in the demesne, where there are 40km of trails.

Castle Leslie (☎ 88109, W www.castle leslie.com) Rooms €90-120 per person, single supplement €25.40 per night. For the ultimate 'Victorian experience' you have to stay at this truly atmospheric castle, whose 14 bedrooms all have original decor. A getaway haven for actors, rock stars and other bohemian types, conversation at the communal four-course dinner (€43.80) need never be dull.

Fortsingleton *(☎ 86054, fax 86120, Emyvale)* Rooms €38.10 per person. For those with shallower pockets this nonsmoking Georgian residence with four-poster beds, 5km up the road, should suffice.

CLONES & AROUND
☎ 047 • pop 2170

The border town of Clones (Cluain Eois), 19km south-west of Monaghan, was the site of an important 6th-century monastery that later became an Augustinian abbey. The bus stop, post office and banks, including a Bank of Ireland branch, are in the central Diamond, or square. The town is the birthplace and home of the Clones Cyclone, former world featherweight champion Barry McGuigan who, after retirement, returned to the limelight for a short-lived reincarnation as a country-and-western singer! Clones is also the setting for Monaghan-born Patrick McCabe's dark novel *The Butcher Boy*.

Things to See & Do
Along with the scant remains of the **abbey** founded by St Tiernach on Abbey St, there is a truncated 22m-high **round tower** in the old cemetery south of town; the layout suggests it may be an early-9th-century example. There's also a fine **high cross** on the Diamond, with beautiful carvings depicting Adam and Eve, Daniel in the lion's den and, on the other side, the marriage at Cana and the miracle of the loaves and fishes. Overlooking it is the Protestant **St Tiernach's Church**.

The Ulster Way in Northern Ireland runs through **Newtownbutler** in Fermanagh, 8km to the north-west of Clones. North of Newtownbutler, there is a **scenic drive** from Derrnawilt to Lisnaskea. South-east of Clones, the road from Newbliss to Cootehill is quite pretty and takes you to the edge of **Bellamont Forest**, which straddles the border with Cavan.

Places to Stay & Eat
There's a dearth of B&Bs in Clones.

Glynch House *(☎/fax 54045, Newbliss)* Rooms from €29.20 per person. Martha O'Grady's Georgian home makes a lavish stopover, 7km from Clones on the Newbliss road (R183).

Lennard Arms Hotel *(☎ 51075, The Diamond, Clones)* Singles/doubles with bathroom €38.10/63.50. A plain, homespun country hotel, it offers simple comfort in its newly refurbished rooms.

Creighton Hotel *(☎ 51055, fax 51284, Lower Fermanagh St, Clones)* Singles/doubles with bathroom €31.75/63.50. Popular with anglers, the hotel has 16 modest but comfortable rooms and is also a nice place for a snack, lunch or full dinner (around €12.70).

Hilton Park *(☎ 56007, fax 56033, Clones)* Singles/doubles from €106/170. For a real treat and to forget the 21st century, try the Hilton Park, 5km south along the L46 towards Scotshouse. This country pile has its own estate, 18-hole golf course and serves top-class food in regal surroundings. Many of the ingredients are grown on the estate's organic farm and dinner costs €34.90 (without wine). There's also self-catering accommodation available in the gate lodge, which sleeps four (from €510 per week).

Getting There & Around
Bus Éireann (☎ 82377) runs buses from Clones through Monaghan and on to Castleblayney, Carrickmacross, Slane and Dublin three-times a day Monday to Saturday. Buses stop in the Diamond. Ulsterbus (☎ 028-6632 2633) has a number of daily buses on a route that takes in Enniskillen, Clones, Monaghan and Belfast. McConnon's (☎ 82020) runs a daily bus between Clones, Monaghan, Castleblayney, Carrickmacross, Slane and Dublin.

You can rent bikes in Clones at Canal Stores (☎ 52125) on Cara St.

CARRICKMACROSS & AROUND
☎ 042 • pop 2617

Carrickmacross (Carraig Mhachaire Rois), Monaghan's second-most-important town, was once a stronghold of the MacMahon clan. It owes its origins to the 3rd earl of Essex, who was a favourite of Elizabeth I and built a castle here in the 1630s. The site is now occupied by the Convent of St Louis. An extensive lace industry helped the early English and Scottish Planters to develop this pleasant little town, which consists of one wide street with some lovely Georgian houses and an old Protestant church.

Things to See & Do
On Market Square is the **Carrickmacross Lace Gallery** *(☎ 966 2506, Market Square; open 10am-1pm & 2pm-3pm Mon & Tues, 10am-1pm & 2pm-5pm Thur May-Oct)*. Run by the local lace cooperative, it has some fine displays and lace for sale. Bustling **Main St** is replete with shops, pubs and some quite elegant Georgian houses, a testimony to the town's wealthier past.

There's **fishing** in many of the lakes around Carrickmacross, including Loughs Capragh, Spring, Monalty and Fea. Contact Jimmy McMahon at the **Carrick Sports Centre** *(☎ 966 1714)* for information on where to fish. Lough Fea has an adjacent 1827 mansion and a demesne with oak parkland. The open **Dún an Rí Forest Park** *(☎ 67320)* with trails and picnic spots is 5km southwest along the R179 Kingscourt road.

Mannan Castle is an enormous and heavily overgrown motte and bailey, about 5km north-west of Carrickmacross in Donaghmoyne. This fortified Norman mound has fragments of a stone castle dating from the 12th century. Both structures were built by the Pipard family, who were given an estate here in 1186 by England's King John.

Places to Stay
Carrickmacross has lots of B&B accommodation.

Shirley Arms (☎ 966 1209, Main St) Singles/doubles with bathroom €44.45/90. This pub offers 10 modest rooms.

Shanmullagh House (☎ 966 3038, Shanmullagh) Singles/doubles €27.95/48.25. This new bungalow in landscaped gardens has five spacious rooms; take the Dundalk road (R178) 3km from town where Shanmullagh House is signposted on the right.

Nuremore Hotel and Country Club (☎ 966 1438, fax 966 1853, Nuremore) Singles/doubles from €114/177. On the out-

skirts of town, this rambling pile has every conceivable amenity, including an 18-hole, championship-length golf course.

Getting There & Away
Nine Bus Éireann (☎ 047-82377) buses daily (six on Sunday) to/from Dublin (1¼ hours) pass through Carrickmacross. There are at least six daily on the Letterkenny–Dublin route, one on the Coleraine–Dublin route and three between Clones and Dublin. Collins (☎ 966 1631), a private bus company, offers two departures daily (one on Sunday) to Dublin (single €5.10). McConnon's (☎ 047-82020) service includes Carrickmacross on its Dublin–Monaghan–Clones route, which also passes through Castleblayney, with two buses a day Monday to Saturday.

The bus stop is outside O'Hanlon's shop on Main St.

INNISKEEN
☎ 042
The village of Inniskeen (Inis Caoin), birthplace of the poet Patrick Kavanagh, is 10km north-east of Carrickmacross. Kavanagh is buried in the local graveyard, where his cross reads: 'And pray for him who walked apart on the hills loving life's miracles.'

Housed in the village's plain chapel is the **Patrick Kavanagh Rural and Literary Resource Centre** *(☎ 937 8560; adult/child €2.55/1.90, literary tour €6.35/3.80; open 11am-5pm Mon-Fri & 2pm-6pm Sat & Sun June-Sept; 11am-5pm Mon-Fri & 2pm-6pm Sun mid-Mar-May, Oct & Nov; 11am-5pm Mon-Fri Dec-mid-Mar)*. It focuses on the acclaimed poet's life and work as well as local and folk history. A local actor takes groups on a literary tour of the area, including Brennan's pub, Kavanagh's local watering hole. Nearby, the forlorn skeletal ruin of a **round tower** is all that is left of the 6th-century **St Daig monastery**.

CASTLEBLAYNEY
☎ 042 • pop 2808
Castleblayney (Baile na Lorgan), about halfway between Carrickmacross and Monaghan on the N2, is nicely situated near Lough Muckno, the county's most expansive

CENTRAL NORTH

and scenic lake. This small town takes its name from Sir Edward Blayney and his family, who built a castle by the lake in 1622 and were responsible for the construction of the plain Georgian courthouse and both the Protestant and former Catholic churches – an uncommon gesture by a landowner at the time.

Blayney's castle was sold in the last century to the Hope family and was renamed after them. In the demesne is the 365-hectare **Lough Muckno Leisure Park** (☎ *974 6356; free; open year round)*, which has lakeshore and woodland trails as well as golf, tennis, cycling, canoeing, sailing, waterskiing, fishing and horse riding (€10 to €25 per hour).

Places to Stay

Rockville House *(☎ 974 6161, Dundalk Rd)* Rooms from €24.75 per person. This is a comfortable, modern house with pleasant rooms and a sauna.

Glencarn Hotel *(☎ 974 6666, fax 974 6521, Monaghan Rd)* Singles/doubles €50.80/99.05. A large, old-fashioned hotel, it has a swimming pool and leisure facilities.

Getting There & Away

Castleblayney is on the main Monaghan–Dublin route, with seven buses daily in each direction. McConnon's (☎ 047-82020), a private bus service, also has a number of daily buses from Clones and Monaghan through Castleblayney and on to Dublin.

County Roscommon

County Roscommon (Ros Comáin) is more a transit route than a destination in itself. But besides the sleepy county town, there are places well worth visiting. Strokestown has one of the better-presented mansions in the country as well as the important Famine Museum. Just south of the Sligo boundary, the town of Boyle is also worth a stop, especially for the unique King House Interpretive Centre.

Much of Roscommon's western border follows the River Suck. About halfway down, a few kilometres inland from Ballyforan, is Dysart (Thomas St on some maps), the ancestral stomping grounds of the illustrious Fallon clan. The remains of their castle are near the town, as is a recently renovated church, parts of which date from the 12th century, in the middle of an ancient cemetery. Roscommon's eastern border is formed by a number of loughs, including the large Lough Ree (or Rea), and the River Shannon, which flows between them. Naturally, fishing is a major draw.

STROKESTOWN & AROUND
☎ 078 • pop 572

Strokestown (Béal na mBuillí), on the N5 between the towns of Longford and Tulsk, is about 18km north-west of Roscommon. It owes its existence to the Mahon family, owners of Roscommon's second-most-important estate. Its incredibly wide main street was designed by one of the early Mahons, who took it upon himself to create Europe's widest street!

Strokestown Park House

At the end of Strokestown's main avenue are three Gothic arches, beyond which is this impressive stately home, the seat of a 12,000-hectare estate granted to Nicholas Mahon by Charles II after the Restoration as a reward for supporting the House of Stuart in the English Civil War *(☎ 33013, fax 33712, ℮ info@ strokestownpark.ie; house & museum adult/ child €8.25/3.80, house, museum & gardens €11.45/5.10, 45-minute house tour €4.45/ 1.90, gardens only €5.70/1.90; open 11am–5.30pm daily Apr–Oct)*.

The original house, completed in 1697, was not considered imposing enough for Nicholas' grandson Thomas, who commissioned Richard Cassels to build him a grand house in the Palladian style, as was the current taste. The only part of the original house to survive Cassels' designs is the still room in the basement. Apart from some alterations made in the mid-19th century, the house has remained unchanged since Cassels' day. The actual estate, however, decreased along with the family's fortunes, and when they eventually sold up to the local garage owner in 1979 the estate had been whittled down to 120 hectares. However, as the estate was never sold at auction, virtually all of the contents were kept intact. It was opened to the public in 1987.

In 1914 Olive Pakenham-Mahon married the heir to the Rockingham estate in Boyle, thus uniting the county's two biggest demesnes. The union lasted only a couple of months as Pakenham was killed in the early days of WWI. His widow maintained the estate until its sale.

David Thomson's novel *Woodbrook* is the perfect book to read after your visit and is available here, and there are paintings by Woodbrook's Phoebe Kirkwood adorning the walls of an upstairs bedroom.

Even children will enjoy the tour, which provides an intriguing glimpse into the Anglo-Irish Ascendancy and takes in a schoolroom and a child's bedroom, complete with 19th-century toys and fun-house mirrors.

In the old stable yards is the fascinating **Irish Famine Museum** (☎ *33013*). The museum is an absolute must for anyone seeking to understand the devastating effects of the potato blight on Ireland in the 1840s. In a marked departure from the traditional silence about the disaster, the museum outlines in vivid detail the horrors of starvation and the irresponsibility of the government, which was too wrapped up in a laissez-faire economic policy to intervene. One exhibit also draws parallels with world hunger and poverty today.

Cruachan Aí Visitor Centre

In Tulsk village, 10km north-west of Strokestown on the N5, is this interpretive centre (☎ *39268; adult/child €3.80/1.25; open 10am-6pm daily year round*). One of the largest of its kind in Europe, it explores the important Celtic royal sites of local Rathcroghan and Carnfree. Surrounding the village are some 60 unmarked megalithic tombs, burial and ceremonial sites of the kings of Connaught, which have remained largely undisturbed for the past 3000 years.

Famine, Suffering & Injustice

When the potato crop failed in the mid-1840s, Major Denis Mahon (landlord of Strokestown at the time) and his land agent simply evicted the hundreds of starving peasants who could no longer contribute to the estate's coffers, and chartered ships to transport them away from Ireland. These overcrowded 'coffin ships', which carried emigrants to the USA and elsewhere, resulted in more suffering and deaths.

In 1847 Major Mahon was shot dead just outside the town, and one of the documents on display in the Irish Famine Museum in Strokestown is a newspaper account of how Patrick Hasty and Owen Beirne committed the deed. Their signed confession looks as suspicious as the ones that convicted the Birmingham Six – exonerated in 1991 – of terrorism in Britain in the 1970s.

According to the legend of Táin Bó Cúailnge (see the boxed text in the Counties Meath & Louth chapter), Cruachan or Rathcroghan was the site of Queen Medb (Maeve) and her lover Cúchulainn's palace. The Oweynagat Cave, believed to be the entrance to the 'Otherworld' is also sited here. There's an audiovisual display in the visitor centre and a map of the sites in the car park. You can walk freely around the sites.

Elphin

Some 10km north-west of Strokestown, Elphin was an important bishopric from the time of St Patrick until 1961, when the seat was moved to Sligo. Ruins of the cathedral, parts of which date from about the 13th century, can be seen in the centre of town. You can visit a restored early-18th-century **windmill** (☎ *078-35181*) and see a demonstration of its use, 1km from Elphin on the Ballinagare road.

Places to Stay

Martin's (☎ *33247, Church St*) Rooms €22.85 per person. This modest, renovated old house is run by Mena Martin.

Lakeshore Lodge (☎ *33966, Clooneen*)

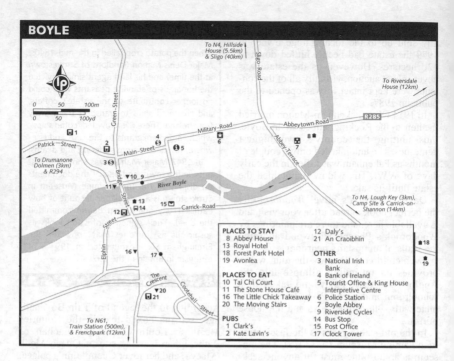

BOYLE

To N4, Hillside House (5.5km) & Sligo (40km)

Sligo Road

To Riversdale House (12km)

Abbeytown Road   R285

Military Road

Green Street

Patrick Street

Main Street

To Drumanone Dolmen (3km) & R294

Bridge Street

River Boyle

Abbey Terrace

To N4, Lough Key (3km), Camp Site & Carrick-on-Shannon (14km)

Carrick Road

Elphin Street

The Crescent

Cootehall Street

To N61, Train Station (500m), & Frenchpark (12km)

PLACES TO STAY		12 Daly's
8 Abbey House		21 An Craoibhín
13 Royal Hotel		
18 Forest Park Hotel		OTHER
19 Avonlea		3 National Irish Bank
		4 Bank of Ireland
PLACES TO EAT		5 Tourist Office & King House Interpretive Centre
10 Tai Chi Court		
11 The Stone House Café		6 Police Station
16 The Little Chick Takeaway		7 Boyle Abbey
20 The Moving Stairs		9 Riverside Cycles
		14 Bus Stop
PUBS		15 Post Office
1 Clark's		17 Clock Tower
2 Kate Lavin's		

Rooms €25.20 per person. On the R371 5km from Strokestown, this modern nonsmoking bungalow is attractively located on the shore of Kilglass Lake. It has a private jetty and boats for hire.

Percy French Hotel *(☎ 33300, fax 33856, Bridge St)* Singles/doubles €44.45/76.20. Strokestown's only hotel is a typical provincial, family-run place in the town centre.

Getting There & Away
The Bus Éireann (☎ 071-60066) express bus from Sligo to Athlone (via Roscommon and Boyle) stops in Strokestown once daily. The Ballina–Dublin bus via Longford and Mullingar stops in Strokestown five-times daily (four on Sunday). The bus stop is outside Hanley's on Main St.

BOYLE & AROUND
☎ 079 • pop 2222
Boyle (Mainistir na Búille) is a garrison town in the north-west of the county at the foot of the Curlew Mountains and on the River Boyle between Lough Key and Lough Gara. Despite its attractions, including the fine Boyle Abbey, the renovated King House Interpretive Centre and the impressive Drumanone Dolmen just outside town, it has surprisingly few distractions for the visitor after dark. Maureen O'Sullivan, the American film actress and mother of Mia Farrow, was born in a house on Main St opposite the Bank of Ireland building in 1911.

History
Boyle grew up around the King-family estate at Rockingham, Roscommon's largest and most powerful demesne. Up to the early 1600s, there was little more than a settlement here. Connaught kings and chieftains such as the MacDermotts and the O'Conors had engaged in a long-running battle to gain control over the area. In 1603, however, Staffordshire-born John King was granted land in Roscommon with a view to 'reduc-

ing the Irish to obedience' through the enforcement of the penal laws.

Over the next 150 years, his descendants proceeded to make their name and fortune, and by 1768 Edward King was made earl of Kingston. In 1730 the stately King House was built, but in 1780 the family moved to the grander Rockingham House, built in what is now Lough Key Forest Park. The majority of the estate was disbanded in the 19th century, leaving just the house, which was burned to the ground by a fire in 1957.

Information

The tourist office (☎ 62145), in King House on the corner where Military Rd meets Main St, opens 10am to 5pm on weekdays, June to mid-September. At other times your call will be diverted to the Galway tourist office, or you can seek assistance from the friendly staff at the interpretive centre in King House. Alternatively check the tourism information board in front of the clock tower in the Crescent, the central square.

There's a National Irish Bank branch with an ATM on the corner of Bridge and Patrick Sts and a Bank of Ireland at the eastern end of Main St. The post office is on Carrick Rd, south of the river.

Boyle Abbey

Beside the N4, to the east of the town centre, is one of the finest Cistercian abbeys in Ireland (☎ 62604; adult/concession €1.25/0.50; open 9.30am-6.30pm daily Apr-Oct). It has remains dating back to the 12th century, when it was founded by monks from Mellifont in County Louth. In 1659 military forces occupied the abbey and turned it into a fort.

The interesting 13th-century nave in the northern part of the abbey has Gothic arches on one side that are narrower than the Romanesque arches on the other. The capitals are also distinctive. On the southern side of the abbey, once the refectory area, there is a fine stone chimney built after the monks left and the abbey became a fortified home. Edward King, whose death by drowning in 1637 inspired English poet John Milton to compose *Lycidas*, is buried here.

Guided tours of this Dúchas-run abbey are available on the hour until 5pm.

King House Interpretive Centre

This interpretive centre is certainly one of the most inspired in the country (☎ 63242, fax 63243, ⓔ kinghouseboyle@hotmail.com, Main St; adult/student/family €3.80/3.20/10.15; open 10am-6pm daily May-Sept; 10am-6pm Sat & Sun Apr & Oct). In a lovely mansion built by Henry King in 1730, it served as a military barracks for the fearsome Connaught Rangers (Wellington called them the 'Devil's Own') from 1788 until Irish independence in 1922, after which it sat derelict until the county council renovated it (1989–95) at a cost of €3.8 million. It contains audiovisual exhibits detailing the turbulent history of the Connaught kings, the chieftains, the town of Boyle and the King family, including a rather grim tale of tenant eviction during the Famine.

Kids will especially enjoy King House. It's very much a hands-on museum where they can try on ancient Irish cloaks, brooches and leather shoes, write with a quill and even 'build' a vaulted ceiling – King House has four floors of them – from specially designed blocks. A tour of King House is an excellent precursor to one of the Famine Museum in Strokestown.

Drumanone Dolmen

This superb dolmen is one of the largest in Ireland, measuring 4.5m by 3.3m, and was constructed before 2000 BC. To get there, follow Patrick St west out of town for 2km, then bear left at the junction sign for Lough Gara for another kilometre, passing under a railway arch. A sign indicates the path across the railway line.

Lough Key Forest Park

This 290-hectare park (☎ 62363; car €3.80 Apr-Sept, free on foot), on the N4 3km east of Boyle, was part of the Rockingham estate, owned by the King family from the late 18th century until it was sold to the Land Commission in 1957. Rockingham House, designed by John Nash, was destroyed by a fire in the same year; all that remains are some stables and outbuildings and a tunnel leading from what was the house to the lake. It's a great spot to have a picnic and children will enjoy the wishing chair, bog gardens, fairy bridge and viewing tower over the lake. There are several marked walking trails you can take and deer roam about in summer.

Lough Key is at the northern limit for cruising on the Shannon. Rowing boats are available for a pricey €7.60 an hour, and fishing is a popular pursuit; record-breaking pike have been caught here. The ruins of a 12th-century abbey can be seen on tiny Trinity Island. On Castle Island, a 19th-century castle stands on the site of 16th-century MacDermott Castle.

Six kilometres from the park, on the N4 towards Carrick-on-Shannon, is **Woodbrook**, the demesne that is the setting for David Thomson's wonderful novel on the Anglo-Irish gentry. It is not open to the public.

Douglas Hyde Interpretive Centre

Frenchpark, some 12km south-west of Boyle on the R361, is home to the Douglas Hyde Interpretive Centre *(☎ 0907-70016, Frenchpark; free; open 2pm-5pm Tues-Fri, 2pm-6pm Sat & Sun May-Sept)*. It's housed in the former Protestant church where Hyde's father was rector. Hyde (1860–1949) was one of the founding members of the Gaelic League in 1893 and was later elected the first president of the Republic in 1937. This Renaissance man published many works of prose and poetry under the pen name An Craoibhín Aoibhinn (Delightful Little Branch), and he is buried in the churchyard; the centre is also known as the Gairdín an Craoibhín (Garden of the Little Branch).

Places to Stay

Lough Key Forest Caravan & Camping Park (☎ 62212) Single tent €3.80, family tent €10.15; electricity €1.90. There's a recreation room, laundrette and children's play area. Indicate your intention to camp to avoid the park's €3.80 admission charge.

Abbey House (☎/fax 62385, Abbeytown Rd) Singles/doubles with bathroom €32.40/50.80. Open Mar-Oct. This large, friendly Georgian house right in the grounds of Boyle Abbey has spacious, modest rooms. Mature gardens and stream are a bonus.

Avonlea (☎ 62538, Dublin Rd) Singles/doubles with bathroom €27.94/48.26. Avonlea is a modern bungalow close to Lough Key Forest Park, on the Carrick road (N4) just south-east of town.

Hillside House (☎ 66075, Doon, Corrigeenroe) Singles/doubles €31/48. This old-fashioned bungalow farmhouse is in a wooded area 5.5km from Boyle; turn right 1km from town on the Sligo road (N4).

Riversdale House (☎ 67012, Knockvicar) Singles/doubles €34.30/50.80. Open Apr-Oct. This Georgian farmhouse, 12km northeast of Boyle on the R285, is the former home of film star Maureen O'Sullivan. It has spacious rooms and evening meals on request.

Royal Hotel (☎ 62016, fax 64949, Bridge St) Singles/doubles €53/108. In the town centre, the 18th-century Royal Hotel offers 16 comfortable rooms. Its *restaurant*, with a Chinese menu, offers lunch and set evening meals (mains €6.50-9).

Forest Park Hotel (☎ 62229, fax 63113, Dublin Rd) Singles/doubles €57/90. This small, family-run hotel, almost opposite Avonlea B&B, offers relatively modern comfort in its 12 rooms.

Places to Eat

They say locally you can be 'oiled in Boyle or boiled in oil' – you can try either option at *The Little Chick Takeaway (The Crescent)*.

An Craoibhín (☎ 62704, Elphin St) Lunch €4.50-5. This small but popular pub is good for a hearty pub lunch.

The Stone House Café (Bridge St) Specials €5.70. Open 9am-7pm Mon-Sat. A cosy place on the river with seats overlooking the water, this was a gate lodge to the now closed Frybrook House. Its fisherman's pie, pasta specials and home-made desserts are probably the best in town.

The Moving Stairs (☎ 63586, The Crescent) Mains €13-17.80. Open 6.30pm-9.30pm Wed-Sat. Try the grilled organic goat's cheese with sesame starter (€5.70) from an interesting menu in colourful surroundings.

Tai Chi Court (☎ *63123, Bridge St*) Mains €8-10.50. Open 5.30pm-11.30pm daily. Overlooking the river, Tai Chi Court serves up reasonable Chinese fare.

Entertainment
Clark's (☎ *62064, Patrick St*) This newly renovated pub has live music on Saturday and set dancing on Tuesday night.

Kate Lavin's (☎ *62855, Patrick St*) Don't visit Boyle without stopping in this authentic old-world pub with its preserved interior and traditional music most nights.

Daly's (☎ *62085, Bridge St*) In the centre of town is this friendly old pub with fires and good Guinness.

Getting There & Away
From almost outside Royal Hotel (and opposite Daly's pub) on Bridge St, the Bus Éireann (☎ 071-60066) express bus leaves four-times daily (once on Sunday) for Sligo (50 minutes) and Dublin (three hours). Boyle station is on Elphin Rd; from there trains (☎ 079-62027) go three-times daily between Sligo (40 minutes) and Dublin (2½ hours) via Mullingar.

Getting Around
You can order a taxi on ☎ 63344 or ☎ 62119. Bikes are available from Riverside Cycles (☎ 63777), just off Bridge St by the river, for €9 per day. It opens 10am to 1pm and 2pm to 6pm daily, except Wednesday and Sunday.

ROSCOMMON
☎ 0903 • pop 3515

The small county town of Roscommon (Ros Comáin), sitting at the crossroads of several major highways, has a few sights of interest that make it worth a stopover. The town gets its name from *ros* (wooded headland) and St Coman, who founded a monastery here in the 8th century.

The local tourist office (☎ 26342), in John Harrison Hall in the Square, opens 10am to 5.30pm Monday to Saturday, June to early September. The post office is next door, and there is a Bank of Ireland opposite Gleeson's Guesthouse in the Square.

Things to See & Do
The Norman **Roscommon Castle** built in 1269 was almost immediately destroyed by Irish forces and rebuilt in 1280. The mullioned windows were added in the 16th century. Though none of the interior remains, the massive walls and round bastions give it an impressive look, standing alone in a field at the northern end of town off Castle St.

At the southern end of town off Circular Rd are the remains of a 13th-century **Dominican priory**, the most notable feature of which is an effigy of the founder, Felim O'Conor, carved around 1300. It's set in the north wall near where the altar once stood. There's also a rare depiction of eight *gallóglí* (mercenary soldiers) in costume of the day, dating from the 15th century.

Roscommon County Museum (☎ *26342, The Square; adult/child €1.90/0.65; open 10am-3pm Mon-Fri year round*) is in John Harrison Hall, a former Presbyterian church with an unusual window in the form of a Star of David supposedly representing the Trinity. The museum contains some vaguely interesting pieces, including an inscribed slab from St Coman's monastery and a medieval sheila-na-gig from Rahara.

The Square's Bank of Ireland used to be the **courthouse**. Opposite is the enormous **old jail**, where executions were carried out by 'Lady Betty' in the mid-18th century. She herself had been condemned to death after confessing to the murder of a lodger in her house – who turned out to be her own son. She escaped death by offering to take over as executioner. Despite planning objections, all but the facade and front block were demolished a decade ago, to make way for a dismal shopping arcade.

Ask the tourist office for a map of the **Suck Valley Way**, a 75km walking trail. The river offers some of the best mixed fishing in Ireland, with rudd, tench, pike and perch in abundance. En route you may pass **La Téne Stone** in Castlestrange, 7km west of town on the R366, an Iron Age spiral-inscribed stone, one of only two in the country from this period.

Places to Stay

Gailey Bay Caravan & Camping Park (☎ *61058, Gailey Bay*) Tent site €6.35, plus €1.25 per person. The site is in Knockcroghery beside Lough Ree about 10km south-east of Roscommon on the N61 to Athlone; a sign points east just near the train station and it's a couple of kilometres up the road. It's a basic site in a nice location on the lake's edge beside the ruins of Gailey Castle. Pitch and putt, and boat hire are available.

Gleeson's Guesthouse (☎ *26954, fax 27425, The Square*) Rooms €38.10-44.45 per person. This listed 19th-century house on the Square has been tastefully restored.

Regan's Guesthouse (☎ *25339, The Square*) Rooms €31.75 per person. Next door to Gleeson's with 10 rooms, this place is slightly cheaper but not nearly as nice.

O'Gara's Royal Hotel (☎ *26317, fax 26225, Castle St*) Singles/doubles with bathroom €50.80/81.30. A busy family-run hotel, it has a lively local bar and disco attached.

Abbey Hotel (☎ *26250, fax 26021, Galway Rd*) Singles/doubles from €76.20/127. This 18th-century manor at the start of the Galway road is the poshest place in town. It can be noisy at the weekend when weddings or discos go on in the function room.

Places to Eat

Gleeson's Restaurant (*see Places to Stay*) Irish breakfast €6.30, lunch from €7. Open 8am-6pm daily. Located in the guesthouse of the same name, Gleeson's serves a full Irish breakfast and lunch specials.

China Palace (☎ *26337, Main St*) Mains €9-12.70. Open 5pm-12.30am Mon-Sat, also 12.30pm-2pm Thur & Fri. Reasonable Chinese fare is served at this place overlooking Main St.

The Manse (*at Gleeson's Guesthouse; see Places to Stay*) Mains €12.70-19. This restaurant is highly recommended by the locals.

O'Gara's Royal Hotel (*see Places to Stay*) Mains €6.35 Open noon-3pm & 6pm-9pm daily. Filling carvery lunches and evening bar snacks are available in the bar.

Knights (☎*/fax 25620, Stone Court, The Square*) Mains €14-23, early-bird 3-course dinner (6pm-7.30pm) €19.05. Try the imaginative meat-oriented menu in the building that originally housed the old jail. Knights has a modern, warm decor and probably the best food in town.

Entertainment

Down the Hatch (☎ *27100, Church St*) This is a small lively pub for people of all ages.

Central Bar (☎ *26219, The Square*) A good mixed-age pub, full of locals. It gets busy at the weekend.

JJ Harlow's (☎ *27505, The Square*) Converted from a family drapery, this old-style bar with snugs attracts a young crowd at the weekend.

Batty O'Brien's (☎ *61122, Knockcroghery*) At the best bar around, you can chat to local character Batty about his world travels. This charming, hippyish pub with pool tables and music most nights is on the main Athlone road, 11km from Roscommon.

Getting There & Around

Bus Éireann (☎ 071-60066) express buses between Westport (2¼ hours) and Dublin (three hours) stop in Roscommon three times daily (once on Sunday). Buses stop in front of Regan's Guesthouse on the Square. Roscommon is also served by train three times daily (four on Friday) on the line from Dublin (two hours) to Westport (1½ hours). The station is in Abbeytown, just west of the town centre, near the Galway road.

You can order a taxi on ☎ 26096.

WESTERN ROSCOMMON

The village of Ballintober (not to be confused with Ballintubber, County Mayo), about 15km north-west of Roscommon off the N60, is dominated by the 14th-century **Ballintober Castle**, built in the early 14th century and once home to the fierce O'Conors of Connaught. Cromwellian forces took the castle in 1652, but it was later restored to the O'Conors – only to be lost again after the defeat of the Catholics at the Battle of the Boyne, 1690. The large central courtyard has polygonal towers at each corner, and the whole edifice is a good example of an early Irish castle.

To the north-west past Castlerea on the N60 is **Clonalis House** (☎ 0907-20014, Castlerea; adult/concession €5.10/2.55; open 11am-5pm Mon-Sat June-mid-Sept). Built in 1878, the house is rather cold and lacks atmosphere, but it does have the harp of Turlough O'Carolan (1630–1738), the great blind harpist and composer (see Turlough O'Carolan Country under Around Carrick-on-Shannon later in this chapter) as well as a copy of the last Brehon Law judgement, which was handed down in 1580.

County Leitrim

Leitrim (Liatroim) stretches 80km from the border with Longford to Donegal Bay in the north-west, with a short coastline of about 5km around Tulloghan. Lough Allen splits the county almost in two. With some of the worst soil fertility in the country, Leitrim was severely underpopulated for much of the last century and allegedly has more pubs per capita than anywhere else in the country! Southern Leitrim's main interest is its lush scenery of lakes and drumlins and a walking or cycling tour of the area would be enjoyable, particularly if you like less tourist-populated areas.

CARRICK-ON-SHANNON
☎ 078 • pop 1868

Carrick-on-Shannon (known simply as Carrick, or in Irish as Cora Droma Rúisc) straddles the border with Roscommon and is the main town in the county, marking the upper limit of navigation on the River Shannon. It is beautifully positioned over the river, and is a major centre for boating. In 1994 the last stretch of the **Shannon-Erne Waterway** was completed with the reopening of the Ballyconnell-Ballinamore Canal, completing 382km of navigable canals and loughs that begin in Limerick and end in Belleek on Upper Lough Erne. The canal has literally put Carrick-on-Shannon on the tourist map, and is one of the main reasons for visiting the town (see Shannon-Erne Waterway later in this section). Aquatic pursuits aside, Carrick is a thriving provincial town with some fine

examples of early-19th-century architecture to be seen in the town centre. Among them, **Hatley Manor**, home of the St George family, the **Old Courthouse**, now seat of the County Council, whose underground tunnel led convicts from the dock to the now demolished jail, and the newly refurbished **Market Yard** are all on St George's Terrace – close to the Clock Tower.

Information
The tourist office (☎ 20170, fax 20089), in the Old Barrel Store at the Marina beside the Landmark Hotel, opens 9am to 8pm daily (till 5pm Saturday and Sunday), June to September, and 9am to 6pm weekdays, March to May. A signposted walking tour (a booklet is available from the tourist office) takes in all the buildings and places of interest in town.

There's an Allied Irish Bank branch at the top of Main St. The post office is on Bridge St opposite Flynn's Corner House bar.

Costello Chapel
At the top of Bridge St, next to Flynn's Corner House, is the sombre little Costello Chapel – reputedly the smallest chapel in Europe. It measures only 5m by 3.6m and was built in 1879 by one distraught Edward Costello after the death of his wife. She is buried on the left side of the chapel under a heavy slab of glass, and her husband was interred on the other side in 1891. The chapel was built on the site of the old courthouse, where 19 men were hanged in the 19th century.

Boating & Fishing
Carrick Craft (☎ 01-278 1666) hires out motorised fishing boats (€50.80/82.55 per half/full day) and two to eight berth cruisers from €381 to €1487 per week. **Moon River** (☎ 21777, The Quay) runs 90-minute cruises on the Shannon at 2.30pm and 4.30pm daily year round (adult/child €9/3.80). The 110-seater boat also doubles up as a floating nightclub of sorts on Saturday night. Contact the tourist office or check the information board on the quay.

The annual **regatta** run by Carrick Rowing Club (☎ 20532) takes place on the first

Sunday in August and draws a big crowd. For information on fishing, contact the **Carrick-on-Shannon Angling Association** (☎ *20489, Gortmor House, Lismakeegan*).

Places to Stay

Camping is free on the Roscommon side of the river bank, though there are no facilities. Tokens for the showers at the nearby Marina can be purchased from the Marina office.

Town Clock Hostel (☎ *20068, Main St*) Dorms €9.50, twin rooms €12.70 per person. Open June-end Sept. This is a basic, small hostel in an old building inside a leafy courtyard at the junction of Main and Bridge Sts.

B&Bs are not in short supply in Carrick. *Aisleigh* (☎/fax *20313, Dublin Rd*) Rooms €24.15 per person. This large modern home, 1km from town, has full facilities including a sauna and fishing tackle hire.

Glencarne Country House (☎/fax *079-67013, Sligo Rd*) Rooms €31.75 per person. The welcoming Mrs Harrington runs this spacious Georgian farmhouse on mature grounds 7km from town on the Boyle road.

Hollywell (☎/fax *21124, e hollywell@ esatbiz.com, Liberty Hill*) Singles/doubles from €44.45/63.50. Hollywell, a beautiful Georgian country house overlooking the river (on the Roscommon side), has four spacious antique-filled rooms and delicious breakfasts. It's undoubtedly the best place to stay in town.

Bush Hotel (☎ *20014, Main St*) Singles/doubles €44.45/95.25. This centrally located, family-run old hotel is a vibrant spot to stay.

Places to Eat

Wheats (☎ *50525, Market Yard*) Snacks €2.50-5. Wheats has healthy home-made breads, salads and wraps to take away.

Coffey's Pastry Case (☎ *20929, Bridge St*) Mains €4.45. On the corner near the bridge is this cheap, self-service coffee shop-cum-bakery that looks like a 1970s TV sitcom set.

The Oarsman Bar and Boathouse Restaurant (☎ *21139, Bridge St*). Mains €6.50-10. Upmarket pub grub and seafood

are offered at this newly renovated cavernous place.

Pyramids (☎ *20333, Main St*) Mains €9.50-14. Open from 12.30pm-2.30pm & 5.30pm-11.30pm Wed-Mon. This cosy place used to be an Egyptian restaurant – hence its name – but now serves top-notch Lebanese cuisine with a good vegetarian selection.

Cryan's Pub (☎ *20409, Bridge St*) Mains €11.50-15.50. An old-fashioned kitsch restaurant with tasselled lamps and banquettes, Cryan's serves all things traditional from bacon and cabbage to sirloin steak and the schoolboys' favourite – sherry trifle.

Entertainment

The Anchorage Bar (☎ *21355, Bridge St*) This is a small, friendly bar with jukebox, toasties and an imposing TV.

Flynn's Corner House (*cnr Main & Bridge Sts*) Flynn's is a great, old-school traditional pub with a good drop of Guinness and live music on Friday night. Savour these authentic pubs before they're modernised.

Moon River (☎ *21777, The Quay*) Admission €9. Departs 10pm Sat. Dancers with sea legs can try this floating nightclub on a 110-seater cruiser (see Boating & Fishing earlier in the section).

Gaiety Cinema (☎ *21869, Bridge St*) Adult/child €4.45/3.80. 8.30pm daily. This no-frills one-screen cinema runs current releases and hosts regular film society screenings and occasional festivals. Ring for details.

Getting There & Away

The bus stop is outside Coffey's Pastry Case on the corner near the bridge and tourist office. The Bus Éireann (☎ *071-60066*) main express bus between Dublin (€11.45, 2¾ hours) and Sligo (€8.90, one hour) stops there four times daily in each direction. There are also buses to Boyle, Longford and Athlone.

The train station (☎ 20036) is a 15-minute walk from the bridge on the Roscommon side of the river. Turn right over the bridge, then left at the service station. Carrick has three trains daily to Dublin (three hours) and Sligo (50 minutes), with an additional one on Friday.

Getting Around

You can hire bicycles from Geraghty's (☎ 21316) on Main St for €10.15/31.75 per day/week; it also rents out fishing rods and tackle. The *Visitors' Guidebook* from the tourist office includes cycling tours.

AROUND CARRICK-ON-SHANNON

The countryside around Carrick, with its quiet lanes and gently undulating landscape, is tailor-made for cycling.

Turlough O'Carolan Country

There are three places to visit in the area that are connected with the famous blind poet, composer and harpist Turlough O'Carolan (1670–1738). He spent most of his time in Mohill, where his patron, Mrs MacDermott-Roe, resided, and a sculpture on the main street of the town commemorates the association. To reach Mohill from Carrick-on-Shannon, follow the N4 to Dublin then turn east onto the R201 shortly after passing Drumsna.

O'Carolan is buried in Kilronan church, which preserves a 12th-century doorway, just over the border in County Roscommon. To reach the church, take the R280 north from Carrick-on-Shannon and at the village of Leitrim turn west on the R284 to Keadue (Keadew on some maps). In Keadue turn west on the R284 to Sligo.

Keadue was a coal-mining town at the foot of the Arigna Mountains until the 1980s and is now a spruced-up 'tidy-town competition' winner. It also has strong associations with the musician and hosts the annual O'Carolan Harp Festival (☎ 078-47204) of traditional music during the last week of July and first week of August.

Drumshanbo

☎ 078 • pop 634

Drumshanbo (Droim Seanbhó), about 9km north of Carrick-on-Shannon on the southern shores of Lough Allen, used to be an iron-smelting town but now is mainly a centre for coarse fishing. Unusually, a number of young people from the hinterland take part in music-related courses there, so this small town has a thriving music scene, including a local samba band! The renowned **Joe Mooney Summer School** *(☎ 41213)* of traditional music takes place annually during the last week of July. There's an interesting audiovisual display on the history and culture of the locality, and a nonfunctioning replica of an ancient Irish sweathouse, at the **Sliabh an Iarainn Visitors Centre** *(☎ 41522, Main St; adult/child €1.25/0.65; open 10am-6pm Mon-Sat, 2pm-6pm Sun Apr-Oct)*.

Drumshanbo Holiday Centre *(☎ 41013, fax 41237, 2 Carrick Rd)* Singles/doubles €19.05/38.10. Mrs Mooney at the southern end of town offers B&B and provides local tourist information.

Conway's *(☎ 41020, The Square)* A genuine old pub with a newspaper counter, Conway's is well worth dropping into for a pint of plain by the Aga stove.

SHANNON-ERNE WATERWAY

The Shannon-Erne Waterway stretches from the River Shannon beside the village of Leitrim, 4km north of Carrick-on-Shannon, through north-western County Cavan to the southern shore of Upper Lough Erne, just over the Northern Ireland border in County Fermanagh.

The 382km-long waterway is a series of rivers and lakes linked by canals. The original canal, which was called the Ballyconnell-Ballinamore Canal, was completed in 1860, but soon fell into disuse with the coming of the railway. The canal was reopened in 1994 and, with its 34 stone bridges and 16 locks, is now busy with boats and pleasure cruisers. The waterway is jointly operated by Dúchas in the Republic and the Department of Agriculture in Northern Ireland.

Before you sail, rental companies give full instructions on how to manoeuvre a boat through the different locks. Before travelling, make sure you have a chart of the waterway with depths and locations of locks; both of the following companies provide this or it is available in bookshops for €9. Rental prices vary according to season.

Carrick Craft *(☎ 078-20236, fax 21336, The Marina, Carrick-on-Shannon)* You can hire 2/4/6/8-berth boats from €266/368/584/698 for three nights or €380/561/1038/1268 for one week, respectively.

Emerald Star *(☎ 078-20234,* e *info@emerald-star.com, The Marina, Carrick-on-Shannon)* 4/6/10-berth boats from €520/863/1752 per week. The 10-berth boat is large and very comfortable.

LEITRIM WAY

The Leitrim Way begins in Drumshanbo and ends in Manorhamilton, a distance of 48km. For more detailed information get a copy of *Way-Marked Trails of Ireland* by Michael Fewer.

County Longford

The history of County Longford (An Longfort) dates back to prehistoric times. St Patrick visited here and for centuries it was the centre of power of the O'Farrell family, who arrived in the 11th century. During the 1798 Rising, the British army under Lord Cornwallis defeated a combined Irish and French army at Ballinamuck, 16km north of Longford. The Potato Famine of the 1840s and 1850s saw massive emigration; many Longford migrants went to Argentina, where one of their descendants, Edel Miro O'Farrell, became president in 1914.

Longford, the county town, is solidly agrarian and prosperous but of little interest to the tourist; many people pass through travelling between Dublin and Mayo or Sligo. Beware of the one-way traffic system through town, which always appears to be congested. **Carrigglas Manor** *(☎ 043-45165; 40-minute house tour €8.90/3.80, museum & garden only €3.80/1.25; open 1.30pm-5pm Mon, Thur & Fri June-Sept; to 6pm Aug)*, 5km north-east, has been the home of the Lefroy family since 1810. You can tour the castellated Gothic manor and visit a Victorian costume and lace museum in the Palladian yard buildings, designed by James Gandon, or stroll in the peaceful 18th-century pleasure gardens.

The 150km **Royal Canal** from Dublin passes through the county to meet the River Shannon near Clondra (or Cloondara) west of Longford. The canal's towpath provides an interesting walking route through the county. The annual **Abbeyshrule Airshow**, during the first weekend in August in Abbeyshrule, 18km south of Longford on the R393, attracts thousands of visitors for its displays of craft, aerobatics and parachuting. For details contact Ted McGoey (☎ 044-57424).

The main attraction for most visitors to County Longford, however, is the fishing around Lough Ree and Lanesborough.

Discreetly hidden 15km south-west of Longford on a broad stretch of bogland is **Corlea Trackway Visitor Centre** *(☎ 043-22386, fax 22442, Keenagh; adult/child €3.20/1.25; open 10am-6pm daily Apr-Sept)*. It's well worth an afternoon's excursion. Here, 1km of Europe's widest timber track way, dating from 148 BC, was discovered in Corlea bog in 1984. Now 18m of the track are on view and an interesting 45-minute tour details the bog's unique flora and fauna as well as the track's discovery and preservation.

County Westmeath

Characterised by lakes and rich pasture land, Westmeath (An Iarmhí) is noted more for its beef than its scenic splendour or historic sites. An exception to the generally monotonous landscape is the area north of Athlone known as Goldsmith country, while the other genuinely interesting places in Westmeath are mostly in the vicinity of Mullingar.

MULLINGAR
☎ 044 • pop 12,492

Mullingar (An Muileann gCearr) is a prosperous market town – with a well used commuter train service each morning and evening to and from Dublin – and much of the surrounding area is rich countryside. There are some fine fishing loughs in the vicinity and a preserved bog that delights naturalists. The town itself is one of the few places outside Dublin that James Joyce visited.

The Royal Canal, linking Dublin with the River Shannon via Mullingar, was con-

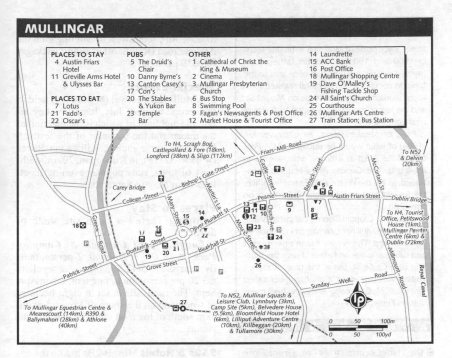

MULLINGAR

PLACES TO STAY	PUBS	OTHER	14 Laundrette
4 Austin Friars Hotel	5 The Druid's Chair	1 Cathedral of Christ the King & Museum	15 ACC Bank
11 Greville Arms Hotel & Ulysses Bar	10 Danny Byrne's	2 Cinema	16 Post Office
	13 Canton Casey's	3 Mullingar Presbyterian Church	18 Mullingar Shopping Centre
PLACES TO EAT	17 Con's	6 Bus Stop	19 Dave O'Malley's Fishing Tackle Shop
7 Lotus	20 The Stables & Yukon Bar	8 Swimming Pool	24 All Saint's Church
21 Fado's	23 Temple Bar	9 Fagan's Newsagents & Post Office	25 Courthouse
22 Oscar's		12 Market House & Tourist Office	26 Mullingar Arts Centre
			27 Train Station; Bus Station

structed in the 1790s as a rival to the Grand Canal. It never managed to compete successfully and, by the 1880s, passenger business had ceased. There was a slight revival during WWII with a turf trade to Dublin, but it finally closed in 1955. Restoration work west of Mullingar is almost complete, with walkways and cycle trails now open; information on these is available from the tourist office.

Information
Midlands-East Tourism (☎ 48650) is in Market House on the corner of Mount and Pearse Sts. It opens 9am to 6pm weekdays, and 10am to 1pm and 2pm to 6pm on Saturday, June to September; and 9.30am to 1pm and 2pm to 5.30pm weekdays the rest of the year.

There's a number of banks on the main street, which changes name five times, including an ACC Bank branch at the start of Oliver Plunkett St. The post office is to the west on Dominick St. There's a laundrette on Oliver Plunkett St, near the roundabout.

Cathedral & Ecclesiastical Museum
The Cathedral of Christ the King was built just before WWII and has large mosaics of St Anne and St Patrick by the Russian artist Boris Anrep. There's a small museum of liturgical objects over the sacristy, entered from the side of the church, which contains vestments worn by St Oliver Plunkett (see the boxed text 'A Moving Head' in the Counties Meath & Louth chapter).

Guided tours (adult/child €1.25/0.65) run between 3pm and 4pm on Wednesday, Saturday and Sunday in July and August. Otherwise call at the church house to the right of the cathedral inside the gates or phone ☎ 48338.

Mullingar Bronze & Pewter Visitors Centre
Mullingar is known for its pewterware, and you can watch artisans turning the silvery-grey metal into cups, bowls and *objets d'art*

The Joyce Connection

James Joyce came to Mullingar in his late teens in 1900 and 1901 to visit his father, John Joyce, a civil servant who had been sent to the town to compile a new electoral register. John Joyce worked in the courthouse on Mount St, and the Joyces stayed at Levington Park House near Lough Owel.

Parts of *Stephen Hero*, an early version (1904) of what would be published as *A Portrait of the Artist as a Young Man*, are set in Mullingar. The Greville Arms Hotel is mentioned, as are the *Westmeath Examiner* office, the Royal Canal and the Columb Barracks on Green Rd.

In *Ulysses*, Leopold Bloom's daughter, Millie, is working in Mullingar, employed in a photographer's shop. This is now Fagan's newsagent and sub-post office on Pearse St near the junction with Castle St, but at the time of Joyce's visits it was owned by a photographer called Phil Shaw. Mullingar also gets a few brief mentions in *Finnegans Wake*.

at the visitor centre (☎ *44948, Great Down, The Downs; shop & showroom open 9.30am-6pm Mon-Fri, 10.30am-5.30pm Sat year round)*. Guided tours are available from 9.30am to 4pm on weekdays (the last tour on Friday is at 12.30pm). The attached Genesis Gift Gallery sells a wide range of crystal, pottery and textile pieces. The centre is about 6km south-east of Mullingar on the Dublin road (N4).

Activities

The **Mullingar Squash and Leisure Club** (☎ *40949, Mullingar Business Park, Lynn Rd)*, offers squash (€7.60 per hour), a sauna and snooker. You can swim at the local **swimming pool** (☎ *40262, off Austin Friars St; adult/child €3.20/1.25)*. **Lilliput Adventure Centre** (☎ *26789, Lilliput House, Lough Ennell)*, 10km south of Mullingar on the N52, offers courses in outdoor sports such as **kayaking, gorge walking** and **abseiling**. A day's mixed-activity package including a night's dormer accommodation costs €34.90.

Mullingar Equestrian Centre (☎ *48331, Athlone Rd)*, south-west of Mullingar on the Athlone road (R390), offers **riding** packages for €19 per hour.

Special Events

The Mullingar Festival (☎ 44044) is held in the second week of July. It's a low-key affair, the highlight of which is the election of the queen and the bachelor of the festival. For some horse racing, Kilbeggan Races (☎ 0506-32176), in Kilbeggan, 20km south-west of town, runs popular evening meetings from May to September.

Places to Stay

Camping There's a camp site south of town.

Lough Ennell Caravan & Camping Park (☎ *48101, Tudenham)*, 2-person/family tent €10.15/12.70, hikers & cyclists €3.20 per person including tent. Open Apr-Sept. The camp site is set in eight hectares of woodland on the shore of Lough Ennell, 5km south of town on the N52 road to Tullamore.

B&Bs & Hotels Most B&Bs are on the approach roads from Dublin and Sligo. It's worth checking out one of the many Georgian houses for an atmospheric slumber.

Petitswood House (☎ *48397, Dublin Rd)* Singles/doubles €25.40/50.80. Mrs Farrell's house, 1km from town, has three comfortable rooms with bathroom and TV.

Lynnbury (☎ *48432, Tullamore Rd)* Rooms €25.40 per person. This 200-year-old Georgian residence with an original tennis court and games room is beautifully located in mature grounds overlooking Lough Ennell, 3km south of town.

Mearescourt (☎ *55112, Rathconrath)* Singles/doubles €50.80/76.20. Four simple, spacious rooms are available in this 18th-century home. Log fires, local history, 80 hectares of parkland and delicious breakfasts will make your stay memorable. Take the R392 to the village of Rathconrath and follow the signs; it's 14km from Mullingar.

Greville Arms Hotel (☎ *48563, fax 48052, Pearse St)* Singles/doubles €63.50/

114.30. This is a busy, old-world country hotel with an excessively patterned interior.

Austin Friars Hotel (☎ 45777, fax 45880, Austin Friars St) Rooms €50.80 per person. This modern, unusually shaped elliptical hotel with a contemporary, colourful decor is in the town centre.

Bloomfield House Hotel (☎ 40894, fax 43767, Tullamore Rd) Singles/doubles €90/140. Nicely located near Lough Ennell, 6km from town, is this rambling, old-fashioned hotel with a swimming pool and leisure centre.

Places to Eat

Con's (☎ 40925, 24 Dominick St) Hot snacks €6.65, roasts €7.55. If you're hungry, try the superb curvery lunches or hearty sandwiches in this busy, newly renovated pub.

Lotus (☎ 32972, Austin Friars St) Mains €11.50-16.50. Open 5.30pm-12.30am daily. This swanky stone-clad Chinese restaurant serves above-average food.

Fado's (☎ 40280, 9 Dominick St) Steaks €15-22, fish dishes €14-19. Open 6pm-10pm daily. Steaks and home-made desserts are the specialities in this new, brightly decorated bistro.

Oscar's (☎ 44909, 21 Oliver Plunkett St) Pasta & pizza €10-11, seafood €12.70. Open 6pm-9.30pm daily. Reputedly the best restaurant in town, this colourful eatery with an Italian propensity offers unusual pizza toppings like Clonakilty black pudding or chilli mango.

Entertainment

The Stables (☎ 40251, 11 Dominick St) A small, popular venue, the Stables hosts DJs on Friday nights and good live music on Saturdays. **The Yukon Bar**, at the front of the Stables, is a peculiar, grungy place popular with young people; apparently the fortune teller, there from 4.30pm to closing on weekdays, is a real draw.

Temple Bar (☎ 48381, 3 Mount St) Named after Dublin's iniquitous drinking quarter, this no-frills bar has traditional and blues sessions on Monday, Wednesday and Sunday and serves late most nights.

Danny Byrne's (☎ 43792, 27 Pearse St)

Newly renovated, this cavernous pub with wooden floors and plush carpet pub has live music at the weekend.

The Druid's Chair (☎ 48526, 9 Pearse St) With a modern Celtic-influenced interior, this is the latest big pub to attract the young with a large disposable income.

Canton Casey's (☎ 42758, Pearse St) Canton Casey's is a museum-quality old-style pub with outdoor benches on Market House's courtyard.

Mullingar Arts Centre (☎ 47777, Lower Mount St, ℮ mgarartscentre@eircom.net) This centre runs an impressive regular program of music, drama and art exhibitions. Ring for details.

Getting There & Away

Bus Éireann (☎ 01-836 6111) runs one daily bus from Galway (three hours) to Dundalk (2¼ hours); five daily (six on Sunday) from Dublin (1½ hours) to Ballina (2¾ hours); three daily to Sligo (2½ hours) coming from Dublin; and four a day Monday to Saturday from Dublin to Longford (one hour). All stop at Mullingar, and they arrive and depart from the train station.

Trains stop at Mullingar (☎ 48274) three or four-times daily in each direction on the line from Dublin (one hour) to Sligo (two hours).

AROUND MULLINGAR
Belvedere House & Gardens

The aptly titled Belvedere ('beautiful view') overlooks Lough Ennell (☎ 044-49060, Mullingar; adult/concession €5/3.20; open 9.30am-7pm daily May-Aug; 10.30am-6pm daily Sept-Oct; 10.30am-4pm daily Nov-Apr). It was the scene of a tale that finds its way into Joyce's Ulysses. Belvedere House was built around 1740 for the recently remarried Lord Belfield, 1st earl of Belvedere, who soon accused his young wife of adultery with his younger brother Arthur and imprisoned her here. She remained under house arrest for 31 years. When the earl's death finally released her, she was dressed in the fashion of three decades earlier. She died still protesting her innocence. Belvedere also sued his brother and had him jailed in London for the rest of his life.

CENTRAL NORTH

Not far from the house, the **Jealous Wall** was deliberately built by the cantankerous Lord Belfield as a ready-made 'ruin' to block a view of the neighbouring house of a second brother, George, with whom he also fell out.

It's worth wandering around the modestly sized house, pleasure gardens and visitor centre with its dramatised film on Belfield's life. An interesting audiovisual display in the recently restored house depicts life in an 18th-century household, and an interactive display details the work of the house's famous architect, Richard Cassels.

Belvedere House is 5.5km south of Mullingar on the N52 road to Tullamore, just before Lough Ennell Caravan and Camping Park.

Locke's Distillery

Some 20km south-west of Mullingar on the N52 road to Tullamore past Belvedere House, Locke's Distillery, in the small town of Kilbeggan, still has a working mill wheel (☎ *0506-32134, Kilbeggan; adult/concession €4.15/2.85; open 9am-6pm daily Apr-Oct; 10am-4pm daily Nov-Mar)*. There is a 35-minute tour of the distillery. Lunch and snacks are served at the adjoining coffee shop, whiskey at the bar.

Crookedwood & Around

Crookedwood, about 5km north-east of Mullingar off the R394, is a small village on the shores of Lough Derravaragh. The lough is associated with the tragic legend of the children of Lir, who were transformed into swans by a jealous stepmother. Two ecclesiastical sites near Crookedwood are worth a visit. Three kilometres to the west is the **Multyfarnham Franciscan friary**. In the present church, the remains of a 15th-century church still stand, and there are outdoor Stations of the Cross set beside a stream.

East of Crookedwood, a small road leads 2km to the ruins of **St Munna's Church**. It dates from the 15th century, replacing a 7th-century church founded by St Munna. This fortified church has a lovely location. Keys to the church are available from the nearby bungalow.

Scragh Bog

Scragh Bog is a nature reserve and home to a rare wintergreen, *Pyrola rotundifolia*, which flowers around willow and beech trees in midsummer. Other, less rare plants include members of the sedge family, orchids and sphagnum species, and there is a profusion of insects. This small bog is 7km north-west of Mullingar near Lough Owel on the N4 road to Longford. The Wildlife Service does not recommend unaccompanied visits, and waterproof boots are a necessity.

Tullynally Castle Gardens

The seat of the Pakenham family and the earldom of Longford is an impressive Gothic revival castle (☎ *044-61159, Castlepollard; adult/concession €5.10/2.55; gardens open 2pm-6pm daily mid-May-Sept)*. It is still home to the Pakenham family. At the time of writing, the family doesn't plan to open the castle to visitors in 2002, but you can still roam the 12 hectares of gardens and parkland including a Chinese and a Tibetan garden and wonderful stretch of yews. To get there, take the N4 north-west out of Mullingar then follow the R394 north-east to Castlepollard. From there the castle and gardens are signposted 2km to the north-west.

Fishing

Trout fishing is popular in the loughs around Mullingar, including Lough Owel, Lough Derravaragh, Lough Glore, White Lake, Lough Lene, Lough Sheelin, Mt Dalton Lake, Pallas Lake (near Tullamore) and Lough Ennell – where in 1894 an 11.9kg trout was landed, still the largest trout ever caught in Ireland. The fishing season runs from 1 March or 1 May (depending on the lake) to 12 October, and all the lakes except Lough Lene are controlled by the Shannon Regional Fisheries Board (☎ 044-48769).

For further information contact **Midlands-East Tourism** (☎ *044-48650)* or the helpful **Dave O'Malley's** (☎ *044-48300, 33 Dominick St)*, both in Mullingar. O'Malley's can provide boats on Lough Owel or Lough Ennell, plus ghillies and permits. For Lough Derravaragh contact Mr Newman (☎ 044-71206); for Lough Owel, Mrs Doolan

Sunset on Mt Mweelrea in the Doolough Valley, County Mayo

Croagh Patrick's memorial

It's easy to see why WB Yeats found inspiration for much of his poetry in County Sligo.

Secluded cottage, County Sligo

Pilgrims climb Croagh Patrick on Reek Sunday as an act of penance

RICHARD CUMMINS

Athlone's cathedral, Westmeath

EOIN CLARKE

The Iron-Age, spiral-inscribed Téne Stone, County Roscommon

GARETH McCORMACK

Time for a sauna? A 19th-century sweathouse on the Leitrim Way

EOIN CLARKE

Jimmy Feeney asks himself why he didn't just buy roof tiles, County Cavan.

(☎ 044-42085); for Lough Sheelin, Mr Reilly (☎ 043-81124); and for Lough Ennell, Mrs Hope (☎ 044-40807) or Mr Roache (☎ 044-40314).

Swimming

Swimming is possible in Loughs Lene, Ennell and Owel, but Derravaragh is very deep and has no shallows.

FORE VALLEY

Just outside the small village of Fore, in the north-east of the county near the shores of Lough Lene, are a group of early-Christian sites that date back to 630, when St Fechin founded a monastery here. There are no visible remains of this early settlement, but there are three later buildings still standing in the valley plain that are closely associated with a legend that 'seven wonders' occurred here. The Fore Valley is a great area to explore by bicycle or on foot.

The Seven Wonders of Fore

The oldest of the three buildings is **St Fechin's Church**, which may well mark the site of the original monastery. The chancel and baptismal font inside are early 13th century, and over the unusually large entrance there is a huge lintel stone carved with a Greek cross. It was supposed to have been put into place through the divine power of St Fechin's prayers and, as such, counts as one of the seven wonders.

A path runs up from the church to the attractive little **Anchorite cell**, which dates back to the 15th century and is another of the seven wonders. The Seven Wonders pub in the village holds the key to the hermit's cell.

Down on the plain, on the other side of the road, there are extensive remains of a 13th-century **Benedictine priory**, built on what was once bog (another wonder). In the next century it was turned into a fortification, hence the castle-like square towers, each of which formed a separate residence, and loophole windows. The western tower is in a dangerous state – keep clear. Two other wonders are a mill without a race and water that flows uphill. The mill site is marked, and legend has it that St Fechin caused water to flow uphill, towards the mill, by throwing his crozier against a rock near Lough Lene, about 1.5km away.

The last two wonders are water that will not boil and a tree with only three branches that will not burn. Both are associated with St Fechin's well, which can be seen on the way to the priory from the road.

To get to the Fore Valley from Mullingar take the N4 north-west out of town and then follow the R394 road north-east to Castlepollard. From there the road to Fore is signposted.

ATHLONE

☎ 0902 • pop 15,544

The county town of Athlone (Baile Átha Luain) has a historical importance, due mainly to its strategic position midway on the River Shannon. An attractive market town, it suffered for many years from heavy traffic congestion on its bridge, but has improved drastically since a much-needed bypass was built in the late 1990s. Though predominantly a garrison town, Athlone is fast gaining a reputation as the culinary hub of the midlands with a plethora of reputable eateries emerging in its so called 'Left Bank' quarter, behind the castle. Many of its tourist attractions are based in the surrounding hinterland, but the town is still quite a nice place to spend an afternoon. A visit to the castle is worth considering, and there are fishing and boat trips along the river to Lough Ree or to the Clonmacnoise monastic site in County Offaly.

Orientation & Information

Athlone is in the far south-west of County Westmeath on the border with Roscommon. It's on the main Dublin–Galway road (N6), and the River Shannon flows northwards through town into Lough Ree. The landmarks here are Athlone Castle and Sts Peter and Paul Cathedral, prominently located on the western bank of the river by the Town Bridge and overlooking Market Square. The castle houses the tourist office, a museum and a heritage centre.

The tourist office (☎ 94630) in the castle grounds opens 9.30am to 5.30pm Monday to Saturday, March to October. The local chamber of commerce has a good information office (☎ 73173) with brochures and pamphlets. Open 9am to 5pm year round, it's at the Jolly Mariner Marina in Coosan, north of the centre on the eastern bank of the Shannon beyond the railway bridge.

The Bank of Ireland is at the start of Northgate St, just up from Custume Place. The post office is on Barrack St beside the cathedral.

Athlone Castle & Museum

The Normans probably had an encampment by the ford over the river before they built a castle here in 1210. In 1690 the castle held out for James II, but the following year the bridge came under Protestant attack again, and this time the Jacobite city fell to the troops under William of Orange's Dutch commander, Ginkel. Major alterations to the castle took place between the 17th and 19th centuries, and the ramp that forms the present entrance is a relatively recent addition. The oldest surviving part is the central keep, where the museum is now housed.

Athlone Museum has two floors: upstairs is the folk collection, and downstairs there are artefacts from prehistoric times *(☎ 92912; adult/concession/child/family €4.45/2.55/1.25/10.15; open 10am-4.30pm Mon-Sat & noon-4.30pm Sun May-Sept).* There's also an old gramophone that belonged to John McCormack (1884–1945), a native of Athlone and one of the greatest tenors of all time. The admission price includes a visit to the **heritage centre**, which has an audiovisual presentation on the town's history and flora and fauna.

Fishing

Just below the Church St end of Town Bridge on the eastern bank of the river opposite the castle, the **Strand Tackle Shop** *(☎ 79277, The Strand)* is the place to go for information, boats and rods. A day's hire of a boat and guide (mostly for pike fishing) will cost around €63.50, depending on where you go. Permits are required for certain areas and are available at the shop.

River Cruises

Several companies offer cruises from Athlone. Every day of the week there are cruises north to Lough Ree (€7.60/5.10). The boats usually depart from The Strand at 2.30pm and 4.30pm; a timetable is available from the tourist office.

MV Ross *(☎ 72892, fax 74386, ⓔ acl@ wmeathtc.iol.ie, Jolly Mariner Marina, Coosan)* Adult/concession/family €7.60/ 4.45/21.60. You can make a group booking or join an existing group on a 90-minute cruise on Lough Ree; ring for details.

Viking Tours (☎ 73383, fax 73392, ⓔ vikingtours@ireland.com, 7 St Mary's Place) Adult/concession & child €12.70/ 7.60. Between July and September, Viking Tours offers a cruise on its Viking ship south to Clonmacnoise (90 minutes), an important early monastic site in County Offaly. It departs from The Strand at 10am several days a week, depending on numbers; ring for a schedule.

Places to Stay

Lough Ree Lodge (☎ 76738, fax 76477, Dublin Rd) Bed in 4-bed dorm €14 per person, singles/doubles €20.30/40.65. Open May-Sept. The closest thing to a hostel in town, the Lough Ree Lodge normally houses students during term-time. It has a simple, clean, basic decor, a large kitchen and a TV/Internet lounge, and also runs a shuttle bus service into town (1km).

Bastion B&B (☎ 94954, fax 93648, ⓔ bastion@iol.ie, 4-6 Bastion St) Singles/doubles €25.40/48.25. A great place to stay in town, over a funky surf and craft shop run by the same brothers, is this friendly, kooky house full of plants, paintings and curios. It has five simple rooms, a games lounge and a famous buffet breakfast.

Shannonside (☎/fax 94773, ⓔ shannon side@eircom.net, West Lodge Rd) Singles/ doubles €33.65/50.80. This is a newly renovated, comfortable house with 10 rooms about 1km from the town centre, with facilities for anglers.

Places to Eat

Some of Athlone's best eateries are located

in the small bohemian area behind the castle, around Bastion St.

A Slice of Life *(☎ 93970, Bastion St)* Mains €4.10. Open 8.30am-6pm Mon-Sat. This small delicatessen and cafe serves really tasty, filling and cheap hot specials or pizza slices and sandwiches.

Ship of Fools *(☎ 98664, 6-8 Bastion St)* Lunch €3-6, dinner €10.50-15. Open for lunch Tues-Sat, dinner Thur-Sun. This cosy, laid-back room with wooden floors and nautical paraphernalia offers you *panini* and hot wraps at lunch and seafood by night.

Saagar *(☎ 70011, Lloyd's Lane)* Mains €6.50-9.50. Open 5.30pm-11pm daily. Head here for excellent Indian food with a good vegetarian selection.

Tribeca *(☎ 98805, 1 Abbey Lane)* Mains €8.50-12.50. Open 5pm-11pm daily. Just off Bastion St in a crooked old stone building, Tribeca is a genuine Italian-American restaurant with great pizza and pasta.

The Olive Grove *(☎ 76946, fax 71248, Bridge St, Custume Place)* Mains €13-18. Open for lunch & dinner Tues-Sun. This colourful, informal place by the river serves loosely Mediterranean cuisine such as trout with raita and polenta or chicken risotto.

The Left Bank Bistro *(☎ 94446, fax 95409, Fry Place)* Mains €9-19. Open 10.30am-9.30pm Mon-Sat May-Sept, 10.30am-6pm Mon-Wed & 10.30am-9.30pm Thur-Sat Oct-Apr. The stylish Left Bank is an airy, relaxed bistro at the bottom end of Bastion St and probably the town's best restaurant. It's extremely popular with businesspeople at lunchtime. Try half a dozen oysters with a glass of fine wine or the halibut and couscous.

Entertainment

Sean's Bar *(☎ 92358, Main St)* Sean's is something of a legend and, dating from 1600, claims to be Ireland's oldest pub. Though they've scrapped the old bus seats, the interior is suitably down-at-heel with log fires, uneven floors and a rickety piano. You can catch live music most nights in summer from the riverside beer garden – miss this pub at your peril.

The Palace Bar *(☎ 92229, Barrack St)* This cavernous bar beside the cathedral has occasional folk music sessions in the upstairs loft venue.

Dean Crowe Theatre *(☎ 92129, fax 98415, e deancrowetheatre@eircom.net, Chapel St)* The sizable, newly refurbished Dean Crowe Theatre runs a broad program of theatrical and musical events year round; ring for details.

Getting There & Away

The bus depot *(☎ 73300)* is beside the train station, and express buses stop there on many routes from the east to the west coast. There are 12 buses daily to Dublin (€9.25, two hours) and Galway (€9.75, 1¼ hours); three daily (one on Sunday) to Westport (€12.25, 2¾ hours) in County Mayo; and one daily (two on Friday) to Mullingar (€7.85, one hour).

From Athlone train station *(☎ 73300)*, there are up to 11 trains daily (seven on Sunday) to Dublin (1½ hours); three daily (four on Friday, two on Sunday) to Westport (2¼ hours); and five to seven daily (four on Sunday) to Galway (1¼ hours). The train station is on the eastern bank on Southern Station Rd. To get there, follow Northgate St up from Custume Place. Its extension, Coosan Point Rd, joins Southern Station Rd near St Vincent's Hospital.

Getting Around

You can order a taxi on ☎ 74400. Bicycles can be hired for €9/38 per day/week from Hardiman's *(☎ 78669)*, opposite the Athlone Shopping Centre on the Dublin road.

AROUND ATHLONE
Lough Ree

Just north of Athlone is Lough Ree, one of the three main lakes formed by the River Shannon. It's celebrated for the early monastic ruins on its many islands and for some excellent trout fishing. The lough is also home to many migratory birds that come here to nest, particularly swans, plover, mallard and curlew. Sailing is popular and the **Lough Ree Yacht Club**, established around 1720, is one of the world's oldest yacht clubs.

MV Goldsmith *(☎ 85163, Ballykeeran)* Adult/child €9/3.80. 2.30pm Sun Apr-Sept.

The 150-seater MV *Goldsmith* tours the lake (2½ hours), numbers permitting, departing from the marina at the Lakeside Hotel and Marina (see under Glasson).

Glasson
☎ 0902

The pretty village of Glasson (Village of the Roses), 8km from Athlone on the N55, is well worth a visit. A stone's throw from Lough Ree and its amenities, it has a couple of very good restaurants, lively pubs and, in what looks like a garden shed, probably the smallest garda station in the country!

You may need a bike or car to get there, though Bus Éireann (☎ 0902-73322) bus No 466 from Athlone to Longford has two services on a Saturday only, stopping outside Grogan's pub.

Places to Stay & Eat Glasson has some good, friendly places to stay.

Glasson Stone Lodge (☎ 76738, fax 76477, Glasson) Singles/doubles from €31.75/50.80. This small, new dormer bungalow in the village centre offers a friendly service and spacious rooms.

Lakeside Hotel and Marina (☎ 85163, fax 85431, @ flynnmo@eircom.net, Ballykeeran) Singles/doubles from €44.45/76.20. Just 1.5km from Glasson on the N55, this is a 10-bedroom, family-run hotel on the lakeshore.

Wineport Restaurant (☎ 85466, fax 85471) Mains €13-22. Open 5pm-10pm Wed-Sat & 12.30pm-9pm Sun. This outstanding restaurant on the lake's edge serves award-winning modern Irish cuisine and carefully chosen wines.

Glasson Village Restaurant (☎ 85001) Mains €13-21. Open 6pm-9.30pm Tues-Sat. People travel for miles to get a table in this restaurant at the northern end of the village. In a beautiful stone cottage that originally housed a garda barracks, it specialises in seafood and local produce. Expensive but worth the treat.

Grogan's (☎ 85158, fax 85685) In the village centre, this pub is the real thing: an authentic old man's bar and lounge with peat fires and a great traditional atmosphere. It also serves good seafood and hearty pub grub all day.

Goldsmith Country

From Athlone, the N55 north-east to County Longford runs close to the eastern side of Lough Ree and through Goldsmith country, so-called because of the area's associations with the 18th-century poet, playwright and novelist Oliver Goldsmith. The gentle aspect of the landscape makes it ideal for cycling. *The Lough Ree Trail: A Signposted Tour* by Gearoid O'Brien, published by Midlands-East Tourism, is available from the tourist offices in Athlone and Mullingar. The tour takes in places associated with Oliver Goldsmith. The whole tour, which goes through Glasson, around the shores of Lough Ree and extends into County Longford, takes a couple of hours.

Places to Stay There are a couple of places to stay in this area.

Lough Ree East Caravan & Camping Park (☎ 78561, fax 77017, @ athlonecamping@eircom.net, Ballykeeran) Tent for 2 adults & car €11.45 plus €3.20/1.25 per adult/child, hikers & cyclists €7.60 per person including tent. A nicely situated small site on the lakeshore, it has basic facilities, including boat hire.

Lake Breeze Lodge (☎/fax 0902-85204, Ballykeeran) Rooms including breakfast €24.15 per person. This friendly, comfortable bungalow with gardens close to the lake is on the road to Glasson.

County Donegal

County Donegal outdoes anywhere else in Ireland for bleakness, dramatic cliffs and hectares of peat bogs – all of which can be great if the weather isn't equally bleak, dramatic and, well, boggy. County Donegal extends farther north than Northern Ireland and is virtually separated from the rest of the Republic by the westwards projection of County Fermanagh.

Roughly one-third of Donegal lies in the Gaeltacht, where Irish is more widely spoken than English. You'll see signs pointing to offices of the Údarás na Gaeltachta, a government agency promoting the social, economic and cultural wellbeing of Irish-speaking areas. In the Gweedore region in particular, it has been instrumental in creating an industrial zone employing hundreds of people.

Tourism in County Donegal is extremely seasonal, and many attractions and most tourist offices open only June (interpreted pretty loosely here) to September – at the latest. Arrive in, say, March and you'll find much of the county shut down.

Although you can get around County Donegal by bus, it's a time-consuming endeavour, especially in winter. This is very much walking and cycling country. When driving, be prepared for switchback roads, suicidal sheep, directions only in Irish, signs hidden behind vegetation, signs pointing the wrong way or no signs at all.

Donegal

☎ 073 • pop 3000

Donegal town, on the River Eske at the top of Donegal Bay, is the principal gateway for the rest of the county. Though there's not a lot to see in the town itself, it's a pleasant, small place where it's well worth spending a little time. The triangular Diamond in the centre, though often choked with traffic in summer and at the weekend, has some good shops selling quality souvenirs and garments.

Highlights

- Wander along the expansive sandy beach at Rossnowlagh
- Explore the spectacular scenery of the small, rugged island of Arranmore
- Walk up Mt Errigal and drink in the views of the Poisoned Glen
- Walk or cycle around Horn Head to watch the bird life and explore the beautiful coastline
- Check out the works of art at Glebe House and Gallery, then visit Tory Island, the inspiration for the artists
- Enjoy the panorama from Grianán of Aileách hilltop fort on Inishowen Peninsula

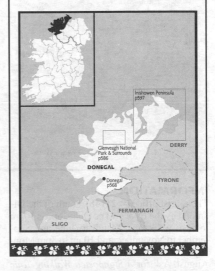

The town's name in Irish, Dún na nGall (Fort of the Foreigner), refers to the Vikings, who had a fort here in the 9th century. Donegal's later importance developed as it was the main seat of the O'Donnell family, which controlled this part of Ireland before the 17th century.

DONEGAL

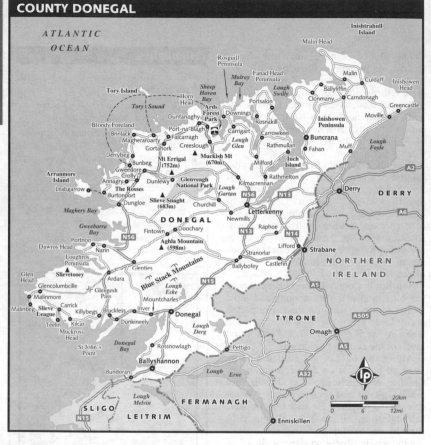

COUNTY DONEGAL

INFORMATION

The tourist office (☎ 21148), south of the Diamond by the Eske on The Quay, opens 10am to 5pm weekdays, March to June and September to November; and 10am to 8pm Monday to Saturday, 9am to 5pm Sunday July and August. Ask for *A Signposted Walking Tour of Donegal Town* to take in the sights.

On the Diamond, the Bank of Ireland, Allied Irish Bank and Ulster Bank all have ATMs and bureaux de change. The post office is on Tirchonaill St, north of the Diamond. The Blueberry Cybercafe (☎ 22933), Castle St, above the Blueberry Tearoom, of-

fers Internet access for €6.30 per hour. It's an honour system: you fill in a chit with your times and pay downstairs.

Four Masters Bookshop (☎ 21526), the Diamond, is the only one in town and has a small selection of maps and travel guides; it doubles as a gift shop.

DONEGAL CASTLE

Dúchas operated Donegal Castle (*☎ 22405, Castle St; adult/concession €3.80/1.60; open 10am-6pm daily mid-Mar-Oct*) is built on a rocky outcrop over the Eske and what remains of this restored castle is impressive.

It was built by the O'Donnells in the 15th century and may well have been burned down by Hugh Roe O'Donnell at the end of the 16th century rather than see it fall into the hands of the English. Sir Basil Brooke, the Englishman who took possession of the castle in about 1623, rebuilt it in Jacobean style. Notice the floral decoration on the corner turret and the decorated fireplace on the 1st floor. Brooke also built the three-storey Jacobean manor house adjoining the castle.

THE DIAMOND OBELISK

In 1474, Red Hugh O'Donnell and his wife, Nuala O'Brien, founded a **Franciscan friary** by the shore south of town. It was accidentally blown up in 1601 by Hugh Roe O'Donnell while laying siege to an English garrison, and little of it remains. What makes it famous is that four of its friars, fearing that the arrival of the English meant the end of Celtic culture, chronicled the whole of known Celtic history and mythology from 40 years before the Flood to AD 1618 in *The Annals of the Four Masters*. The annals remain an important source of early Irish history. The obelisk (1937) in the Diamond commemorates the work, copies of which are displayed in the National Library in Dublin.

DONEGAL RAILWAY HERITAGE CENTRE

The heritage centre *(☎ 22655, Tirchonaill St; adult/concession €1.25/0.65; open 10am-5.30pm Mon-Sat & 2pm-5pm Sun June-Sept; 10am-4pm Mon-Fri Oct-May)*, in the former train station north-east of the town centre, tells the history of the steam railway that ran from Ballyshannon to Derry until 1959.

FISHING

Permits are required for fishing in many of the local rivers. A permit for the Eske, along with licences for salmon and sea trout, is available from Doherty's *(☎ 21119, Main St)*.

SPECIAL EVENTS

The three-day Donegal Town Summer Festival in late June/early July, features a variety of activities including singing, dancing and storytelling, with arts and crafts thrown in for good measure. The tourist office has details.

PLACES TO STAY
Hostels

Donegal Town Independent Hostel *(☎ 22805, Killybegs Rd)* Tents/dorms/private rooms €5.05/10.70/12 per person. Open year round. This clean, friendly IHH/IHO hostel is in a big white building 1km north-west of town off the Killybegs road (N56). It's far enough out to be quiet, but within walking distance of town.

Ball Hill Hostel *(☎ 21174, fax 22605, Ball Hill)* Seniors/juniors €9.50/7.60. Open daily early Apr-Sept, Sat & Sun rest of the year. Ball Hill, a 66-bed An Óige hostel, has a stunning, remote setting at the end of a quiet road, on the shores of Donegal Bay. Stock up on food before arriving. It's about 5km south-west of Donegal Town; follow the Killybegs road (N56) and look out for the signs on the left about 5km out.

B&Bs

Drumcliffe House *(☎ 21200, Killybegs Rd)* Rooms €22.70-31.50 per person. The relaxed atmosphere, fine furnishings and friendly service make this B&B good value. All rooms are en suite, and one has a four-poster bed.

Castle View House *(☎ 22100, Waterloo Place)* Rooms €20.30 per person. Bathrooms are shared in this simple but clean, two-storey B&B overlooking the castle's Jacobean house.

Riverside House *(☎/fax 21083, Waterloo Place)* Rooms €25.40 per person. The building is unprepossessing but inside you'll find all the creature comforts. The bedrooms are nonsmoking.

Eske Villa *(☎ 21187, Marian Villas)* Singles/doubles €38.10/50.80. Friendly Eske Villa has spacious rooms in a quiet location. The breakfast room is adorned with Donegal Parian china.

More B&Bs line Ballyshannon Rd south of town.

Hillcrest Country Home *(☎ 21837, fax 21674, Ballyshannon Rd, Laghey)* Singles/

DONEGAL

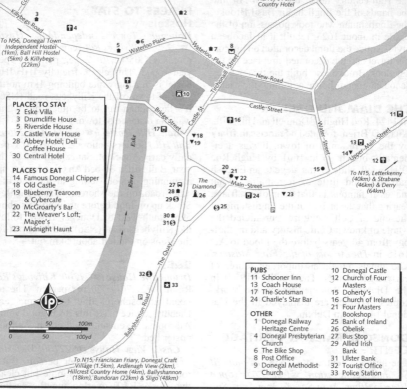

DONEGAL

To Harvey's Point

Coast Road

Killybegs Road

3

4

To Lough Eske &
Harvey's Point
Country Hotel

2

To N56, Donegal Town
Independent Hostel
(1km), Ball Hill Hostel
(5km) & Killybegs
(22km)

5 6

Waterloo Place

7

8

Waterloo Place Street

Tirchonaill Street

New Road

9

10

Bridge Street

Castle St

Castle Street

11

16

Eske

17

18
19

13

14

Upper Main Street

River

20 21
22

15

To N15, Letterkenny
(40km) & Strabane
(46km) & Derry
(64km)

The
Diamond

27
28
29

26

Main Street

24

23

25

30
31

The Quay

Ballyshannon Road

32

33

PLACES TO STAY
2 Eske Villa
3 Drumcliffe House
5 Riverside House
7 Castle View House
28 Abbey Hotel; Deli
    Coffee House
30 Central Hotel

PLACES TO EAT
14 Famous Donegal Chipper
18 Old Castle
19 Blueberry Tearoom
    & Cybercafe
20 McGroarty's Bar
22 The Weaver's Loft;
    Magee's
23 Midnight Haunt

PUBS
11 Schooner Inn
13 Coach House
17 The Scotsman
24 Charlie's Star Bar

OTHER
1 Donegal Railway
   Heritage Centre
4 Donegal Presbyterian
   Church
6 The Bike Shop
8 Post Office
9 Donegal Methodist
   Church

10 Donegal Castle
12 Church of Four
    Masters
15 Doherty's
16 Church of Ireland
21 Four Masters
    Bookshop
25 Bank of Ireland
26 Obelisk
27 Bus Stop
29 Allied Irish
    Bank
31 Ulster Bank
32 Tourist Office
33 Police Station

0   50   100m
0   50   100yd

To N15, Franciscan Friary, Donegal Craft
Village (1.5km), Ardlenagh View (2km),
Hillcrest Country Home (4km), Ballyshannon
(18km), Bundoran (22km) & Sligo (48km)

doubles from €32.40/48.25. Open mid-Apr-Sept. In a small village 4km south of Donegal, Hillcrest has three rooms and is close to a Blue Flag beach.

Ardlenagh View (*☎ 21646, Sligo Rd*) Singles/doubles €38.10/50.80. In a rural, hillside setting 2km south of town, Ardlenagh View has five en suite rooms and panoramic views of Donegal Bay.

Hotels

Central Hotel (*☎ 21027, fax 22295, the Diamond*) Rooms €57.15-76.20 per person. Situated in the heart of town, the Central is a large hotel with its own gym, pool, Jacuzzi and solarium.

Abbey Hotel (*☎ 21014, fax 23660, the Diamond*) Rooms €57.15-69.85 per person. Also central, the three-star Abbey Hotel has 85 en-suite rooms equipped with modern facilities. It's wheelchair accessible.

Harvey's Point Country Hotel (*☎ 22208, fax 22352, Harvey's Point*) Rooms €62.20-95.25 per person. Surrounded by hills and beautifully sited on the shores of Lough Eske this luxury 20-room hotel, 6km north of Donegal town, is signposted from the Diamond.

PLACES TO EAT

Harvey's Point Country Hotel (see Places to Stay) 4-course dinner €38. For a real treat, try the top-quality, French-inspired food at the restaurant here. Reservations and dressy attire are a must.

There are at least half a dozen places to eat within 100m or so of the Diamond.

Old Castle (☎ 21062, Castle St) Mains €8.80-15.10. One of the fancier places in town, this grey-stone pub serves hearty good-value food but only at lunch-time.

McGroarty's Bar (☎ 21049, the Diamond) Mains €6.30-15.10. Sports-oriented McGroarty's is another pub worth checking out for its good snacks, sandwiches and substantial meals served in the rear dining area.

Midnight Haunt (☎ 21111 Main St) Mains €8.80-17. This small upstairs restaurant has a large menu offering Cantonese and other Chinese meals, as well as curries and European dishes.

Blueberry Tearoom (☎ 22933, Castle St) Mains €5.35-7.25. When you taste the freshly prepared food here you can understand why it's so popular. The pies and cakes are particularly good.

The Weaver's Loft (☎ 22660, the Diamond) Meals €5-6.25. On the 1st floor of Magee's store, this is a relaxed, self-service, inexpensive cafe offering sandwiches, salads and light meals.

Deli Coffee House (☎ 21014, the Diamond) Dishes €2.80-5. Open 9am-6pm daily. Near the Abbey Hotel, this is one of the few places open early on Sunday. It serves good breakfasts and well filled baguettes.

Famous Donegal Chipper (☎ 21428, Upper Main St) Fish & chips under €6.30. Open 12.30pm-11.30pm daily. Great fish and chips are on offer at this small takeaway.

ENTERTAINMENT

Numerous music pubs can be found on Main and Upper Main Sts, within a stone's throw of the Diamond.

Coach House (☎ 22855, Upper Main St) A smoky, blokey kind of place where one or two of the regulars might bring along their guitars for an impromptu session.

Schooner Inn (☎ 21671, Upper Main St) This classic Irish pub presents traditional and modern music at the weekend.

The Scotsman (Bridge St) The Scotsman attracts a friendly, local crowd ready to sing or strum at the drop of a pint.

Charlie's Star Bar (☎ 21158, Main St) Quiet during the week, it livens up at the weekend when a young crowd comes to enjoy the live, contemporary music.

SHOPPING

Magee's (☎ 22660, the Diamond) Open 9.45am-6pm Mon-Sat. Well worth a browse, Magee's has its own garment factory and sells its tweed rolls at €25.20 per metre. A mailing service is available. Tweed jackets cost around €252 and skirts €57. Aran sweaters cost around €100.

Donegal Craft Village (☎ 22228, Ballyshannon Rd) Open 9am-6pm Mon-Sat, 11am-6pm Sun. This complex of small art and craft workshops about 1.5km south of town is worth visiting. Pottery, crystal, batik, garments and jewellery are all made on the premises.

GETTING THERE & AWAY

Frequent Bus Éireann (☎ 21101) buses connect Donegal with Derry, Enniskillen and Belfast in the North; Sligo, Galway and Killybegs to the west; Limerick and Cork in the south; and Dublin in the south-east. The bus stop is outside the Abbey Hotel.

Private coaches operated by Feda Ódonaill (also called Busanna Feda; ☎ 075-48114) run to Galway daily, via Ballyshannon, Bundoran and Sligo. They leave from the Donegal tourist office at 9.45am and 5.15pm Monday to Saturday and reach Galway Cathedral (or Eyre Square on Sunday evening) at 1.10pm and 8.45pm. There's an additional departure on Friday at 1.15pm, and on Sunday they leave at 9.45am, 4.15pm and 8.15pm. The fare within County Donegal is €5.05 or €6.30 depending on the distance.

It's also worth checking out McGeehan Coaches (☎ 075-46150), which does Donegal to Dublin (one way €15.10) three to four-times daily (more in summer) and departs from outside the garda (police) station across from the tourist office.

DONEGAL

GETTING AROUND
The Bike Shop (☎ 22515), Waterloo Place, charges €8.80/50.40 per day/week. The owner is friendly and knowledgeable and will help you plan a cycling itinerary.

Around Donegal Town

LOUGH DERG
June to mid-August this small lake due east of Donegal is alive with pilgrims who spend three days on **Station Island** in the middle of the lake where St Patrick is believed to have stayed and fasted. Anyone over the age of 14 is welcome, and some 30,000 turn up every year. But be warned: only genuine pilgrims are allowed on the island. The pilgrimage starts with a 24-hour vigil; one meal (of dry bread and black tea) a day is permitted; and everyone is expected to complete the Stations of the Cross in bare feet on the first day, having fasted from the preceding midnight. The pilgrims reach the island by boat from St Patrick's Purgatory, about 7km north of Pettigo, but outside the pilgrim season there's no regular service to the island.

Further information is available from The Priory (☎ 072-61518, e lochderg@iol.ie, w www.loughderg.org), St Patrick's Purgatory, Pettigo.

Places to Stay
If you're making the pilgrimage to the island you don't need to book accommodation. If you want to stay on the mainland near the lake there are a few B&Bs in the area.

Avondale (☎ 072-61520, fax 61787, Lough Derg Rd, Pettigo) Singles/doubles €25.40/48.25. Open Apr-Sept. A nonsmoking B&B, Avondale has four comfy rooms (two with attached shower).

Hilltop View (☎ 072-61535, Billary, Pettigo) Singles/doubles €25.40/44.45. Open year round. Aptly named, the B&B has four en suite rooms and a garden for guests' use. Billary is just before Pettigo on the Donegal road.

Getting There & Away
Pettigo and Lough Derg are extremely remote, at the end of a road across the moors. During the pilgrim season (1 June to 15 August), a special Bus Éireann service (No 31) leaves Dublin's Busáras at 9am daily Monday to Saturday (10am Sunday), arriving at Lough Derg shore just over 4½ hours later. During the same period bus No 68 leaves Galway at 9am, stopping at Sligo and Ballyshannon – but not Donegal – before reaching Lough Derg at 1.35pm. The first boat leaves at 11am, the last at 3pm.

LOUGH ESKE
This picturesque area north-east of Donegal is good for **fishing**, or for **cycling** or **walking** over the majestic Blue Stack Mountains, from which there are great views. If you're walking, consider using the guide *New Irish Walks: West and North* (Gill & Macmillan), by Tony Whilde & Patrick Simms, or *Hill Walkers' Donegal* (Shanksmare Publications), by David Herman, available from Four Masters Bookshop in Donegal.

Getting There & Away
Leave Donegal from the Diamond on the N56 to Killybegs. About 300m past the bridge, turn right following the signs to Harvey's Point Country Hotel. The ring road eventually joins the N15 to the north-east of Donegal, so it makes a convenient cycling trip. If you hire a bike from the Bike Shop in Donegal, you'll be given a photocopied map.

ROSSNOWLAGH
☎ 072 • pop 50
If you want a beach holiday away from it all, Rossnowlagh (Ross Neamblach), south-west of Donegal, is the place. The sandy Blue Flag beach is stunning, extends for nearly 5km and is a great **surfing** spot.

Ard-na-Mara (☎/fax 51141, Rossnowlagh) Singles/doubles €44.45/69.85. Open Jan-Nov. Nestled in the hillside, Ard-na-Mara has fabulous views of the bay and six rooms with attached showers. It's nonsmoking and accepts credit cards.

Sand House Hotel (☎ 51777, fax 52100, Rossnowlagh) Rooms €63.50-98.40 per person. This small, castellated, luxury hotel is right on the beach with magnificent Atlantic views.

BALLYSHANNON
☎ 072 • pop 2400
This busy, hilly town is set above the River Erne with a small adjunct of shops and houses south of the river connected by a bridge. Ballyshannon (Béal Átha Seanaidh) could be more appealing than Bundoran as a base for exploring the coastline before heading up to Donegal. It's also convenient for trips into the North, with regular buses to Derry and Enniskillen.

Orientation & Information
The centre of Ballyshannon, north of the river, has two main streets converging below the distinctive clock tower of Gallogley Jewellers: Main St runs to the north-west and Market St to the north-east. A little up from Gallogley Jewellers, there's an Allied Irish Bank branch (with an ATM) and a post office at the start of Market St.

Allingham's Grave
The poet William Allingham (1824–89), best remembered for *The Fairies*, was born in Ballyshannon and is buried in the graveyard. It's signposted at the second left up Main St after Dorrian's Imperial hotel. The tombstone is on the left side of the churchyard.

Donegal Parian China Visitor Centre
Parian china is lighter and more translucent than bone china. All the pieces manufactured by Donegal Parian China are on display (and for sale) at the centre (☎ 51826, Ballyshannon; free; open 9am-6pm Mon-Fri year round & 9am-6pm Sat May-Sept; 10am-6pm Sun June-Sept), about 1.5km south-west of Ballyshannon on the Bundoran road (N15). Prices range from around €8 for small pieces to €500 for a full dinner set. Free guided tours, a tearoom, a bureau de change and mail-order service are all laid on.

Abbey Mills
Abbey Mills (☎ 58966, Abbeylands; free;

open 11am-7pm daily June-Sept; 2.30pm-7pm Sun Oct-May) is a heritage centre with an audiovisual display, craft shop and cafe in the restored mills of Abbey Assaroe, founded in the late 12th century by Cistercian monks from Boyle in County Roscommon. To get there, turn left off Main St onto Bridge St, past the Thatch Pub, and take the road to Rossnowlagh (R231). After about 2km, signs indicate Abbey Mills on the left. There are fine views of the Erne Estuary and Donegal Bay.

Places to Stay & Eat
Duffy's Hostel (☎ 51535, Donegal Rd) Tents/dorms €5.05/9.45 per person. Open Mar-mid-Oct. Duffy's is a 20-minute walk up Market St from the bus station. It can be a bit cramped, but there's a conservatory and garden and an attached second-hand bookshop.

There are many B&Bs in the Ballyshannon region.

Rockville House (☎ 51106, Belleek Rd) Singles/doubles €32.95/50.80. B&B here is in a charming, 17th-century house about 500m from the centre overlooking the River Erne.

Dorrian's Imperial (☎ 51147, fax 51001, Main St) Rooms €44.45-62.85 per person. This grand hotel with its 26 rooms, leisure centre and elegant decor is the best in town. Bar food in the hotel's relaxed bar costs between €10 and €17. You can dine more formally in its restaurant.

Devine's Bar (☎ 52981, Market St) Mains €6.30-13.85. This pub has won awards for its freshly prepared food.

Kitchen Bake (Main St) Snacks under €6. At the Kitchen Bake, above a bakery and health-food shop at the junction of Main and Market Sts, you'll find delicious daytime snacks, fresh bread and cakes.

Entertainment
Pubs have live music throughout the summer, but the ideal time to be entertained in Ballyshannon is during the August bank holiday weekend music festival, the first weekend in August.

Two deservedly popular pubs we recommend are **Finn McCool's** (☎ 52677, Main

DONEGAL

St) and the **Thatch Pub** (Bridge St), just off the top of Main St as you turn towards Rossnowlagh.

Getting There & Away
There are regular daily Bus Éireann (☎ 074-21309) buses to Bundoran, Derry, Sligo, Galway, Donegal and Dublin (via Enniskillen, Cavan and Navan). The bus station is between the bridge and the Gallogley Jewellers clock tower.

Feda Ódonaill buses (☎ 075-48114) depart from outside the Olde Distillery pub, which is opposite the bus station, for Donegal, Letterkenny, Dunfanaghy, Gweedore and Crolly at 12.45pm and 6.45pm Monday to Saturday (with extra departures at 4.10pm and 8.30pm on Friday), and at 5.45pm and 11pm on Sunday. For Sligo and Galway they leave from in front of Maggie's Bar, south of the river near the roundabout, at 10am and 5.30pm Monday to Saturday (plus 1.30pm Friday), and 10am, 4.30pm and 8.30pm Sunday.

BUNDORAN
☎ 072 • pop 1700
Bundoran (Bun Dobhráin) is one of Ireland's most popular summer seaside resorts, but the rest of the year it's generally passed by. It's not hard to see why: Main St – East End and West End – is a series of games arcades, fish and chips shops, and tacky souvenir stands. The town is frequented mainly by Catholic Northerners and at night the traditional music in the pubs favours the rebel over the folk song.

The strange cliff-side rock formations on the coast here have whimsical names such as Fairy Bridges and Puffing Hole.

Information
The tourist office (☎ 41350), in a kiosk opposite the Holyrood Hotel, opens 10am to 5pm Monday to Friday mid-March to September; weekends only the rest of the year. The post office is about 120m south of the tourist office; the Allied Irish Bank on Main St has an ATM and bureau de change.

Activities
Just north of the town centre, **Tullan Strand** is a handsome Blue Flag beach with breaks big enough to offer some world-class **surfing**. Surf gear is available from **Fitzgerald's Surfworld** (☎ 41223, Main St), or from the **Donegal Adventure Centre** (☎ 42418, fax 42385, Dinglei Cush), which specialises in surfing tuition but also provides canoeing, cycling and walking programs.

Children enjoy **Waterworld** (☎ 41172, The Promenade; adult/child €6.35/4.45; open 10am-7pm June-Aug; 10am-7pm Sat & Sun Apr, May & Sept) where a slide pool, wave pool and restaurant pack them in by the hundred. The noise level inside probably breaks several EU standards.

Homefield Equestrian Trails (☎ 41288, fax 41049, Bayview Ave; adult/child €15.10/12.60 per hour) organises riding sessions along the beach and instructional courses.

Places to Stay & Eat
Should you decide to give Bundoran a whirl, there are a few options.

Homefield Hostel (☎ 41288, fax 41049, Bayview Ave) Dorms/doubles €15.75/31.50. Rates at this 30-bed, IHH hostel (and equestrian centre, see above) near the beach include breakfast. Meals and bike hire are also available.

You're spoiled for choice when it comes to B&Bs, though few stand out.

Gillaroo Lodge (☎ 42357, fax 42172, West End) Singles/doubles from €29.85/ 48.25. Catering mainly for anglers, this two-storey lodge is in a prime position close to the beach.

Grand Central Hotel (☎ 42722, fax 42656, Main St) Rooms €44-57 per person. A modern, but traditionally decorated hotel in the centre of town, the Grand Central has a gym and weekend entertainment.

There's no shortage of cafes and fast-food places along Main St.

Le Chateaubrianne (☎/fax 42160, Sligo Rd) Set lunch/dinner €19.50/29.60. One of the best restaurants in town, Le Chateaubrianne's cooking combines French and modern Irish cuisine using fresh local seafood and game; it also has some imaginative vegetarian dishes.

Getting There & Away
Bus Éireann (☎ 074-21309) buses stop on Main St outside Pebbles shop. There are direct daily services to Dublin, Derry, Sligo, Galway and Westport. Ulsterbus (☎ 028-9033 3000) has three services daily (one on Sunday) to Belfast and Enniskillen. Feda Ódonaill (☎ 075-48114) buses from Crolly to Galway stop in Bundoran outside the Holyrood Hotel at 10.05am and 5.35pm Monday to Saturday (plus 1.35pm Friday), and also at 10.05am, 4.35pm and 8.35pm on Sunday.

South-Western Donegal

MOUNTCHARLES TO BRUCKLESS
Apart from some pubs and cafes in Mountcharles and Dunkineely, there are few places to eat, so stock up before leaving Donegal or Killybegs.

Mountcharles
☎ 073 • pop 100
The hillside location of Mountcharles (Moin Séarlas), the first settlement along the coastal road (N56) west of Donegal, offers a fine vista of Donegal Bay. About 2km from the centre is a safe, sandy **beach**. Michael O'Boyle's (☎ 35257) boat, the *Martin Óg*, is available for **deep-sea angling** from €19 per day, including rod and tackle. (The boat leaves from the Mountcharles pier; take the first turning on the left as you come into the village from the east.) Mountcharles is the birthplace of Seamus MacManus, a local poet and *seanchaí* (storyteller) who regaled locals with tales around the village pump in the 1940s and 1950s.

Clybawn (☎ 35076, Station Rd) Singles/doubles from €32.40/48.25. Open Apr-Sept. Mrs Harvey operates this comfortable B&B, near the church, with good views of the bay.

The road west to Bruckless passes through the village of **Inver**, which has its own small beach.

Dunkineely
☎ 073 • pop 150
A little farther west at Dunkineely (Dún Cionnfhaolaidh or Dún Cionnaola), a minor road runs down the promontory to the beach at **St John's Point**. There's no sand, but there are good coastal views, and the waters around the point are a prime **diving** site.

Blue Moon Hostel (☎ 37264, Main St) Tent adult/child €3.80/1.25, dorms €8.80. Open year round. Diving information is available at this two-storey IHO hostel, which also offers bicycle hire and can arrange free pick up. Several old pubs are nearby.

Bruckless
☎ 073 • pop 150
Bruckless (An Bhroclais) is about 2km west of Dunkineely. **Horse riding** and **pony trekking** are available at **Deane's Equestrian Centre** (☎/fax 37160, Darney, Bruckless).

Gallagher's Farm Hostel (☎ 37057) Tents/dorms €5.05/10.10 per person. This clean, attractive IHH hostel, with 18 beds in converted farm outbuildings, is halfway between Dunkineely and Bruckless. Campers have separate kitchen facilities from hostellers. The hostel supplies guests with a list of walks in the area.

Bruckless House (☎ 37071, fax 37070) Rooms €45 per person. Open Apr-Sept. Just past the hostel, 18th-century Bruckless House is a cut above the usual B&B.

Getting There & Away
Bus Éireann (☎ 21101) bus No 494 leaves Donegal for Killybegs four-times daily Monday to Saturday, stopping near the Village Tavern in Mountcharles, the Inver post office and Dunkineely Furniture Centre in Dunkineely.

KILLYBEGS
☎ 073 • pop 1630
Killybegs (Ceala Beaga) is Ireland's most important fishing port, and some travellers may be put off by the smell created by the large fishmeal processing plant on the eastern outskirts. The town is also noted for its handmade carpets.

The Bank of Ireland, on Main St just up

from the harbour, has an ATM and bureau de change. The post office is opposite the harbour.

Things to See & Do

A right turn in town up the steep hill brings you to St Catherine's Church, which contains the **tomb of Niall Mór MacSweeney**, who was head of the MacSweeney clan, one of Donegal's ruling families before the Flight of the Earls in 1607. The tombstone is carved with Celtic-style patterns and the figure of a gallowglass. Gallowglasses were Scottish mercenaries who first came to the north and west of Ireland in the late 13th century. At first they were only hired by the big chiefs, but by the late 15th century their descendants were being employed around the country as personal bodyguards and constables.

Several operators offer **fishing** expeditions with the opportunity to catch pollock, cod and whiting. **Brian McGilloway** (☎ 32444, Killybegs) runs fishing trips for €31.50 per person, plus €6.30 for rod and tackle. **The Harbour Store** (☎ 31569, The Harbour), by the wharf, sells fishing gear.

The wild, secluded **Fintra Beach** (also spelled Fintragh), about 3km west, is fun to explore and the water is clean and safe for swimming.

Special Events

The town hosts a huge Sea Angling Open Boat Competition (☎ 31901) in early July.

Places to Stay

If you decide to stay in Killybegs and don't like the smell of fish, pick a guesthouse along Fintra Rd on the western outskirts.

Bannagh House (☎ 31108, Fintra Rd) Rooms €25.40 per person. Open Apr-Oct. This is the first house you come to as you head out on the Fintra Rd, a short walking distance from the town. The front rooms have great views of the harbour. Breakfast includes a choice of yoghurt, fruit and home-made bread.

Oileán Roe House (☎ 31192, Fintra Rd) Singles/doubles €32.40/48.25. Open mid-Mar-Sept. This is a clean, friendly, two-

storey home about 1km from town. It accepts credit cards.

Lismolin Country Home (☎ 31035, fax 32310, Fintra Rd) Singles/doubles €38.10/ 48.25. Open June-Sept. This rather ambitiously named bungalow, also about 1km from town, has five well appointed rooms all with attached shower. The jam and bread at breakfast are home-made.

Bay View Hotel (☎ 31950, fax 31856, Main St) Rooms €57.15-73.65 per person. The Bay View is a large, modern, 40-room hotel that dominates the harbour in the centre of Killybegs.

Places to Eat

Sail Inn (☎ 31130, Main St) Bar food €2.50-6.30, mains €12-19. The Sail Inn has an intimate upstairs restaurant for evening dining, or you can eat snacks or full meals in the colourful downstairs bar where traditional music sessions are held.

Peking Chef (☎ 31894, Main St) Mains €8.80-21.40. Situated at the top rear of Cope House, the restaurant gives the fresh, local seafood an Asian flavour.

Bay View Hotel (see Places to Stay) Mains €9.45-11.35, 3-course set dinner €17. The hotel has a downstairs pub-brasserie and a lovely upstairs restaurant specialising, not surprisingly, in fresh seafood.

Kitty Kelly's (☎ 31925, Kilcar Rd) Mains €7.55-11.35. Open from 6pm Easter-Sept. The restaurant here, 5km west of Killybegs, serves fabulous seafood as well as pasta and traditional Irish dishes in a purple-painted, converted farmhouse. Reservations are recommended.

Getting There & Away

Bus Éireann (☎ 074-21309) bus No 494 from Donegal to Killybegs runs three-times daily (four times in July and August) Monday to Saturday. Bus No 490 heads west to Kilcar and Glencolumbcille once daily Monday to Friday (twice Saturday). In July and August an extra bus runs daily Monday to Saturday, and buses continue to Malinmore twice daily, Monday to Saturday. The bus stop is outside Hegarty's shop.

McGeehan Coaches (☎ 075-46150) runs

a service from Glencolumbcille to Dublin leaving from the Street News store by the harbour at 8.05am and 12.25pm Monday to Saturday, 8.05am and 3.45pm Sunday. Extra buses are laid on in summer.

KILCAR & AROUND
☎ 073 • pop 1300

Kilcar (Cill Chártha) and neighbouring Carrick (An Charraig) are good bases for exploring the Slieve League cliffs and the magnificent indented coastline of south-western Donegal. Kilcar is an important centre for the manufacture of Donegal tweed. Just outside Kilcar is a small, sandy beach.

Information
In Kilcar tourist information is available from the community centre, Aísleann Cill Cartha (☎ 38376), 9am to 5.30pm Monday to Friday year round. It also provides Internet access for €5.05 per hour and genealogical information. There are no banks in either Kilcar or Carrick. The post office in Kilcar is off Main St, past O'Gara's pub.

Studio Donegal
Beside the community centre is Studio Donegal *(☎ 38194, Kilcar; free; open 10am-5.30pm Mon, 9am-5.30pm Tues-Thur, 9.30am-5pm Fri)*, a small tweed factory offering free guided tours. In its shop you can buy tweed by the metre for about €14; you're unlikely to get better prices than this anywhere else in Donegal.

Slieve League
Carrick, 5km north-west of Kilcar, is where you turn off for Teelin and the Bunglass viewing point for Slieve League, the highest cliffs in Europe dropping some 600m into the sea. To drive to the cliff edge, be sure to take the turn-off signposted Bunglass from the Killybegs to Glencolumbcille road (R263) at Carrick, and continue beyond the narrow track signposted Slieve League to the one that's signposted Bunglass.

Walks
There are a number of local walks that take in many prehistoric sites. Three walks that

start in Kilcar are collectively known as the **Kilcar Way.** From Teelin, experienced walkers can spend a day walking north via Bunglass and the somewhat terrifying, cliff-top **One Man's Path** to Malinbeg, near Glencolumbcille. It shouldn't be attempted in windy conditions or if bad weather is likely to impede visibility.

Special Events
On the first weekend in August, Kilcar, like Killybegs, hosts an International Sea Angling Festival, followed almost immediately by the week-long Kilcar Street Festival. Contact the community centre for details.

Places to Stay
Dún Ulún House (☎ 38137, Coast Rd) Tents/dorms/B&B €3.80/12-17/23.30 per person. Dún Ulún House, at the western end of the village, is an agreeable, friendly establishment. The camp site is across the road ensconced in the tiered hillside (with great views); a shower and toilet block is nearby.

Derrylahan Hostel (☎ 38079, fax 38447, Derrylahan, Kilcar) Tent €5, bed in 6-bed dorm €8.80, doubles €25. The equally friendly IHH hostel is some 3km west of the village on a working farm. There's a small library, Internet access, plentiful cooking facilities and a group house accommodating 20 people. If you phone from Kilcar or Carrick, Shaun, the owner, will organise a lift to the hostel for you.

Kilcar Lodge (☎ 38156, Main St) Singles/doubles €33/55.85. Open Apr-Oct. A few metres from the bus stop, the central Kilcar Lodge has four comfy, en suite bedrooms.

Places to Eat
Piper's Rest (☎ 38205, Main St) Mains €6.30-12.60. Much of the conversation is in Gaelic at this thatched pub in Kilcar, which serves good soup, snacks and seafood and has traditional music sessions.

Restaurant Teach Barnaí (☎ 38160, Main St) Mains €11.30-23.90. Excellent food is available at this restaurant, where fresh Irish produce is combined with French and Italian influenced cuisine.

Cúl a Dúin (☎ 39041, Teelin) Meals under

A Tale of Two Priests

While the sexual improprieties of the Catholic clergy in Ireland may grab the headlines, most of the faithful like to think of their priests and nuns as 'living saints' who perform corporal works of mercy and contribute to the development of the community. County Donegal can claim two of them.

When Father James McDyer came to Glencolumbcille from Tory Island in 1952, he was galvanised into action by seeing a community in terminal decay with an emigration rate of 75%. He organised co-operatives, diversified farming practices and promoted tourism. By 1964 emigration dropped to 20%. The Folk Village Museum he established in Glencolumbcille in 1967 – long before such heritage centres had become trendy and substantial EU grants were available to help set them up – is the most tangible evidence of the work of a priest who played a remarkable role in the resurrection of a community.

Another cleric who made his mark on a remote part of rural Donegal was Father Diarmuid Ó Péicín. When the then retired Jesuit missionary visited Tory Island for a day trip in 1980, he encountered a totally dispirited people. A severe storm in 1974 had cut the island off from the mainland and, after it subsided, a number of islanders had migrated to the mainland.

By the time Father Ó Péicín arrived the remaining islanders were convinced that the government was going to abandon the island and move the population to the mainland. The 'lonely rock' they called home would thus go the way of the Blasket Islands (see the County Kerry chapter), abandoned in the 1950s. Father Ó Péicín took up the fight and campaigned both in Ireland and abroad for an electrification and water scheme for Tory, proper sanitation, a regular ferry and a new harbour, all of which were eventually achieved. Although he remained for only four years, his work and spirit encouraged the islanders to fend for themselves.

You can read about Father Ó Péicín's work in his book, *Islanders: The True Story of One Man's Fight to Save a Way of Life.*

€12. This bar serves good pub grub, especially seafood, from May to September. It's owned by the band Altan, whose members sometimes perform here at the weekend.

Getting There & Away
Bus Éireann (☎ 074-21309) bus No 490 connects Kilcar and Carrick with Killybegs and Glencolumbcille once daily Monday to Friday (twice daily Saturday). In July and August an extra bus runs daily Monday to Saturday. McGeehan Coaches (☎ 075-46150) runs a service from Glencolumbcille to Dublin stopping at Carrick outside McGinley's shop at 7.30am and 11.50am Monday to Saturday, 7.30am and 3.10pm Sunday; they stop in Kilcar outside John Joe's pub about 10 minutes later. There are extra buses in summer.

GLENCOLUMBCILLE
☎ 073 • pop 260
Settlement of the area dates back 5000 years and Stone Age remains dot the landscape.

The name in Irish of this collection of tiny settlements – Gleann Cholm Cille (Glen of Columba's Church) – suggests that the 6th-century St Colmcille (alias Columba) lived in the valley here, and the remains of his church can still be seen. Every year at midnight on 9 June – the saint's feast day – the village becomes the focal point of a penitential walkabout.

The name appears as Glencolmcille or Glencolmbkille on some maps.

Information
The Lace House (☎ 30116), Cashel, dispenses information 10am to 6pm Monday to Saturday, 1pm to 5pm Sunday April, June and September to mid-November; 9.30am to 9pm Monday to Saturday, noon to 6pm Sunday July and August. There are no banks but the post office has a bureau de change.

Folk Village Museum
This heritage centre (☎ 30017; *adult/child €2.50/1.90; open 10am-6pm Mon-Sat, noon-*

6pm Sun Easter-Sept), 3km west of the centre, was established by Father James McDyer in 1967 (when he also introduced electricity to the area). It comprises several replicated thatched cottages as lived in by people in the 18th and 19th centuries, with genuine period fittings. Admission includes a tour of the site's buildings. The *shebeen* (illicit drinking place) sells unusual local wines (made from things such as seaweed and fuchsias) alongside marmalade and fudge. The old National School is also open to visitors, and there's a short nature trail up the hill behind.

Malinmore Adventure Centre
Overlooking Malin Bay, this adventure centre *(☎/fax 30123, Malinmore, Glencolumbcille)* offers scuba diving, canoeing, snorkelling, fishing, orienteering, boat trips and other activities. Accommodation packages are available.

Beaches
The beach opposite the folk village can be dangerous due to the undercurrents, but it's worth making the short journey west of Glencolumbcille to **Doonalt**, where there are two sandy beaches. Another beach can be found at the end of the road to Malinbeg, where steps descend to a lovely sheltered cove.

Irish Language & Cultural Courses
***Oideas Gael** (☎ 30248, ✉ oidsgael@iol.ie, Glencolumbcille; weekend courses €50-75 per person, week-long courses €115-165 including accommodation; mid-Mar-Oct)*, at the Foras Cultúir Uladh (Ulster Cultural Foundation), 1km west of the village centre, offers a range of adult courses in the Irish language (beginners welcome) and in traditional culture – from Donegal dancing and marine painting to *bodhrán* (hand-held goatskin drum) playing and tapestry weaving.

Places to Stay
***Dooey Hostel** (☎ 30130, fax 30339, Glencolumbcille)* Tents/dorms/private rooms €5.05/8.80/9.45 per person. This friendly, isolated place is the flagship property of the IHO, and is built into the hillside about 1.5km beyond the village. It offers a range of accommodation, including a group house for 20 people with superb views out over Glen Bay. The hostel has six kitchens and, rather surprising for somewhere so remote, it offers wheelchair access. If you're driving, take the turn beside the Glenhead Tavern; if walking or cycling, take a short cut up the track beside the Folk Village.

***Malinbeg Hostel** (☎ 30006, Malinbeg, Glencolumbcille)* Dorms/private rooms €8.80/11.35 per person. Open year round. This is a new, purpose-built hostel with all mod cons including en-suite rooms. If you call ahead the owners will pick you up.

***Corner House** (☎ 30021, Cashel, Glencolumbcille)* Singles/doubles €32.40/48.25. Each bedroom has its own shower at this cosy B&B.

***Glencolumbcille Hotel** (Óstán Ghleann Cholmcille; ☎ 30003, fax 30222, Glencolumbcille)* Singles/doubles €50/75. You can't fail to spot this yellow-painted, old-world hotel with its 40 brightly furnished, en suite rooms. To get there continue past the Folk Village Museum towards Malinbeg.

Places to Eat
***Lace House Restaurant** (☎ 30444, Cashel, Glencolumbcille)* Mains €5.65-6.25. Open 9.30am-9pm daily. As well as fresh fish and chips, and other standard fare, the restaurant, above the shop of the same name, serves delicious home-made soups and desserts.

***An Chistin** (☎ 30213, Glencolumbcille)* Mains €6.25. Open 12.30am-9.30pm Mon-Fri, 9.30am-9.30pm Sat & Sun. One of the best places to eat is this pleasant cafe at the Ulster Cultural Foundation. It specialises in seafood but also serves good sandwiches, cakes and pastries.

Shopping
***Glencolumbcille Woollen Market** (☎ 39377, Glencolumbcille)* This store is an outlet for Rossan knitwear, manufactured locally, and has a large array of Donegal tweed jackets, caps and ties alongside lamb's-wool scarves and shawls. Also available are Aran sweaters and hand-woven rugs. It's 3km south-west of Cashel on the R263.

Lace House (☎ *30116, Cashel, Glencolumbcille*) As well as dispensing tourist information, the Lace House sells Rossan knitted garments, jackets and rugs.

Getting There & Away

Bus Éireann (☎ 074-21309) bus No 490 leaves for Killybegs at 8.30am Monday to Saturday, plus 11.35am on Saturday. Another bus operates at 12.35pm daily in July and August.

McGeehan Coaches (☎ 075-46150) leave daily from outside Biddy's Pub for Donegal and Dublin (Royal Dublin Hotel on O'Connell St). From Dublin the bus leaves at 2pm and 6pm (with an extra bus at 4pm on Friday), arriving at Glencolumbcille nearly five hours later. Departure from Glencolumbcille is at 7.20am and 11.40am Monday to Saturday, 7.20am and 3pm Sunday. McGeehan also runs to Ardara, Dungloe and Glenties.

ARDARA & AROUND

☎ 075 • pop 650

A small heritage town set in aspic, scenically positioned Ardara (Árd an Rátha) is an important manufacturing centre for knitwear and hand-woven tweed.

Tourist information and Internet access (€1.25 for 10 minutes) are available from the Ardara Heritage Centre (see Things to See & Do following). On the Diamond there's an Ulster Bank with an ATM; the post office is opposite.

Things to See & Do

The road from Glencolumbcille to Ardara goes via the stunning **Glengesh Pass**, a glaciated valley that suddenly opens up before you, with long winding bends carrying the road down to the river. Before entering Ardara, a small road to the left runs down to the tiny village of **Maghera** where you can explore the attractive beach and caves. Be careful, though, as some of them flood when the tide comes in.

The long, narrow **Loughros Peninsula** that extends from Ardara and separates Loughros More Bay from Loughros Beg Bay is well worth walking or cycling.

Ardara Heritage Centre (☎ *41704, the* Diamond; free; open 10am-6pm Mon-Sat, 2pm-6pm Sun, Easter-Sept) tells the story of Donegal's role in the weaving industry and gives you the chance to watch a handloom weaver. An audiovisual presentation upstairs describes the surrounding area, and there's a small cafe.

Special Events

The Ardara Weavers Fair has its origins in the 18th century but went into decline early in the 20th century. It was revived and now takes place over the first weekend in June.

Places to Stay & Eat

Drumbarron Hostel (☎ *41200, the Diamond*) Dorms/private rooms €8.80/10.10 per person. Open year round. Drumbarron, in a Georgian-style, two-storey house, is a very hospitable hostel, with comfortable bunk beds, free hot showers and a large kitchen.

Drumbarron House (☎ *41200, the Diamond*) Singles/doubles €25.40/45.70. Open year round. If you fancy home-made bread and scones for breakfast, then try this delightful, welcoming place just across from the hostel.

Woodhill House (☎ *41112, fax 41516, Ardara*) Rooms €44-57 per person. Signposted off the Diamond, Woodhill is a small hotel about 1.5km from the centre in a quiet, rural setting. It has an excellent restaurant.

The Green Gate (☎ *41546, Ardvally, Ardara*) Singles/doubles €38/50. Run by convivial Frenchman Paul Chatenoud, this fabulously rustic B&B consists of three traditional cottages with all mod cons, and has great all-day breakfasts, an extensive library and sweeping views down to the bay.

Charlie's West End Café (Main St) Mains €3-10. Open 10am-10pm Mon-Thur, 10am-11pm Fri & Sat, 5pm-11pm Sun. A busy cafe at the Killybegs end of Main St, friendly, efficient Charlie's does good all-day breakfasts, as well as soups, sandwiches and meals.

Entertainment

Corner House (☎ *41736, the Diamond*) This bar has live traditional music at the weekend (nightly from June to September) and invites any visiting musicians to join in.

Nancy's Bar (Front St) Nancy's Bar, in a terraced house down by the bridge, is a small, dark pub with lots of atmosphere. It's a good place for a quiet drink.

Shopping

Not unexpectedly, several shops specialise in locally made knitwear, and prices are competitive. You could try *Kennedy's (☎ 41106, Front St)*, up the hill from the Diamond, or *John Molloy (☎ 41133, Killybegs Rd)*, 1km farther out.

Getting There & Away

In July and August, Bus Éireann (☎ 074-21309) bus No 492 from Killybegs stops twice daily Monday to Saturday, in each direction, outside O'Donnell's in Ardara. The rest of the year, these buses run on Tuesday, Thursday and Friday only. June to mid-September McGeehan Coaches (☎ 46150) runs a service from the post office to Dublin at 8.30am and 12.50pm Monday to Saturday, 8.30am and 3.40pm Sunday. The Glencolumbcille to Dublin bus via Glenties stops in Ardara at 8.30am and 12.50pm Monday to Saturday (8.30am only on Sunday).

Getting Around

Don Byrne's of Ardara (☎ 41156), Main St, east of the centre, is part of the Raleigh Rent-a-Bike scheme.

DAWROS HEAD

The landscape of this peninsula north of Ardara consists of numerous tiny lakes surrounded by gentle, rolling hills and makes good walking territory. The twin resort towns of **Narin** and **Portnoo** are packed every summer with holidaymakers from the North and the magnificent Blue Flag beach at Narin is a particularly big crowd-puller. At low tide you can walk out to **Iniskeel Island** where St Connell, a cousin of St Colmcille, founded a monastery in the 6th century, but no trace of it remains.

Signposts off the road from Narin to Rosbeg lead 3km to Lough Doon in the centre of which sits 2000-year-old **Doon Fort**, a fortified oval settlement. To reach it, you need to hire a rowing boat (€5 per hour).

In 1588 the *Duquesa Santa Ana,* part of the Spanish Armada, ran aground off **Tramore Beach**. The survivors temporarily occupied O'Boyle's Island in Kiltoorish Lake, but then marched south through Ardara to Killybegs, where they set sail again in the *Girona*. The *Girona* met a similar fate that year off the Antrim coast in Northern Ireland, with the loss of over 1000 crew.

Places to Stay

Tramore Beach Caravan & Camping Park (☎ 075-51491, fax 51492, Rosbeg) Small/large tents €8.80/11.35. The remote park has 24 tent sites among the sand dunes. Take the road from Ardara to Narin then turn left, following the signposts to Tramore Beach.

Narin and Portnoo have B&Bs that generally open April to September.

Roaninish (☎/fax 075-45207, Narin) Singles/doubles €38.10/55.85. Open June-early Sept. A few minutes' walk from the beach, Roaninish has four pleasant, non-smoking bedrooms (all with showers).

Hazelwood (☎ 075-45151, Portnoo) Singles/doubles €38.75/43.20. Open Apr-Aug. Hazelwood also has four rooms, but only one with attached shower.

Getting There & Away

In July and August, Monday to Saturday, Bus Éireann (☎ 074-21309) bus No 492 departs Killybegs for Portnoo at 10am and 5.05pm. From Portnoo it returns at 12.15pm and 6.15pm.

GLENTIES

☎ 075 ● pop 800

The village of Glenties (Na Gleannta) is on the Owena River at the meeting of two valleys, with the Blue Stack Mountains to the south. The town was home to Patrick MacGill (1891–1963), the 'navvy poet', and a summer school in his honour takes place in August. Glenties was the setting for Brian Friel's film *Dancing at Loughnasa*. It's a popular **fishing** destination and there are several pleasant **walks** in the area.

On the main street there's a Bank of Ireland with an ATM and bureau de change, and a post office.

St Connell's Museum & Heritage Centre

The local-history museum (☎ 51227, Main St; adult/child €2.50/0.65; open 10am-1pm & 2pm-5pm Mon-Fri Apr-Sept), beside the old courthouse at the western end of town, has a small collection of local artefacts. These include an impressive set of early-20th-century bathroom fixtures in the basement, and reminders of the old Glenties to Fintown railway. You can also visit the basement of the courthouse to view the old prison cells.

Places to Stay & Eat

Campbell's Holiday Hostel (☎ 51491, fax 51492, Glenties) Dorms/private rooms €10/12.50 per person. Open Mar-Oct. Clean and spacious, this IHH hostel is on the left behind the museum as you enter from Ardara on the N56. There's a secure car park, a big kitchen-cum-common room with a welcoming fire, and a second kitchen at the other end of the hostel.

Avalon (☎/fax 51292, Glen Rd) Singles/doubles €32.40/48.25. Scenically positioned about 500m from the centre, Avalon has four nonsmoking bedrooms (three with shower). It accepts credit cards and can provide gluten-free food.

Highlands Hotel (☎ 51111, fax 51564, Main St) Singles/doubles €38/70. This relaxed, 20-room hotel dominates the western end of Main St. It serves excellent food (mains €9.45-15) in substantial proportions using fresh produce; the menu includes a few vegetarian choices.

Nighthawks (☎ 51389, Main St) Food €1.65-5. Nighthawks is an above-average, fast-food cafe serving burgers, sandwiches and the like but also does a takeaway pizza service.

Entertainment

Paddy's Bar (☎ 51158, Main St) Paddy's is a lively old pub whose walls reverberate to the sound of traditional music several nights a week.

Limelight (☎ 51118, Main St) Clubbers from around Donegal flock to Glenties' famous nightclub (attached to Molloy's Bar) on Friday and Saturday night.

Getting There & Away

In July and August, Monday to Saturday, Bus Éireann (☎ 074-21309) bus No 492 from Killybegs to Portnoo stops outside the post office in Glenties at 10.45am and 5.50pm. Coming from Portnoo, the bus stops in Glenties at 12.40pm and 6.40pm. The rest of the year, the bus runs Tuesday, Thursday and Friday only.

McGeehan Coaches (☎ 46150) runs a service from Dungloe to Dublin leaving Glenties at 8.15am and 12.30pm Monday to Saturday, 8.15am and 3.30pm Sunday.

INLAND TO THE FINN VALLEY

This part of Donegal is not well travelled – a blessing if you want to get away on your own for some fishing, hill walking or cycling. The **River Finn** is a good salmon river, especially if there has been heavy rain before the middle of June.

There's good **hill walking** on the Blue Stack Mountains and along the Ulster Way, but you need to be equipped with maps and provisions. Finn Farm Hostel (see Places to Stay) dispenses maps and advice and will even arrange a pick-up at the beginning or end of a walk. A long, one-day trek could start from the hostel and end at Campbell's Holiday Hostel in Glenties or Glenleighan Hostel near Fintown.

The main town is **Ballybofey** (Bealach Féich; pronounced bally-**boh**-fay), linked to adjoining **Stranorlar** by an arched bridge over the Finn. There's a small locally run tourist office (☎ 074-31840) in the Ballybofey Balor Theatre on Main St, open 9am to 5pm Monday to Friday. In Ballybofey's Protestant church is the grave of Isaac Butt (1813–79), founder of the Irish Home Rule movement. Fishing gear is available from Mr G's Discount Store, Main St.

Fintown (Baile na Finne), 30km northwest on the hillside overlooking Lough Finn, is a much smaller settlement – just a cluster of houses, a shop, post office, garage and pubs lining the main road. Nevertheless, a renovated part of the narrow-gauge **Fintown Railway** (☎ 075-46280, Fintown) between Fintown and Glenties runs scenic excursions alongside Lough Finn on 5km of track. Trains leave the station 11am to 5pm weekdays and 11am to 6pm at the weekend, July to September; 1pm to 4pm weekdays and 1pm to 5pm on Saturday in June. Fares are adult/child/family €2.50/1.25/7.55.

Places to Stay

Finn Farm Hostel (☎/*fax 074-32261, Cappry, Ballybofey*) Tents/dorms/private rooms €5.65/10.10/11.35 per person. Open year round. This IHH/IHO hostel is on a working farm and is a centre for a community work scheme aimed at reviving dying musical traditions, so if you stay you'll be able to hear the musicians practising. It also offers horse-riding lessons and organised walks. Finn Farm is about 2km from Ballybofey; the turning is signposted simply 'Hostel' off the N15 Donegal road.

Glenleighan Hostel (☎ *075-46141, Glenlieghan, Fintown*) Dorms/private rooms €9.45/10.70 per person. Open year round. This tiny IHO hostel has 12 beds, is beautifully situated above Lough Finn and offers a free pick-up service.

There are B&Bs in both Ballybofey and Stranorlar to the north.

Finn View House (☎ *074-31351, Ballybofey*) Singles/doubles €29.85/48.25. Open Apr-Sept. Finn View is a small, three-room bungalow on the Lifford road.

Kee's Hotel (☎ *074-31018, fax 31917, Stranorlar*) Rooms €57.15-67.30 per person. Kee's is where mail horses were changed on the Derry to Sligo run in the 19th century. Rates include use of the leisure club's swimming pool and sauna.

Jackson's Hotel (☎ *074-31021, fax 31096, Ballybofey*) Rooms €52.70-82.55 per person. You're greeted by an open log fire at reception in this renovated 88-room hotel set in its own gardens.

Places to Eat

The Coffee Bar (☎ *074-31217, Main St, Ballybofey*) Mains €3.70-5. On the second level of McElhinney's Store, this is a busy, inexpensive, self-service place offering sandwiches, salads, snacks and hot meals.

Caife na Locha (*Fintown*) Meals under €7. This small place, run by a women's co-

operative, serves light meals and opens the same hours as the Fintown Railway.

The big hotels offer set dinners costing about €20 to €35.

Entertainment

The Claddagh (☎ *32038, Main St, Ballybofey*) The musicians from Finn Farm also practise at this old pub on a midweek night.

Teá á Céoil (*The Music House; Fintown*) In a small converted farmhouse on the main road, this is the venue of choice in Fintown for music and a pint.

Getting There & Away

Bus Éireann (☎ 074-21309) express bus No 64 between Galway and Derry via Sligo, Donegal and Letterkenny stops up to six-times daily beside the car park at McElhinney's Store in Ballybofey. Local buses connect Ballybofey with Killybegs and Letterkenny.

McGeehan Coaches (☎ 075-46150) runs a Glencolumbcille to Letterkenny bus Monday to Saturday that stops in front of the Fintown post office at 1.25pm (at 5.55pm heading for Glenties, Ardara, Killybegs, Kilcar and Glencolumbcille). There's also a McGeehan Coaches bus from Fintown to Ballybofey at 1.25pm Monday to Saturday, mid-July to August. It stops in Ballybofey en route to Fintown, Killybegs and Glencolumbcille at 5pm.

The Feda Ódonaill (☎ 075-48114) bus from Crolly to Galway stops in Ballybofey outside McElhinney's at 9.15am and 4.45pm from Monday to Saturday (also at 12.45pm on Friday), and at 9.15am, 3.45pm and 7.45pm on Sunday.

North-Western Donegal

The various adjectives used to describe Donegal's scenery – wild, spectacular, dramatic, breathtaking – are nowhere more applicable than in the county's north-west. Despite the absence of large towns, you're rarely far from a village or pub. The stretch

DONEGAL

of land between Dungloe and Crolly is a bleak, rocky Gaeltacht area known as the Rosses (Na Rossa) containing numerous tiny lakes and a coastline of clean, sandy beaches.

The main attraction is the island of Arranmore, reached by ferry from the village of Burtonport. The other accessible island, Tory Island farther to the north, is even more appealing. The coastal area between Bunbeg and Dunfanaghy is absolutely superb, and there are wonderful cycling tours around the Bloody Foreland and Horn Head.

DUNGLOE & AROUND
☎ 075 • pop 990

Dungloe (An Clochán Liath), the capital of the Rosses, makes a good base for exploring the region but is unremarkable itself.

The Bord Fáilte tourist office (☎ 21297), off Main St behind the Bridge Inn, opens 9am to 6pm (closed 1pm to 2pm) Monday to Saturday, 11am to 5pm Sunday June to September. An alternative source of information is the Ireland's Alive office (☎ 22299) on Gweedore Rd. The Bank of Ireland, Main St, has an ATM and bureau de change, and the post office is on Quay Rd off Main St past the Midway Bar.

Fishing for salmon and trout is popular and you can get tackle and permits from Bonner's (☎ 21163) on Main St. The nearest good beach is 6km south-west of Dungloe at **Maghery Bay**.

Special Events

In late July/early August, Dungloe hosts the 10-day Mary from Dungloe Festival, named after a popular 1960s song. Thousands crowd into town for a series of events culminating in a contest to pick the year's 'Mary'. Supposedly, she's selected on the basis of personality, but only women aged 18 to 25 are eligible to enter! The festival is a big, raucous, boozy affair and, although it's sometimes graced by big names such as singers Christy Moore or 'boy-next-door' Daniel O'Donnell, some people might want to avoid Dungloe at this time. If you do want to attend, book a bed well ahead. For more details contact Anne Marie Doherty (☎ 21254, fax 22120).

Places to Stay

Greene's Hostel (☎ 21021, fax 21948, Carnmore Rd) Tent €7.55 (for hitchers and cyclists), dorms/private rooms €10/12.60 per person. Open Mar-Dec. Greene's is a well run, modern IHH hostel where you can hire a bike for €6.30 per day.

Crohy Head Hostel (☎ 21950, Crohy Head) Seniors/juniors €9.55/7.60. Open Easter-Sept. Sitting atop scenic Crohy Head (An Cruach), 8km south-west of Dungloe, this 36-bed, remote An Óige hostel has panoramic views over Boylagh Bay.

Óstán na Rosann (☎ 22444, fax 22400, Mill Rd) Singles/doubles €50.80/66. Just north of town past the Statoil service station, this standard hotel has 48 en suite rooms and a leisure centre with a heated pool.

Places to Eat

Dungloe doesn't offer a great deal of choice.

Riverside Bistro (☎ 21062, Main St) Mains €10-19, pasta €7.95. Open 12.30pm-3pm & 6pm-10pm Tues-Sun. Probably the best place to eat in town, the Riverside is a busy, old-world, candle-lit restaurant serving tasty, wholesome Irish cuisine.

Lucky Jackpot (☎ 21880, Main St) Lunch €7.55, dinner €12.60. Open 12.30pm-3pm & 5pm-10.30pm. This inexpensive Chinese restaurant, up the hill past the garda station, serves noodles and other dishes buffet style.

Courthouse Restaurant (☎ 22000, Main St) Mains €5.70, pizzas €4-7.25. Of the fast-food places this is the standout, with a large self-service area and small bar and takeaway service.

Getting There & Away

Dungloe is served by several private companies but not Bus Éireann.

McGeehan Coaches (☎ 46150) runs a service from Dungloe to Dublin via Glenties and Donegal at 7.45am daily (plus noon Monday to Saturday, and 3pm on Sunday). Mid-July to August it also has a daily bus from Dungloe to Fintown at 11.50am.

O'Donnell Buses (☎ 48356) runs from Dungloe to Belfast (4½ hours) via Burtonport, Bunbeg, Dunfanaghy, Letterkenny and

Derry. Buses leave from in front of Delaney's Hotel on Main St at 7.15am Monday to Saturday and 4.30pm on Sunday.

Derry-based Lough Swilly (☎ 028-7126 2017 in Derry, 074-22863 in Letterkenny) runs a Dungloe–Derry service via Burtonport, Crolly, Bloody Foreland, Falcarragh and Letterkenny three-times daily on weekdays.

Twice weekly, Feda Ódonaill (☎ 48114) runs from Annagry (Anagaire) to Killybegs via Burtonport, Dungloe (8.10am on Monday and 2.40pm on Sunday), Glenties and Ardara. In the other direction it runs twice on Friday only, stopping in Dungloe at 8.15am and 10pm.

BURTONPORT
☎ 075 • pop 280

The otherwise ordinary port village of Burtonport (Ailt an Chorráin) is the embarkation point for Arranmore. Back in 1974, the Atlantis commune was established here by one Jenny James, who practised a form of primal therapy. Her followers became known as 'the Screamers'. Eventually the commune relocated to the Colombian jungle and another group arrived to take its place. The Silver Sisters chose to live a Victorian lifestyle, complete with Victorian dress, and soon bizarre stories were circulating about them. They, too, moved on, allowing Burtonport to sink back into anonymity.

For fishing trips contact Donal O'Sullivan (☎ 42077) at the cabin by the pier.

From mid-July to August, McGeehan Coaches (☎ 46150) runs one bus daily, Monday to Saturday, to Burtonport from Dungloe. For Feda Ódonaill (☎ 48114) buses see Getting There & Away under Dungloe & Around.

ARRANMORE
☎ 075 • pop 900

The small island of Arranmore (Árainn Mhór), 9km by 5km, has some spectacular cliff scenery, sea caves and sandy beaches. It has been inhabited for thousands of years, and a prehistoric fort can be seen on the southern side. The western and northern parts are wild and rugged, with few houses to disturb the sense of isolation. The Arranmore Way circles the island (allow three to four hours) and off the south-western tip is Green Island, a bird sanctuary. There's good fishing in the waters surrounding the island, and in Lough Shure you'll find plenty of rainbow trout.

Places to Stay & Eat
Arranmore Hostel (☎ 20015, fax 20014, Leabgarrow) Dorms/private rooms €10-12/12.60 per person. A few minutes' walk from the ferry, Arranmore is a modern, 30-bed hostel with wheelchair access. Bed linen is included in the price.

Bonner's Ferryboat Restaurant (☎ 20532, Leabgarrow) Rooms €20.15 per person. Bonner's, close to the ferry pier, is a two-storey B&B and has an inexpensive cafe popular with islanders.

Phil Bàn's Bar (☎ 20908, Leabgarrow) Mains €5.05-13.85. The long-established Phil Bàn's, by the ferry pier, is one of several pubs serving decent bar food.

Entertainment
The island's pubs enjoy a 24-hour licence to cater for the local fishing community; they regularly provide traditional music sessions.

Getting There & Away
The Arranmore Ferry (☎ 20532), run by Bonner's, plies the 1.5km from Burtonport to Leabgarrow (adult/child €8.80/4.40 return, 25 minutes). In July and August, there are eight daily crossings (seven on Sunday), starting at 8.30am from Burtonport (noon on Sunday). The rest of the year there are at least five sailings daily (three on Sunday).

GWEEDORE & AROUND
☎ 075 • pop 900

The wonderfully remote, Irish-speaking district of Gweedore (Gaoth Dobhair) has a rugged coastline with many beautiful beaches that attract walkers and cyclists, while its bleak interior contains many small fishing lakes. It's a region in flux: older establishments have closed or been pulled down and a lot of redevelopment is taking place.

Settlements hug the coastline. Derrybeg (Doirí Beaga) and Bunbeg (Bun Beag) virtually run into each other along the R257; Gweedore village, which gives its name to the district, is a few kilometres east on the R258. On the main road in Bunbeg there's an Allied Irish Bank with an ATM and bureau de change, while Derrybeg has a post office. Ferries depart from Bunbeg for Tory Island (see that section later).

Places to Stay & Eat

Backpackers Ireland Seaside Hostel *(☎ 32244, Magheragallon, Derrybeg)* Dorms/ private rooms €8.80/15.75 per person. Open mid-Mar-Oct. A windswept IHO hostel, it lies at the end of the road, near a beach and golf course. Linen is included in the rate and bikes are for hire.

Screag an Iolair Mountain Centre *(☎ 48593, Tor, Crolly)* Dorms/private rooms €10.10/12.60 per person. Open Mar-Oct. Surrounded by a rugged, rocky landscape this beautifully remote, friendly hostel is signposted up in the hills above Crolly, south-west of Gweedore on the N56. It has a large selection of second-hand books and offers a free pick-up service if you don't fancy the 5km walk from the main road.

Bunbeg House *(☎ 31305, Bunbeg)* Rooms €25.20-31.50 per person. Catering largely to anglers and sailors, Bunbeg House is a charming, three-star B&B beside tranquil, picturesque Bunbeg harbour. It has quite a large restaurant, which serves mostly seafood (€5.70-10.80) from 3pm, and offers afternoon tea in a separate tearoom. The turn-off to the harbour is off the main road in the village centre.

An Teach Ban *(☎ 32359, Bunbeg)* Singles/doubles €29.20/45.75. Sitting on the hillside just below the main road (past the Allied Irish Bank towards Derrybeg), it has a commanding view of the bay and clean, nonsmoking rooms.

Fernfield *(☎/fax 31258, Middletown, Derrybeg)* Singles/doubles €25.40/44.45. Open Apr-Oct. Mrs McBride runs an efficient B&B here with its three nonsmoking bedrooms all with showers.

Óstán Gweedore *(☎ 31177, fax 31726, Bunbeg)* Rooms €63.50-95.25 per person. Though the hotel will receive no accolades for its architectural design, it's, nevertheless, a popular, luxury establishment (people come from all over Ireland to use its function room) with great views and only a few minutes' walk from the beach.

Óstán Radharc na Mara *(Seaview Hotel; ☎ 31159, fax 32238, Bunbeg)* Rooms €38-45 per person. On the main road, this modern but traditionally furnished hotel has 40 spacious en suite rooms each with TV and direct-dial phone. Fine bar food is available in ***Tábhairne Hughie Tim*** from 3pm to 9.30pm, or you can dine a la carte in the more formal ***Gola Bistro*** (mains €11-20).

Getting There & Away

Feda Ódonaill (☎ 48114) runs a service twice daily from Gweedore to Letterkenny, Donegal, Sligo and Galway. Buses depart at 7.30am and 2.55pm Monday to Saturday (plus at 10.30am on Friday), and at 7.30am, 2pm and 5.45pm Sunday. They leave Bunbeg from near the turn-off for the harbour. From Galway, buses leave St Nicholas Cathedral at 10am and 4pm daily (plus 1.30pm and 5.30pm on Friday), and at 3pm and 8pm on Sunday from Eyre Square.

DUNLEWY & AROUND

☎ 075 • pop 150

The little hamlet of Dunlewy (Dún Lúiche) sits at the foot of Mt Errigal beside Lough Dunlewy.

Ionad Cois Locha (Dunlewy Lakeside Centre)

The lakeside centre *(☎ 31699, Dunlewy; admission to house & grounds or boat trip adult/child €4.10/2.50, combined ticket €6.95/4.40; open 10.30am-6pm Mon-Sat & 11am-7pm Sun Easter-Oct)* reconstructs the home of Manus Ferry, the last of the local weavers, who died in 1975. Visitors can watch the stages of weaving in operation, then go outside to see assorted farm animals, walk along the lake shore, take a boat ride with a storyteller on board to fill them in on local history, geology and folklore, or go pony trekking. In summer there are traditional music concerts. There's an excellent cafe with a turf fire and craft shop.

Mt Errigal & The Poisoned Glen

You don't need to be an experienced mountaineer to climb Mt Errigal (752m), Donegal's highest peak, but the going can be tough and you should be wary of damp, misty days when visibility may drop with little warning.

There are two paths to the summit: the easier tourist route, which covers 5km and takes roughly two hours to complete; and the more difficult 3.25km walk along the north-western ridge, which involves scrambling over scree for about 2½ hours. Details of both routes are available at the Dunlewy Lakeside Centre.

Stories abound about how the Poisoned Glen got its name. The more prosaic suggest that it's because poisonous Irish spurge once grew here or because the original name – An Gleann Neamhe (The Heavenly Glen) – became corrupted to An Gleann Nimhe (The Poisoned Glen). Another theory is that the British were once camped here, and Irish rebels poisoned the water to kill their horses. More imaginative is the tale of the ancient, one-eyed giant, Balor, who was killed here by his exiled grandson, Lughaidh, whereupon the poison from his eye split the rock and poisoned the glen.

It's possible to walk through the glen, although some of the ground is rough and boggy. From the lakeside centre a return walk along the glen is about 12km and takes from two to three hours.

Places to Stay

Backpackers Ireland Lakeside Hostel (☎ *075-32133, Dunlewy*) Dorms €8.90. Open mid-Mar-Oct. Comfortable bunk beds are available at this 30-bed IHO hostel on the main road in Dunlewy. Bed linen is included in the rate and you can hire bikes.

Errigal Hostel (☎ *075-31180, Dunlewy*) Dorms adult/child €10.15/7.60. Open year round. Sitting in the shadow of Mt Errigal just on the edge of Dunlewy, this simple An Óige hostel is a useful stopover for hikers walking the Ulster Way.

GLENVEAGH NATIONAL PARK

Dunlewy is beside the 14,000-hectare Glenveagh National Park (Pairc Naísúnta Ghleann Bheatha), which is in a lake-filled valley overlooked by the Derryveagh Mountains. Much of the land comprising the park was once farmed by tenants, 244 of whom were evicted by landowner John George Adair in the winter of 1861. A plaque on a gable end at Ardaturr farm commemorates their fate. Adair was responsible for the building of Glenveagh Castle (1870). After the mysterious disappearance of the second owner, the land was bought in 1937 by American Henry McIlhenny, who eventually sold it to the state and later donated the castle and gardens.

Adair's wife, Cornelia, introduced two things that define the national park's appearance: the herd of red deer and the rhododendrons. The latter, despite their beauty in blossom, are seen as a pest, preventing broad-leafed trees from seeding. The park's features include a nature trail through woods of Scots pine and oak to a stretch of blanket bog, a viewing point that's a short walk behind the castle, and several lakes, the largest of which is Lough Beagh. The golden eagle has been reintroduced to the park.

The cleverly designed **Glenveagh Visitor Centre** (☎ *074-37090, Churchill; park admission adult/concession/family €2.55/1.25/ 6.35; visitor centre open 10am-6.30pm Mon-Sat, 10am-7.30pm Sun mid-Apr-Sept; 10am-6.30pm Sat-Thur Oct-early Nov; last admission 90 minutes before closing*) has a useful audiovisual display on the ecology of the park and the infamous Adair. There's also an imaginative toy-theatre representation of the story. The restaurant serves hot food and snacks, and the reception sells the necessary midge repellent, as vital in summer as walking boots and waterproofs are in winter.

The park opens year round; camping is not allowed.

Glenveagh Castle

The castle (☎ *074-37090; adult/child/family €2.55/1.25/6.35; open 10am-6.30pm Mon-Sat & 10am-7.30pm Sun mid-Apr-Sept; 10am-6.30pm Sat-Thur Oct-early Nov*), built by John George Adair in 1870, was modelled in miniature on Scotland's Balmoral. Henry

DONEGAL

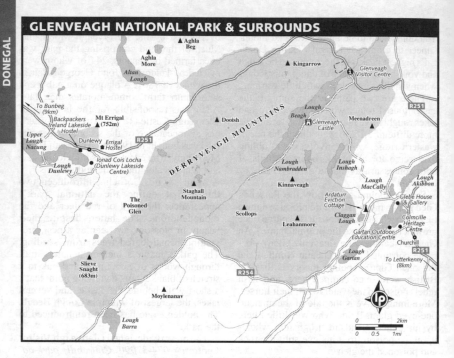

GLENVEAGH NATIONAL PARK & SURROUNDS

McIlhenny made it a comfortable home with lots of reminders of the deer hunting once so important to upper-class life.

A guided tour takes in a series of rooms that look as if McIlhenny just left them. Some of the nicer ones, including the tartan-draped music room and the guest room for female visitors, are in the round tower. The drawing room has a splendid 300-year-old Adams-style fireplace bought by McIlhenny from the Ards estate near Dunfanaghy.

On a dry day the gardens are spectacular. They were nurtured for decades and include a variety of features: a terrace, an Italian garden, a walled kitchen garden, and the Belgian Walk built by Belgian soldiers who stayed here during WWI.

The last guided tours of the castle leave about 45 minutes before closing time. Admission is on top of the national park admission charge. Free minibuses run from the visitor centre to the castle roughly every 15 minutes.

BLOODY FORELAND

Bloody Foreland (Cnoc Fola) gets its name from the red colour of the rocks at sunset, and the road to it is wonderfully remote, scenic and ideal for cycling.

Foreland Heights (☎ 075-31785, Bloody Foreland, Gweedore) Singles/doubles €56.70/65.50 in the high season. Open Apr-Sept. The main thing going for this small, old-fashioned, 12-room hotel is its location at the head of the foreland with magnificent views of the cliffs and ocean.

TORY ISLAND

☎ 074 • pop 250

The remoteness of treeless Tory Island (Oileán Thóraigh), lying about 11km north of the mainland exposed to the harsh elements of the Atlantic, has helped preserve the Irish language and culture of its small community. There's just one pebbly beach, but the cliff walks and a visit to the island's pub or social club make a stay worthwhile.

There are two villages: West Town (An Baile Thiar), containing most of the island's facilities, and East Town (An Baile Thoir).

Things to See & Do
St Colmcille is said to have founded a monastery here in the 6th century. The only remains of this monastic era are near West Town: the **Tau Cross**, a small undecorated T-shaped cross on the pier, and a **round tower**, with a circumference of nearly 16m, built of rounded beach-stones and rough granite, with a round-headed doorway some distance above the ground.

The island is a wondrous place for **birdwatching**: over 100 species of sea bird inhabit the island and among the cliffs in the north-east you can see colonies of puffin. The south-west is topographically quite different – very flat but with some dangerous offshore rocks. It was here that the British gunboat *Wasp* was wrecked in 1884 while on a mission to collect taxes from the islanders. The independent-minded islanders still pay no taxes and elect their own island 'king'.

Tory Island has an indigenous **school of primitive painters**, whose work depicting island life has been exhibited around Europe. The most accomplished was James Dixon, who started painting in his 60s, when he was inspired by (or rather thought he could do better than) the English artist Derek Hill (see Glebe House & Gallery later in this chapter). He died in 1970. You can see and buy their work in the Dixon Gallery near the harbour.

Places to Stay & Eat
The two villages have a number of B&Bs.

Grace Duffy's (☎ 35136, East Town) Singles/doubles from €25.40/45.70. Open May-Oct. This welcoming B&B has three comfy, nonsmoking bedrooms (two with showers) and uses organically grown food. Dinner here costs an extra €11.45.

Óstán Thóraigh (☎ 35920, fax 35613, West Town) Singles/doubles €50/75. Open Apr-Dec. Óstán Thóraigh is a modern, 14-room hotel where you can get good pub food or full meals (€6.30-15).

Caife an Chreagáin (☎ 35856, West Town) Meals under €7. This small cafe serves mainly snacks and light meals.

Entertainment
Club Soisialta Thóraigh (Tory Social Club; ☎ 65121, West Town) One of the island's important social centres, the club regularly presents *ceilidhs* and traditional music sessions.

Óstán Thóraigh (☎ 35920, West Town) The pub here is a relaxed place for a drink and hosts regular traditional music sessions.

Getting There & Away
Donegal Coastal Cruises (Turasmara Teo; ☎ 075-31340) operates a boat service from Bunbeg (☎ 075-31991) and Magheraroarty (☎ 074-35061), which is reached by turning off the N56 at the western end of Gortahork near Falcarragh. The road is signposted Coastal Route/Bloody Foreland.

Boats leave from Bunbeg year round. The boat leaves at 9am daily and returns from Tory at 10.30am between June and October (less frequently from November to May). The boat from Magheraroarty leaves at 11.30am and 5pm daily, June to September (plus 1.30pm in July and August).

On Wednesday in July and August, a boat also leaves Port-na-Blagh (near Dunfanaghy) at 2pm, returning at 6.30pm.

The fare is €18.90 return (bicycles free) but call ahead, as weather and tides can affect sailings.

Getting Around
Bike hire is available from Rothair ar Clós (☎ 65614) in West Town.

FALCARRAGH & AROUND
☎ 074 • pop 900
Falcarragh (An Fál Carrach) is a rather unremarkable resort village, but there's a good beach nearby. Together with neighbouring Gortahork (Gort an Choirce), it has a significant Irish-speaking community. The Bank of Ireland at the eastern end of Main St has an ATM and bureau de change, and the post office is at Main St's western end.

Things to See & Do
You can reach the **beach** (4km away) by

DONEGAL

following signs marked An Trá from either end of Main St. The beach is superb for walking, but swimming is unsafe because of the currents.

The grey bulk of **Muckish Mt** (670m) is a distinctive landmark that dominates the coast between Dunfanaghy and the Bloody Foreland. From the top, on a fine day, there are sweeping panoramic views to Malin Head and Tory Island. It can be climbed from south-east of Falcarragh by way of the inland road through Muckish Gap. Consult *New Irish Walks: West and North*, by Tony Whilde & Patrick Simms, for details.

Places to Stay

Shamrock Lodge Hostel (☎ 35192, Main St) Dorms/private rooms €8.80-10.10/13.85 per person. This IHH-affiliated hostel has 14 beds in the village pub of the same name. It's perfect for those who want a lively nightlife close by, but not if you want to sleep before 1am.

Ferndale (☎ 65506, Falcarragh) Singles/doubles €29.85/48.25. Open May-Sept. Set in a carefully manicured garden only 200m north-west of the centre, Ferndale has four comfy bedrooms, one of which has its own shower.

Cuan-na-Mara (☎ 35327, Ballyness, Falcarragh) Singles/doubles from €30/48. Open June-Sept. Ballyness Bay and Tory Island are visible from this four-room, rural B&B, about 1km from town. The bedrooms are nonsmoking and you can also buy organic food and hire bicycles here.

Entertainment

Falcarragh (and Gortahork) have a number of pubs that come alive at night especially in summer. Two we recommend are *Shamrock Lodge (☎ 35192, Main St)* and *Gweedore Bar (☎ 35293, Main St)*.

Getting There & Away

The Feda Ódonaill (☎ 075-48114) bus from Crolly to Galway stops in front of the phone box on Main St at 7.50am and 3.15pm Monday to Saturday (plus at 10.50am on Friday), reaching Letterkenny about an hour later and Galway at 1.10pm and 8.45pm, respectively.

On Sunday, buses leave at 7.50am, 2.20pm and 6.05pm.

Anthony McGinley's (☎ 075-48167) bus leaves for Dublin at 7.25am daily. Lough Swilly's (☎ 028-7126 2017, 074-22863) Dungloe to Derry bus stops on Main St near the hostel twice daily Monday to Friday (three times on Saturday).

DUNFANAGHY & AROUND
☎ 074 • pop 290

The attractive village of Dunfanaghy (Dún Fionnachaidh) is a popular holiday resort in a small, discreet way. The vast sandy stretches of virtually empty beach are a big draw, and Dunfanaghy makes a good base for trips north to Horn Head, south to Letterkenny or north-west to Tory Island.

The Allied Irish Bank (no ATM) is opposite the Carrig Rua Hotel, and the post office, at the other end of Main St, has a bureau de change open 9am to 5.30pm (closed 1pm to 2pm) weekdays.

Dunfanaghy Workhouse

After the passage of the Poor Law in 1838, workhouses were set up around Ireland to accommodate and employ the destitute in conditions deliberately intended to be uncomfortable. Men, women, children and the sick were separated from one other, and their lives were rigorously governed, with hard work the order of the day. Dunfanaghy's workhouse opened in 1845, just before the onset of the Famine, which caused the number of residents to multiply. By 1847 it was expanded to accommodate some 600 people, double the number originally planned.

The workhouse, west of the centre up past the post office, is now a small **heritage centre** *(☎ 36540, Main St; adult/concession/family €3.15/1.25/8.80; open from 10am-5pm Mon-Sat & noon-5pm Sun Easter-Sept)*, which tells the history of the Famine in a series of audiovisual presentations in different rooms.

Dunfanaghy Gallery *(☎ 36224, Main St; free; open 10am-7pm Mon-Sat)*, just up the road from the heritage centre, started life as a fever hospital. Nowadays it houses art and crafts.

Horn Head

Horn Head (Corrán Binne) has some of Donegal's most spectacular coastal scenery and plenty of bird life. The towering, dramatic headland, with quartzite cliffs over 180m high, can be reached by continuing from the end of the walk described in the following entry, but the route can be perilous at times. Consult the guide *New Irish Walks: West and North*, by Tony Whilde & Patrick Simms, or *Hill Walkers' Donegal*, by David Herman.

An alternative route is to go by bike or car from the Falcarragh end of Dunfanaghy. The road circles the headland and offers tremendous views on a fine day: Tory, Inishbofin, Inishdooey and tiny Inishbeg islands to the west; Sheep Haven Bay and the Rosguill Peninsula to the east; Malin Head to the north-east; and even the coast of Scotland.

Walking

You could easily spend a day walking this area. For an exhilarating walk, take the turning from Dunfanaghy to Tramore Beach and continue along the track down to the dunes by first passing a farm, then crossing a field on a clearly indicated pathway.

The vast, lovely **Tramore Beach** opens up below the sand dunes. Turn right and follow the beach to the end, where you can find a way up onto a path that leads north to **Pollaguill Bay**. From the bay you can continue to the cairn at the end of the bay and follow the coastline for a stupendous view of the 20m **Marble Arch**, carved out by the sea.

Other Activities

Horse riding can be arranged through **Arnold's Hotel** *(see Places to Stay)*, which also offers **bird-watching**, **painting** and **photography** holidays. **Dessie McGilloway** (☎ *66197, Port-na-Blagh)* organises **sea-angling** trips on board the *Lady Port-na-Blagh*.

Places to Stay & Eat

Corcreggan Mill Cottage Hostel (☎ *36409, fax 36092,* e *millhostel@corcreggan.com, Dunfanaghy)* Tent €5.05 per person, dorms €8.80-12.60, private rooms €11.35-13.85

per person. Close to a large, deserted beach, this superior IHH hostel 4km south of Dunfanaghy on the Falcarragh road (N56), offers dorm accommodation in a 200-year-old former kiln house and private rooms in a converted, mahogany railway car. It has three separate kitchens. Buses stop outside.

Rosman House (☎*/fax 36273, Figart, Dunfanaghy)* Singles/doubles €38.10/55.85. The six bedrooms in this modern, clean B&B on a working farm are all en suite and non-smoking and have great views. Credit cards are accepted here.

The Whins (☎*/fax 63481, Kill, Dunfanaghy)* Singles/doubles €35.55/53.30. Dishing up first-rate breakfasts, The Whins is a charming, two-storey B&B set in a beautiful garden and close to a beach and golf course. It also accepts credit cards.

Carrig Rua Hotel (☎ *36133, fax 36277, Main St)* Rooms €45-58 per person. The 22-room hotel is an old-world, friendly place with a relaxed atmosphere. Here, good food is available in the *Highwayman Bar* (mains €7.95-9.45), or in the more formal *Sheep Haven Room Restaurant* (mains €12.50-18) noted for its seafood.

Arnold's Hotel (☎ *36208, fax 36352, Main St)* Rooms €53.35-66.65 per person. Open mid-Mar-early Nov. Arnold's is a big, 32-room hotel overlooking Sheep Haven Bay. French and Asian influences are evident in the fine seafood and other meals (€12-15) served in its bistro and restaurant.

The Mill (☎*/fax 36985, Figart, Dunfanaghy)* Dinner €26-31. Open 7pm-9pm Tues-Sun. If you're looking for a special meal this highly recommended restaurant, at the edge of Dunfanaghy on the Falcarragh road, is hard to beat. Leave some room for dessert. Reservations are necessary.

Dunfanaghy Workhouse (☎ *36540, Main St)* Food under €3. For coffee and delicious home-baked scones, fruitcake or flan, try the tearoom here (which also houses a small art gallery).

Getting There & Away

Feda Ódonaill (☎ 075-48114) buses from Crolly to Galway stop in the square at 8am and 3.25pm Monday to Saturday, plus 11am on Friday. On Sunday they leave at 8am, 2.30pm and 6.15pm.

Anthony McGinley's (☎ 075-48167) buses between Letterkenny and Dublin stop in Dunfanaghy two to three-times daily. Lough Swilly's (☎ 028-7126 2017, 074-22863) Dungloe–Derry bus stops in the square three times daily Monday to Saturday.

DUNFANAGHY TO CREESLOUGH

For places to eat you'd do better in Dunfanaghy or Letterkenny than along the N56 that joins them. If you're hostelling or camping, you can pick up supplies at the supermarkets in Creeslough or Dunfanaghy.

Ards Forest Park

The park *(free; open 10.30am-4pm Sat & Sun Easter-June & Sept; 10.30am-9pm daily July & Aug)*, about 3km south-east of Dunfanaghy off the N56, is a wildfowl sanctuary and has marked nature trails varying in length from about 2km to 13km. It covers the northern shore of the Ards Peninsula and there are walks to its clean beaches. In 1930 the southern part of the peninsula was taken over by Capuchin monks; the grounds of their friary buildings are open to the public.

Doe Castle

The castle *(Caisléan na dTuath; Creeslough)* was once the stronghold of the Scottish MacSweeney family, who were employed by the O'Donnells. Built in the early 16th century it was constantly fought over by the MacSweeney brothers. Early in the 17th century it passed into English hands and was repaired and inhabited until well into the 19th century. The curious slab that rests against the tower near the entrance is thought to be the tomb of one of the MacSweeneys. The castle is picturesquely sited on a low promontory with water on three sides and a moat hewn out of the rock on the landward side. The best view is from the Carrigart to Creeslough road. The castle can only be viewed from outside because of ongoing restoration work, some of the results of which are clearly visible.

It's 5km from Creeslough on the Carrigart road and is clearly signposted.

CREESLOUGH

☎ 074 • pop 250

The small village of Creeslough (An Craoslach), on the N56 near an inlet of Sheep Haven Bay, has an interesting, if ugly, modern church, best viewed against the outline of distant **Muckish Mt** (670m). The mountain can be climbed from Creeslough. A road turns off to the left 2km north-west of the village, by a small derelict shop, on the N56; after 6km along here a rough track begins the ascent. Consult *New Irish Walks: West and North* (published by Gill & Macmillan), by Tony Whilde & Patrick Simms, for details.

Places to Stay & Eat

There are several B&Bs in the Creeslough area.

Hillcrest (☎ *38145, Creeslough)* Singles/doubles from €25/45. Open Apr-Sept. Hospitable Hillcrest, 2km north towards Ards, has four attractive rooms, two of which are en suite.

Stonecutter's Rest (☎ *38001, Creeslough)* Meals €3.15-8.95. Standard but tasty pub grub comes in big portions here, especially the chips.

Getting There & Away

Feda Ódonaill (☎ 075-48114) buses between Galway and Crolly stop in Creeslough twice daily.

Letterkenny & Around

LETTERKENNY

☎ 074 • pop 7600

Letterkenny (Leitir Ceanainn) grew considerably after Derry, 34km north-east, was cut off from its hinterland by the partition of Ireland, and is now Donegal's largest town. There's not a great deal to detain a tourist, although it makes a pleasant enough stop en route to or from Derry. It's also an alternative base to smaller Dunfanaghy in the north, or Dungloe in the west, for exploring the surrounding area.

Orientation & Information

Main St, said to be the longest high street in Ireland, runs from Dunnes Stores at one end to the courthouse at the other and divides into Upper and Lower Main Sts. At the top of Upper Main St there is a Y-junction: High Rd veers left, while Port Rd goes right and down to the bus station and the road out to Derry and Dublin.

The best place for tourist information is the excellent Chamber of Commerce Visitor Information Centre (☎ 24866), on Port Rd in the town centre, which has lots of free literature and advice. It opens 9am to 5pm Monday to Friday. The Bord Fáilte tourist office (☎ 21160), on the Derry road about 1.5km north of town, is geared towards the motorist and can be accessed only via the southbound lane. You could walk there from the roundabout where the buses stop, but it wouldn't be an enjoyable experience. It opens 9am to 7pm Monday to Saturday and 10am to 2pm Sunday in July and August; 9am to 5pm Monday to Friday September to June.

Along Main St are branches of the Allied Irish Bank, Bank of Ireland and Ulster Bank, all with ATMs. The post office is on Upper Main St almost opposite the Central Bar.

You can surf the Internet on the lower floor of Four Lanterns (☎ 20440), a fast-food outlet on Lower Main St, for €1.60 per 15 minutes.

Things to See & Do

The Gothic-style St Eunan's Cathedral (1901) sits west of the centre on Sentry Hill Rd (take Church Lane up from Main St) and contains stained-glass windows and much intricate Celtic carving.

The small, modern Donegal County Museum (☎ 24613, High Rd; free; open 11am-12.30pm & 1pm-4.30pm Tues-Fri, 1pm-4.30pm Sat), on the left past the leisure centre, has a collection of local archaeological finds, including some interesting Iron Age stone heads and early-Christian material. Downstairs there are temporary displays and some telling photos about the realities of life in 19th-century rural Ireland to counterbalance the rather rosy version on display upstairs.

Some salmon and trout rivers and lakes surround Letterkenny. The Letterkenny Anglers Association opens to visitors; membership and permits are available from Brian McCormick's Sports & Leisure (☎ 27833, 56 Upper Main St).

Special Events

The Letterkenny Arts Festival (☎ 27856) is a four-day international festival of music and dance held at the end of August. It features a variety of music, from Celtic rock to folk and jazz, and includes a crafts day and competitions.

Places to Stay

Port Hostel (☎ 25315, fax 24768, Port Rd) Dorms/private rooms €9.45/11.35 per person. Open year round. Port, registered with the IHO, is reached by following the lane beside the An Grianán Theatre round to the end. It's in a quiet spot surrounded by trees. Rates include bed linen.

Arch Hostel (☎ 57255, Upper Corkey, Pluck) Dorms €9.45. Open July-Aug. This remote IHO hostel, in a stable loft 10km from Letterkenny off the Derry road, has only six beds; call ahead to arrange pick up.

Covehill House (☎ 21038, Port Rd) Singles/doubles €27.70/40.30. For B&B try this quiet, pleasant bungalow, set back from Port Rd behind the An Grianán Theatre.

Gallagher's Hotel (☎ 22066, fax 21016, 100 Upper Main St) Rooms €31.75-38.10. Gallagher's is a reasonably priced, central hotel with 27 attractive en suite rooms.

Letterkenny Court Hotel (☎ 22977, fax 22928, 29-45 Upper Main St) Singles/doubles with breakfast €60/88. A finely furnished hotel in the centre of Letterkenny, the Letterkenny Court has both standard bedrooms and apartment-style suites plus two bars and a restaurant.

Places to Eat

Gallagher's Hotel (see Places to Stay) Most mains €5.65-7.30. Open noon-3pm & 6pm-10pm. Gallagher's serves excellent, good-value meals in its bar in huge proportions – if you're really hungry try the massive 'Gallagher's Challenge'.

Yellow Pepper *(☎ 24133, 36 Lower Main St)* Dinner mains €7.25-15.05. Open breakfast, lunch and dinner. This is a fairly stylish eatery serving excellent sandwiches; the extensive evening menu includes a good selection of seafood and vegetarian dishes.

Pat's Pizza *(☎ 21761, Upper Main St)* Pizzas €5-9. Pat's sells delicious, inexpensive pizzas to take away, or you can choose to eat in its unadorned dining area. It also serves kebabs and sandwiches.

Quiet Moment *(☎ 28382, Upper Main St)* Meals €2.50-6.25. This tearoom serves good filling breakfasts, light meals and baguettes in pleasant, comfortable surroundings, though it isn't so quiet when the volume on the radio gets turned up.

Bakersville *(☎ 21887, Church Lane)* Under €4. Delicious bread, scones, cakes and sandwiches are available from this bakery just off Main St, which has a small eating area and does good coffee.

Entertainment

Cottage Bar *(☎ 21338, 49 Upper Main St)* Locals flock to this emerald-green, character-laden pub with its low ceiling, buzzy atmosphere, open fire, bric-a-brac and Thursday night music sessions.

Central Bar *(☎ 24088, 58 Upper Main St)* With its dark, wood-panelled walls and brass rails, this is one of the better pubs for music; it has a separate nightclub at the weekend.

An Grianán Theatre *(☎ 20777, Port Rd)* An Grianán Theatre is both a community theatre and major arts venue for the northwest presenting national and international drama, comedy and music. It also has a good cafe and bar.

Getting There & Away

Letterkenny is a major bus transport hub for north-western Ireland, with a number of bus companies stopping here. The bus station (☎ 22863) is by the roundabout at the junction of Ramelton Rd and the Derry road.

Bus Éireann's (☎ 21309) express bus No 32 runs from Dublin four-times daily (three on Sunday) to Letterkenny via Omagh and Monaghan. The Derry–Galway bus No 64 stops at Letterkenny three-times daily (twice on Sunday) before continuing to Donegal, Bundoran, Sligo, Knock and Galway. The Derry–Cork express bus No 52, via Letterkenny, Sligo, Galway and Limerick, runs twice daily (once on Sunday). The daily service (bus No 69) from Derry to Westport via Donegal, Sligo and Ballina also stops in Letterkenny.

Anthony McGinley (☎ 48167) runs a twice-daily service (three on Friday) from Letterkenny to Dublin. Derry-based Lough Swilly (☎ 028-7126 2017, 074-22863) runs services regularly from Derry to Dungloe, via Letterkenny and Dunfanaghy, as well as direct to Letterkenny.

John McGinley (☎ 35201) buses run twice daily Sunday to Thursday (three times Friday, once Saturday) from Annagry to Dublin through Letterkenny and Monaghan.

The Feda Ódonaill (☎ 075-48114) bus from Crolly to Galway operates twice daily through Letterkenny and continues to Donegal, Bundoran, Sligo and Galway.

Monday to Saturday, McGeehan Coaches (☎ 075-46150) runs a Letterkenny to Glencolumbcille service.

Getting Around

A taxi can be ordered from O'Donnell Cabs (☎ 22444). There's a taxi stand on Main St opposite the square. In summer, you can hire bikes from Church Street Cycles (☎ 26204), near the cathedral, which is part of the Raleigh Rent-a-Bike scheme; bikes cost €12.60/50.40 per day/week.

AROUND LETTERKENNY
Newmills Corn & Flax Mills

In the village of Newmills, 6km south-west of Letterkenny, the restored Dúchas-run mills *(☎ 074-25115, Newmills; adult/concession/family €2.55/1.25/6.35; open 10am-6.30pm, last tour 5.45pm, mid-June-late Sept)* are open to the public. The visitor centre explains the role of corn and flax and how they were produced. There's a riverside walk to a two-room, 19th-century scutcher's cottage and a village forge.

Colmcille Heritage Centre

Colmcille (also known as Columba) was born

Donegal's donkeys jockey for centre stage.

Mountcharles, Co Donegal

Live out your desert-island fantasies at this sandy, sheltered cove near Malinbeg, County Donegal.

It's worth any number of blisters for a view like this from the Urris Hills in County Donegal.

EOIN CLARKE

Curing warts in Newton, Meath

EOIN CLARKE

Ireland's first Cistercian monastery at Mellifont, County Louth

EOIN CLARKE

The view of Carlingford Lough from Slieve Foye in County Louth across to the Mourne Mountains

EOIN CLARKE

Cromwell left his mark on Trim's Yellow Steeple, County Meath.

EOIN CLARKE

Monasterboice, County Louth

in Gartan, 17km north-west of Letterkenny, and the heritage centre (☎ *074-37306, Gartan; adult/concession €1.90/1.25; open 10.30am-6.30pm Mon-Sat, 1pm-6.30pm Sun, Easter, early May-late Sept)*, on the shore of Lough Gartan, is devoted to his life and times, with a lavish display on the production of illuminated manuscripts.

Gartan clay is associated with the birth of Colmcille. The story is that Colmcille's mother, on the run from pagans, haemorrhaged during childbirth and her blood changed the soil's colour from brown to pure white. Ever since, the clay has been regarded as a charm. The clay is found only on townland belonging to the O'Friel family, whose oldest son is the only one allowed to dig it up. Ask nicely and the staff may produce some from under the counter.

On the way to the heritage centre you'll also see signs to the ruins of **Colmcille's Abbey** and to the hillside location of the **saint's birthplace**, marked by a cross erected by Cornelia Adair in 1911 (there are great views of the lake from the latter).

To get to the heritage centre, leave Letterkenny on the R250 road to Glenties and Ardara. A few kilometres out of town, turn right on the R251 to the village of Churchill and follow the signs. Alternatively, from Kilmacrennan on the N56 turn west and follow the signs.

Gartan Outdoor Education Centre

The centre (☎ *074-37032, Gartan, Churchill)*, 18km north-west of Letterkenny, is set in its own 35-hectare estate on the shores of Lough Gartan. It conducts a variety of courses in summer, such as rock climbing, sea canoeing, windsurfing and hill climbing. Courses are run for both adults and children, groups and individuals, and full details are available on request. Including hostel accommodation, weekend multi-skill courses for adults cost from €115.

Glebe House & Gallery

The early-19th-century Glebe House (☎ *074-37071, Churchill; adult/concession/family €2.55/1.25/6.35; open 11am-6.30pm Sat-Thur, Easter & mid-May-Sept)*, on the shore of Lough Gartan, was once a rectory, then a hotel, and was bought by the artist Derek Hill in 1953 for IR£1000. Derek Hill was born in England in 1916 and worked in Germany before travelling to Russia. He visited Armenia with the intrepid explorer Freya Stark and became interested in Islamic art.

Dúchas-operated Glebe House is worth visiting for its works of art alone, and a fascinating guided tour of the house takes about 40 minutes. Landseer, Pasmore, Hokusai, Picasso, Augustus John, Jack B Yeats and Kokoschka are all represented. The kitchen is full of paintings by the Tory Island artists, including a bird's-eye view of West Town by James Dixon (see the Tory Island section earlier in this chapter). The kitchen is done up in a wonderfully folksy style and there's some original William Morris wallpaper in several rooms. Don't miss the unusual bathroom with the forwards-flushing toilet. The gardens are also wonderful.

Doon Well & Rock of Doon

During penal times it was believed that wells had curative properties, and some people still believe this to be true of Doon Well (Tobar a' Duin), judging from the bits of cloth left hanging on the nearby bushes. There are good views from the top of the Rock of Doon (Carraig a' Doon), which is where the O'Donnell kings were inaugurated.

To get here the most straightforward route is to take the signposted turn-off from the N56 just north of Kilmacrennan (the well and rock are about 1.5km north of the village).

Lifford & Around
☎ 074 • pop 1360

About 22km south-east of Letterkenny, along the N14, is the small, picturesque town of Lifford (Leifear). It was once the judicial capital of County Donegal, a position now held by Letterkenny.

Lifford Old Courthouse Visitor Centre

This fine 18th-century courthouse has been converted into a heritage centre (☎ *417 33, Lifford; adult/concession €3.80/1.90; open 9am-5pm Mon-Fri, 10am-5pm Sat &*

2pm-6pm Sun, Easter-Sept) looking at both the historic role of Donegal's Gaelic chieftains and at some of the cases tried in the court and their verdicts.

For those who can't tell their O'Neills from their O'Donnells, some of the information provided in the Clans Room can be pretty heavy going. Descend into the courtroom, though, and the stories of 'Napper' Tandy, 'Half-hanged' McNaughten and other 'criminals' are riveting, and it's amazing how often they ended up being transported to Australia! Descend more stairs and you end up in the chilly cells where there are models of some of the prisoners you've already heard about. Now you hear their side of the story.

Cavanacor House At Rossiger, 3km north of Lifford off the N14, Cavanacor House *(☎/fax 41143, Rossiger; adult/concession €3.20/1.90; open noon-6pm Tues-Sat, 2pm-6pm Sun, Easter-Sept)*, is an attractive 17th-century building, once inhabited by Magdalen Tasker, the great-great-great-grandmother of James Knox Polk, 11th president of the USA from 1845 to 1849. King James II is said to have dined beneath a sycamore in the front garden during the Siege of Derry in 1689. Three rooms in the house are open to visitors, although the gallery at the back housing the paintings and sculptures created by its current owners is probably more interesting. Painting and pottery workshops take place year round and the tearoom serves home baking.

Places to Stay There's little accommodation in Lifford but here are a couple of choices.

***Central Bar** (☎ 45126, Main St)* Rooms €21.45 per person. Open year round. This is the most central accommodation in Lifford. Although above a pub, it's quiet and the rooms are clean and spacious. All rooms have TVs but bathrooms are shared.

***Haw Lodge** (☎ 41397, fax 41985, Sligo Rd)* Singles/doubles from €28/48. Open Mar-Nov. Haw Lodge is a pleasant, non-smoking B&B with private parking and a garden for guests' use.

Getting There & Away Bus Éireann's (☎ 21309) express bus No 32 from Dublin to Letterkenny stops in Lifford up to four-times daily. Local buses connect Lifford with Letterkenny, Ballybofey and Strabane.

North-Eastern Donegal

ROSGUILL PENINSULA

From **Carrigart** (Carraig Airt) it's a 15km journey round this small, beautiful, scenic peninsula along a road marked 'Atlantic Drive'. Carrigart itself has a lovely beach, which is relatively deserted because the camp site at the fishing village of **Downings** to the north draws the crowds. The best beach for swimming is **Trá na Rossan**, and the An Óige hostel nearby is an added attraction. On no account should you swim in Boveeghter or Mulroy Bay – both are unsafe.

There's plenty of social life at night in Downings' pubs, which are often packed with holidaymakers from the North staying at Casey's Caravan Park.

Places to Stay

***Casey's Caravan Park** (☎ 074-55376, fax 55128, Downings)* Tent small/family €12.70/15.25. Open Apr-Sept. Beside a safe, sandy beach the park has limited space for tents so it's best to ring first and check, though it doesn't take bookings.

***Trá na Rosann Hostel** (☎ 074-55374, Downings)* Adult/child €10.15/7.60. Open Easter-Sept. A former hunting lodge, this 34-bed, An Óige hostel is east of the beach. It's 6km from Downings and hitching is the best bet if you're without wheels.

***Mevagh House** (☎ 074-55693, fax 55512, Milford Rd, Carrigart)* Singles/doubles €30.50/48.25. Next to the Esso service station on the edge of the village, Mevagh has large, clean, bright rooms, and breakfast includes a choice of yoghurt and fruit.

***An Crossog** (☎/fax 074-55498, Downings)* Singles/doubles €31.75/50.80. Like Hill House, An Crossog has four comfy rooms (three with showers) and hires out bikes; it also accepts credit cards.

Beach Hotel (☎ 074-55303, fax 55907, Downings) Rooms €33.55-38.10 per person. Open Apr-Oct. Close to the beach in Downings, this family-run hotel has 20 pleasant rooms, most of which are en suite.

Places to Eat

Carrigart is best for food.

North Star (☎ 074-54990, Carrigart) Mains €10-15. This busy bar has surprisingly modern decor and serves good pub grub in plentiful proportions.

Weavers Restaurant & Wine Bar (☎ 074-55204, Carrigart) Mains €8.80-13.85. Open 6.30pm-9.30pm. You can enjoy flavoursome, good-value evening meals in this rustic restaurant.

Getting There & Around

A local bus connects Carrigart and Downings, but it's of limited use for visitors. You really do need your own transport for this area.

FANAD HEAD PENINSULA

The Fanad Head Peninsula is north-east of Letterkenny. On its western side, **Carrowkeel** (Kerrykeel on some maps) has an attractive location overlooking Mulroy Bay and nearby is the 19th-century **Knockalla Fort**, built to warn of any approaching French ships. **Kildooney More portal tomb** is also worth a visit. The small villages of Milford and Rosnakill have little for visitors, but Portsalon does have a beautiful beach.

The Lough Swilly (☎ 028-7126 2017, 074-22863) bus leaves Letterkenny at 10.05am and 6.05pm and reaches Milford an hour later. From Milford it takes a further 10 minutes to Carrowkeel and 35 minutes to Portsalon on the eastern side, handy for the Knockalla camp site (see under Portsalon & Fanad Head later in this section).

The eastern side of the peninsula is more interesting, and both Rathmelton (also spelled Ramelton) and Rathmullan make good bases for a quiet break. Accommodation is relatively limited, so it's wise to book ahead.

Rathmelton
☎ 074 • pop 920

On the eastern side, the first town you come to is the pretty but somewhat faded Rathmelton (Ráth Mealtain). It was founded in the early 17th century by William Stewart and boasts some fine Georgian houses and stone warehouses. When the railway was routed to Letterkenny instead of Rathmelton, a hush descended on the town.

The National Irish Bank, on the Mall by the River Lennon, has a bureau de change but no ATM. The post office is off the Mall on Castle St.

The **Donegal Ancestry Family Research Centre** *(☎ 51266, The Quay; free; open 9am-4.30pm Mon-Thur, 9am-4pm Fri)* houses an exhibition on the history of Ramelton as well as doing genealogical research. Coming from Letterkenny turn right at the river and follow it round for about 400m. The ruined **Tullyaughnish Church**, on the hill, is also worth a visit because of the Romanesque carvings in the eastern wall, which were taken from a far older church on nearby Aughnish Island, on the River Lennon.

Places to Stay & Eat Rathmelton has a number of accommodation and restaurant options.

Lennon Lodge Hostel (☎ 51227, Market Square) Dorms €13. Facilities here include hot showers, central heating, kitchen, laundry, a large common room and TVs in every room. There's also live music in the attached bar Thursday to Sunday nights.

Crammond House (☎ 51055, Market Square) Singles/doubles from €29.85/43.20. Open Apr-Oct. You'll get a warm welcome at this fine Georgian terraced house at the quiet northern end of Rathmelton.

Meadowell (☎ 51125, Burnside Rd) Singles/doubles from €29.85/43.20. Open Mar-Oct. A whitewashed bungalow off the Letterkenny–Rathmullan road, Meadowell is a clean B&B about 500m from the town centre. The bedrooms are nonsmoking.

Mirabeau Steak House (☎/fax 51138, The Mall) Mains €7.25-13.55. The Mirabeau, in a two-storey Georgian house in the town centre facing the river, is Rathmelton's most upmarket restaurant. The cuisine is French with an emphasis on steak and seafood.

Bridge Bar (☎ 51833, Bridgend) Mains €12.35-17.65. On the other side of the river, the Bridge Bar is a lovely old pub with a seafood restaurant whose menu includes such dishes as roasted swordfish.

Getting There & Away Lough Swilly (☎ 028-7126 2017, 074-22863) buses connect Rathmelton with Letterkenny (25 minutes) three-times daily Monday to Saturday.

Rathmullan
☎ 074 • pop 490

Like Rathmelton, quiet Rathmullan (Ráth Maoláin) is a sleepy place that's only now catching up with the modern world, although in the 16th to 18th centuries it was the scene of momentous events.

In 1587, Hugh O'Donnell, the 15-year-old heir to the powerful O'Donnell clan, was tricked into boarding a ship at Rathmullan and taken to Dublin as prisoner. He escaped four years later on Christmas Eve and, after unsuccessful attempts at revenge, died in Spain, aged only 30. In 1607, despairing of fighting the English, Hugh O'Neill, the earl of Tyrone, and Rory O'Donnell, the earl of Tyrconnel, boarded a ship in Rathmullan harbour and left Ireland for good. This decisive act, known as the Flight of the Earls, marked the effective end of Gaelic Ireland and the rule of Irish chieftains. In the aftermath of the earls' departure, large-scale confiscation of their estates took place, preparing for the Plantation of Ulster with settlers from Britain.

Wolfe Tone was captured in Rathmullan following the 1798 Rising.

The sandy area near the pier outside the heritage centre is the only clean part of the town's beach, but there's a strong smell of fish from the quayside warehouse.

Rathmullan Heritage Centre This small heritage centre (☎ 58229, Rathmullan Pier; adult/child €2.55/1.25; open 10am-1pm & 2pm-5pm Thur-Sat, noon-5pm Sun, Easter-Sept), focuses on the Flight of the Earls and will mainly appeal to those with a deep interest in Irish history. It's housed in an early-19th-century fort built by the British when fearing Napoleon's intentions. In lieu of a tourist office, the heritage centre can help with enquiries about local accommodation, sights in the surrounding area and so on.

Rathmullan Priory This Carmelite friary was founded around 1508 by the Mac-Sweeneys, and it was still in use in 1595 when an English commander, George Bingham, raided the place and took off with the communion plate and priestly vestments. The earls left Ireland forever from just outside the priory. Although a ruin, it looks so well preserved because of Bishop Knox's renovation in 1618; he wanted to use it as his own residence.

Places to Stay & Eat Rathmullan has three hotels, all quite different in appearance and style.

Pier Hotel (☎ 58178) Rooms from €19 per person, including breakfast. This 10-room hotel was originally a 19th-century coaching inn and is very much a family establishment. It does bar food as well as full a la carte meals and there are lovely lake views.

Rathmullan House (☎ 58188, fax 58200) Rooms €69-77 per person. About 2km north of town, this genteel, lakeside country house, with an indoor heated swimming pool and sauna, is set in a beautifully wooded garden.

Fort Royal (☎ 58100, fax 58103) Rooms €63-83 per person. In a quiet location by the lake this small, friendly hotel has its own private beach and golf course.

Dinner at the three hotels costs around €30.

An Bonnan Bùi (☎ 58453) Starters €3.15-5.50, mains €9.50-16. Open 6pm-11pm Thur-Mon. Near the Pier Hotel, An Bonnan Bùi's imaginative menu mixes Italian with Portuguese/Brazilian and Middle Eastern dishes.

Getting There & Away The Lough Swilly (☎ 028-7126 2017, 074-22863) bus from Letterkenny arrives in Rathmullan at 10.45am and 6.45pm Monday to Saturday

INISHOWEN PENINSULA

ATLANTIC OCEAN

Malin Head
Banba's Crown
Ballyhillin

Crockalough
(280m)

Glengad
Head

Tullagh Point
Pollan
Bay
Lagg Sand Dunes

Dunaff
Head
Tullagh
Bay
Carrickbrackey
Castle

Malin

Culdaff
Bay
Dunmore Head

Dunaff
Clonmany
Ballyliffin
Trawbreaga
Bay
Culdaff

Clonca Church
& Cross
Bocan
Stone
Circle
Tremone
Bay

Lenan
Head
Mamore
Hill (421m)
Carndonagh
Carrowmore
High Crosses
Gleneely
Kinnagoe
Bay

Gap of
Mamore
Butler's Glen
R238
R244
High Cross
Inishowen
Head

Urris
Hills
Shrove

Dunree
Head
Dunree
Slieve Main
(615m)
Glentogher
R73R
Dunagree
Point
Green Castle

Slieve
Snaght
Greencastle

R238
R240
Cooley
Cross
Moville
Magilligan
Point

O'Docherty's
Keep
Tullyarvan
Mill
DONEGAL
Redcastle

Buncrana

Lough
Swilly
Inis Eoghain 100

Quigley's
Point
Lough Foyle

Fahan
St Mura Cross
Scalp Mountain
(477m)
R238

Inch
Island
Muff
NORTHERN
IRELAND

Inch
Burnfoot
R239

Burt
Bridge
End
Limavady
To Coleraine
(14km)

N13
A2
To Letterkenny
(10km)
Grianán
of
Aileach
A2
Derry
DERRY

0   3   6km
0   2   4mi

en route to Milford, Carrowkeel and Portsalon (morning bus only).

Portsalon & Fanad Head

The appeal of tiny Portsalon (Port an tSalainn), once a popular holiday resort, lies in its long, golden, sandy Blue Flag beach that's safe for swimming.

Knockalla Caravan & Camping Park (☎ *074-59108, Portsalon*) Tent €10.15. Open mid-Mar–mid-Sept. Close to the beach at Portsalon, the park has a kitchen, laundry, shop, games room and outdoor play area for kids.

It's another 8km to the rocky promontory of Fanad Head, the best part of which is the scenic drive there. The lighthouse here overlooks Lough Swilly.

INISHOWEN PENINSULA

The Inishowen (Inis Eoghain) Peninsula, with Lough Foyle to the east and Lough Swilly to the west, reaches out into the Atlantic and extends to Ireland's northernmost point: Malin Head. The landscape is typically Donegal: rugged, desolate and mountainous. Ancient sites abound, but there are also some wonderful beaches and plenty of places where travellers can go off alone. Tourist offices in Donegal, Letterkenny and Derry have free leaflets about walks in the Inishowen area, complete with maps.

The peninsula is a European Special Area of Conservation and home to over 100 species of migrating and indigenous bird life.

The route below follows the road out of Derry up the coast of Lough Foyle to Moville and then north-west to Malin Head, before travelling down the western side to Buncrana. If you're coming from Donegal the peninsula could be approached from the Lough Swilly side by turning off for Buncrana on the N13 road from Letterkenny to Derry. Leaving from Derry, though, the first village in the Republic is Muff. A scenic drive, the **Inis Eoghain 100**, is clearly signposted round the peninsula.

Muff to Moville

The tiny village of Muff (Mugh), only 8km north of Derry, has pubs offering food and music and a fair share of Northern visitors. North-east of Muff along the coast there are larger pubs catering to the same market. **Horse riding** is available at **Lenamore Stables** (☎ *077-84022, Muff*).

North of Muff at **Quigley's Point** (Rinn Mic Coigus) there are good views across Lough Foyle to County Derry.

At the resort town of **Redcastle**, south of Moville, there's a bunch of B&Bs and a hotel. *Fernbank* (☎ *077-83032, fax 83164, Redcastle*) Rooms €25.40 per person. Set back from the main road about 600m south of the village, Fernbank enjoys panoramic views and has four en suite rooms; evening meals are available.

Redcastle Hotel (☎ *077-82073, fax 82214, Redcastle*) Rooms €44-70 per person. On the banks of Lough Foyle just north of the village, this lovely, if slightly tacky, 31-room establishment has all the facilities of a big hotel, including a nine-hole golf course.

Getting There & Away Lough Swilly (☎ 028-7126 2017, 074-22863) runs up to nine buses daily from Derry to Carndonagh via Muff, with almost as many buses to Shrove that also pass through Muff. There's

no Sunday service on either route. Worth considering is Lough Swilly's eight-day Runabout unlimited-travel pass costing €25.20/17.65/12.60 for adults/students/ children.

Moville & Around
☎ 077 • pop 1390

Now a sleepy seaside town, Moville (Bun an Phobail) was once a busy port where emigrants set sail for America. The **coastal walkway** from Moville to Greencastle takes in the stretch of coast where the steamers used to moor. There's **fishing** off the pier for mackerel, mullet and coalfish.

Main St has several banks with ATMs and the post office.

Cooley Cross & Skull House By the gate of the Cooley gravehouse is a 3m-high cross, unusual because of the ringhole in its head through which the hands of negotiating parties are said to have clasped to seal an agreement. In the graveyard the small Skull House still contains some old bones. It may be associated with St Finian, the monk who accused Colmcille of plagiarising one of his manuscripts in the 6th century. He lived in a monastery here that was founded by St Patrick and survived into the 12th century.

Approaching Moville from the south, look out for a turning on the left (if you pass a church, you've gone too far) that has a sign on the corner for the Cooley Pitch & Putt. The graveyard is just over 1km up this road on the right.

Special Events The Foyle Oyster Festival is held in late September and its office (☎ 82042) is on Main St.

Places to Stay & Eat There are several B&Bs in and around Moville.
Barron's Café (☎ *82472, Main St*) Rooms €23 per person. Open year round. Barron's is a central, friendly, renovated B&B where the rooms are all en suite. It also serves good, traditional food including an all-day breakfast (€5).

Bridget McGroarty (☎ *82091, Main St*) Singles/doubles €21.60/38.10. Open Mar-

Sept. Also central, this is a small, cosy place with three rooms and a shared bathroom.

McNamara's Hotel (☎ 82010, fax 82564, Main St) Rooms €43 per person. Restaurant mains €5.30-10.90. Off the bottom of Main St, behind Barron's Café, McNamara's is a family-run, 60-room establishment with lots of old-world character. It has wheelchair access and a good restaurant.

Getting There & Away Lough Swilly (☎ 028-7126 2017, 074-22863) runs four buses daily Monday to Saturday to Moville from Derry.

Greencastle
☎ 077 • pop 590

The popular fishing and holiday village of Greencastle (An Cáisleán Nua), north of Moville, gets its name from the castle built in 1305 by Richard de Burgo, known as the Red Earl of Ulster because of his florid complexion. The Green Castle functioned as a supply base for English armies in Scotland and for this reason was attacked by the Scots under Robert Bruce in the 1320s. In 1555 the castle was demolished, and little of it survives.

The **Inishowen Maritime Museum & Planetarium** *(☎ 81363, Greencastle; museum adult/child €2.50/1.25, planetarium adult/child €2.50/1.25; open 10am-6pm Mon-Sat, noon-6pm Sun June-Sept)*, by the harbour in a former coastguard station, houses an interesting collection of exhibits on the history of local sailing and fishing boats and the Spanish armada; there's also a fascinating, state-of-the-art planetarium.

Kealy's Seafood Bar (☎ 81010, Greencastle) Mains €11-25. Open 12.30pm-3pm & 7pm-9.30pm Thur-Sun (daily in summer). Just near the harbour, Kealy's rather simple exterior belies the fact that it houses a top restaurant serving excellent, fresh, locally caught seafood.

Five Lough Swilly (☎ 028-712 62017, 074-22863) buses travel daily, Monday to Saturday, between Derry and Shrove, passing through Greencastle.

Inishowen Head

A right turn outside Greencastle leads to

Shrove; a sign indicating Inishowen Head is 1km along this road. It's possible to drive or cycle part of the way, but it's also an easy walk to the headland, from where you can see (on a clear day) the Antrim coast as far as the Giant's Causeway. A more demanding walk continues to the sandy beach of **Kinnagoe Bay**. At Shrove, where the road left goes to the headland, a right turn goes to **Dunagree Point** and back to Greencastle, but this loop has little to recommend it.

Culdaff & Around
☎ 077 • pop 500

Several ancient sites surround the sleepy, secluded, resort village of Culdaff (Cúil Dabhcha), which can be visited from the main Moville to Carndonagh road (R238). Culdaff itself is a centre for several water-based activities.

Clonca Church & Cross The carved lintel over the door of this 17th-century building is thought to come from an earlier church. In the north-eastern corner, the rather interesting tombstone was erected by one Magnus MacOrristin and has a sword and hurling stick carved on it. The remains of the cross show the miracle of the loaves and fishes on the eastern face and geometric designs on the sides.

Look for the turn-off to Culdaff, on the right if coming from Moville, on the left after about 6km if coming from Carndonagh. The Clonca Church and Cross are 1.5km on the right behind some farm buildings.

Bocan Stone Circle There are better stone circles in Ireland than this one, which has only a few of some 30 original stones left, but the surrounding views help to conjure up the kind of significance the place must have held some 3000 years ago.

From Clonca Church, continue along the road until you reach a T-junction with a modern church and a cemetery facing you. Turn right here and after about half a kilometre turn left (no sign). The stone circle is inside the first heather-covered field on the left.

The Corncrake Crisis

Once, nights in the Irish countryside were regularly punctuated by the distinctive 'crek, crek' cry of the lovelorn male corncrake. However, due to modern intensive farming practices, in 1988 an all-Ireland survey found only 903 birds still calling and, by the mid-1990s, this number had fallen to just 130. Today the corncrake is a protected bird high on the list of Irish endangered species and survives only in northern Donegal, the Shannon Callows, Mayo and small areas of the western coast.

The corncrake, a dowdy, secretive bird, winters in south-eastern Africa before arriving in Ireland to breed in April. Like so many endangered species, it has habits that render it peculiarly vulnerable to modern life. It nests on small platforms of vegetation on the ground, in fields and undergrowth. After laying their eggs in long grass, females stay with their chicks even as a mowing tractor's blades descend on them. Even if they realise the danger, long centuries of programming make them reluctant to rush for the safety of open ground.

NICKY CAVEN

The Irish Wildbird Conservancy (IWC) offers grants to farmers who delay mowing until August, when the nesting season is over, or cut the grass in 'corncrake-friendly' fashion. There's a 24-hour Corncrake Hotline (☎ 074-65126 in County Donegal, 096-51326 in County Mayo) and you'll see notices in shop windows inviting people to ring in if they hear a corncrake. An IWC officer then visits the site and decides if a nest is in need of protection.

These efforts seem to have had some positive effect. In recent years bird-watchers have reported a rise in the number of singing males and there are around 200 breeding pairs. However, there's a very long way to go before the bird is removed from the endangered-species list.

Carrowmore High Crosses Like the Bocan Stone Circle, these high crosses may prove a little disappointing to some. One is basically a decorated slab showing Christ and an angel, while on the other side of the road there is a taller cross with stumpy arms.

From Bocan Stone Circle and Clonca Church, retrace the route back to the main Carndonagh to Moville road and turn left, then almost immediately right.

Activities Culdaff has a beach that's good for **swimming** and **windsurfing** and, from Bunagee Pier, **sea angling** and **diving** are popular.

Places to Stay & Eat There are a couple of choices in Culdaff.

The Pines Hostel (☎ 79060, *Culdaff*) Dorm beds €9.45. Open year round. This modern, clean, purpose-built hostel, on the Bunagee road close to town, has 18 beds. Bed linen is included in the price and there are bikes for hire.

Ceecliff House (☎ 79120, *fax 79159*, *Culdaff*) Singles/doubles from €28/48. Open year round. Ceecliff, a B&B also on the Bunagee road, offers four rooms (three with bathrooms) and a pleasant garden for guests' use. There's no smoking in the bedrooms. Dinner is available for an extra €15.90.

McGrory's Bar (☎ 79104, e *mcgr@eir com.ie, Culdaff*) Rooms €38-52 per person. This is the place to stay if you want to be near the action. It offers comfortable accommodation and also serves good, local seafood and traditional Irish food. As well, McGrory's hosts regular traditional music sessions on Thursday and Friday from 10pm that continue well into the night, while the attached *Mac's Backroom Bar* often attracts big-name musicians.

Malin Head

At the top of Inishowen Peninsula is Malin Head (Cionn Mhálanna), a familiar name to listeners of radio shipping forecasts throughout the island. The northernmost point of Malin Head – and of Ireland – is rocky Banba's Crown (Fíorcheann Éireann). Malin

Head is one of the few places in Ireland where you can still hear the call of the endangered corncrake in summer. Other birds to look out for are choughs, snow bunting and puffins. The tower on the cliffs was built in 1805 by the British admiralty and later used as a Lloyds signal station. The ugly concrete huts were used by the Irish army in WWII as lookout posts. To the west from the car park a short path leads to **Hell's Hole**, a chasm where the incoming waters crash against the rocky formations. To the east a longer headland walk leads to the **Wee House of Malin**, a hermit's cave in the cliff face.

The pretty Plantation village of **Malin** (Málainn), on Trawbreaga Bay 14km south of Malin Head, is centred on a triangular village green. A circular walk from the green takes in Knockamany Bens, a local hill with terrific views, as well as Lagg Presbyterian Church, the oldest church still in use on the peninsula. Children will love the massive sand dunes at Five Fingers Strand near the church.

Places to Stay & Eat There are two IHO/IHH hostels.

Malin Head Hostel (☎ 077-70309, Malin Head) Dorms/private rooms €8.80/12.60 per person. Open year round. The Malin Head is a clean, friendly hostel with 14 beds. As well as full facilities including free hot showers, you can buy cheap fruit and vegetables from its organic garden and orchard, and receive reflexology and aromatherapy treatments. It also hires out bikes, and local buses stop here.

Sandrock Holiday Hostel (☎ 077-70289, e sandrockhostel@eircom.net, Port Ronan Pier, Malin Head) Dorms €8.80. Open year round. On the western side of the headland beside the ocean, Sandrock is another well run place with 20 beds, free pick up, wheelchair access and bike hire.

Barraicin (☎/fax 077-70184, Malin Head) Singles/doubles from €24/43. Open May-Oct. Mrs Doyle runs this cosy, congenial B&B near Malin Head's only post office.

Malin Hotel (☎ 077-70645, fax 70770, Malin) Rooms €38-45 per person. This charming, traditional hotel, beside the green

in Malin village, serves good food in its restaurant, including fresh, local seafood, and offers entertainment at the weekend.

The Cottage (☎ 077-70257, Malin Head) Meals under €6. Open 11am-6pm daily June-Aug. Just west of Banba's Crown, above Ballyhillin Beach, this thatched tearoom serves tea and tasty snacks, and on Friday evenings hosts traditional music sessions.

Getting There & Away The best way to approach Malin Head is by the R238/242 from Carndonagh, rather than up the eastern side from Culdaff. Lough Swilly (☎ 028-7126 2017, 074-22863) operates a bus that runs on Monday, Wednesday and Friday at 11am between Derry and Malin Head via Carndonagh; on the same days a bus leaves Carndonagh at 3pm for Malin Head. There are three buses from Derry to Malin Head on Saturday.

Carndonagh
☎ 077 • pop 1600

Carndonagh (Cardomhnach), surrounded by hills on three sides, is a busy commercial centre serving the local farming community.

The helpful, locally run Inishowen Tourism office (☎ 74933, e info@visitinishowen.com, w www.visitinishowen.com), on Chapel St south-west of the Diamond, opens 9.30am to 5.30pm Monday to Thursday, to 5pm Friday, September to May; 9.30am to 7pm weekdays, 10am to 6pm Saturday, and noon to 6pm on Sunday, June to August. It also sells fishing licences for all of Donegal. There are three banks on the Diamond and the Allied Irish Bank has an ATM; the post office is off the Diamond near the top of Bridge St.

Once an important ecclesiastical centre, Carndonagh has several early-Christian, stone monuments. At the Ballyliffin end of town, the finely shaped, 7th-century **Donagh Cross** stands erect against the wall of an Anglican church. Either side of the cross are two small pillars, one said to show a man with a sword and shield, possibly Goliath, the other David and his harp. In the graveyard there's a pillar with a carved marigold on a stem and nearby a crucifixion scene.

DONEGAL

Places to Stay & Eat There are a couple of good places to stay and eat in the centre of Carndonagh.

Oregon (☎/fax 74113, New Rd) Rooms €19.05 per person. Open year round. Mrs Doherty runs this simple but pleasant and inexpensive B&B close to the town centre.

Arch Inn (☎ 73209, the Diamond) Under €5. In the main square, the Arch Inn does good soup and sandwiches during the day and hosts a traditional music session on Sunday evening.

Corncrake Restaurant (☎ 74534, Malin Rd) Starters €4.50-5.50, mains €14-17. Open 6pm-10pm daily June-Sept, 6pm-10pm Fri-Sat & 5pm-10pm Sun Oct-May. In a terraced house down from the Diamond, the Corncrake, recognised as one of Ireland's best restaurants, serves traditional Irish food using fresh ingredients and home-grown herbs in an intimate setting. It doesn't accept credit cards; reservations are recommended.

If you're off to Malin Head for the day or going on to the camp site at Clonmany, stock up with provisions at the Centra supermarket in Malin Rd.

Getting There & Away A Lough Swilly (☎ 028-7126 2017, 074-22863) bus leaves Buncrana for Carndonagh at 8.40am on weekdays, plus at 1pm and 5.45pm on Monday and Thursday, 1.45pm and 6.15pm on Friday. On Saturday the buses go at 12.15pm, 2.15pm and 6.15pm. On weekdays they return from Carndonagh at 7.25am, 10am and 4pm. Lough Swilly also runs a bus between Derry and Malin Head via Carndonagh once daily Monday, Wednesday and Friday (three times on Saturday).

North West Busways (☎ 82619) operates a service between Letterkenny and Moville via Buncrana and Carndonagh.

Ballyliffin & Clonmany
☎ 077 • pop 600

The small, seaside resort of Ballyliffin (Baile Lifin) attracts more Irish than overseas visitors, many of whom come to play golf on either of the two 18-hole courses. There's plenty of accommodation in the area. Both villages have post offices but no banks.

About 1km north of Ballyliffin is the lovely, sandy expanse of **Pollan Strand**, but, unfortunately, the crashing breakers make it unsafe for swimming. A walk along the dunes to the north of this beach brings you to **Doagh Island** (now part of the mainland), where the battered ruins of 16th-century **Carrickbrackey Castle** (also spelt Carrickabraghy) face the ocean. Also on the island is the **Doagh Visitor Centre** *(☎ 76493, Doagh Island, Inishowen; adult/child €3.80/1.90; open 10am-5.30pm daily Easter-Oct)*, a reconstructed village of thatched cottages with an emphasis on the story of the Famine. Tea and scones are included in the admission fee.

The other beach is at **Tullagh Strand**. It's great for an exhilarating walk and, although swimming is possible, the current can be strong and it isn't recommended when the tide is going out. From Clonmany there are walks to **Butler's Glen** and **Dunaff Head**.

Places to Stay & Eat There are a few options along the coast here.

Tullagh Bay Camping & Caravan Park (☎ 78997, Tullagh Bay) Tent sites €12.60. Open May-Sept. Five kilometres from Clonmany, this park is ideal for beach-goers as it's just behind Tullagh Strand.

B&Bs line the 2km stretch of road between Ballyliffin and Clonmany.

Ard Donn House (☎ 76156, Ballyliffin) Singles/doubles €27.95/50.80. Open year round. About 500m from the centre of Ballyliffin, this homely B&B uses organic farm produce and has five bedrooms all with attached bathroom.

Ballyliffin Hotel (☎ 76101, fax 76658, Ballyliffin) Singles/doubles €55/75. This is a modern, traditionally furnished hotel near the post office, with excellent food available in the bar.

Strand Hotel (☎ 76017, fax 76486, Ballyliffin) Singles/doubles €45/75. This 12-room hotel is small enough to retain a friendly atmosphere and a personal touch. It offers bar food 12.30pm to 10pm daily.

Entertainment Most pubs and hotels have music in summer.

McFeeley's (☎ 76122, Clonmany) On

weekend nights in this old pub in the centre of Clonmany you can hear both country and traditional music. It serves a good Guinness.

Getting There & Away Lough Swilly (☎ 028-7126 2017, 074-22863) buses run between Clonmany and Carndonagh: see the Carndonagh section earlier in this chapter for times – buses leave/reach Clonmany 20 minutes earlier/later.

Clonmany to Buncrana

There are two routes from Clonmany to Buncrana: the scenic coastal road via the Gap of Mamore and Dunree Head, or the speedier inland road (R238). The **Gap of Mamore** (262m) descends dramatically between Mamore Hill and the Urris Hills into a valley where the road follows the River Owenerk most of the way to Dunree.

Swilly View (☎ 76316, Claggin, Clonmany) Rooms €19.05 per person. Open May-Sept. This aptly named, remote country house, 8km from Clonmany, is close to the Gap of Mamore and offers terrific views of Lough Swilly and the Atlantic Ocean.

The main reason to pause in Dunree (An Dún Riabhach) is to visit the interesting **Fort Dunree Military Museum** (☎ 074-24613, Dunree; adult/child €2.55/1.25; open 10am-6pm Mon-Sat & 1pm-6pm Sun June-Sept), on a windswept, rocky headland overlooking Lough Swilly. In 1798 Wolfe Tone, with the help of the French, planned to arrive at Lough Swilly and march on Derry. The British constructed six forts to guard the lough and the museum tells the whole story. You can easily see fulmar and other birds nesting on the rocks below the fort.

Buncrana

☎ 077 • pop 4000

After Bundoran this must be the most popular resort in Donegal for holidaymakers from the North, but unlike Bundoran it contrives to suggest there's life beyond tourism. In fact, Fruit of the Loom has two knitting mills in Buncrana (Bun Cranncha), though they remain only because of Irish-government inducements. The resort has a 5km-long sandy beach on the shore of Lough Swilly that's safe for swimming, several pubs and a number of places of interest to while away your spare hours.

Ulster Bank, on Upper Main St, and the Allied Irish Bank and Bank of Ireland on Lower Main St, have ATMs and bureaux de change. The post office is on Upper Main St. You can leave your laundry at Valu Clean (☎ 62570), a laundrette on Lower Main St.

Things to See The community-run **Tullyarvan Mill** (☎ 61613, Carndonagh Rd; free; open 10am-5pm May-Sept) is a textile exhibition, craft shop and cafe combined about 1km north of town on the Crana River. It is well worth a visit. The attractively presented exhibition is devoted to the restoration of the mill, local history, and flora and fauna. The place is also worth visiting for its classical and lively traditional music evenings that take place regularly in summer. To find it, head north out of town on the R238 and follow the signs.

At the northern end of the seafront the early-18th-century, six-arched Castle Bridge leads to **O'Docherty's Keep**, a tower house built by the O'Dochertys, the local chiefs, in 1430. It was burned by the English and then rebuilt for their own use. **Buncrana Castle** nearby was built in 1718 by John Vaughan, who also constructed the bridge; Wolfe Tone was imprisoned here following the unsuccessful French invasion in 1798.

Places to Stay & Eat There's no shortage of B&Bs around town, but they can fill up quickly during August.

Town Clock Guest House (☎ 62146, 6 Upper Main St) Rooms with bath €22 per person. This central B&B offers clean and spacious rooms and you don't have to check out until 12.30pm. Breakfast is in the downstairs cafe, which serves good meals all day. At lunchtime during the week it gets packed with hungry schoolchildren.

Lake of Shadows Hotel (☎ 61902, fax 62131, Grianán Park) Singles/doubles €48/70. Old-world character combined with modern facilities make this Victorian hotel a good option. To get here from Main St head down Church St towards the bay.

Ubiquitous *(☎ 62530, 47 Upper Main St)* Mains €12.50-19. The best eatery in terms of choice is this terrific little restaurant and bar complete with jukebox. It provides friendly service and top-quality food, including seafood and vegetarian options, while the bar has a fine selection of beers and wines.

Entertainment Not surprisingly, most entertainment is found in the town's pubs along Main St.

Atlantic Bar *(☎ 20880, Upper Main St)* Dating from 1792, the Atlantic is Buncrana's oldest pub and can be relied on for live music at the weekend.

Óflaitbeartais *(O'Flaherty's; ☎ 61305, Upper Main St)* This large, popular local has a big TV screen for sports and frequently hosts traditional music sessions.

Getting There & Around From Buncrana, Lough Swilly (☎ 028-7126 2017, 074-22863) buses run daily to Derry and Carndonagh. Taxis are available from Town Clock Taxis (☎ 63322).

South of Buncrana

Fahan A monastery was founded in Fahan by St Colmcille in the 6th century, and among its ruins is the beautifully carved, 7th-century **St Mura Cross** stone slab in the graveyard beside the church. Each face is decorated with a cross, and the barely discernible Greek inscription is the only one known from this early-Christian period.

Grianán of Aileách This impressive stone fort atop Grianán Hill in Burt, 18km south of Buncrana and signposted off the N13, offers panoramic views of the surrounding countryside: Swilly and Foyle loughs, Inch Island and distant Derry. The walls are 4m thick and enclose an area 23m in diameter. The fort may have existed at least 2000 years ago, but the site itself has pagan associations that go back to pre-Celtic times.

Between the 5th and 12th centuries it was the seat of the O'Neills before being demolished by Murtogh O'Brien, king of Munster. You might wonder how a fort demolished 800 years ago could look so complete – well, between 1874 and 1878 an amateur archaeologist from Derry reconstructed the fort, and this is mostly what you see today.

The attractive, circular **Burt Church** at the foot of the hill was modelled on the fort by Derry architect Liam McCormack and built in 1967.

The 19th-century church of Christchurch at Burt, on the N13 about 300m south of the turn-off to the fort, houses the **Grianán of Aileách Visitor Centre** *(☎ 077-68512, Burt; adult/child €2.55/1.30; open 10am-6pm daily June-Aug; noon-6pm daily Sept-May)*. It has displays on the hill fort and on the church's history. There's a life-size model of Muirchertach na gCochall Craicinn, a 10th-century ancestor of the O'Neills and king of Aileách from 938 to 943. In 942 he went on an extended tour of Ireland, recorded in verse by Cormacan Eigean. There are also models of members of Christchurch's Victorian congregation and information about the local flora and fauna.

The restaurant here has a lot of character – the bar counter is created out of a Boer War memorial slab, for example – and stays open until 10pm (9pm Sunday). It serves snacks and light meals (€6.30 to €11) during the day, and has an a la carte menu in the evening with plenty of choices, including several vegetarian options.

Inch Island Few tourists make it to tranquil Inch Island, accessible from the mainland by a causeway, but it does have plenty of **bird life** in its western wetlands, two small **beaches** and the remains of an old **fort. Inch Island Stables** *(☎/fax 077-60335)* organises **horse-riding** lessons and trips around the island.

Counties Meath & Louth

Heading north from Dublin along the coast takes you through Counties Meath and Louth before crossing the border into Northern Ireland. This low, coastal landscape is a contrast to the hilly country south of the capital, rising only slightly inland to the plain known in folklore as Murtheimne – where many events mentioned in the Iron Age saga Táin Bó Cúailnge (Cattle Raid of Cooley) took place. The epic's dramatic climax occurred on Louth's beautiful Cooley Peninsula, and many places there owe their names to the legendary heroes and battles of that time. And in Meath and Louth lie some of the most remarkable legacies of the ancient Irish people – the tombs of Newgrange and Loughcrew – as well as the fine monasteries at Monasterboice, Mellifont and Kells, built by early Irish Christians.

It would be wrong, however, to assume that the verdant, settled farmland of these two counties is firmly rooted in the past. Modern Meath is one of Ireland's best examples of the rural success of the Celtic Tiger. Older farming traditions have blended well with a newer, more urbane outlook, which seeks to capitalise on opportunities in tourism and industry. Louth has two major industrial towns, Dundalk and Drogheda, and even in the smaller towns and villages a new thinking has emerged one that pays homage to the more traditional past but is keen to get on with the future.

County Meath

Meath (An Mhí), Dublin's immediate neighbour to the north and north-west, has long been one of Ireland's leading farming counties, a plain of extremely rich soil stretching north to the lakes of Cavan and Monaghan and west before running into the bleak Bog of Allen. Among the huge fields are the solid houses of Meath's former settlers and today's prosperous farmers – many of whom are even wealthier since EU farm-ing policies started offering subsidies for letting land lie fallow.

For a large county, Meath has surprisingly few major settlements. Navan, Trim and Kells are no more than medium-sized towns, while places such as Ashbourne, Dunshaugh-lin and Dunboyne on the southern fringe have become commuter suburbs of Dublin. The county's principal attractions are its ancient

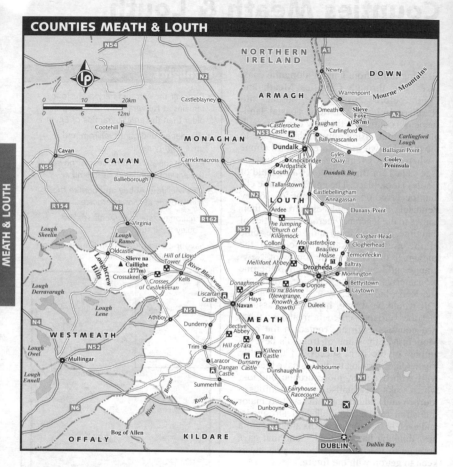

COUNTIES MEATH & LOUTH

sites, and the isolated hills of Tara and Slane have immense historical significance. Also be sure to visit Butterstream Gardens in Trim, which are some of the finest in Ireland.

HISTORY

Meath's rich soil, laid down during the last Ice Age, attracted settlers as early as 8000 BC. They worked their way up the banks of the River Boyne transforming the landscape from forest to farmland. Brú na Bóinne, an extensive prehistoric necropolis dating from around 3000 BC, lies on a meandering section of the Boyne between Drogheda and

Slane. There's a group of smaller passage graves in the Loughcrew Hills near Oldcastle. For 1000 years the Hill of Tara was the seat of power for Irish high kings (*ard rithe*; pronounced **ard** ree-huh), until the arrival of St Patrick in the 5th century. Later, Kells became one of the most important and creative monastic settlements in Ireland and lent its name to the famed Book of Kells, a 9th-century illuminated manuscript now displayed in Trinity College, Dublin.

THE COAST

Meath's mere 10km of coastline includes a

number of small resorts with wide expanses of sand dunes and safe beaches. From the Elizabethan **Maiden Watchtower** in Mornington at the mouth of the Boyne there are fine views of Drogheda, 5km to the west, and the Boyne Estuary.

Laytown is a busy little place with golf, tennis and good windsurfing. It hosts annual horse races on the beach in mid-August. Outside Laytown, on the road to Julianstown (the R150), is **Sonairte National Ecology Centre** (☎ 041-982 7572, The Ninch; adult/student/child €3.20/1.90/1.30; open 9am-5pm Mon-Fri, 11am-5pm Sat, 11am-6pm Sun), beside the River Nanny. It has an organic garden, a nature trail and exhibits displaying the use of wind, water and solar power. In the gift shop you can buy its own wine made from organically grown grapes.

Barely 1km north of Laytown is **Bettystown**, whose claim to fame is that the magnificent 8th-century Tara Brooch was found in a box on the beach here in 1850. The only link between the brooch and Tara is that the magnificent ornamentation and the preciousness of its materials seem to indicate wealth, if not royal, association with the high kings, who were based in Tara. It's now on display in the National Museum, Dublin. There is a long strand on the edge of the village, which is very popular in summer, affording long walks and, if you can overcome the pollution, some pretty good swimming.

Both Laytown and Bettystown are popular holiday destinations for Dubliners and people from Drogheda and Dundalk.

Places to Stay
Tara Guesthouse (☎/fax 041-982 7239, beachfront, Laytown) Room €25.50 per person, breakfast is extra. Overlooking the beach, this guesthouse also serves dinner costing €19.

Neptune Beach (☎ 041-982 7107, fax 982 7412, Bettystown Beach) Rooms cost from €70 per person, including breakfast. A recent refurbishment has really spruced up this beachfront hotel in Bettystown.

Places to Eat
There are a handful of greasy-spoon diners

and fish and chip shops in Bettystown, but there's only one place where you can get really good food.

Bacchus at the Coastguard (☎ 041-982 8251, Bayview, Bettystown) Mains from €11. Open from 6pm Tues-Sat, noon-7pm Sun. On the main road, this is one of the best seafood restaurants in the region. It's beside the shore, and the early-bird dinner (6pm to 7.30pm) costs €25; thereafter it's a la carte. You have to book at the weekend.

Getting There & Away
Bus Éireann (☎ 041-983 5023) runs at least four buses daily along the coast from Drogheda (single/return €3/4.60).

The coast is served by eight trains daily (nine on Friday and four on Sunday) on the Dublin to Belfast line, with the nearest stop at Laytown. From Dublin, it takes 15 minutes and costs single/return €8.90/12.70. Call ☎ 01-836 6222 for timetable information.

DULEEK
☎ 041 • pop 1731
Duleek claims to have had Ireland's first stone church; the town's name comes from *damh liag* (stone house). No trace of the church remains, however. The church's founder was the omnipresent St Patrick (wasn't he a busy man!), and it was built by his disciple St Ciarán sometime around 450. On its way to Armagh for interment, Brian Ború's body lay in state here after his death in 1014 at the Battle of Clontarf, where the Vikings were defeated. After the Battle of the Boyne in 1690, the defeated Jacobite forces retreated to Duleek while their leader, James II, disappeared off to Dublin and then on to France.

The ruins of **St Mary's Priory and tower** date from the 12th century and contain a number of excellent effigies and tombstones, while outside there is a 10th-century high cross. The site was abandoned after Henry VIII's dissolution of the monasteries in 1537. The town square of Duleek has a **wayside cross**, erected in 1601 by Lady Jennet Dowdall in memory of her husband, William Bathe, and herself.

Annesbrook House (☎ 982 3293, fax 982

3024, [e] sweetman@annesbrook.com, off R152 9km south of Duleek) Singles/doubles €51/76.50. Open Mar-Sept. This is a comfortable country house, with rather expensive rooms, surrounded by extensive wooded grounds. The house is a 17th-century building, but the Georgian additions date from a visit paid to Annesbrook by George IV in 1821: the owners felt the entrance wasn't grand enough and quickly added the portico.

There are a couple of pubs in the centre serving lunch.

Greyhound Inn (☎ 982 3208, Main St) Mains from €5. This pub is about the best of a pretty poor lot.

BRÚ NA BÓINNE

There was extensive settlement along the Boyne Valley in prehistoric times, and the necropolis known as Brú na Bóinne (Boyne Palace) was built in the area. This consists of many different sites, the three principal ones being Newgrange, Knowth and Dowth. They were the largest artificial structures in Ireland until the construction of the Anglo-Norman castles.

Over the centuries these tombs decayed, were covered by grass and trees and were plundered by everybody from Vikings to Victorian treasure hunters, whose carved initials can be seen on the great stones of Newgrange. The countryside around them is littered with countless other ancient mounds (or tumuli) and standing stones.

The entire complex, including the three main passage tombs (of which only Newgrange and Knowth are accessible) can only be visited as part of a tour run by the **Brú na Bóinne Visitor Centre** (☎ 041-988 0300, [W] www.heritageireland.ie, Donore; adult/ senior/student €2.50/1.90/1.25 including guided tour; open 9am-7pm daily June-mid-Sept; 9am-5.45pm daily mid-Sept-end Sept; 9.30am-5.30pm daily Oct & Mar-Apr; to 5pm Nov-Feb), south of the River Boyne and 2km west of Donore. This high-quality interpretative centre provoked enormous controversy when it was first opened in the early 1990s, largely because it was deemed an unwelcome and artificial interference in a unique natural setting. Whatever the case

may be, the centre has turned out to be a fairly remarkable place, with an extraordinary series of interactive exhibits on the passage tombs and prehistoric Ireland in general.

You should allow plenty of time to visit this unique place. If you're only planning on taking the guided tour of the interpretative centre, give yourself about an hour. If you plan a visit to Newgrange or Knowth, allow at least two hours. If however, you want to visit all three in one go, you should plan at least half a day. In summer, particularly at the weekend, and during school holidays, the place gets very crowded, and you will not be guaranteed a visit to either of the passage tombs; call ahead to book a tour and avoid disappointment. In summer, the best time to visit is mid-week and/or early in the morning.

Newgrange

Newgrange *(adult/senior/student/family €5.10/3.80/2.55/12.75 for centre & Newgrange, €8.90/6.40/4.20/22.30 for centre, Newgrange & Knowth)* is a huge, flattened, grass-covered mound about 80m in diameter and 13m high. The mound covers the finest Stone Age passage tomb in Ireland and is one of the most remarkable prehistoric sites in Europe. It dates from around 3200 BC, predating the great pyramids of Egypt by some six centuries. The purpose for which it was constructed remains uncertain. It may have been a burial place for kings or a centre for ritual – although the alignment with the sun at the time of the winter solstice also suggests it was designed to act as a calendar.

The name derives from 'new granary' (the tomb did in fact serve as a repository for wheat and grain at one stage), although a belief more popular in the area is that it comes from the Irish for 'Cave of Gráinne', a reference to a Celtic myth taught to every Irish schoolchild: that of The Pursuit of Diarmuid and Gráinne, a story that tells of the illicit love between the wife of Fionn McCumhaill (or Finn McCool), leader of the Fianna, and one of his most trusted lieutenants. When Diarmuid was fatally wounded, his body was brought to Newgrange by the god Aengus in a vain attempt to save him, and the despairing Gráinne followed him into the cave, where she remained long after he died. This suspiciously Arthurian legend (for Diarmuid and Gráinne read Lancelot and Guinevere) is undoubtedly untrue, but it's still a pretty good story. Newgrange also plays another role in Celtic mythology, serving as the site where the hero Cúchulainn was conceived.

Over the centuries, Newgrange, like Dowth and Knowth, deteriorated and was even quarried at one stage. There was a standing stone on the summit until the 17th century. The site was extensively restored in 1962 and again in 1975.

A superbly carved kerbstone with double and triple spirals guards the tomb's main entrance. The front facade has been reconstructed so that tourists don't have to clamber in over it. Above the entrance is a slit or roof box, which lets light in. Another beautifully decorated kerbstone stands at the exact opposite side of the mound. Some experts say that a ring of standing stones encircled the mound, forming a Great Circle about 100m in diameter, but only 12 of these stones remain – with traces of some others below ground level.

Holding the whole structure together are the 97 boulders of the kerb ring, designed to stop the mound from collapsing outwards. Eleven of these are decorated with motifs similar to those on the main entrance stone, although only three of these have extensive carvings.

The white quartzite was originally obtained from Wicklow, 80km to the south, and there is also some granite from the Mourne Mountains in Northern Ireland. Over 200,000 tonnes of earth and stone also went into the mound.

You can walk down the narrow 19m passage, lined with 43 stone uprights, some of them engraved, which leads into the tomb chamber, about one-third of the way into the colossal mound. The chamber has three recesses, and in these are large basin stones that held cremated human bones. Along with the remains would have been funeral offerings of beads and pendants, but these must have been stolen long before the archaeologists arrived.

Above, the massive stones support a 6m-high corbel-vaulted roof. A complex drainage system means that not a drop of water has penetrated the interior in 40 centuries.

At 8.20am during the winter solstice (19 to 23 December), the rising sun's rays shine through the slit above the entrance, creep slowly down the long passage and illuminate the tomb chamber for 17 minutes. There is little doubt that witnessing this is one of the country's most memorable, even mystical, experiences. However, places to experience this annual event are booked up for at least 15 years, and the waiting list is now closed. For the legions of daily visitors there is a simulated winter sunrise for every group taken into the mound.

Knowth

The burial mound of Knowth (Cnóbha; *adult/student/child/family €3.80/2.55/1.60/ 9.55 for centre & Knowth, €8.90/6.40/4.20/ 22.30 for centre, Knowth & Newgrange; open the same hours as Newgrange but only from May to October*), north-west of Newgrange, was built around the same time and seems set to surpass its better-known neighbour, both in the extent and the importance of the discoveries made here. It has the greatest collection of passage-grave art ever uncovered in Western Europe, but it's still under excavation and the interior remains closed to visitors.

Modern excavations started at Knowth in 1962 and soon cleared a 34m passage to the central chamber, much longer than the one at Newgrange. In 1968 a second 40m passage was unearthed on the opposite side of the mound. Although the chambers are separate, they're close enough for archaeologists to hear each other at work. Also in the mound are the remains of six early-Christian souterrains (underground chambers) built into the side. Some 300 carved slabs and 17 satellite graves surround the main mound.

Human activity at Knowth continued for thousands of years after its construction, which accounts for the site's complexity. The Beaker folk, so called because they buried their dead with drinking vessels, occupied the site in the Bronze Age (circa 1800 BC), as did the Celts in the Iron Age around 500 BC. Remnants of bronze and iron workings from these periods have been discovered. Around AD 800 to AD 900 it was turned into a *ráth* (earthen ring fort), a stronghold of the very powerful Uí Néill (O'Neill) clan. In 965, it was the seat of Cormac MacMaelmithic, later Ireland's high king for nine years. The Normans built a motte and bailey here in the 12th century. In about 1400 the site was finally abandoned. Excavations are likely to continue at least for the next decade.

Partly because of the archaeological work and partly because the later buildings on the site weakened the internal structures, making it difficult for anyone to walk along the passage, only the exterior opens for guided tours, which you must join at the Brú na Bóinne Visitor Centre (see above).

Dowth

The circular mound at Dowth (Dubhadh, meaning 'dark') is similar in size to Newgrange – about 63m in diameter – but is slightly taller at 14m high. It has suffered badly at the hands of everyone from road builders and treasure hunters to amateur archaeologists, who scooped out the centre of the tumulus in the 19th century. For a time, Dowth even had a teahouse ignobly perched on its summit. Relatively untouched by modern archaeologists, Dowth shows what Newgrange and Knowth looked like for most of their history. Because it's unsafe, Dowth is closed to visitors, though the mound can be viewed from the road. Excavations began in 1998 and will continue for years to come.

There are two entrance passages leading to separate chambers (both sealed), and a 24m early-Christian souterrain at either end which connect up with the western passage. This 8m-long passage leads into a small cruciform chamber, in which a recess acts as an entrance to an additional series of small compartments, a feature unique to Dowth. To the south-west is the entrance to a shorter passage and smaller chamber.

North of the tumulus are the ruins of **Dowth Castle** and **Dowth House**.

Newgrange Farm

A few hundred metres down the hill to the west of Newgrange tomb is a 135-hectare **working farm** (☎ *041-982 4119, Newgrange; adult/family €4.50/12.70; open 10am-5.30pm Mon-Fri, 2pm-5.30pm Sun, Easter Sat-Sept; also 2pm-5.30pm Sat July & Aug)*, with a large collection of animals on view, displays, a picnic area and a coffee shop. The farm opens for tours.

Places to Stay

There are a couple of really beautiful B&Bs in the area.

Glebe House (☎ *983 6101, fax 984 3469, Dowth)* Rooms €38 per person. This old country house near the Dowth burial mound and 7km west of Drogheda has gorgeous rooms with open, log-burning fireplaces. The breakfast is bountiful and included in the price.

Mattock House (☎/*fax 982 4592, off N51, Newgrange)* Singles/doubles with bathroom €32.50/49. This typical farmhouse about 2km east of Slane, near the Newgrange mound, has large, comfortable rooms and is pretty handy for Brú na Bóinne.

Organised Tours

Brú na Bóinne is one of the most popular tourist attractions in Ireland, and there are a plethora of organised tours transporting busloads of eager tourists to the interpretative centre.

The best of them all, as far as we've discovered, is the tour run by Mary Gibbons (☎ 01-283 9973) from Dublin, which takes in the whole of the Boyne Valley, including Newgrange and the Hill of Tara (see that section later). Eamonn P Kelly, the Keeper of Irish Antiquities at the National Museum in Dublin, described it as 'the authentic tour of Ireland's history'. The expert guides offer a fascinating and expert insight into Celtic and pre-Celtic life in Ireland. It runs from the Dublin Tourism Centre in Suffolk St (see Tourist Offices in the Dublin chapter) at 10.45am to 5.30pm or 6pm on Monday to Wednesday and Friday. It costs €28 (including admission fees).

Bus Éireann's (☎ 01-836 6111, W www .buseireann.ie) Newgrange and the Boyne Valley tours depart Busáras in Dublin at 10am and return at 5.45pm daily except Friday, May to September and Thursday and Saturday only in April (adult/student/child €26/23/13); and 10am to 4.15pm Thursday and Saturday only, October to December (adult/student/child €20.50/18/10.50).

Tir na nÓg Tours (☎ 0800 783 6416, W www.tirnanogtours.com) does a Meath tour that includes the Boyne Valley, Monasterboice, Trim Castle and the Hill of Tara. It departs at 9am daily from the Tir na nÓg offices at 57 Lower Gardiner St and at 9.30am from the Dublin Tourism Centre in Suffolk St. The cost for the day tours is adult/student/child €26/23/13.

Getting There & Away

Newgrange, Knowth and Dowth are all well signposted. Newgrange lies just north of the River Boyne, about 13km south-west of Drogheda and 5km south-east of Slane. Dowth is between Newgrange and Drogheda, while Knowth is about 1km north-west of Newgrange or almost 4km by road.

From Drogheda, Bus Éireann runs a service six-times daily from 10.15am to 4pm (€1.45 single, 20 minutes) that drop you off at the gates of the interpretative centre. Visitors are bussed from the centre to the sites. From Dublin, the nearest you'll get to is Slane (single/return €7.40/10.80, 45 minutes, five buses daily, six on Friday).

SLANE

☎ 041 • pop 688

Built as a manorial village for an important castle, Slane (Baile Shláine) is a charming little place with stone houses and cottages and mature trees. Just south-west of the centre is the massive grey gate to the privately owned Slane Castle. Four identical houses face each other at the junction of the main roads. Local lore has it that they were built for four sisters who had taken an intense dislike to one another and kept watch from their individual residences.

Orientation & Information

Slane is perched on a hillside overlooking the River Boyne, at the junction of the N2 and N51, some 15km west of Drogheda. At the bottom of the hill to the south, the Boyne glides by under a narrow bridge. The hairpin turn on the northern side of the bridge is considered to be one of the most dangerous in the country as there is a steep hill preceding it, with a number of fatal accidents occurring there on an all-too-regular basis. If you are driving, be extra careful.

The helpful community-run tourist office (☎ 988 4055, e info@meathtourism.ie), on Main St opposite the Conyngham Arms Hotel, opens 9.30am to 5pm Monday, Thursday and Saturday year round. On other days, there might be someone available to answer questions, but don't bank on it.

The Hill of Slane

Just above the village, about 1km to the north, is the Hill of Slane. Tradition holds that St Patrick lit a paschal (Easter) fire here in 433 – just a year after his arrival in Ireland – to proclaim Christianity throughout the land. This act was in direct contravention of a decree issued by Laoghaire, the pagan high king of Ireland, that no flame should be lit within sight of the Hill of Tara. The king was furious but was restrained by his druids, who warned that 'the man who had kindled the flame would surpass kings and princes'. Instead, Laoghaire set out to meet Patrick and question him, and all but one of the king's attendants – a man called Erc – greeted him with scorn.

During the encounter, Patrick killed one of the king's guards and summoned an earthquake to subdue the rest. He then plucked a shamrock and used its three leaves to explain the paradox of the Trinity – the union of the Father, the Son and the Holy Spirit in one Godhead. The king made peace and, while he refused to be converted, allowed Patrick to continue his missionary work. Erc was baptised and later named as the first bishop of Slane. On Holy Saturday the local parish priest still lights a fire on the hill.

The Hill of Slane originally had a church associated with St Erc and, later, a round tower and monastery, but only an outline of the foundations remains. Later a motte and bailey was constructed and is still visible on the western side of the hill. A ruined church, tower and other buildings once formed part of an early-16th-century Franciscan friary. On a clear day, from the top of the tower, which is always open, you can see the Hill of Tara and the Boyne Valley, as well (it's said) as seven Irish counties.

St Erc is believed to have become a hermit in old age, and the ruins of a small Gothic church mark the spot where he is thought to have spent his last days, around 512 to 514. It's on the northern river bank, behind the Protestant church on the Navan road, and lies within the private Conyngham estate. It opens to the public only on 15 August.

Slane Castle

Slane Castle, the private residence of Lord Henry Conyngham, earl of Mountcharles, is west of the centre along the Navan road and is best known in Ireland as the setting for major outdoor rock concerts. Bruce Springsteen, Bob Dylan, the Rolling Stones and Guns 'n' Roses have appeared here, and in 2001 U2 played their only Irish concert of the year in the grounds.

Built in 1785 in Gothic Revival style by James Wyatt, the building was altered later by Francis Johnson for the visit of George IV to Lady Conyngham. She was allegedly his mistress, and it's said the road between Dublin and Slane was built especially straight and smooth to speed up the randy king's journeys.

Unfortunately, much of the castle, including some valuable furnishings, was destroyed by fire in 1991, whereupon it was discovered that the earl – a Lloyd's name – was under-insured. Money is now being raised for restoration. The castle and grounds are closed to the public except for the yearly concert, which attracts upwards of 60,000 cider-drinking, rubbish-throwing rock fans; call ☎ 982 4207 for details of Meath's answer to Woodstock.

Ledwidge Museum

Just about 1km east of the village on the Drogheda road is the Ledwidge Museum (☎ 982 4544, Janesville; admission €1.90; open 9am-1pm & 2pm-7pm Apr-Sept; 9am-1pm & 2pm-4.30pm Mon-Fri Oct-Mar).

This labourer's cottage about 1.5km north of Slane was the birthplace of Francis Ledwidge, a poet who died on the battlefield of Ypres in Belgium in 1917 just short of his 30th birthday.

Places to Stay

Slane Farm Hostel (☎/fax 988 4985 ⓔ pad dymacken@eircom.net, Harlinstown House, R163 Navan road) Dorms/doubles €12.70/ 15.25 per person. Just 1km from the castle gates are the stables of Harlinstown House, built by the Marquis of Conyngham in the 18th century for his stable man. They have been converted by the current owners (who reside in the house itself) into this wonderful hostel that has earned rave reviews from our readers.

Boyne View (☎ 982 4121, Slane Village) Singles/doubles €30/49. This elegant Georgian townhouse is down by the river near the bridge; it has three rooms, two en suite.

Conyngham Arms Hotel (☎ 982 4155, fax 982 4205, Slane Village) Singles/doubles €57/95. Near the crossroads in the village, this hotel also has a reasonable restaurant and you can get good snacks in the bar from 10.30am to 7pm.

Places to Eat

Boyle's Licensed Tea Rooms (☎ 982 4195, Main St) From €2. This marvellous tea shop and cafe lies behind an equally beautiful shop front with gold lettering. The menu – written in 12 languages – is strictly of the tea-and-scones type, but people come here for the ambience, which is straight out of the 1940s.

Conyngham Arms Hotel (see Places to Stay) For something more substantial, this place serves traditional, home-made food from noon to 8pm daily. The roast chicken with stuffing, bacon and cabbage (€8.50) is excellent.

Getting There & Away

From Dublin, Slane is on the Letterkenny (five buses daily, six on Friday) and Armagh (up to six daily) routes as well as the less busy routes to Portrush (two daily) and Derry (two to four daily), which sometimes requires a change at Omagh. It takes 45 minutes to get here from Dublin, and the fare is single/return €7.40/10.80. The stop in Slane is in front of the sweet shop on the Derry road. There's a bus service between Slane and Drogheda (€1.45, 35 minutes, six daily, five on Sunday) and Slane and Navan (€1.10, six daily, five on Sunday). The stop is at Conlon's shop near the crossroads. For information of departure and arrival times call Bus Éireann (☎ 01-836 6111) in Dublin.

SLANE TO NAVAN

The 14km journey on the N51 south-west from Slane to Navan follows the Boyne Valley past a number of manor houses, ruined castles, round towers and churches; they're only of moderate interest compared to the fine sites elsewhere in County Meath, though.

Dunmoe Castle lies down a badly signposted cul-de-sac to the south, 4km before reaching Navan. This D'Arcy family castle is a 16th-century ruin with good views of the countryside and of the impressive red-brick **Ardmulchan House** (not open to the public), on the opposite side of the River Boyne. Cromwell is supposed to have fired at the castle from the riverbank in 1649, and local legend holds that a tunnel used to run from the castle vaults under the river. Near Dunmoe Castle is a small overgrown chapel and graveyard, with a crypt containing members of the D'Arcy family. Ardmulchan House, though somewhat dilapidated, is still used as a private residence.

You can't miss the fine 30m round tower and 13th-century church of **Donaghmore**, on the right 2km nearer Navan. The site has a profusion of modern gravestones, but the 10th-century tower with its crucifixion scene above the door is interesting, and there are carved faces near the windows and the remains of the church wall.

NAVAN

☎ 046 • pop 3447

The county town of Navan (An Uaimh) at the confluence of the Boyne and Blackwater Rivers is disfigured by the busy N3 Dublin to Cavan and N51 Drogheda to Westmeath roads, which cut off the rivers from the town. Navan was the birthplace of

Sir Francis Beaufort of the British Navy, who in 1805 devised the internationally accepted scale for wind strengths. The town has a carpet factory, and Europe's largest lead and zinc mine, Tara, is 3km along the Kells road. Frankly, there is little here of any great interest.

Orientation & Information

Market Square is the town hub, with Ludlow, Watergate and Trimgate Sts leading from it in the directions of the former town gates.

The local tourist office (☎ 21581) is in the town library on Railway St, about 500m south-west of Market Square. It opens 9.30am to 12.30pm and 1.30pm to 5pm Monday to Saturday.

There's a map and information point in the town hall car park at the northern end of Watergate St.

The modern post office is past the big shopping centre on Kennedy Rd, which runs off Trimgate St, and there's an Allied Irish Bank branch (with ATM) on the corner of these two streets. The Bizzy Laundry is on Brews Hill, the continuation of Trimgate St. Hi Way (☎ 21910) on Brew's Hill is a pretty good bookshop, with plenty of titles on local history and folklore.

Places to Stay

If you decide to stay in Navan there are several good B&Bs.

Athumley Manor (☎/fax 71388, **e** pboylan@eircom.net, Athumley, Duleek road R153) Singles/doubles €32.50/49. This B&B is the best of the lot; a large, comfortable home with well appointed rooms that are tastefully decorated.

Killyon House (☎ 71224, fax 72766, Dublin road) Singles/doubles €38/63.50. This guesthouse may be modern, but the use of antiques and stylish design ensures that it has a lot of charm.

Places to Eat

The Loft (☎ 71755, 26 Trimgate St) Mains from €10. Open 6pm-11pm Mon-Sat, from 12.30pm Sun. One of the best places around is The Loft, opposite O'Flaherty's, with 'funky food, art and music' every night.

There is an early-bird special before 7pm costing €12.

The Station House *(☎ 25239, Kilmessan)* Dinner around €28. This is one of the most respected restaurants in the area, and for the high quality of its cuisine, it's well worth it.

Ryan's Pub *(☎ 21154, 22 Trimgate St)* From €3. This lovely old pub serves great pub grub, including brown bread with smoked salmon.

Chekhov's Coffee Shop *(☎ 74422, 17 Trimgate St)* From €4. We don't quite get the Russian reference, but no matter: this is a wonderfully cosy place.

Entertainment

O'Flaherty's *(☎ 22810, cnr Railway St & Brews Hill)* is a popular, modern, comfortably furnished pub.

The Lantern *(☎ 23535, 32 Watergate St)* This place delivers an Irish music night on Wednesday.

Hotels are the locations of the town's only nightclubs, which doesn't really say much for them.

Oisin's *(☎ 23119, Ardboyne Hotel, Dublin road)* This is a pretty cheesy nightclub in the Ardboyne Hotel.

Solar *(☎ 73732, Newgrange Hotel, Bridge St)* Chart hits keep the dancefloor pretty full at this hotel nightclub.

Getting There & Away

Buses stop in front of the Mercy Convent on Railway St and in Market Square. Destinations and times are posted, or call Bus Éireann (☎ 01-836 6111) in Dublin for information. Buses run almost hourly to/from Dublin (single/return €8.70/10.80, 45 minutes) on the Dublin–Cavan–Donegal route, which also serves Kells (from Navan: €3/4.60, 15 minutes). Navan is also on the Dundalk to Galway route, with one bus daily stopping also at Drogheda (€3.75/5.60, 35 minutes). From Navan, it takes 1¼ hours to reach Dundalk (€7.90/12.10) and 3¼ hours to get to Galway (€15.25/22.90).

Getting Around

You can order a taxi from Navan Cabs (☎ 23053), and there are ranks on Market Square and in front of the shopping centre on Kennedy Rd. Clarke's Sports (☎ 21130), in the back of the Navan Indoor Market at 39 Trimgate St, is the local Raleigh Rent-a-Bike dealer, with bikes costing €12.70 per day plus a deposit of €63.50. You'd have to negotiate a weekly rate.

AROUND NAVAN

There are some nice **walks** in the area, particularly the one following the towpath that runs along the old River Boyne canal towards Slane and Drogheda. On the southern bank, you can easily go out about 7km as far as Stackallen and the Boyne bridge, passing Ardmulchan House and, on the opposite bank, the ruins of Dunmoe Castle (see the Slane to Navan section, earlier in this chapter, for details). Going beyond the bridge towards Slane is trickier as the path is rough and in some places switches to the opposite side of the bank, with no bridge for you to cross over.

Just west of town is the **Motte of Navan**, a scrub-covered mound that tradition holds to be the burial site of Odhbha, the wife of a Celtic prince who had abandoned her for Tea (pronounced **tay**-ah), the lady who gave her name to Tara. Odhbha followed her husband to Navan and died of a broken heart. In reality, the 16m-high mound was probably formed naturally – a deposit of gravel from the Ice Age – and was then adapted by the Normans as a motte and bailey.

Two kilometres to the south-east of town are the impressive remains of **Athlumney Castle**, built by the Dowdall family in the 16th century with additions made 100 years later. This relatively intact castle was said to have been set alight in 1690 by Sir Lancelot Dowdall, after James' defeat at the Battle of the Boyne. Dowdall vowed that the conqueror, William of Orange, would never shelter in or confiscate his home. He watched the blaze from the opposite bank of the river before leaving for France and then Italy. As you enter the estate, take a right toward the Loreto Convent, where you can pick up the keys to the castle. In the convent yard is another **motte**; at one time it had a wooden tower on it.

Close to the Kells road (N3), 5km north-west of Navan, is the large ruin of a castle that once belonged to the Talbot family. **Liscartan Castle**, is made up of two 15th-century square towers joined by a hall-like room.

TARA

The **Hill of Tara** (Teamhair), has occupied a special place in Irish legend and folklore for millennia, although it's not known exactly when people first settled on this gently sloping hill with its commanding views over the plains of Meath. One of the many mounds on the hill was found to be a Stone Age passage grave from about 2500 BC, and during the Bronze Age people of high rank and status were certainly being buried here.

Much of the pagan significance of Tara seems to have derived from its associations with the goddess Maeve (or Medbh) and the mythical powers of the druids or priest-rulers who reigned over part of the country from here. By the 3rd century, Tara was the seat of the most powerful rulers in Ireland (Cormac Mac Art was the most powerful of them all), a place where the high king and his royal court had their ceremonial residence, feasted and watched over the realm. While Tara's kings may have been more powerful than the others, they would by no means have held sway over all Ireland as there were countless other *rí tuaithe* (petty kings) controlling many smaller areas. Celtic titles were not hereditary, either, so it was not uncommon for the ultimate prize of high king to be won on the battle field.

Tara's remains are not visually impressive. Only mounds and depressions in the grass mark where the Iron Age hill fort and surrounding ring forts once stood, but it remains an evocative, somewhat moving place, especially on a warm summer's evening.

As the focus of Irish political influence and a centre of pagan worship, Tara was targeted by the early Christians. A great pagan *feis* (festival) is thought to have been held around what is now Halloween. On Tara – if not on the Hill of Slane – St Patrick supposedly used the shamrock and its three leaves to explain the Christian Trinity to King Laoghaire in the 5th century. Hence

the adoption of the shamrock as the Irish national symbol.

After the 6th century, once Christianity had taken hold and Tara's pagan significance had waned, the high kings began to desert Tara. The kings of Leinster continued to be based here until the 11th century, however.

In August 1843, Tara saw one of the greatest crowds ever to gather in Ireland. Daniel O'Connell, the 'Liberator' and leader of the opposition to union with Great Britain, held one of his 'monster rallies' at Tara, and up to 750,000 people came to hear him speak.

Tara Visitor Centre

The former Protestant church (with a window by well known artist Evie Hone) houses the Tara Visitor Centre (*☎ 046-25903, Navan; adult/student & child €1.90/0.75; open 9.30am-6.30pm mid-June-mid-Sept; 10am-5pm May-mid-June & mid-Sept-Oct; last admission 45 minutes before closing*), where a 20-minute audiovisual presentation on the site called *Tara: Meeting Place of Heroes* is shown. During the summer the tour from here is a must, as the anecdotes really bring the mounds and relics to life. Tours are available (see Organised Tours, below).

Ráth of the Synods

The names applied to Tara's various humps and mounds were adopted from ancient texts, and mythology and religion intertwine with the historical facts. The Protestant church grounds and graveyard spill onto the remains of the Ráth of the Synods, a triple-ringed fort supposedly where some of St Patrick's early meetings (or synods) took place. Excavations of the enclosure suggest that it was used between AD 200 and AD 400 for burials, rituals and living quarters. Originally the ring fort would have contained wooden houses surrounded by timber palisades.

During a digging session in the graveyard in 1810, a boy found a pair of gold torcs (necklaces of twisted gold bands), now in the National Museum in Dublin. Later excavations brought a surprise when Roman glass, shards of pottery and seals were discovered, showing links with the Roman

Empire, even though the Romans never extended their power into Ireland.

The poor state of the enclosure is due in part to a group of British 'Israelites' who in the 1890s dug the place up looking for the Ark of the Covenant, much to the consternation of the local people. The Israelites' leader claimed to see a mysterious pillar on the enclosure, but unfortunately it was invisible to everyone else. After they failed to uncover anything, the invisible pillar moved to the other side of the road but, before the adventurers had time to start work there, the locals chased them away.

The Royal Enclosure

To the south of the church, the Royal Enclosure (Ráth na Ríogh) is a large, oval Iron Age hill fort, 315m in diameter and surrounded by a bank and ditch cut through solid rock under the soil. Inside the Royal Enclosure are smaller sites.

Mound of the Hostages This bump (Dumha na nGiall) in the northern corner of the enclosure is the most ancient known part of Tara and the most visible of the remains. Supposedly a prison cell for hostages of the 3rd-century king Cormac MacArt, it is in fact a small Stone Age passage grave dating from around 1800 BC and later used by Bronze Age people. The passage contains some carved stonework, but it's closed to the public.

The mound produced a treasure-trove of artefacts, including some ancient Mediterranean beads of amber and faïence (glazed pottery). More than 35 Bronze Age burials were found here, as well as a mass of cremated remains from the Stone Age.

Cormac's House & Royal Seat Two other earthworks found inside the enclosure are Cormac's House (Teach Cormaic) and the Royal Seat (Forradh). Although they look similar, the Royal Seat is a ring fort with a house site in the centre, while Cormac's House is a barrow, or burial mound, in the side of the circular bank. Cormac's House commands the best views of the surrounding lowlands of the Boyne and Blackwater Valleys.

Atop Cormac's House is the phallic **Stone of Destiny** (Lia Fáil), originally located near the Mound of the Hostages and representing the joining of the gods of the earth and the heavens. It's said to be the inauguration stone of the high kings of Tara. The would-be king stood on top of it and, if the stone let out three roars, he was crowned. The mass grave of 37 men who died in a skirmish on Tara during the 1798 Rising is next to the stone.

Enclosure of King Laoghaire

South of the Royal Enclosure is the Enclosure of King Laoghaire (Ráth Laoghaire), a large but worn ring fort where the king – a contemporary of St Patrick – is supposedly buried dressed in his armour and standing upright.

Banquet Hall

North of the churchyard is Tara's most unusual feature, the Banquet Hall, or Teach Miodhchuarta (House of Meadcircling; mead, which was a popular tipple, is fermented from honey). This rectangular earthwork measures 230m by 27m along a north–south axis. Tradition holds that it was built to cater for thousands of guests during feasts. Much of this information about the hall comes from the 12th-century Book of Leinster and the Yellow Book of Lecan, which even includes drawings of it.

Opinions vary as to the site's real purpose. Its orientation suggests that it was a sunken entrance to Tara, leading directly to the Royal Enclosure. More recent research has uncovered graves within the compound, and it's possible that the banks are in fact the burial sites of some of the kings of Tara.

Gráinne's Fort

Gráinne's Fort (Ráth Gráinne) and the northern and southern Sloping Trenches (Claoin Fhearta) off to the north-west are burial mounds. Gráinne was the same daughter of King Cormac who was betrothed to Fionn McCumhaill (Finn McCool) but eloped with Diarmuid ÓDuibhne, one of the king's warriors, on her wedding night and became the subject of the epic The Pursuit of Diarmuid and Gráinne. See Newgrange earlier in this chapter for more about the legend.

Organised Tours

Mary Gibbons Tours (☎ 01-283 9973) have an excellent Boyne Valley tour that includes the Hill of Tara as well as Brú na Bóinne. It departs from the Dublin Tourism Centre in Suffolk St at 10.45am returning at 5.30pm or 6pm on Monday to Wednesday and Friday; it costs €28.

Bus Éireann (☎ 01-836 6111) tours to Newgrange and the Boyne Valley sometimes include a visit to Tara. These depart at 10am and return at 5.45pm Saturday to Thursday, May to September; Thursday and Saturday only in April (adult/student/child €26/23/13); 10am to 4.15pm Thursday and Saturday only, October to December (adult/student/child €20.50/18/10.50). Call for details.

Getting There & Away

Tara is 10km south-east of Navan just off the N3 Dublin to Cavan road. Buses linking Dublin and Navan pass within 1km of the site. There are almost hourly services Monday to Saturday and four on Sunday (€7.40 one way, 40 minutes); ask the driver to drop you off at the Tara Cross and then follow the signs.

AROUND TARA

Five kilometres south of Tara on the Dunshaughlin to Kilmessan road is **Dunsany Castle** (☎ 046-25198, Dunsany; admission €6.35 downstairs, €10.20 downstairs & upstairs bedrooms; open 9am-1pm Mon-Fri May-Aug & Oct-Nov; by arrangement only at the weekend). It's the residence of the lords of Dunsany, former owners of the lands around Trim Castle. The Dunsanys are related to the Plunkett family, the most famous Plunkett being St Oliver, who was executed and whose head is kept in a church in Drogheda (see the boxed text 'A Moving Head' later in this chapter).

There's an impressive private art collection and many other treasures related to important figures in Irish history, such as Oliver Plunkett and Patrick Sarsfield, leader of the Irish Jacobite forces at the siege of

Limerick in 1691. A number of upstairs bedrooms have been restored and are now included in an expanded tour (though the charge to visit these is extra). Maintenance and restoration is ongoing (as it would be in a castle built in 1180!) and different rooms are open to visitors at different times.

Housed in the old kitchen and in part of the old domestic quarters is a boutique that proudly sells the Dunsany Home Collection, featuring locally made table linen and accessories, as well as various articles for the home designed by Lord Dunsany himself, who is something of a well known artist and designer. The boutique opens 10am to 5pm daily, year round.

About 1.5km north-east of Dunsany is the ruined **Killeen Castle** (closed to the public) the seat of another line of the Plunkett family. The 1801 mansion was built around a castle built by Hugh de Lacy, lord of Meath, originally dating from 1180. It comprises a neo-Gothic structure between two 12th-century towers.

According to local lore, the surrounding lands were divided at one point among the two Plunkett branches by a race. Starting at the castles, the wives had to run towards each other and a fence was placed where they met. Luckily for the Killeen women-folk, their castle was on higher ground and they made considerable gains as they ran downhill towards their Dunsany counterparts.

TRIM

☎ 046 • pop 1740

Trim (Baile Átha Troim, Town at the Ford of the Elder Trees) is a rather sleepy little town on the River Boyne, with several interesting ruins. The medieval town was a jumble of streets and once had five gates. At one stage, there were also seven monasteries in the immediate area. In the past, few visitors have paused to inspect the impressive ruins of Trim Castle, Ireland's largest Anglo-Norman structure, which many will recognise as having served as a 'castle double' for York Castle in Mel Gibson's 1996 film Braveheart. The interesting historical irony is that Queen Isabella's real lover, Roger de Mortimer, the

MEATH & LOUTH

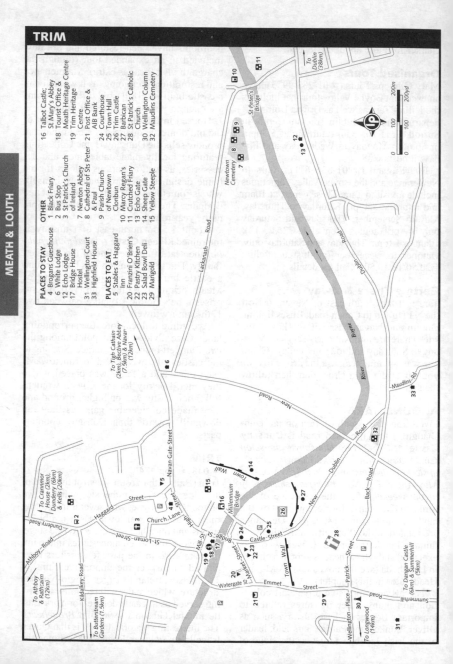

TRIM

PLACES TO STAY
4 Brogans Guesthouse
6 White Lodge
12 Echo Lodge
17 Bridge House
   Hostel
31 Wellington Court
33 Highfield House

PLACES TO EAT
5 Stables & Haggard
   Inn
20 Franzini O'Brien's
22 Pastry Kitchen
23 Salad Bowl Deli
29 Marigold

OTHER
1 Black Friary
2 Bus Stop
3 St Patrick's Church
   of Ireland
7 Newton Abbey
8 Cathedral of Sts Peter
   & Paul
9 Parish Church
   of Newtown
   Clonbun
10 Marcy Regan's
11 Crutched Friary
13 Echo Gate
14 Sheep Gate
15 Yellow Steeple

16 Talbot Castle;
   St Mary's Abbey
18 Tourist Office &
   Meath Heritage
   Centre
19 Trim Heritage
   Centre
21 Post Office &
   AIB Bank
24 Courthouse
25 Town Hall
26 Trim Castle
27 Barbican
28 St Patrick's Catholic
   Church
30 Wellington Column
32 Maudlins Cemetery

earl of March, actually lived in the castle between 1316–20.

According to local history, Elizabeth I considered Trim as a possible site for Trinity College, which eventually ended up in Dublin. The duke of Wellington went to school for a time in Talbot Castle/St Mary's Abbey, which served as a Protestant school in the 18th century. There's a local (and unlikely) belief that he was born in a stable south of the town, which probably arose from the duke's observation that being born in a stable didn't make one a horse, and thus his birth in Ireland didn't make him Irish! A **Wellington column** stands at the junction of Patrick and Emmet Sts. After defeating Napoleon at the Battle of Waterloo, the Iron Duke went on to become prime minister of Great Britain and in 1829 passed the Catholic Emancipation Act, which repealed the last of the repressive penal laws.

Trim was home to the county jail, giving rise to the ditty: 'Kells for brogues, Navan for rogues and Trim for hanging people'.

Information

The tourist office (☎ 37111), on Mill St, opens 9.30am to 5.30pm Monday to Saturday, from noon on Sunday, May to September, and 9am to 5pm Monday to Saturday the rest of the year. Among the brochures for sale is the handy little *Trim Tourist Trail* (€2.50) walking-tour booklet. The post office is at the junction of Emmet and Market Sts, where you'll also find an Allied Irish Bank branch. The post office opens 9.30am to 6pm Monday to Friday and to 1pm on Saturday; the bank opens 10am to 4pm Monday to Wednesday and Friday, and to 5pm on Thursday.

The Power & the Glory

Immediately next to the tourist office in Mill St is the informative **Trim Heritage Centre** (☎ 37227, Mill St; adult/concession €3.20/1.90; open 10am-5pm Mon-Sat, noon 5.30pm Apr-Sept) with an exhibit known as The Power and the Glory, which outlines the medieval history of Trim in audiovisuals. The 20-minute film is shown six-times daily.

The **genealogy & heritage** section (☎ 36633) of the Heritage Centre has now moved to the town hall in Castle St. Here, under the expert guidance of local historian Noel French (who also penned the *Trim Tourist Trail* booklet), there's an extensive genealogical database for people trying to trace Meath ancestors. An initial consultation costs €19, while a full assessment, including your own personalised family tree, costs €89. This office opens 9am to 5pm Monday to Thursday, to 2pm Friday, year round.

Trim Castle

Hugh de Lacy founded Trim Castle (☎ 38619; adult/student €3.20/1.25, castle grounds without the keep €1.30/0.50; open 10am-6pm daily mid-June-mid-Sept only) in 1173, but Rory O'Connor, said to have been the last high king of Ireland, destroyed this motte and bailey within a year. De Lacy did not live to see the castle's replacement, and the building you see today was begun around 1200. It has hardly been modified since then.

Although King John visited Trim in 1210 to bring the de Lacy family into line – hence the building's alternative name of King John's Castle – he never actually slept in the castle. On the eve of his arrival, Walter de Lacy locked it up tight and left town, forcing the king to camp in the nearby meadow.

De Lacy's grandson-in-law, Geoffrey de Geneville, was responsible for the second stage of the keep's construction in the 13th century. De Geneville was a crusader who later became a monk at the Dominican abbey he founded in 1263 just outside the northern wall of the town near Athboy Gate.

In 1399 Henry of Lancaster, later Henry IV, was imprisoned in the Dublin Gate at the southern part of the outer wall by his cousin King Richard II.

Throughout Anglo-Norman times the castle occupied a strategic position on the western edge of the Pale, the area where the Anglo-Normans ruled supreme; beyond Trim was the volatile country where Irish chieftains and lords vied and fought with their Norman rivals for position, power and terrain.

Trim was conquered by Silken Thomas in

1536 and again in 1647 by Catholic Confederate forces, opponents of the English parliamentarians. In 1649 it was taken by Cromwellian forces, and the castle, town walls and Yellow Steeple were badly damaged.

The grassy two-hectare enclosure is dominated by a massive stone keep, 25m tall and mounted on a Norman motte. Inside are three lofty levels, the lowest one divided in two by a central wall. Just outside the central keep are the remains of an earlier wall.

The principal outer curtain wall, some 500m long and for the most part still standing, dates from around 1250 and includes eight towers and a gatehouse. The finest stretch of the outer wall runs from the River Boyne through Dublin Gate to Castle St. The outer wall has a number of sally gates from which defenders could exit to confront the enemy.

Within the northern corner was a church and, facing the river, the Royal Mint, which produced Irish coinage (called 'Patricks' and 'Irelands') into the 15th century. The Russian cannon in the car park is a trophy from the Crimean War and bears the tsarist double-headed eagle.

In 1465, Edward IV ordered that anyone who had robbed or 'who was going to rob' should be beheaded and their heads mounted on spikes and publicly displayed as a warning to other thieves. In 1971, excavations in the castle grounds near the depression south of the keep revealed the remains of 10 headless men, presumably the hapless (or wannabe) criminals.

The castle was closed to the public in 1995, but reopened in 2000 under the care of Dúchas, the Heritage Service. You can now visit the restored keep (by guided tour only) and/or the rest of the castle grounds.

Talbot Castle/St Mary's Abbey

Across the river from the castle are the ruins of the 12th-century Augustinian St Mary's Abbey, rebuilt after a fire in 1368 and once home to a wooden statue of Our Lady of Trim, which was revered by the faithful for its miraculous powers. Cromwell's soldiers set fire to the statue in front of their injured commander, General Croot, a rather poignant slap in the face of Catholic belief (see Maudlins Cemetery under Other Things to See later in this section for more details). Just in case the locals didn't get the symbolism of the gesture, they destroyed the abbey as well. An artists' rendition of the statue is by the roadside in front of the ruins.

Part of the abbey was converted in 1415 into a fine manor house by Sir John Talbot, then viceroy of Ireland. It came to be known as Talbot Castle. The Talbot coat of arms can be seen on the northern wall. Talbot went to war in France, where in 1429 he was defeated by none other than Joan of Arc at Orleans. He was taken prisoner, released and went on fighting the French until 1453. He was known as 'the scourge of France' or 'the whip of the French', and Shakespeare wrote of this notorious man in *Henry VI*:

Is this the Talbot so much feared abroad
That with his name the mothers still their babes?

Talbot Castle was owned in the early 18th century by Esther 'Stella' Johnson, the mistress of Jonathan Swift. She bought the manor house for £65 sterling and lived there for 18 months before selling it to Swift for a tidy £200 sterling. He lived there for a year. Swift was rector of Laracor, 3km south of Trim, from around 1700 until 1745, when he died. From 1713 he was also – and more significantly – dean of St Patrick's Cathedral in Dublin.

Just north of the abbey building is the 40m **Yellow Steeple**, once the bell tower of the abbey, dating from 1368 but damaged by Cromwell's soldiers in 1649. It takes its name from the colour of the stonework at dusk.

A part of the 14th-century town wall stands in the field to the east of the abbey, and includes the **Sheep Gate**, the lone survivor of the town's original five gates. It used to be closed daily between 9pm and 4am, and a toll was charged for sheep entering to be sold at market.

Newtown

About 1.5km east of town on Lackanash Rd, Newtown Cemetery contains an interesting group of ruins. What had been the **parish church of Newtown Clonbun** contains the late 16th-century tomb of Sir Luke Dillon, chief baron of the Exchequer during the reign of Elizabeth I, and his wife Lady Jane Bathe. The effigies are known locally as 'the jealous man and woman', perhaps because of the sword lying between them.

Rainwater that collects between the two figures is claimed to cure warts. Place a pin in the puddle and then jab your wart. When the pin becomes covered in rust your warts will vanish. Some say you should leave a pin on the statue as payment for the cure.

The other ruins here are Newtown's **Cathedral of Sts Peter and Paul**, and the 18th-century **Newtown Abbey** (Abbey of the Canons Regular of St Victor of Paris). The cathedral was founded in 1206 and burned down two centuries later. Parts of the cathedral wall were flattened by a storm in January 1839, which also damaged sections of the Trim Castle wall. The abbey wall throws a superb echo back to **Echo Gate** across the river.

South-east of these ruins and just over the river is the **Crutched Friary**. There are ruins of a keep and traces of a watchtower and other buildings from a hospital set up after the crusades by the Knights of St John of Jerusalem, who wore a red crutch, or cross, on their cassocks. **St Peter's Bridge** beside the friary is said to be the second-oldest bridge in Ireland. *Marcy Regan's* (Lackanash Rd, Newtown Trim), the small pub beside the bridge, claims to be Ireland's second-oldest pub.

Other Things to See

The site of the 13th-century Dominican **Black Friary** lies north of the town, near the junction of the Athboy and Dunderry roads. Only a few mounds remain.

At the other end of town, **Maudlins Cemetery** has a bronze statue of Our Lady of Trim, a later version of a wooden statue put in St Mary's Abbey after its 1368 restoration. The original statue, which was reputed to have miraculous powers, survived the abbey's suppression in 1540 and later came into the possession of a powerful local family. After the sacking of Drogheda in 1649, Cromwell's commander lodged in the house and the statue was burned as firewood.

On the western outskirts of Trim are the award-winning **Butterstream Gardens** (☎ 36017, Kildalkey Rd; admission €4.50; open 11am-6pm daily Apr-Sept), signposted from the centre of town.

Places to Stay

Hostels Trim has an Independent Holiday Hostel (IHH): *Bridge House Hostel* (☎ 31848, fax 0405-46220, 🄴 silversue@ eircom.net, Bridge St) Dorms & rooms €15.90 per person. Open year round. This IHH-affiliated hostel has fairly nice dorm rooms, but, at the same price, the private rooms are a better option.

B&Bs In the centre of Trim is *Brogans Guesthouse* (☎ 31237, fax 37648, 🄴 brogan gh@iol.ie, High St) Singles/doubles €32/ 51. Brogan's has an old-world flavour and has an adjoining bar that serves lunch.

White Lodge (☎/fax 36549, 🄴 whitelodge trim@eircom.net, New Rd) Singles/doubles €33/49. This comfortable B&B is 500m east of the centre at the northern end of New Road.

Echo Lodge (☎ 37945, Steeple Drive, Dublin Rd) Singles/doubles €32/49. This place on the Dublin road is a lovely family home with three nice bedrooms.

Crannmor House (☎ 31635, fax 38087, cranmor@eircom.net, Dunderry Rd) Singles/doubles with bathroom €38/50. This is a converted farmhouse about 2km along the road to Dunderry.

Tigh Cathain (☎/fax 31996, 🄴 marie keane@esatclear.ie, Longwood Rd) Singles/ doubles €32.50/49. This is a country house B&B surrounded by open fields, only 2km west out of Trim.

Hotels To the south of town is *Highfield House* (☎ 36386, fax 38182, 🄴 highfield houseaccom@eircom.net, Maudlins Rd) B&B from €29 per person. This is our favourite place in town, a beautiful early-18th-century house that has been restored to its former elegance. The seven rooms are very well decorated.

Wellington Court (☎ 31516, fax 36002, ⓔ *wellingtoncourt@eircom.net, Summerhill Rd)* Singles/doubles from €50/83.80. Trim's fanciest hotel is this well equipped, 18-room place.

Places to Eat

There's no shortage of somewhere to get a bite in town, with plenty of pubs doing standard pub grub. There are also a couple of pretty good cafes.

Marigold (☎ 36544, Emmet St) Mains from €6. If you want half-decent Chinese food, this is the place. Takeaway is available.

Salad Bowl Deli (☎ 36204, Market St) Dishes under €3.80. For a more substantial lunch, try this place, which serves sandwiches and limited hot plates costing no more than €3.80.

Pastry Kitchen (☎ 38902, Market St) Dishes under €3.80. Like the Salad Bowl next door, this place serves sandwiches and limited hot plates.

Abbey Lodge (☎ 31285, Market St) From €3.80. This nice pub does pretty good grub, from toasted sandwiches to more substantial dishes.

Priory Inn (☎ 36096, Haggard St) Meals from €3.80. Your usual pub fare is available here.

Stables (☎ 31110, Navangate) Mains from €8. This restaurant at the Haggard Inn on Haggard St, is one of the best places to eat in town.

Franzini O'Brien's (☎ 31002, French Lane, off Market St) Mains from €7. This fancy cafe-bar recently opened and has immediately raised the standards of cuisine in Trim. The simple but well prepared food is excellent.

Getting There & Away

Buses stop in front of Tobin's newsagent at the northern end of Haggard St. Buses running between Dublin's Busáras (☎ 01-836 6111) and Granard pass through Trim hourly Monday to Saturday (five times on Sunday) in each direction. It takes just over an hour to get to Trim from Dublin and the fare is single/return €6.75/10.20, although a day return costs only €8.

AROUND TRIM

Some 7.5km north-east of Trim on the way to Navan is **Bective Abbey**, founded in 1147 and the first Cistercian offspring of magnificent Mellifont Abbey in Louth. The remains seen today are 13th- and 15th-century additions and consist of the chapter house, church, ambulatory and cloister. After the suppression of the monasteries in 1543, it was used as a fortified house, and the tower was built.

In 1186, Hugh de Lacy, lord of Meath, began demolishing the abbey at Durrow in County Offaly in order to build a castle. A workman, known both as O'Miadaigh and O'Kearney, was offended by this desecration, lopped off de Lacy's head and fled. Although de Lacy's body was interred in Bective Abbey, his head went to St Thomas Abbey in Dublin. A dispute broke out over who should possess all the bodily remains, and it required the intervention of the pope to, well, pontificate on the matter, with a ruling in favour of St Thomas Abbey.

Some 12km north-west of Trim on the road to Athboy is **Rathcairn**, the smallest Gaeltacht (Irish-speaking) district in Ireland. Rathcairn's population is descended from a group of Connemara Irish speakers, who were settled on an estate here as part of a social experiment in the 1930s.

Six kilometres south of Trim on the road to Summerhill stands **Dangan Castle**, built by the Wellesley family and the boyhood home of the duke of Wellington. The castle is also supposed to have been the birthplace of Don Ambrosio O'Higgins (1720–1801), the Spanish viceroy of Peru and Chile at the end of the 18th century. His son Bernardo O'Higgins went on to become the liberator of Chile, and Santiago's main thoroughfare is named after him (he was also the founder of Argentina's navy, and Buenos Aires has a number of statues in his honour). The mansion's current state is the result of the efforts of Roger O'Conor, its last owner, who set it alight on a number of occasions between 1808 and 1809 for the insurance money.

Summerhill, another 5km farther south, is a pleasant, sleepy little village with a large, tidy green, but there's nothing much to do here except have lunch at *John*

Shaw's (☎ *0405-57427, Summerhill*), a pub-restaurant at the northern edge of the village. Jonathan Swift's connection with the area includes a curious folly in **Castlerichard**, a hamlet 10km west of Summerhill. By the church over the old bridge is a large stone pyramid inscribed with the word 'Swifte'.

Places to Stay

A working farm in the area makes for an interesting overnight option. *Cosy Gibbins Farmhouse* (☎ *0405-57232, Collegelands, Summerhill*) Singles/doubles €32/56. Situated 8km south-east of Summerhill in the hamlet of Collegelands (on the road to Dublin), this place is next to the Forge pub (which is great for a drink!).

KELLS
☎ 046 • pop 2152

While almost every visitor to Ireland pays homage to the magnificent Book of Kells in Dublin's Trinity College, few come to see where it originated, and perhaps with good reason: present-day Kells (Ceanannus Mór) is a dreary place and little remains of the monastic site established here in the 6th century. Still, there are some fine high crosses in various states of preservation, a 1000-year-old round tower, the even older St Colmcille's House, and an interesting display in the gallery of the local church.

After establishing monasteries at Derry, Durrow and, in 559, Kells, St Colmcille (also known as St Columba) went into exile on the remote Scottish island of Iona. In 807, monks from the Iona monastery arrived here after 68 of their brethren were killed in a Viking raid. It's thought that they brought both the remains of their revered saint and an illuminated manuscript of the Gospels with them, bound in vellum and enclosed in a gold case. This extraordinary work of art consequently came to be known as the Book of Kells.

It was stolen two centuries later, but the thief was only after its gold case, and the manuscript was later found buried in a bog. Kells proved to be no safer than Scotland for the monks, however, as Viking raids soon spread to Ireland. Kells was plundered on no less than five different occasions between the 9th and 11th centuries. A century later, the Columbans moved their headquarters to Derry and the monastery was abandoned.

Orientation & Information

The N3 from Dublin to Cavan almost bypasses the town. Turning south at Cross St brings you down to Farrell St, where you'll find most of the pubs and shops (including Maguire's, a newsagent and grocery with disposable mousetraps among other useful items!). The tourist office (☎ 49336) is in the heritage centre (see below) behind the town hall on Headfort Place. It opens 10am to 5.30pm Monday to Saturday (from 1.30pm Sunday), May to September, and 10am to 5pm Tuesday to Saturday (from 1.30pm Sunday) the rest of the year. Kells Hostel is also helpful with queries. There's a Bank of Ireland branch on John St. The post office is on Farrell St.

Kells Heritage Centre

Spread across two detail-packed floors, the town's heritage centre (☎ *49336, Headfort Place; adult/concession €3.80/2.50; open 10am-6pm Mon-Sat, 1.30pm-6pm Sun May-Sept; 10am-5pm Mon-Sat, 1.30pm-5pm Sun Oct-Apr*) has a 12-minute audiovisual on the monastic era which sets the tone for the exhibits. On the ground floor is a replica of the Market Cross (the real one is outside), while upstairs is a rather beautiful copy of the area's most famous object, the Book of Kells. Although you can see the real book in Dublin's Trinity College, it is heavily protected by a shield of glass and you can only see four pages at a time. Here, two touchscreens allow you to leaf interactively through the entire book, giving you a proper sense of the book's awesome beauty. Surrounding the book are various 6th- to 12th-century relics and artefacts as well as a scale model of the town around the 6th century.

Round Tower & High Crosses

The Protestant Church of St Columba (closed to the public), west of the town centre, stands in the grounds of the old monastic settlement. A square belfry dating from the 15th century stands beside the church. Above the doorway is an inscription detailing the addition of the neo-Gothic spire in 1783 by the earl of Bective from a design by Thomas Cooley, the architect of Dublin's City Hall.

The churchyard has a 30m-high, 10th-century round tower on the southern side. It's now without its conical roof but is known to date back at least as far as 1076, when Muircheartach Maelsechnaill, the high king of Tara, was murdered in its confined apartments.

Inside the churchyard are four 9th-century high crosses in various states of repair. The West Cross, at the far end of the compound from the entrance, is the stump of a decorated shaft with scenes of the baptism of Jesus, the Fall of Adam and Eve, and the judgement of Solomon on the eastern face, and Noah's ark on the western face. All that is left of the North Cross is the bowl-shaped base stone.

Near the tower is the best preserved of the crosses, the Cross of Patrick and Columba, with its semi-legible inscription 'Patrici et Columbae Crux' on the eastern face of the base. Above it are scenes of Daniel in the lions' den, the fiery furnace, the Fall of Adam and Eve and a hunting scene. On the opposite side of the cross are the Last Judgement, the crucifixion, and riders with a chariot and a dog on the base. The council has plans to move this cross into the new heritage centre when completed to protect it from the elements.

The other surviving cross is the unfinished East Cross. On the eastern side is a carving of the crucifixion and a group of four figures on the right arm. The three blank, raised panels below these were prepared for carving, but the sculptor apparently never got round to the task.

St Colmcille's House

From the churchyard exit on Church St, St Colmcille's House (free; open 10am-5pm Sat & Sun June-Sept) is left up the hill, among the row of houses on the right side of Church Lane. It is usually open in the summer; otherwise, pick up the keys from Mrs Carpenter (41778) the brown-coloured house at No 1 Lower Church View as you ascend the hill.

This squat, solid structure is a survivor from the old monastic settlement. Its name is

a misnomer, as it was built in the 10th century and St Colmcille was alive in the 6th century. Although its use is unclear, experts have suggested that it was used as a *scriptorium*, a place where monks illuminated books. The original entrance to the 1000-year-old building was over 2m above ground level. Inside, a very long ladder leads to a low attic room under the roof line.

Market Cross

Until recently the Market Cross had stood for centuries in Cross St in the town centre, marking the farthest extent of the 10th-century monastery. It's said that it was moved here by Jonathan Swift, and in 1798 the British garrison executed rebels by hanging them from the crosspiece, one on each arm so the cross wouldn't fall over. Alas, in 1996 the cross met its ignoble fate – in a crass, modern manner. A motorist took a tight turn, reversed and toppled the 1000-year-old thing. It has now been repaired and has been placed outside the heritage centre; originally it was intended to go inside, but local objections to having to pay to see their monument forced a change of plans. Oddly, you can *pay* to see a *replica*, but you'll have to walk by the real thing to do so!

On the eastern side of the Market Cross are Abraham's sacrifice of Isaac, Cain and Abel, the Fall of Adam and Eve, guards at the tomb of Jesus, and a wonderfully executed procession of horsemen. On the western face, the crucifixion is the only discernible image. On the northern side is a panel of Jacob wrestling with the angel.

Places to Stay

Next to Monaghan's Inn is *Kells Hostel* (☎ 49995, fax 40680, e hostels@iol.ie, The Carrick, Cavan Rd) Tent sites €5.10 per person, dorms/rooms €10.20/12.70 per person. This IHH hostel on the Cavan road is 200m uphill from the bus stop. There's a full kitchen and other facilities. You may have to check-in at Monaghan's Inn.

White Gables (☎ 40322, fax 49672, e whitegables@tinet.ie, Headfort Place) Singles/doubles €38.50/76.50. This is a marvellous little B&B set in off the main street and surrounded by a garden. The owner is a cordon bleu chef, so the breakfasts are fantastic.

Headfort Arms Hotel (☎ *40063, fax 40587, John St)* Singles/doubles €57/114.50. This place offers 18 rooms, all well appointed and very neat. It also has a nightclub and restaurant attached.

Boltown House (☎ *43605, fax 43036,* e *boltown@iolfree.ie, off Oldcastle Rd)* Singles/doubles €51/89. About 7km outside of town, this is a large farmhouse with cosy rooms and excellent food, including home-made scones.

Places to Eat

Penny's Place (☎ *41130, Market St)* From €5. Open 9am-6pm Mon-Sat. This is an excellent cafe with home-made food; their brown bread has few equals.

O'Shaughnessy's (☎ *41110, Market St)* From €5. This pub, farther west on Market St serves reasonable sandwiches and lunches.

Monaghan's (☎ *49995, The Carrick, Cavan Rd)* Lunches around €6.50, dinner mains from €8.80. This pub is next to the hostel and serves lunch and dinner.

Entertainment

O'Shaughnessy's *(see Places to Eat)* features lots of rustic timber. ***Blackwater Inn*** (☎ *40386, Farrell St)* has regular Irish music sessions. ***Monaghan's*** *(see Places to Eat)* is favoured by a younger crowd; it often has music at the weekend.

Getting There & Away

Buses stop in front of the church on John St and near the hostel (request stop only). Times are posted at the stop or phone Bus Éireann (☎ 01-836 6111) in Dublin. Buses run from Dublin to Kells (€7.90/12.10, one hour) and Cavan and back almost hourly from 7am to 10pm. Two of the buses are express coaches on their way to and from Donegal. There are also regular services to Navan (€3/4.60, 15 minutes) and Drogheda.

AROUND KELLS
Hill of Lloyd Tower

The 30m tower on the Hill of Lloyd is visible from behind the hostel in Kells, and it's easy to see why it became known as the 'inland lighthouse'. Built in 1791 by the earl of Bective in memory of his father, it has been renovated and if it's open you can climb to the top for €1.90/1.30, or picnic in the surrounding park. The tower is 3km north-west of Kells, off the Crossakeel road.

Crosses of Castlekeeran

Two kilometres farther down the Crossakeel road, signposted to the right, are the Crosses of Castlekeeran. Access is through a farmyard. Three plainly carved, early-9th-century crosses, one in the river, are surrounded by an overgrown cemetery, while at the ruined church in the centre are some early grave slabs and an ogham stone.

LOUGHCREW CAIRNS

North-west of Kells and near Oldcastle, the Loughcrew Hills – of which Slieve (or Sliabh) na Caillighe (279m) is the highest peak – give marvellous views east and south to the plains of Meath and north into the lake country of Cavan. On the summit of three of the hills – Slieve na Caillighe, Carnbane East (194m) and Carnbane West (206m) – are the remains of 30 Stone Age passage graves built around 3000 BC but used up to the Iron Age. In some cases, a large mound is surrounded by numerous, smaller satellite graves. As at Newgrange, larger stones in some of the graves are decorated with spiral patterns. Archaeologists have unearthed bone fragments and ashes, stone balls and beads. Some of the graves look like large piles of stones, while others are less obvious, the cairn having been removed.

To get there from Kells, head north-west on the R163. About 5km from Oldcastle you'll see a sign for Sliabh na Caillighe. Turn right, and at the first house on the right collect the keys to the cairn entrances from Basil Balfe (but ring ☎ 049-41256 first).

If anybody is there to collect it, a deposit of €6.50 (hikers can leave their backpacks as collateral!) is required, and a leaflet about the sites is available. A torch (flashlight) is useful on dull days. Coming from the east, the first group of hills – Patrickstown Cairns – is of little interest; the most interesting and intact remains are on the next two, Carnbane East and Carnbane West.

Carnbane East

Carnbane East has a cluster of sites; Cairn T is the biggest at about 35m in diameter and has numerous carved stones. One of its outlying kerbstones is called the Hag's Chair and is covered in gouged holes, circles and other markings. You need the gate key to enter the passageway and a torch to see anything in detail. It takes about half an hour to climb Carnbane East from the car park. From the summit on a reasonably clear day, you should be able to see the Hill of Tara to the south-east, while the view north is into Cavan, with Lough Ramor to the north-east and Lough Sheelin and Oldcastle to the north-west.

Carnbane West

From the same car park, it takes about an hour to reach the summit of Carnbane West, where Cairn D and L are both some 60m in diameter. Cairn D has been disturbed in an unsuccessful search for a central chamber. Cairn L, north-east of Cairn D, is also in poor condition, though you can enter the passage and chamber, where there are numerous carved stones and a curved basin stone where human ashes were placed.

County Louth

Although the smallest county in Ireland (hence its nickname, the 'Wee County'), Louth is home to the two principal towns of Ireland's north-eastern region.

Drogheda is the more pleasant town of the two, with a bustling town centre and some pretty interesting attractions; it also makes a good base for exploring the Boyne Valley, with its prehistoric sites to the west and the monastic relics to the north.

Dundalk is a border town to the north and a gateway to the lonely but scenic Cooley Peninsula. Its proximity to the border has meant that it has strong affiliations with republicanism, and has been a welcome haven for IRA activists on the run from the Northern authorities.

HISTORY

Humans have lived in this region since about 7000 BC, but Louth's Stone Age relics – like the Proleek Dolmen and passage grave near Dundalk – pale in comparison with the Brú na Bóinne relics in County Meath. Only with the coming of the Iron Age did Louth rival its neighbour.

Louth was part of the ancient kingdom of Oriel, which was the stage for many of the epic tales of Irish mythology. The north of the county and the Cooley Peninsula are the setting for legends of Cúchulainn, one of the most famous heroes of ancient Ireland, who was born and raised around Faughart, just north of Dundalk. Cúchulainn was the lead player in the story of the Táin Bó Cúailnge (Cattle Raid of Cooley), one of the great Celtic epic myths. See the boxed text of that name later in this chapter. *The Táin* by Thomas Kinsella (Dolmen Press) is a modern version of this compelling and bloody tale.

St Patrick introduced Christianity in the 5th century, and numerous religious communities sprang up in the region. The monastery at Monasterboice and the later Cistercian abbey at Mellifont, both near Drogheda, are Louth's most interesting archaeological sites.

Irish society underwent a huge upheaval with the arrival of the Anglo-Normans in the 12th century. Hugh de Lacy's reward for his Irish conquests was the fertile land of Meath and Louth. Mottes, such as the one at Millmount in Drogheda, were first built around this time to defend Anglo-Normans against the hostile Irish.

The Normans' stone castles came later, and smaller satellite castles such as Termonfeckin, north-east of Drogheda, dot the countryside. The Norman invaders were responsible for the development of Dundalk, and for the two towns, on opposite banks of the Boyne, which united in 1412 to become what is now Drogheda.

These new settlers would become some

of the staunchest defenders of Ireland in later centuries, particularly against the English parliamentarians. In 1649, Cromwell's forces massacred the native Irish and Anglo-Norman Catholic defenders of Drogheda for refusing to surrender.

Ireland succumbed to English control in 1690, after the Battle of the Boyne, where the Protestant William of Orange defeated his father-in-law, the English Catholic King James II. James had enlisted the help of the Irish in return for greater religious and political freedom, and his defeat resulted in a new influx of Protestant settlers.

DROGHEDA
☎ 041 • pop 24,460

The historic town of Drogheda hugs a bend on the River Boyne, 5km from the sea. It's a compact settlement, with a small village-like adjunct to the south of the river around Millmount. The town, which is pretty run-down in places, has undertaken a project of urban renewal that has brought new life to the place. The future looks bright for Drogheda, and plans to clean the Boyne (which is filthy around here) will go a long way towards making the town a very attractive spot.

Once fortified, Drogheda still has one

MEATH & LOUTH

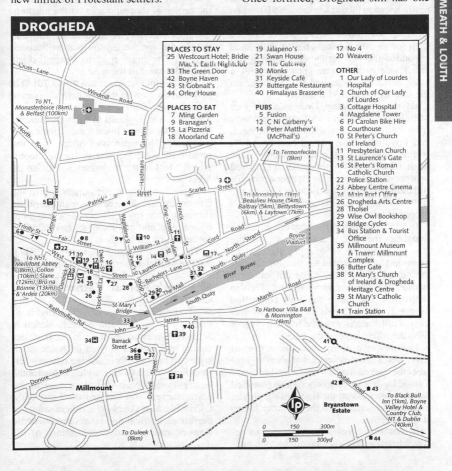

town gate in fine condition, together with some interesting old buildings and the curious hump of Millmount, south of the river. The embalmed head of the Catholic martyr St Oliver Plunkett is housed in St Peter's Roman Catholic Church.

The town's name comes from Droichead Átha (Bridge of the Ford), after the bridge built by the Normans to link the two earlier Viking settlements.

History

There was probably a rough settlement here before the 10th century, but Drogheda really began to take shape around 910, when the Danes built defences to guard a strategic crossing point on the River Boyne. In the 12th century, the Normans built a bridge and expanded the two settlements forming on either side of the river. They also built a large defensive motte-and-bailey castle on the southern side at Millmount.

By the 15th century, Drogheda was one of Ireland's four major walled towns. Many Irish Parliament sessions were held here, and Poyning's Law, passed here in 1494, is the most famous piece of legislation from Irish medieval times. It diminished prospects of home rule or independence for Ireland by granting the English Crown the right to veto any measures the Irish proposed to enact.

In 1465, the Irish Parliament conferred on Drogheda the right to a university, but the plan foundered in 1468, when the earl of Desmond was executed for treason. During the period of the Pale, when only a small portion of the country around Dublin (known as 'The Pale') was fully controlled by the English, Drogheda was a frontier town. Farther north were the fractious Ulster folk, definitely beyond the Pale.

In 1649, the town was the scene of Cromwell's most notorious Irish slaughter (see the boxed text 'The Lord Protector Turned Destructor'). Drogheda also plumped for the wrong side at the Battle of the Boyne in 1690, but surrendered the day after James II was defeated.

It took many years for the town to recover from these events, but in the 19th cen-

tury a number of Catholic churches were built. The massive railway viaduct and the string of quayside buildings hint at the town's brief Victorian industrial boom, when it was a centre for cotton and linen manufacture, and brewing.

For trivia buffs, it was a Drogheda man called Finlay who blew the bugle signalling the start of the Charge of the Light Brigade at Balaclava during the Crimean War (1853–56).

Orientation & Information

Drogheda sits astride the River Boyne with the principal shopping area on the northern bank along West and Laurence Sts. The area south of the river is residential, dull and dominated by the mysterious Millmount mound. The main road to Belfast skirts round the town to the west.

The helpful tourist office (☎ 983 7070) is at the bus station on the southern side of the river. It opens 9.30am to 5.30pm Monday to Saturday, and 11.45am to 5pm on Sunday, March to October (closed Sunday the rest of the year). The main post office is in the middle of West St, next to the Westcourt Hotel. Most of the main banks are also on West St.

There's terrible traffic congestion in the city centre and disc parking is in operation throughout the town. Discs can be bought in newsagents and other shops; they cost 30p for an hour's parking.

The Wise Owl bookshop (☎ 984 2847), on The Mall, has a good range of books.

St Peter's Roman Catholic Church

West St's most impressive building is St Peter's Roman Catholic Church, which is actually two churches in one: the first, designed by Francis Johnston in the classical style and built in 1791, and the newer addition, built in the Gothic style visible today. In a glittering brass-and-glass case in the north transept you can see the head of St Oliver Plunkett (1629–81), executed by the perfidious English and now surrounded by flowers, candles and the attentions of the devout.

A Moving Head

In the northern transept of Drogheda's St Peter's Roman Catholic Church, a relic lurks inside a soaring reliquary of solid brass and unbreakable glass. Closer inspection reveals the leathery head of St Oliver Plunkett, who was hanged by the English in 1681 for his supposed part in the 'Popish Plot'.

Plunkett was born at Loughcrew, near Oldcastle, in 1629, a descendant of Brian Ború, who had defeated the Danes at Clontarf in 1014. In 1645 he was sent to Rome to complete his education and stayed in Italy for 25 years. Ordained in 1654, he became archbishop of Armagh and primate of all Ireland in 1670. In the first three years of his mission he confirmed 48,655 people, ordained many priests and set up what may have been the first integrated Roman Catholic and Protestant school in Drogheda.

But Plunkett lived during a time when the English were particularly paranoid about the supposed threat from Roman Catholicism, and in 1679 he was seized and imprisoned in Dublin, accused of involvement in the 'Popish Plot'. This was an entirely fabricated conspiracy dreamed up by Titus Oates, a ne'er-do-well with a long history of dubious dealings, who claimed in 1678 that he had uncovered a plot to kill Charles II and turn the country over to the Jesuits. Despite Oates' past, he was believed and about 35 men were put to death for supposed involvement. Plunkett was accused of planning the invasion of Ireland by foreign powers and in 1680 he was moved to London's Newgate Prison. Tried and convicted of treason, he was hanged at Tyburn on 1 July 1681. The very next day the plot was revealed as a sham. Oates himself was flogged, pilloried and imprisoned for perjury, only to be pardoned and granted a pension after the revolution of 1688.

At the time of Plunkett's execution, the custom was to quarter the body and then burn the parts. Plunkett's friends obtained permission to remove the body, but only just managed to snatch the head from the fire: scorch marks are still visible on the left cheek and the nose. The head and forearms were placed in tin boxes, and the rest of the body buried in St Giles Cemetery. Later it was exhumed and sent first to a Benedictine monastery in Germany, then to Downside in England. The head, meanwhile, was taken to Rome, then to Drogheda, where the Sisters of Sienna looked after it for the next 200 years.

In 1920 Plunkett was beatified and the head was given to the new parish church of St Peter's, the Oliver Plunkett Memorial Church'. Following a miraculous cure in a Naples hospital which was attributed to Plunkett's intervention, the pope canonised him in October 1975.

In 1990 the priest of St Peter's decided to have the head examined since it was showing signs of decay. At the same time a living descendant of the saint provided a blood sample so that Turin Shroud-style DNA tests could be carried out to verify its authenticity. The tests proved satisfactory and the saint's head was replaced in its reliquary inside an inner capsule containing silica gel, which would make it easier to maintain the correct humidity level. The reliquary was then enclosed in a pedestal shrine over 1m high and with a soaring 9m stone spire. Beside it is displayed the original certificate of authenticity, dated 1682.

St Laurence's Gate

Astride Laurence St, the eastwards extension of the town's main street, is St Laurence's Gate, the finest surviving portion of the city walls and one of only two surviving gates from the original 11.

The 13th-century gate was named after St Laurence's Priory, which once stood outside the gate; no traces of it now remain. The gate consists of two lofty towers, a connecting curtain wall and the entrance to the portcullis. This imposing pile of stone is not in fact a gate but a barbican, a fortified structure used to defend the gate, which was farther behind it. When the walls were completed in the 13th century, they ran for 3km round the town, enclosing 52 hectares.

Millmount Museum & Tower

Across the river from the town, in a village-like enclave amid a sea of dull suburbia, is Millmount, an artificial hill overlooking the

The Great Protector Turns Destructor

Oliver Cromwell (1599–1658) is lauded as being one of the first democrats of England, but in Ireland he is largely reviled for his barbarous treatment of the Irish when he invaded in 1649.

Cromwell didn't much like the Irish. He saw them as treacherous infidels, a dirty race of Roman Catholics who had sided with King Charles I during the Civil War and thus had to be treated with contempt. When 'God's own Englishman' landed his 17,000 troops at Dublin in August 1649, he immediately set out for Drogheda, a strategic fort town and bastion of royalist support. It was his first engagement in Ireland, and he was determined to 'make an example' of the town so as to discourage further resistance.

When Cromwell arrived at the walls of Drogheda, he was met with the resistance of 2500 men. After a week of planning, he called on the town to surrender, which duly refused to do so. Cromwell let fly with artillery, mostly heavy cannon, and after two days the walls were breached.

A pretty straightforward military engagement, it might seem. Had Cromwell simply held the town and put a military governor in command, the taking of Drogheda would have joined an already long list of failed attempts to resist English rule. Instead, Cromwell ordered that everyone who had resisted his troops should be rounded up and executed. Over a period of a few hours, an estimated 3000 were massacred, including priests, women and children. The governor of the town, Sir Arthur Ashton, was beaten to death with his own wooden leg. In one particularly gruesome episode, about 100 terrified locals hid in the tower of St Peter's Church of Ireland; Cromwell's soldiers simply burnt it down, killing everyone inside.

Of the survivors, many were captured and sold into slavery in the Caribbean; the genetic presence of red hair on some Barbadians is commonly attributed to the sexual intermingling of African and Irish slaves.

As for Cromwell's men, they too suffered casualties: according to historians, only 64 men were killed in the sack of Drogheda. To this day, Cromwell's name provokes loathing and hatred in Ireland, nowhere more so than in Drogheda. Hardly surprising really.

---

town. Although it may have been a prehistoric burial mound along the lines of nearby Newgrange, it has never been excavated. There is a tale that it was the burial place of Amergin, a warrior-poet who arrived in Ireland from Spain around 1500 BC. Throughout Irish history, poets have held a special place in society and have been both venerated and feared.

The Normans constructed a motte-and-bailey fort on top of this convenient command post overlooking the bridge. It was followed by a castle, which in turn was replaced by a Martello tower in 1808.

It was at Millmount that the defenders of Drogheda, led by the governor, Sir Arthur Ashton, made their last stand before surrendering to Cromwell (see the boxed text 'The Great Protector Turns Destructor'). Later, an 18th-century English barracks was built round the base, and today this has been converted to house craft-shops, museums and a restaurant, though the courtyard retains the flavour of its former life.

The tower played a dramatic role in the 1922 Civil War, and the Millmount Museum & Tower (☎ 983 3097, Millmount; adult/student €4.50/2.50 for museum & tower; €3.20/2.50 for museum, €2.50/1.90 for tower; open 10am-6pm Mon-Sat & 2.30pm-5pm Sun year round), has a colourful (and somewhat romanticised) painting of its bombardment. The top of the tower offers a fine view over the centre of Drogheda, on the opposite side of the river.

A section of the army barracks is now the Millmount Museum, with interesting displays about the town and its history. Displays include three wonderful late-18th-century guild banners, perhaps the last in the country. There is also a room devoted to Cromwell's siege of Drogheda and the Battle of the

Boyne. The pretty, cobbled basement is full of gadgets and kitchen utensils from bygone times, including a cast-iron pressure cooker and an early model of a sofa bed. There's an excellent example of a coracle. Across the courtyard, the **Governor's House** opens for temporary exhibitions.

You can drive up to the hilltop or climb Pitcher Hill via the steps from St Mary's Bridge.

The 13th-century **Butter Gate**, just northwest of Millmount, is the only genuine town gate to survive. This tower, with its arched passageway, predates the remains of St Laurence's Gate by about a century.

Drogheda Heritage Centre

Just south-east of the Millmount Museum is St Mary's Church of Ireland and churchyard, now home to the Drogheda Heritage Centre (☎ 983 1153, 🖻 reillytom@eircom.net, Mary St; adult/concession €3.20/2.50; open 10am-5pm Mon-Fri, noon-5pm Sat & 2pm-5pm Sun year round), where you can see a pretty bland exhibit on the town's history. It is in this spot that Cromwell was supposed to have breached the city walls, and when the centre first opened there was a minor scandal because Cromwell's death mask was included as part of the display. The audiovisual display that accompanies the exhibit is surprisingly low-key when it comes to discussing the massacre; it is perhaps indicative of the premium that local authorities place on the presence of British tourists that it is so.

Other Buildings

On the corner of West and Shop Sts is **Tholsel**, an 18th-century limestone town hall, now occupied by the Bank of Ireland. Off Hardmans Gardens is the rather charming and more recent **Church of Our Lady of Lourdes**.

North of the centre on William St is **St Peter's Church of Ireland**. This contains the tombstone of Oliver Goldsmith's uncle Isaac, as well as another on the wall depicting two skeletal figures in shrouds, dubiously linked to the Black Death. This is the church whose spire was burned by Cromwell's men, resulting in the death of 100 people seeking sanc-

tuary inside. Today's church (1748) is the second replacement of the original destroyed by Cromwell. It stands in an attractive close approached through lovely wrought-iron gates. Note the old 'Blue School' of 1844 on one side.

On Fair St the modest 19th-century **Courthouse** is being renovated and is home to the sword and mace presented to the town council by William of Orange after the Battle of the Boyne.

Topping the hill behind the main part of town is the **Magdalene Tower**, dating from the 14th century, the belltower of a Dominican friary founded in 1224. Here, England's King Richard II, accompanied by a great army, accepted the submission of the Gaelic chiefs with suitable ceremony in 1395; but peace lasted only a few months and his return to Ireland led to his overthrow in 1399. The earl of Desmond was beheaded here in 1468 because of his treasonous connections with the Gaelic Irish. The tower is reputed to be haunted by a nun.

Organised Tours

The Drogheda Historical Society occasionally runs summer tours of the town; phone the Millmount Museum (☎ 983 3097) to check if anything is scheduled. Harpur House (☎ 983 2736) helps organise tours of Drogheda and the Boyne Valley. The tourist office runs walking tours of historical Drogheda. It also has a leaflet entitled *The Oriel Trail*, which outlines a 150km tour through the county beginning in town.

Places to Stay

Hostels South of the river is *The Green Door* (☎/fax 983 4422, 🖻 greendoorhostel@ hotmail.com, 47 John St) Dorms/doubles/triples €12.70/20.35/16.50 per person. This relatively new hostel, only 150m north of the bus station, has pleasant dorms and family rooms with handcrafted wooden bunks.

B&Bs It's advisable to book ahead between May and October.

Orley House (☎/fax 983 6019, 🖻 orley house@eircom.net, Bryanstown, off Dublin Rd) Singles/doubles €32/71. Orley House is south of the river and 100m off the main Dublin road in the Bryanstown housing estate. Its four bedrooms are all en suite.

St Gobnait's (☎ *983 7844, Dublin Rd*) Singles/doubles with bathroom €32/61. This place is on the main Dublin road near the train station. It's a modern house with three comfortable rooms, all en suite.

Harbour Villa (☎ *983 7441, Mornington Rd*) Singles/doubles with bathroom €28/56. This place is 2km along the river towards the sea on the Mornington road. It overlooks the estuary and has small but pleasant rooms.

Boyne Haven (☎/*fax 983 6700, Dublin Rd*) Singles/doubles with shared bathroom €45/76, with bathroom €51/83. The three rooms all have showers. Further up in scale, this excellent establishment is on the Dublin road.

Hotels Right in the town centre is *Westcourt Hotel* (☎ *983 0965, fax 983 0970, West St*) Singles/doubles €57/114.50. It's worth asking about the special weekend bargain break rate at this more upmarket hotel. Both Mary Robinson and Jack Charlton have visited here.

Boyne Valley Hotel & Country Club (☎ *983 7737, fax 983 9188, Stameen, Dublin Rd*) From €69 per person. This is a 19th-century mansion set way back from the main Dublin road. It has a swimming pool and its own pitch and putt course (an Irish version of par-3 golf).

Places to Eat

Frankly, while Drogheda has plenty of places where you can get a bite, none are particularly memorable. It seems that in Drogheda the onus is simply on eating, rather than eating well.

Restaurants Just opposite St Peter's is *The Gateway* (☎ *983 2755, 15 West St*) From €5. This place has a lunch-of-the-day special (€6.35), which is usually of the chicken-and-chips variety.

Buttergate Restaurant (☎ *983 4759, 9 Barrack St*) Mains €19-26. Open dinner Tues-Sun, lunch Sun. This rather cosy place

is upstairs beside Millmount Museum & Tower, and serves excellent food, with meals before 7pm costing €10.

Himalayas Brasserie (☎ *983 1423, 35 James St*) Mains from €7. This is a pretty good Indian restaurant in the middle of town.

Cafes & Pubs Just north of the river is *Monks* (☎ *984 5630, cnr Shop St & North Quay*) Sandwiches from €4. Open 9am-8pm Mon-Sat. At the southern end of Shop St, on the corner of North Quay, this is a lovely espresso bar and cafe. The coffees are good, and, strangely for Ireland, it is mostly smoke free.

Keyside Café (☎ *984 4878, The Mall*) From €4. This is another good cafe, with an emphasis on modern Irish cuisine.

Jalapeno's (☎ *983 8342, Unit 1, West St*) From €3.80. This pleasant cafe on West St serves really good sandwiches and brews an excellent cup of coffee.

Moorland Café (☎ *983 3951, 96 West St*) From €4. Moorland serves good coffee, snacks and light meals.

La Pizzeria (☎ *983 4208, 15 St Peter's St*) Pizzas under €9.70. Open 6pm-11pm. This busy, Italian-owned joint features pizzas and pasta dishes.

Swan House (☎ *983 7506, Unit 3, West St*) Mains from €6. Open from 5.30pm only. This popular Chinese restaurant also offers takeaways; chicken dishes cost around €8.90.

Black Bull Inn (☎ *983 7139, Dublin Rd*) Mains €8.90-15. About 1km along the Dublin road this pub was once winner of the regional Pub of the Year title and it still gets the local vote. Chinese-style duck costs €12. It has music at the weekend.

Entertainment

Weavers (☎ *983 2816, 82-83 West St*) Weavers always has a youngish crowd and has live music on Wednesday night and DJs at the weekend. It serves some tasty pub food (from €5).

Bridie Macs (☎ *983 0965, West St*) Attached to the Westcourt Hotel, this place also offers a wide range of musical possibilities on Thursday, Friday and Saturday.

C Ní Cairbre (Carberry's; ☎ 984 7569, North Strand) This traditional and old pub is the town's best and most popular watering hole, though you might need infrared glasses because it is so dark inside! There are Irish music sessions on Tuesday night and Sunday afternoon. In theory it opens from 7.30pm; in reality, opening hours vary depending on how the night is going. It gets busy on weekend nights and Sunday afternoon.

Peter Matthew's (McPhail's; ☎ 984 3168, Laurence St) This is Drogheda's alternative to the older bars, attracting a younger crowd who prefer indie and dance music to the more traditional kind.

Earth (☎ 984 5561, Stockwell St) Admission €7. This popular nightclub is located downstairs in the Westcourt Hotel.

No 4 (☎ 984 5044, Stockwell St) Admission €7. Directly opposite Earth, this is a pub that turns into a nightclub after 11pm (free if you're there before 11pm, €7 if you arrive after); it is a favourite of Drogheda's trendy young crowd.

Fusion (☎ 983 5166, 12 George's St) Admission €7. This is the town's other crowd puller, with a fairly animated disco from Thursday to Sunday nights with a mix of 60s, rock, funk and dance music.

Abbey Centre Cinema (☎ 983 0188, Abbey Shopping Centre, off West St) This two-screen cinema is at the back of the shopping centre.

Drogheda Arts Centre (☎ 983 3946, Stockwell Lane) Theatrical and musical events are staged in the municipal building.

Shopping

The Millmount complex (Millmount) This complex has a number of craft studios where you can buy all sorts of *objets d'art*. There's a *jewellery studio (☎ 984 1960)*, a *ceramic potter (☎ 984 6065)*, a *decorative glassworks (☎ 984 5018)* and a studio where you can buy *hand-painted silks (☎ 984 1245)*. Call to arrange a viewing of the work; some of it is of extremely high quality.

Getting There & Away

Bus Drogheda is only 48km north of Dublin, on the main N1 route to Belfast. The Bus Éireann station (☎ 983 5023) is on the corner of John St and Donore Rd just south of the river. This is one of the busiest bus routes in the country, and buses serve Drogheda from Dublin daily every half hour between 7.30am and 4pm, every 15 minutes between 4pm and 7pm; and every half hour thereafter until 11pm. From Dublin it takes roughly 1¼ hours and the fare is €6.35/9.55. Drogheda to Dundalk is another popular route, with hourly buses from 6.45am to 11.45pm daily (€6.35/9.55, 40 minutes).

There is also a daily Dundalk to Galway bus, departing Drogheda at 11.10am Monday to Thursday and Saturday (4.30pm Friday and Sunday). It takes about 4¾ hours to get to Galway (€15.90/24.20), and stops at Athlone along the way, from where you can make connections for Limerick, Sligo and Donegal.

Cheaper is Capital Coaches (☎ 042-934 0025), which has a daily Dundalk to Dublin service through Drogheda; its one-way fare from Drogheda to Dublin is €5.10.

Train Drogheda train station (☎ 983 8749) is just south of the river and east of the town centre, off the Dublin road. Drogheda is on the main Belfast to Dublin line and there are five or six express trains (and many more slower ones) daily each way, with five on Sunday. This is the best line in Ireland, with excellent on-board service. The one-way, off-peak fare from Drogheda to Dublin is €10.20.

The train crosses the river just downstream from Drogheda on Sir John McNeill's mid-19th-century Boyne Viaduct, a fine piece of engineering that dominates the seaward view.

Getting Around

Drogheda itself is infinitely walkable, and many of the surrounding region's interesting sites are within easy cycling distance. PJ Carolan (☎ 983 8242), 77 Trinity St, is part of the Raleigh Rent-a-Bike scheme and offers good bikes costing €12.70 per day. Bridge Cycles (☎ 983 3742), on North Quay near the bridge, rents bikes costing €11.50 per day.

There's a small taxi rank (☎ 985 1839) on Duke St, just off West St. There's a larger one on Laurence St near St Laurence's Gate.

AROUND DROGHEDA

Drogheda makes an excellent base for exploring the Boyne Valley sites to the west – see Brú Na Bóinne in the County Meath section earlier in this chapter for more details. In Louth itself, Mellifont and Monasterboice are two famous and picturesque monastic sites a few kilometres north of Drogheda. Travelling to or from Northern Ireland there's a coastal route, the faster and duller N1 main road route, and a more circuitous inland route via Collon and Ardee, which can include Mellifont and Monasterboice.

Beaulieu House

Five kilometres east of Drogheda on the Baltray road is Beaulieu House, built between 1660 and 1666. The land, which had belonged to the Plunkett family since Anglo-Norman times, was confiscated under Cromwell. This lovely red-brick mansion, with distinctive steep roof and tall chimneys, is thought to have been designed by Sir Christopher Wren (architect of St Paul's Cathedral in London).

In 800 years the estate has been in the possession of only two families, first the Plunketts and then the ancestors of Lord Tichbourne. There's an impressive art collection, but it's a private residence, not open to the public.

Mellifont Abbey

Mellifont Abbey (☎ 041-982 6459, W www .heritageireland.ie, off the R168, Tullyallen; adults/student €1.90/0.75; open 9.30am-6.30pm daily mid-June-mid-Sept; 10am-5pm daily May-mid-June & mid-Sept-Oct), 8km north-west of Drogheda beside the River Mattock, was Ireland's first Cistercian monastery. The name comes from the Latin mellifons (honey fountain). In its prime, Mellifont was the Cistercians' most magnificent and important centre in the country but, while the remains are well worth seeing, they don't really match the site's former significance.

In 1142 St Malachy, bishop of Down,

brought in a new troop of monks from Clairvaux in France to combat the corruption and lax behaviour of the Irish monastic orders. These strait-laced new monks were deliberately established at this remote location, far from any distracting influences. The French and Irish monks failed to get on, and the visitors soon returned to the Continent. However, within 10 years nine more Cistercian monasteries were established and Mellifont was eventually the mother house for 21 lesser monasteries. At one point, as many as 400 monks lived here.

Mellifont not only brought fresh ideas to the Irish religious scene, it also heralded a new style of architecture. For the first time in Ireland, monasteries were built with the formal layout and structure that was being used on the continent. Only fragments of the original settlement remain, but the plan of the extensive monastery can easily be traced. Like many other Cistercian monasteries, the buildings clustered round an open cloister, or courtyard.

To the northern side of the cloister are the remains of a principally 13th-century cross-shaped church. To the south, the chapter house, probably used as a meeting hall by the monks, has been partially floored with medieval glazed tiles, originally found in the church. Here also would have been the refectory, or dining area, the kitchen and the warming room – the only place where the austere monks could enjoy the warmth of a fire. The eastern range would once have held the monks' sleeping quarters.

Mellifont's most recognisable building, and one of the finest pieces of Cistercian architecture in Ireland, is the lavabo, an octagonal washing house for the monks. It was built in the 13th century and used lead pipes to bring water from the river. A number of other buildings would have surrounded this main part of the abbey.

After the dissolution of the monasteries, a fortified Tudor manor house was built on the site in 1556 by Edward Moore, using materials scavenged from the demolition of many of the buildings. In 1603, this house was the scene of a poignant and crucial turning point in Irish history. After the disastrous Battle of

Kinsale, the vanquished Hugh O'Neill, last of the great Irish chieftains, was given shelter here by Sir Garret Moore until he surrendered to the English Lord Deputy Mountjoy. After his surrender, O'Neill was pardoned but, despairing of his position, fled to the continent in 1607 with other old-Irish leaders in the Flight of the Earls. In 1727 the site was abandoned altogether.

The visitor centre next to the site describes monastic life in detail. A back road connects Mellifont with Monasterboice. There is no public transportation to the abbey.

Monasterboice

Just off the N1 road to Belfast, about 10km north of Drogheda, is Monasterboice *(Mainistir Bhuithe; off N1; free; open sunrise-sunset daily)* an intriguing monastic site containing a cemetery, two ancient church ruins, one of the finest and tallest round towers in Ireland and two of the best high crosses. The site can be reached directly from Mellifont via a winding route along narrow country lanes.

Down a leafy country lane and set in sweeping farmland, Monasterboice has a special atmosphere, particularly at quiet times. The original monastic settlement at Monasterboice is said to have been founded by St Buithe, a follower of St Patrick, in the 4th or 5th century, although the site probably had pre-Christian significance. St Buithe's name somehow got converted to Boyne, and the river is named after him. It's said that he made a direct ascent to heaven via a ladder lowered from above. An invading Viking force took over the settlement in 968, only to be comprehensively expelled by Donal, the Irish high king of Tara, who killed at least 300 of the Vikings in the process.

There's a small gift shop outside the compound. There are no set hours but come early or late in the day to avoid the crowds.

High Crosses The high crosses of Monasterboice are superb examples of Celtic art. The crosses had an important didactic use, bringing the gospels alive for the uneducated – cartoons of the Scriptures, if you like. Like Greek statues, they were probably

brightly painted, but all traces of colour have long disappeared.

Muiredach's Cross, the one nearest to the entrance, dates from the early 10th century. The inscription at the foot reads 'Or do Muiredach Lasndernad i Chros' (A prayer for Muiredach for whom the cross was made). Muiredach was abbot here until 922.

The subjects of the carvings have not been positively identified. On the eastern face, from the bottom up, are thought to be: on the first panel, the Fall of Adam and Eve and the murder of Abel; on the second, David and Goliath; on the third, Moses bringing forth water from the rock to the waiting Israelites; and on the fourth, the three wise men bearing gifts to Mary and Jesus. The Last Judgement is at the centre of the cross with the risen dead waiting for their verdict, and farther up is St Paul in the desert.

The western face relates more to the New Testament, and from the bottom depicts the arrest of Christ, Doubting Thomas, Christ giving a key to St Peter, the crucifixion in the centre, and Moses praying with Aaron and Hur. The cross is capped by a representation of a gabled-roof church.

The West Cross is near the round tower and stands 6.5m high, making it one of the tallest high crosses in Ireland. It's much more weathered, especially at the base, and only a dozen or so of its 50 panels are still legible.

The more distinguishable ones on the eastern face include David killing a lion and bear, the sacrifice of Isaac, David with Goliath's head, and David kneeling before Samuel. The western face shows the resurrection, the crowning with thorns, the crucifixion, the baptism of Christ, Peter cutting off the servant's ear in the garden of Gethsemane, and the kiss of Judas.

A third, simpler cross in the north-eastern corner of the compound is believed to have been smashed by Cromwell's forces and has only a few, straightforward carvings. Photographers should note that this cross makes a great evening silhouette picture, with the round tower in the background.

The **round tower**, minus its cap, stands in a corner of the complex. It's still over 30m tall but is closed to the public. In 1097, records suggest, the tower interior went up in flames, destroying many valuable manuscripts and other treasures. The church ruins are later and of less interest.

ARDEE
☎ 041 • pop 3440

How many towns can claim to have two castles in their main street? The sleepy market town of Ardee (Baile Átha Fhirdhia) on the narrow River Dee is 10km north of Collon on the N2. Its long, tidy main street – divided into Bridge, Market and Irish Sts – is dominated by Ardee Castle to the south and Hatch's Castle to the north.

History

For a small town, Ardee has a colourful history. It takes its name from Áth Fhír Diadh (Fear Diadh's Ford), inspired by the well known tale of the combat between Cúchulainn and his half-brother Fear Diadh, or Ferdia, as recorded by the ancient tale of the Táin Bó Cúailnge. After an almighty duel, Cúchulainn fatally wounded his beloved Ferdia with the *gae bolga*, a weapon given to him by the demi-god Lug. Cúchulainn's grief was such that he never fully recovered. It is one of the most tragic and beautiful stories of the Cooley cycle.

In the 12th century, the area was turned into a barony and the town remained in English hands until being taken by the O'Neills in the 17th century. James II had his headquarters here for two months in 1689, prior to the Battle of the Boyne.

Things to See & Do

A square tower dating from the 13th century, **Ardee Castle** *(☎ 685 3805; adult/child €1.30/ 0.60, open 9am-5pm Mon-Sat June-Oct)* was an important outpost on the edge of the English Pale. It later became a courthouse and now houses a museum on the town's history, as well as a coffee shop and craft units. The smaller **Hatch's Castle** also dates from this time and it remained, from Cromwellian times until 1940, in the hands of the Hatch family. It's still a private residence.

The riverbank can be explored around the ford, where there's a well-tended **riverside** walk that has an impressive new bronze sculpture of Cúchulainn and Ferdia.

Places to Stay & Eat

Railway Bar *(☎ 685 3279, e railway _bar57.ardee@oceanfree.net, Market St)* Rooms €23 per person, including breakfast. There are five basic rooms above this pub in the middle of town.

Carraig Mor *(☎/fax 685 3513, e info@ carraigmor.com, Blakestown)* Singles/doubles €32/49. This is a pretty fancy place is 2km south of Ardee on the main Dublin to Donegal road. The five rooms, four en suite, are very well decorated.

Gable's Restaurant *(☎/fax 685 3789, Dundalk Rd)* Singles/doubles €32/51. There are comfortable, neat rooms above this restaurant, which is well considered in the area. There's an excellent set dinner for €28.

Red House *(☎/fax 685 3523, e red house@eircom.net)* Singles/doubles €48/ 60.50, including breakfast. For a real treat, try this elegant Georgian residence, which stands in its own demesne. Take the Dundalk road past Gable's Restaurant and it's about 500m along on the left. Dinner costs another €32.

Smarmore Castle *(☎ 685 7167, fax 685 7650)* Rooms from €127. Four kilometres south of Ardee this is a 14th-century castle recently converted into a hotel.

AROUND ARDEE
The Jumping Church of Kildemock

Three kilometres south-east of town are the remains of the area's oddly named landmark, the Jumping Church of Kildemock. On a thunderous night in February 1715, a storm caused a wall of St Catherine's Church to shift inwards from its foundations. However, rather than settle for this straightforward explanation, locals decided the church had miraculously jumped to exclude the remains of an excommunicated member of the flock who had been buried within its walls. Thus was born the Jumping Church.

Louth

North of Tallanstown (but the turn-off is just

south of town), the county's namesake is an insignificant little place with some mildly interesting remains. **St Mochta's** is a small 11th- or 12th-century church with an enclosure and stone roof. St Mochta, a British follower of St Patrick, founded a monastery here in the early 6th century. Nearby is the church of a 15th-century Dominican friary, sometimes called Louth Abbey.

Ardpatrick

To the east of Louth village are Ardpatrick and Ardpatrick House, home of Oliver Plunkett. There's a mound here where he is supposed to have illegally ordained priests. It was also a good vantage point to spot any advancing English soldiers.

THE COAST ROAD

While the most visually rewarding route between Drogheda and Dundalk is the minor inland road via Mellifont and Collon, the coastal route is also scenic. The latter heads off north under the railway viaduct, passes Baltray with its championship golf course, and continues on quiet country roads to Termonfeckin.

Termonfeckin

A 6th-century monastery was founded in Termonfeckin (Tearmann Féichín) by St Féichín of Cong, County Mayo. All that remains are some gravestones and a 10th-century **high cross**, on the left as you enter the churchyard.

There's also a 15th-century **castle** *(open 10am-6pm)*, or tower house, in a good state of preservation; it has two small corbel-vaulted alcoves and an anticlockwise spiral staircase (most go clockwise). From the village, follow the road to Seapoint Golf Club, take the first left, then the first right. You need to get the key from across the road.

Clogherhead

A couple of kilometres farther north is the busy seaside and fishing centre of Clogherhead (Ceann Chlochair), with a good, shallow Blue Flag beach. Around the town there are enjoyable walks along the coast (partially marred by vistas of caravan parks) or out to **Port Oriel**, an attractive little harbour

with views of the Cooley Peninsula and the Mourne Mountains farther north. During the summer, Port Oriel is home to a fleet of trawlers and smaller fishing boats.

On the southern side of the headland is **Red Man's Cave**. At low tide a reddish fungus becomes visible, covering the cave walls. According to folklore, a group of people fleeing from Cromwell hid in the cave. A barking dog then revealed the hide-out and the people were slaughtered, their blood splashing on the walls, where it remains to this day. The cave is hard to find, so it's sensible to ask a local for directions, but even if you don't find it the walk is satisfying enough.

Annagassan

A minor road (R166), providing picture-book views, continues 12km north to Annagassan (Áth na gCasan), a town on the northern side of Dunany Point, at the junction of the Dee and Glyde Rivers. It's claimed locally that Annagassan is the site of the Vikings' first settlement in Ireland. Records suggest they sacked a monastery here in 842 and may have been responsible for the promontory fort, which is now a low mound overlooking the village.

Castlebellingham

North of Annagassan, the coast road joins the busy main N1 at Castlebellingham, only 12km south of Dundalk. The village grew up around its 18th-century mansion, which is something of a disappointment after the imposing castellated entrance. The mansion is on the site of an earlier castle burned down by James II's troops; the owner, Thomas Bellingham, worked as a guide to William of Orange during his visit to Ireland between 1689 and 1690. The building is now a major hotel: ***Bellingham Castle*** *(☎ 042-937 2176, fax 937 2766,* ⓔ *bellinghamcastle@eir com.net, Castlebellingham)* Singles/doubles €63.50/102 with breakfast.

Buried in the local graveyard is Dr Thomas Guither, a 17th-century physician supposed to have reintroduced frogs to Ireland by releasing imported frog spawn into a pond in Trinity College, Dublin. Frogs, along with snakes and toads, had supposedly

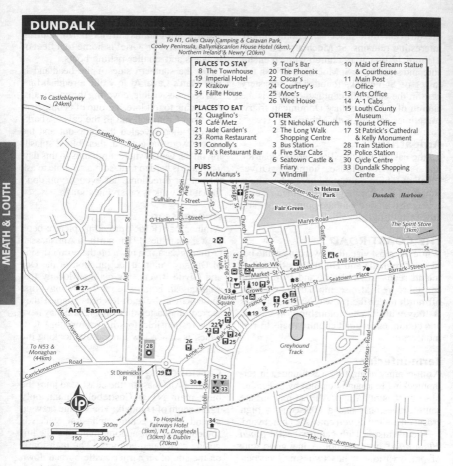

DUNDALK

PLACES TO STAY
8 The Townhouse
19 Imperial Hotel
27 Krakow
34 Fáilte House

PLACES TO EAT
12 Quaglino's
18 Café Metz
21 Jade Garden's
23 Roma Restaurant
31 Connolly's
32 Pa's Restaurant Bar

PUBS
5 McManus's

9 Toal's Bar
20 The Phoenix
22 Oscar's
24 Courtney's
25 Moe's
26 Wee House

OTHER
1 St Nicholas' Church
2 The Long Walk Shopping Centre
3 Bus Station
4 Five Star Cabs
6 Seatown Castle & Friary
7 Windmill

10 Maid of Éireann Statue & Courthouse
11 Main Post Office
13 Arts Office
14 A-1 Cabs
15 Louth County Museum
16 Tourist Office
17 St Patrick's Cathedral & Kelly Monument
28 Train Station
29 Police Station
30 Cycle Centre
33 Dundalk Shopping Centre

received their marching orders from St Patrick 1000 years earlier.

DUNDALK
☎ 042 • pop 25,762
Halfway between Dublin and Belfast, Louth's charmless county town of Dundalk takes its name from Dún Dealgan, a prehistoric fort which was reputedly the home of the hero Cúchulainn (see boxed text 'The Táin Bó Cúailnge' later in this chapter).

The town grew under the protection of a local estate controlled by the de Verdon family, who were granted lands here by King John in 1185. In the Middle Ages, Dundalk was at the northern limits of the English-controlled Pale, strategically located on one of the main highways heading north.

Dundalk is only 13km from the border and widely regarded as a republican stronghold. Indeed, a residential area of the town has been nicknamed 'Little Belfast' for the numbers of Northerners who have settled here, including, most recently, members of the so-called 'Real IRA', a splinter republican group that is opposed to the peace treaty. This group admitted responsibility for the 1998 Omagh bomb, which killed 29 people.

Orientation & Information

Northbound traffic sweeps round to the east of the town centre. The main commercial streets are Clanbrassil and Park Sts. The tourist office (☎ 933 5484) is on Jocelyn St next to Louth County Museum (see later). It opens 9.30am to 1pm and 2pm to 5.30pm (to 6pm in July and August) on weekdays (plus at the weekend in July and August), year round. At other times there are boards and maps with tourist information dotted around town. The Arts Office (☎ 933 2276) in Market Square has details of what's on in the town's entertainment venues, including theatre, cinema and music. It opens 9am to 12.45pm and 2pm to 4.30pm Monday to Friday. The main post office is on Clanbrassil St.

Things to See

The **Courthouse** on the corner of Crowe and Clanbrassil Sts is a fine neo-Gothic building with large Doric pillars which was designed by Richard Morrison, who also designed the courthouse in Carlow. In the front square is the stone **Maid of Éireann**, commemorating the Fenian Rising of 1798.

At the northern end of Church St, **St Nicholas' Church**, or the Green Church, is the burial site of Agnes Burns, elder sister of Robert, the Scottish poet. She married the local rector, and the monument was erected by the townspeople to honour them both. The 15th-century tower to the right of the church entrance is the oldest structure on the site.

The richly decorated **St Patrick's Cathedral** was modelled on King's College Chapel in Cambridge, England. In front of it on Jocelyn St is the **Kelly Monument**, in memory of a local captain drowned at sea in 1858. Also here is the interesting **Louth County Museum** (☎ 932 7056, Jocelyn St; adult/concession €3.80/2.60; open 10.30am-5.30pm Mon-Sat, 2pm-6pm Sun; closed Mon Oct-Apr) with displays depicting the growth of industry in Louth since 1750. Two new floors opened in 1999 and are home to an exhibition on the area's Stone Age past.

At the eastern end of Jocelyn St is the Seatown area of Dundalk with its **castle** (really a friary tower) and a derelict, sail-less **windmill**, the tallest in Ireland. If you arrive

in Dundalk by train you pass the 1820 **garda station** (police station) on St Dominick's Place on the way into town. Its first prisoner is believed to have been its architect, who misappropriated funds and was arrested for nonpayment of bills.

Places to Stay

Fáilte House (☎/fax 933 5152, cnr Hill St & The Long Ave) Singles/doubles from €25.50/49. This excellent B&B is to the south of town.

The Townhouse (☎/fax 932 9898, e the townhouse@eircom.net, 5 Roden Place) Singles/doubles €38/57. From the outside, this place looks like a top-notch guesthouse, but there have been complaints about its cleanliness. It is across the street from St Patrick's Cathedral.

Fairways Hotel (☎ 932 1500, fax 932 1511, e info@fairways.ie, Dublin Rd) Singles/doubles €76/114. This hotel, about 3km out of town on the Dublin road, is modern and plush.

Ballymascanlon House Hotel (☎ 937 1124, fax 937 1598, Carlingford Rd) Singles/doubles €90/142.50 including breakfast. This is a manor-house hotel with a swimming pool, squash courts, a superb 18-hole golf course and other sporting facilities. It's 6km north of Dundalk on the way to Carlingford (see Proleek Dolmen & Gallery Grave in the Around Dundalk section for further details).

Places to Eat

Dundalk has plenty of cheap eateries. *Connolly's* (Long Walk Shopping Centre) From €3. This is a small cafe and delicatessen serving mostly sandwiches and cakes, situated on the ground floor of the shopping centre.

Pa's Restaurant Bar (☎ 933 6602, Dundalk Shopping Centre, The Long Walk) Mains from €5.50. Upstairs in the centre, Pa's is a large restaurant and bar where you can get sandwiches and light meals all day, including some vegetarian ones.

Café Metz (☎ 933 9106, Williamson's Mall) Mains €10-13. This new joint is very trendy, with orange walls, wooden floors and Venetian blinds. The food is excellent, and the menu features such diverse things as roast barbary duck, salmon in filo pastry and a fabulous chowder.

Roma Restaurant (☎ *933 4175, 7 Park St*) From €3. This busy place serves really good curries, burgers, pizzas and sandwiches. Try the pink milkshake: it's so thick it'll push your heart to the limit!

Quaglino's (☎ *933 8567, 88 Clanbrassil St*) Mains from €11; set dinner €32. More upmarket places in town include this Italian restaurant near the post office where a five-course dinner costs €32.

Jade Gardens (☎ *933 0378, 24 Park St*) Mains €11.50-19. This is an excellent Chinese restaurant and the decor is unusually subdued, with low lighting, a black marble floor and an aquarium.

Entertainment

Several good pubs are found around Park St.

Toal's Bar (☎ *933 2759, 7 Crowe St*) This is one of the nicer pubs in town, with plenty of character…and characters.

The Phoenix (☎ *935 2925, 15 Park St*) This bar has an old frontage but has been renovated inside; it is a friendly, locals' kind of place with a terrific atmosphere.

Moe's (☎ *932 9699, 42 Park St*) Dundalk's younger crowd flocks to this long, American-style bar, where the jukebox is always on, and always loud.

Courtney's (☎ *932 6652, 44 Park St*) Across the street, this is a newer bar, but you'd never know it from the old-world atmosphere. It is popular with a younger crowd.

Wee House (☎ *933 5359, Anne St*) This is a very nice bar, with plenty of local atmosphere.

McManus's (☎ *933 1632, 17 Seatown*) This is very much a locals' local, and as such, is quiet and pleasant.

The Spirit Store (☎ *935 2697, George's Quay*) This wonderful little bar about 3km out of town by the harbour was originally your typical harbour saloon, but it has been taken over, painted in bright colours and turned into one of the hippest joints in the area. There's live music throughout the week.

Getting There & Away

Bus Bus Éireann ☎ 041-982 8251 runs an almost hourly service to Dublin and a less frequent one to Belfast. The bus station (☎ 933 4075) is on The Long Walk near the shopping centre. There are plenty of local buses and daily connections to centres nationwide. The one-way fare to Dublin is €7.60. Capital Coaches (☎ 934 0025) runs buses to Dublin; a one-way fare is €5.

Train Clarke Train Station (☎ 933 5521), a few hundred metres west of Park St on Carrickmacross Rd, has 10 trains daily (four on Sunday) on the Dublin to Belfast line.

Getting Around

The Cycle Centre (☎ 933 7159), 44 Dublin St, opposite Dundalk Shopping Centre south of the town centre, rents out bikes for €5.10 per day.

Local taxi companies include A-1 Cabs (☎ 932 6666), 9 Crowe St, and Five Star Cabs (☎ 933 6000), 74 Clanbrassil St.

AROUND DUNDALK
Into Northern Ireland

If you're heading for Derry, take the N53 to the west of town, while for Belfast continue north on the main N1 route. If you're hiking or cycling and want to go directly to the Mourne Mountains, you can, May to September, get a ferry from Omeath to Warrenpoint in County Down (see the Omeath section later in this chapter for details).

The border is about 13km north of Dundalk. It's staffed by a garda and a British soldier (during the day anyway) but you probably won't be stopped. Just north of the border there are a couple of places where you can eat and change money.

Castleroche Castle

Five kilometres north-west of Dundalk on the Castleblayney road, Baron de Verdon's 1230 Castleroche Castle is impressively situated on a pinnacle of rock. The triangular remnants of the building include a twin-towered entrance house and protective wall. One of the windows on the western side is called Fuinneóg an Mhurdair (Murder Window), because the baroness was said to have had the architect thrown from it to prevent similar castles ever being built.

Knockbridge

Five and a half kilometres south-west of Dundalk on the R171, in a field outside the village of Knockbridge, is the **Cloch a Farmore**, an upright stone against which the mortally wounded Cúchulainn is said to have tied himself to remain standing against his enemies. It was not until a cow alighted on his shoulder that they could be persuaded that he was dead and that it was safe to approach him!

In the village itself, the **parish church** has some fine examples of stained-glass windows designed by artisan Harry Clarke and a beautiful replica of the Clogher Cross (the original is in Dublin's National Museum).

Faughart

Faughart (Fochaird), about 4km north-east of Dundalk, has fine views and is reputed to be the birthplace of St Brigid, Ireland's most revered saint after St Patrick. She was the daughter of a local chieftain and settled in Kildare in the 6th century. The grotto and church here mark the spot of a monastery associated with her, and devotions are still carried out on 1 February, her feast day.

In the western corner of the graveyard is the grave of Edward Bruce, a king of Ireland who died in 1318. He was invited to Ireland from Scotland and crowned by the Ulster lords, who hoped he would create trouble for the English in Ireland. He accepted the job, hoping this would relieve English pressure at home on his brother, Robert the Bruce. The hero Cúchulainn is said to have been born near here.

Proleek Dolmen & Gallery Grave

Heading north from Dundalk, turn right after 3km towards Ballymascanlon House Hotel (see Places to Stay in the Dundalk section for details), the start of the Cooley Peninsula ring road. In the grounds of the hotel, up by the 5th green of the golf course (there's a signposted trail for nongolfers), is the fine Giant's Load Proleek Dolmen and Gallery Grave.

Local legends say it's the grave of Para Buí Mór MhacSeóidín, a Scottish giant who came here to challenge Fionn McCumhaill, leader of the fabled Fianna warriors. It dates from 3000 BC, and the 47-tonne capstone sits precariously on three uprights. The pebbles on top are later additions and come from the belief that, if you can land a stone on top, any wish will be granted. Single women who achieve this are guaranteed marriage within a year.

COOLEY PENINSULA

East of Dundalk, the lonely moorlands of the Cooley Peninsula are the setting for a large part of Ireland's most famous fable, the Táin Bó Cúailnge (The Cattle Raid of Cooley); see the boxed text later in this chapter. The low mountains are really a part of Northern Ireland's Mourne Mountains, but are cut off from them physically by the flooded valley of Carlingford Lough and politically by the border, which runs up the centre of the lough. The peninsula is a world of its own and has strong republican traditions.

On a sour note, the Cooley Peninsula was the only part of Ireland to be afflicted by the foot & mouth crisis that so blighted the British countryside in 2001. Virtually the entire area was closed off to the outside world, doing untold damage to the area's tourist potential. At the time of writing Carlingford was only beginning to emerge from its isolation, but it will be a while before the area recoups the huge losses it suffered. That said, you should in no way be concerned while travelling here.

The best way to explore the peninsula is by first circumnavigating it on the ring road, perhaps detouring closer to the sea at **Gyles Quay**, which has a safe beach, before arriving in Carlingford and Omeath.

Gyles Quay Camping & Caravan Park (☎ *937 6262, Greenore, off Coast Rd*) Double tent sites €11.50. Open Mar-Oct. The nearest camping is here, 16km west on the Cooley Peninsula. It has excellent facilities. To get here from Dundalk, travel about 3.5km along the Dundalk–Newry road and turn right onto the coast road; the camp site is signposted about 11km farther along.

The Táin Bó Cúailnge (Cattle Raid of Cooley)

This remarkable tale of greed and war is one of the oldest stories in any European language and the closest thing Ireland has produced to the Greek epics. The story goes that Queen Maeve (Medb), the powerful ruler of Connaught, was jealous because she couldn't match the white bull owned by her husband, Ailill. She heard tales of the finest bull in Ireland, the brown bull of Cooley, and became determined to rectify the situation.

Maeve gathered her armies and headed for Ulster, where she conspired with her druids to place the Ulster armies under a spell. A deep sleep descended on them, leaving the province undefended. The only obstacle remaining was the boy warrior Cúchulainn, who tackled Maeve's soldiers as they tried to ford the river at Ardee in County Louth. Cúchulainn killed many of them and halted their advance. Maeve eventually persuaded Cúchulainn's half-brother and close friend, Ferdia, to take him on, but he was defeated after a momentous battle and died in Cúchulainn's arms.

The struggle continued across Louth and onto the Cooley Peninsula, where many place names echo the ensuing action. Sex rears its head regularly in the Táin, for Maeve was more interested in her chief warrior, Fergus, than in her husband. At various spots in the saga, they sneak off to make love, and in one instance Ailill steals the sword of the distracted Fergus, to shame him and show how careless he is.

While Maeve's soldiers were being despatched in all sorts of ways by Cúchulainn, Maeve had managed to capture the brown bull and spirit it away to Connaught. The wounded Cúchulainn defeated her armies, but the bull was gone. In the end, the brown bull killed Ailill's white bull and thundered around Ireland leaving bits of his victim all over the place. Finally, spent with rage, he died near Ulster at a place called Druim Tarb (Ridge of the Bull). Cúchulainn and Ulster then made peace with Maeve, and thus the saga ended.

Carlingford is probably the best base from which to venture inland over the peninsula's hilltops, soaked in the legends of the Táin Bó Cúailnge, through Windy Gap to the **Long Woman's Grave** and beyond to the picturesque country roads and forests which make the place a haven for walkers.

Carlingford
☎ 042 • pop 647

Near Carlingford (Cairlinn), the peninsula's mountains and views display themselves to dramatic effect. This pretty village, with its cluster of narrow streets and whitewashed houses, nestles on Carlingford Lough, beneath Slieve Foye (587m). After visiting in 1914, the Reverend Laurence Murray wrote of its 'medieval suggestiveness'; that suggestiveness survives today in the street plan and the crumbling walls and towers dotted around the village. Hard though it is to believe, not much of this was appreciated until the late 1980s, when the villagers got together to show what can be done to revive a

dying community. The story of their efforts is vividly told in the heritage centre.

The Mourne Mountains are just a few kilometres north across the lough.

Information There's a small tourist office near the heritage centre. It opens 9am to 5pm on weekdays. At the weekend you can get information from the heritage centre itself. There's a small bank in the town, but it opens on Tuesday and Thursday only.

Holy Trinity Heritage Centre The centre (☎ 937 3454, Churchyard Rd; adult/concession €1.25/0.65; open 11am-5pm Mon-Fri, noon-5pm Sat & Sun) is in the former Holy Trinity Church. The information boards are encased within closeable doors so that the centre can double as a concert hall outside visiting hours. A fine mural shows what the village looked like in its heyday, when the Mint and Taafe's Castle were right on the waterfront. A short video describes the village history and explains what has been done to give it new life in recent years.

King John's Castle Carlingford was first settled by the Vikings, and in the Middle Ages became an English stronghold under the protection of the castle, which was built on a pinnacle in the 11th to 12th centuries to control the entrance to the lough. On the western side, the entrance gateway was constructed to allow only one horse and rider through at a time. King John's name stuck to a remarkable number of places in Ireland, given that he spent little time in or near any of them! In 1210 he spent a couple of days here en route to a nine-day battle with Hugh de Lacy at Carrickfergus Castle in Antrim. It's suggested that the first few pages of the Magna Carta, the world's first constitutional bill of rights, were drafted while he was here.

Other Things to See Near the disused station is **Taafe's Castle**, a 16th-century tower house which stood on the waterfront until the land in front was reclaimed to build the short-lived train line. The **Mint**, in front of the hostel near the square, is of a similar age. Although Edward IV is thought to have granted a charter to a mint in 1467, no coins were produced here. The building has some interesting Celtic carvings round the windows. Near it is the **Tholsel**, the only surviving gate to the original town, although much altered in the 19th century when its defensive edge was softened in the interests of letting traffic through.

West of the village centre are the remains of a **Dominican friary**, built around 1305 and used as a storehouse by oyster fishermen after 1539.

Carlingford is the birthplace of Thomas D'Arcy McGee (1825–68), one of Canada's founding fathers. A bust commemorating him stands opposite Taafe's Castle.

The Táin Trail Carlingford is the starting point for the 40km Táin Trail, making a circuit of the Cooley Peninsula, through the Cooley Mountains. The route is a mixture of surfaced roads, forest tracks and green paths. For more information contact the local tourist office or the office in Dundalk (☎ 933 5484).

Cruises Carlingford Pleasure Cruises (☎ 937 3239) runs one-hour cruises between May and September. The cost is €3.80/1.90 adult/child; there's no set time as departure depends on the tides.

Special Events In mid-August the pubs are packed from morning to midnight when the village is overrun by 20,000 visitors to the Oyster Festival, with funfairs, live bands and buskers alongside the official oyster-opening competitions and tastings.

Almost every weekend from June to September, Carlingford goes event-crazy – there are summer schools, medieval festivals, leprechaun hunts and homecoming festivals.

Places to Stay Carlingford is a nicer place to stay than Dundalk and it has the bulk of accommodation on the peninsula, but options are limited and the village gets busy in summer, especially at the weekend.

Carlingford Adventure Centre & Holiday Hostel (☎ 937 3100, fax 937 3651, Tholsel St) Bed in 2/8-bed dorm €12.70/11.50. This IHH hostel is just off the main street and bedding costs €1.50 extra. The adventure centre exists to teach rock climbing, orienteering, hill walking and windsurfing to groups, so it's a good idea to check whether any large and potentially noisy gaggles of school kids will be staying at the same time as you.

Carlingford's B&Bs are of a high standard, but there aren't many of them, so it's wise to book ahead in summer and at the weekend.

Shalom (☎ 937 3151, ✉ kevinwoods@ eircom.net, Ghan Rd) Singles/doubles with bathroom €32.50/49, including breakfast. This place is along the road towards the pier.

Ghan House (☎/fax 937 3682, Main Rd) Singles/doubles €63.50/102. Two kilometres outside the village on the Dundalk road, this lodging is the best of the lot, a wonderfully atmospheric house with beautifully appointed and comfortable rooms. The breakfast is excellent.

McKevitt's Village Hotel (☎/fax 937 3116, Market Square) Singles/doubles €38/76 including breakfast. This place boasts a good bar and restaurant.

MEATH & LOUTH

Jordan's Townhouse & Restaurant *(☎ 937 3223, fax 937 3827, Newry St)* Singles/doubles €63.50/102. Jordan's has comfortable, spacious and modern B&B rooms.

Places to Eat There are plenty of places with superior seafood on the menu.

Carlingford Arms *(☎ 937 3418, Newry St)* From €7. This place serves hefty helpings of pub food; two people could manage perfectly well with one serving of fish and chips.

PJ's *(☎ 937 3973, Tholsel St)* Mains from €8. This pub, the rear extension of O'Hare's grocery store, serves half a dozen Carlingford Lough oysters with brown bread for €5.

Kingfisher Bistro *(☎ 937 3151, Ghan Rd)* Mains from €9. This is an excellent restaurant that, not surprisingly, keeps the focus on seafood.

Jordan's Restaurant *(☎ 937 3223, Newry St)* Mains from €10. This is a cosy place overlooking the water, and serves surprisingly sophisticated food. The menu ranges from oysters to unusual Irish dishes such as crubeens (pigs' trotters). There's a set dinner but for a la carte count on around €38.10 per person with drinks. It's a good idea to make reservations in summer.

Magee's Bistro *(☎ 937 3106, Tholsel St)* Mains from €4 in cafe, from €10 in restaurant. There are two restaurants in one here; a cheaper cafe-type place and an excellent restaurant, serving delicious seafood (the oysters are superb).

Entertainment There are several good pubs in the village. ***Carlingford Arms*** *(see Places to Eat)* The most popular pub in town, it is a fairly nice place with plenty of room for all of the summer visitors.

Central Bar *(☎ 937 3444, Newry St)* Opposite the Carlingford Arms, the Central has Irish music at the weekend.

PJ's *(see Places to Eat)* Next door, this is a traditional Irish bar with Irish music every Wednesday.

Getting There & Away Monday to Saturday, Bus Éireann *(☎ 933 4075)* runs buses five-times daily to Dundalk, twice daily to Newry. There are no Sunday services.

Omeath
☎ 042 • pop 315

Omeath (Ó Méith), smaller and less busy than Carlingford, lies across Carlingford Lough from County Down's Warrenpoint.

Táin Holiday Village *(☎ 937 5385, fax 937 5417, Ballyoonan)* Tent sites €24.50 for two people, €6.50 for each additional person. Facilities at this family-oriented place include a Jacuzzi and indoor pool (the use of which is included in the site price). It is 2km south of Omeath in Ballyoonan, on the Carlingford road.

Delamare House *(☎ 937 5101, e eileen mcgeown@eircom.net, Ballyoonan)* Singles/doubles with shared bathroom €28/43.50, with bathroom €32/49. Farther south than the Táin Holiday Village is this friendly B&B opposite St Jude's Shrine. It's run by Eileen McGeown and offers large, clean rooms.

Weather permitting, a passenger ferry *(☎ 048-937 2001)* crosses the lough to Warrenpoint in County Down, 1pm to 6pm daily, May to September. A return ticket costs €3.80/2.50.

Northern Ireland

CARRICK-A-REDE
ROPE BRIDGE
...wing important safety informations

Northern Ireland

No visit to Ireland can be complete without a visit north of the invisible border that separates the two political entities on this island. Though important issues remain unresolved and reminders of the Troubles abound, there is a feeling of tremendous optimism in Northern Ireland today – and visitors can't fail to be affected by it. There's absolutely no reason for not visiting Northern Ireland.

HISTORY

With the Industrial Revolution, Belfast and the surrounding counties became the industrial centre of the island, but the wealth generated by Belfast's industrial expansion went primarily to the Protestant community. In the late 19th and early 20th centuries, when Home Rule for Ireland became a possibility, the Protestant citizens of Belfast joined the Ulster Volunteer Force (UVF) in large numbers to resist any such move. The Catholic minority felt increasingly alienated and there were occasional sectarian attacks.

Partition

The Government of Ireland Act of 1920 partitioned Ireland, but the division of the island was rough and ready. The Ulster Unionist leaders demanded only the six of Ulster's nine counties in which they were supported by half or more of the population. South of the dividing line the country was overwhelmingly Catholic, with a small Protestant minority (5%). North of the border, the balance was very different, with a substantial Catholic minority (over 30%), and many southern areas where Catholics were actually in the majority.

The Anglo-Irish Treaty of 1921 was unclear on the future of the North. A Boundary Commission reviewed the borders and made recommendations for minor change; one of those was that Crossmaglen (to become notorious during the Troubles) was due to go to the South. However, nothing was implemented.

On 22 June 1921 the Northern Ireland Parliament came into being, with James Craig as the first prime minister. In 1923 the Civil War in the South ground to an exhausted halt with reluctant acceptance of Ireland's division. Catholic nationalists elected to the new Northern Ireland Parliament took up their seats with equal reluctance and the politics of the North started to become increasingly divided on religious grounds.

Protestant Dominance

The Northern Ireland Parliament sat from 1920 until 1972. The Protestant majority made sure their rule was absolute by systematically excluding Catholics from power. In the early 1970s, when Belfast's population was 25% Catholic, only 2.5% of Belfast Corporation jobs were held by Catholics. In Derry there was discrimination in housing to deny the Catholics a vote; it was not until the 1970s that there was one adult one vote.

The effects of the 1930s depression were more severe in Northern Ireland than elsewhere in the UK, with unemployment averaging 25%. Per capita income was only about 60% of that in Britain, and indicators in every area from housing to public health were considerably worse than in Britain.

In 1922, the bitter struggle going on in the South spilled over the border and serious rioting broke out in Belfast. In 1935, 11 people died in further riots in Belfast. But in spite of all this, Northern Ireland remained relatively peaceful for many years after Partition.

Belfast was heavily bombed in WWII and the first US army forces to land in Europe passed through Belfast on 26 January 1942. The strong support given to Britain's war effort further entrenched British backing of Northern Ireland's continued existence and independence. In 1949 the creation of the Republic of Ireland cut the South's final links with the North. Even though the new Republic's constitution enshrined its eventual goal of regaining the North, this caused little stir. Not until the 1960s did Northern Ireland's basic instability begin to show itself.

Civil Rights

In the 1960s, the government under Prime Minister Terence O'Neill took the first tentative steps towards dealing with the problems of the North's Catholics. A meeting with the South's prime minister and a visit to a Catholic girls' school were hardly earth-shattering moves. Reaction to these symbolic initiatives propelled Reverend Ian Paisley to front stage as the ranting personification of Protestant extremism.

It was in Derry (Londonderry) that Protestant political domination was at its most outrageous. In 1968 Derry's population was split approximately 60% Catholic to 40% Protestant, yet the city's council always had a Protestant majority achieved through electoral boundary rigging and restrictive voting rights. In October 1968 a civil rights march in Derry was violently broken up by the Royal Ulster Constabulary (RUC), and the Troubles, as they became euphemistically known, were under way.

In January 1969, People's Democracy, another civil rights movement, organised a Belfast to Derry march and, just outside Derry, a Protestant mob attacked the marchers. The police stood to one side and then compounded the problem by a sweep through the predominantly Catholic Bogside. Further marches, protests and violence followed, and far from keeping the two sides apart, the police were becoming part of the problem.

Finally, in August 1969, British troops were sent into Derry and then Belfast, to maintain law and order. Though the British army was initially welcomed by the Catholics, it soon came to be seen as a tool of the Protestant majority. Over-reaction by the army, especially through Bloody Sunday, actually fuelled recruitment into the hibernating Irish Republican Army (IRA); the peaceful civil rights movement faded away.

The Troubles

For 25 years the story of the Troubles was one of lost opportunities, intransigence on both sides and fleeting moments of hope.

After 1971, suspected IRA sympathisers could be, and were, interned without trial. On Bloody Sunday (30 January 1972) 13 civilians were killed by British troops in Derry. Northern Ireland's Parliament was abolished in 1972, although substantial progress had been made towards civil rights. A new power-sharing arrangement, worked out in the 1973 Sunningdale Agreement, was killed stone dead by the massive and overwhelmingly Protestant Ulster Workers' Strike of 1974.

While continuing to target people in Northern Ireland, the IRA moved their campaign of bombing to mainland Britain. Their activities were increasingly condemned by citizens and parties on all sides of the political spectrum. Meanwhile, loyalist paramilitaries were running a sectarian murder campaign against Catholics. Passions reached fever pitch in 1981 when republican prisoners in the North went on a hunger strike, demanding the right to be recognised as political prisoners. Ten of them fasted to death, the best known being an elected MP, Bobby Sands.

The waters were further muddied by an incredible variety of parties splintering into sub groups with different agendas. The IRA had split into 'official' and 'provisional' wings, from which sprang more extreme republican organisations such as the Irish National Liberation Army (INLA). Myriad Protestant loyalist paramilitary organisations sprang up in opposition to the IRA, and violence was frequently met with violence, indiscriminate outrage with indiscriminate outrage.

It's easy to line up the 'if onlys' when it comes to the problems of Ireland. If only the Home Rule movement hadn't encountered such violent opposition to Irish independence in the early part of this century, Ireland might be one country today. Northern fears might have been reduced if only the Republic hadn't pandered to them by allowing the Catholic Church's prejudices (on sex, marriage and censorship) to preside over so many corners of life.

Northern Catholics' antipathy to Northern Protestants might have been less if only they had been treated with some fairness between the 1920s and 1990s. Northern fears of Southern impoverishment might have been lower if the Republic's government had not pursued its vision of a rural idyll for longer than was sensible. The British army's unpopularity might have been far less and IRA strength minor if only it hadn't overreacted so extremely to IRA provocation. And the North's unwillingness to countenance any agreement with the South might have been less if only the IRA hadn't been so callously indiscriminate in its violence or, equally frequently, so callously inept.

In 1970 the British home secretary, the hapless Reginald Maudling, was castigated for observing that the best hope for Northern Ireland was to achieve 'an acceptable level of violence'. Twenty years later that was precisely what had been achieved.

1990s to the Present

In the 1990s some external circumstances started to alter the picture. Membership of the EU, economic progress in Ireland and the declining importance of the Catholic Church in the South started to reduce differences between the North and South. Also American interest added an international dimension to the situation, an interest that was to have a profound effect in creating the Good Friday Agreement.

During 1991 and 1992 the various factions met with the British government. Outwardly nothing much seemed to come of this, but behind the scenes individuals, and particularly the Social Democratic and Labour Party (SDLP; a mostly Catholic party) leader, John Hume, continued to beaver away, trying to persuade the main groups that something had to give.

In December 1993, the Downing Street Declaration was signed by British Prime Minister John Major and the Irish Prime Minister Albert Reynolds. It was a crucial element in the peace process, stating that Britain had no 'selfish, strategic or economic interest in Northern Ireland' and enshrining the principle of majority consent at the heart of any talks about constitutional change.

Then, on 31 August 1994, the Sinn Féin leader, Gerry Adams, announced a 'cessation of violence' on behalf of the IRA. In October 1994 the Combined Loyalist Military Command also announced a cease-fire. Most

British troops were then withdrawn to barracks, and roadblocks were removed. There followed an edgy peace while all the parties restated their agendas.

In 1995 the British and Irish governments published two framework documents as a basis for discussion on the way forward. The first, *A Framework for Accountable Government in Northern Ireland*, set out the British government's proposals for restoring democracy through an Assembly, elected by proportional representation. In the second, *A New Framework for Agreement*, the British and Irish governments put forward their joint proposals for relationships within the island and between the two different governments.

Although it was stressed that these were discussion documents and that nothing would be implemented without a referendum first, both sides dug their heels in. The main sticking point was the issue of decommissioning – the Unionist requirement that the IRA show good faith in a final peace settlement by surrendering its weapons before talks began. For their part Sinn Féin and the IRA argued that no arms could be given up until British troops withdrew and political prisoners were freed, and that decommissioning should be part of the final settlement. With the peace process stalled, the IRA declared the cease-fire over when it exploded bombs in Canary Wharf in London on 9 February 1996, killing two people and injuring many more.

In the May 1997 British general election, Tony Blair's Labour Party won a landslide victory and had a new commitment to resolving the problems of Northern Ireland. In June, in the Irish Republic's general election, Fianna Fáil's Bertie Ahern, who had declared that he would talk to Sinn Féin about a new cease-fire, was elected *taoiseach* (prime minister).

In the same month, British officials, led by the new Northern Ireland secretary, Dr Mo Mowlam, promised to admit Sinn Féin to all-party talks in Stormont Castle following any new cease-fire. In the meantime the British and Irish governments had accepted the proposal by George Mitchell, the former US senator brokering the talks, on how to get round the decommissioning impasse.

Talks on the future of Northern Ireland would take place parallel with the talks on decommissioning.

Encouraged by this, and by the decision of Ulster's Loyal Orange Lodges to reroute or cancel some potentially violent 12 July marches celebrating the Battle of the Boyne, the IRA declared another cease-fire from 20 July 1997. Six weeks later Sinn Féin joined the peace talks.

On 10 April 1998 intensive negotiations culminated in the historic Good Friday Agreement. The agreement, which states that the political future of Northern Ireland depends on the consent of the majority of the people of Northern Ireland, was overwhelmingly endorsed by simultaneous referendums held in Northern Ireland and the Republic on 22 May 1998. Just over 71% of people in Northern Ireland voted to accept devolved democracy, while the 94% Yes vote in the Republic accepted the end of Dublin's territorial claim to the North.

Under the agreement the new Northern Ireland Assembly was given full legislative and executive authority over agriculture, economic development, education, environment, finance and personnel, and health and social services. It also established the terms of reference for an independent commission on the future of policing, plans for the release of most paramilitary prisoners, the removal of security installations and a major reduction in the RUC.

On 25 June 1998, 108 Assembly members were elected by proportional representation. David Trimble's UUP won 28 seats; the SDLP, led by John Hume, won 24; the Democratic Unionist Party (DUP), led by Ian Paisley, won 20; Sinn Féin won 18; the Alliance Party won six seats; the UK Unionist Party won five; the Northern Ireland Women's Coalition won two; the Progressive Unionist Party won two; and independents won three seats.

The new Assembly met for the first time on 1 July 1998. David Trimble was elected as first minister (designate) and Seamus Mallon of the SDLP was elected deputy first minister (designate).

Unfortunately the year of the peace agreement was also one of violence, with rioting over the Parades Commission ban on the annual Orange Order parade at Drumcree, Portadown. Escalating loyalist violence culminated in a petrol bomb attack that burned to death three young boys on 12 July.

Then on 15 August 1998 came the single worst atrocity in the entire history of the Troubles, the bombing of Omagh by the Real IRA, a breakaway republican group opposed to the Good Friday Agreement. The 650kg bomb killed 29 people and injured 200. Confused telephone warnings caused the RUC to evacuate people to the very area where the bomb exploded. Swift action by politicians, including a statement by Gerry Adams condemning the bombing, prevented a loyalist backlash. Shortly afterwards the British and Irish governments passed strong new anti-terrorist laws, and cease-fires were declared by the Real IRA (temporary in their case), the INLA and the Loyalist Volunteer Force (LVF).

The issue of paramilitary decommissioning dogged progress with David Trimble refusing to allow Sinn Féin to take up their two ministerial seats in the Assembly before the decommissioning of IRA weapons, and Sinn Féin constantly reiterating that decommissioning was not a precondition to implementing the agreement. This came to a farcical head when the Ulster Unionist Party (UUP) boycotted the Assembly on the very day (15 July 1999) power was supposed to be devolved to Belfast.

Former US Senator George Mitchell, who brokered the peace talks of 1998, returned to Northern Ireland in September 1999 to help resolve the deadlock. Just a few days later, the Independent Commission on Policing for Northern Ireland, chaired by the former Governor of Hong Kong Chris Patten, published its report. The 128-page report, entitled *A New Beginning*, set out 175 recommendations aimed at transforming the Royal Ulster Constabulary (RUC), which had been disproportionately Protestant (currently 92%) and Unionist since its establishment in 1922.

The commission wanted to see the proportion of Catholics in the force raised from 8% to 30% within 10 years (Catholics make

NICKY CAVEN

David Trimble, stalwart of Unionist politics

up 42% of the population). The report also recommended that the RUC be renamed the Northern Ireland Police Service (later amended from 'NIPS' to Police Service for Northern Ireland); that its badge, a harp and crown, be replaced; that the union flag no longer fly from police stations; that the current police authority be replaced; and that police numbers drop from 13,000 to 7500.

On 12 October 1999, in a cabinet reshuffle, the UK Prime Minister Tony Blair appointed Peter Mandelson as Northern Ireland secretary replacing Mo Mowlam. Mowlam was the first woman to hold the post, and many believe that it was her efforts that made the Good Friday Agreement possible.

George Mitchell's review was delivered on 18 November 1999. His plan involved the IRA making a significant statement on decommissioning as soon as the Executive was set up. This face-saving compromise was accepted by the UUP on 27 November and the Assembly returned to business two days later, with power passing back from the UK government on 1 December.

The IRA appointed a representative to the International Body on Decommissioning but this did not satisfy the UUP. David Trimble, under threat from his own party, announced that unless the IRA start decommissioning by February 2000 he would resign. To shore up Trimble's position, Peter Mandelson declared that he would reintroduce direct rule if there were no progress on the matter. Despite furious last-minute negotiations, no

deal came about and, on 11 February, the Assembly was suspended.

In March the expected challenge to Trimble's leadership of the UUP arose but he won by a small margin. In the same month the new Bloody Sunday Enquiry, promised by the Labour Party, began work in Derry. Its task was to examine thousands of documents, approximately 5000 photographs and more than 1000 witnesses to find out the truth behind the massacre.

Fruitless talks continued until 6 May when the IRA released a statement saying that it was ready to begin a process that would 'completely and verifiably' put its arms beyond use. Former ANC official Cyril Ramaphosa and former Finnish president Martti Ahtisaari were chosen to inspect IRA arms dumps and check that the weapons were not being used. This seemed to do the trick and David Trimble expressed cautious optimism.

Another area of confrontation was created on 16 May when the parliamentary bill to reform the RUC was published, with Sinn Féin declaring that it watered down the Patten proposals. On 29 May with David Trimble receiving the backing of his party to return to Stormont and the IRA committing to put arms beyond use, power was returned to Stormont.

At the end of June the arms inspectors reported that they had inspected the arms dumps and concluded that the arms couldn't be used without their detection.

The Orange march at Drumcree in July threatened confrontation but after several days of riots the protests petered out. However feuds between various loyalist paramilitary groups broke out into gang warfare as they vied for power.

In October 2000 a further arms inspection took place but General John de Chastelain of the Independent International Decommissioning Commission (IIDC) declared that no progress had been made on actual disarmament. On 28 October David Trimble decided on a stronger line on decommissioning to head off another leadership challenge. In all the peace process politicking the main players are hostage to the more extreme elements. Sinn Féin, although committed to the peace process, have to keep their supporters on side to prevent any growth in the dissident breakaway republican paramilitary movements. On the Unionist side, the UUP faces leakage of their support to the DUP (and their stated opposition to the Good Friday Agreement) unless they maintain a strong anti-IRA stance.

On 24 January 2001 Peter Mandelson was replaced by Dr John Reid as Northern Ireland secretary. Throughout the first part of 2001 the Assembly carried on its work with much of political life in limbo until the general election, first timetabled for May but delayed due to an outbreak of foot and mouth disease (animal not political) until June.

Although two further arms inspections had verified that the arsenals had not been touched, on 8 May David Trimble dropped a pre-election bombshell of a post-dated letter of resignation. It was to come into effect on 1 July unless the IRA kept its promise to put its arms beyond use by the end of June.

In the British general election on 7 June 2001, Sinn Féin increased its Westminster seats to four and the DUP to five. The UUP lost seats but with six remained the largest party; the SDLP retained their three seats. Thus the gains of the radical parties squeezed out the parties that represented the middle ground.

While support for the DUP comes from disaffected Unionists, increase in support for Sinn Féin comes mainly from the young and those who have never bothered to vote before. The result has changed the political map of Ireland, with a new boundary separating a nationalist west and south of the province from an essentially unionist east and north.

Trimble carried out his threat and stood down as first minister, calling on the British government to back moves to expel Sinn Féin from the power-sharing executive if the IRA did not get rid of its weapons in the next six weeks – giving a deadline of 12 August.

On 8 August 2001 the IRA responded by making a historic announcement that it had presented a scheme to the Decommissioning Commission to put its arms completely beyond use. It was welcomed by most but rejected outright by the UUP leadership as

it gave no timetable for the decommissioning. Angered by this response, the IRA withdrew its proposal a few days later.

In light of these developments, the Northern Ireland secretary, John Reid took the decision to suspend the Assembly for one day, which allows another six-weeks breathing space for further negotiations and a review of the peace process. The same process was enacted again in September and a sequence of rescue talks took place.

With no suggestion of any movement from the IRA, the Ulster Unionist and the Democratic Unionist Ministers resigned. However, the same day there were hints of a historic decision by the IRA, which became reality on 23 October. Their statement read: 'There is a responsibility upon everyone seriously committed to a just peace to do our best to avoid this [collapse of the Assembly]. Therefore, in order to save the peace process, we have implemented the scheme agreed with the IIDC in August. Our motivation is clear. This unprecedented move is to save the peace process and to persuade others of our genuine intentions.'

This meant they were getting rid of weapons but the big questions of whether it was the whole stock, by what irreversible means and whether they'd buy anymore were not answered.

However, it brought most of the Unionists back to the Assembly, the exceptions were two who wouldn't back Trimble's re-election as First Minister. It took some last minute wheeling and dealing to get three non-aligned Alliance party members to support him. Despite a last minute legal challenge by the Democratic Unionist Party, with much to gain from new elections, Trimble was elected First Minister.

ECONOMY

During the 19th century, Northern Ireland was at the forefront of the Industrial Revolution and one of the most prosperous regions of Europe. The decline of traditional industries, such as shipbuilding, textiles and rope making, coupled with the economic dislocation caused by the Troubles, one of the highest birth rates in Europe and discriminatory employment policies, has meant an economy characterised by high unemployment, low incomes and emigration. The region has been heavily subsidised by Britain, the EU and the International Fund for Ireland (IFI), to which the USA has been one of the largest contributors. In addition, security operations have involved high levels of expenditure and employment on defence matters.

Northern Ireland's unemployment rate has fallen to 4.4% (rest of the UK 3.6% to 4%), from a high of 17% in the early 1980s. While this has been aided by the large amounts of money pouring into Northern Ireland since the late 1970s, it also reflects a markedly improved local economy. Apparently there are more BMWs per head of population in Northern Ireland than anywhere outside Germany.

The economic prosperity of the last five years has brought benefits to the Catholic population; there's been a growth in construction and hospitality – both traditional areas of employment; a majority of university students are Catholic and there's a significant Catholic middle class. The proportion of Catholics in the Civil Service is now more in line with their population proportion.

About 46% of all jobs are supported directly or indirectly by the public sector. Agriculture makes up around 6% of employment – three times the UK average – while manufacturing and construction account for a further 23%. The dependence on traditional sectors such as textiles and food remains higher than in the UK.

The first cease-fire in 1994 brought an almost instant dividend in a 20% boom in tourism, but after the collapse of the cease-fires in 1996, tourism figures dropped by approximately 30%. It was not until 1998 that an improvement was seen, with a 4% increase in visitors. Tourism represents about 2% of the economy whereas it's more like 8% in the rest of the UK. Current predictions are that tourism may eventually create 20,000 new jobs and increase its contribution by another 4%, bringing it into line with the Republic where tourism accounts for 6% of GDP.

This will only come as people realise that the North is a safe place to visit and that there are attractions to rival those in the South. Of those that visit Dublin, less than 10% will visit the North, and many of those do a dash from Donegal for a few hours at the Giant's Causeway.

The 1997 cease-fire is continuing to bring about positive economic developments. Foreign investment in 1997–98 was a record £522 million, with an increasing share coming from high-tech sectors such as computer software. Major British retailers, such as Sainsbury's and Tesco, have expanded into Northern Ireland but the major retailing chains selling computers, TVs, cameras and the like have still to make an impact.

The hospitality sector has shown a dramatic improvement, with a sharp rise in hotel space and major investment in bars, restaurants and conference facilities, especially in the centre of Belfast.

While much investment has been in telecommunications and IT, the global turndown which has frozen investment in the South has yet to reach the North. A further marker on the horizon is the decline of EU funding. Northern Ireland is assured of its £940 million funding until 2006, but will then have to start standing on its own feet.

Belfast

pop 279,240

Belfast is a city in recovery, fast rebuilding and reinventing itself. Massive investment during the past few years combined with the optimism of peace has transformed Belfast into something of a boom town.

A string of upmarket hotels, including the Belfast Hilton, opened in the late 1990s and 2000, along with dozens of smart restaurants, bars and cafes. The government-initiated Laganside project has cleaned up the much-neglected River Lagan and is responsible for the regeneration of inner-city areas such as the trendified Cathedral Quarter, the development of spanking-new riverside apartments, the 2235-capacity Waterfront Hall as well as the £91-million Odyssey sporting and cultural complex.

Step into a contemporary bar or restaurant and you'll pick up a sense of excitement and relief, a general feeling and buzz that, after 30 years of conflict, Belfast is joining the rest of the world. Some say that there's more of that buzz in Belfast than Dublin.

The city is home to over quarter of a million people and is compact and easy to get around, with most points of interest within easy walking distance of each other. Like any city worth its salt, Belfast contains some architectural and cultural gems, such as the impressive City Hall and the excellent Linen Hall Library. There are dozens of splendid Victorian pubs to explore and, for a city of its size, Belfast boasts a good nightlife (much of it geared to the student population). It's also pleasantly situated: the Belfast Hills are visible to the west, the rocks and green slopes of Cave Hill loom over the city to the north, and the sweep of Belfast Lough cuts into the city centre from the north-east.

There are, of course, plenty of reminders of the Troubles to be seen, and the deep conflict and passions that have torn Northern Ireland apart over the decades are perhaps more acute in Belfast than anywhere else. But this shouldn't put anyone off visiting. Statistically Belfast has always been a safe

Highlights

- Take a black taxi tour of the murals of West Belfast
- Eat out along the Golden Mile
- Sample the nightlife in the university area
- Hike up Cave Hill for panoramic views
- Enjoy traditional music and beer in Belfast's fabulous pubs
- Visit the new discovery centre, W5, in the Odyssey Complex

city for a visitor; at the height of the Troubles the murder rate was a tenth of New York's. And, although the so-called Peace Line still divides the Catholic and Protestant communities of Belfast, these days the gates remain open most of the time.

HISTORY

Compared with many other cities, Belfast is relatively new with few reminders of its pre-19th-century existence. The city's name comes from Beál Feirste (Mouth of the Sandy Ford), a reference to the River Farset,

BELFAST

which used to flow through the town centre but is now contained inside an underground pipe. In 1177, the Norman John de Courcy built a castle by the River Lagan and a small settlement grew up around it. Both were destroyed 20 years later and the region was controlled for a long time afterwards by the Irish O'Neill family. The city began to develop in earnest in 1611 when Baron Arthur Chichester built a castle and promoted the growth of the settlement.

The first significant waves of foreign settlers were Scottish and English Planters brought in by James I in the early 17th century. They were followed by an influx of Huguenots in the late 17th century. These French Protestants, fleeing from persecution in France, laid the foundations for a thriving linen industry. More Scottish and English settlers arrived and other industries such as rope-making, tobacco, engineering and shipbuilding developed.

Antagonism between Protestants and Catholics only really developed during the 19th century. Prior to this, Belfast had produced many Protestant supporters of an independent Ireland and a fairer society. The United Irishmen, who pushed for increasing independence from England, were founded in Belfast in 1791 and the struggle for fairer trading terms enjoyed both Protestant and Catholic support.

During the 18th and 19th centuries Belfast was the one city in Ireland that really experienced the Industrial Revolution. Sturdy rows of brick terraced houses were built for the factory and shipyard workers. A population of around 20,000 people in 1800 grew steadily to around 400,000 by the start of WWI, by which time Belfast had nearly overtaken Dublin in size.

Queen Victoria visited Belfast in 1849 and her brief foray into the city has been immortalised by a large number of streets and monuments named after her. Belfast was granted city status by Victoria in 1888.

The partition of Ireland after WWI and independence in the South gave Belfast a new role as the capital of Northern Ireland. It also marked the end of the city's industrial growth, although the decline didn't really set in until after WWII. After the initial outbreak of rioting in 1969, Belfast saw more than its fair share of violence and bloodshed, and shocking pictures of extremist bombings and killings, often mirrored by security-force brutality, made Belfast a household name around the world. The mayhem reached its peak in the 1970s and continued through the 1980s and into the 1990s, when the sectarian violence of Belfast simmered down. The cease-fire in 1994 raised hopes but the bombing of Canary Wharf in London in 1996 signalled a return to violence.

The 1997 cease-fire has held, there has been a huge injection of money, especially EU money, and Belfast is reaping the rewards: unemployment is low, house prices are rising faster than in any other UK city and tourism is waiting to boom. There's never been a better time to visit.

ORIENTATION

The city centre is compact, with the imposing City Hall in Donegall Square as a convenient central landmark. Belfast's principal shopping district is north of the square along and off Donegall Place and Royal Ave.

A little farther north, the once run-down area around Donegall St and St Anne's Cathedral forms the Cathedral Quarter. It has its own arts festival and trendy restaurants, bars and clubs are springing up in the red-brick warehouses and old buildings.

Reminders of the Victorian era can be found in the stately buildings surrounding City Hall, in the narrow alleys known as the Entries off Ann and High Sts and in the ornate Grand Opera House and Crown Liquor Saloon on Great Victoria St.

Heading south from Donegall Square, Great Victoria St and Dublin Rd lead to University Rd, where you'll find Queen's University, the Botanic Gardens and the Ulster Museum. There are dozens of restaurants and bars in this area – it's called the Golden Mile – and at night it's the most energetic and cheerful area of a generally hard-working city. Most of the city's accommodation options, including several hostels, are also south of the centre around the university area.

The Europa Bus Centre is behind the

Europa Hotel, in Glengall St, along with the Great Victoria St train station. The Laganside Bus Centre is east of the Albert Memorial Clock Tower, opposite Queen Elizabeth Bridge.

A cross-harbour train link, the Dargan Bridge, runs alongside the Lagan Bridge north of Queen Elizabeth Bridge.

To the east of Donegall Square is Chichester St, which runs down to Oxford St, where you'll find the Royal Courts of Justice, St George's Market, the Belfast Hilton and the Waterfront Hall, a large conference and concert centre. East of the river are Samson and Goliath, the giant cranes dominating the Harland & Wolff shipyards.

West of the centre, the Westlink Motorway divides the city from West Belfast. The (Protestant) Shankill Rd and the (Catholic) Falls Rd run west into West Belfast. The Peace Line built between the two was intended as a safety measure to discourage extremists of either ilk from creating mayhem then scuttling quickly back to their side of the tracks. It's now easy to cross from one side to the other.

Maps
The Belfast Welcome Centre has a good free map of the city centre. The *Collins Belfast Streetfinder* map (£2.99) is more detailed and includes a full index of street names.

INFORMATION
Tourist Offices
The Belfast Welcome Centre (☎ 9024 6609, fax 9031 2424, W www.gotobelfast.com), 47 Donegall Place, near City Hall, opens 9am to 5.30pm Monday to Saturday most of the year. It usually opens 9am to 7pm weekdays, 9am to 5.15pm Saturday and 10am to 4pm Sunday from June to September. Outside these hours, a computer console, accessible from outside, gives details of accommodation and so on. You can pick up information about the whole of Northern Ireland here and book accommodation anywhere in Ireland and Britain. The centre will look after luggage for the day, change money and sell you souvenirs. There's also an Internet cafe here.

Belfast City Council Parks publish a *What's On* booklet giving details of activities, tours, walks and performances in their parks for the year. The Northern Irish Tourist Board publishes a wealth of information covering cycling, horse riding, fishing, sailing, historic homes and gardens plus accommodation choices.

There are tourist information offices in Belfast's two airports; the City Airport branch (☎ 9045 7745) opens 5.30am to 10pm daily, while the International Airport branch (☎ 9442 2888) opens 24 hours.

Bord Fáilte (Irish Tourist Board; ☎ 9032 7888, fax 9024 0201, W www.ireland.travel .ie), 53 Castle St, opens 9am to 5pm weekdays and 9am to 12.30pm Saturday, June to August. It can book accommodation in the South.

Money
There are branches of the major Northern Irish banks in the centre of Belfast. Most open 9.30am to 5.30pm weekdays and some open late Thursday and Saturday morning. There are plenty of ATMs around town; handy ones can be found along Donegall Place and south of the city centre on Shaftesbury Square.

The Belfast Welcome Centre has a bureau de change, as do the main post office on Castle Place and the post office in Shaftesbury Square.

There's a branch of Thomas Cook (☎ 9088 3900) with exchange facilities at 11 Donegall Place and another at the international airport (☎ 9442 2536). The latter opens 5.30am to 9.30pm weekdays and 5.30am to midnight at the weekend. Times vary slightly in winter and during the summer peak to reflect flight activity.

Post & Communications
The main post office on Castle Place opens 9am to 5.30pm weekdays and 9am to 7pm Saturday. Other convenient post offices are in Shaftesbury Square and at the junction of University and Malone Rds.

There are plenty of public telephones, which are divided into coin-only, phonecard-only and those accepting both. Many shops sell pre-paid phonecards.

BELFAST

You can log on to the Internet at Revelations Cafe (☎ 9032 0337, e info@revelations.co.uk), 27 Shaftesbury Square. It opens 8am to 10pm weekdays, 10am to 6pm Saturday and 11am to 7pm Sunday. Access costs £4 per hour, £3 per hour for students. Frequent users can buy a discount card (£10 for four hours).

Belfast Central Library (☎ 9050 9150), Royal Ave, offers Internet access for £2 per hour. See Libraries later in this section for opening hours.

Travel Agencies
The usit NOW travel office (☎ 9032 4073, fax 9023 8845) is at 13b Fountain Centre, College St. Queen's University Travel Centre (☎ 9024 1830), in the Student's Union Building on University Rd, is also run by usit and opens to nonstudents too.

There's a Thomas Cook (☎ 9055 0232) at 11 Donegall Place.

Bookshops
The following bookshops all have a good selection of books on Ireland.

Try Eason's (☎ 9032 8566), 16 Ann St, for books and periodicals.

Waterstone's have two shops, one at 44–46 Fountain St (☎ 9024 0159) and one at 8 Royal Ave (☎ 9024 7355).

The Bookshop at Queen's (☎ 9066 6302), 91 University Rd, opposite Queen's University, is also worth popping into if you're looking for books about the North.

Bookfinders Cafe (☎ 9032 8269), 47 University Rd, is a second-hand bookshop and book-finding service with a gallery and popular cafe at the back.

The Stationery Office Bookshop (☎ 9023 8451), 16 Arthur St, has a selection of maps and guides, one of which is the very useful *25 Walks in and Around Belfast*, by Paddy Dillon.

The Automobile Association (AA; ☎ 0870 550 0600), 108–10 Great Victoria St, sells maps and travel guides.

The Green Cross Art Shop (☎ 9024 3371), 51–53 Falls Rd, has a range of books on Irish issues, mainly giving the republican perspective.

Cultúrlann MacAdam ÓFiaich (The Irish Language and Arts Centre; ☎ 9023 9303), 216 Falls Rd, has some interesting titles on Irish culture, local history and politics.

Libraries
Belfast Central Library (see Post & Communications) opens 9.30am to 8pm Monday and Thursday, 9.30am to 5.30pm Tuesday, Wednesday and Friday, and 9.30am to 1pm on Saturday. See also the Linen Hall Library in the Around the Centre section later in this chapter.

Laundry
Around the university area there's Mike's Laundrette, at 46 Agincourt Ave, and Cleanerette Laundrette, at 160 Lisburn Rd. Globe Drycleaning & Laundrette, at 37 Botanic Ave, incorporates film processing and dry cleaning; it opens 8am to 9pm weekdays, 8am to 6pm Saturday and noon to 6pm on Sunday.

Medical Services
Accident and emergency services are available at the Royal Victoria Hospital (☎ 9024 0503) on Grosvenor Rd, west of the city centre; at the Mater Hospital (☎ 9074 1211), on Crumlin Rd near the junction of Antrim Rd and Clifton St; at the Ulster Hospital (☎ 9048 4511), Upper Newtownards Rd, Dundonald, near Stormont Castle; and at City Hospital (☎ 9032 9241), Lisburn Rd.

For prescriptions, travel vaccinations and so on, you should consult a GP as a temporary resident. All hostels and hotels should have lists of local practitioners.

Unlike in England, Scotland and Wales, the Abortion Act 1967 does not apply in Northern Ireland, so it is illegal. A local GP or the Brook Advisory Centre (☎ 9032 8866), 29a North St, should be able to give initial advice and guidance in the case of an unwanted pregnancy.

Emergency
For national emergency phone numbers see Emergencies in the Facts for the Visitor chapter. Other emergency numbers are the Rape Crisis and Sexual Abuse Centre (☎ 9024

9696), the Samaritans (☎ 0845 790 9090) and Victim Support (☎ 9024 4039).

Dangers & Annoyances

Even at the height of the Troubles, Belfast wasn't a particularly dangerous city for tourists. The violence between the republican and loyalist factions was usually aimed at specific people. As the peace process and cease-fires continue army and police security patrols will become even rarer. You should however keep away from the so-called interface areas after dark as you may be mistaken for one of the other side. At the time of writing there has been a flare up of sectarian violence in the Ardoyne area of North Belfast, so it's only sensible to avoid that area day and night. If in doubt about any area ask at where you're staying.

You're probably safer from 'normal' criminal activity in Belfast than you are in London. Indeed Belfast has, surprisingly, the lowest crime rate in the UK, but this may be due more to control of crime by the paramilitaries and the nonreporting of criminal incidents perpetrated by them than anything else.

As anywhere, you should always lock your car when you leave it and take anything valuable with you. Don't leave your keys in the car even if you're out of it for seconds. A favourite car theft ploy is for someone to entice you to leave your car to check a 'fault', an associate then jumps in, hot wires the car and drives off. If you leave something in the car, make sure it's out of sight and bear in mind that many insurance policies exclude items stolen from cars.

An irritating legacy of the Troubles is the absence of luggage storage facilities at bus and train stations, although lockers have returned to the Great Victoria St train station. Also annoying is when you find the door of a central hotel or shop closed even though there are people inside. Press the buzzer and someone inside will check you out before opening the door. To outsiders fortified police stations can look off putting. Take heart, though: if you need to report a 'normal' crime such as a stolen camera, just march up to the door and press the buzzer. Someone will emerge to help you.

If you want to take photos of fortified police stations, army posts or other military or quasi-military paraphernalia, ask first to be on the safe side.

In the Protestant and Catholic strongholds it's best not to photograph people unawares: always ask first and accept a refusal.

You're unlikely to get into furious political or religious arguments in Belfast pubs because both topics are usually avoided with outsiders. In staunchly single-minded pubs of either persuasion, outsiders are often studiously avoided!

One annoyance for nonsmokers is the high prevalence of smoking in the North. While restaurants are ostensibly segregated you always notice the smoke and pubs, especially small ones, can become much fogged.

AROUND THE CENTRE
Belfast City Hall

The Industrial Revolution transformed Belfast and that rapid rise to muck-and-brass prosperity shows to this day. The fine, white Portland stone City Hall (☎ 9027 0456, Donegall Square; free; one-hour tours at 10.30am, 11.30am & 2.30pm Mon-Fri, 2.30pm Sat, June-Sept; 2.30pm Mon-Sat rest of year) was completed in 1906. Built in the Classical Renaissance style, much to the disdain of architectural purists, it has some fine Italian marble inside and a great deal of pomp and splendour outside. It was built out of the profits of the gas supply company. The first meeting of the Northern Ireland Parliament was held here in 1921 and then at the Union Theological College until Stormont was completed in 1932.

The most noticeable feature of the exterior used to be the huge 'Belfast Says No' banner displayed along the top of the building. It was placed there by the unionist city fathers to show their objections to the Anglo-Irish Agreement, which was signed in 1985 and formed the basis of ongoing consultations between Britain and the Republic over the North. Most unionist city councillors also refused to take part in council affairs while the agreement was in force. In 1988 the City Hall was bombed and the stained-glass windows in the Great Hall

BELFAST

BELFAST

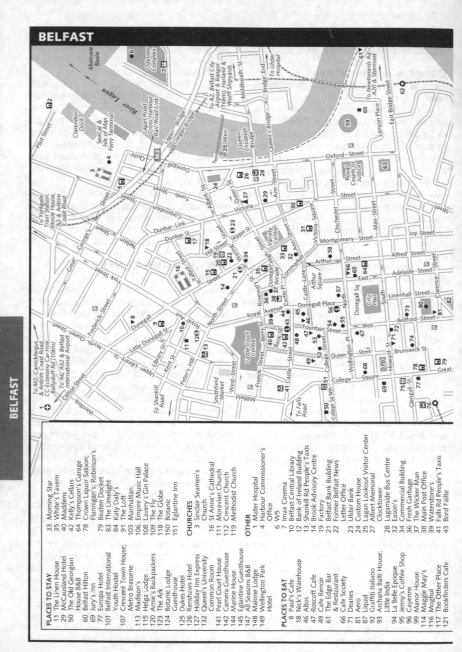

BELFAST

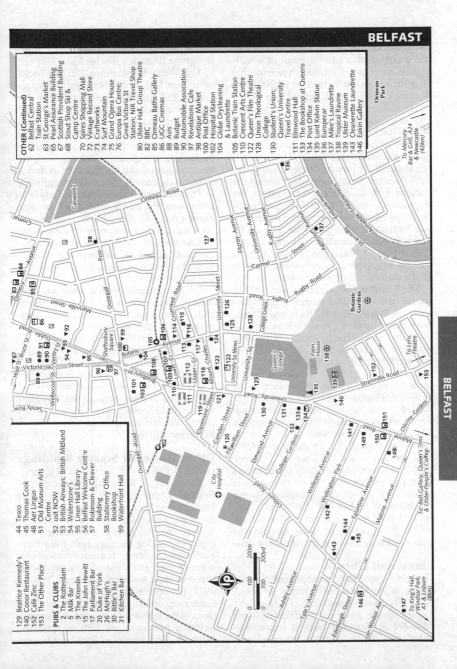

BELFAST

OTHER (Continued)
62 Belfast Central Train Station
63 St George's Market
65 Pearl Assurance Building
67 Scottish Provident Building
68 Scout Shop Ski & Camp Centre
70 Spires Shopping Mall
72 Vintage Record Store
73 Craftworks
74 Surf Mountain
75 Grand Opera House
76 Europa Bus Centre; Great Victoria St Station; NIR Travel Shop
80 Ulster Hall; Group Theatre
82 BBC
85 Ormeau Baths Gallery
86 UGC Cinemas
88 Avis
89 Budget
90 Automobile Association
97 Revelations Cafe
98 Antique Market
100 Post Office
102 Hospital Station
104 Globe Drycleaning & Laundrette
105 Botanic Train Station
110 Crescent Arts Centre
122 Queen's Film Theatre
128 Union Theological College
130 Student's Union; Queen's University Travel Centre
131 Elmwood Hall
133 The Bookshop at Queens
134 Post Office
135 Lord Kelvin Statue
136 Europcar
137 Mike's Laundrette
138 Tropical Ravine
139 Ulster Museum
143 Cleanerette Laundrette
146 Eakin Gallery

PUBS & CLUBS
2 The Rotterdam
9 Milk Bar
9 The Kremlin
15 The John Hewitt
17 Parliament Bar
20 Duke of York
26 McHugh's
30 Bittle's Bar
31 Kitchen Bar
129 Beatrice Kennedy's
140 Conor Restaurant
152 Café Zinc
153 The Other Place

44 Tesco
45 Thomas Cook
48 Aer Lingus
51 Old Museum Arts Centre
52 usit NOW
53 British Airways; British Midland
54 Waterstone's
55 Linen Hall Library
56 Belfast Welcome Centre
57 Robinson & Cleaver Building
58 Stationery Office Bookshop
59 Waterfront Hall

were destroyed. When the building was uncovered after cleaning in 1994, the banner had disappeared, a small symbol of a willingness to consider change. It seems that after the city council elections of 2001 nationalist councillors will control City Hall.

The hall is fronted by a statue of a rather dour and 'we are not amused' Queen Victoria. Statues of city mayors also guard the building on Donegall Square North. At the north-eastern corner of the City Hall grounds is a statue of Sir Edward Harland, the Yorkshire-born marine engineer who founded the Harland & Wolff shipyards. In its prime, the shipyard was one of Belfast's biggest businesses and it still survives, if in a much quieter form under a foreign owner. The yard's most famous construction was the ill-fated *Titanic* (see the boxed text 'Titanic' later in the chapter). A memorial to its victims stands on the eastern side of the City Hall.

The Marquess of Dufferin (1826–1902), whose career included postings as ambassador to Turkey, Russia, Paris and Rome, governor-general of Canada and viceroy to India, has an extremely ornate temple-like memorial flanked by an Indian and a Turkish warrior on the western side of the City Hall. He was responsible for adding Burma (now Myanmar) to the British Empire in 1886. Look out, too, for monuments to the United States of America Expeditionary Force, which arrived in Belfast in January 1942, and to the Boer War.

Among other things on the tour of City Hall you get to see the Council Chamber with its red and blue flashing lights to tell councillors when they've overtalked their allotted 10 minutes; a painting of the proclamation of Edward VII outside City Hall (slashed by a visitor in 1991 and now behind glass); and some highly fanciful images in the grey and white marble of the hall.

Linen Hall Library

Opposite City Hall, on Donegall Square North, is the Linen Hall Library (☎ 9032 1707, W www.linenhall.com, 17 Donegall Square North; free; open 9.30am-5.30pm Mon-Fri, 9.30am-4pm Sat). It was established in 1788 to 'improve the mind and excite a spirit of general inquiry'. It's a wonderful place to come in and research or just to browse through a few books.

The library houses some 260,000 books, more than half of which are part of its important Irish and local-studies collection. The political collection consists of pretty much everything that has been written (some 135,000 publications) about Northern Irish politics since 1966. There's also an extensive performing-arts collection covering Irish theatre and actors, and an important historical collection of early Belfast and Ulster printing.

There's nonmember research access to all collections plus a comprehensive computer-based catalogue. Recent refurbishment has seen the creation of a new reading room, a separate performance/lecture space and complete access for visitors with disabilities. The library has a small *cafe* and all the daily newspapers.

Thomas Russell, the first librarian, was a founding member of the United Irishmen and a close friend of Wolfe Tone – a reminder that this movement for independence from Britain had its origins in Belfast. Russell was hanged in 1803 after Robert Emmet's abortive rebellion. For over a century the library was in the White Linen Hall, which was built from 1784 but demolished to make way for the City Hall. The entrance doorway to the present library is draped with stone linen and topped by the Red Hand of Ulster.

Other Donegall Square Buildings

Donegall Square, with the City Hall squarely in the middle, is undoubtedly the centre of Belfast. If you arrive by local bus you're likely to stop here as most local bus services arrive and depart from around the square.

There are a number of interesting buildings overlooking the City Hall from Donegall Square West, but easily the most magnificent is the wonderfully ornate **Scottish Provident Building**, built from 1897 to 1902. It's decorated with a veritable riot of fascinating statuary, including several allusions to the industries that assured Victorian Belfast's prosperity, as well as sphinxes, dolphins and a variety of lions' heads.

The Red Hand of Ulster

The symbol of the province of Ulster is a striking red hand which you'll see displayed on coats of arms, in stained-glass windows and above the Linen Hall Library entrance on Donegall Square North. It's a symbol that both sides have been happy to use in the past, it's even on a few old graves in the Catholic Milltown cemetery. The story goes that way back in the Middle Ages, when Viking raids were a regular occurrence, a fleet of Norse longboats were approaching land. The chief announced that the land would belong to whoever put his hand on it first, whereupon one Viking sliced off his own hand and threw it forwards, thus beating his competitors. Interestingly this particular Viking must have been left handed as it's the right hand that's always depicted. The O'Neill clan later adopted the red hand as their emblem and it went on to become the symbol of Ulster.

The building was the work of the architectural partnership of Young & MacKenzie, who counterbalanced it in 1902 with the **Pearl Assurance Building** on the Donegall Square East corner. Between these two examples of turn-of-the-20th-century extravagance is the equally fine **Robinson & Cleaver Building**, once the Royal Irish Linen Warehouse and then Belfast's finest department store.

The Entries

The area immediately north of High St was the oldest part of Belfast but suffered considerable damage during WWII bombing. The narrow alleyways known as the Entries run off High St and Ann St in the pedestrianised shopping centre. At one time they were bustling commercial and residential centres: **Pottinger's Entry** had 34 houses in 1822. Today pubs are just about all that survive down these hideaways. The **Morning Star** is one of these wonderful old Belfast bars and it's recommended for food, too.

Joy's Entry is named after Francis Joy who founded the *Belfast News Letter* in 1737, the first daily newspaper in the British Isles. It's still in business. One of his grandsons, Henry Joy McCracken, was executed for supporting the 1798 United Irishmen's revolt.

The United Irishmen were founded in 1791 by Wolfe Tone in Peggy Barclay's tavern in **Crown Entry**. They used to meet in **Kelly's Cellars** (1720) on Bank St, off Royal Ave. **White's Tavern** (1630), on **Wine Cellar Entry**, is the oldest tavern in the city and is still a popular lunchtime meeting spot.

At the western end of Ann St is **Arthur Square**, where five pedestrianised streets meet, with a bandstand, buskers, preachers, hawkers and all sorts of other activities. This was once the central traffic junction in the city but the traffic has long been diverted.

Crown Liquor Saloon

Across from the Europa Hotel is the Crown Liquor Saloon (☎ 9027 9901, *46 Great Victoria St*). It was built by Patrick Flanagan in 1885 and displays Victorian architectural flamboyance at its most extravagant. There's a crown in mosaic on the floor at the front entrance. The story goes that the owners had differing political views. The wife was a unionist and wanted to call the hotel the Crown; the husband, a nationalist, would only accept this if a crown mosaic was laid at the front. This allowed nationalist visitors to walk over the crown and unionists to walk around it. It's an early example of voting with your feet so watch what the other customers do.

This pub is on every visitor's itinerary; you need to get there early to have any hope of standing space, let alone a seat. The exterior is decorated with myriad different coloured and shaped tiles, while the interior has a mass of stained and cut glass, marble, mosaic and mahogany furniture. 'Gas' mantles provide atmospheric lighting.

A long, highly decorated bar dominates one side of the pub, while on the other is a row of ornate wooden snugs. The snugs come equipped with gunmetal plates (from the Crimean War) for striking matches and with bells once connected to the bell board above the standing area. This enabled drinkers to order top-ups without leaving their seats. You can no longer do that, but you can have yourself and your pint beamed to audiences around the world via the Crown's live Internet site (Ⓦ www.belfast telegraph.co.uk/crown).

Above the Crown is **Flannigan's** (☎ 9027 9901), another interesting bar with *Titanic* and other maritime memorabilia.

Grand Opera House

One of Belfast's great landmarks is the Grand Opera House (☎ 9024 1919, *Great Victoria St*), across the road from the Crown Liquor Saloon. Opened in 1895, the Opera House was completely refurbished in the 1970s.

It has suffered grievously at the hands of the IRA. A 450kg truck bomb caused extensive damage in December 1991 and a multi-million pound reconstruction had barely been completed before another well loaded truck was parked outside in May 1993. It has been suggested that as the Europa Hotel next door was the home of the media during the Troubles, the IRA brought the bombs to them so they wouldn't have to leave the bar.

The interior has been restored to over-the-top Victoriana, with purple satin in abundance and swirling wood and plasterwork. It's constantly busy with music shows, operas, plays and ballets.

Albert Memorial Clock Tower & Around

WJ Barre's 1867 Albert Memorial Clock Tower, located in Queen's Square, is not so dramatically out of kilter as the famous tower in Pisa, but is, nevertheless, a leaning tower. At the time of writing it was shrouded with scaffolding and tarpaulins while restoration work was being carried out. Albert will not be straightened but its foundations will be strengthened and damaged stonework repaired.

Looking across the River Lagan from the clock tower, eastern Belfast is dominated by the huge yellow cranes of the Harland & Wolff shipyards. The modern Queen Elizabeth Bridge crosses the Lagan just to the south, but immediately south again is **Queen's Bridge** with its ornate lamps. Completed in 1843, this was Sir Charles Lanyon's (the pre-eminent architect of Belfast in its prime) first important Belfast construction.

Many of the buildings around the clock tower are the work of Lanyon. The white stone building immediately north of the clock tower was completed in 1852 by Lanyon as a head office for the **Northern Bank**. Farther north stands **Clifton House**, built in 1774 by Robert Joy (Henry Joy McCracken's uncle) as a poorhouse and the finest surviving 18th-century building in Belfast. East towards the river is the renovated **Custom House**, built by Lanyon in Italianate style between 1854 and 1857. On the waterfront side the pediment carries sculpted portrayals of Britannia, Neptune and Mercury.

Follow the waterfront round to the ferry terminal and the **Harbour Commissioner's Office** (☎ 9055 4422) in Corporation Square. The office interior features striking marble and stained glass as well as art and sculpture inspired by Belfast's maritime history. The captain's table built for the *Titanic* lives unassumingly here. It was completed behind schedule and never made it on board. Guided tours of the office are available during the Belfast City Summerfest (see Special Events later in this chapter). It's also open during European Heritage Weekend, which usually takes place in October or November.

Sinclair Seamen's Church (☎ 9086 8568, *Corporation Square; free; open during services 2pm-5pm Wed, 11.30am-7pm Sun*), next to the Harbour Commissioner's Office, was built by Charles Lanyon in 1857 and was intended to meet the spiritual needs of sailors coming into the port of Belfast. Part church, part maritime museum, it has a pulpit made from a ship's prow and an organ which sports starboard and port lights.

Ulster Bank & Around

The grandiose 1860 Ulster Bank building survived the wartime bombing that obliterated much of this area. Currently closed to the public, the imposing building has iron railings decorated with the Red Hand of Ulster, cast-iron lamp standards, soaring columns and sculpted figures depicting Britannia, Justice and Commerce. The rooftop figures were by Thomas Fitzpatrick, who was also responsible for the carvings on the Custom House. Inside, the building is even more impressive, with cute blue cherubs playing instruments.

At the junction of Waring and Donegall Sts is the deserted 1822 **Commercial Building**, easily identified by the prominent name of the Northern Whig Printing Company. Opposite is the **Belfast Bank Building**, now occupied by the Northern Bank and the oldest public building in the city (although bearing little relationship to its original design). The building started life as a single-storey market house in 1769, became the Assembly Rooms, with the addition of an upper storey, in 1777 and in 1845 was remodelled by Charles Lanyon to become the bank building.

The former home of the **Belfast News Letter** (59 Donegall St) is an 1873 building decorated with bas-relief portraits of literary figures. The imposing **St Anne's Cathedral** (☎ 9033 2328, Donegall St; admission by donation; open 10am-4.45pm Mon-Fri, 9.30am-3.45pm Sat) was started in 1899 but did not reach its final form until 1981 when the North Transept with its imposing Celtic cross was completed. There are some interesting design features within the cathedral starting with the black and white marble entrance floor. It symbolises the path to eternal life. Follow the black and you come up to a dead end, follow the white and you're all right. If only life were that black and white. The 10 pillars of the nave have capitals carved to represent different aspects of the life in the city including the arts, shipbuilding, science, freemasonry and even one to women. The only tomb in the place is that of Edward Carson.

The **Bank of Ireland Building**, a fine example of 1920s Art Deco, is elegantly placed at the junction of North St and Royal Ave.

Lagan Weir & Lookout

Completed in 1994 at a cost of £14 million, the Lagan Weir was the first stage of Belfast's government-initiated Laganside Development Project, an ambitious scheme involving the regeneration of docklands, other riverside areas as well as the Cathedral Quarter.

Years of neglect and industrial decline had turned the River Lagan, the original lifeblood of the city, into smelly, unsightly mudflats. The weir, along with a program of dredging and aeration, has improved the water quality and increased the depth of the river, so much so that salmon, eels and sea trout now migrate up the river. Fishing stands have even been built along the Annadale Embankment, south-east of the university.

At night the weir is floodlit using special-effect gas-filter blue lights.

The **Lagan Lookout Visitor Centre** (☎ 9031 5444, 1 Donegall Quay; adult/concession £1.50/0.75; Lookout open 11am-5pm Mon-Fri, noon-5pm Sat & 2pm-5pm Sun Apr-Sept; 11am-3.30pm Tues-Fri, 1pm-4.30pm Sat & 2pm-4.30pm Sun Oct-Mar) offers a state-of-the-art explanation of how the weir works and why it was needed, with interactive computers to bring things to life. The centre also has displays on the progress of the entire Laganside Project.

For details of the boat tours that depart from here see the Organised Tours section later in this chapter.

Laganside

The second stage of Belfast's ambitious Laganside Project saw the development of Lanyon Place with the 2235-capacity Waterfront Hall, British Telecom's Riverside Tower and the 'jewel in the crown' of the city, the Belfast Hilton, which opened in 1998. Projects completed since then include several clusters of Nineties-style riverside apartments (almost all sold before completion) and the restoration of listed buildings, such as McHugh's bar and restaurant on Queen's Square, the ornate Victorian warehouses now housing the McCausland Hotel on Victoria St and the Albert Memorial Clock Tower.

Starting at Donegall Quay, near the Lagan Lookout, is an art trail leading you to nine sculptures. The Big Fish, beached outside the Lookout, is the most prominent but then down outside the Waterfront are a herd of bronze sheep and their drover off to market. The Lookout and the Belfast Welcome Centre have a leaflet on the trail.

St George's Market (see the St George's

Market section) has been refurbished and the former gasworks, immediately to the east of Donegall Pass, is still under development. New parks and public spaces linking all these areas are being established and pathways along both banks of the river have been completed. Footbridges linking Lanyon Place to East Bridge St and across to the eastern bank are completed. By the end of 2002 all six of Belfast's bridges will be transformed at night by 'futuristic blue and white lights'.

Odyssey Complex

Opened in early 2001, the Odyssey Complex (W www.odysseyarena.com) is a £91-million sporting and cultural complex built at Abercorn Basin on the eastern side of the river across from Clarendon Dock. The complex features an amazing science centre – W5 – a 10,000-seater sports and entertainment arena, an IMAX cinema and a Hard Rock Cafe. Odyssey is a five-minute walk from the Laganside Bus Centre or the Bridge End train station. There's also a regular shuttle bus operating between the city centre and the Odyssey Arena an hour before doors open, but strangely for only 30 minutes after an event finishes.

W5 Also known as whowhatwherewhenwhy, W5 (☎ 9046 7700, W www.w5online .co.uk; adult/child/family £5/3/14; open 10am-6pm Mon-Fri, noon-6pm Sat & Sun) is the brand new discovery centre in the Odyssey Complex. It's aimed at children of all ages. Of particular interest is a flight of musical stairs, as you walk or run up and down they sing out a particular note. Energetic stair climbing can produce interesting compositions. You can also compose on the 'air harp' by biffing the ends of plastic tubes with a foam rubber bat.

Borrow an eight-year-old and visit the special children's section. Little kiddies put on hard hats and safety vests to build a house and then fed up with that can put on waterproof gear and go and play with water.

Failing all that they have all manner of model building sets where you can design and build things, such as racing cars with motors or reconstruct the *Titanic*.

St George's Market

Elegant St George's Market (☎ 9043 5704, cnr Oxford & May Sts; free; open 7am-3pm Fri) was built in 1896 for the sale of fruit, butter, eggs and poultry, and is the oldest continually operated market in Ireland. Restored at a cost of £3.5 million in 1999, the market now has additional retail and exhibition space. Market day (fresh flowers, fruit, vegetables and fish, plus general household and second-hand goods) is Friday.

The Ha'penny Fair is held on the first Sunday of every month with antique and collectables stalls, arts and crafts plus street entertainers.

SOUTH OF THE CENTRE
University Rd

Heading down University Rd from Bradbury Place, on the right is the 1887 **Moravian Church**. A left turn takes you into Lower Crescent, beside the 1887 **Crescent Church**, with its instantly recognisable skeletal tower. Walking round the green behind the church takes you past mid-19th-century neoclassical terraces, built by Robert Corry, a local entrepreneur, and possibly designed by Charles Lanyon. Across University Rd, WJ Barre's **Methodist Church** of 1865 completes the happy trio of University Rd churches. Continuing along University Rd the next street left is Mount Charles, with a group of stylish **villas** dating from 1842.

Across University Rd from the college building is the modern **Student's Union**, a stark contrast to the exotic **Elmwood Hall**. Built by John Corry, the architect son of Robert Corry, the Italian-inspired church building is now used as a university concert hall.

Ulster Museum

The Ulster Museum (☎ 9038 3000, Stranmillis Rd; bus Nos 69 & 71 from city centre; free; open 10am-5pm Mon-Fri, 1pm-5pm Sat & 2pm-5pm Sun) is set in the Botanic Gardens near the university. As well as galleries on early Ireland, there are good displays on dinosaurs, steam and industrial machines, natural history and Irish painting. There's also a section on Irish linen, an interesting glass collection and several galleries devoted to changing exhibitions.

Items from the 1588 wreck of the *Girona*, a Spanish Armada vessel, are a highlight. The sumptuous gold jewellery found on board includes a ruby-encrusted salamander (mythical creatures who could survive fire – a very real hazard on board a wooden fighting ship) and an inscribed gold ring. Up to 20 Armada ships were wrecked along the coast after being caught in severe autumn storms as they attempted to return to Spain.

The museum was designed in 1911 but not completed until late in the 1920s. An extension was added in 1971 and the complex includes a shop and the *Collections Cafe*, overlooking the Botanic Gardens. The museum also runs a program of weekend activities, lectures, poetry readings, films and talks.

Queen's University

Just over 1km south of the City Hall is the muted red-and-yellow-brick Queen's College building of Queen's University, Northern Ireland's most prestigious university. Catering for around 8000 students, it has a particularly strong reputation in medicine, engineering and law. Although the plan of the college building is based on Magdalen College in Oxford, once again Charles Lanyon was responsible for the design. Queen Victoria was present for the laying of the foundation stone in 1845 and the building was completed in 1849.

The lofty entrance hall leads into the quadrangle. On the southern side a chimney has brickwork spelling out 'VR 1848' (Victoria Regina). Beyond the college building is the Old Library, designed by Lanyon's assistant WH Lynn and built in 1864.

Surrounding the university are quiet, tree-lined streets with small cafes full of students. **University Square**, on the northern side of the campus, dates from 1848 to 1853 and is one of the finest terraced streets in Ireland. It was once known as the Harley St of Belfast and is now owned by the university. Behind the Queen's College building is the colonnaded **Union Theological College**, originally the Presbyterian College. It opened in 1853 and

was also a Lanyon design. From the partition of Ireland it served as the Northern Ireland Parliament until 1932, when Stormont Castle took over.

Botanic Gardens

The well tended Botanic Gardens (☎ *9032 4902, Stranmillis Rd; free; open 8am-sunset)* are a pleasant oasis just a stroll away from the university and the busy Golden Mile area. Once privately owned, the gardens date from 1827. Their centrepiece is the fine cast-iron and curvilinear glass **Palm House** (*open 10am-noon & 1pm-5pm Mon-Fri, 2pm-5pm Sat, Sun & bank holidays; closes at 4pm in winter)*. Built between 1839 and 1852, it houses palms and other hot-house flora. Even with the involvement of Charles Lanyon, the Palm House was essentially the work of Richard Turner of Dublin, who also built glasshouses in the Dublin Botanic Gardens and at Kew Gardens in London, and worked on the 1851 Crystal Palace in London.

Also in the Botanic Gardens is the unique enclosed **Tropical Ravine** (*open same hours as the Palm House)*, which was designed by the garden's curator Charles McKimm and completed in 1889. A raised balcony overlooks a jungle of tropical plants (including ferns, orchids, lilies, bananas and cinnamon) growing in a sunken glen. There's also a pool full of terrapins.

Just inside the gardens at the Stranmillis Rd gate is a statue of Belfast-born Lord Kelvin, who invented the Kelvin scale that measures temperatures from absolute zero (-273°C or 0°K).

Belfast has a number of other parks and gardens in and around the city, all of which are mentioned in the booklet *Parks of Belfast* available from the tourist office.

Sandy Row

Just a block west of Great Victoria St is the curving Sandy Row. This used to be the main road south out of the city and is still a working-class Protestant enclave, wedged in beside the wealthier Golden Mile area. Around here you'll find red-white-and-blue kerbstones and unionist murals, just like on Shankill Rd in West Belfast. Van Morrison

BELFAST

fans may remember that he wandered 'up and down the Sandy Row' on his 1968 album *Astral Weeks*.

ART GALLERIES

Belfast's principal modern-art gallery is the **Ormeau Baths Gallery** (☎ *9032 1402, 18a Ormeau Ave; free; open 10am-6pm Tues-Sat)*, near the BBC building. The spacious galleries show contemporary Irish and international work in all media.

The **Old Museum Arts Centre** (☎ *9023 3332,* W *www.oldmuseumartscentre.org, 7 College Square North; free; open 10am-5.30pm Mon-Sat)*, a fine building dating back to 1831, houses visiting exhibitions of modern art, as well as hosting theatre and dance performances, arts workshops, storytelling and poetry events.

Smaller galleries include the Fenderesky Gallery at the **Crescent Arts Centre** (☎ *9024 2338, 2-4 University Rd; free; open 11.30am-5pm Tues-Sat)*; **Bell Gallery** (☎ *9066 2998, 13 Adelaide Park; free; open 9am-5pm Mon-Thur & 9am-4pm Friday)*, south-west of the university; and **Eakin Gallery** (☎ *9066 8522,* W *www.eakingallery.co.uk, 237 Lisburn Rd; open 9am-5.30pm Mon-Sat)* for modern and traditional Irish art.

WEST BELFAST

The Catholic Falls Rd and the Protestant Shankill Rd in West Belfast have been battlefronts for the Troubles.

Despite its reputation the area is quite safe for visitors. The old Victorian slums and the bulk of the 1960s tower blocks have been replaced by greatly improved public housing. New homes have even appeared in areas close to the wall where not so long ago petrol bombs constantly flew.

A reason for venturing into West Belfast is to see the powerful murals that chart the history of the political conflict as well as the political passions of the moment (see the boxed text 'The Murals of Northern Ireland').

West Belfast grew up around the linen mills that propelled the city into its Industrial Revolution prosperity. It was an area of low-cost, working-class housing and even in the Victorian era was divided along religious lines. The advent of the Troubles in 1968 solidified the sectarian division and the construction of the Westlink Motorway neatly separated the area – and its problems – from central Belfast. Since the start of the Troubles population migrations have exacerbated community divisions.

Getting There & Away

A recommended way to see the Falls and Shankill Rds is by an organised black taxi tour (see Organised Tours later in this chapter). The cabs visit most of the more spectacular murals in and around West Belfast, as well as taking in the Peace Line (where you can write a message on the wall) and other significant sites, such as the new Sinn Féin headquarters and its souvenir-cum-bookshop. It's also a good way of getting a colourful rundown on the history of the area.

There's nothing to stop you visiting under your own steam, either walking or using the People's Taxis along the Falls or Shankill Rds. These recycled London cabs were used by the Catholic and Protestant communities as alternative bus services at the height of the Troubles. Like buses, the taxis pick up and drop passengers as they go. Fares are 60p to £1. Shankill Rd People's Taxis (with orange licence discs) go from North St, Falls Rd People's Taxis (with green licence discs) from Castle St; both sites are close to the modern Castle Court Shopping Centre. The taxis stick to their own roads, but there is a changeover spot on both roads so that passengers can pick up a cab going to the other road.

Alternatively, bus Nos 12 to 15 or 532 to 538 will take you down the Falls Rd; bus Nos 39, 55, 63 and 73 go down the Shankill.

Falls Rd

A short distance west of the centre, the infamous **Divis Flats** take their name from Divis Mountain, the highest summit in the hills around Belfast. They were constructed in the late 1960s during the worldwide mania for high-rise public housing and, as elsewhere in the world, they quickly became 'vertical slums'. During their plan-

The Murals of Northern Ireland

Wander around any of the staunchly loyalist or nationalist areas of Northern Ireland and you'll soon come across the murals. These vivid and often extremely well-painted political messages can be found on ends of houses, on walls or industrial buildings – anywhere there's an empty space.

The mural tradition in the loyalist camp began in 1908, with the appearance of exultant little King Billys celebrating victory at the 1690 Battle of the Boyne. From the mid-1980s, with the signing of the Anglo-Irish Agreement, the dominant image almost to the point of monopoly was of armed loyalists posing with weapons or in action and even the announcement of a loyalist cease-fire in October 1994 did little to change this. These paramilitary murals served to remind supporters and opponents that the armed organisations had not gone away.

By the summer of 2000 some variation in the themes began to appear, with Ulster-Scots Presidents of the United States, St Patrick, the mythological hero Finn McCool and Princess Diana (with a little bit of cleavage) represented on the walls. Heavy-metal group Iron Maiden's 'Eddie' was even recast as an avenging loyalist.

You'll find loyalist murals on and between Shankill and Crumlin Rds, around Newtownards Rd in the east and in Sandy Row and Donegall Pass in the south.

Republicans were late to take up mural painting. One reason for this was the enthusiasm with which public spaces were policed by the RUC. The 'armed struggle' of the IRA was represented, though it never monopolised the imagery to the extent paramilitary images did on the loyalist side. The republican hunger strike of 1981 saw the emergence of hundreds of murals, drawing support for the hunger strikers, one of the most famous, near the Sinn Féin offices on the Falls Rd, being that of Bobby Sands.

After the hunger strike, republican muralists broadened their subject matter to cover wider political issues, Irish legends and historical events. The mural off the Falls Rd commemorating the 150th anniversary of the Potato Famine is particularly powerful; another is the mural celebrating women, children and workers on Ormeau Rd. Elaborate, colourful images from Celtic mythology feature in several by well-known muralist Gerry Kelly, who learned his craft in the Maze, the political prison just to the south of Lisburn.

Republican muralists were also able to point to comparisons between their goals and those of groups elsewhere such as the African National Congress, Palestine Liberation Organization and Sandinistas. In addition, republican murals often related directly to current political issues, such as elections, or other political campaigns, such as opposition to plastic bullets.

With the republican cease-fire of August 1994, the 'armed struggle' images virtually ceased. Initially, the murals stated republican demands in the peace process: prisoner releases, British army withdrawal, disbandment of the RUC, and so on. After the Good Friday Agreement of 1998, the murals came to demand the implementation of the Agreement and, in particular, police reform and the protection of nationalists from sectarian attacks. Look for murals on the Falls Rd, in Ballymurphy, as well as the area around Beechmount Ave, Donegall Rd and Shaw's Rd in West Belfast and on New Lodge Rd in the north.

Bill Rolston, author of the 'Drawing Support' series on murals in Northern Ireland, with additional information by Patrick Horton

BELFAST

ning and construction they were actually welcomed by local residents and churches as an alternative to substandard housing and a way of retaining the local community.

The Troubles quickly turned the flats into the scene of many confrontations between residents and the army. Today most of the flats have been replaced with modern housing, but the Divis still stands. At the start of the Troubles the Irish Republican Socialist Party colonised its roof, winning it the nickname 'The Planet of the IRPS'. When the

British army took their place, this was changed, predictably, to 'The Planet of the Apes'. The top storeys remain occupied by the British army, who come and go by helicopter. There are no plans to tear the block down and, now refurbished, they're quite liked by their occupants.

Across Divis St a huge blue-and-white **mural of the Madonna and Child** decorates the former Brickfields Barracks, the first purpose-built police barracks in Belfast.

From Divis Tower, Divis St runs west, becoming the Falls Rd, which runs in a south-westerly direction through the area known as the Lower Falls.

If you turn right (north) off the Falls Rd into the side streets you'll quickly come up against the **Peace Line**, a rough corrugated-iron wall set up in September 1969 as a 'temporary' barrier to separate Catholics from their Protestant neighbours. In places you could almost lean out of a back window and touch it. There are several gates in the wall, overlooked by cameras, which remain open during the day.

The Falls Rd passes the **Royal Victoria Hospital**, which developed a well earned reputation for dealing with medical emergencies during the 1970s. Look at the blue railings and the way they wave along the front of the hospital and also at the top and bottom where there are alternate yellow 'X's and 'Y's. The railings represent the DNA helix and incorporated into them are eleven laser-cut portraits of people representing life from birth to 100 years.

In a former Presbyterian church, a block or so past the hospital, is the Irish language and cultural centre, **Cultúrlann MacAdam ÓFiaich** (☎ 9023 9303, 216 Falls Rd; open 9am-5.30pm Mon-Fri, 10am-5.30pm Sat). It's a cosy, welcoming place with a wide selection of books on Ireland, Irish music tapes and CDs, and an excellent cafe (see Outside the Centre under Places to Eat later in this chapter). The centre also runs monthly music and poetry events and is a good place to find out what's going on in West Belfast.

All along the Falls you'll come across republican murals, with more murals, slogans

and graffiti in the Ballymurphy area off the Whiterock Rd. Beyond the Lower Falls the road is less interesting until it reaches the **Milltown Cemetery** (see the boxed text 'Sectarian Plots'), the main site for republican burials.

The junction of Glen and Andersonstown Rds marks the end of the Falls Rd with a strongly fortified police/army base looking down the Falls from its position in the fork. It's one of four 'forts' in West Belfast. Andersonstown (Andytown) is about 3km from the centre and beyond here is Twinbrook, another staunchly republican suburb and the former home of Bobby Sands, the first 1981 hunger striker to die. In the development where he lived, one end of a block has been turned into a memorial.

Shankill Rd

Shankill Rd begins not far west of St Anne's Cathedral and runs north-west towards the Crumlin Rd. Although the Shankill has been given less media and tourist attention than the Falls, it's also of interest. The street's name comes from *sean chill* meaning 'old church'. The Shankill feels more a foreboding place, as though under siege, and rather different from the more outward feel of the Falls Rd. Loyalist/Protestant cultures seem to have difficulty in presenting their side of the story whereas the Nationalists/Republicans/Catholics seem a dab hand at 'propaganda'. At the far end of Shankill Rd, look out for **St Matthew's**, a church built in a shamrock shape in 1872.

Beyond Shankill Rd, about half a kilometre up Glencairn Rd, is **Fernhill House: The People's Museum** (☎ 9071 5599, Glencairn Rd; bus No 63 from City Hall; adult/child £2/1; open 9am-5pm Mon-Sat, 1pm-4pm Sun). Set up as a 1930s Shankill house, the museum has exhibitions detailing the Home Rule crisis, the two World Wars and the Orange Order. Unfortunately it seems to be the only celebration of Unionist history and culture open to the public in Belfast.

OUTSIDE THE CENTRE
Harland & Wolff Shipyards

Although you can't easily visit the Harland

Sectarian Plots

Cemeteries always reveal something about the health and wealth of a city. In Belfast's case they also tell us something about the politics.

The City Cemetery, Falls Rd, was opened in 1869 because the Famine had already filled up the other graveyards. Nowadays it covers 99 acres and Travellers, Jews, Protestants and Catholics are all buried here – in their own sections. Much is overgrown and you'll find rare varieties of roses here, planted in the past and left to their own devices while elsewhere they would have died out.

There's humour in death here. There are such epitaphs as 'Beam me up Lord', 'I wish I was fishing' and 'I told you I was sick' to be found on headstones.

There's also concealed sectarianism. When part of the cemetery was allocated to the Catholics, a 3m-high wall was erected to divide the Protestant and Catholic dead. However this wall, like the dead it was to separate, was built underground. The only evidence of it is a mown-grass divide running straight through the old part of the cemetery. Presumably on one side there are Protestant worms and on the other Catholic worms.

Headstone inscriptions show that before partition it was not incongruous to be both a Protestant and an Irish patriot, indeed, many Ulster folk saw themselves as Irish. There are men buried here who fought all over the Empire for the British but yet their headstones or memorials have Irish references. One describes an occupant as a loyal Irish patriot and also lists him as Grandmaster of the Orange Order.

In this cemetery you'll find the men who bankrolled the arming of the Ulster Volunteer Force (UVF) in 1912, those who did the gun running and those who trained the UVF.

The grave of William James Pirrie, who signed the contract for the *Titanic* with the White Star Line on behalf of Harland & Wolff, is here. There's also a memorial to his nephew, who designed the ship, but who was drowned when it sank. Pirrie was sick, stayed at home and lived a while longer.

Milltown cemetery, farther south-west along the Falls Rd, lies under the omnipresent gaze of a large fortified police barracks. Here you'll find the dead republicans, many who died very young, their victims and also victims of the RUC.

Two large green areas stand out, seemingly unused and without headstones. These are the mass graves of victims of the 1918 flu epidemic, which killed 86,000 people. No-one dares reuse this land less any disturbance reactivates the virus. There is however one headstone here marking the grave of a bishop buried among them. It was his request to be buried here because when people prayed for him they'd also be praying for those around him.

There are graves of republicans of every generation, from the civil war of the 1920s, IRA campaigns of the 1940s and the later Troubles. As in life, schisms in the republican paramilitaries are represented in this cemetery. There's an official IRA plot, an Irish National Liberation Association plot and the Provisional IRA plot, which contains the graves of the hunger strikers including Bobby Sands. Likely as not, as you wander around someone will come up to you and show you where to look. They may even tell you their own story, tragic or not.

& Wolff shipyards they certainly dominate eastern Belfast. The giant cranes known as **Samson and Goliath**, one of them over 100m high and 140m long, straddle a 550m-long shipbuilding dock capable of handling ships of up to 200,000 tonnes. The shipyard was founded in 1833, but it was under the Yorkshire engineer Edward Harland, who recruited the German marine draughtsman Gustav Wolff in 1858, that it assumed its leading role in Victorian shipbuilding. There's a statue of Sir Edward Harland by the City Hall. The *Titanic* was built here and more recent constructions have included oil tankers and passenger vessels, including the *Canberra* in 1960.

With substantial British government support the shipyard managed to continue

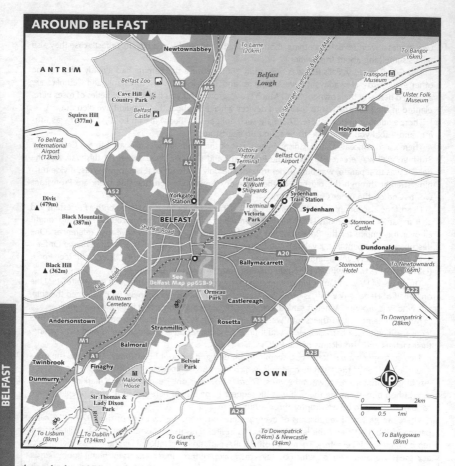

AROUND BELFAST

through the 1970s and 1980s, when most European shipbuilding crumbled before Asian competition. Current employment is at a fraction of its former levels. In its heyday 60,000 people worked here and Harland & Wolff was a prime example of institutionalised employment discrimination – of that huge number only a few hundred would have been Catholic. By the early 1990s workers numbered less than 2000 and now are about 500. Work at the yards is primarily maintenance and repair rather than new construction, but two British navy vessels are being built here.

Stormont Castle

Situated 8km east of the centre, off the A20, Stormont Castle *(Upper Newtownards Rd; bus Nos 16, 17 & 20 from Donegall Square West)* is home to the new Northern Ireland Assembly elected in June 1998. The lavishly restored neoclassical mansion stands at the end of an imposing avenue in the middle of 120 hectares of parkland. Built in 1932, this is where the Northern Ireland Parliament met until 1972, when power was transferred to London.

You can walk in the extensive grounds, but visits to the Parliament buildings must

The *Titanic*

JANE SMITH

Late on 14 April 1912, the world's largest passenger liner hit an iceberg on its maiden voyage to New York. She took just three hours to sink and 1500 of her passengers died.

There is a timeless fascination with the craft as expressed in several films, various *Titanic* societies over the world and even a town named Titanic in the USA. There are still heated debates over design faults, the quality of the hull steel and over what the captain of the *California*, the nearest ship to the disaster, did or might have done if the wireless hadn't been shut down for the night.

In July 1908 Harland & Wolff and the White Star Line signed a contract for two vessels. The keel of No 400 (to become the *Olympic*) was laid in December 1908, the second, to become the *Titanic*, in March 1909. The *Titanic* was designed to be unsinkable, she had double hulls and watertight doors to isolate flooded compartments; with two flooded the ship would still stay afloat. The designers didn't count on an iceberg that would breach six of those compartments.

It took two years to build the *Titanic*. Shipbuilding was a dangerous business; 450 men were injured and 17 killed in building the ship. On 31 May 1911, the same day her sister ship began her maiden voyage to America, the *Titanic* was launched. It took a further year to complete the fitting out.

Two official enquiries, one British the other American, were carried out. They made various recommendations with regard to maritime safety that were quickly implemented (and saved lives during WWI). Then WWI came and interest in the *Titanic* waned until Walter Lord's book, *A Night to Remember,* was published in 1955; it was subsequently made into a film (film buffs say that it is the best). This generated new interest in the disaster that led in 1985 to the discovery of the *Titanic* in its watery grave. There has been rumour of a *Titanic II* being built, but it's just that – a rumour.

What of its sister ship, the *Olympic*? She had an undistinguished career, first as a luxury liner and then war service as a troopship in which she rammed and sank a German submarine. After WWI the *Olympic* took up her old trade again and was eventually withdrawn and scrapped in 1935. Had it not been for that iceberg the same less tragic fate would probably have met the *Titanic*.

Cave Hill Country Park

Cave Hill Country Park (☎ *9077 6925, Antrim Rd; bus Nos 8 to 10 & 45 to 51 from Donegall Square West; free; open 7.30am-dusk daily)* covers 300 hectares of northern Belfast. Walks through the grounds are waymarked and it's a pleasant stroll to the zoo or Belfast Castle. Cave Hill is 355m high; from the top there are panoramic views over Belfast, Belfast Lough and Scotland on a clear day.

The park contains evidence of prehistoric occupation in the form of several *ráths* (circular forts) and a *crannóg* (an artificial island made in a lake). On top of Cave Hill one such ringfort is known as McArt's Fort where members of the United Irishmen, including Wolfe Tone, looked down over the city in 1795 and pledged to struggle for Irish independence.

The peak was originally named after a 9th-century Ulster king, Matudhain, a name that gradually became corrupted to Ben Madigan. Its profile, which dominates the Belfast skyline, is colloquially known as 'Napoleon's Nose'. In previous centuries Cave Hill was a popular site for lighting Halloween bonfires and for rolling hand-painted eggs downhill at Easter. To the north of McArt's Fort are five man-made caves, some of them accessible. To the south side there's a disused limestone quarry.

The country park encompasses two nature

BELFAST

reserves, at Ballyaghagan and Hazelwood. There are five park entrances: beside Belfast Castle and the zoo; at Carr's Glen Linear Park, Ballysillan Rd; at Upper Cave Hill Rd; and in the Upper Hightown Rd.

For children there's the **Cave Hill Adventure Playground** (*☎ 9037 1013; admission £1.30; open daily Apr-Sept; Sat & Sun rest of year*) with all sorts of activities.

Belfast Castle On the slopes of Cave Hill stands Belfast Castle (*☎ 9077 6925,* W *www .belfastcastle.co.uk, Antrim Rd; free; open 9am-10.30pm Mon-Sat, 9am-6pm Sun*). There has been a 'Belfast Castle' since the late 12th century, but this particular model was only built, in the then-fashionable Scottish Baronial style, in 1870. The castle was presented to the City of Belfast in 1934 and became a fashionable venue for weddings after WWII.

Extensive renovation of the castle between 1978 and 1988 left the interior modern and comfortable rather than inspiring. Upstairs is the small Cave Hill Heritage Centre with displays on the folklore, history, archaeology and natural history of the area (there's also a rooftop camera, similar to those on RUC guardposts, you can play with) and the Ben Madigan restaurant (open for Sunday lunch only). Downstairs is the Cellar Restaurant (see Outside the Centre under Places to Eat later in this chapter), an adjoining bar and a small antiques shop.

Legend has it that the castle's residents will experience good fortune only as long as a white cat lives there, a tale commemorated in the formal gardens by nine portrayals of cats in mosaic, painting, sculpture and garden furniture.

Belfast Zoo Belfast Zoo (*☎ 9077 6277, Antrim Rd; adult/concession £5.80/2.90, children under 4 & senior citizens free; open 10am-5pm daily Apr-Sept; 10am-2.30pm daily rest of year*) is an exceptionally good one and has aggressively pursued a policy of building new and large enclosures for its exhibits. The sea lion and penguin pool with its underwater viewing is particularly good. Some of the more unusual animals include

tamarins, spectacled bears and red pandas, but children flock to the meerkats and to the ring-tailed lemur colony.

Malone House and Barnett Demesne

About 5km south of the centre, Malone House (*☎ 9068 1246, Upper Malone Rd; bus Nos 70 & 71 from centre; free; open 9am-5pm Mon-Sat*) is a late-Georgian mansion in the grounds of Barnett Demesne. Built in the 1820s for local merchant William Legge, the house is used for receptions and lectures, has a very good restaurant and the Higgin Gallery, which hosts painting exhibitions.

The surrounding gardens are planted with azaleas and rhododendrons. Some of the paths criss-crossing the 41-hectare estate lead down to the recently reopened Lagan Towpath, which follows the river all the way to Lisburn.

Sir Thomas & Lady Dixon Park

Almost adjoining Barnett Demesne is Sir Thomas and Lady Dixon Park (*Upper Malone Rd; free; open daylight hours year round*), which consists of rolling meadows, woodland, riverside fields and formal gardens. The main drawcard is the spectacular City of Belfast International Rose Garden, which contains more than 20,000 blooms. Among other displays, a spiral-shaped garden traces the development of the rose from early shrub roses up to modern hybrids. The roses are in bloom from late July. The park also contains a walled garden, a Japanese-style garden, a children's playground and a cafe.

ORGANISED TOURS
Walking Tours

The Old Town of 1660–1685 (*☎ 9024 6609*) 1½-hour tour £4. 2pm Sat June-Sept. Departing from the Belfast Welcome Centre, this tour traces the original ramparts of the city and thus the origins of Belfast.

Bailey's Historical Pub Tours (*☎ 9268 3665*) £5. 7pm Thur & 4pm Sat, May-Oct. This tour takes in six of the city's historic pubs, including the fabulous Crown Liquor

Saloon. Tours depart from Flannigan's on Great Victoria St. The very knowledgeable tour guides divulge the secrets of Belfast's pubs and there's the chance to sample the beers and possibly listen to some music.

Belfast City Centre Walk (☎ 9049 1469) 1½-hour tour £4. 2pm Fri July-Sept. This tour wanders around the Victorian city centre and Laganside. It departs from the Belfast Welcome Centre.

Blackstaff Way (☎ 9029 2631) £2. 11am Sat June-Sept. This is a fascinating tour leading through the heart of the city along the route of the Blackstaff River, which was channelled underground in 1881 after becoming so polluted that it was generally referred to as 'The Nuisance'. The tour leaves from the Belfast Welcome Centre.

During the Féile an Phobail (West Belfast Festival) in August and occasionally at other times there are tours of the Falls Rd cemeteries. Check with the Belfast Welcome Centre for details.

Bus Tours

Citybus (☎ 9045 8484) runs two tours. Its 'original' tour has multilingual commentary and runs Monday and Friday for three hours. It takes in the city centre, shipyards, Queen's University, the Ulster Museum, Botanic Gardens and Stormont Castle. It leaves from Castle Place outside the main post office at noon and costs £10.

Citybus also offers a 1¾-hour 'Through the Millennium Tour' (£8), which takes in the city sights, the Shankill and Falls Rds murals, St Anne's Cathedral, the shipyards and Belfast Castle. Tours leave Castle Place at noon daily except Monday and Friday.

Belfast City Tours (☎ 7130 9051) 1½-hour tour £3.50. Daily by arrangement. Northern Ireland Tours and Guides runs a coach tour taking in the city centre, Stormont, Belfast Castle and Harland & Wolff. These are tours for groups (minimum four), but individuals can phone to join an existing tour.

Taxi Tours

Black taxi tours focusing on West Belfast, the murals and some of the major city sights are being offered by an increasing number of local cabbies. These tours are likely to vary a bit in quality and content, but in general they're an intimate (cabs take four to seven people) and entertaining way to see the city, and can easily be tailor-made. Tours are best organised through the Belfast Welcome Centre or any of the city's independent hostels. The original *Black Taxi Tour* (☎ 9064 2264, Ⓦ *www.belfasttours.com*), run by Michael Johnson, has been highly recommended and costs £8 per person with a minimum of three people.

The *Belfast International Youth Hostel* (☎ 9032 4733, 22-32 Donegall Rd) runs its own two-hour tour (£7.50) of West Belfast that has been recommended by several readers. Tours leave at 10.30am daily; booking is required.

Boat Tours

A one-hour cruise on board *The Joyce* (☎ 9033 0844) takes you upstream to Stranmillis, passing many of the new developments on the way. It departs from near the Lagan Weir and costs £4/3 adult/concession; telephone for cruise information.

SPECIAL EVENTS

See also the Public Holidays & Special Events section of the Facts for the Visitor chapter.

The Belfast Marathon takes place on the May bank holiday (the first Monday in May). Runners from across the globe come to compete but it's also a people's event, something to get involved in and run as far and as fast as you want. Contact the Belfast Welcome Centre for details.

St Patrick's Day, 17 March, is a celebration of Ireland's national saint. There are citywide events.

The Cathedral Quarter Arts Festival (☎ 9023 2403, Ⓦ www.cqaf.com) is 12 days of theatre, music, poetry, street theatre and art exhibitions in and around the Cathedral Quarter. It's a brand new festival, held in early May, that's a marker for the new liveliness of the city.

The Belfast City Summerfest (☎ 9032 0202) takes place during May (dates vary from year to year) and includes everything from classical and traditional music concerts to community events and the Lord Mayor's Show. Several buildings are opened to the public for guided tours.

Twelfth of July Orange Parades take place in many parts of Northern Ireland to celebrate the anniversary of the 1690 Battle of the Boyne. Contrary to what many visitors might expect, the vast majority are peaceful and colourful events.

The Belfast Folk Festival (☎ 9074 6021), featuring local, national and international performers, takes place on selected weekends throughout the summer and includes music workshops and *ceilidhs*. Check at the Belfast Welcome Centre, or The Rotterdam bar (see Entertainment later in the chapter), for details.

Féile an Phobail (☎ 9031 3440) takes place in West Belfast during the first week of August. Said to be the largest community festival in Ireland, events include an opening carnival parade, street parties, theatre performances, concerts and historical tours of the City and Milltown cemeteries.

The Belfast Festival at Queen's (☎ 9066 7687), the second-largest arts festival in the UK, is an extravaganza of theatre, music, dance, comedy and visual art taking place in and around Queen's University during three weeks in November.

Halloween, between October 28 and 31, conjures up a 'spectre' of activities over the whole city with a carnival parade, ghost tours and fireworks.

PLACES TO STAY

Accommodation options in Belfast have increased substantially with plenty of new developments to come. At the top end, the Belfast Hilton offers 195 rooms, while there are several hostels for budget travellers to choose from. City B&Bs haven't multiplied as much and so tend to be expensive – £20 per person is the best you're likely to find. Book ahead in the summer or during busy festival times.

Hostels

City Centre There are four hostels in the centre of Belfast.

Arnie's Backpackers (☎ 9024 2867, 63 Fitzwilliam St) Dorms £7-8.50. This long-established hostel is centrally located in the university area. There are decent laundry and cooking facilities, and plenty of lively bars and restaurants nearby.

The Ark (☎ 9032 9626, fax 9032 9647, Ⓦ www.harth.co.uk, 18 University St) Dorms £8.50/9.90 weekdays/weekends. The dorms are comfortable and there's a small sitting room, a kitchen and laundry facilities. Internet access is available, too. The Ark runs a tour to the Giant's Causeway and the Carrick-a-rede rope bridge in season. There's also a Derry visit for £18/59 for a one/two-day tour.

The Ark is in the process of opening an annexe at 74 University St that will have single, double and twin rooms.

Belfast International Youth Hostel (☎ 9031 5435, fax 9043 9699, Ⓦ www.hini .org.uk, 22-32 Donegall Rd) Dorms £8-9, singles/doubles £16/24, breakfast £3. There's a laundry, the Backpackers Coffee House, free linen, free car parking, an Internet console and a kitchen. The walls of the stairwell are lined with paintings of well-known Northern Irish people. See how many you can recognise apart from Van Morrison and George Best. This HINI hostel is between Shaftesbury Square and Sandy Row; some travellers have reported it as being a bit noisy at night. The hostel offers tours of West Belfast (see Organised Tours earlier in the chapter). Their Giant's Causeway tour costs £16.

You can get to all the above hostels by train to Botanic Station, or by bus Nos 69 to 71 from Donegall Square.

The Linen House (Paddy's Backpackers; ☎ 9058 6400, fax 9058 6444, Ⓦ www .belfasthostel.com, 18 Kent St) Beds in 18/8-bed dorms £6.50/7.50, dorms with bathroom £8.50, singles/doubles £15/24. For long-term rates talk to the owner. This, the newest independent hostel, is in a large former linen factory in the rapidly developing Cathedral Quarter, not far from the bottom of the Falls and Shankill Rds. The hostel is spacious with comfortable beds and excellent showers. There are basins in all the rooms, a kitchen and laundry. The hostel comes well recommended by readers. Internet access is available for £0.50 per 15 minutes. The hostel also runs black taxi tours (£7) and day trips to the Giant's Causeway (£16).

Outside the Centre There are a few hostel options farther out of the city.

Queen's Elms (☎ *9038 1608, fax 9066 6680, 78 Malone Rd)* Rooms for UK/international/nonstudents £8.20/9.70/12 per person, doubles £21. Open from the end of June to September and run by the university, this room-only place offers excellent accommodation. Rates include bed linen but not towels and there are cooking and laundry facilities. Rooms may also be available for short periods over Christmas and Easter.

Ulster People's College (☎ *9066 5161, fax 9066 8111, 30 Adelaide Park)* Dorms with continental/cooked breakfast £14/16. This college is off Malone Rd.

B&Bs

The Belfast Welcome Centre makes accommodation reservations for a minimal booking fee. Many B&Bs are in the university area with prices from £22 per person. This area is close to the centre and is well stocked with restaurants and pubs.

The Old Georgian House B&B (☎ *9023 4550, fax 9058 6444, 12 College Square North)* Dorms £12 per person, singles/doubles £22/35 per room, 3-person rooms £45. Full breakfast included. There's laundry and Internet facilities, and black taxi and Giant's Causeway tours available (£7 and £16, respectively).

Helga Lodge (☎ *9032 4820, fax 9032 0653, 7 Cromwell Rd)* Bus No 83 or 85 from Donegall Square. Singles £22-27, doubles £40-50. This large and very comfortable place is just off Botanic Ave. Perhaps there's a political message but the once orange facade is now a tasteful green. Most rooms have their own bathroom, TV and phone.

Botanic Lodge Guesthouse (☎*/fax 9032 7682, 87 Botanic Ave)* Bus No 83, 85 or 86 from Donegall Square. Singles/doubles £25/40, en suite doubles £45, including a full Irish breakfast. This is a handsome place where all rooms have TV and a basin but most bathrooms are shared.

Queen's University Common Room (☎ *9066 5938, fax 9068 1209, 1 College Gardens)* Singles/doubles £19.50-36.50/49.50. The Common Room is another place offering B&B in this popular university area.

Eglantine Guesthouse (☎ *9066 7585, fax 9066 8203, 21 Eglantine Ave)* Singles/doubles £22/44. The rooms have TV but shared bathrooms.

Marine House (☎*/fax 9066 2828, 30 Eglantine Ave)* Singles/doubles from £23/45, including full breakfast. There are cheaper shared-bathroom rooms but most are en suite.

Pearl Court House (☎ *9066 6145, fax 9020 0212, 11 Malone Rd)* Singles/doubles from £28/44, en suite £35/52. This B&B is near Queen's University and you can book an evening meal (£7 to £11).

Camera Guesthouse (☎ *9066 0026, fax 9066 7856, 44 Wellington Park)* Singles with shared bathroom/en suite £24/37, doubles £55. This Edwardian B&B is a very cosy place to stay. It also has self-catering apartments on Wellington Park taking up to six people (from £60 per person, minimum two nights). There's also a five-star town house residence within six minutes' drive of the city centre (from £45 per person, minimum three people and two nights). A breakfast chef and daily housekeeping are provided.

All Seasons B&B (☎ *9068 2814, fax 9038 2128,* e *allseasons@fsmail.net, 356 Lisburn Rd)* Singles/doubles £25/45, including full breakfast. All rooms are en suite with TV. These are nice, airy, well decorated rooms in a new B&B. There's a laundry for guests.

Hotels

Prices are comparatively high except at the weekend when business travellers go home and prices drop. Most established hotels are in the university area with newer places springing up in the regenerated riverside area. Many better hotels provide a trouser press with such uniformity that it would be as much a mark of quality as the star system.

City Centre There's no shortage of hotel beds in Belfast.

Holiday Inn Express (☎ 9031 1909, fax 9031 1910, 106a University St) Doubles & twins £64.95 per room, plus continental breakfast, weekends £55, including full Irish breakfast. This hotel is good value (especially for couples and families) given its close location to the university. Internet access is available.

Madison's (☎ 9050 9800, fax 9050 9808, 59-63 Botanic Ave) Singles/doubles £65/75, including full breakfast. Madison's has large, well designed rooms complete with hair dryer and trouser press. There are two suites for guests with disabilities and there's a swanky bar-restaurant and nightclub.

Crescent Town House (☎ 9032 3349, fax 9032 0646, 13 Lower Crescent) Singles/doubles £80/100, weekends £50/65, including full breakfast. This stylish place is opposite the Empire Music Hall on the corner of Botanic Ave. The Metro Brasserie (see Places to Eat later in this chapter) is downstairs.

Wellington Park Hotel (☎ 9038 1111, fax 9066 5410, e minihotelgroup@talk21.com, 21 Malone Rd) Singles/doubles £95/120 room only, weekends £60/80 including full breakfast. This is another smaller hotel close to the Ulster Museum and Queen's University.

Malone Lodge (☎ 9038 800, fax 9038 8088, W www.malonelodgehotel.com, 60 Eglantine Ave) Singles/doubles from £85/105, weekends £60/80, including full breakfast. This hotel has been recently refurbished.

Renshaws Hotel (☎ 9033 3366, fax 9033 3399, 75 University St) Singles/doubles £49/54, weekends £44/49, including continental breakfast. These big rooms have a phone, TV and trouser press.

Dukes Hotel (☎ 9023 6666, fax 9023 7177, e info@dukes-hotel-belfast.co.uk, 65 University St) Singles/doubles £95/110, weekends £62/72, including full breakfast. Dukes is a three star hotel with good rooms. The Chinese owners have had the feng shui experts in so this place should be full of positive energy.

Jury's Inn (☎ 9053 3500, fax 9053 3511, Fisherwick Place, Great Victoria St) Rooms £68, full breakfast £6.95 extra. This place is close to City Hall in College Square opposite Spires Shopping Mall and is good value. The three-star hotel has 190 rooms that can sleep up to three adults or two adults and two children.

Europa Hotel (☎ 9032 7000, fax 9032 7800, e res@eur.hastingshotels.com, Great Victoria St) Singles/doubles £105/145, weekends £50/70, including breakfast. This hotel is a Belfast landmark – many city directions begin with: 'Do you know the Europa?' Now part of the Hastings Group, it's one of the city's best hotels.

McCausland Hotel (☎ 9022 0200, fax 9022 0220, 34-38 Victoria St) Singles/doubles from £130/150, including breakfast. This elegant hotel opened in January 1999 in two beautifully restored Italianate warehouses originally built for rival firms in the 1850s. Aimed at business travellers, the 60-room 'luxury boutique' hotel has rooms with all the accoutrements. The hotel has a restaurant and a European-style cafe-bar.

Belfast Hilton (☎ 9027 7000, fax 9027 7277, 4 Lanyon Place) Singles/doubles from £160/178, presidential suite £500. An Irish breakfast costs £16.95 (presumably you get the works). Taking pride of place in Belfast is the 195-room Belfast Hilton. The hotel has a top-end restaurant and an extraordinary bar that looks like a set for *Happy Days* on acid.

Outside the Centre There are some top-range hotels just outside the city.

Fitzwilliam International Hotel (☎ 9442 2033, fax 9442 3500, W www.fitzwilliam international.com, Belfast International Airport) Room only £110, B&B at weekends £75. This expensive but excellent place is immediately opposite the terminal at the Belfast International Airport.

Stormont Hotel (☎ 9065 8621, fax 9048 0240, W www.hastingshotels.com, 587 Upper Newtownards Rd) Singles/doubles £110/145 room only, weekends £60/80, including breakfast. The glossy four-star hotel is directly across from the Stormont Assembly building, east of the city centre. Everyone gets a rubber duck to float in the bathtub (must have something to do with the activities of the Assembly).

PLACES TO EAT

Belfast has a surprising number and variety of restaurants, including a couple of the best in all Ireland. Prevented from eating out for many years, Belfast is rapidly catching up with European dining-out habits. New cafes and restaurants are opening up throughout central Belfast.

Golden Mile

Restaurants The biggest choice of restaurants is along the Golden Mile, stretching down Great Victoria St, Dublin Rd, through the university area and onto the Lisburn, Malone and Stranmillis Rds.

Graffiti Italiano (☎ 9024 9269, 50 Dublin Rd) Mains £8-14. Open for dinner daily. You'll get excellent, filling pasta and fish dishes such as seafood spaghetti or steamed mussels here.

Archana Balti House (☎ 9032 3713, 53a Dublin Rd) Mains £5.50-9. Open for dinner daily. This place offers Balti curries and, up to a few years ago, used to win awards, confirming our opinion that the quality of food is not what it should be. Still it remains popular and downstairs the *Little India* (☎ 9058 3040, 53 Dublin Rd) specialises in vegetarian dishes (£4.50 to £5.50) and keeps the same hours – well, they use the same chef.

Moghul (☎ 9032 6677, 62a Botanic Ave) Mains £5.95-7.95, lunch buffet £4.99, thali (6 items) £2.99 Mon-Thur only, set 'high tea' meal £9.95 5.30pm-7.30pm Sun-Wed. This is a more traditional Indian restaurant offering tandoori dishes and a good selection of vegetarian dishes. The weekday lunch buffet from noon to 2pm is good value.

Manor House (☎ 9023 8755, 43-47 Donegall Pass) Mains £10-15, set meals £17. Open for lunch and dinner daily, this restaurant offers excellent Cantonese dishes.

Metro Brasserie (☎ 9032 3349, 13 Lower Crescent) Mains around £9.50, 2/3-course Metro Rush Hour menu £9.95/12.50 6pm to 7.30pm, Mon-Sat. This swish place is in the Crescent Town House hotel and has a tempting menu of main courses.

Beatrice Kennedy's (☎ 9020 2290, 44 University Rd) Mains around £11. Open 5pm-10.30pm Tues-Sat & Sun lunch-time. This restaurant offers a varied and hearty dinner menu – seafood and fresh bread, game terrine or potato salad and pesto.

Café Zinc (☎ 9068 2266, 12 Stranmillis Rd) 3-course meal £12. Open 10am-late Mon-Sun. The Strand offers dishes such as baked stuffed aubergine and Irish lamb noisettes.

Aero (☎ 9024 4844, 44 Bedford St) Mains from £5.25. Open for lunch Mon-Fri, for dinner Mon-Sat. This is a smart new restaurant and bar with an interesting menu and clever view of the attractive red-brick Victoriana outside on Bedford St. In the evening (until 7pm) you can order a two-course pre-theatre menu costing £8.95.

La Belle Epoque (☎ 9032 3244, 61-63 Dublin Rd) Mains £7-12. Open noon-late Mon-Fri, 6pm-late Sat. La Belle has the reputation of being Belfast's most authentic French restaurant.

Cayenne (☎ 9033 1532, 7 Ascot House, Shaftesbury Square) 2/3-course set lunch menus £10/13.50; 3-course a la carte menu £25.50. Open lunch & dinner Mon-Fri, dinner only Sat. Behind an anonymous frosted-glass facade, this accolade-winning restaurant serves superb food in modern surroundings. The chef, Paul Rankin, has a tremendous reputation (and his own TV program).

Fast Food, Cafes & Pubs As well as the restaurants, there are a huge number of cheaper options on the Golden Mile.

Liquid (☎ 9031 4903, 68-72 Great Victoria St) Mains £6-10. Coffee shop open 9.30am-6pm Mon-Sat, upstairs Brasserie 5.30pm-11pm Thur-Sat. Liquid is a blend of American, Mexican and European cuisines.

Jenny's Coffee Shop (☎ 9024 9282, 81 Dublin Rd) Snacks from £3. This is a pleasant little cafe-cum-sandwich bar with dishes such as lasagne and pasta.

Revelations Cafe (☎ 9032 0337, 27 Shaftesbury Square) Snacks around £2.50. Open 9am-10pm Mon-Fri, 10am-6pm Sat, 11am-7pm Sun. You can choose light meals

BELFAST

or cakes and decent coffee while you're browsing the Internet.

Maggie May's (☎ *9032 2662, 50 Botanic Ave)* Light meals £2.95-4.95. Open breakfast-late daily. This place is very popular with students for cheap, healthy food and a great atmosphere. They do a vegetarian fry for breakfast.

The Other Place (☎ *9020 7200 79 Botanic Ave)* Meals £4-8. Open 8am-11pm daily. The cuisine in this extremely popular place is Italian/Mexican. It also serves burgers and chips costing £3.95, with an accompaniment of popular music tracks and lots of student jollity. There's an equally popular branch (☎ *9020 7100, 133 Stranmillis Rd)* open the same hours and with a similar menu.

Bookfinders Cafe (☎ *9032 8269, 47 University Rd)* All meals £3.90. Open 10am-5.30pm Mon-Sat. At the back of the bookshop, this is an excellent place for a quick lunch. It's well known for its repertoire of 40 soups one of which is available daily for £1.75. There's also a range of vegetarian dishes.

Conor Restaurant (☎ *9066 3266, 11a Stranmillis Rd)* Meals £6-14. Open 9.30am-11pm daily. An interesting high-ceilinged building with glass roof illuminates the customers tucking into a varied menu. This is the former studio of William Conor, a Belfast artist.

Flannigan's (☎ *9027 9901)* This pub, above the Crown, does immense breakfasts between 8am and 11.30pm. The menu lists a 'build your own 10 piece breakfast' for £4.95.

City Centre

The centre still quietens down considerably after the shops have closed, but during the day it's lively, with all the pubs, cafes and restaurants doing a roaring trade at lunchtime.

Deanes (☎ *9056 0000, 38 Howard St)* 2-course menu in brasserie/restaurant £20/27. Brasserie open lunch & dinner Mon-Sat, restaurant open 7pm-9.30pm Tues-Sat. If you feel like treating yourself to a grown-up meal while you're in Belfast then book a table at Deanes, the city's only Michelin-starred restaurant. You'll need to book well

ahead for the restaurant upstairs, but you should be able to get a table in the brasserie downstairs. The food, wine, service and ambience are all excellent.

Nick's Warehouse (☎ *9043 9690, 35 Hill St)* Meals £6-13. Open noon-3pm weekdays, 6pm-10pm Tues-Sat. Nick's is an enormous blonde-wood and red-brick bar-restaurant buzzing with happy Belfastians. There's a good wine list and a fresh menu featuring salads and seafood.

The Edge Bar & Restaurant (☎ *9032 2000, Laganbank Rd)* Mains around £7, 4-course lunch/dinner £18/22. This well designed and stylish cafe-bar and restaurant overlooks the river near the Hilton. Booking for dinner is essential; downstairs is a piano bar with an ivory tinkler for pre-dinner drinks.

McHugh's (☎ *9050 9999, 29-31 Queen's Square)* Meals £6-12. Restaurant open for lunch Sun-Fri, dinner on Sat. Farther down the river, this restored pub is similar to The Edge. Serving pub food downstairs and fancier dishes (grilled salmon, Barbary duck) in the restaurant upstairs.

Paul's Cafe *(187 Donegall St)* If you're staying at the Linen House hostel and fancy a fry-up rather than a bowl of cornflakes, try this place nearby.

Cafe Society (☎ *9043 5925, 3 Donegall Square East)* Mains £5-8. Open 8am-5pm Mon-Wed, 8am-8pm Thur, 8am-late Fri-Sat. This is a fine spot for lunch right by City Hall or to listen to jazz on a Friday evening between 6pm and 8pm. They have reasonably priced fresh pasta, pan-fried chicken and vegetarian dishes.

Cafe Renoir (☎ *9032 5592, 5 Queen St)* Meals £3-5. Open 9am-5pm Mon-Sat. They cook everything from fresh ingredients and bake their own bread. With decent coffee and a range of filling vegetarian and wholefood dishes what more do you need?

Roscoff Cafe (☎ *9031 5090, 27-29 Fountain St)* Snacks £1.85-4.65. Open Mon-Sat. Apart from breakfast you can also order excellent sandwiches, salads and a selection of Irish cheeses. The cafe has a good wine list and a takeaway section.

Altos (☎ *9032 3087, Unit 6, Fountain St)*

Mains £5-7.50. Open 10am-5pm Mon-Wed, 10am-8pm Thur, 10am-6pm Fri-Sat. The menu is Mediterranean with traditional Irish influences and challenges the conservative palettes of timid Belfast diners. A giant clock projected onto the back wall means you'll never lose track of time.

Belfast is full of congenial pubs, many of which offer hearty traditional food around the £5 mark.

Bittle's Bar (☎ *9031 1088, 70 Upper Church Lane*) This small pub specialises in traditional dishes such as sausages and champ, and Irish stew.

White's Tavern (☎ *9024 3080, 2-12 Wine Cellar Entry*) This historic pub, between Rosemary and High Sts, serves down-to-earth pub food such as baked potatoes and chicken and broccoli bake.

Duke of York (☎ *9024 1062, 11 Commercial Court*) This is another oldie, popular with journalists from the nearby local papers; it serves sandwiches and excellent solid lunches.

Kitchen Bar (☎ *9032 4901, 16 Victoria Square*) This is a great place for real ale, home-made soups and stews and the house speciality – Paddy's pizza created on a toasted soda-bread base.

Morning Star (☎ *9023 5986, 17 Pottinger's Entry*) Big 24oz steaks cost £14; if you want bigger then you have to give 36 hours' notice, presumably so they can cook a whole beast. The Australian-run restaurant upstairs at the Morning Star has a good reputation. The menu features traditional Irish dishes as well as more unusual things such as kangaroo, emu and crocodile steaks. Downstairs has an excellent buffet (£3.95).

Outside the Centre

Mercury Bar & Grill (☎ *9064 9017, 451 Ormeau Rd*) Open lunch-late daily. South of the centre, this is another of the recent modern bar-restaurant developments that are springing up in the University quarter. It offers an all-day brunch for £4.95, a selection of light meals (such as tempura of field mushrooms) and substantial main courses, and has an excellent wine list. There's live jazz on Sunday.

Ben Madigan Restaurant (☎ *9077 6925, Belfast Castle*) Set lunch £16. Open for Sunday lunch. This restaurant, upstairs in the Belfast Castle, offers Sunday roast overlooking Belfast and Belfast Lough. You'll need to book a couple of days ahead.

Cellar Restaurant (☎ *9077 6925,* e *castlecatering@utvinternet.com, Belfast Castle, Antrim Rd*) Lunch £6-7.50, dinner £11-13. Open lunch & dinner Mon-Sat. Not quite a dungeon setting but this restaurant and bar is downstairs at the castle and caters for morning coffee, lunch, afternoon tea and dinner.

Cultúrlann MacAdam ÓFiaich (☎ *9023 9303, 216 Falls Rd*) Meals from £4. Open 9am-9pm Sun-Wed, 9am-10pm Thur-Sat. If you're exploring West Belfast you may like to drop into the Irish language and arts centre for a browse in the bookshop and some good home-cooked food in the cafe – stews, soups, pizza, baked potatoes and fresh pastries with real maple syrup.

An Cupla Focal (☎ *9023 2608, 145-147 Falls Rd*) Meals £4.25-5.95. Open lunch & dinner daily. This restaurant is a new community business employing people who speak or are learning Irish. The menu is fairly basic. The locals like it but we found that the cooking needs some improvement.

ENTERTAINMENT

Belfast's nightlife has never been busier – sleek new bars opening, old ones changing, the club scene is booming and top-class live music is to be found in dozens of great venues around town. The city is rushing to bypass 30 years of stagnation. This is being reflected in a resurgence of the arts in general – from a growth in community and Irish language-based events to a flourishing visual-arts movement.

The free *The List*, published on Wednesday, covers music events in Northern Ireland although the emphasis is heavily on Belfast. *The Belfast Beat* is a free monthly guide and lists what goes on where each day of the week. On the Internet w www.whereto tonight.com is another useful guide.

The Metro section in the *Irish News* on Friday covers everything from music to art

BELFAST

A Cultural Tour

'There is nothing which has yet been contrived by man by which so much happiness is produced as by a good tavern or inn.'

Samuel Johnson, 1776

Almost any of the pubs in central Belfast could be linked into a pub crawl, but here are some of the more interesting ones.

One should start with the **Crown Liquor Saloon** opposite the Grand Opera House, with its wonderfully ornate Victorian interior (see the Crown Liquor Saloon in the Around the Centre section earlier in this chapter). Catch a seat in the snug if you can and take a pint of Guinness, Ireland's national tonic. One possible reason for the snugs and the bell-call system for more drinks was to preserve the anonymity of those in denial – those who believed wholeheartedly in their religion but had difficulty accommodating the associated doctrine of temperance.

Next stop is **Kelly's Cellars** in Bank St where many Belfast students have drunk their grants before time. Kelley's is Belfast's oldest pub (1720) in Bank St and was a meeting place for Henry Joy McCracken and the United Irishmen planning the 1798 rebellion. The story goes that McCracken hid behind the bar when British soldiers came for him. You could try a pint of McCafferty's in here.

Across the other side of Royal Arcade are the Entries, a set of small streets acting as connecting alleyways to the main thoroughfares. There are a number of good pubs in here. The **Morning Star**, Pottinger's Entry, can be dated back to at least 1810 when it was mentioned in the *Belfast News Letter* as a terminal for the Dublin to Belfast coach. This is an interesting place with a double entry porch. Maybe again those in trouble with their conscience could enter the porch by one entrance, remember their beliefs and stride out through the other porch without even entering the pub. For those without compunction the door opens into an atmospheric place with small snugs. You could try a pint of Ireland's lager, Harp, here.

White's Tavern in Wine Cellar Entry is another historic place and claims to be Belfast's oldest

---

exhibitions and special events. *art.ie* is a new free monthly publication that covers the arts scene throughout the whole of Northern Ireland.

Most of the free publications can be picked up in pubs, clubs and performance venues.

Pubs

There's no shortage of pubs to explore in Belfast. Most offer music of one sort or another – after all, having an entertainment licence means you can stay open until 1.30am. Many of the city-centre pubs are crammed to overflowing at lunchtime as well as in the evening (but there's always room for more) and some of the trendier bars have dress codes (usually no trainers and no jeans).

Traditional Belfast has some fabulous pubs that are as much museums as drinking

places. See also the boxed text 'A Cultural Tour'.

Crown Liquor Saloon (☎ 9024 9476, 46 Great Victoria St) No-one should miss this place, with its wonderfully ornate Victorian interior (see Crown Liquor Saloon in the Around the Centre section earlier in this chapter).

The narrow alleys known as the Entries shelter a plethora of older pubs. Good ones to try include the following.

Morning Star (☎ 9023 5986, 17 Pottinger's Entry) This is a pub with a big sweeping horseshoe bar if you want to mix with the public, or snugs if you want privacy.

White's Tavern (☎ 9024 3080, 2-12 Wine Cellar Entry) This historic place has jazz on Thursday night and traditional Irish music on Friday and Saturday nights.

Kelly's Cellars (☎ 9032 4835, 1 Bank St)

A Cultural Tour

tavern (compared with a pub, a tavern provides food and lodging) and in operation since 1630. In those days the River Blackstaff had not been hidden underground and sailing ships would have been moored adjacent to White's. The murals opposite the pub show life as it would have been at this time. At the turn of the 19th century there were some 15 pubs in these Entries.

Across in Victoria Square is the **Kitchen Bar**, formerly a lodging house for respectable young ladies. In the days of the Empire Theatre next door a large number of the artistes used to come in for a drink and would leave behind one of their publicity photographs. There's a mass of them on the wall and somewhere there's meant to be one of Charlie Chaplin. This is a great spot for real ale so try one of their guest ales.

Bittle's Bar in Upper Church Lane is a most unusual pub for two reasons. Firstly the bar is Belfast's only 'flat iron building', a rather interesting triangular building decorated with gilded shamrocks. This makes the interior of the bar wedge shaped, but more of a feature are the walls, which are covered in paintings of Ireland's literary heroes, all by the one artist, Joe O'Kane. This is a permanent collection of his works which are not for sale and don't appear anywhere else. Pride of the lot on the back wall is a large painting in the genre of 'if all the stars got together in a diner/bar, etc'. This painting depicts Yeats, Joyce, Behan and Beckett at the bar with glasses of Guinness and Wilde pulling the pints on the other side. Try a glass of wheat beer here.

McHugh's in Queen's Square was built in the 1700s but has undergone a massive regeneration. Apart from the maritime memorabilia (two large boiler fronts on one wall) there's the chessboard. This is a political chessboard with model figures of the political players in Northern Ireland. One side lines up the Brits and Protestants featuring the Queen, Ian Paisley, David Trimble and the Archbishop of Canterbury with the RUC as pawns. The Nationalist side includes Gerry Adams, Bill Clinton, Bertie Ahern (the Irish prime minister), a Catholic bishop and IRA paramilitaries as pawns. The owners would like to get the sculptor to make life-sized figures of Gerry Adams and Ian Paisley enjoying a beer together. It may happen in this pub but not in reality.

This is another real-ale pub so finish the tour off with a pint of Belfast Ale.

This pub features folk and blues bands on Friday and Saturday nights.

Duke of York (☎ *9024 1062, 11 Commercial Court*) This pub is hidden away down an alleyway near St Anne's Cathedral. A claim to fame is that the Sinn Féin leader, Gerry Adams, once worked behind the bar here when he was a student.

Kitchen Bar (☎ *9023 4901, 16 Victoria Square*) This is a great spot for real ales, home-cooked food and traditional music sessions.

Maddens (☎ *9024 4114, 74 Smithfield*) This down-to-earth establishment is noted for its lively traditional music.

The John Hewitt (☎ *9023 3768, 51 Donegall St*) This is a new pub in an old tradition. The Hewitt, in its short life so far, has gained a reputation for it, traditional music sessions Wednesday, Saturday and Sunday nights and is also a venue for events in the annual Cathedral Quarter Arts Festival.

The Rotterdam (☎ *9074 6021, 54 Pilot St*) A wonderful small pub with an atmosphere if you don't mind the smoke. There's music most nights and a quiz on Wednesday. In summer the gigs move outside.

Trendy Largely thanks to the student population, Belfast has a growing number of trendy bars.

McHugh's (☎ *9050 9999, 29-31 Queen's Square*) Built in the 1700s and not far from the river on Queen's Square, this is the oldest building in Belfast. Restored at a cost of £2 million, it reopened in October 1998 and is now a very popular bar-restaurant with live music (mostly rock and cover bands) Thursday to Saturday nights and traditional music Wednesday night.

The Globe (☎ *9050 9848, 36 University Rd*) This is a popular student pub with a disco and live music at the weekend.

Eglantine Inn (*The Egg;* ☎ *9038 1994, 32 Malone Rd*) Almost an institution, it's packed with students at the weekend. There is music of one sort or another every night except Tuesday when there's a quiz. Live bands play Sunday and Monday and there's TV for live sports.

Botanic (*The Bott;* ☎ *9050 9740, 23 Malone Rd*) Like the Eglantine, this place is packed with students at the weekend and also features music.

Empire Music Hall (☎ *9024 9276, 42 Botanic Ave*) This is a splendid Victorian building with three entertainment floors presenting a variety of events – revealing comedy Tuesday, Irish music Wednesday, blues Thursday, salsa Friday (with a class at 9pm) – and bands play at the weekend. The *Breakdown Club* once or twice a month attracts top international DJs.

Robinson's (☎ *9024 7447, 38-40 Great Victoria St*) Next door to the Crown, this is a theme pub on four floors with music – from traditional to the latest young bands – most nights. In the basement is *BT1*, a wine and chill-out bar open 5pm to late.

Beaten Docket (☎ *9024 2986, 48 Great Victoria St*). Here's a popular late-night weekend venue for '60s and '70s disco throbbing upstairs in the club.

Lavery's Gin Palace (☎ *9087 1106, 14 Bradbury Place*) This place is popular with an extraordinary range of clients, from students to bikers and hardened drinkers. There's mixed dance music most nights. Downstairs has live bands on several nights. The middle floor bar, the *Gin Palace*, has a DJ every night. Punters going to the top floor on Saturday night can find *Heaven* for the latest dance music. As a calm-me-down, using the brain rather than the body, the quiz night is Tuesday.

Clubs

See also pubs with late-night club events in the previous Pubs section.

Milk Bar (☎ *9027 8876, Tomb St*) This place has music every night of the week

attracting some big name DJs in US house/garage and RnB. Monday is gay night.

Katy Daly's (☎ *9032 5942, 17 Ormeau Ave*) Open noon-1.30am in the week, to 2.30am at the weekend. This place offers live music as well as club nights and there's live music on Saturday afternoon as well. Many big bands get their first break here.

The Limelight (☎ *9032 5942, 19 Ormeau Ave*) Next door to Katy Daly's, this is a popular venue for music especially indie, hiphop, britpop, and alternative sounds.

The Fly (☎ *9050 9750, 5-6 Lower Crescent*) Near the Empire Music Hall, this is a stylish (provided you don't suffer from arachnophobia) bar for young things. Huge metal spiders hunch on the walls behind the bar and dangle from the stairwell. The cocktails (£2.95) are called names such as Fly-by-Night, Flyagra and Flyshagme. There's a DJ on the middle floor every night and an Absolut Vodka Bar with comfy chairs on the top floor. Can this really be Belfast?

The Loft (*Dempsey's;* ☎ *9023 4000, 45 Dublin Rd; admission £5*) This place draws a big crowd on Friday and Saturday nights with a disco and various promotions.

Madison's (*see Places to Stay*) This trendy place has a live band in the cafe-bar Thursday and Sunday evenings; the nightclub opens 10.30am to 2pm Friday to Sunday for mixed dance music.

Manhattan (☎ *9023 3131, 23-25 Bradbury Place*) Downstairs opens normal pub hours but *M-club* upstairs opens 9pm to 1am Thursday and Saturday for some serious clubbing music; on Friday they play '70s music and Monday is 'escape night', with promotions and cheap drinks.

Thompson's Garage (☎ *9032 3762, 3 Patterson's Place*) Although tucked away, this is one of the most popular club venues in town and hosts international DJs. Their policy – stay cool and nobody gets hurt.

Gay & Lesbian Venues

Everybody's welcome at these two venues but the entertainment and ambience is fashioned for their own clientele.

Parliament Bar (☎ *9023 4520, 2 Dunbar St*) Not far from St Anne's Cathedral, this is

Belfast's oldest gay venue. There's a mixture of live bands and club nights throughout the week, with a pop-trivia quiz on Tuesday followed by a late-night disco. Sunday night is karaoke night.

The Kremlin (☎ *9080 9700, 96 Little Donegall St)* Open noon-2am Mon-Wed, noon-3am Thur-Sun. Surmounting the doorway the large figure of Lenin gesticulating to the masses reflects the USSR-kitsch theme of this club. From 'cabaret' to cover bands, there's something every night of the week. Revolution is the big club night on Saturday (4pm to 3am) and Monday is movie night (5pm to 1am).

Music Venues

Odyssey Arena (☎ *9073 9074,* W *www .odysseyarena.com, 2 Queen's Quay)* This is Belfast's new big venue for the big names in the entertainment business.

Waterfront Hall (☎ *9033 4455, Lanyon Place)* This impressive circular hall is one of Belfast's main concert venues. It hosts local, national and international performers from pop-music artists to symphony orchestras.

Ulster Hall (☎ *9032 3900, Bedford St)* Northern Ireland's excellent Ulster Orchestra often plays here. It's also the venue for larger rock-music events (and for lunchtime organ recitals and even boxing bouts) although the new Odyssey Arena may take over some of the events.

King's Hall (☎ *9066 7373, Balmoral)* Another centre for big rock events, it's accessible by bus down Lisburn Rd or by train to Balmoral Station.

Crescent Arts Centre (☎ *9024 2338,* W *www.crescentarts.org, 2-4 University Rd; admission £4-12)* The Crescent hosts some excellent music concerts, from New York jazz to top-rate Irish music. There's a regular Saturday night club (10pm to late, BYO drinks) offering a wide range of music. There are other occasional music events that'll be advertised in *The List* or on their Web site. The Crescent also puts on a literary festival each March called *Between the Lines* and a dance festival, *City Dance,* in June.

Cinemas

Queen's Film Theatre (☎ *9024 4857, 7 University Square Mews)* Near the university, this is a two-screen art-house cinema that screens four films over Friday and Saturday nights starting about 6.30pm.

UGC Cinemas (information line ☎ *0870 155 5176, 9024 5700, Dublin Rd)* With 10 screens this is Belfast's biggest cinema complex. It's at the northern end of Dublin Rd.

Movie House (☎ *9075 5000, Yorkgate Shopping Centre, York St)* This cinema, north of the city centre, has five screens.

Theatre

Grand Opera House (booking office ☎ *9024 1919, 2-4 Great Victoria St)* Booking office opens 8.30am-8pm Mon-Wed, 8.30am-9pm Thur, 8.30am-6.30pm Fri & 8.30am-5.30pm Sat. This venue plays host to a mixture of good theatre, opera and music shows.

Lyric Theatre (☎ *9038 1081,* W *www .lyrictheatre.co.uk, 55 Ridgeway St)* Farther out from the centre, this place has a more serious bent and includes Irish plays in its repertory. The Lyric is a major host for the Belfast Festival at Queen's held in October.

Whitla Hall (☎ *9027 3075, Queen's University, University Rd)* Apart from the Belfast Festival at Queen's, there are occasional music performances at this venue.

Group Theatre (☎ *9032 9685, Bedford St)* This theatre, next door to Ulster Hall, stages work by local companies from September to June.

Factory (☎ *9024 4000, 52 Hill St)* The Factory hosts a variety of different performances.

The Old Museum Arts Centre (☎ *9023 5053, 7 College Square North)* The Old Museum hosts theatre performances and stand-up comedy.

SPECTATOR SPORTS

Rugby, soccer, Gaelic football and hockey are played through the winter, cricket and hurling through the summer. International rugby and soccer matches take place at **Windsor Park** (☎ *9024 4198, off Lisburn Rd),* south of the centre; bus Nos 58 and 59 go that way. You can see Gaelic football and hurling at *Roger Casement Park* (☎ 9070 5868, Andersonstown Rd) in West Belfast. Take bus No 14, 15 or 90. The Sports Council (☎ 9038 1222, ⓦ www.sportni.org) provides information on a range of sporting activities.

The Belfast Giants play ice hockey and draw big crowds at the *Odyssey Arena* (☎ 9073 9074, ⓦ www.odysseyarena.com, 2 Queen's Quay). Their season is September to March.

SHOPPING

Items particular to Northern Ireland that you may like to look out for include fine Belleek china, linen (antique and new) and Tyrone crystal.

The WickerMan (☎ 9024 3550, 14 Donegall Arcade) This shop, off Castle Place, sells a wide range of contemporary Irish crafts and gifts, including silver jewellery, glassware and knitwear.

Craftworks (☎ 9024 4465, 40 Bedford St) Near Ulster Hall, this shop specialises in top-quality work by craftspeople from all over Ulster. You'll find beautifully made designer knitwear, linen shirts, leather-wear, ceramics, *bodhráns* (traditional goatskin drums), textiles and jewellery.

Vintage Record Store (☎ 9031 4888, 54 Howard St) Try this store for a selection of Irish music.

Cultúrlann MacAdam ÓFiaich (☎ 9023 9303, 216 Falls Rd) Another good place to try for Irish music.

St George's Market (☎ 9043 5704, cnr Oxford & May Sts) Open 7am-3pm Fri. This newly restored market sells fresh fruit, vegetables, flowers and fish as well as a variety of other goods. The Ha'penny Fair is held here on the first Sunday of the month with antiques and collectables stalls to browse around while being amused by street entertainers.

Donegall Pass is the antiques shop strip of Belfast. Come here for your brass bedstead, old china or just a browse. Try the *Antique Market* (☎ 9023 2041, 126-128 Donegall Pass). Upstairs opens 9.30am to 5pm Saturday, but downstairs opens all week.

Fresh Garbage (☎ 9024 2350, 24 Rose-mary St) Open 10.30am-5.30pm with a late night (9pm) Thur. Come here for all your club wear, gothic gear and jewellery needs.

For general shopping you'll find everything in the compact central shopping area north of City Hall.

Surf Mountain (☎ 9024 8877, 12 Brunswick St) is good for camping gas cylinders, other camping equipment and surfing gear. The *Scout Shop Ski & Camp Centre* (☎ 9032 0580, 12-14 College Square East) has a huge range of camping equipment for sale.

GETTING THERE & AWAY
Air

There are flights from some regional airports in Britain, including Gatwick, to the convenient Belfast City Airport (☎ 9093 9093), Airport Rd, but everything else (flights from the Republic, Britain, Amsterdam, Brussels and New York) goes to Belfast International Airport (☎ 9448 4848), 30km north-west of the city in Aldergrove by the M2. For details of flights and fares see under Air in the introductory Getting There & Away chapter. Airline offices in Belfast include:

Aer Lingus (☎ 0845 973 7747), 46–48 Castle St
British Airways (☎ 0845 722 2111) 1 Fountain Centre, College St
British Midland (☎ 9024 1188) Suite 2, Fountain Centre, College St

Bus

Belfast has two modern bus stations. The smaller is the Laganside Bus Centre on Oxford St near the river, with bus connections to County Antrim, eastern Down and the Cookstown area. Buses to Larne town, as opposed to the harbour, leave from the Laganside Bus Centre.

Buses to everywhere else in Northern Ireland, the Republic and Larne harbour leave from the bigger Europa Bus Centre on Glengall St, behind the Europa Hotel.

The No 300 service to the International Airport calls at both bus stations.

Pick up regional bus timetables at the bus stations or contact Translink (☎ 9033 3000, ⓦ www.translink.co.uk) for timetable information. For connections to Derry and

Donegal contact the Lough Swilly Bus Company (☎ 7126 2017) in Derry.

Ulsterbus has one-day Freedom of Northern Ireland tickets for £11/5.50 adult/child; three days for £27/13.50 and seven days for £40/20. An all-over Ireland Irish Rover ticket for three days in eight costs £42/21; eight days in 15 costs £83/47 and 15 days in 30 days costs £145/73.

For security reasons there are no left-luggage facilities at Belfast bus stations.

Students are eligible for 15% reductions on Ulsterbus fares of more than £1.15 on production of their ISIC card.

For information on bus fares, durations and frequencies throughout Ireland see under Bus in the introductory Getting Around chapter.

Train

Trains to all destinations, including Larne, Derry, Dublin, Newry, Portadown and Bangor arrive and depart from Belfast Central. Trains also leave Great Victoria St Station for Portadown, Lisburn, Bangor, Larne Harbour and Derry. Great Victoria St is the most central station, while Belfast Central is east of the city centre on East Bridge St.

For tickets and information the NIR Travel Shop (☎ 9023 0671, W www.translink.co.uk) is at Great Victoria St Station next to the Europa Bus Centre. They book ferries, Dublin Rail Breaks and Scotland Rail Breaks (Glasgow and Edinburgh). It opens 9am to 5pm weekdays and 9am to 12.30pm Saturday. Information about local trains is also available from Belfast Central Station (☎ 9089 9411).

There are eight trains Monday to Saturday and five on Sunday between Belfast and Derry. The trip takes just under 2½ hours and a one-way ticket costs £6.70. Belfast to Dublin trains run up to eight times a day (four on Sunday) and take about two hours at a cost of £17 one way.

On Sunday you can buy a £3 go-as-you-please (before 3pm) ticket allowing you to travel all over the Northern Irish train network.

Left-luggage facilities have returned to Great Victoria St station but they seem permanently out of use.

For more information on the train network in Ireland see under Train in the introductory Getting Around chapter.

Boat

The Isle of Man Steam Packet Company and SeaCat operate together (☎ 0870 552 3523, W www.seacat.co.uk) and dock in Donegall Quay, a short distance from the city centre. Services to the Isle of Man only run during summer. SeaCat operates huge catamaran car ferries between Belfast and Troon in Scotland and to Heysham from April to September.

Conventional ferries to and from Scotland dock at Larne, 30km up the coast from Belfast (see Larne in the Counties Derry & Antrim chapter).

Norse Merchant Ferries (☎ 9077 9090) runs a service between Belfast and Liverpool and operates from the Victoria terminal, 5km north of town.

For more information on ferry routes, companies and prices, see the Sea section of the Getting There & Away chapter.

GETTING AROUND

Belfast has that rare thing – an integrated public transport system, with buses and trains linking both airports to the central train and bus stations and to the ferries.

To/From the Airports

Belfast International Airport (☎ 9442 2888) is 30km north of the city. Very frequent buses connect it with the Europa Bus Centre for £5/8 one way/return. A taxi costs about £25.

The more convenient Belfast City Airport (☎ 9093 9093) is only 6km from the centre. You can cross the road from the terminal to Sydenham Halt Station for a train to Botanic Station in the popular university area or Great Victoria St. Citybus No 21 runs between Belfast City Airport and the centre for £1. Bus services run roughly every half-hour weekdays, less frequently at the weekend. A taxi fare to the city centre is about £7.

To/From the Ferry Terminals

Donegall Quay is a short bus ride or walk from the city centre. Trains for Larne Harbour depart from Great Victoria St Station, while buses leave from the Europa Bus Centre.

Bus

Citybus (☎ 9024 6485) operates the bus system in Belfast, which is divided into zones. Very short trips in the centre cost just 50p; in general around the city the standard bus fare is £1, which gets you all the way to Cave Hill or Belfast Zoo. A multijourney ticket costs £3.40 and gives you four rides at slightly lower cost and much greater convenience.

A Day Ticket gives you unlimited travel within the City Zone from 9.30am weekdays or all day at the weekend for £2.80. A seven-day bus pass costs £12.60.

Most local bus services depart from Donegall Square, near the City Hall. Timetables are available from the kiosk on Donegall Square West. Single tickets are bought from the driver but multiple tickets need to be purchased in advance from kiosks on Castle Place or Donegall Square West.

The Centrelink service connects both bus stations, Central Station and Great Victoria St Station with the City Hall and a few central locations. Holders of a valid rail ticket can use the service free of charge.

Belfast has a good system of night buses on Friday and Saturday to enable people to join in the nightlife. Most buses leave from Donegall Square West at 1am and 2am. You can buy tickets (£3) from the driver. For night bus information contact Translink (☎ 9033 3000, W www.translink.co.uk).

Train

A local train connects Great Victoria St Station and Belfast Central Station. Trains run frequently between Belfast Central and Botanic stations until around 11pm. Both trips cost 80p one way.

Car & Motorcycle

If you're driving, the biggest problem is navigating the many one-way streets that Northern Ireland town planners love as a way of dealing with too much traffic for the space available. Signage in the province could be far better. If you're looking for somewhere and if there's a sign for it, then it'll be right at the place you need to turn. You never see

it in time and have to go up the road turn and come back. A good map is advisable for travelling on minor roads out in the country.

Car rental agencies in Belfast include:

Avis
   (☎ 9024 0404) 69–71 Great Victoria St
   (☎ 9045 2017) City Airport
   (☎ 9442 2333) International Airport
Budget
   (☎ 9023 0700) 96–102 Great Victoria St
   (☎ 9045 1111) City Airport
CC Economy Car Hire
   (☎ 9084 0366) 2 Ballyduff Rd
Europcar
   (☎ 9031 3500) 6–24 Agincourt Ave
   (☎ 9442 3444) International Airport
Hertz
   (☎ 9073 2451) City Airport
   (☎ 9442 2533) International Airport
McCausland Car Hire
   (☎ 9033 3777) 21–31 Grosvenor Rd
   (☎ 9442 2022) International Airport

Rates change frequently so ring around (see also Rental under Car & Motorcycle in the Getting Around chapter).

Taxi

For information on People's Taxis in West Belfast see Getting There & Away under the West Belfast section earlier in this chapter. The regular black taxis that travel throughout the city have yellow plates back and front (£2.50 minimum fare) and can be hailed in the street. Minicabs are cheaper and there are plenty around. Companies to call include Stranmillis Taxis (☎ 9020 0400), Value Cabs (☎ 9080 9080) and Sure Cabs (☎ 9076 6666).

Bicycle

Running through Belfast, mostly down the side of the Lagan, is part of the 30km Whiteburn to Lisburn cycle track. It's part of an extensive national cycle network for which the Belfast Welcome Centre can provide details.

McConvey Cycles (☎ 9033 0322), 183 Ormeau Rd, rents out bicycles for £10/50 per day/week. A deposit of £50 is required. The Belfast Welcome Centre has a leaflet outlining cycle routes in Northern Ireland.

Counties Down & Armagh

County Down

County Down is Northern Ireland's sunny south-east, being relatively dry. Neighbouring Belfast delivers hordes of day-trippers to the many seaside resorts, from Bangor to Newcastle and beyond. The shoreline runs from the flat Ards Peninsula, encompassing the drowned drumlins and nature reserves of Strangford Lough, to the Mourne Mountains, which coax the traveller farther south. In the famous lyrics by Percy French, the Mournes 'sweep down to the sea'; they're the highlight of Down. The interior of the county is less scenic, but Hillsborough retains much of its Georgian splendour.

HISTORY

The history of Down goes back 7000 years. The county has its fair share of early monuments: the Giant's Ring near Belfast and the Legananny Dolmen near Ballynahinch are two fine examples.

St Patrick is said to have arrived in Strangford Lough in 432 and died in the area in 461. The whereabouts of his remains is disputed, although Downpatrick Cathedral is the favoured site.

By the time of St Patrick's death, the crusade he had started in Ulster had extended Christianity over Ireland making him one of the few genuinely national heroes. After St Patrick's death, Irish monasteries flourished, surviving repeated Viking attacks.

They were finally to lose out to the Normans, who ousted the Irish monks and built Grey Abbey on the Ards Peninsula and Inch Abbey near Downpatrick. Castles were their main priority, however, and many along the coast survive today.

The Scottish and English settlers who arrived with the Plantation were given large tracts of land previously occupied by the native Irish. They built towns and roads and developed the linen industry in the 17th and 18th centuries.

BELFAST TO BANGOR

Belfast is creeping north-eastwards along the northern shores of County Down, turning many of the small coastal towns into dormitory towns.

Ulster Folk & Transport Museum

This is one of the finest museums in Ireland (*☎ 9042 8428, 153 Bangor Rd; adult/concession/family £5/3/13; park & museum open 10am-5pm Mon-Fri, 10am-6pm Sat & 11am-6pm Sun Mar-June; 10am-6pm*

COUNTIES DOWN & ARMAGH

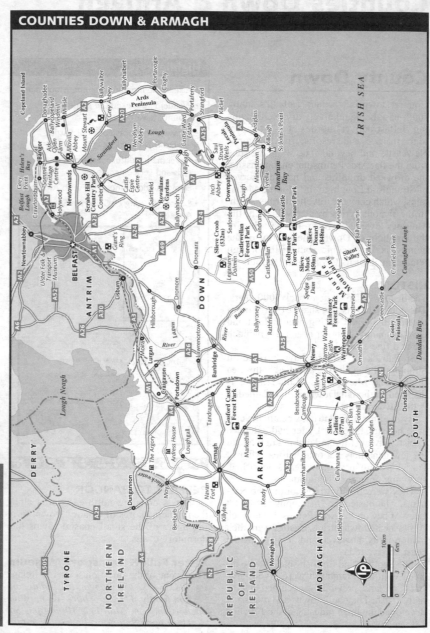

The John Hewitt pub joins in with the Cathedral Quarter Arts Festival.

Belfast's cafe society

The first meeting of the Northern Ireland Parliament was held at imposing Belfast City Hall in 1921.

Admire the flamboyance of Belfast's Crown Liquor Saloon while enjoying a pint in one of its snugs.

Looking across to lofty Slieve Donard (848m), the highest peak of the Mourne Mountains, Co Down

A spot of road bowling, County Armagh

McCartney's of Moira offers traditional fare.

The 35km Mourne Wall, County Down

Mon-Sat & 11am-6pm Sun July-Sept; 10am-4pm Mon-Fri, 10am-5pm Sat & 11am-5pm Sun Oct-Feb). It's 11km north-east of Belfast, near Holywood. Farmhouses, forges, churches and mills have been very carefully reconstructed on the wooded 60-hectare site, with plenty of human and animal extras combining to give strong impressions of Irish life over the past few hundred years. From industrial times, there are complete terraces of 19th-century Belfast and Dromore houses. During the summer activities such as thatching and horse ploughing are demonstrated and in some houses and businesses you'll find characters dressed in the costume of the day practising some sort of craft.

On the opposite side of the road the transport museum is a sort of automotive zoo. The Dalchoolin Transport Galleries display steam locomotives, rolling stock and other paraphernalia. In another section are motorcycles, trams, buses, cars and bicycles. Included in the large automobile collection is a gull-wing stainless-steel car, built in Belfast after former American General Motors whiz kid, John de Lorean, persuaded the British government that to invest £80 million in manufacturing a flash new car would help reduce Northern Ireland's horrifyingly high unemployment. Unfortunately the new car was launched into a market suffering from recession and much of the money vanished into numbered Swiss bank accounts.

In the flight section there's one of the world's first VTOL aircraft (vertical take-off and landing) made by the Belfast firm Shorts. Particularly popular in this section is a *Titanic* display with photographs of its construction and reports of its sinking.

Buses to Bangor stop nearby; the nearest train station is Cultra.

There are car parks for the rural, town and transport sections but after that there's a lot of walking. You'll need at least half a day to do it justice.

There's a fine **coastal walk** of some 6km from Holywood to Helen's Bay, with more pleasant seashore trails continuing north-east to Grey Point.

Crawfordsburn Country Park

Just over 3km west of Bangor, off the B20 at Helen's Bay, this country park *(☎ 9185 3621, Helens Bay; free; open 9am-8pm Apr-Sept; 9am-4.45pm daily rest of year)* has a number of wooded and coastal walks plus a 20th-century gun emplacement with command post and lookout station at Grey Point Fort *(☎ 9185 3621, Bridge Rd South; free guided tours 2pm-5pm Wed-Mon Apr-Sept; 2pm-5pm Sun rest of year).* The large-calibre artillery has been trained on Belfast Lough since before WWI, though never fired in anger.

Phone for details of occasional (free) guided walks. The park is accessible on Belfast to Bangor bus No 2 or by train to Helen's Bay Station, the latter a wonderful little Victorian station dating from 1865 and built by the Marquess of Dufferin, who owned the surrounding estate.

Old Inn (☎ 9185 3255, fax 9185 2775, 15 Main St) £65 per room, including breakfast. This 17th-century building, in the pretty black-and-white village of Crawfordsburn, has bags of character but isn't cheap. Dinner costs around £24.50.

BANGOR
pop 52,440

It's 21km from Belfast to Bangor (Beannchar), a seaside resort and dormitory town for Belfast commuters. The Belfast to Bangor train line was built in the late 19th century to connect the capital with the then flourishing resort. The opening of a 500-berth **marina** in 1995 seems to have lifted the fortunes of Bangor again but there are still some derelict buildings on the front needing restoration. The **Pickie Fun Park**, with mute-swan pedalos, continues the more kitsch tradition of British seaside resorts.

History

The town dates from the 6th century, when the Abbey of St Comgall made Bangor one of the great centres of the early Church. St Comgall was a teacher and friend of St Columbanus and St Colmcille, two of Ireland's most famous saints. Because Bangor was so often their first landfall, the Vikings repeatedly attacked Bangor Abbey, which was abandoned by the 10th century; only one wall remains today. The one priceless surviving relic – The Antiphonary of Bangor, a small 7th-century prayer book, the oldest surviving Irish manuscript – is now housed in Milan's Ambrosian Library.

Orientation & Information

Unusually, Bangor has a Main St and a High St. The bus and train stations are adjacent to Abbey St, at the top of Main St near the post office. At the bottom of Main St is the marina with B&Bs clustered to the east and west on Queen's Parade and Seacliff Rd.

For information call in on the helpful Tower House Tourist Office (☎ 9127 0069, fax 9127 4466, W www.northdown.gov.uk), 34 Quay St, housed in a tower built in 1637 as a fortified customs post. For most of the year it opens 10am to 5pm Monday, 9am to 5pm Tuesday to Friday and 10am to 4pm Saturday September to June (plus 1pm to 5pm Sunday in June and September); 10am to 7pm Monday, 9am to 7pm Tuesday to Friday, 10am to 7pm Saturday and noon to 6pm Sunday in July and August. The office has a bureau de change and books accommodation anywhere in Ireland.

North Down Heritage Centre

Surrounded by Castle Park, this small museum (☎ 9127 1200, fax 9147 8906, Castle Park Ave; free; open 10.30am-4.30pm Tues-Sat, 2pm-4.30pm Sun, to 5.30pm July & Aug) is in the converted laundry, stables and stores of Bangor Castle. It contains an early 9th-century handbell, some ancient swords, a milepost with distances in Irish miles and a facsimile of The Antiphonary of Bangor. There's also an interesting section on the life of Percy French, famous entertainer and writer.

The Heritage Centre has a *restaurant* serving light meals.

Places to Stay

Accommodation can be hard to find so it's wise to book ahead.

Bayview (☎ 9146 4545, fax 9145 4726, 140 Seacliff Rd) £17 per person with shared bathroom plus breakfast. There's also a comfortable guest lounge.

Pierview (☎ 9146 3381, 28 Seacliff Rd) Singles/doubles £15/32, en suite single £18. Some rooms have sea views. The nicest room is at the front on the first floor with a comfy sofa from which to watch the sea.

Snug Harbour (☎/fax 9145 4238, 144 Seacliff Rd) Shared bathroom/en suite £15/17 per person. All rooms have a TV; the tariff includes a cooked breakfast.

Hebron House (☎ 9146 3126, fax 9127 4178, W www.hebron-house.com, 59 Queen's Parade) Singles/doubles from £25/36, evening meal £12. The owners also run the adjacent Bethany Guesthouse; both places are pleasant.

There's another group of B&Bs on Princetown Rd, past Queen's Parade.

Bangor Bay Inn (☎ 9127 0696, fax 9127 1678, e bangorinn@aol.com, 10-12 Seacliff Rd) Singles/doubles £60/85, £45/65 at the weekend, including breakfast. The Bangor, overlooking the marina, has comfortable en suite rooms and a restaurant.

Marine Court Hotel (☎ 9145 1100, fax 9145 1200, W www.marinecourthotel.net, 18-20 Quay St) En suite singles/doubles £80/90, £65/75 at the weekend, including breakfast. A weekend break for two nights (B&B plus a dinner for two) costs £180. The rooms are en suite with satellite TV, phone and, of course, the obligatory trouser press. The Marine Court has a health club and swimming pool free to guests.

Royal Hotel (☎ 9127 1866, fax 9146 7810, W www.the-royal-hotel.com, 26 Quay St) Singles/doubles from £62.50/75, £50/63 at the weekend, including breakfast. The Royal has good rooms with the best overlooking the marina.

Places to Eat

Jenny Watts (☎ 9127 0401, 41 High St) Bar meals £5-6. Good food and service in Bangor's oldest (1780) pub.

Cafe Brazilia (☎ 9127 2763, 13 Bridge St) Snacks £2.60. Open 9am-5pm Mon-Sat. This stylish cafe serves filled baguettes, a variety of light meals, decent coffee and cakes to kill for.

Knuttel's (☎ *9127 4955, 7 Gray's Hill*) 3-course menu £14.95. Open from 6.30pm Tues-Thur, from 6pm Fri & Sat; last orders by 9.30pm. Knuttel's, opposite the marina, serves mainly seafood and traditional meat dishes, such as grilled sirloin steak and pork in sherry sauce.

Shanks (☎ *9185 3313, fax 9185 2493, 150 Crawfordsburn Rd*) Mains £16-36. Open lunch & dinner Tues-Sat. This Michelin-starred restaurant, at the Blackwood Golf Club, has an interior designed by Terence Conran and a mouth-watering menu designed for gourmets (steamed fillet of turbot with toasted hazelnuts, black truffle and celeriac puree). Expect to pay around £20-35 for a three-course meal, or £15.95 for two courses. Booking is essential.

Joseph's Restaurant (☎ *9147 4606, 110 Main St*) From £1.50. Open 9am-5pm Mon-Sat, to 9pm Fri. Above Menary's Department store, this is a good place to come for an Ulster Fry – five items for £1.50. Apart from that there's a wide range of cakes and other light meals.

Entertainment

Boom Boom Rooms (☎ *9146 8830, 17-21 High St*) Admission £3-6. Open 9pm-1am Wed-Fri, 9pm-1.45am Sat. This is a popular dance-music venue featuring house, funk, R'n'B and disco.

Calico Jack's (☎ *9145 1100, 18-20 Quay St*) Open 8pm-1am Thur-Sun. This club is around the side of the Marine Court Hotel. Live bands play on Thursday and a disco is held on the other nights. Calico Jack's is reportedly a good rave on Saturday.

Jenny Watts (see *Places to Eat*). This popular pub has music on Tuesday and Friday to Sunday, with a mix of folk, jazz and easy listening.

Getting There & Away

Ulsterbus Nos 1 and 2 from Belfast depart from the Laganside Bus Centre (☎ 9033 7015) for Bangor. There's a bus each way every 30 minutes or so weekdays and Saturday and two-hourly on Sunday (£2.40). From Bangor, bus No 6 heads for Newtownards, while bus Nos 3 and 7 travel the Ards

Peninsula to Donaghadee and Millisle. These services run roughly hourly.

There's a regular half-hourly train service to Bangor (and the Ulster Folk & Transport Museum) from Belfast Central Station (☎ 9089 9400). Bangor Station (☎ 9127 0141) is on Abbey St.

NEWTOWNARDS & AROUND

Founded as a 6th-century ecclesiastical centre, Newtownards (Baile Nua na hArda) is a quiet and ordinary market-garden town. The Ards Tourist Information Centre (☎ 9182 6846, fax 9182 6681, W www.kingdoms ofdown.com), 31 Regent St, next to the bus station, opens 9.15am to 5pm weekdays and 9.30am to 5pm Saturday. Hours are 9am to 5.15pm Monday to Thursday and 9am to 5.30pm Friday and Saturday in July and August. They operate a bureau de change and offer an extensive collection of local craftwork, much better than the usual souvenir tat. The post office is also on Regent St.

Guided Walking Tours

There are one to 1½-hour guided walks covering Newtownards, the leadmines and Scrabo Country Park. The walks take place between April and October starting at 6.45pm. Booking is essential – call the Ards Tourist Information Centre (☎ 9182 6846).

Scrabo Hill Country Park

This hill-top park, open year round, 2km south-west of town, was once the site of extensive prehistoric earthworks but these were largely removed during construction of the **1857 Memorial Tower** (☎ *9181 1491; free; open 10.30am-6pm Sat-Thur Apr-Sept*) in honour of the 3rd marquess of Londonderry. There's a 12-minute slide show on Strangford Lough every 30 minutes. The summit (after 122 steps) of the 41m tower offers some expansive views of Strangford Lough. In the distance is Belfast, but before that there's the soft undulating landscape with small hills, known as drumlins, created in the last Ice Age when glaciers deposited sandy material.

Somme Heritage Centre

Just over 3km north of town on the A21 is

the Somme Heritage Centre (*☎ 9182 3202, 233 Bangor Rd; adult/child £3.75/2.75; open 10am-5pm Mon-Fri, noon-5pm Sat & Sun July & Aug; 10am-4pm Mon-Thur, noon-4pm Sat & Sun Apr-June & Sept; 10am-4pm Mon-Thur rest of year*). It relates the circumstances leading up to the WWI Somme campaign of 1916 from the perspective of men of the 10th (Irish), 16th (Irish) and 36th (Ulster) divisions. It's a high-tech show with short films and nothing celebratory about the displays, intended as a memorial to the men and women who died. A significant photographic display commemorates the Suffragette Movement and the part that women played in WWI. Future plans are to expand the building and cover WWII.

Bus No 6, Bangor to Newtownards, passes the entrance and there's ample parking space.

Ark Open Farm

Opposite the Somme Heritage Centre, on the other side of the dual carriageway, is the Ark (*☎ 9182 0445, 296 Bangor Rd; adult/concession £2.90/1.90; open 10am-6pm Mon-Sat & 2pm-6pm Sun*), an open farm with displays of rare breeds of sheep, cattle and poultry, alongside a few llamas and a donkey or two.

Other Things to See

There's a ruined 13th-century **Dominican friary** that's not open to the public, on Court St. The little remains of **Movilla Abbey** and its 13th-century church, 1.5km to the east, have been almost swallowed up by the incursion of Movilla Cemetery.

There's some fine 18th- and 19th-century architecture in town, especially along Church St. Most striking is the 18th-century **Market House** (*☎ 9181 0803, Conway Square; free; open 9am-4pm Mon-Sat*), which once housed the town's prison – you can ask to see an original cell. The Market House now houses the local arts centre. In front of Market House a lively **market** takes place every Saturday and a traditional harvest fair in September. The **Market Cross** on High St dates back to the 17th century.

The Lowden Guitar Company (*☎ 9182

0542*), on the Glenford Industrial Estate in Glenford Way, makes guitars for the greats: Eric Clapton, Van Morrison, Richard Thompson and The Edge. Free 15- to 20-minute tours are available 10am to 3.30pm Monday to Thursday and 10am to 1pm Friday. If you've got the sort of cash that rock stars throw away in a day then you can buy a guitar here. Phone in advance to arrange a tour.

Places to Stay

There's no budget accommodation in central Newtownards.

Greenacres (*☎ 9181 6193, 5 Manse Rd*) Singles/doubles with bathroom £22/36, including breakfast. This guesthouse is set in lovely gardens overlooked by the Scrabo Tower.

Ard-Cuan (*☎ 9181 1302, e valkerr@hotmail.com, 3 Manse Rd*) £22 per person, including breakfast. Bathrooms are shared. This B&B, like its neighbour, Greenacres, is in a quiet part of town.

Strangford Arms Hotel (*☎ 9181 4141, fax 9181 1010, e info@strangfordhotel.co.uk, 92 Church St*) Singles/doubles £49/59 Sun-Thur, £39/49 Fri & Sat, including breakfast. All the rooms are en suite. This neat, three-star B&B hotel also has a restaurant, Le Winters.

Places to Eat

Knott's Cake & Coffee Shop (*☎ 9181 9098, 45 High St*) £1.50-5. Open 9am-5pm Mon-Sat. Knott's offers light meals, a range of pastries and home-baked goodies. Knott's is in a large airy and light building with an interesting truss beam roof.

Cafolla's (*☎ 9181 2185, 15 Conway Square*) This place has been serving decent fish and chips (£2.90) for ever.

Roma's (*☎ 9181 2841, w www.romas.co.uk, 4 Regent St*) Lunch specials £5.25, dinner £6.25-12.95, 3-course special 5pm-7pm £7.50. This busy pub serving food all day is the best bet in town for a decent sit-down meal.

Getting There & Away

The Ulsterbus station is on Regent St. There are buses about every half-hour to Bangor and Belfast (£1.50 single) and fewer services along the eastern and western sides of the Ards Peninsula.

STRANGFORD LOUGH

Cut off from the sea by the Ards Peninsula (see the following section), except for a 1km-wide strait (The Narrows) at Portaferry, Strangford Lough (Loch Cuan) is almost a lake. It's 25km long, about 6km wide on average and up to 45m deep. Large colonies of grey seal live here, especially at the southern tip of the peninsula where the exit channel widens out into the sea. Birds abound on the shores and mudflats, including Brent geese wintering from Arctic Canada, eider ducks and many species of wader.

Under water, the muddy lough has a diverse marine biology, which can be studied at closer quarters at Exploris in Portaferry (see Things to See & Do in the Portaferry section later in this chapter). Killer whales and basking sharks have occasionally come into the lough, spent a few days here and caused a sensation. Strangford Lough oysters are a local speciality.

The lough is a great leisure resource with boats and yachts plying their way up and down its sheltered waters. At Portaferry however, 400,000 tonnes of tidal water surge through the strait four-times daily; you can get some idea of the current's remarkable strength just by watching the ferry being whipped sideways by the riptide. There are boat trips around the lough; see Portaferry later in this chapter.

The western side of Strangford Lough isn't as scenic or interesting as the eastern side (see the following Ards Peninsula section), although it's the route followed by the Ulster Way walking trail.

Western Shore

Castle Espie Centre The Wildfowl and Wetlands Centre at Castle Espie (☎ 9187 4146, 78 Ballydrain Rd; adult/concession/ family £3.65/2.25/9.50; open 10.30am-5pm Mon-Sat & 11.30am-6pm Sun Mar-Oct; 11am-4pm Mon-Sat & 11am-4.30pm Sun Nov-Feb) is 2km south-east of Comber, off the Downpatrick road (A22). It's a haven for fledgling ornithologists and for a large gathering of geese, ducks and swans. Many of the birds are so tame they'll take food from your hand. The best time to visit is between May and June, when the grounds are overrun with goslings, ducklings and cygnets.

Trench Farm (☎ 9187 2558, Ringcreevy Rd) B&B £17.50 per person. This place is almost 4km from Comber off the Newtownards road.

Old School House Inn (☎ 9754 1182, fax 9754 2583, W www.theoldschoolhouse inn.com, Ballydrain Rd, Comber) Singles/doubles £45/65 including breakfast. Near Castle Espie, this is the area's best known restaurant. It serves fresh oysters from its own oyster farm and has game in winter. The set dinner costs from £16.95.

Nendrum Monastic Site The site on Mahee Island is connected to the lough's western shore by a causeway which is guarded by the remains of 15th-century Mahee Castle. Nendrum, built in the 5th century under the guidance of St Mochaoi (St Mahee), is earlier than Grey Abbey on the opposite shore. The scant remains provide a clear outline of its early plan. Foundations exist from a number of churches, a round tower, beehive cells and other buildings, as well as three concentric stone ramparts and a monks' cemetery, all in a wonderful country setting. A particularly interesting relic is the vertical stone sundial that has been reconstructed with some of the original pieces. The ruins were only uncovered in 1844 even though the island has long been inhabited.

There's a small **visitor centre** (☎ 9754 2547, adult/concession £0.75/0.40; open 10am-7pm Tues-Sat & 2pm-7pm Sun Apr-Sept; 10am-4pm Sat & 2pm-4pm Sun rest of year). An excellent video compares Nendrum to Grey Abbey and there's some interesting material about the concept of time and how we measure it, presented in child-friendly fashion.

Ballygraffan House (☎ 9187 0622, 102 Killinchy Rd) Shared bathroom/en suite £18/20 including breakfast. It's an extra £1 for a bath for those without en suite. The rooms are well presented and look very comfortable. This B&B is well signposted off the A22 north of Lisbane.

Lisbarnett House (☎ *9754 1589, Killinchey Rd, Lisbane*) Lunch £6-10, dinner £10.95-15.45. Open lunch & dinner Mon-Sat & 12.30pm-9pm Sun. The Lisbarnett has a good local reputation and serves good food, including vegetarian options, with cheery service. There are menu items for children. It does a traditional roast on Sunday.

Killyleagh The A22 continues south to Killyleagh (Cill O Laoch), an old fishing village dominated by the impressive **castle** (closed to the public) of the Hamilton family. Built originally by the Norman John de Courcy in the 12th century, this partly 14th- and 17th-century structure sits on the original motte and bailey and was heavily restored in 1850. Outside the gatehouse, a plaque commemorates Sir Hans Sloane, the naturalist born in Killyleagh in 1660, whose collection was the basis for the founding of the British Museum. The parish church has the tombs of members of the Dufferin family, some of whom lost their lives in the battles of Trafalgar and Waterloo.

Killyleagh Castle (☎ *4482 8261, High St*) Towers from £200 per week. The castle has three gatehouse towers (complete with spiral staircases and roof terraces) available for weekly rental. The two smaller towers sleep four and the larger sleeps five.

Dufferin Coaching Inn (☎ *4482 8229, fax 4482 8755,* **W** *www.dufferincoaching inn.co.uk, 31 High St*) Singles/doubles £37.50/65. These are large, spacious and very nice rooms, a quality that is reflected in the price. The library-cum-reception has many books on the locale and Ireland.

Dufferin Arms (☎ *4482 1182, 35 High St*) Bar meals £4.95, a la carte £8.25-12.25. This pub has an excellent restaurant providing home-cooked food. Music nights (bands) are Thursday, Friday and Saturday, with traditional sessions on Saturday afternoon.

ARDS PENINSULA

The Ards Peninsula (An Aird) slots in between the eastern side of Strangford Lough and the Irish Sea, with Newtownards and

Donaghadee as gateways. From Newtownards the A20 heads south, following the lough shore, passing Mount Stewart and Grey Abbey before arriving at Portaferry, linked by ferry to Strangford on the western shore. The A2 heads back north along the peninsula's seawards side, passing through the fishing port of Portavogie to Millisle and Donaghadee. Relatively flat, the peninsula is about 6km wide and 35km long, with some good beaches. Dotted along the length of the peninsula are the remains of tower houses, built after Henry VI offered a £10 subsidy to anyone constructing a tower to protect the coast in 1429; most date from the 16th century.

Nowadays the Ards is an agricultural region where farmers have diversified into ostrich rearing and daffodil-bulb cultivation. Watch out for dried *dulse*, Ards' edible seaweed, on sale in greengrocers; it tastes much as you'd expect – strong, salty – and is very much an acquired taste.

Mount Stewart House & Gardens

Eight kilometres south-east of Newtownards on the A20, is Mount Stewart (☎ *4278 8387, Portaferry Rd; adult/concession £3.50/1.75; gardens open 11am-6pm daily Apr-Sept, 11am-6pm Sat & Sun Oct, 2pm-5pm Sun Mar; house open 1pm-6pm Easter, weekends & bank holidays Apr & Oct, 1pm-6pm Wed-Mon May-Sept*). The magnificent 18th-century house and gardens were the home of the marquess of Londonderry, though much of the landscaping was carried out in the early 1900s by Lady Edith, wife of the 7th marquess, for the benefit of her children. The 35 hectares form one of the finest gardens in Ireland or Britain and are now in the charge of the National Trust.

These gardens are a cosmopolitan affair, with formal gardens, woodlands and lakes, elegantly populated by a vast collection of plants and statues. On the Dodo Terrace unusual creatures from history (dinosaurs and dodos) and myth (griffins and mermaids) join forces with giant frogs and duck-billed platypuses. The 18th-century owners constructed the Temple of the Winds (open 2pm to 5pm at the weekend from April to October), a folly in the classical Greek style built on a high point above the lough.

The classical house still has lavish plasterwork, marble nudes and valuable paintings (including a portrait of the racehorse Hambletonian by George Stubbs). Kings have stayed here in bedrooms dedicated to the great European cities. Viscount Castlereagh was born here; as British foreign secretary he was responsible for the Act of Union in 1801, dissolving the Dublin Parliament and making Ireland legally a part of Britain.

There's a tearoom for hot drinks, sandwiches and cakes. Monthly Sunday afternoon jazz is played here between April and September. Bus No 10 from Belfast's Laganside Bus Centre and Newtownards passes the gate Monday to Saturday.

Places to Stay You could try this place near Mount Stewart House.

Ballycastle House (☎/fax 4278 8357, 20 Mount Stewart Rd) Singles/doubles £25/40, including top-class breakfast. It has en suite rooms and downstairs is fitted for wheelchair access. This idyllically situated 18th-century farmhouse B&B is off the A20, near Mount Stewart Gardens. Take the first turning left after you pass the Newtownards Sailing Club. There's also a *self-catering cottage* (high season June to August and Christmas) taking a maximum of six people (£260 to £300 per week).

Grey Abbey
pop 697
Grey Abbey, 3km south-east of Mount Stewart, is the location of some fine ruins of a Cistercian abbey (☎ 4278 8581, Church Rd; adult/concession £1/0.50; open 10am-7pm Tues-Sat & 2pm-7pm Sun Apr-Sept). It was founded in 1193 by Affreca, wife of the Norman John de Courcy. The abbey was a daughter house of Holm Cultram Abbey in Cumbria and was used for worship as late as the 18th century. What remains is a characteristic 12th-century Cistercian ground plan consisting of a large cruciform church, two chapels, parts of a refectory, chapter house and rest rooms.

The church was built in early Gothic style even though Romanesque still reigned supreme elsewhere in Ireland. At the far end of the church is a carved tomb possibly depicting Affreca; her husband may be represented by the effigy in the north transept. The grounds overlooked by 18th-century Rosemount House, are awash with trees and flowers on spreading lawns, making this an ideal picnic spot. A sweet-smelling physic (herb) garden has been replanted. The small visitor centre explains Cistercian life with paintings and panels.

The small village of Grey Abbey has a cluster of 18 **antiques shops** that are open 9am to 5pm Wednesday, Friday and Saturday, tucked away in Hoops Courtyard off Main St and on Main St itself.

Places to Stay & Eat There are a couple of options nearby.

The Mervue (☎/fax 4278 8619, ⓔ heron df@yahoo.com, 28 Portaferry Rd) En-suite singles/doubles £17.50/33, including breakfast. Friendly Mervue is 2.5km from Grey Abbey on the road to Portaferry and by the edge of Strangford Lough.

Brimar (☎/fax 4278 8681, 4 Cardy Rd) Rooms with showers £25 per person, including breakfast. Two rooms are self contained with cooking facilities. In association with the Peninsula Equestrian Academy, riding packages are available from £10 an hour.

Ballynester House (☎ 4278 8386, fax 4278 8986, ⓦ www.ballynesterhouse.com, 1a Cardy Rd) Singles/doubles £25/40, including breakfast. This place also has a very nice self-contained unit with full kitchen. It can take a maximum of four people (£200 to £280 per week).

Hoops (☎ 4278 8541, Hoops Courtyard) Meals £3.95. Open 10am-5pm Wed-Sat. This place serves stupendous lunches (excellent roast beef with the works £4.95), wicked cakes and tea in antique silver teapots.

Getting There & Away Ulsterbus Nos 9 and 10 go to Grey Abbey, Portaferry and Ballywalter from Belfast or Newtownards every hour or so.

Portaferry

pop 2324

Portaferry (Port an Pheire), a neat huddle of streets, is the most substantial settlement on the Ards Peninsula. It was originally called Ballyphilip; its new, duller name relates to its position as the terminus for the short ferry ride across the lough to Strangford. The renowned marine biology station on the waterfront uses the lough as an outdoor laboratory. The stone tower above the town is the remains of a windmill. The town itself is a sleepy place that feels like the end of the road, which of course it is. In good weather, you can sit outside the pubs on the waterfront and watch the lough and the ferry go by.

The Portaferry Tourist Information & Visitor Centre (☎ 4272 9882, fax 4272 9822), Castle St, opens 10am to 5pm (to 5.30pm July and August) Monday to Saturday and 1pm to 6pm Sunday between Easter and September. The centre is near the tower house; it changes money and books accommodation.

Things to See & Do You can take a look at the small 16th-century **tower house**, just by the visitor centre, which together with the tower house in Strangford used to control water traffic through The Narrows. Next to the tower house is the outstanding state-of-the-art aquarium, **Exploris** (☎ 4272 8062, W www.exploris.org.uk, Castle St; adult/ concession £3.85/2.70; open 10am-6pm Mon-Fri, 11am-6pm Sat & 1pm-6pm Sun Mar-Aug; closes at 5pm rest of year), concentrating on marine life from Strangford Lough and the Irish Sea. Touch tanks allow visitors to stroke and hold rays, starfish, sea anemones and other sea creatures. Exploris also rehabilitates sick seals. It's likely to be very busy during school holidays.

Diving, **fishing** and **bird-watching** are all popular pastimes. **Des Rogers** (☎ 4272 8297) takes out dive charters (£150 per day) and the youth hostel has a compressor and special drying room. **John Murray** (☎ 4272 8414) organises fishing and bird-watching trips (£35 per hour), as well as cruises on the lough.

Places to Stay There are a number of options in Portaferry.

Barholm Hostel (☎ 4272 9598, fax 4272 9784, e barholm.portaferry@virgin.net, 11 The Strand) Dorms £10.95. This HINI-affiliated hostel, opposite the ferry slipway, is a roomy place with 45 beds, an excellent kitchen, a big conservatory for breakfast and laundry facilities. Breakfast and dinner can be provided with advance notice.

Adair's (☎ 4272 8412, 22 The Square) Singles/doubles £18/36 including, breakfast. Mrs Adair's is in the centre of the village, a modest place without a sign or name to reveal its identity.

Portaferry Hotel (☎ 4272 8231, fax 4272 8999, 10 The Strand) Singles/doubles £57.50/95, weekend break (two nights B&B plus one dinner) £99 per person. This three-star B&B on the seafront has some quaint rooms and a comfy guest lounge. Most rooms look out over the lough.

The Narrows (☎ 4272 8148, e info@ narrows.co.uk, 8 Shore Rd) £43 per person including breakfast, weekend break £95 per person. This comfortable guesthouse is a few steps farther along from the Portaferry Hotel and is also on the seafront. All rooms have a view of the lough.

Places to Eat You could try these places in town.

The Cornstore (☎ 4272 9779, 2 Castle St) Meals £6. Open lunch & dinner Wed-Sun. This restaurant, across from the tower house, specialises in local seafood and is worth a try.

The Narrows (see Places to Stay) Mains £7.95-14.95. Open lunch & dinner. The Narrows offers superb food and wine together with excellent service and brilliant views of the lough. Expect to pay around £20 for an evening meal.

Portaferry Hotel (see Places to Stay) Lunch £4.95-8, dinner £9.95-15. Open for dinner year round, lunch July & Aug only. This place serves delicious seafood (stuffed mussels, fried oysters) as well as bar lunches.

Getting There & Away Ulsterbus Nos 9 and 10 go to Portaferry, Grey Abbey and Ballywalter from Belfast or Newtownards every hour or so. Buses for around the peninsula leave from Newtownards.

The ferry (☎ 4488 1637) sails every half-hour from Portaferry to Strangford between 7.30am and 10.30pm weekdays, 8am to 11pm Saturday and 9.30am to 10.30pm Sunday. The journey time is about 10 minutes and the ferry returns straight away. The single/same-day-return fares are £4.20/6.80 for a car and driver, £2.70/4.20 for motorcyclists and their bikes and £0.85/1.40 for car passengers and those on foot.

Millisle & Around

Millisle (Oileán an Mhuilinn) has a pretty shoreline with a stone wall running out to sea, handy for watching the eider ducks and Brent geese bobbing offshore. About 1.5km north-west along Moss Rd (the B172 to Newtownards) is **Ballycopeland Windmill** (☎ 9186 1413, Moss Rd; bus No 7 from Donaghadee; adult/concession £1/0.50; open 10am-6pm Tues-Sat, 2pm-6pm Sun June-Sept) This is an 18th-century tower mill, in commercial use until 1915, and now restored to working order with an adjacent visitor centre. The windmill is one of only three in Ireland and the only one in the North.

Places to Stay There are places to stay along Ballywater Rd.

The Ballywhiskin Caravan & Camping Park (☎ 9186 2262, fax 9186 2274, 216 Ballywalter Rd) Tent sites £7.50. The park opens year round and has 20 sites.

Mount Erin House (☎ 9186 1979, 46 Ballywalter Rd) Singles/doubles £20/32 with shared bathroom, including breakfast. Nice, flouncily decorated rooms in the traditional UK B&B style. The front room is the nicest.

Seaspray (☎ 9186 2389, 221 Ballywalter Rd) Singles/doubles £20/35, including breakfast. You can't get much nearer the sea than here, hence the name. The Seaspray has very nice rooms, with a lot of attention to service. It is one of the better places to stay along the coast.

Donaghadee

pop 4799

Donaghadee (Domhnach Daoi) is a small, pretty port, encircled by harbour walls designed by John Rennie in 1819 and completed by his son, Sir John Rennie, who designed several of London's bridges. Now it's fast becoming a dormitory town for those working in Belfast; this causes local concern, as the new inhabitants will be unlikely to use local services. In summer it's possible to get a boat out to **Copeland Island**, which was abandoned to the birds at the turn of the 20th century; enquire at the Harbour Office towards the lighthouse or call ☎ 9188 3403.

Grace Neill's dates from 1611 and claims to be Ireland's oldest pub. Among its 17th-century guests was Peter the Great, tsar and later emperor of Russia, who popped by for lunch in 1697 on his grand tour of Europe. In the 19th century, John Keats found the place 'charming and clean' but was 'treated to ridicule, scorn and violent abuse by the local people who objected to my mode of dress and thought I was some strange foreigner'.

Places to Stay & Eat There are a number of options in Donaghadee.

Anathoth (☎ 9188 4004, ✉ sydneymcmaster@talk21.com, 9 Edgewater) Singles/doubles £17/30, including breakfast. One mile out of town on the Millisle Rd, this small B&B has one small room.

The next two B&Bs are opposite each other on Windmill Rd. Take the Newtownards road (A48) from Donaghadee and turn left into Hoggstown Rd. The second left is Windmill Rd; Bridge House is first house on the left. Ring for directions if you get lost.

Bridge House (☎ 9188 3348, 93 Windmill Rd) Singles/doubles £16/32, including breakfast. Guests share a bathroom and the rooms have TV.

Lakeview (☎ 9188 3900, 92a Windmill Rd) Singles/doubles £15/30, including breakfast. Guests share a bathroom and the rooms have TV.

Ballywilliam House (☎/fax 9188 3692, 98a Warren Rd) Singles/doubles £18/36, including breakfast. There's a shared guest-only bathroom. Ballywilliam is on the Donaghadee to Groomsport road near the golf course.

Deans (☎ 9188 2204, 52 Northfield Rd) Singles/doubles £21/38 including breakfast;

bathrooms are shared. Deans is behind the cricket field in the centre of town.

Grace Neill's *(☎ 9188 4595, 33 High St)* Meals £10.55-12.95. Open lunch & dinner Tues-Sat. This bright and pleasant bistro is in a new building at the back of the old pub. It serves modern Italian and French-influenced dishes such as crisp confit of duck with pomme anna, mushrooms, young spinach and white truffle oil for £11.25. The pub also serves bar meals from £4.55.

The Captain's Table *(☎ 9188 2656, 22 The Parade)* Breakfast from £1.50, other meals £2.60. Open 9am-9pm daily. Although primarily a fish and chip shop, this eatery also serves cooked breakfasts, burgers and chicken meals.

LECALE PENINSULA

The Lecale Peninsula is east of Downpatrick at the southern end of Strangford Lough. From Newcastle, the A2 follows the coast east then north to Strangford for the ferry across to Portaferry and the Ards Peninsula. St John's Point, the southern tip of the Lecale Peninsula, is crowned with an automatic lighthouse.

St Patrick was originally kidnapped from Britain by Irish pirates and spent six years tending sheep on Slemish Mt in County Antrim before escaping back to Britain. After religious training, he returned to Ireland to preach the faith in 432 and is said to have landed on Strangford Lough near Saul. Patrick's first church was in a sheep shelter near Saul, north-east of Downpatrick. Using Saul as his base, he made forays out into the country, retiring to Saul after some 30 years of evangelising. He's buried nearby, or so the locals believe.

Strangford

pop 548

The small, quaint fishing village of Strangford (Baile Loch Cuan) is 16km north-east of Downpatrick. The Vikings sailed into the lough and noted the strong tidal currents through the strait – hence the name meaning 'strong fjord'. Most of the village is in a conservation area dominated by **Strangford Castle** *(☎ 9023 5000, Strangford; free; open*

10am-7pm, keys available from Mr Seed at 39 Castle St), another 16th-century tower house. Steps at the end of Castle St (opposite the castle) lead to a network of paths and a fine view of the lough. There's a large and noisy colony of nesting terns on Swan Island, just off the slipway.

See Portaferry in the Ards Peninsula section earlier in this chapter for details of boat cruises on the lough and the car ferry between Strangford and Portaferry.

Places to Stay & Eat Accommodation is rather scarce in Strangford.

Strangford Caravan Park *(☎ 4488 1888, 87 Shore Rd)* Tent & campervan sites £5. There's also a camp site at Castle Ward (see the following section).

The Cuan Hotel *(☎ 4488 1222, W www .thecuan.com, The Square)* Singles/doubles from £34.95/59.90 including breakfast. The hotel is in a corner of the Square and just around the corner from the ferry.

Cuan Bar & Restaurant *(see The Cuan Hotel above)* Bar snacks £4-9, restaurant meals £9-14; 4-course set meal for 2 including wine £39, 4-course Sun lunch £10.95. Open for bar meals daily, restaurant opens for dinner Mon-Sat, plus lunch & high tea Sun. The Cuan has a reputation for excellence and specialises in local seafood.

Lobster Pot *(☎ 4488 1288, 9-11 The Square)* Bar snacks £5-10, restaurant meals £9.50-11.50, table d'hôte menu for 2 including wine £34.50. Open 11.30am-9pm Mon-Sun. The Pot serves excellent seafood (lobster thermidor £22.50) and bar snacks.

Castle Ward Estate

Run by the National Trust, the 280-hectare Castle Ward Estate *(☎ 4488 1204, Park Rd; grounds £3 car, house £3/1.50; gardens open 8am-8pm year round, house open 1pm-6pm Fri-Wed May-Aug; 1pm-6pm Sat & Sun Apr, Sept & Oct)* stretches some 2km alongside the Downpatrick road. It was built in the 1760s by Lord and Lady Bangor – Bernard Ward and wife, Anne – who were quite a pair. Their tastes started poles apart and continued diverging. The result was Castleward House (and a subsequent divorce). Bernard favoured the neoclassical Palladian approach and was victorious in the design of the front facade and the classical staircase. Anne had leanings towards the Strawberry Hill Gothic style, which she implemented on the back facade and in her Gothic boudoir with its incredible fan vaulting. The rest of this great house is a mixture of their different aesthetic tastes.

The grounds have some decent walks with a Greek folly, a fine 16th-century Plantation tower house, Castle Audley by the lough, a Victorian laundry museum, vistas of the lough and a tearoom (open the same hours as the house), which serves light lunches.

Castle Ward Estate Camp Site (☎ *4488 1680, 19 Castle Ward Rd*) Caravans £10, small/large tents £5/10. Open 17 March-end Sept. The entrance is separate from the main entrance and closer to Strangford.

Strangford to Dundrum

A string of castles stretches from Strangford to Dundrum along the A2 road. The majority are large and in good condition.

Kilclief Castle Only 4km south of Strangford, Kilclief Castle (☎ *9023 5000, Strangford; adult/concession £1/0.50; open 10am-7pm Tues-Sat, 2pm-7pm Sun, Apr-Sept)* guards the seawards mouth of the strait. This is the oldest tower house in the county, built in the 15th century by the adulterous bishop of Down. It has some elaborate details and is viewed as the prototype for other castles in the region.

Ardglass Ardglass (Ard Ghlais), 13km south of Strangford, is a fishing village with seven castles or fortified houses from the 14th to 16th centuries. Ardglass Castle (now the golf club clubhouse) and Gowd Castle adjoining it, has Horn and Margaret Castle towers nearby, while King's and Queen's Castles reside on a hilltop above the village. The only one open to the public is **Jordan's Castle** (☎ *4461 2233, Low Rd; adult/concession £0.75/0.40; open 10am-7pm Tues-Sat & 2pm-7pm Sun July & Aug)* a four-storey tower near the harbour. Like others this was built by wealthy merchants at the dawn of

economic development in Ulster. The castle now houses a local museum and a collection of antiques accumulated by its last owner.

On the hill north of the village is a 19th-century **folly** built by Aubrey de Vere Beauclerc as a gazebo for his daughter.

Places to Stay & Eat You could try these places in and around Ardglass.

Coney Island Park (☎ *4484 1210, Killough Rd*) Tents/campervans £4/8. Power hook-up £2. Open 2 Apr-24 Nov. The park is just outside Ardglass on the Killough Rd.

Strand Farm (☎ *4484 1446, 231 Ardglass Rd*) B&B £17 per person. Open Mar-Nov. The Strand is a small B&B on the B1 road from Ardglass to Downpatrick.

Margaret's Cottage (☎/*fax 4484 1080,* e *chrisandsue@margaretscottage.co.uk, Castle Place)* Singles/doubles £18/36. The Cottage has very nice, well decorated rooms, some with sea views of the Isle of Man.

Aldo's (☎ *4484 1315, Castle Place)* Seafood or a la carte £10. Open 5pm-10pm Thur-Sun & Sun lunch. This place comes highly recommended by the locals.

Ardglass Golf Club (☎ *4484 1219, Castle Place)* Bar menu £4-8, restaurant meals £9.75-14.50. The Golf Club is on the waterfront and the bar and restaurant are open to nonmembers. The bar meals menu is varied and a three-course meal in the restaurant gives some choice.

Killough The seaside village of Killough, 4km west of Ardglass, was planned by Castle Ward's Lord Bangor who constructed the dead straight road from here to his estate, 12km to the north. The harbour has long silted up but the village still has a picturesque, vaguely continental feel, the tree-lined streets and buildings around Palatine St and Palatine Square exemplifying this. The Palatines were 17th-century German refugees escaping the Thirty Years' War (1618–48).

A worthwhile **walk** is south to the 10th-century church ruins and nearby lighthouse of St John's Point, a return trip of about 4km.

Clough This small town, at the northern end of a long and narrow inlet, is home to the ruins of yet another castle. **Clough Castle** is a good example of a 13th-century Norman motte and bailey with a small stone keep.

About 2km north of Clough on the A24, in the village of Seaforde, is the **Seaforde Tropical Butterfly House** (☎ *4481 1225, Newcastle Rd; adult/concession £2.50/1.50 for butterfly house or gardens and maze, combined ticket £4.30/2.50, family ticket £12; open 10am-5pm Mon-Sat, 1pm-6pm Sun Easter-Sept)* set in a large walled garden. The butterfly house has hundreds of free-flying tropical butterflies and many safely caged tropical insects and reptiles. There's also a cafe/restaurant here.

Dundrum Four kilometres south of Clough on the shore of Dundrum (Dún Droma) Bay is **Dundrum Castle** (☎ *9054 3037, Dundrum; adult/concession £0.75/0.40; open 10am-7pm Tues-Sat, 2pm-7pm Sun, Apr-Oct)*, built in 1177 by de Courcy on the site of an earlier Irish fortification. De Courcy's castle was made of wood and his successor, de Lacy, added most of the walls in the first years of the 13th century. King John confiscated the castle in 1210 and added the donjon at the highest point, its thick walls still containing the accessible stairway to the top. After a few changes in ownership it was captured by Cromwell who blew it up in 1652.

You can walk up to the castle from the village centre or there's an adjacent car park.

Mourne View House (☎ *4375 1457, 16 Main St)* £28 per person, including breakfast. This place overlooks the quay; the entry is off the street.

Murlough Tavern (☎ *4375 1211, 143 Main St)* Meals £4.50-7.95. Open lunch & dinner daily. This pub offers bar and restaurant meals with some vegetarian options.

Road House Inn (☎ *4375 1209, 157-163 Main St)* Meals £4.50-11.50, lunch specials £5.25. Open noon-9pm. There's pub food here as well as some accommodation.

Buck's Head Restaurant (☎ *4375 1868, 77-79 Main St)* 3-course meal £23.50, 3-course Sun lunch £14.50. Open Tues-Sun Jan-Mar. Fresh mussels and oysters feature on the menu as well as a vegetarian selection. This is the best place to eat in town

DOWNPATRICK
pop 10,260

Downpatrick's name (Dún Pádraig) comes from Ireland's patron saint, who is associated with numerous places in this corner of Down. From Saul and Downpatrick Cathedral he developed the island into a 'land of saints and scholars'.

Downpatrick is the county's administrative centre and capital, 32km south of Belfast. It was settled long before the saint's arrival, his first church here being constructed inside the *dún* (fort) of Rath Celtchair, an earthwork still visible to the south-west of the cathedral. The place later became known as Dún Pádraig, anglicised to Downpatrick in the 17th century.

In the 11th century, St Malachy moved the diocesan seat to Bangor, but the transfer was short-lived. In 1176 the Norman John de Courcy is said to have brought the relics of St Colmcille and St Brigid to Downpatrick to rest with the remains of St Patrick. Later the town declined along with the cathedral until the 17th and 18th centuries, when the Southwell family developed it into more like what we see today. Much of the Georgian architecture is centred on English, Irish and Scotch Sts, which radiate from the town centre, although the best is in the Mall leading up to the cathedral.

Information

The Downpatrick Tourist Information Centre (☎ 4461 2233, fax 4461 2350, W www.kingdomsofdown.com), 53a Market St, is in St Patrick's visitor centre opposite the bus station. It opens 9.30am to 7pm Monday to Saturday and 2pm to 6pm Sunday, mid-June to September, and 9.30am to 5pm weekdays and 10am to 5pm Saturday the rest of the year. You can change money, have accommodation booked or use their fax or postal services here.

Ego Patricius

In the Saint Patrick Centre, Ego Patricius (☎ *4461 9000, W www.saintpatrickcentre .com, Market St; adult/child/family £4.50/ 2.25/11; open 10am-5pm Mon-Sat & 10am-5pm Sun Oct-Mar; 9.30am-5.30pm Mon-*

Sat & 10am-5.30pm Sun Apr-May & Sept; 9.30am-7pm Mon-Sat & 10am-6pm Sun June-Aug) tells the story of Ireland's patron saint. We live in a world shaped by information bites and that's how this interpretive centre's arranged. Press a button for a particular screen and a film re-enactment gives a couple of minutes' story. Touch a computer screen and you enter an animated information maze. In filmed interviews with scholars you discover how much the St Patrick story has been spun and hyped over the years. He was not the sole or first person to bring Christianity to Ireland and the ridding Ireland of snakes story is a later invention.

The best part is the wide-screen film that takes the audience over the landscape of Ireland in a swooping, low-level helicopter ride. All the while, voices explain the importance of St Patrick to the whole of Ireland; even the stentorian tones of Ian Paisley recognise St Patrick, but only in the context of Northern Ireland.

Down Cathedral

The cathedral *(☎ 4461 4922, The Mall; free; open 9am-5pm)* here is a conglomerate of 1600 years of reconstruction. Viking attacks wiped away all trace of the earliest churches and monasteries and the Irish Augustinians who followed produced little before being evicted by the Norman Benedictines. The subsequent Norman cathedral and settlements were destroyed by Edward Bruce in 1315, but the rubble was used in the 15th-century construction, finished in 1512 but lasting only until 1538. After the dissolution of the monasteries it fell into ruins. Today's structure is an 18th- and 19th-century reconstruction with a few additions.

In the grounds are a 9th-century high cross in poor condition and, to the south, a turn-of-the-20th century monolith with the inscription 'Patric'. It has been believed since de Courcy's time that the saint is buried somewhere nearby. According to legend Patrick died in Saul, where angels told his followers to place his body on an ox-cart and that they would guide the cart to where the saint was to be buried. They supposedly halted at the church on the hill of Down, now the site of the cathedral. The interior reveals a bygone era of churchgoing. The private pews are the last of their kind still in use in Ireland. Note the pillar capitals, the eastern window representing the Apostles and the fine 18th-century church organ.

Inch Abbey

This abbey *(☎ 9023 5000; adult/concession £0.75/0.40; abbey open 10am-7pm Tues-Sat Apr-Sept, grounds open year round)*, built by de Courcy for the Cistercians in 1180 over an earlier Irish monastic site, is visible across the river from the cathedral. The English Cistercians had a strict policy of nonadmittance to Irishmen and maintained this until the end in 1541. Much of the remains consist of foundations and low walls only; the groomed setting in the marshes of the River Quoile is its most memorable feature.

To get here head out of town for about 1.5km on the Belfast road, then turn left just before the Abbey Lodge Hotel.

Down County Museum

Downhill from the cathedral is the county museum *(☎ 4461 5218, The Mall; free; open 11am-5pm Mon-Fri, 2pm-5pm Sat & Sun mid-June-mid-Sept; 10am-5pm Tues-Fri, 11am-5pm Sat mid-Sept-mid-June)*, housed in an extensive 18th-century jail. The museum deals with the county history and in a cellblock at the back are models of some of the prisoners incarcerated there. The biggest exhibit of all is outside – a short signposted trail leads to the **Mound of Down**, a good example of a Norman motte and bailey.

The **Mall** itself is the most picturesque street in Downpatrick, with some marvellous 18th-century architecture, including Soundwell School built in 1733 and a courthouse with a finely decorated pediment.

Quoile Countryside Centre

Signposted off Strangford Rd is the small Quoile Countryside Centre *(☎ 4461 5520, ◉ quoilecc@doeni.gov.uk, 5 Quay Rd; free; open 11am-5pm daily Apr-Sept; 1pm-5pm Sat & Sun Oct-Mar)*, an educational centre with lots of information on the local flora and fauna. It's beside the ruins of **Quoile Castle**, a 17th-century tower house that stood on the shores of the Quoile when it was first built. Access to the lower floors is via the countryside centre.

Downpatrick Railway Museum

This working museum (☎ *4461 5779,* W *www.downrail.icom43.net, Market St, trains Sun July-Aug; 1st & 2nd weekends in Sept)* runs steam-hauled trains over the former Belfast to Newcastle line.

Places to Stay

Accommodation in Downpatrick is fairly thin on the ground.

Denvir's Pub (☎ 4461 2012, fax 4461 7002, 14 English St) Singles/doubles £30/ 50, including breakfast. Denvir's is an old coaching inn dating back to 1642. You can see the original fireplace in the restaurant.

Hillside (☎ 4461 3134, 62 Scotch St) Rooms £17 per person. This is the most central B&B in town with three rooms.

Havine Farm (☎ 4485 1242, 51 Bally-donnell Rd) Rooms from £17 per person. This 200-year-old place with three bedrooms is farther afield, about 7km southwest of Downpatrick and 3km north of Tyrella in Ballykilbeg, in a truly rural environment.

Abbey Lodge Hotel (☎ 4461 4511, fax 4461 6415, 38 Belfast Rd) Singles/doubles £45/58, including breakfast. Near Inch Abbey, this two-star hotel has 22 rooms and is about to have its shabby state renovated.

Places to Eat

Iniscora Cafe (☎ 4461 5283, Down Arts Centre, Irish St) Meals £3.25-9. Open 10am-4.30pm Mon-Sat. This is by far the best place to eat in town. It's a fine red-brick Victorian building with a clock tower, hard to miss at the centre of town, at the junction of English, Irish and Scotch Sts.

Harry Afrika's (☎ 4461 7161, 102 Market St) Snacks £3. Open 8.30am-5.30pm Mon-Sat & 10.30am-5.30pm Sun. Immediately opposite the bus station and in the shopping centre, this is a popular diner-style

restaurant offering reasonably priced breakfasts, grills and daily specials.

Denvir's Pub (see Places to Stay) Meals £5.50-11.50. Open lunch & dinner daily. This place serves good wholesome dishes (Irish stew, fresh mussels) featuring fresh organic vegetables. There's music on Thursday and Sunday with a folk club every other Friday.

Abbey Lodge Hotel (see Places to Stay) Set dinner £13, specials £6.25. If you're not looking for anything fancy then this restaurant's menu might do.

Getting There & Away

Ulsterbus Nos 15 and 215 depart regularly from the Europa Bus Centre in Belfast for Downpatrick bus station (☎ 4461 2384), Market St, every half-hour or so (less frequently on Sunday).

AROUND DOWNPATRICK
Saul

Saul (Sabhal) is 3km north-east of Downpatrick off the A2 Strangford road. Upon landing near here in 432, St Patrick made his first convert, Díchú, the local chieftain, who gave St Patrick a sheep barn *(sabhal)* from which to preach. This was the saint's favourite spot and he returned here regularly. West of the village is the supposed site of the barn, with a mock 10th-century church and round tower built in 1932 to mark the 1500th anniversary of his arrival. Beside the church is the surviving wall of a medieval abbey where St Patrick is said to have died. Also in 1932, a massive 10m-high statue was erected on nearby Slieve Patrick, with Stations of the Cross along its ascent.

Struell Wells

Two kilometres east of Downpatrick, behind the hospital, is the final pilgrimage site associated with St Patrick. Since the Middle Ages, the waters from these have been popular cures for all ills, with one well specially set aside for eye ailments. The site's popularity was at its peak in the 17th century and the men's and women's bath houses date from this time.

CENTRAL COUNTY DOWN

South of Belfast is pastoral countryside, with towns such as Craigavon, Lurgan (in neighbouring County Armagh), Saintfield, Ballynahinch, Hillsborough, Moira and Banbridge servicing the region. Hillsborough is a particularly attractive little town. Only Slieve Croob, south-west of Ballynahinch, breaks the flatness of the terrain. Down's greatest megalithic monuments are in this region, including the Giant's Ring and the Legananny Dolmen.

Giant's Ring

This earthwork, only 8km south of Belfast city centre and west of the A24 in Ballynahatty, is a huge prehistoric enclosure nearly 200m in diameter. It encloses nearly three hectares with the **Druid's Altar**, a dolmen from around 4000 BC in the centre. Prehistoric rings were commonly believed to be the home of fairies and consequently treated with respect, but this one was commandeered in the 19th century as a racetrack. The 4m-high embankment was a natural grandstand and course barrier. It's an impressive and atmospheric place.

Rowallane Gardens

Rowallane Gardens *(☎ 9751 0131, Crossgar Rd; adult/concession £3/1.25; open 10.30am-6pm Mon-Fri, noon-6pm Sat & Sun 17 Mar-31 Oct; 10.30am-5pm Mon-Fri rest of year)*, signposted off the A7 2km south of Saintfield, are renowned for spectacular displays of rhododendrons and azaleas in the spring (summer and autumn are brilliant seasons to visit, too). Rowallane House was inherited in 1903 by Hugh Armitage Moore, a distinguished gardener who spent 25 years developing the 21-hectare garden.

The magnificent massed plantings of rhododendrons thrive in a windbreak of Australian laurels, hollies, pines and beech trees. The walled gardens feature rare primulas, blue Himalayan poppies, plantain lilies, roses, magnolias and delicate autumn crocuses.

The tearoom serves hearty lunches, sandwiches, cakes and scones.

Saintfield

pop 2168

The small, quiet town of Saintfield was the scene of the first of two County Down battles in the 1798 Rebellion. The local Presbyterian minister, the Reverend TL Birch, was active in the United Irishmen and had established a branch here in 1791. The rebels held the town for a few days but were defeated at Ballynahinch soon afterwards. The graveyard of the Presbyterian church on Main St contains a memorial plaque and headstones of those killed in battle.

There are several **antiques shops** along Main St well worth browsing in.

March Hare (☎ 9751 9248, 2 Fairview) Meals £3-5. Open 10am-4pm Wed-Sat. This place serves excellent home-made soups, light meals and cakes.

White Horse Inn (☎ 9751 1143, 49 Main St) Mains £4.50-6.80. Open lunch & dinner Mon-Sat. The White Horse offers more substantial meat and fish dishes. Their Beano Expresso Bar is a licensed coffee bar serving home-baked snacks.

Legananny Dolmen

This is perhaps Ulster's most famous Stone Age monument and is found just west of Slieve Croob (532m). The tripod dolmen is less bulky than most and its elevated position gives it the impressive backdrop of the Mourne Mountains to the south. Farther up, the summit presents a much wider panorama of the county.

To reach the mountain, head west from Ballynahinch along the B7 to Dromara, from where there are roads leading southeast across the slopes.

Hillsborough

pop 2407

The gracious small town of Hillsborough (Cromghlinn), 15km south-west of Belfast, was founded in the 1640s by Colonel Arthur Hill, who built a fort here to quell Irish insurgents. Fine Georgian architecture rings the square and runs down Main St.

The Hillsborough Tourist Information Centre (☎ 9268 9717, fax 9268 9773), The Square, is in the Georgian courthouse in the

*This
harbour

347, fax
Rd) Sin-
eakfast.
icensed
wcastle,
ine very

681, fax
els.com,
160, in-
d-brick,
e beach*

Leprechauns & Banshees

Now you see him, now you don't. The leprechaun is a little man no more than 150cm tall with a jaunty feather sticking out of his green cap. Of course he's at pains to hide from you because, as everyone knows, the leprechaun carries a crock of gold. Catch him and you can force him to give it to you. Take your eyes off him for a second and he'll vanish into thin air.

That's the blarney that has spawned many an Irish tea towel. In reality, scholars believe the leprechaun is a reminder of the days when the early Christians neutralised the power of the pagan gods by turning them into 'little people'.

Another mythical figure of Irish folklore is the banshee, from the Gaelic *bean sídhe* (woman of the fairy mound). She is a spirit whose wailing warns of the impending death of a family member, but it's believed by some that she warns families of pure Irish descent only.

centre of the village. It opens 9am to 5.30pm Monday to Saturday, 2pm to 6pm Sunday July and August. The centre changes money and books accommodation. Walking tours (£2.50) leave here at 11am and 2pm Saturday and 3pm on Sunday from June to mid-September.

Things to See At the top of Main St, the most notable building is **Hillsborough Castle** (☎ 9268 1309, *Main St; adult/concession/family £5/3.50/12.50; grounds & state rooms open 11am-4.30pm Sat, 7 Apr-22 Sept*), a rambling, two-storey, late-Georgian mansion built in 1797 and extensively remodelled in the 1830s and 1840s. From 1924 to 1973 it was the official residence of the governor of Northern Ireland and now that of the secretary of state for Northern Ireland (the British government's main representative). The most notable exterior feature is the elaborate wrought-iron gates, dating from 1745, which were originally designed for Richhill Castle near Armagh.

Nearby is the Georgian **Market House** and at the bottom of Main St **St Malachy's Parish Church** (*Main St; free; open daily*) one of Northern Ireland's most splendid churches,

with twin towers at the ends of its transepts and a graceful spire at the western end. Originally dedicated in 1663, St Malachy's was restored and improved in 1774 by the 1st marquess of Downshire, who was also responsible for its fine Snetzler organ. Inside, the nave and transepts are filled with box pews and there are some impressive 18th- and 19th-century wall tablets as well as a 17th-century copy of the Bible in Irish.

Beside the church are the ruins of **Hillsborough Fort** (☎ 9268 3285, *Main St; free; open 10am-7pm Tues-Sat & 2pm-7pm Sun Apr-Sept; 10am-4pm Tues-Sat & 2pm-4pm Sun Oct-Mar*). It was constructed by Colonel Hill in 1650 and remodelled into a Gothic-style tower house in 1758. The fort commanded the strategic pass of Kilwarlin and was used by William of Orange in 1690 on his way south to the Battle of the Boyne.

Places to Stay & Eat There are a couple of good choices in Hillsborough.

Ballykeel House (☎ 9263 8423, *fax 9263 8423, 32 Ballykeel Rd*) B&B £20 per person. The Ballykeel has three rooms, one with en suite. This nonsmoking B&B is out of Hillsborough on the Lisburn road.

White Gables Hotel (☎ 9268 2755, *fax 9268 9532, 14 Dromore Rd*) Singles/doubles £69.50/95 room only Sun-Thur; £55/65 Fri & Sat including breakfast. Some desperately needed maintenance is required to disprove that it's a hotel in decline.

Plough Inn (☎ 9268 2985, *3 The Square*) Bar meals £7-9.50, bistro £5-7. This pub has been offering 'beer and banter' since 1758 and serves excellent food for lunch and dinner. Oysters are a speciality and bar meals are truly global, with Indian, Scandinavian, Turkish, Chinese and Italian dishes.

Hillside (☎ 9268 2765, *21 Main St*) Meals £4.50-20. Bar meals daily; a la carte menu Fri & Sat, restaurant open for dinner Tues-Sat. This place serves good bar food at lunch-time and also has a top-class restaurant with three-course meals starting at £20. The pub serves real ale.

Chimes Coffee Shop (*5b The Square*) Ulster fry £3.45. Open 10am-7pm Mon-Fri, 10am-8pm Sat & 1pm-6pm Sun. The Chimes is a small coffee shop offering light meals and ice creams.

Getting There & Away There are frequent daily services on bus Nos 38 and 238 to Belfast's Europa Bus Centre.

Banbridge & Around

Banbridge (Droíchead na Banna), 15km south-west of Hillsborough, is another Industrial Revolution town. The Gateway Tourist Information Centre (☎ 4062 3322 fax 4062 3114), 200 Newry Rd, is outside town by the A1 junction into Banbridge. It opens 10am to 5pm Monday to Saturday and 2pm to 6pm Sunday, Easter to October; 9am to 7pm Monday to Saturday and 2pm to 6pm Sunday, July and August. The centre operates a bureau de change and books accommodation. There is a cafe here open the same hours.

Things to See & Do Near the centre at the bottom of the hill stands the **statue of Captain Francis Crozier**, complete with some idiosyncratically sculptured polar bears. A native of Banbridge, Captain Crozier was commander of HMS *Terror* in the 1840s and explored the uncharted Antarctic continent. Later he went with Sir John Franklin in search of the elusive Northwest Passage. Franklin died on that voyage in 1847 and Crozier and his crew starved to death a year later, their bodies remaining lost in the Arctic for 10 years. Crozier lived in the fine blue and grey Georgian house across the ▪ from the statue.

▪idge is the start of a **Brontë Home-** ▪▪hich travels the River Bann ▪▪ 12km to the south-east. ▪▪the famous literary

If you want to understand the manufacture of linen you might want to visit the **Ferguson Linen Centre** (☎ 4062 3491, 54 Scarva Rd; admission £2; tours 3pm Mon-Thur). They are the only manufacturers of double damask linen in the world and have been in operation since 1854.

Places to Stay & Eat You could try the following places.

The Mourne View (☎ 4062 6270, fax 4062 4251, 32 Drumnascamph Rd) Singles/doubles with bathroom £22/36, including breakfast and a light supper. This B&B is 4km west of town near Lawrencetown. There are facilities for guests with disabilities and all four rooms are nonsmoking. The lounge room has lovely views of the Mourne Mountains.

Fresh Winds (☎/fax 4062 2943, 30 Ringsend Rd) B&B £20 per person. This place has brightly decorated rooms with large bathrooms.

Harry's Bar (☎ 4066 2794, 7 Dromore St) Meals £6.50-10. Open lunch & dinner Tues-Sat. This place serves good-value meals and bar snacks. Louisiana blackened salmon or venison is the speciality.

Getting There & Away Bus Nos 38 and 238 run regularly from Belfast's Europa Bus Centre via Dromore, Hillsborough and Lisburn; bus No 238 also runs to Newry.

SOUTHERN DOWN & MOURNE MOUNTAINS

The relatively compact yet rather impressive Mourne Mountains have long resisted human settlement. Today they are surrounded on all sides by towns and villages, but crossed only by the B27 road between

offices stock *St Patrick's Vale: The Land of Legend,* which describes 31 walks.

The Silent Valley Park plunges into the range's heart, surrounded by most of the peaks. Ben Crom, Slieve Muck and Slievelamagan are good for strenuous hiking. Westwards is the B27 road, which passes Spelga Dam, a picturesque drive in the evening when the sun goes down behind Eagle Mt and Pigeon Rock Mt. There's good rock climbing in this area.

As in Connemara, the farmers here have produced the characteristic patchwork of small fields with dry-stone walls out of the boulder-strewn landscape. The biggest of the walls, the Mourne Wall, is a different kettle of fish: it was built in the early 20th century to provide employment and to enclose the catchment area of the Silent Valley Reservoir.

Newcastle
pop 7214

From all along the coast the Mournes beckon, and sticking to the coastline will bring you to Newcastle (An Caisleán Nua), 46km from Belfast. This unremarkable town boasts a dramatic setting, with Slieve Donard stretching up behind the town and an attractive 5km crescent of beach.

Information The Newcastle Tourist information Centre (☎ 4372 2222, fax 4372 2400, W www.newcastletic.org), 10–14 Central Promenade, opens 10am to 5pm Monday to Saturday and 2pm to 6pm Sunday, with longer hours in summer. As well as brochures and maps, the office stocks an interesting range of traditional and contemporary crafts. They book accommodation, change money, provide a postal photocopy and fax service.

tains leave from the centre at 10am at the weekend (ring first to double-check). Booking is essential.

Things to See & Do Next to the tourist office, **Tropicana** *(☎ 4372 5034, Central Promenade; adult/child £2.30/1.80; open 11am-5.30pm Mon-Fri, 1pm-6pm Sat & Sun June; 11am-8pm Mon-Fri, 11am-5.30pm Sat & 1pm-6pm Sun July-Aug)* is a family entertainment 'paradise' complete with outdoor heated fun pools and giant slides.

Places to Stay There's a big range of options in Newcastle.

Newcastle Youth Hostel (☎/fax 4372 2133, e newcastle_hini@yahoo.co.uk, 30 Downs Rd) Dorms from £8.50. This central HINI hostel, near the bus station and Slieve Donard Hotel, has 40 beds; the rate includes bed linen. There's a six-bed family apartment from £37 per room. Facilities include a kitchen, laundry and TV room.

Arundel Guesthouse (☎ 4372 2232, 23 Bryansford Rd) Rooms £20 per person. The Arundel has four rooms, all nonsmoking. Evening meals are possible in summer if you give notice.

Beach House (☎ 4372 2345, fax 4372 2817, 22 Downs Rd) Singles/doubles £30/50. This place is right in town opposite the beach. The favourite room is the one at the front with a sea view and its own private bathroom.

Harbour House Inn (☎ 4372 3445, fax 4372 4418, 4 South Promenade) Singles/ doubles with bathroom £27.50/45 guesthouse is south of town by th and has four en suite rooms.

Briers Country House 4372 6633, 39

Burrendale Hotel & Country Club
(☎ *4372 2599, fax 4372 2328,* **W** *www.burrendale.com, 51 Castlewellan Rd)* Singles/
doubles from £65/99. Weekend breaks from
£99 per person – two nights B&B plus one
dinner. This is another upmarket place with
similar prices to Slieve Donard Hotel. A
swimming pool, Jacuzzi, steam room, sauna
and gym are available for residents.

Places to Eat You could try the following
places.

Rooney's (☎ *4372 6239, 36 Downs Rd)*
Meals £5-15, carvery bistro/restaurant. Open
lunch & dinner Mon-Sat & lunch Sun. This
restaurant, down by the beach opposite the
entrance to the Slieve Donard Hotel, is a
good bet.

Seasalt (☎ *4372 5027, 51 Central Promenade)* Light meals £2.50-4.25, 3-course bistro
dinner £17.50. Open 10am-6pm Mon-Thur,
10am-late Fri & Sat; booking needed for
bistro (Fri & Sat) nights. This sunny cafe offers everything from organic soups to homemade beef-and-Guinness pie.

*Burrendale Hotel & Country Club (see
Places to Stay)* Mains £7.50-11.95. Restaurant open lunch & dinner Mon-Sun. The
Burrendale has a high-quality restaurant; try
the baked fillet of sea bass coated with a
lemon and ginger paste and light cream
sauce for £9.20.

*Oak Restaurant (at the Slieve Donard
Hotel; see Places to Stay)* 4-course dinner
specials £23, 3-course lunch specials £16.
Bar snacks are available throughout the day
and the restaurant opens from 6pm nightly.
It also serves Sunday lunch. The Oak is a
place to eat and spend in style.

Getting There & Away The bus station
(☎ 4372 2296), on Railway St, has an
hourly service from Belfast (return £7.90,
1¼ hours) on Ulsterbus Nos 18 and 20
through Ballynahinch.

Getting Around Wiki Wiki Wheels
(☎ 4372 3973), 10b Donard St, near the main
~~roundabout~~, rents out bikes for £6.50 a day.
~~~~ (☎ 4377 8029), on Clarkhill Rd
~~~wellan~~ and also by the bus

station in Newcastle, rents out bikes for
£10/40 per day/week.

Around Newcastle

Newcastle is an ideal base for exploring the
Mourne Mountains and there are three
nearby forest parks for walks, hikes and
pony treks. **Donard Park**, at the southern
edge of town, is the best place from which
to ascend **Slieve Donard**. On a good day the
three-hour effort is well rewarded, with
Down's patchwork of fields, Scotland,
Wales and the Isle of Man on show. Two
cairns near the summit were long believed
to have been cells of St Donard, who retreated here to pray in early Christian times.

The 500-hectare **Tollymore Forest Park**
(☎ *4372 2428, Bryansford; car/motorcycle
£3.80/2; open 10am-sunset)* 3km north-east
of town, has lengthy walks along the
Shimna River and the northern Mournes.
The **visitor centre** (☎ *4372 2428; open
noon-5pm June-Aug; noon-5pm Sat & Sun
Sept-May)* is in a 19th-century church-like
barn that has information on the flora, fauna
and history of the park. Guided walks leave
from outside at 2pm on summer weekends.

Part of the park but with a separate entrance, **Tollymore Mountain Centre** (☎ *4372
2158,* **W** *www.tollymoremc.com, Bryansford; open year round)* runs group courses
on hill walking, rock climbing and canoeing; call to see what's on offer. **hot rock**
(☎ *4372 5354,* **W** *www.hotrockwall.com;
adult/child £3.50/2; open 10am-10pm Mon-
Sat, 10am-6pm Sun)* is a climbing wall run
by the Tollymore Mountain Centre. There's
a cafe, Internet access and equipment hire.

Farther north-east is the slightly smaller
Castlewellan Forest Park (☎ *4377 8664, off
Main St, Castlewellan; car/motorcycle £3.80/
2; open 10am-dusk)* and its lovely lake.
Trout fishing is allowed (daily permit £5).
Fishing from boats is by fly only. The
park entrance is off the main street in
Castlewellan; you could leave your vehicle
there and walk in.

Outside the park is **Mount Pleasant
Horse Trekking Centre** (☎ *4377 8651,*
W *www.mountpleasantcentre.com, Bannonstown Rd; adult/child £10/9 per hour),*

which caters for the experienced rider and the beginner, with various guided treks into the park. Beach rides and horse trekking can also be arranged.

Places to Stay There are plenty of camp sites on offer, though they can fill up at the height of summer.

Castlewellan Forest Park (☎ 4377 8664, fax 4377 1762, off Main St, Castlewellan) Tent sites £7/11 low/high season. Electric hook-up is available for £1.50 a night.

Tollymore Forest Park (☎ 4372 2428, Bryansford) Tent sites £6-10. The camp site is within the forest park.

Mournes Coast Road

The coastal drive south along the A2 around the sweeping Mournes is the most memorable journey in Down. Annalong, Kilkeel, Rostrevor and Warrenpoint offer convenient stopping points, from which you can detour into the mountains. If you take the Head Rd, following the sign for the Silent Valley 1km north of Annalong, you go through the beautiful stone-wall countryside, past the Silent Valley and back to Kilkeel.

Apart from all the wonderful scenery to goggle at, the Mournes are a place to come and do things, energetic or otherwise (see the various entries in the Around Newcastle section). **Mourne Activity Breaks** (☎ 4176 9965, fax 4176 4390, **W** www.mourneactivitybreaks.co.uk, 28 Bridge St, Kilkeel) organises a large number of activities such as cycling, hill walking, horse riding, pottery, fishing and even falconry. Their packages include accommodation.

Annalong The busy little tourist spot of Annalong (Áth na Long), with its shingle beach, is 12km south of Newcastle. Overlooking the harbour is the nicely preserved **Annalong Corn Mill.** Currently closed, it's an 1830 watermill that can still mill flour.

Four Winds (☎ 4376 8345, 237 Kilkeel Rd) B&B £17 per person. The Four Winds has panoramic views of the mountains and the sea.

Glassdrumman Lodge (☎ 4376 8451, fax 4376 7041, 85 Mill Rd) Singles/doubles

from £80/135, including breakfast. This is an expensive but lovely guesthouse, which also serves very good food (£32.50 for a six-course dinner).

Harbour Inn (☎ 4376 8678, 6 Harbour Drive) Pub meals £4-7.50. More down to earth, this place by Annalong's waterfront serves up fish, steaks and pub food.

Kilkeel Nine kilometres farther south is Kilkeel (Cill Chaoil), bigger than Annalong and with a quayside fish market stocked by Northern Ireland's largest fishing fleet. From Kilkeel the B27 ventures north into the mountains. The friendly Kilkeel Tourist Office (☎ 4176 2525, fax 4176 9947, e kdakilkeel@hotmail.com), 28 Bridge St, opens 9am to 1pm and 2pm to 5.30pm Monday to Saturday, year round.

Chestnutt Caravan Park (☎ 4176 2653, 3 Grange Rd) Tent & campervan sites £10 per night. This place is beside a Blue Flag beach and is of a high standard.

Mourne Abbey (☎ 4176 2426, 16 Greencastle Rd) Singles/doubles £16.50/36. The Abbey is only open April to September and is on the Rostrevor side of town.

Sharon Farm (☎ 4176 2521, 6 Ballykeel Rd) Singles/doubles £18/32. This place is about 5km north-west in Ballymartin and is a working farm. You can watch the sheepdogs put in a day's work.

Hill View House (☎ 4176 4269, 18 Bog Rd) Singles £15-17, doubles £36-40, including breakfast. Just off the B27, this establishment is 6km north of Kilkeel and near Silent Valley. There's also a self-contained chalet, sleeping six, for £160 to £200 a week.

Kilmorey Arms Hotel (☎ 4176 2220, fax 4176 5399, **W** www.kilmoreyarmshotel.co.uk, 41-43 Greencastle Rd) Singles/doubles £30/ 40. This homely place also offers a medium-priced menu of familiar a la carte dishes.

Neptune's Larder (☎ 4176 4186, The Harbour) Open 8am-5pm Mon-Sat. This place serves wonderful fish and chips.

Silent Valley Head Rd, just east of keel, leads 6km to the beautiful Sile ley where the Kilkeel River dammed to provide wate

dry-stone **Mourne Wall** surrounds the valley and climbs over the summits of 15 of the nearby peaks. Two metres high and over 35km long, it was built between 1910 and 1922 and outlines the watershed of the springs that feed the two lakes.

At the southern end of the valley is the **Silent Valley Information Centre** (☎ *9074 6581, Silent Valley; car/motorcycle/pedestrian £3/1.50/0.50; open 10am-6pm*). From near the car park there's a bus up the valley to the top of Ben Crom. This operates daily in July and August, but in May, June and September it runs at the weekend only. Otherwise, it's a fine walk.

During July and August, Ulsterbus No 34A (the Mourne Rambler) runs from Newcastle to Silent Valley, with four buses weekdays and three on Saturday.

Greencastle Greencastle (*Caisleán na hOireanaí; ☎ 9054 3037, Cranfield Point; adult/concession £0.75/0.40; open 10am-7pm Tues-Sat & 2pm-7pm Sun Apr-Sept*), on the tip of a promontory across Carlingford Lough, is 6km south-west of Kilkeel. The first **castle** was built in 1261 as a companion to Carlingford Castle on the opposite side of the lough in County Louth. However, the square, turreted remains date from the 14th century. Once the property of the earls of Kildare, it was seized by the Crown and given to the Bagenal family of Newry in the 1550s. They maintained it as a royal garrison until it was destroyed by Cromwell's forces in 1652.

Rostrevor From Kilkeel the 13km journey westwards along Carlingford Lough takes you to Rostrevor (Caislean Ruairi), a pretty Victorian seaside resort at the base of Slievemartin.

Just before entering the town from the north, the road passes a large **obelisk** to Major General Ross. A British commander in the American War of 1812, Ross's achievement was the capture of Washington DC and the burning of the White House. Up until then the presidential residence had been stone grey, but was painted white to cover the smoke and scorch marks left by Ross's men.

To the north-east of the town is **Kilbroney**

Forest Park (☎ *4173 8134, Shore Rd; free; open 9am-5pm daily, to 10pm in summer*), on the northern shores of Carlingford Lough. There's a forest drive and then a footpath to the top of Slievemartin, or a strenuous trek up the steepest side of the mountain. It is possible to camp in the park (tent/campervan sites £6.20/11.25).

Fir Trees (☎ *4173 8105, fax 4173 8563,* ✉ *martin@firtrees-bedandbreakfast.co.uk, 16 Killowen Old Rd*) Singles/doubles £25/20-23, including breakfast. Fir Trees is 3km from Rostrevor and is signposted off the Kilkeel Rd. It has good views of the lough.

There are several bright and welcoming **pubs** in town all offering decent pub food.

Warrenpoint & Around Warrenpoint (An Pointe), at the head of Carlingford Lough, is another spacious and picturesque resort. It's one of the livelier towns around with an active nightlife.

The Warrenpoint Tourist Information Centre (☎ 4175 2256, fax 4175 3022), in the town hall on Church St, opens 9am to 5pm weekdays year round plus the weekend in summer.

Just over 3km west of Warrenpoint is the small **Burren Heritage Centre** (☎ *4177 3378, 15 Bridge Rd; £2/0.50; open 10am-6pm Tues-Sat & 2pm-6pm Sun Apr-Sept; 10am-5pm Mon-Fri Oct-Mar*) explains the court tombs and *crannógs* (artificial islands) of the area, along with a collection of embroidery, tools and bits and pieces rescued from local churches. It has a craft shop and tcaroom attached.

On the Warrenpoint to Newry road you'll see **Narrow Water Castle**, a medieval tower house standing on the shores of the lough and the round tower of the **Clonallan** monastic settlement on the opposite shore.

Weather permitting, a passenger ferry (☎ 4177 2001) crosses the lough to Omeath in County Louth every half hour between 1pm and 6pm daily, June to September. The 10-minute journey costs £2.50/1.50.

Fernhill House (☎ *4177 2677, 90 Clonallan Rd*) Rooms £18.50 per person. Fernhill is about 3km from town up a hill and with great views of the Lough.

Mariann's Place (☎ *4175 2085, 18 Upper*

DOWN & ARMAGH

Dromore Rd) Singles/doubles £22.50/35 with shared bathroom. Mariann's is about half a kilometre from The Square.

Bennett's *(☎ 4175 2314, 21 Church St)* Meals £4-7. Open lunch & dinner daily. Bennett's offers local seafood, steaks and traditional pies in its restaurant or with bar meals.

Rajput *(☎ 4175 3313, 1 Dock St, The Square)* Mains £4.75-10.75. Open 5pm-11pm nightly. The Rajput is above the Victoria pub and serves north Indian cuisine. Like any good Indian restaurant it has a fair number of vegetarian dishes.

Diamonds *(☎ 4175 2053, 9 The Square)* Meals £3.40-10. Open 10am-7pm Mon-Thur, to 10pm Fri & Sat, 12.30pm-10pm Sun. Diamonds has an extensive menu with something to suit most tastes, including vegetarians'.

Newry

pop 22,975

Newry (An tIúr) has long been a frontier town, guardian of the Gap of the North, which lies between the Mourne Mountains to the east and Slieve Gullion to the south-west. Its name derives from a yew tree planted here by St Patrick in an early monastery, of which nothing remains.

A stone castle was built in the town in 1180 by de Courcy, but was repeatedly attacked. Cistercian monks came to shelter near the castle, until their abbey was taken over by Nicholas Bagenal in the 1570s. As grand marshal of all English forces in Ireland, the powerful Bagenal attracted the attention of some of the local rulers. One, Seán 'the Proud' O'Neill, completely destroyed the castle and house in 1566. In 1575 Bagenal used the rubble to construct the first Protestant church built in Ireland since the Reformation. He is buried in the grounds of St Patrick's Church of Ireland on Stream St.

Newry Canal, built in 1740, preceded the English network that led that country into the Industrial Revolution. The canal brought trade and its later demise led to the decline of the town.

Newry is a good base from which to explore the Mourne Mountains, Slieve Gullion Forest Park and the Cooley Peninsula in County Louth.

Information The Newry Tourist Information Centre (☎ 3026 8877), in the town hall, opens 9am to 5pm weekdays (until 8pm July to August) and 10am to 4pm Saturday, June to September.

Newry Museum The small Newry Museum *(☎ 3026 6232, Bank Parade; free; open 10.30am-4.30pm Mon-Fri)*, in the Arts Centre, presents a detailed history of the town and has some intriguing exhibits, including Admiral Nelson's cabin table from HMS *Victory*.

Town Hall The red-brick town hall was built in 1893 on the border of Counties Down and Armagh. So fierce was the rivalry between the two counties that it was erected right on the border – a three-arched bridge over Clanrye River. The cannon outside was captured during the Crimean War (1853–56) and given to the town in memory of the men who volunteered to fight in the war.

Newry Canal You can hardly miss Newry Canal in the centre of town where it parallels Clanrye River, separated from it by a narrow strip of land. It runs 29km north to Lough Neagh and 9.5km south to Carlingford Lough. Victoria Lock, south of the town centre, has been restored for visitors as part of the long-term Newry Canal Restoration Project to restore the whole canal and reopen it to leisure traffic. The towpath between Newry and Portadown is part of the national cycle network (**W** www.national cyclenetwork.org.uk).

Places to Stay & Eat There are a number of good options in Newry.

The Ashton Country Guesthouse *(☎ 3026 2120, 37 Omeath Rd)* Singles/doubles £25/38, including breakfast. Evening meals are possible with notice. The Ashton is a 200-year-old house with large, pleasantly decorated rooms – just the place to lose yourself in relaxation. It's on the road to Omeath some 3½km from town.

Marymount (☎ 3026 1099, e kevin.ohare @talk21.com, Windsor Ave) Singles/doubles £22/36-40, including breakfast. This B&B is up a hill off the road to Belfast. The rooms are pleasant and this would be the best place near the town centre.

Millvale House (☎ 3026 3789, 8 Millvale Rd) Singles/doubles with shared bathroom £25/40, including breakfast. Evening meals are available on request. This place is quite central, near to the railway station, and about 1½km from town on the road to Bessbrook.

Canal Court Hotel (☎ 3025 1234, fax 3025 1177, W www.canalcourthotel.com, Merchants Quay) Singles/doubles £65/100, including breakfast. This is a centrally located, three-star hotel with a restaurant.

Brass Monkey (☎ 3026 3176, 1-4 Sandy St) Meals £5-9. Open lunch & dinner daily. This bar is the best place to eat in town and offers everything from seafood to steak.

Snaubs Coffee Shop (☎ 3026 5381, 15 Monaghan St) Snacks £3.25-5.75. Open 9am-6pm Mon-Sat. Snaubs has a range of vegetarian options plus freshly baked bread and cakes.

Riverside (☎ 3026 7773, 3 Kildare St) Mains £6.50-8. Open for lunch Mon-Sat, dinner every night. This Chinese restaurant does excellent prawn dishes and is also a takeaway.

Getting There & Away From Belfast's Europa Bus Centre bus Nos 38, 45 and 238 run regularly to Newry bus station (☎ 3026 3531) on Edward St. From the Mall in Newry, bus No 39 leaves twice an hour for Kilkeel, passing through Rostrevor and Warrenpoint.

Trains between Dublin and Belfast stop at Newry; the station (☎ 3026 9271) is a fair way from the centre but there are bus connections.

County Armagh

County Armagh, apart from the venerable town of Armagh, has some wonderful prehistoric sites and more modern sights in the surrounding countryside. You could easily spend a week or more here. Apart from small Protestant outposts, such as Bessbrook, County Armagh is strongly Catholic and its nationalist identity is keenly felt.

ARMAGH
pop 14,640

Armagh (Ard Macha) is one of the towns most worth visiting in the North and St Patrick's Trian and the Navan Fort developments were indicative of an effort to boost tourism. 'Were', because at the time of writing the award-winning Navan centre had closed due to lack of funding.

History

This compact little city claims to be one of Ireland's oldest settlements. According to legend the hill now home to the Church of Ireland cathedral was the power base of Queen Macha during the first millennium BC. She gave her name to the city, Ard Macha, meaning 'Macha's height'. St Patrick set up the first Christian church in Ireland here at the base of the hill. Later the local chieftain, a convert to the new religion, gave Patrick the hilltop and a church has been here for over 15 centuries. By the 8th century Armagh was one of Europe's best-known centres of religion, learning and craftwork.

Its fame was its undoing as the Vikings plundered the city 10 times between 831 and 1013. Brian Ború, who died in 1014 near Dublin during the last great battle against the Vikings, was buried on the northern side of the cathedral.

With the Vikings gone, the Irish clans fought each other for the city and the Norman settlement in the 12th and 13th centuries saw more attacks. Religious life continued, with conversion from Celtic Christianity to Catholic customs in the 12th century and the establishment of a Franciscan friary in 1263. What the Vikings and Normans hadn't managed, the Reformation did. The monasteries and educational establishments were destroyed by either English or Irish forces fighting yet again for control of the city. By the 17th century little was left of a once flourishing city.

During the Plantation, Irish landowners were thrown off their lands and settlers

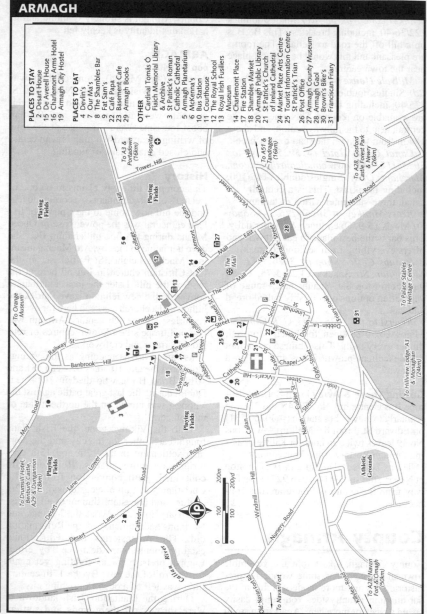

ARMAGH

PLACES TO STAY
2 Desart House
15 De Averell House
16 Charlemont Arms Hotel
19 Armagh City Hostel

PLACES TO EAT
4 Devlin's
7 Our Ma's
8 The Shambles Bar
9 Fat Sam's
22 Café Papa
23 Basement Cafe
29 Armagh Books

OTHER
1 Cardinal Tomás Ó
  Fiaich Memorial Library
  & Archive
3 St Patrick's Roman
  Catholic Cathedral
5 Armagh Planetarium
6 McKenna's
10 Bus Station
11 Courthouse
12 The Royal School
13 Royal Irish Fusiliers
   Museum
14 Charlemont Place
17 Fire Station
18 Shambles Market
20 Armagh Public Library
21 St Patrick's Church
   of Ireland Cathedral
24 Market Place Arts Centre
25 Tourist Information Centre;
   St Patrick's Trian
26 Post Office
27 Armagh County Museum
28 Armagh Gaol
30 Brown's Bike's
31 Franciscan Friary

from England and Scotland took their place. Today's Armagh is a largely Georgian construct and owes its distinctive architecture to Richard Robinson, a Church of Ireland primate. By his arrival in 1765 the town had recovered, economically at least, and had a flourishing linen industry.

Information

The helpful Armagh Tourist Information Centre (☎ 3752 1800, fax 3752 8329, ⓦ www.armagh-visit.com), 40 English St, part of St Patrick's Trian, opens 9am to 5pm Monday to Saturday and 2pm to 5pm (1pm to 5.30pm in summer) Sunday, year round. Note that many things are closed on Sunday.

St Patrick's Church of Ireland Cathedral

The core of the building (☎ 3752 3142, Cathedral Close; admission by donation; open 10am-5pm daily Apr-Oct; 10am-4pm daily Nov-Mar; conducted tours 11.30am & 2.30pm, Mon-Sat) dates to medieval times, but restoration between 1834 and 1840 by Primate Beresford hid what remained of the old stonework between modern masonry. If you ask you might be shown the medieval staircase up to the belfry. The whole appearance is of a modern building. On visiting Armagh a few years after the renovation, the English novelist Thackeray claimed the cathedral as 'neat as and trim as a lady's drawing room'. He went on to remark: 'Future Cockneys setting off from London Bridge after breakfast in an aerial machine may come to hear the morning service here and not remark the faults which have struck a too susceptible tourist of the 19th century.'

Within the church are a section of an 11th-century Celtic Cross that once stood nearby and the Tandragee Idol, being a granite figure dating back to Celtic times. The chapter house has a number of old figures that have yet to be properly displayed.

Near the cathedral, **Vicar's Hill** is one of the oldest terraces in Ireland, built in the 18th century by Richard Cassels (aka Castle) in the Palladian style. The ghost of a green lady is said to haunt the area.

Armagh Public Library

Beside St Patrick's Church of Ireland Cathedral, on the corner of Abbey St, is the wonderful Armagh Public Library (☎ 3752 3142, 43 Abbey St; free; open 9.30am-4pm Mon-Fri), founded in 1771 by Archbishop Richard Robinson and designed by Thomas Cooley. The inscription above the main entrance means 'the medicine shop of the mind'. Step inside and you'd swear that Archbishop Robinson had just swept out another door leaving you to browse among his own personal collection of 17th- and 18th-century books, maps and engravings.

Their collection of books and manuscripts was sadly depleted by the theft of a first edition of Gulliver's Travels annotated by Swift himself. They still have Sir Walter Raleigh's 1614 History of the World, the Claims of the Innocents (pleas to Oliver Cromwell) and a large collection of engravings by Hogarth and others. On the landing outside the library door is an enormous French colour captured by the Armagh Regiment of Militia at the Battle of Ballinamuck in 1798. The flag features the bonnet rouge, the red cap worn by all French revolutionists of the time as the badge of republicanism.

St Patrick's Roman Catholic Cathedral

The other St Patrick's Cathedral (☎ 3752 2802, Cathedral Rd; admission by donation; open until dusk daily) was built between 1838 and 1873. It's built in the Gothic Revival style with huge twin towers dominating the approach up flight after flight of steps. Inside it seems almost Byzantine, with every piece of wall and ceiling covered in brilliantly coloured mosaics. The sanctuary was modernised in 1981 and has a very distinctive tabernacle holder and crucifix that seem out of place among the mosaics and statues of the rest of the church.

Cardinal Tomás Ó Fiaich Memorial Library & Archive

The library (☎ 3752 2981, 15 Moy Rd; free; 9.30am-1pm & 2pm-5pm Mon-Fri) has archives concentrating on Irish language, literature and history.

DOWN & ARMAGH

The Mall

Back along English St (stopping to admire the **Shambles Market** at the corner of English St and Cathedral Rd) and Russell St, you come to the Mall. It's a pleasantly laid-out park that once held horse races, cock fighting and bull baiting, until Archbishop Richard Robinson decided it was a bit low class for a city of learning.

At the northern end of the Mall stands the **courthouse**, now rebuilt after being destroyed by a huge bomb in 1993. It was originally built in 1809 by Armagh man Francis Johnston, who later became one of Ireland's most famous architects. At the southern end of the Mall, exactly in line with the courthouse, is the spooky Armagh Gaol (see that entry below).

Farther along the Mall East is a series of handsome Georgian terraces. **Charlemont Place** is a creation by Francis Johnston and so is the Armagh County Museum's portico, fronting a more workaday building originally put up as a school.

Armagh County Museum

Armagh has one of Ireland's nicer small museums (*☎ 3752 3070, The Mall East; free; open 10am-5pm Mon-Fri, 10am-1pm & 2pm-5pm Sat*). Its showcases are filled with prehistoric axe heads, items found in bogs, old clothes, corn dollies and strawboy outfits, '50s and '60s household goods and icons, and military costumes and equipment. Don't miss the gruesome cast-iron skull that once graced the top of the Armagh gallows. Upstairs is a small art gallery featuring the work of several Irish painters.

Royal Irish Fusiliers Museum

The museum (*☎ 3752 2911, The Mall East; adult/concession £2/1; open 10am-12.30pm & 1.30pm-4pm Mon-Fri*), in the old Sovereign's House near the courthouse, consists of much paraphernalia of war: polished silver and brass, medals and the little personal items that survived from the many battles the fusiliers fought.

Armagh Gaol

The rather forbidding Armagh Gaol, in use until 1988, is no longer open to the public. Built in 1780 to the design of Thomas Cooley it stands opposite the courthouse at the southern end of the Mall.

The building was substantially extended in 1819 and again in 1846. The following year, at the height of the Famine, there were 339 prisoners in the gaol with up to 21 inmates crammed into one cell. At this time the gaol also held dozens of children who had deliberately stolen food in order to escape the appalling conditions of the workhouse.

Public executions took place until 1866; after that prisoners were hanged out of public view in the Hanging Square. Some are buried in the grounds – reputedly under the enormous rhubarb patch.

In the 1920s it became a women's prison and, in the 1970s, C wing was added to house female political prisoners.

Armagh Planetarium

A healthy walk up College Hill from the Mall brings you to **Armagh Planetarium** (*☎ 3752 3689, College Hill; adult/concession £3.75/2.75; open 10am-4.45pm Mon-Fri, 1.15pm-4.45pm Sat & 1.15pm-4.45pm Sun June-Aug; shows at 3pm Mon-Fri June; on the hour from noon-4pm Mon-Fri July-Aug & 2pm, 3pm & 4pm Sat & Sun June-Aug*). It has an interesting Hall of Astronomy displaying astronomical instruments, with lots of hands-on stuff and an Eartharium Gallery designed to give visitors 'a global view of our home'.

Palace Stables Heritage Centre

The heritage centre (*☎ 3752 9629, the Palace Demesne; adult/child/family£3.50/2/9.50; open 10am-5pm Mon-Sat & 2pm-5pm Sun Sept-Mar; 10am-5.30pm Mon-Sat & 1pm-6pm Sun Apr-Aug*), a 10-minute walk out of town off Friary Rd, stands in the grounds of the Palace Demesne, built by Archbishop Robinson when he was appointed primate of Ireland in 1769. As you turn into the demesne, you'll see the ruins of the 13th-century Franciscan friary; much of its stonework was taken to build the demesne walls.

The stables house a set of tableaux meant to illustrate how a guest was entertained in the days of Richard Robinson. You have to go round with a guide (included in ticket price).

The ground-floor lobby of the palace retains some of the grandeur of earlier days, with fine portraits of George III and his wife.

Next to the palace, the Primate's Chapel has fine oak carvings, an elaborate coffered ceiling and stained-glass windows. Beside it, steps lead down to a tunnel. Archbishop Robinson didn't like the smell of cooking, so the kitchen was in an outside building connected to the palace by a tunnel.

St Patrick's Trian

The old Presbyterian church behind the tourist office has been turned into a **heritage centre** (☎ 3752 1801, 40 English St; adult/ concession/family £3.75/2/9.50; open 10am-5pm Mon Sat & 2pm 5pm Sun). It has three exhibitions. The first explores the development of faith within Armagh from its pagan past, St Patrick's adventures here, subsequent schisms in the church and the rise of different sects. An audiovisual display presses the point that there are other religions in the world apart from Christianity. A second exhibition looks at the architectural development of Armagh. For children there's a Land of Lilliput exhibition with a rather wonderful model of Gulliver tied down on the ground while the Lilliputians climb all over him. The story of his adventures in Lilliput is then retold by a gigantic, seemingly real, model of Jonathan Swift's famous creation.

Places to Stay

Gosford Forest Park (☎ 3755 2277, fax 3755 2143, Markethill) Tent sites £6.50/10 in the low/high season. You can camp at this park, which is about 11km south of town on the A28 near Markethill.

Armagh City Hostel (☎ 3751 1800, fax 3751 1801, 39 Abbey St) Dorms £10.50-11.50, twins £12-13 per person. This new HINI hostel, near St Patrick's Church of Ireland Cathedral, is more like a small hotel than a youth hostel. Comfortable twin rooms come complete with en suite bathroom, TV, and tea and coffee facilities. There are also 12 small dorm rooms, a well equipped kitchen, laundry, lounge, reading room and

secure car park. Bike hire is available. It is closed between 11am and 5pm.

Desart House (☎ 3752 2387, 99 Cathedral Rd) Rooms £15 per person, including breakfast. Despite the address the entrance to this B&B is in Desart Lane off Cathedral Rd.

Hillview Lodge (☎ 3752 2000, fax 3752 8276, W www.hillviewlodge.com, 33 Newtownhamilton Rd) Singles/doubles £25/40. This is a modern purpose-built place offering B&B just south of town.

All the following hotels have their own restaurant.

Charlemont Arms Hotel (☎ 3752 2028, fax 3752 6979, W www.charlemontarms hotel.com, 63-65 English St) En suite singles/doubles £45/65, including breakfast. The hotel has been recently renovated, all rooms are en suite and there's a restaurant and wine bar.

De Averell House (☎ 3751 1213, fax 3751 1221, W www.de-averell.com, 47 Upper English St) Singles/doubles £35/59, including breakfast. This three-star Georgian hotel has comfortable rooms and a self-catering apartment; the price depends on how many and for how long. Ask and you might be pleasantly surprised.

Drumsill Hotel (☎ 3752 2009, fax 3752 5624, e info@botanic-inns.com, 35 Moy Rd) Singles/doubles £40/60, including breakfast. This is a small hotel in parklands about 1½km from the city centre.

Places to Eat

The Shambles Bar (☎ 3752 4107, 9 English St) Light meals £4.50. This bar serves a good range of pub grub at lunch-time and a la carte on Friday to Sunday nights.

Café Papa (☎ 3751 1205, 15 Thomas St) Snacks around £4.15. Open 9am-5pm Mon-Thur, 9am-9pm Fri & Sat. This cafe serves decent coffee and gourmet sandwiches. You can bring your own wine here; booking is recommended.

Basement Cafe (☎ 3752 4311, Market Place) Light meals £3.20-5.50. Open 9am-5pm Mon-Sat. The Basement is the place for steak sandwiches and light meals.

Fat Sam's (☎ 3752 5555, 7 Lower English St) Snacks from £1.85. Open 9am-5pm

DOWN & ARMAGH

Mon-Sat. Sam's serves sandwiches, pizzas and breakfasts. Look out for the fibreglass figure of Humphry Bogart outside in his *Casablanca* outfit and there's an invisible pianist tinkling the ivories on a Pianola.

De Averell House (see Places to Stay) Meals around £10. Open 6pm-10pm Wed-Sun. The basement restaurant at this hotel is recommended for dinner or Sunday lunch and it caters well for vegetarians. Booking is recommended.

Our Ma's (☎ 3751 1289, cnr English St & Cathedral Rd) Snacks from £1.50. Open 8am-4pm weekdays, 9am-5pm Sat. This place serves decent snacks and coffee.

Devlin's (☎ 3752 3865, 23 Lower English St) Set meals £5. The restaurant at this pub opens nightly for pub-style grub.

Armagh Books (☎ 3751 1988, 6 Barrack St) Open 9.30am-5.30pm Mon-Sat. This bookshop is also a cafe offering coffee and cakes.

Entertainment

The Shambles, *McKenna's* and *Devlin's*, all in English St, have live bands on Saturday night.

The *Market Place (☎ 3752 1820, ⓦ www.marketplacearmagh.com, Market St)* is the Armagh Theatre and Arts Centre with exhibition galleries, a restaurant, bar and cafe.

Spectator Sports

You may be lucky enough to catch a game of road bowls, a traditional game now only played in Armagh and Cork. Contestants hurl small metal bowls weighing 28oz (0.75kg) along quiet country lanes to see who can make it to the finishing line with the least number of throws. Games usually take place on Sunday afternoon, with championships held in May. Enquire at the Tourist Information Centre.

Getting There & Away

The bus terminal (☎ 3752 2266) is in Lonsdale Rd. There are frequent connections with Belfast, a once-a-day service to Enniskillen (Monday to Saturday) and a service to Dublin. The Belfast to Galway bus No 270 also stops in Armagh. A return fare to Belfast

is £9.50. Bus Nos 40 and 44 run frequently (no Sunday service) to Newry.

Getting Around

Bikes can be hired from **Brown's Bikes** (☎ 3752 2782, 21a Scotch St) for £4/24 per day/week.

AROUND ARMAGH
Navan Fort

A little over 3km west of Armagh is Navan Fort (Emain Macha), the principal archaeological site in Ulster. The Egyptian geographer Ptolemy marked this site on his map of the known world in the 2nd century, naming it Isamnium.

Legend has it that a pregnant woman called Macha was forced to race against the king's horses here; at the end of the race she died giving birth to twins – the name Emain Macha means 'Twins of Macha'. Another legend says that it was the great Queen Macha who began this place, marking out the area with her brooch.

Whatever its origins, the hill was the site for homes and a huge temple during both the Iron and Bronze Ages. Close by is a Bronze Age pond now called the King's Stables where remains of bronze castings have been found.

It's just about walkable from Armagh, or you can take bus No 73 from Mall West.

Unfortunately the impressive visitor centre has closed due to lack of funding.

Orange Order Museum

This Orange Order Museum (☎ 3885 1456, *Main St; free; open by prior arrangement*), 10km north of Armagh in the village of Loughgall, was established in 1961. It contains sashes, banners and weapons from the 1795 Battle of the Diamond between the Protestant Peep o' Day Boys and the Catholic Defenders. This took place at Diamond Hill 5km north-east of the village and led to the founding of the Orange Order.

Ardress House

About 14km north-east of Armagh is the National Trust property Ardress House (☎ 3885 1236, *64 Ardress Rd; adult/concession/fam-*

ily £2.70/1.35/6.75; open 2pm-6pm Sat, Sun & bank holidays Apr-May & Sept; 2pm-6pm Wed-Mon June-Aug), which started life as a farmhouse and was upgraded to a manor house in 1760. Much of the original neo-classical interior remains and the farmyard still functions with a piggery and smithy. The walled garden has been planted with a selection of old apple varieties and there's a small rose garden. There are pleasant walks around the wooded grounds, which are open year round.

The Argory

A fine country house in 130 hectares of woodland above the River Blackwater, The Argory (☎ 8778 4753, Derrycaw Rd, adult/concession £3/1.50; open 2pm-6pm Sat, Sun & bank holidays, Apr May & Sept; 2pm-6pm Wed-Mon June-Aug) retains most of its 1824 fittings; some rooms are lit by acetylene gas from the house's private plant. There are two formal gardens featuring roses, Victorian clipped-yew arbours and a lime walk by the river. It's on Derrycaw Rd off the B28, 3.5km north-east of Moy.

Gosford Castle Forest Park

This relaxing picnic spot (☎ 3755 1277, Markethill; car/adult/concession £3/1.50/0.50; open 10am-dusk daily) has some weird and wonderful poultry on display that children will enjoy. Nature trails work their way around the park and through the trees. In the middle of it all is a vast mock-Norman castle that isn't open to the public. The park is beside the A28, south-east of Armagh near Markethill. Buses to Markethill stop outside.

SOUTH ARMAGH

The notoriety of south Armagh earned it the forbidding epithet of Bandit Country. The intensity of the armed conflict between the IRA and the British army was nowhere more evident or dramatic. At the height of the Troubles many small towns were effectively sealed off by the British military and army helicopters buzzed overhead. The British army is still in evidence, with large observation and communication towers on the tops of several hills, and you'll still hear

low flying helicopters. There are some IRA murals and signs but life has returned to some normality.

Like anywhere else in the North, there's nothing to stop you visiting what is a lovely part of Ireland, steeped in legend and with some fascinating archaeological and ecclesiastical places. Most of the sights are around the Ring of Gullion. This is a ring dyke of rugged hills of volcanic origin encircling 577m-high Slieve Gullion (Sliabh gCuilinn), the mountain where the Celtic warrior Cúchulainn took his name after killing the dog (cú) belonging to the smith Culainn.

Bessbrook

pop 3147

The small town of Bessbrook (An Sruthán) was founded in the mid-19th century by Quaker linen manufacturer John Grubb Richardson to house the workers of his flax mill. The layout of the houses and shops gave the Cadbury family the idea of building Bournville near Birmingham in England. Most buildings are made from local granite and arranged round two squares, each with a green in the middle.

Derrymore House

Just outside the village of Bessbrook is Derrymore House (☎ 3083 8361, Bessbrook; adult/concession/family £2/1/4.50; open 2pm-5.30pm Thur-Sat Easter & May-Aug), an elegant thatched cottage built in 1776 for Isaac Corry who represented Newry in the Irish House of Commons for 30 years. The Act of Union was drafted in the drawing room of the house in 1800. The surrounding parkland was laid out by John Sutherland (1745–1826), one of the most celebrated disciples of Capability Brown.

Killevy Churches

Surrounded by beech trees, these ruined, joined-up churches were built on the site of a 5th-century nunnery founded by St Monenna and plundered by the Vikings in 923. During the Middle Ages a convent of Augustinian nuns was founded but was dissolved in 1542. The eastern church dates from the 15th century, the western from the

12th century. The massive lintel on the western door with the granite jambs may be 200 years older still. Originally, the two churches were nearly a metre apart but became joined at an unknown date.

To the north, the traditional site of St Monenna's grave is marked by a granite slab and a signed walkway leads to a holy well. Heading west out of Camlough, turn left at the crossroads, keeping the lough on the right. A junction on the road points right to the churches and left to Bernish Rock Viewpoint. The churches are 5km from Camlough and can be visited at any time.

Slieve Gullion Forest Park

The coniferous forest, on the B113 about 35km south-east of Armagh, covers the lower slopes of Slieve Gullion (577m) and a gorgeous 13km drive takes in a walk to a lake. The drive emerges from the trees to picturesque views of the Ring of Gullion. Slieve Gullion can be climbed from the south or north. The south approach has a forest road for the first part of the journey, while the north approach is made a little easier because of a rough path all the way. On the summit there are two early-Bronze Age cairns.

Slieve Gullion Courtyard (☎ 3084 8084, fax 3084 8028, 89 Dromintee Rd, Killevy) From £40/50 for a two/eight-person apartment. The Courtyard has ground-floor apartments with rates differing according to season, time of week and size of apartment. Attached is the *Forest Lodge Restaurant*. It opens for dinner on Thursday and Friday, and for lunch and dinner at the weekend. Bar meals cost around £5 and three-course meals cost £12.50. The Courtyard is on the B113 Forkhill Rd, approximately 10km from Newry.

Thí Chulainn Cultural Centre

In the village of Mullach Bán, just west of Slieve Gullion, is Thí Chulainn *(☎ 3088 8828, W www.tichulainn.ie, An Mullach Bán; free; open 10am-4pm Mon-Fri)*, a cul-

tural activities centre that runs an interesting program of traditional music, arts and heritage events. They have an interesting 15-minute video on local history and culture. The **Stray Leaf Folk Club** meets here occasionally.

The nearby pubs in **Forkhill** offer regular traditional music sessions on Tuesday nights and alternate Saturdays; there's a festival of traditional folk singing in October.

Thí Chulainn also has *B&B accommodation* for groups; if you're on your own phone anyway as there might be room.

Crossmaglen
pop 1586

Crossmaglen (Crois Mhic Lionnáin) is a small town near the border with a reputation that should now hopefully be in the past. It's a friendly place known for its excellent music sessions. The large market square here has an open-air market every second Tuesday.

The Crossmaglen Tourist Office (☎ 3086 8900, W www.south-armagh.com), 25-26 The Square, opens 9am to 5pm weekdays.

Places to Stay & Eat *Murtagh's Bar (☎ 3086 1378, e aidmur1964@aol.com, 13 North St)* B&B £20 per person. You can also get dinner here for about £8. Bar meals are available noon to 3pm Monday to Saturday and cost from £4. The *craic* is great.

Ma Kearney's (☎ 3086 8944, 20 Newry St) Bar meals £4.50. Ma's serves bar meals all day and restaurant food for lunch and dinner Monday to Saturday. There's live music on Friday, Saturday and Sunday nights.

Superbite's (☎ 3086 8386, 29-30 The Square) Meals £4-5.50. Open 11.30am-11pm Mon-Sat. Superbite's is a cafe and takeaway dishing up fish and chips, grills and the like.

Getting There & Away Bus No 42 runs regularly Monday to Saturday between Newry and Crossmaglen via Camlough.

Counties Derry & Antrim

Ireland isn't short of fine stretches of coast, but the Causeway Coast from Portstewart in County Derry to Ballycastle in County Antrim, and the Antrim coast from Ballycastle to Belfast, are as magnificent as you could ask for. Most spectacular of all is the surreal landscape of the Giant's Causeway familiar from many a postcard and calendar.

County Derry

The chief attraction of the county is the feisty and historic city of Derry (Doire) nestled by a wide sweep of the River Foyle. North-east along the coast there's good surfing at Portstewart and Portrush, and a fabulous 9km stretch of lonely beach between Castlerock and Magilligan Point. Behind this, from the top of the hills by Binevenagh Lake, is a most astounding view over to Lough Foyle and County Donegal. From Portrush the 214km north-western section of the Ulster Way heads over the gently-rounded Sperrin Mountains.

DERRY
pop 72,330

The handsome city of Derry, the fourth largest in Ireland, is a pleasant surprise to many visitors. Derry has a well founded reputation for musical excellence, from traditional to cutting-edge contemporary. Add to this the resurgence of the arts, peace, an improving economy and the energy and humour of the city's inhabitants, and you have something unbeatable.

There's lots of fascinating history to absorb in Derry, too. A leisurely circuit of the 17th-century city walls is a must, as is a visit to the Tower Museum, which charts the history of the city. And just 6km over the border in Donegal is the Grianán of Aileách, a spectacular stone fort dating back to 1700 BC.

History

There has been a settlement here since the

Highlights

- Discover the feisty city of Derry
- Travel the spectacular Causeway Coast
- Totter across Carrick-a-rede Rope Bridge west of Ballycastle
- Knock back some whiskey at Bushmills Distillery
- Journey to wild Rathlin Island
- Enjoy the astounding view from Binevenagh

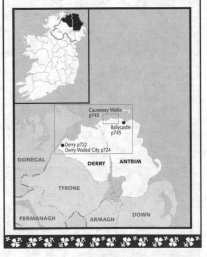

6th century, when St Colmcille (St Columba) founded a monastic community, probably where today's Chapel of St Augustine stands. In the Middle Ages, Derry escaped the worst of the Viking raids and prospered in the 12th and 13th centuries under the Mac Lochlainn dynasty.

Elizabeth I, determined to conquer Ulster, sent an English contingent in 1566 to garrison Derry. In 1600 a second, more lastingly successful attempt to secure the town was made during the Nine Years' War (1594–1603) against the O'Neills and O'Donnells.

COUNTIES DERRY & ANTRIM

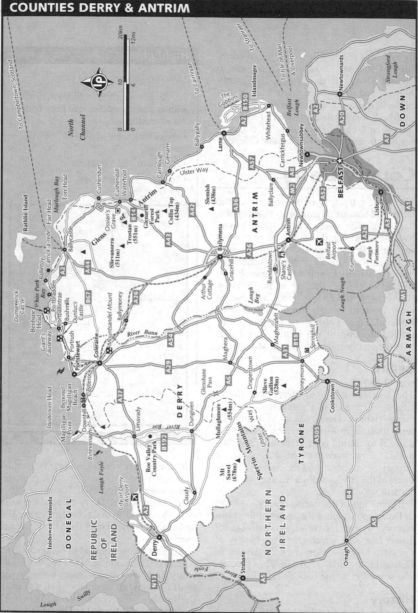

To Campbeltown: Scotland

To Stranraer

North Channel

Rathlin Island

Fair Head
Torr Head
Murlough Bay
Cushendun
Cushendall
Waterfoot
The Gobbins
B150
Islandmagee
To Isle of Man & Liverpool
Strangford Lough
Newtownards
DOWN
A2
A20
Belfast Lough
Whitehead
Carrickfergus
Larne
Ballygally
Carnlough
Glenarm
Ulster Way
Newtownabbey
A7
Antrim
Glens of Antrim
Ossian's Grave
B14
Glenariff Forest Park
Cullin Top (434m)
Slemish (438m)
A42
ANTRIM
A57
BELFAST
A52
Lisburn
A1
A3
Ballycastle
Carrick-a-rede
Ballintoy
White Park Bay
Benbane Head
Giant's Causeway
Dunseverick Castle
Bushmills
Dunluce Castle
Portballintrae
Portrush
Portstewart
B67
Ballymoney
Mountsandel Mount
Coleraine
Trostan (551m)
Slievenorra (511m)
A44
A43
A26
Ballymena
A36
Ballyclare
M2
Antrim
Belfast Airport
Shane's Castle
Crumlin
Lough Portmore
Randalstown
A26
Gracehill
Arthur Cottage
Lough Beg
Lough Neagh
M1
A49
ARMAGH
River Bann
A54
A29
Maghera
Magherafelt
B18
Springhill
A31
Moneymore
Cookstown
A29
A505
A4
Glenshane Pass
A6
Draperstown
Slieve Gallion (528m)
TYRONE
Dungiven
Sperrin Mountains
Ulster Way
Mullaghmore (554m)
Mt Sawel (678m)
River Roe
Limavady
B192
Roe Valley Country Park
Benevenagh
Magilligan Beach
Benone/ Magilligan Point
Downhill
Castlerock
A37
A2
Claudy
B4
A5
DERRY
NORTHERN IRELAND
Inishowen Head
Inishowen Peninsula
DONEGAL
REPUBLIC OF IRELAND
Lough Foyle
City of Derry Airport
A2
Derry
River Foyle
Strabane
N13
Lough Swilly
River Foyle
A5
Omagh

20km
12mi
10
6
0
0

Ess-na-Larach Waterfall, Glenariff Forest Park

Slow-moving traffic in rural County Antrim

County Antrim's spectacular Giant's Causeway is formed from over 38,000 hexagonal basalt columns.

GARETH McCORMACK

Omagh is a useful base for exploring the Sperrin Mountains – if you can find your way through the fog!

GARETH McCORMACK

The evening light on Loch Erne, County Fermanagh, calm after the activities of the day

GARETH McCORMACK

Silhouettes on a crisp winter morning in County Tyrone

Sir Cahir O'Doherty attacked in 1608 and virtually wiped out Derry but in 1609 James I, determined to settle matters for good, granted land to English and Scottish settlers. The wealthy London guilds were put in charge of 'planting' Derry and building the walls.

During the Civil War the city backed Parliament and subsequently William of Orange against James II. In December 1688 Catholic forces led by the earl of Antrim arrived on the other side of the Foyle. They sent emissaries into the city to discuss the crisis; in the meanwhile troops were being ferried across the river. Some apprentice boys on seeing this locked the gates and the great Siege of Derry began.

For 105 days the Protestant citizens of Derry withstood bombardment, disease and starvation. By the time a relief ship burst through and broke the siege, an estimated quarter of the city's 30,000 inhabitants had died.

In the 19th century Derry was one of the main emigration ports to the USA, a fact commemorated by the sculptures of a departing family standing in Waterloo Place. It also played a vital role in the transatlantic trade in shirts; supposedly, local factories provided uniforms for both sides in the American Civil War. To this day Derry still supplies the US president with 12 free shirts every year.

More recently, Derry became a flashpoint for the Troubles. Resentment at the long-running domination and gerrymandering of the council by Unionists boiled over in the civil rights marches of 1968. Simultaneously, attacks on the Catholic Bogside district began and rioting went on for days. The British Army took over from the exhausted Royal Ulster Constabulary (RUC) and accepted the Bogside as a no-go area. For three years until July 1972 and Operation Motorman the Bogside looked after itself, hence the sign 'You Are Now Entering Free Derry'. It took 5000 soldiers with Chieftain tanks to bring down the barriers. In January 1972, Bloody Sunday (see below for details) saw the deaths of 13 Catholic civil-rights marchers at the hands of the army.

Today, the Bogside estate has been rebuilt,

What's in a Name?

Derry's original name was Daire Calgaigh (Oak Grove of Calgach). In the 10th century it was renamed Doire Colmcille (Oak Grove of St Colmcille) for the 6th-century saint who had established the first monastic settlement here. However in 1609 in recognition of the Corporation of London providing the necessary settlers to 'plant' Derry, the city's name was lengthened to Londonderry.

The name is a touchstone for people's political views with Unionists dogmatically asserting the full Londonderry and Nationalists equally firmly shortening it to Derry. Although the city is still officially called Londonderry, the city council was renamed Derry City Council in 1984.

On the radio, to avoid offending anyone, you may hear announcers say both names together – 'DerrystrokeLondonderry' – almost as one word.

Luckily, not everyone takes the Derry/Londonderry controversy too seriously. Some opt instead for the simpler 'Stroke City'!

giving a curiously modern, neat feel to what was once a ghetto. Similarly the Inner City Trust has worked to restore the inner city.

Major developments that have reflected confidence in the future have been the big Foyleside, Quayside and Richmond Shopping Centres and the Millennium Forum.

Bloody Sunday On Sunday 30 January 1972, some 20,000 civilians marched through Derry protesting against internment without trial. It now seems clear that the 1st Battalion of the Parachute Regiment opened fire on unarmed marchers. Thirteen unarmed people were killed, some shot through the back and a 14th died later of injuries. None of those who fired the 108 bullets, or officers in charge, have been brought to trial or even disciplined; records have disappeared and the weapons destroyed. The original Widgery Commission failed to find anyone responsible.

A new enquiry headed by Lord Saville, the Bloody Sunday Enquiry, has been

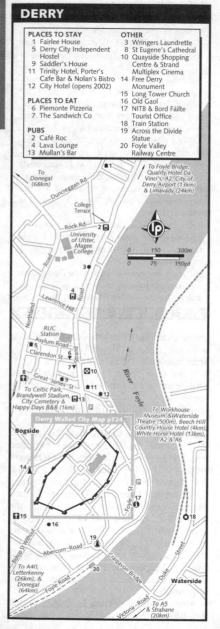

DERRY

PLACES TO STAY
1 Fairlee House
5 Derry City Independent Hostel
9 Saddler's House
11 Trinity Hotel, Porter's Cafe Bar & Nolan's Bistro
12 City Hotel (opens 2002)

PLACES TO EAT
6 Piemonte Pizzeria
7 The Sandwich Co

PUBS
2 Café Roc
4 Lava Lounge
13 Mullan's Bar

OTHER
3 Wringers Laundrette
8 St Eugene's Cathedral
10 Quayside Shopping Centre & Strand Multiplex Cinema
14 Free Derry Monument
15 Long Tower Church
16 Old Gaol
17 NITB & Bord Fáilte Tourist Office
18 Train Station
19 Across the Divide Statue
20 Foyle Valley Railway Centre

underway since March 2000 and may continue for another three years. It sits in the Guildhall Monday to Friday and the public are able to attend.

Nearby, at 39 Shipquay St, is the Bloody Sunday Trust set up to provide support for the families of Bloody Sunday during the enquiry. It opens to the public from 9am to 5pm Monday to Friday (admission by donation) and has a photographic record of that day.

Orientation

The old centre of Derry is the small walled city on the western bank of the River Foyle. At its heart is the square called the Diamond, with Shipquay, Ferryquay, Butcher and Bishop Sts converging on it. The train station is on the eastern side of the River Foyle, while buses stop on the western bank, just outside the walled city. The Craigavon Bridge and, farther downstream, the Foyle Bridge link the two banks of the river.

Information

Tourist Offices The tourist office, near the river at 44 Foyle St, houses both the Northern Ireland Tourist Board (NITB; ☎ 7126 7284, fax 7137 7992, W www.derryvisitor.com) and Bord Fáilte (☎/fax 7136 9501, W www.ireland.travel.ie). It opens 9am to 7pm Monday to Friday, 10am to 6pm Saturday and 10am to 5pm Sunday from July to September; 9am to 5pm Monday to Friday (plus 10am to 5pm Saturday, midMarch to June and October) for the rest of the year. They will book accommodation and have a bureau de change.

Money The banks change euros into pounds and vice versa. The Bank of Ireland and the First Trust Bank on Shipquay St both have ATMs. There's a branch of Thomas Cook (☎ 7185 2552) with exchange facilities at 34 Ferryquay St, open 9am to 5.30pm (8pm Friday) Monday to Saturday. There is a bureau de change in the tourist office.

Post & Communications The main post office is on Custom House St, just north of the city walls. There is another convenient one inside the city walls on Bishop St Within.

Internet Resources The Central Library (see under Libraries later) has free Internet access until 1pm, thereafter at £1.25 per hour. The Derry City Independent Hostel, 4 Asylum Rd, provides Internet access for £4 per hour for nonresidents. An Internet cafe, bean-there.com (☎ 7128 1303, W www.bean -there.com), 20 The Diamond, opens 10am to 7pm Monday to Friday, 10am to 6pm Saturday and 2pm to 6pm Sunday. Costs are £1/2.50/4.50 for 8/30/60 minutes.

Travel Agencies The usit NOW travel office (☎ 7137 1888), 44 Shipquay Place, is also open on Saturday morning.

Bookshops There are several good bookshops in Derry. The Bookworm (☎ 7128 2727), 18-20 Bishop St, is good for material on the Troubles, Derry and Ireland generally.

Foyle Books (☎ 7137 2530), 12a Magazine St, stocks a good selection of secondhand books. Shipquay Books and News (☎ 7137 1747), 10 Shipquay St, is another good bookshop.

Libraries Derry's Central Library (☎ 7127 2300), 35 Foyle St, opens 9.15am to 5.30pm Monday to Friday (on 8pm Monday and Thursday) and 9.15am to 5pm Saturday.

Laundry Derry City Hostel (see Places to Stay for details) operates a wash, dry and fold laundry service for £3.50 for 6kg of dirty clothes. Alternatively, visit glamorous Wringers, 141 Strand Rd, which also has a pool table, electronic games and a snack bar! A wash, dry and fold job for a 5kg load costs £4.

City Walls

Built by 400 workers between 1613 and 1618, the walls were the last complete set of city walls to be constructed in Europe. They are about 8m high and 9m thick, encircle the old city for 1.5km and cost £8357. Their outer design had the purpose of deflecting cannon balls, hopefully back into the attacker's forces; if not, then the earth and rubble filling behind the wall absorbed the damage.

The bastions were built to house cannon that defended the wall. Gunner's Bastion, Coward's Bastion and Water Bastion have been demolished and the original gates (Shipquay, Ferryquay, Bishop's and Butcher's) rebuilt, while three new gates (New, Ferry and Castle) have been added. Derry's sobriquet, the Maiden City, derives from the fact that the walls have never been breached.

City Walk

The walls of Derry are a good place for a wander to understand some of the history of the old city. There are frequent sets of steps so you can get on and off where you want. This walk starts in the centre at the **Diamond**. Derry's Diamond used to house the town hall and three have stood on this site over history. Now the war memorial has taken their place.

From the Diamond, Butcher St, once the street of meat traders leads to **Butcher's Gate**, which was increased in height between 1805 and 1808. Have a look at the inner wall side and you should see a line of larger stones showing the original height.

Passing through Butcher's Gate and going left down Fahan St leads to a set of steps. At the bottom of these, set back from Rossville St, is the Bloody Sunday memorial; the actual incident happened in the enclosed square across the road. See the earlier Bloody Sunday section for more information.

Retracing your steps, turn left after passing through the gate and go down to **Magazine Gate** where a set of steps leads you up onto the wall. This is one of three gates added in 1865 and its road leads to Waterloo St where there's a string of music pubs. The gate is named for the powder magazine that used to be close by. Just by Coward's Bastion is the modern O'Doherty's Tower housing the excellent Tower Museum.

The River Foyle used to come right up to the north-eastern wall so the section from Coward's Bastion to the Water Bastion (demolished 1844) used to have ships moored outside. In the middle is **Shipquay Gate**, a new gate built in 1805 to link the port with the market area. Symbols above the arch show the cornucopia (horn of plenty) and

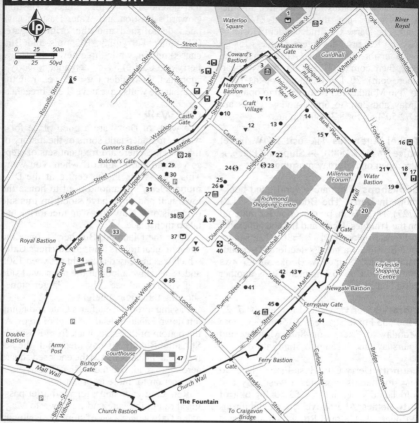

DERRY WALLED CITY

the rod of Mercury (the symbol of trade and commerce).

Just outside the city walls, on reclaimed land, is the red-brick **Guildhall**, originally built in 1890 but rebuilt after a fire in 1908. It was the seat of the old gerrymandering Londonderry Corporation but is now the home of the democratically elected city council.

Turning south-west the walls now come under view from the hills on the other side of the Foyle. This was not lost on the city's enemies and Jacobite cannon fired unimpeded right into the city during the siege.

Where Newmarket St breaches the wall there's a mural. Now mostly out of date, it castigates Western governments for supporting Indonesian aggression in East Timor. Part of the nationalist creed is to lend support to other independence movements.

It was the shutting of the **Ferryquay Gate** by the Apprentice Boys that signalled the start of the 1688/9 siege. In those days there would have been a drawbridge to haul up as well as a padlock on the gate. Both padlock and key can be seen in the Chapter House of St Columb's Cathedral (see that section later for details).

DERRY WALLED CITY

PLACES TO STAY			
29	Derry City Hostel		
30	Tower Hotel (opens 2002)		

PLACES TO EAT
11 Thran Maggies
12 Boston Tea Party
15 Metro Bar
18 McGill's Bistro
21 Cappuccino's
22 Indigo
36 The Sandwich Co
43 Linenhall Bar
44 Fitzroy's

PUBS & CLUBS
4 Peadar O'Donnell's
5 Gweedore Bar
7 Dungloe Bar
8 Fusion

17 Sandino's

OTHER
1 Main Post Office
2 Harbour Museum
3 O'Doherty's Tower; Tower-Museum
6 Bloody Sunday Memorial
9 Soundsaround
10 Foyle Books
13 usit NOW
14 Bloody Sunday Trust
16 Bus Station
19 Central Library
20 St Columb's Hall; Orchard Gallery; Orchard Cinema
23 First Trust Bank (ATM)
24 Bank of Ireland (ATM)
25 Shipquay Books & News

26 Donegal Shop
27 McGilloway Gallery
28 The Nerve Centre
31 Calgach Centre (Fifth Province)
32 First Derry Presbyterian Church
33 Apprentice Boys' Hall
34 Chapel of St Augustine
35 The Bookworm Bookshop
37 Post Office
38 bean-there.com Internet Cafe
39 War Memorial
40 Austins Department Store
41 Antique Market
42 Thomas Cook
45 Playhouse Community Arts Centre
46 Context Gallery
47 St Columb's Cathedral

Above the gate is the image of the Reverend George Walker who was a city leader during the siege. Below in the arches to each side are metal rings. These were used to tether horses that were not allowed into the inner city during market days.

Alongside is Artillery St where cannon balls were made during the siege, the up-ended cannon at the roadside are new but reflect the former redeployment of redundant cannon as hitching posts.

Outside is **The Fountain**, a predominantly Protestant area. The community here is the last significant Protestant enclave on the western bank of the river, the vast majority of Derry's Protestants having moved across the river to the Waterside area or farther afield. The round brick-paved section on the ground is a bonfire site where a 10m-high bonfire is lit on the night before the annual Apprentice Boys march.

Bishop's Gate bisects the southern flank of the wall and was rebuilt for the 100th anniversary of the siege. Bishop Harvey, a keen antiquarian, had a hand in this and requested an 'arch of triumph'. The original gate was lower and had battlements, a drawbridge and portcullis.

During the siege King James II had brought his troops up to this point and demanded the surrender of the city. The defenders replied with gunshots and a cry of 'there'll be no surrender' – still a catchcry of loyalists today.

Outside on Bishop St Without is the one remaining turret of the 1791 **Old Gaol**. Theobald Wolfe Tone, founder of the United Irishmen, spent some time in prison here following the failed rebellion of 1798. On the other side of the road, recent excavations have unearthed artefacts and fortifications dating back to the great siege.

The army towers at the south-western end are potent with listening and watching devices. From the south-western **Double Bastion** there's an excellent overview of the **Bogside** and its famous 'You Are Now Entering Free Derry' monument. This was once the end wall of a row of old houses, but the area was rebuilt and now it stands defiant in the centre of a dual carriageway. The Bogside used to come right up to the city walls but all the houses were removed during the area's rebuilding program.

Standing out from a distance are the murals, one showing a young Bernadette Devlin speaking at a rally, another is taken from a famous photograph of a young boy wearing a gas mask and holding a petrol bomb and another of Bloody Sunday shows

The Derry Skeleton

MATT KING

As you wander around town, you'll soon spot the Derry skeleton, a mournful figure usually with his skull leaned to one side, adorning the city's coat of arms. There are several stories of explanation. One suggests that he's associated with the 1689 Siege of Derry; another that he represents Sir Cahir O'Doherty who sacked Derry in 1608 to avenge an insult. Neither explanation is likely to be right, though, because the skeleton was already gracing the arms in 1600 when the first Plantation of Derry took place.

The most convincing suggestion is that the skeleton represents Walter de Burgo, an Anglo-Norman knight and nephew of the Red Earl, Richard de Burgo. He's said to have fallen out with his cousin William de Burgo, the earl of Ulster, who had him imprisoned in a dungeon in Greencastle in County Donegal. There, he eventually starved to death in 1332. If this story were true, the castle also shown on the coat of arms would probably be Greencastle. In 1311 Edward II granted the Inishowen Peninsula and the island of Derry to Richard de Burgo, thus explaining how his nephew ended up immortalised on the city's coat of arms.

a local priest holding aloft a white handkerchief in an effort to lead some of the injured to safety.

Cannons, given by the London livery companies and reminders of the siege of 1689, still point out over the Bogside.

To the south-west you should see a little of the Foyle, which used to flow through where the Bogside is now. Obviously this was swampy ground hence the current name.

Behind in Society St is the **Apprentice Boys' Hall** and to the front on **Royal Bastion** is an empty plinth. This was once topped by a statue of Reverend George Walker. Here, every Apprentice Boys' march, an effigy of Robert Lundy was burnt. Lundy, the city governor before Walker, fled Derry at the start of the siege and is seen as a traitor by the loyalist community.

In reply, Bogside Catholics used to stoke their fires with old shoes, clothes and anything else to produce an obnoxious smoke, in the hope that the loyalists would be smoked out. The 2.7m statue of Walker, a symbol of unionist domination, was blown up by the IRA in 1973. The restored statue stands in the concrete memorial garden just behind the Apprentice Boys' Hall.

From this point you can see the hills of Donegal, making this one of the few places where you look north to look into the South.

Tower Museum

Just inside Coward's Bastion is the excellent Tower Museum (☎ 7137 2411, Union Hall Place; adult/concession £4.20/1.60; open 10am-5pm Mon-Sat, 2pm-5pm Sun July & Aug; 10am-5pm Tues-Sat & bank holidays Sept-June) which has won major awards. Very well designed exhibits and audiovisuals tell the story of Derry. Items on display include an incredibly well preserved dug-out log boat carbon dated to around the time of St Colmcille's birth in the 520s.

Later there's a wonderful eyewitness account of Shane O'Neill and his soldiers arriving at the court of Elizabeth I to pledge allegiance to the Crown in 1562 (he later reneged):

…armed with hatchets, all bare-headed, their hair flowing in locks on their shoulders, on which were yellow surplices dyed with saffron, or stained with urine, with long sleeves, short coats and thrum jackets, which caused as much staring and gaping among the English people as if they had come from China or America.

Allow a good two hours to do the museum justice.

Art Galleries

There are some interesting galleries in Derry

where you can catch contemporary Irish and international work.

Orchard Gallery (☎ 7126 9675, Orchard St; free; open 10am-6pm Tues-Sat) This gallery presents mainly contemporary works in all media.

Context Gallery (☎ 7137 3538, 5 Artillery St; free; open 10am-5.30pm Tues-Fri & 10am-4.30pm Sat). Context presents an eclectic range of work including performance art.

McGilloway Gallery (☎ 7136 6011, 6 Shipquay St; free; open 10am-5.30pm Mon-Sat) This place also shows modern Irish paintings.

The Fifth Province

The Fifth Province (☎ 7137 3177, Calgach Centre, 4-22 Butcher St, adult/concession £3/1; open 9.30am-4pm Mon-Fri, shows 11.30am & 2.30pm) takes you on a rather extraordinary multimedia trip with hunky Celtic warrior Calgach to discover the fifth province or celebrate your Irishness. Your senses will be bombarded, says the literature and they are. After an introduction to the history of Derry narrated by Richard Harris you sit in a moving 'time chariot' (the best bit) and listen to the handsome Calgach tell tales of Celtic Ireland; finally there's an over-the-top celebration of Irish culture that has you convinced that everyone who emigrated ended up as an astronaut or president of the United States.

St Columb's Cathedral

Standing within the walls of the old city, St Columb's Cathedral (☎ 7126 7313, London St; £1 donation requested; open 9am-5pm Mon-Sat Apr-Oct; 9am-1pm, 2pm-4pm Mon-Sat Nov-Mar), built between 1618 and 1633, was the first Protestant church built in Britain or Ireland after the Reformation. Designed as a fortress (an early example of the 'Church Militant'?) it is now the only siege building left. In a style known as Planter's Gothic, it shares the austerity of many Church of Ireland cathedrals, with dark, carved wooden pews and an open-timbered roof resting on the carved heads of past bishops and deans. The bishop's throne is an 18th-century mahogany chair with beautifully Chinese Chippendale carvings.

In the porch is a hollow cannonball lobbed into the city during the siege by the Jacobites; it carried the terms of surrender, perhaps the first ever airmail letter. The Chapter House contains some drums, paintings, old photos and huge padlocks used to close the city gates in the 17th century.

The flat tombstones in the churchyard are a tradition started during the siege when existing headstones were laid flat to minimise damage.

Other Churches

The Church of Ireland **Chapel of St Augustine**, inside the city walls by Royal Bastion, is thought to have been the site of St Colmcille's 6th-century monastery.

Off Bishop St Without, is St Colmcille's **Long Tower Church** (☎ 7126 2301, Long Tower St; free; open 7.30am-8.30pm Mon-Sat, 7.30am-7pm Sun), Derry's first post-Reformation Catholic church. Built in 1784 in brilliant neo-Renaissance style, it stands on the site of the medieval Tempull Mor (Great Church), which was constructed in 1164. Long Tower was built with the support of the Anglican bishop of the time, Frederick Augustus Harvey, who presented the capitals for the four Corinthian columns framing the ornate high altar.

The Catholic **St Eugene's Cathedral** (☎ 7126 2894, Great James St; open daily) was begun in 1851 as a Catholic response to the end of the Great Famine. Dedicated to St Eugene in 1873 by Bishop Keely, the handsome eastern window is a memorial to the bishop. The bells of St Eugene's still ring every night at 9pm as a reminder of the penal times when Catholics were forbidden to attend mass and were subject to a 9pm curfew.

Guildhall

Just outside the city walls, the redbrick Guildhall (☎ 7137 7335, Guildhall Square; free; open 9am-5pm Mon-Fri) was originally built in 1890 and rebuilt after a fire in 1908. As the seat of the old Londonderry Corporation, which institutionalised the policy of discriminating against Catholics over housing and jobs, it incurred the wrath of nationalists and was bombed twice by the IRA in 1972. The Guildhall is noted for its fine stained-glass windows. Apart from visiting the Saville enquiry (see the earlier Bloody Sunday section for details) there's only the Council Chamber to look around.

Foyle Valley Railway Centre

Down by Craigavon Bridge, the centre (☎ 7126 5234, Foyle Rd; free; on demand excursion adult/concession £3/1.50; open 10am-4.30pm Tues-Sat) stands near what was once the junction of four train lines. At one time Derry had four railways, two standard and two narrow gauge lines. There was one of each size on either banks of the Foyle and were joined via tracks on the lower deck of the Craigavon Bridge. Exhibits inside tell the story of the railways and you can take a 20-minute, 5km-excursion on a train with diesel engine.

Harbour Museum

A small, old-fashioned maritime museum (☎ 7137 7331, Harbour Square; free; open 10am-1pm & 2pm-4.30pm Mon-Fri) with models of ships, a replica of a *currach* – an early open boat with sail – and the bosomy figurehead of the *Minnehaha*, takes up two rooms of the old Londonderry Port Building on Guildhall St.

Workhouse Museum

The new Workhouse Museum (☎ 7131 8328, 23 Glendermott Rd; free; open 10am-4.30pm Mon-Thur & Sat, plus Fri July-Aug) is across the river in the Waterside area in Derry's original 1840–1946 workhouse. Daily life at the workhouse for the up to 800 inmates was designed to encourage them to leave as soon as possible. One of the few exhibits is the grisly horse-drawn hearse used to carry away the workhouse dead.

Other displays detail the Potato Famine, and downstairs the excellent Atlantic Memorial exhibition tells the story of the WWII battle of the Atlantic and the major role that Derry played.

Organised Tours

Walking tours of the inner city depart from the tourist office (see the earlier Tourist Offices section for details). They cost adult/concession £3/1.75 and depart at 2.30pm Monday to Friday November to June; 10.30am and 2.30pm Monday to Friday July to August. They last about 1½ hours.

Northern Ireland Tours and Guides (☎ 7130 9051) runs 1¼-hour Essential Walking Tours of Historic Derry, by arrangement from the Guildhall, June to October. These are tours for groups (£3.50 per person, minimum four) but individuals can phone to check if they can join an existing tour.

McNamara Tours (☎ 7134 5335) runs 1½-hour walking tours at 10am, 1.30pm and 4pm Monday to Saturday, June to September starting at the tourist office. Tours cost adult/concession £3/2.

Foyle Cruises (☎ 7136 2857) run cruises every day on the River Foyle. Day cruises cost adult/child £5/3.50 and depart at noon, 2pm and 4pm, evening cruises cost adult/child £10/7 and depart at 7.30pm.

Special Events

Derry hosts a surprising number of festivals, including the week-long Foyle Film Festival in November; the Gasyard Wall Féile in August, which features concerts, theatre and Irish-language events; and the Féile na Samhna (Irish cultural event), the annual Halloween carnival, which has the entire city dressing up and partying in the streets.

Places to Stay

Accommodation options in Derry are good but booking ahead is advisable in August when festival events are on.

Hostels Be aware that Derry's two hostels have confusingly similar names.

Derry City Hostel (☎ 7128 4100, fax 7128 4101, ℮ info@hini.org.uk, 4-6 Magazine St) Dorms with/without bathroom £7/6.50, B&B singles & doubles £13 per person; prices rise slightly from June to September. This Hostelling International of Northern Ireland (HINI) hostel is in a renovated manor inside the city walls near Butcher's Gate.

Cooking, laundry and currency exchange facilities are available.

Derry City Independent Hostel (Steve's Backpacker's; ☎ 7137 7989, 4 Asylum Rd) 7/3-bed dorms £7.00/8.50 per person, twin rooms £10 per person, fifth night free, continental breakfast included. This small, friendly independent hostel is a short walk north of the walled city. Internet access is free for the first 30 minutes and there are laundry facilities.

Magee College (☎ 7137 1371, fax 7137 5629, University of Ulster, Northland Rd) Rooms £14.10 per person in single bedrooms in five-bedroom self-contained apartments. It's open mid-June to mid-September.

B&Bs You can get to the first two places on bus No D6 or by shared black taxi from Foyle St.

Saddler's House (Joan Pyne's; ☎ 7126 9691, fax 7126 6913, ✉ saddlershouse@btinternet.com, 36 Great James St) En-suite singles/doubles £25/45 including breakfast. About 500m north-west of the bus station, this friendly place is in a lovely 19th-century Victorian house and serves a big breakfast.

Fairlee House (☎ 7137 4551, 86 Duncreggan Rd) Rooms £20-25 per person. This place is farther north again with some en suite rooms.

Happy Days (☎ 7128 7128, fax 7128 7171, ☒ www.happydays.ie, 245 Lone Moor Rd) En-suite rooms £20 per person. Southwest of the walled city near the Brandywell football ground, this place has two rooms and bicycles to rent for £7 per day. To get there take bus no D4 from Foyle St.

Hotels At the time of research two new hotels were being built. Tower Hotel in Butcher St, within the walls, and City Hotel near Queens Quay by the river. Both are due to open in late 2002.

Trinity Hotel (☎ 7127 1271, fax 7127 1277, 22-24 Strand Rd) Singles/doubles £65/85 including breakfast. Weekend £69 per person for two nights B&B plus evening meal. This smart three-star hotel is just north of the city centre. For details of Trinity's restaurants see under Places to Eat.

Quality Hotel Da Vinci's (☎ 7127 9111, fax 7127 9222, ✉ info@davincishotel.com, 15 Culmore Rd) Rooms/breakfast £55/6. As each room has two double beds it only takes four friendly people to make this a very cheap option.

White Horse Hotel (☎ 7186 0606, fax 7186 0371, 68 Clooney Rd) Singles/doubles £40/50 including breakfast. This place is near the airport on the Limavady road. It has a pool, sauna, steam bath, gym and anything else designed to make you exercise.

Beech Hill Country House Hotel (☎ 7134 9279, fax 7134 5366, ☒ www.beech-hill.com, 32 Ardmore Rd) Rooms from £70-90. This elegant 18th-century house is east of the river, out towards Dungiven. The Beech Hill is where Bill Clinton stays when in town and the owner, judging from signed photographs, is also pally with the Kennedys. It has an outstanding restaurant.

Places to Eat

Cappuccino's (☎ 7137 0059, 31 Foyle St) Lunch specials £2.95. Open 8am-6pm Mon-Sat, 9am-1pm Sun. This cosy cafe does a decent £2.95 fry-up for breakfast and has lunch specials such as turnip, bacon and potatoes.

Porter's Cafe Bar (at Trinity Hotel, see Places to Stay) Lunch £3. This is a very popular and thoroughly pleasant place for lunch. Carvery meals cost £3.95.

Nolan's Bistro (at Trinity Hotel, see Places to Stay) Three-course meal £17.50. The Trinity's main restaurant offers a varied dinner menu featuring a couple of interesting vegetarian options.

Nearly all the pubs in town offer reasonably priced pub food and bar snacks.

Linenhall Bar (☎ 7137 1665, 3 Market St) Pub/restaurant meals £3.95/4.75. Open for lunch Mon-Thur, noon-7pm Fri & Sat, 12.30pm-3pm Sun. The Linenhall has a varied menu of pub meals.

Metro (☎ 7126 7401, 3-4 Bank Place) Specials £3.95. The Metro, a popular pub, is a decent place for a feed and there's a large screen for showing televised football if you don't want to miss that important match.

McGill's Bistro (☎ 7130 8273, 24 Foyle St) Main meals £6.95-9.25, 4-course Sunday lunch £6.95. Open noon-5pm Mon-Sat, noon-4pm Sun. Adjoining J&T McGinley's pub, this is an excellent choice for dinner; pan-seared salmon fillet with a herb crust on a bed of champ with a hollandaise dressing costs £7.95.

Indigo (☎ 7127 1011, 27 Shipquay St) Light meals £3.50, mains £4.50. Open noon-11pm daily. This is a bright new cafe-bar-restaurant within the city walls serving light meals and main courses.

Boston Tea Party (15 The Craft Village) Snacks £1-3.25. Open 9am-5.30pm Mon-Sat. In the craft village, off Shipquay St, this place serves pies, soups and sandwiches. The owners cook and prepare everything they sell.

Thran Maggies (☎ 7126 4267, 29-31 The Craft Village) Meals £4.25. Open noon-9.15pm Mon-Sat, noon-5.30pm Sun. Thran (meaning stubborn in Gaelic) Maggies serves up basic Irish dishes at cheap prices. It's licensed and offers a children's menu. Traditional Irish night is on Thursday.

Piemonte Pizzeria (☎ 7126 6828, 2 Clarendon St) Pizza £4, pasta £7. Open 5.30pm-midnight daily. Close to the Derry City Independent Hostel, this is a cheap-and-cheerful place offering pizzas and pasta dishes. It has a BYO licence.

Fitzroy's (☎ 7126 6211, 2-4 Bridge St, 2nd entrance on Carlisle Rd) Meals £3.95-5.50, a la carte £8-14. Open 9.30am-10pm. Popular Fitzroy's does breakfasts from 9.30am to 12.30pm, lunch to 6pm and afternoon snacks from 6pm to 10pm. It has a light breezy atmosphere with snappy service; it's also licensed.

The Sandwich Co (☎ 7126 6771, 61 Strand Rd) Sandwiches & salads £2.75. Open 9am-5pm Mon-Sat. This place serves fresh sandwiches and salads. Another branch on the Diamond has a good selection of sandwiches and cakes.

If you're self-catering *Tesco* (☎ 7137 4400, Quayside Shopping Centre, Strand Rd) supermarket is in the north of the walled city.

Entertainment
Pubs & Clubs Whatever you do in Derry, don't miss an evening in the lively pubs around town. They're friendly and atmos-

pheric; most open until 1am and are within easy walking distance of each other (there are seven within dancing distance on Waterloo St).

Gweedore Bar (☎ 7126 2318, 59-61 Waterloo St) This bar presents live bands every night.

Peadar O'Donnell's (☎ 7126 3513, 61 Waterloo St) Peadar's goes for traditional session music every night starting about 11pm. It is done up as a typical Irish pub-cum-grocer down to shelves of grocery items and a pig's head and hams hanging off the ceiling.

Sandino's (☎ 7130 9297, Water St, off Foyle St) This is a popular venue (named after Nicaraguan guerrilla leader Augusto Sandino) for up-and-coming local bands as well as visiting musicians. There's a live band on Friday and occasionally mid-week, and a traditional session on Sunday afternoon. A film club meets every Tuesday followed by a DJ. A DJ also plays on Saturday night. There are regular theme nights, fund raising nights and political events. Check on Ⓦ www.wheretotonight.com for events.

Mullan's Bar (☎ 7126 5300, 13 Little James St) Another live music venue is Mullan's Bar, featuring jazz, blues and traditional sessions on Wednesday and Thursday nights. There's a DJ for Friday to Sunday. This amazing bar (Northern Ireland does seem to have had a lot of bar designers fuelled by certain substances) was rebuilt after a petrol bomb set the roof on fire during the Troubles – it was a sort of own goal.

Popular club nights (mainly house and '70s and '80s dance music) take place at the following places: *Lava Lounge* (☎ 7126 7529, 113 Strand Rd), *Fusion* (☎ 7126 7600, Waterloo St) and the *Dungloe Bar* (☎ 7126 7716, 41 Waterloo St).

Main Bar and *Spirit Bar* (at Da Vinci's Hotel, see Places to Stay) are two bars out at Da Vinci's. While the Spirit Bar goes in for minimalism, the Main Bar goes in for the monumentalism so loved by Irish bar designers. There's a massive polished wood bar topped with what could only be described as a cut down triumphal arch. The Spirit Bar has a DJ at the weekend.

Café Roc (Earth Complex; ☎ 7136 0556, 1 College Terrace) This nightclub and pub complex has R'n'B, chart hits and music of the '70s to '90s from Tuesday to Sunday. The *Coles Bar* has R'n'B Tuesday and Thursday, and house music Friday and Saturday; the *Equator Room* has house music Tuesday and Friday plus R'n'B on Saturday; the Earth Complex has a student night on Tuesday with a £5 admission charge and £1 drinks. The *Piano Bar* has quieter music for the oldies.

Concerts, Theatre & Arts Centres By publication the new *Millennium Forum* complex (the largest in Ireland) will be open for business. By Bank Place and Newmarket St, this will be a major entertainment venue with an auditorium for dance, drama and music.

Waterside Theatre (☎ 7131 4000, W *www.meg.demon.co.uk, The Ebrington Centre, Glendermott Rd)* This theatre puts on concerts and plays about twice a week.

Magee College (☎ 7137 5679, University of Ulster, Northland Rd) The college holds a variety of arts, theatrical and classical concert performances throughout the year. The tourist office has details (see that section for contact details).

Playhouse Community Arts Centre (☎ 7126 8027, 5 Artillery St) This arts centre is a venue for dance and theatre and is also an exhibition space.

The Nerve Centre (☎ 7126 0562, W *www .nerve-centre.org.uk, 7-8 Magazine St)* This is an arts and multimedia centre started in the late 1980s as an initiative of young musicians and filmmakers. The Nerve has a performance area, theatre/cinema, bar and cafe.

Cinemas If you fancy catching a film, try *Orchard Hall Cinema (☎ 7126 2845, Orchard St)* or *Strand Multiplex (☎ 7137 3900, Quayside Shopping Centre, Strand Rd)*.

Spectator Sports
Derry City Football Club plays soccer at *Brandywell Stadium (☎ 7128 1333, Lone Moor Rd)* south of the walled city. Gaelic football and hurling matches take place at *Celtic Park (☎ 7126 7142, Lone Moor Rd)*.

Shopping
Craft Village (Inner City Trust administration ☎ 7126 0329) Most shops open 9.30am to 5.30pm Monday to Saturday and some open on Sunday in July and August. Tucked off Shipquay St, this place contains craft shops selling Derry crystal, hand-woven cloth, ceramics, jewellery and other local craft items.

Soundsaround (☎ 7128 8890, 22a Waterloo St) This place has an excellent selection of traditional music.

Donegall Shop (☎ 7126 6928, 8 Shipquay St) Just north-east of the Diamond, this place sells garments, tweeds and souvenirs.

Richmond Shopping Centre (☎ 7126 0525, between Ferryquay & Shipquay Sts) This shopping centre within the city walls opens daily.

Foyleside Shopping Centre (☎ 7137 7575, Orchard St) This enormous centre is just outside the eastern city walls.

Austins (☎ 7126 1817, 2 The Diamond) Ireland's oldest department store.

The *antiques market* in Pump St, open 11am-5pm Sat, is a small market with a variety of items on sale.

Getting There & Away
Air City of Derry Airport (☎ 7181 0784) is about 13km east of Derry along the A2 past Eglinton. Ryanair flies twice daily to London's Stansted Airport and British Airways flies to Dublin, Glasgow and Manchester. For more information see The UK in the Air section of the Getting There & Away chapter.

Bus The Ulsterbus station (☎ 7126 2261) is on Foyle St south of the Guildhall.

There are frequent services between Belfast and Derry. Bus No 212, the Maiden City Flyer, is the fastest (one hour 40 minutes), followed by bus No 273, which goes via Omagh (£7.50 single). Bus No 243 to Portstewart, Portrush and the Giant's Causeway leaves at 2.15pm Thursday, Friday and Sunday between July and August. The bus from Derry to Cork leaves at 9am daily, arriving at 7.15pm. The bus from

Cork leaves at 9.15am and arrives in Derry at 8pm.

Bus Éireann (☎ 353-742 1309 in Donegal) operates a Derry to Galway service four-times daily, via Donegal and Sligo. A single to Galway costs £12.

Lough Swilly (☎ 7126 2017) has an office upstairs at the Ulsterbus station, and has buses that connect with County Donegal destinations.

Feda Ódonaill (☎ 353-754 8114 in the Republic, ☎ 0141-637 5673 in Glasgow) runs from Letterkenny to Glasgow via Derry. It leaves Derry bus station at 8.45am, reaching Glasgow around 4pm. The coach from Glasgow leaves at 7.45am from the Citizens' Theatre in Gorbals St and reaches Derry around 3pm. Services run daily in July and August, four-times weekly the rest of the year. The return fare costs £60.

Train From the Northern Ireland Railways station (☎ 7134 2228), on the eastern side of the River Foyle, there are frequent Derry to Belfast services taking about three hours. Trains serve Portrush via Coleraine along a very scenic line. With a valid train ticket there's a free Linkline bus into the town centre from outside the station.

Getting Around
Bus No 143 to Limavady stops near the airport, otherwise a taxi costs about £10.

Local buses leave from Foyle St, by the bus station, where there are also shareable black cabs to outlying suburbs such as Shantallow. The Derry Taxi Association (☎ 7126 0247) and Foyle Taxis (☎ 7126 3905) operate from the city centre to all areas.

The Foyle Valley cycle route passes through Derry on the way to Strabane.

LIMAVADY & AROUND
pop 10,350

Limavady (Léim an Mhadaidh) was granted to Sir Thomas Phillips by James I in 1612, after the last ruling chief, Sir Donnell Ballagh O'Cahan, was found guilty of rebellion. The original Gaelic name means 'Leap of the Dog' and refers to one of the O'Cahans' dogs who jumped a gorge across the

River Roe to bring warning of an unexpected enemy attack.

Today it's a quiet, prosperous small town whose main claim to fame is that one Jane Ross (1810–79) heard a travelling fiddler playing *Londonderry Air* – aka *Danny Boy*, probably the most famous Irish song of all – and noted it down; a blue plaque on the wall of 51 Main St where she lived commemorates the fact.

Information
The tourist office (☎ 7776 0307), in the council building at 7 Connell St, opens 9am to 5pm Monday to Friday (until 5.45pm July and August) and 9.30am to 5.30pm Saturday, April to September; 9am to 5pm Monday to Friday, October to March. Limavady holds a jazz and blues festival in June.

Roe Valley Country Park
This lovely park, about 3km south of Limavady, stretches for 5km either side of the River Roe and is a world-renowned spot for trout and salmon fishing. The area is associated with the O'Cahans, who ruled the valley until the Plantations. The 17th-century settlers saw the flax-growing potential of the damp river valley and the area became an important linen-manufacturing centre. The park's information centre, the Dogleap Centre (☎ 7772 2074), opens 9am to 5pm daily (to 6pm in July and August).

In the **Green House Museum** *(☎ 7772 2226, 41 Dogleap Rd; free; open 1pm-5pm Sat & Sun May-June; 1pm-5pm daily July-Aug)* there are informative old photographs of the flax industry and relics of that time. The weaving shed near the main entrance houses a small museum. The scutch mill, where the flax was pounded, is a 45-minute walk away, along the river, past two watchtowers built to guard the linen when it was spread out in the fields for bleaching.

The park also contains Ulster's first domestic **hydroelectric power station**, opened in 1896. It opens on request at the visitor centre next door. The *cafe (☎ 7772 2920)* opens 10am to 5pm daily (later in summer).

The park is clearly marked off the B192 road between Limavady and Dungiven. Bus

No 146 from Limavady to Dungiven will drop you on the main road, but there's no weekend service. The park is about 30 minutes' walk from the main road.

Places to Stay

Gorteen House Hotel *(☎/fax 7772 2333,* W *www.gorteen.com, 187 Roe Mill Rd)* Singles/doubles £28/44 including breakfast. This reasonable one-star hotel is off Roe Mill Rd, south of Limavady.

Alexander Arms *(☎ 7776 3443, fax 7772 2327, 34 Main St)* £20 per person including breakfast. This pistachio-coloured hotel dates from the 19th century.

Places to Eat

The Lime Tree *(☎ 7776 4300, 30 Catherine St, Limavady)* Lunch £3.95, dinner £9.25, Open noon-2pm & 6pm-9.30pm Wed-Sun. Excellent meals are served here, with an emphasis on seafood. Starters cost from £2.25, main courses include hot wood-smoked salmon with lemon-braised fennel. Light lunches are also available.

Alexander Arms *(see Places to Stay)* Daily lunch special £4.50, evening special £6.25. Open 9am-10.30pm daily. This hotel serves bar food and has a restaurant serving the usual steak and fish pub-style meals.

DOWNHILL & AROUND

The eccentric Anglican bishop of Derry and 4th Earl of Bristol, Frederick Augustus Hervey, built a palatial home at Downhill in 1774. It was burnt down in 1851, rebuilt between 1873 and 1876 and abandoned after WWII. The roof was removed for its scrap value and the remains of the small **castellated building** now stand forlornly on the cliff top.

The major attraction is the curious little **Mussenden Temple** *(free; open noon-6pm Sat & Sun & bank holidays Apr-June & Sept; noon-6pm July-Aug)* built by the energetic bishop to house either his library or his mistress – opinions differ! He conducted an affair with the mistress of Frederick William II of Prussia well into his old age.

It's a pleasant short walk to the temple and the reward is fine views of the beaches at Portstewart and Benone/Magilligan, the hills of Donegal and the shadowy outlines of the Scottish mountains. The beach below is where the bishop challenged his own clergy to race on horseback, rewarding the winners with lucrative parishes. The bishop inscribed a quotation from Lucretius on a frieze: 'It is pleasant to see from the safe shore. The pitching of ships and hear the storm's roar.'

The inscription is thoroughly appropriate on a windy day. The site is about 15km north-east of Limavady. It's owned by the National Trust.

The original demesne covered some 160 hectares, which now forms part of **Downhill Forest**. The beautiful landscaped gardens below the ruins of the house are the work of celebrated gardener Jan Eccles, who became custodian at Downhill at the age of 60 and created the garden over a period of 30 years. She died in 1997 aged 94.

Immediately past the closed-down Downhill Inn, Bishop's Rd forks up to the left leading over the mountains to Limavady, with terrific views from the **Gortmore** picnic area. Even more spectacular views over Lough Foyle, Donegal and the Sperrin mountains are to be found at the top of a vertical escarpment by **Binevenagh Lake**. Just follow the signs for the lake.

Places to Stay On the edge of the beach at Downhill, tucked beneath the sea cliffs, is ***Downhill Hostel*** *(☎ 7084 9077,* W *www .angelfire.com/wa/downhillhostel, 12 Mussenden Rd)* Dorms £7.50 per person, singles/doubles £14/20, family rooms from £28. This beautifully restored 100-year-old house offers very comfortable accommodation in three dorms and four double rooms. There's a well stocked kitchen, laundry facilities and a big lounge with an open fire and a view of the sea. There are no shops in Downhill so bring supplies with you.

You can decorate your own pottery in the hostel pottery and residents have access to the local nature reserve run by the Ulster Wildlife Society.

Castlerock

Castlerock, a small seaside town off the A2, is a train stop on the Coleraine–Derry line.

The late-17th-century **Hezlett House** (☎ *7084 8567, 107 Sea Rd; adult/concession £2/1; open noon-5pm Sat & Sun, bank holidays & Easter, Apr-May & Sept; noon-5pm Wed-Mon June-Aug)* is a single-storey thatched cottage noted for its cruck-truss roof gables of stone and turf strengthened with wooden crucks, or crutches. The interior decoration is Victorian. The house is 8km west of Coleraine at Liffock on the A2.

Hill Farm Riding and Trekking Centre (☎ *7084 8629, 47 Altikeeragh, Castlerock)* offers horse riding from £12 an hour including riding on the beach.

Castlerock Holiday Park (☎ *7084 8381, 24 Sea Rd)* Campervan sites low/high season £8/11. It's open from March to October (low season: March to June, September and October; high season: July and August) but only for campervans.

Benone/Magilligan Beach

Some 9km in length and hundreds of metres wide at low tide, this huge Blue Flag beach, called both Benone and Magilligan, is worth a visit. Bordered by sand dunes and dramatic sea cliffs, the beach sweeps out to Magilligan Point, where a Martello tower stands and from where sailplanes and hanggliders can be seen riding the wind.

Benone Tourist Complex (☎ *7775 0555, fax 7775 0919, 59 Benone Ave)* Tent sites £6-7.70, campervan sites £9.75-13. Adjacent to Benone Beach, this complex has an outdoor heated pool, children's pool and bowling green.

Getting There & Away

Bus From Limavady, Bus No 134 travels to Downhill, Castlerock and Coleraine. No 234 travels to Coleraine, No 146 goes to Dungiven. Bus No 143 runs between Derry and Limavady almost hourly. There's no direct bus to Belfast from Limavady but connections can be made at Coleraine or Dungiven.

Train Castlerock is on the very scenic Derry to Coleraine train line and from the train station it's a pleasant 40-minute walk through the Black Glen to Downhill. From the station head towards the sea, take the first left

on Main St, continue past the caravan park and follow the signs for Bishop's Gate.

COLERAINE
pop 20,720

Although it stands on the banks of the River Bann, Coleraine (Cúil Raithin) is not an attractive town. But Coleraine is an important transport hub for County Derry and you could be waiting here for a bus or train connection. There are plenty of shops catering for the largely Protestant population, who first arrived in 1613 when the land was given by James I to loyal Londoners. The University of Ulster was established just north of town in 1968, much to the chagrin of Derry, which had lobbied hard to win it.

Information

The Coleraine Tourist Information Centre (☎ 7034 4723), Railway Rd, next to Coleraine Leisure Centre, opens 9am to 5pm Monday to Saturday. The centre has an informative leaflet and map on old Coleraine.

Mountsandel Mount

Over 1km south of town, east of the river, is Mountsandel Mount, a mysterious mound that may have been an early-Christian stronghold or a later Anglo-Norman fortification. Just to the north-east of the mound, a 7th millennium BC Mesolithic site has been excavated; post-holes, hearths and pits bear testimony to the early inhabitants of the area. The site is signposted from the Lodge Rd roundabout.

Places to Stay & Eat

There are plenty of accommodation options in Coleraine. The tourist office has a full listing.

Town House (☎ *7034 4869,* e *dale@ townhouse.freeserve.co.uk, 45 Millburn Rd)* Singles/doubles from £17.50/30 including breakfast. This is a large mid-19th-century house with large bedrooms and a homely atmosphere.

Camus House (☎ *7034 2982, 27 Curragh Rd, Castleroe)* Singles/doubles £25/45 including breakfast. This 17th-century house is excellent value and is signposted off the A54, close to the river 5km south of town. It's on site of an 8th-century monastery and there's an old Celtic Cross in the adjacent cemetery. The owner can organise fishing trips.

Pizza Pomodoro (*☎ 7034 4444, 4 The Waterside*) Pizzas from £4.65. Open 4.30pm-11.30pm Mon-Sun. This pizzeria is popular with students and has a BYO licence.

Water Margin at the Boathouse (*☎ 7034 2222, The Boathouse, Hanover Place*) Meals £7.50-12.50. Open lunch & dinner daily. This restaurant offers seafood, vegetarian, European and Chinese dishes.

Getting There & Away
Bus The bus station is part of the train station on Railway Rd. Ulsterbus No 218 travels express between Portrush, Portstewart and Belfast via Coleraine and Antrim. Bus No 234 takes an hour to reach Derry.

Bus No 252, the Antrim Coaster (*☎ 9033 3000*), operates between Belfast and Coleraine twice daily, Monday to Saturday, with train connections between Larne and Belfast. It leaves Larne at 10.15am and 3pm, and departs Coleraine at 9.40am and 3.40pm. The trip takes about three hours.

The open-topped Bushmills Bus (*☎ 9033 3000*), No 177, is a double-decker running (weather permitting) from the Giant's Causeway to Coleraine five-times daily, July and August. The trip takes just over an hour.

Both buses run via Portrush, Portballintrae, Bushmills and the Giant's Causeway.

Train Belfast to Derry trains stop at Coleraine and there's a branch line to Portrush.

DUNGIVEN & AROUND
pop 2812

The small market town of Dungiven (Dún Geimhin) has a couple of ecclesiastical sites and an excellent independent hostel. It's a better base than Limavady if you're travelling between Belfast and Derry or for exploring the Sperrin Mountains. The Ulster Way passes nearby.

Dungiven Priory
The remains of this Augustinian priory, signposted off the A6, date back to the 12th

century, when it replaced a pre-Norman monastery.

The church contains the ornate tomb of Cooey-na-Gal, a chieftain of the O'Cahans who died in 1385. On the tomb are figures of six kilted gallowglasses (armed retainers), mercenaries from Scotland hired by Cooey O'Cahan as minders and earning him the nickname na-Gal ('of the Foreigners'). In the 17th century another foreigner, Sir Edward Doddington, who built the walls of Derry, remodelled the priory and an adjacent small castle built by the O'Cahans. He constructed a private dwelling of which only the foundations remain.

Nearby is a bullaun, a hollowed stone originally used by the monks for grinding grain but now collecting rainwater and used as a site of pilgrimage and prayer by people seeking cures for illnesses.

Maghera Old Church
The church site goes back to a 6th-century monastery plundered by the Vikings in 832. The present ruined nave dates from the 10th century, while the Romanesque door on the western side is two centuries younger. There are interesting motifs on the door jambs and the lintel carries a fine crucifixion scene. In the churchyard there's an unmistakable pillar stone, carved with a ringed cross said to mark the grave of the 6th-century founder, St Lurach.

The town of Maghera is just off the A6 Derry to Belfast road and the best approach is from Dungiven via the Glenshane Pass. Rising to 555m, the road through the Sperrin Mountains offers dramatic views. Bus No 116 runs regularly between Coleraine and Maghera, bus No 278 less frequently.

Places to Stay
Flax Mill Hostel (*☎ 7774 2655, Mill Lane*) Tent sites £3.50; beds with/without breakfast £7.50/5.50 per person. There are three dorms and one double room. Five kilometres north of Dungiven, this idyllic countryside retreat is run by Marion and Herman Baurr, who mill their own flour, grow their own veggies and generate their own electricity. It's signposted off the B192 Limavady road (beware,

there are two Limavady–Dungiven roads). If you're travelling by bus, Marion or Herman will pick you up from Dungiven.

They hold a festival of traditional and folk music in the second weekend of September.

Dungiven Castle (☎ *7774 2428, fax 7774 1968,* Ⓦ *www.dungivencastle.com)* Dorms/doubles £10-12/14. A new hostel in the renovated Dungiven Castle. Although well furnished and equipped it's rather antiseptic and lacks the charm and friendliness of places like the Flax Mill.

Bradagh (*☎/fax 7774 1346, 132 Main St)* Rooms with shared bathroom £14 per person including breakfast.

Places to Eat
Castle Inn (☎ *7774 1369, Upper Main St)* Meals £4.25-6.85. It's reportedly the best place for a pub feed and open every day for lunch and dinner.

Ponderosa Bar and Restaurant (☎ *7774 1987, 974 Glendhane Rd)* Meals £5-8. If you're travelling on to Maghera on the A6 this bar at the top of the Glenshane Pass serves steak, chicken and seafood. It's Ireland's highest pub and featured in *Harry's Game,* the novel by Gerald Seymour.

Entertainment
Murphy's (☎ *7774 1496, 104 Main St)* This pub has traditional sessions on Thursday and bands at the weekend.

Dolphin (☎ *7774 1289, 23 Gortmaghy Rd)* The Dolphin has live music on Friday, Saturday and Sunday nights.

Getting There & Away
Bus No 212 serving Derry and Belfast runs frequently and stops on Main St in Dungiven. Ulsterbus No 146 travels between Limavady and Dungiven.

PLANTATION TOWNS
The rest of inland Derry, south of Dungiven, is strong Protestant territory made up of towns planned and created by London companies with grants of land from William of Orange. In Draperstown, Magherafelt and Moneymore the kerbstones are often painted red, white and blue.

Springhill
Springhill (☎ *8674 8210, Moneymore Rd; adult/concession £2.50/1.25; open 2pm-6pm Sat & Sun Apr-June & Sept; 2pm-6pm Fri-Wed July & Aug)*, 1.5km south of Moneymore on the B18, is an interesting example of early Plantation architecture. The original house was built about 1695 by the Conynghams, who came from Scotland after acquiring the 120-hectare Springhill Estate. It's contemporaneous with Hezlett House, near Castlerock (see that section earlier), but has little in common with that more humble abode. The central block has a high pitched roof, enlarged by the addition of the wings in the 18th century, which give a more solid air of baroque assurance to the house. The barn is also late 17th century. Inside the house is some old oak furniture, a library, a collection of weapons and many costumes.

PORTSTEWART
pop 6459
When the English novelist Thackeray visited Portstewart (Port Stíobhaird) in 1842, he noted the 'air of comfort and neatness'; this still rings true and the place has an air of superiority distinguishing it from Portrush, 6km farther along the coast. A day could easily be passed visiting the excellent beaches in the vicinity (both Portstewart and Portrush have good surf) and the town makes a convenient base for the Giant's Causeway and other coastal attractions.

Orientation & Information
Portstewart consists of one long promenade. To the east it heads along the coast to Portrush and Ballycastle and to the west to the fine Blue Flag beach of Portstewart Strand. Attractions west of town can only be reached via Coleraine.

The tourist office (☎ *7083 2286),* in the library in the red-brick town hall at the western end of town, opens 10am to 4pm Monday to Saturday, July and August.

Things to See & Do
The wide, sweeping **Portstewart Strand** is about a 20-minute walk or a short bus ride along Strand Rd. Vehicles are allowed onto

the firm sand, which can accommodate over 1000 cars. There's a £3 charge if anyone's on duty.

In May the **North-West 200 motorcycle race** is run on a road circuit between Portrush, Portstewart and Coleraine. This classic race is one of the last to be run on closed public roads anywhere in Europe; most such events are now considered too dangerous. It attracts up to 70,000 spectators.

Places to Stay

Camping & Hostels Camp sites are plentiful along the coast road.

Juniper Hill Caravan Park (☎ *7083 2023, 70 Ballyreagh Rd*) Tent/campervan sites £5.50/12. This council-run park, 2.5km east of town on the way to Portrush, has a few tent sites.

Portstewart Holiday Park (☎/*fax 7083 3308, 80 Mill Rd*) Tent sites £10. You'll find this place inland towards Coleraine.

Causeway Coast Hostel (☎ *7083 3789, fax 7083 5314,* e *rick@causewaycoasthos tel.fsnet.co.uk, 4 Victoria Terrace*) Dorms £7, rooms £8.50 per person. This hostel, at the eastern end of town, has four-, six- or eight-bed dorms plus private rooms. It has its own kitchen, laundry and welcoming fires in winter. There's Internet access for guests.

B&Bs & Hotels There are a number of B&Bs at the eastern end of town, at the junction of Victoria Terrace, Hillcrest and Atlantic Circle.

B&Bs include the centrally positioned *Craigmore* (☎ *7083 2120, 26 The Promenade),* offering en suite rooms for £17.50 per person. *Mount Oriel* (☎ *7083 2556, 74 The Promenade)* has rooms with shared bathrooms for £19 per person. At *Akaroa* (☎ *7083 2067, 75 The Promenade)* rooms cost from £18 per person. En suite rooms cost between £20 and £22.

Edgewater Hotel (☎ *7083 3314, fax 7083 2224, 88 Strand Rd*) Singles/doubles £30/60 low season, £37.50/75 high (July & Aug) season. This two-star hotel overlooking Portstewart Strand offers pleasant accommodation.

Places to Eat

There's a well stocked *health food shop* at 62 The Promenade.

Squires (☎ *7083 4103, 18 The Promenade)* Meals £3. Open 9am-10pm daily, Tues-Sun Oct-Mar. Try this place for reasonably priced breakfasts, hot or cold lunches and early evening meals.

Morelli's (see Nino's below) You can hardly miss this neon-lit place midway along The Promenade, which dispenses mouth-watering ice creams and good coffee.

Nino's (☎ *7083 2150, 53-55 The Promenade)* Meals £3.20. Open 9am-11pm daily. Next door to Morelli's, but part of the same complex, Nino's serves hot meals as well as home-made Italian ice cream and usually has a vegetarian special costing around £3.99. Italian coffee comes in all varieties.

The Anchorage (☎ *7083 2003, The Promenade)* Main meals £5.95. This bar place serves decent pub food, opens until late and has live music Thursday to Monday, karaoke on Tuesday and a quiz on Wednesday. The Anchorage also has *accommodation*.

Ashiana (☎ *7083 4455, 12a The Diamond)* Main meals £4.25. Open 5pm-11pm daily. This restaurant has a mixed menu of Indian and European dishes, which includes a good vegetarian selection.

Snappers (☎ *7082 4945, 21 Ballyreagh Rd)* Meals £7. Open lunch & dinner daily. Snappers is a large seafood restaurant on the coast road towards Portrush.

Getting There & Away

Bus Buses leave from The Promenade. Ulsterbus No 218 leaves Portstewart for Belfast, stopping at Coleraine, Ballymoney and Antrim. Bus No 234 leaves several times daily for Derry (once daily at the weekend) and takes an hour. Bus No 140 plies between Coleraine and Portstewart (17 minutes) roughly every half-hour (fewer on Sunday).

See Getting There & Away in the Coleraine section earlier in this chapter for information on the Antrim Coaster and Bushmills Bus services.

Train The nearest station is at Portrush, with connections to the Derry to Belfast train at Coleraine. See Portrush, later in this chapter, for details.

County Antrim

Antrim's (Aontroim's) coastal scenery ranks amongst the most beautiful and distinctive in the world. Everyone is drawn towards the northern coastline, the wide sweeping beaches, small coy harbours and the world-renowned geological formation of the Giant's Causeway.

East of Ballycastle, the distinctive cliffs of Fair Head mark the point where the coast turns southwards and makes its way down to Larne and Belfast Lough. This coastal strip is known as the Glens of Antrim after the series of nine valleys that cut across the range of hills between Ballycastle and Larne. The A2 road runs along the coast for most of the way and it's an exciting route for cyclists and motorcyclists.

Inland Antrim has less to recommend it.

PORTRUSH
pop 5703
The busy little resort of Portrush (Port Rois) bursts at the seams with holidaymakers in summer and on bank holiday weekends. Not surprisingly, many of its attractions are unashamedly focused on families.

Information
The Portrush Tourist Information Centre (☎ 7082 3333, e portrush@nitic.net) is in the Dunluce Centre on Sandhill Drive. It opens 9am to 7pm daily mid-June to September; 9am to 5pm Monday to Friday, noon to 5pm Saturday and Sunday, April to mid-June; noon to 5pm Saturday and Sunday March and October. The centre books accommodation and has a bureau de change.

Portrush Strand has been awarded a Blue Flag for the ecological quality of its beach and lifeguard services.

Things to See & Do
In summer, **boat trips** depart regularly for cruising or fishing; contact the tourist office for a list of operators. For pony trekking

contact the **Maddybenny Riding Centre** (☎ 7082 3394, Maddybenny Farm) or **Hillfarm Riding and Trekking Centre** (☎ 7084 8629, 47 Altikeragh Rd).

Portrush is becoming famous as a **surfing** paradise; surf shops include the friendly **Troggs** (☎ 7082 5476, 8 Bath St), which does board hire (£5 per day) and wet-suit hire (£5 per day), surf reports and general advice.

Waterworld (☎ 7082 2001, The Harbour; admission for water activities £4.25, bowling £12 for 45 minutes; open 10am-8pm Mon-Sat, noon-8pm Sun) by the harbour, has pools, waterslides and spa baths for children to play in (there is a variety of family tickets) and bowling. The Health Suite – sauna, steam room and sunbeds – are all included in the water activities price. There's also a *cafe* in the centre.

The **Dunluce Centre** (☎ 7082 4444, Sandhill Drive; admission £4.50 Mar-Sept; £4 Oct-Feb; open 10am-8pm daily July-Aug; 10am-5pm Sept-June) has a Turbo Tour, a hands-on nature trail with lots of buttons to press and animated shows on local myths and legends.

Places to Stay
Camping & Hostels There are a couple of camping options around Portrush.

Skerries Holiday Park (☎ 7082 2531, fax 7082 2853, 126 Dunluce Rd) Tent/campervan sites £10/12. The Bushmills Bus No 177 runs to this park.

Carrick Dhu Caravan Park (☎ 7082 3712, 12 Ballyreagh Rd) Tent sites £11. This is a smaller place with standard facilities.

Macools (☎ 7082 4845, 5 Causeway View Terrace) Dorms/rooms £7/8 per person. Macools is a welcoming, independent hostel with 18 beds in single-sex dorms with sea views; there is one private room. There's laundry and cooking facilities, Internet access (£4 per hour) and bicycles for rent (£5 per day).

B&Bs & Hotels Places fill up quickly during the summer so it's advisable to book in advance through the tourist office.

Clarmont (☎/fax 7082 2397, e clarmont@talk21.com, 10 Landsowne Cres-

cent) Singles/doubles £25/40-50. These are pleasant rooms, especially those with a sea view, in a B&B with nice touches of the old and the new.

Alexandra (☎/fax 7082 2284, 11 Landsdowne Crescent) Singles/doubles £20/34-40. The single rooms have shared bathrooms while the more expensive doubles have en suites, but all are good.

Belvedere (☎ 7082 2771, 15 Landsdowne Crescent) Standard/en suite rooms £16/19 per person. The Belvedere is good value.

There are also a few B&Bs immediately opposite the station in Eglinton St, including *Glenshane (☎ 7082 4839, ⓔ peterobb sbb@apol.com, 113 Eglinton St)* with en suite singles/doubles costing. £17.50/37. *Atlantic View (☎ 7082 3647, 103 Eglinton St)* costs £15 per person. The top front rooms are better with a sea view.

Magherabuoy House Hotel (☎ 7082 3507, fax 7082 4687, Ⓦ www.maghera buoy.co.uk, 41 Magheraboy Rd) Singles/doubles £60/100. This three-star hotel with plush accommodation can also organise activities such as water skiing, horse riding, surfing, fishing and archery, and you don't have to be a resident.

Eglinton Hotel (☎ 7082 2371, fax 7082 3155, 49 Eglinton St) Singles/doubles £50/68 including breakfast. The rooms are relatively small and pricey in this fairly old hotel.

Places to Eat
Bread Shop & Restaurant (☎ 7082 3722, 21 Eglinton St) Meals £2.95. Next to the post office, the Bread Shop offers decent coffee and light meals.

Ramore Wine Bar (☎ 7082 4313, The Harbour) Main meals £5.95-11.95. Open lunch & dinner daily. Overlooking the harbour, this is Portrush's favourite eating place. The popular *Harbour Bar (☎ 7082 2430, Harbour Rd)* next door and Coast (see below) downstairs are part of the same outfit. The wine bar downstairs has good-value lunch specials, while the pricier restaurant upstairs opens for dinner.

Coast (☎ 7082 3311, The Harbour) Main meals £3.95. Open lunch & dinner Wed-

Mon. Coast does stone-baked pizzas, pastas and the usual steak, chicken and fish dishes.

Don Giovanni's Ristorante (☎ 7082 5516, 9-13 Causeway St) Mains £4.50-7.80. Open 5.30pm-11pm daily. Near the junction with Eglinton and Main Sts, this place with pasta and pizza dishes isn't as expensive as it looks.

Griffin Restaurant (at Magherabuoy House Hotel, see Places to Stay) One/three courses £13/20. Open 7pm-9.30pm. This restaurant has a good reputation for fresh seafood and local game. Also in the hotel is *Cobblers Bistro* (open daily to 9pm) where snacks cost between £4.95 and £8.25.

Beetles Bar & Bistro (☎ 7082 3539, Bushmills Rd) Snacks/chef's specials £4.25/6.50, a la carte £6.95. Part of Kelly's (see Entertainment) this restaurant serves fish, chicken, grills and vegetarian courses.

Entertainment
Rogues (☎ 7082 2946, 54 Kerr St) Just across the road from the Harbour Bar, Rogues has nightly live-music sessions offering traditional music, blues, and rock and roll.

Kelly's (Bushmills Rd) is an exceedingly popular venue and should be, given the effort the owners have put into it. It caters for all ages, the oldies can leave the youngsters in the disco and go off to the restaurants and bars and then all can catch the same taxi home. Plain and small looking from the outside this is an Aladdin's Cave within. One of the owners is an avid antique and arts collector who scours the world for pieces. It's a must-see place if you're anywhere nearby.

The dance-music venues regularly feature DJs from London and Manchester, and attract clients from as far as Belfast. The disco in Kelly's runs 9pm to 1am Wednesday, 9pm to 1am Friday, 9pm to 2am Saturday and until midnight Sunday.

A taxi there from Portrush costs about £5.

Getting There & Away
Bus The bus terminal is near the Dunluce Centre. Bus No 218 leaves several times daily from Portrush for Belfast, travelling via Portstewart, Coleraine, Ballymoney, Ballymena and Antrim. From Monday to Friday bus Nos 139 and 140 run to Coleraine. Bus

No 278 runs daily to Dublin. Bus No 172 runs daily to Bushmills and Ballycastle.

See Getting There & Away in the Coleraine section earlier in this chapter for information on the Antrim Coaster and Bushmills Bus services.

Train Portrush is served by train from Coleraine (15 minutes) roughly every hour. The earliest train leaves Coleraine at 7am, the latest at 11.11pm; from Portrush the times are 6.37am and 11.30pm, respectively. Weekend services are fewer. At Coleraine connections can be made for Belfast or Derry. Contact Translink (☎ 9033 3000) for details.

Getting Around
For taxis call Andy Brown's (☎ 7082 2223) or North West Taxis (☎ 7082 4446). Both companies are near the town hall. A taxi to the Giant's Causeway costs about £10.

PORTBALLINTRAE
During WWI Portballintrae (Port of the Town of Strand) was the only place in the UK to be shelled by a German submarine. Luckily, the result was no worse than a crater on the outskirts of town and the downing of the electric tramlines. In the last few years there has been a tremendous boom in apartment building providing second homes. At £200,000 per apartment no local can afford to compete and several of the town's hotels have closed down and are due to become apartments. Such developments tend to inflict more damage than a few U-boat shells.

Dunluce Castle
The existence of a 1000-year-old souterrain suggests this site, beside the A2 just west of Portballintrae, was used for defensive purposes long before a stone castle was constructed. Parts of the castle (☎ 2073 1938, 87 Dunluce Rd; adult/concession £1.50/0.75; open 10am-6pm Mon-Sat, 2pm-6pm Sun Apr-Sept; 10am-6pm Mon-Sat, noon-6pm Sun June-Aug; 11am-4pm Tues-Sat, 2pm-4pm Sun Oct-Mar) date from the 14th century. In the 16th century, new owners, the Scottish Sorley Boy MacDonnell family, extended the buildings and strengthened defences after a serious artillery attack by the English. In the 17th century a manor house with medieval floor plan and Renaissance embellishments was built inside the walls.

The mainland-facing wall has two openings, holding cannons salvaged from the *Girona*, a Spanish Armada vessel that foundered nearby. Perched 30m above the sea, the castle was of obvious military value and there are extensive remains inside the walls, giving a good idea of what life was like here.

The palatial hall needed two fireplaces, while the kitchen area has ovens, storage space and a drainage system all built into the stone. The lower yard retains the original cobbling and was surrounded by service rooms, some of which collapsed into the sea in 1639; servants and a night's dinner were lost.

The admission price includes an audiovisual display telling the castle's history.

Places to Stay & Eat
Portballintrae Caravan Park *(☎/fax 2073 1478, Ballaghmore Ave)* Tent sites £7. This park has space for 16 tents and is 10 minutes' walk from the beach.

Bushfoot B&B *(☎ 2073 2501,* e *bush foot.bb@virgin.net, 1a Bushfoot Drive)* Singles/doubles £40/70. This homely and well kept B&B is on the outskirts of town on a quiet road.

Manor House *(☎ 2073 2002, fax 2073 0042, 51 Beach Rd)* Singles/doubles £25/36 including breakfast. All rooms are en suite with TV in the only remaining shore-front option.

Anne's Coffee Shop *(☎ 2073 1328, 47 Beach Rd)* Snacks £2.50. Open 9am-5pm Sat & Sun Mar-May; daily May-Aug; Sat & Sun Sept. Anne's produces satisfying snacks during the day.

Getting There & Away
From Monday to Friday bus No 132 between Portrush and Ballymoney stops here twice daily. Bus No 138 runs regularly (except Sunday) to Coleraine and Portrush, while bus No 172 runs several times daily to Portrush and Ballycastle.

See Getting There & Away in the Coleraine section earlier in this chapter for information on the Antrim Coaster and Bushmills Bus services.

BUSHMILLS
pop 1348
Bushmills (Muileann na Buaise) is a small town off the A2 between Portrush and Ballycastle. At its centre is the Diamond, with a grim, grey circular clocktower and war memorial, from where Main St makes its way half a kilometre west to the famous Bushmills Distillery, which is really the only reason for visiting.

Bushmills Distillery
This is the only source of Bushmills whiskey and is the world's oldest licensed, and therefore legal, distillery (☎ 2073 3218, Distillery Rd; adult/child £3.95/1.95; open 9.30am-5.30pm Mon-Sat, noon-5.30pm Sun, last tour at 4pm Apr-Oct; 10am-5pm Mon-Fri, hourly tours 10.30am-3.30pm Nov-Mar). Whiskey was first officially produced here in 1608, but records show distilling taking place hundreds of years earlier. After a tour of the process, you're rewarded with a whiskey-tasting session in which a lucky four get to compare Bushmills whiskeys with other brands. Everybody else still gets a free tasting, but of Bushmills' products. These sessions take place in the 1608 Bar, where an exhibition area has been created in what were once malt kilns.

The **Distillery Kitchen** next to the 1608 Bar does snacks and light lunches.

Places to Stay & Eat
Ballyness Caravan Park (☎/fax 2073 2393, W www.ballynesscaravanpark.com, 36 Catlecatt Rd) Tent/campervan sites £7/12 This brand-new caravan park has won recognition for its eco-friendly site.

Bushmills Inn (☎ 2073 2339, fax 2073 1048, 9 Dunluce Rd) Singles/doubles £78/128 Apr-Sept, £68/118 Oct-Mar. This is a pleasant, quiet place in an old building with lots of interesting things done with wood. There's literally a secret room to find, and that's your clue. There's an attractive **restau-**rant serving everything from sandwiches to full a la carte dinners (two courses £19.85).

The Tramway (☎ 2073 2335, 4 Tramway Drive) En suite singles/doubles £27/40. This basic but tidy B&B is signposted to the left down the Bushmills to Portballintrae Rd.

Ballyness (☎ 2073 1438, 38 Castlecatt Rd) Rooms from £22.50 per person. This B&B is 1km south of the Bushmills distillery on the B66 and is a very agreeable place with a friendly owner.

The Copper Kettle (☎ 2073 2560, 61 Main St) Snacks/lunch specials £2.40/3.70. Open 9am-5pm Mon-Sat, 10am-5pm Sun. The Kettle serves breakfasts, lunch specials, tea, coffee and cakes.

Getting There & Away
Bus No 172 connects Bushmills with Ballycastle, the Giant's Causeway and Portrush, as does bus No 252, the Antrim Coaster, which also goes to Coleraine, Larne and Belfast. Buses drop you off in the Diamond.

GIANT'S CAUSEWAY
The chances are you've seen pictures of the Giant's Causeway (Clochán an Aifir), the North's number-one tourist attraction, long before getting here. A bishop of Derry, a geology convert after seeing Vesuvius erupt, commissioned the paintings of the site that led to its fame. The hexagonal basalt columns are impressive, all 38,000 of them if you count the ones underwater.

The phenomenon is clearly explained in the **Causeway Visitor Centre** (☎ 2073 1855, e causewaytic@hotmail.com, 44 Causeway Rd, B146; audiovisual adult/concession £1/0.50; open 10am-5pm daily, 10am-6pm daily July-Aug) alongside the surprising fact that the Causeway was generally unknown before 1740. The pleasant 1.5km pilgrimage to the actual site is free but minibuses with wheelchair access ply the route every 15 minutes (£1/0.60 return/one way).

Different rock formations have their own names, most invented by the many Victorian guides who made a summer living escorting the tourists. One, Chimney Tops,

The Making of the Causeway

The Mythology

There are several legends that portray the creation of the causeway as a giant-made event. On the Irish side they all accord Fionn McCumhaill (aka Finn McCool) with constructing the Causeway. Some say that he fancied a female giant on the Scottish island of Staffa and built stepping stones to that island, where similar rock formations are found.

Another version has him in arch rivalry with the Scottish giant Benandonner. To tempt Benandonner to combat and give his rival no excuse for not coming to do battle, McCumhaill built the causeway. From this point stories deviate but all end up with McCumhaill asleep in a cot wearing a baby's clothes and bonnet. The Scottish giant crosses the causeway and comes across the 'infant' McCumhaill. Mrs McCumhaill warns Benandonner not to wake McCumhaill's baby. Taking a glance in the cot, Benandonner decides that if this huge baby is Fionn's child then McCumhaill must be immense and thus so much larger than himself. He flees back to Scotland and McCumhaill rips the causeway up.

The Geology

The modern, more prosaic explanation is that red-hot lava erupted from an underground fissure and was forced up into fissures in the existing chalk beds. In doing so it formed an extensive underground lava plateau. This bed of darker rock can be seen today in the dramatic cliffs jutting out to sea. There were three periods of volcanic activity and during the middle one an ancient riverbed at the Causeway was filled with lava. This cooled and contracted with irregular variations resulting in the famous columnar structure. Over the millennia erosion removed the top rocks exposing the formations.

---

was mistaken for Dunluce Castle and shot up by the Spanish Armada in 1588.

Two well established footpaths at different levels start outside the visitor centre and form a circular walk. The less strenuous route is the North Antrim Cliff Path to the Causeway and return by the lower walk.

The cliff top at **Hamilton's Seat** gives an excellent view of the Causeway and the headlands to the west, including Malin Head and Inishowen. Farther east the path continues round Benbane Head, where the headlands become lower until the path reaches the main road near the ruins of Dunseverick Castle (see the following section). The walk from the visitor centre to the castle and back is 16km.

From below the remains of the castle a path winds up and round to the east, ending at Ballintoy. It crosses a number of small wooden bridges before reaching the beach at White Park Bay and the HINI hostel (see The Giant's Causeway to Ballycastle section for details). The whole 16km walk from the Giant's Causeway could be comfortably done in one day.

These walks follow the North Antrim Cliff Path, which actually begins southwest of the visitor centre at Blackrock. A useful map from the visitor centre details the walks, including the rock formations along the way.

Visiting the Giant's Causeway is free of charge but the car park costs £3 (there's free parking on nearby Runkerry Rd). There's a National Trust shop and a cafe on the same site but they close earlier than the centre.

Next to the visitor centre and mainly of interest to children, the **Causeway School Museum** (☎ 2073 1777, Causeway Rd; adult/concession/family £0.75/0.50/2; open 11am-5pm July-Aug) is a listed building designed by Clough William Ellis of Portmeirion fame in North Wales. School groups come here for a living history lesson by sampling early 1900s education.

Places to Stay & Eat

See the following Giant's Causeway to Ballycastle section regarding the *hostels* at White Park Bay and Ballintoy. There are a few B&Bs around.

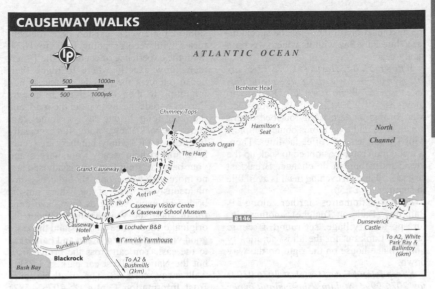

CAUSEWAY WALKS

ATLANTIC OCEAN

Benbane Head

Chimney Tops

Hamilton's Seat

North Channel

Spanish Organ

The Harp

The Organ

Grand Causeway

North Antrim Cliff Path

Causeway Visitor Centre & Causeway School Museum

B146

Dunseverick Castle

Causeway Hotel

Lochaber B&B

Carnside Farmhouse

Runkelly Rd

Blackrock

Bash Bay

To A2 & Bushmills (2km)

To A2, White Park Ray & Ballintoy (6km)

Lochaber (☎ 2073 1385, 107 Causeway Rd) Rooms £14 per person. Lochaber is on the coast road, just 1.5km east of the Causeway and has basic rooms with shared bathrooms.

Carnside Farmhouse (☎ 2073 1337, 23 Causeway Rd) Rooms from £16 per person. Guests share bathrooms.

Causeway Hotel (☎ 2073 1226, fax 2073 2552, 40 Causeway Rd) Singles/doubles £45/65. This two-star hotel is within spitting distance of the Causeway. Otherwise any place in Bushmills, Portballintrae, Portrush or even Ballycastle (see those sections for details) are within reasonable distance. The Causeway's *restaurant* is extremely popular, so it's wise to book in advance. Bar snacks are also available (main meals £8.30, four-course meal £15.50).

There is a *tearoom* in the Causeway Visitor Centre. It serves light meals for around £2.75. You can also buy sandwiches and snacks in two small *shops* outside.

Getting There & Away

The B146 Causeway to Dunseverick road runs parallel to the A2 but closer to the coast and can be joined just east of Bushmills or near White Park Bay. Bus Nos 172 and 252 between Portrush and Ballycastle pass the site. The Causeway Rambler Bus No 376 links Bushmills Distillery with the Causeway Centre, White Park Bay, Ballintoy and Carrick-a-rede. There are seven buses a day from mid-June to mid-September.

See Getting There & Away in the Coleraine section earlier in this chapter for information on the Antrim Coaster service.

GIANT'S CAUSEWAY TO BALLYCASTLE

Dunseverick Castle is spectacularly sited on the B146 (just off the A2) though unfortunately just the ruins of the 16th-century tower remain. Older than Dunluce Castle near Portballintrae, a castle on this site was once the home of Conal Cearnac. This famous wrestler and swordsman was reputed to have been present at Christ's crucifixion and moved the stone at Christ's sepulchre. St Patrick is also said to have visited the castle in the 5th century.

Signposted off the A2 is **Portbradden**, a hamlet with half a dozen pretty harbourside houses and tiny, blue-and-white St Gobban's church, said to be the smallest in Ireland.

Visible from Portbradden and accessible via the next junction off the A2 is the spectacular **White Park Bay** with its wide, sweeping sandy beach.

White Park Bay Hostel (☎ *2073 1745, fax 2073 2034*, Ⓦ *www.whiteparkbayyouthhostel.co.uk, 157 White Park Rd*) Dorms/twin rooms £8.50/12.50. Closed 11am-5pm Oct-Mar. In this modern HINI four-bed dorms are en suite and twin rooms come complete with TV and tea and coffee facilities. There is a common room positioned to soak up the view, and a bureau de change. Breakfast costs £2.50 and an evening meal is available in summer for £4.50.

A few kilometres farther along is **Ballintoy** (Baile an Tuaighe), another picture-postcard village, set round a scenic harbour. Look out for the idiosyncratically out of place house on the right on the way down.

Sheep Island View Hostel (☎ *2076 9391, fax 2076 9994*, Ⓦ *http://sheepisland.hypermart.net, 42a Main St*) En suite dorms/children under 12 years £9/6, breakfast at the nearby Fullerton Arms £13. About 200m past the harbour turn-off this excellent hostel offers beds in small dorms or double rooms. There's a huge kitchen and laundry facilities. The hostel offers a pick-up service from the Giant's Causeway, Bushmills and Ballycastle.

In the grounds a camping barn has more basic singles and doubles for £7.50 with shared bathroom.

Ballintoy House (☎ *2076 2317, 9 Main St*) Rooms and continental/full Irish breakfast £14/17. Ballintoy is an old house dating from 1737 with several decent rooms.

Roark's Kitchen (☎ *2076 3632, Ballintoy Harbour*) Meals £2.50. Open 11am-7pm daily Easter-end Sept, Sat & Sun only the rest of the year. By the harbour, this tiny place serves tea, coffee and light meals. Try the buttered mackerel (£2.75), freshly caught out in the bay.

It's a scary traipse across the **Carrick-a-rede Rope Bridge** (*open 10am-6pm Apr-June & Sept; 10am-8pm July-Aug; last admission 30 minutes before closing*) to a small island with a salmon fishery and hundreds of nesting fulmar and razorbill. A salmon fishery has existed here for centuries with records going back to 1624. With the experience of centuries the fishermen know exactly where to place their net to intercept the passage of the salmon migrating to their home rivers to spawn. Carrick-a-rede means 'rock in the road' and the 20m-long bridge sways some 25m above the rock-strewn water. It's especially frightening if it's windy, but there are secure handrails to help steady your nerves and your balance; stout footwear is advised and no more than two people should cross simultaneously. Workers at the fishery put the bridge up every spring as they have done for the last 200 years though it's not the original bridge. Once on the island there are good views of Rathlin Island and Fair Head to the east. You can cross the bridge free, but the National Trust car park, a 1.25km walk away, costs £3. The small **National Trust Information Centre** (☎ 2073 1582) has an interpretative display plus a leaflet outlining the main places of interest. There's also a *cafe*.

BALLYCASTLE
pop 4000
Ballycastle (Baile an Chaisil), where the Atlantic Ocean meets the Irish Sea, marks the end of the Causeway Coast. It's a pretty, small town, with plenty of 18th- and 19th-century architecture. The beach, of Blue Flag quality, is good but the new harbour with its huge rock barrier doesn't add to the ambience of a seaside town. The Giant's Causeway, Bushmills Distillery and Carrick-a-rede Rope Bridge are all less than 16km away and the Glens of Antrim are due south.

Information
The Ballycastle Tourist Office (☎ 2076 2024) is in the Moyle District Council office at 7 Mary St. It opens 9.30am to 5pm Monday to Friday and 10am to 4pm Saturday for Easter, bank holidays and June to September; and 9.30am to 7pm Monday to Friday, 10am to 6pm Saturday and 2pm to 6pm Sunday, July and August. Pick up a free copy of the *Ballycastle Heritage Trail* leaflet here.

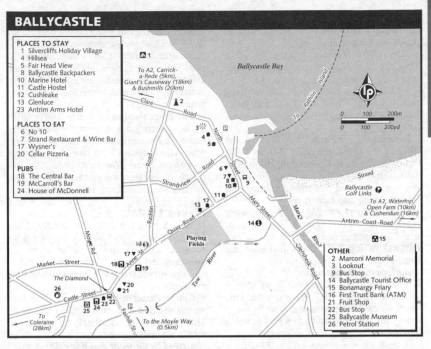

BALLYCASTLE

PLACES TO STAY
1 Silvercliffs Holiday Village
4 Hillsea
5 Fair Head View
8 Ballycastle Backpackers
10 Marine Hotel
11 Castle Hostel
12 Cushleake
13 Glenluce
23 Antrim Arms Hotel

PLACES TO EAT
6 No 10
7 Strand Restaurant & Wine Bar
17 Wysner's
20 Cellar Pizzeria

PUBS
18 The Central Bar
19 McCarroll's Bar
24 House of McDonnell

OTHER
2 Marconi Memorial
3 Lookout
9 Bus Stop
14 Ballycastle Tourist Office
15 Bonamargy Friary
16 First Trust Bank (ATM)
21 Fruit Shop
22 Bus Stop
25 Ballycastle Museum
26 Petrol Station

Ballycastle Bay

To A2, Carrick-a-Rede (5km), Giant's Causeway (18km) & Bushmills (20km)

To Rathlin Island

0   100   200m
0   100   200yd

Clare Road

North Street

Strand

Ballycastle Golf Links

To A2, Watertop Open Farm (10km) & Cushendun (16km)

Strandview Road

Mary Street

Antrim-Coast-Road

Rathlin Road

Glenshesk-Road

Quay-Road

Playing Fields

Tow River

Moyle Rd

Market Street

Anne-St

The Diamond

Castle-Street

To Coleraine (28km)

Faithlin-St

To the Moyle Way (0.5km)

You can also change money and book accommodation here.

Things to See

The tiny **Ballycastle Museum** (☎ 2076 2942, Castle St; free; open 2pm-6pm Mon-Sat July & Aug) is in the town's 18th-century courthouse. The **lookout** on North St has views of the harbour and the cliffs to the east, while down near the harbour is a **memorial** to Guglielmo Marconi (for details see the Rathlin Island section later in this chapter).

The bar in the Antrim Arms has a plaque unveiled by Princess Elettra Marconi Giovanelli in July 1998 commemorating her father's residence in the Antrim Arms during his radio testing in the area in 1898. The bar has a few framed newspaper stories on the hotel/Marconi connection.

Remains of a Franciscan **Bonamargy friary** are 1km east of town on the Ballycastle golf course. The friary was founded around 1500 and used for two centuries. South of

the friary a vault contains the bodies of the MacDonnells, the earls of Antrim, including Sorley Boy MacDonnell from Dunluce Castle. Admission is free.

Special Events

In late May, the Northern Lights Festal is a three-day celebration of Ulster culture. In mid-June there's Fleadh Amhrán agus Rince, a three-day music and dance festival.

The bigger Ould Lammas Fair, on the last Monday and Tuesday of August, dates back to 1606 and is associated with two traditional foods, yellowman and dulse. Yellowman is a hard chewy toffee that's available from a few months before the fair. Dulse is dried seaweed sold salted and ready to eat, although some people toast it. If you're going out for a few beers a few mouthfuls of dulse beforehand encourages the thirst. Always available during the fair, dulse is generally on sale June to September. The fruit shop on the Diamond often stocks both delicacies.

Places to Stay

Camping & Hostels There are a couple of places not far out of town.

Silvercliffs Holiday Village (☎ 2076 2550, fax 2076 2259, W *www.hagansleisure .co.uk, 21 Clare Rd*) Tent/campervan sites £10/12. This is a big caravan and camping park just north-west of town. Facilities include a swimming pool, restaurant, shop, sauna and bar.

Watertop Open Farm (☎ 2076 2576, fax 2076 2175, 188 Cushendall Rd) Tent site £8.50. On the A2 to Cushendun, 10km from Ballycastle, this place has space for a few tents and is a good place for children, with pony trekking and farm tours.

Castle Hostel (☎ 2076 2337, W *www .castlehostel.com, 62 Quay Rd*) Dorms/doubles £7/17 per person. This is a spacious and welcoming hostel; it's just past the Marine Hotel.

Ballycastle Backpackers (☎ 2076 3612, e *am@bcbackpackers.fsnet.co.uk, North St*) Dorms/doubles £6/7.50 per person. This hostel is near the seafront and main bus stop and by the time of publication will have en suite rooms.

B&Bs A very comfortable choice is *Cushleake* (☎/fax 2076 3798, W *www.smooth hound.co.uk/hotels/cushlea.html, 32 Quay Rd*) Singles/doubles £19/30. The Dutch-speaking owner of this period-furnished house hires out bicycles for £7 per day, diving equipment and gives introductory dives.

Glenluce (☎/fax 2076 2914, 42 Quay Rd) £22/20 per person with/without bathroom. The rooms are nicely decorated and there's a veritable art collection of local watercolours in the breakfast room.

Fair Head View (☎ 2076 9376, 26 North St) £14-17 per person including breakfast. The rooms (shared bathrooms) are rather small but good value. For proximity to the sea this place is up the hill from the harbour.

Hillsea (☎/fax 2076 2385, 28 North St) £20 per person including breakfast. Rooms are en suite with TV and tea-making facilities. This place is a little farther uphill than Fair Head View and has the better sea view.

Hotels More than just a place to rest your head is the *Marine Hotel* (☎ 2076 2222, fax 2076 9507, W *www.marinehotel.net, 1 North St*) Singles/doubles £50/75 including breakfast. This place is right on the seafront. Sailing lessons are available through the hotel between Easter and September for £5 per hour.

The hotel also has a *country club* (☎ 2076 2166) offering a swimming pool, Jacuzzi, sauna and steam bath. It's free to residents otherwise it costs £5 per day.

Antrim Arms Hotel (☎ 2076 2284, 75 Castle St) By the time you read this the new owners should be back in the B&B trade.

Places to Eat

Wysner's (☎ 2076 2372, 16 Ann St) Mains £7. Open 8am-5pm Mon-Fri, 8am-8pm Sat & Sun. This is the place to come for sausages and champ; there's also a restaurant upstairs that opens Friday and Saturday evenings.

Cellar Pizzeria (☎ 2076 3037, The Diamond) Meals £4. Open 4.30pm-11pm daily. This place serves reasonably priced pizzas, salads and pasta dishes.

Strand Restaurant and Wine Bar (☎ 2076 2349, 9 North St) Meals £4-11. Open 11am-9pm daily. On the seafront this place serves pub-type meals all day. Go for the smoked haddock fishcakes, they're pretty good.

Number 10 (☎ 2076 8110, 10 North St) Meals £13. Open lunch & dinner (lunch only Sun) June-Sept; dinner Fri & Sat, Sun lunch, rest of the year. This restaurant is reported as offering excellent food, service and ambience. The menu features seafood as well as interesting vegetarian dishes.

Entertainment

The *Marine Hotel* (see Places to Stay) has live music at the weekend during summer and a disco on Saturday night. *The Central Bar* (☎ 2076 3877, 12 Anne St) has regular traditional music sessions on Wednesday and Sunday. *McCarroll's Bar* (☎ 2076 2123, 7 Anne St) has session nights on Thursdays. *House of McDonnell* (☎ 2076 2975, 69 Castle St) has traditional music sessions on Friday night.

Getting There & Away

Bus Nos 131 and 217 link Ballycastle with Belfast and bus No 171 goes to Coleraine but there are no Sunday services. Bus No 172 connects daily with Bushmills and Portrush.

McGinns (☎ 2076 3451), the local private bus company, runs to Belfast's Europa Bus Centre from the Diamond at 4pm on Friday and at 8pm on Sunday. It takes 1½ hours and costs adult/child £7/4 return.

The Antrim Coaster, bus No 252, operates between Larne and Coleraine twice daily, Monday to Saturday using the train to connect to Belfast. It leaves Larne at 10.15am and 3pm and departs Coleraine at 9.40am and 3.40pm. The trip takes about three hours. It stops at Portrush, Portballintrae, Bushmills, the Giant's Causeway, Ballycastle, Cushendun, Cushendall, Carnlough and Glenarm.

RATHLIN ISLAND

pop 113

Only 22km from Scotland's Mull of Kintyre, rugged Rathlin Island (Reachlainn) is only 6km long and nowhere more than 1.5km across. It has a pub, a restaurant, two shops and a handful of accommodation options, along with approximately 100 inhabitants and thousands of seabirds.

The island, which Pliny mentions as Ricnia, was raided by Vikings in 795 and suffered again in 1595 when Sorley Boy MacDonnell sent his family here for safety only to have them massacred by the English along with all the inhabitants. The island's most illustrious visitor was Robert the Bruce, who spent some time in 1306 in a cave on the north-eastern point learning a lesson in fortitude. Watching a spider's resoluteness in repeatedly trying to spin a web gave him the courage to have another go at the English, whom he subsequently defeated at Bannockburn.

Another claim to fame is the fact that Rathlin Island was the first place to have a wireless. Marconi's assistant contacted Rathlin by radio from Ballycastle in 1898 to prove to Lloyds of London that the idea worked.

The bird life at RSPB West Lighthouse Viewpoint (☎ 2076 3948; admission by donation; open only by appointment) at the western end of the island is the chief attraction. Guillemot, kittiwake, razorbill and puffin can be seen here, but by late summer they're no longer nesting or rearing their young, and are difficult to spot from the land. During the summer a minibus takes you there from the ferry harbour but it doesn't run to a timetable so check your return time.

The Boathouse Centre (☎ 2076 3951; open noon-4pm daily May-Aug) south of the harbour sells books and brochures and details the history, culture and ecology of the island.

Places to Stay

You can *camp* for free on the eastern side of Church Bay in a field not far from the harbour.

Soerneog View (☎/fax 2076 3954, Ouig) Dorms £8. South of the harbour overlooking Mill Bay, this place has six hostel beds in three rooms.

Kinramer Cottage (☎ 2076 3948) Dorms £5. This is a basic 'camping barn' where you bring your own food and bedding; you should book in advance. It's an hour's walk from the harbour so ask for directions. You might be able to get a lift with one of the minibuses, see the following Getting Around section for details.

Rathlin Guesthouse (☎/fax 2076 3917, The Quay) Rooms £18 per person including breakfast. Cosy Rathlin's overlooks Church Bay and is five minutes from the ferry terminal.

Manor House (☎/fax 2076 3964, e uravfm@smtp.ntrust.org.uk) Singles/doubles £27/42 including breakfast. Evening meals are available by arrangement. Restored and run by the National Trust, the Manor House is a late-Georgian house south of the harbour with excellent views over to the mainland.

Getting There & Away

A ferry service (☎ 2076 9299, w www.calmac.co.uk) operates daily from Ballycastle except in bad seas so booking and checking up in advance is advisable.

From June to September there are four crossings each way (£8.20 return, 45 minutes). Boats leave Ballycastle at 10am, noon, 4.30pm and 6.30pm (7pm on Friday). Boats leave Rathlin at 8.30am, 11am, 3.30pm and 5.30pm. The winter schedule has boats leaving Ballycastle at 10.30am and 4pm (4.30pm on Friday) and from Rathlin at 9am and 3pm.

Getting Around

Unless you've got a permit you can't take a car to Rathlin. The L-shape of the island is 6.5km long east to west, 4.8km south to north, and it's just over half a kilometre wide at its maximum. If you don't want to walk then you can hire a bicycle (£7 per day) from Soerneog View (☎ 2076 3954), go on Irene's Minibus Tours (☎ 2076 3949) or with McCurdy's Minibus Tours (☎ 2076 3909).

MURLOUGH BAY

Turning off the A2 and taking the Cushendun Scenic Route gives the best access to the scenic coastline between Ballycastle and Cushendun. It's signposted to Torr Head and takes in Murlough Bay, the most stupendous part of the Antrim coastline.

Leave your transport at the first car park – there are three altogether – where a map display sets out the walking possibilities. From the first car park Walk No 1 is to Coolanlough, a 3.5km return trip. From the vantage at Fair Head point, 186m above the sea, Rathlin Island is to the left, while out to sea the peaks of the Isle of Arran can be seen on a clear day beyond the Mull of Kintyre. The walk also takes in Lough na Cranagh and its ancient *crannóg* (artificial island).

The second walk begins from the second car park farther down the road; follow the clear pathway to the west. It leads to some abandoned coal mines, indicated only by arches in the rock, which are probably not safe to explore.

Between the first and second car parks, the remains of a **cross** can be seen, a memorial to Roger Casement, whose family came from this area. Casement, hanged in London in 1916 for enlisting the aid of Germany in the nationalist struggle, made a last request to his cousin: 'Take my body back

with you and let it lie in the old churchyard in Murlough Bay.' It was 50 years before the British released the body.

CUSHENDUN

pop 347

Much of Cushendun (Bun Abhann Duinne) is owned by the National Trust and any new buildings must match existing ones. The distinctive black-and-white houses at the southern end are the work of Clough Williams-Ellis, designer of Portmeirion in North Wales, who came here to work for Lord Cushendun.

The village, on a bay with a small beach, is on the **Ulster Way**. North from Cushendun the walk goes inland before heading down to Murlough Bay and then along the coast to Ballycastle. Going south the walk travels inland nearly all the way to Cushendall.

Places to Stay & Eat

Cushendun Caravan Park (☎ *2176 1254, 14 Glendun Rd)* Tent/campervan site £5.70/ 12.50. Camping is available at this local council-run park.

Cloneymore B&B (☎ *2176 1443, 103 Knocknacarry Rd)* £20 per person. This B&B is just out of Cushendun on the Cushendall Rd. All rooms are en suite and there's one room equipped for visitors with disabilities.

Villa Farmhouse (☎/*fax 2176 1252, 185 Torr Rd)* Singles/doubles £20/36 Sept-June, £25/40 July & Aug; breakfast included. The Farmhouse, north of the village, has a great view over the bay.

Mullarts Apartments (☎ *2176 1221,* 🅔 *mullarts@ldpt.demon.co.uk, 114 Tromra Rd)* From £250 per week for a four-person apartment or from £100 per weekend. These fully self-contained apartments are inside a converted church. There is one ground level apartment with full facilities for visitors with disabilities.

Cushendun Village Tearooms (☎ *2176 1506, 1 Main St)* Snacks £3.50. Open 11am-7pm Mon-Fri Oct-Feb, 11am-7pm daily Mar-Sept. The Tearooms is on the corner near the bridge and serves hot snacks and salads.

Mary McBride's (☎ *2176 1511, 2 Main St)* Bar/restaurant meals £2.95/9.50. Open lunch & dinner. This place offers locally caught seafood and home-made steak-and-Guinness pie. The pub has the smallest bar in Ireland (2.7m by 1.5m) but there's plenty of room in the other bars to drink.

Getting There & Away
Ulsterbus Nos 120 and 150 link Cushendun with Ballymena, Monday to Saturday, with connections to Belfast. Bus Nos 156, 162 and 256 travel to Larne, stopping at towns along the way, five-times daily from Monday to Friday, three-times daily on Saturday and Sunday. From Larne it's a short hop to Belfast.

See Getting There & Away in the Ballycastle section earlier in this chapter for information on the Antrim Coaster bus.

CUSHENDALL
pop 1399
The red sandstone tower at the crossroads of the picturesque little village of Cushendall (Bun Abhann Dalla) was built in the early 19th century by Francis Turnly. From the village the B14 road runs inland to Glenariff Forest Park, the loveliest of Antrim's nine glens.

About 5000 years ago, stone from nearby Tievebulliagh Mountain was the basis of an important stone-axe industry.

Information
The Cushendall Tourist Office (☎ 2177 1180), 24 Mill St, is run by the Glens of Antrim Historical Society. It opens 10am to 1pm and 2pm to 5.30pm Monday to Friday, 10am to 1pm Saturday July to September; 10am to 1pm Tuesday to Saturday during the rest of year.

Layde Old Church
About 1km north of the village, this magical ruined church and churchyard stand beside a fast-flowing stream. The church, believed to have been founded by Franciscans, was used as a parish church from the early 14th century until 1790. The tombstones in the graveyard include MacDonnell memorials and there's a rather pagan-looking one with a hole through it, immediately on the left after you enter the

grounds. You can walk to the church along a lovely cliff-top coastal path, or take the steep coast road (not the A2) that goes north to Cushendun. The church is signposted off the road to the right, but it's difficult to see.

Ossian's Grave
Romantically, but inaccurately, named after the legendary warrior-poet of the 3rd century, this Neolithic court tomb consists of a two-chambered burial ground once enclosed by an oval cairn. The site is signposted off the A2 outside Cushendall on the Cushendun side. You can park at the farm and walk up.

Glenariff Forest Park
Over 800 hectares of woodland make up the park (☎ 2175 8232, 98 Glenariff Rd; cars/motorcycles/pedestrians £3/2/1.50; open 8am–dusk) and the main attraction is **Ess-na-Larach Waterfall**, about half an hour's walk from the visitor centre. There are various other walks, not all clearly marked; the longest is a three-hour circular mountain trail. Views of the valley led the writer Thackeray to exclaim that it was a 'Switzerland in miniature'. By parking at the Manor Lodge restaurant, on the road in, you need only pay the pedestrian fee.

Opposite the park entrance is the start of the **Moyle Way** to Ballycastle, 32km north.

Places to Stay
Glenariff Forest Park (☎ 2175 8232, fax 2175 8828, 98 Glenariff Rd) Tent & campervan sites £10. Camping is possible here, just outside the forest park.

Cushendall Caravan Park (☎ 2177 1699, 62 Coast Rd) Tent site £5.70. On the coast road and overlooking the Moyle, this is a bigger caravan park.

Thornlea Hotel (☎ 2177 1223, fax 2177 1362, 6 Coast Rd) Singles/doubles £30/48 including breakfast. The hotel is to be renovated so quality could improve.

Mountain View (☎ 2177 1246, fax 2177 1996, 1 Kilnadore Rd) Singles/doubles £17/30 including breakfast. All rooms are en suite. This cheap but well-maintained place is up hill off Coast Rd.

Riverside Guest House (☎/fax 2177

DERRY & ANTRIM

1655, e *cushendallBandB@aol.com, 14 Mill St)* Singles/doubles £20/34 including breakfast. This place is centrally located and has cosy rooms with shared bathrooms.

Cullentra House (☎/fax 2177 1762, 16 Cloghs Rd) £17 per person. All rooms are en suite and come with TV, tea making facilities and trouser presses. There are good views of the craggy Antrim coast.

Places to Eat

Gillans Coffee Shop (☎ 2177 1404, 6 Mill St) It serves a great Ulster fry and snacks all day.

Harry's Restaurant (☎ 2177 2022, 10 Mill St) Bar snacks/a la carte £5/7. Open lunch & dinner daily. This is a very popular place, offering good-value meals and big servings. Booking is preferred.

Manor Lodge (☎ 2175 8221, 120 Glen Rd) Meals £7-10, 3-course set menu for two £24.95. Open 10.30am-9pm daily. This restaurant and bar is on a spur road off the road to the park. The Lodge serves grills, seafood and sandwiches in an interestingly decorated 1893 Swiss-style former tearooms.

You could also try the *Glenariff Tea House (☎ 2175 8769, 98 Glenariff Rd)*. It opens 10am to 6pm daily from Easter to September.

Entertainment

Joe McCollam's (Johnny Joe's; ☎ 2177 1992, 23 Mill St) Open from 8pm Mon, Tues & Fri-Sun, 11.30am-11.30pm July & Aug. This tiny bar swells to the sound of traditional Irish music.

Getting There & Away

See the Cushendun section as the buses mentioned also serve Cushendall.

CARNLOUGH
pop 1493

Carnlough is a beautiful little town with a 'pretty as a picture' harbour and fine beach. Many buildings, made of local limestone, were commissioned by the marquess of Londonderry in 1854. The limestone quarries were in use until the early 1960s; the white stone bridge across the village was for trains carrying the stone down to the harbour to be shipped away for export.

The Tourist Information Centre (☎ 2888 5236) is in McKillop's store on 14 Harbour Rd. Opening hours are 10am to 10pm from Easter to September, 10am to 8pm Monday to Saturday. The staff can book accommodation.

Places to Stay

Bay View Caravan Park (☎ 2888 5685, 89 Largy Rd) Tent sites £4. This park looks right over onto the sea and is about 3km north of Carnlough.

Ruby Hill Caravan Park (☎ 2888 5692, 46 Largy Rd) Tent sites £4. This place has limited camping space and, like the Bay View, is about 3km north of Carnlough.

Londonderry Arms Hotel (☎ 2888 5255, fax 2888 5263, 20 Harbour Rd) Singles/doubles from £55/85 (there are often special deals). The marchioness of Londonderry built this prosperous and solid place as a coaching inn in 1848. It was eventually inherited by a distant relation of hers, Winston Churchill, who sold it in 1921 to the present owners. The *Arkle Bar* is named for the very successful Irish horse that won 27 of its 35 races; the bar is decorated with many photographs of Arkle.

Places to Eat

Londonderry Arms Hotel (see Places to Stay) Bar/restaurant meals £3.75/8.95. The hotel serves up locally caught fish, including lobster and wild salmon. They also have a children's menu.

Glencloy Inn (☎ 2888 5226, cnr Harbour Rd & Bridge St) Bar meals £4.25. Open noon-8pm daily. The Glencoy does bar meals and has a restaurant.

Harbour Lights Licensed Restaurant (☎ 2888 5950, 11 Harbour Rd) Lunch £5-7, a la carte £11-14. Open noon-9pm Wed-Sun. Situated by the harbour this restaurant serves all-day breakfasts, teas and delicious light meals.

Getting There & Away

Bus No 128 travels to and from Ballymena five-times daily Monday to Saturday, with connections to Belfast. Bus No 162 between Cushendun and Larne stops at Carnlough.

See Getting There & Away in the Ballycastle section earlier in this chapter for information on the Antrim Coaster bus.

GLENARM
pop 603

Glenarm (Gleann Arma), the oldest village in the glens, is 5km south of Carnlough and the first travelling north from Belfast or Larne. The pavements are made from attractive black and white pebbling. The eyesore of a quarry is about to go as Glenarm goes through a revitalisation courtesy of EU funding. A new harbour is being built providing marina berths and hire boats.

Another major venture will be the Traditional Music centre in the grounds of Glenarm Castle. Importantly it is a cross-cultural venue that will marry the beat of the *bodhrán* and the *lambeg* (the loyalist bands' drum). Apart from performances and festivals there'll be regular workshops.

Glenarm Castle dates from the early 17th century, it was remodelled in the 19th century. It's privately owned and only open to the public on 14 July each year.

Places to Stay & Eat

Margaret's House (☎ 2884 1307, 10 Altmore St) Basic rooms £14 per person including breakfast. If you're coming south turn right at the crossroads for this basic but OK B&B.

Riverside B&B (☎ 2884 1474, 13 Tobermore) Singles/doubles £18/36. The Riverside has good airy rooms.

Drumnagreagh Hotel (☎ 2884 1651, fax 2884 1725, e drumnagreagh@nireland .com, 408 Coast Rd) Singles/doubles £40/60 including breakfast. This is 'location location' with fabulous sea views over to Scotland from some rooms. The *restaurant* opens for lunch and dinner Monday to Saturday plus a Sunday lunch carvery.

Charlies (☎ 2884 1276, 6 Altmore St) Open 11am-8pm daily. Charlies is a tearooms and an emporium of arts and crafts from across the UK and Ireland. Some are rather kitsch but there's also some nice local linen.

Getting There & Away

Bus No 162 runs between Larne and Cushendun, stopping at towns along the way.

See Getting There & Away in the Ballycastle section earlier in this chapter for information on the Antrim Coaster bus.

LARNE
pop 17,580

Arriving from Scotland or down from the spectacular coastline, Larne (Lutharna) with its sectarian graffiti is something of a rude awakening. There's really no reason to linger in Larne and its best attribute is the road north.

Orientation & Information

It's about a 15-minute walk from the ferry terminal via Fleet St and Curran Rd (becoming Main St) to the town's centre.

Inside the ferry terminal there's a small tourist information office with a helpful list of B&B phone numbers.

The main Larne Tourist Information Centre (☎ 2826 0088), on Narrow Gauge Rd, opens 9am to 5pm Monday to Friday October to Easter; 9am to 5pm Monday to Saturday Easter to June and September; and 9am to 6pm Monday to Friday, 9am to 5pm Saturday July and August. As you leave Larne town station, it's in the car park on the far side of the roundabout. The centre has a bureau de change and books accommodation.

Places to Stay & Eat

There are plenty of accommodation options in Larne. The tourist office (see under Orientation & Information) has a full listing.

One of Ireland's better little camp sites is *Carnfunnock Country Park (☎ 2827 0541, Coast Rd)* Tent sites £7. It's nearly 5km north of town off the A2. It's a modest place but well run and pleasantly situated.

Manor Guesthouse (☎ 2827 3305, fax 2826 0505, w www.themanorguesthouse .com, 23 Olderfleet Rd) Singles/doubles £20/36 including breakfast. This is a mid-Victorian house decorated and furnished for the period. Some of the rooms have religious homilies on the wall.

Seaview Guest House (☎/fax 2827 2438,

e) *seaviewhouse@talk21.com, 156 Curran Rd)* Singles/doubles from £17/36. Seaview is a comfortable place to stay and is within walking distance of the harbour.

Captain's Kitchen (☎ 2827 0284, Ferry Terminal) Open 7am-5.30pm daily (until 7.30pm in summer). The Kitchen is in the ferry terminal and is a good fallback for snacks at odd hours.

Carriages (☎ 2827 5132, 105 Main St) Meals £4.95. Open 5pm-11pm daily. This cafeteria-style place serves pizzas, steaks and pasta and also does takeaways.

Dan Campbell's (☎ 2827 7222, 2 Bridge St) Meals £6.95, but buy one meal and you get one free. Dan's is also a pub with nightly entertainment. The usual pub quiz is Thursday night, Karaoke Sundays and music every other night.

Getting There & Away

Bus Bus Nos 256 and 156 provide the regular service to and from Belfast. The earliest bus leaves the bus station (☎ 2827 2345) on Circular Rd at 7.15am and the last one at 7pm. It takes just over an hour and there are only three buses on Sunday. Bus No 162 to Cushendun, stopping at towns along the way, usually operates only between June and September.

See Getting There & Away in the Ballycastle section earlier in this chapter for information on the Antrim Coaster bus that starts and finishes here.

Train Larne has two stations: the main Larne town station (☎ 2826 0604) and Larne Harbour for the ferries. The journey from Belfast Central takes about 50 minutes.

Boat Larne's ferry terminal houses a train station and bus stop, and car hire and bureau de change facilities. P&O Irish Sea (☎ 0870 242 4777) handles the route from Larne to Cairnryan in Scotland; crossings take just over two hours. You can call the Larne Harbour Authority (☎ 2887 2100) for information.

For more information, including fares, see the Sea section in the Getting There & Away chapter.

ISLANDMAGEE

A day trip to Islandmagee (Oileán Mhic Aodha) makes a pleasant excursion. The name is deceptive as this is an 11km by 3km peninsula, not an island. Access is by ferry from Larne or road from Whitehead to the south. Close to the ferry landing point is the **Ballylumford Dolmen** in the front garden of a private home. Also at this northern end is **Brown's Bay** with a big sandy beach.

Brown's Bay Caravan Park (☎ 2826 0088, Brown's Bay) Tent sites £7. Open Apr-Sept. The Larne Tourist Information Centre (see the earlier Larne section for details) handles bookings but if you just turn up a local warden will visit you. The sites are in an enclosed area that is just an extension of the car park.

Taking the picturesque eastern coast road (B150) brings you to **The Gobbins**: more than 2.5km of basalt cliffs with a path cut into the rock. During the 1641 rebellion, the garrison at Carrickfergus, seeking to revenge their fellow Protestants, massacred the Catholic inhabitants of the peninsula, throwing live and dead bodies over the cliffs.

Getting There & Away

The Islandmagee foot passenger ferry leaves Larne Harbour at 7.30am, 8am and then on the hour until 3pm, every half-hour until 5.30pm and then on request by phoning the Larne Harbour Office (☎ 2827 3785). Return trips are immediately after unloading at Islandmagee(adult/child £2/1 return).

CARRICKFERGUS & AROUND

Carrickfergus (Carraig Fhearghais) is a commuter suburb just north of Belfast, noted for its wonderfully situated castle, overlooking the harbour where William of Orange landed on 14 June 1690. There's a commemorative blue plaque on the site and a statue of the king on the seawards side of the castle. The town centre has some attractive 18th-century houses and you can still trace a good part of the 17th-century city walls.

Orientation & Information

The train station is at the northern end of North St. Turn left outside the station and pass under North Gate; the castle is a five-minute walk downhill to the seafront. Ulster-buses stop on Joymount Parade behind the town hall on the seafront.

The Carrickfergus Tourist Information Centre (☎ 9336 6455, fax 9335 0350, W www.carrickfergus.org) is on Antrim St inside the Heritage Plaza. It opens 9am to 5pm Monday to Friday (9am to 6pm April to September); 10am to 6pm Saturday for April to September; noon to 6pm Sunday in July and August. The centre has a bureau de change and books accommodation.

Walking tours (£2.50) of Carrickfergus leave the Knight Ride Centre (see the following section) every Friday at 10am. For details call ☎ 9336 1091.

Carrickfergus Castle

Theatrically sited on a rocky promontory, commanding the entrance to Belfast Lough, this fine castle (☎ 9335 1273, Marine Hwy; adult/child £2.70/1.35, combined castle & knight ride ticket £4.85/2.40; opens 10am-6pm Mon-Sat, 2pm-6pm Sun Apr-Sept; 10am-4pm Mon-Sat, Sun 2pm-4pm Oct-Mar) was built by John de Courcy soon after his 1177 invasion of Ulster. Besieged by King John in 1210 and Edward Bruce in 1315 and briefly captured by the French in 1760, the castle also witnessed a successful attack on a British vessel in 1778 by the American John Paul Jones in the Ranger. The oldest part of the castle, going back to its Anglo-Norman origins, is the inner ward, which is enclosed by a high wall. The keep houses a museum telling the castle's history and the site is dotted with life-sized figures illustrating the castle's history and adding colour to what is undoubtedly Ireland's finest (and first) Norman castle.

Knight Ride

Inside the glassy Heritage Plaza on Antrim St is a smells-and-all ride (☎ 9336 6455, Heritage Plaza; adult/concession £2.70/1.35, combined castle & knight ride ticket £4.85/2.40; open 10am-5.30pm Mon-Sat, noon-5.30pm Sun Apr-Sept; 10am-4.30pm Mon-Sat, noon-4.30pm Sun Oct-Mar) through Carrickfergus' past. It's not as tacky as it first seems. Seated in a giant knight's helmet hanging beneath a monorail you swing out over the atrium and then run back through time, catching quick glimpses of Mary Dunbar's haunted house and the hanging corpses of members of the 18th-century O'Haughan gang. There are then some walk-through historical sections. The ride is wheelchair accessible.

St Nicholas' Church

The church on Albert Rd has pillars in the nave dating back to the church's establishment in the 12th century. Most of the rest dates to 17th-century restoration work, a particularly fine example of which is the Renaissance-style Chichester memorial in the transept known as the Donegal aisle. Stained-glass in the southern side and the nave's western end is 16th-century Irish work. For admission telephone ☎ 9335 5381 or call in at the church office, at 3 Market Place, between 9.30am and noon.

Andrew Jackson Centre

The parents of the 7th US president left Carrickfergus in the second half of the 18th century, hence the Andrew Jackson Centre (☎ 9336 6455, Bonybefore; adult/concession £1.20/0.60; open 10am-1pm & 2pm-4pm Mon-Fri, 2pm-4pm Sat & Sun Apr & May; 10am-1pm & 2pm-6pm Mon-Fri, 2pm-6pm Sat & Sun June-Sept). The Centre is a replica dwelling complete with fireside crane and earthen floor. It has displays on the life of Jackson, the Jackson family in Ulster and Ulster's connection with the USA.

Also here is the **US Rangers Centre**, with a small exhibition on the first US rangers, who were trained during WWII in Carrickfergus before heading for Europe.

The centre is in Boneybefore, 3km north of Carrickfergus. From Monday to Friday you can get a bus to Downshire Rd from where it's a short walk.

Places to Stay & Eat

Langsgarden (☎/fax 9336 6369, 72 Scottish Quarter) Rooms from £18 per person including breakfast. Some rooms have showers or en suites in this sea-front hotel.

***Tramway House** (☎ 9335 5639, 95 Irish Quarter South)* Singles/doubles £18/35 including breakfast, but bathrooms are shared.

***Dobbin's Inn Hotel** (☎/fax 9335 1905, 6-8 High St)* Singles/doubles £44/62 Mon-Thur, £34/52 weekends including breakfast. This inn has been around for over three centuries and has a priest's hole and the original 16th-century fireplace to prove it. The inn's *restaurant* opens 9am to 9pm and serves bar meals and a la carte from £5.

***Courtyard Coffee House** (☎ 9335 1881, 38 Scottish Quarter)* Open lunch Mon-Sat. This cafe serves light lunches as well as rich cakes and has a smaller branch inside Carrickfergus Castle.

***Cafe No 10** (☎ 9336 0306, 10 West St)* This place serves coffee, snacks and grills for around £2.50.

Getting There & Away

Ulsterbus No 166 takes 15 minutes to Belfast's Laganside Bus Centre; bus No 163 takes 30 minutes. There are also regular daily trains from Belfast Central/Botanic Stations.

ANTRIM

pop 20,880

In 1649 Antrim (Aontroim) was burned by General Monro and in 1798 resisted an attack by the United Irishmen. Modern Antrim town is dominated by its shopping centre, but there are a few older buildings, including the fine courthouse, which dates back to 1762.

Belfast International Airport is handy, only 6km to the south.

Information

The very helpful Antrim Tourist Information Centre (☎ 9442 8331, fax 9448 7844, e abs@antrim.gov.uk, w www.antrim.gov.uk) is in the Antrim Business shop, 16 High St. It opens 9am to 5pm Monday to Friday, October to March; 9am to 5pm Monday to Friday and 9am to 2pm Saturday, Easter to June and September; 9am to 5pm Monday to Wednesday, 9am to 6pm Thursday and Friday and 9am to 5pm Saturday during July and August. The centre provides a free self-guided heritage trail leaflet. A free, 90-minute guided tour leaves the centre at 2pm on Friday. The centre books accommodation all over Ireland and has Internet access for £1.50 per 30 minutes.

Things to See & Do

In **Pogue's Entry**, a narrow alley at the end of Church St, a blue plaque marks the tiny, mud-floored home of Alexander Irvine (1863–1941), missionary and writer. His *My Lady of the Chimney Corner* tells the story of his mother's brave struggle to rear nine children in grinding poverty.

Antrim Castle Gardens, behind the courthouse, alongside Sixmilewater River, were originally laid out in the 17th century. Antrim Castle burned down many years ago but the gardens are open to the public.

A 10th-century **round tower**, 27m high, in Steeple Park about 1.5km north of town, is all that remains of a monastery that once stood on the site. The walls are more than 1m thick and the 10th-century dating is strong evidence for linking this and other towers with the Viking raids. Follow the signs for Steeple Industrial Estate, then for the Antrim Borough Council offices.

Antrim is on the edge of Lough Neagh and as expected it's a place to mess about on the water. **Waveriders Watersports Centre** (☎ 9442 8684, 0850 489 470) offers jet skiing (£20 for 20 minutes), canoeing (£10 per hour) and water skiing (£15 per session). They also hire out equipment.

Places to Stay & Eat

***Bro-gra-ni** (☎/fax 9446 2484, 2 Steeple Green)* Singles/doubles £20/35 including breakfast plus tea and coffee whenever needed. The rooms are small but the atmosphere is very friendly.

***The Stables** (☎/fax 9446 6943, 96 Milltown Rd)* Singles/doubles with en suite £30/40 including breakfast. The Stables is about 5km north of Antrim on the Ballymena road in a quiet rural setting.

***Top of the Town** (☎ 9442 8146, 77 Fountain St)* Pub meals £4.25. Open noon to 3pm for lunch Monday to Saturday. Antrim is hardly filled with gourmet restaurants but for a light lunch you could try this place.

Entertainment

Stables *(☎ 9446 5189, 10-16 Castle St)*
There's more to this place than the chocolate box exterior suggests. There are three bars on several levels which are embellished with carved wood and stained-glass windows. It's a place to visit just for the internal architecture apart from the entertainment, which features music from Wednesday to Sunday.

Clotworthy Arts Centre *(☎ 9442 8000, Antrim Castle Gardens, Randalstown Rd; free; gallery open 9.30am-9.30pm Mon-Fri, 10am-5pm Sat, 2pm-5pm Sun July-Aug only)* This centre has a small theatre and hosts changing exhibitions in its gallery.

Getting There & Away

Bus No 120 from Ballymena to Belfast stops in Antrim. There's also bus No 109 to Belfast via Lisburn.

Antrim is on the Derry or Portrush to Belfast train line. Trains to Belfast run 10-times daily.

BALLYMENA & AROUND

The predominantly Protestant town of Ballymena (An Baile Meánach) is the home turf of Ian Paisley, founder/leader of the Free Presbyterian Church and the stridently antinationalist and anti-Catholic Democratic Unionist Party (DUP). The town council was the first to be controlled by the DUP in 1977 and voted unanimously to remove all mention of Darwin's theory of evolution from religious education in Ballymena's schools. The town is also the birthplace of the actor Liam Neeson, of *Schindler's List* and *Michael Collins* fame.

While Ballymena is a pleasant enough town, there's not much reason to linger. The Ballymena Tourist Information Centre (☎ 2563 8494, fax 2563 8495, Ⓦ www.bal lymena.gov.uk), 76 Church St, opens 9am to 5pm Monday to Friday plus 10am to 5pm Saturday from Easter to December.

Arthur Cottage

The ancestors of Chester Alan Arthur, 21st president of the USA, lived in a simple cottage *(☎ 2588 0781, Dreen, Cullybackey;* *adult/concession £2/1; open 10.30am-5pm Mon-Fri, 10.30am-4pm Sat May-Sept)* about 6km north-west of Ballymena, near Cullybackey. Demonstrators in traditional costume bake and quilt on Tuesday, Friday and Saturday at 1.30pm throughout June, July (except on the 12th) and August. Take bus Nos 113 or 115 from Ballymena.

Gracehill

pop 681

In the mid-18th century many Protestant Moravians fled their homeland to escape religious persecution and some settled in Gracehill (Baile Uí Chinnéide), 2km west of Ballymena, in a country not itself renowned for religious tolerance. The Georgian architecture of their elegant village square includes a **church** with separate entrances for men and women worshippers. If you'd like to see inside, visitors are welcome to services at 11am on Sunday. Even the graveyard at the back of the church is laid out for men on the left and women on the right, with the numbered tombstones lying flat either side of the walkway!

Bus No 127 from Ballymena stops at Gracehill. If you're driving, take the A42 past Ballymena's bus and train station; look for a brown sign with a church marked on it and take the turning to the left.

Places to Eat

Galgorm Manor *(☎ 2588 1001, fax 2588 0080, 136 Fenaghy Rd)* 4-course dinner £24.95. Open dinner Tues-Sat, lunch & dinner Sun. About 6km east of Ballymena (turn after the Gracehill roundabout) this place has the best menu on offer in the area (for example, Dundrum oysters, Donegal salmon, steamed chocolate pudding). The Manor also has ***accommodation*** in its 1857 former linen mill.

Getting There & Away

Bus Nos 120, 149, 219 and 220 run south to Belfast, while bus Nos 115, 175 and 143 head north to Derry.

Ballymena is on the Derry or Portrush to Belfast train line. Trains to Belfast run seven times daily.

LISBURN & AROUND

The small town of Lisburn (Lios na gCearrbhach), 12km south-west of Belfast, is most noted as the home of the excellent Irish Linen Centre.

In the early 1600s the Crown gave the Conways a lease to settle Lisburn and in 1627 permission to hold a Tuesday market, which continues to this day. A disastrous fire in 1707 destroyed much of Lisburn but the 17th-century Market House survived to become an assembly hall in the 18th century.

In the 18th and 19th centuries Lisburn grew rich on the proceeds of the linen industry. The modern post office in Linenhall St stands on the site of the old Brown Linen Hall, where unbleached linen used to be sold. In the 18th century John Wesley came here several times, preaching in 1789 at Lisburn's first Methodist church in Market St.

Things are improving for the town. A new leisure complex has opened and there are plans for an arts and performance centre, boat moorings along the Lagan River, new department stores and apartments.

Information

The Lisburn Tourist Information Centre (☎ 9266 0038, fax 9260 7889, [W] www.lisburn.gov.uk) will have moved to Market Square by the time this guide is published; they hope to keep the same telephone number. It opens 9.30am to 5pm Monday to Saturday. Apart from booking accommodation there's a bureau de change.

Irish Linen Centre & Lisburn Museum

The Irish Linen Centre & Lisburn Museum (☎ 9266 3377, *Market Square; free; open 9.30am-5.30pm Mon-Sat & bank holidays*) is housed in the fine 17th-century Market House. It was here from the early days where weavers brought their cloth to sell.

The museum on the ground floor has displays and exhibitions on the cultural and historic heritage of the region, while upstairs the Linen Centre's award-winning permanent Flax to Fabric exhibition details the fascinating history of the linen industry in Northern Ireland – on the eve of WWI

Ulster was the largest linen-producing region in the world, employing some 75,000 people.

There are plenty of audiovisual and hands-on exhibits – you can try your hand at spinning flax and see weavers working on Jacquard looms – and the costume section contains some lovely work.

Other Things to See

Just over 1km north-east of Lisburn is **Hilden Brewery** (☎ *9266 3863, Grand St; tours £4.50; open 10am-5pm Tues-Sat*), Ireland's oldest independent brewery. Hilden, established by Huguenots, is housed in the courtyard of a former linen baron's mansion. The brewery tours, at 11.30am and 2.30pm, are followed by a sample or two of real ale.

With your own transport you could also visit **Ballance House** (☎ *9264 8492, 118a Lisburn Rd, Glenavy; adult/concession £2/0.50; open 11am-5pm Tues-Fri & bank holidays, 2pm-5pm Sat & Sun Apr-Sept*), 8.5km north-west of Lisburn. This farmhouse, birthplace of former New Zealand prime minister John Ballance (1839–93), has been restored to its assumed appearance in 1850 and displays celebrate the province's links with New Zealand.

The **Lagan Valley Leisureplex** (☎ *9267 2121,* [W] *www.lisburn.gov.uk, 12 Lisburn Leisure Park, Governor Rd; adult/child/family £4.10/2.80/11.50; open 3pm-9.50pm Mon-Fri, 11am-8pm Sat & Sun*) is an all round fun place with a pool with water rides, squash courts and other indoor sports. In the same complex is the **Lisburn Omniplex** (☎ 9260 2233) with a 14-screen cinema.

Places to Stay & Eat

Lisburn is an easy visit from Belfast but if you do want to stay there are a few B&Bs around.

Circular Lodge B&B (☎ *9266 5899, 44 North Circular Rd*) Singles/doubles £36/40. The Circular has very pleasant, large rooms in an old house just outside Lisburn's centre.

Strathearn House (☎ *9260 1661, 19 Antrim Rd*) Singles/doubles with shared bathroom £23/40, en suite £30/50. The Strathearn is a pleasant place to stay, near the city centre but not signed.

The Flax about Linen

The manufacture of linen, probably the earliest textile made from plants, was once of vital significance to the Ulster economy. The real boost to linen making in Ulster, though, came with the arrival of Huguenot refugee weavers in the late 17th century.

The flax plant was sown in the north of Ireland from March to May and harvested in mid-August. The first stage in the harvesting was bundling the flax into stacks for open-air drying. The seeds were removed and crushed for linseed oil or kept for the following year's planting. The second stage was a messy and smelly one, entailing the soaking of the bundles of flax in freshwater ponds, or 'lint holes', for up to two weeks. This process of 'retting' softened the outer stem and the 'scutching' could begin.

Scutching separated the dried flax stem; with the introduction of water wheels in the 18th century, large wooden blades pounded and loosened the flax. The fibres were then ready for spinning on a wheel before being woven into lengths of cloth. Some of this unbleached linen was sold as 'brown linen', hence the number of Brown Linen Halls that used to exist.

The next stage was the bleaching, carried out in the open after the cloth had been soaked in water for hours. Huge lengths were stretched out across fields and left in the sunlight. The moisture in the material reacted with the sunlight to produce hydrogen peroxide, which bleached the cloth. The final stage involved the hammering of the cloth by wooden hammers, or beetles, which smoothed out the material and made it ready for selling to the public. Bleached linen was sold through the many White Linen Halls.

At its height the linen industry was so important that Belfast was sometimes referred to as 'Linenopolis'. Flax growing died out in the north towards the end of the 19th century but was reborn during WWI with the demand for parachute material. There was a similar resurgence during WWII, but most of the linen now purchased is made in Scandinavia with the aid of chemicals. In recent years there has been an attempt to reintroduce flax growing in Ulster and you may spot the occasional field of blue flax.

You can visit a beetling mill at Wellbrook outside Cookstown in County Tyrone. For a complete picture of the linen industry and its history, visit the impressive Irish Linen Centre in Lisburn.

Overdale House *(☎ 9267 2275, 150 Belsize Rd)* Singles/doubles £20/40. There's one en suite room that costs extra and the baths here are nicely large.

Tap Room Restaurant *(see Hilden Brewery)* Meals £6-8. Open noon-2.30pm Tues-Sat. You can have a meal in this brewery restaurant. It has a varied menu all of which can be washed down with good beer.

Cafe Crommelin *(see The Irish Linen Centre & Lisburn Museum)* Snacks £3. This cafe in the Irish Linen Centre is a good place to eat. It serves sandwiches, baguettes and a wonderful selection of filled pastries.

Coco's *(☎ 9266 8066, 21 Railway St)* Meals £4. Open 9.30am-4.30pm Mon-Sat. Coco's serves breakfast and lunch specials (such as cheese and cranberry croissant, and Thai fish cakes) and a good selection of coffee and cakes. It also has once-a-month theme nights (8pm to late, £15) featuring cuisines from around the world.

Getting There & Away
Bus Nos 38, 51, 109, 523 and 525 leave frequently from Belfast's Europa Bus Centre. From Lisburn you can catch onwards buses to Hillsborough, Banbridge and Newry. For more information contact the local Ulsterbus office (☎ 9266 2091), 2a Smithfield Square.

Lisburn is on the Belfast to Dublin train line. Trains to Belfast run frequently daily.

Counties Tyrone & Fermanagh

While Tyrone is the larger of these two counties (in fact, it is the biggest county in Northern Ireland), Fermanagh attracts more visitors, with its lakes, rivers and medieval sites. In Tyrone the peaty Sperrin Mountains offer good hiking opportunities. No trains operate in this part of Ireland, but Ulsterbus has services to most towns and the larger villages.

County Tyrone

The attractions of County Tyrone – forest parks, prehistoric sites, the lonely Sperrin Mountains – are sprinkled among some less-than-interesting towns in a way that makes it difficult for visitors to get a feel for the county as a whole. But it's worth the effort of trying to get to know Tyrone, for the county has an illustrious history and its unspoiled countryside is ideal for those wanting to 'get away from it all'.

For centuries County Tyrone had been the territory of the O'Neills, until March 1603, when Hugh O'Neill, earl of Tyrone, finally submitted to the English at Mellifont. This marked the end of Gaelic Ireland. The English and Scottish Planters moved in, introducing linen in the 18th century. Many local people subsequently migrated to America and there are still strong links with the USA today. The huge Ulster American Folk Park near Omagh, sufficient reason in itself for visiting Tyrone, tells the story.

OMAGH
pop 17,280

Sadly, for a long time to come the market town of Omagh (An Óghmagh) will be remembered for the devastating car bomb in 1998 that killed 29 people and injured 200. Planted by the breakaway Real IRA, the bomb was the worst single atrocity in the 30-year history of the Troubles. When Sinn Féin's president, Gerry Adams, denounced the bombing shortly afterwards and stated that: 'The violence we have seen must be, for

Highlights

- Visit the Ulster American Folk Park, one of the best museums in Ireland
- Explore the lonely Sperrin Mountains
- Discover the magic of Celtic and early-Christian archaeological sites around Lough Erne
- Admire the stately homes of Florence Court and Castle Coole near Enniskillen
- Go trout fishing, or just soak up the view, on Lough Erne
- Go underground boating in Marble Arch Caves

all of us now, a thing of the past, over, done with and gone,' he was echoing the feelings of the vast majority.

Situated at the confluence of the Camowen and Drumragh Rivers, which join to form the River Strule, Omagh serves as a useful base for the surrounding area. It also makes a good start or finish to a trip to the Sperrin Mountains or walking a section of the Ulster Way.

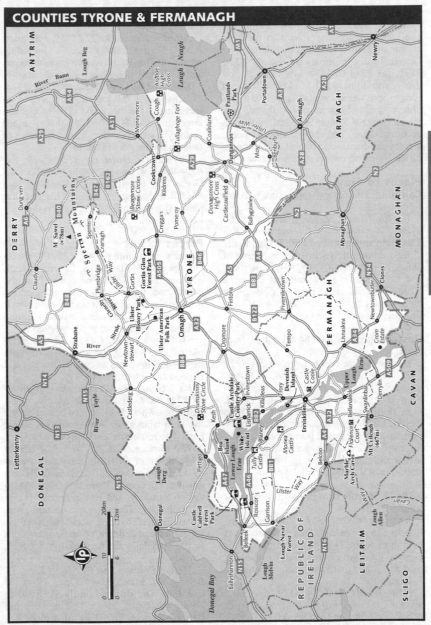

COUNTIES TYRONE & FERMANAGH

TYRONE & FERMANAGH

Orientation & Information

Market St and then High St lead from the confluence of the rivers west to the neo-classical 19th-century courthouse. The Omagh Tourist Information Centre (☎ 8224 7831, fax 8214 0774, W www.omagh.gov .uk/tourism.htm) is at 1 Market St. It opens 9am to 5pm weekdays and 9am to 5pm Saturday, April to September; in July and August it closes at 5.30pm. The staff will book accommodation and change money. There are several banks on High St and the post office is next to the courthouse at No 7.

Places to Stay

Camping The nearest camp site is 10km from town.

Gortin Glen Caravan Park (☎ 8164 8108, fax 8164 7644, 1 Lisnaharney Rd) Tent/caravan site from £4.50/9. This is the closest camp site to town, north-east of Omagh on the B48 Omagh–Gortin road. The camp site is a few minutes from the Ulster Way and campers get a discount at the Omagh Leisure Centre. Bus Nos 92 and 213 (in July and August only) stop nearby.

Hostels There's a good hostel not far from town.

Omagh Independent Hostel (☎/fax 8224 1973, W www.omaghhostel.co.uk, 9a Water-works Rd) Dorms £7 per person. Open Feb-Nov. This spacious and welcoming hostel, 4km north-east of town on the B48 to Gortin, has three rooms adapted for wheelchair access. The hostel is in a lovely peaceful, rural setting and is awash with flowers in the summer. If you ring from the bus station they'll come and pick you up.

B&Bs & Hotels Omagh has a number of simple B&Bs.

Ardmore (☎ 8224 3381, 12 Tamlaght Rd) Rooms £16 per person. This standard B&B with three rooms (with shared bathroom) is close to the town centre. Head for the ring road and Tamlaght roundabout, off which is Tamlaght Rd.

Four Winds (☎ 8224 3554, fax 8225 9923, 63 Dromore Rd) Rooms from £16 per person including an Irish breakfast. Farther

south than Ardmore, this place has three rooms to offer.

Arleston House (☎ 8224 1719, 1 Arleston Park) Singles/doubles £20/36 including breakfast. This B&B has two en-suite rooms and is off the Cookstown road to the east.

Dialinn Country House (☎ 8224 7974, 112 Doogary Rd) Rooms £19.50 per person including a full breakfast. The rooms are large (the double is best) in this spacious country house. It's 3km from the centre of Omagh on the A5 to Dublin.

Silverbirch Hotel (☎ 8224 2520, fax 8224 9061, W www.silverbirchhotel.com, 5 Gortin Rd) En-suite singles/doubles from £44/72 including breakfast. This two-star place with 46 comfortable rooms is the only hotel in town.

Places to Eat

Grant's of Omagh (☎ 8225 0900, 29 George's St) Mains £9-14. Open for lunch & dinner daily. Round the corner from the courthouse, this place is recommended for reasonably priced meals and bar snacks. It has a cosmopolitan menu with an Italian influence. Book ahead at the weekend.

McElroy's (☎ 8224 4441, 30 Castle St) Mains £3.50-13. Food served noon-9pm daily. McElroy's has an extensive menu and is good for pub grub.

La Gondola Restaurant Italiano (☎ 8225 9624, 80 Market St) Mains around £10. The owner/chef has been educating the locals in what good food should be, so eat here. The restaurant also does takeaway.

The Carlton (☎ 8224 7046, 31 High St) Pasta & pizza £4-6.70, restaurant mains £9-12. The Carlton Coffee Bar and Bakery downstairs opens 8.30am to 5.30pm Monday to Saturday, and as a pizzeria 6pm to 10.30pm daily. The restaurant upstairs, with a varied menu covering steak, fish, poultry, vegetarian and children's dishes, opens 6pm to 10.30pm daily and noon to 4pm for Sunday lunch.

Mellon Country Inn (☎ 8166 1224, 134 Beltany Rd) Mains £5-14. Open 10am till late daily. Out of town on the A5 road to Newtownstewart, about 1.5km from the Ulster American Folk Park, this place has an excellent reputation. It also serves bar snacks.

Getting There & Away

Ulsterbus services connect Omagh with a number of towns in the North and in the Republic. Bus No 273 runs frequently to Belfast and Derry. Bus No 274 runs several times daily from Omagh to Dublin (£8.50, 3¼ hours) via Monaghan. A number of other buses leave Omagh for Dungannon (bus No 78) and Enniskillen (bus No 94), where you change for Donegal. Bus No 296 leaves Omagh for Cork (9¼ hours) once a day Monday to Saturday at 10.10am and travels via Longford, Athlone and Cahir.

The bus station (☎ 8224 2711), 3 Mountjoy Rd, is just north of the town centre along Bridge St and across the River Strule.

Getting Around

Conway Cycles (☎ 8076 1258), 157 Lough Macrory Rd, 13.5km towards Cookstown, rents out bicycles for £7/30 per day/week.

AROUND OMAGH
Ulster American Folk Park

Situated 8km north-west of Omagh off the A5, the folk park is one of the best museums in Ireland and an essential visit (☎ 8224 3292, W www.folkpark.com, Mellon Rd; adult/concession/family £6.50/4/18; open 10.30am-6pm Mon-Sat, 11am-5pm Sun & public holidays Apr-Sept; 10.30am-5pm Mon-Fri Oct-Mar; last admission 1½ hours before closing). Thousands of Ulster people left their country to forge a new life across the Atlantic in the 18th and 19th centuries; 200,000 emigrated in the 18th century alone. The American Declaration of Independence was signed by several Ulstermen, and the Exhibition Hall presents many more connections.

The real appeal of the folk park, though, is the outdoor museum. The number of life-sized exhibits is impressive: a forge, a weaver's cottage, a Presbyterian meeting house, a schoolhouse, a log cabin, a 19th-century Ulster street and an early street from western Pennsylvania. Clever use is made of an emigrants' ship and dockside to link the Ulster and USA exhibits.

Costumed guides and craftspeople are on hand to chat and explain the art of spinning, weaving, candle making and so on. The park has been expanded and there are regular theme events such as re-enactments of the American Civil War. There's almost too much to absorb in one visit and at least half a day is needed to do the park justice.

Bus No 97 to Strabane and Derry stops outside the park. On Tuesday and Thursday in July and August only, bus No 213 (the Sperrin Sprinter) leaves Omagh at 1.45pm and stops at the park 20 minutes later, but you'd need to catch bus No 97 back.

Ulster History Park

The story of settlements in Ireland from the Stone Age to the 17th-century Plantation is the theme of this park (☎ 8164 8188, Cullion; adult/concession/family £3.75/2.50/12, joint ticket with Ulster American Folk Park £6.50/4/18; open 10am-6.30pm daily July & Aug; 10am-5.30pm Mon-Sat & 11.30am-7pm Sun Apr-June & Sept; 10am-5pm Mon-Fri Oct-Mar; last admission 1 hour before closing). Reconstructions show a Mesolithic encampment, Neolithic houses, a late-Bronze Age crannóg (artificial island), a 12th-century church settlement complete with a stone round tower, and a Norman motte and bailey. They show what today's ruins would have looked like in their own time. The reception building has a cafe, shop, audiovisual theatre and a model Plantation settlement from the 17th century.

Ulster History Park is about 10km northeast of Omagh off the B48 road to Gortin. Bus No 92 between Omagh and Gortin stops outside Monday to Saturday.

Gortin Glen Forest Park

This park (☎ 8164 8217, Gortin Rd; admission car/motorcycle £2.50/2; open daily till dusk) is mostly planted with conifers and contains a herd of Japanese sika deer as well as other wildlife. It's a park suited for cars and motorbikes and a breathtaking 8km tarmac drive through the forest is the main way to get around. Near the main car park are some wildlife enclosures, an indoor exhibit, a small nature trail and a cafe. Tickets are

TYRONE & FERMANAGH

available from the ranger on duty or from the ticket machine.

There's a manageable day's walk from Gortin Glen Forest Park to the Ulster American Folk Park along a section of the **Ulster Way**. The 16km trip is mostly along small roads and forest tracks, and from the folk park bus No 97 can be caught back to Omagh. The last bus leaves the folk park at 7.30pm. A leaflet and map entitled *The Ulster Way: North-West Section* is available from the tourist office in Omagh.

Fishing

There is fishing along stretches of the three rivers around Omagh – mainly for brown and sea trout and salmon (April to mid-October). Permits, advice and information are available in Omagh from **CA Anderson** (☎ *8224 2311, 64 Market St)*; the entrance is on Drumragh Ave.

SPERRIN MOUNTAINS

In the north-east of the county, the gentle contours of the Sperrin Mountains, some 64km east to west, straddle the border with County Derry. The blanket bog and heather of the open moorland in the upper reaches contrast with the farmland and wooded valleys on the lower slopes. Wildlife is plentiful and trout fishing is a popular activity. The area is also littered with thousands of standing stones and chambered graves.

The mountains reach their highest point at Mt Sawel (678m) behind the **Sperrin Heritage Centre** (☎ *8164 8142, 274 Glenelly Rd, Cranagh; adult/child £2.20/1.30; open 11.30am-5.30pm Mon-Fri, 11.30am-6pm Sat & 2pm-6pm Sun Mar-Oct)*. In the centre, computer presentations and other displays are devoted to the historical, social and ecological aspects of the region. Gold has been found in the mountains and part of the exhibition is devoted to it. You can even try your luck at prospecting in a nearby stream with pans hired from the centre. The centre is also a **tourist information centre**, which will book accommodation, plus there's a cafe.

From Omagh, follow the B48 north-east through Gortin to Plumbridge. From there it's about 13km east on the B47 to Cranagh.

Buses from Omagh go only as far as Plumbridge. From Cookstown take the B162 and B47.

About 20km west of Cookstown on the A505, in Creggan, is the **An Creagán Visitor Centre** (☎ *8076 1112,* W *www.an -creagan.com, Creggan; free; open 11am-6.30pm Apr-Sept; 11am-4.30pm Mon-Fri Oct-Mar)*. It has an interpretive exhibition, rambling and cycling routes, bicycles for rent and a licensed restaurant.

There are some 44 prehistoric monuments within 8km of the centre including the **Beaghmore Stone Circles**. They consist of seven stone circles (the stones are less than 1m high) and a dozen or so stone alignments and burial cairns. The visitor centre has a map of their location.

If you're thinking of **walking** up Mt Sawel, enquire at the Sperrin Heritage Centre about the best route. The climb is easy, but some farmers are more accommodating than others when hikers cross their land. The nearby Ulster Way can be joined at Leagh's Bridge 6km away, roughly halfway along the 55km Dungiven–Gortin section. Another outdoor trip through the Sperrins is on horseback. **Edergole Riding Centre** (☎ *8676 2924, 70 Moneymore Rd, Cookstown)* organises three-day horseback trekking trips through the mountains, or hourly/day rides costing £15/45.

An Clachan (☎ *8076 1112,* W *www.an -creagan.com, Creggan)* 1-3 bedroom self-catering cottages from £150-330 per week, or from £60-110 per weekend/midweek, minimum 3 nights. The cottages are in the grounds of the An Creagán Visitor Centre.

COOKSTOWN
pop 10,470

According to the tourist literature about Cookstown (An Chorr Chríochach), its great advantage is convenient parking. That's not true on Sunday market days when the town's packed to the gunnels.

The Tourist Information Centre (☎ 8676 6727) at The Burnavon, Burn Rd, opens 9am to 5pm weekdays year round, plus 9am to 5pm Saturday and 2pm to 4pm Sunday during July and August, and 10am to 4pm Saturday in June and September. The centre books accommodation, changes money and sells fishing licences.

Places to Stay & Eat
Drum Manor Forest Park *(☎ 8676 2774, Drum Rd, Oaklands)* Tent site £1.70 per person, caravan site low/high season £8/11.50. This is a pleasant place 4km west of Cookstown on the A505, with lakes, a butterfly farm and an arboretum.

Central Inn *(☎ 8676 2255, 27 William St)* Rooms from £18 per person including breakfast. As the name suggests this pub is right in the centre of town.

Edergole *(☎ 8676 2924, 70 Moneymore Rd)* Rooms £20 per person including breakfast. This place is about 3km out of town on the A29 towards Moneymore and has a horse-riding school.

Glenavon House Hotel *(☎ 8676 4949, fax 8676 4396, 52 Drum Rd)* Singles/doubles £60/95 including breakfast. This upmarket hotel has 53 rooms.

Greenvale *(☎ 8676 2243, fax 8676 5539, 57 Drum Rd)* Singles/doubles £35/55 including breakfast. Nearly opposite the Glenavon House Hotel, this is a cheaper place to stay.

The Granary *(☎ 8676 9477, 52 James St)* Meals around £4.25. Open 8am-8pm Mon-Sat & 10am-8pm Sun. This popular cafe offers a variety of dishes, from pancakes or a traditional fry-up for breakfast, to baguettes, sandwiches or fajitas for lunch.

Courtyard *(☎ 8676 2278, 56a William St)* Lunch around £3.50. This is a favourite lunch spot among locals, serving dishes such as chicken curry and vegetarian bakes.

Getting There & Away
Bus No 110 connects Cookstown eight to nine-times daily (three times on Sunday) with Belfast (£5.80, 1¾ hours) via Antrim. Bus No 278 runs once or twice a day Monday to Saturday to Dungannon (20 minutes), Armagh (50 minutes) and, in the Republic, Monaghan and Dublin (four hours). Bus No 80 shuttles regularly between Cookstown and Dungannon, where you can connect with bus No 273 to Belfast, Omagh or Derry.

The bus station *(☎ 8676 6440 or* Translink ☎ 9033 3000)*, on Molesworth St,* opens 9am to 11.30am and 2pm to 4pm (till 5.30pm Wednesday) weekdays.

AROUND COOKSTOWN
No public transport goes directly to the following sights, though buses do pass close by. For bus numbers, times and fares check with the bus station in Cookstown.

Wellbrook Beetling Mill
Beetling, the final stage of linen making, is when the cloth is beaten with wooden hammers, or beetles, to give it a smooth sheen. There were once six such mills at Wellbrook. The hammers were driven by water and one of the mills can be seen in operation *(☎ 8675 1735, 20 Wellbrook Rd; adult/concession £2.50/1.25; open 2pm-6pm Wed-Mon July & Aug; 2pm-6pm Sat, Sun & public holidays Easter, Apr-June & Sept)*. It was literally deafening for those employed here.

Take the A505 Omagh road 5km west to Kildress and turn right at the church; it's about 1km from there.

Tullaghoge Fort
This hill fort was the burial ground of the O'Hagans, chief justices of early Ireland, and the coronation place of the O'Neills as 11th-century kings of Ulster. A 1601 map marks the spot on the hillside where the stone coronation chair stood. The following year the chair was destroyed by General Mountjoy while in pursuit of Hugh O'Neill, the last of the clan to be crowned.

To reach Tullaghoge, leave Cookstown on the A29 Dungannon road south then turn left onto the B520; the fort is 4km southeast of Cookstown.

Ardboe High Cross
The 10th-century Ardboe high cross stands 5.5m high in front of a 6th-century monastery site, now housing the ruins of a 17th-century church. The cross is one of the best preserved in Ulster, with the eastern face showing Old Testament scenes and the western side New Testament ones. On the eastern side try to make out Adam and Eve, the sacrifice of Isaac, Daniel and the lions, the Burning Fiery Furnace, a bishop with people

around him and Christ in glory. The New Testament side has the Magi, the miracle at Cana, the miracle of the loaves and fishes, the entry into Jerusalem, the arrest of Christ and the crucifixion. A lot easier to decipher are some of the 18th-century tombstones in the churchyard.

Ardboe is 16km east of Cookstown on the shore of Lough Neagh. To get there take the B73 through Coagh and turn south just before Newtown Trench.

DUNGANNON
pop 9420

Until 1602, when the castle and town were burned to prevent them falling into the hands of the English, Dungannon (Dún Geanainn) was one of the chief seats of the O'Neill family. Plantation of English and Scottish settlers took place in the 17th and 18th centuries.

In 1969 the town entered the history books when the Civil Rights Association, formed a year earlier to protest against the rampant social and political inequalities suffered by Catholics in Northern Ireland, organised its first march from Coalisland south-west to Dungannon. The crowd of 4000 was met by a police cordon outside the town and, although there was no serious violence, it was the beginning of a new era.

Information

The Killymaddy Tourist Information Centre (☎ 8776 7259, fax 8776 7911, e killy maddy@nitic.net) is inconveniently located some 10km south-west of Dungannon on the A4 Ballygawley road. It opens 9am to 5pm daily year round. In town the council office (☎ 8772 5311) in Circular Rd has some tourist information. You'll find several banks and the post office in the centre on Market Square.

Tyrone Crystal

Just north-east of town, tours are offered at the Tyrone Crystal factory (☎ 8772 5335, Coalisland Rd; tour £2; open 8am-6pm Mon-Sat & 1pm-5pm Sun, tours at 11am, noon, 2pm & 3pm Mon-Fri). They cover the different stages in the production of crystal, starting at the furnace where molten glass is

prepared and then hand-blown. The glass pieces are then quality-checked, bevelled, marked, cut and polished.

The showroom displays what the factory makes, including an etched glass model of a mobile phone and a computer mouse. Some slightly imperfect pieces, not bearing the Tyrone Crystal insignia, cost about 25% less. The tour price is reimbursed if you buy something. To get there take the A45 towards Coalisland. To get there for about 2.5km – it is clearly signposted – or catch bus No 80 heading for Cookstown.

Places to Stay

Killymaddy Tourist Amenity Centre (☎ 8776 7259, fax 8776 7911, e killymaddy @nitic.net, Ballygawley Rd) Tent/caravan site £6/8. This camp site has full facilities in a countryside setting and is next to the tourist information centre.

Dungannon Park (☎ 8772 7327, fax 8772 9169, Moy Rd) Tent/caravan site £6/8. This place is in a quiet location and has good facilities. To get there, take the A29 south towards Armagh for 2.5km and turn left (west) at the signpost.

Mikora Lodge (☎ 8776 7171, 16 Thornhill Rd) Rooms £18 per person including breakfast. The owner of this place, off the A29, will cook you a three-course evening meal (with prior notice) for £8. If you're travelling with a pet, you're both welcome here.

Grange Lodge (☎ 8778 4212, fax 8778 4313, e grangelodge@nireland.com, 7 Grange Rd) Singles/doubles £55/78 including full breakfast. This guesthouse is about 5km south-east of Dungannon; follow the signs for The Grange posted off the Dungannon–Moy road. There's a plush delicacy with a little bit of chintzy kitsch about this house that makes it an interesting place to stay. Parts date from 1698 with Georgian and Victorian renovations.

Oaklin House Hotel (☎ 8772 5151, fax 8772 4953, Parkmount, Moy Rd) En-suite singles/doubles £55/90. This small, musty, two-star hotel has 13 rooms.

Places to Eat

Viscounts Great Food Hall (☎ 8775 3800,

10 Northland Row) Mains £6-14. Open for lunch Mon-Fri, for full dinner menu 2.30pm-9.30pm daily. Set in a converted church, Viscounts offers brunch, a carvery lunch and a la carte dinners. You can eat steaks, pasta, stir-fries and vegetarian dishes in a medieval setting with knights' armour, swords and jousting banners. Booking is essential.

Oaklin House Hotel (see Places to Stay) Mains £7-11, 3-course set lunch £12.95. Open at the weekend for lunch and dinner, this restaurant serves decent steaks and fish.

Getting There & Away
Bus No 80 shuttles regularly between Dungannon and Cookstown (20 minutes) to the north. The No 278 service runs once or twice a day Monday to Saturday south to Armagh and, in the Republic, to Monaghan and Dublin (3½ hours). Bus No 261 journeys between Dungannon and Belfast or Enniskillen. Bus No 273 links Dungannon with Belfast, Omagh and Derry up to eight times daily (four on Sunday). The bus station (☎ 8772 2251) is at the bottom of Scotch St, over the bridge and to the left.

AROUND DUNGANNON
See also under Around Armagh in the Counties Down & Armagh chapter for details of local places of interest.

Peatlands Park
Aimed at a young audience, Peatlands Park Visitor Centre (☎ 3885 1102, 33 Derryhubert Rd, Dungannon; free; open 9am-dusk daily) spills the beans on peat. The bog garden is worth a visit if only to familiarise yourself with the sundew, one of two carnivorous plants indigenous to Ireland. It's a tiny thing, easily missed. Pitcher plants also thrive in the garden, but these were introduced into Ireland over a century ago from Canada.

The park has an open-top, narrow-gauge railway (adult/concession £1/0.50; trains run 1pm-6pm daily June-Aug; 2pm-6pm Sat, Sun & public holidays Easter-May & Sept). Once used for transporting peat, it does a 15-minute circuit of the park for children.

To get to Peatlands Park, which is at The Birches some 11km east of Dungannon,

take exit 13 off the M1 motorway heading towards Belfast.

Benburb Valley Park
The park straddles the River Blackwater, popular for salmon fishing and canoeing. In the park ism the site of **Benburb Castle**, founded by Shane O'Neill, who had a stronghold here long before the English arrived, though nothing remains of it. In 1611 Sir Richard Wingfield added a barn that does still stand. In the 19th century, floors were raised and a private house was incorporated into the building. During WWII, US troops used the place as a hospital and the towers were altered to allow access to the roofs. The castle has been restored along 17th-century lines. About 800m from the castle is **Benburb Valley Heritage Centre** (☎ 9031 1156, 9054 9752, 89 Milltown Rd; admission £1.50; castle & centre open 10am-5pm Mon-Sat Apr-Sept) in a restored linen mill.

Benburb is 11km north-west of Armagh; from Dungannon take the A29 and turn right at Moy onto the B106. The centre is clearly marked; the castle is a short distance farther along.

Donaghmore High Cross
The cross is a hybrid, marrying the base and shaft of one cross with the head and part of another. The join is clearly visible. The carved biblical scenes are similar to those on the Ardboe Cross. On the eastern side are the angel and shepherds, the adoration of the Magi, the miracle at Cana, the miracle of the loaves and fishes, the arrest of Christ and the crucifixion. On the western side are Adam and Eve, Cain and Abel and Abraham and Isaac. The nearby **heritage centre** (☎ 8776 7039, Pomeroy Rd; open 9am-5pm Mon-Fri) is based in a converted 19th-century school.

The cross is 8km north-west of Dungannon on the B43 road to Pomeroy, easily spotted at a road junction in the village of Donaghmore.

Castlecaulfield
Not a castle as such but the remains of a

substantial Jacobean house, Castlecaulfield was built in the early 17th century by Sir Toby Caulfield on the site of an earlier fort belonging to the O'Donnellys.

Over the gatehouse, the Caulfield coat of arms can be made out and this survived the O'Donnellys' act of revenge in 1641 when the house was burned down. The house was rebuilt and, in 1767, it hosted a church service by John Wesley, the founder of Methodism.

From Dungannon, take the A4 west and after about 6km a small road to Castlecaulfield is signposted to the right.

Parkanaur Forest Park

An oak forest is being developed on what was once the Burgess family estate, about 1.5km from Castlecaulfield. The old farm buildings display farm and forest machinery and there are short nature trails.

The white fallow deer in the park are descended from the oldest deer herd in Ireland, dating back to 1595 when a doe and a hart, a gift from Elizabeth I to her goddaughter, were raised at Mallow Castle. The park brought five deer from Mallow in 1978.

Grant Ancestral House

Ulysses S Grant led Union forces to victory in the American Civil War and was later elected the 18th president of the USA for two terms (1869–77). The home of his mother's family has been restored in the style of a typical 19th-century Irish small farm. The furniture is not authentic, but the original field plan of this 4-hectare farm is still there together with various old farming implements.

If you're rushed for time in Tyrone then leave this in favour of places such as the Ulster American Folk Park.

There's an exhibition and cafe at the **visitor centre** (☎ 8555 7133, 45 Dergina; adult/ concession £1/0.50; open noon-5pm Tues-Sat & 2pm-6pm Sun Apr-Sept). Bikes can be hired here too. The site is 20km west of Dungannon. Take the A4 west and turn left at the sign just before the village of Ballygawley.

County Fermanagh

The River Erne wends its way through County Fermanagh – one of the smallest counties in Ireland – into a lake that is 80km long. Where Lough Erne divides between Upper and Lower is the town of Enniskillen, the centre of Fermanagh and a good base for exploration. The town's efficient tourist office serves the whole county.

Lower Lough Erne, the more developed of the lake's 'halves', attracts people for varying reasons: the fishing is superb, there are good facilities for water sports outside Enniskillen, and Devenish and White Islands have fine ecclesiastical remains. A third island, Boa, has a cemetery with a unique stone statue dating back around 2000 years.

Early-Christian missionaries settled in Fermanagh, but the religion penetrated the local pagan culture slowly.

Viking and Norman invaders couldn't subdue the region and the Tudors had difficulty until after 1600 when Enniskillen finally fell to the English. Planters then moved in and quickly established a series of castles around Lough Erne. The town of Enniskillen was transformed into a centre of colonial power, and its strategic importance to the British was measured by its possession of two royal regiments.

At the time of Partition, Fermanagh was reluctantly drawn into Northern Ireland – despite the fact that most of its people were Catholic – and its nationalist spirit has not diminished.

ENNISKILLEN
pop 11,440

The town of Enniskillen (Inis Ceithleann) is a useful centre for activities on Upper and Lower Lough Erne and the antiquities around them. Enniskillen is one of the nicer small towns in Northern Ireland, and has not been messed around by town planners with fetishes for concrete or to accommodate cars. Oscar Wilde and Samuel Beckett were both pupils at the Portora Royal School north-west of the centre.

At the time of writing a new peace centre

TYRONE & FERMANAGH

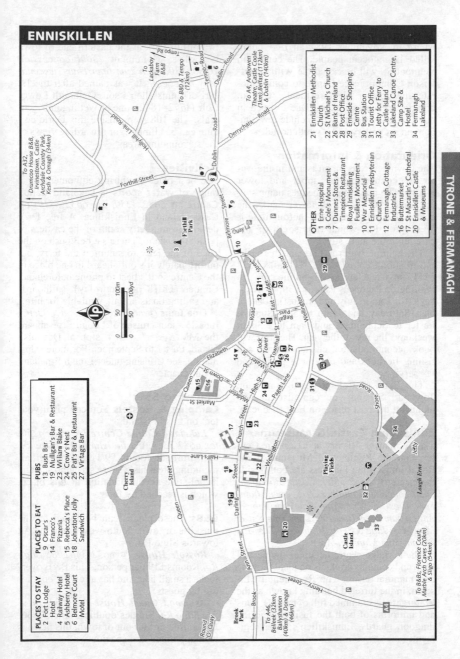

ENNISKILLEN

PLACES TO STAY
2 Fort Lodge Hotel
4 Railway Hotel
5 Ashberry Hotel
6 Belmore Court Motel

PLACES TO EAT
9 Oscar's
14 Franco's Pizzeria
15 Rebecca's Place
18 Johnstons Jolly Sandwich

PUBS
13 Bush Bar
19 Mulligan's Bar & Restaurant
23 William Blake
24 Crow's Nest
25 Pat's Bar & Restaurant
27 Vintage Bar

OTHER
1 Erne Hospital
7 Cole's Monument
8 Dunnes Stores & Timepiece Restaurant
8 Royal Inniskilling Fusiliers Monument
10 War Memorial
11 Enniskillen Presbyterian Church
12 Fermanagh Cottage Industries
16 Buttermarket
17 St Macartin's Cathedral
20 Enniskillen Castle & Museums
21 Enniskillen Methodist Church
22 St Michael's Church
26 Bank of Ireland
28 Post Office
29 Erneside Shopping Centre
30 Bus Station
31 Tourist Office
32 Jetty for Ferry to Castle Island
33 Lakeland Canoe Centre, Camp Site & Hostel
34 Fermanagh Lakeland

was being built in Enniskillen on the site where in November 1987 an IRA bomb killed 11 innocent people. The centre, in Belmont St, will be called the William Jefferson Clinton Peace Centre to commemorate the former US president's role in bringing peace to Ireland. Due to open in mid-2002, the centre will include a restaurant, an art gallery and a youth hostel.

Orientation & Information

The town centre is on an island in the waterway connecting the upper and lower loughs. The main street changes name several times but the clock tower marks the centre. The other principal thoroughfare is Wellington Rd, which runs south of and parallel to the main street.

The helpful, well run Fermanagh Tourist Information Centre (☎ 6632 3110, fax 6632 5511, W www.fermanagh-online.com) in Wellington Rd opens 9am to 5.30pm weekdays (till 7pm in July and August), 10am to 6pm Saturday and 11am to 5pm Sunday, Easter to September; and 9am to 5.30pm weekdays the rest of the year. The staff will book accommodation, change money, sell fishing licences and provide a postal and fax service.

The Bank of Ireland has a branch on Townhall St and you can also change money at the post office on East Bridge St.

Enniskillen Castle & Museums

The Fermanagh History and Heritage Centre, and the Regimental Museum of the Royal Inniskilling Fusiliers are both inside the castle (☎ 6632 5000, Castle Barracks; adult/concession/family £2/1/5; open 10am-5pm Tues-Fri, 2pm-5pm Sat-Mon July & Aug; 10am-5pm Tues-Fri, 2pm-5pm Sat & Mon May-June & Sept; 10am-5pm Tues-Fri & 2pm-5pm Mon Oct-Apr).

The heritage centre occupies the central keep and contains artefacts on local farming and manufacturing. The Regimental Museum, in the turreted building known as the Watergate, is crammed full of medals, guns and uniforms of both the fusiliers and the dragoon guards, Enniskillen's other regiment.

Cole's Monument

In Forthill Park at the eastern end of town is Cole's Monument (adult/concession £0.60/0.30; open 2pm-6pm Thur-Tues mid-May-mid-Sept). It was named after the 1st earl of Enniskillen's son, Galbraith Lowry Cole (1772–1842), one of Wellington's generals. The 108 steps inside this Doric column can be climbed for rewarding views of the surrounding area.

Activities

The best place for hiring equipment for a range of water sports is Lakeland Canoe Centre (☎ 6632 4250, fax 6632 3319) on Castle Island in Enniskillen. A free ferry departs from a jetty south of the castle, opposite the island. There's a bell push on the edge of the jetty to summon the ferry, but unfortunately it's only heard in one place in the Centre so it's best to phone beforehand. Canoes (£8/18 per hour/day), sailboards and sailing boats are all available for hire.

Erne Tours (☎ 6632 2882, Round 'O' Jetty) runs 1¾-hour cruises of Lough Erne aboard the MV Kestrel with a stop at Devenish Island, Easter to September. For more information, see Cruising under Lough Erne later in this chapter.

Places to Stay

Camping & Hostels You can pitch your tent on Castle Island.

Lakeland Canoe Centre (☎ 6632 4250, fax 6632 3319, Castle Island) Tent site £8, dorms/private rooms £9/11 per person, all including breakfast. There's a camp site and hostel-style accommodation at this place, which is reached by ferry.

B&Bs These places can be found on the outskirts of town, south-west along the A4 towards Sligo Rd.

Rossole House (☎ 6632 3462, 85 Sligo Rd) Rooms £19 per person. This B&B overlooks a small lake and has a rowing boat for use by guests.

Ashwood Guest House (☎ 6632 3019, 211 Sligo Rd) Singles/doubles from £22/36. Just a little farther out of town, this place is well appointed and spacious.

On the other side of town B&Bs can be found along the B80 road to Tempo.

Lackaboy Farm *(☎ 6632 2488, fax 6632 0440, Tempo Rd)* Singles/doubles £22/36 including breakfast and supper. Lackaboy is 2km from the centre. Its rooms are a good size and newly equipped.

Drumcoo House *(☎/fax 6632 6672,* e *farrellhj@utvinternet.com, 32 Cherryville)* En-suite singles/doubles £22/40. Drumcoo is by the roundabout on the road north to Castle Archdale and Omagh.

Hotels There are several hotels on the eastern side of town.

Railway Hotel *(☎ 6632 2084, fax 6632 7480, 34 Forthill St)* Singles/doubles from £28.50/60. This 150-year-old B&B hotel is east of town on the road to Omagh and has 19 rooms.

Fort Lodge Hotel *(☎ 6632 3275, fax 6632 0275, 72 Forthill St)* Singles/doubles £35/60 including breakfast. The Fort Lodge is a little farther out of town than the Railway Hotel.

Belmore Court Motel *(☎ 6632 6633, fax 6632 6362,* W *www.motel.co.uk, Tempo Rd)* Singles/doubles from £30/40, continental breakfast £3. East of town, this is a newish place looking more like a row of houses than a motel. Some rooms have a kitchenette.

Ashberry Hotel *(☎ 6632 0333, fax 6632 0348, 14-20 Tempo Rd)* Singles/doubles £45/70 including breakfast. This two-star hotel has comfortable rooms and is fairly central.

Places to Eat

Oscar's *(☎ 6632 7037, 29 Belmore St)* Mains £7.50-13. Open 5pm-10pm daily. This is one of Enniskillen's best restaurants both for food and atmosphere. Named after one Oscar Wilde, a local schoolboy, the restaurant is decorated as a library and the wood-panelled walls bear the pithy sayings of the great man. It has quite a varied menu, including several vegetarian options.

Timepiece Restaurant *(☎ 6632 5132, Forthill St)* Breakfast £2.75. Located in Dunnes Stores on the corner of Forthill St and Castlecoole Rd, Timepiece is definitely the place for a cooked breakfast.

Rebecca's Place *(☎ 6632 4499, Buttermarket)* Snacks £2-4.80. This is a good place to try for sandwiches, salads and pastries while browsing in the Buttermarket.

Franco's Pizzeria *(☎ 6632 4424, Queen Elizabeth Rd)* Mains £7.50-15. Open noon-11pm daily. This popular place on the northern side of town serves pizzas and pasta dishes as well as seafood. It also does takeaways.

Johnstons Jolly Sandwich *(☎ 6632 2277, 3 Darling St)* Open 8am-4.30pm Mon-Sat. Just west of the clock tower in the centre, this place serves good sandwiches and pies.

Mulligan's Bar & Restaurant *(☎ 6632 2059, 33 Darling St)* Mains £4.75-12. Food served noon-8pm. This is a thoroughly pleasant spot for a bite to eat and a pint. It has a varied menu catering for all tastes.

Pat's Bar & Restaurant *(☎ 6632 2040, 1 Townhall St)* Mains £5.50-8. Open 9.30am-7pm (to 9pm in summer) daily. This pub serves morning coffee and lunch specials such as roast beef and fresh trout.

Entertainment

The main street through town has a number of popular pubs.

William Blake *(☎ 6632 2143, 6 Church St)* This Victorian pub has traditional music at the weekend. Some changes may have occurred by the time you read this, with the addition of two restaurants and three bars, one of which one will have an emphasis on music and entertainment. The 1887 bar, we are absolutely assured, will remain untouched.

Crow's Nest *(☎ 6632 5252, 12 High St)* This pub has music nightly and traditional Irish sessions on Monday during the summer. Bar meals are served all day.

Vintage Bar *(☎ 6632 4055, 13 Townhall St)* There's music here Wednesday to Sunday.

Bush Bar *(☎ 6632 5212, 26 Townhall St)* The Bush is a pub with music, including Irish sessions on Friday, Saturday and Sunday.

Ardhowen Theatre *(☎ 6632 5440, Dublin Rd)* Just about every kind of performance takes place at this theatre, about 2km south of the town centre on the Dublin road

(A4). The program includes concerts, local amateur and professional drama and musical productions, pantomime and films.

Shopping

Buttermarket (☎ 6632 4499, off Queen Elizabeth Rd) The best place to shop in Enniskillen is in the refurbished buildings of the old marketplace. A variety of craft shops make and sell their wares, and ceramics and jewellery are the best buys.

Fermanagh Cottage Industries (☎ 6632 2260, 14 East Bridge St) Next to the Presbyterian church, this is another good outlet for crafts.

Erneside Centre (☎ 6632 5705, The Point) This is a modern complex of shops, cafes and a supermarket, across the waterway south of Wellington Rd.

Getting There & Away

Ulsterbus No 261 runs up to 10-times daily (five on Sunday) via Dungannon to Belfast (two hours). Bus No 296 runs to Derry (2½ hours) via Omagh (one hour) and, in the other direction, to Cork (8¼ hours) via Athlone (three hours). The No 262 service runs to Sligo (1½ hours), Ballina (1¼ hours) and Westport (4½ hours). Bus No 99 goes from Enniskillen to Bundoran via Belleek. Bus Éireann's bus No 30 between Dublin (three hours) and Donegal (1¼ hours) calls at Enniskillen five-times daily (four times on Sunday).

The bus station (☎ 6632 2633) is opposite the tourist office on Shore Rd.

Getting Around

Bicycles can be hired at the Lakeland Canoe Centre (☎ 6632 4250) on Castle Island for £10 per day.

AROUND ENNISKILLEN
Sheelin Antique Lace Museum

Just over 6km south-west of Enniskillen in the village of Bellanaleck is the small Sheelin Antique Lace Museum (☎ 6634 8052, W www.irish-lace.com, Bellanaleck; adult/child £2/1; open 10am-6pm daily). It houses a beautiful collection of Irish lace dating from 1850 to 1900. Lace making was a particularly important industry in Fermanagh and the neighbouring counties both before and after the Famine. With trade and agriculture depressed, it was seen as a way of providing employment for women and of relieving poverty. Prior to WWI there were at least 10 lace schools in County Fermanagh. The museum has linen, lace and oil lamps for sale. Next to the museum, the 200-year-old thatched **Sheelin Restaurant** offers lunches, bar snacks and evening meals.

Castle Coole

It's worth visiting this mansion (☎ 6632 2690, Dublin Rd; adult/concession/family £3/1.50/8; open 1pm-6pm Fri-Wed June-Aug; 1pm-6pm Easter, Sat, Sun & public holidays Apr-May & Sept). Designed by James Wyatt, it ranks as probably the purest expression of late-18th-century neoclassical architecture in Ireland. Completed in 1798, over the following two centuries the Portland stone exterior absorbed water to the point that the walls started to crumble.

The National Trust embarked on an expensive rebuilding of the outside walls and redecoration of the interior. The result is now a house that displays the pristine elegance of its original conception. The austerity of the design borders on the sterile; the obsession with symmetry is almost neurotic; and the guided tour shows many examples of form triumphing over substance: fake doors balancing real ones, hollow columns painted to resemble marble ones, keyhole covers on doors that have no keyholes.

The tour first visits the male sanctuary of the library where, as the guide points out, the doors once locked could only be opened from the inside. Most of the furniture is original and the curtain rail is typical of the extravagance of the 2nd earl of Belmore, who decorated the house. The 1st earl spent so much money having the place built that he had nothing left for decorations.

The castle is in a 600-hectare landscaped demesne and its lake is home to a colony of greylag geese. Castle Coole is on the Dublin road (A4), 2.5km south-east of Enniskillen.

Florence Court

This is a Palladian mansion (☎ 6634 8249, *Swanlinbar Rd; adult/concession/family £3/1.50/8; open 1pm-6pm Wed-Mon June-Aug; 1pm-6pm Sat, Sun & public holidays Easter, Apr-May & Sept*). It's named after the wife of John Cole, who settled in the area in the early 18th century. Their son built the present central block and a grandson added the wings. The house was acquired by the National Trust in the 1950s and partly rebuilt after a fire in 1955. It's said that every Irish yew tree has its origin from one in the garden of Florence Court.

Unlike Castle Coole, Florence Court has a lived-in feel and despite the fire much of the original rococo plasterwork remains; the staircase is the best example.

There is a walled garden and a forest park which has a number of walking trails with one leading to the top of Mt Cuilcagh (667m).

The house is almost 13km south-west of Enniskillen; take the A4 Sligo road and turn left onto the A32 Swanlinbar road. Ulsterbus No 192 will drop you about 1.5km from the entrance.

Marble Arch Caves

It's wise to phone ahead and book on the tour (lasting one hour 20 minutes) as the extensive Marble Arch Caves are very popular (☎ 6634 8855, *Marlbank Scenic Loop; adult/concession/child/family £6/4/3/14; open 10am-5pm June-Aug; 10am-4.30pm mid-Mar-May*). The tour starts with a short boat trip on the river running through the caves, while the remainder involves walking through passages scoured out by the river. As it's still an active cave that floods periodically (though not while visitors are there), there's not the abundance of formations that you'd find in other show caves.

During the summer there are occasional free guided walks through the surrounding limestone hills, conducted by the Department of the Environment. Enquire at the tourist office in Enniskillen or contact the Nature Reserve Office (☎ 6862 1588) at Castle Archdale Country Park in Lisnarrick.

The Marble Arch Caves are 16km south-west of Enniskillen near the border. They are reached via the A4 (Sligo road) and the A32 (Swanlinbar road). The site is well signposted.

LOUGH ERNE

Stretching for 80km, Lough Erne is made up of two sections: the Upper Lough in the south and the Lower Lough in the north. The loughs are joined by the River Erne, which begins its journey in County Cavan and flows out to Donegal Bay west of Ballyshannon. The lakes have numerous islands, many containing Celtic and early-Christian archaeological sites (see Around Lough Erne later in this chapter). Coarse and game fish are plentiful, and bird life, especially on Upper Lough Erne, is abundant.

Activities

There's a great deal to do around the area. All the following centres also have accommodation.

Based on Lough McNean Upper, **Corralea Activity Centre** (☎ 6638 6668, W *www.activityireland.com, Belcoo*) hires out bicycles and canoes. It also has instructor-guided activities such as caving, canoeing, climbing, sea surfing and archery from £25 per day.

Similarly, **Lough Melvin Holiday Centre** (☎ 6865 8142, W *www.loughmelvinholidaycentre.com, Garrison*) provides caving, canoeing, walking and fishing activities. A typical price for a weekend including accommodation is £85.

Share Holiday Village (☎ 6772 2122, W *www.sharevillage.com, Smiths Strand, Lisnaskea*) has windsurfing, sailing, canoeing and hill walking.

Fishing The lakes of Fermanagh are renowned for coarse fishing, but trout are found in the northern part of Lower Lough Erne, close to Boa Island and Kesh Bay. The Lough Erne trout fishing season runs from the beginning of March to the end of September. Salmon fishing begins in June and also continues to the end of September. The mayfly season usually lasts a month from the second week in May. There's no closed season for bream, eel, pike, perch, roach or rudd.

A coarse-fishing licence is required for Lough Erne and a game licence for fishing in Lower Lough Erne other than from the shore. These can be purchased from the Fermanagh Tourist Information Centre or from the marina (☎ 6862 8118) in Castle Archdale Country Park, which also hires out day boats. Most rivers in County Fermanagh are privately owned, and information on those where permission to fish is not required is available from the tourist information centre in Enniskillen. It also has a list of ghillies (fishing guides).

The Thatch *(☎ 6865 8181, Main St, Belleek)* organises trips for both fresh water and sea fishing.

Cruising Erne Tours' *(☎ 6632 2882; adult/child £5/2.50)* 56-seater waterbus, the MV *Kestrel*, cruises the lough for 1¾ hours, calling at Devenish Island along the way. It departs from the Round 'O' Quay at Brook Park, just outside Enniskillen on the A46 to Belleek. Tours operate Easter to September (call to check times).

The **Inishcruiser** *(☎ 6772 2122; adult/child £7/6)* offers 1½ to two-hour cruises from the Share Holiday Village south-west of Lisnaskea. Cruises depart at 2.30pm on Sunday between Easter and September; there's an additional 2.30pm cruise on Thursday during July and August.

Boat Hire There are about nine companies in Fermanagh that hire out cruisers. The weekly rates vary from about £400 for a four-berth to about £1100 for an eight-berth boat. A number of companies also rent out day boats at Belleek, Enniskillen, Garrison, Kesh, Killadeas and Newtownbutler. Prices start at about £25 for a four-person rowing boat with outboard engine and £50 for a six-seater with front cabin and diesel inboard engine. The tourist information centre in Enniskillen has a full list of the companies and costs.

Water Sports You can hire sailing boats, paddle boats and canoes at **Drumrush Watersports** *(☎ 6863 1578, fax 6863 2084, Boa Island Rd, Kesh)*. It also instructs in sailing,

water-skiing and jet-skiing, and there's accommodation at the complex.

Lakeland Caravan Park *(☎ 6863 1758, Kesh)* has water-skiing, wakeboarding, canoeing and jet-ski hire (£35 per half-hour).

Horse Riding Drumhoney Stables *(☎ 68 62 1892, Castle Archdale)* offers horse riding for beginners and experienced riders from £12 per ride.

AROUND LOUGH ERNE

There are many ancient religious sites and other antiquities around Lough Erne. In early-Christian times the lough was an important highway from the Donegal coast to inland Leitrim. Churches and monasteries acted as staging posts and in medieval times there was an important pilgrim route to Station Island in Donegal that went via Lough Erne.

The village of Belleek, famous for its chinaware, is just inside the Northern Irish border and easily reached from either side of the lough.

The places below are set out in an anticlockwise tour north from Enniskillen.

Devenish Island

The most extensive of the ancient sites at Lough Erne is Devenish Island (Daimh Inis). A 6th-century monastery, founded here by St Molaise, was sacked by Vikings in 837 in just one of the many incidents of its colourful history. There are church and abbey ruins, fascinating old gravestones, an unusual 15th-century high cross, an excellent small museum and one of the best round towers in Ireland. The 12th-century, 25m-high tower is in perfect condition.

A ferry runs to Devenish Island from Trory Point landing, some 6.5km north of Enniskillen. Take the A32 for Irvinestown and after 5km look for the sign on the left. It's just after a service station and immediately before the junction where roads fork left to Kesh and right to Omagh. The ferry crosses at 10am, 1pm, 3pm and 5pm, Easter to September (adult/child £2.25/1.20 return, five minutes); arrange your return with the ferry operator.

Sheila-na-Gig

The term sheila-na-gig is probably an Anglicisation of Síle na Gcíoch (Sheila of the Teats). It refers to crude carvings of women displaying exaggerated genitalia on the outside of certain medieval churches and buildings. One theory traces their origin back to the exhibitionist figures found in French Romanesque churches that illustrated the ungodly powers threatening men.

MATT KING

Another theory is that they're representations of Celtic war goddesses. Early Irish sagas such as the epic Táin Bó Cúailnge (Cattle Raid of Cooley) refer to women using overt genital display as a weapon to subdue the hero Cúchulainn. This may have encouraged the belief that the Sheilas could ward off evil and hence explain their incorporation into early-Christian architecture.

Other theories are that they may have been connected with some sort of fertility cult or used as a fetish against the evil eye.

Killadeas Churchyard

The **Bishop's Stone** is a remarkable stone carving, dating from between the 7th and 9th centuries, that encapsulates the transition from Celtic Paganism to Christianity. The face that stares out from the front seems quite at odds with the side engraving of a bishop with bell and crozier.

Follow the B82 along the shoreline towards Kesh and look for the sign to the Manor House Country Hotel. About 1km past this sign is a church on the left side of the road; the stone is in the graveyard.

White Island

White Island, near the eastern shore of the lough, has the remains of a small 12th-century **church** containing a line of eight statues thought to date from as early as the 6th century. Nothing remains of the earlier monastic settlement except the trace of the boundary bank on the far side of the church. The most impressive surviving part of the

church is the Romanesque door on its southern side.

The eight **stone figures** are intriguing. The first resembles a sheila-na-gig, while the next is of someone reading a book or holding some object. Number three is obviously ecclesiastical. The next one has been identified as the young David, but the meaning of his hand pointing to his mouth is unknown. Number five is a curly-haired figure holding the necks of two griffin-like birds. Number six has a military appearance, number seven is unfinished and the last one is a single frowning face resembling a death mask.

From April to September a ferry runs across to the island from the marina in Castle Archdale Country Park, which is 16km north of Enniskillen on the Kesh road (B82). The ferry operates every hour on the hour from 10am to 7pm daily (adult/child £3/2 return, 15 minutes). Apart from the ferry to White Island and the marina, the park has extensive grounds for walking through a large area of deciduous trees, watching the red deer and observing the abundant bird life. The grounds were once part of the estate of the now demolished castle.

Drumskinny Stone Circle & Alignment

This Bronze Age circle is made up of 39 stones with a small cairn and an alignment of two dozen stones. The circle is 7km north-east of Kesh and signposted just beyond the junction with the Boa Island road.

Boa Island

At the northern end of the Lower Lough is narrow Boa Island, which is connected at both ends by bridges to the shore. The **Janus figure** (also known as the Lusty Man) in Caldragh graveyard could be 2000 years old, one of the oldest stone statues in Ireland and quite unparalleled. Another more recent stone figure stands beside it.

There's just a small sign to the graveyard, about 1km from the bridge at the western end of the island or 6km from the eastern-end bridge.

TYRONE & FERMANAGH

Castle Caldwell Forest Park

At the entrance to the park is the **Fiddler's Stone** (in the shape of a fiddle), a memorial to a drunk musician who fell off a boat and drowned in 1770. The inscription recorded from the stone before it got too worn to read is:

'To the memory of Denis McCabe Fiddler who fell out of the St Patrick Barge belonging to Sir James Caldwell Bart and Count of Milan and was drowned off this point August ye 13 1770.

Beware ye fiddlers of ye fiddler's fate
Nor tempt ye least ye repent to late
Ye ever have been deemed to water foes
Then shun ye lake till it with whiskey flows
On firm land only exercise your skill
There you may play and drink your fill.'

The castle, built between 1610 and 1619, is nothing but a ruin. The park (open daily) is a nature reserve full of bird life and the main breeding ground of the common scoter duck. There are three colour-coded walks ranging from 1.5km to 4km. The park is about 5km west of Boa Island along the A47.

Belleek

pop 550

Belleek is at the northern end of the Erne–Shannon Waterway that starts in Limerick. There's nothing bleak about Belleek; it's a typical small Irish town with colourfully painted buildings and in summer it's full of flowers. The Black Cat Cove and the Thatch are two particularly nice buildings to visit.

The main reason for stopping is to visit the world-famous Belleek **pottery works** (☎ 6865 9300, Main St; adult/child £2.50/ 1.50; open 9am-6pm daily). It has been producing fine china since 1857. Some of the work is robustly nice while much is twee edging on kitsch, but it's immensely popular.

There are regular tours every half-hour from 9am to 12.15pm and 2.15pm to 4.15pm (till 3.30pm on Friday). The small museum at the visitor centre, the showroom and cafe are open daily.

Also in Belleek is the excellent **ExplorErne Exhibition** (☎ 6865 8866, Erne Gateway Centre; adult/child £1/0.50; open 10am-

4.30pm May-Sept). It tells the story of the Fermanagh lakeland.

Lough Navar Forest

Through this coniferous forest on the western shore, an 11km scenic road leads up to a viewing point that overlooks the lough and the mountains to the north. A section of the Ulster Way passes through the forest. Admission costs £2 per car, and the park is signposted off the A46.

Tully Castle

A signposted left turn off the A46 some 16km south-east of Belleek leads to Tully Castle (adult/child £1/0.50; open 10am-6pm Tues-Sat & 2pm-6pm Sun Apr-Sept). The castle was built in 1613 as a fortified home for a Scottish Planter's family, but was captured and burned by Roderick Maguire in 1641. The bawn (cattle enclosure) has four corner towers and retains a lot of the original paving. The vaulted ground floor has a large fireplace with an equally large staircase leading to the 2nd floor and attics.

Monea Castle

Continuing south on the A46 towards Enniskillen there is a signposted turn to the B81 and Monea Castle to the right. This was built as the best of Fermanagh's Plantation castles around the same time as Tully Castle. It too was captured in the 1641 rising but remained in use until the mid-18th century, when it was gutted by fire. The main entrance has two imposing circular towers topped with built-out squares in a style found in contemporary Scottish castles. There's no charge for viewing the remains. A crannóg sits in the nearby lake.

Crom Estate

Situated on the shores of Upper Lough Erne, south-west of Newtownbutler is the National Trust's Crom Estate (☎ 6773 8118, Newtownbutler; £3 per car; open 10am-6pm Mon-Sat & noon-6pm Sun 17 Mar-30 Sept). The estate covers 760 hectares of woodland, parkland and wetlands. There are numerous walking trails and several ornamental buildings, including the ruins of old Crom Castle, a boathouse and an island folly. There are boats for hire (£5 per hour), seven *self-catering cottages* available (from £195 per week) and *camping* facilities (£4 per night).

Places to Stay
Camping There are numerous camp sites around Lough Erne.

Castle Archdale Caravan Park (☎ 6862 1368, fax 6862 1176, Castle Archdale) Tent/caravan site £10/15. This place is 12km north-east of Enniskillen and is dominated by on-site caravans, but has good facilities. Its restaurant, *Ardale Diner*, opens at the weekend year round and daily in July and August.

Lakeland Caravan Park (☎ 6863 1578, fax 6863 2084, W *www.drumrush.co.uk, Boa Island Rd, Kesh)* Tent/caravan site £8/12. This place is outside Kesh.

Blaney Caravan Park (☎ 6864 1634, W *www.blaneycaravanpark.com, Blaney)* Tent/caravan site £6/11. This caravan park is on the other side of the lough at Blaney, on the A46 to Belleek.

Mullynascarthy Caravan Park (☎ 6772 1040, fax 6772 3378, Gola Rd) Tent/caravan site £6/11. This park is south of Enniskillen and about 2km north-west of Lisnaskea.

Share Holiday Village (☎ 6772 2122, fax 6772 1893, W *www.sharevillage.org, Smiths Strand, Lisnaskea)* Tent/caravan site £7/10. The village also has a range of other accommodation options.

Hostels There's a great hostel not far from Lisnarrick.

Castle Archdale Country Park (☎/fax 6862 8118, Castle Archdale) Dorms £8.50 per person. Open Mar-Oct. This excellent and very peaceful HINI hostel is in converted 18th-century stables. Ulsterbus No 194 from Enniskillen to Pettigo stops outside the park on school days, from where the hostel is a 15-minute walk. Otherwise take the bus to Lisnarrick Corner (four departures daily), which will drop you off about 1.5km from the park.

B&Bs There are plenty of B&Bs along the roads that skirt either side of Lough Erne.

Lakeview Guest House (☎ 6864 1263, Blaney) Singles/doubles £18/32. This farm guesthouse is off the A46 at Blaney and near the lough shore with panoramic views.

Beeches (☎ 6862 8527, e *imeldabyrne@ yahoo.com, Killadeas)* Singles/doubles £20/25. This quiet, friendly and relaxing B&B is right on the shore of Lough Erne. Two of the rooms have superb views over the lough.

The Fiddlestone (☎ 6665 8008, 15 Main St, Belleek) Rooms £18 per person including breakfast. This is a friendly place with five rooms and a lively bar downstairs.

Hotels You'll find some good hotels scattered about the area.

Manor House Country Hotel (☎ 6862 2211, fax 6862 1545, W *www.manor-house -hotel.com, Killadeas)* Singles/doubles £85/ 110. This grandly situated hotel overlooks Lough Erne. In Killadeas on the B82 to Kesh, it has 81 rooms and a leisure complex with spas, saunas, a pool and gym – free to guests. By the time you read this the hotel will be offering lake cruises in its own boat.

Mahon's Hotel (☎ 6862 1656, fax 6862 8344, W *www.mahonshotel.co.uk, 2-10 Mill St, Irvinestown)* Singles/doubles £35/70. The hotel offers weekend packages from £70 per person (for two nights B&B with one dinner). The bar is packed with local people at the weekend.

Drumshane Hotel (☎ 6862 8383, Lisnarrick) Singles/doubles £35/60. Due west of Irvinestown, this is a good 10-room hotel with a *restaurant*. It was under going restoration at the time of writing – the owner has big plans.

Donn Carragh (☎ 6772 1206, fax 6772 1223, Main St, Lisnaskea) Singles/doubles £35/60. This hotel provides reasonable value and is centrally located in Lisnaskea.

Places to Eat
Manor House Country Hotel (see Places to Stay) 5-course set dinner £23. Open for lunch & dinner. The restaurant here has a la carte as well as set dinners. There's traditional and country music at the weekend in summer.

Inishclare Complex (☎ 6862 8550, Killadeas) Meals £18.50-23. Just north of Killadeas, this place has a good restaurant and bistro with great lough views. The complex has the same menu and pricing as the Manor House, which operates it.

The Stables (☎ *6862 1231, 5 Main St, Irvinestown)* Mains £2.50-13. Open noon-10pm Wed-Sun. This is a family-run pub-restaurant with a reputation for good food at reasonable prices. Reservations are recommended for 7pm onwards.

Central Bar (☎ *6862 1249, 38 Main St, Irvinestown)* Mains £4.25. Across the road from The Stables, this place serves food during the day and was a popular watering hole for US pilots during WWII.

Lusty Beg Island (☎ *6863 2032, Lusty Beg Island)* Bar meals £5-12.50, 4-course dinner £19.50. Open Fri-Sun. This place, off Boa Island, serves everything from smoked Irish salmon to baked potatoes. There's a telephone in a blockhouse on the slipway to summon the ferry.

The Thatch (☎ *6865 8181, Main St,* *Belleek)* Meals £2.70-9.50. Open 9am-5pm Mon-Sat. The Thatch serves snacks and real coffee in Belleek's oldest building (late 1700s).

Black Cat Cove (☎ *6865 8942, Main St, Belleek)* Lunch, bar snacks & mains £5-10. The Black Cat is a friendly family-run, traditional Irish pub. It also has music on Tuesday, Wednesday and Thursday from May to September.

Getting There & Away

From Enniskillen, Ulsterbus No 64 runs on Thursday to Belleek (1¼ hours) via Garrison on the western side of Lower Lough Erne. Bus No 99 also goes to Belleek, following the western shoreline through Blaney (15 minutes) past Tully Castle and Lough Navar Forest. On the eastern side bus No 194 runs daily to Irvinestown (35 minutes), Lisnarrick (50 minutes) and Kesh (one hour).

Language

Pronunciation

Irish has three main dialects: Connaught Irish (Galway and northern Mayo), Munster Irish (Cork, Kerry and Waterford) and Ulster Irish (Donegal). The pronunciation guidelines given here (in italics) are an anglicised version of modern standard Irish, which is essentially an amalgam of the three.

Vowels

Irish divides vowels into long (those with an accent) and short (those without) and, more importantly, broad (**a**, **á**, **o**, **ó**, **u** and **ú**) and slender (**e**, **é**, **i** and **í**), which can affect the way preceding consonants are pronounced.

a	as in 'cat'
á	as in 'saw'
e	as in 'bet'
é	as in 'hey'
i	as in 'sit'
í	as the 'ee' in 'see'
o	as in 'son'
ó	as in 'low'
u	as the 'oo' in 'book'
ú	as in 'rule'

Consonants

Though you've probably never seen pairs and clusters such as **mh** and **bhf**, consonants are generally less problematic in Irish than vowels. Most are pronounced as they are in English.

bh	as the 'v' in 'voice'
bhf	as the 'w' in 'well'
c	always hard, as in 'cat'
ch	as the 'ch' in Scottish *loch*
d	as in 'do' when followed by a broad vowel, as the 'j' in 'jug' when followed by a slender vowel
dh	as the 'g' in 'gap' when followed by a broad vowel, as the 'y' in 'year' when followed by a slender vowel
mh	as the 'w' in 'well'

s	as in 'said' when before a broad vowel, as the 'sh' in ship when before a slender vowel and at the end of a word
t	as the 't' in 'toast' when before a broad vowel, as the 'ch' in 'church' before a slender vowel
th	as the 'h' in 'house', as the 't' in 'mat or silent at the end of a word

Greetings & Civilities

Hello.	Dia duit. (lit: God be with you) *dee-a-gwit*
Hello. (reply)	Dia is Muire duit. (lit: God and Mary with you) *dee-as moyra gwit*
Good morning.	Maidin mhaith. *maw-jin wah*
Good night.	Oíche mhaith. *eek-heh wah*
Goodbye.	Slán agat. *slawn agut*
Welcome.	Ceád míle fáilte. (lit: 100,000 welcomes) *kade meela fawltcha*
Thank you.	Go raibh maith agat. *goh rev mut agut*
Thank you very much.	Go raibh míle maith agat. *goh rev meeleh mut agut*
Please.	Le do thoil. *le do hall*
Excuse me.	Gabh mo leithscéal. *gamoh lesh scale*
How are you?	Conas tá tú? *kunas taw too?*
(I'm) fine.	(Tá mé) go maith. *(taw may) goh mah*
What's your name?	Cad is ainm duit? *kod is anim dwit?*
My name is (Sean).	(Sean) is ainm dom. *(Sean) is anim dohm*
Yes/It is.	Tá/Sea. *taw/sheh*

No/It is not.	Níl/Ní hea.
	neel/nee heh
another/one more	ceann eile
	kyawn ella
good, fine, OK	go maith
	goh mah
nice	go deas
	goh dyass

Questions & Comments

Why?	Cén fáth?
	kane faw?
What is this/that?	Cad é seo/sin?
	kod ay shoh/shin?
How much/many?	Cé mhéad?
	kay vade?
Where is...?	Cá bhfuil...?
	kaw will...?
Which way?	Cén slí?
	kane shlee?
I don't understand.	Ní thuigim.
	nee higgim

big	mór
	moor
small	beag
	byawg
expensive	daor
	deer
cheap	saor
	seer
open	oscailte
	uskawlta
closed	dúnta
	doonta
slowly	go mall
	goh mohl
quickly	go tapa
	goh topuh
fine (weather)	go breá
	goh braw
terrible (weather)	go dona
	goh dohna

Getting Around

I'd like to go to…	
Ba mhaith liom dul go dtí…	
baw wah lohm dull go dee...	
I'd like to buy…	
Ba mhaith liom…a cheannach	
bah wah lohm...a kyanukh	

Signs

Toilet	Leithreas
	lehrass
Men	Fir
	fear
Women	Mna
	m'naw
Police	Gardaí
	gardee
Post Office	Oifig An Phoist
	iffig ohn fwisht
Telephone	Telefón/Teileafón
	taylayfon
Town Centre	An Lar
	an lawr

ticket	ticéad
	tickaid
boat	bád
	bawd
ship	long
	lung
car	gluaisteáin/carr
	glooshtawn/car
bus	bus
	bus
train	traein
	trehn
here	anseo
	onshoh
there	ansin
	onshin
stop	stad
	stod
go	ar aghaidh
	err eyeg
bank	banc
	bonk
city	cathair
	kawher
road	bóthar
	bohere
shop	siopa
	shoppa
street	sráid
	shrod
town	baile
	bollyeh
town square	lár an bhaile
	lawr an vallyeh

Accommodation

one night	oíche amháin	
	eek-heh awawn	
one person	duine amháin	
	dinna awawn	
two people	beirt	
	beerch	
bed	leaba	
	leeabaha	
room	seomra	
	showmra	
hotel	óstán	
	oh stahn	
bed & breakfast	loístín oíche	
	leestin eek-heh	

Time & Days

What time is it?	Cén tam é?	
	kane tawm ay?	
7 o'clock	seacht a chlog	
	shocked ah klug	
today	inniu	
	innyu	
tomorrow	amárach	
	amawrok	
hour	uair	
	oor	
minute	nóiméid	
	nomade	
week	seachtain	
	shocktin	
month	mí	
	mee	

Monday	Dé Luaín	*day loon*
Tuesday	Dé Máirt	*day meert*
Wednesday	Dé Ceádaoin	*day kaydeen*
Thursday	Déardaoin	*daredeen*
Friday	Dé hAoine	*day heeneh*
Saturday	Dé Sathairn	*day sahern*
Sunday	Dé Domhnaigh	*day downick*

January	Eanáir	
	ann-ner	
February	Feabhra	
	fiow-ra	

March	Márta
	mortha
April	Aibreán
	ebb-rawn
May	Bealtaine
	balthuna
June	Meitheamh
	me-hiv
July	Iúil
	ool
August	Lúnasa
	loonassa
September	Meán Fómhair
	mian fore
October	Deireadh Fómhair
	djerru fore
November	Samhain
	sowin
December	Nollaig
	null-ig

Numbers

½	leath	*lah*
1	haon	*hayin*
2	dó	*doe*
3	trí	*tree*
4	ceathaír	*kahirr*
5	cúig	*koo-ig*
6	sé	*shay*
7	seacht	*shocked*
8	hocht	*hukt*
9	naoi	*nay*
10	deich	*jeh*
11	haon déag	*hayin jague*
12	dó dhéag	*doe yague*
20	fiche	*feekhe*
21	fiche a haon	*feekhe uh hayin*
30	triocha	*tree-okha*
40	daichead	*day-khayd*
50	caoga	*kowga*
60	seasca	*shaska*
70	seachtó	*shocked-ow*
80	ochtó	*ukth-ow*
90	nócha	*nokha*
100	céad	*kade*
1000	míle	*meeleh*

Appendix – Place Names

Place	Irish Name	Place	Irish Name
Achill	An Caol	Brandon	Cé Bhréannain
Adare	Áth Dara	Bruckless	An Bhroclais
Adrigole	Eadargóil	Bruree	Brú Rí
Allihies	Na hAilichí	Bunbeg	An Bun Beag
Annagry	Anagaire	Buncrana	Bun Cranncha
Annalong	Áth na Long	Bundoran	Bun Dobhráin
Annascaul	Abhainn an Scáil	Bunratty	Bun Raite
Antrim	Aontroim	Burren, The	Boireann
Aran Islands	Oileáin Árainn	Burtonport	Ailt an Chórrain
Ardara	Árd an Rátha	Bushmills	Muileann na Buaise
Ardboe	Ard Bo		
Ardee	Baile Átha Fhirdhia	Cahir	An Cathair
Ardfert	Ard Fhearta	Carlingford	Cairlinn
Ardglass	Ard Ghlais	Carlow	Ceatharlach
Ardmore	Ard Mór	Carndonagh	Cardomhnach
Ards Peninsula	An Aird	Carraroe	An Cheathrú Rua
Arklow	An tInbhear Mór	Carrick	An Charraig
Arlow	Eatharlach	Carrickfergus	Carraig Fhearghais
Armagh	Ard Mhacha	Carrickmacross	Carraig Mhachaire Rois
Arranmore	Árainn Mhór	Carrick-on-Shannon	Cora Droma Rúisc
Athlone	Baile Átha Luain	Carrick-on-Suir	Carraig na Siúire
Athy	Áth Í	Carrigaholt	Carraig an Chabaltaigh
Avoca	Abhóca	Cashel	Caiseal Mumhan
		Castlebar	Caisleán an Bharraigh
Ballina	Béal an Átha	Castleblayney	Baile na Lorgan
Ballinasloe	Béal Átha na Sluaighe	Castlemaine	Caisleán na Mainge
Ballinspittle	Béal Átha an Spidéil	Castletownbere	Baile Chais Bhéara
Ballintober	Bail an Tobair	Cavan	An Cabhán
Ballintoy	Baile an Tuaighe	Céide Fields	Achaidh Chéide
Ballybofey	Bealach Féich	Charleville	Rath Luirc
Ballybunion	Baile an Bhuinneánaigh	Clare	An Clár
Ballycastle	Baile an Chaisil	Clarinbridge	Droichead an Chláirin
Ballyferriter	Baile an Fheirtearaigh	Clear Island	Oileán Cléire
Ballyheigue	Baile Uí Thaidg	Cleggan	An Cloiggean
Ballyliffin	Baile Lifín	Clifden	An Clochán
Ballylongford	Bea Atha Longphuirb	Cloghane	An Clochán
Ballymena	An Baile Meánach	Clones	Cluain Eois
Ballynahinch	Baile na hInse	Clonmacnoise	Cluain Mhic Nóis
Ballyshannon	Béal Átha Seanaidh	Clonmel	Cluain Meala
Ballyvaughan	Baile Uí Bheacháin	Clontarf	Cluain Tarbh
Banbridge	Droichead na Banna	Cobh	An Cobh
Bandon	Droichead na Banndan	Coleraine	Cúil Raithin
Bangor	Beannchar	Cong	Conga
Bansha	An Bháinseach	Connemara	Conamara
Bantry	Beanntraí	Cookstown	An Chorr Chríochach
Belfast	Beál Feirste	Cootehill	An Mhuinchille
Bessbrook	An Sruthán	Cork	Corcaigh
Belmullet	Béal an Mhuirthead	Corofin	Cora Finne
Birr	Biorra	Costello	Casla
Blarney	An Bhlarna	Creeslough	An Craoslach
Blasket Islands	Na Blascaodaí	Crossmaglen	Crois Mhic Lionnáin
Bloody Foreland	Cnoc Fola	Crossmolina	Crois Mhaoiliona
Boyle	Mainistir na Búille	Culdaff	Cúil Dabhcha

Place	Irish Name	Place	Irish Name
Cushendall	Bun Abhann Dalla	Inch	Inse
Cushendun	Bun Abhann Duinne	Inisheer	Inis Oírr
		Inishmaan	Inis Meáin
Dalkey	Deilginis	Inishmór	Inis Mór/Árainn
Derry/Londonderry	Doire	Inishowen	Inis Eoghain
Derrybeg	Doirí Beaga	Innisfree	Inis Fraoigh
Devenish Island	Daimh Inis	Inniskeen	Inis Caoin
Dingle	An Daingean	Inverin	Indreabhán
Donaghadee	Domhnach Daoi	Islandmagee	Oileán Mhic Aodha
Donegal	Dún na nGall		
Downpatrick	Dún Pádraig	Kells	Ceanannas Mór
Dowth	Dubhadh	Kenmare	Neidín
Drogheda	Droichead Átha	Kilcar	Cill Chártha
Drumshanbo	Droim Seanbhó	Kildare	Cill Dara
Dublin	Baile Átha Cliath	Kilfenora	Cill Fhionnúrach
Duleek	Damh Liag	Kilkee	Cill Chaoi
Dundrum	Dún Droma	Kilkeel	Cill Chaoil
Dunfanaghy	Dún Fionnachaidh	Kilkenny	Cill Chainnigh
Dungannon	Dún Geanainn	Killala	Cill Alaidh
Dungarvan	Dún Garbhán	Killaloe	Cill Dalua
Dungiven	Dún Geimhin	Killarney	Cill Airne/Cill Ála
Dungloe	An Clochán Liath	Killybegs	Ceala Beaga
Dunkineely	Dún Cionnfhaolaidh	Killyleagh	Cill O Laoch
Dunlewy	Dún Lúiche	Kilmainham	Cill Mhaigneann
Dunquin	Dún Chaion	Kilmallock	Cill Mocheallóg
Dunree	An Dún Riabhach	Kilronan	Cill Rónáin
		Kilrush	Cill Rois
Easky	Eascaigh	Kingscourt	Dún an Rí
Ennis	Inis	Kinsale	Cionn tSáile
Enniscorthy	Inis Coirthaidh	Kinvara	Cinn Mhara
Enniscrone	Innis Crabhann	Knightstown	Baile An Ridire
Enniskillen	Inis Ceithleann	Knock	Cnoc Mhuire
Ennistymon	Inis Díomáin	Knowth	Cnóbha
Falcarragh	An Fal Cárrach		
Fanore	Fanóir	Lahinch	Leacht Uí Chonchubhair
Fermoy	Mainistir Fhear Muighe	Lanesborough	Béal Átha Liag
Fethard	Fiodh Ard	Larne	Lutharna
		Lauragh	Laith Reach
Galway	Gaillimh	Leenane	An Líonán
Giant's Causeway, The	Clochán an Aifir	Leitrim	Liatroim
Glandore	Cuan Dor	Letterfrack	Leitir Fraic
Glenarm	Gleann Arma	Letterkenny	Leitir Ceanainn
Glenbeigh	Gleann Beithe	Lifford	Leifear
Glencolumbcille	Gleann Cholm Cille	Limavady	Léim an Mhadaidh
Glendalough	Gleann dá Loch	Limerick	Luimneach
Glengarriff	An Gleann Garbh	Lisburn	Lios na gCearrbhach
Glenties	Na Gleannta	Liscannor	Lios Ceannúir
Glenveagh	Gleann Beatha	Lisdoonvarna	Lios Dún Bhearna
Gortahork	Gort an Choirce	Lismore	Lios Mór
Gracehill	Baile Uí Chinnéide	Lispole	Lios Póil
Great Blasket Island	An Blascaod Mór	Listowel	Lios Tuathail
Greencastle	An Cáisleán Nua	Longford	An Longfort
Greencastle	Caisleán na hOireanaí	Loop Head	Ceann Léime
Gweedore	Gaoth Dobhair	Lough Neagh	Loch nEathach
		Loughrea	Baile Locha Riach
Hillsborough	Cromghlinn	Louisburgh	Cluain Cearbán
Holy Island	Inis Cealtra		
Howth	Binn Éadair	Maam Cross	Crois Mám

Place	Irish Name	Place	Irish Name
Malahide	Mullach Ide	Recess	Straith Salach
Malin	Málainn	Roscommon	Ros Comáin
Malin Head	Cionn Mhálanna	Roscrea	Ros Cré
Mallow	Mala	Rossaveal	Ros a' Mhíl
Maynooth	Maigh Nuad	Rosscarbery	Ros O'gCairbre
Mayo	Maigh Eo	Rosses Point	An Ross
Meath	An Mhí	Rosslare	Ros Láir
Millisle	Oileán an Mhuilinn	Rossnowlagh	Ross Neamblach
Mitchelstown	Baile Mhistéala	Rostrevor	Caislean Ruairi
Moira	Maigh Rath	Roundstone	Cloch na Rón
Monaghan	Muineachán		
Monasterboice	Mainistir Bhuithe	Salthill	Bóthar na Trá
Monasterevin	Mainistir Eimhín	Scarriff	An Scairbh
Mt Brandon	Cnoc Bhréannain	Scattery Island	Inis Cathaigh
Mountcharles	Moin Séarbs	Screeb	Scriob
Mountshannon	Baile Uí Bheoláin	Shercock	Searcóg
Moville	Bun an Phoball	Skellig Islands	Oileáin na Scealaga
Muff	Mugh	Skibbereen	Sciobairín
Mullaghmore	An Mullach Mór	Slane	Baile Shláine
Mullingar	An Muileann gCearr	Sligo	Sligeach
Mulrany	An Mhala Raithní	Sneem	An tSnaidhm
		Spanish Point	Rinn na Spáinneach
Naas	An Nás	Spiddal	An Spidéal
Navan	An Uaimh	Strabane	An Srath Bán
Nenagh	An tAonach	Strangford	Baile Loch Cuan
New Quay	Ceibh Nua	Strangford Lough	Loch Cuan
New Ross	Rhos Mhic Triúin	Strokestown	Béal na mBuillí
Newbridge	Droichead Nua	Swords	Sord
Newcastle	An Caisleán Nua		
Newport	Baile Uí Fhiacháin	Tara	Teamhair
Newry	An tIúr	Thurles	Durlas
Newtownards	Baile Nua na hArda	Tipperary	Tiobraid Árann
		Tory Island	Oileán Thóraigh
Ogonnelloe	Tuath Ó gConnaille	Tralee	Trá Lí
Omagh	An Omaigh	Trim	Baile Átha Troim
Oughterard	Uachtar Árd	Tuam	Tuaim
		Tullamore	Tulach Mór
Pettigo	Paiteagó		
Pollotomish	Poll an Tómais	Union Hall	Bréantrá
Portaferry	Port an Pheire		
Portarlington	Cúil an tSúdaire	Valentia Island	Oileán Dairbhru
Portlaoise	Port Laoise	Ventry	Ceann Trá
Portrush	Port Rois	Virginia	Achadh Lir
Portsalon	Port an tSalainn		
Portstewart	Port Stíobhaird	Warrenpoint	An Pointe
		Waterford	Port Láirge
Quin	Chuinche	Waterville	An Coireán
		Westmeath	An Iarmhí
Randalstown	Baile Raghnaill	Westport	Cathair na Mairt
Rathfarnham	Ráth Fearnáin	Wexford	Loch Garman
Rathlin Island	Reachlainn	Wicklow	Cill Mhantáin
Rathmelton	Ráth Mealtain		
Rathmullan	Ráth Maoláin	Youghal	Eochaill

Glossary

An Óige – literally 'The Youth'; Republic of Ireland Youth Hostel Association

An Taisce – National Trust for the Republic of Ireland

Anglo-Norman – Norman, English and Welsh peoples who invaded Ireland in the 12th century

Apprentice Boys – loyalist organisation founded in 1814

ard – literally 'high'; Irish place name

ard rí – Irish for 'high king'

bailey – outer wall of a castle

banshee – female spirit whose wailing warns of impending death

bawn – area surrounded by walls outside the main castle, acting as a defence as well as a place to keep cattle in times of trouble

beehive hut – circular stone building shaped like an old-fashioned beehive

Black and Tans – British recruits to the Royal Irish Constabulary shortly after WWI, noted for their brutality

Blarney Stone – sacred rock in Blarney Castle, County Cork; kissing it is said to bestow the gift of the gab, or allow you to 'gain the privilege of telling lies for seven years'

bodhrán – pronounced **bore**-run; hand-held goatskin drum

Bord Fáilte – literally 'Welcome Board'; Republic of Ireland Tourist Board

botharin – a small lane or roadway; also known as a boreen

Bronze Age – earliest metal-using period, around 2500 BC to 300 BC in Ireland, after the Stone Age and before the Iron Age

B-specials – Northern Irish auxiliary police force, disbanded in 1971

bullaun – stone with a depression, probably used as a mortar for grinding medicine or food and often found on monastic sites

CAC IRA – Continuity Army Council of the IRA, a breakaway group

caher – circular area enclosed by stone walls

cairn – mound of stones heaped over a prehistoric grave

camogie – women's hurling

cashel – stone-walled circular fort; see also *ráth*

cath – literally 'battle'; Irish place name

ceilidh – pronounced **kay**-lee; session of traditional music and dancing

Celts – Iron Age warrior tribes that arrived in Ireland around 300 BC and controlled the country for 1000 years

chancel – eastern end of a church, where the altar is situated, reserved for the clergy and choir

cill – literally 'church'; Irish place name; also known as kill

cillín – literally 'little cell'; a hermitage, or sometimes a small, isolated burial ground

Claddagh ring – ring worn in much of Connaught since the mid-18th century, with a crowned heart between two hands; if the heart points towards the hand then the wearer is taken or married, towards the fingertip means he or she is looking for a mate

clochán – dry-stone beehive hut from the early Christian period

Connaught – one of the four ancient provinces of Ireland

control zone – area of a town centre, usually the main street, where parked cars must not, for security reasons, be left unattended

craic – conversation, gossip, fun, good times; also known as crack

crannóg – artificial island made in a lake to provide habitation in a good defensive position

crios – multicoloured woven woollen belt traditionally worn in the Aran Islands

cromlech – see dolmen

currach – rowing boat made of a framework of laths covered with tarred canvas; also known as a cúrach

Dáil – lower house of the Republic of Ireland Parliament

dairtheach – oratory, a small room set aside for private prayer

DART – Dublin Area Rapid Transport train line

demesne – landed property close to a house or castle

diamond – town square

dolmen – tomb chamber or portal tomb made of vertical stones topped by a huge capstone, dating from around 2000 BC

drumlin – rounded hill formed by retreating glaciers

Dúchas – government department in charge of parks, monuments and gardens in the Republic; formerly known as the Office of Public Works

dún – fort, usually constructed of stone

DUP – Democratic Unionist Party; founded principally by Ian Paisley in 1971 in hardline opposition to Unionist policies

Éire – Irish name for the Republic of Ireland

esker – gravel ridge

Fianna – mythical band of warriors who feature in many tales of ancient Ireland

Fianna Fáil – literally 'Warriors of Ireland'; a major political party in the Republic of Ireland, originating from the Sinn Féin faction opposed to the 1921 treaty with Britain

Fine Gael – literally 'Tribe of the Gael'; a major political party in the Republic, originating from the Sinn Féin faction that favoured the 1921 treaty with Britain. It formed the first government of independent Ireland

fir – literally 'men', singular *fear*; sign on men's toilets

fulacht fiadh – Bronze Age cooking place

gaelscoileanna – Irish-medium school

Gaeltacht – Irish-speaking area

gallery grave – tunnel-shaped burial chamber

gallógli – mercenary soldiers of the 14th to 15th century; also known as gallowglasses

garda – Irish Republic police; plural *gardaí*

ghillie – fishing or hunting guide; also known as a ghilly

gort – literally 'field'; Irish place name

Gothic – style of architecture characterised by pointed arches, common in Ireland from the late 12th to the 16th century

Hibernia – literally 'Land of Winter'; Roman name for Ireland; the Romans had confused Ireland with Iceland

hill fort – a fort formed by a ditch that follows the contour of the hill to surround and fortify the summit, usually dating from the Iron Age

HINI – Hostelling International of Northern Ireland

húicéir – traditional Galway vessel; also known as a hooker

hurling – Irish sport similar to hockey

Iarnród Éireann – Republic of Ireland Railways

INLA – Irish National Liberation Association; formed in 1975 as an IRA splinter group unhappy at the cease-fire

IRA – Irish Republican Army; the largest republican paramilitary organisation, founded 80 years ago with the aim to fight for a united Ireland. In 1969, the IRA split into the Official IRA and the Provisional IRA

IRB – Irish Republican Brotherhood; a secret society founded in 1858 and revived in the early 20th century. It believed in independence, through violence if necessary, and was a precursor to the IRA; also known as the Fenians

Iron Age – in Ireland this lasted from the end of the Bronze Age, around 300 BC (the arrival of the Celts), to the arrival of Christianity, around the 5th century AD

jarvey – driver of a jaunting car

jaunting car – Killarney's traditional horse-drawn transport

keep – main tower of a castle

Lambeg drum – very large drum associated with Protestant loyalist marches

Leinster – one of the four ancient provinces of Ireland

leithreas – toilets

leprechaun – mischievous elf or sprite from Irish folklore

lough – lake, long narrow bay or arm of the sea

loyalist – person, usually a Northern Irish Protestant, insisting on the continuation of Northern Ireland's links with Britain

loyalist orders – loyalist groups committed to the union with the UK; consists mainly of the Orange Order and the Apprentice Boys
LVF – Loyalist Volunteer Force; an extreme loyalist paramilitary group opposed to the current peace process

marching season – parades that take place from Easter and throughout summer to celebrate the victory of Protestant William of Orange in the Battle of the Boyne on 12 July 1690. They are organised by the Orange Order
Mesolithic – also known as the Middle Stone Age; time of the first human settlers in Ireland, about 8000 BC to 4000 BC
mná – literally 'women'; sign on women's toilets
motte – early Norman fortification consisting of a raised, flattened mound with a keep on top; when attached to a bailey it is known as a motte and bailey fort, many of which were built in Ireland until the early 13th century
Munster – one of the four ancient provinces of Ireland

naomh – holy or saint
nationalism – belief in a reunited Ireland
nationalist – proponent of a united Ireland
Neolithic – also known as the New Stone Age; a period characterised by settled agriculture and lasting from around 4000 BC to 2500 BC in Ireland; followed by the Bronze Age
NIR – Northern Ireland Railways
NITB – Northern Ireland Tourist Board
NNR – National Nature Reserves
North, The – the political entity of Northern Ireland, not the northernmost geographic part of Ireland

Ogham stone – ogham (pronounced o-am) was the earliest form of writing in Ireland, using a variety of notched strokes placed above, below or across a keyline, usually on stone
Oireachtas – Parliament of the Republic, consisting of a lower and upper house, the Dáil and Senate
Orange Order – the largest Protestant organisation in Northern Ireland, founded in 1795
óstán – hotel

Palladian – style of architecture developed by Andrea Palladio (1508–80) based on ancient Roman architecture
paramilitaries – armed illegal organisations, either loyalist or republican, usually associated with the use of violence and crime for political and economic gain
Partition – division of Ireland in 1921
passage grave – Celtic tomb with a chamber reached by a narrow passage, typically buried in a mound
penal laws – laws passed in the 18th century forbidding Catholics from buying land, holding public office and so on
Plantation – settlement of Protestant migrants (sometimes known as Planters) in Ireland in the 17th century
poteen – pronounced **pot**-cheen; illegally brewed potato-based firewater
Prod – slang for Northern Irish Protestant
Provisionals – Provisional IRA, formed after a break with the Official IRA; named after the provisional government declared in 1916, they have been the main force combating the British army in the North
PUP – Progressive Unionist Party; a small unionist party; it supports the Good Friday Agreement

ráth – circular fort with earth banks round a timber wall
Real IRA – splinter movement of the IRA opposed to the Good Friday Agreement. The Real IRA was responsible for the Omagh bombing in 1998 in which 29 people died
Red Hand Commandos – loyalist paramilitary group
Red Hand Defenders – breakaway paramilitary loyalist group formed in 1998 by dissident UFF and LVF members
Republic of Ireland – the 26 counties of the South
republican – supporter of a united Ireland
republicanism – belief in a united Ireland, sometimes referred to as militant nationalism
rí – Irish for 'petty king'

ring fort – circular habitation area surrounded by banks and ditches, used from the Bronze Age right through to the Middle Ages

Romanesque – style of architecture seen in 12th-century Irish churches and monasteries; characterised by rounded arches and vaulting

round tower – tall circular tower dating from around the 9th to 11th centuries, built as a lookout and sanctuary during the period when monasteries were frequently subject to Viking raids

RUC – Royal Ulster Constabulary, the former name of the Police Service of Northern Ireland

SDLP – Social Democratic and Labour Party; the largest nationalist party in the Northern Ireland Assembly and instrumental in achieving the Good Friday Agreement

seisún – music session

sept – clan

shamrock – three-leafed plant said to have been used by St Patrick to illustrate the Holy Trinity

shebeen – from the Irish *síbín*; illicit drinking place or speakeasy

sheila-na-gig – literally 'Sheila of the teats'; female figure with exaggerated genitalia, carved in stone on the exteriors of some churches and castles

shillelagh – a stout club or cudgel, especially one made of oak or blackthorn

Sinn Féin – literally 'We Ourselves'; a republican party with the long-term aim of a united Ireland; seen as the political wing of the IRA though it maintains that both organisations are completely separate

slí – hiking trail or way

snug – partitioned-off drinking area in a pub

souterrain – underground chamber usually associated with ring and hill forts; probably provided a hiding place or escape route in times of trouble and/or storage space for goods

South, The – Republic of Ireland

standing stone – upright stone set in the ground, common across Ireland and dating

from a variety of periods; usually the purpose is obscure, though some are burial markers

tánaiste – Republic of Ireland deputy prime minister

taoiseach – pronounced **tea**-shock; Republic of Ireland prime minister

TD – teachta Dála; member of the Republic of Ireland Parliament

teampall – church

Treaty – Anglo-Irish Treaty of 1921, which divided Ireland and gave independence to the South; cause of the 1922–23 Civil War

Tricolour – green, white and orange Irish flag designed to symbolise the hoped-for union of the green Catholic Southern Irish with the orange Protestant Northern Irish

turlough – from the Irish *turlach*; a small lake that often disappears in dry summers

UDA – Ulster Defence Association; the largest loyalist paramilitary group

UDP – Ulster Democratic Party; a small fringe unionist party

UFF – Ulster Freedom Fighters, aka the Ulster Defence Association

Ulster – one of the four ancient provinces of Ireland; a term sometimes used to describe the six counties of the North, despite the fact that Ulster also includes Counties Cavan, Monaghan and Donegal in the Republic

unionism – belief in the political union with Britain

unionist – person who wants to retain Northern Ireland's links with Britain

United Irishmen – organisation founded in 1791 aiming to reduce British power in Ireland

UUP – Ulster Unionist Party; the largest unionist party in Northern Ireland and the majority party in the Assembly; founded by Edward Carson

UVF – Ulster Volunteer Force; a loyalist Northern Irish paramilitary organisation

Volunteers – offshoot of the IRB that came to be known as the IRA

LONELY PLANET

You already know that Lonely Planet produces more than this one guidebook, but you might not be aware of the other products we have on this region. Here is a selection of titles that you may want to check out as well:

Dublin Condensed
ISBN 1 74059 269 7
US$11.99 • UK£5.99

Dublin City Map
ISBN 1 86450 176 6
US$5.99 • UK£3.99

Dublin
ISBN 1 86450 345 9
US$15.99 • UK£8.99

Walking in Ireland
ISBN 0 86442 602 X
US$17.95 • UK£11.99

World Food Ireland
ISBN 1 86450 093 X
US$11.99 • UK£6.99

Europe on a Shoestring
ISBN 1 86450 150 2
US$24.99 • UK£14.99

Read This First: Europe
ISBN 1 86450 136 7
US$14.99 • UK£8.99

Western Europe
ISBN 1 86450 163 4
US$27.99 • UK£15.99

Europe Phrasebook
ISBN 1 86450 224 X
US$8.99 • UK£4.99

Available wherever books are sold

Lonely Planet Guides by Region

Lonely Planet is known worldwide for publishing practical, reliable and no-nonsense travel information in our guides and on our Web site. The Lonely Planet list covers just about every accessible part of the world. Currently there are 16 series: Travel guides, Shoestring guides, Condensed guides, Phrasebooks, Read This First, Healthy Travel, Walking guides, Cycling guides, Watching Wildlife guides, Pisces Diving & Snorkeling guides, City Maps, Road Atlases, Out to Eat, World Food, Journeys travel literature and Pictorials.

AFRICA Africa on a shoestring • Botswana • Cairo • Cairo City Map • Cape Town • Cape Town City Map • East Africa • Egypt • Egyptian Arabic phrasebook • Ethiopia, Eritrea & Djibouti • Ethiopian Amharic phrasebook • The Gambia & Senegal • Healthy Travel Africa • Kenya • Malawi • Morocco • Moroccan Arabic phrasebook • Mozambique • Namibia • Read This First: Africa • South Africa, Lesotho & Swaziland • Southern Africa • Southern Africa Road Atlas • Swahili phrasebook • Tanzania, Zanzibar & Pemba • Trekking in East Africa • Tunisia • Watching Wildlife East Africa • Watching Wildlife Southern Africa • West Africa • World Food Morocco • Zambia • Zimbabwe, Botswana & Namibia
Travel Literature: Mali Blues: Traveling to an African Beat • The Rainbird: A Central African Journey • Songs to an African Sunset: A Zimbabwean Story

AUSTRALIA & THE PACIFIC Aboriginal Australia & the Torres Strait Islands •Auckland • Australia • Australian phrasebook • Australia Road Atlas • Cycling Australia • Cycling New Zealand • Fiji • Fijian phrasebook • Healthy Travel Australia, NZ & the Pacific • Islands of Australia's Great Barrier Reef • Melbourne • Melbourne City Map • Micronesia • New Caledonia • New South Wales • New Zealand • Northern Territory • Outback Australia • Out to Eat – Melbourne • Out to Eat – Sydney • Papua New Guinea • Pidgin phrasebook • Queensland • Rarotonga & the Cook Islands • Samoa • Solomon Islands • South Australia • South Pacific • South Pacific phrasebook • Sydney • Sydney City Map • Sydney Condensed • Tahiti & French Polynesia • Tasmania • Tonga • Tramping in New Zealand • Vanuatu • Victoria • Walking in Australia • Watching Wildlife Australia • Western Australia
Travel Literature: Islands in the Clouds: Travels in the Highlands of New Guinea • Kiwi Tracks: A New Zealand Journey • Sean & David's Long Drive

CENTRAL AMERICA & THE CARIBBEAN Bahamas, Turks & Caicos • Baja California • Belize, Guatemala & Yucatán • Bermuda • Central America on a shoestring • Costa Rica • Costa Rica Spanish phrasebook • Cuba • Cycling Cuba • Dominican Republic & Haiti • Eastern Caribbean • Guatemala • Havana • Healthy Travel Central & South America • Jamaica • Mexico • Mexico City • Panama • Puerto Rico • Read This First: Central & South America • Virgin Islands • World Food Caribbean • World Food Mexico • Yucatán
Travel Literature: Green Dreams: Travels in Central America

EUROPE Amsterdam • Amsterdam City Map • Amsterdam Condensed • Andalucía • Athens • Austria • Baltic States phrasebook • Barcelona • Barcelona City Map • Belgium & Luxembourg • Berlin • Berlin City Map • Britain • British phrasebook • Brussels, Bruges & Antwerp • Brussels City Map • Budapest • Budapest City Map • Canary Islands • Catalunya & the Costa Brava • Central Europe • Central Europe phrasebook • Copenhagen • Corfu & the Ionians • Corsica • Crete • Crete Condensed • Croatia • Cycling Britain • Cycling France • Cyprus • Czech & Slovak Republics • Czech phrasebook • Denmark • Dublin • Dublin City Map • Dublin Condensed • Eastern Europe • Eastern Europe phrasebook • Edinburgh • Edinburgh City Map • England • Estonia, Latvia & Lithuania • Europe on a shoestring • Europe phrasebook • Finland • Florence • Florence City Map • France • Frankfurt City Map • Frankfurt Condensed • French phrasebook • Georgia, Armenia & Azerbaijan • Germany • German phrasebook • Greece • Greek Islands • Greek phrasebook • Hungary • Iceland, Greenland & the Faroe Islands • Ireland • Italian phrasebook • Italy • Kraków • Lisbon • The Loire • London • London City Map • London Condensed • Madrid • Madrid City Map • Malta • Mediterranean Europe • Milan, Turin & Genoa • Moscow • Munich • Netherlands • Normandy • Norway • Out to Eat – London • Out to Eat – Paris • Paris • Paris City Map • Paris Condensed • Poland • Polish phrasebook • Portugal • Portuguese phrasebook • Prague • Prague City Map • Provence & the Côte d'Azur • Read This First: Europe • Rhodes & the Dodecanese • Romania & Moldova • Rome • Rome City Map • Rome Condensed • Russia, Ukraine & Belarus • Russian phrasebook • Scandinavian & Baltic Europe • Scandinavian phrasebook • Scotland • Sicily • Slovenia • South-West France • Spain • Spanish phrasebook • Stockholm • St Petersburg • St Petersburg City Map • Sweden • Switzerland • Tuscany • Ukrainian phrasebook • Venice • Vienna • Wales • Walking in Britain • Walking in France • Walking in Ireland • Walking in Italy • Walking in Scotland • Walking in Spain • Walking in Switzerland • Western Europe • World Food France • World Food Greece • World Food Ireland • World Food Italy • World Food Spain **Travel Literature:** After Yugoslavia • Love and War in the Apennines • The Olive Grove: Travels in Greece • On the Shores of the Mediterranean • Round Ireland in Low Gear • A Small Place in Italy

Lonely Planet Mail Order

onely Planet products are distributed worldwide. They are also available by mail order from Lonely Planet, so if you have difficulty finding a title please write to us. North and South American residents should write to 150 Linden St, Oakland, CA 94607, USA; European and African residents should write to 10a Spring Place, London NW5 3BH, UK; and residents of other countries to Locked Bag 1, Footscray, Victoria 3011, Australia.

INDIAN SUBCONTINENT & THE INDIAN OCEAN Bangladesh • Bengali phrasebook • Bhutan • Delhi • Goa • Healthy Travel Asia & India • Hindi & Urdu phrasebook • India • India & Bangladesh City Map • Indian Himalaya • Karakoram Highway • Kathmandu City Map • Kerala • Madagascar • Maldives • Mauritius, Réunion & Seychelles • Mumbai (Bombay) • Nepal • Nepali phrasebook • North India • Pakistan • Rajasthan • Read This First: Asia & India • South India • Sri Lanka • Sri Lanka phrasebook • Tibet • Tibetan phrasebook • Trekking in the Indian Himalaya • Trekking in the Karakoram & Hindukush • Trekking in the Nepal Himalaya • World Food India **Travel Literature**: The Age of Kali: Indian Travels and Encounters • Hello Goodnight: A Life of Goa • In Rajasthan • Maverick in Madagascar • A Season in Heaven: True Tales from the Road to Kathmandu • Shopping for Buddhas • A Short Walk in the Hindu Kush • Slowly Down the Ganges

MIDDLE EAST & CENTRAL ASIA Bahrain, Kuwait & Qatar • Central Asia • Central Asia phrasebook • Dubai • Farsi (Persian) phrasebook • Hebrew phrasebook • Iran • Israel & the Palestinian Territories • Istanbul • Istanbul City Map • Istanbul to Cairo • Istanbul to Kathmandu • Jerusalem • Jerusalem City Map • Jordan • Lebanon • Middle East • Oman & the United Arab Emirates • Syria • Turkey • Turkish phrasebook • World Food Turkey • Yemen **Travel Literature:** Black on Black: Iran Revisited • Breaking Ranks: Turbulent Travels in the Promised Land • The Gates of Damascus • Kingdom of the Film Stars: Journey into Jordan

NORTH AMERICA Alaska • Boston • Boston City Map • Boston Condensed • British Columbia • California & Nevada • California Condensed • Canada • Chicago • Chicago City Map • Chicago Condensed • Florida • Georgia & the Carolinas • Great Lakes • Hawaii • Hiking in Alaska • Hiking in the USA • Honolulu & Oahu City Map • Las Vegas • Los Angeles • Los Angeles City Map • Louisiana & the Deep South • Miami • Miami City Map • Montreal • New England • New Orleans • New Orleans City Map • New York City • New York City City Map • New York City Condensed • New York, New Jersey & Pennsylvania • Oahu • Out to Eat – San Francisco • Pacific Northwest • Rocky Mountains • San Diego & Tijuana • San Francisco • San Francisco City Map • Seattle • Seattle City Map • Southwest • Texas • Toronto • USA • USA phrasebook • Vancouver • Vancouver City Map • Virginia & the Capital Region • Washington, DC • Washington, DC City Map • World Food New Orleans **Travel Literature**: Caught Inside: A Surfer's Year on the California Coast • Drive Thru America

NORTH-EAST ASIA Beijing • Beijing City Map • Cantonese phrasebook • China • Hiking in Japan • Hong Kong & Macau • Hong Kong City Map • Hong Kong Condensed • Japan • Japanese phrasebook • Korea • Korean phrasebook • Kyoto • Mandarin phrasebook • Mongolia • Mongolian phrasebook • Seoul • Shanghai • South-West China • Taiwan • Tokyo • Tokyo Condensed • World Food Hong Kong • World Food Japan **Travel Literature:** In Xanadu: A Quest • Lost Japan

SOUTH AMERICA Argentina, Uruguay & Paraguay • Bolivia • Brazil • Brazilian phrasebook • Buenos Aires • Buenos Aires City Map • Chile & Easter Island • Colombia • Ecuador & the Galapagos Islands • Healthy Travel Central & South America • Latin American Spanish phrasebook • Peru • Quechua phrasebook • Read This First: Central & South America • Rio de Janeiro • Rio de Janeiro City Map • Santiago de Chile • South America on a shoestring • Trekking in the Patagonian Andes • Venezuela **Travel Literature**: Full Circle: A South American Journey

SOUTH-EAST ASIA Bali & Lombok • Bangkok • Bangkok City Map • Burmese phrasebook • Cambodia • Cycling Vietnam, Laos & Cambodia • East Timor phrasebook • Hanoi • Healthy Travel Asia & India • Hill Tribes phrasebook • Ho Chi Minh City (Saigon) • Indonesia • Indonesian phrasebook • Indonesia's Eastern Islands • Java • Lao phrasebook • Laos • Malay phrasebook • Malaysia, Singapore & Brunei • Myanmar (Burma) • Philippines • Pilipino (Tagalog) phrasebook • Read This First: Asia & India • Singapore • Singapore City Map • South-East Asia on a shoestring • South-East Asia phrasebook • Thailand • Thailand's Islands & Beaches • Thailand, Vietnam, Laos & Cambodia Road Atlas • Thai phrasebook • Vietnam • Vietnamese phrasebook • World Food Indonesia • World Food Thailand • World Food Vietnam

ALSO AVAILABLE: Antarctica • The Arctic • The Blue Man: Tales of Travel, Love and Coffee • Brief Encounters: Stories of Love, Sex & Travel • Buddhist Stupas in Asia: The Shape of Perfection • Chasing Rickshaws • The Last Grain Race • Lonely Planet ... On the Edge: Adventurous Escapades from Around the World • Lonely Planet Unpacked • Lonely Planet Unpacked Again • Not the Only Planet: Science Fiction Travel Stories • Ports of Call: A Journey by Sea • Sacred India • Travel Photography: A Guide to Taking Better Pictures • Travel with Children • Tuvalu: Portrait of an Island Nation

Index

Text

Bold indicates maps.

Boxed Text

MAP LEGEND

BOUNDARIES

.... International
.... Regional
.... Suburb

HYDROGRAPHY

.... Coastline
.... River, Creek
.... Lake
.... Canal

ROUTES & TRANSPORT

.... Freeway
.... Primary Road
.... Secondary Road
.... Tertiary Road
.... Unsealed Road
.... City Freeway
.... City Primary Road
.... City Road
.... City Street, Lane

.... Pedestrian Area
.... Tunnel
.... Train Route & Station
.... Metro & Station
.... Tramway
.... Cable Car or Chairlift
.... Walking Track
.... Walking Tour
.... Ferry Route & Terminal

AREA FEATURES

.... Park, Gardens
.... Urban Area

.... Building
.... Market

.... Beach
.... Cemetery

MAP SYMBOLS

⊕ **DUBLIN** .... City
● **Sligo** .... City or Large Town
● Dysart .... Town
● Ballyforan .... Village

● .... Point of Interest
♦ .... Place to Stay
▲ .... Camp Site
▼ .... Place to Eat
▣ .... Pub, Bar or Club

✈ ✚ .... Airport, Airfield
.... Ancient or City Wall
❸ .... Bank
↗ .... Beach

.... Bird Sanctuary
.... Cave
.... Bus Stop, Bus Station
.... Castle
.... Cathedral or Church
.... Theatre, Cinema
.... Cliff or Escarpment
.... Embassy or Consulate
.... Fountain
.... Hospital
.... Internet Cafe
.... Lighthouse
.... Monument
.... Mountain, Range
.... Museum

.... One-Way Street
.... Parking
.... Pass
.... Police Station
.... Post Office
.... Ruins
.... Shopping Centre
.... Stately Home
.... Surf Beach
.... Swimming Pool
.... Taxi Rank
.... Telephone
.... Toilet
.... Tourist Information
.... Zoo

Note: not all symbols displayed above appear in this book

LONELY PLANET OFFICES

Australia
Locked Bag 1, Footscray, Victoria 3011
☎ 03-8379 8000 fax 03-8379 8111
email: talk2us@lonelyplanet.com.au

USA
150 Linden St, Oakland, CA 94607
☎ 510-893 8555 TOLL FREE: 800 275 8555
fax 510-893 8572
email: info@lonelyplanet.com

UK
10a Spring Place, London NW5 3BH
☎ 020-7428 4800 fax 020-7428 4828
email: go@lonelyplanet.co.uk

France
1 rue du Dahomey, 75011 Paris
☎ 01 55 25 33 00 fax 01 55 25 33 01
email: bip@lonelyplanet.fr
www.lonelyplanet.fr

World Wide Web: www.lonelyplanet.com *or* **AOL keyword: lp**
Lonely Planet Images: lpi@lonelyplanet.com.au